FREE
Online
Support
See Inside Cover

AF889345

Medico Achiever's Series

NEET
Objective
Chemistry

Volume 2

Author
Dr. R.K. Gupta

Co-Authored by
Gaurav Shrivastava

arihant
SUCCESS AND NOTHING LESS

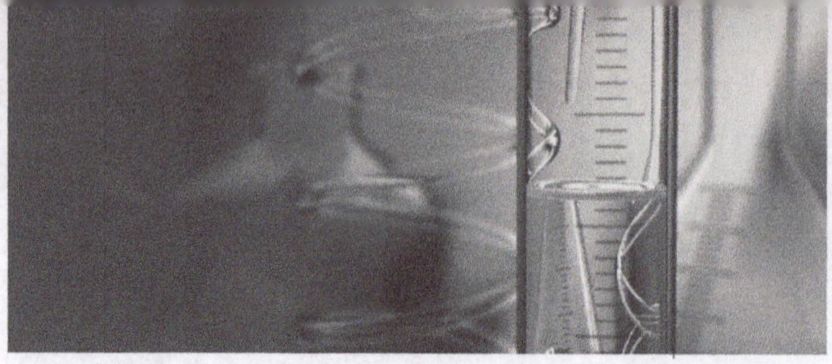

Arihant Prakashan (Series), Meerut

Administrative & Production Offices

Regd. Office

'Ramchhaya' 4577/15, Agarwal Road, Darya Ganj, New Delhi -110002
Tele: 011- 47630600, 43518550

Head Office

Kalindi, TP Nagar, Meerut (UP) - 250002
Tel: 0121-7156203, 7156204

Sales & Support Offices

Agra, Ahmedabad, Bengaluru, Bareilly, Chennai, Delhi, Guwahati, Hyderabad, Jaipur, Jhansi, Kolkata, Lucknow, Nagpur & Pune.

PRICE ₹595.00

PO No : TXT-XX-XXXXXXX-X-XX

Published by Arihant Publications (India) Ltd.

For further information about the books published by Arihant, log on to www.arihantbooks.com or e-mail at info@arihantbooks.com

Follow us on

PRODUCTION TEAM

Project Head	Cover Designer	Inner Designer
Akansha Tomar	Bilal Hashmi	Ankit Tyagi
Page Layouting	*Proof Readers*	*Figure Designer*
Sanjay Yadav	Akhil, Ayush Rai	Mohit

Preface

Mastery on Chemistry is important for students who are planning to make their career in medicine. It specially helps in securing good rank. The competition is no longer easy for a seat in a prestigious medical college today. Present changes in NEET exam Pattern have increased this challenge many a fold. To face this they require an objective approach in their studies. A student can master the concepts and the skills required to tackle the questions asked in different entrances such as NEET (National Eligibility cum Entrance Test) through this approach.

NEET Objective Chemistry books of **Medico achiever's** series are borne out of my experience of teaching chemistry to medical aspirants. The content of these books is framed to provide help in facing present day challenges by future medicos.

The exclusive features of our new magnified edition are

- The Chapter begins via **Overview with NEET connection**. This feature provides 4-way benefits as **Chapter Abstract, Insight of important topics, Suggestions to grip the chapter and NEET analytics** as video support.
- The whole chapter has been divided into smaller modules. Theory part of each module is elaborated with following unparallel features -
  - **Concept Ladder** Focused box matter with enhanced and important info.
  - **Mentor's Tip** Specialised tips, Tricks and advice by the mentor.
  - **NEET Info graphics** Figure enhancement with text for better explanation and visualisation.
- Another speciality of modular theory is its syncing with PYQs through unique features like.
  - **NEET Snapshots** Facts from selected conceptual PYQs with proper elaborations.
  - **NEET Close up** Simulators to sync Numerical PYQs with theory and having skill builders as additional practice tool.
  - **NEET exclusive extra bytes** Important facts from past exams/ topics still important for NEET
- Assignments of the chapters have been divided into three parts:
  - **Step Up Practice** Scientifically designed modular Practice exercise, present just after the theory in each module.
  - **Gear up for NEET** Mixed bag of assorted MCQs with all special format question types as asked in NEET.
  - **Final Check through PYQs** last 10-year PYQs arranged in Modular format.
- The Explanation of all questions is given at the chapter end as hints and Solutions.

Huge efforts have been made from our side to keep this book error free, inspite of that if any error or whatsoever is skipped in the book then that is purely incidental. Please write to us about that so that it can be corrected in the further edition of the book. Further, Suggestions from the respected Teachers & Students are also welcome as these are the foundation stones for the further improvement and success of our book.

Dr. RK Gupta

Email: raghuveshg@gmail.com

Key Features

Learning Objectives

Glimpse of Modular Distribution of Topics.

Learning Objectives

Module-I

- Saturated and Unsaturated Solutions
- Dilute and Concentrated Solutions
- Gaseous Solutions
- Liquid Solutions
- Solid Solutions
- Concentration Terms
- Calculation of Normality and Molarity on Dilution
- Calculation of Normality and Molarity on Mixing

Module-II

- Solubility of Gas in Liquid
- Henry's Law
- Solubility of Solid in Liquid
- Vapour Pressure of Liquid Solutions
- Raoult's Law
- Ideal and Non-Ideal Solution

Module-III

- Relative Lowering of Vapour Pressure
- Elevation in Boiling Point

Chapter overview with NEET connection

Present on the first page of every chapter and contains

- Chapter abstract
- Insight of Important Topics
- Suggestions to grip the chapter in a better way
- NEET analytics as video support

Solutions

Chapter Overview with

NEET Connection

This chapter is useful for the learning of various concentration terms and colligative properties. Without gripping this chapter, it will be difficult to solve various problems related to concentration terms used in other chapters of physical chemistry.

Special format question can be easily formed on following topics of this chapter.

- Expressing concentration of solutions.
- Henry's law
- Raoult's law
- Colligative properties
- van't Hoff factor

For better understanding of this chapter, a grip over Raoult's law concentration of solutions and colligative properties is required.

As the foundation of colligative properties involves calculations. Hence, along with understanding of concepts, a focus on calculation part and basic conversion is also required.

Concept Ladder

Focused Box matter with enhanced and important info to provide better grip over the concept.

Determination of Molar Mass of Solute

If w_2 grams of solute of molar mass M_2 is present in the solution, then $n_2 = \dfrac{w_2}{M_2}$ so above equation will become

$$\pi V = \frac{w_2 RT}{M_2}$$

or $$M_2 = \frac{w_2 RT}{\pi V}$$

where, symbols have their usual meaning.

Concept ladder

Osmotic pressure of a mixture of two liquids can be calculated as

Case I If two solutions of same substance having osmotic pressure of π_1 and π_2 are mixed, then

$$\pi_1 V_1 = \pi_2 V_2 = \pi_R (V_1 + V_2)$$

Case II If number of moles of two solutes are n_1 *and* n_2, which are present in volume V_1 *and* V_2 respectively are mixed then,

$$\pi = \pi_1 + \pi_2 = \left(\frac{n_1 + n_2}{V_1 + V_2}\right) RT$$

Mentor's Tips

Specialised Tips, Tricks and advices by the Mentor for performance enhancement in NEET.

Determination of Molar Mass of Solute

If w_2 gram of solute of molar mass M_2 is dissolved in W_1 gram of solvent then equation (2) is given by

$$\Delta T_f = \frac{K_f \times w_2 \times 1000}{M_2 \times W_1}$$

or $$M_2 = \frac{K_f \times w_2 \times 1000}{\Delta T_f \times W_1}$$

where, M_2 = molar mass of solute

w_2 = mass of solute

W_1 = mass of solvent

Mentor's Tip

- Vapour pressure, boiling point and melting point are not colligative properties.
- Both ΔT_b or ΔT_f is directly proportional to lowering in vapour pressure.

Key Features

NEET Snapshot

Out of molality, molarity, mole fraction and weight percentage only. Molarity is dependent on temperature. ***[NEET 2017]***

All concentration terms those are related with volume show temperature dependency while those which are independent of volume are temperature dependent also because volume is a temperature dependent entity.

NEET Snapshot
Unique element having facts with proper elaborations to sync selected conceptual questions of PYQs with the theory.

NEET Close-up

Example Similar to PYQ Asked in NEET 2024

The Henry's law constant (K_H) values of three gases (X, Y, Z) in water are $144.97, 1.83 \times 10^{-5}$ and 1.67×10^{-6} kbar respectively. The solubility of these gases in water follows the order

(a) $X > Y > Z$ (b) $Y > Z > X$
(c) $X > Z > Y$ (d) $Z > Y > X$

Sol. (*d*) Higher the value of Henry' law constant (K_H) lower is the solubility of gas in water.
So, the order of solubility is $Z > Y > X$.

Skill Builder

The value of Henry' law constant for P, Q, R and S gases are 44, 69, 76 and 40 kbar respectively. The solubility of these gases in water at 293 K follows the order

(a) $P > Q > R > S$ (b) $R > Q > P > S$
(c) $S > P > Q > R$ (d) $Q > R > P > S$

For more practice Refer to Q.5 of step up practice-2.

NEET Close-up
Unparallel concept elevation tool, helpful in syncing PYQs with theory and provide additional practice through skill builders.

NEET Exclusive EXTRA BYTES

Relationship Between Different Colligative Properties

- Osmotic pressure (π) with relative lowering of vapour pressure,
$$\pi = \frac{p^\circ - p}{p^\circ} \times \frac{dRT}{M_1} \; [M_1 = \text{molar mass of the solvent}]$$
- Osmotic pressure (π) with elevation in boiling point (ΔT_b),
$$\pi = \Delta T_b \times \frac{dRT}{1000K_b} \; [d = \text{density of the solution at temperature } T]$$
- Osmotic pressure (π) with depression in freezing point (ΔT_f), $\pi = \Delta T_f \times \frac{dRT}{1000K_f}$
- Elevation in boiling point with relative lowering of vapour pressure,
$$\Delta T_b = \frac{1000K_b}{M_1}\left(\frac{p^\circ - p}{p^\circ}\right) \; [M_1 = \text{molar mass of solvent}]$$
- Depression in freezing point with relative lowering of vapour pressure,
$$\Delta T_f = \frac{1000K_f}{M_1}\left(\frac{p^\circ - p}{p^\circ}\right)$$

NEET Exclusive Extra Bytes
Important facts from Past Exams/ Topics still expected in NEET.

Key Features

Step up Practice

Scientifically designed first practice exercise to check modular learning.

STEP UP Practice 1

1. Which of the following is not the correct match pair?
   (a) Gaseous solution — Camphor in nitrogen gas
   (b) Liquid solution — Oxygen dissolved in water
   (c) Solid solution — Solution of hydrogen in palladium
   (d) Liquid solution — Amalgam of mercury with sodium
2. When a solute is present in trace quantities the expression that is used is
   (a) molality (b) molarity
   (c) mole fraction (d) parts per million
3. For a very diluted solution preferred concentration term is
   (a) percentage of mass (b) molarity
   (c) parts per million (d) molality

11. Given below are two statements one is labelled as Assertion (A) and the other is labelled as Reason (R).
    Assertion (A) The sum of mole fractions of all the component of a solution is unity.
    Reason (R) The mole fraction is a temperature dependent quantity.
    In the light of the above statements, choose the correct answer from the options given below.
    (a) Both A and R are true and R is correct explanation of A.
    (b) Both A and R are true but R is not the correct explanation of A.
    (c) A is true but R is false.
    (d) A is false but R is true.

GEARING UP FOR NEET

1. The concentration of pollutant in ppm, that has been measured at 450 mg per 150 kg of sample is
   (a) 3 ppm (b) 6 ppm
   (c) 3000 ppm (d) 330 ppm
2. Persons are medically considered to have lead poisoning if they have a concentration greater than 10 μg of lead per dicilitre of blood. Concentration in parts per billion is
   (a) 1000 of solvent (b) 100 of solvent
   (c) 10 of solvent (d) 1 of solvent
3. In 4/8 molal solution that contains 0.213 mole of a solute, there is
   (a) 323 g of solvent (b) 513 g of solvent
   (c) 426 g of solvent (d) 216 g of solvent

9. Which of the following pair is correct for a solution showing positive deviations from Raoult's law?
   (a) $\Delta V = +\text{ve}, \Delta H = -\text{ve}$ (b) $\Delta V = +\text{ve}, \Delta H = +\text{ve}$
   (c) $\Delta V = -\text{ve}, \Delta H = -\text{ve}$ (d) $\Delta V = -\text{ve}, \Delta H = +\text{ve}$
10. Which of the following statement is incorrect?
    (a) Raoult's law is a special case of Henry's law in which K_H becomes equal to p°_1.
    (b) Chloroform and diethyl ether shows positive deviation from Raoult's law.
    (c) Azeotropic mixture are binary mixture having same composition in liquid and vapour phase.
    (d) Phenol and aniline show negative deviation from Raoult's law.

Gearing up for NEET

Mixed bag of assorted MCQs with all special format questions types asked in NEET.

Final Check through PYQs

Specialised PYQs section having last 10 years PYQs arranged in modular format to check the preparation levels and gain confidence to face NEET.

Final Check Through PYQs

Module-I Types and Concentration of Solutions

1. In one molal solution that contains 0.5 mole of a solute, there is *[NCERT (New) Pg. 5, NEET 2022]*
   (a) 500 g of solvent
   (b) 100 mL of solvent
   (c) 1000 g of solvent
   (d) 500 mL of solvent
2. Which of the following is dependent on temperature? *[NEET 2017]*
   (a) Molality (b) Molarity
   (c) Mole fraction (d) Weight percentage
3. What is the mole fraction of the solute in a 1.00 m aqueous solution? *[AIPMT 2015]*
   (a) 0.177 (b) 1.770 (c) 0.0354 (d) 0.0177

Module-II Solubility, Vapour Pressure, Raoult's Law

4. The Henry's law constant (K_H) values of three gases (A, B, C) in water are $145, 2\times10^{-5}$ and 35 kbar respectively. The solubility of these gases in water follow the order *[NEET 2024]*
   (a) $B > A > C$
   (b) $B > C > A$
   (c) $A > C > B$
   (d) $A > B > C$
8. Which of the following statements is correct regarding a solution of two compounds A and B exhibiting positive deviation from ideal behaviour? *[NCERT (New) Pg. 13, NEET 2019]*
   (a) Intermolecular attractive forces between A—A and B—B are stronger than those between A—B.
   (b) $\Delta_{mix}H = 0$ at constant T and p.
   (c) $\Delta_{mix}V = 0$ at constant T and p.
   (d) Intermolecular attractive forces between A—A and B—B are equal to those between A—B.

Syllabus

UNIT I SOLUTIONS

Different methods for expressing the concentration of solution - molality, molarity, mole fraction, percentage (by volume and mass both), the vapour pressure of solutions and Raoult's law - Ideal and non-ideal solutions, vapour pressure-composition, plots for ideal and non-ideal solutions: Colligative properties of dilute solutions- a relative lowering of vapour pressure, depression of freezing point, the elevation of boiling point and osmotic pressure, Determination of molecular mass using colligative properties: Abnormal value of molar mass, van't Hoff factor and its significance.

UNIT II ELECTROCHEMISTRY

Electrolytic and metallic conduction, conductance in electrolytic solutions, molar conductivities and their variation with concentration: Kohlrausch's law and its applications. Electrochemical cells-Electrolytic and Galvanic cells, different types of electrodes, electrode potentials including standard electrode potential, half-cell and cell reactions, emf of a Galvanic cell and its measurement: Nernst equation and its applications: Relationship between cell potential and Gibbs' energy change: Dry cell and lead accumulator, Fuel cells.

UNIT III CHEMICAL KINETICS

Rate of a chemical reaction, factors affecting the rate of reactions: concentration, temperature, pressure and catalyst; elementary and complex reactions, order and molecularity of reactions. rate, law rate constant and its units, differential and integral forms of zero and first-order reactions, their characteristics and half-lives, the effect of temperature on the rate of reactions, Arrhenius theory, activation energy and its calculation, collision theory of bimolecular gaseous reactions (no derivation).

UNIT IV *p*-BLOCK ELEMENTS

Group 13 to Group 18 Elements

General Introduction: Electronic configuration and general trends in physical and chemical properties of elements across the periods and down the groups; unique behaviour of the first element in each group.

UNIT V *d*- AND *f*- BLOCK ELEMENTS

Transition Elements

General introduction, electronic configuration, occurrence and characteristics, general trends in properties of the first-row transition elements- physical properties, ionisation enthalpy, oxidation states, atomic radii, colour, catalytic behaviour, magnetic properties, complex formation. interstitial compounds, alloy formation: Preparation, properties, and uses of $K_2Cr_2O_7$, and $KMnO_4$.

Inner Transition Elements

Lanthanoids-Electronic configuration, oxidation states, and lanthanoid contraction.

Actinoids-Electronic configuration and oxidation states.

UNIT VI COORDINATION COMPOUNDS

Introduction to coordination compounds, Werner's theory; ligands. coordination number. denticity, chelation; IUPAC nomenclature of mononuclear co-ordination compounds, isomerism; Bonding-Valence bond approach and basic ideas of Crystal field theory, colour and magnetic properties; Importance of coordination compounds (in qualitative analysis, extraction of metals and in biological systems).

UNIT VII ORGANIC COMPOUNDS CONTAINING HALOGENS

General methods of preparation, properties, and reactions: Nature of C—*X* bond; Mechanisms of substitution reactions.
Uses: Environmental effects of chloroform, iodoform, freons, and DDT.

UNIT VIII ALCOHOLS, PHENOLS, AND ETHERS

General methods of preparation, properties, reactions, and uses.

Alcohols: Identification of primary, secondary, and tertiary alcohols: mechanism of dehydration.

Phenols: Acidic nature, electrophilic substitution reactions: halogenation, nitration and sulphonation. Reimer - Tiemann reaction.

Ethers: Structure.

UNIT IX ALDEHYDES, KETONES & CARBOXYLIC ACIDS

General methods of preparation, properties, reactions, and uses.

Nature of carbonyl group. Nucleophilic addition to $>C=O$ group. relative reactivities of aldehydes and ketones: Important reactions such as- Nucleophilic addition reactions (addition of HCN, NH_3 and its derivatives), Grignard reagent; oxidation: reduction (Wolff Kishner and Clemmensen); the acidity of α-hydrogen, aldol condensation. Cannizzaro reaction. Haloform reaction. Chemical tests to distinguish between aldehydes and ketones.

Carboxylic Acids: Acidic strength and factors affecting it.

UNIT X ORGANIC COMPOUNDS CONTAINING NITROGEN

General methods of preparation. Properties, reactions, and uses.

Amines: Nomenclature, classification, structure, basic character and identification of primary, secondary and tertiary amines and their basic character.

Diazonium Salts: Importance in synthetic organic chemistry.

UNIT XI BIOMOLECULES

General introduction and importance of biomolecules.

Carbohydrates - Classification, aldoses and ketoses: monosaccharides (glucose and fructose) and constituent monosaccharides of oligosaccharides (sucrose, lactose, and maltose).

Proteins - Elementary Idea of a-amino acids, peptide bond, polypeptides. Proteins: primary. secondary, tertiary, and quaternary structure (qualitative idea only), denaturation of proteins, enzymes.

Vitamins - Classification and functions.

Nucleic Acids - Chemical constitution of DNA and RNA. Biological functions of nucleic acids.

Hormones (General introduction).

UNIT XII PRINCIPLES RELATED TO PRACTICAL CHEMISTRY

Detection of extra elements (Nitrogen. Sulphur, halogens) in organic compounds: Detection of the following functional groups; hydroxyl (alcoholic and phenolic), carbonyl (aldehyde and ketones) carboxyl, and amino groups in organic compounds.

- The chemistry involved in the preparation of the following:
  Inorganic compounds; Mohr's salt, potash alum.
  Organic compounds: Acetanilide, p-nitro acetanilide, aniline yellow, iodoform.
- The chemistry involved in the titrimetric exercises - Acids, bases and the use of indicators, oxalic- acid *vs* $KMnO_4$ Mohr's salt vs $KMnO_4$
- Chemical principles involved in the qualitative salt analysis:
  Cations–Pb^{2+}, Cu^{2+}, Al^{3+}, Fe^{3+}, Zn^{2+}, Ni^{2+}, Ca^{2+}, Ba^{2+}, Mg^{2+}, NH_4^+
  Anions–CO_3^{2-} , S^{2-}, SO_4^{2-} , NO_3^- , NO^{2-}, Cl^-, Br^-, I^-(Insoluble salts excluded).

Chemical principles involved in the following experiments:

1. Enthalpy of solution of $CuSO_4$.
2. Enthalpy of neutralisation of strong acid and strong base.
3. Preparation of lyophilic and lyophobic sols.
4. Kinetic study of the reaction of iodide ions with hydrogen peroxide at room temperature.

Content

1. SOLUTIONS **1-51**

Module 1: Types and Concentration of Solutions 2-5

Step Up Practice 1 6-7

Module 2: Solubility, Vapour Pressure, Raoult's Law 8-13

Step Up Practice 2 14-15

Module 3: Colligative Properties (Part I) 15-17

Step Up Practice 3 18-19

Module 4: Colligative Properties (Part II) 20-25

Step Up Practice 4 26-27

- NEET Exclusive Extra Bytes 28
- Gearing Up For NEET 29-33
- Final Check Through PYQs 34-35
- Hints and Solutions 37-51

2. ELECTROCHEMISTRY **52-103**

Module 1: Electrochemical Cell 53-59

Step Up Practice 1 59-60

Module 2: Nernst Equation, Electrochemical Cell and Gibbs Energy of the Reaction 61-64

Step Up Practice 2 64-65

Module 3: Conductors, Conductance of Electrolytic Solutions and Kohlrausch's Law 66-71

Step Up Practice 3 71-72

Module 4: Electrolysis and Electrolytic Cell, Batteries and Corrosion 73-78

Step Up Practice 4 79-80

- NEET Exclusive Extra Bytes 80
- Gearing Up For NEET 81-87
- Final Check Through PYQs 88-90
- Hints and Solutions 91-103

3. CHEMICAL KINETICS **104-146**

Module 1: Chemical Reactions, Rate of a Chemical Reactions 105-107

Step Up Practice 1 108-109

Module 2: Rate Law and Rate Expression, Integrated Rate Equations 110-116

Step Up Practice 2 116-118

Module 3: Theories of Reaction Rate and Effect of Temperature and Catalyst on it 119-123

Step Up Practice 3 123-125

- NEET Exclusive Extra Bytes 125
- Gearing Up For NEET 126-131
- Final Check Through PYQs 132-134
- Hints and Solutions 135-146

4. *p*-BLOCK ELEMENTS **147-204**

Module 1: Boron Family 148-151

Step Up Practice 1 152-153

Module 2: Carbon Family 153-157

Step Up Practice 2 158

Module 3: Nitrogen Family 159-162

Step Up Practice 3 163-164

Module 4: Oxygen Family 164-167

Step Up Practice 4 168-169

Module 5: Halogen Family 169-175

Step Up Practice 5 176-177

Module 6: Noble Gases 177-179

Step Up Practice 6 179-180

- NEET Exclusive Extra Bytes 180
- Gearing Up For NEET 181-186
- Final Check Through PYQs 187-191
- Hints and Solutions 192-204

5. THE *d*- AND *f*- BLOCK ELEMENTS **205-245**

Module 1: The Transition Elements (*d*-Block) 206-212

Step Up Practice 1 213-214

Module 2: Some Important Compounds of *d*-block Elements 215-220

Step Up Practice 2 220-221

Module 3: *f*-Block Elements or Inner Transition Elements 222-226

Step Up Practice 3 227

- NEET Exclusive Extra Bytes 228
- Gearing Up For NEET 229-233
- Final Check Through PYQs 234-236
- Hints and Solutions 237-245

6. COORDINATION COMPOUNDS **246-283**

Module 1: Addition Compounds, Important Terms Related to Coordination Compounds, Nomenclature and Isomerism 247-254

Step Up Practice 1 254-255

Module 2: Bonding in Coordination Compounds (Part-I) 256-259

Step Up Practice 2 260-261

Module 3: Bonding in Coordination Compounds (Part-II) Metal Carbonyls, Importance of Coordination Compounds 261-265
Step Up Practice 3 266
- NEET Exclusive Extra Bytes 267
- Gearing Up For NEET 268-271
- Final Check Through PYQs 272-274
- Hints and Solutions 275-283

7. HALOALKANES AND HALOARENES 284-334
Module 1: Classification, Preparation and Physical Properties of Haloalkanes 285-290
Step Up Practice 1 291-292
Module 2: Chemical Reaction of Haloalkanes 293-298
Step Up Practice 2 299-301
Module 3: Preparation, Physical and Chemical Properties of Haloarenes 301-305
Step Up Practice 3 306-307
Module 4: Polyhalogen Compounds 308-310
- Step Up Practice 4 310
- NEET Exclusive Extra Bytes 311
- Gearing Up For NEET 312-319
- Final Check Through PYQs 320-321
- Hints and Solutions 323-334

8. ALCOHOLS, PHENOLS AND ETHERS 335-393
Module 1: Alcohols (Part I) 336-340
Step Up Practice 1 341-342
Module 2: Alcohols (Part-II) Chemical Reactions of Alcohols 343-347
Step Up Practice 2 347-349
Module 3: Phenols 349-356
Step Up Practice 3 356-358
Module 4: Ethers 358-361
Step Up Practice 4 362-363
- NEET Exclusive Extra Bytes 364
- Gearing Up For NEET 365-373
- Final Check Through PYQs 374-377
- Hints and Solutions 379-393

9. ALDEHYDES, KETONES AND CARBOXYLIC ACIDS 394-447
Module 1: Aldehyde and Ketones : Introduction & Methods of Preparation 395-400
Step Up Practice 1 400-402
Module 2: Aldehydes and Ketones : Chemical Reactions and Uses 402-408
Step Up Practice 2 409-411
Module 3: Carboxylic Acid 412-420
Step Up Practice 3 421-422
- NEET Exclusive Extra Bytes 423
- Gearing Up For NEET 424-429
- Final Check Through PYQs 430-434
- Hints and Solutions 435-447

10. AMINES 448-491
Module 1: Aliphatic Amines 449-454
Step Up Practice 1 455-456
Module 2: Aromatic Amines 457-461
Step Up Practice 2 462-463
Module 3: Diazonium Salts 464-466
Step Up Practice 3 467-468
- NEET Exclusive Extra Bytes 468
- Gearing Up For NEET 469-476
- Final Check Through PYQs 477-479
- Hints and Solutions 480-491

11. BIOMOLECULES 492-532
Module 1: Carbohydrates 493-498
Step Up Practice 1 499-500
Module 2: Proteins 501-505
Step Up Practice 2 505-506
Module 3: Enzymes, Hormones, Vitamins and Nucleic Acids 507-512
Step Up Practice 3 513-514
- NEET Exclusive Extra Bytes 515
- Gearing Up For NEET 516-521
- Final Check Through PYQs 522-523
- Hints and Solutions 525-532

12. PRINCIPLES RELATED TO PRACTICAL CHEMISTRY 533-567
Module 1: Principle of Qualitative Salt Analysis 534-545
Step Up Practice 1 546
Module 2: Chemistry Involved in Titration, Preparation of Inorganic Compounds 547-549
Step Up Practice 2 550-551
Module 3: Qualitative Analysis of Organic Compounds and Chemical Principles Involved in Some Important Experiments 551-556
Step Up Practice 3 556-557
- NEET Exclusive Extra Bytes 557
- Gearing Up For NEET 558-561
- Final Check Through PYQs 562
- Hints and Solutions 563-567

- **Practice Tests (1-3) 568-582**

For deeper insight
Scan the QR Code

Chapter 1

Solutions

Learning Objectives

Module-I

- Saturated and Unsaturated Solutions
- Dilute and Concentrated Solutions
- Gaseous Solutions
- Liquid Solutions
- Solid Solutions
- Concentration Terms
- Calculation of Normality and Molarity on Dilution
- Calculation of Normality and Molarity on Mixing
- Inter-Relation between Different Concentration of Solutions

Module-II

- Solubility of Gas in Liquid
- Henry's Law
- Solubility of Solid in Liquid
- Vapour Pressure of Liquid Solutions
- Raoult's Law
- Ideal and Non-Ideal Solution

Module-III

- Relative Lowering of Vapour Pressure
- Elevation in Boiling Point

Module-IV

- Depression in Freezing Point
- Osmosis and Osmotic Pressure
- Abnormal Molar Mass
- van't Hoff Factor

Chapter Overview with *NEET Connection*

This chapter is useful for the learning of various concentration terms and colligative properties. Without gripping this chapter, it will be difficult to solve various problems related to concentration terms used in other chapters of physical chemistry.

Special format question can be easily formed on following topics of this chapter.

- Expressing concentration of solutions.
- Henry's law
- Raoult's law
- Colligative properties
- van't Hoff factor

For better understanding of this chapter a grip over Raoult's law concentration of solutions and colligative properties is required.

As the foundation of colligative properties involves calculations. Hence, along with understanding of concepts, a focus on calculation part and basic conversion is also required.

Introduction

A solution is a homogeneous mixture of two or more than two components, whose composition can be varied with certain limits.

Generally, the solution contains two components called as solute and solvent.

The component which is present in excess amount is called **solvent** and the component which is present in lesser amount is called as **solute.**
In this chapter, we shall consider only binary solutions, i.e. consisting of two components.

Module 1

Types and Concentration of Solutions

• Saturated and Unsaturated Solutions • Dilute and Concentrated Solutions • Gaseous Solutions • Liquid Solutions • Solid Solutions • Concentration Terms • Calculation of Normality and Molarity on Dilution • Calculation of Normality and Molarity on Mixing • Inter-Relation between Different Concentration of Solutions

Types of Solutions

Solutions are classified on following two basis

1. On the basis of quantity of components, solutions are classified in the following way
   (i) **Saturated solution** It is the solution containing the maximum possible quantity of solute dissolved in a solvent at a certain temperature.
   (ii) **Unsaturated solution** It is the solution in which more amount of solute can be dissolved at a given temperature. It can be further divided into two types, i.e. dilute solutions and concentrated solutions.
      (a) **Dilute solution** Solution containing lower quantity of solute.
      (b) **Concentrated solution** Solution containing higher quantity of solute but still lower than the quantity of a saturated solution.
2. On the basis of physical states of components, there are three types of solutions which are tabulated below.

Types of Solutions

Types of solutions	Solute	Solvent	Examples
Gaseous solutions	Gas	Gas	Mixture of nitrogen and oxygen gases
	Liquid	Gas	Chloroform mixed with nitrogen gas, fog
	Solid	Gas	Camphor in nitrogen gas, dust or smoke
Liquid solutions	Gas	Liquid	Oxygen dissolved in water
	Liquid	Liquid	Ethanol dissolved in water
	Solid	Liquid	Glucose dissolved in water
Solid solutions	Gas	Solid	Solution of hydrogen in palladium
	Liquid	Solid	Amalgam of mercury with sodium
	Solid	Solid	Copper and gold alloy

Expressing Concentration of Solutions

The concentration of a solution is defined as the relative amount of a solute present in a solution.

The concentration of the solution may be expressed in any of the following ways

(i) **Mass percentage** (*w/w*) It is defined as mass of a component present in 100 g of the solution.

Mass percentage of a component

$$= \frac{\text{Mass of the component in the solution}}{\text{Total mass of the solution}} \times 100$$

e.g. 10% *w/w* solution of NaCl in water means that 10 g of NaCl is dissolved in 90 g of water resulting in a 100 g solution.

Example 1. *Calculate the mass percentage of benzene and carbon tetrachloride, if 22 g of benzene is dissolved in 122 g of* CCl_4.

Sol. Total mass of solution = (22 + 122) g = 144 g

$$\text{Mass \% of benzene} = \frac{\text{Mass of benzene in solution}}{\text{Total mass of solution}} \times 100$$

$$= \frac{22}{144} \times 100$$

$$= 15.28\%$$

$$\text{Mass \% of } CCl_4 = \frac{\text{Mass of } CCl_4 \text{ in solution}}{\text{Total mass of solution}} \times 100$$

$$= \frac{122}{144} \times 100$$

$$= 84.72\%$$

(ii) **Volume percentage** (*V/V*) It is defined as volume of a component present in 100 parts by volume of the solution.

Volume percentage of a component

$$= \frac{\text{Volume of the component}}{\text{Total volume of solution}} \times 100$$

(iii) **Mass by volume percentage** (w/V) It is the mass of solute dissolved in 100 mL of the solution.

e.g. A 10% solution of sodium chloride (w/V) means that 10 g of sodium chloride is dissolved in 100 mL of solution. This unit is commonly used in medicine and pharmacy.

(iv) **Parts per million** (ppm) It is defined as the number of parts of the component dissolved in one millionth part (10^6) of the total number of all components of the solution.

$$\text{ppm} = \frac{\text{Number of parts of the component}}{\text{Total number of parts of all components of the solution}} \times 10^6$$

Concentration in ppm can be expressed as mass to mass, volume to volume and mass to volume. The concentration of pollutants in water or atmosphere is often expressed in terms of μ g mL^{-1} or ppm.

(v) **Parts per billion** (ppb) It is the amount of solute, which is dissolved in 10^9 parts of a solution.

$$\text{ppb} = \frac{\text{Number of parts of the component}}{\text{Total number of parts of all components of the solution}} \times 10^9$$

(vi) **Mole fraction** (χ) It is defined as number of moles of one component divided by the total number of moles of all the components present in the solution. It is expressed by χ.

For example, in a binary solution containing two components A and B.

$$\text{Mole fraction of } A(\chi_A) = \frac{n_A}{n_A + n_B}$$

$$\text{Mole fraction of } B(\chi_B) = \frac{n_B}{n_A + n_B}$$

n_A = no. of moles of A, (Solute)

n_B = no. of moles of B, (Solvent)

Sum of mole fraction of solute and solvent is always unity

So, $\chi_A + \chi_B = 1$

Example 2. *What is the mole fraction of glucose in 10% w/w glucose solution ?*

Sol. Number of moles of glucose $(n_B) = \frac{10}{180}$

$= 0.0555$ mol

Number of moles of water $(n_A) = \frac{90}{18} = 5$ mol

$$\text{Mole fraction of glucose} = \frac{n_B}{n_A + n_B}$$

$$= \frac{0.0555}{5.0 + 0.0555} = 0.01$$

(vii) **Molality** (m) It is defined as the number of moles of solute dissolved in 1 kg of solvent. It is denoted by m.

$$m = \frac{\text{Number of moles of solute}}{\text{Mass of solvent (in kg)}}$$

or
$$m = \frac{\text{Mass of solute (in gram)}}{\text{Molar mass} \times \text{Mass of solvent (in kg)}}$$

$$m = \frac{w_B}{m_B \times W_A}$$

where, symbols have their usual meaning.

- If molality of a solution is one, it is called **molal solution.**
- Its unit is mol/kg.

NEET Close-up

Example Similar to PYQ Asked in NEET 2022

In 2 molal solution that contains 0.27 mole of a solute, there is

(a) 300 g of solvent (b) 350 g of solvent
(c) 135 g of solvent (d) 150 g of solvent

Sol. (c) We know that,

$$\text{Molality} = \frac{\text{Number of moles of solute}}{\text{Mass of the solvent (g)}} \times 1000$$

Given that, molality = 2 m

Moles of solute = 0.27 moles

$$\text{Then, } 2 = \frac{0.27}{\text{Mass of the solvent (g)}} \times 1000$$

Mass of the solvent (g) = 135 g of solvent

Skill Builder

In 4 molal solution that contains 3.27 mole for a solute, there is

(a) 817.5 g of solvent (b) 728.31 g of solvent
(c) 823.4 g of solvent (d) 6.23 g of solvent

For more practice Refer to Q. 3 and Q. 5 of Gearing up for NEET.

(viii) **Molarity** (M) It is defined as the number of moles of the solute present in one litre of the solution.

$$\text{Molarity } (M) = \frac{\text{Number of moles of solute}}{\text{Volume of solution (in L)}}$$

$$M = \frac{\text{Mass of solute (in g)}}{\text{Molar mass of solute} \times \text{Volume of solution (in L)}}$$

$$M = \frac{w_B}{m_B \times V \text{ (in L)}}$$

where, symbols have their usual meaning.

- When molarity of a solution is one, it is called **one molar solution.**
- Its unit is mol/L.

Example 3. 4.0 g *of* NaOH *is contained in a* 100 mL *of a solution. Calculate the following.*

(i) *Mole fraction of* NaOH
(ii) *Molality of* NaOH
(iii) *Molarity of* NaOH
[*Density of the solution is* 1.038 g/mL]

Sol. (i) Given,

Volume of the solution = 100 mL

Density = 1.038 g mL^{-1}

Mass of 100 mL of the solution = 1.038 × 100 = 103.8 g

Mass of NaOH = 4.0 g

Mass of water = (103.8 − 4) g = 99.8 g

Number of moles of water $= \frac{99.8}{18} = 5.54$

Mole fraction of NaOH $= \frac{0.1}{0.1 + 5.54} = 0.018$

(ii) Molality of NaOH (m)

$$m = \frac{w_B \times 1000}{m_B \times W_A \text{ (in g)}}$$

$$m = \frac{4 \times 1000}{40 \times 99.8}$$

$$m = 1.002 \text{ m}$$

(iii) Molarity of NaOH

$$M = \frac{w_B \times 1000}{m_B \times V \text{ (in mL)}}$$

$$M = \frac{4 \times 1000}{40 \times 100}$$

Molarity of the solution = 1 M

(ix) **Normality** (N) It is defined as the number of gram equivalents of substance dissolved per litre of the solution.

$$\text{Normality } (N) = \frac{\text{Number of g - equivalent of solute}}{\text{Volume of solution (in L)}}$$

$$= \frac{\text{Mass of solute (in g)}}{\text{Equivalent weight} \times \text{Volume (in L)}}$$

$$N = \frac{\text{Mass of solute } (w) \text{ (in g)}}{\text{Equivalent weight } (E) \times \text{Volume } (V) \text{ (in mL)}} \times 1000$$

$$N = \frac{w_B \times 1000}{E_B \times (V) \text{ (mL)}}$$

where, symbols have their usual meaning.

Unit = gram equivalents per litre.

(x) **Formality** (F) It is the number of gram formula present in a litre of solution for an ionic solute. It is denoted by F.

$$F = \frac{\text{Mass of solute (in gram)}}{\text{Formula mass} \times \text{Volume (in L)}}$$

It is applicable for ionic solids like NaCl.

NEET Snapshot

Out of molality, molarity, mole fraction and weight percentage, only Molarity is dependent on temperature. ***[NEET 2017]***

All concentration terms those are related with volume show temperature dependency while those which are independent of volume are temperature independent also because volume is a temperature dependent entity.

Example 4. *Calculate the formality of a solution of 58.5 g NaCl in 1 L of a solution.*

Sol. Formula mass of NaCl = 58.5 g

Gives mass = 58.5 g

$$\text{Formality} = \frac{\text{Mass of NaCl (in g)}}{\text{Formula mass} \times \text{Volume of solution (in L)}}$$

$$= \frac{58.5}{58.5 \times 1} = 1 \text{ F}$$

Calculation of Normality/Molarity on Dilution

If a solution is diluted from V_1 to V_2, the normality of that solution changes according to the equation

$$\underset{\text{Before dilution}}{N_1V_1} = \underset{\text{After dilution}}{N_2V_2}$$

Similarly, in terms of molarities, it can be given by the equation.

$$\underset{\text{Before dilution}}{M_1V_1} = \underset{\text{After dilution}}{M_2V_2}$$

Concept ladder

- Concentration of one molal aqueous solution is less than that of one molar aqueous solution.
- All concentration terms are thermodynamic intensive property.

Calculation of Normality/Molarity on Mixing

- If a solution of N_1 normality and V_1, volume is mixed with a solution of N_2 normality and V_2, volume of the same solute then normality of the final solution is given by

$$N_1V_1 + N_2V_2 = N_3V_3 \text{ [where, } V_3 = V_1 + V_2]$$

Similarly, in terms of molarities

$$M_1V_1 + M_2V_2 = M_3V_3$$

- If a solution of N_1 normality and V_1, volume is mixed with a solution of N_2 normality and V_2, volume of the different solute then normality of the final solution.

$$N_1V_1 - N_2V_2 = N_3V_3$$

Similarly, in terms of molarities

$$M_1V_1 - M_2V_2 = M_3V_3$$

Inter-Relation between Different Concentration of Solution

(i) Relation between Molality (m) and Mole fraction (χ)

$$m = \frac{\chi_B \times 1000}{\chi_A \times M_A}$$

m = molality

χ_A = mole fraction of solvent

χ_B = mole fraction of solute

M_A = molar mass of the solvent

Example 5. *A 'm' molal solution of a compound in benzene has mole fraction of solute equal to 0.2. The value of 'm' is*

(a) 3.2 (b) 1.2 (c) 4.3 (d) 2.4

Sol. (*a*) Calculation of m

$$m = \frac{\chi_B \times 1000}{\chi_A \times M_A}$$

$$\chi_B = 0.2$$

$$\chi_A = 1 - \chi_B = 0.8$$

$$m = \frac{0.2 \times 1000}{0.8 \times 78} = 3.205 \text{ molal}$$

(ii) Relation between Molality (m) and Molarity (M)

$$M = \frac{md \times 1000}{1000 + mm_B}$$

$$m = \frac{M \times 1000}{1000d - Mm_B}$$

where, M = molarity, m = molality, d = density (g mL^{-1})

m_B = molar mass of solute

Example 6. *Molarity of* H_2SO_4 *is 18 M. If density d is 1.8 g* cm^{-3}, *then its concentration in mol* kg^{-1} *will be*

(a) 50 (b) 500

(c) 18 (d) 5

Sol. (*b*) Molality (m) is related to molarity M by equation,

$$m = \frac{1000M}{1000d - Mm_B}$$

where, m_B is the molar mass of H_2SO_4.

$$m = \frac{1000 \times 18}{(1000 \times 1.8 - 18 \times 98)}$$

= 500 molal or 500 mol/kg

(iii) Relation between Normality and Molarity

Normality = n-factor × molarity

$N = n$-factor × M

(iv) Relation between Molarity (M) and mole fraction of the Solute (χ)

$$M = \frac{\chi_B \times d \times 1000}{\chi_A m_A + \chi_B m_B}$$

where, χ_A = mole fraction of solvent

χ_B = mole fraction of solute

m_A = molar mass of solvent

m_B = molar mass of solute

M = molarity

d = density of the solution (g mL^{-1})

Mentor's TIP

During the determination of mole fraction, if concentration of solution is given in terms of molality, then number of moles of solute will be equal to the concentration of solution.

STEP UP Practice 1

1. Which of the following is not the correct match pair?
(a) Gaseous solution — Camphor in nitrogen gas
(b) Liquid solution — Oxygen dissolved in water
(c) Solid solution — Solution of hydrogen in palladium
(d) Liquid solution — Amalgam of mercury with sodium

2. When a solute is present in trace quantities the expression that is used is
(a) molality (b) molarity
(c) mole fraction (d) parts per million

3. For a very diluted solution preferred concentration term is
(a) percentage of mass (b) molarity
(c) parts per million (d) molality

4. Given below are two statements one is labelled as Assertion (A) and the other is labelled as Reason (R).
Assertion (A) Amalgam of mercury with sodium is an example of solid solution.
Reason (R) Mercury is solvent and sodium is solute in the solution.
In the light of the above statements, choose the correct answer from the options given below.
(a) Both A and R are true and R is the correct explanation of A.
(b) Both A and R are true but R is not the correct explanation of A.
(c) A is true but R is false.
(d) A is false but R is true.

5. At 25°C, the density of 15 M H_2SO_4 is 1.8 g cm^{-3}. Thus, mass percentage of H_2SO_4 in aqueous solution is
(a) 1.8% (b) 60.2%
(c) 2.5% (d) 81.6%

6. 34.2 g of glucose is dissolved in 400 g of water. Percentage by mass of glucose solution is
(a) 8.5% (b) 7.9%
(c) 19.3% (d) 34.2%

7. A chemist prepared a solution by adding 160 g of methanol to 180 g of water. The mole fraction of methanol in the solution is
(a) 0.33 (b) 0.66 (c) 0.25 (d) 0.40

8. If 5.85 g of NaCl is dissolved in 90 g of water, the mole fraction of NaCl is
(a) 0.145 (b) 0.26
(c) 0.35 (d) 0.0196

9. A solution contains 1 mole of water and 4 mole of ethanol. The mole fraction of water and ethanol respectively will be
(a) 0.2 water and 0.8 ethanol
(b) 0.4 water and 0.6 ethanol
(c) 0.6 water and 0.4 ethanol
(d) 0.8 water and 0.2 ethanol

10. If 80 g of NaOH is mixed with 54 g of water to form a solution. Then the mole fraction of water will be
(a) $\frac{2}{5}$ (b) $\frac{1}{5}$ (c) $\frac{3}{5}$ (d) $\frac{4}{5}$

11. Given below are two statements one is labelled as Assertion (A) and the other is labelled as Reason (R).
Assertion (A) The sum of mole fractions of all the component of a solution is unity.
Reason (R) The mole fraction is a temperature dependent quantity.
In the light of the above statements, choose the correct answer from the options given below.
(a) Both A and R are true and R is correct explanation of A.
(b) Both A and R are true but R is not the correct explanation of A.
(c) A is true but R is false.
(d) A is false but R is true.

12. The normality of 0.3 M phosphorus acid (H_3PO_3) is
(a) 0.1 N (b) 0.9 N
(c) 0.03 N (d) 0.6 N

13. 10 N and $\frac{1}{10}$ N, solution, respectively is called
(a) decinormal and decanormal solution
(b) normal and decinormal solution
(c) normal and decanormal solution
(d) decanormal and decinormal solution

14. The amount of anhydrous Na_2CO_3 present in 250 mL of 0.25 M solution is
(a) 6.225 g (b) 66.25 g
(c) 6.0 g (d) 6.625 g

15. The molarity of 0.006 mole of NaCl in 100 mL solution is
(a) 0.600 (b) 0.050
(c) 0.006 (d) 0.06

16. If 1 M and 2.5 L, NaOH solution is mixed with another 0.5 M and 3 L NaOH solution, then molarity of the resultant solution will be .... M.
(a) 1.05 (b) 0.73 (c) 0.80 (d) 0.50

17. Given below are two statements, one is labelled as Assertion (A) and the other is labelled as Reason (R).
Assertion (A) 3.1500 g of hydrated oxalic acid dissolved in water to make 250.0 mL solution will result in 0.1 M oxalic acid solution.
Reason (R) Molar mass of hydrated oxalic acid is 126 g mol^{-1}.
In the light of the above statements, choose the correct answer from the options given below.
(a) Both A and R are true and R is the correct explanation of A.
(b) Both A and R are true but R is not the correct explanation of A.
(c) A is true but R is false.
(d) A is false but R is true.

18. Which of the following should be done in order to prepare 0.4 M NaCl from 100 mL of 0.3 M NaCl?
(a) Add 0.585 g of NaCl (b) Add 20 mL of water
(c) Add 0.1 mol of NaCl (d) Remove 10 mL of water

19. The number of moles of KCl in 1000 mL of 3 molar solution is
(a) 1 (b) 2 (c) 3 (d) 1.5

20. Which of the following modes of expressing concentration is independent of temperature?
(a) Molarity (b) Molality
(c) Formality (d) Normality

21. The molality of a solution is
(a) Number of moles of solute per 1000 mL of the solvent
(b) Number of moles of solute per 1000 g of the solvent
(c) Number of moles of solute per 1000 mL of the solution
(d) Number of gram equivalents of solute per 1000 mL of the solution

22. Which one of the following is an extensive property?
(a) Molar volume (b) Molarity
(c) Number of moles (d) Mole fraction

23. The concentration of a contaminant in ppm (*w*/*w*) that has been measured at 400 mg per 100 kg of sample is
(a) 40 ppm (b) 4 ppm
(c) 4000 ppm (d) 0.4 ppm

24. Normality of 2M sulphuric acid is
(a) 2 *N* (b) 4 *N* (c) $\frac{N}{2}$ (d) $\frac{N}{4}$

25. A solution of $[Al_2(SO_4)_3]$ [d = 1.252 g/mL] contain 22% salt by weight. The molarity, normality and molality of the solution are
(a) 0.805 M, 4.83 N, 0.825 m (b) 0.825 M, 48.3 N, 0.805 m
(c) 4.83 M, 4.83 N, 4.83 m (d) 4.85 M, 4.25 N, 4.82 m

26. The molality of 90% H_2SO_4 solution is [density = 1.8 g/mL]
(a) 91.84 m (b) 18.42 m
(c) 60.18 m (d) 94.32 m

27. If the molarity and molality of a solution of caustic soda are 12.12 M and 94.12 m respectively. Then, the density of the solution will be
(a) 1.213 g/mL (b) 0.421 g/mL
(c) 0.163 g/mL (d) 0.606 g/mL

28. Consider the statements given below.
(i) Normality and molality are extensive properties.
(ii) Normality and molarity are temperature dependent.
(iii) 98% (*w*/*w*) solution of H_2SO_4 means 98 g H_2SO_4 is present in 100 g of solution.
(iv) Normality = *n*-factor × molarity

Total number of correct statement(s) are
(a) 1 (b) 2
(c) 3 (d) 4

29. The molality of 15% (*w*/*V*) solution of H_2SO_4 with density 1.1 g/cm^3, is
(a) 1.23 (b) 2.42
(c) 2.87 (d) 1.61

30. Which of the following pair is not correct regarding molality?
(a) 50 g of glucose dissolved in 250 g of water — 1.11 m
(b) 40 g of ethanol dissolved in 200 g of water — 4.34 m
(c) 30 g of sodium chloride dissolved in 500 g of water — 2.02 m
(d) 25 g of potassium hydroxide (KOH) dissolved in 150 g of water — 2.97 m

31. Consider the statements given below.
(i) Normality of 0.5 M aqueous solution of $H_2C_2O_4.2H_2O$ is 1 N.
(ii) Molality of a solution is dependent on the temperature.
(iii) Molarity of a solution relates moles of solute and mass of solvent in kg.
(iv) Molality of 20% $\left(\frac{m}{m}\right)$ aqueous solution of KI is 1.51 mol/kg.
(v) Molarity and normality of pure water is not same.

Among the given statements the number of correct statements are
(a) 2 (b) 3
(c) 4 (d) 5

32. Which of the following is correct match?
(a) Temperature dependent and extensive property = Molarity
(b) Temperature dependent and intensive property = Molality
(c) Temperature independent and extensive property = Molarity
(d) Temperature independent and intensive property = Molality

33. The correct relationship between molality (m) and molarity (M) of a solution is (d = density in g/mL)
(a) $m = \frac{d}{M} - \frac{1000}{M_{(solute)}}$ (b) $\frac{1}{m} = \frac{M}{d} - \frac{1000}{M_{(solute)}}$
(c) $\frac{1}{m} = \frac{d}{M} - \frac{M_{(solute)}}{1000}$ (d) $\frac{1}{m} = \frac{d}{M} \times \frac{M_{(solute)}}{1000}$

Module 2

Solubility, Vapour Pressure, Raoult's Law

- Solubility of Gas in a Liquid
- Henry's Law
- Solubility of Solid in a Liquid
- Vapour Pressure of Liquid Solutions
- Raoult's Law
- Ideal and Non-ideal Solution

Solubility

It is defined as, maximum amount of a substance that can be dissolved in a specified amount of solvent at a specified temperature.

In this session we will study about the different cases of solubilities.

Solubility of a Gas in a Liquid

All gases are soluble in water as well as in other liquids to a greater or smaller extent, e.g. gases like H_2, O_2, N_2 etc. dissolves in water to a small extent whereas the gases like NH_3, HCl, SO_2 etc., are highly soluble in water.

The solubility of gases in liquids depends upon certain factors which are discussed below

(i) **Nature of the gas** The gases, which can be easily liquified are more soluble in common solvents, e.g. CO_2 is more soluble than H_2 and O_2 in water.

(ii) **Nature of the solvent** The gases which are capable of forming ions in aqueous solutions are much more soluble in water than in other solvents, e.g. gases like HCl and NH_3 are highly soluble in water but not in organic solvents in which they do not ionise.

(iii) **Effect of temperature** The solubility of gases in liquids decreases with an increase in temperature as dissolution is an exothermic process, i.e. it is accompanied by evolution of heat. Thus,

$$\text{Gas} + \text{Solvent} \longrightarrow \text{Solution} + \text{Heat}$$

By applying Le-Chatelier's principle, it is clearly evident that increase of temperature would shift the equilibrium in the backward direction, i.e. the solubility would decrease.

Mentor's TIP

The solubility of some sparingly soluble gases, such as hydrogen and inert gases, increases slightly with increase of temperature especially in the case of non-aqueous solvents such as hydrocarbons, alcohols and acetone.

(iv) **Effect of pressure** The solubility of gases increase with an increase in pressure. As pressure increases, gaseous molecules come closer and get easily solubilised in solvent. Solubility of gas in liquid varying with change in pressure is governed by the Henry's law.

Henry's Law

Henry proposed a quantitative relation between pressure and solubility of a gas in a solvent which is known as **Henry's law**. It states, "The solubility of a gas in a liquid at constant temperature is directly proportional to the partial pressure of the gas present above the surface of liquid or solution."

Alternatively The partial pressure of the gas in vapour phase (p) is proportional to the mole fraction of the gas (χ) in the solution.

$$p \propto \chi \text{ or } p = K_H \chi$$

Here, p = partial pressure of the gas in vapour phase

χ = mole fraction of the gas in the solution

K_H = Henry's law constant.

If we plot a graph between the partial pressure and the mole fraction of the gas in solution, a straight line would be observed.

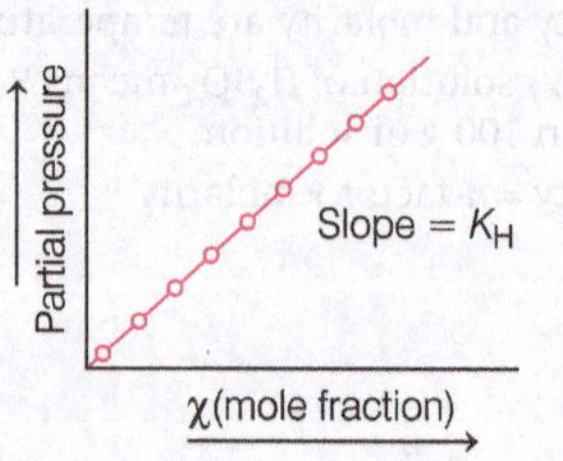

Graph between partial pressure and mole fraction

Different gases have different K_H values at same temperature. It can be understood from the following examples.

Henry's Law Constants for O_2 and N_2 in Water

Temperature (K)	K_H (kbar) for O_2	K_H (kbar) for N_2
293	34.86	76.48
303	46.82	88.84

Thus,

- K_H is a function of nature of the gas.
- Greater the value of K_H, lower is the solubility of the gas in the liquid at the same pressure.
- K_H increases with increase of temperature implying that solubility of gases decreases with increase of temperature at the same pressure.

NEET Close-up

Example Similar to PYQ Asked in NEET 2024

The Henry's law constant (K_H) values of three gases (X, Y, Z) in water are $144.97, 1.83 \times 10^{-5}$ and 1.67×10^{-6} kbar respectively. The solubility of these gases in water follows the order

(a) $X > Y > Z$ (b) $Y > Z > X$
(c) $X > Z > Y$ (d) $Z > Y > X$

Sol. (*d*) Higher the value of Henry' law constant (K_H) lower is the solubility of gas in water.

So, the order of solubility is $Z > Y > X$.

Skill Builder

The value of Henry' law constant for P, Q, R and S gases are 44, 69, 76 and 40 kbar respectively. The solubility of these gases in water at 293 K follows the order

(a) $P > Q > R > S$ (b) $R > Q > P > S$
(c) $S > P > Q > R$ (d) $Q > R > P > S$

For more practice Refer to Q.5 of step up practice-2.

Example 7. *H_2S is a toxic gas used in qualitative analysis. If solubility of H_2S in water is 0.195 mole kg^{-1}, what is the value of K_H?* (Assume $p = 0.987$ bar)

Sol. Number of moles of $H_2S = 0.195$ mol

Number of moles of $H_2O = \frac{1000}{18} = 55.5$ mol

Mole fraction of $H_2S = \frac{0.195}{0.195 + 55.5} = 0.0035$

Pressure exerted by $H_2S = 0.987$ bar

According to Henry's law, $p = K_H \chi$

$$K_H = \frac{p_{H_2S}}{\chi_{H_2S}} = \frac{0.987}{0.0035} = 282 \text{ bar}$$

Applications of Henry's Law

Henry's law finds several applications in industry and explains some biological phenomena. Some of these are

(i) **In production of carbonated beverages.** To increase the solubility of CO_2 in soft drinks and soda water, the bottle is sealed under high pressure.

(ii) **In deep sea diving.** Compressed air cylinder is used by scuba divers to get more oxygen in the blood but N_2 dissolved causes a disease called **decompression sickness.** Hence, air diluted with helium is used.

NEET Snapshot

Helium is used to dilute oxygen in diving apparatus because helium has high solubility in O_2. ***[NEET 2023]***

Helium has much less solubility in oxygen, due to which it prevents decompression sickness or bends caused by formation of nitrogen bubbles in blood.

Hence, the reason is incorrect but the statement written before the reason is correct.

(iii) **In the functioning of lungs.** In the lungs, partial pressure of O_2 is high. It combines with haemoglobin to form oxyhaemoglobin.

In the tissues, partial pressure of O_2 is low. Therefore, O_2 is released from oxyhaemoglobin for functions of the cells.

(iv) **For climbers or people living at high altitude.** At high altitudes, the partial pressure of O_2 is less than that at ground level. Concentration of O_2 in the blood and tissues is so low that they feel weak and are unable to think properly, a disease called **anoxia.**

Limitations

Although, it is an important law of solubility of gases but it is applied only, when

- pressure is not in excess.
- temperature is not at the lowest.
- gases are feebly soluble in solvent.
- the atomic state of gases is similar in both the liquid and gaseous states.

Solubility of a Solid in a Liquid

Every solid does not dissolve in a given liquid, e.g. NaCl and sugar dissolve readily in water while naphthalene and anthracene do not.

The following factors affect the solubility of a solid in a liquid.

(i) **Nature of solute and solvent** Generally, a solid dissolves in a liquid which is chemically similar to it. We can say this conveniently as 'like dissolves like.' In this regard, ionic compounds usually get dissolved in polar solvents, whereas covalent compounds are soluble in non-polar solvents.

(ii) **Effect of temperature** The dissolution can be exothermic or endothermic. The effect of temperature on solubility can be predicted by applying Le-Chatelier's principle. e.g. $NaNO_3$, KNO_3, NaCl, KCl etc. dissolve with the absorption of heat, i.e. their dissolution is **endothermic** ($\Delta_{sol} H > 0$).

Hence, their solubility increases with an increase in temperature.

$Li_2CO_3, Na_2CO_3 \cdot H_2O, Ce_2(SO_4)_3$ etc., dissolve with evolution of heat, i.e. their dissolution is **exothermic** ($\Delta_{sol}H < 0$).

Their solubility decreases with an increase in temperature.

(iii) **Effect of pressure** Pressure does not have any significant effect on solubility of solids in liquids. It is because solids and liquids are highly incompressible and practically remain unaffected by the pressure change.

Vapour Pressure of Liquid Solutions

Liquid solutions are the solutions in which liquid is the solvent. The solute can be a gas, liquid or a solid. We shall discuss the properties of binary solutions, i.e. solution of (i) liquids in liquids and (ii) solids in liquids.

The most important property of liquid-liquid solution is the vapour pressure. Total pressure exerted by the vapour above the liquid surface in equilibrium with the liquid at a given temperature is called **vapour pressure.**

Vapour pressure doesn't depend upon amount of liquid so it is an intensive property.

Vapour Pressure of Liquid-Liquid Solutions

The vapour pressure of liquid in liquid solutions can be explained by using Raoult's law as follows

Raoult's Law

The French Chemist, Francois Marte Raoult's in 1886 studied the vapour pressure of volatile solution.

Raoult's Law for Volatile Solution

This law states that "the partial pressure of any volatile constituent of a solution at a constant temperature is equal to the vapour pressure of pure constituent multiplied by the mole fraction of that constituent in the solution".

Let us assume that a mixture is prepared containing n_A and n_B moles of liquid A and B, respectively.

Further, let p_A and p_B be the partial pressures of A and B, respectively and p_A° and p_B° the vapour pressure in pure state.

Thus, according to Raoult's law,

$$p_A = p_A^\circ \chi_A$$
$$p_B = p_B^\circ \chi_B$$

Raoult's Law for Non-Volatile Solute

At a given temperature, vapour pressure of a non-volatile solute is equal to the partial vapour pressure of the solvent.

$$p_{\text{solution}} = p_{\text{pure solvent}} \times \text{Mole fraction of solvent}$$
$$p_S = p_A^\circ \chi_A$$

or
$$\frac{p_A^\circ - p_S}{p_A^\circ} = \chi_B$$

Here, $p_A^\circ - p_S$ (difference in vapour pressure of pure solvent and solution) represents the lowering in vapour pressure on the formation of solution. Now, by dividing the lowering in vapour pressure with the vapour pressure of the pure solvent, i.e. $(p_A^\circ - p_S)/p_A^\circ$ we get the **relative lowering in vapour pressure.**

The above relation also gives an alternative statement of Raoult's law. Thus, the **Raoult's law in its modified form** may be stated as :

"The relative lowering in vapour pressure of an ideal solution containing the non-volatile solute is equal to the mole fraction of the solute at a given temperature."

Example 8. *Benzene and toluene form nearly ideal solution. At a certain temperature, the vapour pressure of the pure benzene is* 150 torr *and of pure toluene is* 50 torr. *Calculate the vapour pressure of the solution containing equal weights of two substances at this temperature.*

Sol. Let the mass of benzene and toluene in the solution = w gram.

Molar mass of benzene = 78 g mol^{-1}

Molar mass of toluene = 92 g mol^{-1}

Moles of benzene = $\frac{w}{78}$

Moles of toluene = $\frac{w}{92}$

Mole fraction of benzene, $\chi_b = \dfrac{\frac{w}{78}}{\frac{w}{78}+\frac{w}{92}} = 0.541$

Mole fraction of toluene, $\chi_t = 1 - 0.541 = 0.459$

Partial vapour pressure of benzene,

$$p_b = p^\circ_b \times \chi_b$$
$$= 150 \times 0.541 = 81.15 \text{ torr}$$

Partial vapour pressure of toluene $= 50 \times 0.459$
$= 22.95$ torr

Total vapour pressure of solution $= p_b + p_T$
$= 81.15 + 22.95$
$= 104.1$ torr

NEET Close-up

Example Similar to PYQ Asked in NEET 2021

The correct option for the value of vapour pressure of a solution at 55°C with benzene to octane in molar ratio 4 : 3 is .... [At 55°C vapour pressure of benzene is 480 mm Hg and that of octane is 620 mm Hg]

(a) 545 mm Hg (b) 549 mm Hg
(c) 502 mm Hg (d) 540 mm Hg

Sol. (*d*) Molar ratio of benzene to octane, $\frac{n_B}{n_O} = \frac{4}{3}$

Let, $n_B = 4x$ mol, $n_O = 3x$ mol

Total number of moles = $7x$ mol

Mole fraction of benzene,

$$\chi_B = \frac{n_B}{n_B + n_O} = \frac{4x}{7x} = \frac{4}{7}$$

Mole fraction of octane,

$$\chi_O = \frac{n_O}{n_B + n_O} = \frac{3x}{7x} = \frac{3}{7}$$

By using the formula,

Total vapour pressure of solution,

$$p_s = \chi_B p^\circ_B + \chi_O p^\circ_O = \frac{4}{7} \times 480 + \frac{3}{7} \times 620$$

$= 274.28 + 265.71 = 539.99 \approx 540$ mm Hg

Skill Builder

Vapour pressure of a solution at 39°C with benzene to heptane in molar ratio 5 : 2 is [At 39°C vapour pressure of benzene is 496 mm Hg and that of heptane is 627 mm Hg]

(a) 433.24 mm Hg (b) 533.42 mm Hg
(c) 236.12 mm Hg (d) 539.11 mm Hg

For more practice Refer to Q.6 and Q.8 of Gearing up for NEET.

Relation between Dalton's Law and Raoult's Law

According to Dalton's law of partial pressure, the total pressure (p_{Total}) over the solution phase in the container will be the sum of the partial pressures of the components of the solution and is given as

$$p_{\text{Total}} = p_A + p_B$$

Substituting the values of p_A and p_B by using Raoult's law we get

$$p_{\text{Total}} = \chi_A p_A^\circ + \chi_B p_B^\circ$$
$$= (1 - \chi_B) p_A^\circ + \chi_B p_B^\circ$$
$$p_{\text{Total}} = p_A^\circ + (p_B^\circ - p_A^\circ)\chi_B$$

Thus, the following conclusions can be drawn from above equation.

- Total vapour pressure over the solution can be related to the mole fraction of any one component.
- Total vapour pressure over the solution varies linearly with the mole fraction of component *B*.
- Depending on the vapour pressures of the pure components *A* and *B*, total vapour pressure over the solution decreases or increases with the increase of the mole fraction of component *A*.

Raoult's Law as a Special Case of Henry's Law

According to Raoult's law, the vapour pressure of a volatile component in a given solution is proportional to its mole fraction in the solution.

i.e. $p_A \propto \chi_A$ or $p_A = p_A^\circ \cdot \chi_A$ ...(i)

According to Henry's law, in the solution of gas in liquids the partial pressure of the volatile component (gas) is proportional to its mole fraction in the solution.

$p_A \propto \chi_A$ or $p_A = K_H \cdot \chi_A$ ...(ii)

From equations (i) and (ii) it is obvious that, Raoult's law is a special case of Henry's law in which K_H becomes equal to p_A°.

Mentor's TIP

The **difference** and **similarity** between Raoult's law and Henry's law must be noted carefully.

- Both Raoult's law and Henry's law apply to **volatile component** in solution.
- Both state that the vapour pressure of one component is proportional to the mole fraction of that component.
- Raoult's law defines the proportionality constant as the vapour pressure of the pure component, whereas Henry's law defines the proportionality constant as some experimentally determined value.

Vapour Pressure of Solutions of Solids in Liquids

It is an important class of solution that consist of solid dissolved in liquid. Some of the physical properties of these solutions are quite different from the physical properties of pure solvent.

Vapour pressure of a solution of non-volatile solute is lower than that of pure solvent at the same temperature. The decrease in the vapour pressure of solvent depends on the quantity of non-volatile solute present in the solution, irrespective of its nature.

Ideal and Non-ideal Solutions

Liquid-liquid solutions can be classified into ideal and non-ideal solutions on the basis of Raoult's law.

Ideal Solutions

These are the solutions in which solute-solute and solvent-solvent interactions are almost similar to solute-solvent interactions (*A*—*B* = *A*—*A* or *B*—*B* interactions) and such solutions satisfy the following requirements.

- They obey Raoult's law for entire range of concentration at a given temperature.
- $\Delta_{mix}H = 0$
- $\Delta_{mix}V = 0$
- No dissociation or association takes place here.
- No chemical reaction between solute and solvent.
- It does not form azeotrope mixture.

NEET Snapshot

For an ideal solution ΔH_{mix} and ΔV_{mix} is zero, $\Delta p = p_{Observed} - p_{Raoult}$ but $\Delta S_{mix} \neq 0$ ***[AIPMT 2015]***

The entropy of mixing of ideal solutions is positive due to more molecular disorderness of solvent/solute in a solution.

Examples

1. Benzene + Toluene
2. *n*-hexane + *n*-heptane
3. Ethyl bromide + Ethyl iodide
4. Chlorobenzene + Bromobenzene
5. $CCl_4 + SiCl_4$

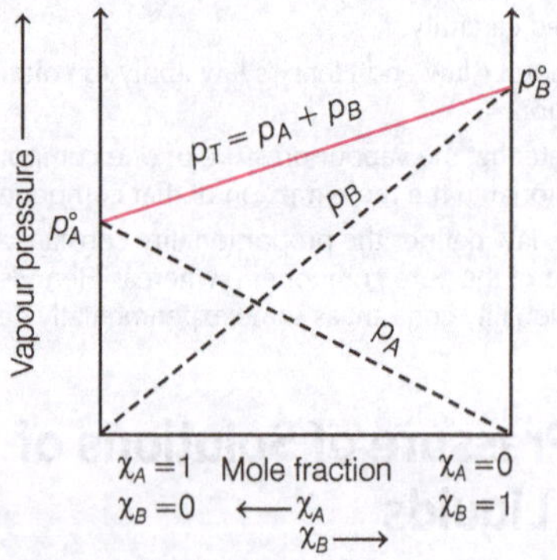

Non-ideal Solutions

Non-ideal solutions are the solutions in which solute-solvent interactions are different from solute-solute and solvent solvent interactions. These solutions do not obey Raoult's law. Such solution satisfy the following requirements for the entire range of concentrations.

1. $\Delta_{mix}H \neq 0$ 2. $\Delta_{mix}V \neq 0$

Types of Non-ideal Solutions

1. Non-ideal Solutions Showing Positive Deviations

When total vapour pressure for any solution is more than what is expected according to Raoult's law then positive deviation is seen. This happens when the new interactions are weaker than the interaction in the pure component (A—B < A—A or B—B interactions).

That is in this case of intermolecular attractive forces between the solute-solvent molecules are weaker than those between the solute-solute and solvent-solvent molecules. This means that in such solutions, molecules of A or B will find it easier to escape than in pure state. This will increase the vapour pressure and result in positive deviation.

$$\Delta_{mix}H = +ve, \Delta_{mix}V = +ve,$$
$$\Delta_{mix}S = +ve, (V.P)_{obs} > (V.P)_{exp}$$
$$p_A > p^\circ{}_A \cdot \chi_A, p_B > p^\circ{}_B \cdot \chi_B; p_T > p^\circ{}_A \chi_A + p^\circ{}_B \chi_B$$

Mixture of ethanol and acetone behave in this manner. In pure ethanol, molecules are hydrogen bonded. On adding acetone, its molecules gets in between the host molecules and break some of the hydrogen bonds between them. Due to weakening of interactions, the solution shows positive deviation from Raoult's law.

Examples

1. Acetone + Carbon disulphide
2. Acetone + Benzene
3. Carbon tetrachloride + Methanol
4. Ethanol + Water

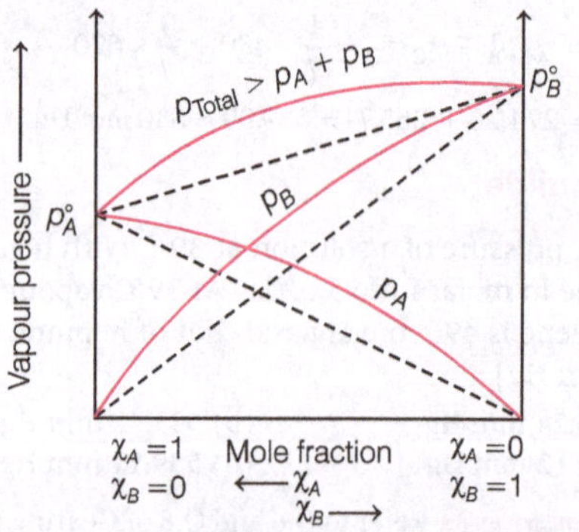

2. Non-ideal Solutions Showing Negative Deviations

When total vapour pressure for any solution is less than that expected from Raoult's law then **negative deviation** is seen. This happens when the new interactions are stronger than the interactions in the pure components (A—B > A—A or B—B interactions).

$$\Delta_{mix}H = -ve, \Delta_{mix}V = -ve,$$
$$\Delta_{mix}S = +ve, (V.P)_{obs} < (V.P)_{exp}$$
$$p_A < p^\circ{}_A \chi_A, p_B < p^\circ{}_B \chi_B; p_T < p^\circ{}_A \cdot \chi_A + p^\circ{}_B \cdot \chi_B$$

A mixture of chloroform and acetone forms a solution with negative deviation from Raoult's law. This is because chloroform molecule is able to form hydrogen bond and acetone molecule as shown.

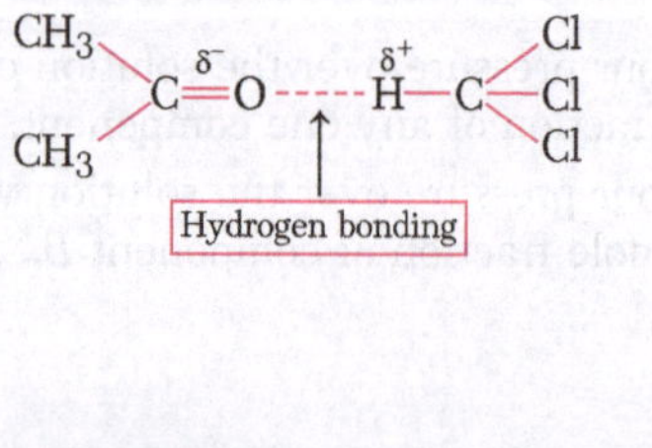

This decrease the escaping tendency of molecules for each component and consequently the vapour pressure decreases resulting in negative deviation from Raoult's law.

Examples

1. Chloroform + Benzene or diethyl ether
2. Acetone + Aniline
3. Nitric acid (HNO_3) + Water
4. Acetic acid + Pyridine

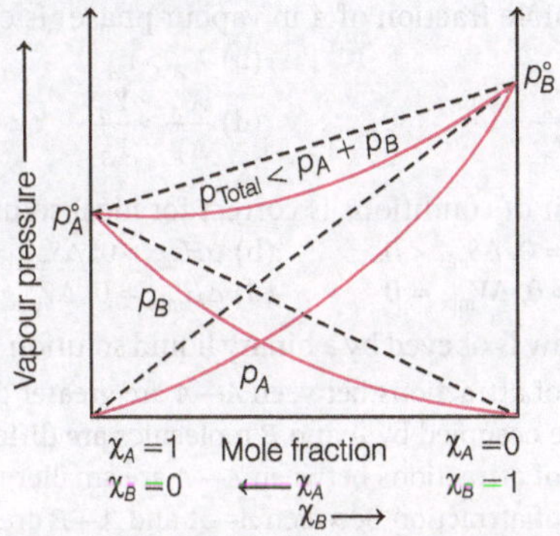

Azeotropic Mixture

It is a mixture of two liquids which boils at one particular temperature like a pure liquid and distils over in the same composition, i.e. these are **constant boiling mixture.**

These are formed by non-ideal solutions and are of two types

(i) **Minimum boiling azeotropes** The solutions whose boiling point is less than either of the two pure components. This is formed by the composition of a non-ideal solution showing the positive deviation from Raoult's law. e.g. Mixture of ethanol (B.P 351.3 K) and water (B.P 373 K) containing 95.4% ethanol forms azeotrope with B.P 351.15 K.

(ii) **Maximum boiling azeotropes** The solution whose boiling point is more than either of the two pure components. This is formed by the composition of a non-ideal solution showing negative deviation e.g. A mixture of nitric acid (B.P 359 K) and water (B.P 373 K) containing 68% nitric acid forms an azeotrope with B.P 393.5 K.

Comparision between Ideal and Non-ideal Solutions

Ideal solution	Positive deviation from Raoult's law	Negative deviation from Raoult's law
(a) Obey Raoult's law at entire range of concentration.	(a) Do not obey Raoult's law.	(a) Do not obey Raoult's law.
(b) $\Delta_{mix}V = 0$; total volume of solution is equal to the sum of volumes of the components.	(b) $\Delta_{mix}V \neq 0$. Volume is increased after dissolution.	(b) $\Delta_{mix}V \neq 0$. Volume is decreased during dissolution.
(c) $\Delta_{mix}H = 0$; neither heat is evolved nor absorbed during dissolution.	(c) $\Delta_{mix}H > 0$. Endothermic dissolution; heat is absorbed.	(c) $\Delta_{mix}H < 0$. Exothermic dissolution; heat is evolved.
(d) *A—A*, *A—B*, *B—B* interactions should be same, i.e. *A* and *B* are identical in shape, size, and character.	(d) *A—B* attractive force should be weaker than *A—A* and *B—B* attractive forces. *A* and *B* have different shape, size.	(d) *A—B* attractive force should be greater than *A—A* and *B—B* attractive froces, *A* and *B* have different shape, size and character.
(e) $p = p_A + p_B = p_A{}^\circ\chi_A + p^\circ{}_B\chi_B$ i.e. $p_T = p_A{}^\circ\chi_A$; $p_B{}^\circ\chi_B$	(e) $p_A > p_A{}^\circ\chi_A$; $p_B > p_B{}^\circ\chi_B$ $\therefore p_A + p_B > p_A{}^\circ\chi_A + p_B{}^\circ\chi_B$	(e) $p_A < p_A{}^\circ\chi_A$; $p_B < p_B{}^\circ\chi_B$ $\therefore p_A + p_B < p_A{}^\circ\chi_A + p_B{}^\circ\chi_B$
(f) Escaping tendency of *A* and *B* should be same in pure liquids and in the solutions.	(f) *A* and *B* escape easily showing higher vapour pressure than the expected value.	(f) Escaping tendency of both components *A* and *B* is lowered showing lower vapour than expected ideally.
Examples Benzene + Toluene *n*-hexane + *n*-heptane Chlorobenzene + Bromobenzene Ethyl bromide + Ethyl iodide *n*-butyl chloride + *n*-butyl bromide	**Examples** Acetone + Ethanol Acetone + CS_2 Water + Methanol Water + Ethanol CCl_4 + Toluene CCl_4 + $CHCl_3$ Acetone + Benzene CCl_4 + CH_3OH Cyclohexane + Ethanol	**Examples** Acetone + Aniline Acetone + Chloroform $CH_3OH + CH_3COOH$ $H_2O + CH_3COOH$ Chloroform + Diethyl ether Water + HCl Acetic acid + Pyridine Chloroform + Benzene

Mentor's TiP

1. Mixture of hydrocarbon + hydrocarbon, alkyl halide + alkyl halide or aryl halide + aryl halide are always ideal solution.
2. Alcohols show a positive deviation and acids show a negative deviation when mixed with water.
3. $\Delta_{mix} S$ is always positive for ideal and non-ideal solution.
4. $\Delta_{mix} G$ is always negative for ideal and non-ideal solution.

STEP UP Practice 2

1. Solubility of a gas in a liquid solvent decreases with
(a) decrease in temperature only
(b) decrease of pressure only
(c) decrease of temperature as well as pressure
(d) increase of temperature and decrease of pressure

2. Which of the following salts shows a decrease in the solubility if the temperature is increased?
(a) NH_4NO_3 (b) $NaNO_3$ (c) NaCl (d) Li_2CO_3

3. The value of Henry's law constant K_H
(a) increases with increase in temperature
(b) is greater for gases with higher solubilities
(c) increases with the atomicity of the gas
(d) first decreases then increases with temperature

4. The solubility of pure He(g) at 25°C and 1 atm is 6.8×10^{-4} mol L^{-1}. If the partial pressure of He(g) in the atmosphere is 0.34 atm, the concentration of He(g) dissolved in water under atmospheric conditions is
(a) 2.313×10^{-4} M (b) 3.712×10^{-3} M
(c) 8.219×10^{-4} M (d) 6.820×10^{-4} M

5. The value of Henry's law constant for helium (He), hydrogen (H_2) and oxygen (O_2) are respectively 144.97 kbar, 69.16 kbar and 34.86 kbar at 293 K. The correct order of their solubility is
(a) $O_2 < He < H_2$ (b) $He < O_2 < H_2$
(c) $He < H_2 < O_2$ (d) $H_2 < He < O_2$

6. If N_2 is bubbled through H_2O at 293 K, millimoles of $N_2(g)$ dissolving in 1 L of water would be
[Assume : $K_H = 70$ kbar, $p_{N_2} = 1$ bar]
(a) 0.65 (b) 0.83 (c) 0.91 (d) 0.77

7. The vapour pressure of pure liquids A and B are 450 mm and 900 mm at 450 K. If total vapour pressure is 800 mm Hg, then the mole fraction of B in vapour phase is
(a) 0.96 (b) 0.88 (c) 0.75 (d) 0.60

8. Given below are two statements, one is labelled as Assertion (A) and the other is labelled as Reason (R).
Assertion (A) If a liquid solute, more volatile than the solvent, is added to the solvent, the vapour pressure of the solution may increase, i.e. $p_S > p°$.
Reason (R) In the presence of a more volatile liquid solute, only the solute will form the vapours not the solvent.
(a) Both A and R are true and R is the correct explanation of A.
(b) Both A and R are true but R is not the correct explanation of A.
(c) A is true but R is false.
(d) A is false but R is true.

9. A mixture contains 1 mole of volatile liquid $A(p_A^\circ = 100$ mm Hg) and 4 moles of volatile liquid $B(p_B^\circ = 90$ mm Hg). If solution behave ideally, total vapour pressure of the distillate is approximately
(a) 90 mm Hg (b) 96 mm Hg
(c) 92 mm Hg (d) 98 mm Hg

10. The vapour pressure of a pure liquid increases when
(a) temperature is decreased (b) temperature is increased
(c) concentration is increased (d) concentration is decreased

11. For an ideal binary liquid solution with $p°_A > p°_B$ which relation between X_A (mole fraction of A in liquid phase) and Y_A (mole fraction of A in vapour phase) is correct?
(a) $X_A = Y_A$ (b) $X_A > Y_A$
(c) $\frac{X_A}{X_B} < \frac{Y_A}{Y_B}$ (d) $\frac{X_A}{X_B} > \frac{Y_A}{Y_B}$

12. Which pair of conditions is correct for ideal solution?
(a) $\Delta H_{mix} = 0, \Delta S_{mix} < 0$ (b) $\Delta H_{mix} > 0, \Delta S_{mix} = 0$
(c) $\Delta H_{mix} > 0, \Delta V_{mix} = 0$ (d) $\Delta H_{mix} = 0, \Delta V_{mix} = 0$

13. Raoult's law is obeyed by a binary liquid solution (AB) when
(a) forces of attractions between A—A are greater than A—B
(b) volume occupied by A and B molecules are different
(c) forces of attractions between A—A are smaller than A—B
(d) forces of attraction between A—A and A—B are identical

14. Which of the following pairs shows a negative deviation from Raoult's law?
(a) Acetone-benzene (b) Acetone-ether
(c) Acetone-chloroform (d) Benzene-methanol

15. Given below are two statements one is labelled as Assertion (A) and the other is labelled as Reason (R).
Assertion (A) Ethanol and water escape easily showing higher vapour pressure than predicted by Raoult's law.
Reason (R) Water and ethanol form non-ideal solution with negative deviation from Raoult's law.
(a) Both A and R are true and R is the correct explanation of A.
(b) Both A and R are true but R is not the correct explanation of A.
(c) A is true but R is false.
(d) A is false but R is true.

16. Which pair shows a positive deviation from Raoult's law?
(a) Acetone-chloroform (b) Benzene-methanol
(c) Water-nitric acid (d) Water-hydrochloric acid

17. Among the given species,
(i) ΔG_{mix} (ii) ΔS_{mix} (iii) ΔP
(iv) ΔH_{mix} (v) ΔV_{mix}
How many of them is less than zero for an ideal solution?
(a) 1 (b) 2 (c) 3 (d) 4

18. Consider the given concentrations
(i) 1 m NaCl (ii) 1 m Urea (iii) 1 m Glucose
(iv) 1 m Sucrose (v) 1 M Water
In how many cases, Raoult's law is not applicable?
(a) 1 (b) 3 (c) 2 (d) 4

19. A maximum boiling azeotrope is a non-ideal solution which
(a) shows negative deviation from Raoult's law
(b) has fixed composition at any pressure
(c) can be completely separated using fractional distillation
(d) shows no deviation from Raoult's law

20. Given below are two statements one is labelled as Assertion (A) and the other is labelled as Reason (R).

Assertion (A) A maxima or minima obtained in the temperature composition curve of an azeotropic mixture of two liquids.

Reason (R) An azeotropic mixture boil at particular temperature without changing its composition.

(a) Both A and R are true and R is the correct explanation of A.
(b) Both A and R are true but R is not the correct explanation of A.
(c) A is true but R is false.
(d) A is false but R is true.

21. Among the given compounds,
(i) Benzene + Toluene
(ii) *n*-hexane + *n*-heptane
(iii) $CCl_4 + CHCl_3$
(iv) Ethyl bromide + Ethyl iodide
(v) HCl + Water

How many compounds form maximum boiling azeotropes?

(a) 3 (b) 1
(c) 4 (d) 2

Module 3

Colligative Properties (Part I)

- Relative Lowering of Vapour Pressure
- Elevation in Boiling Point

The properties of a dilute solution, which depend only upon the number of particles present in a solution and their concentration are called **colligative properties.** (colligative : from Latin : *co* means together, *ligare* means to bind). They depend on the dative fraction of solute and solvent particles but not on the chemical nature of solute, i.e. these are proportional to the number of solute particles in the solution.

There are following four types of colligative properties.

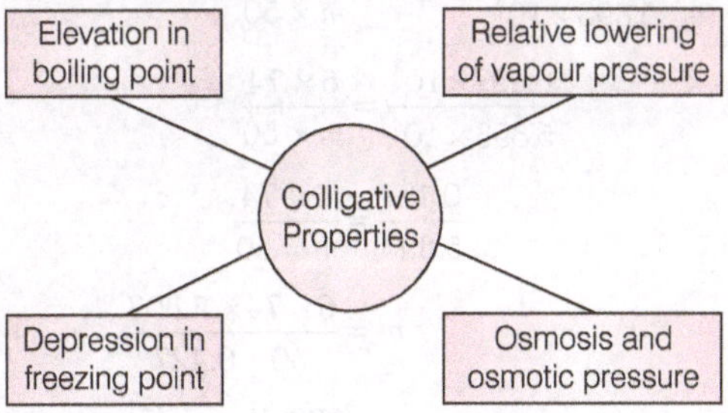

Mentor's TIP

For applying the formulae of colligative properties, the following conditions should be satisfied

- The solution should be very dilute.
- The solute should be non-volatile.
- The solute does not dissociate or associate in the solution.

In the following session we will discuss these properties one by one.

Relative Lowering of Vapour Pressure

When a non-volatile solute is mixed with a volatile solvent, the vapour pressure of solution (p) becomes less than the vapour pressure of pure solvent (p_A°). It is called lowering of vapour pressure.

- The lowering of vapour pressure $= p^\circ{}_A - p_S = \Delta p$
- The ratio of the lowering of vapour pressure and the vapour pressure of pure solvent is defined as the relative lowering of vapour pressure.

$$\frac{p^\circ{}_A - p_S}{p^\circ{}_A} = \text{Relative lowering of vapour pressure}$$

According to Raoult's law,

$$\frac{p^\circ{}_A - p}{p^\circ{}_A} = \chi_B = \frac{n_B}{n_A + n_B}$$

Here, n_A and n_B are the number of moles of solvent and solute respectively, present in the solution.

For a dilute solution $n_B <<< n_A$

$$\frac{p^\circ{}_A - p}{p^\circ{}_A} = \frac{n_B}{n_A}$$

Determination of Molar Mass of Solute

Generally on the basis of Raoult's law, molecular weight of solute in dilute solution can be given by

$$\frac{p^\circ_A - p}{p^\circ_A} = \frac{n_B}{n_A} = \frac{w_B M_A}{W_A M_B}$$

where, w_B = mass of solute, M_B = molar mass of solute

W_A = mass of solvent, M_A = molar mass of solvent

NEET Close-up

Example Similar to PYQ Asked in NEET 2020

If 10 g of a non-electrolyte solute is dissolved in 100 g of *n*-heptane to reduce its vapour pressure to 70%, the molar mass (in g mol^{-1}) of the solute is [Given that, molar mass of *n*-heptane is 100 g mol^{-1}]

(a) 25.21 (b) 25
(c) 30 (d) 23.33

Sol (*d*) Here, relative lowering of given vapour pressure is,

$$\frac{\Delta p}{p^\circ} = 0.3$$

Now, $$\frac{\Delta p}{p^\circ} = \chi_B = \frac{n_B}{n_B + n_A} = \frac{\frac{w_B}{M_B}}{\frac{w_B}{M_B} + \frac{W_A}{M_A}}$$

Given, Mass of solute $(w_B) = 10$ g

Mass of solvent $(W_A) = 100$ g

Molar mass of solute $(M_B) = ?$

Molar mass of solvent (*n*-heptane) $(M_A) = 100$ g/mol

So, $$0.3 = \frac{10/M_B}{\frac{10}{M_B} + \frac{100}{100}} \Rightarrow M_B = 23.33 \text{ g mol}^{-1}$$

Skill Builder

12 g of a non-electrolyte solute is dissolved in 130 g of benzene to reduce its vapour pressure to 80%, the molar mass (in g mol^{-1}) of the solute is [Given that, molar mass of benzene is 78 g mol^{-1}]

(a) 29 (b) 30
(c) 25 (d) 25

For more practice Refer to Q.14 and Q.19 of Gearing up for NEET.

Example 9. *Vapour pressure of water at 20°C is 17.5 mm of Hg and lowering of vapour pressure of a sugar solution is 0.061 mm of Hg. Calculate*

(i) relative lowering of vapour pressure.

(ii) vapour pressure of the solution.

(iii) mole fraction of sugar and water.

Sol. (i) **Calculation of relative lowering of vapour pressure**

Vapour pressure of water $(p^\circ_A) = 17.5$ mm of Hg

Lowering of vapour pressure $(p^\circ_A - p) = 0.061$

∴Relative lowering of vapour pressure,

$$\frac{p^\circ_A - p}{p^\circ_A} = \frac{0.061}{17.5} = 0.00348$$

(ii) **Calculation of vapour pressure of solution**

p = Vapour pressure of solvent − Lowering in vapour pressure

$= 17.5 - 0.061 = 17.439$ mm of Hg

(iii) **Calculation of mole fraction of sugar and water**

Mole fraction of sugar, χ_B (solute)

$$\frac{p^\circ_A - p}{p^\circ_A} = \chi_B$$

Here, $$\frac{p^\circ_A - p}{p^\circ_A} = 0.00348$$

∴Mole fraction of sugar, $\chi_B = 0.00348$

Mole fraction of water,

$$\chi_A = 1 - \chi_B = 1 - 0.00348 = 0.9965$$

Example 10. *A solution containing* 6.0 *gram of benzoic acid in* 50 *gram of ether* $(C_2H_5OC_2H_5)$ *has a vapour pressure equal to* 5.466×10^4 *mm of Hg at 300 K. Given that vapour pressure of ether at the same temperature is* 5.893×10^4 *mm of Hg, calculate the molecular mass of benzoic acid.*

Sol. Vapour pressure of ether (solvent) $= p^\circ$

$= 5.893 \times 10^4$ mm of Hg

Vapour pressure of benzoic acid in ether solution

$= p = 5.466 \times 10^4$ mm of Hg

Molecular mass of solvent $(C_2H_5 - O - C_2H_5)$ $(M) = 74$ g/mol

Mass of solute (benzoic acid) $w = 6$ gram

Mass of solvent (ether) $W = 50$ gram

Let molecular mass of solute (benzoic acid) $= m$

Substituting the values in the relation

$$\frac{p^\circ_A - p}{p^\circ_A} = \frac{w}{m} \times \frac{M}{W}$$

$$\frac{5.893 \times 10^4 - 5.466 \times 10^4}{5.893 \times 10^4} = \frac{6 \times 74}{m \times 50}$$

$$\frac{0.427 \times 10^4}{5.893 \times 10^4} = \frac{6 \times 74}{m \times 50}$$

$$\frac{0.427}{5.893} = \frac{6 \times 74}{m \times 50}$$

$$m = \frac{6 \times 74 \times 5.893}{50 \times 0.427}$$

$$m = 122.55 \text{ g mol}^{-1}$$

Elevation in Boiling Point

The boiling point of a liquid is that temperature at which its vapour pressure becomes equal to the atmospheric pressure. When a non-volatile solute is dissolved in a pure solvent, its vapour pressure is decreased and boiling point increases. The difference in boiling points of the solution and pure solvent is called **elevation of boiling point** (ΔT_b).

- If $T°_b$ is the boiling point of pure solvent and T_b is the boiling point of the solution then, $T_b > T°_b$ and the elevation in boiling point, $\Delta T_b = T_b - T°_b$

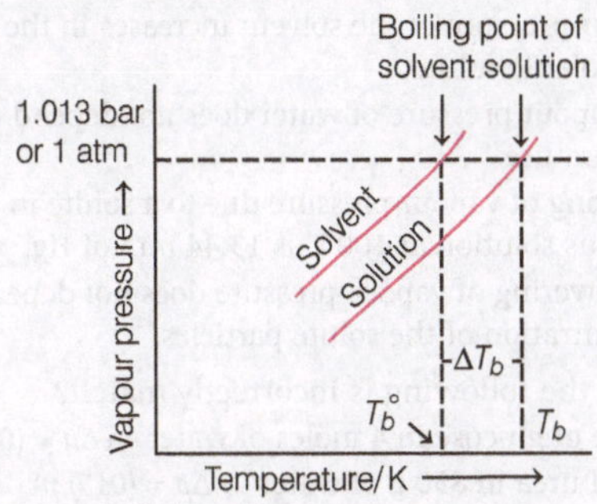

Graph showing ΔT_b elevation of boiling point of a solvent in a solution

The vapour pressure curve for solution lies below the curve for solvent. The diagram shows that ΔT_b denotes the elevation in boiling point of a solvent in solution.

It has been found out experimentally that the elevation in the boiling point (ΔT_b) of a solution is proportional to the molal concentration of the solute in a solution, i.e.

$$\Delta T_b \propto m \text{ or } \Delta T_b = K_b m \quad ...(1)$$

- Here, m (molality) is the number of moles of solute dissolved in 1 kg of solvent and K_b is called **boiling point elevation constant** or **molal elevation constant (Ebullioscopic constant).**

If $m = 1$ then $\Delta T_b = K_b$

Thus, **molal elevation constant** is defined as the elevation in boiling point for 1 molal solution, i.e. a solution containing 1 gram mole of solute dissolved in 1000 g of the solvent.

- The unit of K_b is K kg mol^{-1}.
- The values of K_b which depends upon the nature of the solvent, can be calculated by using,

$$K_b = \frac{R \times M_1 \times (T_b)^2}{1000 \times \Delta_{vap}H}$$

Here, R = gas constant

M_1 = molar mass of the solvent

T_b = boiling point of solution

$\Delta_{vap}H$ = enthalpy for vaporisation.

T_b° = normal boiling point of pure solvent

Determination of Molar Mass of Solute

If w_2 gram of solute of molar mass M_2 is dissolved in W_1 gram of solvent, then equation (1) is given by

$$\Delta T_b = \frac{K_b \times 1000 \times w_2}{M_2 \times W_1}$$

or $$M_2 = \frac{1000 \times w_2 \times K_b}{\Delta T_b \times W_1}$$

Example 11. *A solution containing 0.456 g of camphor (molar mass = 152 g/mol) dissolved in 3.14 g of acetone (BP = 56.30°C), if the molal elevation of acetone is 1.72°C kg mol^{-1}, then calculate the boiling point of the solution.*

Sol. We have, $\Delta T_b = \dfrac{1000 K_b \times w_2}{W_1 \times m_2}$

$$= \frac{1000 \times 1.72 \times 0.456}{3.14 \times 152} = 1.64°C$$

$\therefore$ Boiling point of solution $(T_b) = T°_b + \Delta T_b$

$= 56.30°C + 1.64°C$

$= 57.94°C$

Example 12. *A solution containing 0.730 g of camphor (molar mass =152 g/mol) in 36.8 g of acetone (B.P. 56.30°C) boils at 56.55°C. A solution of 0.564 g of an unknown compound in the same weight of solvent boils at 56.46°C. Calculate the molar mass of the unknown compound.*

Sol. In this problem, the value of K_b is not given. The first data is used to calculate K_b which is to be used to calculate the molar mass in the second data.

(i) **Calculation of K_b for acetone**

$$K_b = \frac{\Delta T_b M_B W_A}{w_B \times 1000}$$

$\Delta T_b = 56.55 - 56.30 = 0.25°C,$

$M_B = 152, w_B = 0.730, W_A = 36.8$ g

$$\therefore \quad K_b = \frac{0.25 \times 152 \times 36.8}{0.730 \times 1000}$$

$= 1.92$ K kg mol^{-1}

(ii) **Calculation of molar mass of unknown compound**

$$M_B = \frac{K_b \times 1000 \times w_B}{\Delta T_b \times W_A}$$

$K_b = 1.92$ K kg mol^{-1}

$\Delta T_b = 56.46 - 56.30 = 0.16°C$

$w_B = 0.564$ g, $W_A = 36.8$ g

$$M_B = \frac{1.92 \times 1000 \times 0.564}{0.16 \times 36.8} = 183.9 \text{ g/mol}$$

STEP UP Practice 3

1. When 5 g of a non-volatile solute is dissolved in 58 g of water, the relative lowering of vapour pressure observed is 0.019. Molecular weight of the substance in g/mol is
(a) 18 (b) 96
(c) 47 (d) 80

2. Which of the following statement is correct?
(a) The vapour pressure of a solvent in solution is more than that of pure solvent.
(b) The lowering of vapour pressure depends only on the identity of the solute particles.
(c) The lowering of the vapour pressure depends on the sum of the mole fraction of same solutes.
(d) Lowering of vapour pressure takes place in both ideal and non-ideal solution.

3. A sample of 30 g of a compound (molar mass 128 g/mol) which is a non-electrolyte is dissolved in 10.0 gram of ethanol. If the vapour pressure of pure ethanol at the temperature used is 0.250 atm, what is the vapour pressure of ethanol in the above solution?
(a) 0.215
(b) 0.123
(c) 1.312
(d) 2.120

4. Given below are the two statements.
Statement I For dilute solutions, relative lowering of vapour pressure may be written as,
$$\frac{p^\circ_1 - p_1}{p^\circ_1} = \frac{n_2}{n_1 + n_2}$$
Statement II The vapour pressure of an aqueous solution of sucrose is less than 1.013 bar at 373.15 K.
In the light of the above statements, choose the correct answer from the options given below.
(a) Both Statement I and Statement II are false.
(b) Statement I is true but Statement II is false.
(c) Statement I is false but Statement II is true.
(d) Both Statement I and Statement II are true.

5. The amount of solute (molar mass 60 g mol^{-1}) that must be added to 186 g of water so that the vapour pressure of water is lowered by 20% is
(a) 124 g (b) 120 g
(c) 130 g (d) 136 g

6. The vapour pressure of pure liquid solvent is 0.60 atm. When a non-volatile solute *B* is added to the solvent, its vapour pressure drops to 0.40 atm. Thus, mole fraction of the compound *B* is
(a) 0.43 (b) 0.41
(c) 0.33 (d) 0.23

7. Select the correct statement from the following.
(a) Vapour pressure of the solvent increases in the presence of non-volatile solute.
(b) The vapour pressure of water does not depend upon the temperature.
(c) Lowering of vapour pressure due to a solute in 1 molal aqueous solution at 100°C is 13.44 mm of Hg.
(d) The lowering of vapour pressure does not depend on the concentration of the solute particles.

8. Which of the following is incorrectly match?
(a) 1 mole of glucose in 4 moles of water $\rightarrow \Delta p = (0.25)\, p^\circ$
(b) 50 g of urea in 850 g of water $\rightarrow \Delta p = (0.17)\, p^\circ$
(c) 40 g of glucose in 350 g of water $\rightarrow \Delta p = (0.011)\, p^\circ$
(d) 80 g of sucrose in 420 g of water $\rightarrow \Delta p = (0.0097)\, p^\circ$

9. The relative lowering of the vapour pressure of an aqueous solution containing a non-volatile solute is 0.0325. The molality of the solution is
(a) 1.805 (b) 0.283
(c) 1.324 (d) 2.314

10. Which of the following statement is incorrect?
(a) The elevation of boiling point depends on the number of solute molecules.
(b) For dilute solutions the elevation of boiling point is directly proportional to the molal concentration of the solute in a solution.
(c) The vapour pressure of a liquid decrease with increase of temperature.
(d) The boiling point of a solution is always higher than that of the pure solvent.

11. A solution containing 0.4316 g of ethylene glycol (molar mass = 62 g/mol) in 40 mL of CCl_4 shows boiling point deviation of 0.502°C. While a solution of 0.8216 g of an unknown solute in the same mass of solvent gave a boiling point elevation of 0.647°C. The molar mass of unknown solute is
(a) 90 g/mol (b) 92 g/mol
(c) 95 g/mol (d) 97 g/mol

12. Which of the following statement is true when a mixture of two immiscible liquids at a constant pressure of 1 atm boils at a temperature ?
(a) Equal to the normal boiling point of more volatile liquid.
(b) Equal to the mean of the normal boiling point of the two liquids.
(c) Greater than the normal boiling point of either of the liquid.
(d) Smaller than the normal boiling point of either of the liquid.

13. A solution containing 5.8 g of a substance in 138 g benzene (b.p. 80°C) boils at 90.77°C. If K_b for 1 L of benzene is 2.18°C, then the molecular weight of the substance will be

(a) 2.31 (b) 4.44
(c) 1.01 (d) 3.30

14. Given below are the two statements.

Statement I ΔT_b is equal to $\frac{K_b Y}{4M}$, when Y g of non-volatile organic substance of molecular mass M is dissolved in 500 g benzene.

Statement II An aqueous solution of glucose boils at 100.01°C, then the number of molecules of glucose in the solution containing 100 g of water is 12.046×10^{20}. (ΔT_b for water = 0.5 K kg mol^{-1})

In the light of the above statements, choose the correct answer from the options given below.

(a) Both Statement I and Statement II are false.
(b) Statement I is true but Statement II is false.
(c) Statement I is false but Statement II is true.
(d) Both Statement I and Statement II are true.

15. Which of the following statement is incorrect?

(a) The unit of boiling point elevation constant is kg mol^{-1}.
(b) The boiling point of liquid is the temperature at which its vapour pressure becomes equal to 760 mm Hg.
(c) When concentration of a salt solution is increased then boiling point increases.
(d) The boiling point of a solution is always higher than the pure solvent.

16. If 0.37 g of a solute, dissolved in 18 g of solvent, is boiled at temperature higher by 0.312°C, than that of the pure solvent, the molar mass of the solute in g/mol (molal elevation constant for the solute is 3.12°C) is

(a) 205.6 (b) 203.21
(c) 198.67 (d) 210.21

17. Given below are the two statements.

Statement I Ebullioscopy is a method of determination of molecular mass by using elevation in boiling point.

Statement II Molecular mass of solute and elevation in boiling point are inversely proportional to each other.

In the light of the above statements, choose the correct answer from the options given below.

(a) Both Statement I and Statement II are false.
(b) Statement I is true but Statement II is false.
(c) Statement I is false but Statement II is true.
(d) Both Statement I and Statement II are true.

18. The boiling point of a solution of 0.12 g of a substance in 20 g of ether was found to be 0.1°C higher than that of pure ether. The molecular weight of the substance will be (K_b = 316°C kg mol^{-1})

(a) 176.2 (b) 180.2
(c) 179.3 (d) 189.6

19. For a dilute solution containing 2.5 g of a non-volatile, non-electrolyte solute in 100 g of water, the elevation in boiling point at 1 atm pressure is 2°C. Assuming concentration of solute is much lower than the concentration of solvent, the vapour pressure (mm of Hg) of the solution is (Take, K_b = 0.76 K kg mol^{-1})

(a) 780
(b) 740
(c) 724
(d) 730

20. Calculate the boiling point of a solution dissolved in 48.5 g of a solute of molecular weight 154 g/mol in 250 g of benzene. [Given, boiling point of pure benzene is 80.1°C and K_b for benzene is 3.61°C m^{-1}]

(a) 178.63 (b) 200.93
(c) 205.11 (d) 197.21

Module 4

Colligative Properties (Part II)

- Depression in Freezing Point
- Osmosis and Osmotic Pressure
- Abnormal Molar Masses
- van't Hoff Factor

Depression in Freezing Point

- The freezing point of a liquid is that temperature at which the liquid and its solid state exist in equilibrium with each other.
- It may be defined as the temperature at which the liquid and solid states of a substance have the same vapour pressure.
- When a non-volatile solute is dissolved in a pure solvent the vapour pressure of the solvent is decreased and freezing point also decreases.
- If T_f° is the freezing point of pure solvent and T_f is the freezing point of its solution then, $T_f < T_f^\circ$.
- The difference in the freezing point of pure solvent and solution is called **depression in freezing point** (ΔT_f).

$$\Delta T_f = T_f^\circ - T_f$$

- Similar to elevation of boiling point, depression in freezing point of a solution is proportional to the molal concentration of the solution, i.e.

$$\Delta T_f \propto m = K_f m \quad ...(2)$$

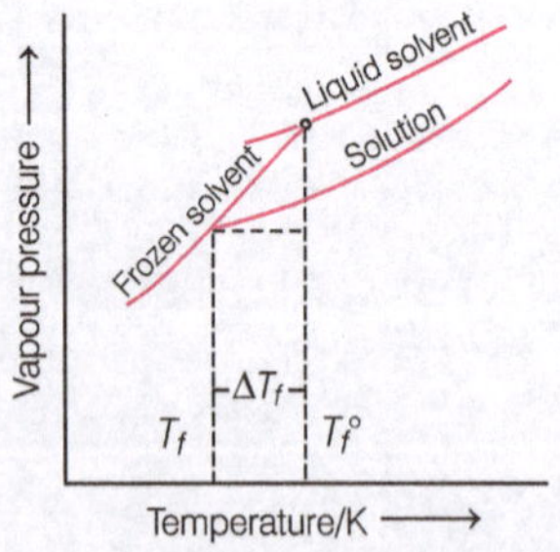

Graph showing ΔT_f, depression in freezing point of a solvent in a solution

where, K_f is called freezing point depression constant, molal depression constant or cryoscopic constant.

If $\quad m = 1$

then $\quad \Delta T_f = K_f$

Thus, **molal freezing point depression constant** is defined as the depression in freezing point for 1 molal solution, i.e. a solution containing 1 gram mole of solute dissolved in 1000 g of solvent.

- The unit of K_f is K kg mol^{-1}.
- The value of K_f that depends upon the nature of the solvent, can be calculated by using

$$K_f = \frac{R \times M_1 \times T_f^2}{1000 \times \Delta_{fus}H}$$

Here, R = gas constant

M_1 = molar mass of the solvent

$\Delta_{fus}H$ = enthalpy for fusion

Determination of Molar Mass of Solute

If w_2 gram of solute of molar mass M_2 is dissolved in W_1 gram of solvent then equation (2) is given by

$$\Delta T_f = \frac{K_f \times w_2 \times 1000}{M_2 \times W_1}$$

or

$$M_2 = \frac{K_f \times w_2 \times 1000}{\Delta T_f \times W_1}$$

where, M_2 = molar mass of solute

w_2 = mass of solute

W_1 = mass of solvent

Mentor's TiP

- Vapour pressure, boiling point and melting point are not colligative properties.
- Both ΔT_b or ΔT_f is directly proportional to lowering in vapour pressure.

Example 13. *Calculate the freezing point of a solution containing* 0.520 g *of glucose* ($C_6H_{12}O_6$) *in* 80.2 gram *of water. For water* K_f = 1.86 K kg mol^{-1}.

Sol. Given,

Mass of solute (glucose), w = 0.520 g

Mass of solvent (water), W = 80.2 g

Molar freezing depression constant, K_f = 1.86 K kg mol^{-1}

Molar mass of the solute ($C_6H_{12}O_6$), m = 180 g mol^{-1}

Calculation of molality

80.2 g of water, contains glucose = 0.520 g

$\therefore$ 1000 g of water, contains glucose = $\frac{1000 \times 0.520}{80.2}$

$\because$ Molality $= \dfrac{1000 \times 0.520}{80.2 \times 180}$

Applying the relation,

$$\Delta T_f = K_f \times \text{molality} = 1.86 \times \frac{1000 \times 0.520}{80.2 \times 180} = 0.067$$

$\therefore$ Freezing point $= 273 - 0.067$

($\because$ Freezing point of water = 273 K)

$= 272.933$ K

Example 14. *Addition of 0.643 g of a compound to 50 mL of benzene (density 0.879 g/mL) lowers the freezing point from 5.51°C to 5.03°C. If K_f for benzene is 5.12 K kg mol^{-1}, calculate the molar mass of the compound.*

Sol. The molar mass, M_B is calculated as

$$M_B = \frac{K_f \times w_B \times 1000}{W_A \times \Delta T_f}$$

$w_B = 0.643$ g,

$W_A = (50 \text{ mL}) \times (0.879 \text{ g/mL}) = 43.95$ g

$K_f = 5.12$ K kg mol^{-1},

$\Delta T_f = 5.51 - 5.03 = 0.48°$

$$M_B = \frac{5.12 \times 0.643 \times 1000}{43.95 \times 0.48} = 156.06 \text{ g/mol}$$

Example 15. *In a cold climate water gets frozen causing damage to the radiator of a Car. Ethylene glycol is used as an antifreezing agent. Calculate the amount of ethylene glycol to be added to 4 kg of water to prevent it from freezing at −6°C. (K_f for water = 1.85 K kg mol^{-1})*

Sol. $$\Delta T_f = \frac{K_f \times 1000 \times w_B}{W_A \times M_B}$$

$$\therefore \quad w_B = \frac{\Delta T_f \times W_A \times M_B}{K_f \times 1000}$$

$K_f = 1.85$ kg mol^{-1}, $W_A = 4 \times 10^3$ g, $M_B = 62$ g mol^{-1},

$\Delta T_f = 0 - (-6) = 6°$C

$$\therefore \quad w_B = \frac{6 \times 4 \times 10^3 \times 62}{1.85 \times 1000} = 804.32 \text{ g}$$

$\therefore$ Amount of ethylene glycol to be added = 804.32 g.

Osmosis

Before discussing about osmotic pressure, let us try to understand osmosis first.

There are many phenomena which we observe in nature or at home like raw mangoes shrivel when pickled in brine, blood cells collapse when suspended in saline water. All these substances are bound by membranes called semipermeable membrane (SPM).

These membranes can be of animal or vegetable origin and these occur naturally such as pig's bladder or parchment or can be synthetic such as cellophane. These appears to be continuous sheets or films yet they contain a network of submicroscopic holes or pores.

When two solutions of different concentrations are separated by a semipermeable membrane, then solvent from the solution of lower concentration, flows to the solution of higher concentration through the semipermeable membrane, until concentrations on both sides become equal. This spontaneous flow of solvent through the semipermeable membrane is called **osmosis.**

Difference between Osmosis and Diffusion

- Diffusion is intermingling of molecules or ions etc., resulting from the random thermal agitation. Thus, there is no restriction to motion of any kind of particles. While in osmosis only solvent molecules can flow through a semipermeable membrane.
- Osmosis takes place through a semipermeable membrane. While for diffusion such things are not required.
- A homogeneous mixture is obtained as a result of diffusion. On the other hand, no mixing is possible in osmosis.
- Diffusion cannot be prevented or stopped. While osmosis can be stopped by applying pressure to the solution.

Concept ladder In osmosis, the solvent flows in both the directions but its net flow is always from the region of lower concentration to the region of higher concentration through a semipermeable membrane.

Osmotic Pressure

The external pressure which must be applied on the solution in order to stop the flow of the solvent into the solution through semipermeable membrane is termed as **osmotic pressure.**

The osmotic pressure of a solution depends on its concentration. Larger the concentration, larger will be the osmotic pressure.

van't Hoff (1887) made a thorough study of the osmotic pressure of the dilute or ideal solution. He concluded that a dilute or ideal solution behave like an ideal gas and the different gas laws are applicable to the dilute solution as well. van't Hoff observed that for dilute solutions, the osmotic pressure (π) is proportional to the molarity, C of the solution at a given temperature T.

Thus, $$\pi = CRT \quad \text{or} \quad \pi = \left(\frac{n_2}{V}\right)RT$$

This equation is known as the van't Hoff equation for osmotic pressure of the solution.

where, π = osmotic pressure, R = gas constant

C = concentration of solution in mol/L

T = temperature

V = volume of solution in litre

n_2 = number of moles of solute

Determination of Molar Mass of Solute

If w_2 grams of solute of molar mass M_2 is present in the solution, then $n_2 = \frac{w_2}{M_2}$ so above equation will become

$$\pi V = \frac{w_2 RT}{M_2}$$

or $$M_2 = \frac{w_2 RT}{\pi V}$$

where, symbols have their usual meaning.

> **Concept ladder** Osmotic pressure of a mixture of two liquids can be calculated as
>
> **Case I** If two solutions of same substance having osmotic pressure of π_1 and π_2 are mixed, then
>
> $$\pi_1 V_1 = \pi_2 V_2 = \pi_R (V_1 + V_2)$$
>
> **Case II** If number of moles of two solutes are n_1 and n_2, which are present in volume V_1 and V_2 respectively are mixed then,
>
> $$\pi = \pi_1 + \pi_2 = \left(\frac{n_1 + n_2}{V_1 + V_2}\right) RT$$

This method is widely used to determine molar masses of proteins, polymers, macromolecules and biomolecules. As they are generally not stable at higher temperatures and polymers have poor solubility. This method has the advantage over other methods as pressure measurement is around the room temperature and the molarity of the solution is used instead of molality.

As compared to other colligative properties, its magnitude is large even for very dilute solutions.

Example 16. *A solution of sucrose (molar mass 342 g/mol) is prepared by dissolving 68.4 g of it per litre of the solution. What is its osmotic pressure at 300 K? (R = 0.082 litre atm K^{-1} mol^{-1})*

Sol. Given, molar mass of the solute = 342 g/mol

Mass of the solute = 68.4 g

Volume (V) of the solution = 1 litre

$T = 300$ K

Osmotic pressure π = ?

$R = 0.082$ litre atm K^{-1} mol^{-1}

$$n, \text{ the no. of moles of solute} = \frac{\text{Mass of solute}}{\text{Molar mass of solute}}$$

or $$n = \frac{68.4}{342}$$

Substituting the values in the equation

$$\pi = \frac{n}{V} RT$$

or $$\pi = \frac{68.4}{342} \times \frac{0.082 \times 300}{1}$$

$$= 4.92 \text{ atm}$$

$\therefore$ Osmotic pressure = 4.92 atm

Important Terminology Related to Osmosis

(i) **Isotonic solution** Two solutions having same osmotic pressure at a given temperature are called isotonic solutions. There is no osmosis between these two solution.

$$\pi_1 = \pi_2$$

$$\frac{n_1}{V_1} RT_1 = \frac{n_2}{V_2} RT_2$$

If $T_1 = T_2$

and $V_1 = V_2$

then $n_1 = n_2$

Thus, equal volume of isotonic solutions will have equal mole of solute under isothermal conditions.

$$\frac{w_1}{m_1} = \frac{w_2}{m_2}$$

If w_1, m_1, w_2 are known then m_2 can be calculated.

Example 17. *How many gram of glucose is present in 0.5 L of solution for its osmotic pressure to be the same as that of 9.2 g of glucose per litre?*

Sol. For isotonic solution, $\pi_1 = \pi_2$

$$\frac{w_1}{m_1 V_1} = \frac{w_2}{m_2 V_2}$$

$$w_1 = \frac{w_2 m_1 V_1}{m_2 V_2} = \frac{9.2 \times 180 \times 0.5}{180 \times 1}$$

$$w_1 = 4.6 \text{ g}$$

(ii) **Hypertonic solution** A solution having more osmotic pressure than the other solution is called hypertonic solution.

(iii) **Hypotonic solution** A solution having less osmotic pressure than the other solution is called hypotonic solution.

(iv) **Reverse osmosis** When a pressure more than the osmotic pressure is applied to the solution, the solvent pass from solution of higher concentration to the solution of lower concentration, through the semipermeable membrane. This type of osmosis is known as reverse osmosis. It is used for the **desalination of sea water.**

When pressure more than osmotic pressure is applied, pure water is squeezed out of the sea water through the membrane. A variety of polymer membranes are available for this purpose. The pressure required for the reverse osmosis is quite high. A workable porous membrane is a film of cellulose acetate placed over a suitable support.

Cellulose acetate is permeable to water but impermeable to impurity and ions present in the sea water.

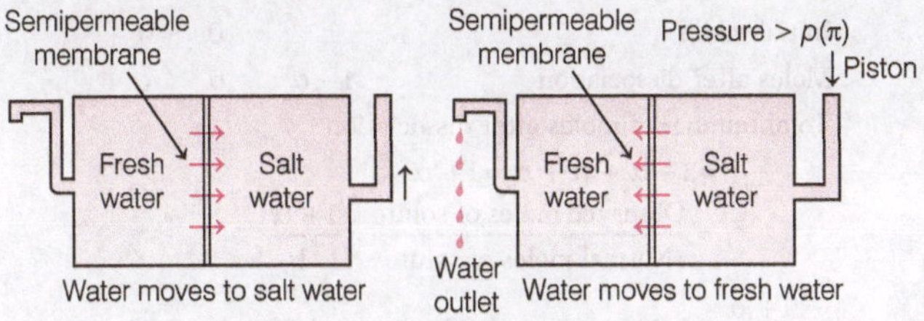

A schematic set up for the reverse osmosis used for desalination of sea water

(v) **Isobaric solutions** At same temperature, the solutions containing equal vapour pressure are known as isobaric solutions.

Applications of Osmosis

- A raw mango placed in concentrated salt solution loses water *via* osmosis and shrivel into pickle.
- Witted flowers revive when placed in fresh water.
- People taking a lot of salt or salty food experience water retention in tissue cells and intercellular spaces because of osmosis. The resulting puffiness or swelling is called **edema.**
- The prevention of meat by salting and of fruits by adding sugar to protect against bacterial action.
- Through the process of osmosis, a bacterium on salted meat or candid fruit loses water, shrivels and dies.

Example 18. *Calculate the osmotic pressure of 20% anhydrous calcium chloride solution at 273 K, assuming that the solution is completely dissociated.* (R = 0.082 L atm K^{-1} mol^{-1}).

Sol. Molar mass of $CaCl_2 = 40 + 71 = 111\,g\,mol^{-1}$

Since, solution is 20%.

$\therefore$ Weight of $CaCl_2$ per litre = 200 g

V = 1 litre

T = 273 K

$$n = \frac{\text{Mass of solute}}{\text{Molar mass of solute}} = \frac{200}{111}$$

Substituting the values in the relation

$$\pi = \frac{n}{V} \times RT$$

We have, $\pi = \dfrac{200}{111} \times \dfrac{0.082 \times 273}{1} = 40.335$ atm

Since, $CaCl_2$ dissolves to give 3 particles for each molecule on complete dissociation ($CaCl_2 \longrightarrow Ca^{2+} + 2Cl^-$)

$\therefore$ Observed osmotic pressure = Normal osmotic pressure × 3

= 40.335 × 3

= 121.00 atm

$\therefore$ Observed osmotic pressure = 121.00 atm

Abnormal Molar Masses

Generally it has been observed that difference in the observed and calculated molecular masses of solute is due to association or dissociation of solute molecules in solution. This change in molar mass is called **abnormal molar mass.**

van't Hoff Factor

It is the ratio of normal molar mass to the abnormal molar mass and is represented by *i*. It also gives relation between observed (abnormal) colligative property and calculated (normal) colligative property.

The factor *i* is defined as

$$i = \frac{\text{normal molecular mass}}{\text{abnormal molecular mass}}$$

or, $$i = \frac{\text{(abnormal) observed colligative property}}{\text{(normal) calculated colligative property}}$$

$$= \frac{\text{actual number of particles in solution}}{\text{number of particles taken}}$$

$$= \frac{\text{Total number of moles of particles after association/dissociation}}{\text{Number of moles of particles before association/dissociation}}$$

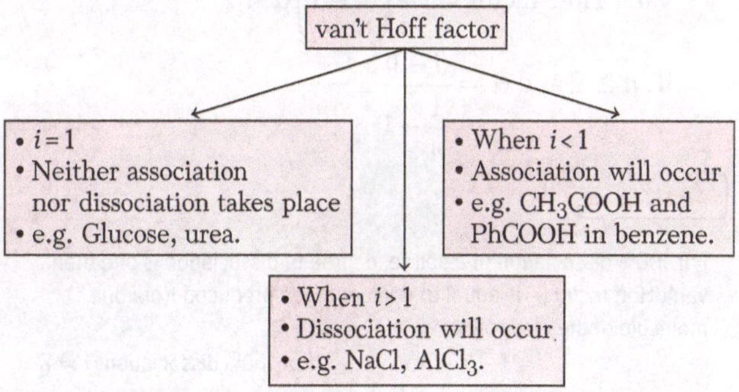

van't Hoff factor can be applied in case of dissociation and association as follows

(i) **In case of dissociation** When substance is an electrolyte, the number of particles increases in solution and the colligative property increases accordingly.

Suppose 1 mole of solute A dissociates to give n ions and α is the degree of dissociation.

	$A \rightleftharpoons$	nB
Initially	1 mol	0
After dissociation	$(1-\alpha)$ mol	$n\alpha$

Total number of moles present in solution

$$= (1-\alpha) + n\alpha = 1 + (n-1)\alpha$$

van't Hoff factor,

$$i = 1 + (n-1)\alpha > 1 \text{ if } n \geq 2$$

and $\alpha = \dfrac{(i-1)}{(n-1)}$

(ii) **In case of association** When substance undergoes association, the number of particles decreases in solution and consequently the value of colligative property decreases. e.g. Molecules of acetic acid dimerise in benzene due to hydrogen bonding.

$$2CH_3COOH \rightleftharpoons (CH_3COOH)_2$$

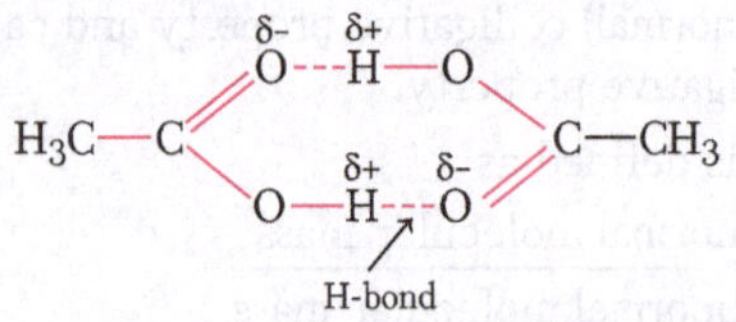

Suppose n molecules associate to form one giant molecule and α is the degree of association.

	nA	$\rightleftharpoons$	$(A)_n$
Initially	1 mol		0
At equilibrium	$(1-\alpha)$ mol		$\dfrac{\alpha}{n}$

Total number of moles in solution

$$= (1-\alpha) + \frac{\alpha}{n} = 1 + \left(\frac{1}{n} - 1\right)\alpha$$

$$\text{van't Hoff factor} = 1 + \left(\frac{1}{n} - 1\right)\alpha < 1$$

$$\text{if, } n \geq 2 \text{ and } \alpha = \frac{(i-1)}{\frac{1}{n} - 1}$$

Mentor's TiP

For 100% dissociation of a solute, degree of dissociation is one then van't Hoff factor (i) is equal to number of ion produced from one molecule of the electrolyte

$$i = 1 - \alpha + n\alpha \quad \text{[For 100\% dissociation } \alpha = 1]$$

$$i = n$$

Example 19. *A solution containing 0.5 g of KCl dissolved in 100 g of water freezes at −0.24°C. Calculate the degree of dissociation of the salt (K_f for water = 1.86° C kg mol^{-1}).*

Sol. Let us first calculate the observed molar mass as

$$M_B = \frac{K_f \times w_B \times 1000}{\Delta T_f \times W_A}$$

$$w_B = 0.5 \text{ g}, W_A = 100 \text{ g},$$

$$\Delta T_f = 0 - (-0.24) = 0.24°\text{C}, K_f = 1.86 \text{ °C kg mol}^{-1}$$

$$\therefore \quad M_B = \frac{1.86 \times 0.5 \times 1000}{0.24 \times 100} = 38.75 \text{ g mol}^{-1}$$

Normal molar mass of KCl = 39 + 35.5 = 74.5 g/mol

$$\text{van't Hoff factor, } i = \frac{\text{Normal molar mass}}{\text{Observed molar mass}} = \frac{74.5}{38.75} = 1.92$$

KCl dissociates as

$$KCl \rightleftharpoons K^+ + Cl^-$$

If α is the degree of dissociation, then

	KCl	K^+	Cl^-
Initial moles	1	0	0
Moles after dissociation	$1-\alpha$	α	α

Total number of moles after dissociation

$$= 1 - \alpha + \alpha + \alpha = 1 + \alpha$$

$$i = \frac{\text{Observed moles of solute}}{\text{Normal moles of solute}} = \frac{1+\alpha}{1}$$

$$\therefore \quad \frac{1+\alpha}{1} = 1.92 \text{ or } 1 + \alpha = 1.92 \quad \text{or} \quad \alpha = 1.92 - 1 = 0.92$$

Degree of dissociation = 92%

Relationship between van't Hoff Factor (i) and Colligative Properties

Relation between van't Hoff factor and different colligative properties is established as follows

- With osmotic pressure,

$$\pi = \frac{n_2}{V} RTi = \frac{w_2}{m_2 V} RTi$$

- With relative lowering of vapour pressure,

$$\frac{p° - p}{p°} = i \frac{w_2 m_1}{m_2 w_1}$$

- With elevation in boiling point,

$$\Delta T_b = i \times K_b \times m$$

- With depression in freezing point,

$$\Delta T_f = i \times K_f \times m$$

All the symbols have their usual meaning and already discussed earlier.

Example 20. *A solution of 2.8 g of CdI_2 (molar mass 365 g mol^{-1}) in 20 g water has elevation in boiling point of 0.20 K. Determine the molecular state of CdI_2 in aqueous solution?*

$$[K_b(H_2O) = 0.52 \text{ K mol}^{-1} \text{ kg}]$$

Sol. To decide molecular state, determine value of i or its molar mass.

(a) If, $i = 1$ and molar mass = calculated molar mass then solute remains without unchanged.

(b) If, $i > 1$ and molar mass < calculated molar mass then solute is ionised.

(c) If, $i < 1$ and molar mass > calculated molar mass then solute is polymerised (dimer, trimer, etc.)

$$\Delta T_b = \frac{1000 K_b w_2}{m_2 w_1} (i)$$

$$i = \frac{\Delta T_b m_2 w_1}{1000 K_b w_2} = \frac{0.20 \times 365 \times 20}{1000 \times 0.52 \times 2.8} = 1.0$$

Thus, CdI_2 remains as CdI_2 (without ionisation) in aqueous solution.

Example 21. *Urea solution is 20% by weight of solution. When water boils at 1 atm pressure and 1 molal glucose solution boils at 100.52°C. The boiling point of urea is*

(a) 2.17°C (b) 102.17°C (c) 100.52°C (d) 200.52°C

Sol. (*b*) Urea and glucose are non-electrolytes hence, $i = 1$

Water boils at 1 atm pressure, it means boiling point of water is 100°C.

$$\Delta T_b \text{ (glucose solution)} = 100.52 - 100.00 = 0.52°\text{C}$$

$$\Delta T_b \text{ (glucose solution)} = mK_b i$$

$$0.52 = 1 \times K_b \times 1$$

$$\therefore \quad K_b = 0.52°\text{C mol}^{-1}\text{ kg}$$

Urea solution is 20% by weight of solution, it means 100 g solution (solute + solvent) has 20 g solute and 80 g solvent

$$\Delta T_b \text{ (urea solution)} = \frac{1000 K_b w_2 i}{m_2 w_1}$$

$$= \frac{1000 \times 0.52 \times 20 \times 1}{60 \times 80} = 2.17°\text{C}$$

$$\therefore \text{Boiling point of urea solution} = 100.00 + 2.17°\text{C}$$

$$= 102.17°\text{C}$$

Example 22. ***Statement I*** *The freezing point of a solution prepared by dissolving* 1.00 *mole of* HF *in* 500 g *water is* −3.8°C.

Statement II *The freezing point of a solution prepared by dissolving* 1.00 *mole of* HCl *in* 500 g *water is* −7.4°C. *Justify.* $K_f(H_2O) = 1.86°\text{C mol}^{-1}$ kg.

In the light of the above statements, choose the correct answer from the options given below.

(a) Both Statement I and Statement II are false.

(b) Statement I is true but Statement II is false.

(c) Statement I is false but Statement II is true.

(d) Both Statement I and Statement II are true.

Sol. (*d*) **For Statement I** $\Delta T_f = mK_f i$

For HF, $m = \frac{1}{0.5} = 2 \text{ mol kg}^{-1}$

$$\Delta T_f = 0 - (-3.8) = 3.8°\text{C}$$

$$\therefore \quad 3.8 = 2 \times 1.86 \times i$$

$$i = \frac{3.8}{2 \times 1.86} = 1.02 \approx 1$$

For Statement II

For HCl,

$$m = \frac{1}{0.5} = 2 \text{ mol kg}^{-1}$$

$$\Delta T_f = 0 - (-7.4) = 7.4°\text{C}$$

$$i = \frac{\Delta T_f}{mK_f}$$

$$= \frac{7.4}{2 \times 1.86} = 1.99 \approx 2$$

Example 23. *Phenol* (C_6H_5OH) *is found to exist as polymer. If there is 100% polymerisation, the number of phenol molecules polymerised in aqueous solution if* 9.4 g *aqueous solution in* 100 g *water freezes at* −0.93°C *is* $K_f(H_2O) = 1.86°\text{C mol}^{-1}$ kg

(a) 0.5 (b) 4

(c) 2 (d) 6

Sol. (*c*) Observed $(\Delta T)_f = 0.93°\text{C}$,

$$\text{Calculated, } \Delta T_f = 1000 K_f \frac{w_2}{m_2 w_1}$$

$$= 1000 \times \frac{1.86 \times 9.4}{94 \times 100} = 1.86°\text{C}$$

$$i = \frac{\text{observed } (\Delta T_f)}{\text{calculated } (\Delta T_f)}$$

$$= \frac{0.93}{1.86} = \frac{1}{2}$$

$$\therefore \quad \frac{1}{n} = \frac{1}{2}$$

$$\Rightarrow \quad n = 2$$

STEP UP Practice 4

1. 3.00 g of a non-electrolyte solute (molar mass 250 g mol^{-1}) was dissolved in 51.2 g of benzene. If the freezing point depression constant, K_f of benzene is 4.12 K kg mol^{-1}, then freezing point of benzene will be lowered by
(a) 1.55 K (b) 0.285 K
(c) 0.966 K (d) 1.65 K

2. What will be the freezing point depression for 0.3 molal solution of benzoic acid in benzene if latent heat of fusion is 50.00 cal g^{-1} and freezing point for benzene is 280 K? (Assume no change in molecular state)
(a) 0.94 K (b) 0.45 K
(c) 0.87 K (d) 0.68 K

3. Which of the following statement is incorrect?
(i) At the freezing point of a substance, the solid phase is in dynamic equilibrium with the liquid phase.
(ii) Depression of freezing point for dilute solution is directly proportional to molarity of the solution.
(iii) Cryoscopic constant depends on the nature of the solvent.
(iv) Molar depression constant is inversely proportional to the enthalpies for the fusion of the solvent.
Choose the correct answer from the given options.
(a) (i), (ii), (iii) (b) (ii) and (iv)
(c) (ii) only (d) (iv) only

4. Given below are the two statements.
Statement I Adding a non-volatile solute to a solvent decreases the freezing point.
Statement II The degree of increase in freezing point is greater for a solute that forms strong ion-dipole interactions with the solvent molecules.
In the light of the above statements, choose the correct answer from the options given below.
(a) Both Statement I and Statement II are false.
(b) Statement I is true but Statement II is false.
(c) Statement I is false but Statement II is true.
(d) Both Statement I and Statement II are true.

5. In the following aqueous solutions, how many of them have same freezing point (K_f = 1.86 K kg/mol)?
(i) 0.1 m KNO_3 (ii) 0.1 m $BaCl_2$
(iii) 0.1 m $AlCl_3$ (iv) 0.1 m $Al_2(SO_4)_3$
(v) 0.1 m NH_4Cl
(a) 1 (b) 2
(c) 3 (d) 4

6. Osmotic pressure of blood is 9.54 atm at 27°C. Number of moles of glucose to be used as 3 L for an intravenous injection that is to have the same osmotic pressure as blood is
(a) 3.15 (b) 1.16
(c) 4.17 (d) 2.20

7. Osmotic pressure of 30% solution of glucose is 1.30 atm and that of 3.43% solution of cane sugar is 4.5 atm. The osmotic pressure of the mixture containing equal volumes of the two solutions will be
(a) 1.9 atm (b) 2.9 atm
(c) 2.5 atm (d) 3.9 atm

8. Which of the following statement is incorrect?
(a) Solvent molecules always flow from higher concentration to lower concentration of solution.
(b) For dilute solutions, the osmotic pressure is proportional to the molarity of the solution.
(c) Measurement of osmotic pressure provides another method of determining molar mass of solutes.
(d) The flow of solvent molecules stop before the equilibrium is attained.

9. Given below are the two statements.
Statement I 1 M solution of glucose has greater osmotic pressure than 1 M solution of KCl at the same temperature.
Statement II The solution which has higher osmotic pressure than its standard solution is known as hypertonic solution.
In the light of the above statements, choose the correct answer from the options given below.
(a) Both Statement I and Statement II are false.
(b) Statement I is true but Statement II is false.
(c) Statement I is false but Statement II is true.
(d) Both Statement I and Statement II are true.

10. Select the correct statement from the following.
(a) Osmotic pressure has large magnitude even for very dilute solutions, as compared to other colligative properties.
(b) Two solutions having different osmotic pressure at a given temperature are called isotonic solutions.
(c) A raw mango placed in concentrated salt solution absorbs water *via* osmosis.
(d) The technique of osmotic pressure is not useful to determine the molar masses of proteins, polymers and other macromolecules.

11. Which of the following is correctly matched?
(a) 0.1 M $Ca(NO_3)_2$ and 0.1 M Na_2SO_4 $\rightarrow$ Isotonic
(b) 0.1 M NaCl and 0.1 M Na_2SO_4 $\rightarrow$ Isotonic
(c) 0.1 M urea and 0.1 M $MgCl_2$ $\rightarrow$ Isotonic
(d) 0.1 M urea and 0.1 M NaCl $\rightarrow$ Isotonic

12. Which of the following statement is incorrect?
(a) Due to osmosis, raw mangoes shrivel when pickled in brine.
(b) Osmotic pressure of a solution is the excess pressure that must be applied to a solution to prevent the flow of solvent.
(c) Another application of osmosis named edema is due to water retention in tissue cells.
(d) Osmotic pressure is useful for determining molar mass of bimolecules, as they are generally stable at higher temperature.

13. Sea water is found to contain NaCl and $MgCl_2$. If NaCl is 90% ionised and $MgCl_2$ is 40% ionised then van't Hoff factor in this case is
(a) 5.0
(b) 2.5
(c) 3.7
(d) 4.8

14. When 55 g of $C_6H_{12}O_6$ is dissolved in 80 g of benzene, a freezing point depression of 3 K is observed. [K_f (benzene) = 1.82 K kg mol^{-1}]. The van't Hoff factor (i) is
(a) 0.2 (b) 0.3
(c) 0.4 (d) 0.5

15. Among the given statements, regarding abnormal molar masses all are true except?
(a) The molar mass that is either lower or higher than the expected or normal value is called abnormal molar mass.
(b) van't Hoff factor more than unity indicates that the solute in solution is associated.
(c) Benzoic acid is dissolved in benzene, its van't Hoff factor will be equal to 0.5.
(d) Abnormal molar mass is the experimentally determined molar mass by assuming that the non-volatile solute is neither associated nor dissociated.

16. Given below are the two statements.
Statement I The van't Hoff factor of 0.005 M aqueous solution of KCl is 1.95, then its degree of ionisation will be 0.95.
Statement II If α is the degree of dissociation of Na_2SO_4, then the value of van't Hoff factor (i) which is used for calculating the molecular mass is $1 + 2\alpha$.
In the light of the above statements, choose the correct answer from the options given below.
(a) Both Statement I and Statement II are false.
(b) Statement I is true but Statement II is false.
(c) Statement I is false but Statement II is true.
(d) Both Statement I and Statement II are true.

17. Among the given species,
(i) $Al_2(SO_4)_3$ (ii) $AlCl_3$ (iii) $Al(NO_3)_3$
(iv) $Al(OH)_3$ (v) $CaCl_2$
How many species, will have same value of van't Hoff factor as that of $K_4[Fe(CN)_6]$?
(a) 2 (b) 3
(c) 1 (d) 4

18. Decimolar solution of potassium ferricyanide, $K_3[Fe(CN)_6]$ has osmotic pressure of 5.39 atm at 37°C. Hence, percent ionisation of the solute is
(a) 35.65% (b) 36.67%
(c) 37.76% (d) 38.85%

19. Among the given species,
(i) 10^{-4} M NaCl
(ii) 10^{-4} M urea
(iii) 10^{-2} M $AlCl_3$
(iv) 10^{-2} M NaCl
(v) 10^{-2} M PCl_3
How many of them have higher boiling point than 10^{-3} M $MgCl_2$?
(a) 1 (b) 2
(c) 3 (d) 4

20. Which of the following is not correctly matched?
(a) 0.1 M $BaCl_2 \rightarrow 3$ ions
(b) 0.1 M $MgSO_4 \rightarrow 2$ ions
(c) 0.1 M NaCl $\rightarrow 2$ ions
(d) 0.1 M Glucose $\rightarrow 4$ ions

21. The values of observed and calculated molar mass of silver nitrate are 102.76 g/mol and 170 g/mol, respectively. The degree of dissociation of silver nitrate is
(a) 68% (b) 60%
(c) 62% (d) 65%

22. Which of the following is not correctly matched, regarding the calculation of van't Hoff factor (i)?
(a) $\pi V \rightarrow \sqrt{in}\, RT$
(b) $\Delta T_f \rightarrow iK_f \cdot m$
(c) $\Delta T_b \rightarrow iK_b \cdot m$
(d) $\dfrac{p^\circ_{\text{solvent}} - p_{\text{solution}}}{p^\circ_{\text{solvent}}} \rightarrow i\left(\dfrac{n}{N+n}\right)$

23. Which of the following is correctly match?
(a) $0 < i < 1 \rightarrow$ No association or dissociation in the solution
(b) $i > 1 \rightarrow$ Association in the solution
(c) $i = 1 \rightarrow$ Dissociation in the solution
(d) $i < 0 \rightarrow$ Impossible

24. Which of the following is correct match?
(a) 0.015 M Glucose $\rightarrow i = 2$
(b) 0.10 M $Na_2SO_4 \rightarrow i = 2$
(c) 0.01 M $KNO_3 \rightarrow i = 3$
(d) 0.015 M Urea $\rightarrow i = 1$

NEET Exclusive EXTRA BYTES

Relationship Between Different Colligative Properties

- Osmotic pressure (π) with relative lowering of vapour pressure, $\pi = \dfrac{p^\circ - p}{p^\circ} \times \dfrac{dRT}{M_1}$ [M_1 = molar mass of the solvent]
- Osmotic pressure (π) with elevation in boiling point (ΔT_b), $\pi = \Delta T_b \times \dfrac{dRT}{1000K_b}$ [d = density of the solution at temperature T]
- Osmotic pressure (π) with depression in freezing point (ΔT_f), $\pi = \Delta T_f \times \dfrac{dRT}{1000K_f}$
- Elevation in boiling point with relative lowering of vapour pressure, $\Delta T_b = \dfrac{1000K_b}{M_1}\left(\dfrac{p^\circ - p}{p^\circ}\right)$ [M_1 = molar mass of solvent]
- Depression in freezing point with relative lowering of vapour pressure, $\Delta T_f = \dfrac{1000K_f}{M_1}\left(\dfrac{p^\circ - p}{p^\circ}\right)$

van't Hoff factor '*i*' for Different Cases of Solutes Undergoing Association and Dissociation

Solute	Example	Association/dissociation (x = degree)	y^*	van't Hoff factor $i = [1 + (y^* - 1)x]$	Abnormal molecular weight (m_2')
Non-electrolyte	urea-glucose, sucrose, etc.	none	1	1	normal molecular weight (m_2)
Electrolyte of type A^+B^-	NaCl, KCl, HCl, CH_3COOH, $FeSO_4$, etc.	$\underset{1-x}{AB} \rightleftharpoons \underset{x}{A^+} + \underset{x}{B^-}$	2	$(1+x)$	$\dfrac{m_2}{(1+x)}$
Electrolyte of type A_2B, AB_2	K_2SO_4, $BaCl_2$, $K_2[PtCl_6]$, etc.	$\underset{1-x}{A_2B} \rightleftharpoons \underset{2x}{2A^+} + \underset{x}{B^{2-}}$ $\underset{1-x}{AB_2} \rightleftharpoons \underset{x}{A^{2+}} + \underset{2x}{2B^-}$	3	$(1+2x)$	$\dfrac{m_2}{(1+2x)}$
Electrolyte of type A_3B, AB_3	Na_3PO_4, $AlCl_3$, $K_3[Fe(CN)_6]$, $FeCl_3$	$\underset{1-x}{A_3B} \rightleftharpoons \underset{3x}{3A^+} + \underset{x}{B^{3-}}$ $\underset{1-x}{AB_3} \rightleftharpoons \underset{x}{A^{3+}} + \underset{3x}{3B^-}$	4	$(1+3x)$	$\dfrac{m_2}{(1+3x)}$
Associated solute	benzoic acid in benzene forming dimer, any solute forming polymer A_n	$2A \rightleftharpoons A_2$ $\underset{(1-x)}{A} \rightleftharpoons \underset{x/2}{\dfrac{1}{2}A_2}$ $nA \rightleftharpoons A_n$ $\underset{(1-x)}{A} \rightleftharpoons \underset{\left(\frac{x}{n}\right)}{\dfrac{1}{n}A_n}$	$\dfrac{1}{2}$ $\dfrac{1}{n}$	$\left(1-\dfrac{x}{2}\right) = \left(\dfrac{2-x}{2}\right)$ $\left[1+\left(\dfrac{1}{n}-1\right)x\right]$	$\dfrac{2m_2}{(2-x)}$ $\dfrac{m_2}{1+\left(\dfrac{1}{n}-1\right)x}$
General	one mole of solute giving y moles of products	$A \rightleftharpoons yB$	y	$[1+(y-1)x]$	$\dfrac{m_2}{[1+(y-1)x]}$

- *y^* = Total mole of product formed after dissociation/association of one mole of reactant.*

GEARING UP FOR NEET

1. The concentration of pollutant in ppm, that has been measured at 450 mg per 150 kg of sample is
(a) 3 ppm (b) 6 ppm
(c) 3000 ppm (d) 330 ppm

2. Persons are medically considered to have lead poisoning if they have a concentration greater than 10 μg of lead per decilitre of blood. Concentration in parts per billion is
(a) 1000 of solvent (b) 100 of solvent
(c) 10 of solvent (d) 1 of solvent

3. In 4/8 molal solution that contains 0.213 mole of a solute, there is
(a) 323 g of solvent (b) 513 g of solvent
(c) 426 g of solvent (d) 216 g of solvent

4. A solution is prepared by mixing 150 mL each of methanol ($d = 0.791$ g/mL) and ethanol ($d = 0.998$ g/mL). If M_1 is molarity of solution described as MeOH solute in EtOH solvent and M_2 is molarity of solution described as EtOH solute in MeOH solvent. Then
(a) $M_2 > M_1$ (b) $M_1 = M_2$
(c) $M_1 + M_2 > 50$ (d) $M_1 > M_2$

5. In 5 molal solution that contains 0.38 mole of a solute, the mass of solvent is
(a) 67 g (b) 76 g
(c) 80 g (d) 79 g

6. The vapour pressure of a solution at 45°C with benzene to hexane in molar ratio 7 : 2 is [At 45°C vapour pressure of benzene is 630 mm Hg and that of hexane is 420 mm Hg]
(a) 583 mm Hg (b) 498 mm Hg
(c) 545 mm Hg (d) 483 mm Hg

7. If the total vapour pressure of the liquid mixtures A and B is given by the equation $p = 270\chi_A + 90$ then the ratio of the vapour pressure of the pure liquids A and B is given by
(a) 4 : 1 (b) 3 : 2
(c) 3 : 1 (d) 6 : 2

8. The value of vapour pressure of a solution at 65°C with benzene to octane in molar ratio 5 : 7 is [At 65°C vapour pressure of benzene is 570 mm Hg and that of octane is 720 mm Hg]
(a) 557.6 mm Hg (b) 530 mm Hg
(c) 630 mm Hg (d) 657.5 mm Hg

9. Which of the following pair is correct for a solution showing positive deviations from Raoult's law?
(a) $\Delta V = +$ ve, $\Delta H = -$ve (b) $\Delta V = +$ ve, $\Delta H = +$ ve
(c) $\Delta V = -$ve, $\Delta H = -$ve (d) $\Delta V = -$ ve, $\Delta H = +$ ve

10. Which of the following statement is incorrect?
(a) Raoult's law is a special case of Henry's law in which K_H becomes equal to $p°_1$.
(b) Chloroform and diethyl ether shows positive deviation from Raoult's law.
(c) Azeotropic mixture are binary mixture having same composition in liquid and vapour phase.
(d) Phenol and aniline show negative deviation from Raoult's law.

11. If vapour pressure of pure liquids A and B are 200 and 600 torr respectively at 25°C. When these two liquids are mixed at this temperature to form a solution in which mole percentage of B is 92, then the total vapour pressure is observed to be 0.98 atm. Which of the following statement is true for this solution?
(a) ΔV_{mix} for the given solutions is more than zero.
(b) ΔH_{mix} for the given solutions is equal to zero.
(c) ΔV_{mix} for the given solutions is equal to zero.
(d) ΔH_{mix} for the given solutions is less than zero.

12. Which of the following pair of given mixtures is correct to be an ideal solution?
(a) NaCl—H_2O (b) C_7H_{16}—C_8H_{18}
(c) C_2H_5OH—C_6H_6 (d) C_7H_{16}—H_2O

13. A solution is obtained by dissolving 12 g of urea (mol. wt. 60) in a litre of water. Another solution is obtained by dissolving 68.4 g of cane sugar (mol. wt. 342) in a litre of water at the same temperature. Then the lowering of vapour pressure in the first solution is
(a) same as that of 2nd solution
(b) nearly one-fourth of the 2nd solution
(c) nearly six times that of 2nd solution
(d) double that of 2nd solution

14. If 5.8 g of a non-electrolyte solute is dissolved in 90 g of oxalic acid to reduce its vapour pressure to 80%, the molar mass (in g mol^{-1}) of the solute is [Given that, molar mass of oxalic acid is 90 g mol^{-1}]
(a) 20.1 (b) 22.9 (c) 25.2 (d) 23.2

15. In water saturated air, the mole fraction of water vapour is 0.23. If the total pressure of the saturated air is 5.2 atm, the partial pressure of dry air is
(a) 3.01 (b) 4.004 (c) 2.113 (d) 4.127

16. Which of the following statements comparing solutions with pure solvent is not correct?
(a) A solution containing a non-volatile solute has a lower vapour pressure than pure solvent.
(b) A solution containing a non-volatile solute has a lower boiling point than pure solvent.
(c) A solution containing a non-volatile solute has a lower freezing point than pure solvent.
(d) A solution will have a greater mass than an equal volume of pure solvent if the solute has a molar mass greater than the solvent.

17. A mixture of gases in a closed vessel at equilibrium contains three different gases : nitrogen (20 moles), hydrogen (45 moles) and ammonia (25 moles). What will be the partial pressure of hydrogen at 40 atm ?
(a) 25 (b) 30 (c) 20 (d) 35

18. The vapour pressure of benzene at 90°C is lowered by 20 mm by dissolving 4 g of a non-volatile substance in 88 g of benzene. The vapour pressure of pure benzene at 80°C is 850 mm. The molecular weight of the substance in g/mol will be
(a) 178 (b) 184.10 (c) 179.21 (d) 187.28

19. If $8\frac{5}{7}$ g of a non-electrolyte solute is dissolved in 140 g of *n*-heptane to reduce its vapour pressure to 90%, the molar mass (in g mol^{-1}) of the solute is [Given that, molar mass of *n*-heptane is 100 g mol^{-1}]
(a) 62 g mol^{-1} (b) 55 g mol^{-1}
(c) 60 g mol^{-1} (d) 56 g mol^{-1}

20. At 150°C the vapour pressure of a solution of 7.85 g of a solute in 100 g of water is 632 mm. If K_b = 0.81°C kg mol^{-1}, the boiling point of this solution will be
(a) 150.12°C (b) 130.01°C
(c) 109.08°C (d) 120.21°C

21. Which of the following is not a correct match?
(a) Hydrogen gas in palladium — A solution of gas in liquid
(b) Sugar solution — A solution of solid in liquid
(c) German silver — A solution of solid in solid
(d) Soda water — A solution of liquid in solid

22. An aqueous solution of a compound *AB* freezes at –0.58°C. At this temperature, *AB* behaves as a non-electrolyte. The same solution boils at 0.23°C at a pressure of 1 atm (for water, $K_f / K_b = 3.7$) we can conclude that compound *AB* at the boiling point of solution
(a) dimerises completely in solution
(b) behaves as a non-electrolyte
(c) dissociates in solution
(d) ionises to the extent of 50%

23. If barium sulphate is considered to be completely dissociated into cations and anions in aqueous solution, the change in freezing point of water (ΔT_f), when 0.02 mole of sodium sulphate is dissolved in 1 kg of water, is
($K_f = 1.38$ K kg mol^{-1})
(a) 0.0658 K (b) 0.0744 K
(c) 0.0186 K (d) 0.0552 K

24. Which of the following is incorrectly matched?
(a) For 1 M $Al_2(SO_4)_3$ solution $\rightarrow \Delta T_f \propto 5$
(b) For 1 M $La(NO_3)_3$ solution $\rightarrow \Delta T_f \propto 4$
(c) For 3 M urea solution $\rightarrow \Delta T_f \propto 3$
(d) For 1.5 M $AlCl_3$ solution $\rightarrow \Delta T_f \propto 5$

25. Elevation in boiling point for 1.5 molal solution of glucose in water is 4 K. The depression in freezing point for 4.5 molal solution of glucose in water is 6 K. What is the ratio of molal elevation constant to molal depression constant?
(a) 3 (b) 2 (c) 5 (d) 6

26. 0.02 (M) solution of an acid *HA* freezes at –0.0305°C. If K_f for water is 1.76 K kg mol^{-1}, the ionisation constant of the conjugate base of the acid will be (consider molarity ≅ molality)
(a) 3.4×10^{-11} (b) 4.3×10^{11} (c) 2.9×10^{-4} (d) 4.1×10^{-11}

27. Which of the following pair is correctly matched?
[Given : $K_f = 1.87$°C kg/mol]
(a) 0.3 m ethylene glycol $\rightarrow \Delta T_f = 0.744$°C
(b) 0.06 m KNO_3 $\rightarrow \Delta T_f = 0.223$°C
(c) 0.1 m glucose solution $\rightarrow \Delta T_f = 0.558$°C
(d) 0.2 m NaCl solution $\rightarrow \Delta T_f = 0.186$°C

28. Consider the separate solution of 0.500 M $C_2H_5OH(aq)$, 0.100 M $Mg_3(PO_4)_2(aq)$, 0.250 M KBr(*aq*) and 0.125 M $Na_3PO_4(aq)$ has osmotic pressure π_1, π_2, π_3 and π_4 respectively at 25°C. Choose the correct option for the osmotic pressure of these solutions, assuming all salts to be strong electrolyte?
(a) $\pi_1 = \pi_2 = \pi_3 = \pi_4$ (b) $\pi_1 > \pi_2 > \pi_3 > \pi_4$
(c) $\pi_3 > \pi_4 > \pi_1 > \pi_2$ (d) $\pi_4 > \pi_2 > \pi_3 > \pi_1$

29. If *A* contains 2% NaCl and is separated by a semipermeable membrane from *B*, which contains 10% NaCl, then which of the following event is true?
(a) Water will flow from *A* to *B*.
(b) Water will flow from *B* to *A*.
(c) NaCl will flow from *A* to *B*.
(d) NaCl will flow from *B* to *A*.

30. Which of the following statements is incorrect?
(a) Osmotic pressure for 0.01 M aqueous solution
$BaCl_2 > KCl > CH_3COOH >$ Sucrose
(b) Osmotic pressure, $\pi = MRT$
(c) The vapour pressure of a component over a solution is proportional to its mole fraction.
(d) Two sucrose solutions of same molality prepared in different solvents have same ΔT_f.

31. Which of the following azeotropes is not correctly matched?
(a) H_2O (43%) + HI (56.7%) $\rightarrow$ Maximum boiling azeotrope, B.P. = 290 K
(b) Chloroform (93.2%) + C_2H_5OH (6.8%) $\rightarrow$ Minimum boiling azeotrope, B.P. = 332.3 K
(c) HNO_3 (68%) + H_2O (32%) $\rightarrow$ Maximum boiling azeotrope. B.P. = 393.5 K
(d) C_2H_5OH (95.5%) + H_2O (4.5%) $\rightarrow$ Minimum boiling azeotrope, B.P. = 351.15 K

32. V_1 mL of an aqueous urea solution having osmotic pressure equal to 2.4 atm is mixed with 'V_2' mL of another aqueous urea solution having osmotic pressure equal to 5.6 atm at same temperature. What will be value of $\frac{V_1}{V_2}$ if resulting solution after mixing has osmotic pressure equal to 2.95 atm?
(a) 3.27 (b) 6.1
(c) 4.81 (d) 4.79

33. π_1, π_2, π_3 and π_4 are the osmotic pressure of 6% (w/V) solution of urea, NaCl, sucrose and KCl respectively at certain temperature. The correct order of their magnitude is
(a) $\pi_4 > \pi_1 > \pi_2 > \pi_3$ (b) $\pi_2 > \pi_4 > \pi_1 > \pi_3$
(c) $\pi_1 < \pi_4 < \pi_2 < \pi_3$ (d) $\pi_4 > \pi_1 > \pi_3 > \pi_2$

34. If van't Hoff factors of aqueous solutions of X, Y and Z are 1.8, 0.8 and 2.5. Then, which of the following relation is correct?
(a) Boiling point : $Z < X < Y$
(b) Freezing point : $Z < X < Y$
(c) Osmotic pressure : $X = Y = Z$
(d) Vapour pressure : $X < Y = Z$

35. For an ideal solution containing a non-volatile solute, which of the following expression is correctly represented?
(a) $\Delta T_b = K_b \times 2M$ (b) $\Delta T_b = K_b \times m$
(c) $\Delta T_b = K_b \times M$ (d) $\Delta T_b = K_b \times 2m$

36. Which of the following is incorrect match ?
(a) 0.01 M $KNO_3 \rightarrow T_b = 0.02K_b + T°_b$
(b) 1.0 M $Na_2SO_4 \rightarrow T_b = 0.3K_b + T°_b$
(c) 0.015 M Glucose $\rightarrow T_b = 0.15K_b + T°_b$
(d) 0.12 M Urea $\rightarrow T_b = 0.12K_b + T°_b$

37. The freezing point depression constant for water is –196°C m^{-1}. If 8.00 g Na_2SO_4 is dissolved in 48.0 g H_2O, the freezing point is changed by –5.38°C, the van't Hoff factor for Na_2SO_4 will be
(a) 1.35 (b) 2.5 (c) 3.01 (d) 2.33

38. A solution of X moles of sucrose in 100 grams of water freezes at –0.3°C. As ice separates the freezing point goes down to 0.35°C. How many grams of ice would have separated?
(a) 15.00 g (b) 14.44 g (c) 15.01 g (d) 14.21 g

39. A 6.21% solution of a substance is isotonic with a 1.5% solution of urea (molar mass = 60 g mol^{-1}) in the same solvent. If the densities of both the solutions are assumed to be equal to 2.0 g cm^{-3}, molar mass of the substance will be
(a) 29 (b) 25 (c) 30 (d) 35

40. Which of the following is correctly match regarding the ratio of i?
(a) NaCl, $MgCl_2$, $K_2SO_4 \rightarrow 2:3:3$
(b) $Al_2(SO_4)_3$, Na_3PO_4, $K_4[Fe(CN)_6] \rightarrow 1:4:2$
(c) Glucose, NaCl, $CaCl_2 \rightarrow 1:3:2$
(d) Urea, Glucose, Fructose $\rightarrow 1:2:1$

Assertion-Reason

Directions (Q. Nos. 41 to 46) Given below are two statements, one is labelled as Assertion (A) and the other is labelled as Reason (R).
(a) Both A and R are true and R is the correct explanation of A.
(b) Both A and R are true but R is not the correct explanation of A.
(c) A is true but R is false.
(d) A is false but R is true.

41. **Assertion** (A) Maximum amount of a solid solute that can be dissolved in a specified amount of a given liquid solvent depend upon pressure.
Reason (R) Solid and liquid are highly incompressible and practically remain unaffected by change in pressure.

42. **Assertion** (A) Total vapour pressure of mixture of 1 mole of A ($p°_A$ = 100 mm Hg) and 3 moles of B ($p°_B$ = 60 mm Hg) is 70 mm Hg it show negative deviation from Raoult's law.
Reason (R) Observed value of total vapour pressure is increased.

43. **Assertion** (A) Boiling point of water is 100°C although water boils below 100°C on mountains.
Reason (R) Boiling point of a liquid is the temperature at which V.P. of liquid becomes equal to 1 atm.

44. **Assertion** (A) The freezing point of a dilute solution of acetamide in glacial acetic acid is 298 K. This is the value when crystals of acetic acid appears first.
Reason (R) CH_3COOH has intramolecular hydrogen bonding.

45. **Assertion** (A) The azeotropic mixture of water (B.P. 100°C) and HCl (B.P. 85°C) boils at 108.5°C. When this mixture is distilled, it is possible to obtain pure water.
Reason (R) Azeotropic mixture is a constant boiling mixture.

46. **Assertion** (A) Benzoic acid is dissolved in benzene then the value of van't Hoff factor is equal to 1.5.
Reason (R) Benzoic acid dissolves in benzene it will be dimerised due to the intermolecular hydrogen bonding.

Statement Type Questions

Directions (Q. Nos. 47 to 51) In the light of the above statements given below, choose the most appropriate answer from the options given.
(a) Both Statement I and Statement II are false.
(b) Statement I is true but Statement II is false.
(c) Statement I is false but Statement II is true.
(d) Both Statement I and Statement II are true.

47. **Statement I** When a solution of $CHCl_3$ is mixed with a solution of acetone, then ΔV_{mix} is negative.
Statement II For an ideal solution, ΔH and ΔV for mixing should be zero.

48. Statement I The latent heat of vaporisation of water is 9700 cal/mol and if the B.P. is 100°C, then K_b of water is 1.025°C.

Statement II Elevation in a boiling point depends upon the number of particles.

49. Statement I The boiling point of 0.1 M urea solution is more than that of 0.1 M KCl solution.

Statement II Elevation of boiling point is directly proportional to the number of species present in the solution.

50. Statement I The direction of osmosis can be reversed if a pressure lower than the osmotic pressure is applied to the solution side.

Statement II Cellulose acetate is impermeable to water but permeable to impurities and ions present in sea water.

51. Statement I The van't Hoff factor (*i*) for an infinitely dilute solution of $NaHSO_4$ is 4.

Statement II The van't Hoff factor (*i*) is directly proportional to the elevation in boiling point.

52. Which of the following statements are incorrect?

A. O_2 + He gas mixture is used by the divers inside the sea.

B. Solubility of gases in liquids decreases with decrease in temperature.

C. Henry's law indicates the relationship between solubility of a gas in liquid and pressure.

D. In a nearly saturated solution, if the dissolution process is exothermic, then the solubility should increase with rise in temperature.

E. Different gases have same K_H values at the same temperature.

Choose the correct answer from the options given below.

(a) B, D and E (b) B and C only
(c) A, C and D (d) A and D only

53. Which of the following statements are correct?

A. van't Hoff factor of Hg_2Cl_2 in its aqueous solution is 1.6 when Hg_2Cl_2 is 80% ionised in the solution.

B. The degree of dissociation of 0.1 M $Mg(NO_3)_2$ solution is 87% if value of (*i*) is 2.75.

C. The value of van't Hoff factor is same for both $Al_2(SO_4)_3$ and $Al(OH)_3$.

D. The degree of ionisation of 0.005 M KCl is 0.97 if the value of van't Hoff factor is 1.95.

E. van't Hoff factor value for glucose is equal to unity.

Choose the correct answer from the options given below

(a) A, D and E (b) B and E only
(c) C and D only (d) A, B and D

54. Which of the following statements are correct?

A. Isotonic solution have the same molar concentration at a given temperature.

B. The molal elevation constant K_b is characteristic of a solvent and indpendent of the solute added.

C. Elevation in boiling point of a molar glucose solution ($d = 1.2\ g\ mL^{-1}$) is $1.20K_b$.

D. Boiling point of 1 molal NaCl solution is twice that 1 molal sucrose solution.

E. The freezing point of 0.1 M KCl solution is more than that of 0.1 M aqueous $AlCl_3$ solution.

Choose the correct answer from the options given below.

(a) E, C and D only (b) C, A and B only
(c) A, B and D only (d) A, B and E only

55. Choose the correct statements from the following.

A. Aquatic species are more comfortable in warm water rather than in cold water.

B. At high altitudes, the partial pressure of oxygen is less than that at the ground level.

C. There is low concentration of O_2 in the blood and tissue of the people living at high altitude.

D. A raw mango placed in concentrated salt solution loses water *via* osmosis and shrivel into pickle.

E. Water movement from soil into plant roots and subsequently into upper portion of the plant is partly due to reverse osmosis.

Choose the correct answer from the options given below.

(a) A, D and E
(b) A, C and D
(c) B, C and D
(d) B and E only

56. Select the incorrect statements from the following.

A. A saturated solution will remain saturated at all temperatures.

B. A plant cell swells when placed in hypertonic solution.

C. The depression in freezing point is directly proportional to molality of the solution.

D. When isotonic solutions are separated by semipermeable membrane no osmosis occurs between them.

E. If the salt concentration is less than (0.9%) (*m*/*V*), then the solution is said to be hypotonic.

Choose the correct answer from the options given below.

(a) A, D and E only (b) D and E only
(c) A and B only (d) B, C and D only

Species Selection Type Questions

57. Among the given solutions,

(i) 100 g of sucrose in 100 mL solution
(ii) 6% by mass of urea in aqueous solution
(iii) 1 M KCl solution
(iv) 9 g of glucose in 59 g aqueous solution
(v) 2% by mass of urea in aqueous solution

In how many case depression in freezing point is equal to cryoscopic constant for water?

(a) 2 (b) 3
(c) 4 (d) 1

58. How many following pairs of solutions can we expect to be isotonic at the same temperature?

(i) 2.5 M KCl and 1 M $Al_2(SO_4)_3$
(ii) 1 M urea and 1 M glucose
(iii) 0.1 M $Ba(NO_3)_2$ and 0.1 M Na_2SO_4
(iv) 250 mL of 0.1 M KCl and 100 mL of 0.1 M $MgCl_2$
(v) 0.1 M NaCl and 0.1 M Na_2SO_4
(vi) 0.1 M $Ca(NO_3)_2$ and 0.1 M $Al_2(SO_4)_3$
(vii) 0.2 M urea and 0.3 M $MgCl_2$

(a) 5 (b) 6
(c) 4 (d) 3

59. Osmosis is involved in one or more processes.

(i) Reverse osmosis
(ii) The membrane allow passage of solute molecules
(iii) Evaporation
(iv) Excretion of urine
(v) Interchange of nutrient and waste products between tissue cells and their surroundings

How many statements are correct?

(a) 3 (b) 2
(c) 1 (d) 4

60. In how many cases, van't Hoff factor remains unchanged?

(i) *Aq.* $SnCl_4$ reacts with *aq.* NH_3
(ii) $PtCl_4$ reacts with *aq.* KCl
(iii) *Aq.* $FeCl_3$ reacts with *aq.* $K_4[Fe(CN)_6]$
(iv) $KMnO_4$ reduced to MnO_2 in alkaline medium
(v) $MnCl_4$ reacts with *aq.* KCl
(vi) *aq.* $ZnCl_2$ reacts with *aq.* NH_3
(vii) *aq.* NaOH reacts with *aq.* $BaCl_2$

(a) 3 (b) 1
(c) 4 (d) 5

61. Consider the following solutions.

(i) $FeCl_3$, 30% ionised
(ii) K_2SO_4, 40% ionised
(iii) $SnCl_4$, 20% ionised
(iv) KCl, 50% ionised
(v) $AgNO_3$, 50% ionised
(vi) $Al(NO_3)_3$, 100% ionised
(vii) $K_4[Fe(CN)_6]$, 20% ionised

In how many cases the van't Hoff factor value is less than 1.8?

(a) 4 (b) 2 (c) 5 (d) 3

62. Among the given solutions.

(i) 1 M acetic acid in benzene
(ii) 1 M Na_3PO_4
(iii) 1 M ammonium phosphate
(iv) 1 M *aq.* glucose
(v) 1 M KNO_3
(vi) 1 M *aq.* sodium chloride
(vii) 1 M NH_4NO_3

How many solutions are hypertonic solutions of 1 M benzoic acid in benzene in nature?

(a) 7 (b) 5
(c) 4 (d) 2

63. Among the given aqueous solutions.

(i) 1 m Urea (ii) 1 m Sucrose
(ii) 1 m Potassium sulphate (iv) 1 m Aluminium sulphate
(v) 1 m Sodium chloride

How many of them have high vapour pressure than 1 m $K_3[Fe(CN)_6]$?

(a) 3 (b) 2 (c) 4 (d) 1

Matching Type Questions

64. Match Column I with Column II.

Column I	Column II
A. Hypertonic	1. Solutions having same osmotic pressure.
B. Isotonic	2. One solution has higher osmotic pressure than the second solution.
C. van't Hoff factor	3. Abnormal molar mass.
D. Hypotonic	4. One solution has less osmotic pressure than the second solution.

Codes

(a) A-2, B-1, C-4, D-3 (b) A-4, B-3, C-2, D-1
(c) A-3, B-4, C-2, D-1 (d) A-2, B-1, C-3, D-4

65. Match Column I with Column II.

Column I	Column II
A. Urea, glucose	1. 2 : 3
B. NaCl, $MgCl_2$	2. 1 : 1
C. $Al_2(SO_4)_3$, Na_3PO_4	3. 1 : 2
D. Glucose, NaCl	4. 1 : 0.8

Codes

(a) A-2, B-1, C-4, D-3 (b) A-4, B-3, C-2, D-1
(c) A-3, B-4, C-2, D-1 (d) A-2, B-1, C-3, D-4

66. Match Column I with Column II.

Column I	Column II
A. Van't Hoff factor, i	1. Ebullioscopic
B. K_b	2. Isotonic solutions
C. Solutions with same osmotic pressure	3. $\frac{\text{Normal molar mass}}{\text{Abnormal molar mass}}$
D Azeotropes	4. Solutions with same composition of vapour above it

Codes

(a) A-3, B-1, C-4, D-2 (b) A-1, B-3, C-2, D-4
(c) A-3, B-1, C-2, D-4 (d) A-3, B-2, C-1, D-4

67. Match the following terms given in Column I with the Column II (van't Hoff factor approx).

Column I	Column II
A. KCl in water	1. 0.5
B. Ethanoic acid in benzene	2. 2
C. K_2SO_4 in water	3. 3
D $C_{12}H_{22}O_{11}$ in water	4. 1

Codes

(a) A-2, B-3, C-1, D-4 (b) A-1, B-3, C-2, D-4
(c) A-2, B-1, C-3, D-4 (d) A-1, B-2, C-3, D-4

Final Check Through PYQs

Module-I Types and Concentration of Solutions

1. In one molal solution that contains 0.5 mole of a solute, there is *[NCERT (New) Pg. 5, NEET 2022]*
(a) 500 g of solvent
(b) 100 mL of solvent
(c) 1000 g of solvent
(d) 500 mL of solvent

2. Which of the following is dependent on temperature? *[NEET 2017]*
(a) Molality (b) Molarity
(c) Mole fraction (d) Weight percentage

3. What is the mole fraction of the solute in a 1.00 m aqueous solution? *[AIPMT 2015]*
(a) 0.177 (b) 1.770 (c) 0.0354 (d) 0.0177

Module-II Solubility, Vapour Pressure, Raoult's Law

4. The Henry's law constant (K_H) values of three gases (A, B, C) in water are 145, 2×10^{-5} and 35 kbar respectively. The solubility of these gases in water follow the order *[NEET 2024]*
(a) $B > A > C$
(b) $B > C > A$
(c) $A > C > B$
(d) $A > B > C$

5. Given below are two statements : one is labelled as Assertion (A) and the other is labelled as Reason (R).
Assertion (A) Helium is used to dilute oxygen in diving apparatus.
Reason (R) Helium has high solubility in O_2.
In the light of the above statements, choose the correct answer from the options given below. *[NEET 2023]*
(a) Both A and R are true and R is the correct explanation of A.
(b) Both A and R are true but R is not the correct explanation of A.
(c) A is true but R is false
(d) A is false but R is true.

6. The correct option for the value of vapour pressure of a solution at 45°C with benzene to octane in molar ratio 3 : 2 is [At 45°C vapour pressure of benzene is 280 mm Hg and that of octane is 420 mm Hg. Assume ideal gas]. *[NCERT (New) Pg. 11, NEET 2021]*
(a) 160 mm of Hg (b) 168 mm of Hg
(c) 336 mm of Hg (d) 350 mm of Hg

7. The mixture which shows positive deviation from Raoult's law is *[NEET 2020]*
(a) benzene + toluene
(b) acetone + chloroform
(c) chloroethane + bromoethane
(d) ethanol + acetone

8. Which of the following statements is correct regarding a solution of two compounds *A* and *B* exhibiting positive deviation from ideal behaviour? *[NCERT (New) Pg. 13, NEET 2019]*
(a) Intermolecular attractive forces between *A*—*A* and *B*—*B* are stronger than those between *A*—*B*.
(b) $\Delta_{mix}H = 0$ at constant *T* and *p*.
(c) $\Delta_{mix}V = 0$ at constant *T* and *p*.
(d) Intermolecular attractive forces between *A*—*A* and *B*—*B* are equal to those between *A*—*B*.

9. In water saturated air the mole fraction of water vapour is 0.02. If the total pressure of the saturated air is 1.2 atm, the partial pressure of dry air is *[NCERT (New) Pg. 12, NEET 2019]*
(a) 1.18 atm (b) 1.76 atm
(c) 1.176 atm (d) 0.98 atm

10. The mixture that forms maximum boiling azeotrope is *[NCERT (New) Pg. 14, NEET 2019]*
(a) ethanol + water
(b) acetone + carbon disulphide
(c) heptane + octane
(d) water + nitric acid

11. Which of the following statements about the composition of the vapour over an ideal 1 : 1 molar mixture of benzene and toluene is correct? Assume that the temperature is constant at 25°C.
(Given, vapour pressure data at 25°C, benzene =12.8, kPa, toluene = 3.85 kPa *[NCERT (New) Pg. 10, NEET 2016]*
(a) The vapour will contain a higher percentage of toluene.
(b) The vapour will contain equal amounts of benzene and toluene.
(c) Not enough information is given to make a prediction.
(d) The vapour will contain a higher percentage of benzene.

12. Which of the following is incorrect for ideal solution? *[NCERT (New) Pg. 13, NEET 2016, Phase II]*
(a) $\Delta H_{mix} = 0$
(b) $\Delta U_{mix} = 0$
(c) $\Delta p = p_{obs.} - p_{\text{calculated by Raoult's law}} = 0$
(d) $\Delta G_{mix} = 0$

13. Which one is not equal to zero for an ideal solution? *[NCERT (New) Pg. 13, AIPMT 2015]*
(a) ΔH_{mix}
(b) ΔS_{mix}
(c) ΔV_{mix}
(d) $\Delta p = p_{observed} - p_{Raoult}$

Module-III Colligative Properties (Part I)

14. If 8 g of a non-electrolyte solute is dissolved in 114 g of n-octane to reduce its vapour pressure to 80%, the molar mass (in g mol^{-1}) of the solute is [Given that, molar mass of n-octane is 114 g mol^{-1}] *[NEET 2020]*
(a) 40 (b) 60
(c) 80 (d) 20

15. At 100°C the vapour pressure of a solution of 6.5 g of a solute in 100 g water is 732 mm. If $K_b = 0.52$, the boiling point of this solution will be *[NCERT (New) Pg. 17, NEET 2016]*
(a) 100°C (b) 102°C
(c) 103°C (d) 101°C

16. The following solutions were prepared by dissolving 10 g of glucose ($C_6H_{12}O_6$) in 250 mL of water (p_1), 10 g of urea (CH_4N_2O) in 250 mL of water (p_2) and 10 g of sucrose ($C_{12}H_{22}O_{11}$) in 250 mL of water (p_3). The right option for the decreasing order of osmotic pressure of these solutions is *[NCERT (New) Pg. 21, NEET 2021]*
(a) $p_2 > p_1 > p_3$ (b) $p_1 > p_2 > p_3$
(c) $p_2 > p_3 > p_1$ (d) $p_3 > p_1 > p_2$

17. Isotonic solutions have same *[NCERT (New) Pg. 22, NEET (Oct.) 2020]*
(a) vapour pressure (b) freezing temperature
(c) osmotic pressure (d) boiling temperature

18. If molality of the dilute solution is doubled, the value of molal depression constant (K_f) will be *[NCERT (New) Pg. 18, NEET 2017]*
(a) doubled (b) halved
(c) tripled (d) unchanged

Module-IV Colligative Properties (Part II)

19. The plot of osmotic pressure (π) *vs* concentration (mol L^{-1}) for a solution gives a straight line with slops 25.73 L bar mol^{-1}. The temperature at which the osmotic pressure measurement is done is (Use $R = 0.083$ L bar $mol^{-1}K^{-1}$) *[NEET 2024]*
(a) 37°C (b) 310°C (c) 25.73°C (d) 12.05°C

20. The van't Hoff factor (i) for a dilute aqueous solution of the strong electrolyte barium hydroxide is *[NCERT (New) Pg. 24, NEET 2016]*
(a) 0 (b) 1 (c) 2 (d) 3

21. The boiling point of 0.2 mol kg^{-1} solution of X in water is greater than equimolal solution of Y in water. Which one of the following statements is true in this case? *[NCERT (New) Pg. 25, AIPMT 2015]*
(a) X is undergoing dissociation in water.
(b) Molecular mass of X is greater than the molecular mass of Y.
(c) Molecular mass of X is less than the molecular mass of Y.
(d) Y is undergoing dissociation in water while X undergoes no change.

22. Which one of the following electrolytes has the same value of van't Hoff factor (i) as that of $Al_2(SO_4)_3$ (if all are 100% ionised)? *[NCERT (New) Pg. 25, AIPMT 2015]*
(a) K_2SO_4
(b) $K_3[Fe(CN)_6]$
(c) $Al(NO_3)_3$
(d) $K_4[Fe(CN)_6]$

23. Of the following 0.10 m aqueous solutions, which one will exhibit the largest freezing point depression? *[AIPMT 2014]*
(a) KCl
(b) $C_6H_{12}O_6$
(c) $Al_2(SO_4)_3$
(d) K_2SO_4

Answers

Step up Practice 1

1 (d)	2 (d)	3 (c)	4 (c)	5 (d)	6 (b)	7 (a)	8 (d)	9 (a)	10 (c)
11 (c)	12 (d)	13 (d)	14 (d)	15 (d)	16 (b)	17 (a)	18 (a)	19 (c)	20 (b)
21 (b)	22 (c)	23 (b)	24 (b)	25 (a)	26 (a)	27 (d)	28 (c)	29 (d)	30 (c)
31 (b)	32 (d)	33 (c)							

Step up Practice 2

1 (d)	2 (d)	3 (a)	4 (a)	5 (c)	6 (d)	7 (b)	8 (c)	9 (c)	10 (b)
11 (c)	12 (d)	13 (d)	14 (c)	15 (c)	16 (b)	17 (a)	18 (a)	19 (a)	20 (a)
21 (b)									

Step up Practice 3

1 (d)	2 (d)	3 (b)	4 (c)	5 (a)	6 (c)	7 (c)	8 (b)	9 (a)	10 (c)
11 (b)	12 (d)	13 (c)	14 (c)	15 (a)	16 (a)	17 (d)	18 (d)	19 (c)	20 (b)

Step up Practice 4

1 (c)	2 (a)	3 (c)	4 (b)	5 (b)	6 (b)	7 (b)	8 (d)	9 (c)	10 (a)
11 (a)	12 (d)	13 (c)	14 (c)	15 (b)	16 (d)	17 (c)	18 (b)	19 (b)	20 (d)
21 (d)	22 (a)	23 (d)	24 (d)						

Gearing up for NEET

1 (a)	2 (b)	3 (c)	4 (d)	5 (b)	6 (a)	7 (a)	8 (d)	9 (b)	10 (b)
11 (a)	12 (b)	13 (a)	14 (d)	15 (b)	16 (b)	17 (c)	18 (d)	19 (c)	20 (c)
21 (a)	22 (c)	23 (d)	24 (d)	25 (b)	26 (a)	27 (b)	28 (a)	29 (a)	30 (d)
31 (a)	32 (c)	33 (b)	34 (b)	35 (b)	36 (c)	37 (d)	38 (b)	39 (b)	40 (a)
41 (d)	42 (d)	43 (a)	44 (c)	45 (d)	46 (d)	47 (d)	48 (c)	49 (c)	50 (a)
51 (c)	52 (a)	53 (b)	54 (d)	55 (c)	56 (c)	57 (d)	58 (d)	59 (a)	60 (b)
61 (d)	62 (a)	63 (a)	64 (a)	65 (a)	66 (c)	67 (c)			

Final Check through PYQs : Module-I

1 (a)	2 (b)	3 (d)

Final Check through PYQs : Module-II

4 (b)	5 (c)	6 (c)	7 (d)	8 (a)	9 (c)	10 (d)	11 (d)	12 (d)	13 (b)

Final Check through PYQs : Module-III

14 (a)	15 (d)	16 (a)	17 (c)	18 (d)

Final Check through PYQs : Module-IV

19 (a)	20 (d)	21 (a)	22 (d)	23 (c)

Hints and Solutions

Step up Practice 1

1. (*d*) Among the given pairs, option (d) is not the correct match as amalgam of mercury with sodium is a solid solution where amalgam of mercury is a solute and sodium is a solvent.
2. (*d*) When solute is present in trace quantities, concentration is expressed in parts per million (ppm).
3. (*c*) For a very diluted solution preferred concentration term is parts per million (ppm).
4. (*c*) A is true but R is false.

   The correct form of R is :

   Mercury is a solute and sodium is solvent in the solution.
5. (*d*) 15 M H_2SO_4 means 15 mol L^{-1}.

   Amount of H_2SO_4 in 1000 mL solution $= 15 \times 98$ g

   Also, 1000 mL $= 1000 \times 1.8$ g H_2SO_4 solution

   So, 100 g solution contains $H_2SO_4 = \frac{15 \times 98 \times 100}{1000 \times 1.8}$

   $= \frac{1470}{1800} \times 100 = 81.6\%$

   Thus, mass percentage of H_2SO_4 = 81.6%.
6. (*b*) Percentage by mass of glucose

   $= \frac{34.2}{434.2} \times 100\%$

   $= 7.87\% \approx 7.9\%$
7. (*a*) Mass of methanol $= 160$ g

   Molar mass of the methanol $= 32$ g/mol

   No. of moles of methanol $= \frac{160}{32} = 5$

   Similarly, no. of moles of water $= \frac{180}{18} = 10$

   Thus, mole fraction of methanol in the solution

   $= \frac{\text{no. of moles of methanol}}{\text{total number of moles in a solutions}} = \frac{5}{15} = 0.33$
8. (*d*) Mass of NaCl = 5.85 g

   Mass of H_2O = 90 g

   No. of moles of NaCl $= \frac{5.85}{58.5} = 0.1$

   No. of moles of $H_2O = \frac{90}{18} = 5$

   Mole fraction of solute $= \frac{n_{\text{solute}}}{n_{\text{solute}} + n_{\text{solvent}}}$

   Mole fraction $= \frac{0.1}{5 + 0.1}$

   $\chi_B = 0.0196$
9. (*a*) Mole fraction of water, $\chi_w = \frac{1}{1+4} = \frac{1}{5} = 0.2$

   and mole fraction of ethanol, $\chi_e = \frac{4}{1+4} = \frac{4}{5} = 0.8$

   So, the mole fraction of water and ethanol will be 0.2 and 0.8 respectively.
10. (*c*) As, 80 g of NaOH is mixed with 54 g of water.

    Moles of NaOH $= \frac{80}{40} = 2$

    Similarly,

    Moles of $H_2O = \frac{54}{18} = 3$

    $\chi_{H_2O} = \frac{n_{H_2O}}{n_{H_2O} + n_{NaOH}}$

    $\chi_{H_2O} = \frac{3}{3+2} = \frac{3}{5}$
11. (*c*) A is true but R is false.

    The correct form of R is :

    The mole fraction does not depend on the temperature.
12. (*d*) H_3PO_3 is dibasic acid as it contains 2 replaceable H atoms.

    Normality = Basicity × Molarity

    Normality $= 2 \times 0.3 = 0.6$ N
13. (*d*) 10 N and 1/10 N, solution is called decanormal and decinormal solution, respectively.
14. (*d*) Molarity

    $= \frac{\text{Mass of anhydrous } Na_2CO_3}{\text{Molar mass of anhydrous } Na_2CO_3 \times \text{Volume (in L)}}$

    $\Rightarrow \quad 0.25 = \frac{\text{Mass of anhydrous } Na_2CO_3}{106 \times 0.25}$

    $w = 106 \times 0.25 \times 0.25$

    $w = 6.625$ g
15. (*d*) Moles of NaCl = 0.006

    Volume of solution $= 100$ mL

    Molarity $(M) = \frac{0.006 \times 1000}{100 \text{ (mL)}}$

    Molarity = 0.06 M

16. (*b*) Mole of 2.5 L of 1 M NaOH $= 2.5 \times 1 = 2.5$

Mole of 3.0 L of 0.5 M NaOH $= 3.0 \times 0.5 = 1.5$

Total moles of NaOH solution $= 2.5 + 1.5 = 4.0$

Total volume of solution $= 2.5 + 3.0 = 5.5$ L

Thus, molarity of resultant solution is given by

$$M = \frac{\text{Total moles of solute}}{\text{Total volume of solution (in L)}}$$

$$4.0 = M \times 5.5$$

$$M = \frac{4.0}{5.5} = 0.73 \text{ M}$$

17. (*a*) Both A and R are true and R is the correct explanation of A.

18. (*a*) Molar mass of NaCl = 58.5 g/mol

No. of moles for 100 mL of 0.3 M is

$$= \frac{100 \times 0.3}{1000} = 0.03 \text{ mole}$$

Similarly,

No. of moles for 100 mL of 0.4 M is

$$= \frac{100 \times 0.4}{1000}$$

$$= 0.04 \text{ mole}$$

So, the moles of NaCl to be added would be

$$0.04 - 0.03 = 0.01 \text{ mole}$$

Thus, 0.01×58.5 g $= 0.585$ g

So, we can say that we need to add 0.585 g of NaCl in order to prepare 0.40 M NaCl from 100 mL of 0.30 M NaCl.

19. (*c*) As we know,

Molarity = Number of moles of solute/Volume of solution (in L)

No. of moles = Molarity × Volume

$$= 3 \times 1 \text{ [Volume} = 1000 \text{ in mL]}$$

$$= 3 \text{ mol}$$

20. (*b*) Molality remains independent of temperature.

21. (*b*) The molality of a solution is the number of moles of solute per 1000 g (1 kg) of the solvent.

22. (*c*) It is number of moles, whose magnitude depends upon the amount of matter hence, it is an extensive property.

23. (*b*) 100 kg $= 10 \times 10^4$ g (sample)

400 mg $= 400 \times 10^{-3}$ g (contaminant)

$$\text{Thus, ppm} = \frac{400 \times 10^{-3}}{10 \times 10^4} \times 10^6$$

$$= 4 \text{ ppm}$$

24. (*b*) Normality of 2 M sulphuric acid is 4 *N*.

25. (*a*) Molar mass of $[Al_2(SO_4)_3]$

$$= 2 \times 27 + 3 \times (32 + 4 \times 16)$$

$$= 342 \text{ g/mol}$$

$$\text{Molarity } (M) = \frac{\left(\frac{22}{342}\right)}{\left(\frac{100}{1.252 \times 1000}\right)} = 0.805 \text{ M}$$

$$\text{Molality } (m) = \frac{\left(\frac{22}{342}\right)}{\left(\frac{78}{1000}\right)} = 0.825 \text{ m}$$

Normality $(N) = 6 \times$ molarity $= 6 \times 0.805 = 4.83$ N

26. (*a*) Given,

The density of solution = 1.8 g/mL

Mass of one litre of solution = 1800 g

$$\therefore \text{Mass of } H_2SO_4 \text{ in the solution} = \frac{1800 \times 90}{100} = 1620 \text{ g}$$

$$\therefore \text{Mass of solvent} = 1800 - 1620 = 180 \text{g}$$

$$\text{So, molality} = \frac{1620}{98} \times \frac{1000}{180} = 91.84$$

27. (*d*) As we know,

$$d = M\left(\frac{1}{m} + \frac{\text{Molar mass of solute}}{1000}\right)$$

$$= 1.212\left(\frac{1}{94.12} + \frac{40}{1000}\right)$$

$$= 1.212\ (0.010 + 0.04)$$

$$d = 0.606 \text{ g mL}^{-1}$$

28. (*c*) Among the given statements, three statements, i.e. (ii), (iii) and (iv) are correct.

29. (*d*) 15% of mass by volume means, 15 g of H_2SO_4 present in 100 mL of solution.

Volume of solution = 100 mL

Density = 1.1 g / cm^3

Mass of solution $= 1.1 \times 100 = 110$ g

$$\text{Now, molality} = \frac{\text{No. of moles of } H_2SO_4}{\text{Mass of solvent (in g)}} \times 1000$$

$$= \frac{15 \text{ g} \times 1000}{98 \times (110 - 15)} = 1.61 \text{ molal}$$

30. (*c*) Among the given pair, option (c) is not correct regarding molality.

Its correct form is :

30 g of sodium chloride dissolved in 500 g of water has 1.02 m (molality).

31. (*b*) Among the given statements, only three statements, i.e. (i), (iv) and (v) are correct while other (ii) and (iii) are incorrect.

Their correct form are :

(i) Molality of a solution does not depend on the temperature.

(ii) Molarity of a solution relates to moles of solutes and volume of solution in litres.

32. (*d*) Molality of the solution does not depend on the temperature and it is an intensive property.

33. (*c*)

Step up Practice 2

1. (*d*) Solubility of a gas in a liquid solvent decreases with increase of temperature and decrease of pressure.

2. (*d*) For Li_2CO_3 salt, solubility decreases with an increase in temperature because the reaction of Li_2CO_3 with water is an exothermic reaction.

3. (*a*) The value of Henry's law constant K_H, increases with increase in temperature.

4. (*a*) Given,

Solubility $(S) = 6.8 \times 10^{-4}$ mol L^{-1}

$$p = 1 \text{ atm}$$

$$p = K_H \times S$$

$$K_H = \frac{p}{S} = \frac{1}{6.8 \times 10^{-4}}$$

$$= 1.470 \times 10^3$$

At atmospheric condition,

Given, $p = 0.34$ atm

Then, $p = K_H S$

$$S = \frac{p}{K_H} = \frac{0.34}{1.470 \times 10^3}$$

$$= 2.312 \times 10^{-4} \text{ M}$$

5. (*c*) Higher the value of Henry's law constant, lower is the solubility of gas in water (or in liquid solvent).

The order of K_H value is

He	>	H_2	>	O_2
144.97 kbar		69.16 kbar		34.86 kbar

Thus, the order of solubility is $He < H_2 < O_2$.

6. (*d*) Given, partial pressure of $N_2 = 1$ bar

K_H for $N_2 = 70$ kbar $= 70 \times 10^3$ bar

According to Henry's law,

Partial pressure $(p) = K_H \times$ mole fraction (χ)

$$\chi_{N_2} = \frac{1}{70 \times 10^3}$$

$$= 0.014 \times 10^{-3}$$

Also, 1 litre of water contains = 55.55 moles

Let the number of moles of nitrogen in the aqueous solution be *a*.

Thus, $\chi_{N_2} = \frac{a}{a + 55.55}$ $[a << 55.55]$

$$0.014 \times 10^{-3} = \frac{a}{55.55}$$

$$a = 0.77 \times 10^{-3}$$

$$a = 0.77 \text{ millimoles}$$

7. (*b*) Given, $p^\circ_A = 450$ mm of Hg

$$p^\circ_B = 900 \text{ mm of Hg}$$

$$p_{total} = 800 \text{ mm of Hg}$$

From Raoult's law, we have

$$p_{total} = p^\circ_A \chi_A + p^\circ_B (1 - \chi_A)$$

$$p_{total} = (p^\circ_A - p^\circ_B)\chi_A + p^\circ_B$$

$$800 = (450 - 900)\chi_A + 900$$

$$800 = -450\chi_A + 900$$

$$-100 = -450\chi_A$$

$$\chi_A = 0.22$$

Therefore, $\chi_B = 1 - \chi_A = 1 - 0.22 = 0.78$

Now, $p_A = p^\circ_A \chi_A = 450 \times 0.22 = 99$

and $p_B = p^\circ_B \chi_B = 900 \times 0.78 = 702$

So, mole fraction of liquid *B* in vapour phase

$$= \frac{p_B}{p_A + p_B}$$

$$= \frac{702}{99 + 702} = 0.876 \approx 0.88$$

8. (*c*) A is true but R is false. The correct form of R is : Both the solute and solvent will form the vapour but vapour phase will become richer in the more volatile component.

9. (*c*) As, $p_{total} = p^\circ_A \chi_A + p^\circ_B \chi_B$

$$= 100 \times \frac{1}{5} + 90 \times \frac{4}{5} = 92$$

$$\chi'_A \text{ (vapours)} = \frac{p^\circ_A x_A}{p_{total}} = \frac{20}{92} = \frac{10}{46}$$

Similarly,

$$\chi'_B \text{ (vapours)} = \frac{72}{92} = \frac{36}{46}$$

So, p_{total} (distillate) $= p^\circ_A \chi'_A + p^\circ_B \chi'_B$

$$= 100 \times \frac{10}{46} + 90 \times \frac{36}{46}$$

$$= 92.17 \approx 92 \text{ mm Hg}$$

10. (*b*) The vapour pressure of a pure liquid increases, when temperature of a pure liquid increases.

11. (*c*) As, $Y_A = \frac{p^\circ_A \times X_A}{p^\circ_A \times X_A + p^\circ_B \times X_B}$

$$Y_A = \frac{X_A}{X_A + X_B \frac{p^\circ_B}{p^\circ_A}} \quad \because p^\circ_A > p^\circ_B$$

$$\therefore \quad \frac{Y_A}{X_A} = \frac{1}{X_A + X_B \dfrac{p^\circ_B}{p^\circ_A}}$$

$$Y_A > X_A \quad \text{...(1)}$$

Similarly,

$$Y_B = \frac{p^\circ_B \times X_B}{p^\circ_A X_A + p^\circ_B X_B} = \frac{X_B}{X_B + X_A \dfrac{p^\circ_A}{p^\circ_B}} \quad \text{...(2)}$$

$$\therefore \quad Y_B > X_B$$

$$\therefore \quad \frac{Y_A}{Y_B} > \frac{X_A}{X_B}$$

12. (*d*) Among the given pairs, only (d), i.e. $\Delta H_{mix} = 0$ and $\Delta V_{mix} = 0$ is correct for ideal solution.

13. (*d*) Raoult's law is obeyed by a binary liquid solution (*AB*) when forces of attractions between *A*—*A* and *A*—*B* are identical.

14. (*c*) Among the given pairs, only acetone-chloroform shows a negative deviation from Raoult's law.

15. (*c*) A is true but R is false.

    The correct form of R is :

    Water and ethanol form non-ideal solution with positive deviation from Raoult's law.

16. (*b*) Among the given pairs, only benzene-methanol shows a positive deviation from Raoult's law.

17. (*a*) Among the given species, only one, i.e. ΔG_{mix} is less than zero for an ideal solution.

18. (*a*) Among the given cases, only one, i.e. (i) Raoult's law is not applicable.

    Because, if the total number of particles of solute changes in the solution due to association or dissociation, Raoult's law is not applicable.

19. (*a*) A maximum boiling azeotrope is a non-ideal solution which show large negative deviation from Raoult's law.

20. (*a*) Both A and R are true and R is the correct explanation of A.

21. (*b*) Among the given compounds, only one, i.e. (v) form maximum boiling azeotropes.

Step up Practice 3

1. (*d*) As we know, $\chi_B = \dfrac{p^\circ_A - p}{p^\circ_A}$

$$\text{So, } 0.019 = \frac{\dfrac{w_B}{M_B}}{\dfrac{w_A}{M_A} + \dfrac{w_B}{M_B}}$$

$$0.019 = \frac{\dfrac{5}{M_B}}{\dfrac{5}{M_B} + \dfrac{58}{18}}$$

$$0.019 = \frac{\dfrac{5}{M_B}}{\dfrac{90 + 58M_B}{18M_B}}$$

$$0.019 = \frac{5}{M_B} \times \frac{18M_B}{90 + 58M_B}$$

$$1.71 + 1.102M_B = 90$$

$$M_B = 80.12 \text{ g/mol} \approx 80 \text{ g/mol}$$

2. (*d*) Among the given statements, only statement (d) is correct while all other, i.e. (a), (b) and (c) are incorrect. Their correct form are
   - The vapour pressure of a solvent in solution is less than that of pure solvent.
   - The lowering of vapour pressure depends only on the concentration of the solute particles.
   - The lowering of the vapour pressure depends on the sum of the mole fraction of different solutes.

3. (*b*) As we know,

$$\frac{p^\circ - p_s}{p^\circ} = \frac{n}{n+N}$$

Given, $p^\circ = 0.250$ atm

$$\text{Thus, } \frac{0.250 - p_s}{0.250} = \frac{\dfrac{30}{128}}{\dfrac{30}{128} + \dfrac{10}{46}} = \frac{0.23}{0.23 + 0.22}$$

$$0.250 - p_s = \frac{0.23 \times 0.250}{0.45} = 0.127$$

$$p_s = 0.250 - 0.127$$

$$p_s = 0.123 \text{ atm}$$

4. (*c*) Statement I is false but Statement II is true.

   The correct form of Statement I is :

   For dilute solutions, relative lowering of vapour pressure may be written as, $\dfrac{p^\circ_1 - p_1}{p^\circ_1} = \dfrac{n_2}{n_1}$

5. (*a*) If $p^\circ = 100$ mm of Hg, $p_s = 100 - 20 = 80$ mm of Hg

$$\text{So, } \frac{p^\circ - p_s}{p^\circ} = \frac{w_2 / M_2}{W_1 / M_1} = \frac{w_2}{M_2} \times \frac{M_1}{W_1}$$

By putting the values,

$$\frac{100 - 80}{100} = \frac{w_2}{60} \times \frac{18}{186}$$

$$w_2 = \frac{20}{100} \times \frac{60 \times 186}{18}$$

$$w_2 = 124 \text{ g}$$

6. (c) According to relative lowering of vapour pressure

$$\frac{\Delta p}{p^\circ} = \chi_B$$

$$\chi_B = \frac{0.60 - 0.40}{0.60} = \frac{0.20}{0.60} = 0.33$$

7. (c) Among the given statements, only statement (c) is correct while other statements (a), (b) and (d) are incorrect.

Their correct form are :

Vapour pressure of the solvent decreases in the presence of non-volatile solute.

The vapour pressure of water depends upon the temperature.

The lowering of vapour pressure depends only on the concentration of the solute particles.

8. (b) Among the given match only (b) is incorrect.

Its correct form is :

50 g of urea in 850 g of water $\rightarrow \Delta p = (0.0173)\, p^\circ$

9. (a) Given,

Relative lowering of vapour pressure = 0.0325

$$\text{So, } 0.0325 = \frac{n_a}{n_a + n_b} \cong \frac{n_a}{n_b}$$

Since, $n_a << n_b$

$$\text{Thus, } 0.0325 = \frac{n_a \times 18}{w_{H_2O}}$$

$$1000 \times \frac{0.0325}{18} = \frac{n_a}{w_{H_2O}} \times 1000$$

$$\text{Molality} = \frac{n_a}{w_{H_2O}} \times 1000$$

$$= \frac{0.0325}{18} \times 1000 = 1.805$$

10. (c) Among the given statements, only statement (c) is incorrect. Its correct form is :

The vapour pressure of a liquid increase with increase of temperature.

11. (b) As we know,

$$\Delta T_b = K_b \cdot m$$

Mass of the solute A in first solution = 0.4316 g

$$\text{No. of moles of solute } A \text{ in first solution} = \frac{0.4316}{62}$$

Suppose the mass of 40 mL of CCl_4 is w g.

For the first solution,

$$\text{Molality} = \frac{0.4316/62}{w} \times 1000 = \frac{431.6}{62w}$$

$$K_b = \frac{0.502}{431.6/62w}$$

As, for second solution,

$$\text{Molality} = \frac{0.8216/M}{w} \times 1000 = \frac{821.6}{wM}$$

$$\text{So, } K'_b = \frac{0.647}{821.6/wM}$$

For the same solvent, $K_b = K'_b$

$$\text{Hence, } \frac{0.502}{431.6/62w} = \frac{0.647}{821.6/wM}$$

So, $M = 91.573 \approx 92$ g/mol

12. (d) Among the given statements, only statement (d) is true, i.e. when a mixture of two immiscible liquids at a constant pressure of 1 atm boils at a temperature that is smaller than the normal boiling point of either of the liquid.

13. (c) As, $\Delta T_b = K_b \times m$

$$\Delta T_b = K_b \times \frac{w_s}{M_s} \times \frac{1}{\text{Mass of solvent (kg)}}$$

$$90.77 = 2.18 \times \frac{5.8}{M} \times \frac{1}{0.138}$$

$$90.77 \times M = \frac{12.644}{0.138}$$

$$M = \frac{12.644}{0.138 \times 90.77} = 1.0094 \approx 1.01 \text{ g mol}^{-1}$$

14. (c) Statement I is false but Statement II is true.

Its correct form is :

ΔT_b is equal to $\frac{2K_b Y}{M}$, when Y g of non-volatile organic substance of molecular mass M is dissolved in 500 g benzene.

15. (a) Among the given statements, only statement (a) is incorrect.

Its correct form is :

The unit of boiling point elevation constant is K kg mol^{-1}.

16. (a) Given, $w_B = 0.37$ g

$$W_A = 18 \text{ g}$$

$$\Delta T_b = 0.312°\text{C}$$

As we know,

$$\Delta T_b = K_b \cdot \frac{w_B}{M_B} \times \frac{1000}{W_A}$$

$$M_B = \frac{K_b \cdot w_B \times 1000}{\Delta T_b \times W_A}$$

$$= \frac{3.12 \times 0.37 \times 1000}{0.312 \times 18}$$

$$= 205.6 \text{ g/mol}$$

17. (*d*) Both Statement I and Statement II are true.

18. (*d*) As we know,

$$M_2 = \frac{K_b \times w_2 \times 1000}{\Delta T_b \times W_1}$$

$$= \frac{3.16 \times 0.12 \times 1000}{0.1 \times 20}$$

$$= \frac{379.2}{2} = 189.6$$

19. (*c*) From elevation in boiling point,

$$\Delta T_b = K_b \times m$$

$$m = \frac{2}{0.76} = \frac{2.5 \times 1000}{M_2 \times 100} \quad \text{...(i)}$$

M_2 = molar mass of the solute

When the concentration of solute is much lower than the concentration of solvent,

$$\frac{p^\circ - p}{p^\circ} = \frac{\text{No. of moles of solute}}{\text{No. of moles of solvent}}$$

$$\frac{760 - p}{760} = \frac{2.5/M_2}{100/18} \quad \text{...(ii)}$$

From Eqs (i) and (ii), $p = 724$ mm.

20. (*b*) As we know,

$$\Delta T_b = K_b \times m$$

$$\Delta T_b = K_b \times \frac{1000 \times w_2}{M_2 \times w_1}$$

$$= \frac{3.61 \times 1000 \times 250}{154 \times 48.5}$$

$$\Delta T_b = 120.83$$

Therefore, the boiling point of the solution is

$$= 80.1 + 120.83 = 200.93^\circ\text{C}$$

Step up Practice 4

1. (*c*) $\Delta T_f = K_f \times \frac{w_1 \times 1000}{w_2 \times M_1}$

where, w_1 = mass of solute

w_2 = mass of solvent

M_1 = molar mass of solute

K_f = freezing point depression constant

$$\Delta T_f = 4.12 \times \frac{3 \times 1000}{51.2 \times 250}$$

$$\Delta T_f = 0.966 \text{ K}$$

2. (*a*) ΔT_0 = freezing point of solvent (280 K)

ΔH_f = latent heat of fusion (50 cal g^{-1})

$$K_f = \frac{RT_0^2}{1000\, \Delta H_f} = \frac{2 \times (280)^2}{1000 \times 50} = 3.136 \text{ K mol}^{-1} \text{ kg}$$

$$\Delta T_f = \text{molality} \times K_f = 0.3 \times 3.136 = 0.94 \text{ K}$$

3. (*c*) Statement (ii) is incorrect while other statements are correct. The correct form of (ii) is as follows

Depression of freezing point for dilute solution is directly proportional to the molal concentration or molality.

4. (*b*) Statement I is true but Statement II is false.

The correct form is as follows

The degree of decrease in freezing point is greater for a solute that forms strong ion-dipole interactions with the solvent molecules.

5. (*b*)

(i) $KNO_3 \longrightarrow K^+ + NO_3^-$ $(i = 2)$

$$\Delta T_f = 2 \times K_f \times 0.1 = 0.2K_f$$

(ii) $BaCl_2 \longrightarrow Ba^{2+} + 2Cl^-$ $(i = 3)$

$$\Delta T_f = 3 \times K_f \times 0.1 = 0.3K_f$$

(iii) $AlCl_3 \longrightarrow Al^{3+} + 3Cl^-$ $(i = 4)$

$$\Delta T_f = 4 \times K_f \times 0.1 = 0.4K_f$$

(iv) $Al_2(SO_4)_3 \longrightarrow 2Al^{3+} + 3SO_4^{2-}$ $(i = 5)$

$$\Delta T_f = 5 \times K_f \times 0.1 = 0.5K_f$$

(v) $NH_4Cl \longrightarrow NH_4^+ + Cl^-$ $(i = 2)$

$$\Delta T_f = 2 \times K_f \times 0.1 = 0.2K_f$$

Hence, KNO_3 and NH_4Cl have same freezing point.

6. (*b*) Volume of the solution, $(V) = 3$ L

Molar mass of solute, $(m) = 180$ g/mol

[Given, Temperature = 27° C = 300 K

Pressure $(\pi) = 9.54$ atm]

Hence, $\pi = CRT = \frac{n}{V} RT = \frac{wRT}{mV}$

$$w = \frac{\pi \cdot m \cdot V}{R \times T}$$

$$= \frac{9.54 \times 180 \times 3}{0.0821 \times 300}$$

$$w = 209.159 \text{ g}$$

$$\text{Number of moles} = \frac{\text{Mass}}{\text{Molar mass}}$$

$$= \frac{209.16}{180} = 1.162 \approx 1.16$$

7. (*b*)

$$\pi_f V_f = \pi_1 V + \pi_2 V$$

$$\pi_f (2V) = 1.30 \times V + 4.5V$$

$$\pi_f = \left(\frac{1.30 + 4.5}{2V}\right) V$$

$$= \frac{5.8}{2} = 2.9 \text{ atm}$$

8. (*d*) Statement (d) is incorrect, while the other statements are correct. The correct form of (d) is as follows :

The flow of solvent molecules stop only when the equilibrium attained.

9. (*c*) Statement I is false but Statement II is true. The correct form of Statement I is as follows

KCl solution has greater osmotic pressure than glucose because KCl dissociates into ions while glucose does not.

For KCl, $\pi = iCRT$, $(i = 2)$

For glucose, $\pi = iCRT$, $(i = 1)$

10. (*a*) The statement (a) is correct while other statements are incorrect. Their correct form are as follows

(b) Isotonic solutions have same osmotic pressure.

(c) A raw mango placed in concentrated salt solution loses water *via* osmosis.

(d) Osmotic pressure method is preferred for the determination of molar masses of proteins, polymers and other macromolecules.

11. (*a*) Option (a) is correctly matched among the given other options.

Solution with equal molar concentrations are isotonic.

So, 0.1 M $Ca(NO_3)_2$ and 0.1 M Na_2SO_4 are isotonic as both gives 3 ions with equal concentrations.

12. (*d*) Statement (d) is incorrect. Its correct form is as follows

The biomolecules are usually not stable at higher temperatures.

13. (*c*) van't Hoff factor for NaCl

$\Rightarrow \quad 1 + x = 1 + 0.9 \Rightarrow 1.9$

van't Hoff factor for $MgCl_2$

$\Rightarrow \quad 1 + 2x = 1 + 2 \times 0.4 = 1.8$

$\therefore$ Total van't Hoff factor = 3.7

14. (*c*) Molality $= \dfrac{55 \times 1000}{180 \times 80} = 3.819$ kg mol^{-1}

$\therefore$ Depression in freezing point

$\Rightarrow \quad 3 = 3.819 \times 1.82 \times i$

$i = 0.432 \approx 0.4$

15. (*b*) Only statement (b) is incorrect, rest all are correct. The correct statement for (b) is as follows

van't Hoff factor more than unity indicates that the solute in solution has dissociated.

16. (*d*) Both Statement I and Statement II are true.

I. $KCl \rightleftharpoons K^+ + Cl^-$ $(n = 2)$

$$\alpha = \frac{i-1}{n-1} = \frac{1.95-1}{2-1} = 0.95$$

II. For Na_2SO_4

$$Na_2SO_4 \longrightarrow \underset{2}{2Na^+} + \underset{1}{SO_4^{2-}}$$

$n = 3$

$i = 1 - \alpha + n\alpha$

$i = 1 - \alpha + 3\alpha$

$i = 1 + 2\alpha$

17. (*c*) Only 1 species $[Al_2(SO_4)_3]$ has same value of van't Hoff factor as that of $K_4[Fe(CN)_6]$.

As, $K_4[Fe(CN)_6] \rightleftharpoons 4K^+ + [Fe(CN)_6]^{4-}, i = 5$

$Al_2(SO_4)_3 \rightleftharpoons 2Al^{3+} + 3SO_4^{2-}, i = 5$

18. (*b*) $\pi = iCRT$, $\pi = 5.39$ atm, $C = 0.1$ M

$i = ?$, $R = 0.0821$ L atm mol^{-1} K^{-1},

$T = 37 + 273 = 310$ K

$5.39 = i \times 0.1 \times 0.0821 \times 310$

$i = 2.1$

$$\alpha\% = \frac{i-1}{n-1} \times 100$$

In $K_3[Fe(CN)_6] \Rightarrow n = 4$

$$\frac{2.1-1}{4-1} = \frac{1.1}{3} \times 100 = 36.67\%$$

19. (*b*) As concentration is increased boiling point of solution also increases, so only two species have higher boiling point than 10^{-3} M $MgCl_2$. i.e. 10^{-4} M NaCl and 10^{-4} M urea.

20. (*d*) Option (d) is not correctly matched, rest are all correctly matched.

0.1 M glucose has only one (1) ion because it is non-volatile, so it has $i = 1$ only.

21. (*d*) $i = \dfrac{\text{Calculated molar mass}}{\text{Observed molar mass}}$

$\Rightarrow \quad \dfrac{170}{102.76} = 1.65$

$\alpha = i - 1 = 1.65 - 1$

$= 0.65 \times 100 = 65\%$

22. (*a*) Option (a) is not correctly matched, other options are correct. The correct form of (a) is as follows

(a) $\pi V = inRT$

23. (*d*) Only the option (d) is correct. Other are incorrectly matched.

(a) $0 < i < 1 \rightarrow$ For association of molecules to form dimer.

(b) $i > 1 \rightarrow$ For strong electrolytes (dissociation).

(c) $i = 1 \rightarrow$ For weak electrolytes and non-electrolytes.

24. (*d*) Statement (d) is correctly matched, while others are not.

The correct match for others are

(a) 0.015 M Glucose $\rightarrow i = 1$

(b) 0.10 M $Na_2SO_4 \rightarrow i = 3$

(c) 0.01 M $KNO_3 \rightarrow i = 2$

Gearing up for NEET

1. (a) 150 kg $=15\times10^4$ g sample

$$450\text{ mg}=450\times10^{-3}\text{ g pollutant}$$

$$\text{Thus, ppm}=\frac{450\times10^{-3}}{15\times10^4}\times10^6=3\text{ ppm}$$

2. (b) Lead $=10\,\mu$g per decilitre or in 0.1 L.

$$=10\,\mu\text{g in }100\text{ mL}$$

Thus, 100 mL blood has lead $=10\times10^{-6}=10^{-5}$ g ion

$$10^9\text{ mL blood has lead}=\frac{10^{-5}\times10^9}{100}=100\text{ ppb}$$

3. (c) We know that,

$$\text{Molality}=\frac{\text{Number of moles of solute}}{\text{Mass of the solvent (g)}}\times1000$$

Given that, molality $=\frac{4}{8}=0.5$

Moles of solute = 0.213

$$\text{Then, }0.5=\frac{0.213}{\text{Mass of the solvent (g)}}\times1000$$

So, mass of the solvent (g) = 426 g

4. (d) Mass of MeOH $=150\times0.791=118.65$

Mass of EtOH $=150\times0.998=149.7$

$$M_1=\frac{118.65\times1000}{32\times300}=12.36$$

$$M_2=\frac{149.7\times1000}{46\times300}=10.85$$

Thus, $M_1>M_2$

5. (b) As,

$$\text{Molality}=\frac{\text{Number of moles of solute}}{\text{Mass of the solvent (g)}}\times1000$$

Given, molality = 5 mol/kg

Moles of solute = 0.38

$$\text{So,}\quad 5=\frac{0.38\times1000}{\text{Mass of the solvent (g)}}$$

Thus, mass of the solvent = 76 g

6. (a) Molar ratio of benzene to hexane

$$\frac{n_B}{n_h}=\frac{7}{2}$$

Mole fraction of benzene,

$$\chi_B=\frac{n_B}{n_B+n_h}=\frac{7x}{9x}=\frac{7}{9}$$

Similarly, Mole fraction of hexane,

$$\chi_h=\frac{n_h}{n_B+n_h}=\frac{2x}{9x}=\frac{2}{9}$$

Total vapour pressure of solution

$$p_S=\chi_B p^\circ_B+\chi_h p^\circ_h$$

$$=\frac{7}{9}\times630+\frac{2}{9}\times420=490+93.33$$

$$=583.33\text{ mm Hg}\approx583\text{ mm Hg}$$

7. (a) As we know,

Total pressure $=p^\circ_A\chi_A+p^\circ_B\chi_B$

$$=p^\circ_A\chi_A+p^\circ_B(1-\chi_A)$$

$$=(p^\circ_A-p^\circ_B)\chi_A+p^\circ_B \quad\text{...(i)}$$

But from the given equation,

$$p=270\chi_A+90 \quad\text{...(ii)}$$

From (i) and (ii) equation,

$$p^\circ_A-p^\circ_B=270$$

$$p^\circ_B=90$$

$$\therefore\quad p^\circ_A=270+90=360$$

$$\text{So,}\quad\frac{p^\circ_A}{p^\circ_B}=\frac{360}{90}=\frac{4}{1}=4:1$$

8. (d) Total vapour of solution,

$$p_S=\chi_B p^\circ_B+\chi_O p^\circ_O\quad\left[\chi_B=\frac{5}{12}\text{ and }\chi_O=\frac{7}{12}\right]$$

$$=\frac{5}{12}\times570+\frac{7}{12}\times720$$

$$=237.5+420$$

$$=657.5\text{ mm Hg}$$

9. (b) $\Delta H_{mix}>0$, endothermic dissolution, heat is absorbed.

$\Delta V_{mix}>0$, volume increased after dissolution.

10. (b) Among the given statement (b) is incorrect. Its correct form is :

Chloroform and diethyl ether shows negative deviation from Raoult's law.

11. (a) According to Raoult's law,

$$p_T=(0.08\times200+0.92\times600)\text{ torr}$$

$$=16+552=568\text{ torr}=0.747\text{ atm}$$

$$p_{exp}=0.98>0.74\text{ atm}$$

Hence, solution show +ve deviation.

So, $\Delta V_{mix}>0$ and $\Delta H_{mix}>0$.

12. (b) Among the given pair, only (b) is correct to be an ideal solution because both are non-polar solution and do not change the strength of intermolecular force of attraction on mixing.

13. (a) In the first solution number of the moles of urea

$$=\frac{\text{Mass of urea}}{\text{Molar mass of urea}}=\frac{12}{60}=0.2$$

In second solution the number of moles of cane sugar

$$=\frac{\text{Mass of cane sugar}}{\text{Mol. wt. of cane sugar}}=\frac{68.4}{342}=0.2$$

So, the lowering of vapour pressure in the first solution is same as that of 2nd solution.

14. (*d*) Here, relative lowering of given vapour pressure is,

$$\frac{\Delta p}{p^\circ} = 0.2$$

Now, $$\frac{\Delta p}{p^\circ} = \chi_B = \frac{n_B}{n_B + n_A} = \frac{\frac{w_B}{M_B}}{\frac{W_B}{M_B} + \frac{W_A}{M_A}}$$

By putting the values,

$$0.2 = \frac{5.8 / M_B}{\frac{5.8}{M_B} + \frac{90}{90}}$$

$$0.2 = \frac{5.8}{M_B} \times \frac{90M_B}{5.8 \times 90 + 90M_B}$$

$$0.2 = \frac{522}{522 + 90M_B}$$

$$104.4 + 18M_B = 522$$

$$M_B = \frac{522 - 104.4}{18} = 23.2 \text{ g mol}^{-1}$$

15. (*b*) Partial pressure of dry air = Total pressure × Mole fraction of dry air

Given, $\chi_{\text{saturated air}} = 0.23$

$$\chi_{\text{dry air}} = 1 - 0.23 = 0.77$$

$$p_{\text{total}} = 5.2 \text{ atm}$$

$\therefore$ $$p_{\text{dry air}} = 5.2 \times 0.77 = 4.004 \text{ atm}$$

16. (*b*) Among the given statements, only (b) is incorrect.

Its correct form is :

A solution containing a non-volatile solute has a higher boiling point than pure solvent.

17. (*c*) Given, $N_2 = 20$ mol

$$H_2 = 45 \text{ mol}$$

$$NH_3 = 25 \text{ mol}$$

Mole fraction of hydrogen gas $= \frac{45}{90} = 0.5$

The partial pressure of hydrogen

$= p_{\text{hydrogen}} \times$ mole fraction of hydrogen gas

$= 40 \times 0.5$

$= 20$ atm

18. (*d*) As we know, $\frac{p_0 - p_s}{p_s} = \frac{w_B \times M_A}{m_B \times W_A}$

$$\frac{20}{(850 - 20)} = \frac{4 \times 88}{m \times 78}$$

$$\frac{20}{830} = \frac{352}{78m}$$

$$m = 187.28 \text{ g/mol}$$

19. (*c*) Given, $\frac{\Delta p}{p^\circ} = 0.1$

So, $$\frac{\Delta p}{p^\circ} = \chi_B = \frac{n_B}{n_B + n_A}$$

$$\frac{\Delta p}{p^\circ} = \frac{\frac{w_B}{M_B}}{\frac{w_B}{M_B} + \frac{w_A}{M_A}}$$

By putting the values,

$$0.1 = \frac{\frac{8.71}{M_B}}{\frac{8.71}{M_B} + \frac{140}{100}}$$

$$0.1 = \frac{8.71}{M_B} \times \frac{100M_B}{8.71 \times 100 + 140M_B}$$

$$87.1 + 14M_B = 871$$

$$M_B = \frac{871 - 87.1}{14} = 55.9 \approx 60 \text{ g mol}^{-1}$$

20. (*c*) From Raoult's law of partial pressure,

$$\frac{p^\circ_A - p_s}{p_s} = \frac{n_B}{n_A}$$

$$\frac{760 - 632}{632} = \frac{w_B \times M_A}{M_B \times W_A}$$

$$0.203 = \frac{7.85 \times 18}{M_B \times 100}$$

$$M_B = \frac{141.3}{20.3} = 6.96 \approx 7$$

$\therefore$ $$\Delta T_b = 0.81 \times \frac{7.85 \times 1000}{7 \times 100} = \frac{6358.5}{700} = 9.08$$

$\therefore$ Boiling point $= 100 + 9.08 = 109.08°C$

21. (*a*) Among the given match, (a) is not a correct match.

Its correct form is :

Hydrogen gas in palladium – A solution of gas in solid.

22. (*c*) As we know, $\Delta T_f = K_f m$

$$0.58 = K_f m \quad \text{...(i)}$$

$$\Delta T_b = iK_b m$$

$$0.23 = iK_b m \quad \text{...(ii)}$$

On dividing Eqs. (i) by (ii), we get

$$\frac{0.58}{0.23} = \frac{K_f}{iK_b}$$

$$\frac{0.58}{0.23} = \frac{3.7}{i}$$

$$i = \frac{3.7 \times 0.23}{0.58} = 1.47$$

Since, van't Hoff factor, $i > 1$, its a case of dissociation.

23. (*d*) Barium sulphate is completely dissociated into cations and anions in aqueous solution is shown as

$$BaSO_4 \longrightarrow Ba^{2+} + SO_4^{2-}$$

So, van't Hoff factor (*i*) for $BaSO_4 = 2$

As, $\Delta T_f = i \times K_f \times m$

$= 2 \times 1.38 \times 0.02$

$\Delta T_f = 0.0552$ K

$[\because m = \frac{0.02 \text{ mol}}{1 \text{ kg}} = 0.02 \text{ mol kg}^{-1}]$

24. (*d*) Among the given match, only (d) is incorrectly matched.

Its corrected match is :

For 1.5 M $AlCl_3$ solution $\rightarrow \Delta T_f \propto 6$

25. (*b*) As we know,

$$\Delta T_b = iK_b m_1 \text{ and } \Delta T_f = iK_f m_2$$

So, $\frac{\Delta T_b}{\Delta T_f} = \frac{K_b}{K_f} \times \frac{m_1}{m_2}$

$$\frac{4}{6} = \frac{K_b \times 1.5}{K_f \times 4.5}$$

$$\frac{K_b}{K_f} = \frac{18}{9} = 2$$

26. (*a*) As we know,

$$\Delta T_f = K_f \times m = 1.76 \times 0.02 = 0.035$$

$$i = \frac{0.0305}{0.035} = 1 + \alpha$$

$$1 + \alpha = 0.871$$

$$\alpha = -0.128$$

As, $K_a = \frac{C\alpha^2}{1-\alpha} = \frac{0.02 \times (-0.128)^2}{1 + 0.128}$

$$= \frac{0.000327}{1.128} = 0.000290$$

$$K_a = 2.9 \times 10^{-4}$$

As, $K_b = \frac{K_w}{K_a} = \frac{1.0 \times 10^{-14}}{2.9 \times 10^{-4}} = 0.34 \times 10^{-10}$

$$K_b = 3.4 \times 10^{-11}$$

27. (*b*) Among the given pair, only (b) is correctly matched while others are incorrect.

Their corrected form are :

0.3 m ethylene glycol $\rightarrow \Delta T_f = 0.558°C$

0.1 m glucose solution $\rightarrow \Delta T_f = 0.186°C$

0.2 m NaCl solution $\rightarrow \Delta T_f = 0.744°C$

28. (*a*) As we know,

Osmotic pressure, $\pi = i \times MRT$

For, 0.500 M $C_2H_5OH(aq)$, $i = 1$

So, $\pi = 0.5RT$

For, 0.100 M $Mg_3(PO_4)_2(aq)$, $i = 5$

So, $\pi \times 5 \times 0.1RT = 0.5RT$

For, 0.250 M $KBr(aq)$, $i = 2$

So, $\pi = 0.5RT$

For, 0.125 M $Na_3PO_4(aq)$, $i = 4$

So, $\pi = 0.5RT$

Hence, all solutions have same osmotic pressure.

29. (*a*) If *A* contains 2% NaCl and is separated by a semipermeable membrane from *B*, which contains 10% NaCl then water will flow from *A* to *B*.

30. (*d*) Among the given statements, only statement (d) is incorrect. It's correct form is :

Two sucrose solutions of same molality prepared in different solvents have different ΔT_f because K_f of solvents is altogether different.

31. (*a*) Among the given match, option (a) is not correctly match. Its corrected form is :

H_2O (43%) + HI (56.7%) $\rightarrow$ Minimum boiling azeotrope, B.P. = 400 K.

32. (*c*) By using, $\pi_1 V_1 + \pi_2 V_2 = \pi_R(V_1 + V_2)$

$$\pi_R = \frac{\pi_1 V_1 + \pi_2 V_2}{(V_1 + V_2)}$$

$$2.95 = \frac{2.4V_1 + 5.6V_2}{V_1 + V_2}$$

$$2.95V_1 + 2.95V_2 = 2.4V_1 + 5.6V_2$$

$$2.95V_1 - 2.4V_1 = 5.6V_2 - 2.95V_2$$

$$0.55V_1 = 2.65V_2$$

$$\frac{V_1}{V_2} = 4.81$$

33. (*b*) Moles of urea $= \frac{6}{60} = 0.1$

Moles of NaCl $= \frac{6 \times 2}{58.5} = 0.205$

Moles of sucrose $= \frac{6}{342} = 0.017$

Moles of KCl (effective) $= 2 \times \frac{6}{74.5} = 0.16$

So, the correct order is $\pi_2 > \pi_4 > \pi_1 > \pi_3$.

34. (*b*) Among the given relation, only (b) is correct match.

35. (*b*) As, $\Delta T_b = i \times K_b \times m$

$i = 1$, for an ideal solution.

36. (*c*) Only (c) is incorrect match.

Its correct form is :

0.015 M Glucose $\longrightarrow T_b = 0.015K_b + T_b^\circ$

37. (*d*) As we know,

$$\Delta T_f = \frac{1000 \times K_f \times w}{m \cdot W} \times i$$

$$\Delta T_f = 0-(-5.38) = 5.38°C$$

So, $5.38 = \dfrac{1000\times 1.96\times 8}{142\times 48}\times i$

On solving, $i = 2.33$

38. (b) As we know,

$$\Delta T_f = m\times K_f$$

$$0.3 = \frac{X\times 1000}{100}\times 1.86$$

Because for non-electrolyte

$$K_f = 1.86 \text{ K kg mol}^{-1}$$

$$X = 0.0161$$

After freezing, $\Delta T_f = m\times K_f$

$$\Delta T_f = \frac{X\times 1000}{(100-y)}\times 1.86 = 0.35$$

$$0.35 = \frac{0.0161\times 1000}{(100-y)}\times 1.86$$

On solving,

Amount of ice $(y) = 14.44$ g ice

39. (b) Solution with the same osmotic pressure are isotonic. Let the molar mass of the substance is M.

$$\pi_1 = C_1RT = C_2RT = \pi_2$$

So, $C_1 = C_2$

As density of the solution are same.

So, $\dfrac{6.21}{M} = \dfrac{15}{60}$

$$M = \frac{60\times 6.21}{15}$$

$$= 24.84 \approx 25$$

40. (a) Among the given match, only (a) is correct match while other are incorrect.

Their correct form are

- $Al_2(SO_4)_3$, Na_3PO_4, $K_4[Fe(CN)_6] \rightarrow 5:4:2$
- Glucose, NaCl, $CaCl_2 \rightarrow 1:2:3$
- Urea, Glucose, Fructose $\rightarrow$ 1: 1 : 1

41. (d) A is false but R is true.

The correct form of A is :

Maximum amount of a solid solute that can be dissolved in a specified amount of a given liquid solvent does not depend upon pressure.

42. (d) A is false but R is true.

The correct form of A is :

Total vapour pressure of mixture of 1 mole of A and 3 moles of B is 70 mm Hg, it shows positive deviation from Raoult's law.

43. (a) Both A and R are true and R is the correct explanation of A.

44. (c) A is true but R is false. The correct form of R is : CH_3COOH has intermolecular hydrogen bonding.

45. (d) A is false but R is true.

The correct form of A is :

The azeotropic mixture of water (B.P 100°C) and HCl (B.P 85°C) boils at 108.5°C.

When this mixture is distilled, neither pure HCl nor pure water is obtained.

46. (d) A is false but R is true.

The correct form of A is :

When benzoic acid is dissolved in benzene then the value of van't Hoff factor is equal to 0.5.

47. (d) Both Statement I and Statement II are true.

48. (c) Statement I is false but Statement II is true.

The correct form of Statement I is :

The latent heat of vaporisation of water is 9700 cal/mole and if the B.P is 100°C, then K_b of water is 0.513°C.

49. (c) Statement I is false but Statement II is true.

The correct form of Statement I is :

The boiling point of 0.1 M urea solution is less than that of 0.1 M KCl solution.

50. (a) Both Statement I and Statement II are false. Their correct form are :

- The direction of osmosis can be reversed if a pressure more than the osmotic pressure is applied to the solution side.
- Cellulose acetate is impermeable to impurities and ions present in sea water and permeable to water.

51. (c) Statement I is false but Statement II is true.

The correct form of Statement I is :

The van't Hoff factor (i) for an infinitely dilute solution of $NaHSO_4$ is 3.

52. (a) Among the given statements, only B, D and E are incorrect while other are correct.

The correct form of B, D and E are :

- Solubility of gases in liquids decreases with increase in temperature.
- In a nearly saturated solution, if the dissolution process is endothermic, then the solubility should increase with rise in temperature.
- Different gases have different K_H values at the same temperature.

53. (b) Among the given statements, only B and E are correct while other are incorrect.

Their correct form are :

- van't Hoff factor of Hg_2Cl_2 in its aqueous solution is 2.6 when Hg_2Cl_2 is 80% ionised in the solution.
- The value of van't Hoff factor is different for both $Al_2(SO_4)_3$ and $Al(OH)_3$.

- The degree of ionisation of 0.005 M *aq.* KCl is 0.95 if the value of van't Hoff factor is 1.95.

54. (*d*) Among the given statements, only A, B and E are correct while other are incorrect.

Their correct form are :

- Elevation in boiling point of a molar glucose solution ($d = 1.2$ g mL^{-1}) is $0.98K_b$.
- Boiling point of 1 molal NaCl solution is not twice that of 1 molal sucrose solution.

Because ΔT_b (NaCl) $= 2K_b$

So, T_b (NaCl) $= (100 + 2K_b)$

and ΔT_b (sucrose) $= K_b$

So, T_b (sucrose) $= (100 + K_b)$

55. (*c*) Among the given statements, only B, C and D are correct while other are incorrect.

Their correct form are :

- Aquatic species are more comfortable in cold water rather than in warm water.
- Water movement from soil into plant roots and subsequently into upper portion of the plant is partly due to osmosis.

56. (*c*) Among the given statements, only A and B are incorrect while other are correct.

The correct form of A and B are :

- A saturated solution will not remain saturated because it depends on temperature and pressure.
- A plant cell shrink when placed in hypertonic solution.

57. (*d*) Among the given solutions, only one solution, i.e. (iv) has depression in freezing point equal to cryoscopic constant for water.

$$\Delta T_f = K_f \times \text{Molality}$$

59 g aqueous solution has 9 g of glucose and 50 g of water

$$\therefore \quad \Delta T_f = K_f \times \frac{\frac{9}{180 \times 50}}{1000}$$

So, $\Delta T_f = K_f$

58. (*d*) Among the given pair of solutions, (i), (ii) and (iii) are isotonic, as they have same osmotic pressure. Osmotic pressure can be calculated by using the formula, $\pi = iCRT$.

59. (*a*) Among the given statements, only three statements, i.e. (i), (iv) and (v) are correct regarding osmosis process.

60. (*b*) i remains unchanged when number of ions before and after complex ion formation remains constant.

Hence, only one, i.e. (vi) among the given cases in which van't Hoff factor remains unchanged.

61. (*d*) Among the given solutions, only three solution, i.e. (iv), (v) and (vi) have van't Hoff factor value less than 1.8.

By using the formula, $i = [1 + (y - 1)\,x]$

$FeCl_3$, 30% ionised $\rightarrow$ 1.9

K_2SO_4, 40% ionised $\rightarrow$ 1.8

$SnCl_4$, 20% ionised $\rightarrow$ 1.8

KCl, 50% ionised $\rightarrow$ 1.5

$AgNO_3$, 50% ionised $\rightarrow$ 1.31

$Al(NO_3)_3$, 100% ionised $\rightarrow$ 1.3

$K_4[Fe(CN)_6]$, 20% ionised $\rightarrow$ 1.8

62. (*a*) All the given solutions are hypertonic solutions of 1 M benzoic acid in benzene in nature.

As, 1 M benzoic acid, $i = 0.5$

(i) 1 M acetic acid, $i = 0.6$

(ii) 1 M Na_3PO_4, $i = 4$

(iii) 1 M $(NH_4)_3PO_4$, $i = 4$

(iv) 1 M *aq.* glucose, $i = 1$

(v) 1 M KNO_3, $i = 2$

(vi) 1 M NaCl, $i = 2$

(vii) 1 M NH_4NO_3, $i = 2$

63. (*a*) Among the given aqueous solutions, only 3 species have high vapour pressure than 1 m $K_3[Fe(CN)_6]$.

$\because$ Vapour pressure $\propto \frac{1}{i}$

As, 1 m urea $\rightarrow i = 1$

1 m sucrose $\rightarrow i = 1$

1 m potassium sulphate $\rightarrow i = 3$

1 m aluminium sulphate $\rightarrow i = 5$

1 m sodium chloride $\rightarrow i = 2$

64. (*a*) The correct match is A-2, B-1, C-4, D-3.

65. (*a*) The correct match is A-2, B-1, C-4, D-3.

66. (*c*) The correct match is A-3, B-1, C-2, D-4.

67. (*c*) The correct match is A-2, B-1, C-3, D-4.

Final Check Through PYQs

1. (*a*) We know that,

$$\text{Molality} = \frac{\text{Number of moles of solute}}{\text{Mass of the solvent (g)}} \times 1000$$

Given that molality = 1

Moles of solute = 0.5

$$1 = \frac{0.5}{\text{Mass of the solvent (g)}} \times 1000$$

Mass of the solvent (g) = 500 g of solvent.

Hence, option (a) is correct.

2. (*b*) Among the given options only molarity is temperature dependent because it involve volume of solution. Volume is dependent on temperature.

$$\text{Molarity } (M) = \frac{\text{Moles of solute}}{\text{Volume of solution (in L)}}$$

Molality, mole fraction and weight percentage does not depend on temperature because they involve masses of solute and solvent.

3. (*d*) Molality $(m) = \dfrac{1000 \times n}{N \times M}$

where, n = number of moles of solute

N = number of moles of solvent

M = molar mass of solvent

Given, $m = 1$

$$\therefore \quad 1 = \frac{1000 \times n}{N \times 18}$$

$$\Rightarrow \quad \frac{n}{N} = \frac{18}{1000}$$

$$\text{or} \quad \frac{n}{n+N} = \frac{18}{1018} = 0.0177$$

4. (*b*) The relation between solubility and Henry's law constant is

$$\text{Solubility} \times \frac{1}{K_H}$$

if $K_H \downarrow$ then solubility increases.

K_H for gas B is lowest $(2 \times 10^{-5}$ kbar)and

A has highest (145 kbar)

Hence, the order of solubility is given by

$$B > C > A.$$

5. (*c*) A is true but R is false.

This is because at normal temperature and pressure helium is practically insoluble in oxygen. However, under extreme conditions very small amount of helium dissolve in oxygen.

6. (*c*) Molar ratio of benzene to octane, $\dfrac{n_B}{n_O} = \dfrac{3}{2}$

Let $n_B = 3x$ mol, $n_O = 2x$ mol

Total number of moles $= n_B + n_O = 3x + 2x = 5x$ mol

Mole fraction of benzene,

$$\chi_B = \frac{n_B}{n_B + n_O} = \frac{3x}{5x} = \frac{3}{5}$$

Mole fraction of octane,

$$\chi_O = \frac{n_O}{n_B + n_O} = \frac{2x}{5x} = \frac{2}{5}$$

Vapour pressure of benzene,

$$p^\circ_O = 420 \text{ mm Hg}$$

Total vapour pressure of solution,

$$p_S = \chi_B p^\circ_B + \chi_O p^\circ_O$$

$$= \frac{3}{5} \times 280 + \frac{2}{5} \times 420 = 3 \times 56 + 2 \times 84$$

$$= 168 + 168 = 336 \text{ mm of Hg}$$

7. (*d*) Let us study the nature of binary solutions made of two volatile liquids

(a) (Benzene + Toluene) Ideal solution, obey Raoult's law.

(b) (Acetone + Chloroform) Non-ideal solution, shows negative deviation from Raoult's law.

(c) (Chloroethane + Bromoethane) Ideal solution, obeys Raoult's law.

(d) (Ethanol + Acetone) Non-ideal solution, shows positive deviation from Raoult's law.

8. (*a*) Solution exhibits positive deviation from ideal behaviour if the intermolecular interactions, i.e. A—B interactions are more weaker than in pure components, i.e. between A—A or B—B. Thus, option (a) is correct. The remaining options are valid only for ideal solutions.

9. (*c*) Partial pressure of dry air = total pressure × mole fraction of dry air

$$\Rightarrow \quad p_{\text{dry air}} = p_{\text{total}} \times \chi_{\text{dry air}}$$

Given, $\chi_{\text{saturated air}} = 0.02$

$$\chi_{\text{dry air}} = 1 - 0.02 = 0.98$$

$$p_{\text{total}} = 1.2 \text{ atm}$$

$$\therefore \quad p_{\text{dry air}} = 1.2 \text{ atm} \times 0.98 = 1.176 \text{ atm}$$

10. (*d*) The solutions that show large negative deviation from Raoult's law forms maximum boiling azeotrope. e.g. Nitric acid and water.

The remaining option containing different mixtures forms minimum boiling azeotrope.

11. (*d*) Since, component having higher vapour pressure will have higher percentage in vapour phase. Benzene has vapour pressure 12.8 kPa which is greater than toluene 3.85 kPa. Therefore, the vapour will contain a higher percentage of benzene.

12. (*d*) $\quad \Delta G_{\text{mix}} = \Delta H_{\text{mix}} - T\Delta S_{\text{mix}}$

For an ideal gas,

$$\Delta H_{\text{mix}} = 0;\ \Delta U_{\text{mix}} = 0;\ \Delta S_{\text{mix}} \neq 0$$

Putting all these values in the expression,

$$\Delta G_{\text{mix}} = \Delta H_{\text{mix}} - T\Delta S_{\text{mix}}$$

$$\Rightarrow \quad \Delta G_{\text{mix}} = 0 - T\Delta S_{\text{mix}}$$

$$\Rightarrow \quad \Delta G_{\text{mix}} \neq 0$$

Thus, option (d) is incorrect.

13. (*b*) For an ideal solution

(i) There will be no change in volume on mixing the two components, i.e. $\Delta V_{\text{mixing}} = 0$

(ii) There will be no change in enthalpy so $\Delta H_{\text{mixing}} = 0$

So, $\Delta S_{\text{mix}} \neq 0$ for an ideal solution.

14. (*a*) Does not match with the options.

Here, relative lowering of given vapour pressure,

$$\frac{\Delta p}{p^\circ} = 0.2$$

Now, $\frac{\Delta p}{p^\circ} = x_B = \frac{n_B}{n_B + n_A} = \frac{\frac{w_B}{M_B}}{\frac{w_B}{M_B} + \frac{W_A}{M_A}}$

p° = vapour pressure of pure solvent (octane)

Mass of solute $(w_B) = 8$ g

Mass of solvent $(W_A) = 114$ g

Molar mass of solute $(M_B) = ?$

Molar mass of solvent (octane) $(M_A) = 114 \text{ g mol}^{-1}$

$$\Rightarrow \quad 0.2 = \frac{8/M_B}{\frac{8}{M_B} + \frac{114}{114}}$$

$$\Rightarrow \quad M_B = 32 \text{ g mol}^{-1}$$

Alternatively,

Let us take a dilute solution,

$$\frac{\Delta p}{p^\circ} \approx \frac{n_B}{n_A} = \frac{w_A \times M_A}{M_B \times W_A}$$

$$\frac{20}{100} = \frac{8}{M_B} \times \frac{114}{114}$$

$$M_B = 40 \text{ g mol}^{-1}$$

15. (*d*) From Raoult's law of partial pressure,

$$\frac{p_A^\circ - p_S}{p_S} = \frac{n_B}{n_A}$$

$$\Rightarrow \quad \frac{760 - 732}{732} = \frac{w_B \times M_A}{M_B \times W_A}$$

$$\Rightarrow \quad \frac{28}{732} = \frac{6.5 \times 18}{M_B \times 100}$$

$$\Rightarrow \quad M_B = 30.6$$

$$\therefore \quad \Delta T_b = 0.52 \times \frac{6.5 \times 1000}{30.6 \times 100} = 110$$

$\therefore$ Boiling point = 100+1.10= 101.1°C ≈ 101°C

16. (*a*) van't Hoff factor for glucose, urea and sucrose is one as all are non-ionic.

Mass of glucose = 10 g

Molar mass of glucose = 180 g mol^{-1}

Number of moles of glucose $= \frac{10}{180} = \frac{1}{18}$ mol = 0.056 mol

Mass of urea = 10 g

Molar mass of urea = 60 g mol^{-1}

Number of moles of urea $= \frac{10}{60} = \frac{1}{6}$ mol = 0.167 mol

Mass of sucrose = 10 g

Molar mass of sucrose = 342 g mol^{-1}

Number of moles of sucrose $= \frac{10}{342} = 0.029$ mol

Osmotic pressure is a colligative property which depends on the amount of solute present in the solution. As the amount of urea is more than that of glucose and sucrose.

Amount of solute : Urea > Glucose > Sucrose

$\therefore$ Osmotic pressure, $p_2 > p_1 > p_3$

17. (*c*) Isotonic solutions have same osmotic pressure (π) at a given temperature

$$\pi = CRT$$

When, two solution have same molar concentration (C) their osmotic pressure will be equal.

18. (*d*) For a dilute solution, the depression in freezing point (ΔT_f) is directly proportional to molality (m) of the solution.

$$\Delta T_f \propto m \text{ or } \Delta T_f = K_f m$$

where, K_f is called molal depression constant or freezing point depression constant or cryoscopic constant.

The value of K_f depends only on nature of the solvent and independent of composition of solute particles, i.e. does not depend on the concentration of solution.

19. (*a*) Osmotic pressure is given by

$$\pi = CRT$$

Plot is between osmotic pressure and concentration i.e. π *vs* C on comparing with $y = mx$

$$\text{Slope, } m = RT$$

$$25.73 = 0.083 \times T$$

$$T = 310 \text{ K or } 37°\text{C}$$

20. (*d*) van't Hoff factor = total number of ions after dissociation

So for $Ba(OH)_2 \rightleftharpoons Ba^{2+}(aq) + 2OH^-(aq)$

van't Hoff factor, $i = 1 + 2 = 3$

21. (*a*) Molality of solution X = Molality of solution Y = 0.2 mol/kg

We know that, elevation in the boiling point (ΔT_b) of a solution is proportional to the molal concentration of the solution i.e., $\Delta T_b \propto m$ or $\Delta T_b = K_b m$

where, m is the molality of the solution and K_b is molal boiling point constant or ebullioscopic constant.

$\therefore$ By elevation in boiling point relation

$$\Delta T_b = iK_b m \text{ or } \Delta T_b \propto i$$

where, i is van't Hoff factor.

Since, ΔT_b of solution X is greater than ΔT_b of solution Y. (Observed colligative property is greatest than normal colligative property).

$\therefore i$ of solution $X > i$ of solution Y

$\therefore$ Solution X undergoing dissociation.

22. (*d*) $Al_2(SO_4)_3 \rightleftharpoons 2Al^{3+} + 3SO_4^{2-}$

Value of van't Hoff factor (i) = 5

(a) $K_2SO_4 \rightleftharpoons 2K^+ + SO_4^{2-}$ $(i = 3)$

(b) $K_3[Fe(CN)_6] \rightleftharpoons 3K^+ + Fe(CN)_6]^{3-}$ $(i = 4)$

(c) $Al(NO_3)_3 \rightleftharpoons Al^{3+} + 3NO_3^-$ $(i = 4)$

(d) $K_4[Fe(CN)_6] \rightleftharpoons 4K^+ + [Fe(CN)_6]^{4-}$ $(i = 5)$

Therefore, $K_4[Fe(CN)_6]$ has same value of i that of $Al_2(SO_4)_3$ i.e. $i = 5$.

23. (*c*) ΔT_f (freezing point depression) is a colligative property and depends upon the van't Hoff factor (*i*), i.e. number of ions given by the electrolyte in aqueous solution.

$$\Delta K_f = i = K_f \times m$$

where, K_f = molal freezing point depression constant

m = molality of the solution

$\therefore$ K_f and m are constant

$\therefore$ $\Delta T_f \propto i$

van't Hoff factor for ionic solution.

(a) $KCl(aq) \rightleftharpoons K^+(aq) + Cl^-(aq)$,

(Total ions = 2 thus, $i = 2$)

(b) $C_6H_{12}O_6 \rightleftharpoons$ no ions $[i = 0]$

because glucose does not give ions.

(c) $Al_2(SO_4)_3(aq) \rightleftharpoons 2Al^{3+} + 3SO_4^{2-}$

[Total ions = 5, thus $i = 5$]

(d) $K_2SO_4(aq) \rightleftharpoons 2K^+ + SO_4^{2-}$

[Total ions = 3, thus, $i = 3$]

Hence, $Al_2(SO_4)_3$ will exhibit largest freezing point depression due to the highest value of *i*.

Skill Builder

- **Sol. of Skill Builder Pg. 3**

(*a*) Molality = $\dfrac{\text{Number of moles of solute}}{\text{Mass of the solvent (g)}} \times 1000$

Given, molality = 4 m

Moles of solute = 3.27 moles

Then, $4 = \dfrac{3.27}{\text{Mass of the solvent (g)}} \times 1000$

Mass of the solvent (g) = 817.5 g of solvent.

- **Sol. of Skill Builder Pg. 9**

(*c*) Higher the value of K_H lower is t he solubility of gas in water so, the correct order of solubility is

$$S > P > Q > R$$

- **Sol. of Skill Builder Pg. 11**

(*b*) Molar ratio of benzene to heptane, $\dfrac{n_B}{n_H} = \dfrac{5}{2}$

Let, $n_B = 5x$ mol and $n_H = 2x$ mol

Total number of moles = $7x$ mol

Mole fraction of benzene, $\chi_B = \dfrac{n_B}{n_B + n_H} = \dfrac{5x}{7x} = \dfrac{5}{7}$

Mole fraction of heptane, $\chi_H = \dfrac{n_H}{n_B + n_H} = \dfrac{2x}{7x} = \dfrac{2}{7}$

By using the formula,

Total vapour pressure of solution,

$$p_s = \chi_B p_B^\circ + \chi_H p_H^\circ$$

$$= \frac{5}{7} \times 496 + \frac{2}{7} \times 627$$

$$= 354.28 + 179.14 = 533.42 \text{ mmHg}$$

- **Sol. of Skill Builder Pg. 16**

(*a*) Now, $\dfrac{\Delta p}{p^\circ} = \chi_B = \dfrac{n_B}{n_B + n_A} = \dfrac{w_B/M_B}{\dfrac{w_B}{M_B} + \dfrac{W_A}{M_A}}$

Given, Mass of solute $(w_B) = 12$ g

Mass of solvent $(w_A) = 130$ g

Molar mass of solute $(M_B) = ?$

Molar mass of solvent (benzene) $(M_A) = 78$ g/mol

So, $0.2 = \dfrac{12/M_B}{12/M_B + 130/78}$

$M_B = 28.8 \approx 29 \text{ g mol}^{-1}$

For deeper insight
Scan the QR Code

Chapter 2

Electrochemistry

Chapter Overview with
NEET Connection

This chapter is useful for the learning of electrochemical cells, cell potential, oxidation reaction, electrolysis etc. Without gripping this chapter it will be difficult to learn and understand the transfer to electrons and energy in various chemical processes.

Special format questions can be easily framed on the following topics of this chapter.

- Electromotive force of the cell
- Application and electrochemical series
- Nernst equation
- Kohlrausch's law
- Faraday's law

For better understanding of this chapter a grip over concept of oxidation-reduction, mole concept, equilibrium quotient, Gibbs free energy, spontaneity and equilibrium constant are required.

As the foundation of this complete chapter involves hefty calculations hence along with the understanding of concepts a focus on calculation part and basic conversion is required.

Learning Objectives

Module-I

- Daniell Cell
- Electrode Potential
- Electromotive Force or Cell Potential
- Electrochemical Series and its Applications

Module-II

- Nernst Equation for Half Cell
- Nernst Equation for Electrochemical Cell
- Equilibrium Constant from Nernst Equation

Module-III

- Conductors
- Conductance of Electrolytic Solution
- Resistance
- Resistivity or Specific Resistance
- Conductance
- Conductivity or Specific Conductance
- Equivalent Conductivity
- Molar Conductivity
- Application of Kohlrausch's law

Module-IV

- Qualitative Electrolysis
- Quantitative Electrolysis
- Batteries
- Fuel Cells

Introduction

Electrochemistry is the branch of chemistry that deals with the study of the production of electricity from chemical energy released during spontaneous redox reactions and the use of electrical energy to bring about non-spontaneous chemical transformations.

A large number of metals, NaOH, Cl_2, F_2 and many other chemicals are produced by electrochemical methods. This chapter deals with the relationship between electrical potential as a quantifiable and quantitative phenomenon. So, let us study about these in detail.

Module 1

Electrochemical Cell

- Daniell Cell
- Electrode Potential
- Electromotive Force or Cell Potential
- Electrochemical Series and its Applications

Electrochemical Cells

It is a device that produces electricity as a result of chemical reaction. In other words, in this device the Gibbs energy of the spontaneous redox reaction is converted into electrical energy.

There are two types of electrochemical cells

1. Galvanic/Voltaic cell
2. Electrolytic cell

Comparison between Galvanic and Electrolytic Cell

Item	Galvanic/Voltaic cell	Electrolytic cell
Metals used for electrode	Two metals with different electrode potentials are used	The same metal can be used for both the cathode and the anode
Charge of the anode	Negative	Positive
Charge of the cathode	Positive	Negative
The electrolyte solution(s)	Are kept separate from one another and are connected only by a salt bridge	The cathode and anode are in the same electrolyte
Energy changes	Chemical potential energy converted to electrical energy	Electrical energy converted to chemical energy
Applications	Electroplating and batteries	Electrolysis, e.g. NaCl

Concept ladder

In a cell, if two electrolytic solutions of different concentrations are in contact with each other, a potential difference develops across the boundary of the two solutions. This potential is called **liquid-junction potential.** Electrolytic concentration cells always have liquid junction.

Galvanic Cells

It is a device used to convert chemical energy produced in a spontaneous redox reaction into electrical energy. These are also called as **voltaic cell.**

A Daniell cell is the best example of a galvanic cell.

In this device, the Gibbs energy of the spontaneous redox reaction is converted into electrical work which may be used for running a motor or other electrical gadgets.

Daniell Cell

- In this cell, anode is made up of Zn-rod which is placed in zinc sulphate solution (oxidation half-cell). Similarly, a Cu-rod is placed in copper sulphate solution taken in another beaker (reduction half-cell).
- In general, electrochemical cell involves the chemical reactions that takes place in two vessels each of which is called **half-cell** or **redox couples.**

  We can construct in numerable number of galvanic cells on the pattern of Daniell cell by taking combinations of different half-cells.
- The two electrodes are connected by a wire and the two solutions are connected by a **salt-bridge.**

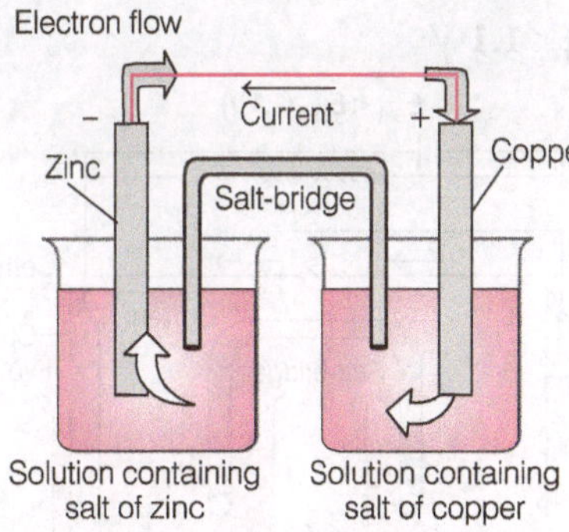

Daniell cell having electrodes of zinc and copper dipping in the solutions of their respective salts

When the Zn and Cu electrodes are joined by wire, following observations are noted.

- Reactions involve in two half-cells are

  At cathode, $Cu^{2+} + 2e^- \longrightarrow Cu(s)$ (Reduction half reaction)

  At anode, $Zn(s) \longrightarrow Zn^{2+} + 2e^-$ (Oxidation half reaction)

- Since, electrons are produced at anode, this electrode is rich in electrons thus also called as **negative electrode.** Whereas, cathode electrode (i.e. Cu-electrode) needs electron for reduction therefore acts as **positive electrode.**
- Thus, in a galvanic cell, the half-cell in which oxidation takes place is called anode and it has a negative potential with respect to the solution.
- The other half-cell in which reduction takes place is called cathode and it has a positive potential with respect to the solution.

Mentor's Tip

The positive (+) sign of the cathode indicates the electrode at which electrons enter the cell and the negative (–) sign of the anode is where the electrons leave the cell.

- There is a flow of electric current in the external circuit from Cu electrode to Zn electrode, i.e. + ve terminal to –ve terminal.
- Zn-rod loses its mass, while Cu-rod gains its mass. Conversely, the concentration of $ZnSO_4$ solution increases while that of $CuSO_4$ solution decreases.
- To maintain the electrical neutrality the cations and anions move through the salt-bridge, this helps to complete the inner circuit.

Functioning of Daniell Cell When External Voltage (E_{ext}) Opposing the Cell Potential is Applied

The standard electrode potential of a Daniell cell is 1.1 V. Following three cases are possible when external voltage (E_{ext}) opposing the cell potential is applied.

(a) When E_{ext} < 1.1 V

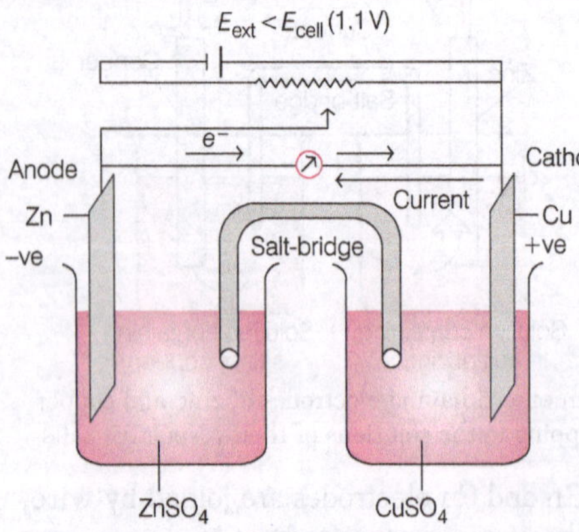

Fig (a)

- Electrons flow from Zn rod to Cu rod hence, current flows from Cu to Zn.
- Zn dissolves at anode and copper deposits at cathode.

(b) When E_{ext} = 1.1 V

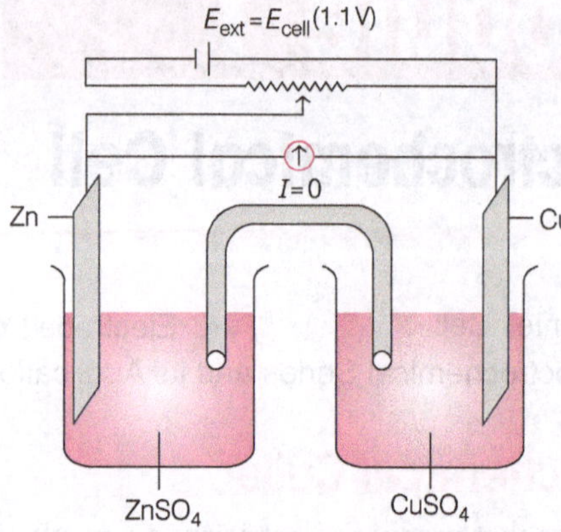

Fig (b)

- No flow of electron or current takes place.
- No chemical reaction takes place.

(c) When E_{ext} > 1.1 V

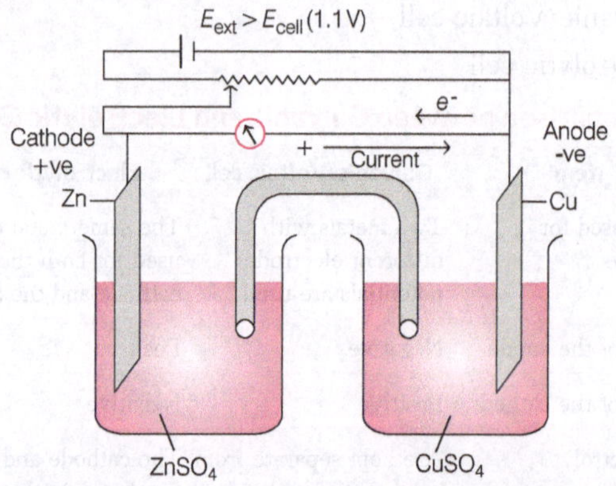

Fig. (c)

- Electrons flow from Cu to Zn and current flows from Zn to Cu.
- Zinc is deposited at the zinc electrode and copper dissolves copper electrode.

Representation of Electrochemical Cell

The following conventions are used in representing an electrochemical cell.

- The electrode on which oxidation takes place is written on the left hand side. While the electrode on which reduction takes place is written on the right hand side.
- The electrode on the left hand side is written by writing the symbol of the metal (or the gas) first followed by the symbol of the ion with its concentration in brackets.
- The electrode on the right hand side is represented by writing the electrolyte first (anion) and then the metal or solid phase.

- Single vertical lines represent the base boundaries of the electrodes.
- Double vertical line represents the salt-bridge.
- C_1 and C_2 (or a_1 and a_2) represents the concentrations that are written within the brackets after the cation.

Thus, a complete Daniell cell can be represented as,

$$Zn|Zn^{2+}(C_1)||Cu^{2+}(C_2)|Cu$$

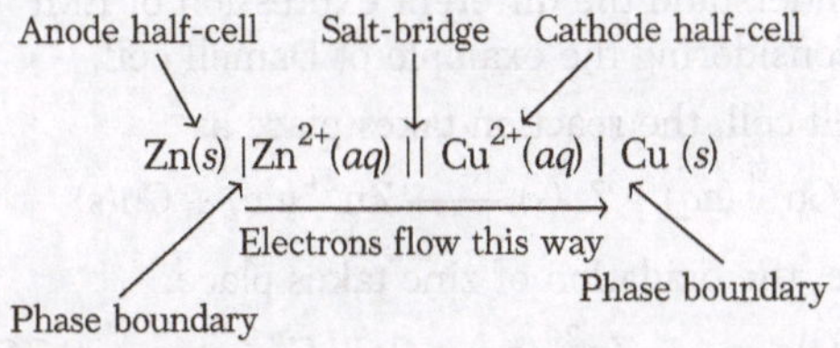

Mentor's TIP

Sometimes we get confused in the nomenclature of electrodes. As a memory aid keep in mind the alphabetical order of the first letter. e.g. A (anode) comes before C (cathode). The cell may be written by arranging each of the pair left-right, anode-cathode, oxidation-reduction, negative and positive in the alphabetical order as

Left anode oxidation negative	Bridge	Right cathode reduction positive

Salt-Bridge

It is a U-shaped glass tube which contains *agar-agar* paste with NH_4NO_3, KNO_3 or KCl as conducting electrolytes. **KCl is not used when electrode is made up of Ag.** This salt-bridge is only used in electrochemical cell.

Significance of salt-bridge The following are the significance of the salt bridge

- It connects the solutions of two half-cells and completes the cell circuits.
- It prevents transference or diffusion of the solutions from one half-cell to the other.
- It keeps the solutions in two half-cells electrically neutral.
- It prevents liquid-liquid junction-potential, i.e. the potential difference which arises between two solutions when in contact with each other.

A broken vertical line or two parallel vertical lines in a cell reaction indicates the salt-bridge.

$$Zn|Zn^{2+}||Cu^{2+}|Cu$$

Electrode Potential

At each electrode-electrolyte interface there is a tendency of metal ions from the solution to deposit on the metal electrode trying to make it positively charged. At the same time, metal atoms of the electrode have a tendency to go into the solution as ions and leaving behind the electrons at the electrode trying to make it negatively charged. Thus, a metal placed in a solution of its ions obtains either a positive or negative charge with respect to the solution. On account of this, a definite potential is developed between the metal and the solution. This potential difference is called **electrode potential.** It depends on the nature of electrode, concentration of ions and temperature.

- **Oxidation potential** It is the tendency of an electrode to get oxidised, i.e. to lose electrons.

  Half cell : $Zn\,|\,Zn^{+2}(aq)$

  Reaction : $Zn \longrightarrow Zn^{+2}(aq) + 2e^-$

  Oxidation potential : $E_{Zn|Zn^{+2}}$ or E_{ox}
- **Reduction potential** It is the tendency of an electrode to get reduced, i.e. to accept electrons.

  Half Cell : $Cu^{+2}(aq)\,|\,Cu$

  Reaction : $Cu^{+2}(aq) + 2e^- \longrightarrow Cu$

  Reduction potential : $E_{Cu^{+2}|Cu}$ or E_{red}

General representation of oxidation and reduction potential

Oxidation potential	$E_{M\|M^{+n}}$
Reduction potential	$E_{M^{+n}\|M}$

Standard Electrode Potential

The potential difference developed between metal electrode and the solution of its ions of unit molarity (1 M) at 25°C (298 K) is called standard electrode potential. It is denoted as $E°$.

Standard electrode potential	$E°_{M\|M^{+n}}$
Standard reduction potential	$E°_{M^{+n}\|M}$

Mentor's TIP

- Electrode potential is an intensive property and state function.
- Electrode potential does not depend upon reaction stoichiometry.
- Reduction potential and oxidation potential of an electrode are numerically equal but have opposite sign.

Measurement of Electrode Potential

The electrode potential is always determined with respect to a standard electrode or reference electrode. Because neither oxidation nor reduction takes place independently that is, no half-cell work independently.

Thus, for indirect measurement of potential of an electrode, we couple the electrode with reference electrode (as its potential is known). The emf (potential difference when no current is drawn from the system) of resulting cell is measured experimentally.

Now, as we know the emf as well as the potential of reference electrode, the potential of other electrode can be easily determined. One of the important reference electrodes, i.e. SHE is discussed below.

Standard Hydrogen Electrode (SHE)

SHE consist of Pt-wire sealed in a glass tube and has a platinum foil attached to it. The foil is coated with finely divided platinum and acts as platinum electrode.

It is dipped into an acid solution containing H^+ ions in 1M concentration (1M HCl). Hydrogen gas is bubbled into the electrode through inlet as shown in figure. The pressure of hydrogen gas is maintained at 1 bar.

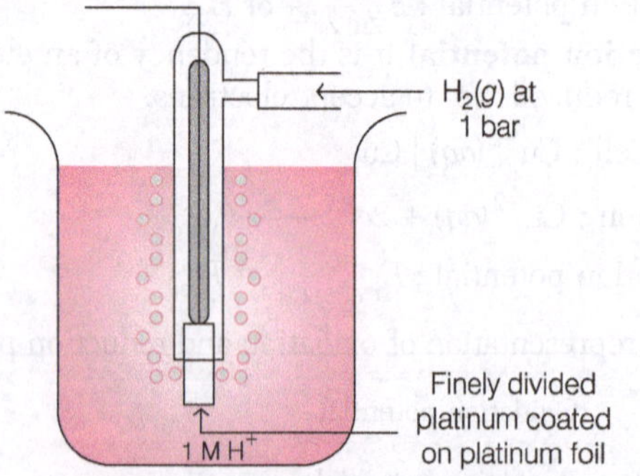

Standard hydrogen electrode (SHE)

H_2 gas gets absorbed on the finely divided platinum. Thus, hydrogen is in contact with H^+ ions of HCl solution at the electrode surface. The assembly so obtained is standard hydrogen electrode.

The following reaction occurs in this half-cell depending upon whether it acts as anode or as a cathode,

- If SHE acts as anode

$$H_2(g) \longrightarrow 2H^+ + 2e^-$$

- If SHE acts as cathode

$$2H^+ + 2e^- \longrightarrow H_2(g)$$

- The SHE potential is taken as zero. The electrode potential of a metal electrode is determined with respect to a standard hydrogen electrode is called standard electrode potential of that electrode.

Concept ladder Pt foil is used in SHE because it is a very good absorber of H_2 gas.

Electromotive Force (emf) of the Cell

The difference in potentials of the two half cells of a cell is known as emf of a cell (E_{cell}). i.e.

$$E^\circ_{cell} = E^\circ_{cathode} - E^\circ_{anode} (\text{value of } E^\circ_{red})$$

$$E^\circ_{cell} = E^\circ_{red.} + E^\circ_{oxi}$$

$$E^\circ_{cell} = E^\circ_{right} - E^\circ_{left}$$

EMF of a cell can be measured by potentiometer or high resistance voltmeter.

EMF of a cell does not depend on size or structure of a cell.

For a spontaneous cell, emf of a cell must be positive. EMF of a cell may be negative but such cells are non-spontaneous and do not produce electricity.

Let us understand the different expression of EMF of a cell by considering the example of Daniell cell.

In Daniell cell, the reaction takes place as

$$Cu^{2+}(aq) + Zn(s) \longrightarrow Zn^{2+}(aq) + Cu(s)$$

At anode, the oxidation of zinc takes place,

$$Zn(s) \longrightarrow Zn^{2+}(aq) + 2e^-; E^\circ_{Zn/Zn^{2+}} = 0.76 \text{ V}$$

At cathode, the reduction of cupric ion takes place,

$$Cu^{2+}(aq) + 2e^- \longrightarrow Cu(s); E^\circ_{Cu^{2+}/Cu} = 0.34 \text{ V}$$

Verifying E°_{cell} using different relationships

- $E^\circ_{cell} = E^\circ_{cathode} - E^\circ_{anode}$ (E°_{red} values)

$= 0.34 - (-0.76)$ $[E^\circ_{anode} = -E^\circ_{Zn/Zn^{2+}} = -0.76 \text{ V}]$

$= 1.10\text{V}$

- $E^\circ_{cell} = E^\circ_{red} + E^\circ_{ox} = E^\circ_{Cu^{2+}/Cu} + E^\circ_{Zn/Zn^{2+}}$

$= 0.34 + 0.76$ (as reaction takes place)

$= 1.10\text{V}$

- $E^\circ_{cell} = E^\circ_{right} - E^\circ_{left}$

$= 0.34 - (-0.76)$ $[E^\circ_{left} = -E^\circ_{Zn/Zn^{2+}} = -0.76 \text{ V}]$

$= 1.10 \text{ V}$

As value of E°_{cell} is same in all the case, hence, any of these relationships can be used to calculate EMF of a cell.

Example 1. *In a simple electrochemical cell, which is in the standard state, the half cell reactions with their appropriate reduction potentials are given below*

$$Pb^{+2}(aq) + 2e^- \longrightarrow Pb(s); \quad E^\circ = -0.13 \text{ V}$$

$$Ag^+(aq) + e^- \longrightarrow Ag(s); \quad E^\circ = 0.80 \text{ V}$$

(i) *What is the cell reaction for the cell?*

(ii) *Calculate the emf of the cell.*

Sol. (i) The reduction potential of $Ag^+ \mid Ag$ electrode is more than that of $Pb^{+2} \mid Pb$.

Therefore, reduction will occur at silver electrode and oxidation will occur at lead electrode and the cell reaction will be.

$$2Ag^+(aq) + Pb(s) \longrightarrow 2Ag(s) + Pb^{+2}(aq)$$

(ii) $E^\circ_{cell} = E^\circ_C - E^\circ_A$

$= 0.80 - (-0.13) = 0.93 \text{ V}$

Concept ladder

Different Types of Electrodes

S. No.	Name of Electrode	Anode	Cathode
1.	Hydrogen electrode	$Pt(s) \mid H_2(g) \mid H^+(aq)$ $E_{OP} = E^\circ_{OP} - \frac{0.0591}{2} \log \frac{[H^+]^2}{p_{H_2}}$	$H^+(aq) \mid H_2(g) \mid Pt(s)$ $E_{RP} = E^\circ_{RP} - \frac{0.0591}{2} \log \frac{p_{H_2}}{[H^+]^2}$
2.	Metal-metal ion electrode	$M(s) \mid M^{+n}(aq)$ $E_{OP} = E^\circ_{OP} - \frac{0.0591}{n} \log [M^{+n}]$	$M^{+n}(aq) \mid M(s)$ $E_{RP} = E^\circ_{RP} - \frac{0.0591}{n} \log \frac{1}{[M^{+n}]}$
3.	Calomel electrode	$Hg(l), Hg_2Cl_2(s) \mid Cl^-(aq)$ $E_{OP} = E^\circ_{OP} - \frac{0.0591}{2} \log \frac{1}{[Cl^-]^2}$	$Cl^-(aq) \mid Hg_2Cl_2(s), Hg(l)$ $E_{RP} = E^\circ_{RP} - \frac{0.0591}{2} \log [Cl^-]^2$
4.	Redox electrode	$Pt(s) \mid Fe^{+2}(aq), Fe^{+3}(aq)$ $E_{OP} = E^\circ_{OP} - \frac{0.0591}{1} \log \frac{[Fe^{+3}]}{[Fe^{+2}]}$	$Fe^{+3}(aq), Fe^{+2}(aq) \mid Pt(s)$ $E_{RP} = E^\circ_{RP} - \frac{0.0591}{1} \log \frac{[Fe^{+2}]}{[Fe^{+3}]}$
5.	Metal insoluble salt anion electrode	$Ag(s) \mid AgCl(s) \mid Cl^-(aq)$ $E_{OP} = E^\circ_{OP} - \frac{0.0591}{1} \log \frac{1}{[Cl^-]}$	$Cl^-(aq) \mid AgCl(s) \mid Ag(s)$ $E_{RP} = E^\circ_{RP} - \frac{0.0591}{1} \log [Cl^-]$

Electrochemical Series

After measuring the potential of various electrode *versus* hydrogen electrode, a series of standard electrode potential has been established which is known as **electrochemical series** or **activity series** or **electromotive series.** In this series, the reduction potentials of various electrodes have been arranged in the increasing order. (See Table).

Electrochemical Series

Element	Electrode reaction (Reduction)	Standard reduction potential (in Volt)	Element	Electrode reaction (Reduction)	Standard reduction potential (in Volt)
Li	$Li^+ + e^- \rightarrow Li$	−3.05	Sn	$Sn^{+2} + 2e^- \rightarrow Sn$	−0.14
K	$K^+ + e^- \rightarrow K$	−2.925	H_2	$2H^+ + 2e \rightarrow H_2$	0.00
Ca	$Ca^{2+} + 2e^- \rightarrow Ca$	−2.87	Cu	$Cu^{+2} + e^- \rightarrow Cu$	+0.337
Na	$Na^+ + e^- \rightarrow Na$	−2.714	I_2	$I_2 + 2e^- \rightarrow 2I^-$	+0.535
Mg	$Mg^{+2} + 2e^- \rightarrow Mg$	−2.37	Ag	$Ag^+ + e^- \rightarrow Ag$	+0.799
Al	$Al^{+3} + 3e^- \rightarrow Al$	−1.66	Hg	$Hg^{+2} + 2e^- \rightarrow Hg$	+0.885
Zn	$Zn^{+2} + 2e^- \rightarrow Zn$	−0.7628	Br_2	$Br_2 + 2e^- \rightarrow 2Br^-$	+1.08
Cr	$Cr^{+3} + 3e^- \rightarrow Cr$	−0.74	Cl_2	$Cl_2 + 3e^- \rightarrow 2Cl^-$	+1.36
Fe	$Fe^{+2} + 2e^- \rightarrow Fe$	−0.44	Au	$Au^{+3} + 3e^- \rightarrow Au$	+1.50
Cd	$Cd^{+2} + 2e^- \rightarrow Ni$	−0.403	F_2	$F_2 + 2e^- \rightarrow 2F^-$	+2.87
Ni	$Ni^{+2} + 2e^- \rightarrow Ni$	−0.25			

Increasing tendency to accept electrons (↓)

Increasing tendency to lose electrons (↑)

Activity decreases (↓)

Characteristics

- The substances which are stronger reducing agents than hydrogen are placed above hydrogen in the series and have negative values of standard reduction potentials.
- All those substances which have positive values of reduction potentials and placed below hydrogen in the series are weaker reducing agents than hydrogen.
- The substances which are stronger oxidising agents than H^+ ion are placed below hydrogen in the series.
- The metals on the top (having high negative values of standard reduction potentials) have the tendency to lose electrons readily. These are active metals.
- The non-metals on the bottom (having high positive values of standard reduction potentials), have the tendency to accept electrons readily. These are active non-metals.

Applications

The important applications of electrochemical series are

(i) **To compare relative strength of oxidising and reducing agent** Greater is the reduction potential, more easily is the substance (element or ion) reduced and stronger oxidising agent it is. e.g. F_2 has the highest reduction potential and Li^+ ions has the lowest reduction potential this means that F_2 is reduced most easily whereas Li^+ ions are reduced with great difficulty.

Thus, F_2 is the strongest oxidising agent and Li^+ ions are the weakest oxidising agents.

(ii) **To compare the relative activities of metals** A metal with greater oxidation potential can displace metals with lower oxidation potential from their salt solution. In other words, a metal with high negative reduction potential can displace metals with less negative reduction potentials from their salt solution.

This concept is very useful in displacement reactions, e.g. oxidation potentials of Al, Mn, Zn, Cr and Fe are in the order

$$Al > Mn > Zn > Cr > Fe$$

Thus, their reactivity is same as of the above order.

(iii) **To calculate the emf of the cell** The emf of the cell can be determined by knowing the electrode potential from the series as

$$E^\circ_{cell} = E^\circ_{right} - E^\circ_{left}$$

(If standard reduction potential are given)

(iv) **To predict the product of electrolysis** The ion which is stronger oxidising agent is discharged first at cathode.

(v) **Help in extraction of metals from their ores.**

(vi) **To predict whether a metal can liberate hydrogen from acid or not.** The metals which have negative reduction potentials (or present above hydrogen) can only liberate hydrogen from the acids.

(vii) **To predict the feasibility of a redox reaction** In general a redox reaction is feasible only if the species which has higher reduction potential is reduced, while the species which has lower reduction potential is oxidised, otherwise redox reaction is not feasible.

NEET Close-up

Example Similar to PYQ Asked in NEET 2022

Given below are the half-cell reactions,

$$Mn^{2+} + 2e^- \longrightarrow Mn, E^\circ_{cell} = -1.18 \text{ V}$$

$$2(Mn^{3+} + 2e^- \longrightarrow 2Mn^{2+}), E^\circ_{cell} = +1.51 \text{ V}$$

The E° for $3Mn^{2+} \longrightarrow Mn + 2Mn^{3+}$ will be

(a) –2.69 V, the reaction will occur
(b) –2.69 V, the reaction will not occur
(c) –0.33 V, the reaction will not occur
(d) –0.33 V, the reaction will occur

Sol. (*b*) For the given half-cell reaction.

$$Mn^{2+} + 2e^- \longrightarrow Mn, E^\circ = -1.18 \text{ V} \quad ...(i)$$

$$2Mn^{3+} + 2e^- \longrightarrow 2Mn^{2+}, E^\circ = +1.51 \text{ V} \quad ...(ii)$$

Subtracting Eq. (ii) from Eq. (i), we get

$$3Mn^{2+} \longrightarrow Mn + 2Mn^{3+}$$

$$E^\circ = -1.18 - (+1.51) = -2.69 \text{ V}$$

Since, the value of E° is –ve, therefore the reaction is non-spontaneous.

Skill Builder

Determine the standard reduction potential for the half-cell reaction, $Cl_2 + 2e^- \longrightarrow 2Cl^-$

Given, $Pt^{2+} + 2Cl^- \longrightarrow Pt + Cl_2, E^\circ_{cell} = -0.15 \text{ V}$

$Pt^{2+} + 2e^- \longrightarrow Pt, E^\circ_{cell} = +1.20 \text{ V}$

(a) –1.35 V (b) 1.05 V (c) –1.05 V (d) 1.35 V

For more practice Refer to Q.15 in step up practice 1 and Q.11 in Gearing up for NEET.

Example 2. *Predict what will happen if molecular bromine* (Br_2) *is added to solution containing* NaCl *and* NaI *at* 25°C. *Assume all species are in their standard states.*

$$I_2(s) + 2e^- \longrightarrow 2I^-(1M); E^\circ = 0.53 \text{ V}$$

$$Br_2(l) + 2e^- \longrightarrow 2Br^- \ (1 \text{ M}); E^\circ = 1.07 \text{ V}$$

$$Cl_2(1 \text{ bar}) + 2e^- \longrightarrow 2Cl^- \ (1 \text{ M}); E^\circ = 1.36 \text{ V}$$

Sol. Standard reduction potentials have been given. Based on these values oxidising nature of Br_2 relative to Cl_2 and I_2 can be compared.

E°_{red} of $I_2 < Br_2 < Cl_2$. Hence, oxidising power of $Cl_2 > Br_2 > I_2$. Thus, $Br_2(l)$ can oxidise I^- to I_2 but cannot oxidise Cl^- to Cl_2,

i.e. $2I^-(aq) + Br_2(l) \longrightarrow 2Br^-(aq) + I_2(s)$

is spontaneous, but

$$2Cl^-(aq) + Br_2(l) \longrightarrow 2Br^-(aq) + Cl_2(g)$$

is non-spontaneous. However, if $E^\circ_{cell} > 0$ then cell reaction is spontaneous.

Example 3. *Arrange the following oxidising agent in order of increasing strength under standard-state conditions $Br_2(l)$, $Fe^{3+}(aq)$, $Cr_2O_7^{2-}(aq)$ given.*

$$Cr_2O_7^{2-} + 14H^+ + 6e^- \longrightarrow 2Cr^{3+} + 7H_2O, \ E^\circ_1 = 1.33 \text{ V}$$

$$Br_2(l) + 2e^- \longrightarrow 2Br^-(aq), E^\circ_2 = 1.06 \text{ V}$$

$$Fe^{3+}(aq) + e^- \longrightarrow Fe^{2+}(aq), E^\circ_3 = 0.77 \text{ V}$$

Sol. E° values given are standard reduction potentials. We find that $E^\circ_1 > E^\circ_2 > E^\circ_3$.

Thus, $Cr_2O_7^{2-}$ has the maximum tendency to be reduced, hence, it is the best oxidising agent, order being $Fe^{3+} < Br_2 < Cr_2O_7^{2-}$.

Mentor's TiP

More positive value of the E°_{red} implies its greater tendency to be reduced hence, bettter oxidising agent.

Example 4. *If* $Co^{3+} + e^- \longrightarrow Co^{2+}; E^\circ = 1.82$ V

$$2H_2O \longrightarrow O_2(g) + 4H^+ + 4e^-; E^\circ = -1.23 \text{ V}$$

Explain Co^{3+} is not stable in aqueous solution.

Sol. $4 \times [Co^{3+} + e^- \longrightarrow Co^{2+}]; E^\circ = 1.82$ V

$$2H_2O \longrightarrow O_2(g) + 4H^+ + 4e^-; E^\circ = -1.23 \text{ V}$$

$$\text{Net}: 4Co^{3+} + 2H_2O \longrightarrow 4Co^{2+} + O_2(g) + 4H^+; \ E^\circ = 0.59 \text{ V}$$

Cell reaction is spontaneous (E° = +ve), hence Co^{3+} is reduced to Co^{2+} thus, unstable in aqueous solution.

Concept ladder Electrochemical cells are extensively used for determining the pH of solutions, solubility product, equilibrium constant and other thermodynamic properties and for potentiometric titrations.

STEP UP Practice 1

1 Which of the following is incorrect match about galvanic cell?

(a) Charge of the cathode $\longrightarrow$ Positive

(b) Metals used $\longrightarrow$ Same metal can be used for both the cathode and the anode.

(c) Energy change $\longrightarrow$ Chemical potential energy converted to electrical energy.

(d) Charge of the anode $\longrightarrow$ Negative

2 Select the incorrect statement.

(a) In a galvanic cell, a spontaneous chemical reaction generates an electric current.

(b) In an electrolytic cell, an electric current drives a non-spontaneous reaction.

(c) In a galvanic cell, cell reaction is exothermic.

(d) Current flows from anode to cathode in galvanic cell.

3 Consider the following statements.

Statement I In Daniell cell, when $E_{ext.}$ (opposite) is less than 1.1 V then Zn dissolves at cathode and copper deposits at anode.

Statement II To maintain the electrical neutrality the cations and anions move through the salt-bridge, this helps to complete the inner circuit.

In the light of the above statements, choose the most appropriate answer from the options given below.

(a) Both Statement I and Statement II are false.

(b) Statement I is true but Statement II is false.

(c) Statement I is false but Statement II is true.

(d) Both Statement I and Statement II are true.

4 Which of the following is correctly match?

(a) Galvanic cell $\rightarrow$ Chemical energy is converted into electrical energy.

(b) Galvanic cell $\rightarrow$ Chemical energy is converted into heat.

(c) Galvanic cell $\rightarrow$ Electrical energy is converted into heat.

(d) Galvanic cell $\rightarrow$ Electrical energy is converted into chemical energy.

5 In the galvanic cell,

$$Fe(s) + 2Fe^{3+}(aq) \longrightarrow 3Fe^{2+}(aq)$$

(a) $Fe(s)$ is at the cathode because it is in contact with $Fe^{2+}(aq)$

(b) $Fe(s)$ is at the cathode because it is in contact with $Fe^{3+}(aq)$

(c) $Fe(s)$ cannot be used at cathode since it would directly react with Fe^{3+}, and short-circuit the cell

(d) salt-bridge contains Fe^{2+} and Fe^{3+} ions

6 For the cell reaction,

$$Cu(s) + Cl_2(aq) \longrightarrow Cu^{2+}(aq) + 2Cl^-(aq)$$

Cell notation is

(a) $Cu(s)|Cu^{2+}(aq)||Cl^-(aq)|Cl_2(g)|C(s)$

(b) $C(s)|Cl^-(aq)|Cl_2(g)||Cu^{2+}(aq)|Cu(s)$

(c) $Cu(s)|Cu^{2+}(aq)||Cl^-(aq)|Cl_2(g)$

(d) $Cu(s)|Cu^{2+}(aq)||Cl_2(aq)|Cl^-(aq)$

7 Electrochemical cell stops working after sometime because
(a) electrode potential of both the electrodes becomes zero
(b) the reaction reverts its direction
(c) one of the electrode completely vanishes
(d) electrode potential of both the electrodes equalise

8 For the reaction,

$$Cd^{2+}(aq) + Zn(s) \longrightarrow Zn^{2+}(aq) + Cd(s)$$

The correct cell representation is
(a) $Zn(s)|Cd(s)||Zn^{2+}(aq)|Cd^{2+}(aq)$
(b) $Cd(s)|Cd^{2+}(s)||Zn(s)|Zn^{2+}(aq)$
(c) $Cd^{2+}(aq)|Zn^{2+}(aq)||Cd(s)|Zn(s)$
(d) $Zn(s)|Zn^{2+}(aq)||Cd^{2+}(aq)|Cd(s)$

9 Select the correct match regarding salt-bridge.
(a) Salt-bridge contains $\longrightarrow$ Calomel
(b) Salt-bridge contains $\longrightarrow$ H_2O
(c) Salt-bridge contains $\longrightarrow$ Corrosive sublimate
(d) Salt-bridge contains $\longrightarrow$ *agar-agar* paste

10 Electrical potential of a cell is
(a) an intensive property
(b) an extensive property
(c) an isothermal property
(d) an isobaric property

11 Consider the following statements.
Statement I The electrode potential is always determined with respect to a standard electrode or reference electrode.
Statement II The potential of individual half-cell cannot be measured.
In the light of the above statements, choose the most appropriate answer from the options given below.
(a) Both Statement I and Statement II are false.
(b) Statement I is true but Statement II is false.
(c) Statement I is false but Statement II is true.
(d) Both Statement I and Statement II are true.

12 Select the correct match.
(a) Calomel electrode $\rightarrow$ $ZnCl_2$
(b) Calomel electrode $\rightarrow$ $CuSO_4$
(c) Calomel electrode $\rightarrow$ $HgCl_2$
(d) Calomel electrode $\rightarrow$ Hg_2Cl_2

13 In which of the following cells the emf will be independent of the activity of the chloride ion?
(a) $Zn|ZnCl_2(aq)||KCl(aq)|Pt(Cl_2)$
(b) $Zn|ZnCl_2(aq)||KCl(aq)|AgCl(s), Ag$
(c) $Ag, AgCl(s)|KCl(aq)|Pt(Cl_2)$
(d) $Hg, Hg_2Cl_2(s)|KCl(aq)||AgNO_3(aq)|Ag$

14 $Cu^+ + e^- \longrightarrow Cu, \quad E° = x_1$ V
$Cu^{2+} + 2e^- \longrightarrow Cu, \quad E° = x_2$ V, then for
$Cu^{2+} + e^- \longrightarrow Cu^+$, $E°$ (volt) will be
(a) $x_1 - 2x_2$
(b) $x_1 + 2x_2$
(c) $x_1 - x_2$
(d) $x_2 - x_1$

15 For the electrochemical cell having, $E°_{(M^+/M)} = 0.55$ V and $E°_{X/X^-} = 0.44$ V. From this data, one can deduce that
(a) $M + X \longrightarrow M^+ + X^-$ is the spontaneous (feasible) reaction, $E°_{cell} = 0.11$ V
(b) $M^+ + X^- \longrightarrow M + X$ is the spontaneous (feasible) reaction, $E°_{cell} = 0.11$ V
(c) $E°_{cell} = 0.77$ V
(d) $E°_{cell} = 0.36$ V

16 If, $Sn^{2+} + 2e^- \longrightarrow Sn;\ E° = -0.14$ V
$Sn^{4+} + 2e^- \longrightarrow Sn^{2+};\ E° = 0.13$ V
then,
(a) Sn^{2+} is unstable and disproportionates to Sn^{4+} and Sn
(b) Sn^{2+} is stable and disproportionation reaction is not spontaneous
(c) Sn^{4+} is easily reduced to Sn
(d) Sn^{2+} is stable and disproportionation reaction is spontaneous

17 Consider the following species,
(i) *aq.* NaCl
(ii) *aq.* $AgNO_3$
(iii) *aq.* $ZnSO_4$
(iv) *aq.* $Cd(NO_3)_2$
(v) *aq.*$CaCl_2$
How many of them will turn blue when placed in the copper vessel?
(a) 3
(b) 4
(c) 1
(d) 2

18 Standard reduction potentials at 25°C or $Li^+|Li$, $Ba^{2+}|Ba$, $Na^+|Na$ and $Mg^{2+}|Mg$ are –3.05, –2.90, –2.71, and –2.37 V respectively. Which one of the following is the strongest oxidising agent?
(a) Na^+
(b) Li^+
(c) Ba^{2+}
(d) Mg^{2+}

19 Which of the following species is correct match with the given property?
(a) $Pb^{2+} < Ni^{2+} < Cr^{3+} < Al^{3+} \longrightarrow$ Oxidising ability
(b) $Al^{3+} < Cr^{3+} < Ni^{2+} < Pb^{2+} \longrightarrow$ Oxidising ability
(c) $Cr^{3+} < Al^{3+} < Ni^{2+} < Pb^{2+} \longrightarrow$ Oxidising ability
(d) $Ni^{2+} < Pb^{2+} < Al^{3+} < Cr^{3+} \longrightarrow$ Oxidising ability

20 Consider the following reactions with their $E°$ values,
(i) $Fe^{2+} + 2e^- \longrightarrow Fe;\ E° = -0.44$
(ii) $Cr^{3+} + 3e^- \longrightarrow Cr;\ E° = -0.76$
(iii) $Cu^{2+} + 2e^- \longrightarrow Cu;\ E° = +0.52$
(iv) $I_2 + 2e^- \longrightarrow 2I^-;\ E° = +0.54$
(v) $Na^+ + e^- \longrightarrow Na;\ E° = -2.71$
How many of them are stronger reducing agent than H^+/H_2 couple?
(a) 3
(b) 1
(c) 4
(d) 2

Module 2

Nernst Equation, Electrochemical Cell and Gibbs Energy of the Reaction

- Nernst Equation for Half-Cell
- Equilibrium Constant from Nernst Equation
- Nernst Equation for Electrochemical Cell

Nernst Equation

In electrochemistry, the Nernst equation is an equation that can be used (in conjunction with other information) to determine the equilibrium reduction potential of a half cell in an electrochemical cell. It can also be used to determine the total voltage (EMF) of a full electrochemical cell. It is named after the German chemist who first formulated it, Walther Nernst.

According to thermodynamics,

$$\Delta G = \Delta G^\circ + RT \ln Q$$

$$(-\Delta G = nFE \text{ and } -\Delta G^\circ = nFE^\circ)$$

$$-nFE = -nFE^\circ + RT \ln Q$$

$$E_{\text{cell}} = E^\circ_{\text{cell}} - \frac{2.303\,RT}{nF} \log Q$$

$$E_{\text{cell}} = E^\circ_{\text{cell}} - \frac{2.303\,RT}{nF} \log \frac{[P]}{[R]}$$

The above equation is called **Nernst equation.**

where, E° = standard electrode potential

R = gas constant ($8.314\ \text{JK}^{-1}\ \text{mol}^{-1}$)

T = temperature (298 K)

F = Faraday (96500 coulomb)

n = number of moles of e^- gained, lost or transferred in balanced equation.

$$\frac{2.303\,RT}{F} = 0.059\ \text{V}$$

$$E_{\text{cell}} = E^\circ_{\text{cell}} - \frac{0.059}{n} \log \frac{[P]}{[R]}$$

Nernst Equation for Half-Cell

Electrode reaction may be reduction reaction or oxidation reaction

$$E_{\text{electrode}} = E^\circ_{\text{electrode}} - \frac{0.059}{n} \log \frac{[P]}{[R]}$$

This is called Nernst equation for electrode potential. Thus, for

$$Zn^{+2} + 2e^- \longrightarrow Zn \text{ (Reduction reaction)}$$

$$E_{\text{red}} = E_{Zn^{+2}|Zn} = E^\circ_{Zn^{+2}|Zn} - \frac{0.059}{2} \log \frac{[Zn]}{[Zn^{+2}]}$$

But concentration of solid is taken as unity

$$E_{Zn^{+2}|Zn} = E^\circ_{Zn^{+2}|Zn} - \frac{0.059}{2} \log \frac{1}{[Zn^{+2}]}$$

and for $Zn \longrightarrow Zn^{+2} + 2e^-$ (Oxidation reaction)

$$E_{\text{oxi}} = E_{Zn|Zn^{+2}} = E^\circ_{Zn|Zn^{+2}} - \frac{0.059}{2} \log \frac{[Zn^{+2}]}{[Zn]}$$

$$E_{Zn|Zn^{+2}} = E^\circ_{Zn|Zn^{+2}} - \frac{0.059}{2} \log [Zn^{+2}]$$

Example 5. *If E° for copper electrode is +0.34 V, what will be the E.M.F value when the solution in contact with it is 0.1 M in copper ions? How does E.M.F. for copper electrode change when concentration of Cu^{2+} ion in the solution is decreased?*

Sol. EMF of the cell can be calculated by using Nernst equation as

$$Cu^{+2} + 2e^- \longrightarrow Cu$$

$$E = E^\circ - \frac{0.059}{2} \log \frac{1}{[Cu^{+2}]}$$

when $[Cu^{2+}] = 0.1$ M

$$E = 0.34 - \frac{0.059}{2} \log \frac{1}{(0.1)}$$

$$= 0.34 - \frac{0.059}{2} \times 1 = 0.3105\ \text{V}$$

Example 6. *Write the Nernst equation for different electrodes.*

(i) *Electrode* : $M(s) \longrightarrow M^+(aq) + e^-$

(ii) *Electrode* : $Cu^{+2}(aq) + 2e^- \longrightarrow Cu(s)$

(iii) *Electrode* : Pt, H_2/H^+

(iv) *Electrode* : H^+/H_2, Pt

(v) *Electrode* : Cl^-/Cl_2, Pt

Sol. (i) $E_{oxi} = E^\circ_{oxi} - \frac{0.059}{1}\log[M^+]$

(ii) $E_{red} = E^\circ_{red} - \frac{0.059}{2}\log\frac{1}{[Cu^{+2}]}$

(iii) Balanced half-cell reaction in the given electrode is

$$H_2(g) \longrightarrow 2H^+(aq) + 2e^-$$

$$E_{oxid} = E^\circ_{oxid} - \frac{0.059}{2}\log\frac{[H^+]^2}{p_{H_2}}$$

(iv) Balanced half-cell reaction in the given electrode is

$$2H^+(aq) + 2e^- \longrightarrow H_2(g)$$

$$E_{red} = E^\circ_{red} - \frac{0.059}{2}\log\frac{P_{H_2}}{[H^+]^2}$$

(v) Balanced half-cell reaction in the given electrode is

$$Cl_2(g) + 2e^- \longrightarrow 2Cl^-(aq)$$

$$E_{red} = E^\circ_{red} - \frac{0.059}{2}\log\frac{[Cl^-]^2}{p_{Cl_2}}$$

Nernst Equation for EMF of a Cell

Let us consider a hypothetical redox reaction.

$$A(s) + B^{n+}(aq) \longrightarrow A^{n+}(aq) + B(s)$$

The Nernst equation may be written as

$$E_{cell} = E^\circ_{cell} - \frac{2.303\,RT}{nF}\log\frac{[A^{n+}][B]}{[A][B^{n+}]}$$

For solid $[A] = [B] = 1$

$$E_{cell} = E^\circ_{cell} - \frac{2.303\,RT}{nF}\log\frac{[A^{n+}]}{[B^{n+}]}$$

At 298 K, the equation becomes

$$E_{cell} = E^\circ_{cell} - \frac{0.059}{n}\log\frac{[A^{n+}]}{[B^{n+}]}$$

In general,

$$E_{cell} = E^\circ_{cell} - \frac{2.303RT}{nF}\log\frac{[\text{Products}]}{[\text{Reactants}]}$$

e.g. For Daniell cell,

$$Zn(s) + Cu^{2+}(aq) \longrightarrow Zn^{2+}(aq) + Cu(s)$$

$$E_{cell} = E^\circ_{cell} - \frac{0.059}{2}\log\frac{[Zn^{2+}][Cu(s)]}{[Cu^{2+}][Zn(s)]}$$

$$= E^\circ_{cell} - \frac{0.059}{2}\log\frac{[Zn^{2+}]}{[Cu^{2+}]} \quad [\because [Cu(s)] = 1, [Zn(s)] = 1]$$

NEET Close-up

Example Similar to PYQ Asked in NEET 2022

For the redox reaction

$$Zn(s) + Cu^{2+}(0.1\text{ M}) \longrightarrow Zn^{2+}(1\text{ M}) + Cu(s)$$

taking place in a cell, E°_{cell} is 1.10 volt. E_{cell} will be .... V if $2.303\frac{RT}{F} = 0.059$

(a) 2.14 (b) 1.80 (c) 1.07 (d) 0.82

Sol. (c) $E = E^\circ - \frac{0.059}{n}\log\frac{[Zn^{2+}]}{[Cu^{2+}]}$

$= 1.10 - \frac{0.059}{2}\log\frac{1}{0.1}$

$= 1.10 - 0.0295\log 10 = 1.07\text{ V}$

Skill Builder

The EMF of the cell in which the following reaction. $Zn(s) + Ni^{2+}(0.1\text{ M}) \rightleftharpoons Zn^{2+}(1.0\text{ M}) + Ni(s)$ occurs, is found to be 0.5105 V at 298 K. The standard e.m.f. of the cell is .... V.

(a) 0.4810 (b) 0.54
(c) 0.5696 (d) – 0.5105

For more practice Refer to Q.9 and Q.18 in step up practice 2.

Example 7. *Write the Nernst equation and calculate the emf of the following cell at 298 K.*

$$Cu(s) \mid Cu^{+2}(0.130\text{ M}) \parallel Ag^+(1.0\times10^{-4}\text{ M}) \mid Ag(s)$$

Given : $E^\circ_{(Cu^{2+}\mid Cu)} = 0.34\text{ V}$

and $E^\circ_{(Ag^+\mid Ag)} = 0.80\text{ V}$

Sol. The electrode reactions and cell reaction are respectively :

$$Cu(s) \longrightarrow Cu^{2+}(aq) + 2e^-$$

$$2Ag^+(aq) + 2e^- \longrightarrow 2Ag(s)$$

$$Cu(s) + 2Ag^+(aq) \longrightarrow Cu^{2+}(aq) + 2Ag(s)$$

Nernst equation is :

$$E_{cell} = E^\ominus_{cell} - \frac{0.059}{n}\log\frac{[Cu^{2+}]}{[Ag^+]^2}$$

$$E^\ominus = E^\ominus_{(Ag^+/Ag)} - E^\ominus_{(Cu^{2+}\mid Cu)}$$

$= 0.80 - 0.34$

$= 0.46\text{ V}$

$$E_{cell} = 0.46 - \frac{0.059}{2}\log\frac{(0.130)}{(1.0\times10^{-4})^2}$$

$= 0.46 - \frac{0.059}{2}\log 1.30\times10^7$

$= 0.46 - 0.21$

$= 0.25\text{ V}$

Equilibrium Constant from Nernst Equation

Nernst equation may also be used to calculate the equilibrium constant for a cell reaction. Let us consider an hypothetical equation,

$$aA + bB \longrightarrow cC + dD$$

The Nernst equation can be written as,

$$E_{cell} = E^{\circ}_{cell} - \frac{RT}{nF}\ln\frac{[C]^c[D]^d}{[A]^a[B]^b} \quad ...(i)$$

At equilibrium, $E_{cell} = 0$ and

$$\frac{[C]^c[D]^d}{[A]^a[B]^b} = K_C = K_{eq} \text{ (equilibrium contant)}$$

Thus, equation (i) becomes

$$0 = E^{\circ}_{cell} - \frac{RT}{nF}\ln K_{eq}$$

$$\left[\frac{2.303\ RT}{F} = 0.059 \text{ at } 25°\text{C}\right]$$

$$E^{\circ}_{cell} = \frac{0.059}{n}\log K_{eq}$$

Thus, the above equation gives a relationship between equilibrium constant of the reaction and standard potential of the cell in which that reaction takes place. Thus, equilibrium constants of the reaction, which is difficult to measure otherwise, can be calculated from the corresponding $E^{\ominus}$ value of the cell.

Example 8. *Calculate the value of the equilibrium constant for the following cell reaction :*

$$4Br^- + O_2 + 4H^+ \longrightarrow 2Br_2 + 2H_2O$$

Given that : $E^{\ominus}_{cell} = 0.16$ V.

Sol. $E^{\ominus}_{cell}$ is related to equilibrium constant, K_C as

$$E^{\ominus}_{cell} = \frac{0.059}{n}\log K_C$$

or $$\log K_C = \frac{nE^{\circ}_{cell}}{0.059}$$

In this reaction, four electrons are transferred so that $n = 4$

$$\log K_C = \frac{4 \times 0.16\text{ V}}{0.059\text{ V}} = 10.8$$

$$K_C = 6.31 \times 10^{10}$$

NEET Close-up

Example Similar to PYQ Asked in NEET 2019

For a cell involving one electron $E^{\circ}_{cell} = 1.05$ V at 298 K, the equilibrium constant for the cell reaction is

$\left[\text{Given that } \frac{2.303RT}{F} = 0.059\text{V at } T = 298\text{K}\right]$

(a) $1.0 \times 10^{17.79}$
(b) $1.0 \times 10^{0.056}$
(c) 1.0×10^{10}
(d) 1.0×10^{30}

Sol. (a) $E^{\circ}_{cell} = \frac{2.303RT}{nF}\log K$

Given, $E^{\circ}_{cell} = 1.05$ V, $n = 1$

$$1.05 = \frac{0.059}{1}\log K$$

$$\frac{1.05}{0.059} = \log K$$

$$17.79 = \log K$$

$$K = 10^{17.79}$$

Skill Builder

For a cell involving two electrons $E^{\circ}_{cell} = 1.07$ V at 298 K, the equilibrium constant for the cell reaction is

$\left[\text{Given that } \frac{2.303RT}{F} = 0.059\text{V at } T = 298\text{K}\right]$

(a) 10^{10}
(b) $10^{18.13}$
(c) $10^{36.27}$
(d) $10^{1.07}$

For more practice Refer to Q15, in step up Practice-2

Electrochemical Cell and Gibbs' Energy of the Reaction

The free energy change of the reaction in any state, ΔG (when equilibrium has not been attained) is related to the standard free energy change of the reaction, $\Delta G°$ (which is equal to the difference in free energies of formation of the products and reactants both in their standard states). According to the equation,

$$\Delta G = \Delta G° + RT\ln Q$$

where, Q is the reaction quotient.

When equilibrium is attained, there is no further free energy change, i.e. $\Delta G = 0$ and Q becomes equal to equilibrium constant. Hence, the above equation becomes,

$$\Delta G° = -RT\ln K_{eq}$$

$$\Delta G° = -2.303\ RT\log K_{eq}$$

In case of galvanic cells, Gibbs energy change ΔG is related to the electrical work done by the cell.

$$\Delta G = -nFE_{cell}$$

where, n = number of electrons involved

F = Faraday constant

E_{cell} = emf of the cell

If reactants and products are in their standard states

$$\Delta G^\circ = -nFE^\circ_{cell}$$

Mentor's TiP

- If E_{cell} is positive, reaction occurs spontaneously in the forward direction.
- If E_{cell} is negative, the reaction occurs spontaneously in the reverse direction.
- If a cell reaction is reversed, E_{cell} sign changes.
- $\Delta_r G$ is an extensive thermodynamic property and the value depends on n.

Example 9. *Calculate the cell emf and ΔG for the cell reaction at 25°C.*

$$Zn(s) | Zn^{2+} (0.0004\ M) || Cd^{2+} (0.2\ M) | Cd(s)$$

E° values at 25°C : $Zn^{2+} | Zn = -0.763$ V;

$Cd^{2+} | Cd = -0.403$ V

$F = 96500\,C, R = 8.314\ JK^{-1}\ mol^{-1}$.

Sol. Cell is

$$Zn(s) | Zn^{2+} (0.0004\ M) || Cd^{2+} (0.2\ M) | Cd(s)$$

$$Zn(s) + Cd^{2+}(aq) \longrightarrow Zn^{2+}(aq) + Cd(s)$$

$$E^\ominus_{cell} = E^\ominus_{(Cd^{2+}/Cd)} - E^\ominus_{(Zn^{2+}/Zn)}$$

$$= -0.403 - (-0.763) = 0.36\ V$$

According to Nernst equation,

$$E = E^\ominus - \frac{0.059}{2} \log \frac{[Zn^{2+}]}{[Cd^{2+}]}$$

$$[Zn^{2+}] = 0.0004\ M, \ [Cd^{2+}] = 0.2\ M$$

$$E = 0.36 - \frac{0.059}{2} \log \frac{0.0004}{0.2}$$

$$= 0.36 - \frac{0.059}{2} \log 2 \times 10^{-3}$$

$$E_{cell} = 0.36 - \frac{0.059}{2} \times (-2.6990)$$

Cell emf = 0.44 V

Now, $\Delta G = -nFE$

$n = 2$ mol, $F = 96500$ C, $E = 0.44$ V

$\Delta G = -2 \times 96500\ C \times 0.44\ V$

$= -84920$ Coulomb × Volt $= -84.920$ kJ

STEP UP Practice 2

1 Nernst equation is not useful in determining

(a) emf of a cell

(b) equilibrium constant

(c) spontaneity of a cell reaction

(d) cell potential

2 For the given cell,

Ag | $AgNO_3$ (1 M) || $AgNO_3$ (2 M) |Ag, E_{cell} is

(a) 0.0591V

(b) (0.0591 × 0.3010) V

(c) 0.0591 × 2 V

(d) zero

3 Which of the following changes will increase the emf of the cell?

$$Co(s) | CoCl_2(M_1) || HCl\ (M_2) | Pt(H_2, g)$$

(a) Decrease the volume of $CoCl_2$ solution from 100 mL to 200 mL

(b) Increase M_2 from 0.01 M to 0.50 M

(c) Increase the pressure of the $H_2(g)$ from 1.00 to 2.00 atm

(d) Increase M_1 from 0.01 M to 0.50 M

4 Following behaves as SHE at a pressure of Pt, H_2 | H_2O

(a) 1 bar (b) 10^{-14} bar

(c) 10^7 bar (d) 10^{14} bar

5 Which of the following emf is correctly match regarding the given cell ; Pt $- H_2$ | H^+ | $H_2 -$Pt is
p_1 p_2

(a) $E_{cell} = \frac{RT}{F} + \log_e \frac{p_1}{p_2}$ (b) $E_{cell} = \frac{RT}{F} \log \frac{p_1}{p_2}$

(c) $E_{cell} = \frac{RT}{F} - \log_e \frac{p_2}{p_1}$ (d) $E_{cell} = \frac{RT}{2F} \log_e \frac{p_1}{p_2}$

6 Which has maximum potential (numerical value) for the half-cell reaction ?

$$2H^+ + 2e^- \longrightarrow H_2$$

(a) 1.0 M HCl (b) A solution having pH 4

(c) Pure water (d) 1.0 M NaOH

7 For the following half-cell reactions, E° values are also given

$Mn^{2+} + 2H_2O \longrightarrow MnO_2 + 4H^+ + 2e^-, E^\circ = -1.23$ V

$MnO_4^- + 4H^+ + 3e^- \longrightarrow MnO_2 + 2H_2O, E^\circ = +1.70$ V

Select the correct statement(s).

(a) Mn^{2+} reacts with MnO_4^- in acid solution to form MnO_2.

(b) $Mn(MnO_4)_2$ is stable in acid solution.

(c) MnO_2 disproportionates to Mn^{2+} and MnO_4^- in acid solution.

(d) Mn^+ on reaction with MnO_4^- forms 2MnO in acidic medium.

8 $E^\circ_{Al^{3+}/Al} = -1.66$ V and K_{sp} of $Al(OH)_3 = 1.0 \times 10^{-33}$. Reduction potential of the above couple at pH = 14 is
(a) − 2.31 V (b) + 2.31 V
(c) −1.01 V (d) + 1.01 V

9 Consider the given data
Half-cell reaction and $E°$ values
1. $Cr_2O_7^{2-} + 14H^+ + 6e^- \rightleftharpoons 2Cr^{3+} + 7H_2O$; +1.33 V
2. $Cr^{3+} + 3e^- \rightleftharpoons Cr$; − 0.74 V
3. $Cu^+ + e^- \rightleftharpoons Cu$; + 0.52 V
4. $Cu^{2+} + 2e^- \rightleftharpoons Cu$; + 0.34 V

$E°$ for the reaction,
$2Cr(s) + 3Cu^{2+}(aq) \rightleftharpoons 2Cr^{3+} + 3Cu$ is
(a) −1.08 V (b) −0.70 V (c) 1.08 V (d) 2.50 V

10 The reaction,
$Cu^{2+}(aq) + 2Cl^-(aq) \longrightarrow Cu(s) + Cl_2(g)$ has $E^\circ_{cell} = -1.02$ V.
This reaction
(a) can be made to produce electricity in a voltaic cell
(b) can be made to occur in an electrolysis cell
(c) occurs whenever Cu^{2+} and Cl^- are brought together in an aqueous solution
(d) can occur in acidic but not in basic solution

11 For the following cell reaction,
$Pb(s) + Hg_2SO_4(s) \rightleftharpoons PbSO_4(s) + 2Hg(l)$; $E^\circ_{cell} = 0.92$ V
$K_{sp}(PbSO_4) = 2 \times 10^{-8}$, $K_{sp}(Hg_2SO_4) = 1 \times 10^{-6}$;
Hence, E_{cell} is
(a) 0.92 V (b) 0.89 V (c) 1.04 V (d) 0.95 V

12 Consider the following relations,
(i) $E^\circ_{cell} = \frac{RT}{nF} \ln K$ (ii) $E^\circ_{cell} = \frac{2.303RT}{nF} \log K$
(iii) $E^\circ_{cell} = -2.303\,RT \ln K$ (iv) $\ln K = \frac{nFE^\circ_{cell}}{RT}$
(v) $E^\circ_{cell} = -nF \ln K$
How many of them represent the correct relation between the EMF and equilibrium constant of the cell?
(a) 2 (b) 1 (c) 4 (d) 3

13 In the electrolysis of aqueous sodium chloride solution which of the half-cell reaction will occur at anode ?
(a) $Na^+(aq) + e^- \longrightarrow Na(s)$; $E^\ominus_{cell} = -2.71$ V
(b) $2H_2O(l) \longrightarrow O_2(g) + 4H^+(aq) + 4e^-$; $E^\ominus_{cell} = 1.23$ V
(c) $H^+(aq) + e^- \longrightarrow \frac{1}{2} H_2(g)$; $E^\ominus_{cell} = 0.00$ V
(d) $Cl^-(aq) \longrightarrow \frac{1}{2} Cl_2(g) + e^-$; $E^\ominus_{cell} = 1.36$ V

14 Consider the following statements.
Statement I Electrical work done in one second is equal to electrical potential multiplied by total charge passed.
Statement II The reversible work done by a galvanic cell is equal to decrease in its Gibbs energy.
In the light of the above statements, choose the most appropriate answer from the options given below.
(a) Both Statement I and Statement II are false.
(b) Statement I is true but Statement II is false.
(c) Statement I is false but Statement II is true.
(d) Both Statement I and Statement II are true.

15 For a reaction, $A + B^{2+} \longrightarrow B + A^{2+}$ at 25°C, $E° = 0.2955$ V. Hence, K_{eq} is
(a) 10 (b) 10^{10}
(c) −10 (d) 10^{-10}

16 Consider the following statements.
Statement I E°_{cell} for the reaction, $2H_2O \longrightarrow H_3O^+ + OH^-$ at 25°C is −0.8277 V. The value of K for the reaction is 10^{-14}.
Statement II $\Delta G°$ and K are independent on electrode potential.
In the light of the above statements, choose the most appropriate answer from the options given below.
(a) Both Statement I and Statement II are false.
(b) Statement I is true but Statement II is false.
(c) Statement I is false but Statement II is true.
(d) Both Statement I and Statement II are true.

17 For the reactions,
I. $MnO_4^- + 8H^+ + 5e^- \longrightarrow Mn^{2+} + 4H_2O$, $E° = 1.51$V
II. $MnO_2 + 4H^+ + 2e^- \longrightarrow Mn^{2+} + 2H_2O$, $E° = 1.23$ V
then for the reaction,
III. $MnO_4^- + 4H^+ + 3e^- \longrightarrow MnO_2 + 2H_2O$, $E°$ is
(a) 1.70 V (b) 5.09 V (c) 0.28 V (d) 0.84 V

18 Select the correct match.
(a) $\Delta_r G° = -nRT \ln K$
(b) $\Delta_r G° = \frac{-RT}{nF} \ln K$
(c) $\Delta_r G° = \frac{-nRT}{F} \ln K$
(d) $\Delta_r G° = -RT \ln K$

19 Which of the following statements is correct ?
(a) E_{cell} and $\Delta_r G$ of cell reaction both are extensive properties.
(b) E_{cell} and $\Delta_r G$ of cell reaction both are intensive properties.
(c) E_{cell} is an intensive property while $\Delta_r G$ of cell reaction is an extensive property.
(d) E_{cell} is an extensive property while $\Delta_r G$ of cell reaction is an intensive property.

20 Which of the following statements about the spontaneous reaction occuring in a galvanic cell is always true?
(a) $E^\circ_{cell} > 0$, $\Delta G° < 0$ and $Q < K_{eq}$
(b) $E^\circ_{cell} > 0$, $\Delta G° < 0$ and $Q > K_{eq}$
(c) $E^\circ_{cell} > 0$, $\Delta G° > 0$ and $Q > K_{eq}$
(d) $E^\circ_{cell} < 0$, $\Delta G° < 0$ and $Q < K_{eq}$

Module 3

Conductors, Conductance of Electrolytic Solutions and Kohlrausch's Law

- Conductors
- Conductance of Electrolytic Solutions
- Resistance
- Resistivity or Specific Resistance
- Conductance
- Conductivity or Specific Conductance
- Equivalent Conductivity
- Molar Conductivity
- Application of Kohlrausch's Law

Conductors

Substances which allow electric current to flow through them are known as **conductors,** e.g. metals like Fe, Ag, Cu. Whereas, the substances which do not allow the passage of electricity through them are called insulators, e.g. plastics.

Types of Conductors

Conductors are of two types

1. Metallic Conductors or Electronic Conductors

These are metallic substances that conduct electric current due to the mobility of free electrons, without undergoing any chemical change, e.g. metals like Cu, Ag, Fe, non-metals like graphite, some minerals etc.

Mentor's TiP

Hg is a metallic conductor and it is liquid at room temperature.

2. Electrolytic Conductors (or Electrolytes)

The substance in solution or in the molten state conducts electric current and is simultaneously decomposed is called an electrolytes. The extent or degree of dissociation of different electrolytes in solution is different. Electrolytes can be broadly categorised into two types, i.e. strong and weak electrolytes.

(i) **Strong electrolytes** Substances which are largely dissociated and form a highly conducting liquid in water are strong electrolytes. e.g. Mostly salts are strong electrolyte except the weakly ionized salts ($CdBr_2$, $HgCl_2$) mineral acids like HCl, H_2SO_4, HNO_3, etc. and bases like NaOH, KOH, etc. are strong electrolytes. The strong electrolytes are almost 100% ionised at normal dilution.

(ii) **Weak Electrolytes** Substances which dissociate only to a small extent in aqueous solution forming low conducting liquid are weak electrolytes. e.g. All organic acids (except sulphonic acids), inorganic acids like HCN, H_2CO_3, etc., and bases like NH_3, amines, etc., are weak electrolytes.

Difference between Electronic Conductor and Electrolytic Conductors

Electronic conductors or Metallic conductors	Electrolytic conductors
Passage of current by movement of electrons in the metallic lattice, e.g. Cu, Ag, etc.	Passage of current by ions in molten state or in aqueous solution of electrolytes, e.g. NaCl (*aq*) or NaCl (fused).
Passage of current brings in only physical changes.	Passage of current brings in physical as well as chemical changes.
It generally shows no transfer of matter.	It involves transfer of matter in the form of ions.
It generally shows an increase in resistance during the passage of current due to increase in temperature thermal motion of metal ions hindering the flow of electrons increases with increase in temperature	It generally shows a decrease in resistance due to decrease in viscosity of the medium and degree of hydration of ions with increase in temperature.
The conducting power of metals is usually high.	The conducting power of electrolytic conductors is relatively low.

Conductance of Electrolytic Solutions

Just like metallic conductors, electrolytic solutions also obey Ohm's law, which states that,

"The current flowing through a conductor is directly proportional to the potential difference across it."

Resistance (R)

The hinderance provided by the medium in the flow of current is called **resistance.**

From Ohm's law, $V \propto I$

$$\boxed{V = RI} \quad \text{(where, } R = \text{resistance)}$$

Unit of resistance is Ω (ohm).

Resistivity or Specific Resistance (ρ)

Resistance provided by unit volume of the medium is called, resistivity.

For any medium, Resistance ∝ length

Also, $$\text{resistance} \propto \frac{1}{\text{area}}$$

So, $$R \propto \frac{\text{length}}{\text{area}}$$

$$R = \rho \frac{l}{a}$$

where, ρ is called **resistivity** or **specific resistance**

If $l = 1$ cm, $a = 1$ cm^2, then $R = \rho$, its unit is ohm-cm.

Cell Constant (G^*)

It is the ratio of distance between electrode (l) and total surface area (a) of the electrodes.

$$G^* = \frac{l}{a}$$

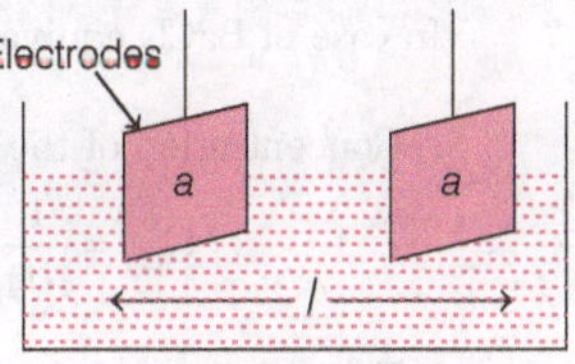

Electrolytic cell

Unit of cell constant = m^{-1}, cm^{-1}

This cell constant is a function of the electrode areas, the distance between the electrodes and the electrical field pattern between the electrodes.

$$\text{Cell constant} = \frac{\text{Resistance}}{\text{Resistivity}}$$

NEET Close-up

Example Similar to PYQ Asked in NEET 2023

The conductivity of centimolar solution of KCl at 25°C is 0.125 ohm^{-1} cm^{-1} and the resistance of the cell containing the solution at 25°C is 40 ohm. The value of cell constant is-

(a) 2.43 cm^{-1} (b) 3.41 cm^{-1} (c) 4.68 cm^{-1} (d) 5 cm^{-1}

Sol. (*d*) Given, conductivity (κ) = 0.125 Ω^{-1} cm^{-1}

Resistance = 40 Ω and Cell constant = ?

We know that, $\kappa = \frac{1}{R} \times \frac{l}{a}$

Cell constant $= \frac{l}{a} = \kappa \times R = 0.125 \times 40 = 5$ cm^{-1}

Skill Builder

What is the cell constant if the conductivity of 0.001 M NaCl solution at 298 K is 0.146×10^{-3} S cm^{-1}? If the resistance of a conductivity cell containing 0.001 M NaCl solution at 298 K is 1000 Ω.

(a) 2.129 cm^{-1} (b) 0.219 cm^{-1}
(c) 0.292 cm^{-1} (d) 0.146 cm^{-1}

For more practice Refer to Q.5 in step up practice 3.

Conductance (G)

The property of a medium which tells about ease with which current flows through the medium is called conductance.

By definition, conductance $(G) = \frac{1}{\text{resistance } (R)}$

Unit of conductance (G) = ohm^{-1}, mho, Siemens (S)

Conductivity or Specific Conductance (κ)

The reciprocal of specific resistance is called specific conductance, i.e. the conductance of a solution of 1 cm length and having 1 cm^2 area of cross section. It is denoted by κ (kappa).

$$\text{Conductivity} = \frac{1}{\text{resistivity}}$$

$$\kappa = \frac{1}{\rho}$$

Unit of κ is ohm^{-1}cm^{-1} or Siemens cm^{-1} (S cm^{-1}) or mho cm^{-1}.

1 ohm^{-1}cm^{-1} = 100 ohm^{-1}m^{-1}

Example 10 *When a certain conductivity cell was filled with 0.020 M KCl which has specific conductivity of 0.2768 Ω^{-1} m^{-1}, it had a resistance of 82.40 Ω at 25°C. With 0.0025 M K_2SO_4, it has a resistance of 326.0 Ω. Calculate*

(i) *the cell constant.* (ii) *conductivity of K_2SO_4 solution.*

Sol. (i) Caliberation of the cell has been done using 0.020 M KCl solution.

$$\text{Specific conductance} = \frac{\text{Cell constant}}{\text{Resistance } (R)}$$

∴ cell constant = specific conductance × resistance

$= 0.2768 \times 82.4$

$= 22.81$ m^{-1}

(ii) Thus, specific conductance of K_2SO_4 solution.

$$= \frac{22.81}{326} = 0.07\,\Omega^{-1}\,\text{m}^{-1}\ (\text{S m}^{-1})$$

Equivalent Conductivity (Λ_{eq})

The conductance of all the ions produced from 1 gram equivalent of the electrolyte such that electrolyte is kept between two electrodes at 1 cm apart.

$$\text{Equivalent conductivity} = \frac{\text{Conductance}}{\text{Gram equivalent of electrolyte}}$$

$$\Lambda_{eq} = \frac{G}{\text{g.eq}}$$

$$= \frac{\kappa(a/l)}{N\frac{V(\text{cc})}{1000}} = \frac{\kappa(a/l)}{N(a.l)} \times 1000$$

$$\Lambda_{eq} = \frac{\kappa}{Nl^2} \times 1000$$

As $l = 1$, cm then $\Lambda_{eq} = \frac{\kappa \times 1000}{N}$

Its unit is mho-cm^2- eq^{-1}. (S cm^2 eq^{-1})

1 S cm^2 eq^{-1} = 10^{-4} S m^2 eq^{-1}

Example 11. *The resistance of* 0.01 N NaCl *solution at* 298 K *is* 200 ohm. *Cell constant of the conductivity cell is unity. Calculate the equivalent conductance.*

Sol. Calculation of specific conductance,

$$\text{Specific conductance, } \kappa = \frac{1}{R} \times \text{cell constant}$$

$$= \frac{1}{200 \text{ ohm}} \times 1 \text{ cm}^{-1}$$

$$= 5 \times 10^{-3} \text{ ohm}^{-1} \text{ cm}^{-1}$$

Calculation of equivalent conductance

$$\Lambda_e = \frac{\kappa \times 1000}{\text{Normality}}$$

$$= \frac{5 \times 10^{-3} \times 1000}{0.01}$$

$$= 5 \times 10^2 \text{ ohm}^{-1} \text{ cm}^2 \text{ eq}^{-1}$$

Molar Conductivity (Λ_m)

Molar conductivity of a solution is the conductance provided by 1 mole of electrolyte such that electrolyte is kept between two electrode at 1 cm apart.

$$\Lambda_m = \frac{\text{Conductance}}{\text{Mole of electrolyte}} = \frac{G}{n} = \frac{\kappa(a/l)}{N\frac{V(cc)}{1000}}$$

where, M = molarity V = volume

$$= \frac{\kappa(a/l)}{M(al)} \times 1000$$

When, $l = 1$ cm then $\Lambda_m = \frac{\kappa \times 1000}{M}$

Unit of Λ_m is mho cm^{2}mol^{-1} (S cm^{2}mol^{-1}).

Mentor's TiP

Relation between molar conductivity and equivalent conductivity,

$$\Lambda_{eq} = \frac{\Lambda_m}{\text{number of ion} \times |\text{Charge on an ion}|}$$

Ion may be cation or anion.

Example 12. *The conductivity of a solution containing* 1 gram *of anhydrous* $BaCl_2$ *in* 200 cm^3 *of water has been found to be* 0.0058 mho cm^{-1}. *What are the molar conductivity and equivalent conductivity of the solution ? (At. wt. of* Ba = 137 *and* Cl = 35.5*).*

Sol. Conductivity = 0.0058 mho cm^{-1}

Molecular mass of $BaCl_2$ = 137 + 2 × 35.5 = 208

As 1 gram of $BaCl_2$ is present in 200 cm^3 of the solution, therefore,

$$\text{Molar concentration, } (C) = \frac{1}{208} \times \frac{1}{200} \times 1000 \text{ mol L}^{-1}$$

$$= 0.0240 \text{ mol L}^{-1}$$

$$\text{Molar conductivity, } \Lambda_m = \kappa \times \frac{1000}{C} = 0.0058 \times \frac{1000}{0.0240}$$

$$= 241.67 \text{ ohm}^{-1} \text{ cm}^2 \text{ mol}^{-1}$$

$$\text{In case of BaCl}_2 \text{ equivalent weight} = \frac{\text{Mol. wt.}}{2} = \frac{208}{2} = 104$$

∴ Concentration of the solution in gram equivalent per litre

$$C_{eq.} = \frac{1}{104} \times \frac{1}{200} \times 1000 = 0.0480$$

$$\therefore \text{Equivalent conductivity, } \Lambda_{eq} = \kappa \times \frac{1000}{C_{eq}}$$

$$= 0.0058 \times \frac{1000}{0.480}$$

$$= 12.083 \text{ ohm}^{-1} \text{ cm}^2 \text{ eq}^{-1}$$

Factors Affecting Conductivity

The conductivity of electrolytes can be affected by the following factors.

(i) **Interionic attraction** If interionic attraction between solute molecules is higher than conductivity becomes lower.

(ii) **Polarity of solvent** If solvent is more polar than its ionisation and conductivity will be greater.

(iii) **Viscosity of medium** On increasing viscosity of medium, conductivity decreases.

(iv) **Temperature** On increasing the temperature of electrolytic solution, conductivity increases.

(v) **Concentration of the solution** All types of conductivities are affected by changing the concentration. Their respective variations with concentration are discussed below

(a) **Effect of concentration on specific conductivity** Conductivity always decreases with decrease in concentration (i.e. with dilution) of both the strong and weak electrolytes. This is due to the fact that the number of ions that carry current in a unit volume of solution always decreases with decrease in concentration.

(b) **Effect of concentration on molar and equivalent conductivity** On decreasing the concentration of electrolytic solution, molar conductivity and equivalent conductivity increases. It is because on progressively decreasing the concentration the dissociation of electrolytes goes on increasing. Thus, the number of ions goes on increasing.

Variation of Conductivity and Molar Conductivity with Concentration

Depending upon the values of molar conductivity, the electrolytes can be divided into two groups namely strong electrolytes and weak electrolytes.

For Strong Electrolyte

Strong electrolytes are completely ionised in all concentrations. For strong electrolytes, Λ_m increases slowly with dilution. It is found to vary with concentration according to the Debye-Huckel-Onsager equation.

$$\Lambda_m = \Lambda_m^\circ - [A + B\Lambda_m^\circ]\sqrt{C}$$

where, A is called Debye-Huckel constants and C is the molar concentration (mol L^{-1}).

Λ_m° is the molar conductivity at infinite dilution called as **limiting molar conductivity**.

Concept ladder

In Debye-Huckel Onsager equation, the expression of A and B are as follows

$$A = \frac{82.4}{(DT)^{1/2}\eta}, \quad B = \frac{8.20 \times 10^5}{(DT)^{3/2}}$$

D and η are the dielectric constant and coefficient of viscosity of the medium respectively at temperature T (K).

Interpretation of Limiting Molar Conductivity

This equation found to hold good at low concentrations. Thus, if we plot molar conductivity (Λ_m) against $\sqrt{C}$, a linear graph is obtained with negative slope. Whereas, it is not linear for higher concentrations as shown in Figure in which KCl has been taken as an example of a strong electrolyte. This decrease of the slope is not due to a change in the number of ions with concentration, but due to change in the interionic attractions.

At high concentrations, there are greater number of ions per unit volume which increases attraction between cation (K^+) and anion (Cl^-). Attraction between ions reduces the conducting ability of the ions hence, Λ_m falls with increasing concentration.

If solution is diluted (concentration is decreased), there is decrease in ionic attractions hence, molar conductivity increases with decrease in concentration.

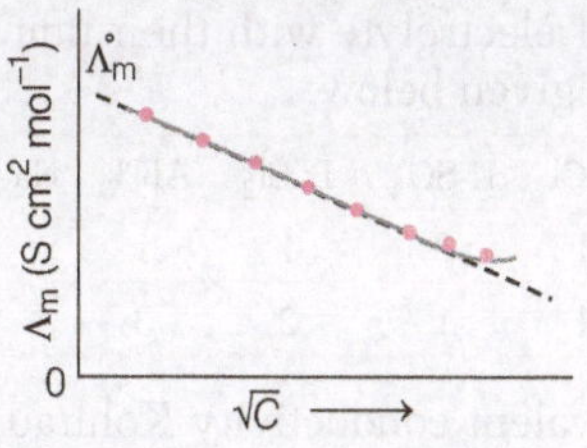

Variation of Λ_m with $\sqrt{C}$ for strong electrolytes (KCl)

The value of limiting molar conductivity can be obtained by extrapolating the curve to $\sqrt{C} = 0$.

For Weak Electrolyte

In case of weak electrolytes (as CH_3COOH, NH_4OH, AgCl etc.), ionisation is very small as compared to strong electrolytes, hence, Λ_m (or Λ_{eq}) of a weak electrolyte is low.

In very low concentration range, the degree of ionisation rises sharply hence Λ_m increases sharply when the solution is diluted in lower concentration range.

In this region, the graph of weak electrolyte becomes parallel to the Y-axis. So, the limiting molar conductivity of a weak electrolyte cannot be determined by the extrapolation of the plot. It is rather determined by applying the **Kohlrausch law** of independent migration of ions.

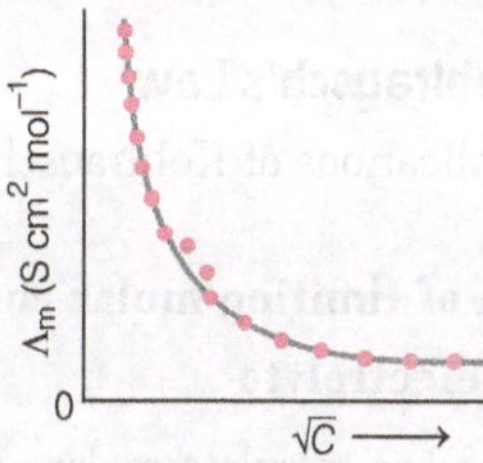

Variation of Λ_m with $\sqrt{C}$ for weak electrolyte (CH_3COOH)

Limiting Conductivity for Weak Electrolytes and Kohlrausch's Law

At infinite dilution each ion makes a definite contribution towards molar conductivity (or equivalent conductivity) of the electrolyte irrespective of the nature of the other ions present.

In other words, we can say that the **limiting molar conductivity** of an electrolyte is the sum of the limiting molar conductivities of the cation and the anion each multiplied with the number of ions present in one formula unit of the electrolyte.

Mathematically, Λ_m° for $A_xB_y = x\lambda^\circ_{(A)^{y+}} + y\lambda^\circ_{(B)^{x-}}$

where, Λ_m° = limiting molar conductivity of electrolyte

$\lambda^\circ_{(A)^{y+}}$ and $\lambda^\circ_{(B)^{x-}}$ are the limiting molar conductivities of cation (A^{y+}) and anion (B^{x-}) respectively.

The multiplication of number of ions with molar conductivity of a particular ion is called **molar ionic conductance** of that particular ion.

Some example of electrolyte with their number of ions per formula unit are given below.

Electrolyte	HCl	K_2SO_4	$BaCl_2$	$AlCl_3$	Na_3PO_4	$Fe_2(SO_4)_3$
x	1	2	1	1	3	2
y	1	1	2	3	1	3

In terms of equivalent conductivity Kohlrausch's law is defined as "The limiting equivalent conductivity (or equivalent conductivity at infinite dilution) is the sum of the equivalent conductivities of cations and anions", i.e.

$$\Lambda^\circ_{eq} = \lambda^\circ_a + \lambda^\circ_c$$

where, λ°_c and λ°_a are called limiting ionic conductivities for cation and the anion respectively.

Example 13. *Calculate molar conductance of $CaCl_2$ at infinite dilution if limiting equivalent conductivities of Ca^{+2} and Cl^- is x and y $S\,cm^2\,eq^{-1}$ respectively.*

Sol. Equivalent conductance of $CaCl_2$ will be

$$\Lambda^\circ_{eq} = \lambda^\circ_{Ca^{+2}} + \lambda^\circ_{Cl^-} = x + y$$

$$\Lambda^\circ_m = n_f \times \Lambda^\circ_{eq}$$

$$\Lambda^\circ_m = 2 \times \Lambda^\circ_{eq}$$

$$\Lambda^\circ_m = 2\,(x + y)$$

Applications of Kohlrausch's Law

Some important applications of Kohlrausch's law are as follows

(i) **Determination of limiting molar conductivity (Λ°_m) for weak electrolyte**

This law is helpful to calculate molar conductance at infinite dilution for weak electrolytes. Suppose, we have to calculate the limiting conductance for CH_3COOH. Then, according to Kohlrausch's law

$$\Lambda^\circ_{(CH_3COOH)} = \Lambda^\circ_{(CH_3COO^-)} + \Lambda^\circ_{(H^+)} \quad ...(i)$$

This equation can be obtained by the knowledge of molar conductance at infinite dilution for some strong electrolytes, i.e.

$$\Lambda^\circ_{(CH_3COO^-Na^+)} = \Lambda^\circ_{(CH_3COO^-)} + \Lambda^\infty_{(Na^+)} \quad ...(ii)$$

$$\Lambda^\circ_{(HCl)} = \Lambda^\circ_{(H^+)} + \Lambda^\circ_{(Cl^-)} \quad ...(iii)$$

$$\Lambda^\circ_{(NaCl)} = \Lambda^\circ_{(Na^+)} + \Lambda^\circ_{(Cl^-)} \quad ...(iv)$$

The above Eq. (i) can be obtained by adding Eqs. (ii) and (iii) and subtracting Eq. (iv) from the sum, i.e.

$$\Lambda^\circ_{(CH_3COOH)} = \Lambda^\circ_{(CH_3COONa)} + \Lambda^\circ_{(HCl)} - \Lambda^\circ_{(NaCl)}$$

NEET Close-up

Example Similar to PYQ Asked in NEET 2019

If the molar conductivities at infinite dilution of NaCl, HCl and CH_3COONa are 126.4, 426.1 and 91.0 $ohm^{-1}\,cm^2\,mol^{-1}$ respectively, what will be the molar conductivity of acetic acid at infinite dilution?

(a) 208.7 $ohm^{-1}\,cm^2\,mol^{-1}$ (b) 643.5 $ohm^{-1}\,cm^2\,mol^{-1}$
(c) 390.7 $ohm^{-1}\,cm^2\,mol^{-1}$ (d) 420.7 $ohm^{-1}\,cm^2\,mol^{-1}$

Sol. (c) According to Kohlrausch Law,

$$\Lambda^\circ \text{ for } CH_3COOH = \lambda^\circ_{CH_3COO^-} + \lambda^\circ_{H^+}$$

$$\Lambda^\circ \text{ for NaCl} = \lambda^\circ_{Na^+} + \lambda^\circ_{Cl^-} = 126.4\ ohm^{-1}\,cm^2 \quad ...(i)$$

$$\Lambda^\circ \text{ for HCl} = \lambda^\circ_{H^+} + \lambda^\circ_{Cl^-} = 426.1\ ohm^{-1}\,cm^2 \quad ...(ii)$$

$$\Lambda^\circ \text{ for } CH_3COONa = \lambda^\circ_{CH_3COO^-} + \lambda^\circ_{Na^+} = 91.0\ ohm^{-1}\,cm^2 \quad ...(iii)$$

Adding equations (ii) and (iii) and subtracting (i), we get,

$$\lambda^\circ_{CH_3COOH} = \lambda^\circ_{CH_3COO^-} + \lambda^\circ_{Na^+} + \lambda^\circ_{H^+} - \lambda^\circ_{Cl^-} - \lambda^\circ_{Na^+} + \lambda^\circ_{Cl^+}$$

$$= 426.1 + 91.0 - 126.4\ ohm^{-1}\,cm^2$$

$$\lambda^\circ_{CH_3COO^-} + \lambda^\circ_{H^+} = 390.7\ ohm^{-1}\,cm^2\,mol^{-1}$$

$$\lambda^\circ \text{ for } CH_3COOH = 390.7\ ohm^{-1}\,cm^2\,mol^{-1}$$

Skill Builder

From the following molar conductivities at infinite dilution:

Λ°_m for $Ba(OH)_2 = 457.6\ ohm^{-1}\,cm^2\,mol^{-1}$

Λ°_m for $BaCl_2 = 240.6\ ohm^{-1}\,cm^2\,mol^{-1}$

Λ°_m for $NH_4Cl = 129.8\ ohm^{-1}\,cm^2\,mol^{-1}$

Calculate Λ°_m for NH_4OH.

(a) 258.1 $ohm^{-1}\,cm^2$ (b) 356.8 $ohm^{-1}\,cm^2\,mol^{-1}$
(c) 156.2 $ohm^{-1}\,cm^2\,mol^{-1}$ (d) 451.2 $ohm^{-1}\,cm^2\,mol^{-1}$

For more practice Refer to Q.18 and Q.20 step up of practice 3.

(ii) **In the calculation of degree of dissociation** For calculating degree of dissociation (α) of weak electrolyte, formula used is

$$\alpha = \frac{\Lambda^C_m}{\Lambda^\circ_m}$$

where, α = degree of dissociation
Λ^C_m = molar conductance at any concentration
Λ°_m = limiting molar conductance

(iii) **In the calculation of ionisation or dissociation constant (K_a) for weak binary electrolyte** For a weak electrolyte, dissociation constant can be formulated as,

$$K_a = \frac{C\alpha^2}{1-\alpha} = \frac{C\Lambda^2_m}{\Lambda^\circ_m(\Lambda^\circ_m - \Lambda_m)}$$

where, C = concentration of electrolyte
Λ°_m = limiting molar conductivity
Λ_m = molar conductivity

Example 14. *The conductivity of a 0.01 M solution of acetic acid at 298 K is 1.65×10^{-4} S cm^{-1}. Calculate*

(i) molar conductivity of the solution

(ii) degree of dissociation of CH_3COOH

(iii) dissociation constant for acetic acid.

Given that $\lambda^\circ_{(H^+)} = 349.1$ and $\lambda^\circ_{(CH_3COO^-)} = 40.9$ S cm^2 mol^{-1}

Sol. (i) Calculation of molar conductivity of solution.

$$\Lambda = \frac{\kappa \times 1000}{C}$$

$$\kappa = 1.65 \times 10^{-4} \text{ S cm}^{-1}, C = 0.01 \text{ M}$$

$$\therefore \quad \Lambda = \frac{1.65 \times 10^{-4} \times 1000}{0.01} = 16.5 \text{ S cm}^2 \text{ mol}^{-1}$$

(ii) Calculation of degree of dissociation of acetic acid.

$$\alpha = \frac{\Lambda^C}{\Lambda^\circ}$$

$$\Lambda^\circ_{(CH_3COOH)} = \lambda^\circ_{(H^+)} + \lambda^\circ_{(CH_3COO^-)}$$

$$= 349.1 + 40.9 = 390 \text{ S cm}^2 \text{ mol}^{-1}$$

$$\therefore \quad \alpha = \frac{16.5}{390} = 0.0423$$

(iii) Calculation of dissociation constant, K

Acetic acid dissociation as:

$$CH_3COOH \rightleftharpoons CH_3COO^- + H^+$$

	CH_3COOH	CH_3COO^-	H^+
Initial conc.	c	0	0
Equilibrium conc.	$C(1-\alpha)$	$C\alpha$	$C\alpha$

$$\text{Dissociation constant, } K = \frac{[CH_3COO^-][H^+]}{CH_3COOH} = \frac{C\alpha \times c\alpha}{C(1-\alpha)}$$

$$\text{or} \quad K = \frac{C\alpha^2}{1-\alpha}$$

$$\text{Substituting the values, } K = \frac{0.01 \times (0.0423)^2}{1 - 0.0423} = 1.87 \times 10^{-5}$$

STEP UP Practice 3

1. The conductivity of electricity through the electrolyte solution is due to

(a) movement of molecules of electrolyte
(b) movement of ions of electrolyte
(c) movement of particles of the solvent
(d) movement of separate atoms

2. Which of the statement about solutions of electrolytes is not correct?

(a) Conductivity of solution depends upon size of ions
(b) Conductivity depends upon viscosity of solution
(c) Conductivity does not depend upon solvation of ions present in solution
(d) Conductivity of solution increases with temperature

3. Cell constant is maximum in case of a

(a) wire of length 100 cm and area 100 cm^2
(b) wire of length 10 cm and area 10 cm^2
(c) one centimeter cube of a material
(d) equal in all cases

4. The cell constant of a conductivity cell ....

(a) changes with change of electrolyte
(b) changes with change of concentration of electrolyte
(c) changes with temperature of electrolyte
(d) remains constant for a cell

5. The specific conductance of 0.1 N KCl solution at 23°C is $0.012 \Omega^{-1}$ cm^{-1}. The resistance of cell containing the solution at the same temperature was found to be 55 Ω. The cell constant will be

(a) 0.142 cm^{-1}
(b) 0.66 cm^{-1}
(c) 0.918 cm^{-1}
(d) 1.12 cm^{-1}

6 Variation of resistance (R) with increase in cell constant (l/a) gives graph of the type

(a)
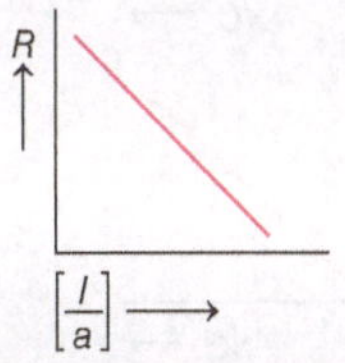

(b)
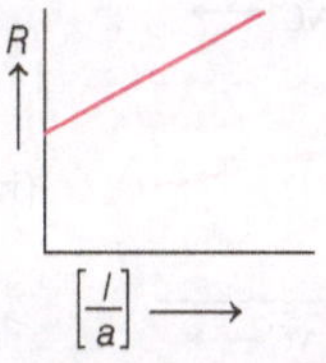

(c)
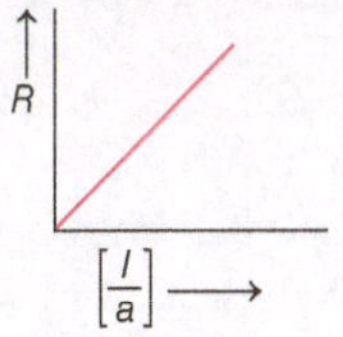

(d)
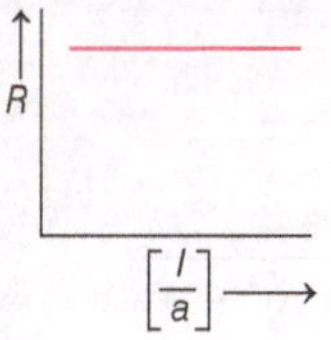

7. Consider the following statements.

Statement I Conductivity of all electrolytes solutions decreases on dilution.

Statement II On dilution number of ions per unit volume decreases.

In the light of the above statements, choose the most appropriate answer from the options given below.

(a) Both Statement I and Statement II are false.
(b) Statement I is true but Statement II is false.
(c) Statement I is false but Statement II is true.
(d) Both Statement I and Statement II are true.

8. When a certain conductivity cell was filled with 0.01 M solution of KCl, it had a resistance of 160 Ω at 25°C and when filled with 0.005 M NaOH, it had a resistance of 190 Ω. If specific resistance of KCl solution is 700 Ω-cm, specific conductance of NaOH solution is

(a) $0.00120 \Omega^{-1}$ cm^{-1}
(b) $0.00170 \Omega^{-1}$ cm^{-1}
(c) $0.00180 \Omega^{-1}$ cm^{-1}
(d) $0.00190 \Omega^{-1}$ cm^{-1}

9. Which of the following is correctly matched regarding the unit of molar conductance?
(a) Molar conductance $\longrightarrow$ ohm^{-1} cm mol^{-1}
(b) Molar conductance $\longrightarrow$ mho cm^2 mol^{-1}
(c) Molar conductance $\longrightarrow$ ohm cm^2 mol^{-1}
(d) Molar conductance $\longrightarrow$ ohm^{-1} cm^{-1} mol^{-1}

10. 0.1 M aqueous solution of a dibasic acid is diluted such that its equivalent conductance is five times. Hence, final concentration is
(a) 0.01 N (b) 0.02 N (c) 0.04 N (d) 0.055 N

11 Consider the following statements.
Statement I Λ_m for weak electrolytes shows a sharp increase when the electrolytic solution is diluted.
Statement II For weak electrolytes degree of dissociation increases with dilution of solution.
In the light of the above statements, choose the most appropriate answer from the options given below
(a) Both Statement I and Statement II are false.
(b) Statement I is true but Statement II is false.
(c) Statement I is false but Statement II is true.
(d) Both Statement I and Statement II are true.

12 Consider the following graphs,

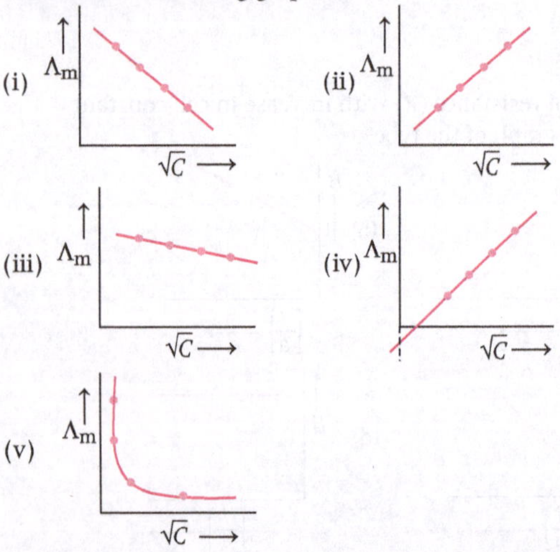

How many graph represent the variation of Λ_m with $\sqrt{C}$ for CH_3COOH?
(a) 1 (b) 2 (c) 4 (d) 3

13 0.1 M H_2SO_4 is diluted to 0.01 M H_2SO_4. Hence, its molar conductance will be
(a) 10 times (b) $\frac{1}{10}$th (c) 100 times (d) 10000 times

14 0.04 N solution of a weak acid has specific conductance 4.23×10^{-4} mho cm^{-1} and degree of dissociation is 0.0612. The equivalent conductance (ohm^{-1} cm^2 equiv^{-1}) of weak acid at infinite dilution is
(a) 1.72 (b) 17.29 (c) 142.27 (d) 172.79

15 The molar conductivity of strong electrolytes
(a) does not change on dilution
(b) increases on dilution slightly
(c) decreases on dilution
(d) depends on density of electrolyte itself

16 Which of the following is correctly matched?
(a) $\Lambda^\circ_{m(NH_4OH)} = \Lambda^\circ_{m(NaOH)} + \Lambda^\circ_{m(NH_4Cl)} - \Lambda^\circ_{(HCl)}$
(b) $\Lambda^\circ_{m(NH_4OH)} = \Lambda^\circ_{m(NH_4Cl)} + \Lambda^\circ_{m(NaOH)} - \Lambda^\circ_{(NaCl)}$
(c) $\Lambda^\circ_{m(NH_4OH)} = \Lambda^\circ_{m(NH_4Cl)} + \Lambda^\circ_{m(NaCl)} - \Lambda^\circ_{(NaOH)}$
(d) $\Lambda^\circ_{m(NH_4OH)} = \Lambda^\circ_{m(NaOH)} + \Lambda^\circ_{m(NaCl)} - \Lambda^\circ_{(NH_4Cl)}$

17 Consider the following compounds,
(i) HCN (ii) HCOOH (iii) CH_3NH_2 (iv) KCl
(v) CH_3COOH
In how many cases Λ_m values *vs* $\sqrt{C}$ shows a straight line?
(a) 4 (b) 1 (c) 2 (d) 3

18 For pure water degree of dissociation of water is 1.9×10^{-9}
$\Lambda^\infty_m (H^+) = 350$ S cm^2 mol^{-1}
$\Lambda^\infty_m (OH^-) = 200$ S cm^2 mol^{-1}
Hence, molar conductance of water is
(a) 1.045×10^{-6} S cm^2 mol^{-1} (b) 1.045×10^{-9} S cm^2 mol^{-1}
(c) 1.045×10^{-10} S cm^2 mol^{-1} (d) 1.04×10^{-14} S cm^2 mol^{-1}

19 Equivalent conductance at infinite dilution of $BaCl_2$, H_2SO_4 and HCl(*aq*) solutions are x_1, x_2 and x_3 respectively. Equivalent conductance of $BaSO_4$ solution is
(a) $x_1 + x_2 - x_3$ (b) $x_1 - x_2 - x_3$
(c) $x_1 + x_2 - 2x_3$ (d) $x_1 - 2x_2 + x_3$

20 Which of the following is correctly matched?
(a) $\Lambda^\infty_m (BaSO_4) \longrightarrow \Lambda^\infty_m$ of $(BaCl_2 + H_2SO_4 - HCl)$
(b) $\Lambda^\infty_m (BaSO_4) \longrightarrow \Lambda^\infty_m$ of $(2BaCl_2 + 2H_2SO_4 - HCl)$
(c) $\Lambda^\infty_m (BaSO_4) \longrightarrow \Lambda^\infty_m$ of $(BaCl_2 + H_2SO_4 - 2HCl)$
(d) $\Lambda^\infty_m (BaSO_4) \longrightarrow \Lambda^\infty_m$ of $(BaCl_2 + 2H_2SO_4 - HCl)$

21 Which of the following relationship is not correct?
(a) Conductivity (κ) $\longrightarrow$ Observed conductance (G) $\times$ Cell constant
(b) Molar conductance (Λ_m) $\longrightarrow \frac{\kappa \times 1000}{\text{Concentration}}$
(c) Degree of dissociation (α) = $\frac{\Lambda^c_m}{\Lambda^\circ_m}$
(d) Resistivity = $\frac{RA}{l}$

22 Equivalent conductance of 1 M CH_3COOH is 10 Ω^{-1} cm^2 equiv^{-1} and at infinite dilution 200 Ω^{-1} cm^2 equiv^{-1}. Hence, percentage ionisation of CH_3COOH is
(a) 5% (b) 2%
(c) 4% (d) 1%

23 Consider the following relation,
(i) $K_a = \frac{C\alpha^2}{1-\alpha}$ (ii) $K_a = \frac{C\Lambda^2_m}{\Lambda^\circ_m(\Lambda^\circ_m - \Lambda_m)}$
(iii) $\Lambda_m = \frac{\kappa A}{l}$ (iv) $\Lambda_m = \Lambda^\circ_m + AC^{\frac{1}{2}}$
(v) $\Lambda^\circ_m = V_+\lambda^\circ_+ + V_-\lambda^\circ_-$
How many relations are correct?
(a) 1 (b) 2 (c) 4 (d) 3

Module 4

Electrolysis and Electrolytic Cell, Batteries and Corrosion

• Qualitative Electrolysis • Quantitative Electrolysis • Batteries • Fuel Cells

Electrolysis and Electrolytic Cell

The phenomenon in which passage of current through an electrolyte (molten or solution) brings in chemical changes involving electronation (reduction) as well as de-electronation (oxidation) of ions is known as **electrolysis.**

- Electrolysis is a non-spontaneous process ($\Delta G > 0$).
- The apparatus used to carry out electrolysis is known as **electrolytic cell.**

Diagram and Working of an Electrolytic Cell

The three primary components of electrolytic cells are :

- Cathode (which is negatively charged for electrolytic cells)
- Anode (which is positively charged for electrolytic cells)
- Electrolyte

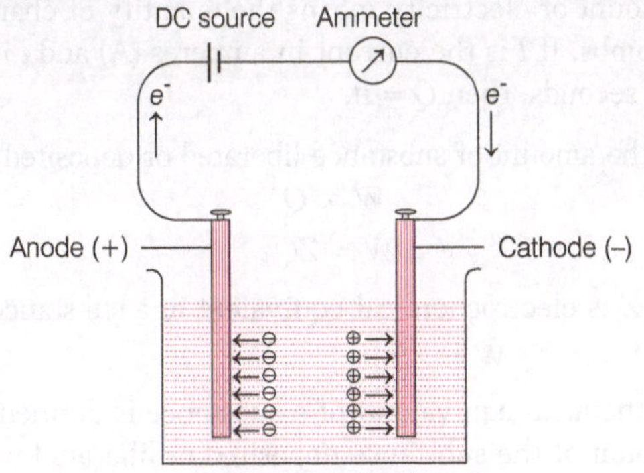

Electrolytic cell

Concept ladder An electrolytic solution provides the medium for the exchange of electrons between the cathode and the anode.

During electrolysis cations of electrolyte are discharged on cathode and anions of electrolyte on anode.

$$AB \rightleftharpoons A^+ + B^-$$

At anode : $B^- \longrightarrow B + e^-$ (oxidation)

At cathode : $A^+ + e^- \longrightarrow A$ (reduction)

During electrolysis oxidation takes place at anode (+ve pole) and reduction takes place at cathode (-ve pole).

During electrolysis anode acts as oxidising agent while cathode acts as reducing agent.

The minimum potential required to discharge the ion on the appropriate electrode is termed as discharge potential.

- More discharge potential indicate less tendency to deposite ions.
- The values for discharge potential are different for different ions.

(i) **For cation** In general, cations which is stronger oxidising agent (have high value of standard reduction potential) is discharged first at the cathode. The increasing order of decomposition of few cations is

$$\xrightarrow[\text{Increasing order of decomposition}]{K^+, Ca^{2+}, Na^+, Mg^{2+}, Al^{3+}, Zn^{2+}, Fe^{2+}, H^+, Cu^{2+}, Ag^+, Au^{3+}}$$

(ii) **For anion** The anion which is stronger reducing agent (have lower value of standard reduction potential) is liberated first at anode. The increasing order of discharge of few anions is

$$\xrightarrow[\text{Increasing order of discharge}]{SO_4^{2-}, NO_3^{2-}, \bar{OH}, Cl^-, Br^-, I^-}$$

Types of Electrolysis

Following are the types of electrolysis.

(i) **Qualitative electrolysis** Study of possible products formed at cathode and anode during electrolysis.

(ii) **Quantitative electrolysis** Study of amount/moles/volume of the products formed at cathode and anode during electrolysis.

Qualitative Electrolysis

Some examples of electrolysis are discussed below

1. Electrolysis of Molten NaCl

$$NaCl(molten) \longrightarrow Na^+ + Cl^-$$

At anode, $2Cl^- \longrightarrow Cl_2\uparrow + 2e^-$

At cathode, $2Na^+ + 2e^- \longrightarrow 2Na\ (l)$

Thus, Cl_2 and Na are the products of electrolysis of molten NaCl.

2. Electrolysis of Aqueous NaCl Solution (Using Inert Electrode)

In aqueous solution of NaCl, $Na^{\oplus}$, $Cl^{\ominus}$, $H^{\oplus}$ (from water) and $\overset{\ominus}{O}H$ (from water) ions are free to move for the conduction of the electric current. When electric current is passed, $Na^{\oplus}$ and $H^{\oplus}$ ions are attracted to cathode and $Cl^{\ominus}$ and $\overset{\ominus}{O}H$ ions attracted to anode. The solution now contains four ions $Na^{\oplus}$, $Cl^{\ominus}$ (from NaCl), $H^{\oplus}$, $\overset{\ominus}{O}H$ (from water) and there is race amongst them for their discharge at their respective electrodes.

The following electrode reactions are possible:

At cathode,

$$Na^+(aq) + e^- \longrightarrow Na(s)\ ;\ E^\circ_{Na^{\oplus}|Na} = -2.71\ V$$

$$2H_2O(l) + 2e^- \longrightarrow H_2(g) + 2\overset{\ominus}{O}H(aq)\ ;\ E^\circ_{H_2O|H_2} = -0.83\ V$$

At anode,

$$2Cl^{\ominus}(aq) \longrightarrow Cl_2(g) + 2e^-\ ;\ E^\circ_{Cl^{\ominus}|Cl_2} = -1.36\ V$$

$$2H_2O(l) \longrightarrow O_2(g) + 4H^{\oplus}(aq) + 4e^-\ ;$$

$$E^\circ_{H_2O|O_2} = -1.23V$$

Overall reaction :

$$2Na^{\oplus}(aq) + 2Cl^{\ominus}(aq) \longrightarrow Na(s) + Cl_2(g)$$

In this electrolysis, H_2 at cathode and Cl_2 at anode are given off.

3. Aqueous NaCl Solution (Using Hg Electrodes) (Active Electrode)

Possible reactions

At cathode,

$$Na^{\oplus}(aq) + e^- \longrightarrow Na(s);\ E^\circ_{Na^{\oplus}|Na} = -2.71\ V$$

$$2H_2O(l) + 2e^- \longrightarrow H_2(g) + 2\overset{\ominus}{O}H(aq);\ E^\circ_{H_2O|H_2} = -0.83\ V$$

At anode,

$$2Cl^{\ominus}(aq) \longrightarrow Cl_2(g) + 2e^-;\ E^\circ_{Cl^{\ominus}|Cl_2} = -1.36\ V$$

$$2H_2O(l) \longrightarrow O_2(g) + 4H^{\oplus}(aq) + 4e^-;\ E^\circ_{H_2O|O_2} = -1.23\ V$$

When Hg electrodes are used instead of Pt, $Na^{\oplus}(aq)$ gets deposited which further reacts with Hg to form sodium amalgam.

$$Na(s) + Hg(s) \longrightarrow NaHg(s)$$

4. Electrolysis of H_2SO_4

For dilute H_2SO_4,

At anode, $2H_2O(l) \longrightarrow O_2(g) + 4H^+(aq) + 4e^-$

At cathode, $2H^+(aq) + 2e^- \longrightarrow H_2(g)$

For concentrated H_2SO_4,

At anode, $2SO_4^{2-}(aq) \longrightarrow S_2O_8^{2-}(aq) + 2e^-$

At cathode, $2H^+(aq) + 2e^- \longrightarrow H_2(g)$

Quantitative Electrolysis

Michael Faraday showed (in 1830) that the amount of substance produced at electrode by electrolysis depends on the quantity of charge passed through the cell.

For example, passage of 1 mole of electrons through a cell yields 1 mole (23.0 g) of sodium at the cathode

$$\underset{1\ mol}{Na^+(l)} + e^- \longrightarrow \underset{1\ mol}{Na(l)}$$

Quantitative aspects of electrolysis are governed by **Faraday's law of electrolysis.**

1. First Law of Electrolysis

It states that "the amount of any substance that is deposited or liberated at an electrode is directly proportional to the quantity of electricity passing through the electrolytic cell."

The amount of electricity means the quantity of charge (Q) in coulombs. If I is the current in amperes (A) and t is the time in seconds, then $Q = It$.

If W is the amount of substance liberated or deposited, then

$$W \propto Q$$

$$W = ZQ$$

where, Z is electrochemical equivalent of a substance

$$\Rightarrow \quad W = ZIt$$

Electrochemical equivalent of a substance is defined as the amount of the substance deposited or liberated when an ampere current is passed for one second.

$$W = Z \times I \times t$$

$$I = 1\,A$$

$$t = 1\,s$$

$$W = Z$$

$$Z = \frac{E}{96500}$$

E = Equivalent weight of the substance

$$Z = \frac{\text{molar mass}}{\text{valency} \times 96500}$$

Unit = gram/Coulomb

Example 15. *The electrochemical equivalent for zinc (atomic weight = 65.4 g/mol) is*

(a) 3.4×10^{-4} (b) 3.8×10^{-4}
(c) 3.6×10^{-4} (d) 7.2×10^{-3}

Sol. (*a*) $Zn^{+2} + 2e^- \longrightarrow Zn$

$$Z = \frac{65.4}{96500 \times 2} \approx 0.00034 \text{ g/C}$$

$$Z = 3.4 \times 10^{-4} \text{ g/C}$$

2. Second Law of Electrolysis

When the same quantity of electricity is passed through different electrolyte the weights of different substance liberated at the electrodes are directly proportional to their equivalents or equivalent weights.

e.g. $CuSO_4$ solution and $AgNO_3$ solution connected in series if the same quantity of electricity is passed then

$$\frac{\text{Weight of Cu deposited}}{\text{Weight of Ag deposited}} = \frac{\text{Eq. weight of Cu}}{\text{Eq. weight of Ag}}$$

$$W \propto E$$

$$\frac{W_1}{W_2} = \frac{E_1}{E_2}$$

Example 16. *How many moles of electrons are required to*
(i) reduce 1 mole of MnO_4^- to Mn^{2+}
(ii) produce 10.0 g of Al from molten Al_2O_3

Sol. Moles of electrons required :

(i) $MnO_4^- + 5e^- \longrightarrow Mn^{2+}$

1 mole of MnO_4^- will be reduced by 5 moles of electrons.

(ii) $Al^{3+} + 3e^- \longrightarrow Al$

3 mole of electrons are required to produce 1 mole or 27 g of Al

$\therefore$ 10 g of Al will be produced by $= \frac{3}{27} \times 10$
$= 1.11$ mol electrons

NEET Close-up

Example Similar to PYQ Asked in NEET 2024

Match Column-I with Column-II.

Column I (Conversion)		Column II (Number of Faraday required)
A. 2 mol H_2O to O_2	1.	2F
B. 2 moles of MnO_4^- to Mn^{2+}	2.	6F
C. 3 moles of Ca from molten $CaCl_2$	3.	10F
D. 2 moles of FeO to Fe_2O_3	4.	4F

Codes

	A	B	C	D		A	B	C	D
(a)	2	1	4	3	(b)	4	1	3	2
(c)	2	4	1	3	(d)	4	3	2	1

Sol. (*d*) The correct match is A-4, B-3, C-2, D-1.

A. $2H_2O \longrightarrow O_2 + 4H^+ + 4e^-$
So 2 moles of H_2O will require 4F charge.

B. $8H^+ + MnO_4^- + 5e^- \longrightarrow Mn^{2+} + 4H_2O$
So, 2 moles of MnO_4^- required 10F charge.

C. $CaCl_2 + 2e^- \longrightarrow Ca + 2Cl^-$
3 moles of Ca will require 6F.

D. $2FeO + H_2O \longrightarrow Fe_2O_3 + 2H^+ + 2e^-$
So, 2 moles of FeO will require 2F charge.

Skill Builder

Match Column I with Column II.

Column I (Conversion)		Column II (Number of Faraday required)
A. 1 gram magnesium from molten $MgCl_2$	1.	4F
B. 20 g calcium from $CaCl_2$	2.	3F
C. Deposition of 1 mol of H	3.	1F
D. Deposition of 4 g of H_2	4.	2F

Codes

	A	B	C	D		A	B	C	D
(a)	2	1	4	3	(b)	4	1	3	2
(c)	2	4	1	3	(d)	4	3	2	1

For more practice Refer to Q. 14 in step up Practice 4 and Q.50, 51 of Gearing up for NEET.

Example 17. *A current of 3 ampere is passed for 20 minutes through a voltameter containing a solution of sodium chloride. What is the amount of chlorine produced at the anode?*

Sol. $I = 3$ ampere and $t = 20$ minutes or 1200 seconds

$$Q = I \times t$$
$$= 3 \times 1200 = 3600 \text{ coulombs}$$

We know that,

96500 coulombs of electricity deposit = 1 g eq. of chlorine = 35.5 g of chlorine

Hence, 3600 coulombs of electricity deposit

$$= \frac{35.5}{96500} \times 3600 \text{ g} = 1.32 \text{ g}$$

Mentor's TiP

To determine the amount of current necessary to produce a known quantity of substance in a given amount of time use the following steps.

1. Find the quantity of substance produced/or consumed in moles.
2. Write the equation for the half-cell reaction that takes place.
3. Calculate the number of moles of electrons required.
4. Convert the moles of electrons into coulombs of charge.
5. After that calculate the current required.

Example 18. *What amount of current is required to produce* 400.0 L *of hydrogen gas, measured at STP, from the electrolysis of water in* 1 *hour* (3600 s)?

Sol. (i) First of all, calculate the number of moles of H_2. (Remember, at STP, 1 mole of any gas occupies 22.4 L)

$$400.0 \text{ L } H_2 \times \frac{1 \text{ mole } H_2}{22.4 \text{ L } H_2} \approx 17.9 \text{ mole } H_2$$

(ii) Now, write the equation for the half-reaction that takes place.

Hydrogen is produced during the reduction of water at the cathode.

The equation for this half-reaction is :

$$4e^- + 4H_2O(l) \longrightarrow 2H_2(g) + 4OH^-(aq)$$

(iii) Now, calculate the number of moles of electrons.

According to the stoichiometry of the equation, 4 mole of e^- are required to produce 2 moles of hydrogen gas, or 2 moles of e^- s for every one mole of hydrogen gas.

$$17.9 \text{ mole } H_2 \times \frac{2 \text{ mole } e^-}{1 \text{ mole } H_2} = 35.8 \text{ mole } e^-$$

(iv) Convert the moles of electrons into coulombs of charge.

$$35.8 \text{ mole } e^- \times \frac{1\text{F}}{1 \text{ mole } e^-} = 35.8 \text{ F};$$

$$35.8 \text{ F} \times \frac{96500 \text{ C}}{1\text{F}} = 3.45 \times 10^6 \text{C}$$

(v) Calculate the current required.

$$I \times 3600 \text{ s} = 3.45 \times 10^6 \text{ C}$$
$$I \approx 958 \text{ C/s} = 958 \text{ Ampere}$$

Batteries

Any cell or batteries that we employ as a source of electrical energy is basically an electrochemical cell. If a number of cells are arranged in a series then this arrangement is collectively called as **battery.**

In this, the anode of each cell connected to the cathode of the adjacent cell and the voltage provided by the battery is the sum of the individual cell voltages. These batteries can be classified as follow

1. Primary Batteries

In these type of batteries, redox reactions occur only once and the battery becomes dead after sometime. They cannot be recharged or used again, e.g. dry cell like leclanche cell, mercury cell.

(i) Leclanche Cell

It is called dry cell as it has constituents in dry powdered or paste form and not in solution form. The components of this cell are

At anode Zinc metal container.

At cathode Inert graphite rod surrounded by powdered MnO_2 and carbon black.

Electrolyte moist paste of NH_4Cl and $ZnCl_2$ in starch.

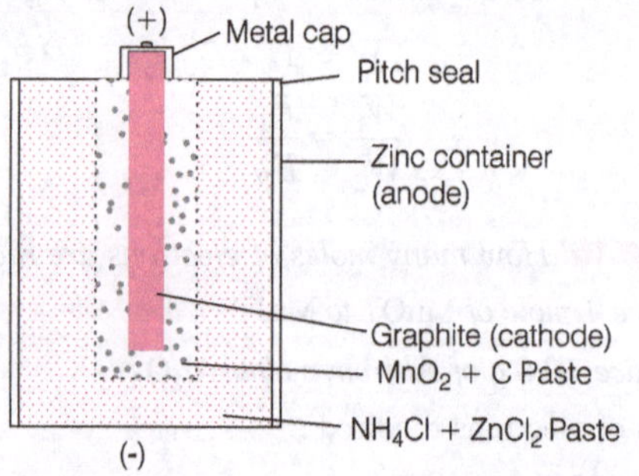

The dry cell

Reactions Involved

At anode, $Zn(s) \longrightarrow Zn^{2+}(aq) + 2e^-$

At cathode, $2MnO_2(s) + 2NH_4^+(aq) + 2e^- \longrightarrow Mn_2O_3(s) + 2NH_3(g) + H_2O(l)$

Net reaction

$$Zn(s) + 2NH_4^+(aq) + 2MnO_2(s) + 2e^- \longrightarrow Mn_2O_3(s) + 2NH_3(aq) + H_2O(l)$$

Ammonia produced in the reaction forms of a complex with Zn^{2+} to give $[Zn(NH_3)_4]^{2+}$.

$$Zn^{2+}(aq) + 4NH_3(aq) \longrightarrow [Zn(NH_3)_4]^{2+}(aq)$$

Mentor's TiP

In the reaction at cathode, manganese is reduced from the + 4 oxidation state to the + 3 oxidation state.

(ii) Mercury Cell

These cells are suitable for low current devices like hearing aids, watches etc. It has

At anode Zinc and mercury amalgam

At cathode Paste of carbon and HgO

Electrolyte Paste of KOH and ZnO.

Reactions Involved

At anode,

$$Zn(Hg) + 2OH^-(aq) \longrightarrow ZnO(s) + H_2O(l) + 2e^-$$

At cathode,

$$HgO(s) + H_2O(l) + 2e^- \longrightarrow Hg(l) + 2OH^-(aq)$$

Net reaction

$$Zn(Hg) + HgO(s) \longrightarrow ZnO(s) + Hg(l)$$

Net reaction does not involve any ion, i.e. OH^- hence, cell potential is independent of OH^- concentration. Therefore, the cell gives a constant potential of 1.35V.

2. Secondary Batteries

- It is a chemical device in which energy may be stored in the form of chemical energy and it may be drawn out when required.
- It can be recharged by passing an electric current through them.
- It can be used over and over again.
- It acts as an accumulator or storage cell.
- It shows reversible reactions.

(i) Nickel-Cadmium Batteries

Nickel-cadmium or 'Ni-Cad' batteries are rechargeable storage batteries. They have longer life but are more expensive.

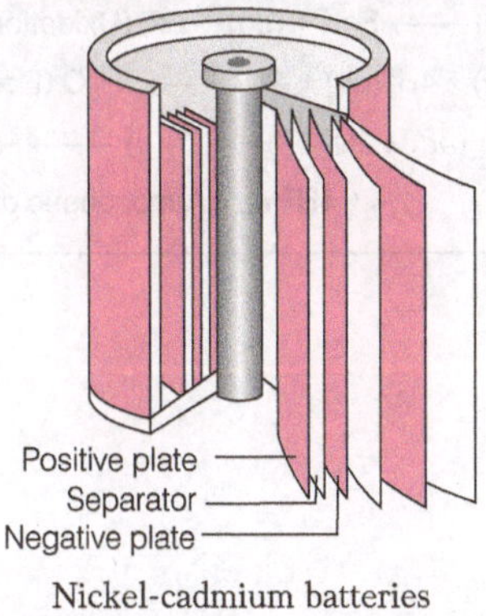

Nickel-cadmium batteries

At anode cadmium metal,

At cathode nickel (III) compound like NiO(OH) supported on nickel.

Electrolyte KOH

Reactions involved during discharge

At anode $Cd(s) + 2OH^-(aq) \rightleftharpoons Cd(OH)_2(s) + 2e^-$

At cathode

$$NiO(OH)(s) + H_2O(l) + e^- \longrightarrow Ni(OH)_2(s) + OH^-(aq)$$

Net reaction

$$Cd(s) + 2NiO(OH)(s) + 2H_2O(l) \underset{\text{Recharging}}{\overset{\text{Discharging}}{\rightleftharpoons}} Cd(OH)_2(s) + 2Ni(OH)_2(s)$$

When cell is recharging, the reactions are reversed.

(ii) Lead-Storage Batteries

A typical 12-V battery consists of six cells connected in series, each cell providing a potential of about 2 V.

At anode A series of lead grids packed with spongy lead

At cathode A series of grids packed with lead dioxide.

Electrolyte An aqueous solution of H_2SO_4, 38% by weight.

- **Discharge of battery** When the cell gets discharged, (providing current), it acts as an electrochemical cell. The reactions involved are

  At anode $Pb(s) + SO_4^{2-}(aq) \longrightarrow PbSO_4(s) + 2e^-$

  At cathode

  $$PbO_2(s) + 4H^+(aq) + SO_4^{2-}(aq) + 2e^- \longrightarrow PbSO_4(s) + 2H_2O(l)$$

  Net reaction

$$Pb(s) + PbO_2(s) + 2H_2SO_4(aq) \longrightarrow 2PbSO_4(s) + 2H_2O(l)$$

Mentor's Tip

In lead storage batteries there is no need for the cell to have separate anode and cathode compartments because the oxidising and reducing agents are both solids (PbO_2 and Pb). They are kept away from coming in contact by the presence of insulating spaces between the grids.

Characteristics

Following are the characteristic of lead storage battery.

- Sulphuric acid is consumed during discharging and when the concentration of H_2SO_4 falls to 1.20 g L^{-1} it requires recharging.
- **Recharging the battery** A "run-down" lead storage battery can be recharged by using an external source of direct current to drive the cell reaction in the reverse non-spontaneous direction.

  Actually, it forces the electrons to flow in opposite direction resulting in the deposition of Pb on the anode and PbO_2 on the cathode. In this case battery behaves like electrolytic batteries.

Fuel Cells

A fuel cell is a galvanic cell in which one of the reactants is a traditional fuel such as CH_4 or H_2 or CO.

Reactants are not contained within the cell but instead are continuously supplied from an external reservoir.

- **Electrodes** are made of porous carbon impregnated with metallic catalysts (Pt, Ag or metal oxide).
- **Electrolyte** Concentrated KOH or NaOH
- **Catalysts** Generally Pt or Pd

Reactions involved The fuel (gaseous H_2) and the oxidising agent (gaseous O_2) do not react directly but instead of flow into separate cell compartments where H_2 is oxidised at the anode and O_2 is reduced at the cathode.

At anode

At cathode $2H_2(g) + 4OH^-(aq) \longrightarrow 4H_2O(l) + 4e^-$

$$O_2(g) + 2H_2O(l) + 4e^- \longrightarrow 4OH^-(aq)$$

Net reaction $2H_2(g) + O_2(g) \longrightarrow 2H_2O(l)$

Catalyst used in this cell, increases the rate of electrode reactions.

Advantages

- Fuel cells are pollution free cell, light in weight and have high reliability.
- Efficiency of fuel cell is very high (about 70%).

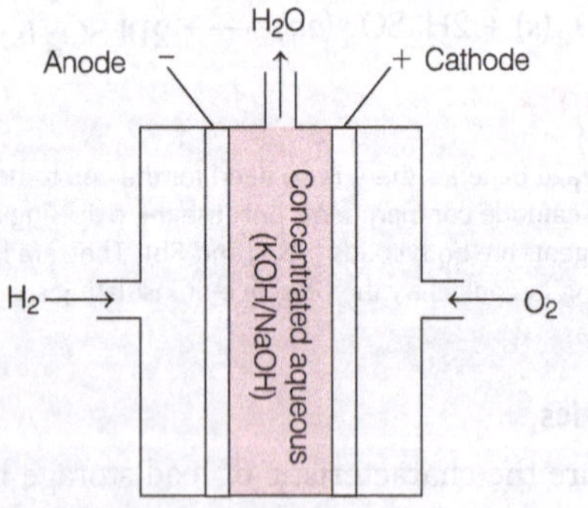

Fuel cell

Disadvantages

- It is very difficult to handle gaseous fuels.
- Catalyst used are very costly.
- Electrode preparation is very difficult and time taking.

Uses

The primary use of this kind of cells is in space craft, where by-product (H_2O) can be used for other purposes as well. These cells are also used in other vehicles like electric cars, submarines etc.

Corrosion

Corrosion is the oxidative deterioration of a metal, such as conversion of iron to rust $[Fe_2O_3 \cdot xH_2O]$, tarnishing of silver (due to formation of Ag_2O), development of a green coating on copper and bronze.

Corrosion is basically an electrochemical phenomenon. A metal is oxidised by loss of electrons to oxygen and forms metal oxide.

NEET Infographic

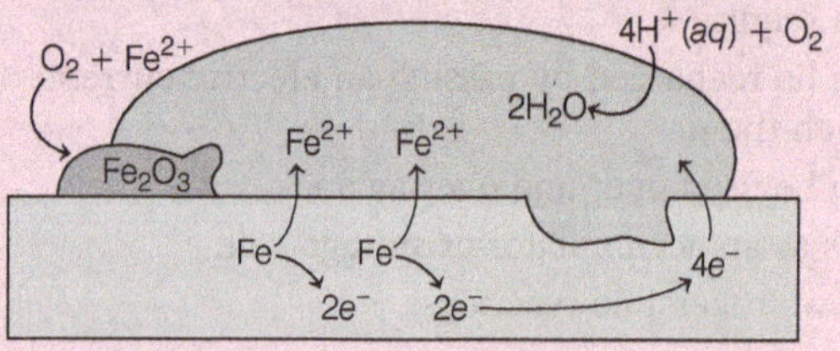

A water droplet on the surface of iron forms an electrochemical cell which leads to rusting atmospheric oxygen plays a major part in the corrosion.

1. $Fe(s) \longrightarrow Fe^{2+}(aq) + 2e^-$ (Oxidation)
2. $O_2(g) + 4H^+(aq) + 4e^- \longrightarrow 2H_2O$ (Reduction)
3. $2Fe^{2+}(aq) + 2H_2O(l) + \frac{1}{2}O_2(g) \longrightarrow Fe_2O_3(s) + 4H^+(aq)$ (Atmospheric oxidation)

STEP UP Practice 4

1 When a dilute aqueous Li_2SO_4 solution is electrolysed, the products formed at the anode and cathode, respectively are
(a) S and Li (b) O_2 and Li
(c) SO_2 and H_2 (d) O_2 and H_2

2 When $Na_2SO_4(aq)$ is electrolysed between Pt electrodes, the reaction that occurs at cathode is
(a) $Na^+ + e^- \longrightarrow Na$
(b) $H^+ + e^- \longrightarrow \frac{1}{2} H_2$
(c) $2OH^- \longrightarrow \frac{1}{2} O_2 + H_2O + 2e^-$
(d) $2H_2O + 2e^- \longrightarrow H_2 + 2OH^-$

3. The current in a given wire is 1.8 A. In 1.36 min, the number of coulombs transferred in wire is
(a) 136.44 C (b) 138.88 C
(c) 146.88 C (d) 150.66 C

4. 1 A of current is passed to supply 72000 C of charge in
(a) 10 h (b) 5 h
(c) 10 h (d) 20 h

5. The electric charge for electrode deposition of gram equivalent of a substance is
(a) 1 A per second
(b) 96500 C per second
(c) 1 A for 1 h
(d) charge on one mole of electrons

6. 1 g equivalent of Na metal is formed from electrolysis of fused NaCl. Number of moles of Al formed by the same current from fused Na_3AlF_6 will be
(a) 1 (b) 3
(c) 1/3 (d) 2

7. Same quantity of current is passed through molten NaCl and molten cryolite containing Al_2O_3. If 4.6 g of sodium were liberated in one cell, the mass of aluminium liberated in other cell was
(a) 0.9 g (b) 2.7 g
(c) 1.8 g (d) 3.6 g

8. Which of the following is correctly matched regarding the electrolysis of water?
(a) 1F charge produce $\longrightarrow$ one mole of oxygen
(b) 1F charge produce $\longrightarrow$ one g atom of oxygen
(c) 1F charge produce $\longrightarrow$ 22.4 litres of oxygen
(d) 1F charge produce $\longrightarrow$ 8 g of oxygen

9. For $M^{2+} + 2e^- \longrightarrow M$, 0.275 g of metal M is deposited at the cathode due to passage of 1 A of current for 965 s. Hence, atomic weight of the metal M is
(a) 27.5 g (b) 55.0 g
(c) 110.0 g (d) 13.7 g

10. A steady current of 30.0 A for 70.2 min corresponds to a passage of
(a) 1.26×10^5 electrons (b) 1.31 Coulombs
(c) 1.26×10^5 Faradays (d) 1.31 Faradays

11. In a process of electrolysis, MnO_4^- is converted into MnO_2. By 1 Faraday, one mole of MnO_4^- will give
(a) 1 mol of MnO_2 (b) 0.5 mol of MnO_2
(c) 0.66 mol of MnO_2 (d) 0.33 mol of MnO_2

12. Consider the following statements.
Statement I 1 Faraday of electricity deposits 1 g equivalent of Ag or Cu or Al.
Statement II 1 mole of electrons are required to reduce 1 mole of Ag^+ or Cu^{2+} or Al^{3+} ion.
In the light of the above statements, choose the most appropriate answer from the options given below
(a) Both Statement I and Statement II are false.
(b) Statement I is true, but Statement II is false.
(c) Statement I is false, but Statement II is true.
(d) Both Statement I and Statement II are true.

13. How many coulombs are required for the oxidation of 1 mole H_2O to O_2?
(a) 3.86×10^5 C (b) 9.65×10^4 C
(c) 1.93×10^5 C (d) 4.825×10^4 C

14. 1 mole each of $AgNO_3$, $CuSO_4$ and $AlCl_3$ is electrolysed. Number of Faradays required are in the ratio of
(a) 1 : 1 : 1 (b) 1 : 2 : 3 (c) 3 : 2 : 1 (d) 1 : 3 : 1

15. How many Faradays are required to reduce one mole of MnO_4^- to Mn^{2+}?
(a) 1 (b) 5 (c) 3 (d) 2

16. $Ag \mid \underset{\text{1 L solution}}{Ag^+ (1\,M)} \parallel \underset{\text{1 L solution}}{Ag^+ (2M)} \mid Ag$, 0.5 F of electricity in the LHS (anode) and 1 F electricity in the RHS (cathode) is first passed making them independent electrolytic cells at 298 K. EMF of the cell after electrolysis will be
(a) increased (b) decreased
(c) no change (d) time is also required

17. Consider the following statements.
Statement I Mercury cell does not give steady potential.
Statement II In the cell reaction, ions are not involved in solution.
In the light of the above statements, choose the most appropriate answer from the options given below
(a) Both Statement I and Statement II are false.
(b) Statement I is true, but Statement II is false.
(c) Statement I is false, but Statement II is true.
(d) Both Statement I and Statement II are true.

18 Consider the following species,

(i) Zinc (ii) MnO_2

(iii) 38% H_2SO_4 (iv) NH_4Cl

(v) Platinum (catalyst)

How many of them are present in dry cell?

(a) 2 (b) 4 (c) 3 (d) 1

19 In H_2-O_2 fuel cell, the reaction occurring at cathode is

(a) $2H_2(g) + O_2(g) \longrightarrow 2H_2O(l)$

(b) $2H_2(g) + 4OH^-(aq) \longrightarrow 4H_2O(l) + 4e^-$

(c) $O_2(g) + 2H_2O(l) + 4e^- \longrightarrow 4OH^-(aq)$

(d) $2H_2 + \frac{1}{2}O_2(g) \longrightarrow 2H_2O(l)$

20 Which of the following cells has a constant voltage throughout its life?

(a) Leclanche cell

(b) Daniell cell

(c) Mercury cell

(d) Electrolytic cell

NEET Exclusive EXTRA BYTES

- While dealing with Daniell cell strictly activity should be used instead of concentration. It is directly proportional to concentration the proportionality constant is called **activity coefficient**. In dilute solutions, activity coefficient is one and therefore activity is equal to concentration.
- While writing the half-cell reaction, the reduced species is written with anode before oxidised species. Similarly, we write the cathode with oxidised species before reduced species.
- If the $E°$ value is large and positive that means a strong oxidising agent and a weak reducing agent is present in the half-cell.
- The positive values of $E°_{cell}$ shows that overall reaction is spontaneous. It should be remembered that we do not multiply the potentials by the numbers used to balance the electron transfer.
- The concentration of pure solids and pure liquids do not appear in the expression for Q.
- **Transport number** or transference number is defined as the fraction of the current carried by an ion.

$$\text{Transport number} = \frac{\text{current carried by ion}}{\text{total current carried}}$$

Transport no. of cation + Transport no. of anion = 1

- **Calomel electrode** is generally used reference electrode but it comes in the category of **secondary reference electrode** (primary reference electrode is standard hydrogen electrode).
- In this electrode a paste of mercury and mercurous chloride is placed at the bottom of the tube over this paste, KCl solution is filled and a glass sealed platinum wire is used for electrical contact. The potential of electrode depends upon KCl solution.
- On the basis of concentration of KCl, the calomel electrode is named differently. e.g. If KCl solution is saturated, electrode is called **SCE** (Saturated Calomel Electrode).

GEARING UP FOR NEET

1. In the Daniell cell constructed in the laboratory, the voltage observed was 0.9 V instead of 1.1 V of the standard cell. A possible explanation is
(a) $[Zn^{2+}] > [Cu^{2+}]$
(b) $[Zn^{2-}] < [Cu^{2-}]$
(c) the Zn electrode has twice the surface of Cu electrode
(d) mol ratio of $Zn^{2+} : Cu^{2+}$ is 2:1

2. For the cell, $Zn \mid Zn^{2+} (1M) \| Cu^{2+} (1 M) \mid Cu$,
E°_{cell} is 1.10 V, $E^\circ_{Cu^{2+}/Cu} = 0.34$ V and for the cell $Cu \mid Cu^{2+} (1M) \| Ag^+ (1M) \mid Ag$, $E^\circ_{cell} = 0.46$ V hence, E°_{cell} of the cell
$$Zn \mid Zn^{2+} (1M) \| Ag^+ (1M) \mid Ag \text{ is}$$
(a) − 0.04 V (b) + 0.04 V
(c) + 0.30 V (d) + 1.56 V

3. An electrochemical cell is set up as
$Pt(H_2) \mid HCl(0.1\ M) \| CH_3COOH(0.1\ M) \mid Pt(H_2)$
The emf of this cell will not be zero, because
(a) the temperature is constant
(b) pH of 0.1 M HCl and 0.1 M CH_3COOH is not same
(c) acids used in two compartments are different
(d) emf depends on molarities of acids used

4. During the electrolysis of aqueous zinc nitrate
(a) O_2 and H_2 evolved at the cathode
(b) zinc plates out at the anode
(c) hydrogen gas H_2 is evolved at the anode
(d) oxygen gas O_2 is evolved at the anode

5. Given, $E^\circ_{Ag^+/Ag} = 0.80$ V, $E^\circ_{Mg^{2+}/Mg} = -2.37$ V,
$E^\circ_{Cu^{2+}/Cu} = 0.34$ V, $E^\circ_{Hg^{2+}/Hg} = 0.79$ V
Which of the following statement is correct?
(a) $AgNO_3$ can be stored in copper vessel
(b) $Cu(NO_3)_2$ can be stored in magnesium vessel
(c) $CuCl_2$ can be stored in silver vessel
(d) $HgCl_2$ can be stored in copper vessel

6. Consider the following half-cell reactions,
$$Cu^{2+} + 2e^- \longrightarrow Cu; \quad E^\circ = 0.34 \text{ V}$$
$$Zn^{2+} + 2e^- \longrightarrow Zn; \quad E^\circ = -0.76 \text{ V}$$
$$SO_4^{2-} + 4H^+ + 2e^- \longrightarrow SO_2 + 2H_2O; \ E^\circ = 1.17 \text{ V}$$
Hence, select the correct statement(s).
(a) Cu reacts with dil. H_2SO_4 forming H_2 and SO_2
(b) Cu reacts with concentrated H_2SO_4 forming SO_2
(c) Zn reacts with concentrated H_2SO_4 forming SO_2
(d) Both (b) and (c)

7. A certain electrode has a reduction potential of 0.100 V when measured against a standard calomel electrode (anode); $E^\circ_{calomel} = -0.244$ V. Potential *versus* SHE is
(a) − 0.344 V (b) − 0.144 V (c) + 0.144 V (d) + 0.344 V

8. It is not advisable to
(a) stir copper sulphate solution with a zinc spoon
(b) stir silver nitrate solution with a copper spoon
(c) Both (a) and (b)
(d) stir iron sulphate solution with a copper spoon

9. Which cell will measure standard electrode potential of copper electrode?
(a) $Pt\ (s) \mid H_2(g, 0.1 \text{ bar}) \mid H^+ (aq, 1\ M) \| Cu^{2+} (aq, 1\ M) \mid Cu$
(b) $Pt\ (s) \mid H_2(g, 1 \text{ bar}) \mid H^+ (aq, 1\ M) \| Cu^{2+} (aq, 2\ M) \mid Cu$
(c) $Pt\ (s) \mid H_2(g, 1 \text{ bar}) \mid H^+ (aq, 1\ M) \| Cu^{2+} (aq, 1\ M) \mid Cu$
(d) $Pt\ (s) \mid H_2(g, 0.1 \text{ bar}) \mid H^+ (aq, 0.1\ M) \| Cu^{2+} (aq, 1\ M) \mid Cu$

10. Which of the following is/are function(s) of salt-bridge?
(a) It completes the electrical circuit with electrons flowing from one electrode to other through external wires and a flow of ions between the two compartments through salt-bridge.
(b) It prevents the accumulation of the ions.
(c) It does not prevents the diffusion of solution from one cell to the other.
(d) It maximises the liquid-liquid junction potential.

11. Given below are the half-cell reactions,
$$Mn^{2+} + 2e^- \longrightarrow Mn, \ E^\circ = -1.28 \text{ V}$$
$$2(Mn^{3+} + e^- \longrightarrow Mn^{2+}), \ E^\circ = +2.51 \text{ V}$$
The E° for $3Mn^{2+} \longrightarrow Mn + 2Mn^{3+}$ will be
(a) −2.69 V, the reaction will not occur
(b) −2.69 V, the reaction will occur
(c) −3.79 V, the reaction will not occur
(d) −3.79 V, the reaction will occur

12. A solution containing one mole per litre each of $Cu(NO_3)_2$, $AgNO_3$, $Hg_2(NO_3)_2$ and $Mg(NO_3)_2$ is being electrolysed using inert electrodes. The values of standard reduction potentials are
$E^\circ_{Ag^+/Ag} = +0.80$ V, $E^\circ_{Hg_2^{2+}/Hg} = +0.79$ V
$E^\circ_{Cu^{2+}/Cu} = +0.34$ V, $E^\circ_{Mg^{2+}/Mg} = -2.37$ V

with increasing voltage, the sequence of deposition of metals on the cathode will be
(a) Ag, Hg, Cu, Mg
(b) Mg, Cu, Hg, Ag
(c) Ag, Hg, Cu
(d) Cu, Hg, Ag

13. If for the half-cell reactions $E°$ values are known

$$Cu^{2+} + e^- \longrightarrow Cu^+, E° = 0.15 \text{ V}$$
$$Cu^{2+} + 2e^- \longrightarrow Cu, E° = 0.34 \text{ V}$$

Predict which exists in aqueous solution?
(a) Copper (I) sulphate
(b) Copper (II) sulphate
(c) Copper (III) sulphate
(d) Copper (I) Sulphate and copper (II) sulphate

14. If $E°_{Fe^{2+}/Fe}$ is x_1, $E°_{Fe^{3+}/Fe}$ is x_2 then $E°_{Fe^{3+}/Fe^{2+}}$ will be
(a) $3x_2 - 2x_1$ (b) $x_2 - x_1$
(c) $x_2 + x_1$ (d) $2x_1 + 3x_2$

15. For the cell,
$Hg|Hg_2Cl_2|Cl^-(0.1 \text{ M})||Cl^-(0.01 \text{ M})|Pt(Cl_2)$, $E°_{cell}$ is 1.10 V.
Hence, E_{cell} is
(a) 1.1591 V (b) −1.1591V
(c) 1.0409 V (d) −1.0409 V

16. For the half-cell, $Cl^-/Pt(Cl_2)$, $(E - E°)$
(a) increases as $[Cl^-]$ increases
(b) decreases as $[Cl^-]$ increases
(c) remains constant as $[Cl^-]$ increases
(d) cannot be predicted

17. For the half-cells,
Cu^+/Cu, $E° = +0.52$ V ; Cu^{2+}/Cu^+, $E° = +0.16$ V hence, $E°$ for the disproportionation reaction

$$2Cu^+ \longrightarrow Cu^{2+} + Cu \text{ would be}$$

(a) 0.36 V (b) 0.78 V
(c) 0.84 V (d) − 0.36 V

18. In the following electrochemical cell

$$\underset{\ominus}{Zn \mid Zn^{2+}} \,||\, \underset{\oplus}{H^+ \mid Pt(H_2)}$$

$E°_{cell} = E_{cell}$. This will be when
(a) $[Zn^{2+}] = [H^+] = 1$ M and $p_{H_2} = 1$ atm
(b) $[Zn^{2+}] = 0.01$ M, $[H^+] = 0.1$ M and $p_{H_2} = 1$ atm
(c) $[Zn^{2+}] = 1$ M, $[H^+] = 0.1$ M and $p_{H_2} = 0.01$ atm
(d) $[Zn^{2+}] = [H^+] = 0.02$M and $p_{H_2} = 0.1$ atm

19. The $E°_{M^{3+}/M^{2+}}$ values for Cr, Mn, Fe and Co are −0.41 V, +1.57 V, +0.77 V and 1.97 V respectively. For which one of these metals the change in oxidation state from +2 to +3 is easiest?
(a) Cr (b) Mn
(c) Fe (d) Co

20. For $Pt(H_2)|H_2O$, electrode potential at 298 K and 1 atm is
(a) −0.2364 V (b) −0.4137 V
(c) 0.4137 V (d) 0.00 V

21. $2Ag^+(aq) + Cu(s) \longrightarrow Cu^{2+}(aq) + 2Ag(s)$
The standard potential for this reaction is 0.46 V. Which change will increase the standard potential the most?
(a) Doubling the $[Ag^+]$
(b) Halving the $[Cu^{2+}]$
(c) Doubling the size of the Cu(*s*) electrode
(d) Standard potential is considered only for 1 M solutions

22. $Zn|Zn^{2+}(10^{-4} \text{ M})||H_2O|\underset{1 \text{ bar}}{Pt(H_2)}$, $E°_{cell} = 0.76$ V at 298 K.
Hence, E_{cell} is
(a) 0.93 V (b) 0.23 V (c) 0.46 V (d) 0.64 V

23. Electrode potential for Mg electrode varies according to the equation

$$E_{Mg^{2+}/Mg} = E°_{Mg^{2+}/Mg} - \frac{0.0591}{2}\log\frac{1}{[Mg^{2+}]}$$

The graph of $E_{Mg^{2+}/Mg}$ *vs* $\log[Mg^{2+}]$ is

(a)
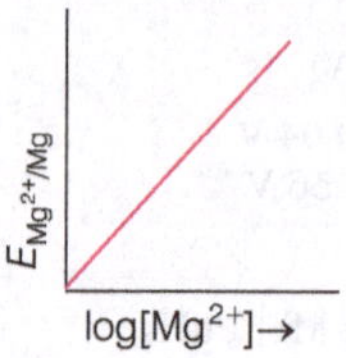

(b)
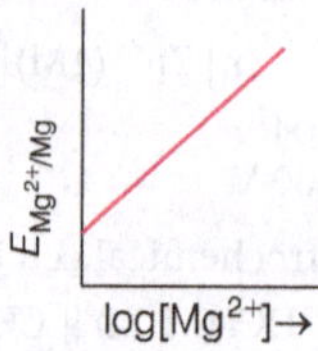

(c)
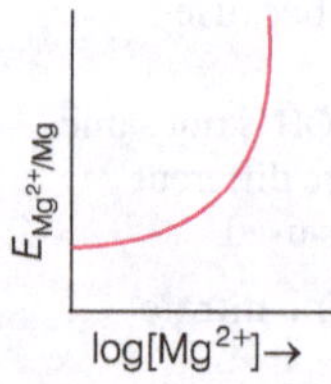

(d)
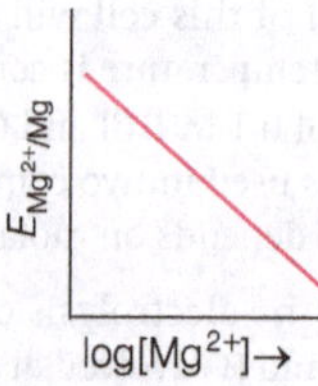

24. Consider the half-cell reaction,

$$O_2(g) + 4H^+(aq) + 4e^- \longrightarrow 2H_2O$$

By what factor are *n*, *Q*, *E* and *E°* changed, if all the stoichiometric coefficients are multiplied by the factor two?

	n	*Q*	*E*	*E°*
(a)	Doubled	Squared	No change	No change
(b)	Doubled	No change	Doubled	No change
(c)	Doubled	Doubled	Doubled	No change
(d)	Doubled	Doubled	Doubled	Noubled

25. The standard reduction potentials of Cu^{2+}/Cu and Cu^+/Cu are 0.339 V and 0.518 V respectively. The standard electrode potential of Cu^{2+}/Cu^+ half-cell is
(a) 0.16 V (b) − 0.179 V
(c) − 0.16 V (d) +0.179 V

26. For the calomel half-cell, Hg, $Hg_2Cl_2 | Cl^-(aq)$ values of electrode potentials are plotted at different log $[Cl^-]$ variation is represented by

(a) 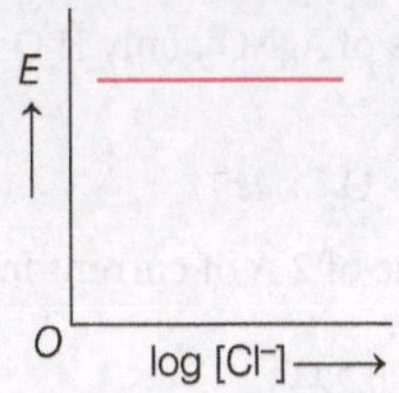

(b) 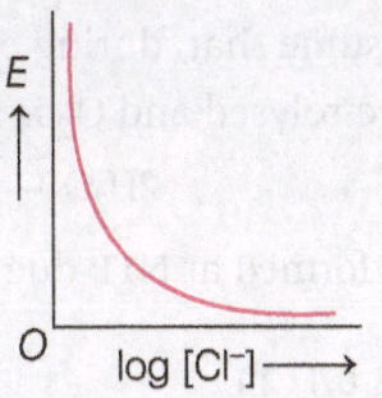

(c) 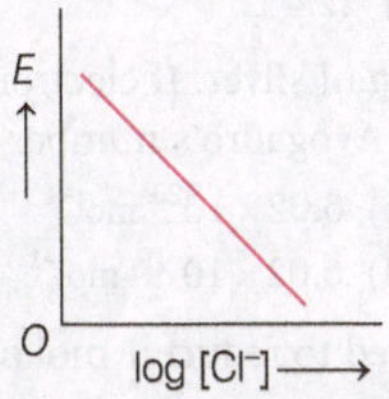

(d) 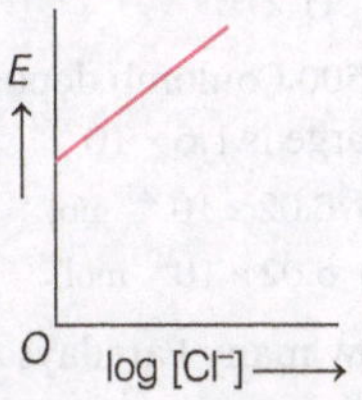

27. $Cu^{2+} + 2e^- \longrightarrow Cu$, For this between log (Cu^{2+}) *versus* E_{red} is a straight line of intercept 0.34 V then electrode potential of the half-cell Cu/Cu^{2+} (0.1 M) will be

(a) $0.34 + \frac{0.0591}{2}$
(b) $-0.34 - \frac{0.0591}{2}$
(c) 0.34
(d) $-0.34 + \frac{0.0591}{2}$

28. For the half-cell given below.

$Pt(H_2) | pH = 2$
1 atm

Half-cell potential is

(a) 0.0591 V
(b) 0.0295 V
(c) 0.1182 V
(d) 0.00 V

29. $Zn + Cu^{2+}(aq) \rightleftharpoons Cu + Zn^{2+}(aq)$ reaction quotient is $Q = \frac{[Zn^{2+}]}{[Cu^{2+}]}$. Variation of E_{cell} with log Q is of the type with $OA = 1.10$ V. E_{cell} will be 1.1591 V when

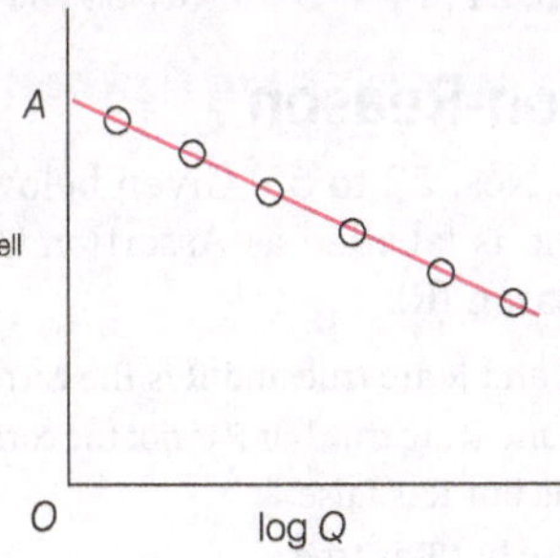

(a) $\frac{[Cu^{2+}]}{[Zn^{2+}]} = 0.01$
(b) $\frac{[Zn^{2+}]}{[Cu^{2+}]} = 0.01$
(c) $\frac{[Zn^{2+}]}{[Cu^{2+}]} = 0.1$
(d) $\frac{[Zn^{2+}]}{[Cu^{2+}]} = 1$

30. $10Cl^-(aq) + 2MnO_4^-(aq) + 16H^+(aq) \rightleftharpoons 5Cl_2(g) + 2Mn^{2+}(aq) + 8H_2O(l)$

For this reaction, $E° = 0.15$ V at 298 K.

Hence, equilibrium constant is

(a) 2.4×10^{25}
(b) 4.9×10^{12}
(c) 1.2×10^5
(d) 3.4×10^2

31. For the galvanic cell,

$Cu | Cu^{2+}(0.01\ M) || Ag^+(0.1\ M) | Ag$, $E°_{cell}$ is 0.46 V at 298 K.
⊖ ⊕

Hence, E_{cell} is

(a) 0.460 V
(b) 0.519 V
(c) 0.401 V
(d) 0.430 V

32. Oxidation potential for the following half-cell reactions are

$Zn \rightleftharpoons Zn^{2+} + 2e^-; E° = 0.76$ V

$Fe \rightleftharpoons Fe^{2+} + 2e^-; E° = +0.44$ V

The emf for the cell reaction,

$Fe^{2+}(aq) + Zn \longrightarrow Zn^{2+}(aq) + Fe$ will be

(a) −120 V
(b) + 0.32 V
(c) − 0.32 V
(d) −1.20 V

33. $AgNO_3(aq)$ was added to an *aq*. KCl solution gradually and the conductivity of the solution was measured. The plot of conductance (Λ_C) *vs* the volume of $AgNO_3$ is

(a) 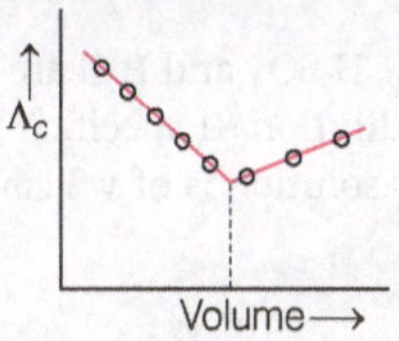

(b) 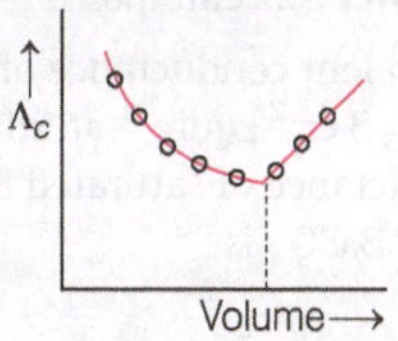

(c) 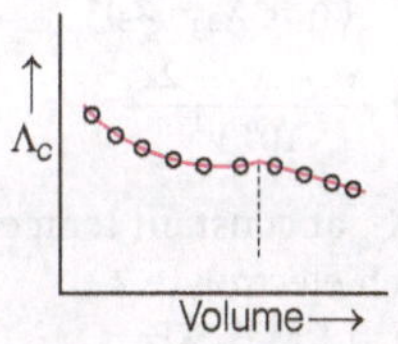

(d) 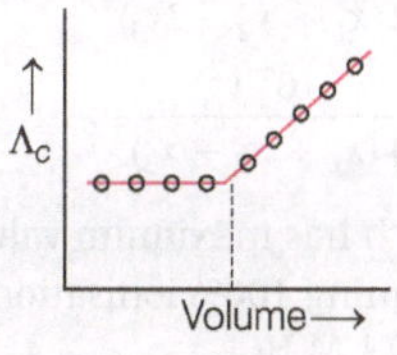

34. The resistance of 0.1 N solution of salt is found to be $2.5 \times 10^3\ \Omega$. The equivalent conductance of solution (cell constant = $1.15\ cm^{-1}$) in $\Omega^{-1}\ cm^2\ equiv^{-1}$ is

(a) 3.8
(b) 4.6
(c) 6.4
(d) 7.6

35. Λ^{∞}_{AgCl} can be obtained

(a) by extrapolation of the graph Λ and $\sqrt{C}$ to zero concentration
(b) by known values of Λ^{∞} of $AgNO_3$, HCl and HNO_3
(c) by known value of $\lambda^{\circ}_{Ag^+} - \lambda^{\circ}_{Cl^-}$
(d) by extrapolation of the graph $\sqrt{\Lambda_m}$ and $\sqrt{C}$ to zero

36. Ionic conductances of H^+ and SO_4^{2-} at infinite dilution are x and y S cm^2 $equiv^{-1}$. Hence, equivalent conductance of H_2SO_4 at infinite dilution is

(a) $x + y$
(b) $2(x + y)$
(c) $2x + y$
(d) $x + 2y$

37. The molar conductance of Ba^{2+} and Cl^- are respectively 127 and 76 Ω^{-1} cm^2 M^{-1} at infinite dilution. The equivalent conductance (in Ω^{-1} cm^2 M^{-1}) of $BaCl_2$ at infinite dilution will be

(a) 139.5 (b) 203
(c) 279 (d) 101.5

38. Equivalent conductance of NaCl, HCl and C_2H_5COONa at infinite dilution are 126.45, 426.16 and 91 Ω^{-1} $equiv^{-1}cm^2$, respectively. The equivalent conductance of C_2H_5COOH is

(a) 201.28 Ω^{-1} $equiv^{-1}$ cm^2 (b) 390.71 Ω^{-1} $equiv^{-1}$ cm^2
(c) 698.28 Ω^{-1} $equiv^{-1}$ cm^2 (d) 540.48 Ω^{-1} $equiv^{-1}$ cm^2

39. Which of the following facts about electrolytic conduction is incorrect?

(a) Λ_m decreases with increase in $\sqrt{C}$ due to increase in interionic attraction between ions.
(b) For weak electrolytes, there is rapid increase in the degree of ionisation with dilution hence, interionic attraction decreases and Λ_m or Λ_{eq} increases rapidly in lower concentration range.
(c) Λ_m^∞ can be obtained by extrapolation to $\sqrt{C} = 0$.
(d) Weak electrolytes have lower degree of dissociation at lower concentrations.

40. Equivalent conductance of $BaCl_2$, H_2SO_4 and HCl are x_1, x_2 and x_3 S cm^2 $equiv^{-1}$ at infinite dilution. If specific conductance of saturated $BaSO_4$ solution is of y S cm^{-1}, then K_{sp} of $BaSO_4$ is

(a) $\dfrac{10^3\, y}{2(x_1 + x_2 - 2x_3)}$ (b) $\dfrac{10^6\, y^2}{(x_1 + x_2 - x_3)^2}$

(c) $\dfrac{10^6\, y^2}{4(x_1 + x_2 - x_3)^2}$ (d) $\dfrac{x_1 + x_2 - 2x_3}{10^6\, y^2}$

41. Which has maximum value of Λ_{eq} at constant temperature assuming 100% ionisation of each electrolyte ?

(a) 0.1 M HCl (b) 0.1 M H_2SO_4
(c) 0.1 M H_3PO_4 (d) Equal

42. 500 mL of an aqueous solution contains 0.1 mole of the solute *AB*, if its specific conductance is x S cm^{-1}, its molar conductance will be .... S cm^2 mol^{-1}.

(a) $10x$ (b) $5000x$
(c) x (d) $200x$

43. A certain current liberates 0.500 g of H_2 in 2.00 h. How many gram of oxygen can be liberated by the same current in the same time?

(a) 0.500 g (b) 8.00 g
(c) 4.00 g (d) 16.00 g

44. A 0.200 M KOH solution is electrolysed for 1.5 h using a current of 8.00 A. How many moles of O_2 were produced at the anode?

(a) 0.48 mol (b) 0.224 mol
(c) 0.112 mol (d) 2.24×10^{-2} mol

45. For reducing 1 mole of $Cr_2O_7^{2-}$ to Cr^{3+} the charge required is

(a) 3×96500 C (b) 6×96500 C
(c) 0.3 F (d) 0.6 F

46. Assume that, during electrolysis of $AgNO_3$, only H_2O is electrolysed and O_2 is formed as,

$$2H_2O \longrightarrow 4H^+ + O_2 + 4e^-$$

O_2 formed at NTP due to passage of 2 A of current for 965 s is

(a) 0.112 L (b) 0.224 L
(c) 11.2 L (d) 22.4 L

47. 96500 Coulomb deposits 107.9 g of silver. If electronic charge is 1.6×10^{-19} C, value of Avogadro's number is

(a) 6.02×10^{-23} mol^{-1} (b) 6.02×10^{23} mol^{-1}
(c) 6.02×10^{19} mol^{-1} (d) 6.02×10^{-19} mol^{-1}

48. How many Faradays are required to reduce 1 mol of $Cr_2O_7^{2-}$ to Cr^{3+} in acidic medium?

(a) 2 (b) 3
(c) 5 (d) 6

49. A current of 5.00 A flowing for 30.00 min deposits 3.048 g of zinc at the cathode. Hence, equivalent weight of zinc is

(a) 65.4 g (b) 130.8 g
(c) 32.7 g (d) 16.85 g

50. The quantity of charge required to obtain one mole of aluminium from Al_2O_3 is ....

(a) 1 F (b) 6 F
(c) 3 F (d) 2 F

51. Consider the following electrolytes,

1. $AgNO_3$ 2. $CuSO_4$ 3. $AlCl_3$ 4. $Bi_2(SO_4)_3$

The quantity of electricity needed to electrolyte separately 1 M solutions of these electrolytes will be (F is Faraday)

(a) 1 F, 2 F, 3 F, 6 F (b) 2 F, 3 F, 6 F, 1 F
(c) 3 F, 6 F, 2 F, 1 F (d) 6 F, 3 F, 2 F, 1 F

Assertion-Reason

Direction (Q. Nos. 52 to 55) Given below are two statements, one is labelled as Assertion (A) and the other is labelled as Reason (R).

(a) Both A and R are true and R is the correct explanation of A.
(b) Both A and R are true but R is not the correct explanation of A.
(c) A is true but R is false.
(d) A is false but R is true.

52. **Assertion** (A) KCl, NaCl and NH_4Cl cannot be used as the salt-bridge in a cell containing silver.

Reason (R) A salt-bridge contains concentrated solution of an inert electrolyte like KCl, KNO_3, K_2SO_4 or solidified solution of such an electrolyte in *agar-agar* and gelatin.

53. **Assertion** (A) A standard hydrogen electrode is also called reversible electrode.

Reason (R) Standard hydrogen electrode can act both as anode as well as cathode in an electrochemical cell.

54. **Assertion** (A) At standard conditions (25°C, 1 atm, 1 M concentrations), the Nernst equation reduces to the standard cell potential equation.

Reason (R) The Nernst equation incorporates the standard reduction potential and the reaction quotient to calculate the cell potential under any given conditions.

55. **Assertion** (A) Kohlrausch's law applies only to strong electrolytes.

Reason (R) Strong electrolytes completely dissociate into ions in solution.

Statement Type Questions

Directions (Q. Nos. 56-61) In the light of the above statements, choose the correct answer from the options given below.

(a) Both Statement I and Statement II are false.
(b) Statement I is true, but Statement II is false.
(c) Statement I is false, but Statement II is true.
(d) Both Statement I and Statement II are true.

56. **Statement I** When acidified zinc sulphate solution is electrolysed between zinc electrodes, it is zinc that is deposited at the cathode and hydrogen evolution does not take place.

Statement II The electrode potential of zinc is more negative than hydrogen as the over-voltage for hydrogen evolution on zinc is quite large.

57. **Statement I** Copper sulphate can be stored in zinc vessel.

Statement II Zinc is less reactive than copper.

58. **Statement I** Cu is less reactive than hydrogen.

Statement II $E^{\ominus}_{Cu^{2+}/Cu}$ is negative.

59. **Statement I** E°_{cell} should have a positive value for the cell to be feasible.

Statement II $E_{cathode} < E_{anode}$

60. **Statement I** Equivalent conductance increases with dilution for an electrolyte solution.

Statement II The number of ions in one litre of electrolyte increases with dilution.

61. **Statement I** Cell constant is the emf of a cell.

Statement II Cell constant is determined by using saturated KCl solution.

62 Select the correct statements from the following.

A. The molar conductivity at infinite dilution of an electrolyte can be represented as the sum of individual ions (cations and anions) of the electrolyte.

B. The change in Λ_m with dilution is due to increase in the degree of dissociation.

C. Λ°_m can be obtained by extrapolation of Λ°_m to zero concentration.

D. Degree of dissociation can be obtained by the ratio of molar conductivity Λ_m to the limiting molar conductivity, at any concentration C.

E. Kohlrausch law is only applicable for the calculation of limiting molar conductivity of weak electrolyte.

Choose the correct answer from the options given below.

(a) A, B and D (b) B and E
(c) B, C and E (d) A, B, C and D

63 Select the incorrect statements from the following.

A. In the primary batteries, the reaction occurs only once and after use over a period of time battery becomes dead.

B. In mercury cell, zinc-mercury amalgam and a paste of HgO and carbon is used as cathode and anode respectively.

C. In lead storage battery, during the discharging phase, sulphuric acid is formed as product in overall cell reaction.

D. A nickel-cadmium cell has shorter life than the lead storage cell.

E. Fuel cells are galvanic cells that are designed to convert the energy of combustion into electrical energy.

Choose the correct answer from the options given below.

(a) A and E (b) B, C and D
(c) A, B, C and D (d) C, D and E

64. Select the incorrect statements from the following.

A. In the primary batteries, the reaction occurs only one time.

B. Leclanche cell are used in transistors and clocks.

C. In leclanche cell the reaction occurring at anode is

$$Zn^{2+} + 2e^- \longrightarrow Zn(s)$$

D. In mercury cell, the electrolyte is a paste of KOH and ZnO.

E. Mercury cells are suitable for high current devices.

Choose the correct answer from the options given below.

(a) A, B and D (b) C and E
(c) C and D (d) B and E

65. Select the correct statements from the following.

A. Λ^{∞}_m of strong electrolytes as well as weak electrolytes can be obtained by Kohlrausch's law as

$$\Lambda^{\infty}_m = x_+ \lambda^{\infty}_+ + y_- \lambda^{\infty}_-$$

B. Λ^{∞}_m of weak electrolytes as well as strong electrolytes is obtained by extrapolation to $\sqrt{C} \to 0$.

C. In weak electrolytes, the change in Λ_m with dilution is due to increase in the degree of dissociation.

D. Weak electrolytes fully dissociate into ions when dissolved in water.

E. For acetic acid, it is possible to determine the value of its dissociation constant once we know the Λ°_m and Λ_m at a given concentration C.

Choose the correct answer from the options given below :
(a) A, C and E (b) A, D and E
(c) B, D and C (d) A, B and C

66 Select the correct statements from the following.
A. 0.2 M HCl solution is diluted to 0.02 M HCl, its molar conductivity will be 1/10 times of the initial concentration.
B. The ionisation constant (K_a) of weak acid in terms of molar conductance and Λ_m° (limiting molar conductivity of very dilute solution) is $K_a = \frac{(\Lambda_m^\circ)}{(\Lambda_m^\circ - \Lambda_m)}$
C. For strong electrolytes, Λ_m increases slowly with dilution.
D. Conductance of an ion in the solution is inversely proportional to its size in the solution.
E. The Debye-Huckel Onsager equation is expressed as $\Lambda_m^\circ = \Lambda_m - A\sqrt{c}$.

Choose the correct answer from the options given below
(a) A, B and E (b) D and C
(c) C, D and E (d) B, C and D

Species Selection Type Questions

67 Consider the following substances.
(i) Na (ii) Hg (iii) S (iv) Pt
(v) Graphite
How many of them can be used as electrodes in electrolytic cells having aqueous solutions?
(a) 4 (b) 2 (c) 3 (d) 1

68 Consider the following species in their standard states,
(i) Br^- (ii) Zn^{2+} (iii) Co^{3+} (iv) Fe^{2+}
(v) Au^{3+}
How many of them are weaker reducing agent than H^+/H_2 couple?
(a) 1 (b) 4 (c) 2 (d) 3

69 Consider the following reactions.
(i) $H_2O_2 + 2H^+ + 2e^- \longrightarrow 2H_2O$
(ii) $H_2O_2 + 2e^- \longrightarrow O_2 + 2H^+$
(iii) $H_2O_2 + 2e^- \longrightarrow 2HO^-$
(iv) $H_2O_2 + 2OH - 2e^- \longrightarrow O_2 + 2H_2O$
(v) $PbS + 4H_2O_2 \longrightarrow PbSO_4 + 4H_2O$
In how many reactions, H_2O_2 has positive value of electrode potential ?
(a) 2 (b) 3
(c) 4 (d) 1

70 Consider the following relations.
(i) $\lambda^\infty_{(A^+)} + \lambda^\infty_{(B^-)}$ (ii) $\lambda^\infty_{(A^+)}, \lambda^\infty_{(B^-)}$
(iii) $2\lambda^\infty_{(A^+)} + \frac{1}{2}\lambda^\infty_{(B^-)}$ (iv) $2\lambda^\infty_{(A^+)} + \lambda^\infty_{(B^-)}$
(v) $\lambda^\infty_{(A^+)} - \frac{1}{2}\lambda^\infty_{(B^-)}$

How many of them represent the limiting value of molar conductivity of A_2B electrolyte, according to Kohlrausch law?
(a) 4 (b) 3
(c) 1 (d) 2

71 Consider the following compounds.
(i) $Ca(NO_3)_2$ (ii) NaCl
(iii) KNO_3 (iv) NH_4OH
(v) $FeSO_4$ (vi) HCN
(vii) CH_3COOH
How many of them are strong electrolyte?
(a) 3 (b) 6
(c) 5 (d) 4

Matching Type Questions

72 Match electrode in Column I with its presentation in Column II.

	Column I		Column II
A.	Electrode reversible with respect to cation	1.	$Pt/Fe^{2+}, Fe^{3+}$
B.	Electrode reversible with respect to anion	2.	$Pt, H_2 \mid H^+ (a=1)$ 1 bar
C.	Redox electrode	3.	Ag | AgCl (s), HCl (aq)
D.	Reference electrode	4.	Ag | $AgNO_3$

Codes

	A	B	C	D		A	B	C	D
(a)	4	3	1	2	(b)	3	2	4	1
(c)	2	4	1	3	(d)	4	1	3	2

73 Match the items of Column I and Column II on the basis of data given below.
$E^\ominus_{F_2/F^-} = 2.87$ V, $E^\ominus_{Li^+/Li} = -3.5$ V,
$E^\ominus_{Au^{3+}/Au} = 1.4$ V, $E^\ominus_{Br_2/Br^-} = 1.09$ V

	Column I		Column II
A.	F_2	1.	Metal is the strongest reducing agent
B.	Li	2.	Non-metal which is the best oxidising agent
C.	Au^{3+}	3.	Anion that can be oxidised by Au^{3+}
D.	Br^-	4.	Metal ion which is an oxidising agent

Codes

	A	B	C	D		A	B	C	D
(a)	2		3	4	(b)	2	1	4	3
(c)	1	3	2	4	(d)	2	3	1	4

74 Match the terms in Column I with corresponding units Column II.

	Column I		Column II
A.	Transport number	1.	$cm^2\ V^{-1}\ s^{-1}$
B.	Ionic mobility	2.	$\Omega^{-1}\ cm^2\ mol^{-1}$
C.	Ionic conductivity	3.	cm^{-1}
D.	Cell constant	4.	unitless

Codes

	A	B	C	D		A	B	C	D
(a)	4	1	3	2	(b)	2	1	4	3
(c)	3	1	4	2	(d)	4	1	2	3

75 Match the physical term in Column I with the unit in Column II.

	Column I		Column II
A.	Conductance	1.	Siemen $m^2\ mol^{-1}$
B.	Resistivity	2.	Siemen
C.	Conductivity	3.	Siemen m^{-1}
D.	Molar conductivity	4.	Ohm metre

Codes

	A	B	C	D		A	B	C	D
(a)	1	2	4	3	(b)	3	4	1	2
(c)	2	4	3	1	(d)	3	4	2	1

76 Match the items of Column I and Column II.

	Column I		Column II
A.	κ	1.	$i \times t$
B.	Λ_m	2.	$\Lambda_m / \Lambda_m^\circ$
C.	α	3.	$\dfrac{\kappa}{C}$
D.	Q	4.	$\dfrac{G^*}{R}$

Codes

	A	B	C	D		A	B	C	D
(a)	4	3	2	1	(b)	3	4	1	2
(c)	2	1	4	3	(d)	3	2	1	4

77 Match the terms given in Column I with the items given in Column II.

	Column I		Column II
A.	Λ_m	1.	Intensive property
B.	E°_{cell}	2.	Depends on number of ions/volume
C.	κ	3.	Extensive property
D.	$\Delta_r G_{cell}$	4.	Increase with dilution

Codes

	A	B	C	D		A	B	C	D
(a)	1	4	2	3	(b)	2	3	4	1
(c)	3	4	1	2	(d)	4	1	2	3

78 Match the items of Column I and Column II.

	Column I		Column II
A.	Leclanche cell	1.	Cell reaction : $2H_2 + O_2 \longrightarrow 2H_2O$
B.	Ni-Cd cell	2.	Does not involve any ion in solution and is used in hearing aids
C.	Fuel cell	3.	Rechargeable
D.	Mercury cell	4.	Reaction at anode, $Zn \longrightarrow Zn^{2+} + 2e^-$

Codes

	A	B	C	D		A	B	C	D
(a)	2	1	3	4	(b)	2	4	1	3
(c)	3	4	2	1	(d)	4	3	1	2

79 Match the items of Column I and Column II.

	Column I		Column II
A.	Lead storage battery	1.	Maximum efficiency
B.	Mercury cell	2.	Prevented by galvanisation
C.	Fuel cell	3.	Gives steady potential
D.	Rusting	4.	Pb is anode, PbO_2 is cathode

Codes

	A	B	C	D		A	B	C	D
(a)	1	2	4	3	(b)	2	4	1	3
(c)	3	1	4	2	(d)	4	3	1	2

Final Check Through PYQs

Module-I Electrochemical Cell

1. Given below are half-cell reactions

$MnO_4^- + 8H^+ + 5e^- \longrightarrow Mn^{2+} + 4H_2O,$

$$E^\circ_{Mn^{2+}/MnO_4^-} = -1.510 \text{ V}$$

$\frac{1}{2}O_2 + 2H^+ + 2e^- \longrightarrow H_2O, E^\circ_{O_2/H_2O} = +1.223 \text{ V}$

Will the permanganate ion, MnO_4^- liberate O_2 from water in the presence of an acid? *[NEET 2022]*

(a) No, because $E^\circ_{cell} = -0.287$ V

(b) Yes, because $E^\circ_{cell} = +2733$ V

(c) No, because $E^\circ_{cell} = -2733$ V

(d) Yes, because $E^\circ_{cell} = +0.287$ V

2. Identify the reaction from following having top position in EMF series (Standard reduction potential) according to their electrode potential at 298 K. *[NEET 2020]*

(a) $Mg^{2+}\ 2e^- \longrightarrow Mg(s)$ (b) $Fe^{2+} + 2e^- \longrightarrow Fe(s)$

(c) $Au^{3+}\ 2e^- \longrightarrow Au(s)$ (d) $K^+ + 1e^- \longrightarrow K(s)$

3. The standard electrode potential (E°) values of (Al^{3+}/Al, Ag^+/Ag, K^+/K and Cr^{3+}/Cr are -1.66 V, 0.80V, 2.93 V and -0.74 V, respectively. The correct decreasing order of reducing power of the metal is *[NCERT (New) Pg. 34, NEET 2019]*

(a) Ag > Cr > Al > K (b) K > Al > Cr > Ag

(c) K > Al > Ag > Cr (d) Al > K > Ag > Cr

4. In the electrochemical cell

$Zn|ZnSO_4$ (0.01 M)||$CuSO_4$(1.0M) Cu, the emf of this Daniel cell is E_1. When the concentration of $ZnSO_4$ is changed to 1.0 M and that of $CuSO_4$ changed to 0.01 M, the emf changes to E_2. From the followings, which one is the relationship between E_1 and E_2?

(Given, $\frac{RT}{F} = 0.059$) *[NCERT (New) Pg. 36, NEET 2017, 2003]*

(a) $E_1 = E_2$ (b) $E_1 < E_2$

(c) $E_1 > E_2$ (d) $E_2 = 0 \neq E_1$

Module-II Nernst Equation, Electrochemical Cell and Gibbs Energy of the Reaction

5. Find the emf of the cell in which the following reaction takes place at 298 K

$Ni(s) + 2Ag^+(0.001\text{ M}) \longrightarrow Ni^{2+}(0.001\text{ M}) + 2Ag(s)$

(Given that, $E^\circ_{cell} = 1.05$ V, $\frac{2.303\,RT}{F} = 0.059$ at 298 K)

[NCERT (New) Pg. 39, NEET 2022]

(a) 1.385 V (b) 0.9615 V

(c) 1.05 V (d) 1.0385 V

6. For a cell involving one electron $E^\circ_{cell} = 0.59$ V at 298 K, the equilibrium constant for the cell reaction is *[NCERT (New) Pg. 39, NEET 2019]*

$\left[\text{Given that } \frac{2.303RT}{F} = 0.059 \text{ V at } T = 298 \text{ K}\right]$

(a) 1.0×10^2 (b) 1.0×10^5

(c) 1.0×10^{10} (d) 1.0×10^{30}

7. For the cell reaction,

$$2Fe^{3+}(aq) + 2I^-(aq) \longrightarrow 2Fe^{2+}(aq) + I_2(aq)$$

$E^\circ_{cell} = 0.24$ V at 298 K. The standard Gibbs energy ($\Delta_r G^\circ$) of the cell reaction is [Given that Faraday constant $F = 96500$ C mol^{-1}]

[NCERT (New) Pg. 40, NEET 2019]

(a) -23.16 kJ mol^{-1}

(b) 46.32 kJ mol^{-1}

(c) 23.16 kJ mol^{-1}

(d) -46.32 kJ mol^{-1}

8. The pressure of H_2 required to make the potential of H_2-electrode zero in pure water at 298 K is *[AIPMT 2016, Phase I]*

(a) 10^{-12} atm (b) 10^{-10} atm

(c) 10^{-4} atm (d) 10^{-14} atm

Module-III Conductors, Conductance of Electrolytic Solutions and Kohlrausch's Law

09. The conductivity of centimolar solution of KCl at 25°C is 0.0210 ohm^{-1} cm^{-1} and the resistance of the cell containing the solution at 25°C is 60 ohm. The value of cell constant is *[NEET 2023]*

(a) 3.28 cm^{-1} (b) 1.26 cm^{-1}
(c) 3.34 cm^{-1} (d) 1.34 cm^{-1}

10. The molar conductance of NaCl, HCl and CH_3COONa at infinite dilution are 126.45, 426.16 and 91.0 S cm^2 mol^{-1} respectively. The molar conductance of CH_3COOH at infinite dilution is
Choose the right option for your answer. *[NEET 2021]*

(a) 201.28 S cm^2 mol^{-1} (b) 390.71 S cm^2 mol^{-1}
(c) 698.28 S cm^2 mol^{-1} (d) 540.48 S cm^2 mol^{-1}

11. The molar conductivity of 0.007 M acetic acid is 20 S cm^2 mol^{-1}. What is the dissociation constant of acetic acid ? Choose the correct option.
$[\overset{\circ}{\lambda}_{H} = 350 \text{ S cm}^2 \text{ mol}^{-1}, \overset{\circ}{\lambda}_{CH_3COO^-} = 50 \text{ S cm}^2 \text{ mol}^{-1}]$
[NCERT (New) Pg. 45, NEET 2021]

(a) 1.75×10^{-4} mol^{-1} L^{-1} (b) 2.50×10^{-4} mol^{-1} L^{-1}
(c) 1.75×10^{-5} mol^{-1} L^{-1} (d) 2.50×10^{-5} mol^{-1} L^{-1}

12. Following limiting molar conductivities are given as

$\overset{\circ}{\lambda}_{m(H_2SO_4)} = x$ S cm^2 mol^{-1}

$\overset{\circ}{\lambda}_{m(K_2SO_4)} = y$ S cm^2 mol^{-1}

$\overset{\circ}{\lambda}_{m(CH_3COOK)} = z$ S cm^2 mol^{-1}

$\overset{\circ}{\lambda}_{m}$ (in S cm^2 mol^{-1}) for CH_3COOH will be
[NCERT (New) Pg. 47, NEET 2019]

(a) $x - y + 2z$ (b) $x + y - z$
(c) $x - y + z$ (d) $\frac{(x - y)}{2} + z$

13. The molar conductivity of a 0.5 mol/dm^3 solution of $AgNO_3$ with electrolytic conductivity of 5.76×10^{-3} S cm^{-1} at 298 K is
[NCERT (New) Pg. 47, AIPMT 2016, Phase II]

(a) 2.88 S cm^2/mol (b) 11.52 S cm^2/mol
(c) 0.086 S cm^2/mol (d) 28.8 S cm^2/mol

Module-IV Electrolysis and Electrolytic Cell, Batteries and Corrosion

14. Match Column I with Column II. *[NEET 2024]*

	Column I (Conversion)		Column I (Number of Faraday required)
A.	1 mole of H_2O to O_2	1.	3F
B.	1 mol of MnO_4^- to Mn^{2+}	2.	2F
C.	1.5 mol of Ca from moles $CaCl_3$	3.	1F
D.	1 mole of FeO to Fe_2O_3	4.	5F

Codes
(a) A-2, B-4, C-1, D-3 (b) A-3, B-4, C-1, D-2
(c) A-2, B-3, C-1, D-4 (d) A-3, B-4, C-2, D-1

15. Mass in grams of copper deposited by passing 6.6484 A current through a voltmeter containing copper sulphate solution for 100 seconds is *[NEET 2024]*
(Given : Molar mass of Cu : 63 g mol^{-1} 1F = 96487 C)

(a) 3.15 g (b) 0.315 g
(c) 31.5 g (d) 0.0315 g

16. The number of Faradays (*F*) required to produce 20 g of calcium from molten $CaCl_2$ (Atomic mass of Ca = 40 g mol^{-1}) is *[NCERT (New) Pg. 52, NCERT 2020]*

(a) 2 (b) 3 (c) 4 (d) 1

17. On electrolysis of dilute sulphuric acid using platinum (Pt) electrode, the product obtained at anode will be *[NEET 2020]*

(a) oxygen gas (b) H_2S gas
(c) SO_2 gas (d) hydrogen gas

18. In a typical fuel cell, the reactants (*R*) and product (*P*) are *[NEET 2020]*

(a) $R = H_2(g), O_2(g); P = H_2O_2(l)$
(b) $R = H_2(g), O_2(g); P = H_2O(l)$
(c) $R = H_2(g), O_2(g), Cl_2(g); P = HClO_4(aq)$
(d) $R = H_2(g), N_2(g); P = NH_3(aq)$

19. During the electrolysis of molten sodium chloride, the time required to produce 0.10 mol of chlorine gas using a current of 3 amperes is

(a) 55 minutes *[NCERT (New) Pg. 52, AIPMT 2016, Phase II]*
(b) 110 minutes
(c) 220 minutes
(d) 330 minutes

20. The number of electrons delivered at the cathode during electrolysis by a current of 1 ampere in 60 seconds is (charge on electron = 1.60×10^{-19} C)

(a) 6×10^{23} *[NCERT (New) Pg. 52, AIPMT 2016, Phase II]*
(b) 6×10^{20}
(c) 3.75×10^{20}
(d) 7.48×10^{23}

21. Zinc can be coated on iron to produce galvanised iron but the reverse is not possible. It is because *[AIPMT 2016, Phase II]*

(a) zinc is lighter than iron
(b) zinc has lower melting point than iron
(c) zinc has lower negative electrode potential than iron
(d) zinc has higher negative electrode potential than iron

22. Aqueous solution of which of the following compounds is the best conductor of electric current? *[NCERT (New) Pg. 49, AIPMT 2015]*

(a) Acetic acid, $C_2H_4O_2$ (b) Hydrochloric acid, HCl
(c) Ammonia, NH_3 (d) Fructose, $C_6H_{12}O_6$

23. A device that converts energy of combustion of fuels like hydrogen and methane, directly into electrical energy is known as *[AIPMT 2015]*

(a) fuel cell (b) electrolytic cell
(c) dynamo (d) Ni-Cd cell

24. When 0.1 mole of MnO_4^{2-} is oxidised, the quantity of electricity required to completely oxidise MnO_4^{2-} to MnO_4^- is *[AIPMT 2014]*

(a) 96500 C (b) 2×96500 C
(c) 9650 C (d) 96.50 C

25. The weight of silver (At. wt. = 108) displaced by a quantity of electricity which displaces 5600 mL of O_2 at STP will be *[AIPMT 2014]*

(a) 5.4 g (b) 10.8 g
(c) 54.0 g (d) 108.0 g

Answers

Step up Practice 1

1 (b)	2 (d)	3 (c)	4 (a)	5 (c)	6 (a)	7 (d)	8 (d)	9 (d)	10 (a)
11 (d)	12 (d)	13 (c)	14 (d)	15 (b)	16 (b)	17 (c)	18 (d)	19 (b)	20 (a)

Step up Practice 2

1 (d)	2 (b)	3 (b)	4 (b)	5 (d)	6 (d)	7 (a)	8 (a)	9 (c)	10 (b)
11 (d)	12 (d)	13 (d)	14 (d)	15 (b)	16 (b)	17 (a)	18 (d)	19 (c)	20 (a)

Step up Practice 3

1 (b)	2 (c)	3 (d)	4 (c)	5 (b)	6 (c)	7 (d)	8 (a)	9 (b)	10 (c)
11 (d)	12 (a)	13 (a)	14 (d)	15 (b)	16 (b)	17 (b)	18 (a)	19 (c)	20 (c)
21 (c)	22 (a)	23 (c)							

Step up Practice 4

1 (d)	2 (d)	3 (c)	4 (d)	5 (d)	6 (c)	7 (c)	8 (d)	9 (b)	10 (d)
11 (d)	12 (b)	13 (c)	14 (b)	15 (b)	16 (c)	17 (c)	18 (b)	19 (c)	20 (c)

Gearing up for NEET

1 (a)	2 (d)	3 (b)	4 (d)	5 (c)	6 (d)	7 (d)	8 (c)	9 (c)	10 (c)
11 (c)	12 (c)	13 (b)	14 (d)	15 (a)	16 (b)	17 (a)	18 (b)	19 (a)	20 (c)
21 (d)	22 (c)	23 (b)	24 (a)	25 (a)	26 (d)	27 (d)	28 (c)	29 (b)	30 (a)
31 (a)	32 (b)	33 (d)	34 (b)	35 (b)	36 (a)	37 (c)	38 (b)	39 (d)	40 (c)
41 (a)	42 (b)	43 (c)	44 (c)	45 (b)	46 (a)	47 (b)	48 (d)	49 (c)	50 (c)
51 (a)	52 (b)	53 (a)	54 (d)	55 (d)	56 (c)	57 (a)	58 (b)	59 (b)	60 (d)
61 (c)	62 (a)	63 (b)	64 (b)	65 (a)	66 (b)	67 (b)	68 (d)	69 (a)	70 (c)
71 (d)	72 (a)	73 (b)	74 (d)	75 (c)	76 (a)	77 (d)	78 (d)	79 (d)	

Final Check through PYQs : Module-I

1 (d)	2 (c)	3 (b)	4 (c)

Final Check through PYQs : Module-II

5 (b)	6 (c)	7 (d)	8 (d)

Final Check through PYQs : Module-III

9 (b)	10 (b)	11 (c)	12 (d)	13 (b)

Final Check through PYQs : Module-IV

14 (a)	15 (b)	16 (d)	17 (a)	18 (b)	19 (b)	20 (c)	21 (d)	22 (b)	23 (a)
24 (c)	25 (d)								

Hints and Solutions

Step up Practice 1

1. (*b*) Among the given match, (b) is incorrect match.

   Its correct match is:

   Two metals with different reaction potentials are used for galvanic cell.

2. (*d*) Among the given statements, statement (d) is incorrect.

   Its correct form is :

   In galvanic cell, current flows from cathode to anode.

3. (*c*) Statement I is false but Statement II is true.

   Its corrected form is:

   In Daniell cell, when E_{ext} (opposite) is less than 1.1 V then Zn dissolves at anode and copper deposits at cathode.

4. (*a*) In galvanic cell, chemical energy is converted into electrical energy.

5. (*c*) 6. (*a*) 7. (*d*)

8. (*d*) The correct cell representation of the given reaction is

$$Zn(s)|Zn^{2+}(aq)||Cd^{2+}(aq)|Cd(s)$$

9. (*d*) *Agar-Agar* is a gelatin, it is used in salt-bridge along with KCl electrolyte.

10. (*a*) Electrical potential of a cell is an intensive property.

11. (*d*) Both Statement I and Statement II are true.

12. (*d*) Mercurous chloride, Hg_2Cl_2 is used in colomel electrode.

13. (*c*) $Ag + Cl^- \longrightarrow AgCl + e^-$

$$\frac{1}{2}Cl_2 + e^- \longrightarrow Cl^-$$

$$\overline{Ag + \frac{1}{2}Cl_2 \longrightarrow AgCl}$$

14. (*d*)

15. (*b*) The given reaction, $M^+ + X^- \longrightarrow M + X$ is the spontaneous (feasible) reaction, and emf for (b) reaction is positive and $= E^\circ_{red}(M) + E^\circ_{ox}(X)$

$$= 0.55 + (-0.44)$$
$$= 0.11\text{ V}$$

16. (*b*) A cell reaction is spontaneous, if $E^\circ_{cell} = +\text{ve}$

$$Sn^{2+} \longrightarrow Sn^{4+} + 2e^-;\quad E^\circ = -0.13\text{ V}$$
$$Sn^{2+} + 2e^- \longrightarrow Sn;\quad E^\circ = -0.14\text{ V}$$
$$2Sn^{2+} \longrightarrow Sn^{4+} + Sn;\quad E^\circ_{cell} = -0.27\text{ V}$$

   Thus, (a) is not possible.

17. (*c*) Among the given species, only one, i.e. (ii) will turn blue when placed in the copper vessel because Ag comes after Cu in electrochemical series.

   Thus, Cu is more reactive and can replace Ag from its solution.

$$2AgNO_3 + Cu \longrightarrow \underset{\text{(Blue)}}{Cu(NO_3)_2} + 2Ag$$

18. (*d*) More negative values of $E^\circ_{M^{n+}/M}$ represents better reducing agent and more positive values of $E^\circ_{M^{n+}/M}$ represents better oxidising agent.

19. (*b*) Among the given match, (b) is correctly match with the given property.

   Higher the value of reduction potential (high positive), stronger will be oxidising capacity.

20. (*a*) Among the given reactions with their E° values, only three, i.e. (i), (ii) and (v) are stronger reducing agent that H^+/H_2 couple.

   A negative E° means that the redox couple is a stronger reducing agent than the H^+/H_2 couple.

Step up Practice 2

1. (*d*) Nernst equation can not be used to calculate the cell potential when a current in flowing through the anode.

2. (*b*) At anode, $Ag \longrightarrow Ag^+ + e^-$

   At cathode, $1e^- + Ag^+ \longrightarrow Ag$

$$\underset{C_1}{Ag^+(aq)} \longrightarrow \underset{C_2}{Ag^+(aq)}$$

$$\therefore\quad E^\circ_{cell} = 0$$

$$E_{cell} = E^\circ_{cell} - \frac{0.0591}{1}\log\frac{[Ag^+]C_2}{[Ag^+]C_1}$$
$$= -0.0591 \times \log 0.5$$
$$= (0.0591 \times 0.3010)\text{ V}$$

3. (*b*) $Co + 2H^+ \longrightarrow Co^{2+} + H_2$

$$Q = \frac{[Co^{2+}]}{[H^+]^2}$$

$$E = E^\circ - \frac{0.0591}{2}\log\frac{[Co^{2+}]}{[H^+]^2}$$

   E will increase, when $[H^+]$ increases or $[Co^{2+}]$ decreases, i.e. increase M_2 from 0.01 M to 0.50 M.

4. (*b*) Instead of H^+(1 M), H_2O has been taken

$$Pt, H_2(g) \mid \underset{\ominus}{H_2O}$$

$$[H^+] = 10^{-7}\text{ M}$$

Oxidation takes place being at anode

$H_2(g) \longrightarrow 2H^+(aq) + 2e^-$

$$E = E° - \frac{0.0591}{2}\log\frac{[H^+]^2}{p_{H_2}}$$

$$0 = 0 - \frac{0.0591}{2}\log\frac{(10^{-7})^2}{p_{H_2}}$$

$$\frac{(10^{-7})^2}{(p_{H_2})} = 1$$

$\therefore\ p_{H_2} = 10^{-14}$ bar

5. (d) $H_2 \longrightarrow 2H^+ + 2e^-$

$2H^+ + 2e^- \longrightarrow H_2$

$$E_{cell} = E°_{OPH} + E°_{RPH} + \frac{RT}{2F}\log_e\frac{[p_{H_2}]_1}{[p_{H_2}]_2}$$

$$= \frac{RT}{2F}\log_e\frac{p_1}{p_2}$$

6. (d) $2H^+ + 2e^- \longrightarrow H_2$; $K = \frac{1}{[H^+]^2}$

$$E = E° + \frac{0.0591}{2}\log[H^+]^2$$

$$= E° + 0.0591\log[H^+]$$

$$= E° - 0.0591\text{ pH} = -0.0591\text{ pH}$$

(a) $E = 0.0591\log 1 = 0$

(b) $E = -0.0591 \times 4 = -0.2364$ V

(c) $E = +0.0591 \times \log 10^{-7} = -0.4137$ V

(d) 1.0 M NaOH = 1.0 M $[OH^-] = 10^{-14}$ M $[H^+]$

$\therefore\ E = 0.0591\log 10^{-14} = -0.8274$ V

7. (a) $2MnO_4^- + 3Mn^{2+} + 2H_2O \longrightarrow 5MnO_2 + 4H^+$;

$E° = 0.47$ V

Thus, cell reaction in which Mn^{2+} on reaction with MnO_4^- forms MnO_2 in acidic medium.

8. (a) pH = 14, pOH = 0

$\therefore\ [OH^-] = 1$ M

$K_{sp}[Al(OH)_3] = 1.0 \times 10^{-33}$

$[Al^{3+}][OH^-]^3 = 1 \times 10^{-33}$

$\therefore\ [Al^{3+}] = 1 \times 10^{-33}$ M

$Al^{3+}(aq) + 3e^- \longrightarrow Al(s)$

$$K = \frac{1}{[Al^{3+}]} = 1 \times 10^{33}$$

$$\therefore\ E = E° - \frac{0.059}{3}\log K$$

$$= -1.66 - \frac{0.059}{3}\log 1 \times 10^{33} = -2.31\text{ V}$$

9. (c) Half-cell reactions in (1) and (3) are of no use; from (2) and (4)

3 × (4) + 2(2) we get required equation

$\therefore\ E°_{cell} = 0.34 + 0.74 = 1.08$ V

$E°$ values are additive, when equal number of electrons are involved.

10. (b) When $E°_{cell} < 0$ electrolysis takes place.

11. (d)

$Pb(s) \rightleftharpoons Pb^{2+}(aq) + 2e^-$

$Hg_2^{2+}(aq) + 2e^- \longrightarrow 2Hg(l)$

$Hg_2^{2+}(aq) + Pb(s) \longrightarrow Pb^{2+}(aq) + 2Hg(l)$

$$\therefore\ K = \frac{[Pb^{2+}]}{[Hg_2^{2+}]}$$

$[Pb^{2+}]$ in LHS is from $PbSO_4$.

$\therefore\ [Pb^{2+}] = \sqrt{K_{sp}(PbSO_4)} = \sqrt{2 \times 10^{-8}}$

$= 1.41 \times 10^{-4}$ M

$[Hg_2^{2+}]$ in RHS is from Hg_2SO_4.

$\therefore\ [Hg_2^{2+}] = \sqrt{K_{sp}(Hg_2SO_4)} = \sqrt{1 \times 10^{-6}} = 1 \times 10^{-3}$ M

$$\therefore\ K = \frac{1.41 \times 10^{-4}}{1 \times 10^{-3}} = 1.41 \times 10^{-1}$$

$$\therefore\ E = E° - \frac{0.0591}{2}\log 1.41 \times 10^{-1}$$

$= 0.92 + 0.025 = 0.945\text{ V} \approx 0.95$V

12. (d) Among the given relations, only three, i.e. (i), (ii) and (iv) are the correct representation of the EMF and equilibrium constant of the cell.

13. (d) In case of electrolysis of aqueous NaCl oxidation reaction occurs at anode as follows

$Cl^-(aq) \longrightarrow \frac{1}{2}Cl_2(g) + e^-$; $E° = 1.36$ V

$2H_2O(l) \longrightarrow O_2(g) + 4H^+(aq) + 4e^-$; $E°_{cell} = -1.23$ V

But due to lower $E°_{cell}$ value, water get oxidised in preference of $Cl^-(aq)$. However, the actual reaction taking place in the concentrated solution of NaCl is (d) and not (b), i.e. Cl_2 is produced and not O_2.

This unexpected result is explained on the basis of the concept of 'overvoltage', i.e. water needs greater voltage for oxidation of O_2 (as it is kinetically slow process) than that needed for oxidation of Cl^- ions to Cl_2. Thus, the correct option is (d) not (b).

14. (d) Both Statement I and Statement II are true.

15. (b) $E° = \frac{2.303\,RT}{nF}\log K_{eq}$

$$0.2955 = \frac{0.0591}{2}\log K_{eq}$$

$\therefore\ K_{eq} = 10^{10}$

16. (b) Statement I is true but Statement II is false.

Its corrected form is :

$\Delta G°$ and K are dependent on electrode potential.

17. (a) For reaction involving different electrons

$$\Delta G_3 = \Delta G_1 - \Delta G_2$$

$$-n_3FE_3° = (-n_1FE°_1) - (-n_2FE°_2)$$

$$n_3E°_3 = n_1E°_1 - n_2E°_2$$

$$E°_3 = \frac{5 \times 1.51 - 2 \times 1.23}{3} = 1.70 \text{ V}$$

18. (d)

19. (c) E_{cell} is an intensive property as it does not depend upon mass of species (number of particles) but $\Delta_r G$ of the cell reaction is an extensive property because this depends upon mass of species (number of particles).

20. (a) For spontaneous reaction occuring in a galvanic cell is

$$E^\circ_{cell} > 0, \Delta G < 0 \text{ and } Q < K_{eq}.$$

Step up Practice 3

1. (b)

2. (c) Solution consisting of electrolytes is known as electrolytic solution and conductivity of electrolytic solution depends upon the following factors.

(a) **Size of ions** As ion size increases, ion mobility decreases and conductivity decreases.

(b) **Viscosity of solution** Greater the viscosity of the solvent lesser will be the conductivity of the solution.

(c) **Solvation of ions** Greater the solvation of ions of an electrolyte lesser will be the electrical conductivity of the solution.

(d) **Temperature of medium** Conductivity of solution increases with increase in temperature.

3. (d)

4. (d) Cell constant is defined as the ratio of length of object and area of cross section.

$$G^* = \frac{l}{A}$$

Since, l and A remain constant for any particular object, hence value of cell constant always remains constant.

5. (b) Specific conductance = conductance × cell constant

$$0.012 = \frac{1}{55} \times \text{cell constant}$$

∴ Cell constant = 0.66 cm^{-1}

6. (c)

7. (d) Both Statement I and Statements II are true.

Since, conductivity depends upon number of ions per unit volume. Therefore, the conductivity of all electrolytes decreases on dilution due to decrease in number of ions per unit volume.

8. (a) Resistance = specific resistance × cell constant

$$(R)_{KCl} = (S)_{KCl} \times \text{(cell constant)}$$

$$(R)_{NaOH} = (S)_{NaOH} \times \text{(cell constant)}$$

$$\frac{(R)_{KCl}}{(R)_{NaOH}} = \frac{(S)_{KCl}}{(S)_{NaOH}}$$

$$\Rightarrow \frac{160}{190} = \frac{700}{(S)_{NaOH}}$$

$$\therefore (S)_{NaOH} = 831.25 \text{ ohm-cm}$$

$$\kappa = \frac{1}{S} = \frac{1}{831.25} \Omega^{-1}\text{cm}^{-1}$$

∴ Specific conductance $(\kappa)_{NaOH} = 1.20 \times 10^{-3} \Omega^{-1} \text{ cm}^{-1}$
$\approx 0.00120 \Omega^{-1}\text{cm}^{-1}$

9. (b) Among the given match, (b) is correctly match regarding the unit of molar conductance.

10. (c) Equivalent conductance is five times, hence, dilution is also five times.

$$\therefore \quad 0.1\text{M} \times V \equiv M' \times 5 \text{ V}$$

$$\therefore \quad M' \text{ (final)} = 0.02 \text{ M}$$

$$= 0.04 \text{ N (due to dibasic acid)}$$

11. (d) Both Statement I and Statement II are true.

12. (a) Among the given graph, only one, i.e. (v) represent the variation of Λ_m with $\sqrt{c}$ for CH_3COOH.

13. (a)

14. (d) Equivalent conductance of 0.04 N weak acid

$$= \frac{1000 \times 4.23 \times 10^{-4}}{0.04}$$

$$= 10.575 \ \Omega^{-1} \text{ cm}^2 \text{ equiv}^{-1}$$

Also, α (degree of dissociation) $= \frac{\Lambda^C_{eq}}{\Lambda^\circ_{eq}}$

$$0.0612 = \frac{10.575}{\Lambda^\circ_{eq}}$$

$$\Lambda^\circ_{eq} = 172.79 \ \Omega^{-1} \text{ cm}^2 \text{ equiv}^{-1}$$

15. (b)

16. (b) $\Lambda^\circ_{m\,(NH_4Cl)} = \Lambda^\circ_{m\,(NH_4^+)} + \Lambda^\circ_{m\,(Cl^-)}$

$$\Lambda^\circ_{m\,(NaOH)} = \Lambda^\circ_{m\,(Na^+)} + \Lambda^\circ_{m\,(OH^-)}$$

$$\Lambda^\circ_{m\,(NaCl)} = \Lambda^\circ_{m\,(Na^+)} + \Lambda^\circ_{m\,(Cl^-)}$$

$$\Lambda^\circ_{m\,(NH_4Cl)} + \Lambda^\circ_{m\,(NaOH)} - \Lambda^\circ_{m\,(NaCl)} = \Lambda^\circ_{m\,(NH_4OH)}$$

17. (b) Among the given compounds, in only, one i.e. (iv) Λ_m values *vs* $\sqrt{C}$ shows a straight line.

18. (a) $\Lambda^\circ_{H_2O} = \Lambda^\circ_{H^+} + \Lambda^\circ_{OH^-} = 550 \text{ S cm}^2 \text{ mol}^{-1}$

$$\alpha = \frac{\Lambda_m}{\Lambda^\circ_m}$$

$$\therefore \quad \Lambda_m = \alpha \times \Lambda_m = 1.9 \times 10^{-9} \times 550$$

$$= 1.045 \times 10^{-6} \text{ S cm}^2 \text{ mol}^{-1}$$

19. (c) $\Lambda_{BaSO_4} = \Lambda_{BaCl_2} + \Lambda_{H_2SO_4} - \Lambda_{HCl}$

$$= x_1 + x_2 - 2x_3$$

20. (c) Λ^∞_m $BaSO_4$ is equal to Λ^∞_m of $(BaCl_2 + H_2SO_4 - 2HCl)$.

21. (c) Among the given relationship, (c) is not correctly matched. Its correct match is :

Degree of dissociation $(\alpha) = \frac{\Lambda^C_m}{\Lambda^\circ_m}$

22. (a) $\alpha = \frac{\Lambda^C_{eq}}{\Lambda^\circ_{eq}} = \frac{10}{200} = 0.05$, % ionisation = 5%

23. (c) Among the given relations, only four, i.e. (i), (ii), (iii) and (v) are correct while (iv) is incorrect.
Its correct relation is

$$\Lambda_m = \Lambda^\circ_m - AC^{1/2}$$

Step up Practice 4

1. (d) Reduction potential of water > Reduction of Li.
So, at cathods water gets reduced to give H_2 gas. Similarly, oxidation potential of water < oxidation potential of sulphate ion. So, at anode water gets oxidised to give O_2 gas.

2. (d) *Aq.* Na_2SO_4 solution on electrolysis procedures O_2 gas at anode H_2 gas at cathode.
At anode, $2H_2O \longrightarrow O_2 + 4H^+ + 4e^-$
At cathode, $2H_2O + 2e^- \longrightarrow H_2 + 2OH^-$

3. (c) Quantity of electricity $= it = 1.8 \times 1.36 \times 60$ C
$= 146.88$ C

4. (d) Quantity of electricity $= it$
$72000 = 1 \times t$
$t = 72000\text{ s} = 20\text{ h}$

5. (d) The electric charge for electrode deposition of 1 g equivalent of a substance is one Faraday. It is equal to 96500 coulombs. It corresponds to the amount of charge on 1 mole electrons.

6. (c) By Faraday's law,
Eq. of Na = Eq. of Al

$$\left(\frac{w}{\text{At. wt.}/n}\right)_{Na} = \left(\frac{w}{\text{At.wt.}/n}\right)_{Al}$$

[For Al, $n = 3$ and Na, $n = 1$]

$1 \times 1 = n_{Al} \times 3$

Moles of Al $= \frac{1}{3}$

7. (c) $\frac{w(\text{Al})}{w(\text{Na})} = \frac{\text{equivalent weight of Al}}{\text{equivalent weight of Na}}$

$\frac{w(\text{Al})}{4.6} = \frac{9}{23}$

$\therefore \quad w = 1.8$ g

8. (d) Electrolysis of water :

$$2H_2O \rightleftharpoons 4H^+ + 4e^- + O_2$$

4F charge will produce = 1 mole of O_2 = 32 g O_2.

1F charge will produce $= \frac{32}{4} = 8$ g of O_2.

9. (b) $w = \frac{\text{atomic weight}}{96500 \times \text{electron}} \times i \times t$

Atomic weight = 55 g

10. (d) $q = it = 30 \times 70.2 \times 60\text{ C} = 126360$ C
$= \frac{126360}{96500}$ C
$= 1.31$ F

11. (d) $\underset{+7}{MnO_4^-} \longrightarrow \underset{+4}{MnO_2}$
Thus, electrons gained = 3
Thus, 1 mole of MnO_4^- gives $\frac{1}{3}$ mole of MnO_2
= 0.33 mol

12. (b) Statement I is true but Statement II is false.
Its correct form is :
1 mole of electrons are required to reduce 1 mole of Ag^+ or $\frac{1}{2}$ mole of Cu^{2+} or $\frac{1}{3}$ mole of Al^{3+} ions.

13. (c) $\underset{1\text{ mol}}{H_2O(l)} \longrightarrow \frac{1}{2}O_2(g) + 2H^+ + 2e^-$
Moles of electrons exchanged = 2
Charge carried by 1 mole of electrons = 96500 C
Thus, charge carried by 2 moles of electrons
$= 2 \times 96500$ C
$= 1.93 \times 10^5$ C

14. (b) $Ag^+ + e^- \longrightarrow Ag$
$Cu^{2+} + 2e^- \longrightarrow Cu$
$Al^{3+} + 3e^- \longrightarrow Al$
Thus, number of Faradays required by 1 mole each of Ag^+, Cu^{2+} and Al^{3+} = 1 : 2 : 3

15. (b) $MnO_4^- \xrightarrow{+5e^-} Mn^{2+}$
Thus, MnO_4^- requires 5F to convert into Mn^{2+}.

16. (c) $E = E^\circ + \frac{0.0591}{1}\log\frac{[Ag^+]_R}{[Ag^+]_L}$
$= 0 + 0.0591 \log 2$
$= 0.0591 \times 0.301$ V
After current is passed $[Ag^+]_R = 1$ M
$[Ag^+]_L = 0.5$ M
Hence, no change in emf takes place.

17. (c) Statement I is false but Statement II is true.
The correct form of statement I is :
Mercury cell gives steady potential.

18. (b) Among the given species, only four, i.e. (i), (ii), (iii) and (iv) are present in dry cell while Pt present as a catalyst in fuel cells.

19. (c) In, H_2-O_2 fuel cell the reaction occurring at cathode is

$$O_2(g) + 2H_2O(l) + 4e^- \longrightarrow 4OH^-(aq)$$

20. (c) Mercury cell has a constant voltage throughout its life.

Gearing Up for NEET

1. (a) $E_{cell} = E^{\circ}_{cell} - \frac{0.0591}{2} \log \frac{[Zn^{2+}]}{[Cu^{2+}]}$

$= 1.1 - \frac{0.0591}{2} \log \frac{[Zn^{2+}]}{[Cu^{2+}]}$

$E_{cell} < 1.1$ V if, $\frac{[Zn^{2+}]}{[Cu^{2+}]} > 1$

2. (d) For first cell,

$E^{\circ}_{cell} = E^{\circ}_{Zn/Zn^{2+}} + E^{\circ}_{Cu^{2+}/Cu}$

$1.10 = E^{\circ}_{Zn/Zn^{2+}} + 0.34$

$\therefore \quad E^{\circ}_{Zn/Zn^{2+}} = 0.76$ V

For second cell,

$E^{\circ}_{cell} = E^{\circ}_{Cu/Cu^{2+}} + E^{\circ}_{Ag^{+}/Ag}$

$0.46 = -0.34 + E^{\circ}_{Ag^{+}/Ag}$

$E^{\circ}_{Ag^{+}/Ag} = 0.80$ V

For third cell,

$E^{\circ}_{cell} = E^{\circ}_{Zn/Zn^{2+}} + E^{\circ}_{Ag^{+}/Ag}$

$0.76 + 0.80 = 1.56$ V

3. (b) Since, CH_3COOH is a weak acid and emf is dependent on pH, also pH of 0.1 M HCl < pH of 0.1 M CH_3COOH.

4. (d)

5. (c) Reducing nature varies as Mg > Cu > Hg > Ag, hence $CuCl_2$ can be stored in silver-vessel.

6. (d) $Cu + 2H^{+}(\text{dil. } H_2SO_4) \longrightarrow Cu^{2+} + H_2$

$E^{\circ}_{cell} = E^{\circ}_{Cu/Cu^{2+}} + E^{\circ}_{SHE} = -0.34$ V

Thus, (a) is not feasible.

$Cu + SO_4^{2-} + 4H^{+} \longrightarrow Cu^{2+} + SO_2 + 2H_2O$

$E^{\circ}_{cell} = -0.34 + 1.17 = 0.83$ V

$E^{\circ}_{cell} > 0$

Thus, (b) is feasible.
Similarly, (c) is feasible.

7. (d) $E^{\circ}_{calomel} + E^{\circ}_{X} = 0.10$

$E^{\circ}_{X} = 0.344$ V

Since, $E^{\circ}_{SHE} = 0.00$ V

$E_{electrode\ vs\ SCE} = 0.100$

$E_{SCE\ vs\ SHE} = -0.244$

$E_{electrode\ vs\ SHE} = 0.100 + (-0.244) = -0.144$

Hence, E°_{X} (w.r.t.) = 0.344 V

8. (c) Zn is more reactive in first case, copper is more reactive in second case.

9. (c) Standard electrode potential of copper electrode can be calculated by constructing a concentration cell composed of two half-cell reactions in which concentration of species on left hand and right hand side are unity. In such case, cell potential is equal to standard electrode potential.

$\underbrace{Pt(s)|H_2(g, 1\text{ bar})|H^{+}(aq, 1\text{ M})}_{\text{Oxidation half-cell reaction}} \Big\| \underbrace{Cu^{2+}(aq, 1\text{ M})|Cu}_{\text{Reduction half-cell reaction}}$

10. (c)

11. (c) The given reactions is

$Mn^{2+} + 2e^{-} \longrightarrow Mn, E^{\circ} = -1.28$ V ...(i)

$2Mn^{3+} + 2e^{-} \longrightarrow 2Mn^{2+}, E^{\circ} = +2.51$ V ...(ii)

Adding Eq. (ii) with Eq. (i), we get

$3Mn^{2+} \longrightarrow Mn + 2Mn^{3+}$

$E^{\circ} = -1.28 + (-2.51)$
$= -3.79$ V

Since, the value of E° is –ve, therefore the reaction is non-spontaneous (not-feasible).

12. (c) Reducing power of Mg > Cu > Hg > Ag

Thus, Cu^{2+}, Hg^{2+} and Ag^{+} are reduced to metals and Mg remain as oxidised part.

13. (b) $2 \times [Cu^{+} \longrightarrow Cu^{2+} + e^{-}]; \quad E^{\circ} = -0.15$ V

$Cu^{2+} + 2e^{-} \longrightarrow Cu; \quad E^{\circ} = 0.34$ V

$Cu^{+} \longrightarrow Cu^{2+} + Cu; \quad E^{\circ} = 0.19$ V

In aqueous solution, Cu^{+} disproportionates to Cu^{2+} and Cu.

Thus, Cu^{+} is not stable but Cu^{2+} is stable.

14. (d)

15. (a) $2Hg(l) + 2Cl^{-}(aq) \longrightarrow Hg_2Cl_2(s) + 2e^{-}$

$Cl_2(g) + 2e^{-} \longrightarrow \underset{R}{2Cl^{-}(aq)}$

$\underset{(L)}{2Cl^{-}(aq)} \longrightarrow \underset{(R)}{2Cl^{-}(aq)}$

$K = \frac{[Cl^{-}]_R^2}{[Cl^{-}]_L^2} = \frac{(0.01)^2}{(0.1)^2} = 0.01$

$E_{cell} = E^{\circ}_{cell} - \frac{0.0591}{2} \log K$

$= 1.10 - \frac{0.0591}{2} \log (0.01)$

$= 1.1591$ V

16. (b) $Cl_2 + 2e^{-} \longrightarrow 2Cl^{-}$

$K = [Cl^{-}]^2$

$\therefore \quad E = E^{\circ} - \frac{0.0591}{2} \log [Cl^{-}]^2$

$(E - E^{\circ}) = -0.0591 \log [Cl^{-}]$

$(E - E^{\circ}) = 0.0591 \log \left[\frac{1}{Cl^{-}}\right]$

Thus, as $[Cl^{-}]$ increases, $(E - E^{\circ})$ decreases.

17. (a) I. $Cu^+ + e^- \longrightarrow Cu; E_1^\circ = 0.52$ V

II. $Cu^{2+} + e^- \longrightarrow Cu^+; E_2^\circ = 0.16$ V

III. $2Cu^+ \longrightarrow Cu^{2+} + Cu; E_3^\circ = ?$

Reverse the equation (II) and then add both the reaction.

$$E_3^\circ = E_1^\circ + E_2^\circ \Rightarrow E_3^\circ = 0.52 + (-0.16)$$

$$\therefore \ E_3^\circ = 0.36 \text{ V}$$

18. (b) $Zn + 2H^+ \longrightarrow Zn^{2+} + H_2$ hence, $(E - E^\circ) = 0$

$[H^+] = 0.1$ M

$$[Zn^{2+}] = 0.01 \text{ M} \Rightarrow K = \frac{[Zn^{2+}]}{[H^+]^2} = 1$$

Hence, $(E - E^\circ) = 0$

19. (a) More negative value of E°_{red} indicates better reducing agent, then easily oxidised. Thus, oxidation of Cr^{2+} and Cr^{3+} is the easiest.

20. (c) $H_2 \longrightarrow 2H^+ + 2e^-$

$Q = [H^+]^2 = 10^{-14}$ M in H_2O

$$E = E^\circ - \frac{0.0591}{2} \log 10^{-14}$$

$$= 0 + 0.0591 \times 7 = 0.4137 \text{ V}$$

21. (d)

22. (c)

$$Zn \longrightarrow Zn^{2+} + 2e^-$$

$$2H^+ + 2e^- \longrightarrow H_2$$

overall, $Zn + 2H^+ \longrightarrow Zn^{2+} + H_2 \quad K = \dfrac{[Zn^{2+}][H_2]}{[Zn][H^+]^2}$

In H_2O, $[H^+] = 1 \times 10^{-7}$ M under standard condition (298 K, 1 bar)

$$K = \frac{(10^{-4})(1)}{(1)(10^{-7})^2} = 10^{10}$$

$$\therefore \ E = E^\circ - \frac{0.0591}{2} \log K = 0.76 - \frac{0.0591}{2} \log 10^{10}$$

$$= 0.4645 \text{ V}$$

23. (b) Electrode potential for Mg electrode varies according to the equation,

$$E_{Mg^{2+}/Mg} = E^\circ_{Mg^{2+}/Mg} - \frac{0.059}{2} \log \frac{1}{[Mg^{2+}]}$$

$$E_{Mg^{2+}/Mg} = E^\circ_{Mg^{2+}/Mg} + \frac{0.059}{2} \log [Mg^{2+}]$$

$$E_{Mg^{2+}/Mg} = \frac{0.059}{2} \log [Mg^{2+}] + E^\circ_{Mg^{2+}/Mg}$$

This equation represents equation of straight line. It can be correlated as,

$$\underset{Y}{E_{Mg^{2+}/Mg}} = \underset{m}{\left(\frac{0.059}{2}\right)} \underset{X}{\log [Mg^{2+}]} + \underset{+C}{E^\circ_{Mg^{2+}/Mg}}$$

So, intercept $(C) = E^\circ_{Mg^{2+}/Mg}$.

Thus, equation can be diagramatically represented as,

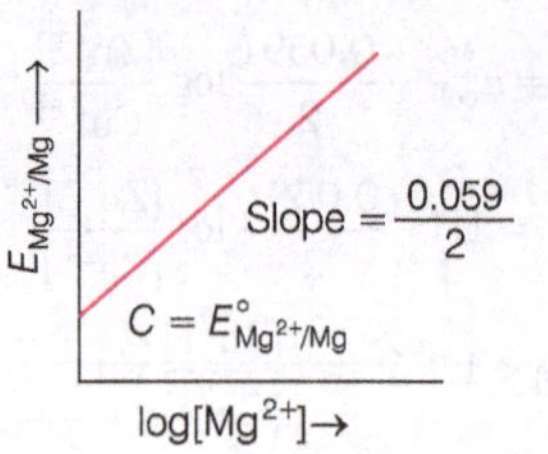

24. (a)

25. (a) I. $Cu^{2+} + 2e^- \longrightarrow Cu; \quad E^\circ_1 = 0.339$ V, $n_1 = 2$

II. $Cu^+ + e^- \longrightarrow Cu; \quad E^\circ_2 = 0.518$ V, $n_2 = 1$

III. $Cu^{2+} + e^- \longrightarrow Cu^+; \ E^\circ_3 = ?,$ $n_3 = 1$

I - II = III

$$\therefore \ \Delta G^\circ_{III} = \Delta G^\circ_I - \Delta G^\circ_{II}$$

$$-n_3FE_3^\circ = -n_1FE_1^\circ + n_2FE_2^\circ$$

$$\therefore \ E_3^\circ = \frac{n_1E_1^\circ - n_2E_2^\circ}{n_3}$$

$$= \frac{0.678 - 0.518}{1}$$

$$= 0.160 \text{ V}$$

26. (d) Half-cell reaction is

$$2Hg(l) + 2Cl^-(aq) \longrightarrow Hg_2Cl_2(s) + 2e^-$$

$$\therefore \ K = \frac{1}{[Cl^-]^2}$$

$$E = E^\circ - \frac{0.0591}{2} \log \frac{1}{[Cl^-]^2}$$

$$E = E^\circ + 0.0591 \log [Cl^-] \quad \text{... (i)}$$

Thus, E increases as $[Cl^-]$ increases.

By comparing, the equation (i) with straight line equation, we get $m = +0.0591$ and intecept $C = E^\circ$. So, the graph obtained is shown in option (d).

27. (d)According to Nernst equation,

$$E = E^\circ - \frac{0.0591}{n} \log Q$$

$$E_{Cu/Cu^{2+}} = E^\circ_{Cu/Cu^{2+}} - \frac{0.0591}{2} \log [Cu^{2+}]$$

If $\log [Cu^{2+}] = 0$, i.e. $[Cu^{2+}] = 1$

then, $E_{Cu/Cu^{2+}} = E^\circ_{Cu/Cu^{2+}}$

Also, $E^\circ_{Cu/Cu^{2+}} = -E^\circ_{Cu^{2+}/Cu} = -0.34$

So, for oxidation cell, emf is

$$E_{Cu/Cu^{2+}} = -0.34 - \frac{0.0591}{2} \log(0.1)$$

$$= -0.34 + \frac{0.0591}{2} \text{ (as, } n \text{ is 2 here)}$$

28. (c) $Pt(H_2) \mid pH = 2$

$$H_2(g) \rightleftharpoons 2H^+ + 2e^-$$

$$K = [H^+]^2 = (10^{-2})^2 = 10^{-4}\text{ M}$$

$$E = E^\circ - \frac{0.0591}{2}\log 10^{-4} = 0.1182\text{ V}$$

29. (b) As we know,

$$E_{cell} = E^\circ_{cell} - \frac{0.0591}{2}\log\left[\frac{Zn^{2+}}{Cu^{2+}}\right]$$

Given, $OA = 1.10\text{ V} = E^\circ_{cell}$ and $E_{cell} = 1.1591$

$$\text{So, } 1.1591 = 1.10 - \frac{0.0591}{2}\log\left[\frac{Zn^{2+}}{Cu^{2+}}\right]$$

$$\log\left[\frac{Zn^{2+}}{Cu^{2+}}\right] = -2$$

$$\frac{[Zn^{2+}]}{[Cu^{2+}]} = 10^{-2} = 0.01$$

30. (a) $E^\circ = \frac{0.0591}{n}\log K$

$$0.15 = \frac{0.0591}{10}\log K$$

$$K = 2.4 \times 10^{25}$$

31. (a) $Cu + 2Ag^+ \longrightarrow 2Ag + Cu^{2+}$

$$K = \frac{[Cu^{2+}]}{[Ag^+]^2} = \frac{0.01}{(0.1)^2} = 1$$

$$\therefore \quad E = E^\circ \frac{0.0591}{2}\log K$$

$$= 0.46 - \frac{0.0591}{2}\log 1 = 0.46\text{ V}$$

32. (b) $Zn \rightleftharpoons Zn^{2+} + 2e^-;\ E^\circ_1 = 0.76\text{ V}$ ... (i)

$Fe^{2+} + 2e^- \rightleftharpoons Fe;\ E^\circ_2 = -0.44\text{ V}$ ... (ii)

After adding Eq. (i) with Eq. (ii) then we get,

$$Fe^{2+} + Zn \longrightarrow Zn^{2+} + Fe;\ E^\circ_3 = ?$$

So, $E^\circ_3 = E^\circ_1 + E^\circ_2 = 0.76 - 0.44 = +0.32\text{ V}$

33. (d)

34. (b) Equivalent conductance

$$= \frac{1000 \times \text{conductance} \times \text{cell constant}}{\text{concentration}}$$

$$= 1000 \times \frac{1}{2.5 \times 10^3} \times \frac{1.15}{0.1} = 4.6$$

35. (a)

36. (a) $\Lambda^\circ_{eq} = \lambda^\infty_{H^+} + \lambda^\infty_{SO_4^{2-}} = (x + y)$

37. (c) $\Lambda_m = \lambda_{Ba^{+2}} + 2 \times \lambda_{Cl^-}$

$$= 127 + 2(76)$$

$$= 279$$

38. (b) $\Lambda^\circ_{CH_3CH_2COOH} = \Lambda^\circ_{CH_3CH_2COONa} + \Lambda^\circ_{HCl} - \Lambda^\circ_{NaCl}$

$$= 390.71\ \Omega^{-1}\text{ equiv}^{-1}\text{ cm}^2$$

39. (d) Its correct form is :

Weak electrolytes have lower degree of dissociation at higher concentrations.

40. (c) $\Lambda^\circ_{BaSO_4} = \Lambda^\circ_{BaCl_2} + \Lambda^\circ_{H_2SO_4} - \Lambda^\circ_{HCl} = (x_1 + x_2 - x_3)$

Equivalent conductance of $BaSO_4$

$$\Lambda^\circ_{BaSO_4} = \frac{1000 \times \text{specific conductance}}{\text{solubility (in saturated solution)}}$$

$$(x_1 + x_2 - x_3) = \frac{1000\,y}{\text{Solubility}}$$

$$\therefore \quad \text{Solubility } (BaSO_4) = \frac{1000\,y}{(x_1 + x_2 - x_3)}\text{ N}$$

$$= \frac{1000\,y}{2(x_1 + x_2 - x_3)}\text{ M}$$

$$BaSO_4 \rightleftharpoons Ba^{2+} + SO_4^{2-}$$

$$K_{sp}(BaSO_4) = [Ba^{2+}][SO_4^{2-}]\text{ M}^2$$

$$= \frac{10^6\,y^2}{4(x_1 + x_2 - x_3)^2}$$

41. (a) Λ_{eq} depends upon concentration, temperature, nature of electrolyte and mobility of ions. As we know, conductance α mobility of ions and mobility of ions 2 smaller size of ion.

Hence, 0.1 M HCl has maximum value of Λ_{eq} at constant temperature.

42. (b) Concentration of solute = 0.1 mole in 0.5 L = 0.2 M

$$\text{Molar conductance} = \frac{1000 \times \text{specific conductance}}{\text{molarity}}$$

$$= \frac{1000 \times x}{0.2} = 5000x\text{ S cm}^2\text{mol}^{-1}$$

43. (c) $2H^+ + 2e^- \longrightarrow H_2(g)$

$$\text{Equivalent weight of } H_2 = \frac{2}{2} = 1$$

$$2O^{2-} \longrightarrow O_2 + 4e^-$$

$$\text{Equivalent weight of } O_2 = \frac{32}{4} = 8$$

By Faraday's second law of electrolysis,

$$\frac{\text{weight of } O_2}{\text{weight of } H_2} = \frac{\text{equivalent weight of } O_2}{\text{equivalent weight of } H_2}$$

$$\text{weight of } O_2 = \frac{8 \times 0.5}{1} = 4\text{ g}$$

44. (c) Electrolysis of H_2O takes place as follows

At anode, $2H_2O \longrightarrow 4H^+ + O_2 + 4e^-$

$$w = zit = \frac{32}{4 \times 96500} \times 8 \times 1.5 \times 3600\text{ g}$$

$$= 3.58\text{ g} \approx 3.69 = 0.112\text{ mol}$$

45. (*b*) $Cr_2O_7^{2-} + 6e^- \longrightarrow 2Cr^{3+}$
6 mol
$Q = 6 \times 96500$ C

46. (*a*) $w(O_2) = zit = \frac{32 \times 2 \times 965}{4 \times 96500}$
$= 0.16$ g $= 0.005$ mol
$= 0.112$ L at NTP

47. (*b*) Number of moles of Ag $= \frac{107.9}{107.9} = 1$
Number of Ag atoms $= 1 \times N_0$ (where, N_0 is the Avogadro's number)
Total charge $= N_0 \times 1.6 \times 10^{-19}$ C
$\therefore \; N_0 \times 1.6 \times 10^{-19} = 96500$
(charge carried by 1 mole of electrons)
$\therefore \; N_0 = \frac{96500}{1.6 \times 10^{-19}} = 6.02 \times 10^{23}\ \text{mol}^{-1}$

48. (*d*) In acidic medium,
$Cr_2O_7^{2-} + 14H^+ + 6e^- \longrightarrow 2Cr^{3+} + 7H_2O$
Thus, $n = 6$
Hence, 6F charge is required to reduce 1 mole of $Cr_2O_7^{2-}$ to Cr^{3+} in acidic medium.

49. (*c*) Amount of zinc $= 3.048$ g
$Zn^{2+} + 2e^- \longrightarrow Zn(s)$
$w = Zit$
where, Z = electrochemical equivalent $\left(= \frac{\text{atomic weight}}{\text{electrons} \times 96500}\right)$
i = current in amperes
t = time in seconds
$3.048 = \frac{A}{2 \times 96500} \times 5 \times 30 \times 60$
$A = 65.36\ \text{g mol}^{-1}$
$\therefore$ Equivalent weight $= \frac{A}{2} = 32.68$ g equivalent^{-1}
≈ 32.7 g equivalent^{-1}

50. (*c*) The quantity of charge required to obtain one mole of aluminium from Al_2O_3 is equal to the number of electron required to convert Al_2O_3 to Al.
$Al^{3+}(aq) \xrightarrow{+3e^-} Al(s)$
Hence, total 3F is required.

51. (*a*)

52. (*b*) Both A and R are true but R is not the correct explanation of A.
The correct explanation of A is :
KCl, NaCl and NH_4Cl cannot be used as a salt-bridge in a cell containing silver as one of the electrodes because they react with it to form a ppt. of AgCl.

53. (*a*) Both A and R are true and R is the correct explanation of A.

54. (*d*) A is false but R is true. The correct form of A is :
At standard conditions, the Nernst equation doesn't reduce to the standard cell potential equation instead it represents the cell potential under non-standard conditions.

55. (*d*) A is false but R is true. The correct form of A is :
Kohlrausch's law is applicable for both strong and weak electrolyte.

56. (*c*) Statement I is false but Statement II is true. Its correct form is :
When acidified zinc sulphate solution is electrolysed between zinc electrodes. It is zinc that is oxidised at anode while the hydrogen is reduced at the cathode.

57. (*a*) Both Statements I and Statement II are false.
Copper sulphate can not be stored in zinc vessel as zinc is more reactive than copper due to negative value of standard reduction potential of Zn.

58. (*b*) Statement I is true but Statement II is false.
Electrode potential of Cu^{2+}/Cu is + 0.34 V and electrode potential of $2H^+/H_2$ is 0.00 V.
Hence, correct reason is due to positive value of Cu^{2+}/Cu it looses electron to H^+ and get reduces, while H_2 gas evolves out.

59. (*b*) Statement I is true but Statement II is false.
Correct form of statement II is $E_{\text{cathode}} > E_{\text{anode}}$.

60. (*d*) Both Statement I and Statement II are ture.

61. (*c*) Statement I is false but Statement II is true.
Correct form of Statement I is :
Cell constant is a constant physical quantity of an electrolytic cell and is equal to distance between electrodes divided by cross-section area.

62. (*a*) Among the given statements, A, B and D are correct whereas C and E are incorrect.
Their correct form are
- Λ_m° can not be obtained by extrapolation of Λ_m to zero concentrations in weak electrolyte.
- Kohlrausch law is applicable for the calculation of limiting molar conductivity of any (weak and strong) electrolyte.

63. (*b*) Among the given statements, B, C and D are incorrect whereas A and E are correct.
The correct form of B, C and D are :
- In mercury cell, mercury amalgam and a paste of HgO and carbon are used as anode and cathode respectively.
- In lead storage battery, during the discharging phase, sulphuric acid is consumed in overall cell reaction.
- A nickel-cadmium cell has longer life than the lead storage battery.

64. (*b*) Among the given statements. Only C and E are incorrect while other are correct. Their correct form are

- In leclanche the reaction occuring at anode is

$$Zn(s) \longrightarrow Zn^{2+} + 2e^-$$

- Mercury cells are suitable for low current devices like hearing aids, watches etc.

65. (*a*)Among the given statements, only A, C and E are correct while B and D are incorrect.

Their correct forms are

- Λ_m^∞ of strong electrolytes can be obtained by extrapolation to $\sqrt{C} \to 0$ not for weak electrolytes.
- Weak electrolytes are partially dissociate into ions when dissolved in water.

66. (*b*) Among the given statements, D and C are correct whereas A, B and E are incorrect.

Their correct form is :

- 0.2 M HCl solution is diluted to 0.02 M HCl, its molar conductivity will be 10 times of the initial concentration.
- The ionisation constant (K_a) of weak acid in terms of molar conductance and Λ_m° (limiting molar conductivity) of very dilute solution is

$$K_a = \frac{C(\Lambda_m^2)}{\Lambda_m^\circ(\Lambda_m^\circ - \Lambda_m)}$$

The Debye-Huckel Onsager equation is expressed as

$$\Lambda_m = \Lambda_m^\circ - A\sqrt{C}$$

67. (*b*) Among the given substances, only inert electrode, i.e. (iv) and (v) can be used as electrodes in electrolytic cells having aqueous solutions.

68. (*d*) Among the given species, only three, i.e. (i), (iii) and (v) are weaker reducing agent than H^+/H_2 couple.

69. (*a*) Among the given reactions, only two, i.e. (ii) and (iv) has positive value of electrode potential.

70. (*c*) Among the given relations, only one, i.e. (iv) represent the limiting value of molar conductivity of A_2B electrolyte, according to Kohlrausch law.

71. (*d*) Among the given compounds, only four, i.e. (i), (ii), (iii) and (v) are strong electrolyte while others are weak electrolyte.

72. (*a*) The correct match is A-4, B-3, C-1, D-2.

73. (*b*) The correct match is A-2, B-1, C-4, D-3.

A. F_2 is a non-metal and best oxidising agent because SRP of F_2 is +2.87 V.

B. Li is a metal and strongest reducing agent because SRP of Li is -3.05 V.

C. Au^{3+} is a metal ion which is an oxidising agent as SRP of Au^{3+} is +1.40 V.

D. Br^- is an anion that can be oxidising by Au^{3+} as Au^{3+} ($E° = 1.40$) is greater than Br^- ($E° = 1.09$ V).

74. (*d*) The correct match is A-4, B-1, C-2, D-3.

75. (*c*) The correct match is A-2, B-4, C-3, D-1.

76. (*a*) The correct match is A-4, B-3, C-2, D-1.

77. (*d*) The correct match is A-4, B-1, C-2, D-3.

A. Λ_m (molar conductivity) is the conductivity due to number of ions furnished by one mole of electrolyte. As dilution increases number of ions present in the solution increases hence molar conductivity increases.

B. E_{cell}° of any atom/ion does not depend upon number of atom/ion, hence E_{cell}° of any atom/ion is an intensive properties.

C. κ represents specific conductivity which depends upon number of ions present in per unit volume.

D. $\Delta_r G_{cell}$ is an extensive property as it depends upon number of particles (species).

78. (*d*) The correct match is A-4, B-3, C-1, D-2.

79. (*d*) The correct match is A-4, B-3, C-1, D-2.

Final Check through PYQs

1. (*d*)

Reduction

$$MnO_4^- + 8H^+ + 5e^- \longrightarrow Mn^{2+} + 4H_2O$$

$$E^\circ_{Mn^{2+}/MnO_4^-} = -1.510 \text{ V}$$

$$1/2O_2 + 2H^+ + 2e^- \longrightarrow 2H_2O$$

Reduction

$$E^\circ_{O_2/H_2O} = +1.223 \text{ V}$$

Reaction at cathode (reduction)

$$2MnO_4^- + 16H^+ + 10e^- \longrightarrow 2Mn^{2+} + 8H_2O;$$

Reaction at anode (oxidation) $E^\circ_{RP} = 1.510$ V

$$5H_2O \longrightarrow \frac{5}{2}O_2 + 10H^+ + 10e^-;$$

$$E^\circ_{OP} = -1.223 \text{ V}$$

The overall reaction is

$$2MnO_4^- + 6H^+ \longrightarrow 2Mn^{2+} + \frac{5}{2}O_2 + 3H_2O$$

$$E^\circ = E^\circ_{MnO_4^-/Mn^{2+}} - E^\circ_{O_2/H_2O}$$

$$E^\circ = 1.510 - 1.223 = 0.287 \text{ V}$$

Here, since the value of $E°$ is positive, the reaction is spontaneous. Hence, MnO_4^- will liberate O_2.

2. (c) Let us consider the segment of EMF series (standard reduction potential) of the given reduction half-cell reactions :

Reduction half reaction	E/V at 298K
(a) $Mg^{2+} + 2e^- \longrightarrow Mg$	− 2.36
(b) $Fe^{2+} + 2e^- \longrightarrow Fe$	− 0.44
(c) $Au^{3+} + 3e^- \longrightarrow Au$	+ 140
(d) $K^+ + e^- \longrightarrow K$	− 2.93

Hence, option (c) is correct.

3. (b) More negative the value of standard reduction potential, higher is the reduction power.

i.e. Reducing power $\propto \dfrac{1}{\text{standard reduction potential}}$

Thus, the correct decreasing order of reducing power of the metal is

$$\underset{(E^\circ_{K^+/K} = -2.93\text{V})}{K} > \underset{(E^\circ_{Al^{3+}/Al} = -1.66\text{ V})}{Al} >$$
$$\underset{(E^\circ_{Cr^{3+}/Cr} = -0.74\text{ V})}{Cr} > \underset{(E^\circ_{Ag^+/Ag} = 0.80\text{ V})}{Ag}$$

4. (c) For the electrochemical cells,

$Zn|ZnSO_4\ (0.01M)||CuSO_4(1M)|Cu$

Cell reaction :

$$Zn + Cu^{2+} \longrightarrow Zn^{2+} + Cu;\ n = 2$$

$$E_1 = E^\circ - \frac{0.059}{2}\log\frac{Zn^{2+}}{Cu^{2+}} = E^\circ - \frac{0.059}{2}\log\frac{0.01}{1}$$

$$E_1 = E^\circ - \frac{0.059}{2}\log\frac{1}{100} = (E^\circ + 0.059)$$

For cell,

$Zn|ZnSO_4(1M)||CuSO_4(0.01M)|Cu$

$$E_2 = E^\circ - \frac{0.059}{2}\log\frac{1}{0.01}$$

$$E_2 = E^\circ - \frac{0.059}{2}\log 100$$

$$= (E^\circ - 0.059) \Rightarrow E_1 > E_2$$

5. (b) Given, $E^\circ_{cell} = 1.05$ V

$$\frac{2.303\ RT}{F} = 0.059$$

$$[Ni^{2+}] = 0.001\ M = 10^{-3}\ M$$
$$[Ag^+] = 0.001\ M = 10^{-3}\ M$$

Using Nernst equation,

$$E_{cell} = E^\circ_{cell} - \frac{0.059}{n}\log\frac{[Ni^{+2}]^1}{[Ag^+]^2}$$

$$= 1.05 - \frac{0.059}{2}\log\frac{(10^{-3})}{(10^{-3})^2}$$

$$= 1.05 - \frac{0.059}{2}\log 10^3 = 1.05 - \frac{0.059}{2}\times 3$$

$$= 1.05 - 0.0885;\ E_{cell} = 0.9615$$

6. (c) $E^\circ_{cell} = \dfrac{2.303RT}{nF}\log K$

Given : $E^\circ_{cell} = 0.59$ V, $n = 1$

$$0.59 = \frac{0.059}{1}\log K$$

$$\frac{0.59}{0.059} = \log K$$

$$10 = \log K \Rightarrow K = 10^{10}$$

7. (d) The relation between E°_{cell} and $\Delta_r G^\circ$ is as follows

$$\Delta_r G^\circ = -nFE^\circ_{cell}$$

For the cell reaction,

$$2Fe^{3+}(aq) + 2I^-(aq) \longrightarrow 2Fe^{2+}(aq) + I_2(aq);\ n = 2$$

Given, $F = 96500$ C mol^{-1}, $E^\circ_{cell} = 0.24$ V

Now, we know that $\Delta_r G^\circ = -n\,FE^\circ_{cell}$

On substituting the given values in above equation we get

$$\Delta_r G^\circ = -2\text{ mol} \times 96500\text{ C mol}^{-1} \times 0.24\text{ J mol}^{-1}$$
$$= -46320\text{ J mol}^{-1} = -46.32\text{ kJ mol}^{-1}$$

Hence, option (d) is correct.

8. (d) From the question, we have an equation

$$2H^+ + 2e^- \longrightarrow H_2(g)$$

According to Nernst equation,

$$E = E^\circ - \frac{0.0591}{2}\log\frac{p_{H_2}}{[H^+]^2}$$

$$= 0 - \frac{0.0591}{2}\log\frac{p_{H_2}}{(10^{-7})^2} \qquad [\because [H^+] = 10^{-7}]$$

∴ For potential of H_2 electrode to be zero, p_{H_2} should be equal to $[H^+]^2$, i.e. 10^{-14} atm.

$$\therefore \qquad \log\frac{10^{-14}}{(10^{-7})^2} = 0$$

9. (b) Given, conductivity $(\kappa) = 0.0210\ \Omega^{-1}\text{cm}^{-1}$

Resistance = 60 Ω

Cell constant = ?

We know that,

$$\kappa = \frac{1}{R}\times\frac{l}{a}$$

$$\text{Cell constant} = \frac{l}{a} = \kappa \times R$$
$$= 0.0210 \times 60 = 1.26\text{ cm}^{-1}$$

10. (b) Molar conductance of NaCl,

$$\lambda^\circ_{NaCl} = 126.45\text{ S cm}^2\text{ mol}^{-1}$$

Molar conductance of HCl,

$$\lambda^\circ_{HCl} = 426.16\text{ S cm}^2\text{ mol}^{-1}$$

Molar conductance of $CH_3CO\overset{-}{O}\overset{+}{Na}$,

$$\lambda^\circ_{CH_3COONa} = 91.0\text{ S cm}^2\text{ mol}^{-1}$$

According to Kohlrausch's law;

$$\lambda^\circ_{HCl} = \lambda^\circ_{H^+} + \lambda^\circ_{Cl^-} \qquad \text{...(i)}$$

$$\lambda^\circ_{NaCl} = \lambda^\circ_{Na^+} + \lambda^\circ_{Cl^-} \quad \text{...(ii)}$$

$$\lambda^\circ_{CH_3COONa^+} = \lambda^\circ_{Na^+} + \lambda^\circ_{CH_3COO^-} \quad \text{...(iii)}$$

$$\lambda^\circ_{CH_3COOH} = \lambda^\circ_{CH_3COO^-} + \lambda^\circ_{H^+}$$

$$\lambda^\circ_{CH_3COOH} = (\lambda^\circ_{CH_3COO^-} + \lambda^\circ_{Na^+}) + (\lambda^\circ_{H^+} + \lambda^\circ_{Cl^-}) - (\lambda^\circ_{Na^+} + \lambda^\circ_{Cl^-})$$

$$\lambda^\circ_{CH_3COOH} = \lambda^\circ_{CH_3COONa^+} + \lambda^\circ_{HCl} - \lambda^\circ_{NaCl}$$

$$\lambda^\circ_{CH_3COOH} = 91.0 + 426.16 - 126.45$$

$$\lambda^\circ_{CH_3COOH} = 390.71 \text{ S cm}^2 \text{ mol}^{-1}$$

11. (*c*) $\lambda_{CH_3COOH} = 20 \text{ S cm}^2 \text{ mol}^{-1}$

Concentration of CH_3COOH, $C = 0.007$ M

$$\lambda^\circ_{H^+} = 350 \text{ S cm}^2 \text{ mol}^{-1}$$

$$\lambda^\circ_{CH_3COO^-} = 50 \text{ S cm}^2 \text{ mol}^{-1}$$

According to Kohlrausch's law,

$$\lambda^\circ_{CH_3COOH} = \lambda^\circ_{H^+} + \lambda^\circ_{CH_3COO^-}$$

$$\lambda^\circ_{CH_3COOH} = 350 + 50 = 400 \text{ S cm}^2 \text{ mol}^{-1}$$

Degree of dissociation,

$$\alpha = \frac{\lambda_{CH_3COOH}}{\lambda^\circ_{CH_3COOH}}$$

$$\alpha = \frac{20}{400} = \frac{1}{20} = 0.05 = 5 \times 10^{-2}$$

	CH_3COOH	$\rightleftharpoons$	CH_3COO^-	+	H^+
$t = 0$	C		0		0
$t = t_{eq}$	$C - C\alpha$		$C\alpha$		$C\alpha$

Equilibrium constant,

$$K = \frac{C^2\alpha^2}{C(1-\alpha)} = \frac{C\alpha^2}{1-\alpha}$$

As $\alpha << 1; 1 - \alpha \approx 1$

$$K = C\alpha^2 = 0.007 \times (0.05)^2$$

$$= 0.007 \times 25 \times 10^{-4}$$

$$= 1.75 \times 10^{-5} \text{ mol L}^{-1}$$

12. (*d*) Given

$$\lambda^\circ_{m(H_2SO_4)} = 2\lambda^\circ_{H^+} + \lambda^\circ_{SO_4^{2-}}$$

$$= x \text{ S cm}^2 \text{mol}^{-1} \quad \text{...(i)}$$

$$\lambda^\circ_{m(K_2SO_4)} = 2\lambda^\circ_{K^+} + \lambda^\circ_{SO_4^{2-}}$$

$$= y \text{ S cm}^2 \text{mol}^{-1} \quad \text{...(ii)}$$

$$\lambda_m(CH_3COOK) = \lambda^\circ_{CH_3COO^-} + \lambda^\circ_{K^+}$$

$$= z \text{ S cm}^2 \text{mol}^{-1} \quad \text{...(iii)}$$

To find :

$$\lambda^\circ_{m(CH_3COOH)} = \lambda^\circ_{CH_3COO^-} + \lambda^\circ_{H^+}$$

The above equation can be obtained by

$$\text{Eq. (iii)} + \frac{\text{Eq. (i)}}{2} - \frac{\text{Eq. (ii)}}{2}$$

$$\therefore \lambda^\circ_{m(CH_3COOH)} = \lambda^\circ_{m(CH_3COOK)} + \frac{\lambda^\circ_{m(H_2SO_4)}}{2} - \frac{\lambda^\circ_{m(K_2SO_4)}}{2}$$

$$= \left(z + \frac{x}{2} - \frac{y}{2}\right) \text{S cm}^2 \text{ mol}^{-1}$$

$$= \left(\frac{x-y}{2} + z\right) \text{S cm}^2 \text{ mol}^{-1}$$

13. (*b*) Given, concentration of solution,

$$M = 0.5 \text{ mol / dm}^3$$

Electrolytic conductivity,

$$\kappa = 5.76 \times 10^{-3} \text{ S cm}^{-1}$$

Temperature, $T = 298$ K

$\therefore$ Molar conductivity,

$$\lambda_m = \frac{\kappa \times 1000}{M}$$

$$= \frac{5.76 \times 10^{-3} \times 1000}{0.5}$$

$$= 11.52 \text{ S cm}^2/\text{mol}$$

14. (*a*) The correct match is A-2, B-4, C-1, D-3.

A. $2H_2O \longrightarrow O_2 + 4H^+ + 4e^-$

1 mol H_2O will require 2F charge.

B. $8H^+ + MnO_4^- + 5e^- \longrightarrow Mn^{2+} + 4H_2O$

1 mol of MnO_4^- will require 5F charge.

C. $CaCl_2 + 3e^- \longrightarrow Ca + 2Cl^-$

1.5 mol of Ca will require 3F charge.

D. $2FeO + H_2O \longrightarrow Fe_2O_3 + 2H^+ + 2e^-$

1 mole of FeO will require 1F charge.

15. (*b*) Given, current, $i = 9.6487$ A

$$1F = 96487 \text{ C}$$

$$t = 100 \text{ sec}$$

$$W = \frac{E(it)}{96487}$$

$$W = \frac{63/2 \times 9.6487 \times 100}{96487}$$

$$W = 0.315 \text{ g of Cu}$$

16. (*d*) $\underset{\text{Molten}}{CaCl_2} \rightleftharpoons Ca^{2+} + 2Cl^-$

At cathode (Reduction) $Ca^{2+} + 2e^- \longrightarrow Ca$

According to Faraday's first law,

Charge passed in Faraday = Gram equivalent of product

$$= \frac{\text{Given mass}}{\text{Atomic mass}} \times \text{no. of } e^- \text{ released}$$

$$= \frac{20}{40} \times 2 = 1 \text{ F}$$

So, one Faraday (*F*) is required for the process.

17. (*a*) Dilute H_2SO_4 contains H_2SO_4 and H_2O and they show electrolytic dissociation as,

$$\underset{\text{Strong electrolyte as it is dilute}}{H_2SO_4} \longrightarrow 2H^+ + SO_4^{2-}$$

$$H_2O \rightleftharpoons H^+ + OH^-$$

Reaction at cathode (Pt)

$$2H^+ + 2e^- \longrightarrow H_2\uparrow$$

Reaction at anode (Pt)

$$4\overline{O}H - 4e^- \longrightarrow O_2\uparrow + 2H_2O$$

We get, O_2 gas at anode.

18. (*b*) The reaction takes place in a fuel cell is

$$\underbrace{\underset{\text{[at anode]}}{2\overset{0}{H_2}(g)} + \underset{\text{[at cathode]}}{\overset{0}{O_2}(g)}}_{\text{Reactants } R} \longrightarrow \underbrace{2\overset{+1}{H_2}\overset{-2}{O}(l)}_{\text{Product (P)}}$$

Heat energy [gets converted into electrical energy]

Hence, option (b) is the correct.

19. (*b*) Given, $w = 0.10 \text{ mol} = (0.10 \times 71)$ g,

$i = 3$ A, $E = 35.5$

The following reactions occured,

At cathode,

$$2H_2O \xrightarrow{+2e^-} H_2 + 2OH^-$$

At anode, $\underset{35.5 g}{2Cl^-} \xrightarrow{-2e^-} \underset{71 g}{Cl_2}$

$$W = \frac{EIT}{96500} \quad \text{... (i)}$$

Putting all values in expression (i) we get

$$(0.10 \times 71) = \frac{35.5}{96500} \times 3 \times t$$

or $t = 6433$ s

or $t = 107.22 \text{ min} \simeq 110 \text{ min} \quad \left[1 \text{ s} = \frac{1}{60} \text{ min}\right]$

20. (*c*) From Faraday's first law of electrolysis,

$$\frac{w}{E} = \frac{it}{96500} \quad \text{...(i)}$$

Given, $i = 1$ A; $t = 60$ s

Putting these values in Eq. (i), we get

$$\frac{w}{E} = \frac{1 \times 60}{96500}$$

or $\frac{w}{E} = \frac{6}{9650}$

= Number of mole of electrons

∴ Number of electrons

$$= \frac{6}{9650} \times 6.022 \times 10^{23} = 3.75 \times 10^{20}$$

21. (*d*) $Zn^{2+} + 2e \longrightarrow Zn; \; E° = -0.76$ V

$Fe^{2+} + 2e^- \longrightarrow Fe; \; E° = -0.44$ V

Here, in galvanised iron, Zn has higher negative reduction potential means Zn takes electrons given by iron and itself gets reduced.

Thus, Zn works as anode and protects iron from rusting by making iron as cathode.

22. (*b*) Since, HCl is strong acid and dissociates completely. Hence, it conducts electricity best in its aqueous solution.

23. (*a*) Fuel cell is a device that converts energy of combustion of fuels like hydrogen and methane, directly into electrical energy.

24. (*c*) $MnO_4^{2-} \xrightarrow{[1 \text{ mol } e^- = 1 \text{ F}]} MnO_4^-$

As per the equation, for 1 mole of MnO_4^{2-}, 1 F of electricity is required. Thus, for 0.1 mole of MnO_4^{2-}, 0.1 F of electricity is required.

Since, 1 F = 96500 C

∴ 0.1 F = 0.1 × 96500 C

= 9650 C

Hence, 9650 C of electricity is required to completely oxidise MnO_4^{2-} to MnO_4^-.

25. (*d*) Since, 22400 mL volume is occupied by 1 mole of O_2 at STP.

Thus, 5600 mL O_2 means $= \frac{5600}{22400}$ mol O_2

$= \frac{1}{4}$ mol O_2

∴ Weight of $O_2 = \frac{1}{4} \times 32 = 8$ g

According to given question,

Equivalents of Ag = Equivalents of O_2

$$= \frac{\text{Weight of Ag}}{\text{Equivalent weight of Ag}}$$

$$= \frac{\text{Weight of } O_2}{\text{Equivalent weight of } O_2}$$

$$\frac{w_{Ag}}{\frac{M_{Ag}}{1}} = \frac{w_{O_2}}{\frac{M_{O_2}}{4}}$$

∴ $\frac{w_{Ag}}{108} \times 1 = \frac{8}{32} \times 4$

$[\because 2H_2O \longrightarrow O_2 + 4H^+ + 4e^-]$

⇒ $w_{Ag} = 108$ g

Skill Builder

- **Sol. of Skill Builder Pg. 58**

(*d*) The given reaction is

$$Pt^{2+} + 2Cl^- \longrightarrow Pt + Cl_2;\ E^\circ_{cell} = -0.15\ V$$

On reversing the above reaction,

$$Pt + Cl_2 \longrightarrow Pt^{2+} + 2Cl^-;\ E^\circ_{cell} = 0.15\ V$$

Also, $Pt^{2+} + 2e^- \longrightarrow Pt;\ E^\circ_{cell} = 1.20\ V$

Now, $E^\circ_{cell} = E^\circ_{cathode} - E^\circ_{anode}$

$$E^\circ_{Cl_2/2Cl^-} = 0.15 - (-1.20) = 1.35\ V$$

- **Sol. of Skill Builder Pg. 62**

(*b*) $$E = E^\circ - \frac{0.059}{n}\log\frac{[Zn^{2+}]}{[Ni^{2+}]}$$

$$0.5105 = E^\circ - \frac{0.059}{2}\log\left(\frac{1}{0.1}\right)$$

$$E^\circ = 0.5105 + \frac{0.059}{2}$$

$$E^\circ = 0.54\ V$$

- **Sol. of Skill Builder Pg. 63**

(*c*) At 298 K, $$E^\circ_{cell} = \frac{0.059}{n}\log K$$

$$1.07 = \frac{0.059}{2}\log K$$

$$\frac{2 \times 1.07}{0.059} = \log K$$

$$\frac{2.14}{0.059} = \log K$$

$$36.27 = \log K$$

$$K = 10^{36.27}$$

- **Sol. of Skill Builder Pg. 67**

(*d*) Conductivity, $\kappa = 0.146 \times 10^3\ S\ cm^{-1}$

Resistance, $R = 1000\ \Omega$

Cell constant $= \kappa \times R = 0.146 \times 10^{-3} \times 1000 = 0.146\ cm^{-1}$

- **Sol. of Skill Builder Pg. 70**

(*b*) According Kohlrausch's law,

Λ°_m for $NH_4OH = \lambda^\circ_{NH_4^+} + \lambda^\circ_{OH^-}$

Λ°_m for $Ba(OH)_2 = \lambda_{Ba^{2+}} + \lambda_{OH^-}$

$= 457.6\ ohm^{-1}cm^2\ mol^{-1}$ ... (i)

Λ°_m for $BaCl_2 = \lambda_{Ba^{2+}} + \lambda_{Cl^-}$

$= 240.6\ ohm^{-1}cm^2 mol^{-1}$ ... (ii)

Λ°_m for $NH_4Cl = \lambda_{NH_4^+} + \lambda_{Cl^-}$

$= 129.8\ ohm^{-1}cm^2 mol^{-1}$ ... (iii)

Adding equations (i) and (iii) and subtracting from (ii), we get

$$\lambda^\circ_{NH_4^+} + \lambda^\circ_{Cl^-} = \lambda_{Ba^{2+}} + \lambda_{OH^-} + \lambda_{NH_4^+} + \lambda_{Cl^-} - \lambda_{Ba^{2+}} - \lambda_{Cl^-}$$

$= 457.6 + 129.8 - 240.6$

$= 356.8\ ohm^{-1}cm^2\ mol^{-1}$

- **Sol. of Skill Builder Pg. 75**

(*d*) The correct match is A-4, B-3, C-2, D-1

A. For 1 gram magnesium from $MgCl_2$ (molten)

$$Mg^{2+} + 2e^- \longrightarrow Mg$$

So, 1 gram magnesium requires 2F charge.

B. $Ca^{2+} + 2e^- \longrightarrow Ca$

for 40 g, 2F is required. So, for 20g 1F is required.

C. $Al^{3+} + 3e^- \longrightarrow Al$

for depositing 1 mol of Al, 3F is required.

D. $2H^+ + 2e^- \longrightarrow H_2(g)$

So, for 4 g of H_2, 4F is required.

For deeper insight
Scan the QR Code

Chapter 3

Chemical Kinetics

Learning Objectives

Module-I

- Chemical Reactions
- Rate of a Chemical Reaction
- Average and Instantaneous Rate
- Factors Affecting Rate of Reaction

Module-II

- Rate Law and Rate Constant
- Characteristic of Rate Constant
- Molecularity of a Reaction
- Order of a Reaction
- Integrated Rate Equations
- Half-life Period
- Pseudo First Order Reactions

Module-III

- Collision Theory
- Transition State Theory
- Effect of Temperature and Catalyst on Reaction Rate
- Arrhenius Equation

Chapter Overview with
NEET Connection

This chapter is useful for the learning of rate of chemical reactions. The other chapters which we have already studied like thermodynamics and chemical equilibrium are also related to rate of chemical reactions.

All these chapters are interconnected with each other with chemical equations in their core. But the individual importance in gripping chemistry of each of them is variable.

Special format questions can be easily framed on the following topics of this chapter.

- Graphical interpretation of rate
- Integrated rate equations
- Arrhenius equation
- Molecularity and order of a reaction
- Half-life period

For better understanding of this chapter, a grip over chemical reactions and basics like speed, velocity are required.

As the foundation of order, half-life and Arrhenius equation involves calculation, so along with conceptual understanding, a focus on calculation part and basic unit conversions are also required.

Introduction

The feasibility of a reaction can be predicted with the help of thermodynamic principles. Likewise relative amounts of reactants and products at equilibrium position of the reaction can also be predicted from chemical equilibrium.

However, the thermodynamic principles do not provide any information regarding the speed of a given reaction, i.e. how much time a given feasible reaction will take for its completion. It can only be predicted by chemical kinetics.

Module 1

Chemical Reactions, Rate of a Chemical Reaction

- Chemical Reactions
- Rate of a Chemical Reaction
- Average and Instantaneous Rate
- Factors Affecting Rate of Reaction

All these questions can be answered by branch of chemistry, which deals with the study of reaction rates and their mechanisms, called **chemical kinetics.** The word kinetics is derived from the Greek word *kinesis* meaning movement.

In this chapter, we shall be dealing with average and instantaneous rate of reaction and the factors affecting them. Some elementary ideas about the collision theory of reactions rates are also given. Let us first learn about the reaction rate.

Chemical Reactions

When one or more substances undergo a change which result in the formation of a new product, it is called **chemical reactions.** There are different types of chemical reactions, which are discussed as follows

Types of Chemical Reactions

Depending upon reaction rates or speeds, chemical reactions can be classified in the following ways.

(i) **Instantaneous or fast reactions** These reactions proceed at very fast speed. They occur as soon as the reactants are brought together. So, it is practically impossible to measure the speed of such reactions. e.g. Neutralisation reactions, precipitation reactions etc.

(ii) **Extremely slow reactions** These type of reactions proceed at very low speed. So, it is also very difficult to measure the speed of these reactions. e.g. Rusting of iron, etc.

(iii) **Moderately slow reactions** These type of reactions proceed with a measurable speed at room temperature. Thus, these reactions are utilised in the study of chemical kinetics. e.g. Inversion of cane sugar, decomposition of ammonium nitrate etc.

Depending upon number of steps, chemical reactions are classified in the following ways

(i) **Elementary reactions** The reactions taking place in one step are called elementary reactions.

(ii) **Complex reactions** The reactions which do not take place in one step are called complex reactions. In these reactions, all the atoms, ions or molecules as represented in the balanced chemical equation may not come together to collide simultaneously. Such reactions occur in a sequence of a number of steps.

e.g. $4HBr + O_2 \longrightarrow 2H_2O + 2Br_2$

Step I $HBr + O_2 \xrightarrow{\text{Slow}} HOOBr$

Step II $HOOBr + HBr \xrightarrow{\text{Fast}} 2HOBr$

Step III $[HOBr + HBr \xrightarrow{\text{Fast}} H_2O + Br_2] \times 2$

$$4HBr + O_2 \longrightarrow 2H_2O + 2Br_2$$

Rate of a Chemical Reaction

The change in concentration of any one of the reactants or products per unit time is called **rate of a reaction.** It can be expressed as

"The rate of disappearance or decrease in concentration of any one of the reactant."

Or

"The rate of appearance or increase in concentration of any one of the products".

Consider a hypothetical reaction, assuming that the volume of the system remains constant.

$$nA \longrightarrow mB$$

When $t = t_1$ $[A_{t_1}]$ $[B_{t_1}]$

When $t = t_2$ $[A_{t_2}]$ $[B_{t_2}]$

Rate of consumption of $A = -\dfrac{\Delta[A]}{\Delta t}$

Rate of formation of $B = +\dfrac{\Delta[B]}{dt}$

Rate of a reaction

$$= \frac{1}{n}\left[\frac{\text{decrease in the concentration of reactant}}{\text{time taken}}\right]$$

$$\text{or } \frac{1}{m}\left[\frac{\text{increase in the concentration of product}}{\text{time taken}}\right]$$

$$\text{Rate of reaction} = \frac{1}{n}\frac{[A_{t_2}]-[A_{t_1}]}{[t_2-t_1]} = -\frac{1}{n}\frac{\Delta[A]}{\Delta t}$$

$$= \frac{1}{m}\frac{[B_{t_2}]-[B_{t_1}]}{[t_2-t_1]} = +\frac{1}{m}\frac{\Delta[B]}{\Delta t}$$

Here, n and m are the stoichiometric coefficients of A and B, respectively.

Mentor's Tip

- The rate expression
  - The negative sign indicates that the concentration of reactants decreases with time.
  - The positive sign indicates that the concentration of products increases with time.
- The concentration change may be positive or negative but the rate of reaction is always positive.

Types of Rate of Reaction

The rate of reaction can be classified into following two types

Average Rate of Reaction

It is defined as the change in concentration of reactant or product during large interval of time.

e.g. For a reaction,

$$PCl_5 \longrightarrow PCl_3 + Cl_2$$

$$r_{avg} = -\frac{\Delta[PCl_5]}{\Delta t} = +\frac{\Delta[PCl_3]}{\Delta t} = +\frac{\Delta[Cl_2]}{\Delta t}$$

Instantaneous Rate of Reaction

It is defined as rate of reaction at any particular instant of time. It is equal to the small change in concentration (dx) in small interval of time (dt).

e.g. For a reaction, $R \longrightarrow P$

$$r_{avg} = -\frac{\Delta[R]}{\Delta t} = \frac{\Delta[P]}{\Delta t}$$

$$\lim_{\Delta t \to 0} r_{inst} = \frac{-d[R]}{dt} = \frac{d[P]}{dt}$$

Example 1 *The concentrations of a reactant R at different times are given below.*

t (s)	$[R]$(molL^{-1})
0	160×10^{-3}
5	80×10^{-3}
10	40×10^{-3}
20	10×10^{-3}
30	2.5×10^{-3}

Calculate the average rate of reaction, $R \longrightarrow P$ during different intervals of time.

Sol. The average rate of reaction can be calculated as

$$r_{av} = -\frac{[R]_2-[R]_1}{\Delta t}$$

$[R_1]$	$[R_2]$	t_1	t_2	r_{av} (mol L^{-1} s^{-1})
160×10^{-3}	80×10^{-3}	0	5	$-\frac{(80-160)\times 10^{-3}}{5-0} = 16 \times 10^{-3}$
80×10^{-3}	40×10^{-3}	5	10	$-\frac{(40-80)\times 10^{-3}}{10-5} = 8 \times 10^{-3}$
40×10^{-3}	10×10^{-3}	10	20	$-\frac{(10-40)\times 10^{-3}}{20-10} = 3 \times 10^{-3}$
10×10^{-3}	2.5×10^{-3}	20	30	$-\frac{(2.5-10)\times 10^{-3}}{30-20} = 0.75 \times 10^{-3}$

It can be seen that the average rate decreases from 16×10^{-3} to 0.75×10^{-3} mol L^{-1} s^{-1} during the time interval 0 to 30 s.

Rate of Reaction in the form of Stoichiometry

The rate of a reaction can be expressed in terms of each reactant and product.

For a general reaction,

$$aA + bB \longrightarrow cC + dD$$

The rate expression may be expressed as

$$\text{Rate} = -\frac{d[A]}{a\,dt} = -\frac{d[B]}{b\,dt} = +\frac{d[C]}{c\,dt} = +\frac{d[D]}{d\,dt}$$

- Stoichiometric coefficient does not involve in the expression of disappearance rate of reactant and formation rate of product.
- Stoichiometric coefficient must be involved in the expression of rate of a reaction.
- During this change, concentration is divided by stoichiometric coefficient to maintain uniformity.

Let us write instantaneous rate expression for the reaction,

(a) $2NO(g) + O_2(g) \longrightarrow 2NO_2(g)$

$$\text{Rate} = \frac{-d[NO]}{2dt} = \frac{-d[O_2]}{dt} = \frac{d[NO_2]}{2\,dt}$$

(b) $N_2 + 3H_2 \longrightarrow 2NH_3$

$$\text{Rate} = -\frac{d[N_2]}{dt} = \frac{-d[H_2]}{3\,dt} = \frac{d[NH_3]}{2dt}$$

For a gaseous reaction at constant temperature, concentration is directly proportional to the partial pressure of a species.

Hence, rate can also be expressed as rate of change in partial pressure of the reactant or the product.

Mentor's Tip

Symbol 'Δ' is used for a large change, i.e. for average rate whereas symbol d is used for a small change, i.e. for instantaneous rate.

Units of the Rate of a Reaction

Generally, the unit of rate is concentration time^{-1}. i.e. If concentration is in mol L^{-1} and time is in seconds then unit will be mol L^{-1} s^{-1}.

However, in gaseous reaction, when the concentration of gases is expressed in terms of their partial pressures, the unit of the rate equation will be **atm s^{-1}**.

Example 2 *Express the rate of the following reactions:*

(i) $PCl_5 \longrightarrow PCl_3 + Cl_2$ *(ii)* $2NO_2 \longrightarrow 2NO + O_2$

in terms of the concentration of reactants and products.

Sol. (i) For the reaction, $PCl_5 \longrightarrow PCl_3 + Cl_2$

$$\text{Rate of reaction} = -\frac{d[PCl_5]}{dt} = \frac{d[PCl_3]}{dt} = \frac{d[Cl_2]}{dt}$$

(ii) For the reaction, $2NO_2 \longrightarrow 2NO + O_2$

$$\text{Rate of reaction} = -\frac{1}{2}\frac{d[NO_2]}{dt} = \frac{1}{2}\frac{d[NO]}{dt} = \frac{d[O_2]}{dt}$$

Example 3. *Ammonia and oxygen react at high temperature as :*

$$4NH_3(g) + 5O_2(g) \longrightarrow 4NO(g) + 6H_2O(g)$$

In an experiment, the rate of formation of NO is 3.6×10^{-3} Ms^{-1}. *Calculate*

(i) the rate of disappearance of ammonia and

(ii) the rate of formation of water vapour.

Sol. For the reaction, $4NH_3(g) + 5O_2(g) \longrightarrow 4NO(g) + 6H_2O(g)$

$$\text{Rate} = \frac{1}{4}\frac{-d[NH_3]}{dt} = \frac{1}{5}\frac{-d[O_2]}{dt} = \frac{1}{4}\frac{d[NO]}{dt} = \frac{1}{6}\frac{d[H_2O]}{dt}$$

(i) Rate of disappearance of ammonia

= Rate of appearance of NO $= 3.6 \times 10^{-3}$ mol L^{-1} s^{-1}

(ii) Rate of formation of water vapour $= \frac{d[H_2O]}{dt}$

From the rate equation, $\frac{1}{6}\frac{d[H_2O]}{dt} = \frac{1}{4}\frac{d[NO]}{dt}$

$$\therefore \quad \frac{d[H_2O]}{dt} = \frac{6}{4} \times 3.6 \times 10^{-3} = 5.4 \times 10^{-3} \text{ mol L}^{-1}\text{ s}^{-1}$$

Factors Affecting the Rate of Reaction

Reaction rate is affected by following factors :

(i) **Concentration of reactants** Reaction rate usually increases when concentration of reactant increases due to increase in collision frequency.

Mentor's Tip

For a general reaction, $aA + bB \longrightarrow cC + dD$
The representation of rate of reaction in terms of concentration can be given by Rate $= k[A]^x[B]^y$ which we will discuss in detail in module 2.

(ii) **Pressure** Rate of gaseous reactions is affected by pressure. While there is no effect of pressure on reaction rate in solid or liquid phases.

(iii) **Temperature** The rate of chemical reaction usually increases on increasing the temperature.

(iv) **Nature of reactants** The nature of bonds in a molecule influences the rate of reaction at which it changes into products.

(v) **Physical state of reactants** Physical state of reactants has also considerable effect on rate of reaction.

e.g Reaction rate in solid phase < liquid phase < gas phase

- Homogeneous reactions occur faster than heterogeneous reactions.
- Solid reactant in powdered form becomes more reactive due to more surface area.

(vi) **Presence of catalyst** A positive catalyst increases the rate of reaction by lowering the energy barrier.

(vii) **Presence of light** There are many chemical reactions whose rate are influenced by radiations. Such reactions are called photochemical reactiokns.

e.g. Photosynthesis, fading of colour in sunlight, formation of picture on a photographic plate.

- For such reactions, rate is almost unaffected by temperature but depends on intensity of light.
- Rate of reaction $\propto$ intensity of light.

NEET Close-Up

Example Similar to PYQ Asked in NEET 2023

For a certain reaction, the rate $= k[A]^3[B]$, when the initial concentration of A is tripled keeping concentration of B constant, the initial rate would

(a) decrease by a factor of 10 (b) increase by a factor of 19
(c) increase by a factor of 27 (d) decrease by a factor of 30

Sol. (c) Given, rate $(r) = k[A]^3[B]$ ...(i)

$$r_1 = k[3A]^3[B] \quad \text{...(ii)}$$

Dividing Eqs. (i) by (ii) we get,

$$\frac{r}{r_1} = \frac{k[A]^3[B]}{k[3A]^3[B]} = \frac{1}{27} \Rightarrow r_1 = 27r$$

Thus, the initial rate would increase by a factor of 27.

Skill Builder

For a certain reaction, the rate $= k[A]^2[B]^2$, when the initial concentration of B is doubled keeping concentration of A constant, the initial rate would

(a) decrease by a factor of nine (b) increase by a factor of six
(c) increase by a factor of nine (d) increase by a factor of four

For more practice Refer to Q. 18 of Step up Practice 1 and Q.6 of Gearing up for NEET.

STEP UP Practice 1

1. Which of the following expressions is correct for the rate of reaction given below?

$$5Br^-(aq) + BrO_3^-(aq) + 6H^+(aq) \longrightarrow 3Br_2(aq) + 3H_2O(l)$$

(a) $\frac{\Delta[Br^-]}{\Delta t} = 5\frac{\Delta[H^+]}{\Delta t}$

(b) $\frac{\Delta[Br^-]}{\Delta t} = \frac{6}{5}\frac{\Delta[H^+]}{\Delta t}$

(c) $\frac{\Delta[Br^-]}{\Delta t} = \frac{5}{6}\frac{\Delta[H^+]}{\Delta t}$

(d) $\frac{\Delta[Br^-]}{\Delta t} = 6\frac{\Delta[H^+]}{\Delta t}$

2. Observe the following reaction.

$$A(g) + 4B(g) \longrightarrow 5C(g)$$

The rate of disappearance of $B\left\{\frac{-d[B]}{dt}\right\}$ is 2×10^{-3} mol L^{-1} min^{-1}.

What is the value of $\frac{-d[A]}{dt}$ in mol L^{-1} min^{-1}?

(a) 3×10^{-3} (b) 2×10^{-5}
(c) 5×10^{-4} (d) 4×10^{-4}

3. $2N_2O_5 \longrightarrow 4NO_2 + O_2$

If $-\frac{\Delta[N_2O_5]}{\Delta t} = k_1[N_2O_5]$, $\frac{\Delta[NO_2]}{\Delta t} = k_2[N_2O_5]$,

$\frac{\Delta[O_2]}{\Delta t} = k_3[N_2O_5]$, then

(a) $k_1 = k_2 = k_3$ (b) $2k_1 = k_2 = 4k_3$
(c) $2k_1 = 4k_2 = k_3$ (d) $k_1 = 2k_2 = 3k_3$

4. Consider the following statements.

Statement I For $3A \longrightarrow 2B$, rate of disappearance of A, reaction $\frac{-d[A]}{dt}$ is equal to $+\frac{2}{3}\frac{d[B]}{dt}$.

Statement II For reaction, $N_2(g) + 3H_2(g) \longrightarrow 2NH_3(g)$

The relationship between $\frac{d[NH_3]}{dt}$ and $\frac{-d[N_2]}{dt}$ is $\frac{d[NH_3]}{dt} = \frac{-2d[N_2]}{dt}$.

In the light of the above statements, choose the most appropriate answer from the options given below.

(a) Both Statement I and Statement II are false.
(b) Statement I is true, but Statement II is false.
(c) Statement I is false, but Statement II is true.
(d) Both Statement I and Statement II are true.

5. Consider the reaction, $B + 3D \longrightarrow 4A + 2C$; following reaction rates are given below as:

(i) $\frac{1}{2}\frac{d[C]}{dt} = \frac{-1}{3}\frac{d[D]}{dt}$ (ii) $\frac{-d[A]}{2dt} = \frac{-d[B]}{dt}$

(iii) $\frac{1}{4}\frac{d[A]}{dt} = \frac{-d[B]}{dt}$ (iv) $\frac{-d[C]}{3\,dt} = \frac{d[D]}{dt}$

(v) $-\frac{1}{3}\frac{d[D]}{dt} = \frac{1}{4}\frac{d[A]}{dt}$

How many of them does not express the reaction rate?

(a) 3 (b) 1
(c) 4 (d) 2

6. Rate of reaction in terms of the pressure of the reactant (assume rate as an extensive property) may be expressed in terms of $\frac{dn}{dt}$ as (where, n = number of moles of CH_3CHO)

$$CH_3CHO \longrightarrow CO + CH_4$$

(a) $-\frac{V}{RT}\frac{dp_{CH_3CHO}}{dt}$ (b) $-\frac{1}{RT}\frac{dp_{CH_3CHO}}{dt}$

(c) $-\frac{1}{RTV}\frac{dp_{CH_3CHO}}{dt}$ (d) $\frac{n_{CH_3CHO}}{V}\frac{dp_{CH_3CHO}}{dt}$

7. On increasing the pressure four fold, the rate of the elementary reaction of $2H_2S + O_2 \longrightarrow$ products, would increase

(a) 27 times (b) 4 times
(c) 16 times (d) 64 times

8. The rate of disappearance of SO_2 in the reaction $2SO_2 + O_2 \longrightarrow 2SO_3$ is 1.60×10^{-3} g/L/s then the rate of formation of SO_3 is

(a) 1.28×10^{-3} g/L/s
(b) 2.00×10^{-3} g/L/s
(c) 0.64×10^{-3} g/L/s
(d) 0.80×10^{-3} g/L/s

9. The rate of the reaction, $2NO + Cl_2 \longrightarrow 2NOCl$ is given by the rate equation, rate = $k[NO]^2[Cl_2]$. The value of the rate constant can be increased by

(a) increasing the concentration of NO
(b) increasing the temperature
(c) increasing the concentration of the Cl_2
(d) decreasing the temperature

10. Consider the reaction,

$$N_2(g) + 3H_2(g) \longrightarrow 2NH_3(g)$$

The equality relationship between $\frac{d[NH_3]}{dt}$ and $\frac{-d[H_2]}{dt}$ is

(a) $+\frac{d[NH_3]}{dt} = -\frac{2}{3}\frac{d[H_2]}{dt}$ (b) $+\frac{d[NH_3]}{dt} = +\frac{2}{3}\frac{d[H_2]}{dt}$

(c) $\frac{d[NH_3]}{dt} = -\frac{3d[H_2]}{dt}$ (d) $\frac{d[NH_3]}{dt} = -\frac{1}{3}\frac{d[H_2]}{dt}$

11. Consider the reaction,

$$2N_2O_5 \longrightarrow 4NO_2 + O_2$$

$$\frac{-d}{dt}[N_2O_5] = k[N_2O_5]$$

$$\frac{d[NO_2]}{dt} = k'[N_2O_5]$$

$$\frac{d[O_2]}{dt} = k''[N_2O_5]$$

(i) $k' = 2k$ (ii) $k'' = k$

(iii) $k' = -2k$ (iv) $k'' = \frac{k'}{4}$

(v) $-k' = k$

The number of correct relationship(s) between k, k' and k'' is

(a) 3 (b) 2 (c) 4 (d) 1

12. The rate of formation of SO_3 in the following reaction. $2SO_2 + O_2 \longrightarrow 2SO_3$ is 15 g s^{-1}. The rate of disappearance of O_2 will be

(a) 3 g/s (b) 100 g/s
(c) 5 g/s (d) 2 g/s

13. The average rate and instantaneous rate of a reaction are equal

(a) at the start (b) at the end
(c) in the middle
(d) when two rate have time interval $\Delta t \rightarrow 0$

14. For the reaction,

$$A(g) + 2B(g) \longrightarrow C(g) + D(g)$$

$$\frac{dx}{dt} = k[A][B]^2$$

Initial pressure of A and B are respectively 0.60 atm and 0.80 atm. At a time when pressure of C is 0.20 atm, rate of the reaction, relative to the initial value is

(a) $\frac{1}{6}$ (b) $\frac{1}{48}$ (c) $\frac{1}{4}$ (d) $\frac{1}{24}$

15. Consider the following statements.

Statement I The average rate of a reaction is calculated from the slope of a graph.

Statement II For average rate determination, a graph is plotted between [*c*] (concentration of reactants) versus time (*t*).

In the light of the above statements, choose the most appropriate answer from the options given below.

(a) Both Statement I and Statement II are false.
(b) Statement I is true, but Statement II is false.
(c) Statement I is false, but Statement II is true.
(d) Both Statement I and Statement II are true.

16. Which of the following statement is correct?

(a) Average rate cannot be used to predict the rate of a reaction at a particular instant.
(b) Unit of rate of reaction is concentration^{-1} time^{-1}.
(c) Rate of reaction does not depend upon the experimental conditions such as concentration of reactants, temperature and catalyst.
(d) Average rate does not depends upon the change in concentration of reactants or products and the time taken for that change to occur.

17. Which of the following statements is incorrect?

(a) In gaseous reactions, when the concentration of gases is expressed in terms of their partial pressures (in atm), then unit of the rate equation will be atm s^{-1}.
(b) Average rate does not depends upon the change in concentration of reactants or products.
(c) Change in concentration of reactants is a negative quantity.
(d) The speed of a reaction can be defined as the change in concentration of a reactant or product in unit time.

18. For a certain reaction, the rate = $k[A]^3[B]^2$, when the initial concentration of A is doubled and the initial concentration of B is tripled, then the initial rate would

(a) decrease by a factor of 27.
(b) increase by a factor of 72.
(c) increase by a factor of 84.
(d) decrease by a factor of 72.

Module 2

Rate Law and Rate Expression, Integrated Rate Equations

- Rate Law and Rate Constant
- Characteristics of Rate Constant
- Molecularity of a Reaction
- Order of a Reaction
- Integrated Rate Equations
- Half-Life Period
- Pseudo First Order Reactions

Rate Law and Rate Constant

The rate of a chemical reaction at a given temperature may depend on the concentration of one or more reactants and products.

The representation of rate of reaction in terms of concentration of the reactants is known as **rate law**. It is also called as **rate equation** or **rate expression.**

Consider a general reaction,

$$aA + bB \longrightarrow cC + dD$$

where, a, b, c and d are the stoichiometric coefficients of reactants and products.

The rate expression for this reaction is

$$\text{Rate} \propto [A]^x [B]^y$$

$$\text{Rate} = k[A]^x [B]^y \quad \text{...(i)}$$

k = velocity constant or rate constant.

Here, the exponents x and y may or may not be equal to the stoichiometric coefficients, a and b of the reactants.

Thus, rate law is the expression (based on the law of mass action) in which reaction rate is given in terms of molar concentration of reactants with each term raised to some power, which may or may not be same as the stoichiometric coefficient of the reacting species in a balanced chemical equation.

The equation (i) can also be written as

$$\frac{-d[R]}{dt} = k[A]^x [B]^y$$

This form of equation is known as **differential rate equation.**

Now, if the concentration of each of the reactants involved in the reaction is unity, i.e. $[A] = [B] = 1$, then on substituting these values in the above expression, we get

Rate of reaction $= k \times 1 \times 1 = k$

Thus, the rate constant of reaction at a given temperature may be defined as the rate of the reaction when the concentration of each of the reactants is unity. It is also called as **specific reaction rate.**

Examples of rate law or rate expression

(i) $2NO(g) + O_2(g) \longrightarrow 2NO_2(g)$

(ii) $CHCl_3 + Cl_2 \longrightarrow CCl_4 + HCl$

(iii) $CH_3COOC_2H_5 + H_2O \longrightarrow CH_3COOH + C_2H_5OH$

Experimental rate expression

$\text{Rate} = k[NO]^2[O_2]$

$\text{Rate} = k[CHCl_3][Cl_2]^{1/2}$

$\text{Rate} = k[CH_3COOC_2H_5]^1[H_2O]^0$

Thus, rate law for an reaction cannot be predicted by merely looking at the balanced chemical equation, i.e. theoretically but must be determined experimentally.

Characteristics of Rate Constant

- It is a characteristic constant for a reaction at a given temperature. For a reaction, higher value of k indicates higher rate of reaction.
- It is independent of concentration of reactants and time taken in reaction.
- Different reactions have different value of k.
- The rate law may not depend on the concentration of every reactant or product of the reaction.
- Value of rate constant depends upon temperature and catalyst.
  - It increases with increase in temperature for endothermic reaction as well as exothermic reaction.
  - Positive catalyst increases the rate constant while negative catalyst decreases the rate constant.
  - Quantitative dependence of temperature and catalyst can be given by Arrhenius equation.

NEET Close-up

Example Similar to PYQ Asked in NEET 2022

For a first order reaction, $A \longrightarrow$ Products, initial concentration of A is 0.5 M, which becomes 0.005 M after 10 minutes. Rate constant for the reaction in min^{-1} is

(a) 0.3512 (b) 0.2342
(c) 0.5310 (d) 0.4606

Sol. (*d*) Given,

Initial concentration $[A]_0 = 0.5$ M

Conc. after 10 min $[A]_t = 0.005$ M

Using rate constant formula for Ist order reaction,

$$k = \frac{2.303}{t} \log \left(\frac{A_0}{A_t}\right)$$

$$= \frac{2.303}{t} \log \left(\frac{0.5}{0.005}\right)$$

$$k = \frac{2.303}{10} \times 2 = 0.4606$$

Skill Builder

For the first order reaction $A \longrightarrow$ Products, initial concentration of A is 0.43 M, which becomes 0.0043 M after 20 min. Rate constant for the reaction in min^{-1} is

(a) 0.23 (b) 0.64
(c) 0.56 (d) 0.60

For more Practice Refer to Q. 16 of Gearing up for NEET.

Unit of Rate Constant

Since, the dimension of rate is concentration/time and the SI units for concentration are mol m^{-3}, mol dm^{-3}, or mol L^{-1} and second (s) for time.

Let us consider a hypothetical reaction,

$$nA \longrightarrow \text{Product}$$

$$\text{Rate} = k[A]^n; \; k = \frac{\text{Rate}}{[A]^n}$$

Thus, the dimension of k is equal to

$$\frac{\text{concentration / time}}{[\text{concentration}]^n} = [\text{concentration}]^{1-n}[\text{time}]^{-1}$$

$$= \left[\frac{\text{mol}}{\text{L}}\right]^{1-n} s^{-1}$$

where, n = order of reaction.

Concept ladder

For gaseous reactions, concentrations are expressed in terms of pressure in the unit of atmosphere. Thus, the rate has the unit of atm per second.

Differences between Rate of Reaction and Rate Constant

Rate of reaction	Rate constant
It is the speed with which reactants are converted into products.	It is the proportionality constant in the rate law.
It is measured as the rate of reaction decrease in the concentration of reactants or increase in the concentrations, of products with time.	It is equal to the rate of reaction when the concentrations of reactants are unity.
It depends upon the initial concentrations of reactants or products.	It is independent of the initial concentrations of reactants or products.
Its unit is always mol L^{-1} $time^{-1}$.	Its unit depend upon the order (n) of reaction as, $(\text{conc.})^{1-n}$ $time^{-1}$ or $(\text{mol/L})^{1-n}$ $time^{-1}$.

Molecularity of a Reaction

It is defined as the number of reacting species molecules, atom or radicals, that participate in an elementary reaction or in the slowest step of a complex reaction which must collide simultaneously in order to bring about a chemical reaction.

Depending on the number of participating molecules, the reaction can be unimolecular, bimolecular, trimolecular, etc.

Reactions (Elementary)	No. of participating molecule(s)	Molecularity
$N_2O_4 \longrightarrow 2NO$	One molecule	1 (Unimolecular)
$H_2 + I_2 \longrightarrow 2HI$	Two molecule	2 (Bimolecular)
$2SO_2 + O_2 \longrightarrow 2SO_3$	Three molecule	3 (Trimolecular)

Characteristics of Molecularity of Reaction

- It is a theoretical concept.
- It is always a whole number, i.e. molecularity can not be zero, negative and fractional.

- Molecularity greater than three is rare because more than three molecules may not mutually collide with each other.
- For complex reactions which occur in many steps, the number of particles that collide in a particular steps is called molecularity of that step. Overall molecularity of complete reaction has no significance in multiple step reactions.

Order of a Reaction

The order of a reaction is equal to the number of reacting molecules whose concentration shows observable change during course of reaction.

- Sum of powers of concentration terms involved in experimental rate law expression becomes equal to order of reaction(n).
- Consider a reaction : $aA + bB \longrightarrow$ product, its experimental rate law expression is $r = k[A]^x[B]^y$
order with respect to $A = x$
order with respect to $B = y$
overall order of reaction $= x + y$

Characteristics of Order of Reaction

- It is an experimentally determined quantity. It cannot be calculated by balanced form of reaction.
- It may be zero, fractional, positive and negative but infinite and imaginary values of order of reaction are not possible.
- For elementary reaction (simple or single step reaction) order and molecularity remain same.
- For complex multiple step reactions, order of reaction is meant for the reaction and not for its individual steps.
- Order is decided by reaction mechanism. Slowest step is used to write experimental rate expression, called **rate determining step** (rds).
- If a reactant is taken in excess in a complex reaction then order with respect to it becomes zero.

NEET Snapshot

The overall order of the reaction : $X + Y_2 \longrightarrow 2XY$ will be given by the slowest step in the reaction mechanism, i.e. $X + Y_2 \rightleftharpoons XY + Y$ ***[NEET 2017]***

The slowest step in a reaction mechanism is called as rate determining step (RDS) as it effectively limits the overall rate of a reaction, thus is responsible for determining overall order of a complex reaction.

Differences Between Molecularity and Order of Reactions

Molecularity	Order
The number of reacting species which must collide simultaneously in order to bring about a chemical reaction is called molecularity of a reaction.	The sum of powers of the concentrations of the reactants in the rate law expression is called the order of the chemical reaction.
Molecularity is always a whole number value.	Order of reaction may be zero, whole number or fractional values and even negative.
Molecularity is a theoretical concept.	Order of reaction is determined experimentally.
Molecularity is applicable to elementary reaction only. For complex reactions, it has no meaning.	Order of reaction is applicable to elementary as well as complex reactions.
For elementary reactions, molecularity can be obtained from the stoichiometry of the equations.	For simple reactions, order of reaction may not be equal to the number of molecules of the reactants as seen from the balanced equation.

Example 4 *The gas-phase reaction of nitric oxide and bromine yield nitrosyl bromide.*

$$2NO(g) + Br_2(g) \longrightarrow 2NOBr(g)$$

The rate law is, rate $= k[NO]^2[Br_2]$

Calculate the reaction order with respect to each of the reactants and what is the overall reaction order?

Sol. Rate law is, rate $= k[NO]^2[Br_2]$

hence, w.r.t NO, order $= 2$ and w.r.t Br_2, order $= 1$

Overall reaction order $= 2 + 1 = 3$

Example 5

(i) *If concentrations of A and B are expressed in terms of mol dm^{-3} and time in min, calculate the unit for the rate constant for the following elementary reaction.*

$$A + B \longrightarrow AB$$

(ii) *What is the unit for a zero order reaction? (Concentrations are expressed in mol L^{-1} and time in seconds).*

Sol. (i) For the reaction,

$$A + B \longrightarrow AB$$

$$\text{Rate} = k[A][B],\ n = 1 + 1 = 2$$

The rate is change in concentration with time. The time and concentration are expressed in min and mol dm^{-3} respectively.

$$k = (\text{mol dm}^{-3})^{1-n}(\text{min}^{-1})$$

or $$= (\text{mol dm}^{-3})^{-1}(\text{min}^{-1})$$

$$= \mathbf{mol^{-1}\ dm^3 min^{-1}}$$

(ii) For zero order ($n = 0$) reaction, the rate is independent of the concentration:

$$\text{Rate} = k \Rightarrow (\text{mol}^{-1}\text{L})^{1-n}(\text{s}^{-1})$$

$\therefore$ Unit of $k = \textbf{mol L}^{-1}\textbf{s}^{-1}$

Integrated Rate Equations

It is difficult to determine the rate law and the order of reaction using differential rate equation. This is because, it is not always covenient to determine the instantaneous rate, as it is measured by determination of slope of the tangent at point '*t*' in concentration *vs* time plot.

Thus, we can integrate the differential rate equation to give a relation between concentrations at different times and rate constant.

The integrated rate equations are different for the reactions of different reaction orders.

1. Zero Order Reaction

The reaction in which rate of reaction is directly proportional to the zero power of product of concentrations of reactants, is known as zero order reaction.

For the reaction, $A \longrightarrow$ Product

	A	Product
At $t = 0$	a	0
At $t = dt$	$a - x$	x

$$\therefore \quad [A]_0 = a$$
$$[A] = a - x$$
$$\text{Rate} = -\frac{d[A]}{dt} = k[A]^0 = k$$

or
$$\frac{dx}{dt} = k$$

- Since, the rate is independent of concentration, the plot of rate *versus* concentration will be a straight line parallel to the concentration axis.
- Integrated rate equation,

$$-\frac{d[A]}{dt} = k[A]^0 = k$$

Integrating both sides,

$$-\int d[A] = k\int dt$$

Assume $[A] = [A]_0$ at $t = 0$

and $[A] = [A]_t$ at time t

$$\therefore \quad -[A]_t = kt + I \qquad \text{...(i)}$$

I = Integration constant

If $t = 0$, $[A]_t = [A]_0$

$$\therefore \quad -[A]_0 = I$$

Substituting the value of I in equation (i)

$$\therefore \quad -[A]_t = kt - [A]_0$$
$$\therefore \quad [A]_0 - [A]_t = kt$$

$\therefore$ For zero order reaction,

$$[A]_t = [A]_0 - kt \qquad \text{...(ii)}$$

Since,
$$[A]_0 - [A]_t = x$$
$$x = kt$$
$$k = \frac{x}{t}$$

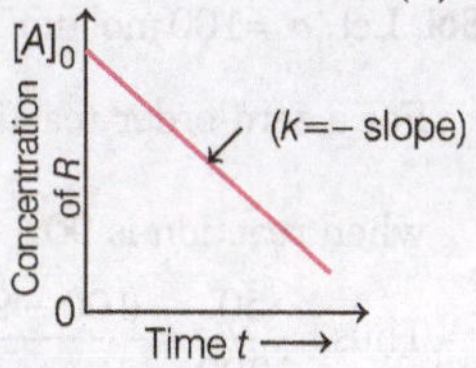

Graphically, equation (ii) is represented as given slope $= -k$ (rate constant) and intercept equal to $[A]_0$.

- Some examples of zero order reactions are

(a) $$2NH_3(g) \xrightarrow[1130\,K]{Pt} N_2(g) + 3H_2(g)$$

$$\text{Rate} = k[NH_3]^0 = k$$

In this reaction, Pt is a catalyst. At very high pressure, the metal surface gets saturated with gas molecules and any further change in experimental conditions has no effect on concentration of NH_3 on the surface of the catalyst and rate remains independent of $[NH_3]$.

(b) $$H_2(g) + Cl_2(g) \xrightarrow{h\nu} 2HCl$$

(c) $$2HI \xrightarrow{Gold} H_2 + I_2$$

- Unit of rate constant, $k = \left(\frac{\text{mol}}{\text{L}}\right)\frac{1}{\text{s}} = \text{mol L}^{-1}\text{s}^{-1}$
- **Half-life time period** ($t_{1/2}$) The time required to reduce the concentration of the reactant to half of its initial value is called half-life time period. It is denoted by ($t_{1/2}$).

For zero order reaction, if concentration of product is $\frac{[A]_0}{2}$ at time $t_{1/2}$ then

$$k = -\frac{[A]_0 - [A]_t}{t} = \frac{[A_0] - \left[\frac{A_0}{2}\right]}{t_{1/2}}$$

$$\boxed{t_{1/2} = \frac{[A]_0}{2k}} \qquad \text{...(v)}$$

Therefore, $t_{1/2}$ for zero order reaction is directly proportional to the initial concentration of the reactant.

Mentor's TiP

- Rate of zero order reaction does not depend upon the concentration of the reactant.
- The unit of rate and rate constant for zero order reactions are same.
- Zero order reaction for 100% completion takes two half-life.

$$\boxed{t_{100\%} = 2t_{50\%}}$$

$t_{1/2}$ is also written as $t_{50\%}$.

Example 6 *A zero order reaction is 50% completed in 20 minutes. How much time will it take to complete 90%?*

Sol. Let, $a = 100 \text{ mol dm}^{-3}$.

For a zero-order reaction, $k = \frac{x}{t} = \frac{(100-50)\,(\text{mol dm}^{-3})}{20 \times 60\ (\text{s})}$

when reaction is 90% complete, $x = 90$. Therefore,

Thus, $\frac{50}{1200} = \frac{(100-90)}{t}$

or $t = \frac{10 \times 1200}{50} = 240 \text{ s} = 4 \text{ min}$

NEET Close-up

Example Similar to PYQ Asked in NEET 2020

The half-life for a zero order reaction having 0.05 M initial concentration of reactant is 150 s. The rate constant (in $\text{mol L}^{-1}\text{s}^{-1}$) for the reaction is

(a) 1.57×10^{-5} (b) 1.67×10^{-4} (c) 1.72×10^{-4} (d) 1.38×10^{-5}

Sol. (*b*) For a zero order reaction,

$$t_{1/2} = \frac{1}{k} \times \frac{[A]_0}{2}$$

$$k = \frac{[A]_0}{2 \times t_{1/2}} = \frac{0.05 \text{ M}}{2 \times 150 \text{ s}}$$

$$= 0.000166 \text{ Ms}^{-1}$$

$$= 1.67 \times 10^{-4} \text{ mol L}^{-1}\text{ s}^{-1}$$

Skill Builder

The half-life for a zero-order reaction having 0.061 M initial concentration of reactant is 200 s. The rate constant (in $\text{mol L}^{-1}\text{ s}^{-1}$) for the reaction is

(a) 2.37×10^{-6} (b) 1.71×10^{-3}

(c) 1.52×10^{-4} (d) 1.81×10^{-2}

For more Practice Refer to Q. 12 of Step up practice-2 and Q. 9, 10 of Gearing up for NEET.

2. First Order Reaction

A reaction is said to be of first order if its rate is determined by the change of one concentration term only. It means rate is directly proportional to the concentration of one reactant raised to first order.

Consider a hypothetical equation,

	A	$\longrightarrow$ Product
Concentration at $t = 0$	$a = [A]_0$	0
Concentration at $t = t$	$(a-x) = [A]_t$	x

where, a or $[A]_0$ is the concentration of 'A' at initial time and $(a-x)$ or $[A]_t$ is the concentration of 'A' after time t.

∴ Differential rate equation can be written as,

$$\therefore \quad -\frac{dx}{dt} = k(a-x)$$

or $$-\frac{d[A]}{dt} = k[A]_t \quad \text{...(i)}$$

- Integrated rate equation is

$$k = \frac{2.303}{t}\log_{10}\frac{a}{(a-x)}$$

or $$k = \frac{2.303}{t}\log\frac{[A]_0}{[A]_t} \quad \text{...(ii)}$$

- Some examples of first order reaction

$$2N_2O_5 \longrightarrow 4NO_2 + O_2$$

$$SO_2Cl_2 \longrightarrow SO_2 + Cl_2$$

Concept ladder All natural and artificial radioactive decay of unstable nuclei take place by first order kinetics.

$${}^{226}_{88}\text{Ra} \longrightarrow {}^{4}_{2}\text{He} + {}^{222}_{86}\text{Rn}$$

- Unit of rate constant for first order reaction is **time^{-1}**, i.e. **s^{-1}**.
- For a typical 1st order gas phase reaction,

$$A(g) \longrightarrow B(g) + C(g)$$

Let p_i be the initial pressure of A and p_t the total pressure at time 't'. Integrated rate equation for such a reaction is given by

$$k = \frac{2.303}{t}\log\frac{p_i}{2p_i - p_t}$$

- Since, the rate directly depends upon the concentration, the plot of rate *versus* concentration will be a straight line passing through the origin.
- If $\log_{10}(a-x)$ is plotted against time t, a straight line is obtained with slope $\frac{-k}{2.303}$ and intercept $\log a$.

$$\Rightarrow \quad \log\frac{a-x}{a} = -\frac{kt}{2.303}$$

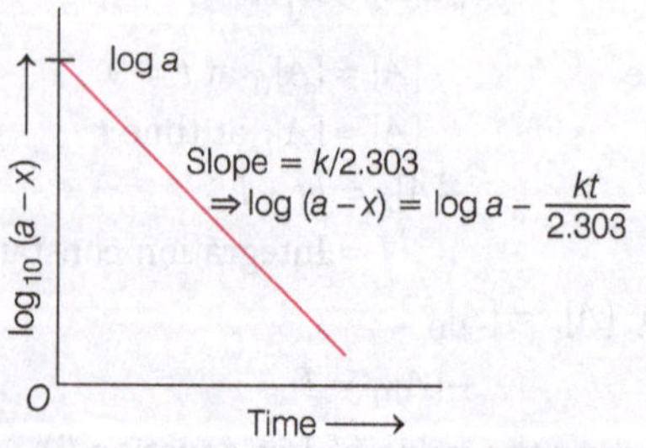

Plot of log $(a-x)$ *vs* time for a first order reaction

- If initial concentration of the reactant is not known, rate constant k can be derived by taking its concentration at two time intervals.

  Let $[A]_1 = (a - x_1)$ = concentration of A at time t_1

  $[A]_2 = (a - x_2)$ = concentration of A at time t_2

$$\therefore \quad \frac{kt_2}{2.303} = \log_{10} a - \log_{10}(a - x_2)$$

$$\frac{kt_1}{2.303} = \log_{10} a - \log_{10}(a - x_1)$$

$$\therefore \quad k = \frac{2.303}{(t_2 - t_1)} \log \frac{(a - x_1)}{(a - x_2)}$$

$$k = \frac{2.303}{(t_2 - t_1)} \log \frac{[A]_1}{[A]_2}$$

- **Half-life period** $(t_{1/2})$ From the definition of half-life period, $t = t_{1/2}$, then $(a - x) = \frac{a}{2}$, putting this value in rate equation.

  For first order, we get

$$t_{1/2} = \frac{2.303}{k} \log\left(\frac{a}{a - (a/2)}\right) = \frac{2.303}{k} \log 2$$

$$\boxed{t_{1/2} = \frac{0.693}{k}}$$

Mentor's TiP

- Half-life of first order reaction does not depend upon initial concentration of reactant.
- First order reaction for 100% completion takes infinite half-lives.
- First order reaction for 99.9% completion takes ten half-lives.

Example 7 *A first order reaction is 20% complete in 10 minutes. Calculate the time for 75% completion of the reaction.* [log 2 = 0.3]

Sol. For the first order reaction,

$$k = \frac{2.303}{t} \log \frac{[A]_0}{[A]}$$

If $[A]_0 = a, [A] = a - \frac{a \times 20}{100} = 0.80\,a, t = 10$ min

$$\therefore \quad k = \frac{2.303}{10} \log \frac{a}{0.80a} = \frac{2.303}{10} \log \frac{10}{8}$$

$$= \frac{2.303}{10} \times (1 - 3 \times 0.3)$$

$$= 2.303 \times 10^{-2}\ \text{min}^{-1}$$

$\Rightarrow$ For first order reaction,

$$t_{75} = 2 \times t_{50} = 2 \times \frac{0.693}{k}$$

$$= \frac{2 \times (2.303 \times \log 2)}{2.303 \times 10^{-2}} = 60\ \text{min}$$

Example 8 *A first order reaction has a rate constant of $15 \times 10^{-3}\ s^{-1}$. Calculate the time taken by 5.0 g of reactants to reduce to 3.0 g.* [log 2 = 0.30, log 3 = 0.47]

Sol. From first order equation,

$$t = \frac{2.303}{k} \log \frac{a}{a - x}$$

Given, $k = 15 \times 10^{-3}\ s^{-1}, a = 5\,g, (a - x) = 3\,g$

$$\Rightarrow \quad t = \frac{2.303}{15 \times 10^{-3} s^{-1}} \log \frac{5}{3} = \frac{2.303}{15 \times 10^{-3}} \log \frac{10}{6}$$

$$t = \frac{2.303}{15 \times 10^{-3}} \times (1 - 0.3 - 0.47) = 35.3\ s$$

Example 9 *Calculate the half-life period of a first order reaction where the specific reaction rate is*

(i) $200\ s^{-1}$ (ii) $2\ \text{min}^{-1}$ (iii) $5\ \text{yr}^{-1}$

Sol. For the first order reaction,

$$t_{1/2} = \frac{0.693}{k}$$

(i) $k = 200\ s^{-1}$

$$\therefore \quad t_{1/2} = \frac{0.693}{200} = 3.465 \times 10^{-3}\ s$$

(ii) $k = 2\ \text{min}^{-1}$

$$\therefore \quad t_{1/2} = \frac{0.693}{2} = 0.3465\ \text{min}$$

(iii) $k = 5\ \text{yr}^{-1}$

$$\therefore \quad t_{1/2} = \frac{0.693}{5} = 0.1386\ \text{yr}$$

Pseudo First Order Reactions

In reactions with order one or two, generally, the molecularity and order of reaction is same. But in pseudo first order reactions values of order and molecularity are not same. e.g.

- Hydrolysis of methylacetate in presence of dilute HCl.

$$CH_3COOCH_3 + H_2O \xrightarrow[(H_3O^+)]{\text{Dil. HCl}} CH_3COOH + CH_3OH$$

  Here, the stoichiometric equation shows that it is a bimolecular reaction and its order must also be two, i.e. rate of reaction must be

$$\frac{dx}{dt} = k'[CH_3COOCH_3][H_2O]$$

But experiments showed that this reaction obeys first order rate equation, although two molecules are taking part in reaction. This can be explained by the fact that here H_2O is in excess, hence the changes in concentration of water is negligible and its concentration remains nearly constant.

So, the rate of reaction depends only on the concentration of ester, and rate of reaction is one

$$\frac{dx}{dt} = k[CH_3COOCH_3]$$

$\therefore \quad [H_2O] = \text{constant}$

This reaction is thus, pseudo first order or pseudo unimolecular reaction.

- Inversion of cane sugar takes place according to the reaction :

$$\underset{\text{Sucrose}}{C_{12}H_{22}O_{11}} + H_2O \xrightarrow{\text{Dil. HCl}} \underset{\text{Glucose}}{C_6H_{12}O_6} + \underset{\text{Fructose}}{C_6H_{12}O_6}$$

Here, two molecules are taking part in the reaction and is bimolecular, but experiments show that it is a first order reaction.

As water is in excess, rate of reaction depends only on the concentration of sucrose.

$$\frac{dx}{dt} = k[C_{12}H_{22}O_{11}]$$

This is also a pseudo first order reaction.

For zero order	For first order

(a) Plot of rate of reaction *vs* concentration

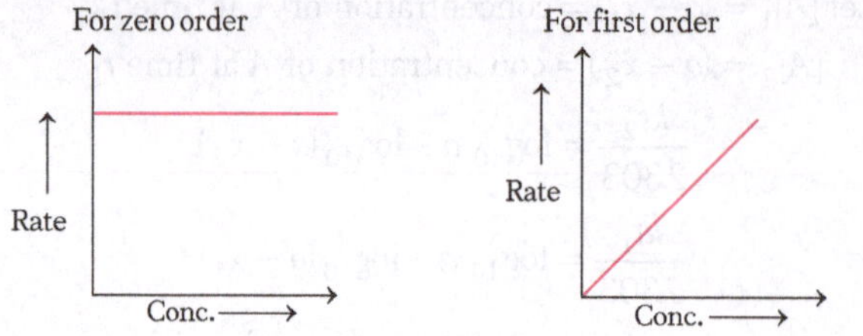

(b) Plot from integrated rate equations

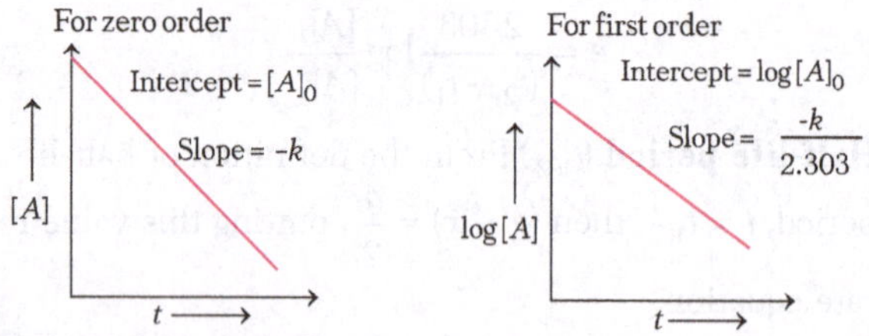

(c) Plot of half-life *vs* initial concentration

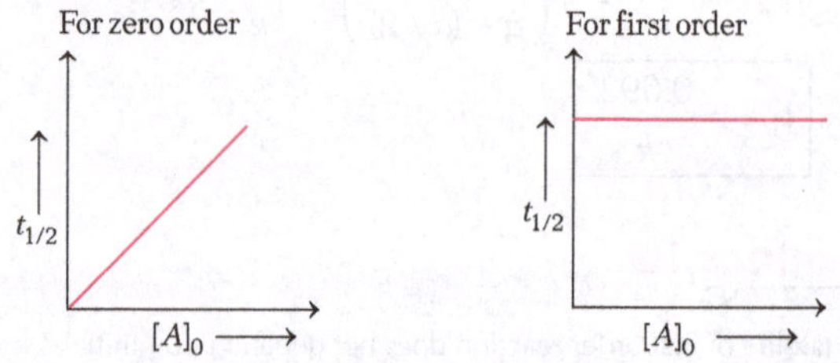

STEP UP Practice 2

1. The rate law for the reaction,
$RCl + NaOH \longrightarrow ROH + NaCl$ is given by, Rate $= k[RCl]$.
The rate of the reaction will be
(a) doubled on decreasing the concentration of sodium hydroxide.
(b) halved on reducing the concentration of alkyl halide to one half.
(c) decreased on increasing the temperature of the reaction.
(d) unaffected by increasing the temperature of the reaction.

2. Consider the following statements.
Statement I In rate laws, the exponents for concentration do not necessarily match the stoichiometric coefficients.
Statement II It is the mechanism and not the balanced chemical equation for the overall change that governs the reaction rate.
In the light of the above statements, choose the most appropriate answer from the options given below.
(a) Both Statement I and Statement II are false.
(b) Statement I is true, but Statement II is false.
(c) Statement I is false, but Statement II is true.
(d) Both Statement I and Statement II are true.

3. Which of the following is not a correct statement?
(a) Rate law can be deduced from the stoichiometry of the reaction.
(b) The representation of rate of reaction in terms of concentration of the reactants is known as rate law.
(c) Rate law for any reaction cannot be predicted by merely looking at the balanced chemical equation.
(d) Rate law is also called as rate equation or rate expression.

4. Consider an elementary reaction, $aG + bH \longrightarrow$ Products. When concentrations of both the reactants G and H are doubled, the rate increases by eight times. However, when concentration of G is doubled keeping the concentration of H fixed, the rate is doubled. The overall order of the reaction is
(a) 0 (b) 1 (c) 2 (d) 3

5. If in the fermentation of sugar in an enzymatic solution that is initially 0.12 M the concentration of the sugar is reduced to 0.06 M in 10 h and to 0.03 M in 20 h, then, order of the reaction is
(a) 0 (b) 1 (c) 2 (d) 3

6. Which of the following statements is not correct about order of a reaction?
(a) It can be a fractional number.
(b) It is an experimentally determined quantity.
(c) It is always equal to the sum of the stoichiometric coefficients of reactants in the balanced chemical equation for a reaction.
(d) The order of a reaction is the sum of the powers of molar concentration of the reactants in the rate law expression.

7. Which of the following is the not a correct match for the unit of rate constant?
(a) Zero order $\longrightarrow$ mol L^{-1} s^{-1}
(b) First order $\longrightarrow$ s^{-1}
(c) Second order $\longrightarrow$ mol^{-1} L^{-1} s^{-1}
(d) Third order $\longrightarrow$ mol^{-2} L^2 s^{-1}

8. Consider the following statements.
Statement I Order and molecularity of a reaction are not always same.
Statement II Order is determined experimentally and molecularity is the sum of the stoichiometric coefficient of rate determining elementary step.
In the light of the above statements, choose the most appropriate answer from the options given below.
(a) Both Statement I and Statement II are false.
(b) Statement I is true, but Statement II is false.
(c) Statement I is false, but Statement II is true.
(d) Both Statement I and Statement II are true.

9. Which of the following is the correct match for a given rate law expression, $r = k[A]^{3/2}[B]^{-1}$?
(a) Order of a reaction $\longrightarrow \frac{3}{2}$
(b) Order of a reaction $\longrightarrow$ Zero
(c) Order of a reaction $\longrightarrow \frac{1}{2}$
(d) Order of a reaction $\longrightarrow \frac{5}{2}$

10. For a reaction following first-order kinetics, which of the following statement is correct?
(a) The time taken for the completion of 50% of the reaction is called half-life period.
(b) A plot of the reciprocal of the concentration of the reactants against time gives a straight line.
(c) The degree of dissociation is equal to $1 + e^{-kt}$.
(d) A plot of $\frac{[A]_0}{[A]}$ *versus* time gives a straight line.

11. Which of the following is not a correct match for zero order reaction where x is concentration and t is time?
(a) Zero order reaction $\longrightarrow \left(\frac{dx}{dt}\right) = k[A]^0$
(b) Zero order reaction $\longrightarrow x = kt$
(c) Zero order reaction $\longrightarrow \log x = \log t + \log k$
(d) Zero order reaction $\longrightarrow \frac{1}{x} = \frac{1}{t} + \frac{1}{k}$

12. The half-life for a zero-order reaction having 0.2 M initial concentration of reactant is 80s. The rate constant (in mol $L^{-1}s^{-1}$) for the reaction is
(a) 1.25×10^{-3} (b) 228×10^{-3}
(c) 1.45×10^{-3} (d) 1.85×10^{-3}

13. Consider the following graphical representations.

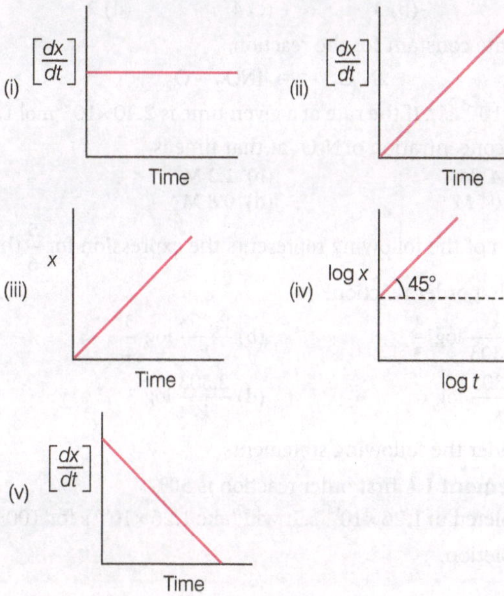

How many of them is (are) correct graphical representation(s) for the zero order reaction?
(a) 1 (b) 2 (c) 4 (d) 3

14. The half-life period for a zero order reaction is
(a) proportional to initial concentration
(b) independent of initial concentration
(c) inversely proportional to initial concentration
(d) inversely proportional to the square of the initial concentration

15. For the reaction, $A(g) \longrightarrow B(g) + C(g)$
rate law is $-\frac{d[A]}{dt} = k[A]$
At the start, pressure is 100 mm Hg and after 10 min, pressure is 120 mm Hg. Hence, rate constant (min^{-1}) is
(a) $\frac{2.303}{10}\log\frac{6}{5}$ (b) $\frac{2.303}{10}\log 5$
(c) $\frac{2.303}{10}\log\frac{5}{4}$ (d) $\frac{2.303}{10}\log\frac{5}{6}$

16. A reaction of first order completed 90% in 90 min, hence, it is completed 50% in approximately
(a) 50 min
(b) 54 min
(c) 27 min
(d) 62 min

17. Consider the following reactions.
(i) $2H_2O_2 \longrightarrow 2H_2O + O_2$

(ii) 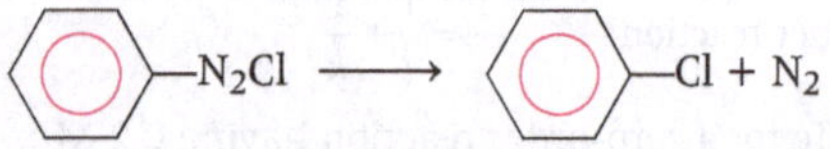

(iii) $CH_3COOC_2H_5 + H_2O \longrightarrow CH_3COOH + C_2H_5OH$
(iv) $CH_3COOC_2H_5 + NaOH \longrightarrow CH_3COONa + C_2H_5OH$
(v) $2N_2O_5 \xrightarrow{CCl_4} 4NO_2 + O_2$

How many of them is/are not first order reaction(s)?
(a) 1 (b) 3 (c) 4 (d) 2

18. The rate constant for the reaction,

$$2N_2O_5 \longrightarrow 4NO_2 + O_2$$

is 3×10^{-5} s^{-1}. If the rate at a given time is 2.40×10^{-5} mol L^{-1} s^{-1}, then concentration of N_2O_5 at that time is
(a) 1.4 M (b) 1.2 M
(c) 0.04 M (d) 0.8 M

19. Which of the following represents the expression for $\frac{5}{6}$ th life of a first order reaction?
(a) $\frac{k}{2.303} \log \frac{4}{3}$ (b) $\frac{2.303}{k} \log \frac{3}{4}$
(c) $\frac{2.303}{k} \log 6$ (d) $\frac{2.303}{k} \log 3$

20. Consider the following statements.
Statement I A first order reaction is 50% completed in 1.26×10^{14} s. It will take 1.26×10^{15} s for 100% completion.
Statement II Half-life period of first order reaction is 10 min. Starting with 10 mol L^{-1}, then rate after 20 min is 0.0693×2.5 min^{-1}.

In the light of the above statements, choose the most appropriate answer from the options given below.
(a) Both Statement I and Statement II are false.
(b) Statement I is true, but Statement II is false.
(c) Statement I is false, but Statement II is true.
(d) Both Statement I and Statement II are true.

21. The ratio $t_{7/8} : t_{1/2}$ for the first order reaction is
(a) 3 (b) 5
(c) 2 (d) 7

22. The rate of a first order reaction is 0.04 mol L^{-1} s^{-1} at 10 min and 0.03 mol L^{-1} s^{-1} at 20 min. Thus, half-life of the reaction is
(a) 24.1 min
(b) 34.8 min
(c) 50.1 min
(d) 48.2 min

23. For the reaction, $H_2(g) + Br_2(g) \longrightarrow 2HBr(g)$, the reaction rate $= k[H_2][Br_2]^{1/2}$. Which statement is correct about this reaction?
(a) The reaction is of second order.
(b) Molecularity of the reaction is $\frac{3}{2}$.
(c) The unit of k is s^{-1}.
(d) Molecularity of the reaction is 2.

24. Which of the following statements is not correct about molecularity of a reaction ?
(a) It can be obtained from balanced chemical equation.
(b) It can be more than three, which is very common.
(c) It cannot be fractional.
(d) It may or may not be equal to the order of reaction.

Module 3

Theories of Reaction Rate and Effect of Temperature and Catalyst on it

- Collision Theory
- Effect of Temperature and Catalyst on Reaction Rate
- Transition State Theory
- Arrhenius Equation

Theories of Reaction Rate

Following theories are given to explain the rate of reaction.

Collision Theory

Collision theory was developed by Max-Trautz and William Lewis in 1916-18 which provides a greater insight into the energetic and mechanism aspects of reactions. It is based on kinetic theory of gases.

The fundamental aspect of the collision theory of reaction rates is that for reaction to occur, reacting species like, molecules, atoms or ions must collide first. Increased concentrations of reacting species result in greater number of collisions per unit time. However, not all collisions result in reaction, i.e. not all collisions are effective collisions.

The number of collisions per second per unit volume of the reaction mixture is known as collision frequency (Z).

Factors affecting effective collisions,

(i) For a collision to be effective, the reacting species must

(a) **possess at least a certain minimum energy, i.e. threshold energy** which is defined as the minimum amount of energy which the colliding molecules must possess so as to make the chemical reaction to take place.

(b) **have proper orientation towards each other at the time of collision** If colliding molecules have improper orientations, they do not react even though they may possess sufficient energy.

We know that, the average kinetic energy of a collection of molecules is proportional to the absolute temperature. At high temperatures, more molecules possess sufficient energy to react.

Reaction, $NO + N_2O \longrightarrow NO_2 + N_2$

(ii) The minimum additional energy required by the molecule to attain threshold energy is called **activation energy**, which is required by the species during collision as a result of interchange of energies.

$$E_a = E_{(\text{threshold energy})} - E_{(\text{reactants})}$$

The fraction of collisions (f) with an energy equal to or greater than the activation energy E_a is given as,

$$f = e^{-E_a/RT}$$

where, $e^{-E_a/RT}$ is called **Boltzmann factor.**

The fraction of collisions having proper orientation for conversion of reactants to products is called the **probability or steric factor, P.**

For the reaction, $A + BC \longrightarrow AB + C$, the value of P is expected to be about 0.5 because A has a nearly 50 : 50 probability of colliding with each of B and C, of BC.

Collision rate $= Z_{AB}[A][BC]$

where, Z_{AB} is a constant related to **collision frequency** (in the unit of $M^{-1}\ s^{-1}$)

and reaction rate $= P \times$ collision rate $\times f$

$$= PZ_{AB}[A][B] \times f$$

Thus, rate constant, $k = PZ_{AB}f = PZ_{AB}e^{-E_a/RT}$

Thus, in collision theory, activation energy and proper orientation of the molecules together determine the criteria for an effective collision and hence rate of a chemical reaction.

NEET Snapshot

Out of heat of reaction, threshold energy, collision frequency and activation energy only collision frequency changes whenever there is an increase in concentration of the reactant. ***[NEET 2020]***

Collision frequency is the number of collisions per second per unit volume of reaction mixture. Thus, it involves a concentration term. Hence, it varies directly with the concentration of reactant. While other do not involve any concentration terms hence posses no effect.

Collision theory also has certain drawbacks as it considers atoms/molecules to be hard spheres and ignores their structural aspect.

Transition State Theory

To occur the reaction, some covalent bonds must break so that others can be formed. This can occur only if the molecules collide with enough kinetic energy to overcome the stabilisation potential energy of the bond.

The process of conversion of reactant into product (assuming both of the chances : Exothermic and Endothermic) is shown in figure given below.

(i) **Exothermic reaction**

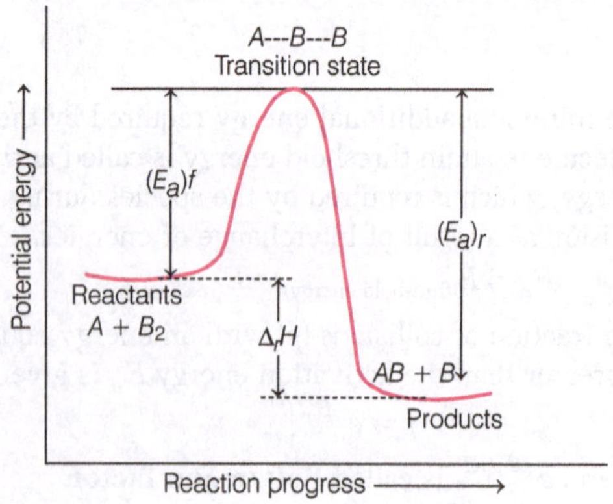

(ii) **Endothermic reaction**

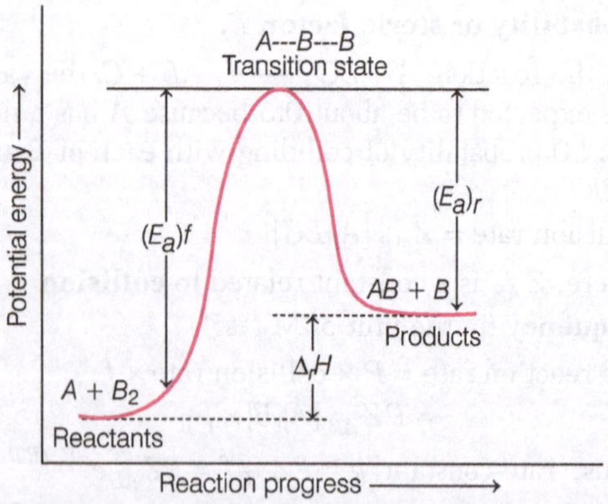

Potential energy profile for the reaction $A + B_2 \longrightarrow AB + B$ showing the energy barrier between the reactants and products.

As the reaction progresses, kinetic energy of the reactants is first converted into potential energy of the transition state and then transformed into kinetic energy of the products. At each point along the profile, the total energy is conserved.

According to the transition state theory,

- The reactants pass through a short-lived, high-energy intermediate state, called a **transition state,** before the products are formed.

$$\underset{\substack{\text{Reactants} \\ A+B_2}}{A+B-B} \longrightarrow \underset{\substack{\text{Transition state} \\ AB_2}}{A\cdots B\cdots B} \longrightarrow \underset{\substack{\text{Products} \\ AB+B}}{A-B+B}$$

- The activation energy E_a is the additional energy that must be absorbed by the reactants in their ground states to allow them to reach the transition state.
- The activated complex is supposed to be in equilibrium with the reactant molecules. This complex though unstable, has a transient existence and its potential energy is maximum. Finally, it decomposes into products.
- If A and B_2 molecules do not possess the necessary amount of energy (E_a), above their ground states when they collide, reaction cannot occur.

  If they possess sufficient energy to "climb the energy barrier" (to reach the transition state), the reaction can proceed. When the atoms go from the transition state arrangement to the product molecules, energy is released. This type of reaction is called **exothermic reaction.**
- If the reaction results in a net absorption of energy, the amount less than E_a is given off when the transition state is converted to products and the reaction is **endothermic**.
- When the reverse reaction occurs, an increase in energy equal to the reverse activation energy, $E_{a(\text{reverse})}$ is required to convert the AB product molecules to the transition state. As you can see from the potential energy diagrams,

$$E_{a(\text{forward})} - E_{a(\text{reverse})} = \Delta H_{\text{reaction}}$$

Effect of Temperature and Catalyst on the Reaction Rate

These are explained as follows

Effect of Temperature

Most of the chemical reactions are accelerated by increase in temperature. It has been found that for a chemical reaction with rise in temperature by 10°C, the rate constant is nearly doubled. The effect of temperature is usually expressed in terms of temperature coefficient. Mathematically,

$$\text{Temperature coefficient } (n) = \frac{\text{Rate constant at } (T+10)^\circ}{\text{Rate constant at } T^\circ}$$

Explanation

At a particular temperature T, all the molecules of reactants do not have the same kinetic energy. Only the fraction of molecules having particular kinetic energies at a particular temperature remains constant. The distribution of kinetic energy may be described by plotting the fraction of molecules (N_E / N_T) with a given kinetic energy (E) *versus* kinetic energy. This is called Maxwell's distributions of energies. Here, N_E is the number of molecules with energy E and N_T is the total number of molecules.

The peak of the curve represents the kinetic energy possessed by the maximum fraction of molecules and is known as **most probable kinetic energy**. Small number of molecules possess either very low or very high kinetic energy. Most of the molecules have intermediate kinetic energies between the highest kinetic energy and the lowest kinetic energy.

On raising temperature, the maxima of the curve shifts to higher kinetic energy value and the curves spreads to the right such that there is a greater proportion of molecules with much higher energies. However, the total area under the curve must be constant, since total probability must be one at all times.

We can determine E_a (activation energy) with the Maxwell Boltzmann distribution curve.

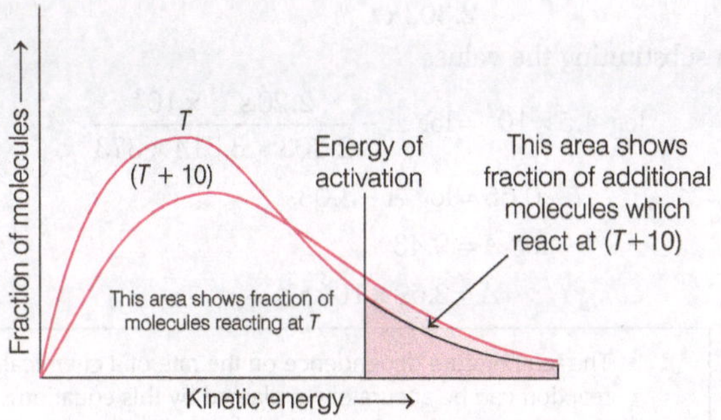

Distribution curve showing temperature dependence of rate of a reaction

Increasing the temperature of the substance increases the fraction of molecules which collide with energies greater than E_a. It is clear from above figure that in the curve at $(T + 10)$, the area showing the fraction of molecules having energy equal to or greater than activation energy gets doubled leading to doubling rate of a reaction.

Arrhenius Equation

Variation of rate constant k with temperature T (K) is given by Arrhenius equation.

It was first proposed by Dutch chemist, J.H. van't Hoff but Arrhenius provided its physical justification and interpretation.

It is based on the two theories of reaction rates, i.e. collision theory and transition state theory.

$$k = Ae^{-E_a/RT} \quad \text{...(i)}$$

where, A is called the Arrehenius factor or frequency factor or the pre-exponential factor.

E_a is an activation energy and $e^{-E_a/RT}$ is referred as Boltzmann factor.

'A' has same unit as the rate constant because, at $T \to \alpha$, $k_{max} = A$. Collectively A and E_a are called the Arrhenius parameters of the reaction.

> **Concept ladder** Activation energy can never be zero. If $E_a = 0$, then according to Arrhenius equation the value of k will become equal to A. A is energy of collision between molecules which leads to a chemical reaction. This can never be true.

Calculation of Activation Energy

Two methods for the calculation of activation energy are given below.

(i) Graphical Method

By taking logarithm on both sides of Eq. (i),

$$\log k = \log_e A - \frac{E_a}{RT}$$

$$\log_{10} k = \log_{10} A - \frac{E_a}{2.303RT} \quad \text{...(ii)}$$

Comparing it with $y = c - mx$

The plot between $\log_{10} k$ and $(1/T)$ is a straight line and is given by

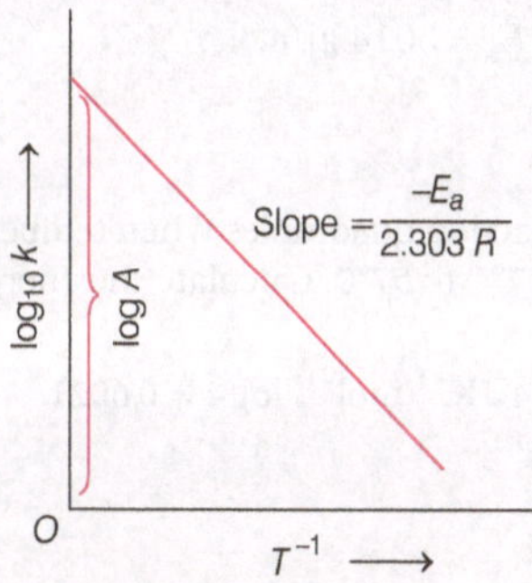

Plot of $\log_{10} k$ *vs* $1/T$

$$\text{Slope} = -\frac{E_a}{2.303R} \text{ (slope has negative value)}$$

The intercept of the line will give the value of log A.

(ii) Experimental Method

Now at temperature T_1 and T_2 rate constants are k_1 and k_2 respectively, hence from Eq. (i) we get

$$\log_{10} k_2 = \log_{10} A - \frac{E_a}{2.303RT_2} \quad \text{...(iii)}$$

and

$$\log_{10} k_1 = \log_{10} A - \frac{E_a}{2.303RT_1} \quad \text{...(iv)}$$

By subtracting Eq. (iv) from Eq. (iii) we get,

$$\therefore \quad \log_{10}\left(\frac{k_2}{k_1}\right) = \frac{E_a}{2.303R}\left[\frac{1}{T_1} - \frac{1}{T_2}\right] \quad \text{[Here, } T_2 > T_1]$$

This relation is used when rate constant at two different temperature are given.

Example 10 *The pre-exponential factor for the free radical addition of chlorine is $2 \times 10^{13}\ s^{-1}$. Find the rate constant of this reaction at STP.*

Sol. For free radical addition reaction, (photochemical reaction)

$$E_a = 0.$$
$$k = Ae^{-E_a/RT} \text{ (if } E_a = 0)$$
$$k = A = 2 \times 10^{13}\ s^{-1}.$$

NEET Close-up

Example Similar to PYQ Asked in NEET 2024

The rate of a reaction tripled when temperature changes from 27°C to 57°C. Calculate the energy of activation.

Given, $R = 8.314\ JK^{-1}mol^{-1}$, $\log 3 = 0.477$

(a) 30.14 kJ mol (b) 3.014 kJ/mol
(c) 301.4 kJ/mol (d) 3014 kJ/mol

Sol. (*a*) Given $\frac{r_2}{r_1} = 3 = \frac{k_2}{k_1}$

Now, $$\log_{10}\left(\frac{k_2}{k_1}\right) = \frac{E_a}{2.303R}\left[\frac{1}{T_1} - \frac{1}{T_2}\right]$$

$$\log_{10}(3) = \frac{E_a \times 1000}{2.303 \times 8.314}\left(\frac{1}{300} - \frac{1}{330}\right)$$

$$E_a = 30.14 \text{ kJ/mol}$$

Skill Builder

The rate of a reaction quadruples when temperature changes from 37°C to 57°C. Calculate the energy of activation.

Given, $R = 8.314\ JK^{-1}\ mol^{-1}$, $\log 4 = 0.6021$

(a) 68.73 kJ/mol
(b) 43.14 kJ/mol
(c) 25.60 kJ/mol
(d) 37.24 kJ/mol

For more practice Refer to Q.15 of Gearing up for NEET.

Example 11 *Calculate the activation energy for a reaction when a change of temperature from 20°C to 30°C exactly triples the reaction rate constant?* [log 3 = 0.477)

Sol. Given, $T_1 = 273 + 20 = 293$ K; $k_1 = k$ (say)

$T_2 = 273 + 30 = 303$ K; $k_2 = 3k$

On substituting these values in the equation,

$$\log\frac{k_2}{k_1} = \frac{E_a}{2.303R}\left(\frac{T_2 - T_1}{T_1T_2}\right), \text{ we get}$$

$$\log\frac{3k}{k} = \frac{E_a}{2.303 \times 8.314}\left(\frac{303 - 293}{303 \times 293}\right)$$

$$\Rightarrow \quad E_a = 81083 \text{ J mol}^{-1}$$

or $$E_a = 81.083 \text{ kJ mol}^{-1}$$

Example 12 *The rate constant values of a reaction are $1.5 \times 10^7\ s^{-1}$ at 50°C and $4.5 \times 10^7\ s^{-1}$ at 100°C. What will be the value of Arrhenius parameters A and E_a?* [log 3 = 0.477, log 4.5 = 0.65, log 1.5 = 0.17, $10^{9.43} = 2.69 \times 10^9$]

Sol. According to Arrhenius equation,

$$\log\frac{k_2}{k_1} = \frac{E_a}{2.303R}\left[\frac{T_2 - T_1}{T_1T_2}\right]$$

$k_1 = 1.5 \times 10^7\ s^{-1}$, $k_2 = 4.5 \times 10^7\ s^{-1}$, $T_1 = 323$ K, $T_2 = 373$ K

Substituting the value in above equation,

$$\log\frac{4.5 \times 10^7}{1.5 \times 10^7} = \frac{E_a}{2.303 \times 8.314}\left[\frac{373 - 323}{373 \times 323}\right]$$

$$\Rightarrow \quad 0.477\ s^{-1} = \frac{E_a}{2.303 \times 8.314} \times \frac{50}{373 \times 323}$$

$$E_a = 2.20\ s^{-1} \times 10^4\ \text{J mol}^{-1}$$

Calculation of A

$$k = Ae^{-E_a/RT}$$

$$\Rightarrow \quad \log k = \log A - \frac{E_a}{2.303RT}$$

On substituting the values

$$\log 4.5 \times 10^7 = \log A - \frac{2.20\ s^{-1} \times 10^4}{2.303 \times 8.314 \times 373}$$

$$\Rightarrow \quad 7 - 0.65 = \log A - 3.08$$

$$\therefore \quad \log A = 9.43$$

or $$A = 2.69 \times 10^9\ s^{-1}.$$

Concept ladder

- The temperature dependence on the rate of a chemical reaction can be accurately explained by this equation.

If E_a increases ⇒ E_a/RT increases ⇒ $-E_a/RT$ decreases ⇓
Reaction slows down ⇐ k decreases ⇐ $e^{-E_a/RT}$ decreases

- When $T \to \infty$, $k = Ae^0$ or rate constant becomes equal to Arrhenius or frequency factor.
- Larger is the activation energy, smaller is the value of rate constant.
- Larger the activation energy, greater the effect of a given temperature rise on rate constant (k).

Effect of Catalyst

Catalysts (say, positive catalysts) are substances that can be added to reacting species to increase the rate of reaction. A catalyst does take part in the reaction, but all of it is regenerated in later steps.

When the added substance reduces the rate of reaction, it is called **inhibitor**. The action of the catalyst can be explained by intermediate complex theory.

According to this theory, a catalyst participates in a chemical reaction by forming temporary bonds with the reactants resulting in an intermediate complex. This has a transitory existence and decomposes to yield products and the catalyst. Thus, a catalyst does not appear in the balanced equation for the reaction. They allow reactions to occur *via* alternative pathways that increases the reaction rate by lowering activation energy as depicted in figure.

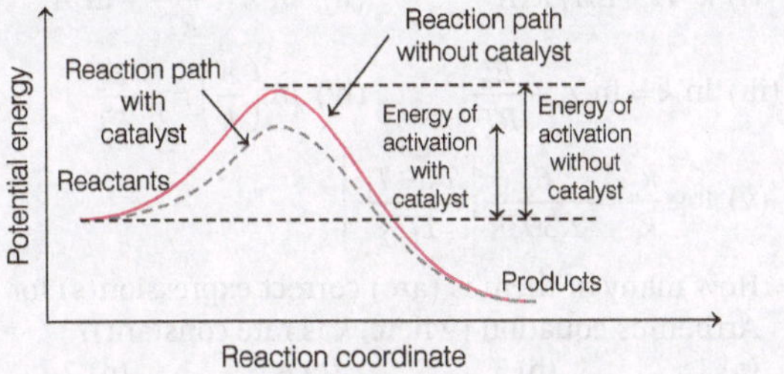

Effect of catalyst on activation energy

Characteristics

- A small amount of the catalyst can catalyse a large amount of reactions.
- A catalyst does not alter Gibbs' energy (ΔG) of a reaction.
- It catalyses the spontaneous reactions but does not catalyse non-spontaneous reactions.
- It does not change the equilibrium constant of a reaction.

NEET Snapshot

The addition of a catalyst during a chemical reaction alters activation energy. ***[NEET 2016]***

The addition of a catalyst reduces the height of barrier by providing an alternative path for the reaction and lowers the activation energy. It does not alter internal energy, enthalpy and entropy.

STEP UP Practice 3

1. Which of the following statements is incorrect about the collision theory of chemical reaction ?
(a) It considers reacting molecules or atoms to be hard spheres and ignores their structural features.
(b) Number of effective collisions determines the rate of reaction.
(c) Collision of atoms or molecules possessing sufficient threshold energy results into the product formation.
(d) Molecules should collide with sufficient threshold energy and proper orientation for the collision to be effective.

2. The rate constant is given by the equation,
$$k = P \cdot Z \times e^{-E_a/RT}.$$
Which factor should decrease for the reaction to proceed more rapidly?
(a) k (b) E_a
(c) Z (d) P

3. Consider the following statements.
Statement I The rate of a chemical reaction increases as the temperature is increased.
Statement II The collision frequency between the reactant molecules increases on increasing temperature.
In the light of the above statement, choose the most appropriate answer from the options given below.
(a) Both Statement I and Statement II are false.
(b) Statement I is true, but Statement II is false.
(c) Statement I is false, but Statement II is true.
(d) Both Statement I and Statement II are true.

4. A reaction takes place by the following mechanism,
$$A + BC \longrightarrow 'X'$$
$$'X' \longrightarrow AC + B$$
The potential energy profile for this is shown below.

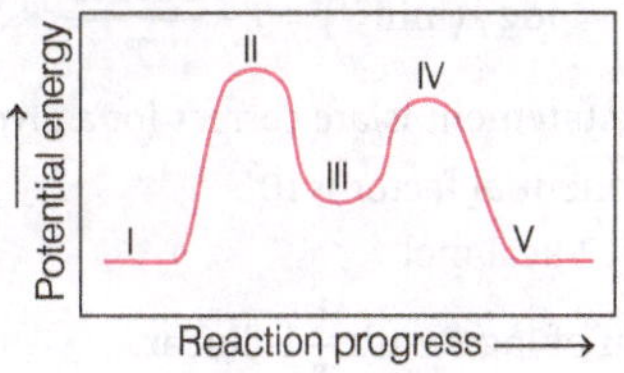

Transition states are shown by
(a) Both I and V (b) Both II and IV
(c) II, III and IV (d) Only III

5. $A \longrightarrow B$, $\Delta H = -10\,\text{kJ mol}^{-1}$, $E_a = 50\,\text{kJ mol}^{-1}$ then E_a of $B \longrightarrow A$ will be
(a) 40 kJ mol^{-1} (b) 50 kJ mol^{-1}
(c) −50 kJ mol^{-1} (d) 60 kJ mol^{-1}

6. For the following reaction,
$$A \rightleftharpoons B + 10\,\text{kcal}$$
increase in temperature will
(a) increase rate of the forward as well as backward reaction
(b) increase rate of the forward reaction but decreases that of backward reaction
(c) decrease rate of the forward reaction but increases that of the backward reaction
(d) decrease rate of forward as well as backward reactions

7. In a zero order reaction, for every 10°C rise of temperature the rate is doubled. If the temperature is increased from 10°C to 100°C, rate of reaction will become
(a) 256 times (b) 1024 times
(c) 128 times (d) 512 times

8. Which of the following is correctly matched for the temperature coefficient of a reaction (α_T)?
(a) $\alpha_T = \dfrac{k_{t+10}}{k_t}$ (b) $\alpha_T = \dfrac{r_t + 10}{r_t}$
(c) $\alpha_T = \dfrac{t_k}{t_k + 10}$ (d) $\alpha_T = \dfrac{E_a - k_{t+10}}{E_a + K_t}$

9. Which of the following is correctly matched, when temperature of a reaction is changed from T_1 and T_2, half-life is found to decrease?
(a) $T_1 > T_2 \longrightarrow$ reaction is always endothermic.
(b) $T_2 > T_1 \longrightarrow$ reaction is always exothermic, R
(c) $T_1 > T_2 \longrightarrow$ reaction is always exothermic = 2 cal/mol/K
(d) $T_2 > T_1 \longrightarrow$ reaction can be exothermic or endothermic.

10. The activation energy of a reaction is 10 kcal/mol. The increase in the rate constant when its temperature is raised from 400 to 405 K is approximately [Antilog (0.067) = 1.166, R = 2 cal/mol/K]
(a) 18% (b) 12.2%
(c) 15% (d) 16.6%

11. Rate constant k varies with temperature as given by equation, [R = 2 cal/mol/K]
$$\log k(\text{min}^{-1}) = 5 - \frac{2000\,\text{K}}{T}$$
How many statement is/are correct for a given reaction?
(i) Pre-exponential factor is 10^5.
(ii) E_a is 9.212 kcal/mol
(iii) Variation of $\log k$ with $\dfrac{1}{T}$ is linear.
(iv) Variation of $\log k$ with $\dfrac{1}{T}$ is parabola.
(v) The value of activation energy (E_a) is 40.31 kJ/mol.
(a) 2 (b) 3
(c) 1 (d) 4

12. Which of the following is the correct unit of A in Arrhenius equation for a first order reaction?
(a) Unit of $A \longrightarrow \text{mol L}^{-1}\text{s}^{-1}$
(b) Unit of $A \longrightarrow \text{JK}^{-1}\text{s}^{-1}$
(c) Unit of $A \longrightarrow \text{s}^{-1}$
(d) Unit of $A \longrightarrow \text{JK}^{-1}\text{L}^{-1}\text{s}^{-1}$

13. Consider the given expressions,
(i) $k = e - \Delta H/RTA$ (ii) $\ln k = \dfrac{\Delta E_a}{RT} + \ln A$
(iii) $\ln k = \ln A - \dfrac{E_a}{RT}$ (iv) $\ln\left(\dfrac{A}{k}\right) = -\dfrac{E_a}{RT}$
(v) $\log \dfrac{k_2}{k_1} = \dfrac{E_a}{2.303R}\left[\dfrac{T_2 - T_1}{T_1 T_2}\right]$
How many of them is (are) correct expression(s) for Arrhenius equation (where, k is rate constant)?
(a) 1 (b) 3 (c) 4 (d) 2

14. Consider the Arrhenius equation given below and mark the correct option.
$$k = A\,e^{-\frac{E_a}{RT}}$$
(a) Rate constant increases exponentially with increasing activation energy and decreasing temperature.
(b) Rate constant decreases exponentially with increasing activation energy and decreasing temperature.
(c) Rate constant increases exponentially with decreasing activation energy and decreasing temperature.
(d) Rate constant increases exponentially with decreasing activation energy and increasing temperature.

15. The activation energy of a reaction at a given temperature, TK is found to be 2.303 RT J mol^{-1}. The ratio of rate constant to the Arrhenius factor is
(a) 0.01 (b) 0.1
(c) 0.02 (d) 0.001

16. Reactant R gives two reactions and forms two products B and C with activation energy E_{a_1} and E_{a_2} respectively. If $E_{a_2} = 2E_{a_1}$, then which of the following is correct match for the rate constant k_1 and k_2?
(a) $k_2 = k_1 e^{E_{a_1}/RT}$ (b) $k_2 = k_1 e^{E_{a_2}/RT}$
(c) $k_1 = Ak_2 e^{E_{a_1}/RT}$ (d) $k_1 = 2k_2 e^{E_{a_2}/RT}$

17. For a reaction, the rate constant is expressed as, $k = A \cdot e^{-60000/T}$. The energy of the activation is [R = 2 cal/mol/K]
(a) 12×10^4 cal/mol (b) 3×10^4 cal/mol
(c) 8×10^3 cal/mol (d) 6×10^4 cal/mol

18. For the decomposition of hydrogen iodide at 130°C, the fraction of molecules having energy equal to or greater than activation energy can be given as
(a) $10^{-\frac{E_a}{921.2R}}$ (b) $10^{-\frac{E_a}{2.303R}}$
(c) $10^{\frac{-E_a}{928.1R}}$ (d) $10^{-\frac{E_a}{1930R}}$

19. The rate of a reaction, (a) doubles on increasing the temperature from 300 to 310 K. By how much, the temperature of reaction (*b*) should be increased from 300 K so that rate doubles if activation energy of the reaction (*b*) is twice to that of reaction (*a*).
(a) 9.84 K
(b) 4.92 K
(c) 2.45 K
(d) 19.67 K

20. The rate of a chemical reaction generally increases rapidly even for small temperature increase because of rapid increase in the
(a) collision frequency
(b) fraction of molecules with energies in excess of the activation energy
(c) kinetic energy
(d) average kinetic energy of molecules

21. In presence of catalyst, E_a is lowered by 2 kcal/mol at 27°C. $[R = 2 \text{ cal/mol/K}, e^{3.33} = 27.97]$
Hence, rate will be
(a) 20 times (b) 14 times
(c) 28 times (d) 2 times

22. Consider the following statements.
Statement I The enthalpy of reaction remains constant in the presence of a catalyst.
Statement II A positive catalyst participating in the reaction forms different activated complex and lowers down the activation energy but the difference in energy of reactant and product remains the same.
In the light of the above statement, choose the most appropriate answer from the options given below.
(a) Both Statement I and Statement II are false.
(b) Statement I is true, but Statement II is false.
(c) Statement I is false, but Statement II is true.
(d) Both Statement I and Statement II are true.

23. Which of the following statements is not correct for a positive catalyst ?
(a) It catalyses the forward and backward reactions to the same extent.
(b) It alters ΔG of the reaction.
(c) It is a substance that does not change the equilibrium constant of a reaction.
(d) It provides an alternate mechanism by reducing activation energy between reactants and products.

24. Consider the following statements.
Statement I A positive catalyst enhances the rate of a reaction.
Statement II The energy of activation of the reaction is lowered in presence of a positive catalyst.
In the light of the above statement, choose the most appropriate answer from the options given below.
(a) Both Statement I and Statement II are false.
(b) Statement I is true, but Statement II is false.
(c) Statement I is false, but Statement II is true.
(d) Both Statement I and Statement II are true.

NEET Exclusive EXTRA BYTES

Plots for Diffferent Order Reactions

For second order	For third order

(a) Plot of rate of reaction *vs* concentration

(b) Plot from integrated rate equations

(c) Plot of half-life *vs* concentration

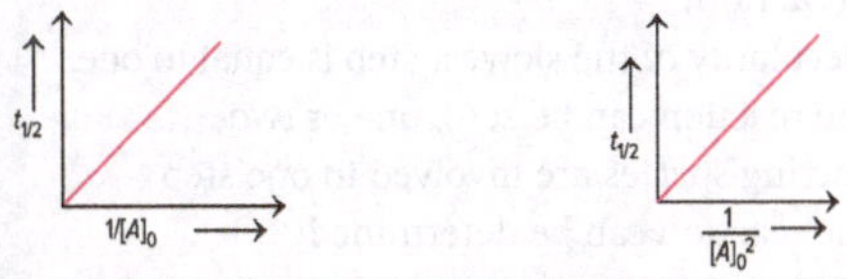

Important points related to Arrhenius equation

- The temperature dependence on the rate of a chemical reaction can be accurately explained by this equation.

If T increases ⇒ E_a/RT decreases ⇒ $-E_a/RT$ increases ⇒ $e^{-E_a/RT}$ increases ⇒ k increases ⇒ Reaction speeds up

- When $T \to \infty$, $K = Ae^{\circ}$ or rate constant becomes equal to Arrhenius or frequency factor.
- Variation of k leads to variation of rate of reaction of the same degree since for a rate of reaction $= K[\text{conc.}]^n$.
- Larger is the activation energy, smaller is the value of rate constant.

If E_a increases ⇒ E_a/RT increases ⇒ $-E_a/RT$ decreases ⇒ $e^{-E_a/RT}$ decreases ⇒ k decreases

- Larger the activation energy, greater the effect of a given temperature rise on rate constant (k).

GEARING UP FOR NEET

1. A reaction follows the given concentration-time graph. The rate for this reaction at 20 s will be (approximately)

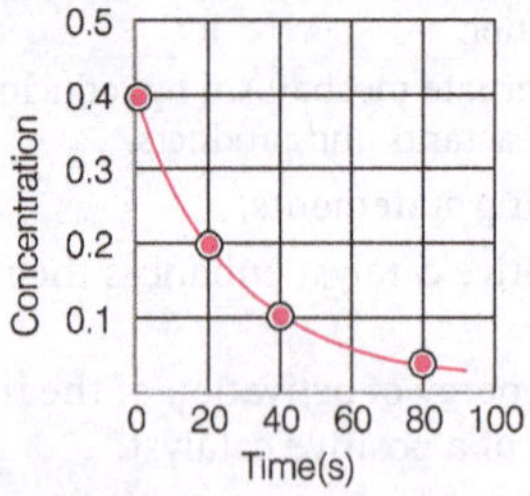

(a) 7×10^{-3} M s^{-1} (b) 8×10^{-3} M s^{-1}
(c) 2×10^{-2} M s^{-1} (d) 5×10^{-3} M s^{-1}

2. Consider the reaction, $A \longrightarrow B$. The concentration of both the reactants and the products varies exponentially with time. Which of the following graph correctly describes the change in concentration of reactants and products with time?

(a)

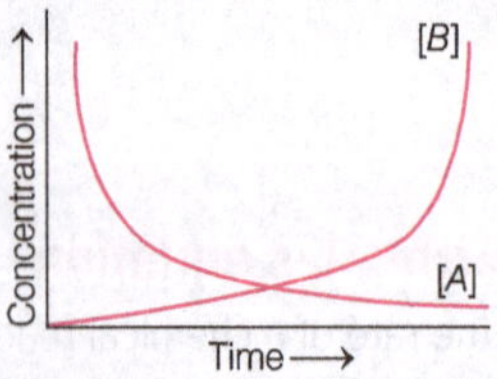

(b)

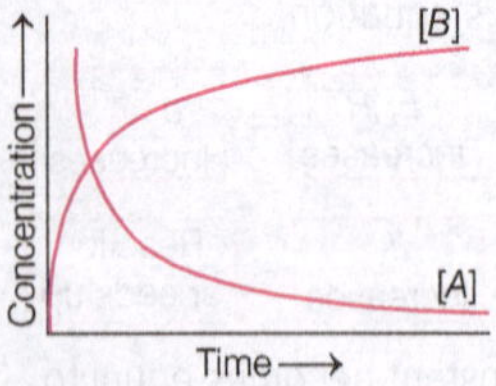

(c)

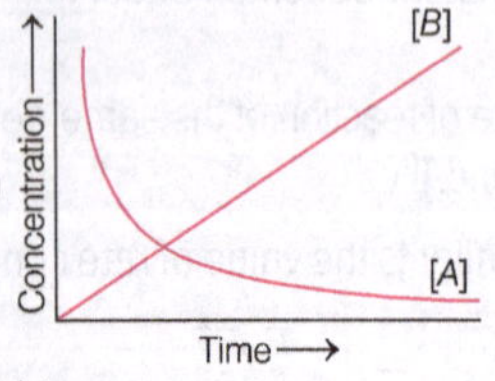

(d)

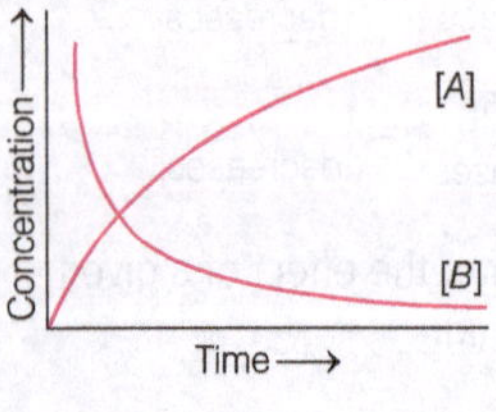

3. For a given reaction $A \rightarrow$ Product, rate is 1×10^{-4} Ms^{-1} when $[A] = 0.01$ M and rate is 1.41×10^{-4} Ms^{-1} when $[A] = 0.02$ M. Hence, rate law is

(a) $\frac{-d[A]}{dt} = k[A]^2$ (b) $\frac{-d[A]}{dt} = k[A]$

(c) $\frac{-d[A]}{dt} = \frac{k}{4}[A]$ (d) $\frac{-d[A]}{dt} = k[A]^{1/2}$

4. $A \rightarrow$ Product and $\left(\frac{dx}{dt}\right) = k[A]^2$, if $\log\left(\frac{dx}{dt}\right)$ is plotted against $\log [A]$, then graph is of the type

(a)

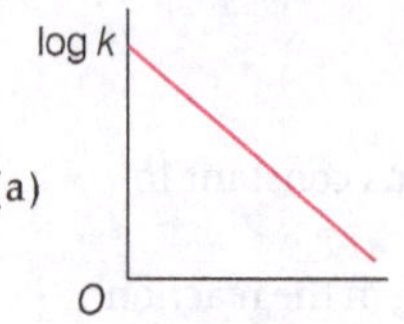

(b)

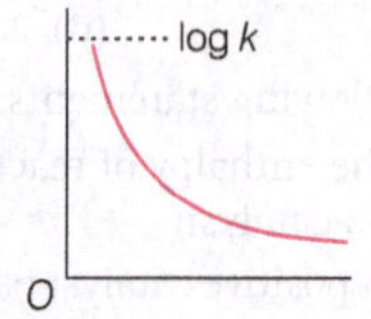

(c)

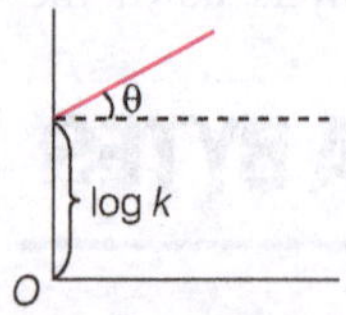

(d)

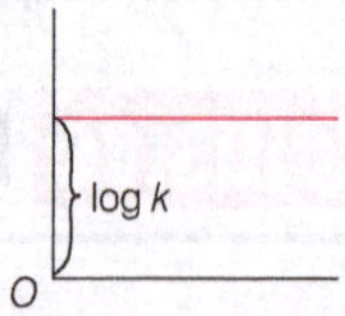

5. In the complex reaction,

$$N_2 + 3H_2 \rightleftharpoons 2NH_3$$

(i) $\left(\frac{dx}{dt}\right) = 1 \times 10^2 M^{-3}$

(ii) $[N_2][H_2]^3 = 1 \times 10^{-3} M^{-1} [NH_3]^2$

Now, $\frac{[N_2][H_2]^3}{[NH_3]^2} = 10^{-5}$ M^{-2} if $\left(\frac{dx}{dt}\right)$ is

(a) 0 (b) 1×10^5 (c) 1×10^{-5} (d) 1×10^{-3}

6. In a reaction $A + B \longrightarrow C$, the rate expression is $R = k[A]^2[B]$. If the concentration of both the reactants is tripled at constant volume then the rate of the reaction will be increased by

(a) 9 times (b) 27 times
(c) 81 times (d) 243 times

7. For a unimolecular reaction,

(a) the order and molecularity of the slowest step is equal to one.
(b) molecularity of the reaction can be zero, one or two
(c) more than one reacting species are involved in one step.
(d) molecularity of the reaction can be determined experimentally only.

8. For a reaction, $2NO + 2H_2 \longrightarrow N_2 + 2H_2O$, the possible mechanism is

$$2NO \overset{k_{eq.}}{\rightleftharpoons} N_2O_2$$

$$N_2O_2 + H_2 \xrightarrow[k']{\text{Slow}} N_2O + H_2O$$

$$N_2O + H_2 \xrightarrow[k'']{\text{Slow}} N_2 + H_2O$$

Which of the following pair is correct for the given reaction?
(a) Rate = $k[N_2O_2]$, order = 1 (b) Rate = $k[N_2O_2][H_2]$, order = 2
(c) Rate = $k[N_2O_2]^2$, order =2 (d) Rate = $k[NO]^2[H_2]$, order =3

9. The $t_{90\%}$ for a zero order reaction having 0.36 M initial concentraion of reactant is 150 s. The rate constant (in mol $L^{-1}s^{-1}$) for the reaction is
(a) 2.4×10^{-4} (b) 5.1×10^{-4} (c) 3.6×10^{-3} (d) 4.1×10^{-3}

10. The $t_{75\%}$ for a zero order reaction having 0.08 M initial concentration of reactant is 180 s. The rate constant (in mol $L^{-1}s^{-1}$) for the reaction is
(a) 2.5×10^{-6} (b) 5.1×10^{-4}
(c) 4.8×10^{-3} (d) 1.1×10^{-4}

11. For the reaction of the zeroth order, variation of log T_{50} with log a (where, T_{50} is half-life period and a is the initial concentration) is given by

(a) 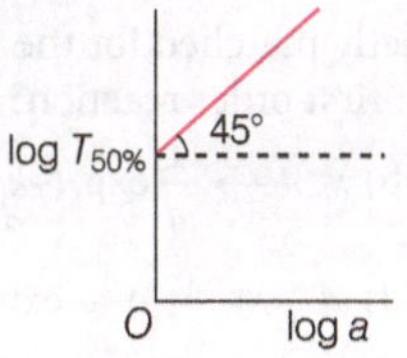

(b) 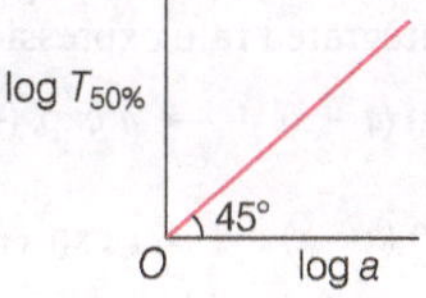

(c) 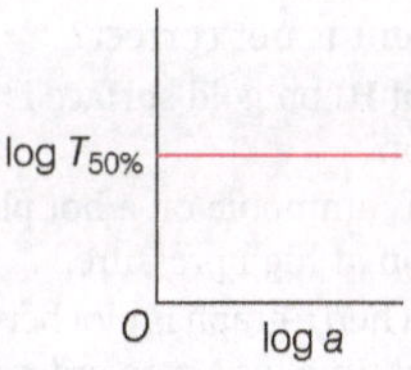

(d) 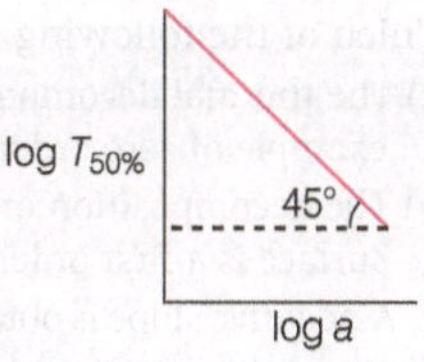

12. Consider the following reaction, the total number of the relations which represents the first order reaction is

(i) $t_{1/2} = \frac{0.693}{k}$ (ii) $t_{1/2} = 0.693 + k$

(iii) $t_{1/2} = \frac{2303}{k} \log 2$ (iv) $k = \frac{1}{t} \ln \frac{a}{a-x}$

(v) $k = -\frac{2.303}{t} \log \frac{a}{a-x}$ (vi) $k = \frac{1}{t} - \frac{x}{a(a-x)}$

(vii) $t_{1/2} = \frac{2.303}{k} \log 3$

(a) 2 (b) 4 (c) 3 (d) 5

13. Consider a first order reaction,

$$(A) \longrightarrow \text{Product}$$

Concentration of A, changes from 0.1 M to 0.025 M in 40 min. Find the rate of reaction, when concentration of A is 0.01 M.

(a) 3.47×10^{-4} M min^{-1} (b) 3.47×10^{-5} M min^{-1}
(c) 1.73×10^{-4} M min^{-1} (d) 1.73×10^{-5} M min^{-1}

14. In a first order reaction, $A \longrightarrow P$, the ratio of $a/(a-x)$ was found to be 8 after 60 min. If the concentration is 0.1 M then the rate of reaction is
(a) 2.226×10^{-3} mol L^{-1} min^{-1} (b) 3.466×10^{-3} mol L^{-1} min^{-1}
(c) 4.455×10^{-3} mol L^{-1} min^{-1} (d) 5.532×10^{-3} mol L^{-1} min^{-1}

15. The rate of a reaction twice when temperature changes from 30°C to 40°C. Calculate the energy of activation.
(a) 23.3 kJ/mol
(b) 233 kJ/mol
(c) 2330 kJ/mol
(d) 54.47 kJ/mol

16. For a first order reaction, $A \longrightarrow$ Products, initial concentration of A is 0.32 M, which becomes 0.032 M after 9 minutes. Rate constant for the reaction in min^{-1} is
(a) 0.312 (b) 0.256
(c) 1.312 (d) 1.031

17. Which of the following rate expression is correctly matched with their order for a certain reaction repressive?
(a) Rate = $k[A]^{1/2}[B]^{3/2} \longrightarrow 3$
(b) Rate = $k[A]^{3/2}[B]^{-1} \longrightarrow -\frac{1}{2}$
(c) Rate = $k[A]^{-5/3}[B]^2 \longrightarrow \frac{1}{3}$
(d) Rate = $k[A]^1[B]^{1/2} \longrightarrow \frac{2}{3}$

18. Consider the data given below for the given reaction.

$$2A + B_2 \longrightarrow 2AB$$

Exp. No.	[A]	[B_2]	Rate (Ms^{-1})
1	0.50	0.50	1.6×10^{-4}
2	0.50	1.00	3.2×10^{-4}
3	1.0	1.00	3.2×10^{-4}

The rate equation for the above data is
(a) rate $= k[B_2]$ (b) rate $= k[A]$
(c) rate $= k[B_2]^2[A]$ (d) rate $= k[A][B_2]^2$

19. Which of the following relation between half reaction time ($t_{1/2}$) and initial concentration of reactant for $(n-1)$ order reaction is correctly matched?
(a) $t_{1/2} \propto [R]_0$ (b) $t_{1/2} \propto [R]_0^{2-n}$
(c) $t_{1/2} \propto [R]_0^{n+1}$ (d) $t_{1/2} \propto [R]_0^{n-2}$

20. Which of the following is not correctly matched?
(a) In graph of ln [R] *vs* $t \longrightarrow$ slope is $(-k)$ for first order reaction
(b) In graph of ln k *vs* $\frac{1}{T} \longrightarrow$ slope is $\left(\frac{-E_a}{R}\right)$ for Arrhenius equation
(c) In graph of $\frac{[R]_0}{[R]}$ *vs* $t \longrightarrow$ slope is $\left(\frac{2.303}{k}\right)$ for first order reaction
(d) In Graph of $t_{1/2}$ *vs* $[A]_0 \longrightarrow$ slope is $\left(\frac{1}{2k}\right)$ for zero order reaction

21. For the decomposition of N_2O into N_2 and O in the presence of gaseous argon. The value of

$$k = (5.0 \times 10^{11}\ \text{L mol}^{-1}\text{s}^{-1})e^{-29000(K)/T}$$

Hence, E_a (energy of activation) is [$R = 1.98$ cal/mol/K]

(a) 5.0×10^{11} kcal/mol (b) 29000 kcal/mol
(c) 57 kcal/mol (d) –29000 cal/mol

22. The slope of Arrhenius plot $\left(\ln k \text{ vs } \frac{1}{T}\right)$ of first order reaction is -7.1×10^3 K. The value of E_a of the reaction is [Given, $R = 8.314\ \text{JK}^{-1}\text{mol}^{-1}$]

(a) 65.01 kJ mol^{-1} (b) 59.03 kJ mol^{-1}
(c) 45.02 kJ mol^{-1} (d) 55.01 kJ mol^{-1}

23. Which of the following is correctly matched regarding the time required for 100% completion of a zero order reaction?

(a) $t_{100\%} \longrightarrow ak$ (b) $t_{100\%} \longrightarrow \frac{a}{2k}$
(c) $t_{100\%} \longrightarrow \frac{a}{k}$ (d) $t_{100\%} \longrightarrow \frac{2k}{a}$

24. A first order reaction is 50% complete in 30 minutes at 27°C and in 10 minutes at 47°C. The reaction rate constant at 27°C and the energy of activation of the reaction are respectively. [log 3 = 0.477]

(a) $k = 0.0231\ \text{min}^{-1}$, $E_a = 43.84$ kJ mol^{-1}
(b) $k = 0.017\ \text{min}^{-1}$, $E_a = 52.54$ kJ mol^{-1}
(c) $k = 0.693\ \text{min}^{-1}$, $E_a = 43.84$ kJ mol^{-1}
(d) $k = 0.0231\ \text{min}^{-1}$, $E_a = 28.92$ kJ mol^{-1}

25. Which of the following is correctly matched for a zero order reaction?

(a) $t_{3/4} \longrightarrow \frac{3}{2}t_{1/2}$ (b) $t_{1/2} \longrightarrow \frac{5}{2}t_{3/4}$
(c) $t_{1/2} \longrightarrow 2t_{3/4}$ (d) $t_{3/4} \longrightarrow (t_{1/2})^2$

26. For an exothermic chemical process occurring in two steps as follows,

(i) $A + B \longrightarrow X$ (slow) (ii) $X \longrightarrow AB$ (fast)

In how many of the following graph, the process of the reaction is (are) truely described?

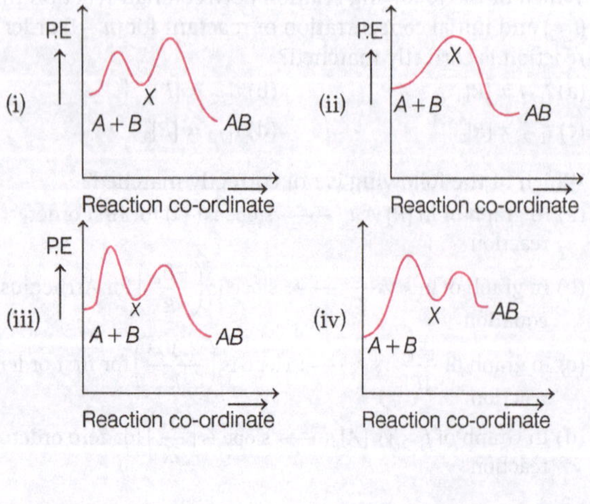

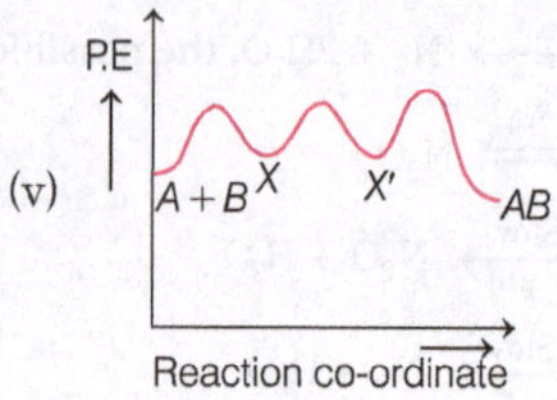

(a) 1 (b) 2 (c) 3 (d) 4

27. Two reactions with different activation energies have the same rate at room temperature. Which statement correctly describes the rates of these two reactions at the higher temperature?

(a) The reaction with the greater activation energy will be faster.
(b) The reaction with the smaller activation energy will be faster.
(c) The two reactions will have the same rate.
(d) Temperature range is also required.

28. The energies of activation for forward and reverse reactions for $A_2 + B_2 \rightleftharpoons 2AB$ are 260 kJ mol^{-1} and 280 kJ mol^{-1} respectively. The presence of a catalyst lowers the activation energy of both (forward and reverse) reaction by 100 kJ mol^{-1}. The magnitude of enthalpy change of the reaction ($A_2 + B_2 \longrightarrow 2AB$) in the presence of a catalyst will be (in kJ mol^{-1})

(a) 420 (b) 540
(c) 20 (d) 120

29. Which of the following is correctly matched for the integrated rate expression for a first order reaction?

(a) $(a - x) \longrightarrow a\ \text{exp.}(-k_1t)$ (b) $x \longrightarrow \frac{1}{a}\ \text{exp.}(-k_1t)$
(c) $(a - x) \longrightarrow t\ \text{exp.}(+k_1t)$ (d) $(a - x) \longrightarrow a\ \text{exp.}\left(-\frac{k_1}{t}\right)$

30. Which of the following statement is not correct?

(a) The thermal decomposition of HI on gold surface is an example of zero order reaction.
(b) The decomposition of gaseous ammonia on a hot platinum surface is a first order reaction at high pressure.
(c) A negative slope is obtained, when a graph is plot between the concentration of reactant and time for a zero order reaction.
(d) Zero order reaction means that the rate of the reaction is proportional to zero power of the concentration of reactants.

31. Graph between log k and $\frac{1}{T}$ (k is rate constant in s^{-1} and T is the temperature in K) is a straight line. If $OX = 5$ and slope of the line $= -\frac{1}{2.303}$ then E_a is [$R = 2$ cal/mol/K]

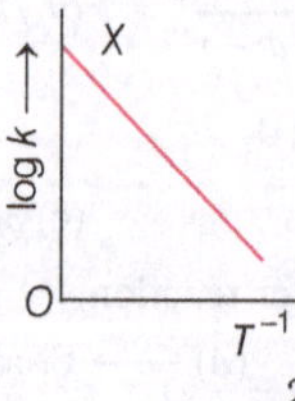

(a) 2.303×2 cal/mol (b) $\frac{2}{2.303}$ cal/mol
(c) 2 cal/mol (d) 2.303 cal/mol

32. Which of the following statements is not correct regarding the given reaction, $H_2(g) + I_2(g) \longrightarrow 2HI(g)$?
(a) According to Arrhenius, this reaction can take place only when a molecule of hydrogen and a molecule of iodine collide to form an unstable intermediate.
(b) The energy required by reactant molecules to form the intermediate of the given reaction is called activation energy.
(c) The final enthalpy of the given reaction does not depend upon the nature of reactants and products.
(d) All the molecules in the reacting species do not have the same kinetic energy.

33. Which of the following is correctly matched w.r.t. first order reaction?
(a) $t_{0.75} \longrightarrow 4t_{0.5}$ (b) $t_{0.75} \longrightarrow 2t_{0.5}$
(c) $t_{0.75} \longrightarrow 1.3t_{0.5}$ (d) $t_{0.75} \longrightarrow 1.5t_{0.5}$

34. Select the incorrect statement.
(a) Larger the value of E_a, smaller the value of rate constant (k).
(b) Larger the value of E_a, greater is the effect on the value of k for a given temperature change.
(c) At lower temperature, increase in temperature cause more change in the value of k than at higher temperature.
(d) k is affected by change in concentration.

Assertion-Reason

Directions (Q. Nos. 35 to 38) Given below are two statements, one is labelled as Assertion (A) and the other is labelled as Reason (R).
(a) Both A and R are true and R is the correct explanation of A.
(b) Both A and R are true but R is not the correct explanation of A.
(c) A is true but R is false.
(d) A is false but R is true.

35. **Assertion** (A) If 50% of a zero order reaction is completed in 100 s, then 75% of reaction will be completed in150 s.
Reason (R) The rate constant of a zero order reaction increases with time.

36. **Assertion** (A) If 50% of a reaction occurs in 100 s and 75% of the reaction occurs in 200 s, then the order of this reaction will be one.
Reason (R) Half-life of the given reaction is independent of conentration and follows the relation, $t_{3/4} = \frac{t_{1/2}}{2}$.

37. **Assertion** (A) Acidic hydrolysis of methyl ethanoate is a pseudo first order reaction.
Reason (R) Water is present in large excess therefore its concentration remains constant throughout the reaction.

38. **Assertion** (A) For a chemical reaction with rise in temperature by 10°, the rate constant is nearly doubled.
Reason (R) At $(t+10)$, the fraction of molecules having energy equal to or greater than activation energy gets doubled.

Statement Type Questions

Directions (Q. Nos. 39 to 43) In the light of the below statements, choose the correct answer from the options given below.
(a) Both Statement I and Statement II are false.
(b) Statement I is true, but Statement II is false.
(c) Statement I is false, but Statement II is true.
(d) Both Statement I and Statement II are true.

39. **Statement I** For the reaction, $2A + B \longrightarrow$ Products, Rate $\propto [A][B]$ If the concentration of B is doubled, then the half-life will not change but if the concentration of A is doubled, the rate of reaction increases by two times.
Statement II For the reaction of order $=2$ $2A + B \longrightarrow$ Products with same conditions, the unit of rate constant is $mol^{-1} Ls^{-1}$.

40. **Statement I** Half-life for zero order reaction is directly proportional to initial concentration of the reactant.
Statement II The half-life period of a first order reaction is 69.3 s, then the rate constant of the reaction will be $0.01 s^{-1}$.

41. **Statement I** The rate of a reaction normally increases by a factor of 2 or 3 for every 10°C rise in temperature.
Statement II Increase in temperature increases the number of collisions.

42. **Statement I** Rate constant determined from Arrhenius equation are fairly accurate for simple as well as complex molecules.
Statement II Reactant molecules do not undergo any chemical change irrespective of their orientation during collision.

43. **Statement I** In collision theory, activation energy and proper orientation of the molecules together determine the criteria for an effective collision.
Statement II Collision theory also consider the structural aspect of atoms/molecules.

44. Which of the following statements are correct?
A. For a zero order reaction, the unit of rate and rate constant are same.
B. The unit of rate of reaction changes with order of reaction.
C. The unit of rate constant for a reaction is $mol^{1-n}L^{1-n}s^{-1}$, where, n is order of the reaction.
D. Any quantity raised to power zero is equal to unity.
E. The integrated rate equations can be determined for zero order chemical reactions.

Choose the correct answer from the options given below.
(a) A, D and E
(b) C and D
(c) A, B and C
(d) C, D and E

45. Which of the following statements are correct?

A. For first order reaction, $t_{1/2}$ is inversely proportional to rate constant.

B. A plot between ln [k] and t for a first order reaction gives positive slope.

C. If concentration of the reactant is doubled, half-life period remains same in the zero order reaction.

D. For a first order reaction, $t_{1/2}$ is independent of initial concentration of the reacting species.

E. For a first order reaction, half-life period is constant.

Choose the correct answer from the options given below.

(a) B, C and D (b) A and E
(c) A, D and E (d) C and D

46. Consider the following statements w.r.t zero order reaction.

I. The rate of the reaction is independent of temperature.

II. Rate law expression, $R = k[A]^0$ and unit of k is s^{-1}.

III. The rate constant of reaction is independent of reactant concentration.

IV. The rate of the reaction is independent of reactant concentration.

Choose the correct statement.

(a) III and IV (b) I and II
(c) II and IV (d) I and III

47. Which of the following statements are incorrect?

A. The word catalyst should not be used when the added substance reduces the rate of reaction.

B. A small amount of the catalyst can catalyses a large amount of reactants.

C. Catalyst catalyses the non-spontaneous reaction.

D. A catalyst can alter the equilibrium constant of a reaction.

E. A catalyst increase the rate of a reaction without itself undergoing any permanent chemical change.

Choose the correct answer from the option given below.

(a) B and A (b) C and D
(c) B, C and E (d) A, C and D

48. Select the incorrect statement from the following.

A. Formation of methanol from bromoethane does not depends upon the orientation of reactant molecules.

B. For effective collisions, another factor P, called the probability or steric factor is introduced in the formula $Z_{AB}e^{-E_a/RT}$.

C. According to collision theory, the reactant molecules are assumed to be large in size.

D. All the molecules which collide with one other are effective collisions.

E. Rate $= Z_{AB}e^{-E_a/RT}$ for collision in which $e^{-E_a/RT}$ is the fraction of molecules with kinetic energy equal to or greater than E_a.

Choose the correct answer from the options given below:

(a) B and E (b) A, C and D
(c) C and B (d) B, D and E

Species Selection Type Questions

49. Consider the following expression for the first order reaction,

(i) $k = \frac{2.303}{t}\log\left(\frac{A_0}{A_t}\right)$ (ii) $k = \frac{t}{2.303}\log\left(\frac{A_0}{A_t}\right)$

(iii) $k = \frac{t}{2.303}\log\left(\frac{A_t}{A_0}\right)$ (iv) Rate $= k[A]$

(v) $k = -\frac{2.303}{t}\log\left[\frac{A_0}{A_t}\right]$

How many expression is not correct for first order reaction?

(a) 3 (b) 4 (c) 2 (d) 1

50. Consider the given relation for a first order reaction, if (E_a : activation energy), k_1 = rate constant at temperature T_1 and k_2 = rate constant at temperature T_2

(i) $\log\frac{k_1}{k_2} = \frac{2.303E_a}{R}\left(\frac{T_2 - T_1}{T_1T_2}\right)$

(ii) $\log\frac{k_2}{k_1} = \frac{E_a}{2.303R}\left(\frac{T_2 - T_1}{T_1T_2}\right)$

(iii) $\ln k_2 - \ln k_1 = \frac{E_a}{RT_1} - \frac{E_a}{RT_2}$

(iv) $\ln\frac{k_1}{k_2} = \frac{E_a}{R}\left[\frac{1}{T_1} - \frac{1}{T_2}\right]$

(v) $\log\frac{k_2}{k_1} = -\frac{E_a}{2.303\,R}\left[\frac{1}{T_2} - \frac{1}{T_1}\right]$

How many of them are correct relation for a first order reaction?

(a) 2 (b) 1 (c) 4 (d) 3

51. Consider the following graphs.

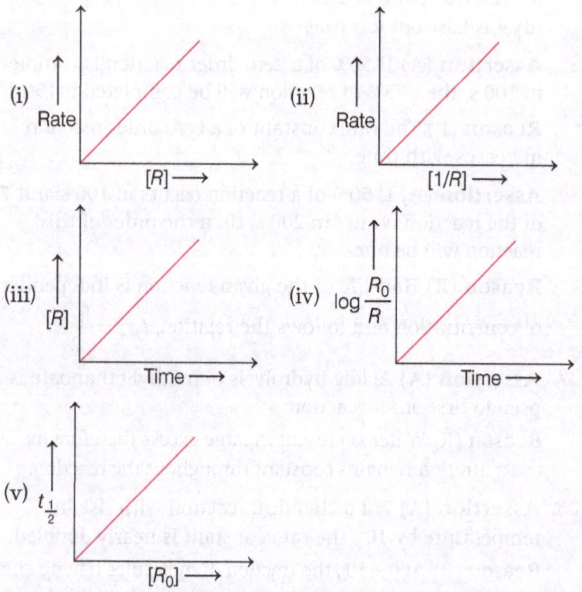

How many of them is the graphical representation for the first order reaction [$R \rightarrow D$].

(a) 2 (b) 4 (c) 3 (d) 5

Matching Type Questions

52. Match the items of Column I and Column II.

Column I	Column II
A. Diamond to graphite	1. Short interval of time
B. Instantaneous rate	2. Ordinarily rate of conversion is imperceptible
C. Average rate	3. Long duration of time

Codes
(a) A-2, B-1, C-3
(b) A-1, B-2, C-3
(c) A-3, B-2, C-1
(d) A-1, B-3, C-2

53. Match the Column I and Column II.

Column I (Rate expression)	Column II (Order of a reaction)
A. Rate $= k[A]^{1/2}[B]^{3/2}$	1. 1/2
B. Rate $= k[A]^{3/2}[B]^{-1}$	2. $-\frac{1}{2}$
C. Rate $= k[A]^{-5/3}[B]^{2}$	3. 2
D. Rate $= k[A]^{-1}[B]^{1/2}$	4. 1/3

Codes
(a) A-4, B-1, C-3, D-2
(b) A-3, B-4, C-2, D-1
(c) A-3, B-1, C-4, D-2
(d) A-4, B-1, C-2, D-3

54. Match the Column I and Column II.

Column I (Graph)	Column II (Slope)
A. $\ln = [R]$ *vs* t [Order =1]	1. $-E_a/R$
B. $\ln k$ *vs* $1/T$	2. $k/2$
C. $\log [R_o]/[R]$ *vs* t [Order =1]	3. $-k$
D. $t_{1/2}$ *vs* $[A]_0$ [Order = 0]	4. $k/2.303$

Codes
(a) A-2, B-4, C-1, D-3
(b) A-2, B-1, C-4, D-3
(c) A-3, B-4, C-1, D-2
(d) A-3, B-1, C-4, D-2

55. Match Column I with Column II.

Column I (Rate)	Column II (Unit)
A. $k[NH_3]^0$	1. $L^{1/2}mol^{-1/2}s^{-1}$
B. $k[H_2O_2][I^-]$	2. mol $L^{-1}s^{-1}$
C. $k[CH_3CHO]^{3/2}$	3. s^{-1}
D. $k[C_2H_5Cl]$	4. L $mol^{-1}s^{-1}$

Codes
(a) A-3, B-2, C-1, D-4
(b) A-2, B-4, C-1, D-3
(c) A-4, B-1, C-3, D-2
(d) A-3, B-4, C-1, D-2

Final Check Through PYQs

Module-I Chemical Reactions and Rate of Chemical Reactions

1. For a certain reaction, the rate $= k[A]^2[B]$, when the initial concentration of A is tripled keeping concentration of B constant, the initial rate would **[NEET 2023]**
(a) increase by a factor of six.
(b) increase by a factor of nine.
(c) increase by a factor of three.
(d) decrease by a factor of nine.

2. For the chemical reaction,
$N_2(g) + 3H_2(g) \longrightarrow 2NH_3(g)$ the correct option is **[NCERT (New) Pg. 65, NEET 2019]**
(a) $3\frac{d[H_2]}{dt} = 2\frac{d[NH_3]}{dt}$ (b) $-\frac{1}{3}\frac{d[H_2]}{dt} = -\frac{1}{2}\frac{d[NH_3]}{dt}$
(c) $-\frac{d[N_2]}{dt} = 2\frac{d[NH_3]}{dt}$ (d) $-\frac{d[N_2]}{dt} = \frac{1}{2}\frac{d[NH_3]}{dt}$

Module-II Rate Law, Rate Expression and Integrated Rate Equations

3. The given graph is a representation of kinetics of a reaction. **[NEET 2022]**

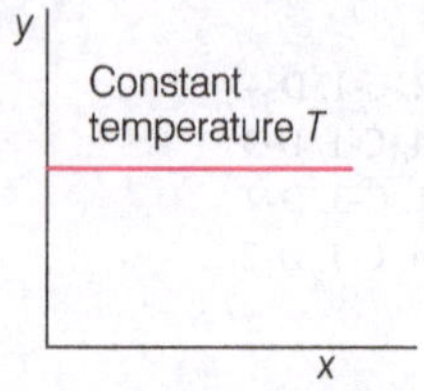

The y and x axes for zero and first order reactions, respectively are
(a) zero order (y = concentration and x = time), first order (y = rate constant and x = concentration).
(b) zero order (y = rate and x = concentration), first order ($y = t_{1/2}$ and x = concentration).
(c) zero order (y = rate and x = concentration), first order (y = rate and $x = t_{1/2}$).
(d) zero order (y = concentration and x = time), first order ($y = t_{1/2}$ and x = concentration).

4. For a first order reaction $A \rightarrow$ products, initial concentration of A is 0.1 M, which becomes 0.001 M after 5 minutes. Rate constant for the reaction in min^{-1} is **[NCERT (New) Pg. 66, NEET 2022]**
(a) 0.9212 (b) 0.4606
(c) 0.2303 (d) 1.3818

5. The rate constant for a first order reaction is $4.606 \times 10^{-3}\ s^{-1}$. The time required to reduce 2.0 g of the reactant to 0.2 g is **[NCERT (New) Pg. 66, NEET 2020]**
(a) 200 s
(b) 500 s
(c) 1000 s
(d) 100 s

6. The half-life for a zero order reaction having 0.02 M initial concentration of reactant is 100 s. The rate constant (in mol $L^{-1}\ s^{-1}$) for the reaction is **[NCERT (New) Pg. 67, NEET 2020]**
(a) 1.0×10^{-4} (b) 2.0×10^{-4} (c) 2.0×10^{-3} (d) 1.0×10^{-2}

7. A first order reaction has a rate constant of $2.303 \times 10^{-3}\ s^{-1}$. The time required for 40 g of this reactant to reduce to 10 g will be [Given that, $\log_{10} 2 = 0.3010$] **[NCERT (New) Pg. 67, NEET 2019]**
(a) 230.3 s (b) 301 s (c) 2000 s (d) 602 s

8. If the rate constant for a first order reaction is k, the time (t) required for the completion of 99% of the reaction is given by **[NEET 2019]**
(a) $t = 6.909/k$ (b) $t = 4.606/k$
(c) $t = 2.303/k$ (d) $t = 0.693/k$

9. When initial concentration of the reactant is doubled, the half-life period of a zero order reaction **[NEET 2018]**
(a) is tripled (b) is doubled
(c) is halved (d) remains unchanged

10. Mechanism of a hypothetical reaction, $X_2 + Y_2 \longrightarrow 2XY$ is given below. **[NCERT (New) Pg. 71, NEET 2017]**
(i) $X_2 \longrightarrow X + X$ (fast) (ii) $X + Y_2 \rightleftharpoons XY + Y$ (slow)
(iii) $X + Y \longrightarrow XY$ (fast)
The overall order of the reaction will be
(a) 2 (b) 0
(c) 1.5 (d) 1

11. A first order reaction has a specific reaction rate of $10^{-2}\ s^{-1}$. How much time will take for 20 g of the reactant to reduce to 5 g? **[NEET 2017]**
(a) 238.6 s (b) 138.6 s
(c) 346.5 s (d) 693.0 s

12. The decomposition of phosphine (PH_3) on tungsten at low pressure is a first-order reaction. It is because the **[NCERT (New) Pg. 72, NEET 2016]**
(a) rate is proportional to the surface coverage
(b) rate is inversely proportional to the surface coverage
(c) rate is independent of the surface coverage
(d) rate of decomposition is very slow

13. The rate of a first order reaction is $0.04 \text{ mol L}^{-1} \text{ s}^{-1}$ at 10 s and $0.03 \text{ mol L}^{-1} \text{ s}^{-1}$ at 20 s after initation of the reaction. The half-life period of the reaction is **[NCERT (New) Pg. 76, NEET 2016]**
(a) 34.1s
(b) 44.1s
(c) 54.1 s
(d) 24.1 s

14. The rate constant of the reaction $A \rightarrow B$ is 0.6×10^{-3} mole per per litre second. If the concentration of A is 5 M, then concentration of B after 20 min is **[NEET 2015]**
(a) 1.08 M
(b) 3.60 M
(c) 0.36 M
(d) 0.72 M

15. When initial concentration of a reactant is doubled in a reaction, its half-life period is not affected. The order of the reaction is **[CBSE AIPMT 2015]**
(a) zero
(b) first
(c) second
(d) more that zero but less than first

Module-III Theories of Reaction Rate and Effect of Temperature and Catalyst on it

16. Which plot of $\ln k$ vs $\frac{1}{T}$ is consistentwith Arrhenius equation? **[NEET 2024]**

(a) 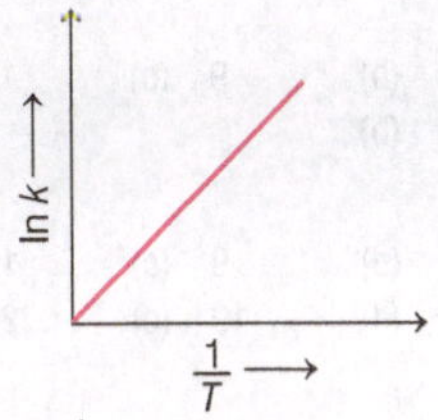

(b) 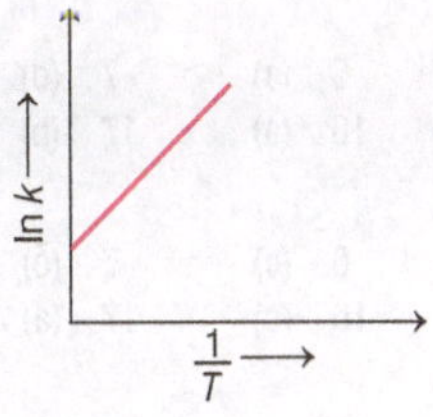

(c) 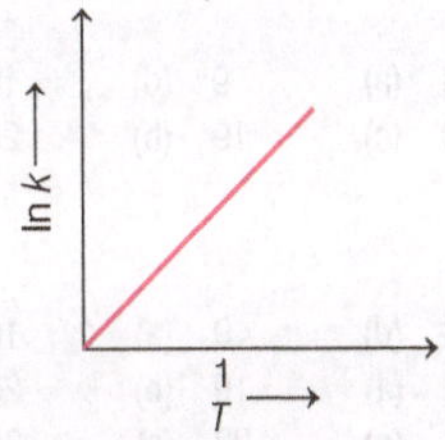

(d) 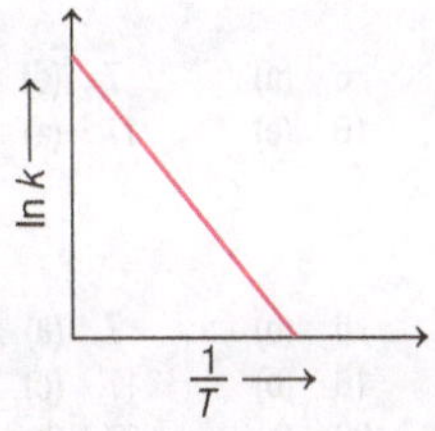

17. Activation energy of any chemical reaction can calculated if one knows the value of **[NEET 2024]**
(a) rate constant at standard temperature
(b) probability of collision
(c) orientation of reactant molecules during collision
(d) rate constant at two diferent temperature

18. The rate of a reaction quadruples when temperature changes from 27°C to 57°C. Calculate the energy of activation. **[NEET 2024]**
[Given : $R = 8.314 \text{ JK}^{-1} \text{ mol}^{-1}$, $\log 4 = 0.6021$]
(a) 38.04 kJ/mol (b) 380.4 kJ/mol
(c) 3.80 kJ/mol (d) 3804 kJ/mol

19. Given below are two statements is one labelled as Assertion A and the other is labelled as Reason R.
Assertion (A) A reaction can have zero activation energy.
Reason (R) The minimum extra amount of energy absorbed by reactant molecules so that their energy becomes equal to threshold value, is called activation energy.
In the light of the above statements, choose the correct answer from the options given below. **[NCERT (New) Pg. 79, NEET 2023]**
(a) Both A and R are true and R is the correct explanation of A.
(b) Both A and R are true but R is not the correct explanation of A.
(c) A is true but R is false.
(d) A is false but R is true.

20. For a reaction, $A \rightarrow B$, enthalpy of reaction is -4.2 kJ mol^{-1} and enthalpy of activation is 9.6 kJ mol^{-1}. The correct potential energy profile for the reaction is shown in option. **[NCERT (New) Pg. 79, NEET 2021]**

(a) 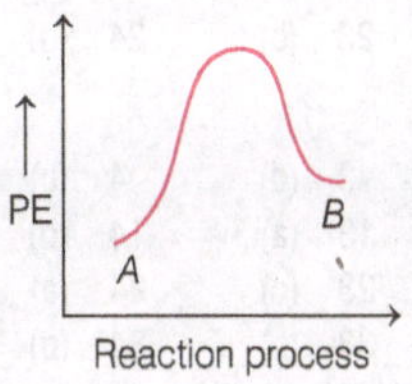

(b) 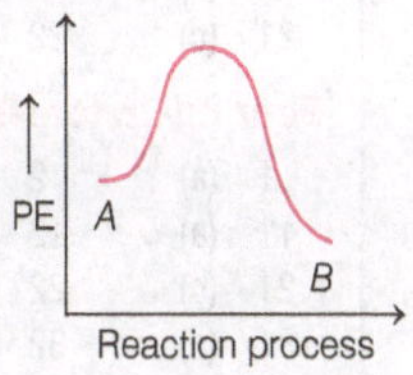

(c) 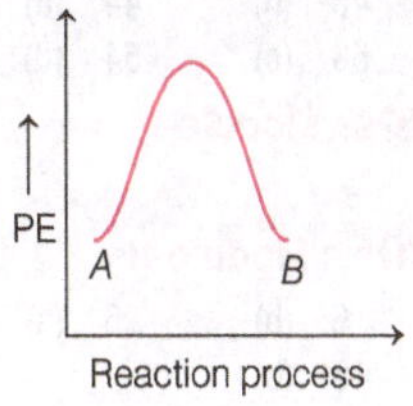

(d) 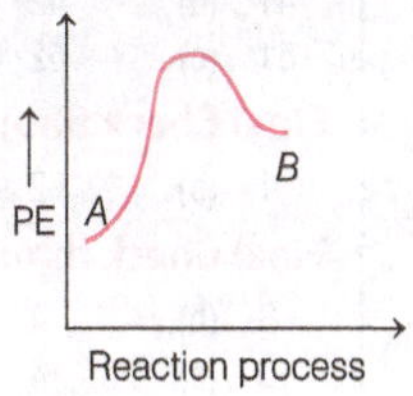

21. The slope of Arrhenius plot $\left(\ln k \text{ vs } \frac{1}{T}\right)$ of first order reaction is -5×10^3K. The value of E_a of the reaction is [Given, $R = 8.314 \text{ JK}^{-1} \text{ mol}^{-1}$] **[NEET 2021]**
(a) 41.5 kJ mol^{-1} (b) 83.0 kJ mol^{-1}
(c) 166 kJ mol^{-1} (d) -83 kJ mol^{-1}

22. An increase in the concentration of the reactants of a reaction leads to the change in **[NCERT (New) Pg. 83, NEET 2020]**
(a) heat of reaction (b) threshold energy
(c) collision frequency (d) activation energy

23. In collision theory of chemical reaction, Z_{AB} represents **[NEET 2020]**
(a) the fraction of molecules with energies greater than E_a
(b) the collision frequency of reactants, A and B
(c) steric factor
(d) the fraction of molecules with energies equal to E_a

24. For a reaction, activation energy $E_a = 0$ and the rate constant at 200 K is $1.6 \times 10^6 s^{-1}$.
The rate constant at 400 K will be [Given that, gas constant $R = 8.314\,JK^{-1}mol^{-1}$] **[NEET 2019]**
(a) $3.2 \times 10^4 s^{-1}$
(b) $1.6 \times 10^6 s^{-1}$
(c) $1.6 \times 10^3 s^{-1}$
(d) $3.2 \times 10^6 s^{-1}$

25. Which one of the following statements is not correct? **[NEET 2017]**
(a) Catalyst does not initiate any reaction.
(b) The value of equilibrium constant is changed in the presence of a catalyst in the reaction equilibrium.
(c) Enzymes catalyse mainly biochemical reaction.
(d) Coenzymes increase the catalytic activity of enzyme.

26. The addition of a catalyst during a chemical reaction alters which of the following quantities? **[NEET 2016]**
(a) Internal energy (b) Enthalpy
(c) Activation energy (d) Entropy

27. The activation energy of a reaction can be determined from the slope of which of the following graphs? **[AIPMT 2015]**
(a) $\ln k$ *vs* T (b) $\dfrac{\ln k}{T}$ *vs* T (c) $\ln k$ *vs* $\dfrac{1}{T}$ (d) $\dfrac{T}{\ln K}$ *vs* $\dfrac{1}{T}$

Answers

Step up Practice 1

1 (c)	2 (c)	3 (b)	4 (c)	5 (d)	6 (a)	7 (d)	8 (b)	9 (b)	10 (a)
11 (b)	12 (a)	13 (d)	14 (a)	15 (d)	16 (a)	17 (b)	18 (b)		

Step up Practice 2

1 (b)	2 (d)	3 (a)	4 (d)	5 (b)	6 (c)	7 (c)	8 (d)	9 (c)	10 (a)
11 (d)	12 (a)	13 (d)	14 (a)	15 (c)	16 (c)	17 (a)	18 (d)	19 (c)	20 (c)
21 (a)	22 (a)	23 (d)	24 (b)						

Step up Practice 3

1 (c)	2 (b)	3 (d)	4 (b)	5 (d)	6 (a)	7 (d)	8 (a)	9 (d)	10 (d)
11 (b)	12 (c)	13 (d)	14 (d)	15 (b)	16 (c)	17 (a)	18 (c)	19 (b)	20 (b)
21 (c)	22 (d)	23 (b)	24 (d)						

Gearing up for NEET

1 (a)	2 (b)	3 (d)	4 (c)	5 (a)	6 (b)	7 (a)	8 (d)	9 (a)	10 (d)
11 (a)	12 (c)	13 (a)	14 (b)	15 (d)	16 (b)	17 (c)	18 (a)	19 (b)	20 (c)
21 (c)	22 (b)	23 (c)	24 (a)	25 (a)	26 (a)	27 (b)	28 (c)	29 (a)	30 (b)
31 (c)	32 (c)	33 (b)	34 (d)	35 (c)	36 (c)	37 (a)	38 (a)	39 (d)	40 (d)
41 (d)	42 (b)	43 (b)	44 (a)	45 (c)	46 (a)	47 (b)	48 (b)	49 (a)	50 (d)
51 (c)	52 (a)	53 (c)	54 (d)	55 (b)					

Final Check through PYQs : Module-I

1 (b)	2 (d)

Final Check through PYQs : Module-II

3 (b)	4 (a)	5 (b)	6 (a)	7 (d)	8 (b)	9 (b)	10 (c)	11 (b)	12 (a)
13 (d)	14 (d)	15 (b)							

Final Check through PYQs : Module-III

16 (d)	17 (d)	18 (a)	19 (d)	20 (b)	21 (a)	22 (c)	23 (b)	24 (b)	25 (b)
26 (c)	27 (c)								

Hints and Solutions

Step up Practice 1

1. (c) Given, chemical reaction is

$$5Br^-(aq) + BrO_3^-(aq) + 6H^+(aq) \longrightarrow 3Br_2(aq) + 3H_2O(l)$$

Rate law expression for the above equation can be written

$$-\frac{1}{5}\frac{\Delta[Br^-]}{\Delta t} = -\frac{\Delta[BrO_3^-]}{\Delta t}$$

$$= \frac{-1}{6}\frac{\Delta[H^+]}{\Delta t} = \frac{+1}{3}\frac{\Delta[Br_2]}{\Delta t}$$

$$\Rightarrow \quad -\frac{\Delta[Br^-]}{\Delta t} = -\frac{5\,\Delta[BrO_3^-]}{\Delta t} = \frac{-5}{6}\frac{\Delta[H^+]}{\Delta t}$$

$$\Rightarrow \quad \frac{\Delta[Br^-]}{\Delta t} = \frac{5}{6}\frac{\Delta[H^+]}{\Delta t}$$

2. (c) Given reaction,

$$A(g) + 4B(g) \longrightarrow 5C(g)$$

$$\frac{-d[A]}{dt} = \frac{1}{4}\frac{d[B]}{dt}$$

$$\frac{-d[A]}{dt} = -\frac{1}{4} \times 2 \times 10^{-3} = 0.5 \times 10^{-3}$$

$$= 5 \times 10^{-4} \text{ mol L}^{-1}\text{ min}^{-1}$$

3. (b) Based on the given reaction,

$$-\frac{1}{2}\frac{\Delta[N_2O_5]}{\Delta t} = \frac{1}{4}\frac{\Delta[NO_2]}{\Delta t} = \frac{\Delta[O_2]}{\Delta t}$$

$$\frac{k_1}{2}[N_2O_5] = \frac{k_2}{4}[N_2O_5] = k_3[N_2O_5]$$

$$\therefore \quad 2k_1 = k_2 = 4k_3$$

Hence, option (b) is correct.

4. (c) Statement I is false but Statement II is true.

The correct form of Statement I is :

For $3A \longrightarrow 2B$, $\frac{-d[A]}{dt}$ is equal to $+\frac{3}{2}\frac{d[B]}{dt}$.

5. (d) Among the given expression, only two, i.e. (ii) and (iv) do not express the reaction rate of the given reaction.

6. (a) By using, $pV = nRT$

$$p_{CH_3CHO} = \frac{n}{V}RT$$

$$\therefore \quad -\left(\frac{dp_{CH_3CHO}}{dt}\right) = \left(\frac{dn}{dt}\right)\frac{RT}{V}$$

$$\therefore \quad \frac{dn}{dt} = \frac{V}{RT}\frac{dp_{CH_3CHO}}{dt}$$

7. (d) For given elementary reaction,

$$2H_2S + O_2 \longrightarrow \text{products}$$

$$\text{Rate} = [p_{H_2S}]^2\,[p_{O_2}] \text{ and}$$

$$(\text{Rate})_{new} = [4p_{H_2S}]^2[4p_{O_2}]$$

$$= 64\,[p_{H_2S}]^2[p_{O_2}]$$

$$= 64 \text{ (initial rate)}$$

8. (b) The rate of disappearance of SO_2,

$$\frac{-d[SO_2]}{dt} = 1.60 \times 10^{-3} \text{ g/L/s}$$

$$r = -\frac{1}{2}\frac{d[SO_2]}{dt} = \frac{1}{2}\frac{d[SO_3]}{dt} = \frac{-d[O_2]}{dt}$$

$$= \frac{1}{64} \times 1.60 \times 10^{-3} \text{ mol/L/s}$$

$$= 2.5 \times 10^{-5} \text{ mol/L/s}$$

$$\Rightarrow \quad \frac{d[SO_3]}{dt} = 2.5 \times 10^{-5} \text{ mol/L/s}$$

$$= 80 \times 2.5 \times 10^{-5} \text{ g/L/s}$$

$$= 2 \times 10^{-3} \text{ g/L/s}$$

9. (b) The value of the rate constant can be increased only by increasing the temperature.

10. (a) If we write rate of reaction in terms of concentration of NH_3 and H_2 then,

$$\text{Rate of reaction} = \frac{1}{2}\frac{d[NH_3]}{dt} = -\frac{1}{3}\frac{d[H_2]}{dt}$$

$$\text{So,} \quad \frac{d[NH_3]}{dt} = -\frac{2}{3}\frac{d[H_2]}{dt}.$$

11. (b) Among the given relation, only two relation are correct between k, k' and k''.

For the given reaction,

$$2N_2O_5 \longrightarrow 4NO_2 + O_2$$

Rate law expression for this reaction is

$$-\frac{1}{2}\underset{(k)}{\frac{d[N_2O_5]}{dt}} = +\frac{1}{4}\underset{(k')}{\frac{d[NO_2]}{dt}} = +\underset{(k'')}{\frac{d[O_2]}{dt}}$$

$$\text{So,} \quad -\frac{1}{2}k = \frac{1}{4}k' = k''$$

$$\Rightarrow \quad k' = -2k \text{ and } k'' = \frac{k'}{4}$$

12. (a) $2SO_2 + O_2 \longrightarrow 2SO_3$

$$r_{SO_3} = 15 \text{ g/s} = \frac{15}{80} \text{ mol/s}$$

$$\text{Also,} \quad \frac{r_{O_2}}{1} = \frac{r_{SO_3}}{2}$$

$$r_{O_2} = \frac{15}{80} \times \frac{1}{2} \text{ mol/s}$$
$$= \left(\frac{15}{160}\right) \times 32 \text{ g/s} = 3 \text{ g/s}$$

13. (*d*) The average rate and instantaneous rate of a reaction are equal when two rate have time interval $\Delta t \to 0$.

14. (*a*) $\left(\frac{dx}{dt}\right)_0 = k(0.60)(0.80)^2 = 0.384\,k$

$$A(g) + 2B(g) \longrightarrow C(g) + D(g)$$

0.60	0.80	0	0
$(0.60 - x)$	$(0.80 - 2x)$	x	x

$x = 0.2$ atm

$\therefore$ $[A] = 0.4$ atm

$[B] = 0.4$ atm

$\therefore$ $\left(\frac{dx}{dt}\right)_t = k(0.4)(0.4)^2 = 0.064\,k$

$\therefore$ $\left(\frac{dx}{dt}\right)_t \Big/ \left(\frac{dx}{dt}\right)_0 = \frac{0.064k}{0.384k} = \frac{1}{6}$

15. (*d*) Both Statement I and Statement II are true.

16. (*a*) Among the given statements, only (a) is correct. While other statements (b), (c) and (d) are incorrect.

Their correct forms are

- Unit of rate of reaction is concentration time^{-1}.
- Rate of reaction depends upon the experimental conditions such as concentration of reactants, temperature and catalyst.
- Average rate depends upon the change in concentration of reactants or products and the time taken for that change to occur.

17. (*b*) Among the given statements, only (b) is incorrect.

Its correct form is :

Average rate depends upon the change in concentration of reactants or products.

18. (*b*) Given, rate $(r) = k[A]^3[B]^2$ ...(i)

$r_1 = k[2A]^3[3B]^2$ ...(ii)

Dividing Eqs. (i) by (ii) we get,

$$\frac{r}{r_1} = \frac{k[A]^3[B]^2}{k[2A]^3[3B]^2}$$
$$\frac{r}{r_1} = \frac{1}{8 \times 9}$$
$$r_1 = 72r$$

Step up Practice 2

1. (*b*) As rate $= k[RCl]$, on decreasing the concentration of RCl to half, the rate will also be halved.

2. (*d*) Both Statement I and Statement II are true.

3. (*a*) Among the given statements, only statement (a) is incorrect.

Its correct form is :

Rate law for any reaction must be determined experimentally.

4. (*d*) $\left(\frac{dx}{dt}\right) = k[G]^a[H]^b$

$$8\left(\frac{dx}{dt}\right) = k[2G]^a[2H]^b \quad \text{...(i)}$$
$$2\left(\frac{dx}{dt}\right) = k[2G]^a[H]^b \quad \text{...(ii)}$$

$\therefore$ $2 = (2)^a$

$\Rightarrow$ $a = 1$

$\Rightarrow$ $8 = (2)^a(2)^b$

$4 = (2)^b$

$\Rightarrow$ $b = 2$

Thus, overall order $= 1 + 2 = 3$.

5. (*b*) 0.12 M $\longrightarrow$ 0.06 M 10 h (50% reaction)

0.12 M $\longrightarrow$ 0.03 M 20 h (75% reaction)

Time of 75% reaction $= 2 \times$ time of 50% reaction which is the property of first order reaction.

6. (*c*) Order of reaction is an experimentally determined quantity. It cannot be calculated by balanced form of reaction.

7. (*c*) Among the given match, only (c) is not a correct match.

Its correct match is :

Second order $\longrightarrow$ mol^{-1} L s^{-1}.

8. (*d*) Both Statement I and Statement II are true.

9. (*c*) Among the given match, only (c) is correctly matced for a given rate law expression, $r = k[A]^{3/2}[B]^{-1}$

$\Rightarrow$ Order of a reaction is $\Rightarrow \frac{3}{2} - 1 = \frac{1}{2}$.

10. (*a*) Among the given statements, only statement (a) is correct for a reaction following first order kinetics while other statements are incorrect.

11. (*d*) Among the given match, (d) is not correctly matched about zero order reaction.

12. (*a*) For a zero-order reaction,

$$t_{1/2} = \frac{a_0}{2k}$$
$$k = \frac{a_0}{2 \times t_{1/2}} = \frac{0.2}{2 \times 80}$$
$$= 1.25 \times 10^{-3} \text{ mol L}^{-1}\text{s}^{-1}$$

13. (*d*) Among the given graphical representation, only three (i), (iii) and (iv) represent the zero order reaction.

14. (*a*) The half-life period for a zero order reaction is proportional to initial concentration.

15. (*c*) Reactants and products are in gaseous state thus,

$$A(g) \longrightarrow B(g) + C(g)$$

At $t = 0$ p_i 0   0

At $t = t$ $(p_i - x)$ x x

Total pressure at time (t),

$$p_t = p_i - x + x + x = p_i + x$$

$$\therefore \quad x = (p_t - p_i)$$

and $(a - x) = p_i - (p_t - p_i) = 2p_i - p_t$

Given, $p_i = a = 100$ mm Hg

$p_t = 120$ mm Hg

$\therefore \quad (a - x) = 2p_i - p_t = 80$ mm

$$\therefore \quad k = \frac{2.303}{10} \log \frac{100}{80}$$

or $$\frac{2.303}{10} \log \frac{5}{4} \text{ min}^{-1}$$

16. (*c*) $k = \dfrac{2.303}{t} \log\left(\dfrac{a}{a - x}\right)$

$$k = \frac{2.303}{90} \log\left(\frac{100}{100 - 90}\right) \quad \text{...(i)}$$

$$k = \frac{2.303}{90} \log 10$$

$$\Rightarrow \quad k = \frac{2.303}{90} \text{ min}^{-1} \quad \text{...(ii)}$$

Also, $$k = \frac{2.303}{t_{50\%}} \log \frac{100}{100 - 50}$$

$$= \frac{2.303}{t_{50\%}} \log 2 \quad \text{...(iii)}$$

From Eqs. (ii) and (iii),

$$\therefore \quad \frac{2.303 \log 2}{t_{50}} = \frac{2.303}{90}$$

$$\therefore \quad t_{50} = \log 2 \times 90 = 0.3 \times 90 = 27 \text{ min}$$

17. (*a*) Among the given reactions, only one reaction [iii] is not of first order.

18. (*d*) The given reaction is

$$2N_2O_5 \longrightarrow 4NO_2 + O_2$$

The unit of rate constant indicates it is a first-order reaction.

$$\text{Rate} = k[N_2O_5]$$

Given, $$k = 3 \times 10^{-5} \text{ s}^{-1}$$

$$\text{Rate} = 2.4 \times 10^{-5} \text{ mol L}^{-1} \text{ s}^{-1}$$

By putting the values,

$$2.4 \times 10^{-5} = 3.0 \times 10^{-5} [N_2O_5]$$

$$\Rightarrow \quad \frac{8}{10} = [N_2O_5]$$

$$[N_2O_5] = 0.8 \text{ mol L}^{-1}$$

19. (*c*) For $\dfrac{5}{6}$th life, $x = \dfrac{5a}{6}$

$$\therefore \quad t_{5/6} = \frac{2.303}{k} \log \frac{a}{a - \frac{5a}{6}}$$

$$= \frac{2.303}{k} \log \frac{a}{\frac{a}{6}} = \frac{2.303}{k} \log 6$$

20. (*c*) Statement I is false but Statement II is true

Correct form of Statement I is :

A first order reaction is 50% completed in 1.26×10^{14} s. It will take infinite time for 100% completion.

Statement II $r\,(\text{min}^{-1}) = k \times \left(10 \times \dfrac{1}{2^{20/10}}\right)$

$$= \frac{0.693}{t_{50}} \times \frac{10}{2^2} = \frac{0.693}{10} \times 2.5$$

$$= 0.0693 \times 2.5 \text{ min}^{-1} \quad \left[\because \frac{a}{a_0} = \frac{1}{2^n} = \frac{1}{2^{T/t_{50}}}\right]$$

21. (*a*) $t_{7/8} = \dfrac{2.303}{k} \log \dfrac{a}{a - \frac{7}{8}a}$

$$= \frac{2.303}{k} \log \frac{a}{\frac{a}{8}} = \frac{2.303}{k} \log 2^3$$

$$t_{1/2} = \frac{2.303}{k} \log \frac{a}{\left(a - \frac{a}{2}\right)} = \frac{2.303}{k} \times \log 2$$

$$\therefore \quad \frac{t_{7/8}}{t_{1/2}} = \frac{\frac{2.303}{k} \log 2^3}{\frac{2.303}{k} \log 2} = 3$$

22. (*a*) Given, $t_1 = 10$ min, $t_2 = 20$ min

$[R_1] = 0.04$ mol/Ls, $[R_2] = 0.03$ mol/Ls

For first order reaction,

$$\text{Rate } (k) = \frac{2.303}{t_2 - t_1} \log \frac{[R_1]}{[R_2]}$$

By putting the values,

$$k = \frac{2.303}{10} \log\left(\frac{0.04}{0.03}\right)$$

$$k = 0.02877 \text{ min}^{-1}$$

Now, the half-life for the first order reaction,

$$t_{1/2} = \frac{0.693}{k} = \frac{0.693}{0.02877}$$

$$= 24.087 \approx 24.1 \text{ min}$$

23. (*d*) Among the given statements, only statement (d) is correct while other statements are incorrect.

$$H_2(g) + Br_2(g) \longrightarrow 2HBr(g)$$

The molecularity of the reaction is $1+1=2$

Rate of reaction $= k[H_2][Br_2]^{1/2}$

Order of reaction $= 1 + \frac{1}{2} = \frac{3}{2}$

Unit of $k = \text{mol}^{-1/2}\ \text{L}^{1/2}\text{s}^{-1}$.

24. (*b*) Among the given statements, only statement (b) is not correct about molecularity of a reaction. Molecularity more than three is rare.

Step up Practice 3

1. (*c*) Among the given statements, only statement (c) is incorrect about the collision theory of chemical reaction.

2. (*b*) The rate constant is given by the equation, $k = P \cdot Z \times e^{-E_a/RT}$ then, the factor E_a should decrease for the reaction to proceed more rapidly.

3. (*d*) Both Statements I and Statement II are true.

4. (*b*) In the given graph transition states are shown by II and IV positions.

5. (*d*) $\Delta H(A \rightarrow B) = -10\ \text{kJ}$ (exothermic reaction)

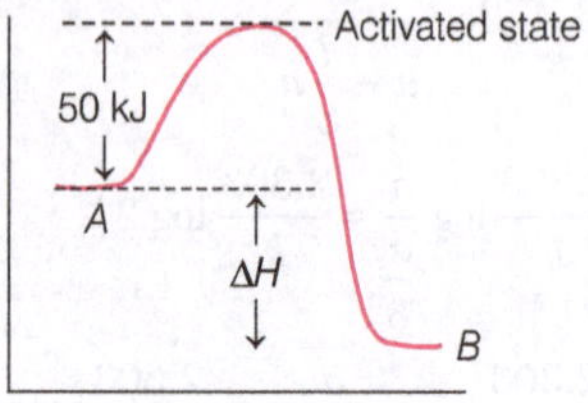

$\therefore\ \Delta H(B \rightarrow A) = 10\ \text{kJ}$

$E_a(A \rightarrow \text{activated state}) = 50\ \text{kJ}$

$\therefore\ E_a\ (B \rightarrow \text{activated state}) = 50 + 10 = 60\ \text{kJ mol}^{-1}$

6. (*a*) For the given reaction, as the temperature increases, the rate of the forward as well as backward reactions also increase.

7. (*d*) For 10°C rise in temperature, $n = 1$

So, rate $= (2)^n = (2)^1 = 2$

When temperature is increased from 10°C to 100°C, change is $= 100 - 10 = 90°\text{C}$

$n = 9$

Rate $= (2)^9 = 512$ times

8. (*a*) Among the given match, only (a) is correct match for the temperature coefficient of a reaction.

9. (*d*) Among the given match, only (d) is correctly matched. When temperature of a reaction is changed from T_1 and T_2, half-life is found to decrease (i.e. rate of the reaction increases), then $T_2 > T_1$ and reaction can be exothermic or endothermic.

10. (*d*) From Arrhenius equation,

$$\log \frac{k_2}{k_1} = \frac{E_a}{2.303R}\left[\frac{T_2 - T_1}{T_1T_2}\right]$$

$$= \frac{10000}{2.303 \times 2}\left(\frac{5}{400 \times 405}\right) = \frac{50000}{746172}$$

$$\log \frac{k_2}{k_1} = 0.067$$

$$\frac{k_2}{k_1} = 1.166$$

or $\quad \frac{k_2}{k_1} - 1 = 1.166 - 1$

$$\frac{k_2 - k_1}{k_1} = 0.166$$

$$k_2 - k_1 = 0.166\ k_1$$

i.e. k_2 increases by 16.6%

11. (*b*) Among the given statements, only three statements (i), (ii) and (iii) are correct while statements (iv) and (v) are incorrect.

- $\log k\ (\text{min}^{-1}) = 5 - \frac{2000\text{K}}{T}$

$$\log_{10} k = \log_{10} A - \frac{E_a}{2.303RT}$$

- $\log_{10} A = 5, A = 10^5$
- $\frac{E_a}{2.303R} = 2000$

$$E_a = 2000 \times 2.303 \times 0.002\ \text{kcal/mol}$$
$$= 9.212\ \text{kcal/mol}$$

- Equation represents straight line.

12. (*c*) Among the given match, only option (c) represents the correct unit of A in Arrhenius equation for a first order reaction. Because, A is a constant having the same unit as the rate constant, i.e. s^{-1}.

13. (*d*) Among the given expressions, only two (iii) and (v) are correct while other (i), (ii) and (iv) are incorrect for Arrhenius equation (where, k is rate constant).

14. (*d*) According to Arrhenius equation,

$$k = Ae^{-E_a/RT}$$

which indicates that as activation energy decreases rate constant increases and as temperature increases rate of reaction increases.

15. (*b*) $\log k - \log A = -\frac{E_a}{2.303RT}$

$$\log\left(\frac{k}{A}\right) = -\frac{2.303RT}{2.303RT} = -1 = \log(10^{-1})$$

$$\frac{k}{A} = 1 \times 10^{-1} = 0.1$$

16. (*c*) Among the given match, only (c) is correct for the k_1 and k_2.

Given, $\quad R \xrightarrow{k_1} B, E_{a_1}$

$\quad R \xrightarrow{k_2} C, E_{a_2}$

As we know,

Here : $k_1 = A_1 e^{-E_{a1}/RT}$ and $k_2 = A_2 e^{-E_{a2}/RT}$

$$\frac{k_1}{k_2} = \left(\frac{A_1}{A_2}\right) e^{\frac{-E_{a1}+E_{a2}}{RT}}$$

Now, $\frac{A_1}{A_2}$ = constant $= A$ and $E_{a_2} = 2E_{a_1}$

$$\frac{k_1}{k_2} = Ae^{\frac{-E_{a1}+2E_{a1}}{RT}} \Rightarrow \frac{k_1}{k_2} = Ae^{\frac{Ea_1}{RT}}$$

$$k_1 = Ak_2 e^{Ea_1/RT}$$

17. (*a*) As we know,

$$k = A \cdot e^{\frac{-E_a}{RT}} \quad \text{...(i)}$$

given, $$k = A \cdot e^{\frac{-60000}{T}} \quad \text{...(ii)}$$

On comparing both the equations we get,

$$-\frac{E_a}{RT} = \frac{-60000}{T}$$

$$E_a = 60000 \times 2 = 12 \times 10^4 \text{ cal/mol}$$

18. (*c*) In Arrhenius equation, the fraction of molecules $= e^{-\frac{E_a}{RT}}$

$$= 10^{-E_a/2.303RT} = 10^{-\frac{E_a}{2.303 \times R \times 403}} = 10^{-\frac{E_a}{928.1R}}$$

19. (*b*) Given, $T_{a_1} = 300$ K

$T_{a_2} = 310$ K

$T_{b_1} = 300$ K

$T_{b_2} = x$

$E_b = 2E_a$

So, $$E_a\left(\frac{1}{T_{a_1}} - \frac{1}{T_{a_2}}\right) = E_b\left(\frac{1}{T_{b_1}} - \frac{1}{T_{b_2}}\right)$$

$$E_a\left(\frac{1}{300} - \frac{1}{310}\right) = 2E_a\left(\frac{1}{300} - \frac{1}{x}\right)$$

$$\frac{1}{300} - \frac{1}{x} = \frac{1}{18600}$$

$$\frac{1}{x} = \frac{1}{300} - \frac{1}{18600}$$

$$\Rightarrow \quad x = 304.92$$

So, increase in temperature of B from 300 K is 4.92 K.

20. (*b*) The rate of a chemical reaction generally increases rapidly even for small temperature increase because of rapid increase in the fraction of molecules with energies in excess of the activation energy.

21. (*c*) $k = Ae^{-E_a/RT}$ in absence of catalyst and $R = k[A]$

$k' = Ae^{-(E_a-2)/RT}$ in presence of catalyst and $R' = k'[A]$

$$\because \quad \frac{R'}{R} = \frac{k'}{k} = e^{2/RT}$$

$$= e^{2/0.002 \times 300} = e^{3.33} = 27.94 \approx 28$$

22. (*d*) Both the Statements I and Statements II are true.

23. (*b*) Among the given statements, only statement (b) is incorrect for the catalyst.

Its correct form is :

Catalyst does not alter Gibbs free energy as it is related to reaction quotient.

24. (*d*) Both Statements I and Statements II are true.

Gearing up for NEET

1. (*a*) From the graph, it is evident that it is a first order reaction.

Let, the reaction be

$A \rightarrow$ Product

So, $$\text{rate} = k[A] \quad \text{...(i)}$$

where, k = rate constant

$$\frac{k}{2.303} = \frac{1}{t}\log\frac{[A]_0}{[A]_t}$$

From the graph,

At $t = 0$, $[A]_0 = 0.4$

At $t = 205$, $[A]_t = 0.2$

So, $k = \frac{1}{20}(2.303)\log\frac{[0.4]}{[0.2]} = \frac{0.693}{20}$

Now, from equation (i) at $t = 20$ s

$$r = \frac{0.693}{20}[0.2]$$

$$= 6.93 \times 10^{-3} = 7 \times 10^{-3} \text{ ms}^{-1}$$

2. (*b*) $A \longrightarrow B$

Concentration of reactants and products varies exponentially with respect to time.

(i) Concentration of reactant (here, A) decreases exponentially with respect to time.

(ii) Concentration of product (here, B) increases exponentially with respect to time.

3. (*d*) $$\frac{-d[A]}{dt} = k[A]^n$$

$$1 \times 10^{-4} = k[0.01]^n$$

$$1.41 \times 10^{-4} = k[0.02]^n$$

$$(1.41) = (2)^n$$

$$(2)^{1/2} = (2)^n$$

$$n = \frac{1}{2}$$

$$\therefore \quad \frac{-d[A]}{dt} = k[A]^{1/2}$$

4. (*c*) Given, $\frac{dx}{dt} = k[A]^2$

$$\log\left(\frac{dx}{dt}\right) = \log k + 2\log A$$

On comparing with equation of straight line $y = mx + c$, we get intercept $\log k$ and slope $= \tan\theta = 2$.
Thus, graph given in option (c) is correct.

5. (*a*) $N_2 + 3H_2 \underset{K_b}{\overset{K_f}{\rightleftharpoons}} 2NH_3$

$$\left(\frac{dx}{dt}\right)_{net} = K_f[N_2][H_2]^3 - K_b[NH_3]^2 \quad ...(i)$$

Also, $\frac{[NH_3]^2}{[N_2][H_2]^3} = \frac{K_f}{K_b}$

or $\frac{[N_2][H_2]^3}{[NH_3]^2} = \frac{K_b}{K_f}$

$$= \frac{1\times10^{-3}}{1\times10^{2}} = 1\times10^{-5}$$

$\Rightarrow$ $[N_2][H]^3 = 1\times10^{-5}\,[NH_3]^2\,M^2$

From Eqn. (i)

$$\left(\frac{dx}{dt}\right) = 1\times10^{2}M^{-3}\times10^{-5}[NH_3]^2M^2 - 1\times10^{-3}\,[NH_3]^2\,M^{-1}$$

Thus, $\left(\frac{dx}{dt}\right) = 0$

Hence, option (a) is correct.

6. (*b*) Given, $R = k[A]^2[B]$

when, $A = [3A], B = [3B]$

then, $R' = k[3A]^2[3B]$

$= 9\times 3k[A]^2[B] = 27k[A]^2[B]$

$R' = 27R$

Thus, the rate will become 27 times higher.

7. (*a*) For a unimolecular reaction, both order and molecularity are one and slowest step is the rate determining step.

8. (*d*) Among the given pair, only (d) is correct for the given reaction.

$\Rightarrow$ $r = k'[N_2O_2][H_2]$

Again, $k_{eq} = \frac{[N_2O_2]}{[NO]^2}$

$\Rightarrow$ $r = k'\times[k_{eq}\times(NO)^2]\times[H_2]$

$\therefore r = k[NO]^2[H_2]$ and $n = 3$

9. (*a*) For a zero order reaction,

$$t = \frac{1}{k}(a_0 - a)$$

$$t_{90\%} = \frac{1}{k}\times\frac{a_0}{10} \qquad \left[\because \text{at } t_{90\%},\ a = \frac{9}{10}a_0\right]$$

$$k = \frac{a_0}{10\times t_{90}}$$

$$= \frac{0.36}{10\times150} = 0.00024$$

$$k = 2.4\times10^{-4}\ \text{mol L}^{-1}\text{s}^{-1}$$

10. (*d*) For a zero order reaction,

$$t = \frac{1}{k}(a_0 - a) \qquad \left[\because \text{At } t_{75\%},\ a = \frac{3}{4}a_0\right]$$

$$t_{75\%} = \frac{1}{k}\times\frac{1}{4}a_0$$

$$k = \frac{a_0}{4\times t_{75\%}} = \frac{0.08}{4\times180}$$

$$= \frac{0.08}{720} = 0.00011$$

$$k = 1.1\times10^{-4}\ \text{mol L}^{-1}\text{s}^{-1}$$

11. (*a*) $T_{50\%} \propto \left(\frac{1}{a}\right)^{n-1}$

$$T_{50\%} \propto a \quad (n = 0)$$

$$T_{50\%} = ka$$

$$\log T_{50\%} = \log a + \log k$$

Thus, a graph between $\log T_{50}$ and $\log a$ is a straight line of slope 45° and intercept, $\log a$.

12. (*c*) Among the given relations, only three relations, i.e. (i), (iii) and (iv) represent the first order reaction.

13. (*a*) $k = \frac{2.303}{40}\log\frac{0.1}{0.025} = 0.03466\ \text{min}^{-1}$

$$\frac{dx}{dt} = k[A] = 0.03466\times 0.01$$

$$= 3.47\times10^{-4}\ \text{M min}^{-1}$$

14. (*b*) $k = \frac{2.303}{t}\log\left(\frac{a}{a-x}\right)$

$$= \frac{2.303}{60}\log 8$$

$$= 0.03466\ \text{min}^{-1}$$

$$\left(\frac{dx}{dt}\right) = k[A] = 0.03466\times 0.1$$

$$= 3.466\times10^{-3}\ \text{mol L}^{-1}\ \text{min}^{-1}$$

15. (*d*) Rate is doubled, i.e. $r_2 = 2r_1$

We know,

$$\frac{r_2}{r_1} = 2 = \frac{k_2}{k_1}$$

Now,

$$\log\frac{k_2}{k_1} = \frac{E_a}{2.303R}\left[\frac{1}{T_1} - \frac{1}{T_2}\right]$$

$$\log_{10}2 = \frac{E_a\times1000}{2.303\times8.314}\left[\frac{1}{303} - \frac{1}{313}\right]$$

$$E_a = 54.47\ \text{kJ/mol}$$

16. (b) Given, initial concentration, $[A]_0 = 0.32$ M

Conc. after 9 min, $[A]_t = 0.032$ M

Using rate constant formula for I[st] order reaction,

$$k = \frac{2.303}{t} \log \left[\frac{A_0}{A_t}\right]$$

$$= \frac{2.303}{9} \log \left[\frac{0.32}{0.0321}\right]$$

$$= \frac{2.303}{9} \times 1 = 0.256$$

17. (c) Among the given match, only (c) is correctly matched with its order while other are incorrect. Their corrected forms are

- Rate $= k[A]^{1/2}[B^{3/2}]$; Order $= \frac{1}{2} + \frac{3}{2} = 2$
- Rate $= k[A]^{3/2}[B]^{-1}$; Order $= \frac{3}{2} - 1 = \frac{1}{2}$
- Rate $= k[A]^1[B]^{1/2}$; Order $= 1 + \frac{1}{2} = \frac{3}{2}$

18. (a) $$r = k[A]^x [B_2]^y$$

$$1.6 \times 10^{-4} = k[0.5]^x [0.5]^y \quad ...(i)$$

$$3.2 \times 10^{-4} = k[0.5]^x [1.0]^y \quad ...(ii)$$

$$3.2 \times 10^{-4} = k[1.0]^x [1.0]^y \quad ...(iii)$$

Divide Eqs. (ii) by (i)

$$2 = 2^y$$

$$y = 1$$

Divide Eqs. (iii) by (ii)

$$1 = 2^x$$

$\Rightarrow$ $$x = 0$$

So, $$r = k[A]^0 [B_2]^1$$

$$r = k[B_2]$$

19. (b) Among the given relation, only (b) is correctly matched between half reaction time $t_{1/2}$ and initial concentration of reactant for $(n-1)$ order reaction.

$$\Rightarrow \quad t_{50} \propto [R]_0^{(1-\text{order})}$$

20. (c) Among the given match only (c) is not correctly matched.

Its correct form is :

Graph between $\log \frac{[R]_0}{[R]}$ vs t gives a slope $\left(\frac{k}{2.303}\right)$.

21. (c) Given, $k = 5.0 \times 10^{11} \cdot e^{-\frac{29000(K)}{T}}$

As we know, $k = A \cdot e^{-\frac{E_a}{RT}}$

$$\frac{-E_a}{RT} = \frac{-29000}{T}$$

$$E_a = 29000 \times 1.98$$

$$= 57.42 \text{ kcal mol}^{-1} \approx 57 \text{ kcal mol}^{-1}$$

22. (b) Arrhenius equation, $k = Ae^{-\frac{E_a}{RT}}$

$$\ln k = \ln A - \frac{E_a}{R}\left(\frac{1}{T}\right)$$

$\Rightarrow -\frac{E_a}{R}$ is the slope of Arrhenius plot and

$\ln A$ is the intercept.

$\Rightarrow$ Slope $= -7.1 \times 10^3$ K

$$R = 8.314 \text{ JK}^{-1} \text{mol}^{-1}$$

So, $$-\frac{E_a}{R} = -7.1 \times 10^3 \text{ K}$$

$$E_a = 7.1 \times 10^3 \times 8.314$$

$$= 59.0294 \times 10^3 \text{ J mol}^{-1} = 59.03 \text{ kJ mol}^{-1}$$

23. (c) Among the given matched, only (c) is correctly matched regarding the time required for 100% completion of a zero order reaction.

As, for zero order reaction, $[A] = -kt + [A]_0$

where, $[A]_0$ = initial concentration $= a$

$[A]$ = remaining concentration $= a - a = 0$ at t_{100}

On putting the value of $[A]_0$ and $[A]$, we get,

$$t = \frac{a}{k}$$

24. (a) Since, $t_{1/2} = \frac{0.693}{k}$, $\therefore k = \frac{0.693}{t_{1/2}}$

Given, $t_{1/2} = 30$ min at 27°C and $t_{1/2} = 10$ min at 47°C

$$\therefore \quad k_{27°C} = \frac{0.693}{30} \text{ min}^{-1} = 0.0231 \text{ min}^{-1}$$

and $$k_{47°C} = \frac{0.693}{10} \text{ min}^{-1} = 0.0693 \text{ min}^{-1}$$

We know that,

$$\log \frac{k_{47°C}}{k_{27°C}} = \frac{E_a}{2.303R} \times \frac{(T_2 - T_1)}{T_2 \times T_1}$$

$$\therefore \quad E_a = \frac{2.303\, R \times T_1 \times T_2}{(T_2 - T_1)} \log \frac{k_{47°C}}{k_{27°C}}$$

$$E_a = \frac{2.303 \times 8.314 \times 10^{-3} \times 300 \times 320}{(320 - 300)} \log \frac{0.0693}{0.0231}$$

$$= 43.84 \text{ kJ mol}^{-1}$$

25. (a) Among the given match, only (a) is correctly matched for a zero order reaction.

For a zero order reaction, $A = [A]_0 - kt$

$$t_{1/2} = \frac{[A]_0}{2k}; \; t_{3/4} = \frac{3}{2}\frac{[A]_0}{2k}$$

$$\frac{t_{3/4}}{t_{1/2}} = \frac{3}{2} \Rightarrow t_{3/4} = \frac{3}{2} t_{1/2}$$

26. (a) Among the given graph, only one, i.e. (iii) describes the process of the given reaction.

As, first step is slow (requires large activation energy and the second step is fast (less activation energy) and overall reaction is exothermic.

So, product energy level should be less as compared to reactants.

27. (*b*)

28. (*c*) Presence of catalyst does not change the reaction enthalpy.

$$\Delta_r H^\ominus = (E_a)_f - (E_a)_r$$
$$= [(260) - (280)]\,\text{kJ mol}^{-1}$$
$$= -20\,\text{kJ mol}^{-1}$$

29. (*a*) Among the given match, option (a) is correctly matched for the integrated rate expression for a first order reaction.

30. (*b*) The decomposition of gaseous ammonia on a hot platinum surface is a zero order reaction at high pressure.

31. (*c*) $\log k = \log_{10} A - \dfrac{E_a}{2.303\,RT}$

$$\text{Slope} = -\frac{E_a}{2.303\,R} = -\frac{1}{2.303}$$

$\therefore \quad E_a = R = 2$ cal/mol

32. (*c*) Among the given statements, only (c) is incorrect while other are correct statements regarding the given reaction, $H_2(g) + I_2(g) \longrightarrow 2HI(g)$.

Its corrected form is :

The final enthalpy of the given reaction depends upon the nature of reactants and products.

33. (*b*) Among the given match, only (b) is correctly matched w.r.t. a first order reaction.

Because 75% of the reaction involves two half-lives while 50% of the reaction involves just one half-life.

34. (*d*) Among the given statement, statement (d) is incorrect. Its corrected form is :

k is not affected by the change in concentration.

35. (*c*) A is true but R is false.

The correct form of R is :

The rate constant of a zero order reaction does not depend on time.

36. (*c*) A is true but R is false.

The correct form of R is :

Half-life of the given reaction is independent of concentration and follows the relation, $t_{3/4} = 2 \times t_{1/2}$.

37. (*a*) Both A and R are true and R is the correct explanation of A.

38. (*a*) Both A and R are true and R is the correct explanation of A.

39. (*d*) Both Statement I and Statement II are true.

40. (*d*) Both Statement I and Statement II are true.

41. (*d*) Both Statement I and Statement II are true.

42. (*b*) Statement I is true but Statement II is false.

Its correct form is :

Reactant molecules undergoes chemical change irrespective of their orientation during collision.

43. (*b*) Statement I is true but Statement II is false.

Its correct form is :

Collision theory has a drawback that it ignores the structural aspect of atoms/molecules.

44. (*a*) Among the given statements, only A, D and E are correct while other are incorrect.

Their corrected form are as follows

- The unit of rate of reaction does not change with order of reaction.
- The unit of rate constant for a reaction is $\text{mol}^{1-n}\text{L}^{n-1}\text{s}^{-1}$, where, *n* is order of the reaction.

45. (*c*)

46. (*a*) Statements given in III and IV are correct while I and II are incorrect.

47. (*b*)

48. (*b*) Among the given statements, only A, C and D are incorrect while the statement B and E are correct.

The corrected forms of A, C and D are

- Formation of methanol from bromoethane depends upon the orientation of reactant molecules.
- According to collision theory, the reactant molecules are assumed to be hard spheres.
- Only those collisions in which molecules collide with sufficient energy and proper orientation are effective collisions.

49. (*a*) Among the given expression, only three, i.e. (ii), (iii) and (v) are not correct for first order reaction.

50. (*d*) Among the given relations, only three, i.e. (ii), (iii) and (v) are correct relation for a first order reaction.

51. (*c*) Among the given graphs only three i.e. (i), (iii) and (iv) represent first order reaction while others not.

52. (*a*) The correct match is A-2, B-1, C-3.

53. (*c*) The correct match is A-3, B-1, C-4, D-2.

54. (*d*) The correct match is A-3, B-1, C-4, D-2.

55. (*b*) The correct match is A-2, B-4, C-1, D-3.

Final Check Through PYQS

1. (*b*) Given, rate $(r) = k[A]^2[B]$ ...(i)

$$r_1 = k[3A]^2[B] \quad \text{...(ii)}$$

Dividing Eq. (i) by (ii), we get

$$\frac{r}{r_1} = \frac{k}{k}\frac{[A]^2[B]}{[3A]^2[B]}$$

$$\frac{r}{r_1} = \frac{1}{9} \Rightarrow r_1 = 9r$$

The initial rate would increase by a factor of nine.

2. (*d*) According to the chemical reaction,

$$\text{Rate of reaction} = \frac{-d[N_2]}{dt} = -\frac{1}{3}\frac{d[H_2]}{dt} = \frac{1}{2}\frac{d[NH_3]}{dt}$$

3. (*b*)

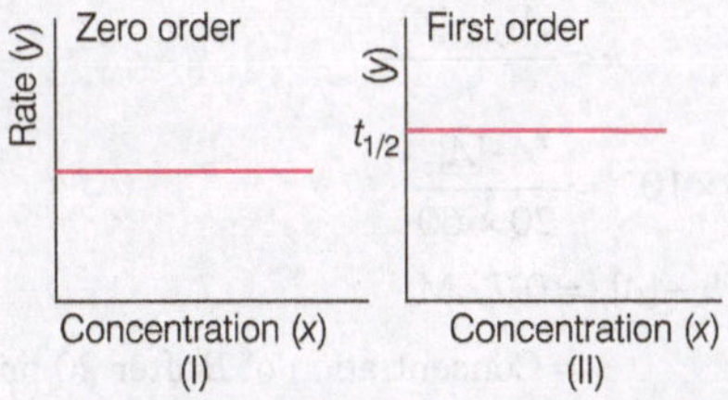

Here, graph I is of zero order if y-axis is representing rate and x represents concentration. For zero order, reaction rate is independent of concentration and remains constant.

While II graph represents first order if y is half-life ($t_{1/2}$) and x is concentration. Here, $t_{1/2}$ is independent of concentration.

Hence, option (b) is correct, i.e. zero order (y = rate and x = concentration), first order ($y = t_{1/2}$ and x = concentration).

4. (*a*) Given, Initial concentration $[A_0] = 0.1$ M

Concentration after 5 min $[A_t] = 0.001$ M

$t = 5$ minutes

Using rate constant formula for 1st order reaction

$$k = \frac{2.303}{t}\log\left(\frac{A_0}{A_t}\right) = \frac{2.303}{5}\log\left(\frac{0.1}{0.001}\right)$$

$$k = \frac{2.303 \times 2}{5} = 0.9212\ \text{min}^{-1}$$

Hence, the rate constant for the reaction is

$$k = 0.9212\ \text{min}^{-1}.$$

5. (*b*) For a first order reactions

Rate constant $(k) = 4.606 \times 10^{-3}\ \text{s}^{-1}$

Initial amount $(a_0) = 2$ g

Final amount $(a) = 0.2$ g

So, time required,

$$t = \frac{2.303}{k}\log\frac{a_0}{a} = \frac{2.303}{4.606 \times 10^{-3}} \times \log\frac{2}{0.2} = 500\ \text{s}$$

6. (*a*) For a zero order reaction,

$$t = \frac{1}{k}(a_0 - a)$$

$$\Rightarrow \quad t_{50\%} = \frac{1}{k} \times \frac{a_0}{2} \qquad [\because \text{At } t_{50\%}, a = a_0/2]$$

$$\Rightarrow \quad k = \frac{a_0}{2 \times t_{50\%}} = \frac{0.02\ \text{M}}{2 \times 100\ \text{s}}$$

$$= 1 \times 10^{-4}\ \text{Ms}^{-1}$$

$$= 1 \times 10^{-4}\ \text{mol L}^{-1}\ \text{s}^{-1}$$

7. (*d*) For first order reaction,

$$t = \frac{2.303}{k}\log\frac{a}{a-x} \qquad \text{...(i)}$$

Given: $k = 2.303 \times 10^{-3}\ \text{s}^{-1}$

$$a = 40\ \text{g}$$

$$a - x = 10\ \text{g}$$

On substituting the given values in Eq. (i) ,

$$t = \frac{2.303}{2.303 \times 10^{-3}}\log\frac{40}{10} = 10^3 \log 2^2$$

$$= 2 \times 10^3 \times \log 2$$

$$= 2 \times 10^3 \times 0.3010 = 602\ \text{s}$$

8. (*b*) Let the initial concentration $(a) = 100$

After time t, final concentration $(a - x) = 100 - 99 = 1$

We know that,

$$t = \frac{2.303}{k}\log\frac{a}{a-x}$$

On substituting the given values in above Eq., we get

$$t = \frac{2.303}{k}\log\frac{100}{1}$$

$$= \frac{2.303}{k}\log 10^2$$

$$= \frac{2.303}{k} \times 2\log 10 = \frac{4.606}{k}$$

Thus, option (b) is correct.

9. (*b*) For zero order reaction,

$$t_{1/2} = \frac{[R]_0}{2k}$$

where, $[R]_0$ = initial concentration of the reactant.

k = rate constant.

Thus, $t_{1/2}$ for zero order reaction is directly proportional to the initial concentration of the reactant.

$$t_{1/2} \propto [R]_0$$

$\therefore$ For zero order reaction, when the concentration of reactant is doubled, the half-life ($t_{1/2}$) will also get doubled.

10. (*c*) Since, the reaction (ii) is the slowest step, so the rate of this reaction will be reaction rate for the main reaction.

$\because$ $\qquad \text{Rate} = k[X][Y_2] \qquad$ ...(i)

(k = rate constant)

Assume, step (i) is reversible

So, equilibrium constant $k_{eq} = \dfrac{[X]^2}{[X_2]}$

$$[X]^2 = k_{eq}[X_2],$$

$$[X] = k_{eq}^{1/2}[X_2]^{1/2} \quad \text{...(ii)}$$

From Eq. (i) and Eq. (ii)

$$\text{Rate} = k\, k_{eq}^{1/2}[X_2]^{1/2}[Y_2]$$

Let $k\, k_{eq}^{1/2} = k$

$$\therefore \quad \text{Rate} = k[X_2]^{0.5}[Y_2]^1$$

Hence, the order of the reaction is $= \frac{1}{2} + 1 = \frac{3}{2} = 1.5$

11. (*b*) For a first order reaction,

$$\text{Rate constant } (k) = \frac{2.303}{t} \log \frac{a}{a-x}$$

where, a = Initial concentration

$a - x$ = Concentration after time 't'

t = Time in sec

Given, $a = 20$ g

$a - x = 5$ g,

$k = 10^{-2}\ s^{-1}$

$$\therefore \quad t = \frac{2.303}{10^{-2}} \log \frac{20}{5} = 138.6\ s$$

12. (*a*) $PH_3 \xrightarrow{\text{Tungsten}} P + \frac{3}{2} H_2$

This is an example of surface catalysed unimolecular decompositon.

For the above reaction, rate is given as

$$\text{Rate} = \frac{k\, \alpha\, p}{1 + \alpha p}$$

where, p = partial pressure of adsorbing substrate (adsorbent).

At low pressure, $\alpha p << 1$ or Rate $= k\, \alpha p$

$\because (\alpha p + 1)$ can be neglected.

Thus, the decomposition is predicted to be first order.

13. (*d*) Given, order of reaction = 1

Rate of reaction at 10 s = 0.04 mol $L^{-1}\ s^{-1}$

Rate of reaction at 20 s = 0.03 mol $L^{-1}\ s^{-1}$

$\therefore$ Half-life period $(t_{1/2})$ = ?

Using the formula

$$k = \frac{2.303}{(t_2 - t_1)} \log \frac{A_{t_1}}{A_{t_2}}$$

$$= \frac{2.303}{10} \log \frac{0.04}{0.03}$$

$$= \frac{2.303}{10} \times 0.1249$$

$$k = 0.0287\ s^{-1}$$

We know that,

$$t_{1/2} = \frac{0.693}{k}$$

$$= \frac{0.693}{0.0287\ s^{-1}} = 24.1\ s$$

14. (*d*) For a zero order reaction, unit of rate constant is mole per litre per second.

Hence, we can easily calculate concentration of B after 20 minutes by the following formula

$$k = \frac{[A]_0 - [A]_t}{t}$$

$$\Rightarrow \quad 0.6 \times 10^{-3} = \frac{5 - [A]_t}{20 \times 60}$$

$$5 - [A]_t = 0.72\ M$$

= Concentration of B after 20 min.

15. (*b*) For a first order reaction,

$$t_{50} = \frac{0.693}{k}$$

i.e. For a first order reaction, half-life is independent of initial concentration of reactant.

Then the order of the reaction is first.

16. (*d*) According the Arrhenius equation,

$$k = A e^{-E_a/RT}$$

$$\ln k = \ln A - \frac{E_a}{RT}$$

$$\ln k = -\frac{E_a}{R}\left(\frac{1}{T}\right) + \ln A$$

Compare it with $y = mx + C$

$\ln k \rightarrow y$ and $\frac{1}{T} \rightarrow x$

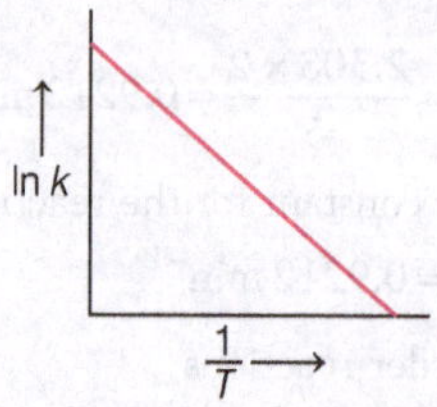

Hence, option (d) match the correct graph.

17. (*d*) Formula for calculating activation energy is given by

$$\log_{10}\left(\frac{k_2}{k_1}\right) = \frac{E_a}{2.303R}\left[\frac{1}{T_1} - \frac{1}{T_2}\right]$$

Here, k_1 is rate constant at T_1 and k_2 is rate constant at T_2.

18. (*a*) Given, rate is quadruples, i.e. $r_2 = 4r_1$,

We know, $\frac{r_2}{r_1} = 4 = \frac{k_2}{k_1}$

Now, $\log_{10}\left(\frac{k_2}{k_1}\right) = \frac{E_a}{2.303R}\left[\frac{1}{T_1} - \frac{1}{T_2}\right]$

[where, $T_1 = 300$ K, $T_2 = 330$ K]

$$\log_{10}(4) = \frac{E_a \times 1000}{2.303 \times 8.314}\left[\frac{1}{300} - \frac{1}{330}\right]$$

$$E_a = 38.04 \text{ kJ/mol}$$

19. (*d*) A is false but R is true.

When a reaction have zero activation energy, the initial energy of the reactant will be equal to the activation energy of the reaction. That means every collision results into a chemical reaction which is not possible.

Mathematically,

If $E_a = 0$, then according to Arrhenius equation.

$$k = Ae^{-E_a/RT} = Ae^0 = A$$

20. (*b*) The enthalpy of reaction is negative, - 4.2 kJ mol^{-1}. The reaction is an exothermic reaction i.e. the energy of product *B*, is less than the energy of reactant *A*. So, the potential energy profile for the reaction is

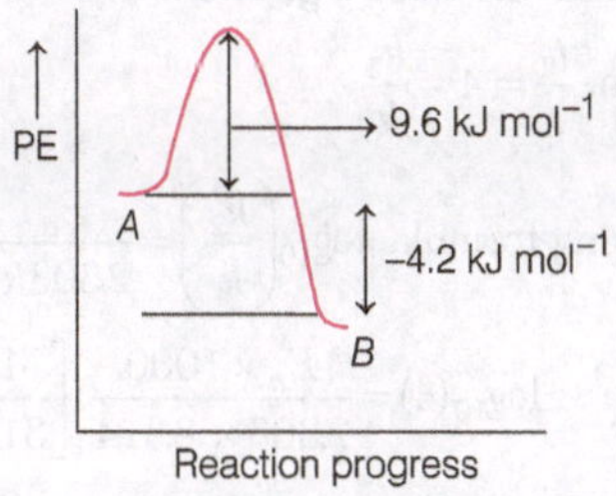

21. (*a*) According to Arrhenius equation,

$$k = Ae^{-E_a/RT}$$

$$\ln k = \ln A - \frac{E_a}{R}\left(\frac{1}{T}\right)$$

and $\frac{-E_a}{R}$ is the slope of Arrhenius plot $\left(\ln k \; vs \frac{1}{T}\right)$

ln *A* is the intercept

$$\text{Slope} = -5 \times 10^3 \text{ K}$$

$$R = 8.314 \text{ J K}^{-1} \text{ mol}^{-1}$$

So, $$-\frac{E_a}{R} = -5 \times 10^3 \text{ K}$$

$$\Rightarrow \quad E_a = 5 \times 10^3 \times R$$

$$= 5 \times 10^3 \times 8.314$$

$$= 41.57 \times 10^3 \text{ J mol}^{-1}$$

$$\approx 41.5 \text{ kJ mol}^{-1}$$

22. (*c*) Collision frequency is directly proportional to number of reacting molecules that means higher the concentration of reactant molecule, higher will be the probability of collision. Hence, the collision frequency increases.

23. (*b*) From collision theory of chemical reaction, Arrhenius equation we get, $k = A \times e^{-E_a/RT}$

where, k = rate constant,

$e^{-E_a/RT}$ = fraction of molecules with energy greater than E_a at *TK* [option-(a)].

A = Arrhenius factor or frequency factor = $P \times Z_{AB}$

when, P = steric factor [option-(c)]

Z_{AB} = collision frequency of reactants, *A* and *B*

= number of effective binary collisions between *A* and *B* in one second in unit volume [option-(b)].

Hence, option (b) is the correct.

24. (*b*) Given, $E_a = 0$, $T_1 = 200$ K

$$k_1 = 1.6 \times 10^6 \text{ s}^{-1}$$

$$T_2 = 400 \text{ K}$$

$$R = 8.314 \text{ JK}^{-1} \text{ mol}^{-1}$$

According to Arrhenius equation,

$$\log \frac{k_2}{k_1} = \frac{E_a}{2.303R}\left[\frac{1}{T_1} - \frac{1}{T_2}\right]$$

On substituting the given values in above equation,

$$\log \frac{k_2}{1.6 \times 10^6} = \frac{0}{2.303 \times 8.314}\left[\frac{1}{200} - \frac{1}{400}\right]$$

$$\log\left(\frac{k_2}{1.6 \times 10^6}\right) = 0$$

$$\Rightarrow \quad \frac{k_2}{1.6 \times 10^6} = 10^0 = 1$$

$$k_2 = 1.6 \times 10^6 \text{ s}^{-1} \text{ at 400K}$$

Thus, option (b) is correct.

25. (*b*) For a reversible reaction, catalyst accelerates the speed of forward as well as backward reaction to the same extent.

Hence, it does not disturb the equilibrium, i.e. does not change the equilibrium constant of the reaction but helps to attain the equilibrium faster.

26. (*c*) A positive catalyst provides a new reaction path with a lower energy barrier (lowering activation energy).

27. (*c*) By Arrhenius equation, $k = Ae^{-E_a/RT}$

where, E_a = energy of activation

Taking log on both sides,

$$\ln k = \ln A - \frac{E_a}{RT} \quad \text{...(i)}$$

$$\log k = -\frac{E_a}{2.303R} + \log A \quad \text{...(ii)}$$

Compare the above equation w.r.t. straight line equation of $y = mx + C$

Thus, if a plot of log *k* *vs* $\frac{1}{T}$ is a straight line, the validity of the equation is confirmed.

Slope of the line $= -\dfrac{E_a}{2.303\,R}$

Thus, by measuring the slope of the line, the value of E_a can be calculated.

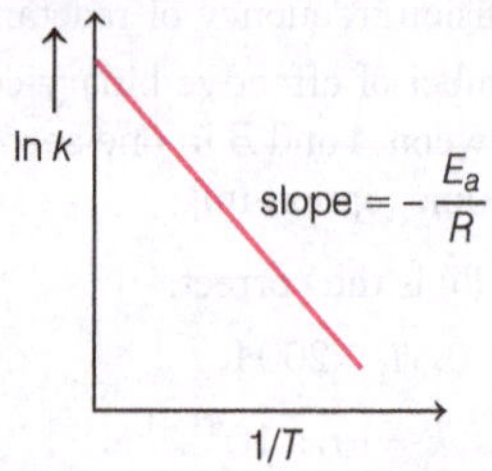

Skill Builder

■ Sol. of Skill Builder Pg. 107

(*d*) Given, rate $(r) = k[A]^2[B]^2$ ... (i)

$r_1 = k[A]^2\,[2B]^2$ ... (ii)

Dividing Eq. (i) by (ii) we get,

$$\frac{r}{r_1} = \frac{k[A]^2[B]^2}{k[A]^2[2B]^2} = \frac{1}{4}$$

$$r_1 = 4r$$

Thus, the initial rate would increase by a factor of 4.

■ Sol. of Skill Builder Pg. 111

(*a*) Given, Initial concentration $[A]_0 = 0.43$ M

Concentration after 20 min. $[A]_t = 0.0043$ M

Using rate constant formula for first order reaction,

$$k = \frac{2.303}{t}\log\frac{[A]_0}{[A]_t}$$

$$= \frac{2.303}{20}\log\frac{[0.43]}{[0.0043]} = \frac{2.303}{20} \times 2 = 0.23$$

■ Sol. of Skill Builder Pg. 114

(*c*) For a zero order reaction, $t_{1/2} = \dfrac{1}{k}[A]_0$

$$t_{5_{1/2}} = \frac{1}{k} \times \frac{[A]_0}{2}$$

$$k = \frac{[A]_0}{2 \times t_{1/2}} = \frac{0.061\text{ M}}{2 \times 200\text{ s}}$$

$$= 0.000152\ \text{Ms}^{-1}$$

$$= 1.52 \times 10^{-4}\ \text{mol L}^{-1}\,\text{s}^{-1}$$

■ Sol. of Skill Builder Pg. 122

(*c*) Given, $\dfrac{r_2}{r_1} = 4 = \dfrac{k_2}{k_1}$

Now, using formula, $\log_{10}\left(\dfrac{k_2}{k_1}\right) = \dfrac{E_a}{2.303R}\left[\dfrac{1}{T_1} - \dfrac{1}{T_2}\right]$

$$\log_{10}(4) = \frac{E_a \times 1000}{2.303 \times 8.314}\left[\frac{1}{310} - \frac{1}{330}\right]$$

$$E_a = 25.60\ \text{kJ/mol}$$

For deeper insight
Scan the QR Code

Chapter 4

p-Block Elements

Learning Objectives

Module-I Group-13
- General and Physical Properties
- Chemical Properties
- Anomalous Behaviour of Boron

Module-II Group-14
- General and Physical Properties
- Chemical Properties
- Anomalous Behaviour of Carbon

Module-III Group-15
- General and Physical Properties
- Chemical Properties
- Anomalous Behaviour of Nitrogen

Module-IV Group-16
- General and Physical Properties
- Chemical Properties
- Anomalous Behaviour of Oxygen

Module-V Group-17
- General and Physical Properties
- Chemical Properties
- Anomalous Behaviour of Fluorine

Module-VI Group-18
- General and Physical Properties
- Chemical Properties
- Uses of Noble Gases

Chapter Overview with NEET Connection

This chapter is useful for the learning about elements and their reactions. Without gripping this chapter, it will be difficult to learn and understand the various properties and reactions of different elements.

Special format questions can be easily framed on the following topics of this chapter.

- Nature of oxide
- Inert pair effect
- Structure and compounds of xenon
- Anomalous behaviour of 2nd period elements
- Oxyacids of N, S, P and Cl

For better understanding of this chapter a grip over periodic table and different periodic properties is required especially, electronic configuration, oxidation state, ionisation enthalpy and electron affinity.

Introduction

Elements in which the last electron enters in the outermost *p*-orbitals are called ***p*-block elements.** Since, *p*-orbitals can accommodate a maximum of 6 electrons, hence *p*-block contains 6 group of elements. The groups 13 (III A), 14 (IVA), 15 (VA), 16 (VI A) (or chalcogens), 17 (VII) A (or halogens) and group 18 (zero or noble gases) belong to *p*-block.

p-block elements can be either **metals, metalloids** or **non-metals.** The general valence shell electronic configuration of these elements is $ns^2\ np^{1\text{-}6}$, where $n = 1, 2, 3...$ with the exception of He which has $1s^2$ configuration. This chapter is completely dedicated to all these elements.

Module 1

Boron Family

- General and Physical Properties
- Chemical Properties
- Anomalous Behaviour of Boron

Group 13 Elements : The Boron Family

Group 13 (earlier called IIIA) marks the beginning of the *p*-block elements. There are six elements in this group, namely **boron** (B), **aluminium** (Al), **gallium** (Ga), **indium** (In), **thallium** (Tl) and **ununtrium** (Uut). Uut is now known as **nihonium** (Nh).

The first element that is boron is non-metal but other members of the family show metallic properties. Nh (metal) is radioactive in nature.

Boron is very less abundant in earth's crust and is found mainly in the form of borax. It occurs in two isotopic forms *viz*, $_5B^{10}$ (19%) and $_5B^{11}$(81%). Aluminium is the third most abundant element and the most abundant metal in earth's crust. Gallium, indium and and thallium are less abundant elements and do not show commercial applications.

General and Physical Properties

The variations of general and physical properties of group 13 elements are given below.

Electronic Configuration

The general electronic configuration of the elements of boron family is ns^2np^1 or $ns^2np_x^1np_y^\circ np_z^\circ$, where, $n = 2$ to 7.

Electronic configuration of each element of the group 13 is listed in table.

Electronic Configurations of Elements of Group 13

Element	Atomic number	Electronic configuration
Boron (B)	5	[He] $2s^2 2p^1$
Aluminium (Al)	13	[Ne] $3s^2 3p^1$
Gallium (Ga)	31	[Ar] $3d^{10} 4s^2 4p^1$
Indium (In)	49	[Kr] $4d^{10} 5s^2 5p^1$
Thallium (Tl)	81	[Xe] $4f^{14} 5d^{10} 6s^2 6p^1$
Nihonium (Nh)	113	[Rn] $5f^{14} 6d^{10} 7s^2 7p^1$

Concept ladder

In ground state of general valence shell electronic configuration of group 13 there is just one unpaired electron allowing them to form just one bond while in the excited state there are three unpaired e^- allowing them to form three bonds.

Atomic and Ionic Radii

In general, the atomic and ionic radii of the group 13 elements are smaller than elements of previous groups in respective periods. This is because the effective nuclear charge increases while going from left to right in a period. On moving down the group, the atomic radii as well as ionic radii increase because of the successive addition of one extra shell.

There is a deviation at gallium in case of atomic radii. Atomic radii of Ga is lesser as compared to Al. This is because the ten extra *d*-electrons present in Ga atom do not screen the nucleus effectively. Consequently, electrons of Ga are more attracted by nucleus. Thus, the order of atomic radii of the group members can be written as

$$B < Ga < Al < In < Tl$$

Density

In general, density increases on moving down the group. However, Al shows exceptionally low increase in density. Due to its unexpected larger molar volume.

So, the order of density is $B < Al < Ga < In < Tl$

Melting and Boiling Points

The melting point decreases considerably on moving down the group upto gallium (Ga) and then increases again in the case of indium (In) and thallium (Tl).

The melting point of Ga is so low that it could exist in liquid state during summer. Boiling point decreases regularly on moving down the group as interatomic attraction decreases down the group.

Order of melting point $Ga < In < Tl < Al < B$

Order of boiling point $Tl < In < Ga < Al < B$

Ionisation Energy

The first ionisation energy of 13th group elements are rather low as compared to the corresponding ionisation energies of group 2 elements but higher than group 1 elements. The second and third ionisation energies are considerably higher.

The general order of first ionisation energy in this group is

$$In < Al < Ga < Tl < B$$

However, there is no regular pattern of change in ionisation energies down the group. It first decreases from B to Al, then increases from Al to Ga, again decreases from Ga to In and again increases from In to Tl.

The decrease from B to Al is due to increase in size while the observed discontinuity in ionisation enthalpy between Al to Tl is due to inability of *d*- and *f*-electrons which have low screening effect, to compensate the increase in nuclear charge.

The sum of three successive ionisation energies for B is very high. Boron does not form B^{3+} ion, due to its very small size.

Concept ladder B forms only covalent compounds on account of its high ionisation enthalpy while Al forms covalent compounds in anhydrous state and ionic compounds in aqueous solutions.

Inert Pair Effect

It is the reluctance of the *s*-electrons of the valence shell to take part in bonding. It arises due to poor or ineffective shielding of the ns^2 electrons of the valence shell by the intervening *d*- and *f*-electrons. In group 13 elements, inert pair effect is more pronounced in Tl.

Oxidation States

Boron and aluminium show + 3 oxidation state in their compounds while rest of the members show + 1 as well as + 3 oxidation states.

The stability of + 3 oxidation states decreases while going down the group, i.e.

$$B^{3+} > Al^{3+} > Ga^{3+} > In^{3+} > Tl^{3+}$$

However, stability of + 1 oxidation state increases on going down the group, i.e. $Ga^+ < In^+ < Tl^+$.

Such a presence of two oxidation states in *p*-block elements is due to the **inert pair effect.**

Thallium (Tl) with oxidation state of + 1 shows resemblance with alkali metals in compound formation, e.g. TlOH, is highly soluble and strong base, like NaOH. Tl_2CO_3 resembles with Na_2CO_3 and K_2CO_3.

Gallium exhibits both + 1 and + 3 oxidation states.

Ga^{3+} is more stable than Ga^+, hence Ga^+ salts act as strong reducing agent.

Metallic Character

Boron is the only non-metal in the group, while all the other members are metals. The metallic or electropositive character increases from boron to aluminium, which is most electropositive element of the group.

The metallic character then decreases from aluminium to thallium and the last three members, i.e. Ga, In and Tl are weakly metallic. The overall order of electropositive character is B < Tl < In < Ga < Al.

In Ga to Tl, d^{10} and f^{14} (in case of Tl) do not shield the nuclear charge effectively and thus these metals are less electropositive.

Reducing Character

The reducing power of group 13 elements decreases down the group from aluminium to thallium as the electrode potential values for M^{3+}/M increase. Thus, the reducing power follows the trend

$$Al > Ga > In > Tl$$

Chemical Properties

Important reactions of group 13 elements are given below.

Reaction with Air and Water

Boron is very unreactive at ordinary temperature. It does not react with water and its crystalline form is also inert towards air but its amorphous form reacts with oxygen only when heated.

$$4B\,(s) + 3O_2\,(g) \xrightarrow{\Delta} 2B_2O_3\,(s)$$

Boron also reacts with nitrogen at very high temperature

$$2B + N_2 \xrightarrow{\Delta} 2BN$$

BN (boron nitride), have structure similar to graphite. Hence, it is also called as **inorganic graphite.**

Aluminium is quite reactive, even at lower temperature. It reacts with water and oxygen to form oxide.

$$2Al(s) + 3H_2O\,(l) \longrightarrow Al_2O_3 + 3H_2(g)\uparrow$$

Al_2O_3 formed, covers the surface of the metal and thus, **protects** it from further reaction with water. Reaction of Al with O_2 is exothermic and is called **thermite reaction.**

$$2Al\,(s) + \frac{3}{2}O_2(g) \longrightarrow Al_2O_3(s), \quad \Delta H = -1670 \text{ kJ}$$

The thermite reaction evolves so much heat energy that it can be dangerous. Thermite reaction finds applications in the metallurgical extraction of other metals from their oxides.

Ga and In do not react with water and oxygen individually as these are less reactive, however thallium forms TlOH in moist air.

$$4Tl + 2H_2O + O_2 \longrightarrow 4TlOH$$

Reaction with Halogens

Group 13 elements form trihalides of MX_3 type (where, M is the group member and X is the halogen). All the halides of group 13 elements are known except thallium iodide (TlI_3).

$$2M + 3X_2 \longrightarrow 2MX_3$$

The halides of boron (BX_3) are covalent . The fluorides of rest of the group member are ionic while other trihalides of these elements (i.e. Al, Ga, In and Tl) are covalent in anhydrous form, e.g. anhydrous $AlCl_3$ is covalent but gets hydrolysed to give $Al^{3+}(aq)$ ions in water.

In all the trihalides of this group, have trigonal planar geometry and elements have sp^2-hybridisation.

All the trihalides of this group act as Lewis acids and their electron accepting tendency follows the order

$$B > Al > Ga > In$$

Concept ladder

- The relative strength of Lewis acids of boron trihalides increases in the order $BF_3 < BCl_3 < BBr_3 < BI_3$.
- This order can be explained on the basis of the tendency of the halogen atom to back donate its electrons to the boron atom and makes it less electron deficient.
- Amongst the trihalides of group 13, BF_3 and $AlCl_3$ are widely used as Lewis acid catalysts.

Reaction with Acids

Boron reacts only with hot concentrated oxidising acid at high temperature.

e.g. $2B(s) + 6HNO_3(aq) \xrightarrow{\Delta} 2H_3BO_3(aq) + 6NO_2(g)$

Aluminium and other metals of the group reacts with other acids to liberate hydrogen gas.

$$2M + 6HCl \longrightarrow 2M^{3+} + 6Cl^- + 3H_2\uparrow$$

(where, M = Al, Ga, In, Tl)

However, aluminium becomes passive during reaction with concentrated nitric acid due to formation of protective layer of alumina (Al_2O_3).

(i) $Al + 4HNO_3 \longrightarrow Al(NO_3)_3 + 2H_2O + NO$

(ii) $4Al(NO_3)_2 \longrightarrow \underset{\text{(Protective layer)}}{2Al_2O_3} + 8NO_2 + O_2$

Tl dissolves in acids forming univalent cation and becomes passive in HCl due to the formation of water soluble TlCl.

NEET Close-up

Example Similar to PYQ Asked in NEET 2023

Which of the following is not a Lewis acid?

(a) BBr_3 (b) BF_3 (c) $[BH_4]^{\ominus}$ (d) BCl_3

Sol. (c) In $[BH_4]^{\ominus}$, no vacant 2p-orbital is present on B (sp^3) to accept the electron pair, hence it does not behave as a Lewis acid.

Skill Builder

Which of the following is a Lewis acid?

(a) Cl^- (b) H_2O
(c) $AlCl_3$ (d) HF

For more practice Refer to Q.8 of step up practice 1.

Reaction with Alkalies

Except indium and thallium all other elements react with alkali solutions to evolve dihydrogen

$$2M(s) + 2NaOH(aq) + 2H_2O \longrightarrow 2NaMO_2(s) + 3H_2(g)$$

(where, M = Al or Ga)

Al also reacts with aqueous alkali and liberates dihydrogen with sodium tetrahydroxyaluminate.

$$2Al(s) + 2NaOH(aq) + 6H_2O(l) \longrightarrow \underset{\text{Sodium tetrahydroxyaluminate (III)}}{2Na^+[Al(OH)_4]^-(aq)} + 3H_2(g)$$

Formation of Hydrides

Group 13 elements do not react directly with hydrogen, however a large number of hydrides of this group are known. Boron forms hydrides with general formula B_nH_{n+4} (e.g. B_2H_6) and B_nH_{n+6} (e.g. B_4H_{10}). These are collectively called **boranes.**

Aluminium forms polymeric hydride $(AlH_3)_n$ called alane. It decomposes on heating above 200°C into its constituent element. GaH_3 is very less stable, while InH_3 and TlH_3 are extremely unstable.

Formation of Oxides and Hydroxides

The group 13 elements form the oxide and hydroxide with general formula M_2O_3 and $M(OH)_3$ respectively, having + 3 oxidation state in each case.

Boron being non-metal, forms acidic oxide, while aluminium and gallium forms amphoteric oxides and the rest of two metals forms basic oxides. The increasing order of basic character is

$$B_2O_3 < Al_2O_3 < Ga_2O_3 < In_2O_3 < Tl_2O_3$$

Hydroxides of this group follow same trend of basicity as shown by the oxide.

Concept ladder

Among group 13 elements, only boron forms several oxyacids, all of which are obtained by adding one or more H_2O molecules to one or more B_2O_3 molecules as

$$B_2O_3 + 3H_2O \longrightarrow \underset{\text{Orthoboric acid}}{2H_3BO_3} \text{ or } 2B(OH)_3$$

$$B_2O_3 + H_2O \longrightarrow \underset{\text{Metaboric acid}}{2HBO_2}$$

$$2B_2O_3 + 3H_2O \longrightarrow \underset{\text{Tetraboric acid}}{H_2B_4O_7}$$

$$2B_2O_3 + 3H_2O \longrightarrow \underset{\text{Pyroboric acid}}{H_6B_4O_9}$$

$$3B_2O_3 + 2H_2O \longrightarrow \underset{\text{Hexaboric acid}}{H_4B_6O_{11}}$$

$$4B_2O_3 + 3H_2O \longrightarrow \underset{\text{Octaboric acid}}{H_6B_8O_{15}}$$

Anomalous Behaviour of Boron

Boron because of its small size, high electron density, high electronegativity and non-availability of *d*-electrons exhibits the following anomalous properties.

- Boron is a typical non-metal, while other members of the group are metals.
- Its melting and boiling points are higher than the other members of the group.
- It forms only covalent compounds while other members can form covalent as well as ionic compounds. The maximum covalency of B is four while that of Al is six.
- Only boron exhibits allotropy and exists in crystalline as well as amorphous forms.
- Its oxides and hydroxides have acidic nature while that of other members have amphoteric and basic nature.
- Its hydrides are quite stable while that of other members are not so stable.
- Like non-metals, it combines with metals to form metal borides (e.g. Mg_3B_2) while other members form alloy with metals.
- It does not decompose steam while other members do so.
- Dilute acids have no action on B. Other members of group 13, liberate H_2 when react with dilute acids.

Mentor's Tip

Boron is a semi-metal which behaves as a non-metal due to its very small size. However, it should be noted that in NCERT boron is given as a non-metal.

Diborane (B_2H_6)

It is the simplest electron deficient hydride of boron. It is colourless highly toxic gas with b.p. of 180 K.

Diborane react with NH_3 in 1: 2 ratio at high temperature to form borazine.

$$\underset{1}{3B_2H_6} + \underset{2}{6NH_3} \xrightarrow{\text{High temperature}} \underset{\text{Borazine}}{2B_3N_3H_6} + 12H_2$$

$B_3N_3H_6$ is called **'inorganic benzene'** because its structure shows similarity with benzene, with delocalised electrons (II) and aromatic character (III).

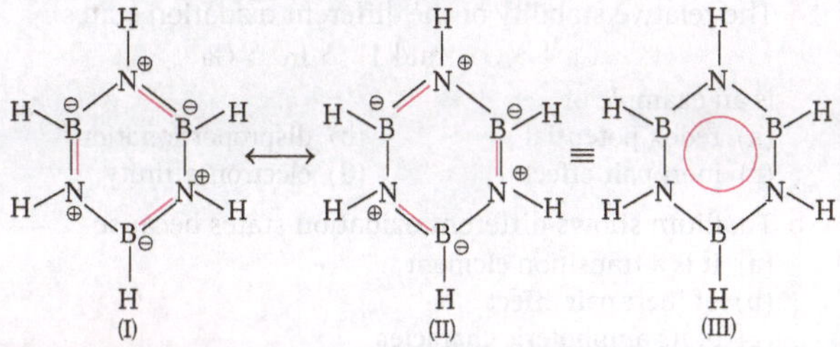

Borazine

NEET Snapshot

In diborane both the boron atoms are *sp*^{2}-hybridised. *[NEET 2022]*

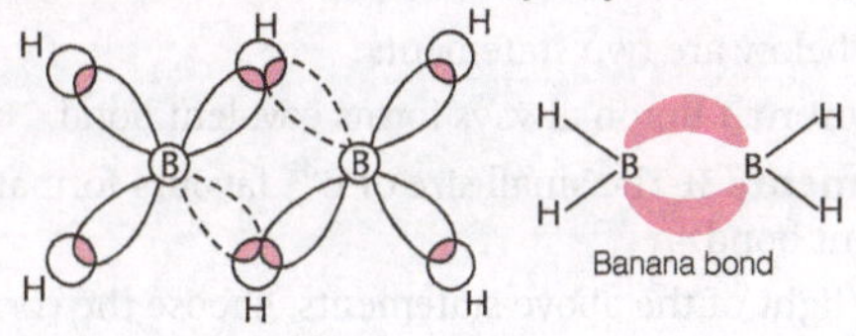

Structure of diborane

During the bonding in diborane, each B-atom uses sp^3-hybridised (still $\bar{e}$-deficient) orbital.

The four terminal B—H bonds (2c—2e) lie in same plane while the two bridge B ··· H ··· B bonds (3c—2e) lie above and below the plane.

The (3c— 2e) bridge bonds are also known as banana bonds. Hence the statement given is the incorrect statement.

STEP UP Practice 1

1 Which of the following group 13 elements has the highest density?
(a) Al (b) Ga
(c) In (d) Tl

2 Stabilities of adducts formed with boron-halides are in order
(a) $BF_3 < BCl_3 < BBr_3$
(b) $BBr_3 < BCl_3 < BF_3$
(c) $BCl_3 < BBr_3 < BF_3$
(d) $BF_3 < BBr_3 < BCl_3$

3 What is the correct order of electron accepting tendency of group 13 elements ?
(a) B < Al < Ga < In (b) Al < B < Ga < In
(c) B > Al > Ga > In (d) Al > B > Ga > In

4 The relative stability of the different oxidation states

$$Ga^{3+} > Ga^{+} \text{ and } Tl^{+} > In^{+} > Ga^{+}$$

is an example of
(a) redox potential (b) disproportionation
(c) inert pair effect (d) electron-affinity

5 Thallium shows different oxidation states because
(a) it is a transition element
(b) of inert pair effect
(c) of its amphoteric character
(d) of its higher reactivity

6 Which of the following group 13 elements has lowest value of electronegativity?
(a) B (b) Tl (c) Al (d) In

7 Given below are two statements.
Statement I Boron always forms covalent bond.
Statements II The small size of B^{3+} favours formation of covalent bond.
In the light of the above statements, choose the correct answer from the options given below.
(a) Both Statement I and Statement II are false.
(b) Statement I is true, but Statement II is false.
(c) Statement I is false, but Statement II is true.
(d) Both Statement I and Statement II are true.

8 Which of the following is a Lewis acid ?
(a) $AlCl_3$ (b) $MgCl_2$
(c) $CaCl_2$ (d) $BaCl_2$

9 Which of the following oxides is correctly matched with the given nature?
(a) $Al_2O_3 \longrightarrow$ Basic
(b) $Ga_2O_3 \longrightarrow$ Amphoteric
(c) $In_2O_3 \longrightarrow$ Acidic
(d) $Tl_2O_3 \longrightarrow$ Acidic

10 Aluminium is not used
(a) in silvery paints
(b) for making utensils
(c) as a reducing agent
(d) as an oxidiser in metallurgy

11 The element which exists in liquid state for a wide range of temperature and can be used for measuring high temperature is
(a) B (b) Al (c) Ga (d) In

12 Consider the following elements,
(i) B^{3+} (ii) Al^{3+}
(iii) Ga^{3+} (iv) In^{3+}
(v) Tl^{3+}
How many of them does not act as oxidising agent?
(a) 3 (b) 4
(c) 2 (d) 1

13 Which of the following product is correctly matched with the given reaction?
(a) $4B + 3O_2 \xrightarrow[\text{(ii) } 3H_2O]{\text{(i) } \Delta} H_6B_4O_9$
(b) $Mg + N_2 \xrightarrow[\text{(ii) } H_2O]{\text{(i) } \Delta} NH_3 + Mg(OH)_3$
(c) $Ga + N_2 \xrightarrow[\text{(ii) } H_2O]{\text{(i) } \Delta} Ga(OH)_3 + NH_3$
(d) $Al + N_2 \xrightarrow[\text{(ii) } H_2O]{\text{(i) } \Delta} N_2\uparrow + Al(OH)_2$

14 Aqueous solution of borax reacts with 2 moles of acids. This is because of
(a) formation of 2 moles of $B(OH)_3$
(b) formation of 2 moles of $[B(OH)_4]^{2-}$
(c) formation of 1 mole each of $B(OH)_3$ and $[B(OH)_4]^{2-}$
(d) formation of 2 moles each of $[B(OH)_4]^-$ and $B(OH)_3$, in which only $[B(OH)_4]^-$ reacts with acid

15 Which one of the following statements is correct ?
(a) The hydroxide of aluminium is more acidic than boron.
(b) The hydroxide of boron is basic while aluminium is amphoteric.
(c) The hydroxide of boron is acidic, while aluminium is amphoteric.
(d) The hydroxides of boron and aluminium are amphoteric.

16 Which of the following statements about H_3BO_3 is not correct?
(a) It is strong tribasic acid.
(b) It is prepared by acidifying an aqueous solution of borax.
(c) It has a layer structure in its crystalline solid state in which planar BO_3 units are joined by hydrogen bonds.
(d) It acts as a Lewis acid by accepting hydroxyl ion.

17 Orthoboric acid H_3BO_3 behaves as a weak monobasic acid. It gives products H_3O^+ and 'P' on dissolving in water. The product 'P' is
(a) $H_2BO_2^+$ (b) $H_2BO_2^-$
(c) $[B(OH)_4]^-$ (d) $[B(OH)_4]^+$

18 Given below are two statements.

Statement I In aqueous solution, $AlCl_3$ forms dimer Al_2Cl_6.

Statement II The high enthalpy of hydration is sufficient to break the covalent dimer into $[M(H_2O)_6]^{3+}$ and Cl^- ions.

In the light of the above statements, choose the correct answer from the options given below.

(a) Both Statement I and Statement II are false.
(b) Statement I is true but Statement II is false.
(c) Statement I is false but Statement II is true.
(d) Both Statement I and Statement II are true.

19 Which of the following statements is not true, for both B and Al?

(a) They burn in oxygen to give oxides at high temperature.
(b) Their halides are Lewis acids.
(c) They combine with nitrogen to form nitrides.
(d) They react with HCl to form chlorides.

20 Consider the following compounds.

(i) $Na_2B_4O_7$ (ii) $NaBO_2$ (iii) Na_3BO_3
(iv) H_2 (v) B_2O_3

How many of them is (are) formed when boron is fused with NaOH?

(a) 3 (b) 4 (c) 2 (d) 1

Module 2

Carbon Family

- General and Physical Properties
- Chemical Properties
- Anomalous Behaviour of Carbon

Group 14 Elements : The Carbon Family

Group 14 (earlier called IVA) contains six elements **carbon** (C), **silicon** (Si), **germanium** (Ge), **tin** (Sn), **lead** (Pb) and **flerovium** (Fl).

These are collectively said to form carbon family after the name of the first element, carbon.

Out of these **carbon** (C) is non-metal, **silicon** (Si) and **germanium** (Ge) are metalloids while **tin** (Sn) and **lead** (Pb) are metals and Fl is a synthetic radio-metal.

General and Physical Properties

The variations of general and physical properties of group 14 elements are given below:

Electronic Configuration

The general electronic configuration of group 14 elements are ns^2np^2 or $ns^2np_x^1np_y^1np_z^\circ$ where, $n = 2$ to 7

Electronic configuration of each element of group is listed in table.

Electronic Configurations of Elements of Group 14

Element	Atomic number	Electronic configuration
Carbon (C)	6	$[He]2s^22p^2$
Silicon (Si)	14	$[Ne]3s^23p^2$
Germanium (Ge)	32	$[Ar]3d^{10}4s^24p^2$
Tin (Sn)	50	$[Kr]4d^{10}5s^25p^2$
Lead (Pb)	82	$[Xe]4f^{14}5d^{10}6s^26p^2$
Flerovium (Fl)	114	$[Rn]5f^{14}6d^{10}7s^27p^2$

Atomic Radii

The atomic or covalent radii of the group 14 elements, increases with increase in atomic number. However, this increase, is not uniform. When we move from C to Si, the covalent radius increases sharply and then from Si to Pb small increase in radii is observed.

From Si to Pb the slight increase occur because of the poor shielding of the valence electrons (by the intervening of *d* and *f*-electrons in case of Ge, Sn and Pb).

The atomic radii of these elements are smaller than the corresponding elements of group 13 due to increased effective nuclear charge, which exerts a stronger attractive influence on the outer electrons and hence, the covalent radius decreases.

Density

The density of the elements of group 14 increases down the group as expected. This is due to large increase in atomic mass as compared to increase in the atomic size. However, diamond, an allotrope of carbon, has higher density than silicon. It is due to the fact that diamond has dense network structure.

The order of density is Si < C < Ge < Sn < Pb.

Melting and Boiling Points

The melting and boiling points of group 14 elements are much higher than those of group 13 elements due to the strong inter atomic binding forces in their solid as well as liquid states. There is a gradual decrease in both melting and boiling points of the group members while going down the group.

This is due to increase in the size of atoms and decrease in interatomic forces of attraction. However, melting point of tin is lower than that of lead.

- Order of melting point C > Si > Ge > Pb > Sn
- Order of boiling point Si > Ge > Sn > Pb

Ionisation Energy

The first and second ionisation energies decrease down the group from C to Sn as expected, but they increase slightly when we move to Pb.

The decreasing order is C > Ge > Si > Pb > Sn.

The decrease in the 1st and 2nd ionisation energies from C to Sn is because of the increase in atomic size down the group. The increase in the ionisation energies from Sn to Pb is due to the poor shielding effect of the 4*f* and 5*d*-electrons.

On the other hand, both the 3rd and the 4th ionisation energies vary irregularly. On account of high ionisation energies, simple M^{4+} ions of the group are not known. The tendency to form negative ions by gaining electrons is observe only in carbon. For C and Si, stable divalent compounds, MX_2 are very rare.

Concept ladder The only stable divalent metal ion formed by group 14 elements is Pb^{2+}.

Oxidation States

The most common oxidation state shown by the group 14 members are +4. C and Si rarely form compounds with +2 oxidation state of these elements. However, Ge, Sn and Pb show both +2 and +4 oxidation states, depending on whether ns^2 pair is involved in bonding or not, i.e. a case of inert pair effect.

As we go down the group, inertness of ns^2 pair increases hence, tendency to exhibit +2 oxidation state increases and that of +4 oxidation state decreases. Thus, stability order is

$$Ge^{4+} > Sn^{4+} > Pb^{4+} \text{ and } Ge^{2+} < Sn^{2+} < Pb^{2+}$$

Also, stability of $Sn^{2+} < Sn^{4+}$ and $Pb^{2+} > Pb^{4+}$

Thus, Sn^{2+} salts are better reducing agents than Sn^{4+} and Pb^{4+} salts are better oxidising agents than Pb^{2+}.

Electronegativity

Carbon has higher electronegativity as compared to other elements of the group. As a result, it can accept (gain) electrons and can form negative ions of the kind C_2^{2-} in acetylides and C^{4-} in methanides, while the other elements in the group are unable to do so.

Electronegativities of group 14 elements is more than the corresponding group 13 elements.

The value of electronegativity decreases down the group as expected, with Ge as an exception whose electronegativity is nearly same as that of Si and Sn. This could be due to the higher effective nuclear charge in case of Ge.

The general order of electronegativity can be written as

$$C(2.5) > Si\ (1.8) \sim Ge\ (1.8)\ Sn\ (1.8) < Pb\ (1.9)$$

Element	C	Si	Ge	Sn	Pb
Electronegativity (Pauling scale)	2.5	1.8	1.8	1.8	1.9

Catenation

The property of self-linking of atoms of an element through covalent bonds to form straight or branched chains and rings of different sizes is called **catenation.**

The tendency of an element to form chains depend upon the strength of the element-element bond. Amongst the group 14 elements, C—C bond strength is maximum therefore, it shows maximum tendency for catenation. This is due to smaller size and higher electronegativity of C-atom and unique strength of C—C bonds.

Down the group, catenation tendency decreases due to decrease in element-element bond strength.

Catenation tendency is highest in carbon while silicon has second highest tendency of catenation among all elements of carbon family and the decreasing element-element tendency of catenation is as follows

$$C >> Si > Ge \approx Sn$$

Concept ladder
- Pb does not show catenation.
- Catenation power of carbon family is higher than boron family and nitrogen family as well.

Given below is the general formulae of hydrides to have an idea about the catenation property of the group 14 members.

Element	General formula of hydrides	Common name	Known number of hydride (n)
Carbon (C)	C_nH_{2n+2}	Alkane	$n = 1$ to 100
Silicon (Si)	Si_nH_{2n+2}	Silane	$n = 1$ to 8
Germanium (Ge)	Ge_nH_{2n+2}	Germane	$n = 1$ to 9
Tin (Sn)	Sn_2H_{2n+2}	Stannane	$n = 1$ or 2

Allotropy

All the elements of the carbon family with the exception of lead exhibit allotropy and this tendency decreases from C to Pb. It is due to decreasing element-element bond energy.

Bond	C — C	Si — Si	Ge — Ge	Sn — Sn
Bond energy (kJ/mol)	348	297	260	240

Concept ladder

Solid compounds of carbon with elements other than hydrogen are generally called **carbides**.

On the basis of type of bonding involved, carbides are of following three types.

- Ionic or salt-like carbides — Be_2C, Al_4C_3 (methanides) CaC_2 (acetylides)
- Interstitial carbides — Tungsten carbide
- Covalent carbides — Silicon carbide (SiC) and B_4C

Chemical Properties

Some important chemical reactions of group 14 elements are given below

Reaction with Oxygen

When heated in oxygen, these elements form two types of oxides *viz* monoxides of formula MO, e.g. CO, SiO, GeO, SnO and PbO and dioxides of formula MO_2, e.g. CO_2, SiO_2, GeO_2, SnO_2 and PbO_2.

Except SiO and GeO all monoxides are stable. SiO exists only at high temperature where it is thought to be formed by reduction of SiO_2 with Si.

$$SiO_2 + Si \xrightarrow{\text{High temperature}} 2SiO$$

Oxides in higher oxidation states of the elements are generally more stable than those in lower oxidation states.

Acidic character of dioxides decreases and basic character of dioxides increases while moving down the group.

Oxides	Nature	Oxides	Nature
CO_2	Acidic	SnO, SnO_2	Amphoteric
SiO_2	Acidic	PbO, PbO_2	Amphoteric
GeO, GeO_2	Acidic	Pb_3O_4	Amphoteric

CO_2 is monomeric but SiO_2 has a three dimensional network structure.

All these dioxides dissolve in alkalies forming carbonates, silicates, germinates, stannates and plumbates respectively.

$$MO_2 + 2NaOH \longrightarrow Na_2MO_3 + H_2O$$

The dioxides of Sn and Pb also dissolve in acids, thus show their amphoteric nature.

$$SnO_2 + 4HCl \longrightarrow SnCl_4 + 2H_2O$$
$$PbO_2 + 4HCl \longrightarrow PbCl_2 + Cl_2 + 2H_2O$$

PbO_2 is a powerful oxidising agent. Lead also forms Pb_3O_4 (red lead or sindoor) which is a mixed oxide of $PbO_2 \cdot 2PbO$. The other oxide of Pb is Pb_2O_3 called lead sesquioxide. Among the monoxides. CO is neutral, GeO is distinctly acidic, SnO and PbO are amphoteric.

Red form of PbO is called ***Litharge*** and its yellow form is called ***Massicot.***

NEET Close-up

Example Similar to PYQ Asked in NEET 2020

Which of the following oxides is not acidic in nature?

(a) Pb_3O_4 (b) SiO_2
(c) GeO (d) GeO_2

Sol. (*a*) Among the given oxide, Pb_3O_4 is not acidic instead it is an amphoteric oxide.

Skill Builder

Which of the following oxides is not acidic in nature?

(a) CO_2 (b) PbO_2
(c) SiO_2 (d) GeO_2

For more practice Refer to Q. 6 of step up practice 2.

Reaction with Halogens

The elements of group 14 form MX_4 and MX_2 type halides (where, X = F, Cl, Br and I).

Formation of Tetrahalides

All tetrahalides, (except SnF_4 and PbF_4) are covalent in nature and central atoms are sp^3-hybridised with tetrahedral geometry.

Further, the thermal stability of tetrahalides of the same element decreases with increase in molecular mass of the tetrahalide, i.e.

$$MF_4 > MCl_4 > MBr_4 > MI_4$$

The stability of halides of different elements with same halogen decreases with increasing atomic number.

$$CX_4 > SiX_4 > GeX_4 > SnX_4 > PbX_4$$

$PbBr_4$ is unstable and PbI_4 does not exist because Pb^{4+} being a strong oxidant does not survive in presence of strong reductants Br^- and I^- and is immediately reduced to Pb^{2+} with release of Br_2 and I_2 respectively.

Tetrahalides of Ge, Sn and Pb behave as oxidising agents and the oxidising character of M^{4+} species increases in the order.

$$GeCl_4 < SnCl_4 < PbCl_4$$

The tetrahalides of all the elements except carbon form complexes when dissolved in halogen acids due to presence of vacant *d*-orbitals and thus act as Lewis acid.

Concept ladder

- The tetrahalide of carbon, i.e. CCl_4 cannot be hydrolysed by water since it cannot expand its covalency beyond 4 due to the absence of *d*-orbitals.
- The tetrachlorides of other elements, i.e. $SiCl_4$, $GeCl_4$, $SnCl_4$ and $PbCl_4$ are easily hydrolysed due to presence of vacant *d*-orbitals which accepts OH^- from water molecules. The ease of hydrolysis follows the sequence
$$SiCl_4 < GeCl_4 < SnCl_4 < PbCl_4$$
- Silicon chloride, due to availability of *d*-orbitals easily undergoes the hydrolysis and form silanol.
- Other chlorides ($GeCl_4$, $SnCl_4$, $PbCl_4$) of this group form respective oxide upon hydrolysis.
$$MCl_4 + 2H_2O \longrightarrow MO_2 + 4HCl$$

Formation of Dihalides

Heavier members of this family (i.e. from Ge to Pb) also form dihalides, MX_2, stability of which increases on moving down the group from Ge to Pb.

Thus, the dihalides of tin and lead are stable. Dihalides are generally ionic in nature and behave as reducing agents, the reducing character (of M^{2+} species) decreases in the order

$$GeCl_2 > SnCl_2 > PbCl_2$$

Considering the thermal and chemical stability, GeX_4 is more stable than GeX_2 whereas PbX_2 is more stable than PbX_4.

Reaction with Acid

- C, Si, Ge remain unaffected by dilute acid. Sn dissolves in dilute HNO_3 forming $Sn(NO_3)_2$. Pb dissolves slowly in dilute HCl forming $PbCl_2$ (sparingly soluble) and quite readily in dilute HNO_3 forming $Pb(NO_3)_2$.
$$Pb + 2HCl(\text{dil.}) \xrightarrow{\Delta} PbCl_2 + H_2\uparrow$$
$$3Pb + 8HNO_3(\text{dil.}) \longrightarrow 3Pb(NO_3)_2 + 2NO + 4H_2O$$
However, Pb does not dissolve in dilute H_2SO_4 due to formation of $PbSO_4$ coating on its surface.
- Carbon in form of diamond remains unaffected by concentrated acids.
- In the presence of hot concentrated HF/HNO_3 graphite forms carbon dioxide. Si is oxidised and changes to SiF_4 by hot concentrated HNO_3/HF. Ge dissolves slowly in hot concentrated H_2SO_4 and HNO_3. Sn also dissolves in concentrated acids. Pb does not dissolve in concentrated HCl due to formation of $PbCl_2$ coating.

Reaction with Water

C, Si and Ge do not decompose water. Sn decomposes steam to form SnO_2 and H_2.

$$Sn + 2H_2O \xrightarrow{\Delta} SnO_2 + 2H_2$$

Pb is not affected by water probably due to the formation of a protective film of lead oxide on its surface.

However, in presence of air and CO_2, lead dissolves forming $Pb(OH)_2$ which gives poisonous Pb^{2+} ions. This reaction is called **plumbo solvency**. It is due to this reason lead pipes are not used for carrying water.

Uses

- Light weight composites of the high strength are obtained by embedding graphite fibres in plastic material.
- Activated charcoal because of its highly porous nature is used to adsorb poisonous gases.
- Carbon black is used as a black pigment in black ink and as filler in automobile tyres.
- Coke is a good fuel and is a good reductant, widely used in metallurgy.

Anomalous Behaviour of Carbon

Carbon due to its very small size, high electronegativity, catenation, high bond enthalpy and absence of *d*-orbitals possesses some properties which are quite different from the other members of the group.

Some of these unique properties are listed below.

- Carbon has unusually high tendency of catenation, due to this carbon have highest number of compounds.
- Melting and boiling points of carbon are very high with respect to other members of the group. Further, because of smallest atomic radius and lowest atomic volume, carbon is the hardest element of group 14.
- Due to high tendency of $p\pi$-$p\pi$ multiple bond formation, carbon forms double and triple bond with its own atoms

(e.g. C═C, C≡C) or with other atom (e.g. C═O, C≡N). Other members do not show this tendency, they rather form $p\pi$-$d\pi$ bonding.

- Carbon has a maximum covalency of four while other group members show covalency upto 6.
- Carbon does not react with alkalies while other members react with alkalies such as NaOH, KOH etc.

Allotropes of Carbon

The properties of catenation and $p\pi$-$p\pi$ bond formation allow carbon to exist in multiple allotropic forms.

The crystalline and amorphous forms are

S. No.	Crystalline	Amorphous
(i)	Diamond	Coal
(ii)	Graphite	Charcoal
(iii)	Fullerene	Lamp black or carbon black

Diamond

Diamond is the purest form of carbon (crystalline) and one of the hardest substances with very high density as well as high refractive index. It has a three dimensional structure in which sp^3-hybridised C-atoms are arranged tetrahedrally. The C—C bond distance in diamond molecule is 1.54Å. Each C-atom lies at the centre of a regular tetrahedron and is linked to four C-atoms lying at the corners of the tetrahedron as shown in the figure.

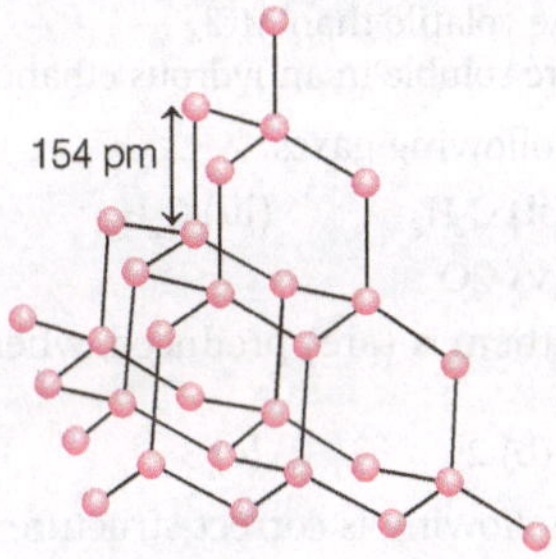

The crystal structure of diamond

The strong covalent bond between C-atoms, is the reason for hardness, high density and unusually high melting point (3500°C highest in the periodic table) of diamond. It is good conductor of heat but bad conductor of electricity.

Graphite

It is a soft, opaque, grey coloured allotrope with two dimensional structure. Each two dimensional sheet of graphite is made up of hexagonal rings [Figure (a)] involving 3 out of the 4 valence electrons of C participate in bonding, thus the hybridisation of each C-atom is sp^2. The fourth electron remains free and can conduct electricity.

The two dimensional sheet or layers [Figure (b)] are held together by weak van der Waals' forces, which is the cause of less compact, soft and lubricating texture of graphite.

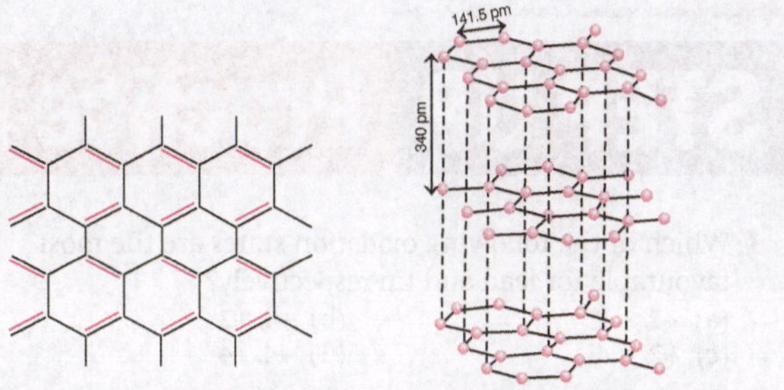

(a) The structure of a graphite sheet (b) Layered structure of graphite

Structure of graphite

Concept ladder Graphite is thermodynamically more stable than diamond and its ($\Delta_f H° = 0$) free energy of formation is 1.9 kJ less than diamond. However, entropy of graphite is more than diamond.

Fullerenes

Fullerenes are the recently discovered allotropes of carbon also called Buckminster fullerenes. These are cage like spheroidal molecules (e.g. C_{60}, C_{70} etc.)

C_{60} or the bucky ball consists of 60 C-atoms arranged in 20 six-membered and 12 five-membered rings of C-atoms, giving it an appearance of a soccer ball. Every ring in this structure is aromatic.

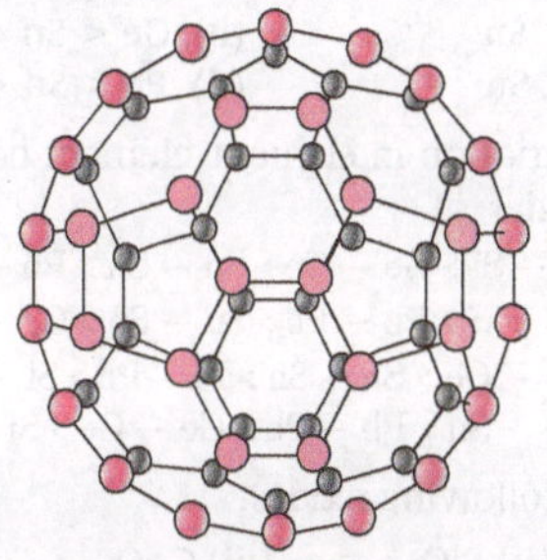

Structure of C_{60}, Buckminster fullerene

Each C-atom in C_{60} is sp^2-hybridised forming σ-bonds with three other C-atoms. The fourth electron remains free and responsible for its conductivity.

Amorphous forms of Carbon

Coal, charcoal, lamp black or carbon black, belong to this category. Carbon black is obtained by burning hydrocarbons in a limited supply of air. Charcoal and coke are obtained by heating wood and coal respectively at high temperatures in the absence of air or limited supply of air.

$$CH_4 + O_2 \longrightarrow \underset{\text{Carbon black}}{C} + 2H_2O$$

NEET Snapshot

ZSM-5 is a type of zeolite that is used to convert alcohols into gasoline. *[NEET 2020]*

Zeolites are the minerals that mainly contains aluminium and silicon compounds and their general formula is $M_x Al_x Si_{1-x} O_2 \cdot yH_2O$.

Zeolites are widely used as a catalyst in petrochemical industries for cracking of hydrocarbons and isomerisation.

STEP UP Practice 2

1 Which of the following oxidation states are the most favourable for lead and tin respectively?
(a) +2, + 2 (b) +4, +2
(c) +2, + 4 (d) +4, +4

2 Which of the following statements is correct with respect to the property of elements in the carbon family with an increase in the atomic number?
Their
(a) atomic size decreases
(b) stability of +2 oxidation state increases
(c) metallic character decreases
(d) ionisation energy increases

3 The stability of dihalides of Si, Ge, Sn and Pb increases steadily in the sequence
(a) $PbX_2 < SnX_2 < GeX_2 < SiX_2$
(b) $GeX_2 < SiX_2 < SnX_2 < PbX_2$
(c) $SiX_2 < GeX_2 < PbX_2 < SnX_2$
(d) $SiX_2 < GeX_2 < SnX_2 < PbX_2$

4 Amongst the elements of group 14, the reducing power of the tetravalent species increases in the order
(a) Ge < Pb < Sn (b) Ge < Sn < Pb
(c) Pb < Ge < Sn (d) Pb < Sn < Ge

5 The correct variation in element-element bond energy follows the order
(a) C − C > Si − Si > Ge − Ge > Sn − Sn > Pb − Pb
(b) Si − Si > C − C > Pb − Pb > Sn − Sn > Ge − Ge
(c) C − C > Ge − Ge > Sn − Sn > Pb −Pb > Si − Si
(d) C − C > Sn − Sn > Pb − Pb > Ge − Ge > Si − Si

6 Consider the following oxides.
(i) CO_2 (ii) SiO_2 (iii) GeO_2
(iv) SnO_2 (v) PbO_2
How many of them is (are) not acidic in nature?
(a) 2 (b) 1
(c) 4 (d) 3

7 The element that does not show catenation is
(a) Ge (b) Sn
(c) Si (d) Pb

8 Which of the following is correct match regarding the behaviour of CO_2 in water?
(a) CO_2 in water ⟶ weak monobasic acid, $H—OCO_2H$
(b) CO_2 in water ⟶ weak dibasic acid, H_2CO_3
(c) CO_2 in water ⟶ weak diacidic base, $CO(OH)_2$
(d) CO_2 in water ⟶ weak monoacidic base, $HO—CO_2H$

9 Which of the following oxides is amphoteric in nature?
(a) GeO_2 (b) GeO
(c) SnO (d) CO_2

10 Given below are two statements.
Statement I Diamond is an insulator and graphite is a conductor of electric current .
Statement II C-atoms are sp^3-hybridised in graphite as well as in diamond.
In the light of the above statements, choose the correct answer from the options given below.
(a) Both Statement I and Statement II are false.
(b) Statement I is true but Statement II is false.
(c) Statement I is false but Statement II is true.
(d) Both Statement I and Statement II are true.

11 Graphite is a soft solid lubricant extremely difficult to melt. The reason for this anomalous behaviour is that graphite
(a) is a non-crystalline substance
(b) is an allotropic form of diamond
(c) has molecules of variable molecular masses like polymers
(d) has carbon atoms arranged in large plates of rings of strongly bound carbon atoms with weak interplate bonds

12 A metal (*M*) of group 14 forms chlorides in its +2 and +4 oxidation states. Which of the following statements about these chlorides is correct?
(a) MCl_2 is more ionic than MCl_4.
(b) MCl_2 is more easily hydrolysed than MCl_4.
(c) MCl_2 is more volatile than MCl_4 .
(d) MCl_2 is more soluble in anhydrous ethanol than MCl_4.

13 Consider the following gases.
(i) CH_4 (ii) C_2H_2 (iii) C_2H_6
(iv) CO_2 (v) CO
How many of them is (are) produced, when Al_4C_3 is hydrolysed?
(a) 4 (b) 2 (c) 3 (d) 1

14 Which of the following is correct structure of anion of pyrosilicates?
(a) 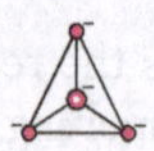 (b) 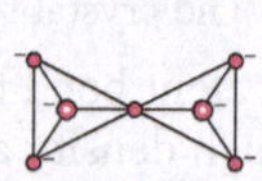
(c) 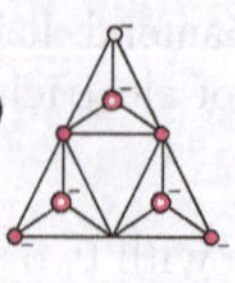 (d) 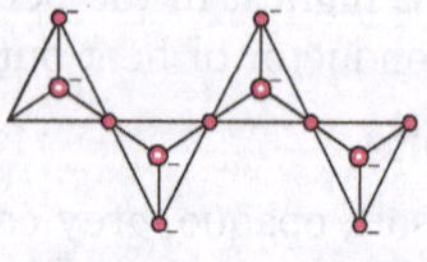

15 Silicon has a strong tendency to form polymers like silicones. The chain length of silicone polymer can be controlled by adding
(a) $MeSiCl_3$ (b) Me_2SiCl_2 (c) Me_3SiCl (d) Me_4Si

Module 3

Nitrogen Family

- General and Physical Properties
- Chemical Properties
- Anomalous Behaviour of Nitrogen

Group 15 Elements : The Nitrogen Family

Group 15 of the periodic table contains six elements namely, **nitrogen** (N), **phosphorus** (P), **arsenic** (As), **antimony** (Sb), **bismuth** (Bi) and **moscovium** (Mc). They are commonly known as pnictogens (pnicogen) meaning choking.

The first two elements, N and P are non-metals, arsenic and antimony are metalloids, whereas bismuth is a metal (Mc is a synthetic ratio-metal).

General and Physical Properties

The variations of general and physical properties of group 15 elements are given below:

Electronic Configuration

These elements contain five electrons in their valence shell. The general electronic configuration of this group is ns^2np^3 or $ns^2np_x^1np_y^1np_z^1$, where, $n = 2$ to 7.

Electronic configuration of each element of group 15 is listed in table given below.

Electronic Configurations of Elements of Group 15

Element	Atomic number	Electronic configuration
Nitrogen (N)	7	$[He]2s^2 2p^3$
Phosphorus (P)	15	$[Ne]3s^2 3p^3$
Arsenic (As)	33	$[Ar]3d^{10} 4s^2 4p^3$
Antimony (Sb)	51	$[Kr]4d^{10} 5s^2 5p^3$
Bismuth (Bi)	83	$[Xe]4f^{14} 5d^{10} 6s^2 6p^3$
Moscovium (Mc)	115	$[Rn]5f^{14} 6d^{10} 7s^2 7p^3$

Physical Appearance

Nitrogen is gaseous in nature and exist as a diatomic molecule (N≡N). Phosphorus exist as tetraatomic molecule in the gaseous state, whereas in solid state, it exists in different allotropic forms. Arsenic, antimony and bismuth are solids.

Atomic Radii

On moving down the group, i.e. from N to Bi, atomic radii (covalent radii) increases due to addition of extra principal energy shell in each succeeding element.

Group 15 elements have shorter atomic radii than those of corresponding elements of carbon family but larger than those of chalcogens due to increase in effective nuclear charge from left to right in a period.

Ionisation Enthalpy

The ionisation values of elements decrease down the group due to gradual increase in atomic size. Nitrogen, being the first member of this group has very high value, due to its small atomic size.

Element	N	P	As	Sb	Bi
IE_1 (kJ mol^{-1})	1402	1012	947	834	703

Metallic Nature

The metallic nature of elements increases down the group. Hence, nitrogen and phosphorus are non-metals, arsenic and antimony are metalloids and bismuth is a typical metal.

Electronegativity

The elements of nitrogen family are electronegative in nature. The value of electronegativity, in general decreases on moving down the group from nitrogen to bismuth. Nitrogen is the most electronegative element in group 15.

Element	N	P	As	Sb	Bi
Electronegativity	3.0	2.1	2.0	1.9	1.9

Melting and Boiling Points

Elements of group 15 do not show a regular trend in the values of melting and boiling points. Melting point first increases from N to As and then decreases to Sb and Bi (this is because of their tendency to form three covalent bond instead of five covalent bond due to inert pair effect). Boiling point first increases from N to Sb but boiling point of Bi is less than Sb.

The correct order for melting and boiling points are given below

Melting point N< P< Bi< Sb< As

Boiling point N< P< As< Bi< Sb

> **Concept ladder** All the members of group 15 (except Bi) show the phenomenon of allotropy. Nitrogen exists in two solid and one gaseous allotropic forms. Phosphorus exists in several allotropic forms such as white, red, scarlet, violet and black phosphorus. Arsenic exists in three allotropic forms, i.e. grey, yellow and black. Similarly, antimony (Sb) exists as metallic, α- or yellow and black or β-antimony.

Oxidation States

All the elements of group 15 have five electrons in their valence shell. Thus, oxidation states of these elements are +3 and +5. On moving down the group, stability of +5 oxidation state decreases and that of +3 oxidation state increases due to **inert pair effect,** i.e. **reluctance** of *s*-electrons to participate in bonding.

Therefore, Bi^{3+} is more stable than Bi^{5+} As a result, Bi^{5+} salts are very rare and are good oxidising agents

$$Bi^{5+} + 2e^- \longrightarrow Bi^{3+}$$

As^{3+} salts are good reducing agents,

$$As^{3+} \longrightarrow As^{5+} + 2e^-$$

Nitrogen shows $-\frac{1}{3}$, -2, -3, 0, +1, +2, +3, +4 and +5 oxidation states in $N_3H, N_2H_4, NH_3, N_2, N_2O$, NO, N_2O_3, N_2O_4 and N_2O_5 respectively due to its high electronegativity, small size and strong tendency to form $p\pi$ - $p\pi$ bonds.

Chemical Properties

Chemical properties of group-15 elements are discussed below.

Reaction with Hydrogen

Elements of group 15 react with hydrogen to form hydrides of formula : MH_3 (M is sp^3). All the hydrides are volatile, poisonous and foul smelling gases. These are pyramidal in shape.

> **Concept ladder** The trihydrides of group 15 elements are prepared from binary metal compounds (nitrides) such as Mg_3N_2, Zn_3As_2, Mg_3Sb_2 etc. by the action of water or dilute acids.
> e.g. $Mg_3N_2 + 6H_2O \longrightarrow 3Mg(OH)_2 + 2NH_3$
> $Zn_3As_2 + 6HCl \longrightarrow 3ZnCl_2 + 2AsH_3$

On moving down the group from NH_3 to BiH_3 following trends are observed.

Properties of hydride	Order with reason
Bond angle	$NH_3 > PH_3 > AsH_3 > SbH_3 > BiH_3$
Down the group the bond angles gradually decrease due to decrease in bond pair-bond pair repulsion.	
Basic character	$NH_3 > PH_3 > AsH_3 > SbH_3 \geq BiH_3$
This is due to the decrease in the availability of the lone pair of electrons on the central atoms.	
Boiling points	$BiH_3 > SbH_3 > NH_3 > AsH_3 > PH_3$
Except for ammonia, the boiling point increases down the group due to increase in molecular size resulting in increased van der Waals' force of atttraction. The abnormally high boiling point of NH_3 is due to the association of molecules through weaker intermolecular hydrogen bonding.	
Melting points	$NH_3 > SbH_3 > AsH_3 > PH_3$
NH_3 has the highest melting point this is due to intermolecular H-bonding. The other hydrides of this group do not show this H-bonding. Hence, their melting point are lower than NH_3.	
Thermal stability	$NH_3 > PH_3 > AsH_3 > SbH_3 > BiH_3$
Due to increase in size of central atoms, strength of *M*—H bond decreases.	
Reducing and acidic characters	$NH_3 < PH_3 < AsH_3 < SbH_3 < BiH_3$
This is due to the decrease in the stability of hydrides and increase in ionisation of hydrides that increases the reducing character and acidic character.	

> **Mentor's TiP**
> - Ammonia is highly soluble in H_2O because it form H-bonds with H_2O while PH_3 and other hydrides are insoluble because they do not form H-bonds with water.
> - Dipole moment of hydrides of group 15 elements decrease as the electronegativity of the central atom decreases down the group.

Reaction with Halogens

Elements of group 15 react with halogens to form trihalides (MX_3) and pentahalides (MX_5). All trihalides except that of nitrogen are stable. In case of nitrogen, only NF_3 is stable and inert.

- Trihalides are sp^3-hybridised (central atoms) with distorted tetrahedral geometry and pyramidal shape. Pentahalides are sp^3d-hybridised (central atoms) with trigonal bipyramidal geometry.

- Trihalides are less covalent than pentahalides as $M(+5)$ are more polarising than $M(+3)$ [Fajans' rule].
- Nitrogen does not form pentahalides due to non-availability of d-orbitals. The pentahalide of phosphorus, i.e. PCl_5 is unstable and decomposes to give PCl_3 and Cl_2.

Concept ladder

- Trihalides are easily hydrolysed than pentahalides. Ease of hydrolysis decreases down the group. Therefore, NCl_3 is easily hydrolysed but $SbCl_3$ and $BiCl_3$ are partly hydrolysed. NF_3 and PF_3 do not undergo hydrolysis.
- For NX_3, basic character increases as the electronegativity of halogen decreases that allows the availability of the lone pair of electrons are as follows

$$NF_3 < NCl_3 < NBr_3 < NI_3$$

- The Lewis acidic strength increases with increase in electronegativity of the central atom.

$$PCl_3 > AsCl_3 > SbCl_3$$

- The trihalides of P, As and Sb especially, fluorides and chlorides act as Lewis acids, since they can accept a lone pair of electrons from halide ion.

$$PF_3 + F_2 \longrightarrow PF_5$$
$$SbF_3 + 2F^- \longrightarrow [SbF_5]^{2-}$$
$$SbCl_3 + 2Cl^- \longrightarrow [SbCl_5]^{2-}$$

Reactivity Towards Oxygen

All the elements of this group form two types of oxides, i.e. M_2O_3 and M_2O_5 called trioxides and pentoxides.

Various Oxides Formed by Group 15 Elements

S.No.	Oxidation state	N	P	As	Sb	Bi
1.	+1	N_2O	–	–	–	–
2.	+2	NO	–	–	–	–
3.	+3	N_2O_3	P_2O_6	As_2O_3	Sb_2O_3	Bi_2O_3
4.	+4	N_2O_4	P_4O_8	–	–	–
5.	+5	N_2O_5	P_4O_{10}	As_2O_5	Sb_2O_5	Bi_2O_5

On moving down the group, acidic character decreases. This is because down the group, metallic character increases. Trioxides of N and P are acidic, trioxides of As and Sb are amphoteric and that of Bi is basic in nature. All the pentoxides are however, acidic but the acidity decrease as we move down the group.

Thus, N_2O_5 is the strongest acidic oxide while Bi_2O_5 is the weakest. The acidic strength decreases in the order

$$N_2O_5 > P_2O_5 > As_2O_5 > Sb_2O_5 > Bi_2O_5$$

Mentor's TIP

All the pentaoxide (except P_2O_5) can readily loose oxygen to form lower oxides, thus they act as a strong oxidising agents.

Anomalous Behaviour of Nitrogen

Nitrogen differs from rest of the members of the group because of its small size, high electronegativity, high ionisation energy, absence of vacant d-orbitals and capacity to form $p\pi$-$p\pi$ multiple bonds.

The properties that are different from other members are as follows

- Nitrogen is a gas while others are solid.
- It exists as diatomic molecule with triple bond while others form single bond.
- Nitrogen is chemically inert under ordinary conditions due to high bond dissociation energy, while others are reactive due to presence of single bond.
- Nitrogen does not show penta valency because of non-availability of d-orbitals. Therefore, NCl_3 exists but NCl_5 does not.
- Because of its high electronegativity, nitrogen is distinctly non-metallic while the other two members (As, Sb) are metalloids and bismuth is distinctly a metal.
- Nitrogen exhibits a large number of oxidation states such as −3 to +5. Other elements do not exhibit such a variety of oxidation states.
- Hydride of nitrogen (NH_3) is stable while the hydrides of other elements are not stable. Moreover, only hydrides of nitrogen form H-bonding while other members do not.
- Nitrogen forms oxides such as N_2O, NO, N_2O_4. Oxides such as NO formed by other elements. Nitrogen forms oxides that are monomeric such as N_2O, NO, N_2O_4. P forms 3 dimeric oxides such as ($P_4O_6, P_4O_8, P_4O_{10}$), As and Sb form 2 dimeric oxides only whereas Bi forms monomeric oxide.

Oxides of Nitrogen

Nitrogen combines with oxygen under different conditions to form several oxides. These oxides show wide range of oxidation states from +1 to +5. All of the oxides are covalent in nature.

Some important information regarding these oxides are as follows

Name	Oxidation state of nitrogen	Properties	Resonance structure (Lewis dot form)	Bond parameters
Dinitrogen monoxide or dinitrogen oxide or nitrous oxide [Nitrogen (I) oxide] (N_2O) (Laughing gas)	+1	Colourless gas, neutral	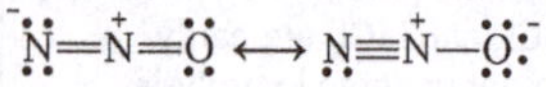	N—N—O 113 pm 119 pm Linear
Nitrogen monoxide or nitric oxide [Nitrogen (II) oxide] (NO)	+2	Colourless gas, neutral, paramagnetic in gaseous state	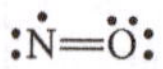	N—O 115 pm Linear
Dinitrogen trioxide [Nitrogen (III) oxide] (N_2O_3)	+3	Blue solid, acidic	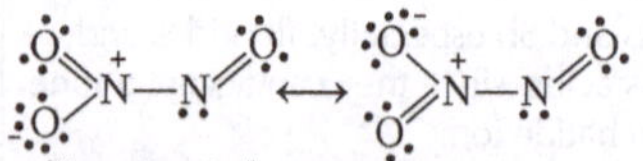 (Unsymmetrical)	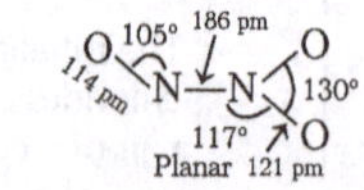
Nitrogen dioxide [Nitrogen (IV) oxide] (NO_2)	+4	Brown gas, reactive, paramagnetic, acidic	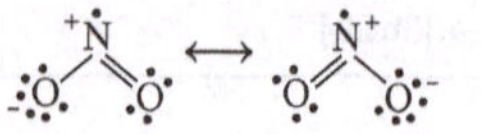	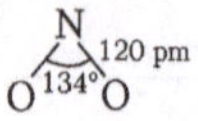
Dinitrogen tetraoxide [Nitrogen (IV) oxide] (N_2O_4)	+4	Colourless exists both in solid and liquid state with NO_2 in equilibrium, acidic.	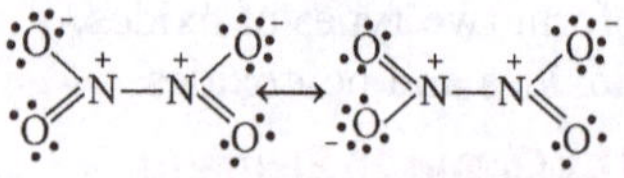	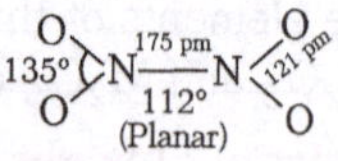
Dinitrogen pentaoxide [Nitrogen (V) oxide] (N_2O_5)	+5	Unstable as gas. In the solid state exists as $[NO_2]^+$ $[NO_3]^-$, colourless, acidic.	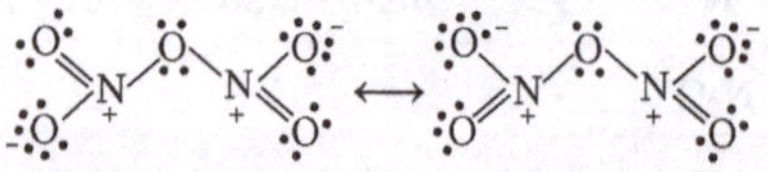	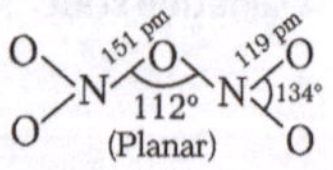

Mentor's TiP

- NO_2 is a reddish brown gas at room temperature. On cooling, it condenses to give first a yellow liquid and then a colourless solid due to dimerisation.
- NO_2 is paramagnetic but N_2O_4 is diamagnetic.

Oxoacids of Nitrogen

Nitrogen forms several oxoacids such as $H_2N_2O_2$, HNO_2, HNO_3 and HNO_4 that are given in the following table.

Name of oxoacid	Molecular formula	Structure	Oxidation state of N	Basicity	Nature
Hyponitrous acid	$H_2N_2O_2$	HO—N=N—OH exists as *trans*-isomer dipole moment being zero	+1	2(dibasic)	Highly explosive
Nitrous acid	HNO_2	HO—N̈=O	+3	1(monobasic)	Unstable weak acid
Nitric acid	HNO_3	H—O—N(→O)=O	+5	1(monobasic)	Stable, strong acid
Pernitric acid	HNO_4	O=N(→O)—O—O—H	+5	1(monobasic)	Unstable and explosive

STEP UP Practice 3

1 The most abundant uncombined element present in atmosphere is
(a) Ca (b) Mg (c) Al (d) N

2 Which of the following is incorrectly matched regarding the oxidation state of underlined element?
(a) $\underline{N}_2O \longrightarrow +1$ (b) $\underline{N}O \longrightarrow +2$
(c) $\underline{N}_2O_3 \longrightarrow +3$ (d) $\underline{N}_2O_5 \longrightarrow +4$

3 Which of the following is arranged in the increasing order of enthalpy of vaporisation?
(a) $NH_3 < PH_3 < AsH_3$ (b) $AsH_3 < PH_3 < NH_3$
(c) $NH_3 < AsH_3 < PH_3$ (d) $PH_3 < AsH_3 < NH_3$

4 Which of the following elements does not show allotropy?
(a) Nitrogen (b) Bismuth (c) Antimony (d) Arsenic

5 $NH_4Cl(s)$ is heated in a test tube. Vapours are brought in contact with red litmus paper, which changes to blue and then to red. It is because of
(a) formation of NH_4OH and HCl
(b) formation of NH_3 and HCl
(c) greater diffusion of NH_3 than HCl
(d) Both (b) and (c)

6 Which of the following is correctly matched regarding the conversion of atmospheric nitrogen in plants?
(a) Atmospheric nitrogen $\longrightarrow$ Carbohydrate
(b) Atmospheric nitrogen $\longrightarrow$ Proteins
(c) Atmospheric nitrogen $\longrightarrow$ Glycerol
(d) Atmospheric nitrogen $\longrightarrow$ Fats

7 Compound *A* undergoes hydrolysis to produce a colourless gas with rotten fish smell. The gas gives a vortex ring. The gas is
(a) PH_3 (b) P_2O_3 (c) P_2O_5 (d) P_2S_5

8 Which of the following is least basic?
(a) NF_3 (b) NCl_3 (c) NBr_3 (d) NI_3

9 Given below are two statements.
Statement I $(SiH_3)_3N$ is planar while $(CH_3)_3N$ is pyramidal.
Statement II (*lp-bp*) repulsion in $(CH_3)_3N$ makes it pyramidal and in case of $(SiH_3)_3N$ lone pair on N-atom is transferred to empty *d*-orbital of Si, thus minimize the repulsion.
In the light of the above statements, choose the correct answer from the options given below.
(a) Both Statement I and Statement II are false.
(b) Statement I is true but Statement II is false.
(c) Statement I is false but Statement II is true.
(d) Both Statement I and Statement II are true.

10 Consider the following compounds.
(i) NH_4Cl (ii) NaOH
(iii) $NaNO_2$ (iv) NH_4OH
(v) $NaNO_3$
The total number of compounds, which is/are used to prepared pure N_2 gas in the laboratory is
(a) 4 (b) 1 (c) 3 (d) 2

11 Both NF_3 and NCl_3 are covalent but they differ in the extent of hydrolysis because
(a) NF_3 is more stable than NCl_3 and hydrolysis product of NF_3, that is HOF, does not exist
(b) dipole moment of NF_3 is greater than that of NCl_3
(c) electronegativity of F is greater than that of Cl
(d) Cl can expand its octet by using *d*-orbitals

12 Nitrogen differs from P, As, Sb and Bi in the following properties
(a) it forms diatomic molecule
(b) it is not able to extend its coordination number beyond four
(c) nitrogen does not function as a Lewis acid whereas P, As, Sb and Bi do so
(d) N differs in all the properties given above

13 N_2O (laughing gas) finds use in the following except.
(a) As a propellant for whipped ice-cream
(b) As an anaesthetic
(c) For the preparation of N_3H
(d) As fuel for rockets

14 Which of the following is most acidic oxide ?
(a) N_2O_5 (b) P_2O_5 (c) As_2O_5 (d) Sb_2O_5

15 Given below are two statements.
Statement I N_2H_4 is kinetically stable compound.
Statement II Two N-atoms are bonded by a triple bond in N_2H_4.
In the light of the above statements, choose the correct answer from the options given below.
(a) Both Statement I and Statement II are false.
(b) Statement I is true but Statement II is false.
(c) Statement I is false but Statement II is true.
(d) Both Statement I and Statement II are true.

16 Only *pπ-pπ* multiple bonding is present in
(a) oxides of nitrogen (b) oxides of phosphorus
(c) halides of nitrogen (d) halides of phosphorus

17 Which of the following structures is exhibited by solid crystalline PCl_5?
(a) Bi pyramidal moieties
(b) Octahedral and tetrahedral ions
(c) Square pyramidal moieties
(d) Pentagonal moieties

18 Consider the following compounds.
(i) P_4 (ii) N_4 (iii) PCl_5
(iv) NCl_5 (v) PO_2
How many of them do not exist?
(a) 3 (b) 4 (c) 2 (d) 5

19 Which of the following is correctly matched regarding the number of P—O—P bonds in cyclo tri-metaphosphoric acid?

(a) P—O—P bonds ⟶ zero
(b) P—O—P bonds ⟶ two
(c) P—O—P bonds ⟶ three
(d) P—O—P bond ⟶ four

20 Choose the incorrect match with the given oxidation state.

(a) Orthophosphoric acid ⟶ +5
(b) Pyrophosphoric acid ⟶ +5
(c) Orthophosphorus acid ⟶ +5
(d) Tri-metaphosphoric acid ⟶ +5

21 Strong reducing behaviour of H_3PO_2 is due to

(a) low oxidation state of phosphorus
(b) presence of two — OH group and one P — H bond
(c) presence of one — OH group and two P—H bonds
(d) Both (a) and (c)

22 Which of the following statements is wrong?

(a) Single N—N bond is stronger than the single P—P bond.
(b) PH_3 can act as a ligand in the formation of coordination compound with transition elements.
(c) NO_2 is paramagnetic in nature.
(d) Covalency of nitrogen in N_2O_5 is four.

23 The structural formula of hypophosphorus acid is

(a) 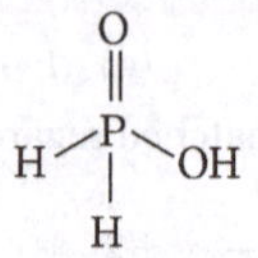
(b) 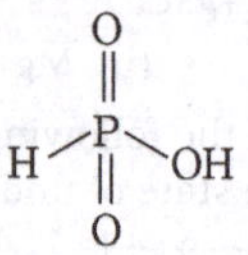
(c) 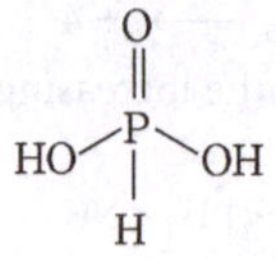
(d) 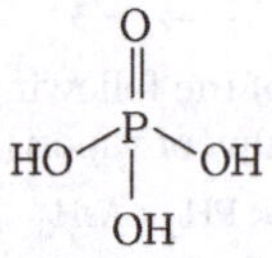

Module 4

Oxygen Family

- General and Physical Properties
- Chemical Properties
- Anomalous Behaviour of Oxygen

Group 16 Elements : The Oxygen Family

Group 16 of the periodic table contains six elements namely, **oxygen** (O), **sulphur** (S), **selenium** (Se), **tellurium** (Te), **polonium** (Po) and livermorium (Lv). Oxygen is the most abundant of all element the earth. The first four elements are non-metals while the last element, polonium is a **radioactive metal** (Lv is a synthetic radio-metal). These non-metallic elements are commonly referred to as **chalcogens** (meaning ore forming) because many metal ores occur as oxides, sulphides etc. They are also known as members of **oxygen family**.

General and Physical Properties

The general and physical properties of group 16 elements are as follows

Electronic Configuration

The general electronic configuration of all the elements of this group is ns^2np^4 or $ns^2np_x^2np_y^1np_z^1$, where, $n = 2$ to 7.

Electronic configuration of each element of group 16 listed in table.

Electronic Configurations of Elements of Group 16

Element	Atomic number	Electronic configuration
Oxygen (O)	8	$[He]2s^2 2p^4$
Sulphur (S)	16	$[Ne]3s^2 3p^4$
Selenium (Se)	34	$[Ar]3d^{10} 4s^2 4p^4$
Tellurium (Te)	52	$[Kr]4d^{10} 5s^2 5p^4$
Polonium (Po)	84	$[Xe]4f^{14} 5d^{10} 6s^2 6p^4$
Livermorium (Lv)	116	$[Rn]5f^{14} 6d^{10} 7s^2 7p^4$

Physical State

Oxygen occurs as diatomic molecule O_2 and is therefore, a gas while sulphur occurs as polyatomic molecule S_8 and therefore, is a solid. All other elements also exist as solids.

Atomic Radii

Atomic radii increase gradually on moving down the group, i.e. from O to Po. This occurs due to an increase in the number of electronic shells.

Ionisation Energy

It decreases down the group due to increase in size. Ionisation enthalpy of elements of this group is lower as compared to those of group-15 elements in the corresponding periods. Because of the fact that group 15 elements have extra stable half-filled *p*-orbital configurations.

Electronegativity

It decreases from O to Po as the atomic size increases. Oxygen is the second most electronegative element after fluorine.

Due to high electronegativity, the elements of oxygen family (except Po) form ionic compounds with metals and covalent compounds with non-metals.

Electron Affinity

Electron affinity of group-16 elements decreases as the atomic size increases. However, electron affinity of O is least in group 16. This is because of the small size and high charge density on O atom.

Melting and Boiling Points

Melting and boiling points show a regular increase from oxygen to tellurium. There is a large difference in melting and boiling points of oxygen and sulphur that can be explained on the basis of their structure.

Oxygen exists mostly as a discrete diatomic molecule while sulphur and selenium exist as polyatomic molecules, e.g. S_8, Se_8, etc., where the atoms are bonded by covalent bonds associated with high dissociation energy.

Concept ladder

- Like the elements of groups 14 and 15, all the elements of group 16 show allotropy. Allotropes are the different forms of the same element, where the atoms combine in different ways, so at the same temperature and pressure they can exist in different forms. Thus, oxygen exists in two allotropic forms O_2 and O_3 (ozone).
- Sulphur occurs in a number of allotropic forms such as rhombic (α) sulphur, monoclinic (β) sulphur, plastic (γ) sulphur, colloidal (δ) sulphur. All these allotropes are non- metallic in character.
- Selenium exists in two forms, i.e. red form which is non-metallic and grey form which is metallic in nature.
- Tellurium also exists in two forms, i.e. non-metallic and metallic (more stable) form. While allotropes of polonium are α and β forms, which are metallic in nature.

Oxidation States

Elements of group 16 exhibit a number of oxidation states which are as follows

Element	Oxidation state
O	-2, -1,
S	-2, +2, +4, +6
Se	-2, +2, +4, +6
Te	-2, +2, +4, +6
Po	+2, +4

The stability of −2 oxidation state decreases down the group. Oxygen mainly exhibits −2 oxidation state (except in OF_2, where it shows +2, as electronegativity of $F > O$.

Stability of +4 oxidation state increases and that of +6 oxidation state decreases down the group due to inert pair effect.

NEET Close-up

Example Similar to PYQ Asked in NEET 2024

Among group-16 elements, + 6 oxidation state is possible with

(a) S and Se only
(b) S and Te only
(c) Se and Te only
(d) S, Se and Te

Sol. (*d*) Among the given elements, S, Se and Te has + 6 oxidation states.

Skill Builder

Among group-16 elements, which one shows −1 oxidation state?

(a) S (b) Te
(c) O (d) Po

For more practice Refer to Q.29 of Gearing up for NEET.

Chemical Properties

The chemical properties shown by group 16 elements are as follows

Reaction with Hydrogen

Group 16 elements react with H_2 to form binary hydrides of general formula $H_2\ddot{M}\!:$ (where, $M = O, S, Se, Te, Po$).

$$M + H_2 \longrightarrow H_2M$$

H_2O is liquid at room temperature but all other hydrides are colourless and foul smelling toxic gases.

Characteristics of these hydride are discussed below.

Properties of hydride	Order	Reason
Bond angle	$H_2O > H_2S > H_2Se > H_2Te$	Due to bond pair-bond pair repulsion decreases down the group.
Covalent character	$H_2O < H_2S < H_2Se > H_2Te$	Difference in electronegativity of M–H decreases down the group.
Thermal stability	$H_2O > H_2S > H_2Se > H_2Te$	Due to increase in size of central atom, strength of M–H bond decreases down the group.
Reducing character	$H_2S < H_2Se < H_2Te$	Due to strength of M–H bond decreases down the group.
Acidic character	$H_2O < H_2S < H_2Se < H_2Te$	Due to strength of M–H bond decreases down the group.
Melting and Boiling points	$H_2S < H_2Se < H_2Te < H_2O$	H_2O has the highest melting and boiling point due to stronger intermolecular H-bonding.

NEET Snapshot

The decreasing order of pK_a value of group 16 elements is $H_2O > H_2S > H_2Se > H_2Te$. ***[NEET 2021]***

- The pK_a value is inversely proportional to acidic strength. So on increasing the acidic character, the pK_a value decreases.
- On moving down the group, bond dissociation enthalpy of hydrides of group 16 elements decrease, hence acidity increase and the pK_a values decrease.

Reaction with Oxygen

They react with oxygen to form oxides of types MO_2 and MO_3 and in some cases MO is also formed.

Different Oxides of 16 Group Elements

Type of oxide	O	S	Se	Te	Po
Monoxide	—	SO	—	TeO	PoO
Dioxide	O_2	SO_2	SeO_2	TeO_2	PoO_2
Trioxide	O_3	SO_3	SeO_3	TeO_3	PoO_3
Heptoxide	—	S_2O_7			

Some important characteristics of oxides of group 16th elements are given below.

- O_3 and SO_2 are gases but SeO_2 is solid. On moving from SO_2 to TeO_2, reducing property decreases. As a result, TeO_2 acts as an oxidising agent. MO_3 type oxide are formed by sulphur, selenium and tellurium but tendency to form MO_3 type of oxides decreases down the group due to inert pair effect.
- These oxides are acidic in nature, i.e. form acids with water and this nature decreases down the group due to decrease in electronegativity and increase of metallic character.

  Hence, order of acidic nature of oxides is

$$SO_3 > SeO_3 > TeO_3$$

Reaction with Halogen

They react with halogens to form various types of halides such as MX_6, MX_4 and MX_2. Oxygen forms halides only with fluorine (OF_2) and its compounds with rest of the halogens are called **oxides** (not halides) as its electronegativity is more than any other halogen. Other elements form halides of different oxidation number, i.e. + 1, + 2, + 4 and + 6.

$$M + 3F_2 \longrightarrow MF_6$$
$$2M + Cl_2 \longrightarrow M_2Cl_2$$
$$M_2Cl_2 + Cl_2 \longrightarrow 2MCl_2$$
$$M + 2Cl_2 \longrightarrow MCl_4$$

Different Oxidation Numbers of Group 16 Elements and their Respective Halides

Halides	X	Oxidation numbers
S_2X_2	F, Cl, Br, I	+1
SX_2	F, Cl	+2
SX_4	F	+4
SX_6	F	+6
Se_2X_2	Cl, Br	+1
SeX_2, TeX_2	Cl, Br	+2
SeX_4, TeX_4	F, Cl, Br	+4
TeX_4	I	+4
SeX_6, TeX_6	F	+6

Some important characteristic of 16th group halides are as follows

- For same element the stability of the halides decreases in the order F > Cl > Br > I.
- SF_6 is thermodynamically inert, non-toxic gas. Inertness of SF_6 is due to the presence of sterically protected sulphur atom. SF_6 is used as a gaseous insulator in high voltage generators.

Mentor's TiP

All the elements of group 16 except oxygen form tetrafluorides and hexa fluorides.

Anomalous Behaviour of Oxygen

Oxygen, the first member of 16th group, differs in some important ways from other group members.
This is due to its

- small size,
- high electronegativity and
- non-availability of *d*-orbitals for bonding.

The main points of difference between oxygen and other members of 16th group are given below.

- Oxygen exists as O_2 (diatomic) gas while all other members are solid.
- Oxygen is paramagnetic while others are not (S_2 is also paramagnetic).
- Compounds of oxygen are ionic and polar covalent due to its high electronegativity.
- Oxygen exhibits – 2 oxidation state while other members show + 6 oxidation states (in general).
- Oxygen form $p\pi$-$p\pi$ bonds while sulphur forms $d\pi$-$p\pi$ bonds.
- Only hydride of oxygen is non-poisonous, i.e. H_2O, while other hydrides are poisonous gases.

Oxoacids of Sulphur

Sulphurous Acid Series

(a)	H_2SO_3	S (+ 4)	Sulphurous acid	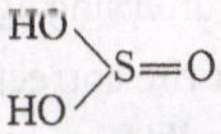
(b)	$H_2S_2O_5$	S (+ 5) *S (+ 3)	Disulphurous acid or Pyrosulphurous acid	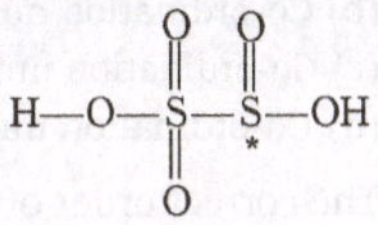
(c)	$H_2S_2O_4$	S (+ 3)	Dithionous acid	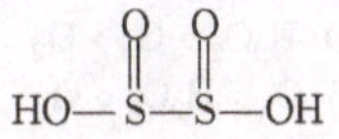

Sulphuric Acid Series

(a)	H_2SO_4	S (+ 6)	Sulphuric acid	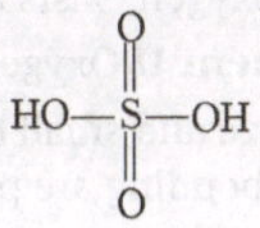
(b)	$H_2S_2O_3$	S (+ 4) *S(0)	Thiosulphuric acid	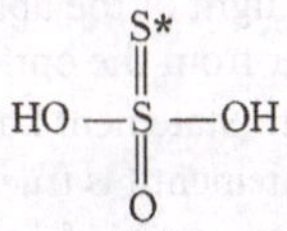
(c)	$H_2S_2O_7$	S (+ 6)	Pyrosulphuric acid (oleum)	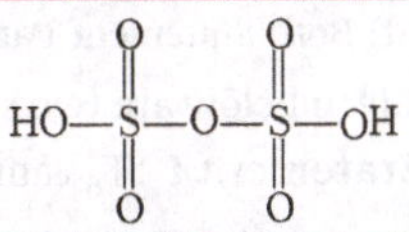

Peroxo Acid Series

(a)	H_2SO_5	S (+ 6)	Peroxomono-sulphuric acid (Caro's acid)	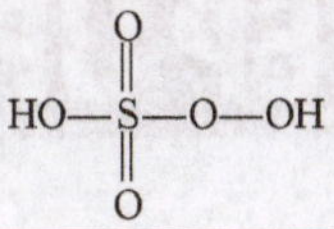
(b)	$H_2S_2O_8$	S (+ 6)	Peroxodisulphuric acid (Marshall's acid)	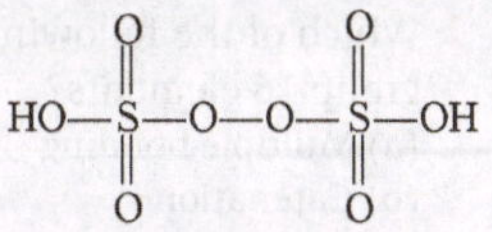

Thionic Acid Series

(a)	$H_2S_2O_6$	S (+5)	Dithionic acid	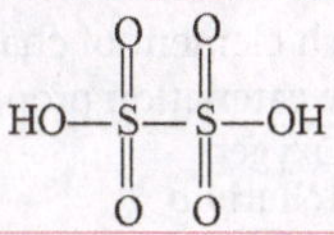
(b)	$H_2S_nO_6$	S (+5) S* (0)	Polythionic acid	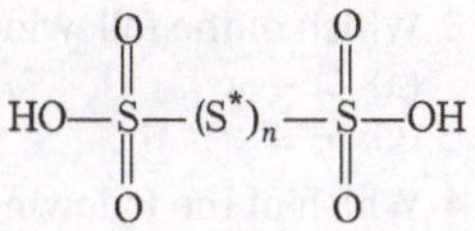

NEET Close-up

Example Similar to PYQ Asked in NEET 2020

Which of the following oxoacids of sulphur has —S—O—S— linkage?

(a) Sulphurous acid (b) Peroxidisulphuric acid
(c) Pyrosulphuric acid (d) Sulphuric acid

Sol. (c) The structure of pyrosulphuric acid is

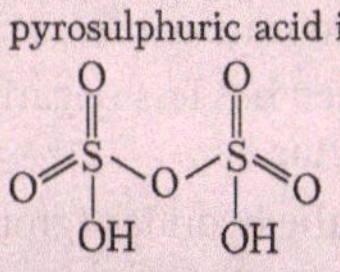

Thus, it has –S–O–S– linkage among all the given oxoacids.

Skill Builder

Which of the following oxoacids of sulphur has one S=O bond?

(a) Peroxodisulphuric acid (b) Sulphurous acid
(c) Sulphuric acid (d) Pyrosulphuric acid

For more practice Refer to Q. 16 of Gearing up for NEET.

The elements of group 16 are very useful. For example sulphuric acid is a very important industrial chemical. A nation's industrial strength can be judged by the quantity of H_2SO_4 it produces and consumes.

STEP UP Practice 4

1 Which of the following physical property not possessed by group 16 elements?
(a) Multiple bonding
(b) Catenation
(c) Allotropy
(d) High viscosity

2 Which element of chalcogens has maximum tendency to show catenation property?
(a) Oxygen (b) Sulphur
(c) Tellurium (d) Polonium

3 Which of the following bonds has the least bond energy?
(a) Se—Se (b) Te—Te
(c) S—S (d) O—O

4 Which of the following elements does not show an oxidation state higher than +2?
(a) Oxygen (b) Sulphur
(c) Selenium (d) Tellurium

5 Tetrafluorides of elements of group-16 have hybridisation and geometry respectively
(a) sp^3 and trigonal pyramidal
(b) sp^3d and tetrahedral
(c) sp^3d and trigonal bipyramidal
(d) sp^3 and tetrahedral

6 Given below are two statements.
Statement I Oxygen has less negative electron gain enthalpy than sulphur.
Statement II All the hydrides (group-16) except water possess reducing property and this reducing character decreases from H_2S to H_2Te.
In the light of the above statements, choose the correct answer from the options given below.
(a) Both Statement I and Statement II are false.
(b) Statement I is true but Statement II is false.
(c) Statement I is false but Statement II is true.
(d) Both Statement I and Statement II are true.

7 A group 16 element exists in metallic lattice. It also exists in two crystalline allotropic forms. The metal is
(a) sulphur
(b) polonium
(c) selenium
(d) tellurium

8 The absorption of UV radiation by O_3
(a) protects the inhabitants of our planet from injurious radiation
(b) maintains an equilibrium between the concentrations of O_2 and O_3
(c) makes both the functions effective
(d) makes no function effective

9 Water is much less volatile than H_2S because
(a) H_2O has a bond angle of nearly 150°
(b) hydrogen is loosely bonded with the sulphur
(c) S-atom is less electronegative than O-atom
(d) S-atom is more electronegative than O-atom

10 Among CH_4, NH_3 and H_2O, acidity of H_2O is maximum because
(a) oxygen contains two lone pairs of electrons
(b) bond angle in H_2O is less than 109°28′ due to VSEPR
(c) oxygen is more electronegative than C or N
(d) H_2O is an associated liquid

11 In presence of H_2O, SO_2 acts as
(a) an oxidising agent (b) a reducing agent
(c) a hydrolysing agent (d) a redox reagent

12 Pick out the correct match.
(a) Co-ordination number of oxygen in liq. $H_2O \longrightarrow 2$
(b) Co-ordination number of oxygen in liq. $H_2O \longrightarrow 3$
(c) Co-ordination number of oxygen in liq. $H_2O \longrightarrow 4$
(d) Co-ordination number of oxygen in liq. $H_2O \longrightarrow 5$

13 The correct order of O—O bond length in O_2, H_2O_2 and O_3 is
(a) $H_2O_2 > O_3 > O_2$ (b) $O_2 > H_2O_2 > O_3$
(c) $O_3 > H_2O_2 > O_2$ (d) $O_2 > O_3 > H_2O_2$

14 Given below are two statements.
Statement I Both rhombic and monoclinic sulphur exist as S_8 but oxygen exists as O_2.
Statement II Oxygen forms $p\pi - p\pi$ multiple bond due to small size and small bond length but both $p\pi - p\pi$ and $d\pi - p\pi$ bonding are possible in sulphur compounds.
In the light of the above statements, choose the correct answer from the options given below.
(a) Both Statement I and Statement II are false.
(b) Statement I is true, but Statement II is false.
(c) Statement I is false, but Statement II is true.
(d) Both Statement I and Statement II are true.

15 Given below are two statements.
Statement I SF_6 cannot be hydrolysed but SF_4 can be.
Statement II Six F-atoms in SF_6 prevent the attack of H_2O on sulphur atom of SF_6.
In the light of the above statements, choose the correct answer from the options given below.
(a) Both Statement I and Statement II are false.
(b) Statement I is true, but Statement II is false.
(c) Statement I is false, but Statement II is true.
(d) Both Statement I and Statement II are true.

16 Consider the following compounds.
(i) Sulphur trioxide (ii) Hydrogen peroxide
(iii) Sulphur dioxide (iv) Ozone
(v) Hydrogen sulphide
How many them can act as a bleaching agent?
(a) 1 (b) 3
(c) 2 (d) 4

17 Which of the followign property is not correctly matched with the given compound?
(a) $H_2SO_4 \longrightarrow$ Reducing agent
(b) $H_2SO_4 \longrightarrow$ Dehydratign agent
(c) $H_2SO_4 \longrightarrow$ Sulphonating agent
(d) $H_2SO_4 \longrightarrow$ Highly viscous

18 $Na_2S_2O_3$ is used in photography for fixing the negative. It removes the AgBr by
(a) complex formation $Na_3[Ag(S_2O_3)_2]$
(b) oxidation of AgBr to Br_2
(c) reduction of AgBr to Ag
(d) formation of a double salt

19 Which of the following compounds is correctly matched with the given linkage?
(a) $H_2S_2O_7 \longrightarrow 1$ (S—O—S linkage)
(b) $H_2S_2O_8 \longrightarrow 1$ (S—O—S linkage)
(c) $H_2SO_4 \longrightarrow 2$ (S—O—S linkage)
(d) $H_2SO_3 \longrightarrow 1$ (S—O—S linkage)

20 Aqueous hypo solution on reaction with aqueous $AgNO_3$ gives
(a) yellow ppt. changing to black
(b) white ppt. changing to black
(c) orange ppt. changing to blue
(d) no ppt.

21 Consider the following acids,
(i) $H_2S_2O_3$ (ii) $H_2S_4O_6$ (iii) H_2SO_5
(iv) $H_2S_2O_8$ (v) H_2SO_4
How many of them is (are) peroxy acids?
(a) 4 (b) 3 (c) 1 (d) 2

22 The correct formula of Caro's acid is
(a) H_2SO_3 (b) H_2SO_5 (c) $H_2S_2O_8$ (d) $H_2S_2O_7$

Module 5

Halogen Family

• General and Physical Properties • Chemical Properties • Anomalous Behaviour of Fluorine

Group 17 Elements : Halogen Family

Group 17 consists of six elements, namely **fluorine** (F), **chlorine** (Cl), **bromine** (Br), **iodine** (I), **astatine** (At) and the recently discovered element, **tennessine** (Ts), earlier called ununseptium-Uus). These are collectively called **halogens** due to their property of forming salts (*Greek halo*-means salt).

The first four members (F, Cl, Br and I) are non-metals and show similar properties. However, not much is known about the rest two members (At and Ts) except that astatine (At) is radioactive.

General and Physical Properties

The various general and physical properties of group 17 elements are given below.

Electronic Configuration

The general electronic configuration of group 17 elements is ns^2np^5 or $ns^2np_x^2np_y^2\ np_z^1$ where, $n = 2$ to 7

Electronic configuration of each element of group 17 is listed in the table given below.

Electronic Configurations of Elements of Group 17

Element	Atomic number	Electronic configuration
Fluorine (F)	9	$[He]2s^2 2p^5$
Chlorine (Cl)	17	$[Ne]3s^2 3p^5$
Bromine (Br)	35	$[Ar]3d^{10} 4s^2 4p^5$
Iodine (I)	53	$[Kr]4d^{10} 5s^2 5p^5$
Astatine (At)	85	$[Xe]4f^{14} 5d^{10} 6s^2 6p^5$
Tennessine (Ts)	117	$[Rn]5f^{14} 6d^{10} 7s^2 7p^5$

Physical State

Halogens exist as diatomic covalent molecules, held together by weak van der Waals' forces of attraction. Strength of these forces increases as the size of halogens increase from F to I. Hence, F_2 and Cl_2 exist as gases at room temperature, Br_2 is a liquid whereas I_2 exists as a solid.

Atomic and Ionic Radii

The atomic or covalent radii of group 17 elements increases down the group as the atomic number increases. The similar trend is found in case of ionic radii as well. The increase in radius is due to the addition of an extra shell of electrons as we go down in a group.

Elements	F	Cl	Br	I
Covalent radius (pm)	64	99	114	133
Ionic radius (pm) [X^-]	133	184	196	220

Ionisation Energy

The first ionisation energy decreases down the group as expected.

$$F > Cl > Br > I$$

This is due to increase in atomic size on moving down the group. As the size increases, it is easier to pull an electron out from the outermost shell.

Electron Affinity

Halogens have seven electrons in their valence shell, they have a very strong tendency of gaining an electron to acquire a stable noble gas configuration.

Therefore, they have very high negative electron affinities. In fact, their electron affinities are the highest in their respective periods. The order follows as

$$Cl > F > Br > I$$

Concept ladder The smaller electron affinity of fluorine than that of chlorine is a consequence of the small size of fluorine and high charge density.

Electronegativity

It decreases on moving down in the group, making fluorine the most and iodine the least electronegative among the halogens.

$$F > Cl > Br > I$$

As a result of decrease of electronegativity, non-metallic character decreases from F to I. As we go across the *p*-block elements in a period, the electronegativity increases reaching maximum at the halogen group.

Thus, halogens are the most electronegative elements in their respective periods and fluorine is the most electronegative element in the periodic table.

Oxidation States

The most common oxidation state of halogens is −1. However, Cl, Br and I exhibit +1, +3, +5 and +7 oxidation states as well. Fluorine being most electronegative element and devoid of *d*-orbitals does not show oxidation state other than −1 (except in **HOF** which is very unstable).

While different other oxidation states shown by the other group members are possible due to presence of *d*-orbitals in them, in which *p*-electrons can be excited to *d*-orbitals.

Bond Dissociation Energy

Bond dissociation energies of halogen molecules decreases down the group as the size of atom increases. The bond dissociation energy of fluorine (F—F) is lower than those of chlorine (Cl—Cl) and bromine (Br—Br) because of inter electronic repulsion present in the small atom of fluorine.

X_2	F_2	Cl_2	Br_2	I_2
Bond dissociation energy (kJ mol^{-1})	158.8	242.6	192.8	151.1

Hence, bond energy decreases in the order

$$Cl_2 > Br_2 > F_2 > I_2$$

Oxidising Power

Halogens are strong oxidising agents as they have strong tendency to accept an electron. The electron gain enthalpy of fluorine is less negative than that of chlorine but still it is the strongest oxidising agent. This is due to its **low bond dissociation energy** and **high heat of hydration** as compared to those of chlorine. The order of oxidising power is $F_2 > Cl_2 > Br_2 > I_2$.

Concept ladder

- F_2 has the most negative $\Delta G°$ value, i.e. −730 kJ mol^{-1}, hence it is the strongest oxidising agent and can oxidise Cl^-, Br^- and I^- to Cl_2, Br_2 and I_2 respectively.
- F_2 can also oxidise H_2O to O_2,

$$F_2 + H_2O \longrightarrow 2HF + \frac{1}{2}O_2$$

Bond Length in X_2 Molecule

As the size of the halogen atom increases, the bond length of *X*—*X* bond in X_2 molecule increases from F_2 to I_2.

$$F_2 < Cl_2 < Br_2 < I_2$$

X–*X* bond	F–F	Cl–Cl	Br–Br	I–I
Bond length (pm)	143	199	228	266

Solubility

Halogens being non-polar in molecular form are readily soluble in organic solvents like hexane. However, they're not as much soluble in polar solvents like water. Their solubility in water decreases down the group as

$$F_2 > Cl_2 > Br_2 > I_2$$

Fluorine reacts with water violently. Chlorine and bromine are fairly soluble, while iodine is least soluble.

> **Concept ladder**
> I_2 is least soluble in water but more soluble in aqneous KI solution due to the formation of polyhalide ion, I_3^- which increases the solubility of iodine in water.
> $$I_2(s) + KI(aq) \longrightarrow KI_3 \longrightarrow K^+(aq) + I_3^-(aq)$$

Melting and Boiling Points

The melting and boiling points of halogens increase down the group. This trend is in accordance with their increasing atomic size. As the size increases, interparticle attraction increases, which further increase the melting and boiling points.

Order of boiling point is $F_2 < Cl_2 < Br_2 < I_2$.

Order of melting point is $F_2 < Cl_2 < Br_2 < I_2$.

Colours

All these halogens are coloured. F_2 is yellow, Cl_2 is greenish yellow, Br_2 is reddish brown and I_2 is violet. The colour is because of absorption of energy from visible light by halogen molecules for exicitation of outer electron from the highest occupied π^* molecular orbital to the lowest unoccupied σ^* molecular orbital.

Chemical Properties

Halogen group is one of the most reactive groups in the periodic table. Having high electron affinity and low bond enthalpy, these can react with most of elements in the periodic table.

However, the order of reactivity of the group members decreases down the group as F > Cl > Br > I.

Having high oxidising power, halogens can oxidise even noble metals (like Ag, Au, Pt) and some noble gases (like Kr, Xe, Rn). Reactivity and chemical properties of halogens are discussed as follows

Reaction with Oxygen

All the halogens are known to form oxides of varying oxidation states but most of them are unstable. Stability of particular type of oxide increases down the group as

$$F < Cl < Br < I$$

- Fluorine forms two oxides $\overset{+2}{OF_2}$ and $\overset{+1}{O_2}F_2$. Among them OF_2 is thermally stable at 298 K. These oxides are essentially oxygen fluorides. This is because of the higher electronegativity of fluorine than oxygen.
- Chlorine, bromine and iodine form oxides in which the oxidation states of these halogens range from +1 to +7.

Some of the known oxides of halogens with oxidation state of the respective halogen (atom) are as follows

F : OF_2 (−1), O_2F_2 (−1)

Cl : Cl_2O (+1), ClO_2 (+4), Cl_2O_6 (+5, +7+6), Cl_2O_7(+7)

Br : Br_2O (+1), BrO_2 (+4), BrO_3 (+6)

I : I_2O_4 (+4), I_2O_5 (+5), I_2O_7 (+7)

General characteristics of oxides of halogen

- Oxides of Cl, Br and I are acidic and their acidic character increases as the percentage of oxygen increases in them.
- The structure of OF_2 is similar to that of H_2O. Due to greater electronegativity of fluorine than oxygen, the bond pairs in OF_2 lie nearer to the fluorine atom.

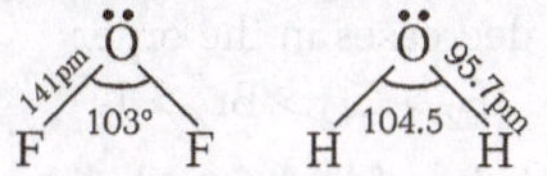

But in H_2O, electronegativity of O is greater than H, the bond pair lie nearer to O-atom.

- The structure of O_2F_2 is similar to that of H_2O_2 involving sp^3-hybridisation.

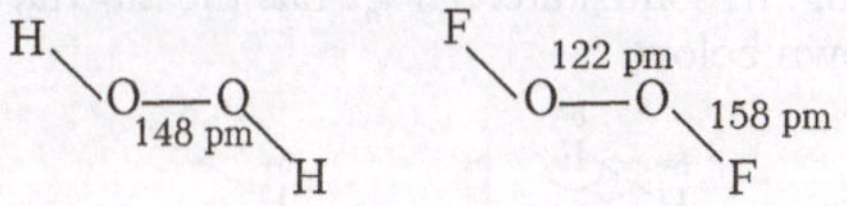

In this case, the bond length of O—O bond in O_2F_2 is shorter than H_2O_2 because F is much more electronegative than O, therefore it attracts the *lp* of electrons on the O-atom towards itself, which result in decrease in *lp-lp* repulsion between the two O-atom in O—O bond.

O_2F_2 oxidises plutonium to PuF_6 and the reaction is used in removing plutonium as PuF_6 from spent nuclear fuel.

- Out of three oxides of iodine, I_2O_5 is the most stable oxide. It is the anhydride of iodic acid (HIO_3). It dissolve in water to produce iodic acid. It is also a good oxidising agent and used in estimation of CO from mixture of gases.

Structure of Oxides of Chlorine

Name	Formula	Oxidation state of chlorine	Hybridisation of chlorine	Structure
Chlorine monoxide	Cl_2O	+1	sp^3	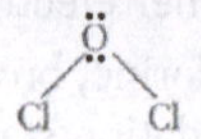
Chlorine dioxide	ClO_2	+3	sp^2	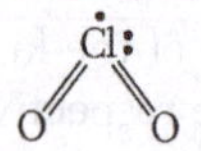
Chlorine hexoxide	Cl_2O_6	+5, +7	sp^3	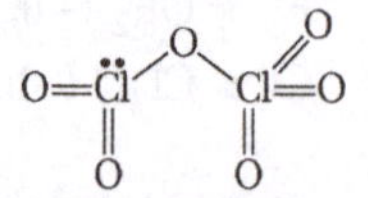
Chlorine heptoxide	Cl_2O_7	+7	sp^3	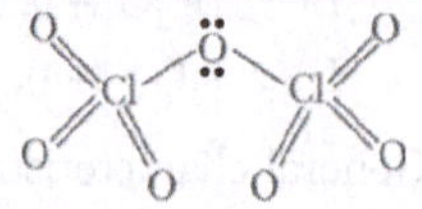

Reaction with Hydrogen

Halogens react with hydrogen to form hydrogen halide.

$$X_2 + H_2 \longrightarrow 2HX \quad \text{(where, } X = \text{F, Cl, Br or I)}$$

Fluorine reacts violently with hydrogen while iodine gives very poor yield with hydrogen. The affinity of halogens toward hydrogen decreases in the order

$$F_2 > Cl_2 > Br_2 > I_2$$

General characteristics of hydrogen halides are as follows

(i) **Physical state** HF is a low boiling liquid and others are colourless, irritating gases at room temperature. HF exists as an associated molecules $[HF]_n$, due to the presence of very strong intermolecular hydrogen bonding. In solid state, $[HF]_n$ has the *zig-zag* structure as shown below.

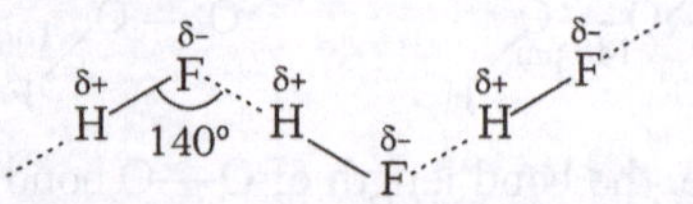

(ii) **Boiling point** It increases as we move down in the group due to increase in magnitude of van der Waals' forces of attraction as the size of halogen increase. Boiling point of HF is also normally high due to H-bonding, HF > HI > HBr > HCl.

(iii) **Dipole moment** The order of dipole moment is as follow

$$\underset{1.86\text{ D}}{HF} > \underset{1.11\text{ D}}{HCl} > \underset{0.79\text{ D}}{HBr} > \underset{0.38\text{ D}}{HI}$$

As the electronegativity of the halogen decreases down the group, dipole moment of halogen halide also decreases in the same order.

(iv) **Percentage of ionic character** It increases in the order HI < HBr < HCl < HF.

As the electronegativity of the halogen decreases down the group, ionic character also decreases in the same direction.

(v) **Bond length** It increases in the order

$$\underset{91.7\text{pm}}{HF} < \underset{127.4\text{ pm}}{HCl} < \underset{141.4\text{ pm}}{HBr} < \underset{160.9\text{ pm}}{HI}$$

With the increase in the size of the halogen atom, bond length increases in the same direction.

(vi) **Bond strength or bond dissociation energies** It increases in the order

$$HI < HBr < HCl < HF$$

It increases with decrease in the bond length. In simple words, shorter the bond length, higher is the bond strength.

(vii) **Thermal stability** It increase in the order

$$HI < HBr < HCl < HF$$

Thermal stability increases with increase in the bond dissociation energy or bond strength.

Concept ladder

- $\Delta_f G°$ of HF, HCl and HBr are large and negative, suggesting that for them $H_2 + X_2 \rightarrow 2HX$ goes to completion.
- For HI (g), $\Delta_f G°$ is small and positive suggesting the HI should dissociate

$$2HI(g) \longrightarrow H_2(g) + I_2(g)$$

to some extent. However, because of the high activation energy the dissociation occurs only very slowly in the absence of a catalyst. As a result, HI(*g*) is quite stable at room temperature. Thus, at room temperature, decomposition of HI(*g*) is kinetically controlled (rather than thermodynamically controlled).

(viii) **Acidic strength** It increases in the order

$$HF < HCl < HBr < HI$$

Higher is the bond dissociation energy, lower is the degree of ionisation hence, weaker is the acid. Since, the bond dissociation decreases down the group, therefore ionisation of halogen halide increases in same order.

Liquid HF has been used as a non-aqueous solvent. It undergoes self ionisation.

$$2HF \rightleftharpoons [H_2F]^+ + F^-$$

Acid-base reactions occur in this solvent system. However, the solvent itself has a very strong tendency to donate protons. Mineral acids like HNO_3, H_2SO_4 and HCl, behave as bases when dissolved in HF, as they accept proton from HF.

$$\underset{\text{Base}}{HCl} + \underset{\text{Acid}}{HF} \rightleftharpoons \underset{\text{Acid}}{H_2Cl^+} + \underset{\text{Base}}{F^-}$$

$$\underset{\text{Base}}{H_2SO_4} + \underset{\text{Acid}}{HF} \rightleftharpoons \underset{\text{Acid}}{H_3SO_4^+} + \underset{\text{Base}}{F^-}$$

$$\underset{\text{Base}}{HNO_3} + \underset{\text{Acid}}{HF} \rightleftharpoons \underset{\text{Acid}}{H_2NO_3^+} + \underset{\text{Base}}{F^-}$$

$HClO_4$ (perchloric acid) however behaves as an acid in liquid HF which acts like a base

$$\underset{\text{Acid}}{HClO_4} + \underset{\text{Base}}{HF} \rightleftharpoons \underset{\text{Acid}}{H_2F^+} + \underset{\text{Base}}{ClO_4^-}$$

(ix) **Reducing power** It depends upon the ease with which they decomposes to give H_2 and X_2.

$$2HX \longrightarrow H_2 + X_2$$

Reducing power increases in the order

$$HF < HCl < HBr < HI$$

As the bond dissociation energy decreases down the group, the ease of decomposition increases and hence reducing character increases in same direction.

Reaction with Alkalies

Fluorine reacts with alkalies at different conditions. Reaction involved are as follows

$$2F_2 + \underset{\text{Cold dil.}}{2NaOH} \longrightarrow 2NaF + OF_2 + H_2O$$

$$2F_2 + \underset{\text{Hot conc.}}{4NaOH} \longrightarrow 4NaF + O_2 + 2H_2O$$

While reaction involving other halogens (Cl_2, Br_2, I_2) are as follows

$$X_2 + \underset{\text{Cold dil.}}{2NaOH} \longrightarrow NaX + \underset{\text{Hypohalite}}{NaOX} + H_2O$$

$$3X_2 + \underset{\text{Hot conc.}}{6NaOH} \longrightarrow 5NaX + \underset{\text{Halate}}{NaXO_3} + 3H_2O$$

Reaction with Metals

Most of the metals react with halogens to form metal halides as $2M + nX_2 \longrightarrow 2MX_n$

(Here, M = metal, n = oxidation state of metal, X = F, Cl, Br or I)

The ionic character of halides decreases as the size of halogen ion increases $MF_n > MCl_n > MBr_n > MI_n$.

Moreover, the ionic character decreases (and hence the covalent character increases) as the oxidation state of metals combining a halogen increases. Thus, for chlorides of metals with different oxidation state, the ionic character decreases as $MCl > MCl_2 > MCl_3 > MCl_4$.

Reaction with Some Non-Metals

(i) **With phosphorus** Phosphorus exhibits an oxidation state of +3, when reacts with F_2, Cl_2, Br_2 and I_2.

$$2P + 3X_2 \longrightarrow 2PX_3 \quad \text{(Here, } X = \text{F, Cl, Br, I)}$$

However, phosphorus forms halides with the oxidation state of +5 only with F_2, Cl_2 and Br_2.

$$2P + 5X_2 \longrightarrow 2PX_5 \quad \text{(Here, } X = \text{F, Cl, Br)}$$

(ii) **With sulphur** Sulphur forms halides of different oxidation states with different halogens except the iodine. Sulphur does not form a stable compound with iodine. Different reactions involving sulphur and halogens are as follows

Different oxoacids of halogens are as follows

$$3F_2 + S \longrightarrow SF_6$$

$$2Cl_2 + S \longrightarrow SCl_4$$

$$X_2 + 2S \longrightarrow S_2X_2 \quad \text{(Here, } X = \text{Cl, Br)}$$

Concept ladder

Different halogens react with water in different manners. These reactions represent relative oxidising power of halogens. Fluorine oxidises water to give oxygen gas.

$$F_2 + 2H_2O \longrightarrow 4H^+F^- + O_2$$

Chlorine and bromine form hydrohalic acid and hypohalous acid, upon reactions with water.

$$X_2 + H_2O \longrightarrow HX + HOX \quad \text{(Here, } X = \text{Cl, Br)}$$

Whereas iodine does not give reaction with water spontaneously

$$I_2 + H_2O \longrightarrow \text{No reaction}$$

Oxoacids of Halogens

Properties	HOX Hypohalous acid	HXO_2 Halous acid	HXO_3 Halic acid	HXO_4 Perhalic acid
	HOF	–	–	–
	HOCl	$HClO_2$	$HClO_3$	$HClO_4$
	HOBr	–	$HBrO_3$	$HBrO_4$
	HOI	–	HIO_3	HIO_4
Anhydride	X_2O	X_2O_3	X_2O_5	X_2O_7
Oxidation state of X	+I	+III	+V	+VII
Oxidising power	strong	⟵	⟵	weak
Acid strength*	weak	⟶	⟶	strong
Thermal stability	weak	⟶	⟶	good
Hydrolysis of anion	maximum	⟵	⟵	minimum
Structure of anion	(OCl^-) linear	(ClO_2^-) angular	(ClO_3^-) trigonal pyramidal	(ClO_4^-) tetrahedral

**Acid strength of one type oxoacid increases as size of halogen atom decreases.*

Important Oxyacids of Chlorine and their Structures

Name	Formula	Oxidation state of chlorine	Anionic part	Shape and structure
Hypochlorous acid	HClO	+1	Hypochlorite, ClO^-	Angular 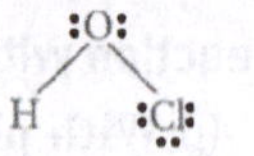
Chlorous acid	$HClO_2$	+3	Chlorite, ClO_2^-	Angular 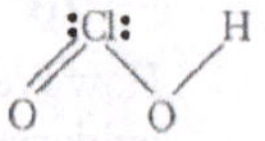
Chloric acid	$HClO_3$	+5	Chlorate, ClO_3^-	Pyramidal 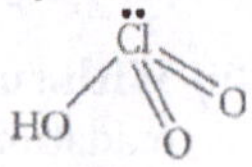
Perchloric acid	$HClO_4$	+7	Perchlorate, ClO_4^-	Tetrahedral 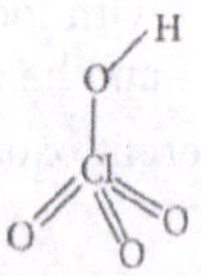

NEET Close-up

Example Similar to PYQ Asked in NEET 2019

The correct structure of perchloric acids is

(a) 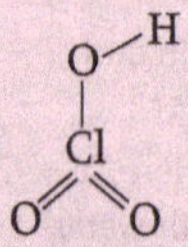

(b) 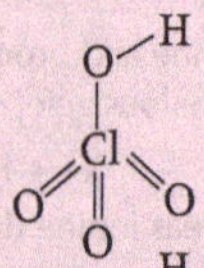

(c) 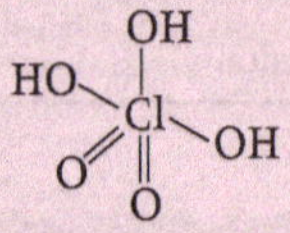

(d) 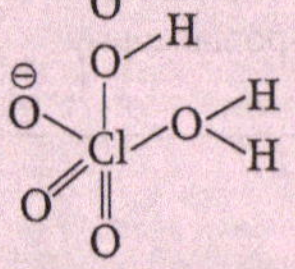

Sol. (*b*) The correct strucure of perchloric acid is

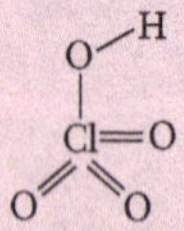

Skill Builder

The correct structure of chlorous acid is

(a) 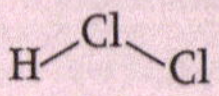

(b) 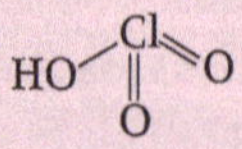

(c) 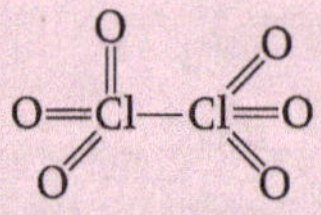

(d) 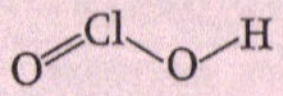

For more practice Refer to Q.13 of step up practice 5.

Reaction with a Different Halogen (Interhalogen Compounds)

Interhalogens are the compounds that are formed by two different halogens. Depending upon the ratio in which two halogens combine, they are known to be of four types *viz.* larger and more electropositive halogen (X) always be the central atom. XY, XY_3, XY_5 and XY_7 of which X is of higher atomic number as shown.

XY	XY_3	XY_5	XY_7
ClF	ClF_3	ClF_5	
BrF	BrF_3	BrF_5	
ICl	ICl_3 (I_2Cl_6)	IF_5	IF_7 (only)
IBr			
BrCl			

Concept ladder Interchalogen compounds are used as a fluorinating agents. e.g. ClF_3 and BrF_3 are used for the production of UF_6 in the enrichment of ^{235}U.

Nomenclature

They are named as halogen halides. The halogen with positive oxidation state is named as such while, the halogen with negative oxidation state is named as halide.

e.g. BrCl — Bromine chloride
ICl_3 — Iodine trichloride

Chemical Properties

(i) **Reactivity** These compounds are generally more reactive than the halogens (except F_2). Their order is as follows

$ClF_3 > BrF_3 > IF_7 > ClF > BrF_3 > IF_5 > BrF > IF_3 > IF$

Reason The X—Y bond between two dissimilar electronegative elements is weaker than the bond between two similar atoms . This occurs because overlapping of orbitals of two dissimilar atoms is less effective than the overlapping of orbitals of similar atoms.

(ii) **Thermal stability** As the size difference or the electronegativity difference between the two halogen atoms decreases, thermal stability also decreases. As the size of central atom increases, stability of the interhalogen compound increases. General order of thermal stability follows as

Thermal stability	IF >	BrF >	ClF >	ICl >	IBr >	BrCl
Electronegativity difference	1.5	1.2	1.0	0.5	0.3	0.2

(iii) **Hydrolysis** Interhalogen compounds, when undergo hydrolysis gives halide ion derived from the smaller or more electronegative halogen (Y) along with a hypohalite (XY) or halite (XY_3) or halate (XY_5) or perhalate (XY_7) anion derived from the larger halogen.

$$ClF + H_2O \longrightarrow HF + HClO$$

(iv) Interhalogen compound fluorinate many metal oxides, metal halides and metals.

Formula, Name, Physical Properties and Structure of Interhalogen Compounds

Type of interhalogen compound	Formula and name	Physical state and colour at ordinary temperatures	Shape	Structure
$:\ddot{X}Y$	ClF- chlorine fluoride	Gas, colourless	Linear	$X—Y$
	BrF-bromine fluoride	Liquid below 293 K, pale-brown gas above 293 K		
	BrCl-bromine chloride	Liquid, reddish yellow		
	ICl-iodine chloride	Solid, rubby red		
	IBr-iodine bromide	Solid, brown like iodine		
$:\ddot{X}Y_3$	ClF_3- chlorine trifluoride	Liquid below 261 K, colourless gas above 261 K	T-shaped	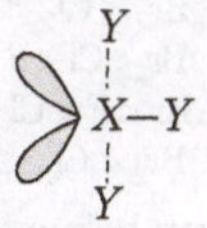
	BrF_3- bromine trifluoride	Liquid, colourless		
	$BrCl_3$- bromine trichoride	Solid, orange		
$:XY_5$	ClF_5- chlorine pentafluoride	Gas, colourless	Square pyramidal	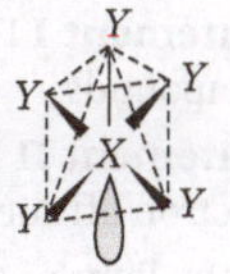
	BrF_5- bromine pentafluoride	Liquid, colourless		
	IF_5- Iodine pentafluoride	Liquid, colourless		
XY_7	IF_7 -iodine heptafluoride	Gas, colourless	Pentagonal bipyramidal	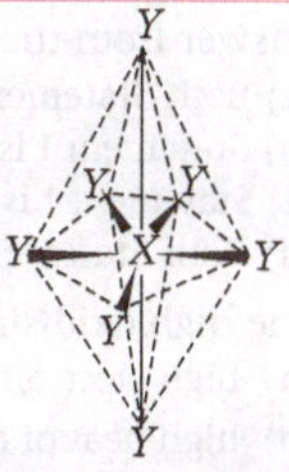

Anomalous Behaviour of Fluorine

It differs from other elements of the group because of its exceptionally small atomic and ionic size and low fluorine—fluorine bond dissociation energy. The result of these differences is that fluorine is the most electronegative element in the periodic table and a powerful oxidant.

Some of the differences between fluorine and other halogens are discussed as follows

- It is more reactive than other halogens because of low F—F bond energy.
- Due to its high electronegativity, the bond between fluorine and other elements is very strong, so its compounds are more stable. Some of them are inert, e.g. SF_6.
- Fluorine is almost invariably monocoordinate (coordination number = 1).
- It always has oxidation state of −1 in its compounds.
- Fluorine is the strongest oxidising agent and oxidises the elements to their highest oxidation state, e.g. in IF_7, iodine has oxidation state of +7.
- Fluorides are more ionic.
- Fluorine forms strong hydrogen bonds resulting in the properties of hydrogen fluoride being anomalous (at high bp).
- Fluorine forms fumes in moist air and decomposes water to give oxygen, whereas other halogens are sparingly soluble in water and react partly to give hydrohalic and hypohalous acids.

$$2F_2 + 2H_2O \longrightarrow 2HF + O_2$$
$$X_2 + H_2O \rightleftharpoons HOX + HX$$

- Fluorine reacts with alkalies to yield oxygen difluoride, OF_2

$$2F_2 + \underset{\text{(Cold dil.)}}{2NaOH} \longrightarrow OF_2 + 2NaF + H_2O$$

Mentor's Tip

Apart from fluorine all other halogens react with alkalies to yield a solution of hypohalite ions, which may disproportionate as

$$Cl_2 + \underset{\text{(Cold dil.)}}{2NaOH} \longrightarrow NaClO + NaCl + H_2O$$

Uses

- It is used in the preparation of UF_6, which is used in the gaseous diffusion process for separating isotopes of uranium (U-235 and U -238).
- It is used in the preparation of teflon.

STEP UP Practice 5

1 The general electronic configuration of the valence shell of a halogen atom is
(a) ns^2np^3 (b) ns^2np^4
(c) ns^2np^5 (d) ns^2np^6

2 Which of the following atoms has the highest ionisation energy ?
(a) F (b) Cl
(c) Br (d) I

3 Which of the following arrangements does not truly represent the property indicated against it?
(a) $Br_2 < Cl_2 < F_2$: Oxidising power
(b) $Br < Cl < F$: Electronegativity
(c) $Br < F < Cl$: Electron affinity
(d) $Br_2 < Cl_2 < F_2$: Bond energy

4 Given below are two statements.
Statement I Fluorine has only –1 oxidation state in compounds
Statement II Fluorine has maximum electronegativity and electron affinity in the periodic table.
In the light of the above statements, choose the correct answer from the options given below.
(a) Both Statement I and Statement II are false.
(b) Statement I is true but Statement II is false.
(c) Statement I is false but Statement II is true.
(d) Both Statement I and Statement II are true.

5 The high oxidising power of fluorine is due to
(a) high electron affinity
(b) high heat of dissociation and low heat of hydration
(c) low heat of dissociation and high heat of hydration
(d) high heat of dissociation and high heat of hydration

6 Which is the strongest oxidising agent out of the following?
(a) I_2 (b) Cl_2
(c) Br_2 (d) F_2

7 Dipole moment and ionisation constant are maximum in case of ... and ... respectively
(a) HF, HF (b) HF, HI
(c) HI, HF (d) HI, HI

8 Which of the following statements is incorrect ?
(a) All halogens form oxyacids.
(b) All halogens show –1, +1, +3, +5, +7 oxidation states.
(c) Hydrofluoric acid forms H_2SiF_6 when it attacks glass.
(d) Oxidising power is in order : $F_2 > Cl_2 > Br_2 > I_2$.

9 Given below are two statements.
Statement I HI cannot be prepared by the reaction of KI with concentrated H_2SO_4.
Statement II HI has lowest H—*X* bond strength among the halogen acids.
In the light of the above statements, choose the correct answer from the options given below.
(a) Both Statement I and Statement II are false.
(b) Statement I is true but Statement II is false.
(c) Statement I is false but Statement II is true.
(d) Both Statement I and Statement II are true.

10 Dissociation of HI into H_2 and I_2 is
(a) kinetically controlled
(b) thermodynamically controlled
(c) kinetically as well as thermodynamically controlled
(d) neither kinetically nor thermodynamically controlled

11 Consider the following compounds,
(i) $Ca(OCl)_2$ (ii) NaCl
(iii) Conc. H_2SO_4 (iv) $NaHSO_4$
(v) NaOH
How many of them is (are) used to dry HCl gas?
(a) 1 (b) 4
(c) 3 (d) 2

12 Which of the following correctly represents the composition of *aqua-regia*?
(a) 1 part conc. HCl, 3 parts conc. H_2SO_4 (V/V)
(b) 1 part conc. HCl, 3 parts conc. HNO_3 (V/V)
(c) 3 parts conc. HCl, 1 part conc. H_2SO_4 (V/V)
(d) 3 parts conc. HCl, 1 part conc. HNO_3 (V/V)

13 The corrcet structure of chloric acid is
(a) 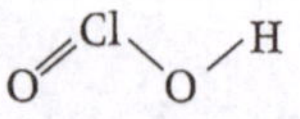

(b) 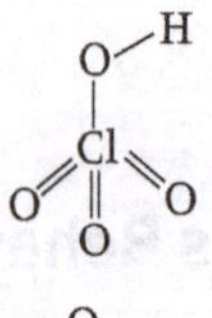

(c) 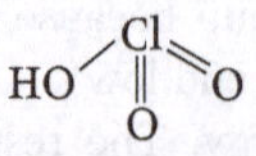

(d) 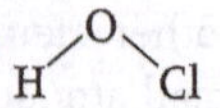

14 Select the incorrect statement.
(a) ClO_2 and Cl_2O are used as bleaching agents for paper pulp and textiles.
(b) OCl^- (hypohalites) salts are not used as a detergent.
(c) OCl^- disproportionates in an alkaline medium.
(d) BrO_3^- is oxidised to Br_2 by Br^- in an acidic medium.

15 Select the incorrect statement.
(a) Cl_2O_6 is diamagnetic in solid state.
(b) ClO_3 is paramagnetic and exists in liquid state.
(c) Cl_2O_6 is the anhydride of $HClO_3$.
(d) ClO_3 forms dimer due to one unpaired electron on C-atom.

16 The tetrahedral arrangement of perchlorate ion is due to
(a) presence of a lone pair of electrons
(b) trigonal bipyramidal shape of the ion
(c) sp^3-hybridisation of Cl atom in ClO_4^-
(d) sp^2-hybridisation of Cl atom in ClO_4^-

17 Which of the following is not a correct match?
(a) Perphosphoric acid $\longrightarrow$ Peroxy acid
(b) Pernitric acid $\longrightarrow$ Peroxy acid
(c) Perdisulphuric acid $\longrightarrow$ Peroxy acid
(d) Perchloric acid $\longrightarrow$ Peroxy acid

18 Which of the following products is not correctly matched with the given reaction?
(a) $2KI + Br_2 \longrightarrow 2KBr + I_2$
(b) $2KBr + I_2 \longrightarrow 2KI + Br_2$
(c) $2KBr + Cl_2 \longrightarrow 2KCl + Br_2$
(d) $2H_2O + 2F_2 \longrightarrow 4HF + O_2$

19 Which one of the following oxoacids of chlorine is the least oxidising in nature?
(a) HClO (b) $HClO_2$ (c) $HClO_3$ (d) $HClO_4$

20 Acidic strength of oxoacids of halogen is in order
(a) HOF > HOCl > HOBr > HOI
(b) HOI > HOBr > HOCl > HOF
(c) HOI > HOCl > HOBr > HOF
(d) HOCl > HOBr > HOI > HOF

21 Consider the following compounds,
(i) ICl_3 (ii) BrF_5 (iii) IF_7 (iv) $BrCl_7$ (v) ClF
How many of them is (are) interhalogen compound(s) which is (are) abundant?
(a) 3 (b) 4 (c) 2 (d) 1

Module 6

Noble Gases

- General and Physical Properties
- Chemical Properties
- Uses of Noble Gas

Group 18 Elements : Noble Gases

Group 18 or zero group of periodic table contains seven elements collectively known as noble gases. These are **helium** (He), **neon** (Ne), **argon** (Ar), **krypton** (Kr), **xenon** (Xe), **radon** (Rn) and oganesson (Og). They are also known as **inert gases** as they have stable electronic configuration due to which they are inert in nature at normal condition. However, some of these such as xenon, forms compounds under specific conditions.

General and Physical Properties

These are monoatomic, colourless, odourless and tasteless gases. They are sparingly soluble in water and have low melting and boiling points due to presence of weak dispersion forces. Some of the trends in properties of group 18 of the periodic table are as follows.

Electronic Configuration

The general electronic configuration of this group is ns^2np^6 or $ns^2\ np_x^2\ np_y^2\ np_z^2$. (except helium for which it is $1s^2$). Due to presence of completely filled valence shell, these gases are highly stable.

Atomic Radii

Atomic radii increase with increase in atomic number, i.e. down the group from He to Rn due to addition of extra principal shell in each succeeding element. Atomic radii of these elements correspond to van der Waals' radii.

Element	He	Ne	Ar	Kr	Xe
Atomic radius (pm)	120	160	190	200	220

Ionisation Energy and Electron Gain Enthalpy

The noble gases have high values of ionisation energy and have large positive value of electron gain enthalpy due to presence of fully-filled valence shells with electronic configuration ns^2np^6.

They have no tendency to add or lose electron thus, lack chemical reactivity as compared to other elements of periodic table.

Down the group the ionisation enthalpies decrease due to increase in atomic radii and shielding effect. Also, on moving down the group atomic size increases and electron affinity becomes less positive.

Boiling Point

Noble gases are low boiling gases. Boiling point increases down the group due to increase in magnitude of van der Waals' radii.

Trend of boiling points down the group is shown below.

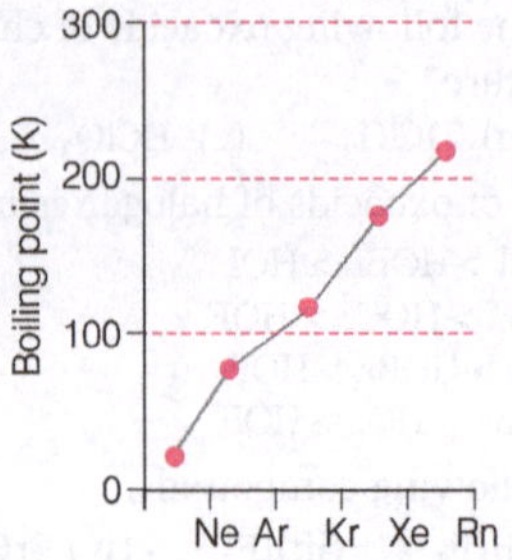

Helium has the lowest boiling point amongst all elements and its behaviour as a liquid is most unusual. It has no triple point that is there is no single combination of temperature and pressure at which the solid, the liquid and the gas phases will co-exist.

At about 2K, helium undergoes a transition to another form of helium, labelled as He_{II}. It will creep up the walls of the container in which it is placed and thus it exists in two phases in liquid helium, one of which has an extremely low viscosity.

NEET Snapshot

Noble gases have very high melting and boiling points. ***[NEET 2021]***

The boiling and melting point of noble gases are very low. As, the van der Waals' forces or interatomic forces of noble gases are weak and they are liquified at very low temperature which results in low melting and boiling point.

Hence, the statement given in the begining is incorrect.

Heat of Vaporisation

They have very low values of heat of vaporisation due to presence of weak van der Waals' forces of attraction. Values of heat of vaporisation increases with increase in atomic number, i.e. down the group.

Element	He	Ne	Ar	Kr	Xe
Heat of vaporisation (kJ mol^{-1})	0.08	1.7	6.5	9.1	12.7

Concept ladder

Heat of vaporisation increases down the group, this indicates that there is an increase in polarisability of elements of larger electronic clouds.
The order of polarisability is as follows
$He < Ne < Ar < Kr < Xe$

Chemical Properties

Noble gases are chemically inert in nature. Therefore, they do not have tendency to lose or add electrons. This is because of completely filled valence shells, high ionisation enthalpies and positive electron gain enthalpies.

Hence, noble gases do not form compounds.

But in 1962, **Neil Bartlett** prepared a red compound $O_2^+[PtF_6]^-$ by reacting platinum hexafluoride (PtF_6) with dioxygen.

$$O_2(g) + PtF_6(g) \longrightarrow \underset{\text{Dioxygen hexafluoro platinate (V)}}{O_2^+[PtF_6]^-(s)}$$

He found that the ionisation enthalpy of xenon (1170 kJ/mol) is fairly close to molecular oxygen (1175 kJ/mol). Therefore, he was able to form compound of xenon.

$$Xe + PtF_6 \longrightarrow \underset{\text{Xenon hexafluoro platinate}}{Xe^+[PtF_6]^-}$$

As a results, number of compounds of xenon with fluorine and oxygen are formed, like xenon fluorides, xenon oxides and xenon oxyfluorides. Their structures are given below:

Compounds of xenon	Hybridisation	Geometry
XeF_2	sp^3d	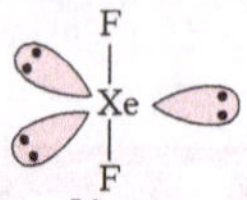 Linear
XeF_4	sp^3d^2	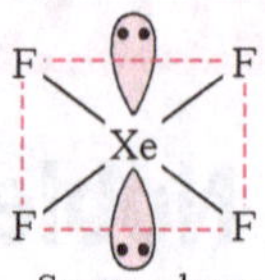 Square planar
XeF_6	sp^3d^3	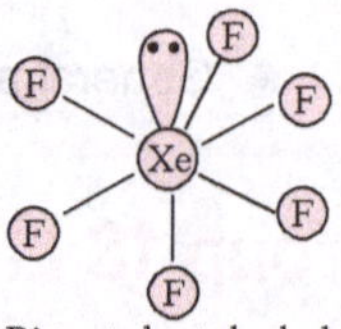 Distorted octahedral
XeO_3	sp^3	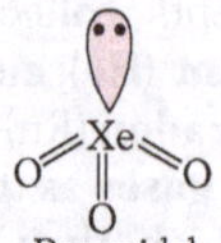 Pyramidal
XeO_4	sp^3	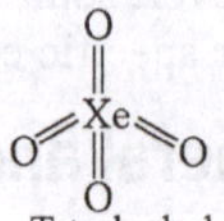 Tetrahedral
$XeOF_4$	sp^3d^2	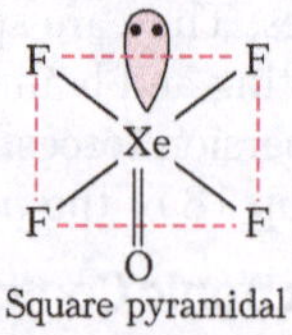 Square pyramidal

Concept ladder

Noble gases form a number of compounds in which the gases are entrapped in the cavities of crystal lattices of some organic and inorganic compounds.

Such compounds are called **clathrates** or **cage compounds** or **host-guest compounds**, e.g. $Xe \cdot 6H_2O$, quinol clathrate.

The organic or inorganic compound with cavities is called **host** and the gas entrapped in them is called **guest.** He and Ne do not form such compounds because of small size. Only Ar, Kr and Xe form clathrates.

Uses of Noble Gas

There are many uses of noble gases. Some of the uses are summarised in the table given below.

Noble gas	Uses	Reasons
Helium	1. Filling balloons for meteorological observations	Non-flammable, 93% lifting power as compared to flammable H_2
	2. He/O_2 mixture use for deep-sea breathing, instead of N_2/O_2 mixture	Low solubility in blood, prevents nitrogen narcosis and "bends"
	3. Diluent use for gaseous anaesthetics	Non-flammable, non-reactive
	4. He/O_2 mixtures use for respiratory patients	Low density, flows easily through restricted passages
	5. Heat transfer medium for nuclear reactions	Transfers heat readily, does not become radioactive, chemically inert
	6. (Liquid He) To maintain very low temperature in research (cryogenics)	Extremely low boiling point
Neon	Neon signs	Even at low Ne pressure, moderate electric current causes bright orange-red glow, can be modified by coloured glass or mixing with Ar or Hg vapour.
Argon	1. Inert atmosphere for welding	Chemically inert
	2. Filling incandescent light bulbs	Inert, prevents vaporisation of tungsten and blackening of bulbs
Krypton	Airport runway and approach lights	Gives longer life to incandescent lights than Ar but more expensive
Xenon	Xe and Kr mixture in high intensity, short exposure photographic flash tubes	Both have fast response to electric current
Radon	Radiotherapy of cancerous-tissues	Radioactive

STEP UP Practice 6

1 Which of the following configurations represents a noble gas?

(a) $1s^2 2s^2 2p^6 3s^2$ (b) $1s^2 2s^2 2p^6 3s^1$
(c) $1s^2 2s^2 2p^6$ (d) $1s^2 2s^2 2p^6 3s^2 3p^6 4s^2$

2 Which has same electronic configuration as of noble gas?

(a) Ag^{3+} (b) Cu^{3+} (c) Pb^{4+} (d) Ti^{4+}

3 Consider the folliowing underline compounds.

(i) $\underline{P}Cl_6^-$ (ii) $\underline{P}Cl_5$ (iii) $\underline{Br}F_3$ (iv) $\underline{Xe}F_2$ (v) $\underline{Xe}OF_4$

How many of them have sp^3d-hybidisation?

(a) 2 (b) 1 (c) 4 (d) 3

4 In the preparation of compounds of Xe, Bartlett had taken $O_2^+[PtF_6]^-$ as a base compound. This is because

(a) both O_2 and Xe have same size
(b) both O_2 and Xe have same electron gain enthalpy
(c) both O_2 and Xe have almost same ionisation enthalpy
(d) both Xe and O_2 are gases

5 Variable oxidation state is shown by

(a) He (b) Ne (c) Ar (d) Xe

6 Thermal stability of hydrates of group 18 elements

(a) increases down the group
(b) decreases down the group
(c) remains unchanged
(d) first increases up to Ar and then decreases

7 Isolation and separation of inert gases from air depends on

(a) viscosity (b) surface tension
(c) boiling point (d) melting point

8 Deep sea divers used a mixture of which gases to respirate?

(a) Oxygen and argon (b) Oxygen and helium
(c) Oxygen and nitrogen (d) Oxygen and hydrogen

9 For advertisement, the coloured discharged tubes contain

(a) He (b) Ne
(c) Ar (d) Kr

10 Helium accumulates in the earth's crust through

(a) α-decay of radioactive element
(b) thermonuclear reactions
(c) β-decay of radioactive element
(d) γ-decay of radioactive element

11 What is X in the following reaction?

$$^{226}_{88}Ra \longrightarrow {}^{222}_{86}Rn + X$$

(a) ^1_1H (b) ^2_1H
(c) ^4_2He (d) ^3_1H

12 Which of the following is the correct match with the given structures?

(a) $XeF_2 \longrightarrow$ Square planar
(b) $XeF_4 \longrightarrow$ Pyramidal
(c) $XeO_3 \longrightarrow$ Linear
(d) $XeOF_4 \longrightarrow$ Square pyramidal

13 Given below are two statements.

Staement I XeF_6 can be used as an oxidising agent.

Statement II Oxidation state of Xe in XeF_6 is +6.

In the light of the above statements, choose the correct answer from the options given below.

(a) Both Statement I and Statement II are false.
(b) Statement I is true, but Statement II is false.
(c) Statement I is false, but Statement II is true.
(d) Both Statement I and Statement II are true.

14 The forces acting between noble gas atoms are

(a) van der Waals' forces
(b) ion-dipole forces
(c) dipole-dipole forces
(d) magnetic force

15 Given below are two statements.

Statement I The hybridisation of XeF_2 is sp^3d.

Statement II The hybridisation of XeF_4 and XeF_6 are sp^3d^2 and sp^3d^3 respectively.

In the light of the above statements, choose the correct answer from the options given below.

(a) Both Statement I and Statement II are false.
(b) Statement I is true, but Statement II is false.
(c) Statement I is false, but Statement II is true.
(d) Both Statement I and Statement II are true.

16 The $[XeF]^+$ ions are attached to anion $[AsF_6]^-$

(a) with a linear F-bridge
(b) with an angular F-bridge
(c) with H-bond
(d) with tetrahedral F-bridge

17 Which of the following is an incorrect match?

(a) $XeF_6 \longrightarrow$ 1, non-bonding electron pair on Xe
(b) $XeF_4 \longrightarrow$ 2, non-bonding electron pair on Xe
(c) $XeF_2 \longrightarrow$ 3, non-bonding electron pair on Xe
(d) $XeOF_4 \longrightarrow$ 2, non-bonding electron pair on Xe

NEET Exclusive EXTRA BYTES

- Boron forms only covalent compounds whereas aluminium can form both covalent and ionic compounds. For example, anhydrous $AlCl_3$ is covalent while hdyrated $AlCl_3$ is ionic. When anhydrous $AlCl_3$ is hydrated, the hydration energy released is sufficient to overcome the ionisation enthalpy of Al.
- Thallium trichloride ($TlCl_3$) decomposes to TlCl and Cl_2 above 313 K. In this way $TlCl_3$ acts as an oxidising agent.

$$TlCl_3 \xrightarrow[> 313\text{ K}]{\text{Heat}} TlCl + Cl_2$$

- Carbon is unaffected by alkalis. However, Si reacts slowly with cold aqueous NaOH solution, and readily with hot solution.

$$Si + 2NaOH + H_2O \longrightarrow Na_2SiO_3 + 2H_2$$

- Sn and Pb are slowly attacked by cold alkali and rapidly by hot alkali, giving stannates $Na_2[Sn(OH)_6]$ and plumbates $Na_2[Pb(OH)_6]$.
- Hydrazoic acid (N_3H) is fairly strong acid, stronger than CH_3COOH but weaker than mineral acids. Azide ion, (N_3^-) is linear and functions as a ligand in complexes of transition metals like halide ion (pseudo halide). Hydrazoic acid behave both as an oxidising as well as a reducing agent. One of the resonance structure for HN_3 is $H—\ddot{N}=\overset{+}{N}=\ddot{N}\!:^-$
- The name sulphur has been derived from Sanskrit word "Sulveri" meaning killer of copper. Sulphur is also called as **brimestone**.
- In I_7^- and IF_6^- central atom I undergoes sp^3d^3-hybridisation giving a distorted octahedral structure with one lone pair of **electrons** on I.
- When Cl_2 is passed over iodine, at first monochloride ICl (dark liquid) is formed which further reacts with Cl_2 to give trichloride (ICl_3) which is a yellow solid. ICl is a good conductor of electricity in fused state.
- XeO_3 explodes violently when dry and its explosion power is 22 times more than TNT.

GEARING UP FOR NEET

1 Stability of trivalent cations of group IIIA will be in order

(a) $Ga^{3+} < In^{3+} < Tl^{3+}$ (b) $Ga^{3+} > In^{3+} > Tl^{3+}$
(c) $Ga^{3+} = In^{3+} = Tl^{3+}$ (d) $Tl^{+} < In^{+} < Ga^{+}$

2 The geometry of a complex species can be understood from the knowlege of type of hydridisation of orbitals of central atom. The hybridisation of orbitals of the central atom in $[B(OH)_4]^-$ and the geometry of the complex are respectively.

(a) sp^3, tetrahedral (b) sp^3, square planar
(c) sp^3d^2, octahedral (d) dsp^2, square planar

3 Aluminium vessels should not washed with materials containing washing soda since

(a) washing soda is expensive
(b) washing soda is easily decomposed
(c) washing soda reacts with aluminium to form soluble aluminate salt
(d) washing soda react with aluminium to form in soluble aluminium oxide

4 Alum is found to contain hydrated monovalent cation $[M(H_2O)_6]^+$, trivalent cation $[M'(H_2O)_6]^{3+}$ and SO_4^{2-} in the ratio of

(a) 1 : 1 : 1 (b) 1 : 2 : 3 (c) 1 : 3 : 2 (d) 1 : 1 : 2

5 Standard electrode potential values, $E°$ for Al^{3+}/Al is -1.66 V and that of Tl^{3+}/Tl is $+1.26$ V. On the basis of this data, which of the following statements is wrong?

(a) Al has high tendency to form Al^{3+} *(aq)* ions.
(b) Tl^{3+} is not only unstable in solution but is a powerful oxidising agent also.
(c) Tl^{+} is more stable in solution than Tl^{3+}.
(d) Aluminium is less electropositive than thallium.

6 The exhibition of highest coordination number depends on the availability of vacant orbitals in the central atom. Which of the following elements is not likely to act as central atom in MF_6^{3-}?

(a) B (b) Al
(c) Ga (d) In

7 Which of the following statements is not correct?

A. Al is covalent in all its compound.
B. Al is a light metal of great tensile strength.
C. Al is a powerful reducing agent.
D. Al react with steam to form Al_2O_3.
E. Al dissolves in dilute HCl and liberates chlorine.

Choose the correct answer from the options given below.

(a) B and C only (b) D and E only
(c) C and D only (d) A and E only

8 Which of the following has the highest first ionisation energy?

(a) Oxygen (b) Nitrogen
(c) Boron (d) Carbon

9 Pb_3O_4 reacts with HNO_3 forming nitrate and oxide which are

(a) $Pb(NO_3)_4$ form PbO_2 and PbO remains unreacted
(b) $Pb(NO_3)_2$ from PbO and PbO_2 remains unreacted
(c) $Pb(NO_3)_2$ and $Pb(NO_3)_4$ and PbO remains unreacted
(d) PbO_4 remains insoluble in HNO_3

10 Catenation, i.e. linking of similar atoms depends on size and electronic configuration of atoms.

The tendency of catenation in group 14 elements follows the order.

(a) $C > Si > Ce > Sn$
(b) $C >> Si > Ge \approx Sn$
(c) $Si > C > Sn > Ge$
(d) $Ge > Sn > Si > C$

11 Select the incorrect statement about hydrides of group 15 elements.

(a) The central atom in the hydride MH_3 is sp^2-hybridised.
(b) NH_3 readily forms NH_4^+ salts with H^+.
(c) The tetrahedron is distorted due to repulsion between the lone pair of electrons and the bond pairs.
(d) The bond energy of the M—H bond decreases from NH_3 to BiH_3 because of increase in the size of the atom.

12 A colourless salt gives a white ppt. (soluble in ammonium acetate) and a brown coloured pungent gas on reaction with conc. H_2SO_4. Salt is

(a) $Ba(NO_3)_2$ (b) $Pb(NO_3)_2$
(c) $NaNO_3$ (d) NH_4NO_3

13 Maximum number of covalent bonds formed by an atom of N and P respectively are

(a) 3, 5 (b) 3, 6
(c) 4, 5 (d) 4, 6

14 What is the role of phosphate ion in a detergent?

(a) It reduces pH of the water.
(b) It increases pH of the water.
(c) It removes Ca^{2+} and Mg^{2+} ions from water that causes hardness.
(d) It increases its solubility in water.

15 A black compound of manganeese reacts with a halogen acid to give greenish yellow gas. When excess of this gas reacts with NH_3, an unstable trihalide is formed. In this process the oxidation state of nitrogen changes from ....
(a) –3 to +3 (b) –3 to 0
(c) –3 to +5 (d) 0 to –3

16 Which of the following oxoacids of sulphur has —S—S— linkage?
(a) Peroxomonosulphuric acid (b) Peroxodisulphuric acid
(c) Dithionic acid (d) Pyrosulphuric acid

17 When PCl_5 reacts with sulphuric acid, sulphuryl chloride is formed as the final product. This shows that sulphuric acid
(a) has two hydroxyl groups in its structure
(b) is a derivative of sulphur dioxide
(c) is a dibasic acid
(d) has greater affinity for water

18 Which of the following acids forms three series of salts?
(a) H_3PO_2 (b) H_3BO_3
(c) H_3PO_4 (d) H_3PO_3

19 A substance which gives a canary yellow precipitate, when boiled with an excess of nitric acid and ammonium molybdate and reddish yellow precipitate with $AgNO_3$ is
(a) orthophosphate (b) pyrophosphate
(c) metaphosphate (d) hypophosphate

20 HNO_3 in pure state is colourless but it is often of yellow coloured. It is due to
(a) unstable structure of HNO_3, which immediately changes to NO_2^-
(b) photochemical decomposition of HNO_3 into NO_2 in presence of sunlight
(c) interaction of atmospheric gases with HNO_3
(d) conversion of HNO_3 into NO_2^+

21 Aqueous solutions of hydrogen sulphide and sulphur dioxide when mixed together yield
(a) sulphur trioxide and water
(b) sulphurous acid
(c) sulphur and water
(d) hydrogen peroxide and sulphur

22 The element which is radioactive in nature is
(a) S (b) Te (c) Se (d) Po

23 A bottle completely filled with conc. H_2SO_4 is left unstoppered for several days and we observe spontaneous overflow of acid. It is due to
(a) change in temperature
(b) hygroscopic nature of H_2SO_4
(c) absorption of air by H_2SO_4
(d) dehydration of H_2SO_4

24 A chalcogen combines directly with hydrogen to form a hydride but with a great difficulty. On burning in air, this chalcogen forms a solid polymeric dioxide and it also has the highest electrical resistance amongst the metals. This chalcogen is
(a) sulphur (b) selenium
(c) polonium (d) tellurium

25 Select the correct statements about oxygen family (group-16).
A. The tendency for catenation decreases markedly as we go down the group.
B. Maximum coordination number of oxygen is four due to lack of *d*-orbitals but that of other elements of group 16 is six due to presence of *d*-orbitals.
C. The tendency to form multiple bonds with C, N and O decreases as going down the group from S to Te.
D. Preferably, SO_2 is an oxidising while TeO_2 is a reducing agent.
E. All hexafluorides are solid in nature at 298 K, 1 atm.
Choose the correct answer from the options given below.
(a) B, D and E (b) A, B and C
(c) A, C and D (d) C, D and E

26 Hot conc. H_2SO_4 acts as moderately strong oxidising agent. It oxidises both metals and non-metals. Which of the following elements is oxidised by conc. H_2SO_4 into two gaseous products?
(a) Cu (b) S
(c) C (d) Zn

27 Sulphur dioxide levels in the atmosphere can be reduced by using
(a) catalytic converters in industry
(b) static electricity to attract it in factory chimneys
(c) more efficient car engines
(d) low sulphur fuels

28 Affinity for hydrogen decreases in the group from fluorine to iodine. Which of the halogen acids should have highest bond dissociation enthalpy?
(a) HF (b) HCl
(c) HBr (d) HI

29 Among group 16 elements, which one does not show +4 oxidation state?
(a) Te (b) O
(c) Se (d) S

30 Which of the following statements is incorrect?
(a) Basic nature of X^- is in order $F^- > Cl^- > Br^- > I^-$.
(b) Among all halogen halides, HI is the strongest acid.
(c) The ionic character of *M*—*X* bond decreases in the order *M*—F > *M*—Cl > *M*—Br > *M*—I.
(d) Bromine and iodine are sparingly soluble in various organic solvents such as chloroform, CCl_4 etc.

31 $HClO_4$, HNO_3 and HCl all are very strong acids in aqueous solution. In glacial acetic acid medium, their acid strength is such that
(a) $HClO_4 > HNO_3 > HCl$ (b) $HNO_3 > HClO_4 > HCl$
(c) $HCl > HClO_4 > HNO_3$ (d) $HCl > HClO_4 > HNO_3$

32 Oxidation of hydrogen halide, *HX* affords a method for the industrial and laboratory preparation of the halogen, X_2 in the free state in respect to all of the following except
(a) fluorine (b) chlorine
(c) bromine (d) iodine

33 Which one of the following is the weakest base as per the Bronsted concept?
(a) $[ClO_4]^-$ (b) $[ClO_3]^-$
(c) $[ClO_2]^-$ (d) $[ClO]^-$

34 Reduction potentials of some ions are given below. Arrange them in decreasing order of oxidising power.

Ion	ClO_4^-	IO_4^-	BrO_4^-
Reduction potential ($E^\ominus$/V)	$E^\ominus = 1.19$ V	$E^\ominus = 1.65$ V	$E^\ominus = 1.74$ V

(a) $ClO_4^- > IO_4^- > BrO_4^-$ (b) $IO_4^- > BrO_4^- > ClO_4^-$
(c) $BrO_4^- > IO_4^- > ClO_4^-$ (d) $BrO_4^- > ClO_4^- > IO_4^-$

35 Select the incorrect statement from the following.
(a) Helium has the lowest melting point and boiling point.
(b) Helium can diffuse through rubber, PVC and even glass.
(c) Ar, Kr and Xe form clathrate.
(d) The noble gases have large negative value of electron gain enthalpy.

36 Inert atmosphere for welding of metal is obtained by using
(a) Ar, He (b) N_2, He
(c) O_2, N_2 (d) Ar, N_2

37 Clathrates compounds are not formed by which of the following pairs?
(a) He,Ne (b) Kr, Xe
(c) He, Kr (d) He, Xe

38 Select the correct statements from the following.
A. XeF_2, XeF_4 and XeF_6 are coloured crystalline solids and sublime readily at 298 K.
B. XeF_2 is hydrolysed to give Xe, HF and O_2.
C. XeF_6 has seven electron pairs, around Xe.
D. Hydrolysis of XeF_4 and XeF_6 with water gives finally XeO_2F_2.
E. Partial hydrolysis of XeF_6 with water gives oxyfluorides.

Choose the correct answer from the options given below.
(a) A, B and C (b) B, C and D
(c) B, C and E (d) D, C and E

39 An alkaline solution $HXeO_4^-$ disproportionates into
(a) XeO_6^{4-} and Xe (b) XeO_4^{2-} and XeO_3
(c) XeO_3 and Xe (d) XeO_6^{4-} and XeO_3

40 Among the given compounds, the maximum distortion will take place in
(a) XeF_2 (b) XeF_4
(c) XeF_6 (d) XeO_3

41 Basic character of fluorides increases in the order
(a) $XeF_6 < XeF_4 < XeF_2$
(b) $XeF_2 < XeF_4 < XeF_6$
(c) $XeF_2 = XeF_4 < XeF_6$
(d) $XeF_2 > XeF_4 < XeF_6$

42 Consider the following transformation.
I. $XeF_6 + NaF \longrightarrow Na^+[XeF_7]^-$
II. $2PCl_5(s) \longrightarrow [PCl_4]^+ + [PCl_6]^-$
III. $[Al(H_2O)_6]^{3+} + H_2O \longrightarrow [Al(H_2O)_5OH]^{2+} + H_3O^+$

Possible transformations are
(a) I, II and III (b) Both I and III
(c) Both I and II (d) Both II and III

43 Which of the following statements regarding helium is incorrect?
(a) It is used to produce and sustain powerful superconducting magnets.
(b) It is used as a cryogenic agent for carrying out experiments at low temperatures.
(c) It is used to fill gas balloons instead of hydrogen because it is lighter and non-inflammable.
(d) It is used in gas-cooled nuclear reactors.

Assertion-Reason

Direction (Q. 44 to 49) Given below are two statements, one is labelled as Assertion (A) and the other is labelled as Reason (R).
(a) Both A and R are true and R is the correct explanation of A.
(b) Both A and R are true but R is not the correct explanation of A.
(c) A is true but R is false.
(d) A is false but R is true.

44 **Assertion** (A) If aluminium atoms replace a few silicon atoms in three dimensional network of silicon dioxide, then the overall structure will acquire a positive charge.

Reason (R) Aluminium is trivalent whereas silicon is tetravalent.

45 **Assertion** (A) Inhalation of carbon monoxide may cause death.

Reason (R) CO has a 300-fold greater affinity for blood hemoglobin than does oxygen.

46 **Assertion** (A) Sn^{4+} is a reducing while Pb^{4+} is an oxidising agent.

Reason (R) Due to the inability of ns^2 electrons of the valence shell to participate in bonding.

47 **Assertion** (A) The pentavalent oxide of group-15 element, E_2O_5 is less acidic than trivalent oxide E_2O_3 of the same element.

Reason (R) The acidic character of trivalent oxide of group 15 elements E_2O_3, decreases down the group.

48 **Assertion** (A) The correct order of boiling points of group 15 hydrides is $BiH_3 > SbH_3 > NH_3 > AsH_3 > PH_3$.
Reason (R) The van der Waals' force in SbH_3 dominates the H-bonding in NH_3.

49 **Assertion** (A) NaCl reacts with conc. H_2SO_4 to give colourless fumes with pungent smell. But on adding MnO_2 the fumes becomes greenish yellow.

Reason (R) MnO_2 reduces HCl to chlorine gas which is greenish yellow.

Statements Type Questions

Direction (Q. Nos. 50 to 56) In the light of the below statements, choose the correct answer from the options given below.

(a) Both Statement I and Statement II are false.
(b) Statement I is true but Statement II is false.
(c) Statement I is false but Statement II is true.
(d) Both Statement I and Statement II are true.

50 **Statement I** $AlCl_3$ forms dimer Al_2Cl_6 but it dissovles in H_2O furming $[Al(H_2O)_6]^{3+}$ and Cl^- ions.

Statement II Aqueous solution of $AlCl_3$ in acidic due to hydrolysis.

51 **Statement I** PbF_2 is less stable than PbF_4 as effective nuclear charge on *s*-orbital electrons is lower due to poor shielding of *d*-orbitals.

Statement II PbF_4 is a good fluorinating agent as Pb is a heavy metal and F is a smaller size atom.

52 **Statement I** Both H_3PO_3 and H_3PO_4 have the same number of hydrogen atoms but H_3PO_4 is dibasic acid and H_3PO_3 is a tribasic acid.

Statement II 1mole of H_3PO_3 is neutralised by 2 moles of NaOH while 1 mole of H_3PO_4 is neutralised by 3 moles of NaOH.

53 **Statement I** $S_3O_6^{2-}$ (trithionate) has no S—S bond.

Statement II It is a conjugate base of $HS_3O_6^-$.

54 **Statement I** Hydrofluoric acid forms two series of salts KHF_2, K_2F_2.

Statement II Hydrofluoric acid is a tribasic acid due to hydrogen bonding.

55 **Statement I** Bond dissociation energy of F_2 is smaller than that of Cl_2.

Statement II Bond dissociation energy order is

$$F_2 < Cl_2 < Br_2 < I_2.$$

56 **Statement I** He and Ne do not form clathrates.

Statement II They are difficult to polarise due to smaller size.

57 Select the correct statements from the following.

A. Cyclic silicates having three Si-atoms contain 6 Si—O—Si linkages.
B. The structural unit of silicates is SiO_2^{4-}.
C. In silicates the silicon atom is bonded to four oxygen atom in tetrahedron form.
D. $(Si_2O_5)_n^{2n-}$ is the general formula of double chain silicate.
E. Silicates contains silicon and oxygen atoms.

Choose the correct answer from the options given below

(a) A and B (b) C and E
(c) C, D and E (d) B, C and D

58 Which of the following statements are incorrect?

A. The strong fluorinating agent, O_2F_2 oxidises plutonium to PuF_6.
B. Chlorine water on standing loses its yellow colour due to the formation of HCl and H_2SO_4.
C. Due to high electronegativity and small size, fluorine forms only one oxoacid.
D. The compound IF_7 is a colourless gas and has pentagonal bipyramidal molecular structure.
E. The interhalogen compounds are all covalent molecules and are paramagnetic in nature.

Choose the correct answer from the options given below.

(a) B and E (b) C and D
(c) A and C (d) C and E

59 Select the correct statements about noble gases.

A. XeF_6 can be prepared by the interaction of XeF_4 and O_2F_2 at 143 K.
B. They generally do not form ionic compounds.
C. They have variable oxidation states in their compounds.
D. They have very high melting and boiling points.
E. XeO_3 is a colourless explosive solid and has a square pyramidal molecular structure.

Choose the correct answer from the options given below.

(a) B, D and E (b) A and C
(c) B and D (d) A, B and C

Species Selection Type Questions

60 Consider the following elements.

(i) B (ii) Ga (iii) Al (iv) In (v) Tl

How many of them have pseudo noble gas configuration in their penultimate shell?

(a) 1 (b) 3
(c) 4 (d) 2

61 Consider the following compounds.

(i) H_3BO_3 (ii) B_2O_3 (iii) O_2 (iv) H_2O_3
(v) $B_2(CH_3)_4H_2$ (vi) H_2 (vii) H_2O_2

How many of them is/are formed when diborane is instantly hydrolysed by water?

(a) 2 (b) 1
(c) 4 (d) 5

62 Consider the following compounds.

(i) Pyrophosphoric acid (ii) Hypophosphoric acid
(iii) Orthophosphoric acid (iv) Metaphosphoric acid
(v) Phosphoric acid (vi) Phosphinic acid
(vii) Pyrophosphorus acid

How many of them have —P—O—P— linkage in their structure?

(a) 4 (b) 3 (c) 1 (d) 5

63 Consider the following oxoacids of phosphorus,

(i) $H_4P_2O_7$ (ii) $H_4P_2O_8$
(iii) $H_4P_2O_6$ (iv) $H_4P_2O_5$
(v) H_3PO_2

How many of them are tetrabasic in nature?

(a) 2 (b) 3 (c) 4 (d) 1

64 Consider the following oxoacids of sulphur,

(i) $H_2S_2O_3$ (ii) H_2SO_4
(iii) $H_2S_2O_4$ (iv) $H_2S_2O_7$
(v) $H_2S_4O_6$

How many of them does not contain bond between sulphur atoms?

(a) 1 (b) 4 (c) 3 (d) 2

65 Consider the following compounds,

(i) ClO_2 (ii) Cl_2O_7 (iii) Cl_2O
(iv) Cl_2O_6 (v) HOCl (vi) ClO_4^-
(vii) $HClO_2$

How many of them is/are the anhydride of $HClO_4$?

(a) 3 (b) 5
(c) 4 (d) 1

66 Consider the following compounds,

(i) XeF_4 (ii) XeF_6
(iii) XeO_3 (iv) XeF_2
(v) XeO_2F_2

How many of them can not be stored in glass vessels?

(a) 2 (b) 1
(c) 3 (d) 4

67 Consider the following compounds.

(i) XeO_2F_2 (ii) XeF_6
(iii) XeF_2 (iv) XeO_3
(v) XeF_4 (vi) $XeOF_4$
(vii) XeO_2

How many of them have one lone pairs of electrons on Xe atom?

(a) 4 (b) 5 (c) 3 (d) 2

Matching Type Questions

68 Match the compounds in Column I with their uses in the Column II.

	Column I (Compounds)		Column II (Uses)
A.	Boric acid	1.	In Friedel-Craft acylation
B.	Borax	2.	Mild antiseptic
C.	Aluminium chloride	3.	Washing powder
D.	Sodium peroxoborate	4.	Buffer

Codes

	A	B	C	D		A	B	C	D
(a)	1	2	3	4	(b)	4	3	2	1
(c)	2	4	1	3	(d)	3	1	4	2

69 Match the types of borates in Column I with their formula in Column II.

	Column I (Types of borates)		Column II (Formula)
A.	Metaborate	1.	$NaBO_3 \cdot 4H_2O$
B.	Orthoborates	2.	$Mg_2B_2O_5$
C.	Pyroborates	3.	$K_3(BO_2)_3$
D.	Perborate	4.	$Ca_3(BO_3)_2$

Codes

	A	B	C	D		A	B	C	D
(a)	3	4	2	1	(b)	1	2	3	4
(c)	2	1	3	4	(d)	4	2	3	1

70 Match the items in Column I with their formula in Column II.

	Column I (Compounds)		Column II (Formula)
A.	Tetraboric acid	1.	$B_3N_3H_6$
B.	Borax	2.	$Ga(OH)_3$
C.	Borazine	3.	$H_2B_4O_7$
D.	Amphoteric	4.	$Na_2B_4O_7 \cdot 10H_2O$

Codes

	A	B	C	D		A	B	C	D
(a)	1	4	3	2	(b)	3	4	1	2
(c)	2	1	3	4	(d)	4	2	4	3

71 Match the acids (in Column I) with number of acid salts formed by them (in Column II).

	Column I		Column II
A.	Hypophosphorus acid	1.	One
B.	Orthophosphorus acid	2.	Two
C.	Orthophosphoric acid	3.	Zero
D.	Mellitic acid	4.	Six

Codes

	A	B	C	D		A	B	C	D
(a)	3	1	2	4	(b)	1	3	2	1
(c)	3	1	4	2	(d)	1	2	3	4

72 Match the species given in Column I with their corresponding properties given in Column II.

	Column I		Column II
A.	SO_2	1.	Sulphonating agent
B.	$H_2S_2O_8$	2.	Precipitating agent
C.	H_2S	3.	Oxidising agent
D.	SO_3	4.	Reducing agent

Codes

	A	B	C	D		A	B	C	D
(a)	4	3	2	1	(b)	1	2	3	4
(c)	1	3	2	4	(d)	4	3	1	2

73 Match the species in given Column I with their structural features in Column II.

Column I	Column II
A. SO_3	1. sp^2-hybridised atom (s)
B. H_2SO_5	2. Sulphur in different oxidation states
C. $S_2O_3^{2-}$	3. No (S—S) linkage
D. S_3O_9	4. Peroxy linkage

Codes

	A	B	C	D		A	B	C	D
(a)	1	4	2	3	(b)	1	4	3	2
(c)	4	1	2	3	(d)	4	1	3	2

74 Match the species in Column I with the best satisfied corresponding properties in Column II.

Column I	Column II
A. Fluorine (F_2)	1. Exists in liquid state
B. Chlorine (Cl_2)	2. Least (X—X) bond energy
C. Bromine (Br_2)	3. Maximum electron gain enthalpy
D. Iodine (I_2)	4. Best oxidising agent

Codes

	A	B	C	D		A	B	C	D
(a)	4	3	1	2	(b)	4	3	2	1
(c)	3	4	1	2	(d)	3	4	2	1

75 Match the species in Column I with the corresponding properties in Column II.

Column I	Column II
A. Cl_2O_4	1. Anhydride of $HClO_3$ and $HClO_4$
B. Cl_2O_6	2. Paramagnetic
C. ClO_2	3. Anhydride of $HClO_2$ and $HClO_3$
D. Cl_2O_2	4. Unstable and explodes on heating

Codes

	A	B	C	D		A	B	C	D
(a)	3	1	2	4	(b)	3	1	4	2
(c)	1	3	2	4	(d)	1	3	4	2

76 Match the items of Column I and Column II and mark the correct option.

Column I	Column II
A. Its partial hydrolysis does not change oxidation state of central atom.	1. He
B. It is used in modern diving apparatus.	2. XeF_6
C. It is used to provide inert atmosphere for filling electrical bulbs.	3. XeF_4
D. Its central atom is in sp^3d^2-hybridisation.	4. Ar

Codes

	A	B	C	D		A	B	C	D
(a)	2	1	4	3	(b)	1	2	4	3
(c)	2	1	3	4	(d)	1	2	3	4

Final Check Through PYQs

Module I Boron Family

1 Amongst the given options which of the following molecules/ions acts as a Lewis acid? ***[NCERT (Old) Pg. 311, NEET 2023]***

(a) H_2O (b) BF_3 (c) OH^- (d) NH_3

2 Taking stability as the factor, which one of the following represents correct relationship? ***[NEET 2023]***

(a) $TlI_3 > TlI$

(b) $AlCl > AlCl_3$

(c) $TlI > TlI_3$

(d) $TlCl_3 > TlCl$

3 Which of the following statements is not correct about diborane? ***[NCERT (Old) Pg. 313, NEET 2022]***

(a) The four terminal B — H bonds are 2-centre-2 electron bonds.

(b) The four terminal hydrogen atoms and the two boron atoms lie in one plane.

(c) Both the boron atoms are sp^2-hybridised.

(d) There are two 3-centre-2-electron bonds.

4 BF_3 is planar and electron deficient compound. Hybridisation and number of electrons around the central atom, respectively are ***[NEET 2021]***

(a) sp^2 and 8 (b) sp^3 and 4

(c) sp^3 and 6 (d) sp^2 and 6

5 Match the following and identify the correct option. ***[NCERT (Old) Pg. 313, 319, NEET 2020]***

Column I	Column II
A. $CO(g) + H_2(g)$	1. $Mg(HCO_3)_2 + Ca(HCO_3)_2$
B. Temporary hardness of water	2. An electron deficient hydride
C. B_2H_6	3. Synthesis gas
D. H_2O_2	4. Non-planar structure

Codes

	A	B	C	D
(a)	3	2	1	4
(b)	3	4	2	1
(c)	1	3	2	4
(d)	3	1	2	4

6 Aluminium chloride in acidified aqueous solution forms a complex '*A*', in which hybridisation state of Al is '*B*'. What are '*A*' and '*B*', respectively? ***[NCERT (Old) Pg. 311, NEET (Odisha) 2019]***

(a) $[Al(H_2O)_6]^{3+}$, d^2sp^3 (b) $[Al(H_2O)_6]^{3+}$, sp^3d^2

(c) $[Al(H_2O)_4]^{3+}$, sp^3 (d) $[Al(H_2O)_4]^{3+}$, dsp^2

7 Which one of the following elements is unable to form MF_6^{3-} ion? ***[NCERT (Old) Pg. 312, NEET 2018]***

(a) Ga (b) Al

(c) In (d) B

8 Boric acid is an acid because its molecule ***[NCERT (Old) Pg. 313, NEET 2016, Phase II]***

(a) contains replaceable H^+ ion

(b) gives up a proton

(c) accepts OH^- from water releasing proton

(d) combines with proton from water molecule

9 AlF_3 is soluble in HF only in presence of KF. It is due to the formation of ***[NEET 2016, Phase II]***

(a) $K_3[AlF_3H_3]$

(b) $K_3[AlF_6]$

(c) AlH_3

(d) $K[AlF_3H]$

10 The stability of +1 oxidation state among Al, Ga, In and Tl increases in the sequence ***[NCERT (Old) Pg. 310, AIPMT 2015]***

(a) Ga < In < Al < Tl

(b) Al < Ga < In < Tl

(c) Tl< In < Ga < Al

(d) In < Tl < Ga < Al

Module II Carbon Family

11 Match Column I with Column II. ***[NCERT (Old) Pg. 319, 318, 317, NEET 2023]***

	Column I		Column II
A.	Coke	1.	Carbon atoms are sp^3-hybridised.
B.	Diamond	2.	Used as a dry lubricant.
C.	Fullerene	3.	Used as a reducing agent.
D.	Graphite	4.	Cage like molecules.

Codes

	A	B	C	D		A	B	C	D
(a)	4	1	2	3	(b)	3	1	4	2
(c)	3	4	1	2	(d)	2	4	1	3

12 Choose the correct statement. ***[NCERT (Old) Pg. 317, 318, NEET 2022]***

(a) Diamond is covalent and graphite is ionic.
(b) Diamond is sp^3-hybridised and graphite is sp^2-hybridised.
(c) Both diamond and graphite are used as dry lubricants.
(d) Diamond and graphite have two dimensional network.

13 Which of the following oxides is amphoteric in nature? ***[NEET (Oct.) 2020]***

(a) SnO_2 (b) SiO_2
(c) GeO_2 (d) CO_2

14 Identify the correct statements from the following

1. $CO_2(g)$ is used as refrigerant for ice-cream and frozen food.
2. The structure of C_{60} contains twelve, six membered carbon rings and twenty, five membered carbon rings.
3. ZSM-5, a type of zeolite, is used to convert alcohols into gasoline.
4. CO is colourless and odourless gas. ***[NEET (Sep.) 2020]***

(a) (1) and (3) only (b) (2) and (3) only
(c) (3) and (4) only (d) (1), (2) and (3) only

15 Which of the following is not correct about carbon monoxide? ***[NCERT (Old) Pg. 319, NEET 2020]***

(a) It reduces oxygen carrying ability of blood.
(b) The carboxyhaemoglobin (haemoglobin bound to CO) is less stable than oxyhaemoglobin.
(c) It is produced due to incomplete combustion.
(d) It forms carboxyhaemoglobin.

16 Which of the following compounds is used in cosmetic surgery? ***[NCERT (Old) Pg. 322, NEET Odisha 2019]***

(a) Zeolites (b) Silica
(c) Silicates (d) Silicones

17 Which of the following is incorrect statement? ***[NCERT (Old) Pg. 316, NEET (National) 2019]***

(a) $SiCl_4$ is easily hydrolysed
(b) GeX_4 (X =, F, Cl, Br, I) is more stable than GeX_2
(c) SnF_4 is ionic in nature
(d) PbF_4 is covalent in nature

18 It is because of inability of ns^2 electrons of the valence shell to participate in bonding that ***[NCERT (Old) Pg. 316, NEET 2017]***

(a) Sn^{2+} is oxidising while Pb^{4+} is reducing
(b) Sn^{2+} and Pb^{2+} are both oxidising and reducing
(c) Sn^{4+} is reducing while Pb^{4+} is oxidising
(d) Sn^{2+} is reducing while Pb^{4+} is oxidising

Module III Nitrogen Family

19 Which of the following oxoacids of phosphorus has strongest reducing property? ***[NCERT (Old) Pg. 185, NEET (Odisha) 2019]***

(a) $H_4P_2O_7$ (b) H_3PO_3
(c) H_3PO_2 (d) H_3PO_4

20 Identify the incorrect statement related to PCl_5 from the following. ***[NCERT (Old) Pg. 183, NEET 2019]***

(a) Two axial P— Cl bonds make an angle of 180° with each other.
(b) Axial P— Cl bonds are longer than equatorial P— Cl bonds.
(c) PCl_5 molecule is non-reactive.
(d) Three equatorial P— Cl bonds make an angle of 120° with each other.

21 The correct order of N-compounds in its decreasing order of oxidation states is ***[NCERT (Old) Pg. 177, NEET 2018]***

(a) $HNO_3 > NH_4Cl > NO > N_2$
(b) $HNO_3 > NO > NH_4Cl > N_2$
(c) $HNO_3 > NO > N_2 > NH_4Cl$
(d) $NH_4Cl > N_2 > NO > HNO_3$

22 Which oxide of nitrogen is not a common pollutant introduced into the atmosphere both due to natural and human acitivity? ***[NCERT (Old) Pg. 175, NEET 2018]***

(a) N_2O (b) NO_2
(c) N_2O_5 (d) NO

23 Which is the correct statement for the given acids? ***[NCERT (Old) Pg. 185, NEET 2016, Phase I]***

(a) Phosphinic acid is a monoprotic acid while phosphonic acid is a diprotic acid
(b) Phosphinic acid is a diprotic acid while phosphonic acid is a monoprotic acid
(c) Both are triprotic acids
(d) Both of diprotic acids

24 Among the following, which one is a wrong statement? ***[NCERT (Old) Pg. 173, NEET 2016, Phase II]***

(a) PH_5 and $BiCl_5$ do not exist.
(b) $p\pi$ - $d\pi$ bonds are present in SO_2.
(c) SeF_4 and CH_4 have same shape.
(d) IF_2^+ has bent geometry.

Module-IV Oxygen Family

25 Among group 16 elements, which one does not show–2 oxidation state? *[NEET 2024]*
(a) O (b) Se (c) Te (d) Po

26 Given below are two statement.
Statement I The boiling point of hydrides of group-16 elements of follow the order $H_2O > H_2Te > H_2Se > H_2S$.
Statement II On the basis of molecular mass, H_2O is expected to have lower boiling point than the other memebrs of the group but due to the presence of extensive H-bonding in H_2O, it has higher boiling point. *[NEET 2024]*
In the light of the above statements, choose the correct answer from the options given below.
(a) Both Statement I and Statement II are true.
(b) Both Statement I and Statement II are false.
(c) Statement I is true but Statement II is false.
(d) Statement I is false but Statement II is true.

27 Match Column I with Column II.

Column I (Oxoacids of sulphur)	Column II (Bonds)
A. Peroxodisulphuric acid	1. Two S–OH, four S =O, one S–O–S
B. Sulphuric acid	2. Two S–OH, one S =O,
C. Pyrosulphuric acid	3. Two S–OH, four S =O, one S–O–O–S
D. Sulphurous acid	4. Two S–OH, two S =O

Codes *[NEET 2023]*
(a) 3 4 1 2 (b) 1 3 4 2
(c) 3 4 2 1 (d) 1 3 2 4

28 Given below are two statements.
Statement I The boiling points of the following hydrides of group 16 elements increases in the order

$$H_2O < H_2S < H_2Se < H_2Te$$

Statement II The boiling points of these hydride increases with increase in molar mass. *[NCERT (Old) Pg. 187, NEET 2022]*
In the light of the above statements, choose the correct answer from the options given below.
(a) Both Statement I and Statement II are false.
(b) Statement I is true, but Statement II is false.
(c) Statement I is false, but Statement II is true.
(d) Both Statement I and Statement II are true.

29. In which one of the following arrangements the given sequence is not strictly according to the properties indicated against it? *[NEET 2021]*
(a) $HF < HCl < HBr < HI$: Increasing acidic strength
(b) $H_2O < H_2S < H_2Se < H_2Te$: Increasing pK_a values
(c) $NH_3 < PH_3 < AsH_3 < SbH_3$: Increasing acidic character
(d) $CO_2 < SiO_2 < SnO_2 < PbO_2$: Increasing oxidising power

30 Which of the following oxoacids of sulphur has —O—O— linkage? *[NEET 2020]*
(a) H_2SO_4, sulphuric acid
(b) $H_2S_2O_8$, peroxodisulphuric acid
(c) $H_2S_2O_7$, pyrosulphuric acid
(d) H_2SO_3, sulphurous acid

31 Identify the correct formula of oleum from the following. *[NEET (Odisha) 2019]*
(a) $H_2S_2O_7$ (b) H_2SO_3
(c) H_2SO_4 (d) $H_2S_2O_8$

32 Which is the correct order of thermal stability for H_2E (E = O, S, Se, Te and Po)? *[NEET (National) 2019]*
(a) $H_2O < H_2S < H_2Se < H_2Te < H_2Po$
(b) $H_2Po < H_2Te < H_2Se < H_2S < H_2O$
(c) $H_2Se < H_2Te < H_2Po < H_2O < H_2S$
(d) $H_2S < H_2O < H_2Se < H_2Te < H_2Po$

33 In which pair of ions both the species contain S—S bond? *[NEET 2017]*
(a) $S_2O_7^{2-}$, $S_2O_8^{2-}$ (b) $S_4O_6^{2-}$, $S_2O_3^{2-}$
(c) $S_2O_7^{2-}$, $S_2O_3^{2-}$ (d) $S_4O_6^{2-}$, $S_2O_7^{2-}$

34 How concentrated sulphuric acid is a moderately strong oxidising agent. Which of the following reaction does not show oxidising behaviour? *[NEET 2016, Phase II]*
(a) $Cu + 2H_2SO_4 \longrightarrow CuSO_4 + SO_2 + 2H_2O$
(b) $3S + 2H_2SO_4 \longrightarrow 3SO_2 + 2H_2O$
(c) $C + 2H_2SO_4 \longrightarrow CO_2 + 2SO_2 + 2H_2O$
(d) $CaF_2 + H_2SO_4 \longrightarrow CaSO_4 + 2HF$

35 Nitrogen dioxide and sulphur dioxide have some properties in common. Which property is shown by one of these compounds, but not by the other? *[AIPMT 2015]*
(a) Forms' acid rain.
(b) Is a reducing agent.
(c) Is soluble in water.
(d) Is used as a food preservative.

Module-V Halogen Family

36 Given below are two statements one is labelled as Assertion (A) and the other is labelled as Reason (R).
Assertion (A) ICl is more reactive than I_2.
Reason (R) I—Cl bond is weaker than I—I bond.
In the light of the above statements, choose the most appropriate answer from the options given below. *[NCERT (Old) Pg. 206, NEET 2022]*
(a) Both A and R are true and R is the correct explanation of A.
(b) Both A and R are true but R is not the correct explanation of A.
(c) A is true but R is false.
(d) A is false but R is true.

37 Given below are two statements.

Statement I Acid strength increases in the order given as HF << HCl << HBr << HI.

Statement II As the size of the elements F, Cl, Br and I increases down the group. the bond strength of HF, HCl, HBr and HI decreases and so the acid strength increases.

In the light of the above statements, choose the correct answer from the options given below. ***[NCERT (Old) Pg. 201, NEET 2021]***

(a) Both Statement I and Statement II are false.
(b) Statement I is true, but Statement II is false.
(c) Statement I is false, but Statement II is true.
(d) Both Statement I and Statement II are true.

38 Match the compounds of Xe in Column I with the molecular structure in Column II. ***[NEET (Oct.) 2020]***

	Column I		Column II
A.	XeF_2	1.	Square planar
B.	XeF_4	2.	Linear
C.	XeO_3	3.	Square pyramidal
D.	$XeOF_4$	4.	Pyramidal

Codes

	A	B	C	D		A	B	C	D
(a)	2	1	3	4	(b)	2	4	3	1
(c)	2	3	1	4	(d)	2	1	4	3

39 The correct structure of tribromooctaoxide is ***[NEET (National) 2019]***

(a) 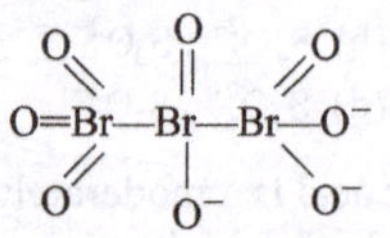
(b) 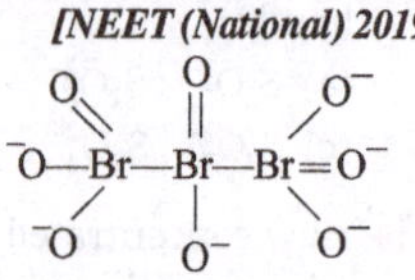
(c) 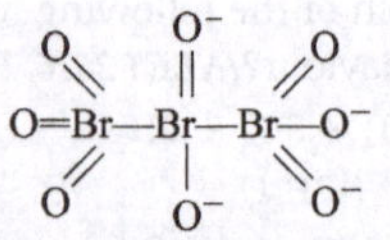
(d) 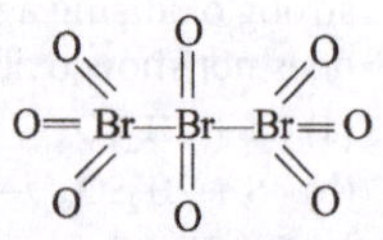

40 Which of the following statements is not true for halogens? ***[NCERT (Old) Pg. 201, NEET 2019]***

(a) All fluorine show positive oxidation states.
(b) All are oxidising agents.
(c) All form monobasic oxyacids.
(d) Chlorine has the highest electron gain enthalpy.

41 In the structure of ClF_3, the number of lone pairs of electrons on central atom 'Cl' is ***[NCERT (Old) Pg. 206, NEET 2018]***

(a) four (b) two (c) one (d) three

42 Match the interhalogen compounds of Column I with the geometry in Column II and assign the correct code. ***[NCERT (Old) Pg. 206, NEET 2017]***

	Column I		Column II
A.	XX'	1.	T-shape
B.	XX'_3	2.	Pentagonal bipyramidal
C.	XX'_5	3.	Linear
D.	XX'_7	4.	Square-pyramidal
		5.	Tetrahedral

Codes

	A	B	C	D		A	B	C	D
(a)	4	3	2	1	(b)	3	4	1	2
(c)	3	1	4	2	(d)	1	4	3	2

43 Which of the following pairs of compounds is isoelectronic and isostructural? ***[NEET 2017]***

(a) $BeCl_2$, XeF_2 (b) TeI_2, XeF_2
(c) IBr_2^-, XeF_2 (d) IF_2, XeF_2

44 Among the following, the correct order of acidity is ***[NCERT (Old) Pg. 205, NEET 2016, Phase I, AIPMT 2005]***

(a) $HClO < HClO_2 < HClO_3 < HClO_4$
(b) $HClO_2 < HClO < HClO_3 < HClO_4$
(c) $HClO_4 < HClO_2 < HClO < HClO_3$
(d) $HClO_3 < HClO_4 < HClO_2 < HClO$

45 Which one of the following order is correct for the bond dissociation enthalpy of halogen molecules? ***[NCERT (Old) Pg. 201, NEET 2016, Phase I]***

(a) $Cl_2 > Br_2 > F_2 > I_2$ (b) $Br_2 > I_2 > F_2 > Cl_2$
(c) $F_2 > Cl_2 > Br_2 > I_2$ (d) $I_2 > Br_2 > Cl_2 > F_2$

46 Match the compounds of Xe in Column I with the hybridisation and shape given in Column II and mark the correct option. ***[NCERT (Old) Pg. 210, NEET 2016, Phase I]***

	Column I		Column II
A.	XeF_6	1.	Distorted octahedral
B.	XeO_3	2.	Square planar
C.	$XeOF_4$	3.	Pyramidal
D.	XeF_4	4.	Square pyramidal

Codes

	A	B	C	D		A	B	C	D
(a)	1	2	4	3	(b)	4	3	1	2
(c)	4	1	2	3	(d)	1	3	4	2

47 The correct geomtry and hybridisation for XeF_4 are ***[NEET 2016, Phase III]***

(a) octahedral, sp^3d^2
(b) trigonal bipyramidal, sp^3d
(c) planar triangle, sp^3d^3
(d) square planar, sp^3d^2

48 The variation of the boiling point of the hydrogen halides in the order HF > HI > HBr > HCl. What explains the higher boiling point of hydrogen fluoride? ***[AIPMT 2015]***

(a) The electronegativity of fluorine is much higher than for other elements in the group.
(b) There is strong hydrogen bonding between HF molecules.
(c) The bond energy of HF molecules is greater than in other hydrogen halides.
(d) The effect of nuclear shielding is much reduced in fluorine which polarises the HF molecule.

49 Which of the statements given below is incorrect? ***[AIPMT 2015]***

(a) Cl_2O_7 is an anhydride of perchloric acid.
(b) O_3 molecule is bent.
(c) ONF is isoelectronic with NO_2^-.
(d) OF_2 is an oxide of fluorine.

Module-VI Noble Gases

50 Noble gases are named because of their inertness towards reactivity. Identify an incorrect statement about them. ***[NEET 2021]***

(a) Noble gases are sparingly soluble in water.
(b) Noble gases have very high melting and boiling points.
(c) Noble gases have weak dispersion forces.
(d) Noble gases have large positive values of electron gain enthalpy.

Answers

Step up Practice 1

1 (d)	2 (a)	3 (c)	4 (c)	5 (b)	6 (c)	7 (d)	8 (a)	9 (b)	10 (d)
11 (c)	12 (b)	13 (a)	14 (d)	15 (c)	16 (a)	17 (c)	18 (c)	19 (d)	20 (c)

Step up Practice 2

1 (c)	2 (b)	3 (d)	4 (d)	5 (a)	6 (a)	7 (d)	8 (b)	9 (c)	10 (b)
11 (d)	12 (a)	13 (d)	14 (b)	15 (c)					

Step up Practice 3

1 (d)	2 (d)	3 (d)	4 (b)	5 (d)	6 (b)	7 (a)	8 (a)	9 (d)	10 (d)
11 (a)	12 (d)	13 (b)	14 (a)	15 (b)	16 (a)	17 (b)	18 (a)	19 (c)	20 (c)
21 (d)	22 (a)	23 (a)							

Step up Practice 4

1 (d)	2 (b)	3 (b)	4 (a)	5 (c)	6 (b)	7 (b)	8 (c)	9 (c)	10 (c)
11 (b)	12 (c)	13 (a)	14 (d)	15 (d)	16 (b)	17 (a)	18 (a)	19 (a)	20 (b)
21 (d)	22 (b)								

Step up Practice 5

1 (c)	2 (a)	3 (d)	4 (b)	5 (c)	6 (d)	7 (b)	8 (b)	9 (d)	10 (a)
11 (a)	12 (d)	13 (c)	14 (b)	15 (c)	16 (c)	17 (d)	18 (b)	19 (d)	20 (a)
21 (b)									

Step up Practice 6

1 (c)	2 (d)	3 (d)	4 (c)	5 (d)	6 (a)	7 (c)	8 (b)	9 (b)	10 (a)
11 (c)	12 (d)	13 (d)	14 (a)	15 (d)	16 (a)	17 (d)			

Gearing up for NEET

1 (b)	2 (a)	3 (c)	4 (d)	5 (d)	6 (a)	7 (d)	8 (b)	9 (b)	10 (b)
11 (a)	12 (b)	13 (a)	14 (d)	15 (a)	16 (c)	17 (a)	18 (c)	19 (a)	20 (b)
21 (c)	22 (d)	23 (b)	24 (d)	25 (b)	26 (c)	27 (d)	28 (a)	29 (b)	30 (d)
31 (a)	32 (a)	33 (a)	34 (c)	35 (d)	36 (a)	37 (a)	38 (c)	39 (a)	40 (c)
41 (a)	42 (a)	43 (a)	44 (d)	45 (a)	46 (a)	47 (d)	48 (a)	49 (c)	50 (d)
51 (c)	52 (c)	53 (c)	54 (b)	55 (b)	56 (d)	57 (b)	58 (a)	59 (d)	60 (b)
61 (a)	62 (c)	63 (b)	64 (d)	65 (d)	66 (b)	67 (a)	68 (c)	69 (a)	70 (b)
71 (a)	72 (a)	73 (a)	74 (a)	75 (a)	76 (a)				

Final Check through PYQs : Module-I

1 (b)	2 (c)	3 (c)	4 (d)	5 (d)	6 (b)	7 (d)	8 (c)	9 (b)	10 (b)

Final Check through PYQs : Module-II

11 (b)	12 (b)	13 (a)	14 (c)	15 (b)	16 (d)	17 (d)	18 (d)

Final Check through PYQs : Module-III

19 (c)	20 (c)	21 (c)	22 (a)	23 (a)	24 (c)

Final Check through PYQs : Module-IV

25 (d)	26 (a)	27 (a)	28 (a)	29 (b)	30 (b)	31 (a)	32 (b)	33 (b)	34 (d)
35 (d)									

Final Check through PYQs : Module-V

36 (a)	37 (d)	38 (d)	39 (d)	40 (a)	41 (b)	42 (c)	43 (c)	44 (a)	45 (a)
46 (d)	47 (d)	48 (b)	49 (d)						

Final Check through PYQs : Module-VI

50 (b)

Hints and Solutions

Step up Practice 1

1. (*d*) Density of group 13 elements increases down the group, so Tl will have highest density among the given elements.

2. (*a*) Lewis acid character of $BF_3 < BCl_3 < BBr_3$ as $p\pi$-$p\pi$ back bonding is strongest in BF_3.
Thus, stability of the adduct formed is in same order.

3. (*c*) Electron accepting tendency of group 13 elements decreases down the group.
Thus, the correct order is B > Al > Ga > In.

4. (*c*) As we go down the group, stability of +1 oxidation state increases and that of +3 oxidation state decreases.

Thus, $Tl^+ > In^+ > Ga^+$

$Ga^{3+} > In^{3+} > Tl^{3+}$

$Ga^{3+} > Ga^+$

This is an example of inert pair effect.

5. (*b*) Tl shows different oxidation state that is +1 and +3 due to inert pair effect.

6. (*c*) Amongst groups 13 elements, Al has lowest electronegativity of 1.5. B has 2.0, Ga-1.6, In-1.7 and Tl-1.8.

7. (*d*) Both Statement I and Statement II are true.

8. (*a*) Alkaline earth metals form ionic chloride whereas aluminium chloride is covalent. Despite of sharing electrons with chlorine, the octet of aluminium is incomplete. To complete the octet, it needs electrons and thus, acts as a Lewis acid.

$_{13}Al = 2, 8, 3$ and $_{17}Cl = 2, 8, 7$

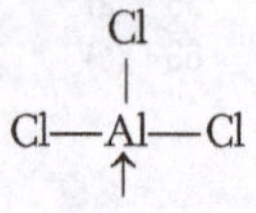

Octet incomplete

9. (*b*) Among the given match, (b) is correctly matched while other are incorrect.
Their correct match are
- $Al_2O_3 \longrightarrow$ Amphoteric
- $In_2O_3 \longrightarrow$ Basic
- $Tl_2O_3 \longrightarrow$ Basic

10. (*d*) Since, Al is a good reducing agent, it can not be used as an oxidiser in metallurgy.

11. (*c*) In gallium, the crystal structure is different, suggesting that Ga consists of almost discrete Ga_2 molecules, that's why its melting point is lowest. Ga exists as liquid from 30°C upto 2000°C and hence, it is used in high temperature thermometry.

12. (*b*) Among the given elements, only four, i.e. (i), (ii), (iii) and (iv) do not act as an oxidising agent.
Tl^{3+} can easily gain $2e^-$ and gets converted into Tl^+ and acts as an oxidising agent.

13. (*a*) Among the given match, only (a) is correctly match, while other are incorrect.
The reaciton proceeds as follow

$$4B + 3O_2 \xrightarrow{\Delta} 2B_2O_3 \xrightarrow{3H_2O} \underset{\text{(Pyroboric acid)}}{H_6B_4O_9}$$

14. (*d*) Aqueous solution of borax

$$Na_2B_4O_7 + 7H_2O \longrightarrow \underset{\text{Weak acid}}{2B(OH)_3} + \underset{\text{Base}}{2Na[B(OH)_4]}$$

The base formed, i.e. $[B(OH)_4]^-$ reacts with acid but not the $B(OH)_3$. Hence, option (d) is correct.

15. (*c*) Boron hydroxide $B(OH)_3$ or boric acid (H_3BO_3) is acidic while aluminium hydroxide $Al(OH)_3$ is amphoteric.

16. (*a*) Among the given statements, (a) is not correct about H_3BO_3.
Its correct form is :
H_3BO_3 is a weak monobasic and weak Lewis acid.

17. (*c*) The reaction proceeds as follows

$$B(OH)_3 + 2H_2O \longrightarrow B(OH)_4^- + H_3O^+$$

18. (*c*) Statement I is false but Statement II is true.
Its correct form is :
$AlCl_3$ forms dimer Al_2Cl_6 is gaseous state but it dissolves in H_2O forming $[Al(H_2O)_6]^{3+}$ and $3Cl^-$ ions.

19. (*d*) Boron does not react with HCl but Al reacts with HCl, $2Al + 6HCl \longrightarrow 2AlCl_3 + 3H_2$

20. (*c*) Among the given compounds, only two, i.e. (iii) and (iv) are formed when boron is fused with NaOH.
The reaction proceeds as follows

$$2B + 6NaOH \longrightarrow 2Na_3BO_3 + 3H_2\uparrow$$

Step up Practice 2

1. (*c*) Most favourable oxidation states of lead and tin are +2 and +4 respectively. Lead shows +2 state due to inert pair effect.

2. (*b*) In carbon family the stability of +2 oxidation state increases on moving down the group in the periodic table with an increase in atomic number due to inert pair effect.

3. (*d*) The stability of dihalides of group 14 elements increases down the group due to increase in inert pair effect impact.

4. (d) Reducing power of tetravalent species/ion for group 14 elements decreases down the group due to increase in impact of inert pair effect.

5. (a) Bond energy of group 14 elements decreases on moving down the group due to increase in size.

6. (a) Among the given oxides, only two, i.e. (iv) and (v) are not acidic in nature.

- $SnO_2 \longrightarrow$ Amphoteric
- $PbO_2 \longrightarrow$ Amphoteric

7. (d) On moving down the group, catenation tendency decreases due to decrease in element bond strength. Catenation tendency in group 14-element is highest in carbon while silicon has second highest tendency of catenation among all elements of family due to higher bond energy. The decreasing tendency of catenation among group 14 elements is as follows

$$C >> Si > Ge \approx Sn$$

However, Pb does not show catenation.

8. (b) CO_2 in water behaves as a weak dibasic acid.

$$CO_2 + H_2O \longrightarrow H_2CO_3 \longrightarrow 2H^+ + CO_3^{2-}$$

9. (c) Among the given oxides, SnO is an amphoteric oxide while others are acidic in nature.

10. (b) Statement I is true but Statement II is false.

Its correct form is :

C-atoms in diamond are sp^3-hybridised while in case of graphite they are sp^2-hybridised.

11. (d) 12. (a)

13. (d) Among the given gases, only one, i.e. (i) is liberated, when Al_4C_3 is hydrolysed.

$$Al_4C_3 + 12HOH \longrightarrow 3CH_4\uparrow + 4Al(OH)_3$$

14. (b) In pyrosilicates ($Si_2O_7^{6-}$), one of the oxygen atom is shared by two silicon atoms.

15. (c) The product obtained by the hydrolysis of Me_3SiCl contains only one —OH group which when subjected to polymerisation makes the polymer incapable for further polymerisation and hence controls the chain length.

Step up Practice 3

1. (d) The most abundant uncombined element present in atmosphere is N.

2. (d) Among the given match, (d) is not a correct match with respect to the given oxidation state.

Its correct match is

$$N_2O_5 \longrightarrow +5$$

3. (d) In $NH_3(l)$ there is intermolecular H-bonding. Thus, it has maximum heat of vaporisation.

In PH_3, there is no H-bonding.

Thus, it is in gaseous state it has minimum heat of vaporisation.

Thus, correct order is $PH_3 < AsH_3 < NH_3$.

4. (b) Among the given elements, bismuth does not show allotropy

5. (d)

6. (b) In plants, atmospheric nitrogen is converted into proteins.

7. (a)

8. (a) Fluorine is the most electronegative element, thus tendency of N-atom to donate lone pair of $\bar{e}s$ (to behave as Lewis acid) is least.

9. (d) Both Statement I and Statement II are true.

10. (d) Among the given compounds, only two, i.e. (i) and (iii) are used to prepare pure N_2 gas in the laboratory.

11. (a) 12. (d) 13. (b)

14. (a) Electronegativity of N is highest amongst P, As and Sb.

∴ Thus, N_2O_5 is most acidic oxide.

15. (b) Statement I is true but Statement II is false.

Its correct form is :

- Two N-atoms are bonded by single bond in N_2H_4.
- Structure of N_2H_4 is 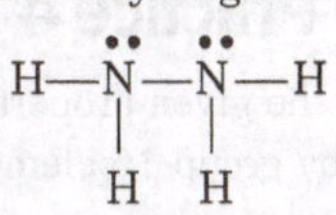

16. (a) There are only valence p-orbitals in N and O. Thus, there is $p\pi$-$p\pi$ bonding is present in oxides of nitrogen.

17. (b) $2PCl_5 \rightleftharpoons [PCl_4]^{\oplus} + [PCl_6]^{\ominus}$

Solid	Tetrahedral	Octahedral
(P : sp^3d)	(P : sp^3)	(P : sp^3d^2)

18. (a) Among the given compounds, only three, i.e. (ii), (iv) and (v) do not exist.

19. (c) The cyclo tri-metaphosphoric acid $(HPO_3)_3$ is

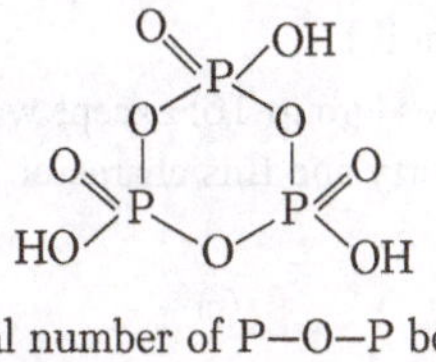

Thus, the total number of P—O—P bonds in cyclo tri-metaphosphoric acid is three.

20. (c) Among the given match, (c) is the incorrect match with the given oxidation state.

Its correct match is :

Orthophosphorus acid (H_3PO_3) has +3 oxidation state.

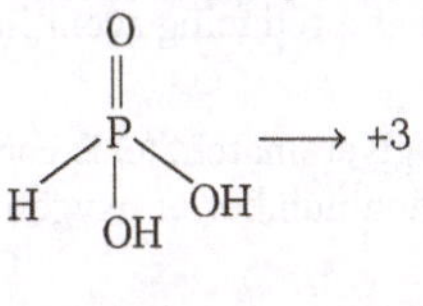

21. (d) Strong reducing behaviour of $\overset{+1}{H_3PO_2}$ is due to presence of two P—H bonds and one P—OH bond and +1 oxidation state of P-atom.

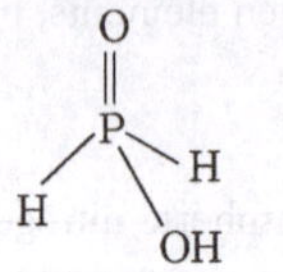

Hypophosphorus acid
(Monobasic)

H atoms also show reducing behaviour.

22. (a) Among the given statements, (a) is incorrect. Its correct form is

Single N—N bond is weaker than the single P—P bond.

That's why phosphorus shows allotropy but nitrogen does not.

23. (a) The structure of hypophosphorus acid (H_3PO_2) is

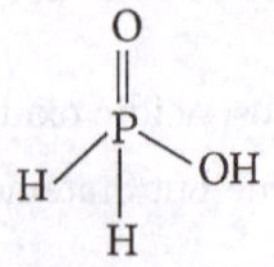

Step up Practice 4

1. (d) Among the given properties, high viscosity is not possessed by group-16 elements.
2. (b) Sulphur has the maximum tendency to show catenation property.
3. (b) Among the given bonds, Te—Te has the least bond energy.
4. (a)
5. (c) Tetrafluorides of elements of group-16 have sp^3d hybridisation and trigonal bipyramidal structure respectively.
6. (b) Statement I is true but statement II is false.

   Its correct form is :

   All the hydrides (group-16) except water possess reducing property and this character increases from H_2S to H_2Te.
7. (b) 8. (c) 9. (c)
10. (c) Oxygen is more electronegative than C or N, thus bonding pair is pulled by oxygen making ionisation of H_2O easier and thus making it more acidic than NH_3 and CH_4.
11. (b) $SO_2 + 2H_2O \longrightarrow H_2SO_4 + 2H$

    Thus, SO_2 acts as a reducing agent in the presence of H_2O.
12. (c) Among the given match, (c) is correctly match. The co-ordination number of oxygen in liq. H_2O is 4 (O is sp^3).
13. (a)

		Bond order
O=O	(double bond)	2
H—O—O—H	(single bond)	1
$O=O\rightarrow O$	(between double bond and single bond)	1.5

Larger the bond order, smaller the bond length.
Thus, (O—O) bond length in $H_2O_2 > O_3 > O_2$.

14. (d) Both Statement I and Statement II are true.
15. (d) Both Statement I and Statement II are true.
16. (b) Among the given compounds (ii), (iii) and (iv) act as a bleaching agent except (i) and (v) that act as an oxidising agent and a reducing agent.
17. (a) Among the given match, (a) is incorrectly matched while other are correctly matched.

    Its correct match is H_2SO_4 an oxidising agent.
18. (a) AgBr is soluble in $Na_2S_2O_3$ due to complex formation $Na_3[Ag(S_2O_3)_2]$.

    $$AgBr + 2Na_2S_2O_3 \longrightarrow Na_3[Ag(S_2O_3)_2] + NaBr$$
19. (a) Among the given compounds, (a) is correctly matched with the given linkage while other are incorrect. It is because $H_2S_2O_8$, H_2SO_4 and H_2SO_3 all has zero S—O—S linkage.
20. (b) The reaction proceeds as follow

    $$2AgNO_3 + \underset{\text{(Hypo sol)}}{Na_2S_2O_3} \longrightarrow \underset{\text{White}}{Ag_2S_2O_3} + 2NaNO_3$$

    $$Ag_2S_2O_3 + H_2O \longrightarrow \underset{\text{Black}}{Ag_2O} + H_2SO_4$$
21. (d) Among the given acids, only two, i.e. (iii) and (iv) are peroxy acids.
22. (b) The correct formula of Caro's acid is H_2SO_5.

Step up Practice 5

1. (c) The general electronic configuration of the valence shell of a halogen atom is ns^2np^5.
2. (a) Fluorine has the highest ionisation energy due to its its small size.
3. (d) Br—Br 158 kJ mol^{-1}

   Cl—Cl 210 kJ mol^{-1}

   F—F 126 kJ mol^{-1}

   Thus, $F_2 < Br_2 < Cl_2$
4. (b) Statement I is true but Statement II is false.

   Its correct form is :

   Fluorine has maximum electronegativity but its electron affinity is less than that of chlorine.
5. (c)
6. (d) F_2 is the strongest oxidising agent due to its lower heat of dissociation and higher heat of hydration.

7. (b) HF has maximum dipole moment, HI is the strongest acid hence has highest ionisation constant.

8. (b) Only fluorine shows (-1) oxidation state due to lack of d-orbital.

9. (d) Both Statement I and Statement II are true.

10. (a) Dissociation of HI into H_2 and I_2 is kinetically controlled.

11. (a) Among the given compounds, only, one i.e. (iii) is used to dry HCl gas.

12. (d)

13. (c) The correct structure of chloric acid is

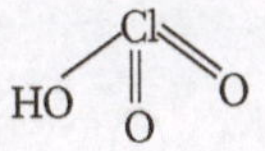

14. (b) Its correct statement is :

OCl^- (hypohalites salt) are used as a bleaching agent.

15. (c) Cl_2O_6 (dimer of ClO_3) is a mixed anhydride of $HClO_3$ and $HClO_4$.

$$Cl_2O_6 + H_2O \longrightarrow HClO_3 + HClO_4$$

Thus, statement (c) is incorrect.

16. (c) The tetrahedral arrangement of perchlorate ion is due to sp^3-hybridisation of the Cl-atom in ClO_4^- ion.

17. (d) Among the given match, (d) is not correct match.

Its correct match is :

Perchloric acid, 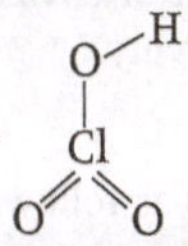 is not a peroxy acid because it does not contain —OOH bond.

18. (b) Among the given match, (b) is not corectly matched with the given reaction.

As, reactivity order (oxidising power) is

$$F > O > Cl > Br > I$$

So, I cannot replaced Br hence the reaction is not feasible according to the given product.

19. (d) $HClO_4$ has Cl in maximum oxidation state.

Thus, is not further oxidised, i.e. least oxidising in nature.

20. (a) The correct order is

$$HOF > HOCl > HOBr > HOI$$

21. (b) Among the given compounds, only four, i.e. (i), (ii), (iii) and (v) are interhalogen compounds, as $BrCl_7$ does not exist.

Step up Practice 6

1. (c) The electronic configuration, i.e. $1s^2 2s^2 2p^6$ represents a noble gas.

2. (d) Among the given elements, only Ti^{4+} has same electronic configuration as of noble gas, i.e. Ar (argon).

3. (d) Among the given compounds, only three, i.e. (ii), (iii) and (iv) have sp^3d-hybridisation.

4. (c) Bartlett had taken $O_2^+[PtF_6]^-$ as a base compound because O_2 and Xe both have almost same ionisation enthalpy. The ionisation enthalpies of noble gases are the highest in their respective periods due to their stable electronic configurations.

5. (d) Xe forms compounds (XeF_2, XeF_4, XeF_6) of variable oxidation states.

6. (a) Thermal stability of hydrates of group 18 elements increases down the group.

7. (c) Isolation and separation of inert gases from air depends upon boiling point.

8. (b) 9. (b)

10. (a) $$\underset{\text{(Radioactive)}}{{}^{226}_{88}Ra} \longrightarrow \underset{(\alpha\text{-particles})}{{}^{4}_{2}He} + {}^{222}_{86}Rn$$

11. (c) $${}^{226}_{88}Ra \longrightarrow {}^{222}_{86}Rn + {}^{b}_{a}X$$

$86 + a = 88$, thus $a = 2$

$222 + b = 226$, thus $b = 4$

Thus, ${}^{b}_{a}X$ is ${}^{4}_{2}He$.

12. (d) Among the given match, (d) is correct match while other are incorrect match with given structure.

Their correct matchings are

- $XeF_2 \longrightarrow$ Linear
- $XeF_4 \longrightarrow$ Square planar
- $XeO_3 \longrightarrow$ Pyramidal

13. (d) Both Statement I and Statement II are true.

14. (a) The forces acting between noble gas atoms are van der Waals' forces.

15. (d) Both Statement I and Statement II are true.

16. (a) The $[XeF]^+$ ions are attached to anion $[AsF_6]^-$ through a linear F-bridge.

$$XeF_2 + MF_5 \longrightarrow [XeF]^+ [MF_6^-] \quad (M = As, Sb, P)$$

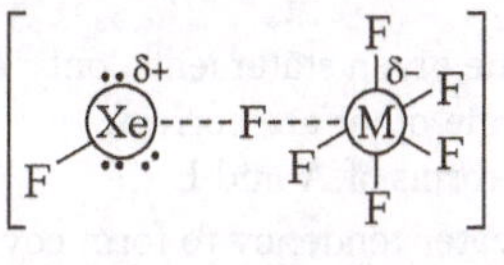

17. (d) Among the given, (d) is incorrect match.

Its correct match is :

$:XeOF_4 \longrightarrow$ 1, non-bonding electron pair on Xe.

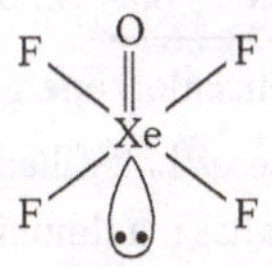

[1, non-bonding electron pair]

Gearing Up for NEET

1. (b) Stability of trivalent cations of group 13 elements decrease down the group and as such the correct order will be

$$Ga^{3+} > In^{3+} > Tl^{3+}$$

2. (a) Structure of $B(OH)_4^-$ is

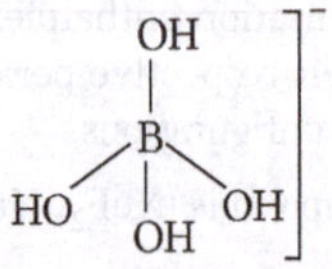

4 bond pairs + 0 lone pair
Hybridisation (B) – sp^3; Geometry– Tetrahedral

3. (c) Washing soda (Na_2CO_3) produces NaOH with water which reacts with aluminium to form soluble sodium meta-aluminate and thus damages the aluminium vessels.

$$Na_2CO_3 + H_2O \longrightarrow 2NaOH + CO_2$$

$$2NaOH + 2Al + 6H_2O \longrightarrow \underset{\text{(Sodium meta-aluminate)}}{2Na[Al(OH)_4]} + 3H_2$$

4. (d) $\underbrace{K_2SO_4 \cdot Al_2(SO_4)_3 \cdot 24H_2O}$
$\downarrow$
$[M_2SO_4 \cdot M'_2(SO_4)_3 \cdot 24H_2O]$

$$2K^+ : 2Al^{3+} : 4SO_4^{2-}$$
$$1 \quad : \quad 1 \quad : \quad 2$$

5. (d) The negative values of $E°$ for Al^{3+}/Al suggest that Al has strong tendency to form $Al^{3+}(aq)$ ions. On the other hand, positive value of $E°$ for Tl^{3+}/Tl suggests that Tl does not have high tendency to form Tl^{3+} ions. Since, Al can form Al^{3+} ions more easily than Tl does to form Tl^{3+} ions. Therefore, Al is more electropositive than Tl.

6. (a) Among the given elements, Boron has lowest atomic number, i.e. 5 and do not have vacant *d*-orbitals. The element, *M* in the complex ion MF_6^{3-} has a coordination nubmer of six. Boron can show maximum coordination number of 4. Thus, B can not form complex of the type MF_6^{3-}.

7. (d) Among the given statements, only A and E are incorrect while other are correct.
The correct forms of A and E are
- Al has greater tendency to form covalent compounds and a little tendency to form ionic compounds.
- Al dissolves in dilute HCl and liberates dihydrogen.

8. (b) B C N O [2nd period]
$\longrightarrow$
Size decreases, Ionisation energy increases
But nitrogen posseses half-filled ($2p^3$) electronic configuration so it has maximum first ionisation energy.

9. (b) Pb_3O_4 is a mixed oxide of Pb : $2PbO \cdot PbO_2$.

$$2PbO \cdot PbO_2 + 4HNO_3 \longrightarrow 2Pb(NO_3)_2 + 2H_2O + PbO_2$$

10. (b) The tendency to form long, open or closed chains by combination of some atoms in themselves is known as catenation.
The catenation is maximum in carbon and decreases down the group.

$$C >> Si > Ge \approx Sn$$

This is due to high bond energy of C—C bonds.
Down the group, size increass and electronegativity decreases, thereby, tendency to show catenation decreases.

11. (a) $:NH_3$ (M = N)

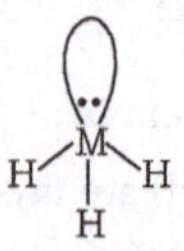

There is a lone pair on central atom resulting in sp^3-hybridised $\ddot{M}H_3$, where $M = a$ group 15 element.

12. (b) $Pb(NO_3)_2 + H_2SO_4 \longrightarrow \underset{\text{White ppt.}}{PbSO_4} + 2HNO_3$
(soluble in $CH_3CO\bar{O}N\overset{+}{H_4}$)

$$\Rightarrow PbSO_4 + 2CH_3COONH_4 \longrightarrow (NH_4)_2SO_4 + (CH_3COO)_2Pb$$

13. (a) The maximum number of covalent bonds formed by N and P are 3, 5 respectively.

14. (d)

15. (a) The reaction proceeds as follow

$$MnO_2 + 4HCl \longrightarrow MnCl_2 + \underset{\text{(Greenish yellow gas)}}{Cl_2 \uparrow} + 2H_2O$$

$$\overset{(-3)}{NH_3} + 3Cl_2 \longrightarrow \overset{(+3)}{NCl_3} + 3HCl$$

Thus, the oxidation state of nitrogen changes from −3 to +3.

16. (c) The structure of dithionic acid is

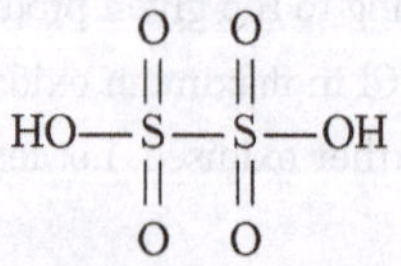

It has —S—S— linkage among the given oxoacid.

17. (a) $SO_2(OH)_2 + PCl_5 \longrightarrow SO_2Cl_2 + 2HCl + POCl_3$
Formation of SO_2Cl_2 indicates that there are two —OH groups in H_2SO_4.

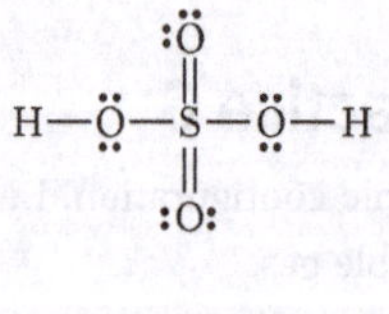

18. (*c*) Structure of H_3PO_4 is

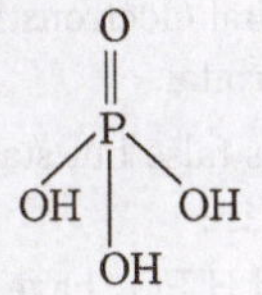

It has 3 OH groups, i.e. has three ionisable H-atoms and hence forms three series of salts. These three possible series of salts are as follows,

$$NaH_2PO_4, Na_2HPO_4 \text{ and } Na_3PO_4$$

19. (*a*) It is analytical qualitative test of phosphate ion.

$$\underset{\text{(Orthophosphate)}}{PO_4^{3-}} \xrightarrow{(NH_4)_2MoO_4 + HNO_3} \underset{\text{Yellow ppt.}}{\underline{(NH_4)_3PO_4 \cdot 12MoO_3}}$$

$$PO_4^{3-} \xrightarrow{AgNO_3} \underset{\text{Reddish yellow ppt.}}{Ag_3PO_4}$$

20. (*b*)

21. (*c*) The reaction proceeds as follows,

$$2H_2S + SO_2 \xrightarrow{\Delta} \underset{\text{(Sulphur)}}{3S} + \underset{\text{(Water)}}{2H_2O}$$

22. (*d*) Among the given elements, polonium (Po) is radioactive in nature.

23. (*b*)

24. (*d*) Among the given chalcogens, Se and Te react with H_2 with great difficulty.

Since, Te has the highest electrical resistance than Se. So, the chalcogens is tellurium.

25. (*b*) Among the given statements, only A, B and C are correct while the other statements D and E are incorrect.

Their correct forms are :

- Preferably SO_2 is a reducing while TeO_2 is an oxidising agent.
- All hexafluorides are gaseous in nature, at 298 K, 1 atm.

26. (*c*) Carbon (C) is the element oxidised by conc. H_2SO_4 to give two gaseous products, i.e. CO_2 and SO_2.

The reaction proceeds as follows,

$$C(s) + 2H_2SO_4(aq) \longrightarrow 2H_2O(l) + CO_2(g) + 2SO_2(g)$$

27. (*d*)

28. (*a*) The decreasing order of bond dissociation energy is $HF > HCl > HBr > HI$.

29. (*b*) Among group-16 elements, oxygen does not show +4 oxidation state due to lack of *d*-orbitals.

30. (*d*) Its correct statement is :

Bromine and iodine are only sparingly soluble in water but soluble in various organic solvents such as chloroform, CCl_4 and carbon disulphide etc.

31. (*a*) The correct acid strength order is

$HClO_4 > HNO_3 > HCl$.

32. (*a*) As F_2 is the strongest oxidising agent, chemical oxidation of a F^- salt or HF into F_2 is not possible.

33. (*a*) If acid is strong, conjugate base is weak.

Base	ClO_4^-	ClO_3^-	ClO_2^-	ClO^-
Acid	$HClO_4$	$HClO_3$	$HClO_2$	HClO
Oxidation number of halogen	+7	+5	+3	+1

Acidic strength : Maximum ⟵ ⟶ Basic strength : Maximum

More is the oxidation number of Cl more will be the acidity (when, basicity is constant). Hence, $HClO_4$ is more acidic.

Thus, ClO_4^- is the weakest (Bronsted) base.

34. (*c*) Greater the SRP value of species, higher will be its oxidising power of the oxidised form.

Thus, the correct order is $BrO_4^- > IO_4^- > ClO_4^-$

Species	E°_{cell} $(XO_4^-/?)$
ClO_4^-	1.19V
IO_4^-	1.65V
BrO_4^-	1.74V

Here, SRP = standard reduction potential.

Thus, the correct order is $BrO_4^- > IO_4^- > ClO_4^-$.

35. (*d*) Among the given statements, only (d) is incorrect while other are correct. Its correct form is :

The noble gases have large positive value of electron gain enthalpy.

36. (*a*) Inert atmosphere for welding of metal is obtained by using Ar, He.

37. (*a*) Clathrates compounds are not formed by He, Ne.

38. (*c*) Among the given statements, only B, C and E are correct while the other statements A and D are incorrect.

Their correct forms are :

- XeF_2, XeF_4 and XeF_6 are colourless crystalline solids and sublime readily at 298 K.
- Hydrolysis of XeF_4 and XeF_6 with water gives finally XeO_3.

39. (*a*) The reaction proceeds as follows,

$$\underset{+6}{HXeO_4^-} + 2OH^- \longrightarrow \underset{+8}{XeO_6^{4-}} + \underset{0}{Xe} + H_2O + O_2$$

Thus, XeO_6^{4-} disproportionates to XeO_6^{4-} (by oxidation) and Xe (by reduction).

40. (c)

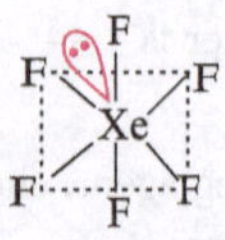

XeF_6
Distorted octahedral
[Octa bond pairs, 1 lone pair]

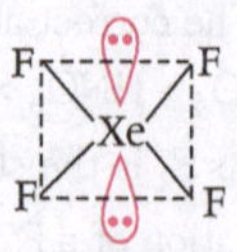

XeF_4
Square planar
[4 bond pairs, 2 lone pairs]

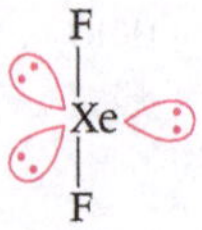

XeF_2
Linear
[2 bond pairs, 3 lone pair]

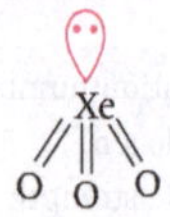

XeO_3
Pyramidal
[3 bond pairs, 1 lone pair]

41. (a) The correct increasing order of fluorides is

$$XeF_6 < XeF_4 < XeF_2.$$

Due to the presence of 3 lone pairs and two F atoms ($-I$ effect) in XeF_2 has maximum basic character than XeF_4.

42. (a) I. XeF_6 form complex with NaF.

Thus, I is true.

II. PCl_5 in the solid state exists as $[PCl_4]^+$ and $[PCl_6]^-$.

Thus, II is also true.

III. $[Al(H_2O)_6]^{3+}$ is a proton donor.

Thus, III is also true.

43. (a) Statement (a) is incorrect regarding helium.

Helium is used for the purpose of cooling down in the super conducting magnet.

44. (d) A is false but R is true.

The correct form of A is :

If aluminium atoms replace a few silicon atoms in three dimensional network of silicon dioxide, then the overall structure will acquire a negative charge.

45. (a) Both A and R are true and R is the correct explanation of A.

46. (a) Both A and R are true and R is the correct explanation of A.

47. (d) A is false but R is true.

The correct form of A is :

The pentavalent oxide (E_2O_5) is more acidic than trivalent oxide (E_2O_3) of group 15 elements.

48. (a) Both A and R are true and R is the correct explanation of A.

49. (c) A is true but R is false. The correct form of R is : MnO_2 oxidises HCl to chlorine gas which is greenish yellow.

50. (d) Both Statement I and Statement II are true.

51. (c) Statement I is false but Statement II is true. The correct form of Statement I is :

PbF_2 is more stable than PbF_4 as effective nuclear charge on *s*-orbital electrons is higher due to poor shielding of *d*-orbital.

52. (c) Statement I is false but statement II is true.

Its correct form is :

Both H_3PO_3 and H_3PO_4 have the same number of hydrogen atoms but H_3PO_4 is a tribasic acid and H_3PO_3 is a dibasic acid.

53. (c) Statement I is false but Statement II is true.

Its correct form is :

$S_3O_6^{2-}$ (trithionate) has S—S bond.

Its structure is shown as

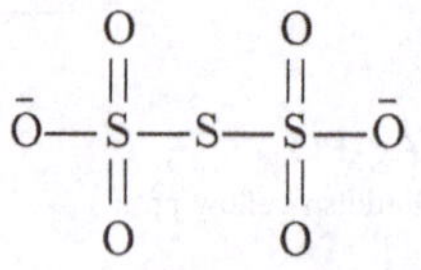

54. (b) Statement I is true but Statement II is false.

Its correct form is :

HF is a dibasic acid due to hydrogen bonding.

55. (b) Statement I is true but Statement II is false.

Its correct form is :

The bond dissociation energy order is

$$Cl_2 > Br_2 > F_2 > I_2.$$

56. (d) Both Statement I and Statement II are true.

57. (b) Among the given statements only C and E are correct, while statements A, B and D are incorrect. The correct form of these statements are :

- Cyclic silicates having three Si-atoms ($Si_3O_9^{6-}$) contains three Si—O—Si linkage.
- The basic structural unit of silicates is SiO_4^{4-}.
- General formula of double chain silicate is $(Si_4O_{11})_n^{6n-}$.

58. (a) Among the given statements, only B and E are incorrect while other are correct. Their correct form are

- Chlorine water on standing loses its yellow colour due to the formation of HCl and HOCl.
- The interhalogen compounds are all covalent molecules and are diamagnetic in nature.

59. (d) Among the given statements, only A, B and C are correct while the other statements are incorrect.

Their correct form are

- They have very low melting and boiling points.
- XeO_3 is a colourless explosive solid and has a pyramidal molecular structure.

60. (b) Among the given elements, only three, i.e. (ii), (iv) and (v) have pseudo noble gas configuration in their penultimate shell because they have 18 electrons in their penultimate shells.

61. (*a*) Among the given compounds, only two, i.e. (i) and (vi) are formed when diborane is instantly hydrolyzed by water.

The reaction proceeds as follows

$$B_2H_6(g) + 6H_2O(l) \longrightarrow 2H_3BO_3(aq) + 6H_2(g)$$

62. (*c*) Among the given compounds, only one, i.e. (i) have —P—O—P— linkage in their structure.

63. (*b*) Among the given compounds, only three, i.e. (i), (ii) and (iii) are tetrabasic compounds.

64. (*d*) Among the given oxoacid of sulphur, only two, i.e. (ii) and (iv) do not contain bond between sulphur atoms.

65. (*d*) Among the given compounds, only one, i.e. (ii) is the anhydride of $HClO_4$.

$$2HClO_4 \longrightarrow H_2O + Cl_2O_7$$

66. (*b*) Among the given compounds, only one, i.e. (ii) can not be stored in glass vessels because it reacts with SiO_2 of the glass to give highly explosive XeO_3.

67. (*a*) Among the given compounds, only four, i.e. (i), (ii), (iv) and (vi) have one lone pair of electrons on Xe atom.

- $XeO_2F_2 \rightarrow$ 1 lone pair
- $XeF_6 \rightarrow$ 1 lone pair
- $:XeF_2 \rightarrow$ 3 lone pairs
- $:XeO_3 \rightarrow$ 1 lone pair
- $:XeF_4 \rightarrow$ 2 lone pairs
- $XeOF_4 \rightarrow$ 1 lone pair
- $:XeO_2 \rightarrow$ 2 lone pairs

68. (*c*) The correct match is A-2, B-4, C-1, D-3.

69. (*a*) The correct match is A-3, B-4, C-2, D-1.

70. (*b*) The correct match is A-3, B-4, C-1, D-2.

71. (*a*) The correct match is A-3, B-1, C-2, D-4.

72. (*a*) The correct match is A-4, B-3, C-2, D-1.

73. (*a*) The correct match is A-1, B-4, C-2, D-3.

74. (*a*) The correct match is A-4, B-3, C-1, D-2.

75. (*a*) The correct match is A-3, B-1, C-2, D-4.

76. (*a*) The correct match is A-2, B-1, C-4, D-3.

Final Check Through PYQs

1. (*b*) Among the given options, BF_3 molecule acts as a Lewis acid.

As it is an electron deficient molecule and have the tendency to accept the electron pair.

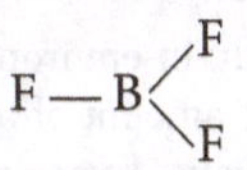

BF_3 has six electrons around B that means its octet is not complete.

2. (*c*) Among the given relation TlI > TlI_3 is correct. As in group 13 element + 1 oxidation state becomes more and more stable as we go down the group, i.e. Al < Ga < In < Tl. This is because of the presence of intervening *d* and *f*-orbitals which do not shield the nucleus efficiently.

Consequently effective nuclear charge increases, that holds the *ns*-electrons tightly, so that they do not participate in bonding (inert pair effect). Thus, in Tl (+ 1) oxidation state is more predominant whereas the +3 is strongly oxidising nature.

3. (*c*) The incorrect statement about diborane is option (c) because in diborane boron has sp^3-hybridisation and it is non-planar.

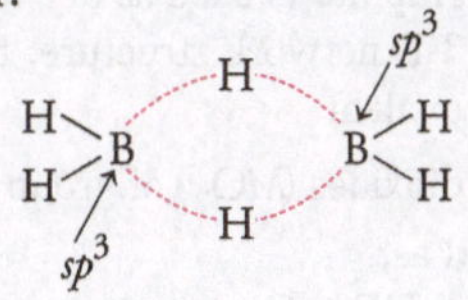

4. (*d*) In BF_3, hybridisation is sp^2 and number of electrons are 6 for the central atom (B).

5. (*d*) A-(3) Mixture of CO and H_2 gases is known as water gas or synthesis gas.

B-(1) Temporary hardness of water is due to the presence of bicarbonates of calcium and magnesium.

C-(2) Diborane (B_2H_6) is an electron deficient hydride.

D-(4) H_2O_2 is non-planar molecule having open book like structure.

6. (*b*) $AlCl_3 \xrightarrow{\text{Acidified } aq. \text{ sol.}} \underset{sp^3d^2}{[Al(H_2O)_6]^{3+}}$

7. (*d*) Boron belongs to 2nd period and it does not have vacant *d*-orbitals. Hence, it is unable to expand its valency to form MF_6^{3-}.

8. (*c*) Boric acid can be considered as an acid because its molecule accepts OH^- from water, releasing proton.

$$\underset{\text{Acid}}{H_3BO_3} + \underset{\text{Base}}{2H_2O} \rightleftharpoons \underset{\text{Conjugate base}}{[B(OH)_4]^-} + \underset{\text{Conjugate acid}}{H_3O^+}$$

Remember In the given options of the question, (a), (b) and (c) are correct as all of these sentences have more or less similar meaning but here (c) option is the most appropriate one as it gives complete explanation of the fact that how boric acid can be combined with water.

9. (*b*) AlF_3 forms $K_3[AlF_6]$ when dissolved in HF in the presence of KF as shown below:

$$AlF_3 + 3KF \xrightarrow{HF} K_3[AlF_6]$$

10. (*b*) Al < Ga < In < Tl

This is due to inert pair effect or tendency of ns^2electrons which do not participate in bond formation. This tendency of + 3 oxidation state decreases on moving down the group while the stability of + 1 oxidation state increases.

11. (*b*) The correct match is A-3, B-1, C-4, D-2.

12. (*b*) The correct statement is option (b). It is because in diamond, each carbon is bonded with four other carbon atoms. So, hybridisation of carbon atom is sp^3. In graphite each carbon atom is bonded with three other carbon atoms.

So, hybridisation of carbon atom in graphite is sp^2.

Hence, diamond is sp^3-hybridised and graphite is sp^2-hybridised. Rest all other options are incorrect. It is because only graphite is used as dry lubricants. Diamond has 3-D network structure. Both diamond and graphite are covalent.

13. (*a*) Nature of dioxides (MO_2) of group 14 elements can be represented as,

CO_2 SiO_2 GeO_2 SnO_2 PbO_2

Acidic oxides (CO_2, SiO_2) | Amphoteric oxides (GeO_2, SnO_2, PbO_2)

Hence, option (a) is correct.

14. (*c*) 3 and 4 are correct statements, whereas 1 and 2 are incorrect.

1. Dry ice or $CO_2(s)$ [not $CO_2(g)$] is used as refrigerant for ice-cream and frozen food.
2. C_{60} contains 20 hexagones (not 12) and 12 pentagones (not 20).
3. ZSM-5, a type of zeolite, is used to convert alcohols directly into gasoline. It is true.
4. CO is a colourless and odourless gas. It is true.

15. (*b*) The carboxyhaemoglobin (haemoglobin bound to CO), is about 300 times more stable than oxyhaemoglobin.

16. (*d*) Silicones are used in cosmetic surgery.

17. (*d*) All the tetrahalides of group 14 elements are covalent in nature and sp^3-hybridised with tetrahedral geometry. Exceptions are SnF_4 and PbF_4 which are ionic in nature.

Thus, statement (d) is incorrect while the remaining statements are correct.

18. (*d*) Due to inert pair effect, Pb(II) is more stable than Pb(IV) and Sn (IV) is more stable than Sn(II).

So, P(IV) is easily reduced to Pb(II) and acts as an oxidising agent whereas Sn(II) is easily oxidised to Sn(IV) and acts as reducing agent.

19. (*c*) +1 oxidaiton state of P-atom and two P—H bonds found in phosphorus acids have reducing properties. Thus, reducing property is directly proportional to number of P—H bonds.

The structures of given oxoacids of phosphorus are as follows

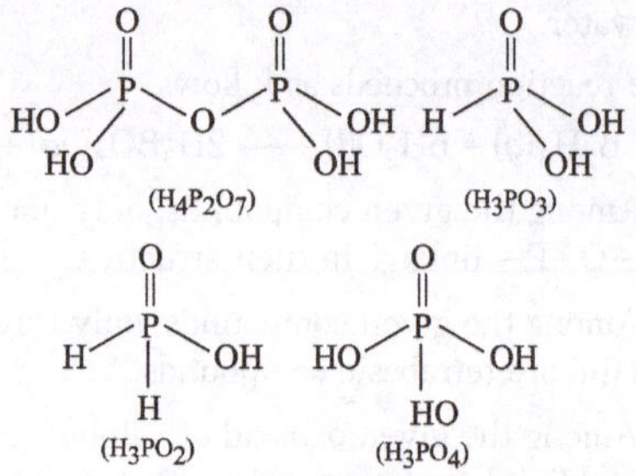

H_3PO_2 contains 2P—H bonds which is maximum among the given options. Thus, H_3PO_2 has strongest reducing property.

20. (*c*) In gaseous and liquid phases, PCl_5 has a trigonal bipyramidal structure with sp^3d-hybridisation (P).

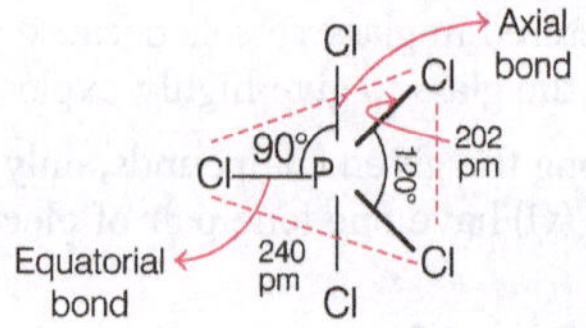

Due to presence of longer and weaker axial bonds, PCl_5 is a reactive molecule. Hence, statement in option (c) is incorrect.

21. (*c*) Let the oxidation state of nitrogen in each of the given N-compounds be *x*.

(i) $HNO_3 : +1 + x + 3(-2) = 0$

$x = +5$

$\therefore$ Oxidation state of N in HNO_3 is +5.

(ii) $NO : x + 1(-2) = 0$

$x = +2$

$\therefore$ Oxidation state of N in NO is +2.

(iii) $NH_4Cl : x + 4(+1) + 1(-1) = 0$

$x = -3$

$\therefore$ Oxidation state of N in NH_4Cl is −3 .

(iv) $N_2 : x = 0$

[$\because N_2$ is present in elemental state]

$\therefore$ Oxidation state of N in N_2 is 0.

Thus, the correct decreasing order of oxidation states of given N compounds will be

$$\overset{+5}{H N O_3} > \overset{+2}{NO} > \overset{0}{N_2} > \overset{-3}{NH_4Cl}$$

22. (*a*) Nitrous oxide (N_2O), nitrogen dioxide (NO_2) and nitric oxide (NO) are the common pollutant introduced into the atmosphere.

N_2O occurs naturally in environment. NO and NO_2 causes considerable amount of air pollution. They are given off in car exhaust fumes and when fossil fuels are burnt as well as produced during thunderstroms. In each case NO is formed first and then NO_2.

23. (*a*) Phosphinic acid

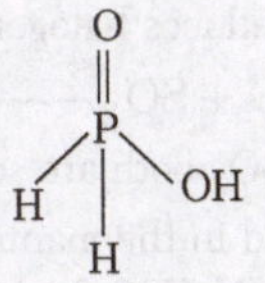

Phosphonic acid

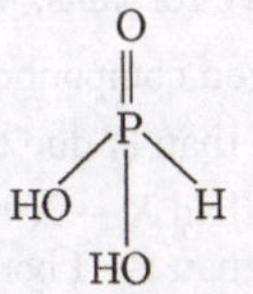

Due to the presence of one replaceable proton in phosphinic acid, it is monoprotic acid and due to presence of two replaceable protons in phosphonic acid, it is diprotic acid.

24. (*c*) PH_5 does not exist due to

(i) axial P—H bond formation (σ-bond) by $3d_z^{'}2$ (P) and 1*s*(H) is not possible (ii) very less electronegativity difference between P and H. Hydrogen is slightly more electronegative than phosphorus, thus could not hold significantly the sharing electrons. On the other hand, $BiCl_5$ does not exist due to inert pair effect, Bi(*v*) is unstale.

⇒ On moving down the group, +5 oxidation state becomes less stable while +3 oxidation state becomes more stable.

⇒ In SO_2, *p*π(*o*)-*d*π(*s*) and *p*π(*o*)-*p*π(*s*) both types of bonds are present.

⇒

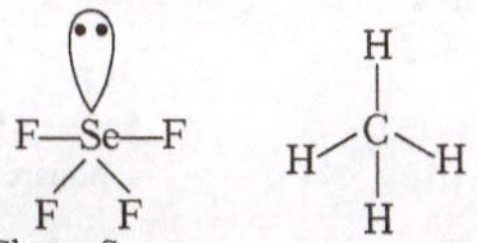

Shape-*See-saw*

Thus, SeF_4 and CH_4 do not have same shape.

⇒ IF_2^+ has bent geometry.

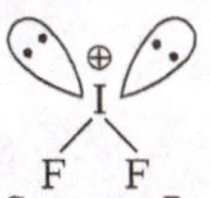

Geometry-Bent

Thus, option (c) is inccorrect statement.

25. (*d*) Po does not show −2 oxidation state due to its metallic nature.

26. (*a*) Both Statement I and Statement II are true.

Boiling point order

$$H_2O > H_2Te > H_2Se > H_2S$$

Water has maximum boiling point due to presence of high extent of H-bonding even though its molecular mass is minimum among these hydrides.

27. (*a*) The correct match is A-3, B-4, C-1, D-2.

Structure of given oxoacids of sulphur are as follows

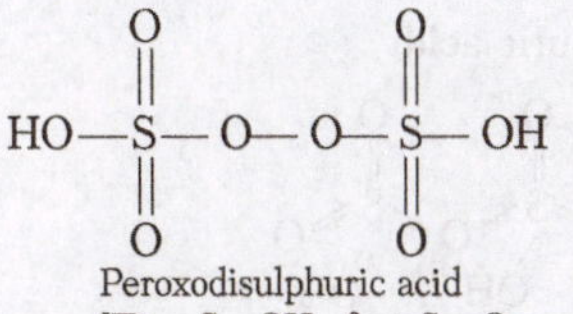

Peroxodisulphuric acid [Two, S—OH, four S=O bonds one S—O—O—S bond]

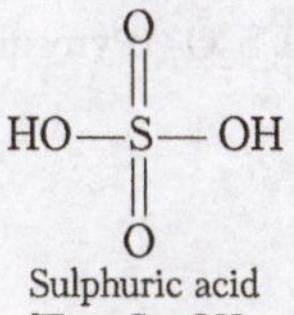

Sulphuric acid [Two, S—OH, two S=O bonds]

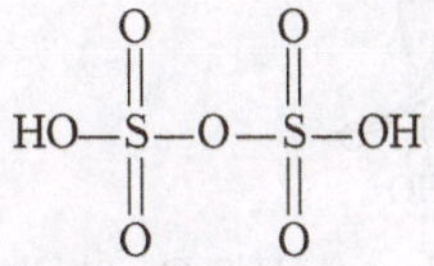

Pyrosulphuric acid [Two, S—OH, four, S=O bond, one S—O—S bond]

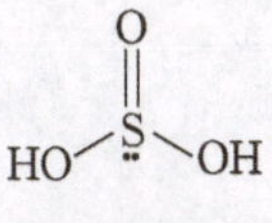

Sulphurous acid [Two, S—OH, one S=O bonds]

28. (*a*) **Statement I** The correct order of boiling points of group 16th hydride is $H_2S < H_2Se < H_2Te < H_2O$

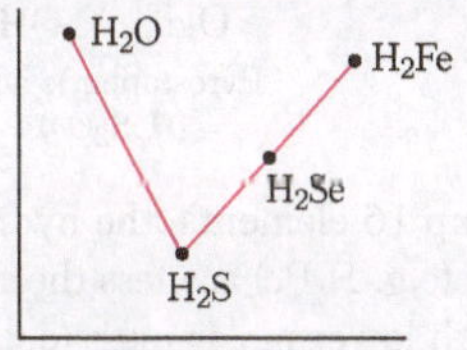

Statement II Boiling point increases with increase in molar mass but H_2O has a higher boiling point due to presence of hydrogen bond. Hence, both Statement I and Statement II are false.

So, option (a) is correct.

29. (*b*) HF < HCl < HBr < HI; Down the group, size of atom increases, bond length increases and bond enthalpy decreases. So, acidic strength increases.

∴ The given sequence is correct.

$H_2O > H_2S > H_2Se > H_2Te$, pK_a is inversely proportional to acidic strength. So, pK_a decreases.

∴ The given sequence is incorrect.

$NH_3 < PH_3 < AsH_3 < SbH_3$; Acidic character increases down the group,

∴ The given sequence is correct.

$CO_2 < SiO_2 < SnO_2 < PbO_2$; On moving down the group oxidising power increases.

∴ The given sequence is correct.

30. (*b*) The structure of given sulphur oxoacids are

- H_2SO_4 (Sulphuric acid) ⇒

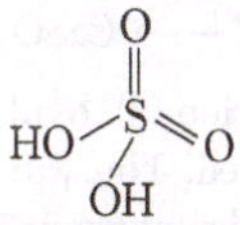

- $H_2S_2O_8$ (Peroxodisulphuric acid) ⇒

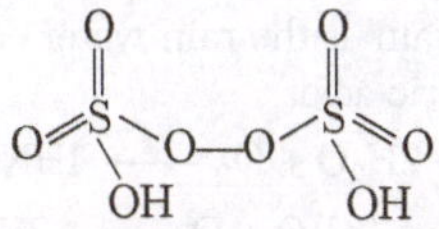

Hints and Solutions

- $H_2S_2O_7$ (Pyrosulphuric acid)

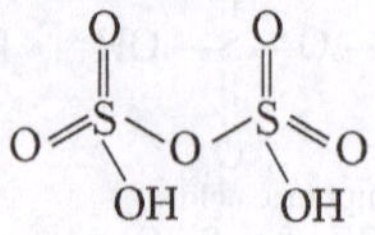

- H_2SO_3 (Sulphurous acid) ⇒

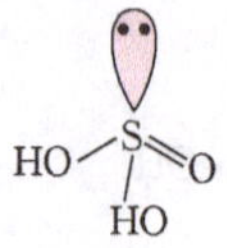

31. (*a*) The correct formula of oleum is $H_2S_2O_7$ which is also known as pyrosulphuric acid.

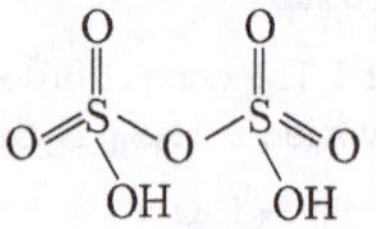

Pyrosulphuric acid ($H_2S_2O_7$)

32. (*b*) For group 16 elements, the hydrides with higher molar mass (e.g. H_2Po) are less thermally stable than hydride with lower molar mass (e.g. H_2O). This is due to the increase in size of central atom, which results to weakening of *M*—H bond due to increased bond length.

Thus, the correct order of thermal stability for H_2E (E = O, S, Se, Te and Po) is as follows

$$H_2Po < H_2Te < H_2Se < H_2S < H_2O$$

33. (*b*) $S_4O_6^{2-}$ and $S_2O_3^{2-}$ have S–S bond.

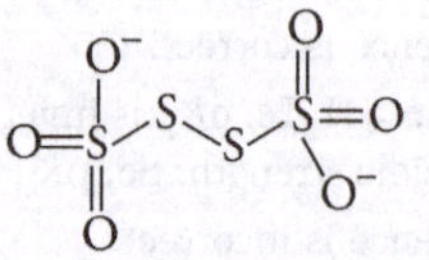

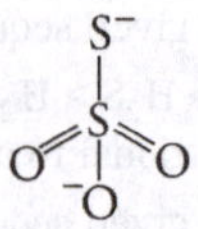

1

($S_4O_6^{2-}$) (Tetrathionate) Thiosulphate ion ($S_2O_3^{2-}$)

34. (*d*) (a) $\overset{0}{Cu} + 2H_2SO_4 \longrightarrow \overset{+2}{Cu}SO_4 + SO_2 + 2H_2O$

(b) $3\overset{0}{S} + 2H_2SO_4 \longrightarrow 3\,\overset{+4}{S}O_2 + 2H_2O$

(c) $\overset{0}{C} + H_2SO_4 \longrightarrow \overset{+4}{C}O_2 + 2SO_2 + 2H_2O$

(d) $\overset{+2}{Ca}\overset{-1}{F_2} + H_2SO_4 \longrightarrow \overset{+2}{Ca}SO_4 + 2\,H\overset{-1}{F}$

In reaction of option (d), oxidation number of elements remains unchanged. Thus, in this reaction, H_2SO_4 does not act as an oxidising agent.

35. (*d*) Nitrogen dioxide and sulphur dioxide forms acid rain. 'Acid rain' is the rain water containing sulphuric acid and nitric acid.

(a) $NO_2 + 2H_2O + O_2 \longrightarrow 4HNO_3$

$2SO_2 + 2H_2O + O_2 \longrightarrow 2H_2SO_4$

(b) NO_2 and SO_2 act as a good reducing agent. e.g. SO_2 reduces halogens to halogen acid.

$$Cl_2 + 2H_2O + SO_2 \longrightarrow 2HCl + H_2SO_4$$

(c) NO_2 and SO_2 both are soluble in water.

(d) SO_2 is used in the manufacture of sodium bisulphite ($NaHSO_3$) which is used as a preservative for jams, jellies and squashes.

36. (*a*) In interhalogen compounds of group 17th(XY_n), ICl is more reactive than I_2 due to its polarity. Also, X—Y bond is weaker than X—X bond except F_2. So I— Cl bond is weaker than I—I bond.

Hence, both A and R are true and R is the correct explanation of A.

37. (*d*) The order of acidic strength is

$$HF << HCl << HBr << HI$$

As we move down the group, the size of atom increases.

Thus, the bond length also increases and bond enthalpy decreases.

So, it becomes easier to break H–X bond on moving down the group. This results the increase in the acidic strength.

So, both Statement I and Statement II are true.

38. (*d*)

(A) $:\ddot{X}eF_2$ (B) $:\ddot{X}eF_4$

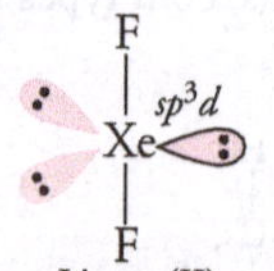

Linear (II)

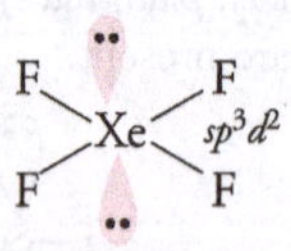

Square planar (I)

(C) $\ddot{X}eO_3$ (D) $\ddot{X}eOF_4$

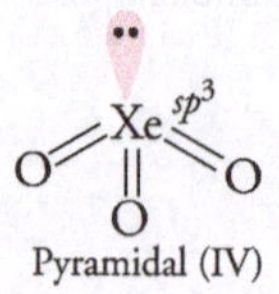

Pyramidal (IV)

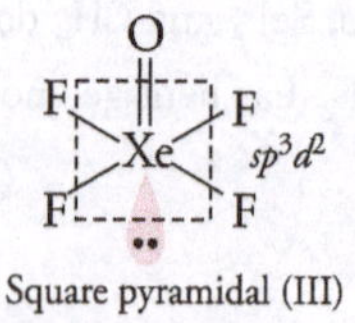

Square pyramidal (III)

Hence, option (d) is correct match.

39. (*d*) The correct structure of tribromooctaoxide is

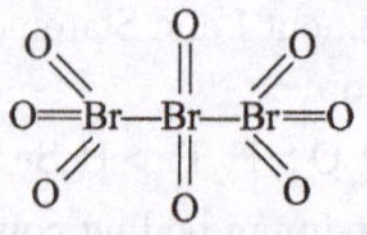

In this compound, Br exhibits variable oxidation states. The oxidation state of Br from left to right are + 6, + 4 and + 6, respectively.

40. (*a*) Fluorine is the most electronegative element and cannot exhibit any positive oxidation state. Other

halogens have d-orbitals and therefore, can expand their octets and show +1, +3, +5 and +7 oxidation states. Thus, option (a) is incorrect.

41. (*b*) The central atom Cl has seven electrons in the valence shell. Three of these will form electron pair bonds with three fluorine atoms leaving behind two *lp* of electrons.

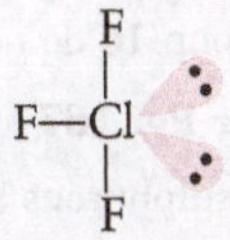

Thus, there are three bond pairs and two lone pairs of electrons.

42. (*c*) Two different halogens may react to form interhalogen compounds are

XX' (ClF, BrF, BrCl, IF, ICl) Linear

XX'_3 (ClF_3, BrF_3, IF_3, ICl_3) T-shaped

XX'_5 (ClF_5, $BrCl_5$, IF_5) Square-pyramidal

XX'_7 (IF_7) Pentagonal bipyramidal

43. (*c*) Isoelectronic species have equal number of valence electrons. Both IBr_2^- and XeF_2 are linear and number of valence electrons present in both the species is same, i.e. they are also isoelectronic.

S. No.	Compounds	Number of valence electrons	Geometry
1.	$BeCl_2$	2 + 14 = 16	Linear
2.	XeF_2	8 + 14 = 22	Linear
3.	TeI_2	6 + 14 = 20	Bent or V-shape
4.	IBr_2^-	7 + 14 + 1 = 22	Linear
5.	IF_3	7 + 21 = 28	T-shape

44. (*a*) As the oxidation state of halogen increases, (i.e. Cl, in this case) acidity (all are being monobasic acids) of oxyacids increases.

HClO : Oxidation state of Cl = +1

$HClO_2$: Oxidation state of Cl = +3

$HClO_3$: Oxidation state of Cl = +5

$HClO_4$: Oxidation state of Cl = +7

Therefore, the correct order of acidity would be

$$HClO < HClO_2 < HClO_3 < HClO_4$$

45. (*a*) As the size increases, bond dissociation enthalpy becomes lower.

Also, as the size of atoms get smaller, ion pairs on the two atoms get close enough together to experience repulsion in case of F_2, this repulsion is larger and bond becomes weaker.

Hence, the correct order is $Cl_2 > Br_2 > F_2 > I_2$.

46. (*d*) The correct match is A-1, B-3, C-4, D-2

The structure of the xenon compounds are represented below.

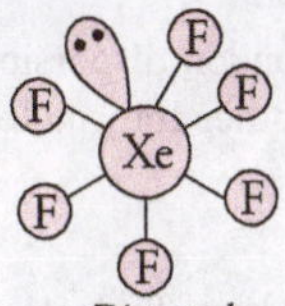

Distorted octahedral (XeF_6)

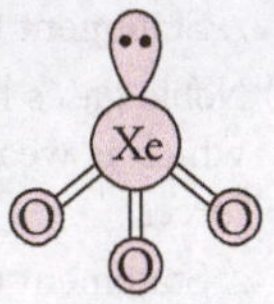

Pyramidal (XeO_3)

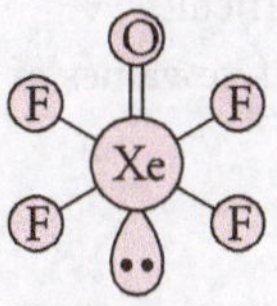

Square pyramidal ($XeOF_4$)

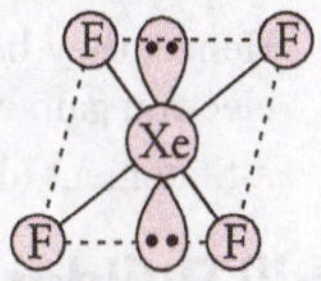

Square planar (:XeF_4)

47. (*d*)

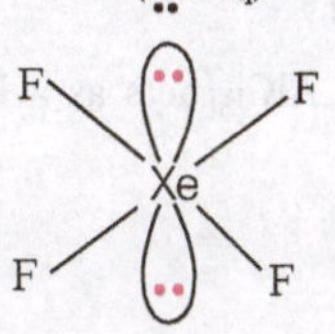

Geometry-square planar

Hybridisation — sp^3d^2(Xe)

Thus, option (a) is correct.

48. (*b*) Since, there is a strong hydrogen bonding between HF molecules, bp of HF is highest here.

$$HF > HI > HBr > HI$$

49. (*d*)

(a) Cl_2O_7 is an anhydride of perchloric acid

$$2HClO_4 \xrightarrow[-H_2O]{\Delta} Cl_2O_7$$

(b) Shape of O_3 molecule is bent.

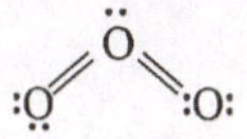

(c) Number of electrons in ONF = 24

Number of electrons in NO_2 = 24

∴ ONF and NO_2 both are isoelectronic.

(d) OF_2 is a fluoride of oxygen because electronegativity of fluorine is more than that of oxygen.

OF_2 = Oxygen difluoride

50. (*b*)

(a) Noble gases or inert gases are sparingly soluble in water as they are non-polar in nature. For solubility the thumb rule is "Like dissolves like".

∴ Statement (a) is correct.

(b) Nobles gases have weak interatomic forces (van der Waals' forces). So, they have low melting and boiling points.

∴ Statement (b) is incorrect.

(c) Noble gases have weak London dispersion forces which is weaker than all other intermolecular forces.

∴ Statement (c) is correct.

(d) The last shell of noble gas have 8 electrons. They have stable electronic configuration. So, addition of an electron is difficult.

Hence, they have large positive values of electron gain enthalpy.

∴ Statement (d) is correct.

Skill Builder

- **Sol. of Skill Builder Pg. 150**

(*c*) Among the given options, $AlCl_3$ acts as a Lewis acid.

- **Sol. of Skill Builder Pg. 155**

(*b*) Among the given oxide, PbO_2 is amphoteric in nature.

- **Sol. of Skill Builder Pg. 165**

(*c*) Oxygen mainly exhibit −2 oxidation state (except in OF_2). However, in the case of peroxides, the oxidation number corresponding to oxygen is −1 while other elements of group-16 do not show −1 oxidation state.

- **Sol. of Skill Builder Pg. 167**

(*b*) The structure of sulphurous acid is

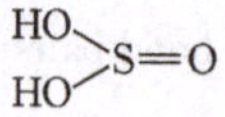

Thus, among the given oxoacids, sulphurous acid contain one S=O bond.

- **Sol. of Skill Builder Pg. 174**

(*d*) The correct structure of chlorous acid is

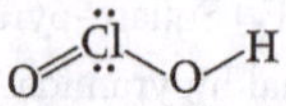

For deeper insight
Scan the QR Code

Chapter 5

The *d*- and *f*-Block Elements

Learning Objectives

Module-I

- Transition Elements (*d*-Block)
- Position in Periodic Table
- Electronic Configurations
- General Properties of Transition Elements (*d*-Block)

Module-II

- Oxides and Oxoanion of Metals
- Potassium Dichromate
- Potassium Permanganate

Module-III

- Inner Transition Elements (*f*-Block)
- Electronic Configuration of Lanthanoids
- General Characteristics of Lanthanoids
- Electronic Configuration of Actinoids
- General Characteristics of Actinoids
- Comparison in Lanthanoids and Actinoids
- Some Applications of *d*- and *f*-block Elements

Chapter Overview with *NEET Connection*

This chapter is the foundation stone towards advanced inorganic chemistry. Without gripping this chapter, it will be difficult to learn and understand the chapter like coordination compounds.

Special format questions can be easily framed on the following topics of this chapter

- Electronic configurations of *d*- and *f*-block
- Ionisation potential of *d*-block
- Important compounds of *d*-block
- Lanthanide contraction

For better understanding of this chapter a grip over general properties of periodic table and concept of oxidation-reduction is required.

Introduction

The elements positioned between *s*-block (group 1 and 2) and *p*-block (group 13-18) elements are classified as *d*-block and *f*-block elements. The *d*-block of the periodic table contain the elements of the group 3-12 and are also called **transition metals.**

The *f*-block elements are present in group 3 (periods 6 and 7) only and are also called **inner-transition elements.** The *f*-block elements are further classified as **lanthanoides** (lying in 6th period) and **actinoides** (lying in 7th period).

In this chapter, we will study about the general characteristics of transition elements with special emphasis on the trends of 3*d* transition metals.

Module 1

The Transition Elements (*d*-Block)

- Transition Elements (*d*-Block)
- Position in the Periodic Table
- Electronic Configurations
- General Properties of the Transition Elements (*d*-Block)

Transition Elements (*d*-Block)

These are the elements which have incomplete filled $(n-1)$ *d*-subshells either in neutral atom or in their ions. The transition metals typically have incompletely filled $(n-1)$ *d*-subshells or readily give rise to ions with incompletely filled $(n-1)$ *d*-subshells.

The group 12 (II B) metals Zn, Cd and Hg do not have this characteristic electronic configuration. They have completely filled $(n-1)$ *d*-orbitals hence, are regarded as pseudo transition metals.

Mentor's TIP

In *d*-block elements, the electrons are added in the penultimate shell, expanding it from 8 to 18 electrons while in *s*-and *p*-block the electrons are added to the outermost shell of the atoms.

Position in the Periodic Table

The *d*-block occupies the large middle section of the periodic table flanked between *s*- and *p*-block in the periodic table. The *d*-orbitals of the penultimate energy level of atoms receive electrons giving rise to four rows of the transition metals, i.e. 3*d*, 4*d*, 5*d* and 6*d*.

Electronic Configurations

The general electronic configuration of outer orbitals of *d*-block elements is $(n-1)d^{1-10}ns^{0-2}$.

In 3*d* transition series, Cr and Cu show anomalous configuration because of half-filled configuration in Cr and completely filled configuration in Cu which are more stable. Their expected and observed electronic configurations are given below.

	Expected configuration	Observed configuration
Cr	[Ar] $3d^4 4s^2$	[Ar] $3d^5 4s^1$
Cu	[Ar] $3d^9 4s^2$	[Ar] $3d^{10} 4s^1$

The transition elements are classified into different series. These series with elements and their outer shell electronic configurations (ground state) are discussed in table given below.

Transition Elements, at a Glance

Series name	Group-3	Group-4	Group-5	Group-6	Group-7	Group-8	Group-9	Group-10	Group-11	Group-12
	(III B)	(IV B)	(V B)	(VI B)	(VII B)	VIII B			(I B)	(II B)
3*d*-series	Sc-21 ($3d^1 4s^2$)	Ti-22 ($3d^2 4s^2$)	V-23 ($3d^3 4s^2$)	Cr-24 ($3d^5 4s^1$)	Mn-25 ($3d^5 4s^2$)	Fe-26 ($3d^6 4s^2$)	Co-27 ($3d^7 4s^2$)	Ni-28 ($3d^8 4s^2$)	Cu-29 ($3d^{10} 4s^1$)	Zn-30 ($3d^{10} 4s^2$)
4*d*-series	Y-39 ($4d^1 5s^2$)	Zr-40 ($4d^2 5s^2$)	Nb-41 ($4d^4 5s^1$)	Mo-42 ($4d^5 5s^1$)	Tc-43 ($4d^6 5s^1$)	Ru-44 ($4d^7 5s^1$)	Rh-45 ($4d^8 5s^1$)	Pd-46 ($4d^{10} 5s^0$)	Ag-47 ($4d^{10} 5s^1$)	Cd-48 ($4d^{10} 5s^2$)
5*d*-series	La-57 ($5d^1 6s^2$)	Hf-72 ($5d^2 6s^2$)	Ta-73 ($5d^3 6s^2$)	W-74 ($5d^4 6s^2$)	Re-75 ($5d^5 6s^2$)	Os-76 ($5d^6 6s^2$)	Ir-77 ($5d^7 6s^2$)	Pt-78 ($5d^9 6s^1$)	Au-79 ($5d^{10} 6s^1$)	Hg-80 ($5d^{10} 6s^2$)
6*d*-series	Ac-89 ($6d^1 7s^2$)	Rf-104 ($6d^2 7s^2$)	Db-105 ($6d^3 7s^2$)	Sg-106 ($6d^4 7s^2$)	Bh-107 ($6d^5 7s^2$)	Hs-108 ($6d^6 7s^2$)	Mt-109 ($6d^7 7s^2$)	Ds-110 ($6d^8 7s^2$)	Rg-111 ($6d^{10} 7s^1$)	Cn-112 ($6d^{10} 7s^2$)

General Properties of the Transition Elements (d-Block)

Nearly all transition elements resemble in their physical and chemical properties as they have similar ns^2 orbital electronic configuration in the outermost energy shell.

Some of the general properties of the transition elements are discussed below.

Physical Properties

- They are hard metals, have high tensile strength, ductility, malleability and are good conductors of heat and electricity.
- They have high melting and boiling points and form alloys with other metals.
- Their reactivity decreases with the increase in their atomic number.

1. Metallic Character

All the transition elements are metals having hcp, ccp or bcc lattices. Metallic bonding is caused due to the presence of one or two electrons in the outermost energy level (*ns*) and also unpaired $(n-1)$ *d*-electrons. Greater the number of unpaired *d*-electrons, stronger is the metallic bonding and metals will be hard, e.g. Cr, Mo and W.

Thus, transition elements are more metallic than the representative elements. On the other hand, absence of unpaired electrons results in a weak metallic bonding and the metals will be soft, e.g. Zn, Cd and Hg.

2. Melting and Boiling Points

These metals have very high melting and boiling points due to stronger metallic bonding. The melting points of the transition elements first rise to a maximum and then fall as the atomic number increases. Manganese and technetium have abnormally low melting points.

The metallic bond strength increases upto the middle of a particular series with increasing number of unpaired electrons. Thus, Cr, Mo and W have maximum number of unpaired *d*-electrons and have highest melting points in their respective series. Tungsten has the highest melting point (3683 K) among the *d*- block elements.

As there are no unpaired electrons in Zn, Cd and Hg, they have low melting points. Hg is liquid at ordinary temperature with lowest melting point (234 K) among the transition metals.

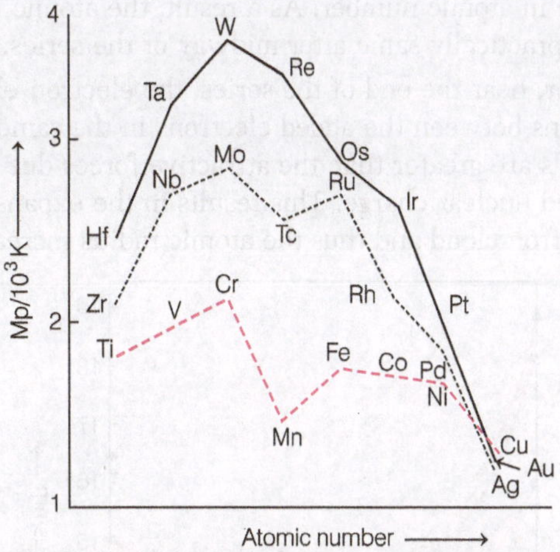

Trends in melting points of transition elements

3. Enthalpy of Atomisation

Transition elements (except Zn, Cd and Hg) are much harder and less volatile. They exhibit high enthalpies of atomisation. The maximum value lies at about middle of each series indicating that interatomic interaction increases with the number of unpaired *d*-electrons. The metals of 4*d* and 5*d* transition series have greater enthalpies of atomization than the corresponding elements of the first (3*d*) series. This is due to much more frequent metal-metal bonding in their compounds.

Order of enthalpy of atomisation ($\Delta_a H°$) of 3*d* series is

$$Zn < Mn < Sc < Cu < Cr < Fe < Co < Ni < Ti < V$$

4. Density

Density of these elements generally increases with decrease in metallic radius coupled with increase in atomic mass. Thus, from Ti to Ni the significant increase in density may be noted.

Order of density (3*d* series):

$$Sc < Ti < V < Cr < Mn < Fe < Co < Ni < Cu > Zn$$

Density increases (Sc to Cu)   Density decreases (Cu to Zn)

In *d*-block series, Os and Ir have highest density and in 3*d*-series, Cu has the highest density.

Atomic and Ionic Radii

- The atomic and ionic radii for transition elements are smaller than their corresponding *s*-block elements and are greater than their corresponding *p*-block elements.
- In a series, the atomic radii first decrease with increase in atomic number upto the middle of the series, then become constant and at the end of the series show a slight increase.
- This is due to the fact that in the begining, the atomic radius decreases as the nuclear charge increases. But with the increase in the *d*-electrons, screening effect increases which counter balances the increased nuclear charge due to

increase in atomic number. As a result, the atomic radii remain practically same after midway of the series.

- However, near the end of the series, the electron-electron repulsions between the added electrons in the same *d*-orbitals are greater than the attractive forces due to increased nuclear charge. This results in the expansion of the electron cloud and thus the atomic radius increases.

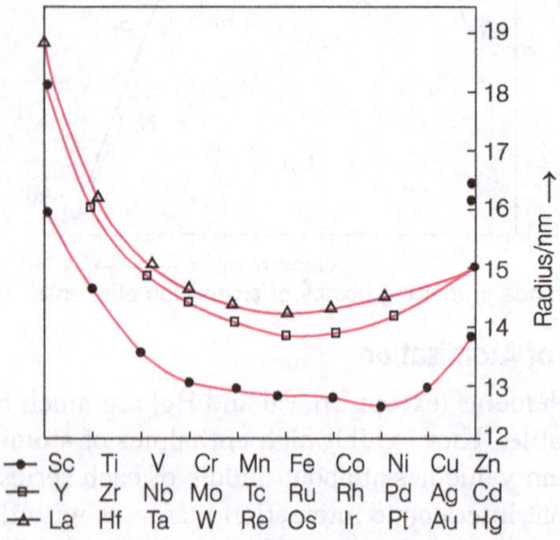

Trends in atomic radii of transition elements.

- The atomic radii increase down the group from first transition series to the second transition series but the atomic radii of the second and third transition series are almost same.
- The increase in the atomic radii down the group of the second transition series is due to the increase in the number of shells in the atoms.
- But the similarity in the atomic radii of the elements of second and third transition elements is due to lanthanoid (lanthanide) contraction.
- Ionic radii of transition elements are different in different oxidation states. In general, the ionic radii decrease with increase in oxidation state and *vice versa*.
- The ionic radii of M^{2+} cations decrease with the increase in atomic number.

Mentor's Tip

Zr and Hf have very similar physical and chemical properties because of their similar radii which makes their separation difficult.

Electronic Configurations of Some Transition Metal Ions

Element	Sc	Ti	V	Cr	Mn	Fe	Co	Ni	Cu	Zn
Atomic number	21	22	23	24	25	26	27	28	29	30
Electronic configuration										
M	$3d^1 4s^2$	$3d^2 4s^2$	$3d^3 4s^2$	$3d^5 4s^1$	$3d^5 4s^2$	$3d^6 4s^2$	$3d^7 4s^2$	$3d^8 4s^2$	$3d^{10} 4s^1$	$3d^{10} 4s^2$
M^+	$3d^1 4s^1$	$3d^2 4s^1$	$3d^3 4s^1$	$3d^5$	$3d^5 4s^1$	$3d^6 4s^1$	$3d^7 4s^1$	$3d^8 4s^1$	$3d^{10}$	$3d^{10} 4s^1$
M^{2+}	$3d^1$	$3d^2$	$3d^3$	$3d^4$	$3d^5$	$3d^6$	$3d^7$	$3d^8$	$3d^9$	$3d^{10}$
M^{3+}	[Ar]	$3d^1$	$3d^2$	$3d^3$	$3d^4$	$3d^5$	$3d^6$	$3d^7$	–	

Ionisation Enthalpies

- The ionisation energies of transition elements usually lie between those of *s*-and *p*-block elements.
- Their ionisation energy increases in a period with atomic number. This is due to increase in nuclear charge with atomic number which accompanies the filling of the inner *d*-orbitals.
- First ionisation energy, $(IE)_1$ of 5*d*-elements are higher than those of the 3*d* and 4*d*-elements. This is due to greater effective nuclear charge acting on outer valence electrons because of the weak shielding of the nucleus by 4*f*-electrons. The ionisation energies of the 3*d* elements are irregular.
- The $(IE)_1$ in general, increases but the magnitude of the increase in the $(IE)_2$ and $(IE)_3$ for the successive elements is much higher along a series.

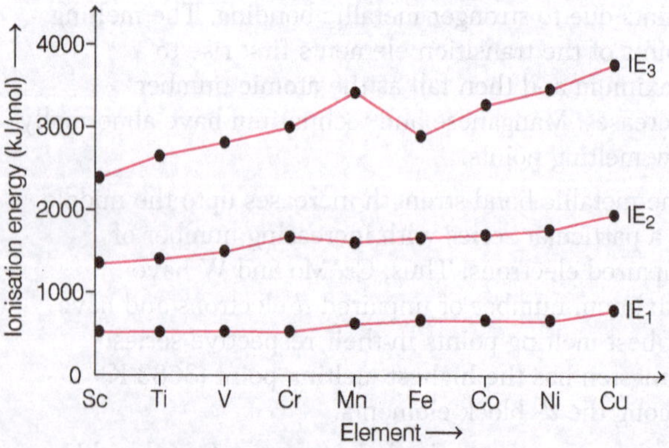

Variation of the first, second and third ionisation energies for the first transition metals.

- When an electron is ionised from any transition element, say from iron ($Z = 26$) of $3d$-series, the effective nuclear charge experienced by the $3d$-electrons is greatly enhanced over that of any $4s$-electron.

  Thus, ionisation of two or more electrons from an atom of a transition element will take place with the removal of *s*-electrons in preference to the *d*-electrons.

  Thus, ionisation energies increase only slightly along the $3d$-series.
- A general trend of increasing values of $(IE)_2$ is expected as the effective nuclear charge increases because one *d*-electron does not shield another electron from the influence of nuclear charge because *d*-orbitals differ in direction.
- The magnitude of ionisation energies give an idea about the relative stabilities of various oxidation states of transition elements. e.g. Ni (II) compounds are thermodynamically more stable than platinum (II) while platinum (IV) compounds are relatively more stable than nickel (IV) compounds.

(in J/mol)	$(IE)_1 + (IE)_2$	$(IE)_3 + (IE)_4$	Total
Ni	2.49×10^3	8.80×10^3	11.29×10^3
Pt	2.66×10^3	6.70×10^3	9.36×10^3

- The three terms responsible for the value of ionisation enthalpy are attraction of each electron towards the nucleus, repulsion between the electrons and the exchange energy.

Oxidation States

A characteristic property of the transition metals is their ability to exhibit several oxidation states differing usually by units of one. This is due to the fact that $(n-1)d$ electrons may get involved along with *ns*-electrons in bonding, as electrons in $(n-1)d$-orbitals are in an energy state comparable to *ns*-electrons.

The stability of a given oxidation state depends on the nature of the element with which the transition metal is combined.

The highest oxidation states are found in the compounds of transition elements with most electronegative elements like F and O (stronger oxidising in nature).

The different oxidation states of $3d$-series are given below.

- Oxidation states of the 1st row transition metals. (Oxidation states given in brackets are very rare).

Sc	Ti	V	Cr	Mn	Fe	Co	Ni	Cu	Zn
								I	
	(II)	II	II	II	II	II	II	II	II
III	III	III	III	(III)	III	III	(III)		
	IV	IV	IV	IV	(IV)	(IV)	(IV)		
		V	(V)	(V)					
			VI	VI	VI				
				VII					

- The elements which give the highest number of oxidation states occur in or near the middle of the series.
- The most common oxidation state of $3d$-series transition metals is +2 (except Sc). Highest oxidation state of $3d$-series elements is +7. *d*-Block metals can also show zero oxidation state when it form complex with CO ligand. The transition metal ions having d^0 (Sc^{+3}, Ti^{+4}, V^{+5}, Mn^{+7}), d^5 (Mn^{+2}) and d^{10} (Zn^{+2}) configurations are most stable.
- Low oxidation states are found when a complex has ligands capable of showing π-acceptor character in addition to the σ-bonding. For example, in $Ni(CO)_4$ and $Fe(CO)_5$, the oxidation state of nickel and iron is zero.

Mentor's TIP

Highest oxidation state of *d*-block elements is +8, which is seen in Os (76) (as in OsO_4) but with respect to halogens, the highest oxidation state of *d*-block elements is +6, i.e. CrF_6.

Trends in Stability of Higher Oxidation States

The stable halides of the $3d$ series of transition metals is given below.

Oxidation No.									
+6			CrF_6						
+5		VF_5	CrF_5						
+4	TiX_4	VX_4^I	CrX_4	MnF_4					
+3	TiX_3	VX_3	CrX_3	MnF_3	FeX_3^I	CoF_3			ZnX_2
+2	TiX_2^{III}	VX_2	CrX_2	MnX_2	FeX_2	CoX_2	NiX_2	CuX_2^{II}	
+1								CuX^{III}	

$X = F \rightarrow I$; $X^I = F \rightarrow Br$, $X^{II} = F$, Cl; $X^{III} = Cl \rightarrow I$

The highest oxidation number are achieved in TiX_4 (tetrahalides), VF_5 and CrF_6. The ability of fluorine to stabilise the highest oxidation state is due to either higher lattice energy as in case of CoF_3 or higher bond enthalpy terms for the higher covalent compounds e.g. VF_5 and CrF_6.

Another feature of fluorides is their instablity in the lower oxidation states, e.g. VX_2 and the same applies to CuX. The ability of oxygen to stabilise the highest oxidation state is demonstrated in the oxides.

Oxides of 3*d* Metals

Oxid. No.	Groups 3	4	5	6	7	8	9	10	11	12
+7					Mn_2O_7					
+6				CrO_3						
+5			V_2O_5							
+4		TiO_2	V_2O_4	CrO_2	MnO_2					
+3	Sc_2O_3	Ti_2O_3	V_2O_3	Cr_2O_3	Mn_2O_3 $Mn_3O_4^*$	Fe_2O_3 $Fe_3O_4^*$	$Co_3O_4^*$			
+2 +1		TiO	VO	CrO	MnO	FeO	CoO	NiO	CuO Cu_2O	ZnO

[*Mixed Oxides]

The ability of oxygen to form multiple bonds to metals explains its superiority. In the covalent oxide, Mn_2O_7, each Mn is tetrahedrally surrounded by four O atoms including a Mn—O—Mn bridge. The ability of oxygen to stabilise these higher oxidation states exceeds that of fluorine. Thus, the highest Mn fluoride is MnF_4 whereas the highest oxide is Mn_2O_7.

Trends in the M^{3+}/M^{2+} Standard Electrode Potential

The $E^\circ_{(M^{3+}/M^{2+})}$ value shows the varying trends. Sc has the lowest value due to stability of Sc^{3+} which has a noble gas configuration. Quantitatively, the stability of transition metal ions in different oxidation states in solution can be determined on the basis of electrode potential data.

Lower the electrode potential (i.e. more negative the standard reduction potential) of the electrode, more stable is the oxidation state of the transition metal ion in aqueous solution. Electrode potential values depend upon energy of sublimation of the metal, the ionisation enthalpy and the hydration enthalpy.

All the elements of the first transition series, except copper, have negative values and can react with acids (H^+) producing hydrogen. E° values (M^{2+}/M) for first row (3*d*-series) transiton metals are given below:

Standard Electrode Potential (E°/V)

Element	Ti	V	Cr	Mn	Fe	Co	Ni	Cu	Zn
$E^\circ_{(M^{2+}/M)}$ in volts (V)	- 1.63	- 1.18	- 0.90	- 1.18	- 0.44	- 0.28	- 0.25	+ 0.34	- 0.76
$E^\circ_{(M^{3+}/M^{2+})}$ in volts (V)	- 0.37	- 0.26	- 0.41	+ 1.57	+ 0.77	+ 1.97	-	-	-

NEET Snapshot

The stability of Cu^{2+} is more than Cu^+ salts in aqueous solution, due to hydration energy. *[NEET 2023]*

Cu^+ undergoes disproportionation reaction in aqueous solution.

$$2Cu^+(aq) \longrightarrow Cu^{2+} + Cu(s)$$

The high stability of Cu^{2+} ion in aqueous solution is due to negative enthalpy of hydration, $\Delta_{hyd}H^\circ$ which easily compensates the energy required. Thus, making the process spontaneous.

Chemical Reactivity and E° Values

Transition metals vary widely in their chemical reactivity. Many of them are sufficiently electropositive to dissolve in mineral acids, although a few are noble, i.e. they are unaffected by single acids. All the elements of 3*d*-series are good reducing agents except copper.

However, they are weaker reducing agent than *s*-block elements.

- More negative the value of the electrode potential for the couple M^{n+}/M, usually more is the reducing power of the element.

  Similarly, more positive is the value of electrode potential for the couple M^{n+}/M, usually more is the oxidising power of the element. Electrode potential is a measure of the electropositive character and the reactivity of the metals.
- In general along a period, there is a decrease in electropositive character. The reactivity of metals also decreases along a period.
- Although, most of the transition metals have negative electrode potential and can react with acid but these are inert or less reactive with acids due to formation of protective layers.

  e.g. Despite a negative standard reduction potential Cr is quite inert chemically because of the formation of chromium (III) oxide, Cr_2O_3 on its surfaces. This fact finds application of Cr to use as a protective and non-corrosive plating on other metals.

Magnetic Properties

Due to the presence of unpaired electrons in the $(n-1)$ *d*-orbitals, most of the transition metal ions and their compounds are paramagnetic, i.e. they are attracted by magnetic field.

These transition elements which has paired electrons are diamagnetic, i.e. they are weakly repelled by the magnetic field, greater is the number of unpaired electron in an ion, greater is its paramagnetic nature and paramagnetism.

Magnetic moment produced due to spin of electrons or unpaired electrons is measured in terms of Bohr Magneton (B.M.) or μ_B and is given by

$$\text{Magnetic moment } (\mu) = \sqrt{n(n+2)} \text{ B.M.}$$

n = number of unpaired electron.

The above relation is also called **"spin only"** formula. Using spin only formula, the 'μ' values for various number of unpaired electrons is given below:

Calculated Magnetic Moment (B.M.)

Ion	Sc^{3+}	Ti^{3+}	Ti^{2+}	V^{2+}	Cr^{2+}	Mn^{2+}	Fe^{2+}	Co^{2+}	Ni^{2+}	Cu^{2+}	Zn^{2+}
Electronic configuration	d^0	d^1	d^2	d^3	d^4	d^5	d^6	d^7	d^8	d^9	d^{10}
No. of unpaired electron(s)	0	1	2	3	4	5	4	3	2	1	0
Magnetic moment	0	1.73	2.83	3.87	4.90	5.92	4.90	3.87	2.83	1.73	0

NEET Close-up

Example Similar to PYQ Asked in NEET 2024

Spin only magnetic moment is same for which of the following ions?

A. Ti^{2+} B. Mn^{2+} C. V^{3+}
D. Cr^{3+} E. Sc^{2+}

Choose the most appropriate answer from the options given below.

(a) B, C and D (b) B and E
(c) A and C (d) A, C and D

Sol. (c) Spin only magnetic moment is given by

$$\mu_s = \sqrt{n(n+2)} \text{ BM}$$

where, n = number of unpaired electrons.

A. $Ti^{2+} \rightarrow 3d^2, n = 2, \mu = \sqrt{8}$ BM

B. $Mn^{2+} \rightarrow 3d^5, n = 5, \mu = \sqrt{35}$ BM

C. $V^{3+} \rightarrow 3d^2, n = 2, \mu = \sqrt{8}$ BM

D. $Cr^{3+} \rightarrow 3d^3, n = 3, \mu = \sqrt{15}$ BM

E. $Sc^{2+} \rightarrow 3d^1, n = 1, \mu = \sqrt{3}$ BM

Hence, A and C have same value of magnetic moment.

Skill Builder

Spin only magnetic moment is same for which of the following ions?

A. Fe^{3+} B. Co^{3+} C. Ti^{2+}
D. Ni^{2+} E. Fe^{2+}

Choose the most appropriate answer from the options given below.

(a) A and D (b) A and B
(c) C and E (d) C and D

For more practice Refer to Q. 20 of Step up Practice-1.

Formation of Coloured Ions

When an electron from a lower energy *d*-orbital is excited to a higher energy *d*-orbital (*d*-*d* transition), the energy of excitation corresponds to the frequency of light absorbed. This frequency generally lies in the visible region.

The colour observed corresponds to the complementary colour of the light or wavelength absorbed. The frequency of the light absorbed is determined by the nature of the ligand.

For example, in case of hydrated Cu^{2+} salts (where H_2O is the ligand), red wavelength is absorbed and the complementary colour greenish blue. $[Ti(H_2O)_6]^{3+}$ ion is purple as it absorbs yellow wavelength.

The colours of some of 3*d* metal ions are

Ions	Colour
Sc^{3+}, Ti^{4+}, Zn^{2+}	Colourless
Ti^{3+}	Purple
V^{4+}, Cr^{2+}, Cu^{2+}	Blue
V^{3+}, Fe^{2+}, Ni^{2+}	Green
V^{2+}, Cr^{3+}, Mn^{3+}	Violet
Mn^{2+}	Pink
Fe^{3+}	Yellow
Co^{3+}, Co^{2+}	Blue, Pink

Concept ladder

In the series, Sc (+III), Ti (+IV), V (+V), Cr (+VI) and Mn (+VII), all have empty *d*-orbitals, hence *d*–*d* transition is impossible and they should be colourless. But VO_2^{2+} (pale yellow), CrO_4^{2-} (deep yellow) and MnO_4^- (dark purple) are coloured in aqueous solutions. The colours arise by **charge transfer**, e.g. in MnO_4^-, an electron is momentarily transferred from O to the metal $3d^0$ orbital and thus oxygen changes from O^{2-} to O^- and manganese from Mn(+VII) to Mn(+VI).

Formation of Complex Compounds

Transition metal ions form a large number of complexes in which the central metal ion is linked to a number of ligands. This is because of the following characteristic properties of transition metals:

- They have high nuclear charge and small size, i.e. charge/size ratio (charge density) is large.
- They have empty *d*-orbitals to accept the lone pairs of electrons donated by the ligands.
  Thus, in complexes metal ions behave as Lewis acids and ligands behave as Lewis bases.

Complexes can be linear (*sp*-hybridisation), square planar (dsp^2-hybridisation), tetrahedral (sp^3-hybridisation), octahedral (d^2sp^3-hybridisation) or trigonal bipyramidal (sp^3d-hybridisation). [Hybridisation of the metal in the coordination sphere].

Catalytic Properties

Many transition metals (like Fe, Co, Ni, Pt, Mo etc.) and their compounds are used as catalysts due to ability to show variable oxidation states, available vacant *d*-orbitals and large surface area available for adsorption.

Catalyst at a solid surface involves the formation of bonds between reactant molecules and atoms of the surface of catalyst. This has the effect of increasing the concentration of the reactants at the catalyst surface and also weakening of the bonds in the reacting molecules (the activation energy is lowered). Also because, transition metal ions can change their oxidation states, they become more effective as catalysts.

For example, Fe(III) catalyses the reaction between I^- and $S_2O_8^{2-}$.

$$2I^- + S_2O_8^{2-} \xrightarrow{Fe^{3+}} I_2 + 2SO_4^{2-}$$

Mechanism :

$$2Fe^{3+} + 2I^- \longrightarrow I_2 + 2Fe^{2+}$$
$$2Fe^{2+} + S_2O_8^{2-} \longrightarrow 2Fe^{3+} + 2SO_4^{2-}$$

So, actually Fe^{3+} oxidises I^- to I_2.

Formation of Interstitial Compounds

Transition metals can trap some small atoms like hydrogen, boron, carbon, nitrogen, etc., in vacant spaces in their crystal lattice forming interstitial compounds. Carbon and nitrogen always occupy octahedral holes; hydrogen is smaller and occupies tetrahedral holes. As only transition metals form such compounds, the *d*-electrons are, therefore, presumably involved in the bonding.

The structure of the metal often changes during the formation of such compounds. The composition of these compounds is generally non-stoichiometric.

For example, *wustite* contains Fe and O atoms and the composition varies between $Fe_{0.84}O$ and $Fe_{0.94}O$. Therefore, ferrous oxide should be written with a bar over the formula FeO to indicate that the ratio of Fe and O atoms is not exactly 1 : 1. $VH_{0.56}$, $TiH_{1.7}$ are other examples of non-stoichiometric compounds.

Characteristics of interstitial compounds.

- They have high melting points, higher than those of pure metals.
- They are chemically inert.
- They are less malleable and ductile.
- Interstitial compounds are neither ionic nor covalent.
- They are very hard and retain metallic conductivity.

Mentor's TIP

Cementite (Fe_3C) is an interstitial carbide and it used for making railway track.

Alloy Formation

An alloy is a blend of metals prepared by mixing the components. Alloys are heterogeneous solid solutions (colloids) in which the atoms of one metal are distributed randomly among the atoms of the other. Because of similar radii and other characteristics of transition metals, alloys are readily formed by these metals.

Alloys are generally harder, have higher melting points and more resistant to corrosion than the individual metals. Metals such as Cr, V, Mo, W and Mn are used in the production of alloy steels and stainless steels. Alloys containing mercury as one of the constituent elements are called amalgams.

Alloys of transition metals with non transition metals such as brass (copper-zinc) and bronze (copper-tin) etc., are also of considerable industrial importance.

Concept ladder

Transition metals and their compounds as catalyst

Fe/Mo	Mo Promoted Fe used in Haber-Bosch process of NH_3.
$TiCl_4$	Used as Ziegler-Natta catalyst in production of polyethene (HDPE).
Ni	Hydrogenation process.
Pt	Ostwald process for HNO_3 from NH_3.
V_2O_5	Used in contact process of H_2SO_4.
$CuCl_2$	Deacon's process of manufacturing Cl_2 from HCl.

Some important alloys of transition metals

Rolled gold	Cu + Al
Invar	Fe + Ni
Alnico	Fe + Al + Ni + Co
Stainless steel	Fe + Ni + Cr
German silver	Ni + Cu + Zn
20 carat gold	Au + Cu
24 carat gold	100% Au

STEP UP Practice 1

1. Transition elements exhibit variable valencies because they release electrons from the folllowing orbitals
(a) *ns* and *np* orbitals
(b) $(n-1)d$ and *ns* orbitals
(c) $(n-2)$ *d* and *np* orbitals
(d) $(n-1)$ *d* orbitals only

2. Transition elements, the elements of *d* block are named as because their characterstics are
(a) like that of *p* and *d*-block elements
(b) the members of IA group
(c) in between *s* and *p*-block elements
(d) like that of inactive elements

3. Consider the following electronic configurations,
(i) $Fe^{2+} = [Ar]\ 3d^6 4s^0$ (ii) $Ni = [Ar]\ 3d^8 4s^2$
(iii) $Cu = [Ar]\ 3d^9 4s^2$ (iv) $Cr = [Ar]\ 3d^5 4s^1$
(v) $V^{2+} = [Ar]\ 3d^3 4s^0$
How many of the above electronic configurations is (are) correct?
(a) 4 (b) 1 (c) 2 (d) 3

4. In the series V ($Z = 23$) to Zn ($Z = 30$) which element has least enthalpy of atomisation?
(a) Zn (b) V
(c) Cr (d) Co

5. Which one of the following transition metal ions has the lowest density?
(a) Copper (b) Scandium
(c) Nickel (d) Iron

6. Which of the following sets of elements have almost same atomic radii?
(a) Sc, V, Cr (b) V, Ni, Zn
(c) Ni, Cu, Zn (d) Fe, Co, Ni

7. Given below are two statements.
Assertion (A) The second ionisation energies of $_{23}V$, $_{24}Cr$ and $_{25}Mn$ are in the order V < Cr < Mn.
Reason (R) Ionisation energies slightly increases along a period with increase in atomic number.
In the light of the above statements, choose the correct answer from the options given below.
(a) Both A and R are true but R is not the correct explanation of A.
(b) Both A and R are true and R is the correct explanation of A.
(c) A is true but R is false.
(d) A is false but R is true.

8. The transition element which shows the highest oxidation state is
(a) Cu (b) Mn (c) W (d) Os

9. Which of the following elements show +2, +3 and +4 oxidation states ?
(a) Sc, Ti (b) Fe, Ni
(c) Ti, Ni (d) Zn, Ni

10. Which of the following underlined metals is correctly matched with its oxidation state?
(a) $\underline{Mn}O_4^- \longrightarrow +6$ (b) $\underline{Cr}O_4^{2-} \longrightarrow +7$
(c) $\underline{Zn}O_2^{2-} \longrightarrow +2$ (d) $\underline{Cr}O_5 \longrightarrow +10$

11. Magnetic moment of a divalent ion in aqueous solution of an element with atomic numbers 25 is
(a) 2.84 BM (b) 3.87 BM
(c) 4.90 BM (d) 5.92 BM

12. The number of unpaired electrons in gaseous species of Mn^{3+}, Cr^{3+} and V^{3+} respectively are
(a) 4, 9 and 2 (b) 3, 3 and 2
(c) 4, 3 and 2 (d) 3, 3 and 3

13. Consider the following statements.
Statement I The $E^\circ_{(M^{2+}/M)}$ value of copper is negative (– 0.34 V).
Statement II Copper (s) has high heat of atomisation and low enthalpy of hydration of Cu^{2+}.
In the light of the above statements, choose the most appropriate answer from the options given below.
(a) Both Statement I and Statement II are false.
(b) Statement I is true but Statement II is false.
(c) Statement I is false but Statement II is true.
(d) Both Statement I and Statement II are true.

14 The incorrect statement for a transition element is
(a) it shows magnetic property
(b) it has variable valency
(c) it has tendency of formation of coloured ions
(d) it has completely filled *d*-orbitals in its ground state or in its stable oxidation states.

15. Highest oxidation state of manganese in fluoride is +4 (MnF_4) but highest oxidation state in oxides is +7(Mn_2O_7) because
(a) fluorine is more electronegative than oxygen
(b) fluorine does not possess *d*-orbitals
(c) fluorine stabilises lower oxidation state
(d) in covalent compounds, fluorine can form single bond only while oxygen forms double bond

16 Which one of the following ionic species will impart colour to an aqueous solution?
(a) Ti^{4+} (b) Cu^+ (c) Zn^{2+} (d) Cr^{3+}

17 Consider the following statements.

Statement I Most of the compounds of the transition elements are coloured in the solid and solution state.

Statement II During *d-d* transition, the *d*-electrons absorb certain radiation from the visible region of the spectrum.

In the light of the above statements, choose the most appropriate answer from the options given below.

(a) Both Statement I and Statement II are false.
(b) Statement I is true but Statement II is false.
(c) Statement I is false but Statement II is true.
(d) Both Statement I and Statement II are true.

18 Which of the following is paramagnetic as well as coloured ion?

(a) Cu^+ (b) Cu^{2+}
(c) Sc^{3+} (d) Ti^{4+}

19 Select the incorrect statement.

(a) Ionisation energies of 5*d*-elements are greater than those of 3*d* and 4*d*-elements.
(b) Cu(I) is diamagnetic while Cu(II) is paramagnetic.
(c) $[Ti(H_2O)_6]^{3+}$ is coloured while $[Sc(H_2O)_6]^{3+}$ is colourless.
(d) Transition elements cannot form complexes.

20 Spin only magentic moment is same for which of the following ions?

A. Fe^{2+} B. Co^{2+} C. Ni^{2+}
D. Mn^{3+} E. Co^{3+}

Choose the most appropriate answer from the options given below.

(a) A, D and E (b) B, C and D
(c) A and D (d) A and E

21 Ti^{2+} is purple while Ti^{4+} is colourless, because

(a) there is zero upaired electron in Ti^{4+}
(b) Ti^{2+} has $3d^2$ configuration
(c) Ti^{4+} has $3d^2$ configuration
(d) Ti^{4+} is a very small cation when compared to Ti^{2+} and hence, does not absorb any radiation

22 Given below are two statements.

Assertion (A) Transition metals are good catalysts.

Reason (R) V_2O_5 or Pt is used in the preparation of H_2SO_4 by contact process.

In the light of the above statements, choose the correct answer from the options given below.

(a) Both A and R are true and R is the correct explanation of A.
(b) Both A and R are true but R is not the correct explanation of A.
(c) A is true but R is false.
(d) A is false but R is true.

23 Given below, catalyst and corresponding process are matched. The incorrect match is

(a) V_2O_5 ⟶ Haber-Bosch process
(b) Ni in the presence of hydrogen ⟶ Vegetable oil to ghee
(c) Finely divided iron ⟶ Haber's process
(d) $[TiCl_4 + Al(CH_3)_3]$ ⟶ Polymerisation

24 Select the incorrect characteristics of interstitial compounds.

(a) They have high melting points, higher than those of pure metals.
(b) They are chemically inert.
(c) They are more malleable and ductile.
(d) They are neither ionic nor covalent.

25 Given below, metals and corresponding alloys are matched. The mismatch is

(a) Cu + Zn ⟶ Brass
(b) Cu + Sn ⟶ Bronze
(c) Ni + Cu + Zn ⟶ Stainless steel
(d) Cu + Al ⟶ Rolled gold

Module 2

Some Important Compounds of *d*-block Elements

• Oxides and Oxoanions of Metals • Potassium Dichromate ($K_2Cr_2O_7$) • Potassium Permanganate ($KMnO_4$)

Oxides and Oxoanions of Metals

These oxides are generally formed by the reaction of metals with oxygen at higher temperatures. All the metals except Sc form MO type of oxides which are basic.

- While moving along a period from Sc to Zn basic nature decreases and acidic nature increases.

Sc_2O_3	TiO_2	V_2O_5	Cr_2O_3	MnO_2	Fe_2O_3	Co_2O_3	NiO	CuO	ZnO
A	*A*	*A*	*A*	*A*	*B*	*B*	*B*	*B*	*A*

A : Amphoteric *B* : Basic

This behaviour differs when oxidation states are different. With increase in the oxidation state of a given transition metal, covalent character of its compound increases and thus acidic character also increases.

	MnO	Mn_3O_4 ($MnO \cdot Mn_2O_3$)	Mn_2O_3	MnO_2	MnO_3	Mn_2O_7
Oxidation state of Mn	+2	+8/3	+3	+4	+6	+7
Nature of oxide	Basic	Amphoteric	Amphoteric	Amphoteric	Weakly acidic	Strongly acidic

- The basic and amphoteric oxides dissolve in non-oxidising acids and form hexaaquo ions $[M(H_2O)_6]^{n+}$.
- The acidic oxides like CrO_3 and Mn_2O_7 dissolve in water to form the oxyacids. These oxides also react with bases to form oxosalts.

$$CrO_3 + H_2O \longrightarrow \underset{\text{(Chromic acid)}}{H_2CrO_4} \quad \text{(yellow)}$$

$$CrO_3 + 2KOH \longrightarrow K_2CrO_4 + H_2O$$

$$2CrO_3 + H_2O \longrightarrow \underset{\text{(Dichromic acid)}}{H_2Cr_2O_7} \quad \text{(orange)}$$

$$2CrO_3 + 2KOH \longrightarrow \underset{\text{Potassium dichromate}}{K_2Cr_2O_7} + H_2O$$

$$Mn_2O_7 + H_2O \longrightarrow \underset{\text{(Permanganic acid)}}{2HMnO_4} \quad \text{(purple)}$$

$$Mn_2O_7 + 2KOH \longrightarrow 2KMnO_4 + H_2O$$

- As we move along a given transition series, +2 oxidation state of the metals becomes more and more stable and hence the tendency of these metals to lose electrons increases hence, reducing nature of the metal oxide increases. VO and CrO are strong reducing agents.
- Characteristics of oxides and ions of vanadium and chromium have been summarised in table given below.

Characteristics of Oxides and Some Ions of V and Cr

O.S.	Oxide/ Hydroxide	Behaviour	Ion	Name of ion	Colour of ion
+2	VO	Basic	V^{2+}	Vanadium (II) (vanadous)	Violet
+3	V_2O_3	Basic	V^{3+}	Vanadium (III) (vanadic)	Green
+4	VO_2	Amphoteric	VO^{2+}	Oxovanadium (IV) (vanadyl)	Blue
			$V_4O_9^{2-}$	Hypovanadate (vanadite)	Brown
+5	V_2O_5	Amphoteric	VO_2^+	Dioxovanadium (V)	Yellow
			VO_4^{3-}	Orthovanadate (V)	Colourless
+2	CrO $Cr(OH)_2$	Basic	Cr^{2+}	Chromium (II) (chromous)	Light blue
+3	Cr_2O_3 $Cr(OH)_3$	Amphoteric	Cr^{3+} $Cr(OH)_4^-$	Chromium (III) (chromic) Chromite	Violet Green
+6	CrO_3 $CrO_2(OH)_2$ $H_2Cr_2O_7$	Acidic	CrO_4^{2-} $Cr_2O_7^{2-}$	Chromate Dichromate	Yellow Orange

Potassium Dichromate [$K_2Cr_2O_7$]

The preparation and properties of $K_2Cr_2O_7$ are as follows

Preparation

$K_2Cr_2O_7$ is obtained from chromite ore [$FeCr_2O_4$ or $FeO \cdot Cr_2O_3$] in the following steps

***Step* I** Chromite ore is fused with molten Na_2CO_3 in the presence of air to give Na_2CrO_4 and Fe_2O_3. Fe_2O_3 is water insoluble while Na_2CrO_4 is water soluble hence, separation can easily be done by filtration.

$$4FeCr_2O_4 + 8Na_2CO_3 + 7O_2 \xrightarrow{1100^\circ C} \underset{\substack{\text{Water soluble}\\\text{(Yellow solution)}}}{8Na_2CrO_4} + \underset{\text{Water insoluble}}{2Fe_2O_3} + 8CO_2\uparrow$$

***Step* II** Aqueous solution of Na_2CrO_4 is acidified and $Na_2Cr_2O_7$ is formed.

$$2Na_2CrO_4 + \underset{\text{Dil.}}{H_2SO_4} \longrightarrow Na_2Cr_2O_7 + Na_2SO_4 + H_2O$$

***Step* III** Sodium dichromate ($Na_2Cr_2O_7$) is more soluble and less stable than $K_2Cr_2O_7$ hence, $Na_2Cr_2O_7$ changes to $K_2Cr_2O_7$ on reaction with KCl (saturated solution). On cooling concentrated solution of $K_2Cr_2O_7$, orange crystals are obtained.

$$Na_2Cr_2O_7 + 2KCl \longrightarrow \underset{\text{Orange crystals}}{K_2Cr_2O_7\downarrow} + 2NaCl$$

Structure

A dichromate ion is made up of two chromate ions. Each of the chromate groups has a tetrahedral structure.

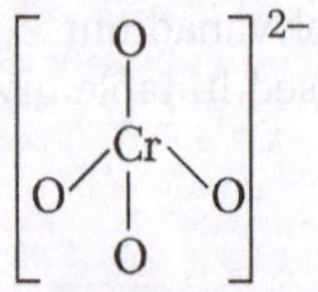

Chromate ion

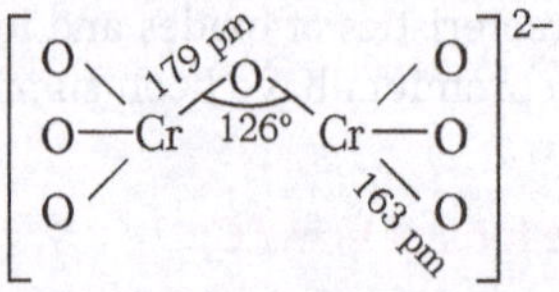

Dichromate ion

NEET Snapshot

The oxidation state of Cr in CrO_4^{2-} (chromate) and $Cr_2O_7^{2-}$ (dichromate) are same and it is +6. ***[NEET 2020]***

The ionic charges on chromate and dichromate ion is –2 and the oxidation state of oxygen is –2. Also, the oxidation state of chromium in both chromate and dichromate ion is +6.

Physical Properties

- It is orange-red coloured crystal, having melting point of 699 K. It is moderately soluble in cold water but highly soluble in hot water.
- It is generally used as primary standard in the volumetric analysis because it is very stable at room temperature.

Chemical Properties

(i) Effect of Heat

When potassium dichromate strongly heated, it decomposes to give oxygen.

$$\underset{\text{Orange red}}{4K_2Cr_2O_7(s)} \xrightarrow{\Delta} \underset{\text{Yellow}}{4K_2CrO_4(s)} + \underset{\text{Dark green}}{2Cr_2O_3(s)} + 3O_2(g)$$

(ii) Action of Alkalies and Concentrated Sulphuric Acid

- In cold conc., red crystals of chromic anhydride (or chromium trioxide) are formed.

$$K_2Cr_2O_7 + \underset{\text{(Cold and conc.)}}{2H_2SO_4} \longrightarrow 2CrO_3 + 2KHSO_4 + H_2O$$

- On heating the mixture, chromium (III) sulphate is formed.

$$\underset{\text{Yellow}}{2K_2Cr_2O_7} + 8H_2SO_4 \xrightarrow{\Delta} 2K_2SO_4 + \underset{\text{Green}}{2Cr_2(SO_4)_3} + 8H_2O + 3O_2$$

- On adding an alkali, the concentration of H^+ ions decreases or we can say pH of the solution increases. In that case yellow colour chromate solution is formed.
While, on adding acid, the concentration of H^+ ions increases or we can say pH of the solution decreases. This results to an orange solution containing $Cr_2O_7^{2-}$ ions.

$$\underset{\text{Orange}}{Cr_2O_7^{2-}} + \underset{(pH>7)}{2OH^-} \longrightarrow \underset{\text{Yellow}}{2CrO_4^{2-}} + H_2O$$

$$\underset{\text{Yellow}}{2CrO_4^{2-}} + \underset{(pH<7)}{2H^+} \longrightarrow \underset{\text{Orange}}{Cr_2O_7^{2-}} + H_2O$$

Thus, chromates and dichromates are interconvertible in aqueous solution depending upon pH of the solution.

Concept ladder

Reason for inter conversion In dichromate solution, the orange-red $Cr_2O_7^{2-}$ ions are invariably in equilibrium with yellow CrO_4^{2-} ions.

$$\underset{\text{Orange-red}}{Cr_2O_7^{2-}} + H_2O \rightleftharpoons \underset{\text{Yellow}}{2CrO_4^{2-}} + 2H^+$$

Thus, on the basis of Le-Chatelier's principle

- When the conc. of OH^- is increased, then forward reaction proceeds faster resulting to more yellow coloured CrO_4^- ion.
- Similarly when acid is added, conc. of H^+ ions is increased resulting to faster backward reaction.

(iii) Oxidising Nature

Sodium and potassium dichromates are strong oxidising agents, the sodium salt has a greater solubility in water.

$K_2Cr_2O_7$ is a good oxidising agent in acidic medium.

$$K_2Cr_2O_7 + 4H_2SO_4 \longrightarrow K_2SO_4 + Cr_2(SO_4)_3 + 4H_2O + 3[O]$$

or $\underset{\text{Orange}}{Cr_2O_7^{2-}} + 14H^+ + 6e^- \longrightarrow \underset{\text{Green}}{2Cr^{3+}} + 7H_2O$

The reaction is spontaneous ($E° > 0$) and $Cr_2O_7^{2-}$ is used as a primary standard in volumetric (titrimetric) analysis.

$$Cr_2O_7^{2-} \equiv 6e^-;$$

$\therefore$ Eq. wt. $[Cr_2O_7^{2-}]$ (as an oxidising agent)

$$= \frac{\text{Mol. wt.}}{\text{Electron transfer}} = \frac{294}{6} = 49$$

Means one sixth of the molecular weight of $K_2Cr_2O_7$ dissolved in 1 litre of water would give one normal (1N) solution (containing 1g-equivalent of $K_2Cr_2O_7$)

Thus, acidified potassium dichromate will oxidise iodides to iodine, sulphides to sulphur, tin (II) to tin (IV) and iron (II) salts to iron (III). The half reactions are noted below.

$$6I^- \longrightarrow 3I_2 + 6e^-$$
$$3Sn^{2+} \longrightarrow 3Sn^{4+} + 6e^-$$
$$3H_2S \longrightarrow 6H^+ + 3S + 6e^-$$
$$6Fe^{2+} \longrightarrow 6Fe^{3+} + 6e^-$$

The full ionic reaction is (for Fe^{2+} ion) :

$$Cr_2O_7^{2-} + 14H^+ + 6Fe^{2+} \longrightarrow 2Cr^{3+} + 6Fe^{3+} + 7H_2O$$

Concept ladder

$K_2Cr_2O_7$ when heated with conc. H_2SO_4 and soluble or ionic chlorides (like NaCl, KCl) gives deep red vapour of CrO_2Cl_2. This test is called as **chromyl-chloride test.** It is used to identify Cl^- in inorganic salt-analysis. But AgCl, $PbCl_2$, $SnCl_4$, HgCl or $HgCl_2$ (more covalent in nature) does not show chromyl chloride test.

Uses

- In volumetric analysis, it is used as a standard solution for the estimation of Fe^{2+}, I^- etc.
- In organic reactions, it is used as an oxidising agent.
- It is used in preparation of chrome alum.

$$K_2Cr_2O_7 + H_2SO_4 + 3SO_2 \xrightarrow{\Delta} \underbrace{K_2SO_4 + Cr_2(SO_4)_3}_{\text{Crystallises as}}$$

$$\downarrow + H_2O$$

$$\underset{\text{Chrome alum}}{[KCr(SO_4)_2 \cdot 12H_2O]_2}$$

- In calico printing and dyeing. It is deep purple compound used for leather tanning.
- In photography.
- In hardening of gelatine flim.

Potassium Permanganate [$KMnO_4$]

The preparation and properties of $KMnO_4$ are as follows.

Preparation

$KMnO_4$ is prepared from MnO_2 (pyrolusite) in the following steps

***Step* I** When MnO_2 is fused with KOH and $KClO_3$ or KNO_3, potassium manganate (K_2MnO_4) is formed which is indicated by its dark green colour.

In this reaction, $KClO_3$ and KNO_3 acts as an oxidising agent.

$$\underset{\text{Brown}}{3MnO_2} + 6KOH + KClO_3 \xrightarrow{\Delta} \underset{\text{Green}}{3K_2MnO_4} + KCl + 3H_2O$$

The fused mass is extracted with water and solution is green (MnO_4^{2-}).

***Step* II** When Cl_2 gas is passed, K_2MnO_4 is oxidised to $KMnO_4$ (purple).

$$\underset{\text{Green}}{2K_2MnO_4} + Cl_2 \longrightarrow 2KCl + \underset{\text{Purple}}{2KMnO_4}$$

or, K_2MnO_4 disproportionates in a neutral or acidic solution to give permanganate.

$$3MnO_4^{2-} + 4H^+ \longrightarrow 2MnO_4^- + MnO_2 + 2H_2O$$

Commercially, it is prepared by the alkaline oxidation fusion of MnO_2 followed by the electrolytic oxidation of manganate (VI).

At anode, $\underset{\text{Manganate ion}}{MnO_4^{2-}} \longrightarrow \underset{\text{Permanganate ion}}{MnO_4^-} + e^-$

At cathode, $2H^+ + 2e^- \longrightarrow H_2$

In laboratory, a manganese (II) ion salt is oxidised by peroxodisulphate to permanganate

$$2Mn^{2+} + 5S_2O_8^{2-} + 8H_2O \longrightarrow 2MnO_4^- + 10SO_4^{2-} + 16H^+$$

Potassium permanganate forms dark purple (almost black) crystals which are isostructural with $KClO_4$.

NEET Close-up

Example Similar to PYQ Asked in NEET 2022

If MnO_2 is fused with KOH and oxidised with air or KNO_3, the oxidation number of Mn changes from

(a) + 2 to + 4 (b) + 4 to + 6
(c) + 6 to + 2 (d) + 4 to + 4

Sol. (*b*) The reaciton is proceed as

$$\underset{(+4)}{MnO_2} \xrightarrow[\text{With air or } KNO_3]{\text{Fused with KOH, oxidised}} \underset{\substack{\text{(Manganate ion)} \\ (+6)}}{MnO_4^{2-}}$$

Skill Builder

If $KMnO_4$ is reduced by oxalic acid in an acidic medium, then oxidation number of Mn changes from

(a) +7 to +2 (b) + 7 to + 4
(c) + 4 to + 2 (d) + 6 to + 4

For more practice Refer to Q. 23 of Gearing up for NEET.

Structure

In permanganate ion (MnO_4^-), manganese is sp^3-hybridised and hence four oxygen atoms are arranged tetrahedrally.

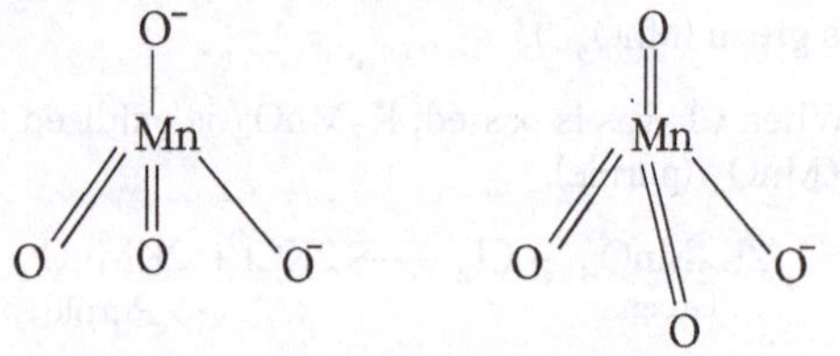

Manganate ion (Green) Permanganate ion (Purple)

Thus, both manganate and permanganate ions are tetrahedral where bonding takes place by overlap of *p*-orbital of oxygen with *d*-orbitals of manganese. The given manganate is paramagnetic but the permanganate is diamagnetic.

NEET Snapshot

MnO_4^{2-} ions exhibit *d-d* transition and paramagnetism while MnO_4^-, $Cr_2O_7^{2-}$ and CrO_4^{2-} will not. *[NEET 2018]*

The ions having d^0 or d^{10} configuration are incapable to show *d-d* transition, so they are colourless, e.g. Mn^{7+}, Cr^{6+} and Cu^+ etc.
In MnO_4^{2-} ion, Mn^{+6} has d^1 configuration hence it exhibits *d-d* transition.

Physical Properties

- It exists as deep purple black prisms with a greenish lustre which becomes dull in air due to reduction.
- It is moderately soluble in water at room temperature and more soluble in hot water.

Chemical Properties

(i) Effect of Heat

When heated to 513 K, it readily decompose to give potassium manganate, manganese (IV) oxide and oxygen.

$$2KMnO_4 \xrightarrow{513\,K} K_2MnO_4 + MnO_2 + O_2$$

(ii) Effect of Conc. H_2SO_4

- With cold conc. H_2SO_4, it gives a green oily compound (Mn_2O_7) which is highly explosive in nature.

$$2KMnO_4 + \underset{\text{Cold conc.}}{2H_2SO_4} \longrightarrow \underset{\text{Green}}{Mn_2O_7} + 2KHSO_4 + H_2O$$

$$2Mn_2O_7 \xrightarrow{\Delta} 4MnO_2 + 3O_2$$

- With warm conc. H_2SO_4

$$4KMnO_4 + \underset{\text{Warm conc.}}{6H_2SO_4} \longrightarrow 2K_2SO_4 + 4MnSO_4 + 6H_2O + 5O_2$$

(iii) Stability in Acidic Medium

Permanganate solutions are intrinsically unstable in acidic solution and decompose slowly. Decomposition is catalysed by sunlight, so $KMnO_4$ solution should be stored in dark bottles and they must be standardised at the moment of its use in volumetric analysis.

$$4MnO_4^- + 4H^+ \longrightarrow 4MnO_2 + 3O_2 + 2H_2O$$

(iv) Oxidising Property

$KMnO_4$ is a good oxidising agent. The actual oxidising action depends upon the use of the $KMnO_4$ in (A) neutral (B) alkaline or (C) acidic medium.

A. **In neutral solution** It acts as moderate oxidising agent.

$$2KMnO_4 + H_2O \longrightarrow 2KOH + 2MnO_2 + 3O$$

$$MnO_4^- + 2H_2O + 3e^- \longrightarrow MnO_2 + 4OH^-$$

During the course of reaction, alkali is generated which make the medium weakly alkaline (even though we started with neutral solutions).

Hence eq. wt. of $KMnO_4$ in neutral or weakly alkaline medium $= \dfrac{\text{mol. wt}}{3} = \dfrac{158}{3} = 52.67$

Some oxidising properties of $KMnO_4$ in the neutral medium.

- H_2O_2 is oxidised to O_2

$$2MnO_4^- + 3H_2O_2 \longrightarrow 2MnO_2 + 3O_2 + 2OH^- + 2H_2O$$

- $S_2O_3^{2-}$ is oxidised to SO_4^{2-}

$$8MnO_4^- + 3S_2O_3^{2-} + H_2O \longrightarrow 8MnO_2 + 6SO_4^{2-} + 2OH^-$$

- Mn^{2+} is oxidised to MnO_2

$$2MnO_4^- + 3Mn^{2+} + 2H_2O \longrightarrow 5MnO_2 + 4H^+$$

- It oxidises hydrogen sulphide to sulphur

$$2KMnO_4 + 4H_2S \longrightarrow 2MnS + S + K_2SO_4 + 4H_2O$$

NEET Close-up

Example Similar to PYQ Asked in NEET 2019

When neutral or faintly alkaline $KMnO_4$ is treated with thiosulphate then thiosulphate is oxidised to 'X'. 'X' is

(a) SO_4^{2-} (b) SO_3^-
(c) SO^{2-} (d) $2SO_2$

Sol. (a) When neutral or faintly alkaline $KMnO_4$ is treated with thiosulphate then thiosulphate is oxidised almost quantitatively to sulphate.

The reaction is proceed as

$$8MnO_4^- + 3S_2O_3^{2-} + H_2O \longrightarrow 8MnO_2 + 6SO_4^{2-} + 2OH^-$$

Skill Builder

When acidic solution of $KMnO_4$ is treated with sulphurous acid, sulphite is oxidised to 'Z'. 'Z' is

(a) $S_2O_3^{2-}$ (b) H_2SO_4
(c) SO_2^{2-} (d) SO

For more practice Refer to Q. 12 of Step up Practice-2

B. **In acidic medium** It acts as a strong oxidising agent.

$$2KMnO_4 + 3H_2SO_4 \longrightarrow K_2SO_4 + 2MnSO_4 + 3H_2O + 5O$$

$$\underset{\text{(Purple)}}{MnO_4^-} + 8H^+ + 5e^- \longrightarrow \underset{\text{(Colourless or extremely light pink)}}{Mn^{2+}} + 4H_2O$$

- The purple colour of MnO_4^- acts as its own indicator (self) in titrations.
- Since, in above reaction, MnO_4^- ion gains 5 electrons or 5 atoms of oxygen are available for two molecules of $KMnO_4$.

Thus, equivalent weight of MnO_4^-

$$= \frac{\text{mol. wt.}}{5} \text{ in acidic medium.}$$

Some oxidising properties of $KMnO_4$ in acidic medium are given below.

- It oxidises ferrous sulphate to ferric sulphate (i.e. ferrous salt to ferric salt).

$$2KMnO_4 + 8H_2SO_4 + 10FeSO_4 \longrightarrow K_2SO_4 + 2MnSO_4 + 5Fe_2(SO_4)_3 + 8H_2O$$

or $$2MnO_4^- + 16H^+ + \underset{\text{Green}}{10Fe^{2+}} \longrightarrow 2Mn^{2+} + 8H_2O + \underset{\text{Yellow}}{10Fe^{3+}}$$

- It oxidises oxalates or oxalic acid to CO_2

$$2KMnO_4 + 3H_2SO_4 + 5C_2H_2O_4 \longrightarrow K_2SO_4 + 2MnSO_4 + 8H_2O + 10CO_2$$

or $$2MnO_4^- + 16H^+ + 5C_2O_4^{2-} \longrightarrow 2Mn^{2+} + 8H_2O + 10CO_2$$

- It oxidises potassium iodide to iodine.

$$2KMnO_4 + 3H_2SO_4 + 10KI \longrightarrow K_2SO_4 + 2MnSO_4 + 5H_2O + 5I_2$$

or $$2MnO_4^- + 16H^+ + 10I^- \longrightarrow 2Mn^{2+} + 8H_2O + 5I_2$$

- It also oxidises H_2O_2 to O_2.

$$2KMnO_4 + 3H_2SO_4 + 5H_2O_2 \longrightarrow K_2SO_4 + 2MnSO_4 + 8H_2O + 5O_2$$

or $$2MnO_4^- + 6H^+ + 5H_2O_2 \longrightarrow 2Mn^{2+} + 8H_2O + 5O_2$$

- It oxidises nitrites (NO_2^-) to nitrates [NO_3^-].

$$2KMnO_4 + 3H_2SO_4 + 5KNO_2 \longrightarrow K_2SO_4 + 2MnSO_4 + 3H_2O + 5KNO_3$$

or $$2MnO_4^- + 6H^+ + 5NO_2^- \longrightarrow 2Mn^{2+} + 3H_2O + 5NO_3^-$$

- It oxidises sulphur dioxide to sulphurous acid.

$$2KMnO_4 + 5SO_2 + 2H_2O \longrightarrow K_2SO_4 + 2MnSO_4 + 2H_2SO_4$$

or $$2MnO_4^- + 5SO_2 + 2H_2O \longrightarrow 5SO_4^{2-} + 2Mn^{2+} + 4H^+$$

- It oxidises hydrogen halide (HX, where X = Cl, Br, I) to dihalogen (X_2).

$$2KMnO_4 + 3H_2SO_4 + 10HX \longrightarrow K_2SO_4 + 2MnSO_4 + 8H_2O + 5X_2$$

or $$2MnO_4^- + 16H^+ + 10X^- \longrightarrow 2Mn^{2+} + 8H_2O + 5X_2$$

- It oxidises ethyl alcohol to aldehyde.

$$2KMnO_4 + 3H_2SO_4 + 5CH_3CH_2OH \longrightarrow K_2SO_4 + 2MnSO_4 + 5CH_3CHO + 8H_2O$$

- Sulphurous acid or sulphite is oxidised to a sulphate or sulphuric acid.

$$5SO_3^{2-} + 2MnO_4^- + 6H^+ \longrightarrow 2Mn^{2+} + 3H_2O + 5SO_4^{2-}$$

C. **In alkaline medium** In strongly alkaline medium, first potassium manganate is formed from $KMnO_4$ which further is reduced to MnO_2.

$$2KMnO_4 + 2KOH \longrightarrow 2K_2MnO_4 + H_2O + O$$

or $$MnO_4^- + e^- \longrightarrow MnO_4^{2-}$$

$$2K_2MnO_4 + 2H_2O \longrightarrow 2MnO_2 + 4KOH + 2[O]$$

Equivalent weight (in strongly basic medium)

$$= \frac{\textbf{mol. wt.}}{1} = 158$$

It oxidises potassium iodide to potassium iodate

$$2KMnO_4 + H_2O + KI \longrightarrow 2MnO_2 + 2KOH + KIO_3$$

Uses

- Alkaline (cold and dilute) $KMnO_4$ is called **Baeyer's reagent** and is used to test **unsaturation** (non aromatic, C=C and C≡C) in an organic compound, where it decolorises $KMnO_4$ (purple coloured).

$$CH_2{=}CH_2 + H_2O \xrightarrow[\text{(O) 273 K}]{KMnO_4/OH^-} \underset{\displaystyle OH}{CH_2}-\underset{\displaystyle OH}{CH_2}$$

- $KMnO_4$ is also widely used as a disinfectant and germicide.
- A very dilute solution of $KMnO_4$ is used for washing wounds and gargling of mouth sore.
- It is also used for purifying water and treat stinking wells.
- Being a good oxidising agent, it is also used for bleaching of wool, cotton, silk etc.
- It is used in volumetric analysis (as a secondary standard solution) for the estimation of ferrous salts, oxalates, iodides and hydrogen peroxides.

Concept ladder $KMnO_4$ is not used as primary standard solution. This is due to the fact that it is difficult to obtain it in the pure state and free from traces of MnO_2. That's why it is always first standardised with a standard solution of oxalic acid.

STEP UP Practice 2

1. In $Cr_2O_7^{2-}$, every Cr is linked to
(a) two O atoms (b) three O atoms
(c) four O atoms (d) five O atoms

2. When MnO_2 is fused with KOH and $KClO_3$, a coloured compound is formed, the product and its colour is
(a) K_2MnO_4, green (b) $KMnO_4$, purple
(c) Mn_2O_3, brown (d) Mn_3O_4 black

3. Which is not the true statement about $KMnO_4$?
(a) Its solution is unstable in acidic medium.
(b) Its small quantity added to conc. H_2SO_4, a green coloured solution containing MnO_3^+ ions is formed
(c) MnO_4^- changes to Mn^{2+} in basic solution.
(d) It is self-indicator in Fe^{2+} or $C_2O_4^{2-}$ titration.

4. Which of the following is incorrectly matched about dichromate and chromate ion?
(a) Dichromate ion ⟶ Cr—O—Cr bond angle of 126°.
(b) Chromate ion ⟶ Tetrahedral geometry
(c) Chromate ion ⟶ Oxidation state of Cr is +6.
(d) Dichromate ion ⟶ Oxidation state of Cr is +3.

5 Which of the following statements is incorrect?
(a) When moving along a period from Sc to Zn, basic nature decreases and acidic nature increases.
(b) The basic and amphoteric oxides dissolve in non-oxidising acids and form hexaaqua ions.
(c) The basic oxides like CrO_3 and Mn_2O_3 dissolve in water to form the oxoacids.
(d) VO and CrO both are strong reducing agents.

6. In alkaline H_2O_2, $Cr_2O_7^{2-}$ changes to tetraperoxo species ... having oxidation number of Cr as ...
(a) CrO_4^{2-}, +6 (b) CrO_5, +6 (c) CrO_8^{3-}, +5 (d) CrO_8^{3-}, +11

7. Consider the following statements.
Statement I Chromium can be used as a protective and non-corrosive plating on other metals.
Statement II Due to atmospheric oxidation, chemically a inert layer of Cr_2O_3 is formed.
In the light of the above statements, choose the most appropriate answer from the options given below.
(a) Both Statement I and Statement II are false.
(b) Statement I is true but Statement II is false.
(c) Statement I is false but Statement II is true.
(d) Both Statement I and Statement II are true.

8. $K_2Cr_2O_7$ on heating with aqueous NaOH, gives
(a) CrO_4^{2-} (b) $Cr(OH)_3$ (c) $Cr_2O_7^{2-}$ (d) $Cr(OH)_2$

9. Consider the following statements.
Statement I Green solution of potassium manganate (VI), K_2MnO_4 turns purple and brown solid is precipitated when CO_2 is bubbled into it.
Statement II K_2MnO_4 changes to K_3MnO_8 by CO_2.
In the light of the above statements, choose the most appropriate answer from the options given below.
(a) Both Statement I and Statement II are false.
(b) Statement I is true but Statement II is false.
(c) Statement I is false but Statement II is true.
(d) Both Statement I and Statement II are true.

10. Traces of MnO_4^- in conc. H_2SO_4 may change to
(a) Mn_2O_7 (b) MnO_3^+ (c) MnO_2 (d) MnO_4^{2-}

11. What would happen, when a solution of potassium chromate is treated with an excess of dilute nitric acid?
(a) Cr^{3+} and $Cr_2O_7^{2-}$ are formed.
(b) $Cr_2O_7^{2-}$ and H_2O are formed.
(c) CrO_4^{2-} is reduced to +3 state of Cr.
(d) CrO_3 and CO_2 are formed.

12. When acidic solution of $KMnO_4$ is treated with nitrite, then nitrite is oxidised to '*P*'. '*P*' is
(a) NO_2^- (b) $N_2O_3^-$
(c) NO (d) NO_3^-

13. $KMnO_4$ spot cannot be bleached by
(a) H_2O_2 / H^+ (b) SO_2 / H^+
(c) $C_2O_4^{2-}$ / H^+ (d) $C_2O_7^{2-}$ / H^+

14. Which of the following reactions is incorrectly matched with the product formed in these reactions?
(a) $4K_2Cr_2O_7(s) \xrightarrow[\Delta]{\text{Strongly heated}}$ Oxygen
(b) $K_2Cr_2O_7 \xrightarrow[2H_2SO_4]{\text{Cold and Conc.}}$ Chromium dioxide
(c) $2K_2Cr_2O_7 \xrightarrow{H_2SO_4,\ \Delta}$ Chromium (III) sulphate
(d) $Na_2Cr_2O_7 \xrightarrow{KCl}$ Potassium dichromate (orange crystal)

15. $K_2Cr_2O_7 \xrightarrow{\Delta} K_2CrO_4 + O_2 + X$. In the above reaction X is
(a) CrO_3 (b) Cr_2O_7
(c) Cr_2O_3 (d) CrO_5

16. What are the species, *A* and *B* in the following reactions respectively?
$$CrO_3 + H_2O \longrightarrow A \xrightarrow{OH^-} B$$
(a) H_2CrO_4, $H_2Cr_2O_7$ (b) $H_2Cr_2O_7$, Cr_2O_3
(c) CrO_4^{2-}, $Cr_2O_7^{2-}$ (d) H_2CrO_4, CrO_4^{2-}

17. The reaction of $K_2Cr_2O_7$ with NaCl and conc. H_2SO_4 gives
(a) CrO_2Cl_2 (b) Cr_2O_3
(c) $CrCl_3$ (d) $CrOCl_2$

18. Consider the following statements.
Statement I Potassium dichromate on strongly heating decomposes to give oxygen.
Statement II Potassium dichromate on action with concentrated HCl, Cl_2 gas is evolved and chromyl chloride is obtained.
In the light of the above statements, choose the most appropriate answer from the options given below.
(a) Both Statement I and Statement II are false.
(b) Statement I is true but Statement II is false.
(c) Statement I is false but Statement II is true.
(d) Both Statement I and Statement II are true.

19. In dilute alkaline solution MnO_4^- changes to
(a) MnO_4^{2-}
(b) MnO_2
(c) Mn_2O_3
(d) MnO

20. In cold acidic medium, H_2O_2 changes $K_2Cr_2O_7$ to CrO_5 (deep blue solution in ether) having two peroxylinkage. Oxidation number of Cr in CrO_5 is
(a) +10 (b) −10
(c) +4 (d) +6

21. Given below are two statements.
Assertion (A) Aqueous soution of $K_2Cr_2O_7$ is preferred as a primary standard in volumetric analysis over $Na_2Cr_2O_7$ aqueous solution.
Reason (R) $K_2Cr_2O_7$ has a higher solubility in water than $Na_2Cr_2O_7$.
In the light of the above statements, choose the correct answer from the options given below.
(a) Both A and R are true and R is the correct explanation of A.
(b) Both A and R are true but R is not the correct explanation of A.
(c) A is true but R is false.
(d) A is false but R is true.

22. Consider the following conversions.
(i) $Fe^{2+} \longrightarrow Fe^{3+} + e^-$
(ii) $I^- \longrightarrow IO_3^-$
(iii) $I^- \longrightarrow I_2$
(iv) $H_2S \longrightarrow S$
(v) $H_2O \longrightarrow OH^-$
How many of them can be carried out by both acidified $K_2Cr_2O_7$ and acidified $KMnO_4$?
(a) 4 (b) 1
(c) 2 (d) 3

23. One of the products formed when $K_2Cr_2O_7$ reacts with conc. H_2SO_4 in cold is
(a) CrO_3 (b) $Cr_2(SO_4)_3$
(c) Cr_2O_3 (d) CrO_4Cl_2

Module 3

f-Block Elements or Inner Transition Elements

- Inner Transition Elements
- Electronic Configuration of Lanthanoids
- General Characteristics of Lanthanoids
- Electronic Configuration of Actinoids
- General Characteristics of Actinoids
- Comparision in Lanthanoids and Actinoids
- Some Applications of *d*-and *f*-Block Elements

The Inner-Transition Elements (*f*-Block Elements)

The elements in which differentiating electron enters in $(n-2)f$ subshell are called *f*-**block elements.** They are also called **inner-transition elements** because in periodic table they are placed inside the transition elements.

These elements are divided into two series

(i) 4*f*-series or lanthanoids (ii) 5*f*-series or actinoids

4*f*-series or Lanthanoids or First Inner Transition Series

Fourteen elements of the first row (4*f*-series) from cerium ($Z = 58$) to lutetium ($Z = 71$) which follow lanthanum ($Z = 57$) (a 5*d*-block element of group 3) in the periodic table are called **lanthanoids** or **lanthanones.** These elements are characterised by successive filling of 4*f*-orbitals in their electronic configuration.

Electronic Configurations of Lanthanum and Lanthanoids

The general electronic configuration of these elements is $[Xe]4f^{1-14}\ 5d^{0-1}\ 6s^2$. Members of this series along with their electronic configurations are summarised in table.

Electronic Configuration of Lanthanoids

Element	Symbol	Atomic number	Outer configuration
Lanthanum	La	57	$[Xe]5d^1 6s^2$ [*d*-block]
Cerium	Ce	58	$[Xe]4f^1 5d^1 6s^2$
Praseodymium	Pr	59	$[Xe]4f^3 6s^2$
Neodymium	Nd	60	$[Xe]4f^4 6s^2$
Promethium	Pm	61	$[Xe]4f^5 6s^2$
Samarium	Sm	62	$[Xe]4f^6 6s^2$
Europium	Eu	63	$[Xe]4f^7 6s^2$
Gadolinium	**Gd**	**64**	$[Xe]4f^7 5d^1 6s^2$
Terbium	Tb	65	$[Xe]4f^9 6s^2$
Dysprosium	Dy	66	$[Xe]4f^{10} 6s^2$
Holmium	Ho	67	$[Xe]4f^{11} 6s^2$
Erbium	Er	68	$[Xe]4f^{12} 6s^2$
Thulium	Tm	69	$[Xe]4f^{13} 6s^2$
Ytterbium	Yb	70	$[Xe]4f^{14} 6s^2$
Lutetium	**Lu**	**71**	$[Xe]4f^{14} 5d^1 6s^2$

General Characteristics of Lanthanoids

Some of the general characteristics of lanthanoids are discussed below.

Physical State

- All are silvery white (except Eu and Yb which are pale yellow) soft metals having tensile strength and are good conductor of heat and electricity.
- The hardness increases with increasing atomic number, samarium being steel hard.
- They have typical metallic structure.
- They have higher density values which increases with increase in atomic number.
- They have high melting point with no regularity.

Atomic Size, Ionic Size and Lanthanoid Contraction

There is a regular decrease in the atomic and ionic radii of lanthanoid from La to Lu. This decrease in radii is a unique feature and is known as **lanthanoid contraction.** It is due to greater effect of the increased nuclear charge than that of the screening effect.

Consequence of lanthanoid contraction

- As a result of lanthanoid contraction, the normal increase in size from Sc $\rightarrow$ Y $\rightarrow$ La disappears for the lanthanoides and the pairs of elements such as Zr and Hf, Nb and Ta, Mo and W etc., have nearly same size. The properties of these elements are very similar.
- The similarities in properties within these pairs make their separation very difficult. However, due to this contraction, their ability to form complexes varies slightly. This slight variation is utilised to separate lanthanoids by ion-exchange method.
- Due to lanthanoid contraction, the elements of 5*d* and 4*d*-transition series resemble each other much more closely than to that of 4*d* and 3*d* series.
- Covalent character of hydroxides of lanthanoids increases as the size decreases, from La^{3+} to Lu^{3+} but basic strength decreases, i.e. $La(OH)_3$ is most basic whereas $Lu(OH)_3$ is least basic.
- Tendency to form stable complexes from La^{3+} and Lu^{3+} increases as the size decreases in that order.

Ionisation Enthalpy

These elements have low ionisation enthalpy and thus, have high electropositive character.

Oxidation States

Lanthanoids have limited oxidation states because there is a large gap in the energy of 4*f* and 5*d*-subshells. Most stable oxidation state of lanthanoids is +3 but some of them also show +2 and +4 oxidation states in solution or in solid compounds.

- In aqueous solution Eu^{2+}, Sm^{2+}, Tm^{2+} and Yb^{2+} ions are present but they revert back to +3 oxidation state. Hence, they are good reducing agents.
- Similarly Pr, Ce, Tb, Dy, in aqueous solution are present in +4 oxidation state but they revert back to +3 oxidation state. Hence, they are good oxidising agents.

Colour

Several trivalent (M^{3+}) lanthanoid ions are coloured in solid state as well as in aqueous solution. Colour of member of this series arise due to *f*-*f* electronic transition, as *f*-subshells are partially filled. However, absorption bonds are narrow, probably because of the excitation within *f*-level.

Generally, lanthanoid ions with xf electrons have a similar colour to those with $(14-x)f$ electrons, e.g. La^{3+} and Lu^{3+} are colourless, Eu^{3+} and Tb^{3+} are pale pink etc.

Magnetic Properties

Many lanthanoid ions are paramagnetic due to the presence of unpaired electrons in the 4*f*-orbitals (except Ce^{4+}, Lu^{3+} and Yb^{2+}). There is difference in calculating the magnetic moment of these elements with respect to transition elements. Here, both spin as well as orbital moments give contribution and μ_{eff} is calculated.

$$\mu_{eff} = \sqrt{4s(s+1) + l(l+1)}\ \text{BM}$$

where, l is orbital (azimuthal) quantum number and s is the spin quantum number.

The Colour and Magnetic Moment of Lanthanoid (III) Ions

Ion	Colour (Aqua complex)	Electronic configuration	*N* (unpaired electrons)	Magnetic moment of *N* unpaired electrons/μ BM	
				Calculated (Only total spin) $\sqrt{N(N+2)}$	Observed
La^{3+}	Colourless	$4f^0$	0	00	0
Ce^{3+}	Colourless	$4f^1$	1	1.73	2.3 - 2.5
Pr^{3+}	Green	$4f^2$	2	2.83	3.4 - 3.6
Nd^{3+}	Lilac	$4f^3$	3	3.87	2.5 - 3.6
Pm^{3+}	Yellow	$4f^4$	4	4.90	2.70
Sm^{3+}	Yellow	$4f^5$	5	5.92	1.5 - 1.6
Eu^{3+}	Pale pink	$4f^6$	6	6.93	3.4 - 3.6
Gd^{3+}	Colourless	$4f^7$	7	7.94	7.8 - 8.0
Tb^{3+}	Pale pink	$4f^8$	6	6.93	9.4 - 9.6
Dy^{3+}	Yellow	$4f^9$	5	5.92	10.4 - 10.5
Ho^{3+}	Pale yellow	$4f^{10}$	4	4.90	10.3 - 10.5
Er^{3+}	Rose-red (pink)	$4f^{11}$	3	3.87	9.4 - 9.6
Tm^{3+}	Pale-green	$4f^{12}$	2	2.83	7.1 - 4.4
Yb^{3+}	Colourless	$4f^{13}$	1	1.73	4.4 - 4.9
Lu^{3+}	Colourless	$4f^{14}$	0	0.00	0

NEET Close-up

Example Similar to PYQ Asked in NEET 2024

The pair of lanthanoid ions which are diamagnetic is

(a) La^{3+} and Lu^{3+} (b) Sm^{3+} and Ho^{3+}
(c) Dy^{3+} and Lu^{3+} (d) Yb^{3+} and Ce^{3+}

Sol. (*a*) $La^{3+} = [Xe]\ 4f^0 5d^0 6s^0$ and $Lu^{3+} = [Xe] 4f^{14} 5d^0 6s^0$

Both ions do not contain any unpaired electron. Hence, these are diamagnetic.

Skill Builder

The pair of lanthanoid ions which are diamagnetic is

(a) Pm^{2+} and Tb^{3+} (b) Er^{2+} and Tm^{2+}
(c) Yb^{2+} and Ce^{4+} (d) Sm^{2+} and Tb^{3+}

For more practice Refer to Q.30 Gearing up for NEET.

Complex Formation

Lanthanoid ions have very less tendency to form complexes. This is because of their low charge density, i.e. charge to size ratio. They form complexes with strong chelating agents like EDTA, β-diketones, oxime etc. But do not form π-bonded organometallic compounds.

Alloy Formation

They form alloys easily with other metals (especially with iron). An alloy of lanthanoid metal is **misch-metal.** It has lanthanoid metals (95%) and iron about 5% with traces of S, C, Ca and Al. It is used in the production of bullets, shells and lighter flint.

Chemical Reactivity

In their chemical behaviour, in general, the earlier members of the series are quite reactive similar to calcium but with increasing atomic number they behave more like aluminium.

- They are highly electropositive and reactive. All of them burn in air to form oxides Ln_2O_3 and nitrides LnN (cerium gives CeO_2). Powdered cerium is even pyrophoric. Yttrium usually forms a protective oxide coating on it and remains unattacked by air even at 1273 K.
- They combine with H_2 on gentle heating and form hydrides, have a defect lattice and are non-stoichiometric.
- They form trihalides on burning with halogens but Ce and Tb give CeF_4 and TbF_4 respectively. Complex fluorides of Pr(IV), Nd(IV) and Dy(IV) are also formed.
- They react with H_2O to form hydroxide and liberate H_2 gas.

$$\underset{\text{(In general, Ln)}}{Ln} + H_2O \longrightarrow Ln(OH)_3 + H_2\uparrow$$

- The hydroxides, $M(OH)_3$ are ionic and basic. They are less basic than $Ca(OH)_2$. The basic strength decreases from $Ce(OH)_3$ to $Lu(OH)_3$.
- Lanthanoids (in general, Ln) on reaction with carbon at high temperature (approx. 2500°C) form carbides of the type Ln_3C, Ln_2C_3 and LnC_2.
- Non-availability of d-electrons for π-bonding does not favour the formation of carbonyls by most of the lanthanoids. However, an unstable $Nd(CO)_6$ has been prepared.
- The reaction with acids are very vigorous, but do not dissolve in alkalies.
- They are also stable in HF and H_3PO_4 owing to the formation of a protective film of insoluble salts.

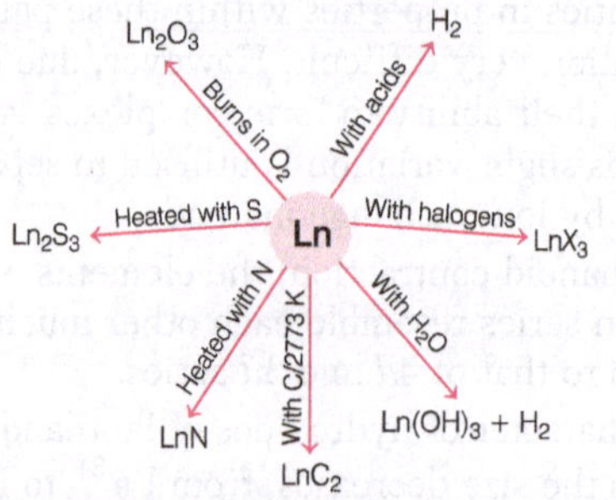

Chemical reactions of the lanthanoids

> **Concept ladder** Europium and ytterbium dissolve in liquid ammonia at 195 K forming blue coloured solutions which give spectra, characteristic of M^{2+} and ammoniated electrons.

Uses

- The best single use of the lanthanoids, i.e. for the prodution of alloy steels for plates and pipes.
- They are used in the production of alloys like misch-metal.
- Mixed oxides of lanthanoids are used as catalysts in petroleum cracking.

5f-Series or Actinoids or Second Inner-Transition Series

- In 5f-series elements, the differentiating electron occupies 5f-orbital, thus these elements are said to belong to 5f-series. These are also called **actinoids** because of their close resemblance in properties with actinium.
- This series includes 14-elements from Th to Lr following actinium in the seventh period of the periodic table. Most of them are radioactive and therefore have the greatest importance in the study of **nuclear chemistry**.
- Elements with atomic numbers greater than 92 (atomic number of uranium) are called the **transuranium elements.** All these elements are man-made and radioactive, i.e. they are produced in the laboratory through artificial nuclear reactions.
- The latter members could be prepared only in nanogram quantities.

Electronic Configurations

- The general electronic configuration of actinoids is $[Rn]5f^{1-14}6d^{0-2}7s^2$. The electrons are formally added to $5f$ but not from, thorium ($Z = 90$) but from Pa($Z = 91$) onward.
- The irregularities in the electronic configurations of the actinoids like those in lanthanoids is due to the extra stabilities of f^0, f^7 and f^{14} occupancies of the $5f$-orbitals. Members of this series along with their electronic configurations are tabulated in table.
- The **allocation** of electrons to the $5f$ or $6d$-orbitals in the actinide atoms is more uncertain than the allocation to the $4f$ or $5d$-orbitals in the lanthanoid atoms. It is because the external shielding of the $5f$-electrons is less than that of the $4f$-electrons.
- In simple words, $5f$ is less deeply burried than $4f$, thus, $4f$ electrons can participate in bonding to a far greater extent.

Electronic Configurations of Actinium and Actinoids

Name	Symbol	Atomic No.	Configuration
Actinium	Ac	89	$[Rn]6d^1 7s^2$ [d-block]
Thorium	Th	90	$[Rn]5f^0 6d^2 7s^2$
Protactinium	Pa	91	$[Rn]5f^2 6d^1 7s^2$
Uranium	U	92	$[Rn]5f^3 6d^1 7s^2$
Neptunium	Np	93	$[Rn]5f^4 6d^1 7s^2$
Plutonium	Pu	94	$[Rn]5f^6 6d^0 7s^2$
Americium	Am	95	$[Rn]5f^7 6d^0 7s^2$
Curium	**Cm**	**96**	$\mathbf{[Rn]5f^7 6d^1 7s^2}$
Berkelium	Bk	97	$[Rn]5f^9 6d^0 7s^2$
Californium	Cf	98	$[Rn]5f^{10} 6d^0 7s^2$
Einsteinium	Es	99	$[Rn]5f^{11} 6d^0 7s^2$
Fermium	Fm	100	$[Rn]5f^{12} 6d^0 7s^2$
Mendelenium	Md	101	$[Rn]5f^{13} 6d^0 7s^2$
Nobelium	No	102	$[Rn]5f^{14} 6d^0 7s^2$
Lawrencium	**Lr**	**103**	$\mathbf{[Rn]5f^{14} 6d^1 7s^2}$

NEET Close-up

Example Similar to PYQ Asked in NEET 2016

The electronic configuration of Np (Atomic No. 93), Pu (Atomic No. 94), Am (Atomic No. 95) are

(a) $[Rn]\,5f^5 6d^1 7s^2$, $[Rn]\,5f^4 7s^2$, $[Rn]\,5f^6 7s^2$
(b) $[Rn]\,5f^4 6d^1 7s^2$, $[Rn]\,5f^6 7s^2$, $[Rn]\,5f^7 7s^2$
(c) $[Rn]\,5f^5 7s^2$, $[Rn]\,5f^7 7s^2$, $[Rn]\,5f^3 7s^2$
(d) $[Rn]\,5f^3 6d^2 7s^2$, $[Rn]\,5f^1 6d^1 7s^2$, $[Rn]\,5f^6 7s^2$

Sol. (b) The correct electronic configurations are given as

$$_{93}Np = [Rn]\,5f^4 6d^1 7s^2$$
$$_{94}Pu = [Rn]\,5f^6 7s^2$$
$$_{95}Am = [Rn]\,5f^7 7s^2$$

Skill Builder

The elecronic configuration of Tm (Atomic No. 69, Er (Atomic No. 68), Ho (Atomic No. 67) are

(a) $[Xe]\,4f^{14} 5d^1 6s^2$, $[Xe]\,4f^9 5d^1 6s^2$, $[Xe]\,4f^{11} 5d^1 6s^2$
(b) $[Xe]\,4f^9 5d^2 6s^2$, $[Xe]\,4f^{11} 5d^2 6s^1$, $[Xe]\,4f^{10} 5d^1 6s^2$
(c) $[Xe]\,4f^{11} 6s^2$, $[Xe]\,4f^{13} 6s^2$, $[Xe]\,4f^{14} 6s^2$
(d) $[Xe]\,4f^{13} 6s^2$, $[Xe]\,4f^{12} 6s^2$, $[Xe]\,4f^{11} 6s^2$

For more practice Refer to Q. 33 in Gearing up for NEET.

General Characteristics of Actinoids

Some of the general characteristics of actinoids are discussed below.

Physical State

- They are silvery white in appearance and display a variety of structures.
- Generally, actinoids have high density (except thorium and americium).

Atomic, Ionic Size and Actinide Contraction

- Like lanthanoids, the atomic and ionic size of actinoids too decreases gradually from Th to Lr. This is called as **actinoide contraction.**
- It is due to poor shielding effect of the $5f$-electrons which result in increase in effective nuclear charge (which causes contraction in size of the electron cloud).

Ionisation Enthalpy

The ionisation enthalpies of the early actinoids, though not accurately known but the lower than for the early lanthanoids. The $5f$ electrons will be more effectively shielded from the nuclear charge than the $4f$ electrons to the corresponding lanthanoids. The outer electrons are less firmly held, they are available for bonding in the actinoids.

Oxidation States

The actinoids in general show +3 oxidation state. There is also a greater range of oxidation states due to comparable energies of $5f$, $6d$ and $7s$ levels.

- The maximum oxidation state increases from +4 in Th to +5, +6 and +7 respectively in Pu, U and Np and then decreases in succeeding elements.
- The actinoids resemble the lanthanoids in having more compounds in +3 state than in +4 state but they tend to hydrolyse.
- U^{3+} in aqueous solution evolves hydrogen on standing; aqueous solutions of Np^{3+} and Pu^{3+} are stable, but are easily oxidised to Np^{4+} and Pu^{4+}. All the other trivalent ions up to No^{3+} are stable.
- U^{4+} and Np^{4+} are stable to water, but are slowly oxidised by air to UO_2^{2+} and NpO_2^{2+}.

Oxidation States of Actinium and Actinoids

Ac	Th	Pa	U	Np	Pu	Am	Cm	Bk	Cf	Es	Fm	Md	No	Lr	Ds
+3		+3	+3	+3	+3	+3	+3	+3	+3	+3	+3	+3	+3	+3	+3
	+4	+4	+4	+4	+4	+4	+4	+4							
		+5	+5	+5	+5	+5									
			+6	+6	+6	+6									
				+7	+7										

> **Concept ladder**
> Actinoids ion are generally coloured because of the *f-f* electronic transition (charger transfer). But those ion having $5f^0$, $5f^7$ and $5f^{14}$ electronic configuration are colourless.

Magnetic Properties

The variation in the magnetic susceptibility of the actinoids with the number of unpaired $5f$ electrons is roughly parrallel to the corresponding results for the lanthanoids, the latter have higher values.

Chemical Reactivity

- These are highly reactive metals, especially when finely divided.
- The action of boiling waer on them, for example, gives a mixture of oxide and hydride and combination with most non-metals takes place at moderate temperature.
- HCl reacts with all actinoids.
- Most of them are slightly affected by HNO_3 owing to the formation of protective oxide layer. However, alkalies have no action.

Comparison in Lanthanoids and Actinoids

Elements of these two series have not remarkable similarities and dissimilarities in between them. Some of them are listed below in table.

Comparative Study on Actinoids and Lanthanoids

Lanthanoids	Actinoids
These exhibit mainly +3 oxidation state. In addition to +3 oxidation state, the lower oxidation state of +2 and higher oxidation state of +4 are noticed.	These also exhibit +3 oxidation state. In addition to +3 states, higher oxidation state +3 to +7 are also noticed.
These show lanthanoid contraction.	These show actinoid contraction.
These are separated by ion exchange behaviour.	These also show ion exchange behaviour.
Most of the ions of lanthanoids elements are colourless.	Most of the ions of actinoids are coloured.
These possess lesser tendency for complexation.	These possess greater tendency for complexation.
These do not give oxocations.	These give oxocations, e.g. UO_2^{2+} etc.
Their compounds are less basic in nature.	Their compounds are more basic in nature.
These are non-radioactive (only promethium shows radioactivity)	All these are radioactive.
They are referred to as rare earth metals.	Elements beyond $_{92}U$ are referred as transuranium elements.
Their magnetic nature can be easily explained.	Their magnetic nature can not be easily explained.
Their chemical and physical nature has been studied thoroughly.	Chemical and physical nature of these elements beyond $_{92}U$ has not been studies considerably.

Some Applications of *d*- and *f*-Block Elements

- Iron and steels are the most important construction materials.
- Some compounds are manufactured for special purposes such as TiO for the pigment industry and MnO_2 for use in dry battery cells.
- Ag and Au are restricted to collection items and the contemporary UK copper coins and copper coated steel.
- The silver UK coins are a Cu/Ni alloy.
- They are essential catalysts in the chemical industry.
- The photographic industry relies on the special light sensitive properties of AgBr.

STEP UP Practice 3

1. The electronic configuration of ytterbium (Atomic no. 70) is
(a) $[Xe]4f^{13}5d^1 6s^2$
(b) $[Xe]\,4f^{14}6s^2$
(c) $[Xe]\,4f^{13}6s^2$
(d) $[Xe]\,4f^{12}5d^2 6s^2$

2. For which lanthanide, + 2 and + 3 oxidation states are common ?
(a) La (b) Nd
(c) Ce (d) Eu

3. Which one of the following elements shows maximum number of different oxidation states in its compounds?
(a) Eu (b) La
(c) Gd (d) Am

4. Consider the following statements.
Statement I Ionic radii of Ta and Nb are same.
Statement II The lanthanide contraction decreases the sizes with the increase in atomic number.
In the light of the above statements, choose the most appropriate answer from the options given below.
(a) Both Statement I and Statement II are false.
(b) Statement I is true but Statement II is false.
(c) Statement I is false but Statement II is true.
(d) Both Statement I and Statement II are true.

5. Which of the following element is not a lanthanoid?
(a) Er (b) Pu
(c) Tm (d) Tb

6. The correct order of ionic radii of Y^{3+}, La^{3+}, Eu^{3+} and Lu^{3+} is
(Atomic number of Y = 39, La = 57, Eu = 63, Lu = 71)
(a) $Lu^{3+} < Eu^{3+} < La^{3+} < Y^{3+}$
(b) $La^{3+} < Eu^{3+} < Lu^{3+} < Y^{3+}$
(c) $Y^{3+} < La^{3+} < Eu^{3+} < Lu^{3+}$
(d) $Y^{3+} < Lu^{3+} < Eu^{3+} < La^{3+}$

7. The main reason for larger number of oxidation state exhibited by the actinoids than that of corresponding lanthanoids, is
(a) lesser energy difference between $5f$ and $6d$-orbitals than between $4f$ and $5d$-orbitals
(b) larger atomic size of actinoids than the lanthanoids
(c) more energy difference between $5f$ and $6d$-orbitals than between $4f$ and $5d$-orbitals
(d) greater reactive nature of the actinoids than the lanthanoids

8. Which of the following lanthanoid ions is diamagnetic?
[Atomic number Pr = 50, Eu = 63, Tb = 65, Yb = 70]
(a) Pr^{2+} (b) Eu^{2+}
(c) Tb^{2+} (d) Yb^{2+}

9. Which of the following factors may be regarded as the main cause of lanthanoid contraction?
(a) Greater shielding of $5d$-electrons by $4f$-electrons.
(b) Poorer shielding of $5d$-electrons by $4f$-electrons.
(c) Effective shielding of one $4f$-electrons by another in the subshell.
(d) Poor shielding of one of $4f$-electrons by another in the subshell.

10. Which of the following oxidation states is the most common among the lanthanoides?
(a) +3 (b) +4 (c) +2 (d) +5

11. Misch-metal is
(a) an alloy of lanthanoids and copper
(b) an alloy of lanthanoids and nickel
(c) an alloy of lanthanoids, iron and carbon
(d) an alloy of calcium and copper

12. Which of the following elements is incorrectly matched with the number of unpaired electrons?
(a) $Er^{2+} \longrightarrow$ 3 unpaired electrons
(b) $Gd^{2+} \longrightarrow$ 8 unpaired elecrons
(c) $Nd^{2+} \longrightarrow$ 4 unpaired electrons
(d) $Tb^{3+} \longrightarrow$ 6 unpaired electrons

13. Which of the following exhibits only +3 oxidation state?
(a) U (b) Th
(c) Ac (d) Pa

14. Am^{3+} (a trivalent actinoid ion) with atomic number 95 has electronic configuration
(a) $5f^6 7s^0$ (b) $5f^7 7s^2$
(c) $5f^5 7s^1$ (d) $5f^4 7s^1$

15. Consider the following statements.
Statement I Actinide form relatively less stable complexes as compared to lanthanoids.
Statement II Actinoids can utilise their $5f$-orbitals alongwith $6d$-orbitals in bonding but lanthanoids do not use their $4f$-orbital for bonding.
In the light of the above statements, choose the most appropriate answer from the options given below.
(a) Both Statement I and Statement II are false.
(b) Statement I is true but Statement II is false.
(c) Statement I is false but Statement II is true.
(d) Both Statement I and Statement II are true.

16. Consider the following actinoids,
(i) U (ii) Np (iii) Am
(iv) Cm (v) Pu
How many actinoid show(s) +7 oxidation state?
(a) 4 (b) 3
(c) 2 (d) 1

NEET Exclusive EXTRA BYTES

- First member of each transition series, i.e. Sc, Y, La and Ac do not show variable oxidation states. They show only +3 oxidation state.
- Most stable oxidation state for Cu is +2, Ag is +1 and for Au is +3.
- The monovalent Cu^+, Ag^+ and Au^+ salts are insoluble in water and colourless except Cu_2O which is red. The red colour is due to charge transfer transitions.
- Mercury is the only transition metal which is liquid at room temperature. This is due to the very high ionisation enthalpy making it difficult for electrons to participate in metallic bonding.
- $K_2Cr_2O_7$ is preferred over $Na_2Cr_2O_7$ for use in volumetric analysis (titrations) because the Na-compounds are hygroscopic while the compounds of K are not. Thus, $K_2Cr_2O_7$ can be used as a primary standard.
- In $KMnO_4$ titrations, only sulphuric acid is found to be suitable for making the solution acidic because it (dilute) does not react with $KMnO_4$.
- HCl cannot be used in $KMnO_4$ titrations for acidifying the solution as it reacts with $KMnO_4$ to give Cl_2 and introduces an error into the results.
- Heavier transition metal –1 show strong tendency to form strong $M—M$ bonds than their light congeners. For example, in $Re_2Cl_8^{4-}$ there is a strong quadruple bond between Re—Re.
- The adsorption of H_2 by transition metals such as Pt, Pd, Ni etc., is called occlusion and is due to the interstitial hydride formation.

GEARING UP FOR NEET

1. Nickel has an atomic number 28. The correct electronic configuration of Ni^+ is
(a) $1s^2 2s^2 2p^4 3s^2 3p^8 3d^{10}$
(b) $1s^2 2s^2 2p^6 3s^2 3p^6 3d^8 4s^1$
(c) $1s^2 2s^2 2p^4 3s^2 3p^8 4s^2$
(d) $1s^2 2s^2 3s^2 3p^8 3d^{10}$

2. Which of the following pair of elements has $(n-1)d^{10} ns^2$ electronic configuration?
(a) Fe, Co, Ni
(b) Cu, Ag, Au
(c) Zn, Cd, Hg
(d) Sc, Y, La

3. Which of the following elements has the highest ionisation enthalpy?
(a) Scandium
(b) Vanadium
(c) Copper
(d) Zinc

4. The atomic number of V, Cr, Mn and Fe are 23, 24, 25 and 26 respectively. Which of the following has highest value of their second ionisation enthalpy?
(a) V
(b) Cr
(c) Mn
(d) Fe

5. The radii of the elements from chromium ($Z = 24$) to copper ($Z = 29$) are very close to one another. This is due to
(a) lanthanide contraction
(b) the fact that successive addition of *d*-electrons screen the outer electrons (4*s*) from the inward pull of the nucleus
(c) increase in radii due to increase in *n* is compensated by decrease in radii due to increase in *Z*
(d) atomic radii do not remain constant but decrease in a normal gradation.

6. The basic character of the transition metal monoxides follows the order
(Atomic number Ti = 22, V = 23, Cr = 24, Fe = 26)
(a) TiO > FeO > VO > CrO
(b) TiO > VO > CrO > FeO
(c) TiO > CrO > TiO > FeO
(d) CrO > VO > FeO > TiO

7. VO_2 is an amphoteric oxide and in acidic medium it forms
(a) VO^{2+}
(b) VO_2^+
(c) V^{3+}
(d) VO_2^{2+}

8. Which of the following compounds is an amphoteric hydroxide?
(a) $Cr(OH)_2$
(b) $Fe(OH)_2$
(c) $Cr(OH)_3$
(d) $Fe(OH)_3$

9. The pair of compounds having metals in their highest oxidation states is
(a) $MnO_2, FeCl_3$
(b) $[MnO_4]^-, CrO_2Cl_2$
(c) $[Fe(CN)_6]^{3-}, [Co(CN)_3]$
(d) $[NiCl_4]^{2-}, [CoCl_4]^-$

10. Which of the following metals has more than one oxidation state?
(a) Zn
(b) Mn
(c) Sr
(d) Ca

11. Among the following pairs of ions, the lower oxidation state in aqueous solutions is more stable than the other in
(a) Ti^+, Ti^{3+}
(b) Cu^+, Cu^{2+}
(c) Cr^{2+}, Cr^{3+}
(d) V^{2+}, VO^{2+}

12. Which of the following statements is incorrect?
(a) The transition metals with the exception of Zn, Cd and Hg are very hard and have low volatility.
(b) Once the d^5 configuration is exceeded, the tendency to involve all the 3*d* electrons in bonding decreases.
(c) In the highest oxidation states, the transition metals show basic character and form cationic complexes.
(d) In the highest oxidation states of the first five transition elements (Sc to Mn), all the 4*s* and 3*d* electrons are used for bonding.

13. In which of the following oxoanions, the oxidation state of the central atom is not the same as that of its group number in the periodic table?
(a) MnO_4^-
(b) $Cr_2O_7^{2-}$
(c) VO_4^{3-}
(d) FeO_4^{2-}

14. Generally, transition elements form coloured salts due to the presence of unpaired electrons. Which of the following compounds will be coloured in solid state?
(a) Ag_2SO_4
(b) CuF_2
(c) ZnF_2
(d) Cu_2Cl_2

15. There are three unpaired electrons in $[Co(H_2O)_6]^{2+}$ and calculated value of magnetic moment is 3.87 B.M which is quite different from the experimental value of 4.40 B.M. This is because of
(a) increase in number of unpaired electrons
(b) some contribution of the orbital motion of the electrons to the magnetic moment
(c) change in orbital spin of the electron
(d) *d*-*d* transition

16. Which one of the following has the least magnetic moment?
(a) Co^{2+} (b) Ni^{2+} (c) Fe^{2+} (d) Cu^{2+}

17. Magnetic moment of Cr (Z = 24), Mn^{+} (Z = 25) and Fe^{2+} (Z = 26) are x, y, z. They are in order
(a) $x < y < z$ (b) $x = y < z$
(c) $z < x = y$ (d) $x = y = z$

18. The magnetic moment is associated with its spin angular momentum and orbital angular momentum. Spin only magnetic moment value of Cr^{3+} ion is
(a) 2.87 BM (b) 3.87 BM
(c) 3.47 BM (d) 3.57 BM

19. Which pair of the compounds is expected to show similar colour in aqueous medium?
(a) $FeCl_3$ and $CuCl_2$ (b) $VOCl_2$ and $CuCl_2$
(c) $VOCl_2$ and $FeCl_2$ (d) $FeCl_2$ and $MnCl_2$

20. Which of the following plays a major role in the formation of complex compound?
(a) Transition metals
(b) Lanthanoides and actinoides
(c) Representative elements
(d) *p*-block elements

21. Which of the following pairs of elements cannot form an alloy?
(a) Zn, Cu (b) Fe, Hg
(c) Fe, C (d) Hg, Na

22. Interstitial compound is formed by
(a) Mg and Al (b) Co, Ni and Mg
(c) Fe, Ni and Al (d) Fe, Co and Ni

23. In the preparation of $KMnO_4$, pyrolusite (MnO_2) is first converted to potassium manganate (K_2MnO_4). In this conversion, the oxidation state of manganese changes from
(a) +6 to +2 (b) +4 to +6
(c) +2 to +4 (d) +3 to +1

24. Oxidation state of Mn in MnO_4^- is +7 indicating all electrons are paired in Mn but MnO_4^- is coloured. It is due to
(a) charge transfer from ligand to metal
(b) presence of unpaired electrons in *d*-orbitals in oxygen
(c) charge transfer from metal to ligand
(d) oxidation state of Mn in MnO_4^- is +6

25. $Cr_2O_7^{2-} + X \xrightarrow{H^+} Cr^{3+} + H_2O +$ Oxidised product of 'X'. 'X' in the above reaction cannot be
(a) $C_2O_4^{2-}$ (b) Fe^{2+}
(c) SO_4^{2-} (d) S^{2-}

26. Consider the following reaction,
$$3MnO_4^{2-} + 2H_2O \rightleftharpoons 2MnO_4^- + MnO_2 + 4OH^-$$
the reagent that facilitates the removal of OH^- ions to ensure the completion of the conversion of K_2MnO_4 is
(a) KOH (b) CO_2
(c) SO_2 (d) HCl

27. Chromium ion is formed by the reaction between KI and acidified potassium dichromate solution. The change in oxidation state of chromium in this reaction is from
(a) +6 to +4 (b) +7 to +3
(c) +7 to +4 (d) +6 to +3

28. The atomic number of potassium is 19 and that of manganese is 25. Although the colour of MnO_4^- is dark violet yet the K^+ is colourless. This is due to the fact that
(a) Mn is a transition element, while K^+ is not
(b) $[MnO_4]^-$ is negatively charged, while K^+ has a positive charge
(c) The effective atomic number of Mn in $[MnO_4]^-$ is 26; while for K^+, the atomic number is 18.
(d) The Mn in a high positive oxidation state allows charge transfer transitions.

29. When acidified $K_2Cr_2O_7$ solution is added to Sn^{2+} salt then Sn^{2+} changes to
(a) Sn (b) Sn^{3+}
(c) Sn^{4+} (d) Sn

30. The pair of lanthanoid ions which are diamagnetic and paramagnetic respectively.
(a) Pr^{2+} and Pr^{3+} (b) Dy^{2+} and Gd^{3+}
(c) Nd^{2+} and Pm^{3+} (d) Yb^{2+} and Eu^{3+}

31. $Cr_2O_7^{2-} \xrightarrow{pH = x} CrO_4^{2-} \xrightarrow{pH = y} Cr_2O_7^{2-}$
pH values x and y can be
(a) 4 and 5 (b) 4 and 8
(c) 8 and 4 (d) 8 and 9

32. In reduction of dichromate by Fe(II), the number of electrons involved per chromium atom is
(a) 2 (b) 3
(c) 4 (d) 1

33. The electronic configuration of Tb (Atomic no. 65), Nd (Atomic no. 60) and Sm (Atomic no. 62) are
(a) $[Xe]4f^3 6s^2$, $[Xe]4f^9 6s^2$, $[Xe]4f^7 6s^2$
(b) $[Xe]4f^9 6s^1$, $[Xe]4f^5 6s^2$, $[Xe]4f^5 6s^1$
(c) $[Xe]4f^6 6s^2$, $[Xe]4f^9 6s^2$, $[Xe]4f^7 6s^1$
(d) $[Xe]4f^9 6s^2$, $[Xe]4f^4 6s^2$, $[Xe]4f^6 6s^2$

34. The lanthanoid contraction is responsible for the fact that
(a) Zn and Y have about the same radii
(b) Zr and Nb have similar oxidation state
(c) Zr ahd Hf have about the same radii
(d) Zr and Zn have the same oxidation state

35. Which of the following statements concerning lanthanoides elements is false?
(a) Lanthanoides are separated from one another by ion-exchange method.
(b) Ionic radii of trivalent lanthanides steadily increases with increase in the atomic number.
(c) All lanthanides are highly dense metals.
(d) More characteristic oxidation state of lanthanoides elements is +3.

36. Which of the following is incorrectly matched with their oxidation state?
(a) Mn in MnO_2 $\longrightarrow$ +4
(b) Most stable oxidation state of Cr $\longrightarrow$ +6
(c) Most stable oxidation state of Mn in oxides $\longrightarrow$ +6
(d) Characteristic oxidation state of lanthanoids $\longrightarrow$ +3

37. Which of the following compounds/elements is incorrectly matched with their uses?
(a) Lanthanoid oxide $\longrightarrow$ *X*-ray screen
(b) Misch metal $\longrightarrow$ Lanthanoid metal + iron
(c) Magnesium based alloy is constituent of $\longrightarrow$ Bullets
(d) Mixed oxides of lanthanoids are employed $\longrightarrow$ Petroleum cracking

Assertion-Reason

Directions (Q. Nos. 38 to 43) Given below are two statements, one is labelled as Assertion (A) and the other is labelled as Reason (R).
(a) Both A and R are true and R is the correct explanation of A.
(b) Both A and R are true but R is not the correct explanation of A.
(c) A is true but R is false.
(d) A is false but R is true.

38. **Assertion** (A) The metals of 4*d* and 5*d* has greater enthalpies of atomisation than the corresponding elements of the 3*d*-series.
Reason (R) The metal-metal bond in 4*d* and 5*d* series are stronger than those in the 3*d*-series.

39. **Assertion** (A) In acidic medium, $K_2Cr_2O_7$ exists as $Cr_2O_7^{2-}$ while in basic medium it is converted to CrO_4^{2-}.
Reason (R) $K_2Cr_2O_7$ is hygroscopic in nature and changes colour on reaction with water.

40. **Assertion** (A) In a solution of potassium chromate if a strong acid is added it changes its colour from yellow to orange.
Reason (R) The colour change is due to the change in oxidation state of chromium.

41. **Assertion** (A) Hydrochloric acid is not used to acidify a $KMnO_4$ solution in volumetric analysis of Fe^{2+} and $C_2O_4^{2-}$.
Reason (R) Part of the oxygen produced from $KMnO_4$ and HCl is used up in oxidising HCl to Cl_2.

42. **Assertion** (A) Acidified $K_2Cr_2O_7$ solution turns green when Na_2SO_3 is added to H_2SO_4.
Reason (R) In the given reaction, $Cr_2(SO_3)_3$ is formed.

43. **Assertion** (A) The green manganate is diamagnetic but the purple permanganate is paramagnetic in nature.
Reason (R) MnO_4^{2-} contains one unpaired electron while in MnO_4^- all electrons are paired.

Statement Type Questions

Directions (Q. Nos. 44 to 50) In the light of the above statements, choose the correct answer from the options given below.
(a) Both Statement I and Statement II are false.
(b) Statement I is true, but Statement II is false.
(c) Statement I is false, but Statement II is true.
(d) Both Statement I and Statement II are true.

44. **Statement I** The +7 state for Mn is not represented in simple halide but MnO_3F is known and beyond Mn, no metal has a trihalide except FeX_3 and CoF_3.
Statement II The ability of fluorine to stabilise the highest oxidation state is either due to higher lattice energy as in the case of CoF_3.

45. **Statement I** The highest Mn-fluoride is MnF_3, whereas the highest oxide is Mn_2O_7.
Statement II In Mn_2O_7, each Mn is tetrahedrally surrounded by O's including a Mn—O—Mn bridge.

46. **Statement I** Mn^{3+} and Co^{3+} ions are strongest oxidising agents in aqueous solutions.
Statement II The ions Ti^{2+}, V^{2+} and Cr^{2+} are strong oxidising agents and will liberate hydrogen from a dilute acid.

47. **Statement I** Oxidising power of the oxides is in order.
$$VO_2^+ < Cr_2O_7^{2-} < MnO_4^-$$
Statement II Stability of the reduced species is in order
$$V^{3+} < Cr^{3+} < Mn^{2+}$$

48. **Statement I** Potassium permanganate forms dark purple crystals which are isostructural with those of $KClO_4$.
Statement II A manganese (II) ion salt is reduced by peroxodisulphate to permanganate.

49. **Statment I** In the reaction,
$$FeCr_2O_4 + 4Na_2CO_3 + O_2 \xrightarrow{\text{Fusion}} [X] \xrightarrow[H_2O]{H^+} [Y] \xrightarrow[H_2O_2]{H^+} [Z]$$
in all three compounds, i.e. *X*, *Y* and *Z*, the chromium is in +6 oxidation state.
Statement II Saturated solution of [*Y*] gives a bright orange compound, chromic anhydride with concentrated H_2SO_4.

50. **Statement I** The purple colour of $KMnO_4$ is due to the charge transfer transition.
Statement II The intense colour, in most of the transition metal complexes is due to *d*-*d* transition.

51. Which of the following statements are correct?
A. The *d*-orbitals of the transition elements protrude to the periphery of an atom more than the other orbitals (i.e. *s* and *p*).
B. The transition metals and their compounds also exhibit catalytic property and paramagnetic behaviour.
C. Generally, greater the number of valence electrons, stronger is the resultant bonding.
D. The transition metals with very low enthalpy of atomisation tend to be inert in their reactions.
E. The metals of the second and third series have greater enthalpies of atomisation than the corresponding elements of the first series.
Choose the correct answer from the option given below.
(a) C, D and E
(b) A, B and D
(c) A, B, C and E
(d) A, B and C

52 Select the incorrect statements from the following.
A. The elements which give the highest number of oxidation states occur in or near the middle of the series.
B. The only oxidation state of zinc is +3 (no *d* electrons are involved).
C. The maximum oxidation states of reasonable stability correspond in value to the sum of the *s* and *d*-electrons upto manganese.
D. In non-transition elements, the oxidation states normally differ by a unit of one.
E. Cr(VI) in the form of dichromate in acidic medium is a strong oxidising agent, whereas MoO_3 and WO_3 are not.
Choose the correct answer from the options given below:
(a) D and E (b) A, B and C
(c) B, D and E (d) B and D

53. Which of the following statements are correct?
A. The frequency of the light absorbed is determined by the nature of the ligand.
B. The transition metals form a larger number of complex compounds due to the comparatively larger sizes of the metal ions.
C. Catalysts at a solid surface involve the formation of bonds between reactant molecules and atoms of the surfaces of the catalyst.
D. The transition metal ions can change their oxidation states, they become less effective than catalysts.
E. Fe(III) behave as catalyst in the reaction between iodide and persulphate ions.
Choose the correct answer from the options given below
(a) B, D and E (b) A and C
(c) C, D and B (d) A, C and E

54. Select the incorrect statements form the following.
A. The chromates and dichromates are interconvertible in aqueous solution depending upon pH of the solution.
B. Sodium and potassium dichromates are strong oxidising agents and the sodium salt has a lesser solubility in water.
C. The acidified potassium dichromate will oxidise iodides to iodine and tin (III) to tin (IV).
D. When the solution of sodium dichromate treated with potassium chloride, yellow crystals of potassium dichromate crystallise out.
E. The structure of chromate ion is tetrahedral.
Choose the correct answer from the options given below.
(a) A, D and E
(b) C and D
(c) B, C and D
(d) A, B and C

55 Select the correct statements from the following.
A. The $E°$ value for Ce^{4+}/Ce^{3+} is +1.74 V which suggests that it can oxidise water.
B. Eu^{2+} is formed by losing the two *s*-electrons and its f^{14}-configuration accounts for the formation of this ion.
C. Tb^{IV} has half-filled *f*-orbitals and it is a reductant.
D. The lanthanoid ions other than the f^0 type and the f^{14}type are all paramagnetic.
E. The carbides Ln_3C, Ln_2C_3 and LnC_2 liberate oxygen from dilute acids and burn in halogens to form halides.
Choose the correct answer from the options given below.
(a) A, B and D (b) C and E
(c) B, D and E (d) A, C and D

Species Selection Type Questions

56. Consider the following elements.
(i) Cu (ii) Ag
(iii) Au (iv) Zn
(v) Hg (vi) Co
(vii) Cd
The number of elements which do not show the characteristic properties of *d*-block elements?
(a) 4 (b) 3
(c) 5 (d) 6

57. Consider the following species.
(i) MnO_4^- (ii) $Cr(CN)_6^{3-}$
(iii) NiF_6^{2-} (iv) CrO_2Cl_2
(v) V_2O_6
The number of species which have +6 oxidation state is
(a) 2 (b) 4
(c) 3 (d) 1

58. Consider the following electronic configurations.

(i) Ce : [Xe] $4f^2 6s^2$ (ii) Pm : [Xe] $4f^5 6s^2$

(iii) Yb : [Xe] $4f^{14} 5d^1 6s^2$ (iv) Nd : [Xe] $4f^4 6s^2$

(v) Bk : [Rn] $5f^7 7s^2$ (vi) Cf : [Rn] $5f^7 6d^1 7s^2$

(vii) Pa : [Rn] $5f^2 6d^1 7s^2$

How many of them are incorrect electronic configurations?

(a) 5 (b) 3 (c) 4 (d) 2

Matching Type Questions

59. Match the elements with their electronic configurations.

Column I (Elements)		Column II (Electronic configurations)	
A.	Samarium	1.	$5f^{14} 6s^2$
B.	Dysprosium	2.	$5f^{12} 6s^2$
C.	Fermium	3.	$4f^{10} 6s^2$
D.	Nobelium	4.	$4f^6 6s^2$

Codes

(a) A-1, B-2, C-3, D-4 (b) A-4, B-3, C-2, D-1
(c) A-4, B-2, C-1, D-2 (d) A-3, B-1, C-1, D-1

60. Match the compounds with their uses/property.

Column I (Compounds)		Column II (Uses)	
A.	MnO_2	1.	Cu/Ni alloy
B.	Silver UK coins	2.	Dry battery cells
C.	Iron catalyst	3.	Polymerisation of alkynes
D.	Ni complexes	4.	Haber's process

Codes

(a) A-1, B-2, C-3, D-4
(b) A-3, B-2, C-4, D-1
(c) A-2, B-1, C-4, D-3
(d) A-2, B-3, C-4, D-1

61. Match the metals with their properties.

Column I (Metal)		Column II (Properties)	
A.	Os	1.	lowest density
B.	Sc	2.	highest melting point
C.	Zn	3.	shows +8 oxidation state
D.	Mn	4.	5 unpaired electrons

Codes

(a) A-3, B-1, C-2, D-4
(b) A-4, B-2, C-3, D-1
(c) A-2, B-1, C-3, D-4
(d) A-1, B-2, C-3, D-4

62. Match the metal ions with their magnetic moments.

Column I [Ions]		Column II [Magnetic moments (BM)]	
A.	Zn^{2+}	1.	$\sqrt{24}$
B.	Ti^{+}	2.	0
C.	Mn^{3+}	3.	$\sqrt{15}$
D.	Cu^{2+}	4.	$\sqrt{3}$

Codes

(a) A-1, B-2, C-3, D-4
(b) A-2, B-3, C-4, D-1
(c) A-4, B-2, C-1, D-2
(d) A-2, B-3, C-1, D-4

Final Check Through PYQs

Module-I *d*-block Elements

1 'Spin only' magnetic moment is same for which of the following ions? ***[NEET 2024]***

A. Ti^{3+} B. Cr^{2+} C. Mn^{2+} D. Fe^{2+} E. Sc^{3+}

Choose the most appropriate answer from the options given below :

(a) B and D only (b) A and E only
(c) B and C only (d) A and D only

2 The $E°$ value for the Mn^{3+}/Mn^{2+} couple is more positive than that of Cr^{3+}/Cr^{2+} or Fe^{3+}/Fe^{2+} due to change of ***[NEET 2024]***

(a) d^5 to d^4 configuration (b) d^5 to d^2 configuration
(c) d^4 to d^5 configuration (b) d^3 to d^5 configuration

3 The stability of Cu^{2+} is more than Cu^+ salts in aqueous solution due to ***[NCERT (New) Pg. 100, NEET 2023]***

(a) enthalpy of atomisation (b) hydration energy
(c) second ionisation enthalpy (d) first ionisation enthalpy

4 The calculated spin only magnetic moment of Cr^{2+} ion is ***[NCERT (New) Pg. 102, NEET 2020]***

(a) 4.90 BM (b) 5.92 BM (c) 2.84 BM (d) 3.87 BM

5 Identify the incorrect statement. ***[NEET 2020]***

(a) The transition metals and their compounds are known for their catalytic activity due to their ability to adopt multiple oxidation states and to form complexes.
(b) Interstitial compounds are those that are formed when small atoms like H, C or N are trapped inside the crystal lattices of metals.
(c) The oxidation states of chromium in CrO_4^{2-} and $Cr_2O_7^{2-}$ are not the same.
(d) Cr^{2+} (d^4) is a stronger reducing agent than Fe^{2+} (d^6) in water.

6 Match the followings aspects with the respective metal.

Column I (Aspects)	Column II (Metal)
A. The metal which reveals a maximum number of oxidation states	1. Scandium
B. The metal although placed in 3*d* block is considered not as a transition element.	2. Copper
C. The metal which does not exhibit variable oxidation states	3. Manganese
D. The metal which in +1oxidation state in aqueous solution undergoes disproportionation	4. Zinc

Codes ***[NEET 2020]***

(a) A-1, B-4, C-2, D-3 (b) A-3, B-4, C-1, D-2
(c) A-3, B-1, C-4, D-2 (d) A-2, B-4, C-1, D-3

7 Match the catalyst with the process

Column I (Catalyst)	Column II (Process)
A. V_2O_5	1. The oxidation of ethyne to ethanal
B. $TiCl_4 + Al(CH_3)_3$	2. Polymerisation of alkynes
C. $PdCl_2$	3. Oxidation of SO_2 in the manufacture of H_2SO_4
D. Nickel complexes	4. Polymerisation of ethylene

Which of the following is the correct option? ***[NEET 2019]***

Codes

(a) A-3, B-4, C-1, D-2 (b) A-1, B-2, C-3, D-4
(c) A-1, B-3, C-2, D-4 (d) A-3, B-1, C-4, D-2

8 Match the metal ions given in Column I with the spin only magnetic moments of the ions given in Column II and assign the correct code. ***[NCERT (New) Pg. 102, NEET 2018]***

Column I	Column II
A. Co^{3+}	1. $\sqrt{8}$ BM
B. Cr^{3+}	2. $\sqrt{35}$ BM
C. Fe^{3+}	3. $\sqrt{3}$ BM
D. Ni^{2+}	4. $\sqrt{24}$ BM
	5. $\sqrt{15}$ BM

Codes

(a) A-4, B-1, C-2, D-3 (b) A-1, B-2, C-3, D-4
(c) A-4, B-5, C-2, D-1 (d) A-3, B-5, C-1, D-2

9 The number of *d*-electrons in Fe^{2+} ($Z = 26$) is not equal to the number of electrons in which one of the following? ***[AIPMT 2015]***

(a) *p*-electrons in Cl ($Z = 17$)
(b) *d*-electrons in Fe ($Z = 26$)
(c) *p*-electrons in Ne ($Z = 10$)
(d) *s*-electrons in Mg ($Z = 12$)

10 Magnetic moment 2.84 BM is given by (At. No. Ni = 28, Ti = 22, Cr = 24, Co = 27) ***[NCERT (New) Pg. 102, AIPMT 2015, 2014]***

(a) Ni^{2+} (b) Ti^{3+}
(c) Cr^{3+} (d) Co^{2+}

Module-II Some Important Compounds of d-Block Elements

11 Which of the following statements are incorrect?

A. All the transition metals except scandium form *MO* oxides which are ionic.

B. The highest oxidation number corresponding to the group number in transition metal oxides is attained in Sc_2O_3 to Mn_2O_7.

C. Basic character increases from V_2O_3 to V_2O_4 to V_2O_5.

D. V_2O_4 dissolves in acids to give VO_4^{3-} salts.

E. CrO is basic but Cr_2O_3 is amphoteric.

Choose the correct answer from the options given below *[NCERT (New) Pg. 105, NEET 2023]*

(a) B and D (b) C and D (c) B and C (d) A and E

12 In the neutral or faintly alkaline medium, $KMnO_4$ oxidises iodide into iodate. The change in oxidation state of manganese in this reaction is from *[NCERT (New) Pg. 108, NEET 2022]*

(a) + 6 to + 4 (b) + 7 to + 3
(c) + 6 to + 5 (d) + 7 to + 4

13 The manganate and permanganate ions are tetrahedral, due to *[NCERT (New) Pg. 107, NEET 2019]*

(a) there is no π-bonding
(b) the π-bonding involves overlap of *p*-orbitals of oxygen with *p*-orbitals of manganese
(c) the π-bonding involves overlap of *d*-orbitals of oxygen with *d*-orbitals of manganese
(d) the π-bonding involves overlap of *p*-orbitals of oxygen with *d*-orbitals of manganese

14 When neutral or faintly alkaline $KMnO_4$ is treated with potassium iodide, iodide ion is converted into '*X*'. '*X*' is *[NEET 2019]*

(a) I_2 (b) IO_4^- (c) IO_3^- (d) IO^-

15 Which one of the following ions exhibits *d-d* transition and paramagnetism as well? *[NCERT (New) Pg. 102, NEET 2018]*

(a) MnO_4^- (b) $Cr_2O_7^{2-}$ (c) CrO_4^{2-} (d) MnO_4^{2-}

16 Name the gas that can readily decolourise acidified $KMnO_4$ solution. *[NEET 2017]*

(a) CO_2 (b) SO_2 (c) NO_2 (d) P_2O_5

17 $HgCl_2$ and I_2 both when dissolved in water containing I^- ions the pair of species formed is *[NEET 2017]*

(a) HgI_2, I_3^- (b) HgI_2, I^-
(c) HgI_4^{2-}, I_3^- (d) Hg_2I_2, I^-

18 Which one of the following statements is correct when SO_2 is passed through acidified $K_2Cr_2O_7$ solution? *[NCERT Pg. 106, NEET 2016, Phase I]*

(a) The solution is decolourised.
(b) SO_2 is reduced.
(c) Green $Cr_2(SO_4)_3$ is formed.
(d) The solution turns blue.

19 Which of the following processes does not involve oxidation of iron? *[AIPMT 2015]*

(a) Rusting of iron sheets.
(b) Decolourisation of blue $CuSO_4$ solution by iron.
(c) Formation of $Fe(CO)_5$ from Fe.
(d) Liberation of H_2 from steam by iron a high temperature.

20 Assuming complete ionisation, same moles of which of the following compounds will require the least amount of acidified $KMnO_4$ for complete oxidation? *[AIPMT 2015]*

(a) $FeSO_4$ (b) $FeSO_3$
(c) FeC_2O_4 (d) $Fe(NO_2)_2$

21 The pair of compounds that can exist together is *[AIPMT 2014]*

(a) $FeCl_3, SnCl_2$ (b) $HgCl_2, SnCl_2$
(c) $FeCl_2, SnCl_2$ (d) $FeCl_3$, KI

22 In acidic medium, H_2O_2 changes $Cr_2O_7^{-2}$ to CrO_5 which has two (—O—O—) bonds. Oxidation state of Cr in CrO_5 is *[NCERT Pg. 106, AIPMT 2014]*

(a) + 5 (b) + 3
(c) + 6 (d) – 10

23 The reaction of aqueous $KMnO_4$ with H_2O_2 in acidic conditions gives *[NCERT Pg. 107, AIPMT 2014]*

(a) Mn^{4+} and O_2
(b) Mn^{2+} and O_2
(c) Mn^{2+} and O_3
(d) Mn^{4+} and MnO_2

Module-III f-Block Elements or Inner Transition Elements

24 The pair of lanthanoid ions which are diamagnetic is *[NEET 2024]*

(a) Ce^{4+} and Yb^{2+} (b) Ce^{3+} and En^{2+}
(c) Gd^{3+} and Eu^{3+} (b) Pm^{3+} and Sm^{3+}

25 Gadolinium has a low value of third ionisation enthalpy because of *[NCERT Pg. 110, NEET 2022]*

(a) high exchange enthalpy
(b) high electronegativity
(c) high basic character
(d) small size

26 The incorrect statement among the following is *[NEET 2021]*

(a) actinoid contraction is greater for element to element than lanthanoid contraction.
(b) most of the trivalent lanthanoid ions are colourless in the solid state.
(c) lanthanoids are good conductors of heat and electricity.
(d) actinoids are highly reactive metals, especially when finely divided.

27 Zr ($Z = 40$) and Hf ($Z = 72$) have similar atomic and ionic radii because of *[NCERT (New) Pg. 109, NEET 2021]*
(a) belonging to same group
(b) diagonal relationship
(c) lanthanoid contraction
(d) having similar chemical properties

28 The reason for greater range of oxidation states in actinoids is attributed to *[NCERT (New) Pg. 112, NEET 2017]*
(a) the radioactive nature of actinoids
(b) actinoid contraction
(c) $5f$, $6d$ and $7s$ levels having comparable energies
(d) $4f$ and $5d$ levels being close in energies

29 The electronic configurations of Eu (Atomic no. 63), Gd (At. no. 64) and Tb (At. no. 65) are *[NCERT (New) Pg. 110, NEET 2016]*
(a) $[Xe]\,4f^6 5d^1 6s^2$, $[Xe]\,4f^7 5d^1 6s^2$ and $[Xe]\,4f^9 6s^2$
(b) $[Xe]\,4f^6 5d^1 6s^2$, $[Xe]\,4f^7 5d^1 6s^2$ and $[Xe]\,4f^8 5d^1 6s^2$
(c) $[Xe]\,4f^7 6s^2$, $[Xe]\,4f^7 5d^1 6s^2$ and $[Xe]\,4f^9 6s^2$
(d) $[Xe]\,4f^7 6s^2$, $[Xe]\,4f^8 6s^2$ and $[Xe]4f^8 5d^1 6s^2$

30 Which one of the following statements related to lanthanons is incorrect? *[NEET 2016, Phase II]*
(a) Europium shows +2 oxidation state.
(b) The basicity decreases as the ionic radius decreases from Pr to Lu.
(c) All the lanthanons are much more reactive than aluminium.
(d) Ce (+4) solutuion are widely used as oxidising agent in volumetric analysis.

31 Because of lanthanoid contraction, which of the following pairs of elements have nearly same atomic radii? (Numbers in the parenthesis are atomic numbers). *[NCERT (New) Pg. 110, AIPMT 2015]*
(a) Ti (22) and Zr (40)
(b) Zr (40) and Nb (41)
(c) Zr (40) and Hf (72)
(d) Zr (40) and Ta (73)

32 Gadolinium belongs to 4f series. It's atomic number is 64. Which of the following is the correct electronic configuration of gadolinium? *[NCERT (New) Pg. 110, AIPMT 2015]*
(a) $[Xe]4f^8 6d^2$
(b) $[Xe]4f^9 5s^1$
(c) $[Xe]4f^7 5d^1 6s^2$
(d) $[Xe]4f^6 5d^2 6s^2$

33 Reason of lanthanoid contraction is *[NCERT (New) Pg. 110, AIPMT 2014]*
(a) negligible screening effect of f-orbitals
(a) increasing nuclear charge
(b) decreasing nuclear charge
(d) decreasing screening effect

Answers

Step up Practice 1

1 (b) 2 (c) 3 (a) 4 (a) 5 (b) 6 (d) 7 (d) 8 (d) 9 (c) 10 (c)
11 (d) 12 (c) 13 (c) 14 (d) 15 (d) 16 (d) 17 (d) 18 (b) 19 (d) 20 (a)
21 (a) 22 (b) 23 (a) 24 (c) 25 (c)

Step up Practice 2

1 (c) 2 (a) 3 (c) 4 (d) 5 (c) 6 (c) 7 (d) 8 (a) 9 (b) 10 (b)
11 (b) 12 (d) 13 (d) 14 (b) 15 (c) 16 (d) 17 (a) 18 (b) 19 (a) 20 (d)
21 (c) 22 (d) 23 (a)

Step up Practice 3

1 (b) 2 (d) 3 (d) 4 (d) 5 (b) 6 (d) 7 (b) 8 (d) 9 (b) 10 (a)
11 (c) 12 (a) 13 (c) 14 (a) 15 (c) 16 (c)

Gearing up for NEET

1 (b) 2 (c) 3 (d) 4 (b) 5 (b) 6 (b) 7 (a) 8 (c) 9 (b) 10 (b)
11 (a) 12 (c) 13 (d) 14 (b) 15 (b) 16 (d) 17 (c) 18 (b) 19 (b) 20 (a)
21 (b) 22 (d) 23 (b) 24 (a) 25 (c) 26 (b) 27 (d) 28 (d) 29 (c) 30 (d)
31 (c) 32 (b) 33 (d) 34 (c) 35 (b) 36 (c) 37 (a) 38 (a) 39 (c) 40 (c)
41 (a) 42 (c) 43 (d) 44 (d) 45 (c) 46 (b) 47 (d) 48 (b) 49 (d) 50 (d)
51 (c) 52 (d) 53 (d) 54 (c) 55 (a) 56 (b) 57 (a) 58 (c) 59 (b) 60 (c)
61 (a) 62 (d)

Final Check through PYQs : Module-I

1 (a) 2 (c) 3 (b) 4 (a) 5 (c) 6 (b) 7 (a) 8 (c) 9 (a) 10 (a)

Final Check through PYQs : Module-II

11 (b) 12 (d) 13 (d) 14 (c) 15 (d) 16 (b) 17 (c) 18 (c) 19 (c) 20 (a)
21 (c) 22 (c) 23 (b)

Final Check through PYQs : Module-III

24 (a) 25 (a) 26 (b) 27 (c) 28 (c) 29 (c) 30 (c) 31 (c) 32 (c) 33 (a)

Hints and Solutions

Step up Practice 1

1. (*b*) Transition elements exhibit variable valencies because they release electrons from the $(n-1)\,d$ and *ns*-orbitals.

2. (*c*) The elements of *d*-block are named as transition elements because their characteristics are in between *s* and *p*-block elements.

3. (*a*) Among the given electronic configurations, only four, i.e. (i), (ii), (iv) and (v) are correct while (iii) is incorrect.

   The correct electronic configuration of Cu is
   $$Cu = [Ar]\,3d^{10}\,4s^1$$

4. (*a*) In general, greater the number of unpaired electrons, greater is the number of bonds and therefore, greater is the strength of these bonds, thus higher will be enthalpy of atomisation. Hence, among the given metals, Zn has least enthalpy of atomisation due to the absence of unpaired electrons ($3d^{10}$).

5. (*b*) Density of transition metals increases from left to right, so among the given transition metal ions, scandium has the lowest density.

6. (*d*) Among the given sets of elements, Fe, Co and Ni have almost same atomic radii.

	Fe	Co	Ni
Atomic radii (pm)	126	125	124

7. (*d*) A is false but R is true. The correct form of A is The second ionisation energies of $_{23}V$, $_{24}Cr$ and $_{25}Mn$ are in the order of V < Mn < Cr.

8. (*d*) Highest oxidation state of *d*-block element is + 8 and is exhibited by Os (as in OsO_4).

9. (*c*) Among the given metals, only Ti and Ni show +2, +3 and +4 oxidation state. While
   $$Fe \longrightarrow +2, +3, +4, +6$$
   $$Sc \longrightarrow +3$$
   $$Zn \longrightarrow +2$$

10. (*c*) Among the given options, (c) is correctly matched while all other are incorrect. Their correct matchings are as follows,
    - $MnO_4^- \longrightarrow +7$
    - $CrO_4^{2-} \longrightarrow +6$
    - $CrO_5 \longrightarrow +6$

11. (*d*) Atomic number $(Z = 25)$ = Mn atom

    Electronic configuration of Mn $= [Ar]\,3d^5\,4s^2$

    Electronic configuration of $Mn^{2+} = [Ar]\,3d^5$
    $$\mu = \sqrt{n(n+2)}\ \text{BM}$$
    where, n = number of unpaired electrons = 5.
    $$\mu = \sqrt{5(5+2)}$$
    $$= \sqrt{35}\ \text{BM}$$
    $$= 5.92\ \text{BM}$$

12. (*c*) The number of unpaired electrons in the given species Mn^{3+}, Cr^{3+} and V^{3+} are 4, 3 and 2 respectively.

    We know,
    $$Mn \longrightarrow 3d^5\,4s^2 \Rightarrow Mn^{3+} = 3d^4$$
    $$Cr \longrightarrow 3d^5\,4s^1 \Rightarrow Cr^{3+} = 3d^3$$
    $$V \longrightarrow 3d^3\,4s^2 \Rightarrow V^{3+} = 3d^2$$

13. (*c*) Statement I is false but Statement II is true.

    The correct form of Statement I is:

    The $E^\circ_{(M^{2+}/M)}$ value of copper is positive (+0.34 V), accounts for its inability to liberate H_2 from acids.

14. (*d*) Among the given statements, statement (d) is incorrect for transition element.

    Its correct form is :

    Transition elements have partially filled *d*-orbitals in their ground state or in their stable oxidation states.

15. (*d*) Highest oxidation state of manganese in fluoride is +4 (MnF_4) but highest oxidation state in oxides is +7(Mn_2O_7). The reason is that in covalent compounds, fluorine can form single bond while oxygen forms double bond.

16. (*d*) Maximum number of unpaired electrons

    Cr^{3+} = | ↿ | ↿ | ↿ | | | d^3

    Due to presence of unpaired electrons, *d*-*d* transition can take place and thus, it will impart colour in aqueous solution.

17. (*d*) Both statement I and Statement II are true.

18. (*b*) Electronic configuration of Cu^{2+} is $[Ar]\,3d^9$.

    Thus, it has one unpaired electron.

    Hence, it is coloured and paramagnetic in nature.

19. (*d*) Among the given statements, statement (d) is incorrect while other are correct.

    Its correct form is:

    Transition element have vacant *d*-orbitals, they exhibit variable valencies and thus can form complexes.

20. (*a*) The ions having same number of unpaired electrons have same value of magnetic moment.

A. $Fe^{2+} \Rightarrow 3d^6 \Rightarrow$ 4 unpaired electrons

B. $Co^{2+} \Rightarrow 3d^7 \Rightarrow$ 3 unpaired electrons

C. $Ni^{2+} \Rightarrow 3d^8 \Rightarrow$ 2 unpaired electrons

D. $Mn^{2+} \Rightarrow 3d^4 \Rightarrow$ 4 unpaired electrons

E. $Co^{3+} \Rightarrow 3d^6 \Rightarrow$ 4 unpaired electrons

Hence, A, D and E have same value of magnetic moment.

21. (*a*) Ti(22) : [Ar] $4s^2 3d^2$

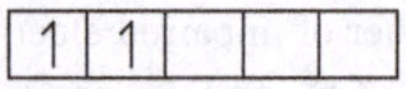

Ti^{2+} = [Ar] $3d^2$ and Ti^{4+} = [Ar] $3d^0$

Ti^{2+} has two unpaired electrons in 3*d* and thus *d*-*d* transition is possible due to absorption of light in visible region. But this is not possible in Ti^{4+} as it has absence of unpaired electrons.

22. (*b*) Both A and R are true but R is not the correct explanation of A.

The correct explanation of A is

Due to large surface area and variable valencies, transition metals form intermediate activated complexes easily, hence they are used as a good catalysts.

23. (*a*) Among the given option, (a) is incorrect match with their process.

It's correct match is $V_2O_5 \longrightarrow$ Contact process.

24. (*c*) Interstitial compounds are less malleable and ductile.

25. (*c*) Among the given option (c) is incorrect match with their alloy formation.

Its corrected match is :

Ni + Cu + Zn $\longrightarrow$ German silver

Step up Practice 2

1. (*c*) In $Cr_2O_7^{2-}$, every Cr is linked to four O atoms as shown in structure.

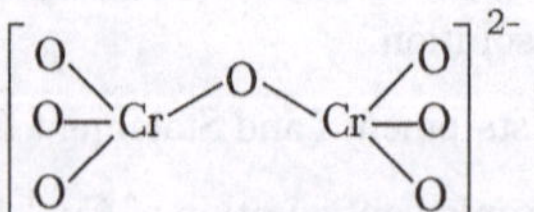

$(Cr_2O_7^{2-})$

2. (*a*) When MnO_2 is fused with KOH and $KClO_3$, a green coloured compound K_2MnO_4 is formed.

The reaction proceeds as

$$\underset{\text{(Brown)}}{3MnO_2} + 6KOH + KClO_3 \xrightarrow{\Delta} \underset{\text{(Green)}}{3K_2MnO_4} + 3H_2O$$

3. (*c*) Among the given statements, (c) is not true about $KMnO_4$.

The correct form is MnO_4^- changes to MnO_4^{2-} or MnO_2 in basic medium.

4. (*d*) Among the given match, (d) is incorrectly match.

Its correct match is:

Dichromate ion $\longrightarrow$ oxidation state of Cr is +6.

5. (*c*) Among the given statements, (c) is incorrect.

Its correct form is:

The acidic oxides like CrO_3 and Mn_2O_3 dissolve in water to form the oxoacids.

6. (*c*) Tetraperoxo species, $[Cr(O_8)]^{3-}$

Let the oxidation state of Cr be *x*.

Then, oxidation number of Cr = $x - 8 \times (-1) = -3$

$x = +5$

7. (*d*) Both Statement I and Statement II are true.

8. (*a*) The reaction can be written as

$$K_2Cr_2O_7 + 2NaOH \longrightarrow 2CrO_4^{2-} + H_2O$$

9. (*b*) Statement I is true but statement II is false.

The correct form of statement II is

K_2MnO_4 changes to $KMnO_4$ by CO_2.

The reaction can be written as

$$3K_2MnO_4 + CO_2 + 2H_2O \longrightarrow \underset{\text{(Purple)}}{2KMnO_4} + \underset{\text{(Brown)}}{MnO_2(s)} + 4KHCO_3$$

10. (*b*) The reaction is proceed as

$$MnO_4^- + H_2SO_4 \longrightarrow \underbrace{MnO_3^+ + HSO_4^-}_{\text{Green}}$$

11. (*b*) The reaction can be written as

$$\overset{+6}{CrO_4^{2-}} + 2H^+ \longrightarrow \overset{+6}{Cr_2O_7^{2-}} + H_2O$$

12. (*d*) When acidic solution of $KMnO_4$ is treated with nitrite, then nitrite is oxidised to nitrate (NO_3^-).

The reaction is given as

$$5NO_2^- + 2MnO_4^- + 6H^+ \longrightarrow 2Mn^{2+} + 5NO_3^- + 3H_2O$$

13. (*d*) Among the given, $KMnO_4$ spot cannot be bleached by $C_2O_7^{2-}/H^+$ while with other reagents $KMnO_4$ reacts and oxidise them.

In these reactions, purple colour of solution disappears due to reduction of permanganate solution.

14. (*b*) Among the given reaction, (b) is incorrectly matched with the product formed in the reaction.

Its correct match is:

$$K_2Cr_2O_7 \xrightarrow[\text{2H}_2\text{SO}_4]{\text{Cold and conc.}} \underset{\text{(Chromium trioxide or chromic anhydride)}}{2CrO_3} + 2KHSO_4 + H_2O$$

15. (*c*) Potassium dichromate on heating gives oxygen and chromic oxide (Cr_2O_3).

$$4K_2Cr_2O_7 \xrightarrow{\Delta} 4K_2CrO_4 + 3O_2 + \underset{(X)}{2Cr_2O_3}$$

16. (d) $CrO_3 + H_2O \longrightarrow \underset{(A)}{H_2CrO_4} \xrightarrow{OH^-} \underset{(B)}{CrO_4^{2-}}$

17. (a) $4NaCl + \underset{\text{(Conc.)}}{3H_2SO_4} + K_2Cr_2O_7 \longrightarrow$

$$\underset{\text{Chromyl chloride}}{2CrO_2Cl_2} + K_2SO_4 + 2Na_2SO_4 + 3H_2O$$

18. (b) Statement I is true but Statement II is false.

The correct form of Statement II is:

Potassium dichromate on action with concentrated HCl, Cl_2 gas is evolved and chromic chloride is obtained. The reaction can be written as

$$K_2Cr_2O_7 + 14HCl \longrightarrow 2KCl + \underset{\text{(Chromic chloride)}}{2CrCl_3} + 7H_2O + 3Cl_2\uparrow$$

19. (a) The reaction of MnO_4^- in dilute alkaline solution can be written as

$$MnO_4^- + 3e^- + 2H_2O \longrightarrow MnO_4^{2-} + 4OH^-$$

20. (d) The structure of CrO_5 is

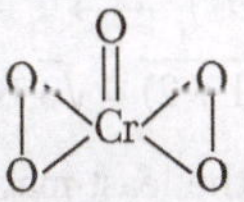

Oxidation number of Cr in CrO_5 is +6.

$$x + 1 \times (-2) + 4(-1) = 0 \Rightarrow x = +6$$

21. (c) A is true but R is false.

The correct form of R is

$Na_2Cr_2O_7$ has a higher solubility in water than $K_2Cr_2O_7$ due to smaller size of sodium ions, as compared to potassium ions.

22. (d) Among the given conversions, only three, i.e. (i), (iii) and (iv) can be carried out by both acidified $K_2Cr_2O_7$ and acidified $KMnO_4$, while (ii) and (v) can be carried out only by acidified $KMnO_4$.

23. (a) $K_2Cr_2O_7 + 2H_2SO_4 \xrightarrow{\text{Cold}} 2CrO_3 + 2KHSO_4 + H_2O$

CrO_3 is highly acidic and oxidising. It is the anhydride of chromic acid.

Step up Practice 3

1. (b) The electronic configuration of Ytteribium is $[Xe]\,4f^{14}6s^2$.

2. (d) Among the given lanthanides, Eu can show +2 and +3 oxidation states.

3. (d) Among the given elements, 'Am' shows maximum number of different oxidation states.

As, Am has +3, +4, +5, +6 oxidation state.

4. (d) Both Statement I and Statement II are true.

5. (b) Among the given elements, Pu is not a lanthanoid while, Pu belongs to the actinoids series with atomic number 94.

6. (d) The correct order of ionic radii of Y^{3+}, La^{3+}, Eu^{3+} and Lu^{3+} is

$$Y^{3+} < Lu^{3+} < Eu^{3+} < La^{3+}$$

As, Y belongs to 5th period and La belongs to 6th period. Ionic radii increases from Y^{3+} to La^{3+} down the group due to lanthanoid contraction. Again, ionic radii follows the order,

$$Lu^{3+} < Eu^{3+} < La^{3+}.$$

7. (b) The main reason for larger number of oxidation state exhibited by the actinoids than that corresponding lanthanoids, is larger atomic size of actinoids than the lanthanoids.

8. (d) Among the given lanthanoids, Yb^{2+} is diamagnetic because it has no unpaired electron while other have unpaired electrons and they are paramagnetic in nature.

9. (b) The main cause of lanthanoid contraction is the poorer shielding of 5d-electrons by 4f-electrons.

10. (a) The most common oxidation state among the lanthanoids is +3.

11. (c) Misch-metal which consists of a lanthanoid metal (~95%) and iron (~5%) and traces of S, C, Ca and Al.

12. (a) Among the given match, (a) is incorrectly match with the number of unpaired electrons

Its correct match is:

$Er^{2+} \longrightarrow 4f^{12} \longrightarrow$ 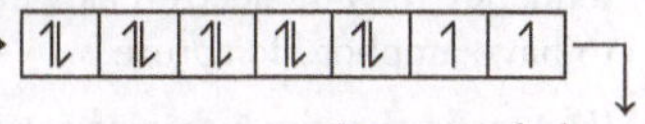

2 unpaired electrons

while others are correctly matched.

13. (c) Among the given elements, Ac exhibit only +3 oxidation states.

As, $\quad Ac(89) = Rn6d^17s^2$

14. (a) The trivalent actinoid ion (Am^{3+}) has electronic configuration $\rightarrow 5f^67s^0$ with atomic number 95.

15. (c) Statement I false but statement II is true.

The correct form of Statement I is:

Actinoids form relatively more stable complexes as compared to lanthanoids.

16. (c) Among the given actinoids only two, i.e. Np and Pu, show +7 oxidation state while 'U' and 'Am' show +3, +4, +5, +6 and Cm shows +3, +4 oxidation state.

Gearing up for NEET

1. (b) The electronic configuration of Ni with an atomic number 28 is

$$1s^22s^22p^63s^23p^63d^84s^2$$

and Ni^+ has electronic configuration

$$1s^22s^22p^63s^23p^63d^84s^1$$

2. (c) Among the given elements, Zn, Cd and Hg has $(n-1)\,d^{10}ns^2$ electronic configuration.

3. (d) Ionisation enthalpy shows only a little variation on moving along the period of d-block elements. The first ionisation enthalpy of zinc, cadmium and mercury are

higher than the other elements in their respective series because of the fully-filled $(n-1)d^{10}ns^2$ electronic configuration.

4. (b) Among the given elements, Cr has highest value of their second ionisation enthalpy due to half-filled configuration of Cr^+ion ($3d^5$).

5. (b) The radii of the elements from chromium ($Z=24$) to copper ($Z=29$) are very close to one another. This is due to the fact that successive addition of d-electrons screen the outer electrons (4s) from the inward pull of the nucleus.

6. (b) The correct order of the basic character of the transition metal monoxide is

$$TiO > VO > CrO > FeO$$

As, the size of metal ion decreases from Ti to Fe, the basic character of their monoxide decreases.

7. (a) In acidic medium, VO_2 is converted into VO^{2+} and the reaction proceeds as follows

$$VO_2 + 2H^+ \longrightarrow VO^{2+} + H_2O$$

8. (c) Among the given compounds, $Cr(OH)_3$ is an amphoteric hydroxide as Cr in +3 oxidation state (d^3) has tendency to gain electron as well as to loose electron as to have amphoteric nature.

9. (b) Among the given pair of compounds, only $[MnO_4]^-$ and CrO_2Cl_2 having metals in their highest oxidation states.

In $[MnO_4]^-$, Mn has +7 oxidation state and in CrO_2Cl_2, Cr has +6 oxidation state.

10. (b) Among the given metals, only Mn shows variable oxidation states as +2, +3, +4, +5, +6, +7.

11. (a) Ti^+ ($3d^2 4s^1$) is more stable than Ti^{3+} ($3d^1$) because of hall-filled stable configuration. Thus, Ti^{3+} changes to Ti^+ thereby acting as oxidising agent.

12. (c) Among the given statements, (c) is incorrect statement. Its correct form is : When the transition metals are in their highest oxidation state, they have no longer tendency to loose their electrons, thus they are not basic but show acidic character and form anionic complexes.

13. (d) In FeO_4^{2-}, the oxidation state of Fe is not same as that of its group number in the periodic table.

Oxo-anion	Electronic configuration	Group number
• MnO_4^-	+7,	$[Ar]3d^5 4s^2 = 7$
• $Cr_2O_7^{2-}$	+6,	$[Ar]3d^5 4s^1 = 6$
• VO_4^{3-}	+5,	$[Ar]3d^3 4s^2 = 5$
• FeO_4^{2-}	+6,	$[Ar]3d^6 4s^2 = 8$

14. (b) Transition elements form coloured salts due to the presence of unpaired electrons. In CuF_2, Cu(II) contain one unpaired electron hence, CuF_2 is coloured in solid state.

15. (b) $\mu_{cal} = \sqrt{n(n+2)}$, where, $n=3$, $\mu_{cal} = 3.87$ BM

The experimental value of magnetic moment is 4.40 B.M due to some contribution of the orbital motion of electron to the magnetic moment.

16. (d) Greater the number of unpaired d-electrons, more is the magnetic moment and magnetic moment can be obtained by using the formulas, $\sqrt{n(n+2)}$.

where, n = number of unpaired electrons.

For, $Co^{2+}(3d^7) \longrightarrow$ 3 unpaired electrons

$\mu = \sqrt{3(3+2)} = \sqrt{15}$ BM

$Ni^{2+}(3d^8) \longrightarrow$ 2 unpaired electrons

$\mu = \sqrt{2(2+2)} = \sqrt{8}$ BM

$Fe^{2+}(3d^6) \longrightarrow$ 4 unpaired electrons

$\mu = \sqrt{4(4+2)} = \sqrt{24}$ BM

$Cu^{2+}(3d^9) \longrightarrow$ 1 unpaired electrons

$\mu = \sqrt{1(1+2)} = \sqrt{3}$ BM

Thus, Cu^{2+} has the least magnetic moment.

17. (c) The number of unpaired electrons in Cr, Mn^+ and Fe^{2+} are 6, 6 and 4 respectively.

Hence, the magnetic moment of Cr, Mn^+ and Fe^{2+} will not be equal.

So, $z < x = y$ where x, y and z are the magnetic moment of Cr, Mn^+ and Fe^{2+} respectively.

18. (b) The number of unpaired electrons in Cr^{3+} is 3.

The spin only magnetic moment value of $Cr^{3+}(3d^3)$ ion is calculated as $= \sqrt{n(n+2)}$ $(n=3)$

$= \sqrt{3(3+2)}$

$= \sqrt{15} = 3.87$ BM

19. (b) In $VOCl_2$, the oxidation number of V is +4.

In $CuCl_2$, the oxidation number of Cu is +2.

Thus, $V^{4+} = 3d^1$ $(n=1)$ and $Cu^{2+} = 3d^9$ $(n=1)$

Both metals have one unpaired electron. The metal ion salts having similar number of unpaired electron in d-orbitals. Thus, show similar colour in aqueous medium.

20. (a) The transition metals form a large number of complex compounds. This is due to the comparatively smaller sizes of the metal ions, their high nuclear charges and the availability of vacant d-orbitals for bond formation.

21. (b) Fe, Hg cannot form an alloy.

Mercury has the property of dissolving nearly all metals, forming liquid or solid solutions called amalgams but it does not dissolve iron or platinum. Thus, iron and platinum cannot form alloy (amalgam) with mercury.

22. (d) Transition metals such as Fe, Co and Ni form interstitial compounds.

23. (b) The reaction proceeds as follows.

$$\overset{+4}{MnO_2} \longrightarrow K_2\overset{+6}{MnO_4}$$

Thus, in this conversion, the oxidation state of manganese changes from +4 to +6.

24. (a) MnO_4^- is coloured due charge transfer from O to Mn, i.e. ligand → metal charge transfer.

25. (c) The given reaction can be written as

$$Cr_2O_7^{2-} + X \xrightarrow{H^+} Cr^{3+} + H_2O + \text{Oxidised product of } X.$$

X in the above reaction cannot be SO_4^{2-} as in SO_4^{2-}, S is present in the highest oxidation state (+6) and can not be oxidised further.

26. (b) HCl and SO_2 are reducing agents. So, they can reduce MnO_4^-. CO_2 is neither strongly oxidising nor reducing agent and it will provide only acidic medium. It can shift the reaction in forward direction and the reaction can go to completion.

27. (d) The reaction can be written as

$$K_2\overset{+6}{Cr_2}O_7 + 7H_2SO_4 + 6KI \longrightarrow 4K_2SO_4 + \overset{+3}{Cr_2}(SO_4)_3 + 3I_2 + 7H_2O$$

Thus, the change in oxidation state of chromium in the given reaction is form +6 to +3.

28. (d)

29. (c) When acidified $K_2Cr_2O_7$ solution is added to Sn^{2+} salt then Sn^{2+} changes to Sn^{4+}.

The reaction is given below.

$$\overset{+6}{Cr_2}O_7^{2-} + 14H^+ + 3Sn^{2+} \longrightarrow 2Cr^{3+} + 3Sn^{4+} + 7H_2O$$

(Reduction: $Cr_2O_7^{2-} \to Cr^{3+}$; Oxidation: $Sn^{2+} \to Sn^{4+}$)

30. (d) $Yb^{2+} = [Xe]4f^{14}6s^0$ and $Eu^{3+} = [Xe]4f^66s^0$

The ion Yb^{2+} does not contain any unpaired electron hence it is diamagnetic and the ion Eu^{3+} contains six unpaired electrons hence, it is paramagnetic in nature.

31. (c) The reaction proceeds as follows

- $Cr_2O_7^{2-} + 2OH^- \longrightarrow 2CrO_4^{2-} + H_2O$
  In this reaction, pH > 7 (x > 7)
- $2CrO_4^{2-} + 2H^+ \longrightarrow Cr_2O_7^{2-} + H_2O$
  In this reaction, pH < 7 (y < 7)

Thus, the pH values x and y can be 8 and 4.

32. (b) The reaction can be written as

$$Cr_2O_7^{2-} + 6e^- + 14H^+ \longrightarrow 2Cr^{3+} + 7H_2O$$

The no. of electrons transfered per Cr atom = 3

33. (d) The correct electronic configuration is given as

$_{65}Tb = [Xe]4f^96s^2$, $_{60}Nd = [Xe]4f^46s^2$, $_{62}Sm = [Xe]4f^66s^2$

34. (c) The lanthanoid contraction is responsible for the fact that Zr and Hf have about the same radius.

35. (b) In lanthanoid series, the ionic radii of trivalent ions decreases with increase in the atomic number due to lanthanoid contraction.

36. (c) Among the given match, only (c) is incorrectly matched with their oxidation state.

Its correct match is :

Most stable oxidation state of Mn in oxides ⟶ + 7.

37. (a) Among the given match, (a) is incorrectly match.

Its correct match is:

Lanthanoids oxide ⟶ Television screen

38. (a) Both A and R are true and R is the correct explanation of A.

39. (c) A is true but R is false. The correct form of R is: $K_2Cr_2O_7$ changes colour only with change in pH of aqueous solution.

40. (c) A is true but R is false.

The correct form of R is:

The colour change is due to the change of chromate ions to dichromate ions and there is no change in the oxidation state of chromium, which is +6.

41. (a) Both A and R are true and R is the correct explanation of A.

42. (c) A is true but R is false.

The correct form of R is :

The reaction can be written as

$$K_2Cr_2O_7 + 3Na_2SO_3 + 4H_2SO_4 \longrightarrow 3Na_2SO_4 + K_2SO_4 + Cr_2(SO_4)_3 + 4H_2O$$

Acidified $K_2Cr_2O_7$ solution turns green when Na_2SO_3 is added to it, this is due to the formation of $Cr_2(SO_4)_3$ instead of $Cr_2(SO_3)_3$.

43. (d) A is false but R is true.

The correct form of A is:

The green manganate is paramagentic but the purple permanganate is diamagnetic in nature.

44. (d) Both Statement I and Statement II are true.

45. (c) Statement I is false but Statement II is true.

The correct form of Statement I is:

The highest Mn fluoride is MnF_4, whereas the highest oxide is Mn_2O_7.

46. (b) Statement I is true but Statement II is false.

The correct form of Statement II is:

The ions Ti^{2+}, V^{2+} and Cr^{2+} are strong reducing agents and will liberate hydrogen from a dilute acid, e.g.

$$2Cr^{2+} + 2H^+ \longrightarrow 2Cr^{3+} + H_2(g)$$

47. (d) Both Statement I and Statement II are true.

48. (*b*) Statement I is true but Statement II is false.
The correct form of Statement II is A manganese (II) ion salt is oxidised by peroxodisulphate to permanganate.

49. (*d*) Both Statement I and Statement II are true.

50. (*d*) Both Statement I and Statement II are true.

51. (*c*) Among the given statements, A, B, C and E are correct while the statement D is incorrect.
Its correct form is:
The transition metals with very high enthalpy of atomisation tend to be inert in their reactions.

52. (*d*) Among the given statements, only B and D are incorrect while A, C and E are correct. The correct froms of B and D are
- The only oxidation state of zinc is +2 (no *d* electrons are involved).
- In non-transition elements, the oxidation states normally differ by a unit of two.

53. (*d*) Among the given statements, only A, C and E are correct while B and D are incorrect.
The correct forms of B and D are
- The transition metals form a larger number of complex compounds due to the comparatively smaller sizes of the metal ions.
- The transition metal ions can change their oxidation states, they become more effective as catalysts.

54. (*c*) Among the given statements, only B, C and D are incorrect while the statement A and E are correct.
The correct forms of B, C and D are
- Sodium and potassium dichromates are strong oxidising agents, the sodium salt has a greater solubility in water.
- The acidified potassium dichromate will oxidise iodides to iodine and tin (II) to tin (IV).
- When the solution of sodium dichromate treated with potassium chloride, orange crystals of potassium dichromate crystallise out.

55. (*a*) Among the given statements, only A, B and D are correct while the statements C and E are incorrect.
Their correct forms are as follows
- Tb^{IV} has half-filled *f*-orbitals and it is an oxidant.
- The carbides Ln_3C, Ln_2C_3 and LnC_2 liberate hydrogen from dilute acids and burn in halogens to form halides.

56. (*b*) Among the given elements, only three, i.e. (iv), (v) and (vii) do not show the characteristic properties of *d*-block elements.

57. (a) Among the given species, only two, i.e. (iv) and (v) have +6 oxidation state while other have different oxidation state which are shown below.
- $MnO_4^- \longrightarrow +7$
- $Cr(CN)_6^{3-} \longrightarrow +3$
- $NiF_6^{2-} \longrightarrow +4$

58. (*c*) Among the given electronic configuration, only four, i.e. (i), (iii), (v) and (vi) are incorrect while other are correct. The correct electronic configurations, of (i), (iii), (v) and (vi) are as follows
- $Ce \rightarrow [Xe]\, 4f^1 5d^1 6s^2$
- $Yb \rightarrow [Xe]\, 4f^{14} 6s^2$
- $Bk \rightarrow [Rn]\, 5f^9 7s^2$
- $Cf \rightarrow [Rn]\, 5f^{10} 7s^2$

59. (*b*) The correct match is A-4, B-3, C-2, D-1.

60. (*c*) The correct match is A-2, B-1, C-4, D-3.

61. (*a*) The correct match is A-3, B-1, C-2, D-4.

62. (*d*) The correct match is A-2, B-3, C-1, D-4.

Final Check Through PYQS

1. (*a*) Spin only magnetic moment is given by

$$\mu_s = \sqrt{n(n+2)}$$

where, n = number of unpaired electrons.

A. $Ti^{3+} \longrightarrow 3d^1, n = 1$

$$\mu_s = \sqrt{1(1+2)} = \sqrt{3}$$

B. $Cr^{+2} \longrightarrow 3d^4, n = 4$

$$\mu_s = \sqrt{4(4+2)} = \sqrt{24}$$

C. $Mn^{+2} \longrightarrow 3d^5, n = 5$

$$\mu_s = \sqrt{5(5+2)} = \sqrt{35}$$

D. $Fe^{+2} \longrightarrow 3d^6, n = 4$

$$\mu_s = \sqrt{4(4+2)} = \sqrt{24}$$

E. $Sc^{3+} \longrightarrow 3d^0, n = 0, \mu = 0$

Thus, B and D have same magnetic moment.

2. (*c*) $E° = +$ ve for Mn^{+3}/Mn^{+2}

$$Mn = 25 \longrightarrow 3d^5 4s^2$$
$$Mn^{+2} \longrightarrow 3d^5$$
$$Mn^{+3} \longrightarrow 3d^4$$

Thus, $E°$ value for Mn^{+3}/Mn^{+2} is more positive.

3. (*b*) In aqueous solution, copper (I) undergoes disproportionation reaction.

$$2Cu^+(aq) \longrightarrow Cu^{2+} + Cu(s)$$

the highest stability of Cu^{2+} ion is more than Cu^+ in aqueous solution is due to negative enthalpy of hydration.

4. (*a*) Electronic configuration of Cr^{2+} ion is

Cr^{2+} : $[Ar]3d^4$ or [Ar] | 1 | 1 | 1 | 1 | |
($3d^4$)

It has four (n = 4) unpaired electrons.

∴Spin only magnetic moment

$$(\mu) = \sqrt{n(n+2)} \text{ BM}$$
$$= \sqrt{4(4+2)} \text{ BM}$$
$$= 4.90 \text{ BM}$$

5. (*c*) Statements in options (a), (b) and (d) are correct. Statement in option (c) is incorrect because oxidation states of Cr in CrO_4^{2-} (chromate) and $Cr_2O_7^{2-}$ (dichromate) are same which is +6.

i.e. $\overset{x}{Cr}O_4^{2-} \Rightarrow x + 4(-2) = -2 \Rightarrow x = +6$

$\underset{y}{Cr_2}O_7^{2-} \Rightarrow 2y + 7(-2) = -2 \Rightarrow y = +6$

6. (*b*)

(A) Mn shown six oxidation states in its compounds, *viz*, $+2, +3, +4, +5, +6$ and $+7 \Rightarrow (3)$

(B) Zn is not considered as transition element like Cd and Hg because of fully-filled (d^{10}-configuration) $\Rightarrow$ (4)

(C) Sc does not exhibit variable oxidation states. Only +3 state is shown by Sc in its compounds $\Rightarrow$ (1)

(D) Cu^+ shows disproportionaton in aqueous solution as,

$$2Cu^+ \longrightarrow Cu^0 + Cu^{2+} \Rightarrow (2)$$

7. (*a*)

A. V_2O_5 –(3) Oxidation of SO_2 in the manufacture of H_2SO_4 by contact process.

B. $TiCl_4 + Al(CH_3)_3$ - (Ziegler-Natta catalyst)- (4) Polymerisation of ethylene.

C. $PdCl_2$–(1) Oxidation of ethyne to ethanal.

D. Nickel complexes–(2) Polymerisation of alkynes.

Thus, the correct match is

(A) → (3), (B) → (4), (C) → (1), (D) → (2).

8. (*c*) The electronic configuration of Co^{3+} is $[Ar]3d^6$.

Here, $n = 4$

$$\mu = \sqrt{4(4+2)} = \sqrt{24} \text{ BM}$$

The electronic configuration of Cr^{3+} is $[Ar]3d^3$.

Here, $n = 3$

$$\mu = \sqrt{3(3+2)} = \sqrt{15} \text{ BM}$$

The electronic configuration of Fe^{3+} is $[Ar]3d^5$.

Here, $n = 5$

$$\mu = \sqrt{5(5+2)} = \sqrt{35} \text{ BM}$$

The electronic configuration of Ni^{2+} is $[Ar]3d^8$.

Here, $n = 2$

$$\mu = \sqrt{2(2+2)} = \sqrt{8} \text{ BM}$$

So, the correct option is (c).

9. (a) Electronic configuration of

$Fe^{2+} = 1s^2 2s^2 2p^6 3s^2 3p^6 3d^6$

$Fe^{2+} = 3d^6$ (number of '*d*' electrons = 6)

The electronic configuration of $Cl = 1s^2 2s^2 2p^6 3s^2 3p^5$

Total *p* electrons is 11, which are not equal to number of '*d*' electrons in Fe^{+2}.

The electronic configuration of $Ne = 1s^2 2s^2 2p^6$

p-electrons in neon = 6

The electronic configuration of $Mg = 1s^2 2s^2 2p^6 3s^2$

s-electrons in magnesium = 6

10. (*a*) Magnetic moment, $\mu = \sqrt{n(n+2)}$ BM

where, n = number of unpaired electrons

$\mu = 2.84$ (given)

$\therefore \quad 2.84 = \sqrt{n(n+2)}$ B.M

$(2.84)^2 = n(n+2) \quad \Rightarrow \quad 8 = n^2 + 2n$

$n^2 + 2n - 8 = 0$

$n^2 + 4n - 2n - 8 = 0 \quad \Rightarrow n(n+4) - 2(n+4) = 0$

$n = 2$

$Ni^{2+} = [Ar]3d^8 4s^0$ (two unpaired electrons)

$Ti^{3+} = [Ar]3d^1 4s^0$ (one unpaired electron)

$Cr^{3+} = [Ar]3d^3$, (three unpaired electrons)

$Co^{2+} = [Ar], 3d^7, 4s^0$ (three unpaired electrons)

So, only Ni^{2+} has 2 unpaired electrons and thus has a magnetic moment of 2.84 BM.

11. (*b*) Among the given statements, C and D statements are incorrect. Their correct forms are as follows

- Basic character decreases from V_2O_3 to V_2O_4 to V_2O_5. In general, the oxides in lower oxidation states of metals are basic and in their higher oxidation states they are acidic.
- V_2O_4 dissolves in acids to give VO_2^+ salts.

12. (*d*) The reaction that takes place in the given condition is as follows

$$\underset{+7}{KMnO_4} + I^- \xrightarrow[\text{Weak alkaline medium}]{\text{Neutral}} \underset{+4}{MnO_2} + IO_3^-$$

So, the change in oxidation state of manganese in this reaction is from + 7 to + 4.

Hence, option (d) is correct option.

13. (*d*) The structures of manganate and permanganate ions are as follows

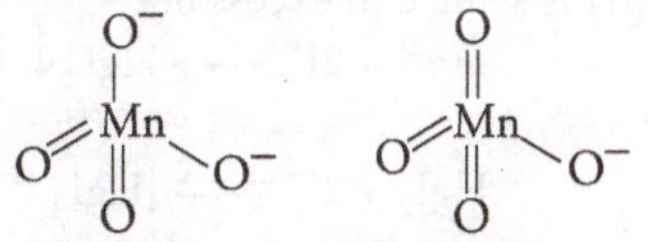

Manganate (MnO_4^{2-}) Permanganate (MnO_4^-)

The manganate and permanganate ions are tetrahedral and contain π-bonds of $d\pi$(Mn) - $p\pi$(O)-type, oxygen does not have any *d*-orbital.

Hence, the π-bonding takes place by overlap of *p*-orbitals of oxygen and *d*-orbitals of manganese.

14. (*c*) When neutral or faintly alkaline $KMnO_4$ is treated with potassium iodide, $KMnO_4$ is converted into MnO_2 while iodide (I^-) ion is converted into IO_3^- (iodate).

The reaction takes place as follows

$$KMnO_4 + I^- + \bar{O}H \longrightarrow MnO_2 + \underset{'X'}{IO_3^-} + H_2O$$

15. (*d*) The complex which contains unpaired electrons exhibit *d-d* transition and paramagnetism.

(i) In MnO_4^-,

The electronic configuration of Mn^{+7} is $[Ar]3d^0$.

Number of unpaired electrons = 0

Therefore, it will be diamagnetic and will not show *d-d* transition.

(ii) In $Cr_2O_7^{2-}$,

The electronic configuration of Cr^{+6} is $[Ar]3d^0$.

Number of unpaired electrons = 0

So, it will be diamagnetic and will not show *d-d* transition.

(iii) In CrO_4^{2-},

The electronic configuration of Cr^{+6} is $[Ar]3d^0$.

Number of unpaired electrons = 0

Therefore, it is also diamagnetic and will not show *d-d* transition.

(iv) In MnO_4^{2-},

The electronic configuration of Mn^{+6} is $[Ar]3d^1$.

Number of unpaired electron = 1

Since, it contains one unpaired electron so it will exhibit both *d-d* transition and paramagnetism.

16. (*b*) SO_2 gas can readily decolourise acidified $KMnO_4$ solution because $KMnO_4$ is an oxidising agent and SO_2 act as reducing agent.

$$\underset{\text{(Purple)}}{2MnO_4^-} + 5SO_2 + 2H_2O \longrightarrow \underset{\text{(Colourless)}}{2Mn^{2+}} + 5SO_4^{2-} + 4H^+$$

17. (*c*) $HgCl_2$ and I_2 both when dissolved in water containing I^- ions, the pair of species formed is HgI_4^{2-} and I_3^-. In aqueous solution, I_2 reacts with I^- and maintains the following equilibrium.

$$I_2 + I^- \rightleftharpoons I_3^-$$

Hg^{2+} gives ppt. of HgI_2 on reaction with I^-.

But HgI_2 is soluble in excess of I^-

$$Hg^{2+} + 2I^- \longrightarrow \underset{\text{Red ppt.}}{HgI_2 \downarrow} + 2Cl^-$$

$$HgI_2 + 2I^- \rightleftharpoons [HgI_4]^{2-}$$

18. (*c*) When SO_2 is passed through acidified $K_2Cr_2O_7$ solution, green chromium sulphate is formed. In this reaction, oxidation state of Cr changes from +6 to +3.

$$K_2\overset{+6}{Cr_2}O_7 + H_2SO_4 + 3SO_2 \longrightarrow K_2SO_4 + \overset{+3}{Cr_2}(SO_4)_3 + H_2O$$

The appearance of green colour is due to the reduction of chromium metal from Cr^{+6} to Cr^{+3}.

19. (*c*) The following equations can be written from the given reactions.

(a) $\overset{0}{Fe} + \underbrace{H_2O + O_2}_{\text{from air}} \longrightarrow \overset{III}{Fe_2}O_3 \cdot xH_2O]$

(b) $\overset{0}{Fe} + CuSO_4 \longrightarrow \overset{II}{Fe}SO_4 + Cu$

(c) $\overset{0}{Fe} + 5CO \longrightarrow \overset{0}{Fe}(CO)_5$

(d) $\overset{0}{Fe} + \underset{\text{Steam}}{H_2O} \longrightarrow \overset{III}{Fe_2}O_3 + H_2$

$\therefore$ Formation of $Fe(CO)_5$ from Fe does not involve oxidation of iron because there is no change in oxidation state.

20. (*a*) $FeSO_4$ will require the least amount of acidified $KMnO_4$ for complete oxidation as in SO_4^{2-} as sulphur is already present in its highest oxidation state.

$$Fe^{2+} \longrightarrow Fe^{3+}$$

and $SO_4^{2-} \longrightarrow$ No oxidation (least $KMnO_4$)

$$SO_3^{2-} \longrightarrow SO_4^{2-}\ (+4 \rightarrow +6)$$

$$C_2O_4^{2-} \longrightarrow CO_2\ (+3 \rightarrow +4) \times 2e^-$$

$$NO_2^- \longrightarrow NO_3^-\ (+3 \rightarrow +5)$$

21. (*c*) The compounds with lower oxidation number and which cannot reduced or-oxidised by one another can exist together. Thus, $FeCl_2$ and $SnCl_2$ can exist together as Fe^{2+} cannot be reduced by Sn^{2+}.

22. (*c*) The structure of CrO_5 is

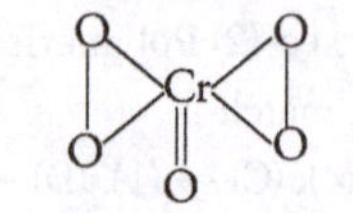

Hence, CrO_5 has two (—O—O—) linkage.

Now suppose the oxidation number of Cr is x then,

$$x + (-1 \times 4) + (-2) \times 1 = 0 \Rightarrow x = +6$$

23. (*b*) The reaction of aqueous $KMnO_4$ with H_2O_2 in acidic medium is as follows

$$3H_2SO_4 + 2KMnO_4 + 5H_2O_2 \longrightarrow 5O_2 + 2MnSO_4 + 8H_2O + K_2SO_4$$

In the above reaction, $KMnO_4$ oxidises H_2O_2 to O_2 and itself, i.e. $[MnO_4^-]$ gets reduced to Mn^{2+} ion as $MnSO_4$. Hence, aqueous solution of $KMnO_4$ with H_2O_2 yields Mn^{2+} and O_2 in acidic conditions.

24. (*a*) $Ce^{+4} = [Xe]\,4f^0 6s^0$ and $Yb^{+2} = [Xe]\,4f^{14} 6s^0$

Both ions do not contain any unpaired electrons. Hence, these are diamagnetic.

25. (*a*) The electronic configuration of gadolinium is

$$Gd = [Xe]\,4f^7 5d^1 6s^2.$$

$$Gd^{3+} = [Xe]\,4f^7$$

After removal of 3rd electron, it will attain half-filled electronic configuration. Due to which $4f$ will have high exchange energy. So, Gd has low value of third ionisation energy. Hence, option (a) is correct.

26. (*b*) The shielding effect of $5f$-orbitals in actinoids is poor than the shielding effect of $4f$-orbitals. So, the effective nuclear charge on valence electrons is more in actinoids. Hence, actinoid contraction is greater than lanthanoid contraction.

∴ Statement (a) is correct.

Trivalent lanthanoid ions are coloured in the solid state due to presence of f-electrons.

∴ Statement (b) is incorrect.

Lanthanoids are inner transition metals. So, they are good conductors of heat and electricity.

∴ Statement (c) is correct.

The surface area increases when actinoids are finely divided which results in exposure of more reactant molecules to react. Hence, rate increases and so, actinoids are highly reactive metals when finely divided.

∴Statement (d) is correct.

27. (c) $Zr\ (Z=40) \rightarrow 1s^2\ 2s^2\ 2p^6 3s^2 3p^6\ 3d^{10} 4s^2 4p^6 4d^2 5s^2$

$Hf\ (Z=72) \rightarrow 1s^2 2s^2 2p^6 3s^2 3p^6 3d^{10} 4s^2 4p^6 4d^{10}$
$5s^2 5p^6 4f^{14} 5d^2 6s^2$

Hf is a post lanthanoid element. Due to presence of 4f-orbitals which have poor shielding effect, the effective nuclear charge on valence shell electrons is more which result in the decrease of the size of Hf. This effect is known as lanthanoid contraction.

Thus, Zr and Hf have similar atomic and ionic radii due to lanthanoid contraction.

28. (c) The reason for greater range of oxidation states in actinoids is attributed to the 5f, 6d and 7s levels having comparable energies.

The 5f-orbitals extend into space beyond the 7s and 6p-orbitals and participate in bonding. This is in direct contrast to the lanthanoides where the 4f-orbitals are buried deep inside the atom, totally shielded by outer orbitals and thus unable to take part in bonding.

29. (c) Electronic configuration of $_{63}Eu = [Xe]_{54}\ 4f^7 6s^2$

Electronic configuration of $_{64}Gd = [Xe]_{54}\ 4f^7 5d^1 6s^2$

Electronic configuration of $_{65}Tb = [Xe]_{54}\ 4f^9 6s^2$

30. (c) Considering the given statements.

(a) $Eu(63) = 4f^7 5d^0, 6s^2$; $Eu^{2+} = 4f^7$. Thus, it shows +2 state.

(b) In lanthanoids series, ionic radius decreases and covalent character increases, thus basicity decreases due to lanthanoid contraction.

(c) Lanthanons are less reactive than aluminium due to high ionisation potential. The reason for this high ionisation potential is lanthanoid contraction.

(d) Ce^{4+} is a good oxidising agent, it is easily converted to Ce^{3+}.

Thus, (c) is incorrect.

31. (c) Because of the lanthanoid contraction Zr (atomic radii 160 pm) and Hf (atomic radii 158 pm) have nearly same atomic radii.

Lanthanoid contraction is associated with the intervention of the 4f orbitals which are filled before the 5d-series of elements starts. The filling of 4f orbitals before 5d-orbitals results in regular decrease in atomic radii which compensates the expected increase in atomic size with increasing atomic number. As a result of this lanthanoid contraction, the elements of second and third transition series have almost similar atomic radii.

32. (c) $_{64}Gd = [Xe]\,4f^7\ 5d^1\ 6s^2$

33. (a) Lanthanoid contraction is the regular decrease in atomic and ionic radii of lanthanides. This is due to the imperfect shielding [or poor screening effect] of f-orbitals due to their diffused shape which enable to counter balance the effect to the increased nuclear charge. Hence, the net result is a contraction in size of lanthanoids.

Skill Builder

- **Sol. of Skill Builder Pg. 211**

(d) Spin only magnetic moment is given by

$\mu = \sqrt{n(n+2)}$ BM, n = number of unpaired electrons.

A. $Fe^{3+} \rightarrow 3d^5, n=5, \mu = \sqrt{35}$ BM

B. $Co^{3+} \rightarrow 3d^6, n=4, \mu = \sqrt{24}$ BM

C. $Ti^{2+} \rightarrow 3d^2, n=2, \mu = \sqrt{8}$ BM

D. $Ni^{2+} \rightarrow 3d^8, n=2, \mu = \sqrt{8}$ BM

E. $Fe^{2+} \rightarrow 3d^6, n=4, \mu = \sqrt{24}$ BM

Hence, option (d) is correct

- **Sol. of Skill Builder Pg. 218**

(a) The reaction takes place as follows

$$\underset{(+7)}{2MnO_4^-} + 16H^+ + 5C_2O_4^{2-} \longrightarrow \underset{(+2)}{2Mn^{2+}} + 8H_2O + 10CO_2$$

- **Sol. of Skill Builder Pg. 219**

(b) Sulphurous acid or sulphuric is oxidised to a sulphate or sulphuric acid (Z).

$$5SO_3^{2-} + 2MnO_4^- + 6H^+ \longrightarrow 2Mn^{2+} + 3H_2O + \underset{(Z)}{5SO_4^{2-}}$$

- **Sol. of Skill Builder Pg. 223**

(c) $Yb^{2+} = [Xe]4f^{14}6s^0$ and $Ce^{4+} = [Xe]4f^0 5d^0 6s^0$

Both ions do not contain any unpaired electron. Hence, these are diamagnetic.

- **Sol. of Skill Builder Pg. 225**

(d) The correct electronic configuration is given as

$_{69}Tm = [Xe]\,4f^{13} 6s^2$

$_{68}Er = [Xe]\,4f^{12} 6s^2$

$_{67}Ho = [Xe]\,4f^{11} 6s^2$

For deeper insight
Scan the QR Code

Chapter 6

Coordination Compounds

Learning Objectives

Module-I

- Addition Compounds
- Important Terms Related to Coordination Compounds
- Nomenclature of Coordination Compounds
- Isomerism in Coordination Compounds

Module-II

- Werner's Theory
- Valence Bond Theory (VBT)

Module-III

- Crystal Field Theory (CFT)
- Colour in Coordination Compounds
- Magnetic Properties of Coordination Compounds
- Organometallic Compounds
- Importance of Coordination Compounds

Chapter Overview with *NEET Connection*

Coordination compounds are the backbone of modern inorganic and bio-inorganic chemistry. The chemistry of coordination compounds is an important and challenging area of modern drug and synthetic industries.

Special format questions can be easily framed on the following topics of this chapter.

- IUPAC nomenclature and isomerism
- Hybridisation and geometry of complexes
- Magnetic properties
- Colour

For better understanding of this chapter a grip over *d*- and *f*-block elements and preliminary knowledge about ligands is required.

New concepts of chemical bonding and molecular structure have provided insights into the functioning of these compounds as vital components of biological systems.

Introduction

Some metals, especially transition metals, have tendency to form large number of compounds. These compounds are formed by either combination of two or more simpler compounds of metals or by combination of few groups to a metal ion. These are combinedly known as **addition compounds** and play important role in natural processes as well as in our daily life.

Module 1

Addition Compounds, Important Terms Related to Coordination Compounds, Nomenclature and Isomerism

- Addition Compounds
- Nomenclature of Coordination Compounds
- Important Terms Related to Coordination Compounds
- Isomerism in Coordination Compounds

Addition Compounds

When solution having two or more stable compounds, combine in a simple molecular (stoichiometric) proportions, they form a new compound called **addition** or **molecular compounds.**

e.g. $Fe(CN)_2 + 4KCN \longrightarrow Fe(CN)_2 \cdot 4KCN$

$K_2SO_4 + Al_2(SO_4)_3 + 24H_2O \longrightarrow K_2SO_4 \cdot Al_2(SO_4)_3 \cdot 24H_2O$

These addition compounds can be divided into two types

(i) **Double salts or lattice compounds** The addition compounds which dissociate and lose their identity in solution are called **double salts.**

e.g. Mohr's salt $[FeSO_4 \cdot (NH_4)_2SO_4 \cdot 6H_2O]$

Potash alum $[KAl(SO_4)_2 \cdot 12H_2O]_2$

Carnallite $KCl \cdot MgCl_2 \cdot 6H_2O$

(ii) **Coordination or complex compounds** The addition compounds which do not dissociate and retain their identity in solution are called **complex** or **coordination compounds.**

e.g. $K_2[PtCl_6]$, $K_4[Fe(CN)_6]$

Transition metals form large number of complex compounds with anions or neutral molecules.

In complex compounds, metal ion acts as a Lewis acid while the other groups attached to it act as Lewis bases.

Concept ladder

Both the double salts and coordination compounds are formed by combination of heavy elements. But basic difference in both the compounds is that double salts dissociate into ions when dissolved in water whereas complex ions do not dissociate. For instance, Mohr salt, $FeSO_4 \cdot (NH_4)_2SO_4 \cdot 6H_2O$ on dissolving in water dissociates into Fe^{2+}, NH_4^+ ions while complex ion such as $[Fe(CN)_6]^{4-}$ does not dissociate into Fe^{2+} and CN^- ions.

Example 1. *Which of the following pairs contains complex compound and double salt respectively?*

(a) $FeSO_4$, $K_4[Fe(CN)_6]$

(b) $[Cu(NH_3)_4]SO_4$, $FeSO_4 \cdot 7H_2O$

(c) $[Cu(NH_3)_4]SO_4$, $K_2SO_4 \cdot Al_2(SO_4)_3 \cdot 24H_2O$

(d) $MgSO_4 \cdot 7H_2O$, $CuSO_4$

Sol. (c) Among the given options $[Cu(NH_3)_4]SO_4$, is a complex compound while $K_2SO_4 \cdot Al_2(SO_4)_3 \cdot 24H_2O$ is a double salt.

Important Terms Related to Coordination Compounds

Some of the important terms related to coordination compounds are as follows

Complex Ion or Coordination Entity

It is a metal ion with a Lewis base attached to it through coordinate bonds, e.g. $[Fe(CN)_6]^{4-}$.

Complex ion can be represented as

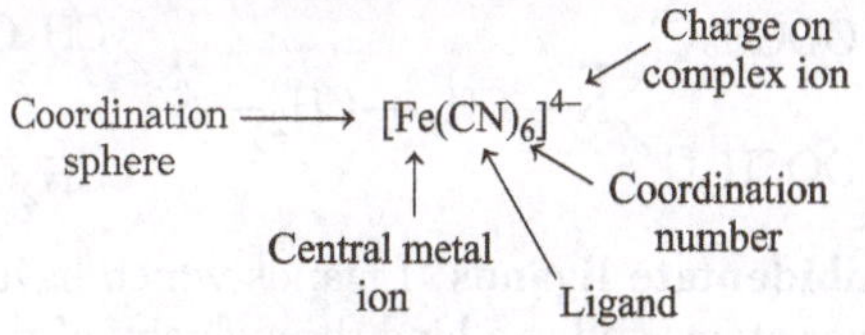

Different types of complex ions are as follows

- Complex ion which bears positive charge is called **cationic complex ion,** e.g. $[Co(NH_3)_6]^{3+}$.
- Complex ion which bears negative charge is called **anionic complex ion,** e.g. $[Ag(CN)_2]^-$.
- Complex ion which has no charge is called **neutral complex,** e.g. $[Ni(CO)_4]$.

Central Metal Atom/Ion

The atom (or ion) to which a fixed number of groups or ions are bonded in definite geometrical arrangement, is called central metal ion.

e.g. In $[Fe(CN)_6]^{3-}$, Fe^{3+} is the central metal ion.

Ligands

The groups of ions or molecules which are bonded to central metal ion are known as ligands. They donate pair of electrons to metal ion. Therefore, are also called Lewis bases.

e.g. In $[Fe(CN)_6]^{3-}$, CN^- ion acts as ligand.

Ligands can be further divided on the basis of number of donor atoms present.

(i) **Mono or unidentate ligands** Ligands which have only one donor atom and donates one electron pair to central metal ion are called monodentate ligands.

e.g. NH_3, H_2O, Cl^- etc.

(ii) **Bidentate ligands** Ligands which can bind metal ion through two donor atoms are called bidentate ligands.

e.g. Oxalate $(C_2O_4^{2-})$, ethane-1, 2-diamine

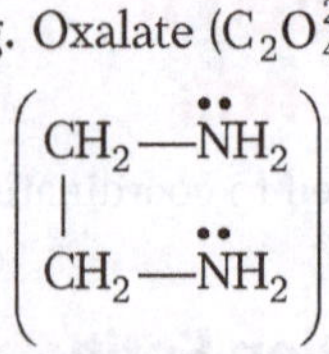

etc.

(iii) **Polydentate ligands** Ligands which have more than two donor atoms are called polydentate ligands. e.g. $EDTA^{4-}$ (ethylene diamine tetraacetate ion) is a hexadentate ligand.

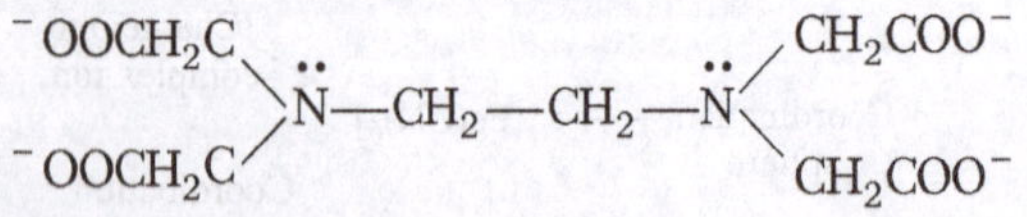

(iv) **Ambidentate ligands** Ligands which have two donor atoms and can bind through any of the atom is called ambidentate ligand.

e.g. NO_2^- (nitrite ion) can bind through nitrogen as well as through oxygen. Other examples are CN^-, SCN^- etc.

(v) **Chelating ligands** When a di- or polydentate ligand binds to a central metal ion and forms a ring, then it is called chelating ligands.

They usually form five or six membered rings called **chelates**.

e.g.

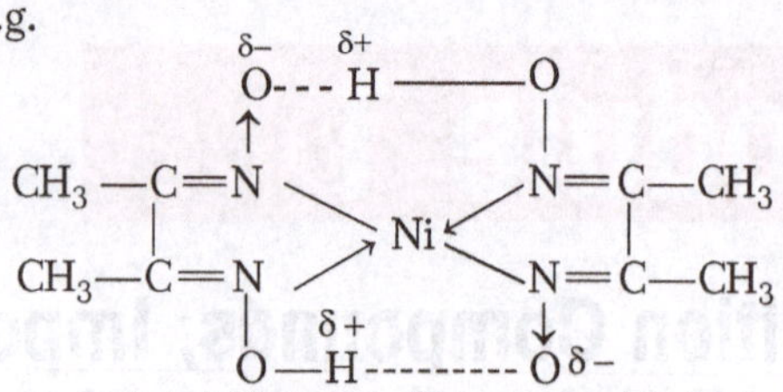

Nickel (II) dimethyl glyoximate (chelate)
[*bis*-(dimethylglyoximato)nickel (II)]

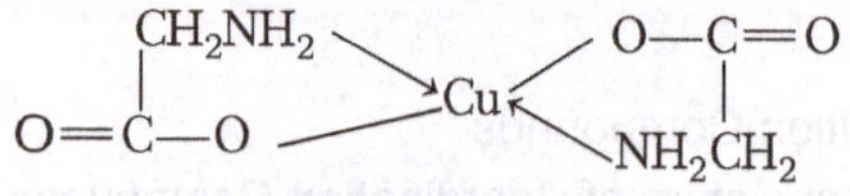

Copper (II) glycinate (chelate)
[*trans*-diglycinatocopper (II)]

The number of such donor groups present in a single ligand that bind to central metal atom is called **denticity**.

Coordination Sphere

The central atom/ion and the ligands attached to it are enclosed in square brackets and are collectively called as coordination sphere. It represents single entity in coordination compounds. The ionisable groups are written outside the bracket and are called counter **ions**.

e.g. $[Co(NH_3)_6]^{2+}$ is a coordination sphere.

Coordination Polyhedron

It is the spatial arrangement of the ligand atoms which are directly attached to the central atom/ion is called coordination polyhedron.

e.g. $[Co(NH_3)_6]^{3+}$ is octahedral, $Ni(CO)_4$ is tetrahedral and $[PtCl_4]^{2-}$ is square planar.

Coordination Number

It is the number of donor atoms of ligands to which a central metal ion is directly bonded.

e.g. In $[Ni(NH_3)_4]^{2+}$, here coordination number of Ni is 4.

In case of polydentate ligands,

C.N. = number of ligand × denticity of ligand

e.g. In $[Fe(C_2O_4)_3]^{3-}$, coordination number of Fe is 6.

Mentor's TIP

Always remember, π-bonds are not involved in the determination of coordination number in non-organometallic compounds.

Oxidation Number

It is the charge present on central metal atom/ion if all the ligands bonded to it are removed along with pairs of electrons that are shared with the central atom/ion.

e.g. Oxidation number of Cu in $[Cu(NH_3)_4]^{2+}$ is +2, as NH_3 is a neutral ligand, in $[Cu(CN)_4]^{3-}$ oxidation number of Cu is +1 as CN is an anionic ligand ($\bar{C}N$).

Homoleptic and Heteroleptic Complexes

Complexes in which a metal is bound to only one kind of donor group are known as homoleptic complexes. e.g. $[Co(NH_3)_6]^{3+}$ whereas complexes in which a metal is bound to more than one kind of donor groups are known as heteroleptic complexes. e.g. $[Co(NH_3)_4Cl_2]^+$.

NEET Snapshot

$[Co(NH_3)_6]^{3+}$ is a homoleptic complex whereas $[Co(NH_3)_4Cl_2]^+$ is a heteroleptic complex because only one kind of ligands are present in $[Co(NH_3)_6]^{3+}$, whereas $[Co(NH_3)_4Cl_2]^+$ contains more than one kind of ligand. ***[NEET 2024]***

Homoleptic complexes have same kind of ligands while heteroleptic complexes have different kind of ligands.

Nomenclature of Coordination Compounds

Nomenclature is important in coordination chemistry. The formulas and names adopted for coordination entities are based on the recommendation of International Union of Pure and Applied Chemistry (IUPAC).

Formulas of Mononuclear Coordination Entities

The following rules are applied while writing the formulas.

- The central atom is listed first.
- The ligands are then listed in alphabetical order.
- The formula for the entire coordination entity is enclosed in square brackets.
- There should be no space between the ligands and the metal within a coordination sphere.
- The charge of the cation(s) is balanced by the charge of the anion(s).

Naming of coordination compounds are done as per some rules set by the IUPAC. These rules are as follows

- Coordination compounds contain two parts : cation and anion. Cations are named before anions.

  e.g. In $K_4[Fe(CN)_6]$, K^+ is a cation, it is named before the anion $[Fe(CN)_6]^{4-}$. Hence, IUPAC name of compound is potassium hexacyanidoferrate(II).
- If more than one type of ligands are present then they are written in alphabetical order.
- Names of anionic ligands ending with 'ide' changes to 'ido', 'ite' changes to 'o' 'ate' changes to 'o'.
- Positive ligands end with '**ium**' and neutral ligands like H_2O, NH_3 are given names such as aqua, ammine respectively.

  In latest trend **e** is simply replaced by **o.**

Name of Some Common Ligands

Neutral ligands		Negative ligands	
Formula	**Name of ligand**	**Formula**	**Name of ligand**
$\underline{O}H_2$	aqua		
$\underline{N}H_3$	ammine	$\underline{F}^-$ (fluoride)	fluorido
$\underline{C}O$	carbonyl	$\underline{Cl}^-$	chlorido
$\underline{N}O$	nitrosyl	$\underline{Br}^-$	bromido
$\underline{N}H_2CH_3$	methylamine	$\underline{I}^-$	iodido
$\underline{N}C_5H_5$ or Py	pyridine	$\underline{O}^{2-}$ (oxide)	oxo
$\underline{N}(C_2H_5)_3$	triethylamine	$\underline{O}H^-$ (hydroxide)	hydroxido
$\underline{N}(CH_3)_3$	trimethylamine	$^*\underline{C}N^-$ (cyanide)	cyanido
$\underline{P}(C_6H_5)_3$	triphenyl phosphine	$^*\underline{N}C^-$	isocyanido
$\underline{P}H_3$	phosphine	$\underline{S}^{2-}$	sulphido
(positive ligands) NO_2^+	Nitronium	$S\underline{O}_4^{2-}$	Sulphato
$NH_2—NH_3^+$	Hydrozinium	$C_2\underline{O}_4^{2-}$	oxalato
NO^+	Nitrosonium	$^*\underline{N}O_2^-$ $^*ON\underline{O}^-$ $C\underline{O}_3^{2-}$	nitrito-N nitrito-O carbonato

Underlined atoms are electron donating and ambident ligands.

Concept ladder The 2004 IUPAC drafts recommends that anionic ligands will end with "*ido*" so that chloro would become chlorido, *cyano* would become cyanido etc.

- If several ligands of same types are present, prefixes di, tri, tetra etc., are used. When the name of ligand (denticity ≥ 2) involves a number then prefixes *bis*, *tris*, *tetrakis* are used and name of ligands is placed in brackets, e.g. compound $[Co(en)_3]Cl_3$ is named as *tris* (ethane-1, 2-diamine) cobalt (III) chloride.

  Here, *tris* is used to indicate three ligands since **en** (ethane-1, 2-diamine) also carries **di** in its name.
- In complex ion, ligands are named first followed by name of central metal ion with its oxidation state in Roman numeral (Hall's notation).

- If complex ion is cation, the name of central metal ion remains the same. e.g.
  - $[Fe(NH_3)_6]Cl_3$ hexammineiron(III) chloride
  - $[CoCl(NH_3)_5]^{2+}$ pentaamminechlorocobalt(III) ion
- If complex ion is anion, the name of central metal ion ends with '-ate'. e.g.
  - $[ZnCl_4]^{2-}$ tetrachloridozincate(II) ion
  - $[AlH_4]^-$ tetrahydridoaluminate(III) ion
  - $K_4[Fe(CN)_6]$ potassium hexacyanidoferrate(II)
- The neutral complex molecule is named similar to that of complex cation.
- Ambidentate ligands are named as follows
  - *M*—NO_2 (NO_2 joined to metal *M* through N is **nitrito-N**).
  - *M*–ONO (NO_2 joined to metal *M* through O is **nitrito-O**).

  Similarly, the SCN group may be named thiocyanato-S [to indicate S coordinated to metal *M*] and thiocyanato-N [to indicate N coordinated to metal *M*]
- The ligands and metal ion inside coordination sphere are written without any space. While oxidation number and the ion outside are separated by single space. e.g. $[Co(NH_3)_5SO_4]Br \Rightarrow$ (pentaamminesulphatocobalt(III) bromide).

Naming of Coordination Compounds Having Cationic Complex Ion

In the following examples, complex ion exists as cation

- $[Fe(NH_3)_6]Cl_3$ hexammineiron(III) chloride
- $[CoCl(NH_3)_5]^{2+}$ pentaamminechloridocobalt(III) ion
- $[CoSO_4(NH_3)_4]NO_3$ tetraamminesulphatocobalt(III) nitrate

Naming of Coordination Compounds Having Anionic Complex Ion

In the following examples, complex ion exists as anion

- $K_2[Cr(CN)_2(O)_2(O_2)NH_3]$ potassium amminedicyanidodioxoperoxochromate (VI)
- $[Zn(NCS)_4]^{2-}$ tetrathiocyanato-N-zincate(II) ion (N indicates that ligand joined to metal ion through N-side)

Naming of Coordination Compounds Having Organic Ligands

In the following examples, organic ligands have been used

- $[Pt(py)_4][PtCl_4]$ tetrapyridineplatinum(II) tetrachloridoplatinate(II)
- $[Cr(en)_3]Cl_3$ *tris*-ethane-1, 2-diamine chromium (III) chloride
- $[Pt(en)_2]^{2+}$ *bis*-ethane-1, 2-diamine platinum (II) ion
- $[Cr(\eta^6\text{-}C_6H_6)_2]$ *bis*(benzene) chromium(0)
- $[Fe(\eta^5\text{-}C_5H_5)_2]$ *bis*(cyclopentadienyl)iron(II) [It is ferrocene]

NEET Close-up

Example Similar to PYQ Asked in NEET 2022

The IUPAC name of the complex $[Co(NH_3)_4Br_2][ZnCl_4]$ is
(a) tetraamminedibromocobalt (III) tetrachlorozincate (II)
(b) tetraamminedibromocobalt (II) tetrachlorozincate (II)
(c) tetraamminedibromocobalt (III) tetrachlorozincate (III)
(d) tetraamminedibromocobalt (II) tetrachlorozincate (III)

Sol. (*a*) In this complex, charges on complex cation and complex anion are +1 and −2 respectively. Therefore, the oxidation states of cobalt and zinc can be calculated as

Complex cation	Complex anion
$[Co(NH_3)_4Br_2]^+$	$[ZnCl_4]^{-2}$
$x+0-2=+1$	$x-4=-2$
$x=+3$	$x=+2$

Therefore, oxidation states of cobalt and zinc are +3 and +2 respectively. Therefore, the name of the complex is tetrammminedibromocobalt (III) tetrachlorozincate (II).

Skill Builder

The IUPAC name of the complex $[Co(NH_3)_6][Cr(NH_3)_2Cl_4]_3$ is
(a) hexaamminecobalt (I) diammine tetrachlorochromate (III)
(b) hexaamminecobalt (II) diammine tetrachlorochromate (II)
(c) hexaamminecobalt (III) diammine tetrachlorochromate (II)
(d) hexaamminecobalt (II) diammine tetrachlorochromate (III)

For more practice Refer to Q. 11 and 12 of Step up Practice 1.

Isomerism in Coordination Compounds

Compounds which have same molecular formula but different arrangements of atoms or molecules or structures having different properties are known as **isomers**. This phenomenon is called **isomerism.**

It is classified into two types namely.

(i) Structural isomerism (ii) Stereoisomerism

Structural Isomerism

The isomers which differ in their linkages, distribution of ligands around central metal atom are called **structural isomers**. The phenomenon is called structural isomerism. These are further divided into following types.

Ionisation Isomerism

Isomers which give different ions in solution or in molten state when ionised are called **ionisation isomers.** There is an interchange of anions between the coordination sphere of the metal ion and the ions outside the sphere. In other words, when the counter ion in a complex salt is itself a potential ligand and can displace a ligand which can then become the counter ion.

e.g. $[Co(NH_3)_5(SO_4)]Br$ — Red (pentaamminesulphatocobalt (III) bromide)

$[Co(NH_3)_5Br]SO_4$ — Violet (pentaamminebromidocobalt (III) sulphate)

- SO_4^{2-} inside coordination sphere and Br^- outside it
- gives yellow ppt. of AgBr with Ag^+, ionisation being as $[Co(NH_3)_5SO_4]^+ + Br^-$

- Br^- inside coordination sphere and SO_4^{2-} outside it.
- gives white ppt. of $BaSO_4$ with Ba^{2+}, ionisation being as $[Co(NH_3)_5Br]^{2+} + SO_4^{2-}$

Other examples are

$[Pt(NH_3)_4SO_4](OH)_2$ and $[Pt(NH_3)_4(OH)_2]SO_4$

$[Co(NH_3)_5NO_2]SO_4$ and $[Co(NH_3)_5SO_4]NO_2$

$[Cr(NH_3)_5SO_4]Br$ and $[Cr(NH_3)_5Br]SO_4$

Linkage Isomerism

When the ligand is attached to the central metal ion of a complex in different ways, it gives rise to linkage isomerism. Such ligands are called ambidentate ligands, e.g. nitrite ion has electron pairs available for coordination on both N and O atoms.

$[Co(NH_3)_5ONO]Cl_2$ — pentaamminenitrito-o-cobalt (III) chloride (red), decomposes in acids

and $[Co(NH_3)_5NO_2]Cl_2$ — pentaamminenitrito-N-cobalt (III) chloride (yellow), stable in acids

Concept ladder Irradiation with ultraviolet light of the yellow isomer results in inter- conversion into red isomer. This isomerisation reverses on warming.

Coordination Isomerism

When both the positive and negative ions are complex ions, isomerism may be caused by the interchange of ligands between the anion and cation. This arises only if cationic and anionic metals have same C.N. and charge.

e.g. $[Cr(NH_3)_6]^{3+}\ [Co(CN)_6]^{3-} \Rightarrow$
hexaamminecobalt(III) hexacyanidochromate(III)
$[Co(NH_3)_6]^{3+}\ [Cr(CN)_6]^{3-} \Rightarrow$
hexaamminechromium(III) hexacyanidocobaltate(III)
Both above complex have same charge ; same C.N. = 6

Coordination Position Isomerism

In polynuclear complexes, on interchange of ligands between the different metal nuclei gives rise to position isomerism.

e.g.

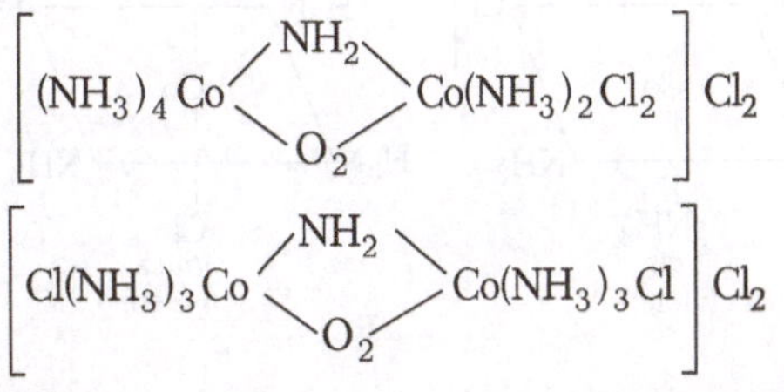

Hydrate (Solvate) Isomerism

Hydrate isomers are isomers of a complex that differ in the placement of water molecules in the complex. e.g. $CrCl_3 \cdot 6H_2O$ have following hydrate isomers.

$[Cr(H_2O)_6]Cl_3$ – violet (anhydrous)
$[Cr(H_2O)_5Cl]Cl_2 \cdot H_2O$ – light green (monohydrate)
$[Cr(H_2O)_4Cl_2]Cl \cdot 2H_2O$ – dark green (dihydrate)

This is closely related to ionisation isomerism and principle is the same except that H_2O (a neutral ligand) is present in this case. While in case of ionisation isomerism anionic ligand is present.

NEET Close-up

Example Similar to PYQ Asked in NEET 2024

Match the following Column I with Column II.

Column I (Complex)	Column II (Type of isomerism)
A. $[Co(NO_2)(NH_3)_5]Cl_2$	1. Linkage isomerism.
B. $[Cr(NH_3)_6]\ [Co(CN)_6]$	2. Ionisation isomerism
C. $[PtCl_2(NH_3)_4]Br_2$	3. Solvate isomerism
D. $[Cr(H_2O)_5]Cl_3$	4. Coordination isomerism

Codes

(a) A-4, B-1, C-2, D-3
(b) A-1, B-4, C-2, D-3
(c) A-2, B-4, C-1, D-3
(d) A-3, B-4, C-1, D-2

Sol. (b) The correct match is A-1, B-4, C-2, D-3.

A. $[Co(NH_3)_5(NO_2)]Cl_2$ is an example of linkage isomerism, it arises in a compound containing ambidentate ligand.

B. $[Cr(NH_3)_6]\ [Co(CN)_6]$ is an example of coordination isomerism. it arises from interchange of ligands between cationic and anionic entities of different metal ions present in a complex.

C. $[PtCl_2(NH_3)_4]Br_2$ is an example of ionisation isomerism. This form of isomerism arises when the counter ion in a complex salt is itself a potential ligand and can displace a ligand which can become counter ion.

D. $[Cr(H_2O)_5]Cl_3$ is an example of solvate isomerism, in this isomerism water is involved as a solvent.

Skill Builder

Match the following Column I with Column II.

Column I (Complex)	Column II (Type of isomerism)
A. $[Cr(SCN)(NH_3)_5]Cl$	1. Coordination isomerism
B. $[Cu(NH_3)_4]\ [PtCl_4]$	2. Ionisation isomerism
C. $[CoCl(NH_3)_5]SO_4$	3. Solvate isomerism
D. $[Co(H_2O)_5Cl]Cl_2 . H_2O$	4. Linkage isomerism

Codes

(a) A-2, B-4, C-1, D-3
(b) A-3, B-2, C-4, D-1
(c) A-1, B-2, C-3, D-4
(d) A-4, B-1, C-2, D-3

For more practice Refer to Q. 13 of Step up Practice 1.

Stereoisomerism

Isomers which have same molecular formula but different spatial arrangements are called stereoisomers. This phenomenon is known as stereoisomerism.

It is divided into two types namely

(i) Geometrical isomerism (ii) Optical isomerism

Geometrical Isomerism

Isomerism which occurs in heteroleptic complexes due to different relative arrangements of ligands around the central metal atom is known as geometrical isomerism.

Geometrical isomers are of two types

(i) ***cis*-isomer** When two similar ligands occupy adjacent positions to each other are called *cis*-isomer.

(ii) ***trans*-isomer** When two similar ligands are present at opposite position to each other are called *trans*-isomer. *cis*- and *trans*- position are indicated in figures:

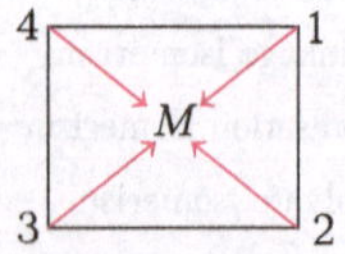

Square planar

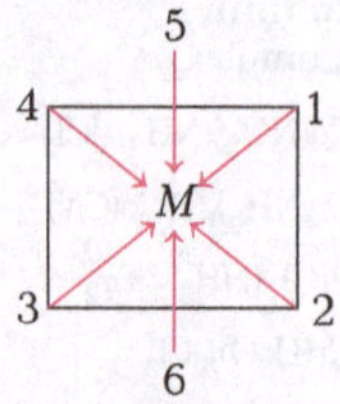

Octahedral

***cis*-position** : (1,2), (2,3), (3,4), (1,4) — (1,2), (2,3), (3,4), (1,4), (1,5), (4,5), (3,5), (2,5), (1,6), (2,6), (3,6) and (4,6)

***trans*-position** : (1,3) and (2,4) — (1,3), (2,4) and (5,6)

Geometrical Isomerism in Coordination Number 4

Complex compound with coordination number 4 posses two geometry that are tetrahedral and square planar.

Coordination number	Hybridisation (of central metal atom/ion)	Geometry
4	sp^3	Tetrahedral
4	dsp^2	Square planar

Tetrahedral Complexes

These complexes do not show geometrical isomerism as all the bond angles are 109°28'. So, here *cis-trans* form do not exist.

Mentor's TIP

- Pt and Pd with coordination number 4 are always square planar.
- Complex with coordination number 4 having bidentate ligand are always square planar.
- Square planar complex with *AA* type (symmetrical bidentate ligand) do not give geometrical isomerism.

Square Planar Complexes

- Complexes of type MA_4, MA_3B and MAB_3 do not show geometrical isomerism, where *A* and *B* are monodentate ligands.
- Complexes of formula MA_2B_2 and MA_2BC types have two geometrical isomers, where *A* and *B* are monodentate ligands. e.g.
  - $[PtCl_2(NH_3)_2]$ resembles MA_2B_2 in formula and exists in two isomeric forms:

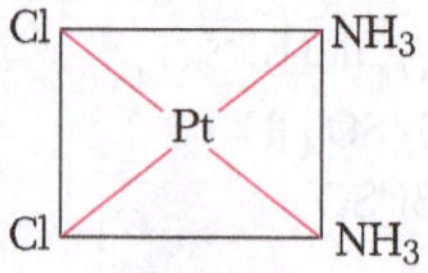

cis-isomer (orange yellow)

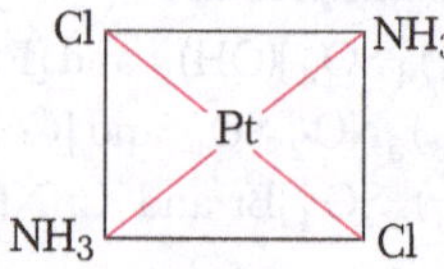

trans-isomer (pale yellow)

  - $[PtCl(NH_3)(py)_2]$ resembles MA_2BC and exists in two isomeric forms:

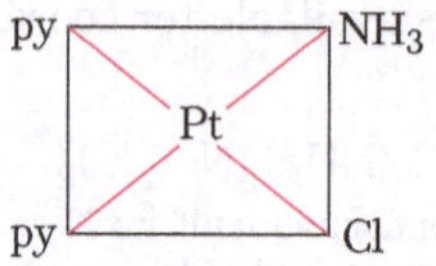

cis

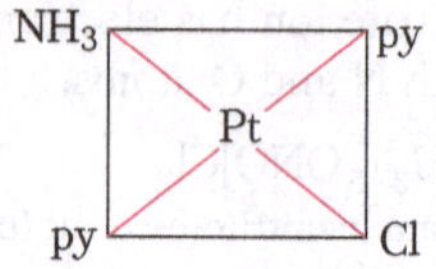

trans

- Complexes of formula *MABCD* exist in three isomeric forms.

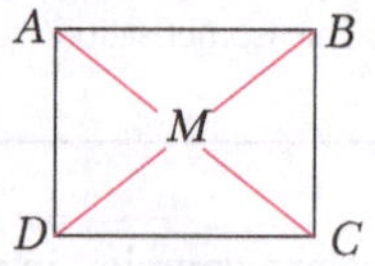

(i)

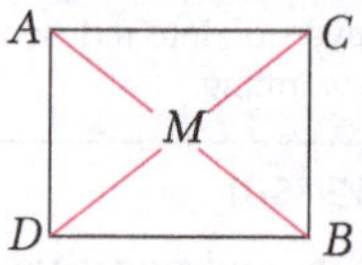

(ii)

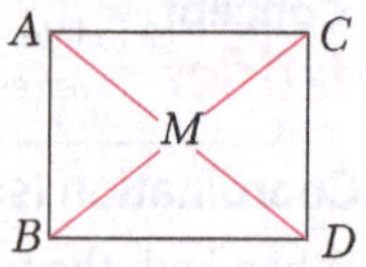

(iii)

e.g. $[Pt(NO_2)(NH_2OH)(NH_3)(py)]$ exists in 3 isomeric forms. $A = NO_2$, $B = NH_2OH$, $C = NH_3$, $D = py$

- Complexes of formula $[M(AB)_2]$ exist in two isomeric forms, here *AB* is unsymmetrical bidentate ligand.

Geometrical Isomerism in Coordination Number 6

- Complexes with formula MA_6 and MA_5B do not show geometrical isomerism, where both *A* and *B* are monodentate ligands.
- Complexes with formula MA_4B_2 or $MA_2B_2C_2$ exhibit geometrical isomerism. e.g.
  - $[Co(NH_3)_4Cl_2]^+$ can exist as

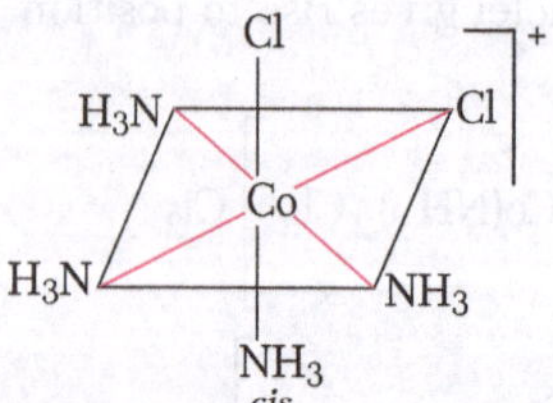

cis (violet)

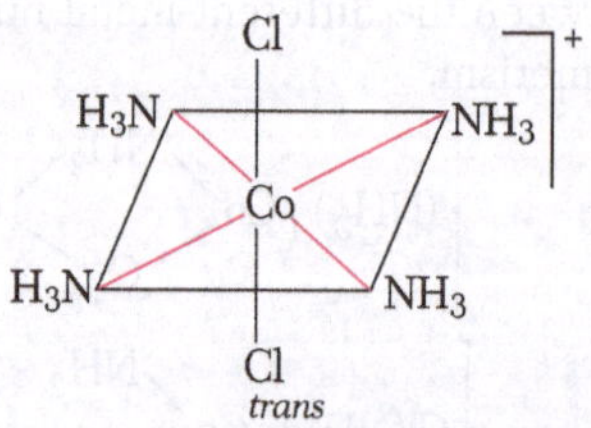

trans (green)

- $[Pt(NH_3)_2Cl_2Br_2]$ can exist as

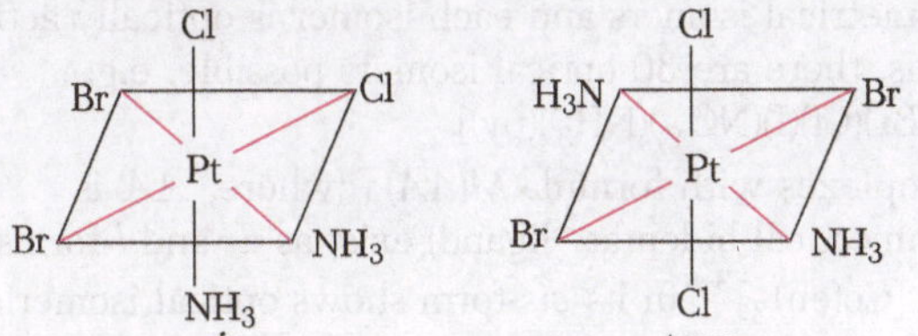

cis *trans*

- Complexes with formula MA_3B_3 exhibit *facial* and *meridional* isomerism. If each trio of donor atoms occupy adjacent position at the corners of an octahedral *face*, it is called ***facial* (*fac*–) isomer.**

When the positions are around the meridian of the octahedron, the isomer is called ***meridional* (*mer*–) isomer.** e.g. $[Co(NO_2)_3(NH_3)_3]$.

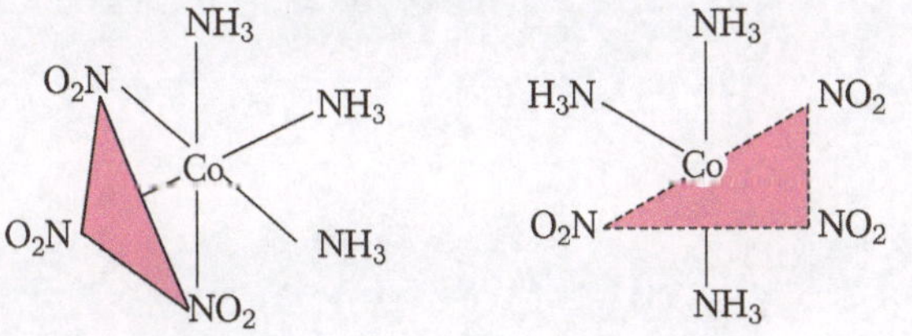

fac- *mer-*

The facial (*fac*) and meridional (*mer*) isomers of $[Co(NH_3)_2(NO_2)_3]$.

- Complexes with formula *MABCDEF* exist in 15 isomeric forms but practically only three of them have been isolated, e.g. $[Pt(Br)(Cl)(I)(NO_2)(NH_3)(py)]$.
- Complexes with formula $M(AA)_2B_2$, $M(AA)_2BC$ also exhibit geometrical isomerism (where, *AA* is a symmetrical bidentate ligand). e.g. $[Co(en)_2Cl_2]^+$.

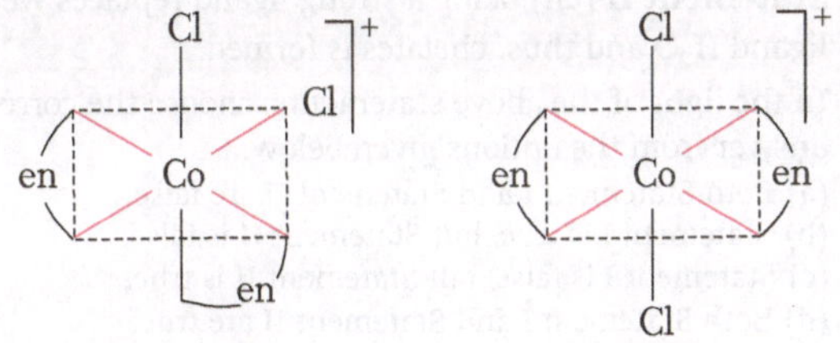

cis-isomer *trans*-isomer

- Complexes with formula $M(AB)_3$ (where, *AB* is an unsymmetrical bidentate ligand) also exhibit geometrical isomerism, e.g. $[Cr(gly)_3]$.

Optical Isomerism

Complexes which are non-superimposable on their mirror images and do not possess the plane of symmetry are called **optical isomers** and the phenomenon is known as **optical isomerism.** They have same chemical properties but differ in action towards plane polarised light.

The molecules or ions that cannot be superimposed are called chiral.

The optically active complex which rotates plane polarised light to left is laevorotatory (*l* or –) and which rotates to right is dextrorotatory (*d* or +). These '*d*' and '*l*' isomers of a complex are called **enantiomorphs** or **enantiomers.**

Optical Isomerism in Tetrahedral and Square Planar Complexes

Complexes with coordination number 4 (tetrahedral and square planar) do not give optical isomerism due to the presence of plane of symmetry.

Mentor's TiP

[*M* (*abcd*)] tetrahedral complex gives optical isomerism due to the absence of plane of symmetry.

Optical Isomerism in Octahedral Complexes

It is common in octahedral complexes involving bidentate ligands. These are as follows

- Complex with formula $M(A-A)_2B_2$ can exist as *cis* and *trans* isomers. But only *cis*-isomer can have *d*- and *l*-optical isomers. *trans*-form is optically inactive due to presence of plane of symmetry. e.g. $[Co(en)_2Cl_2]^+$.

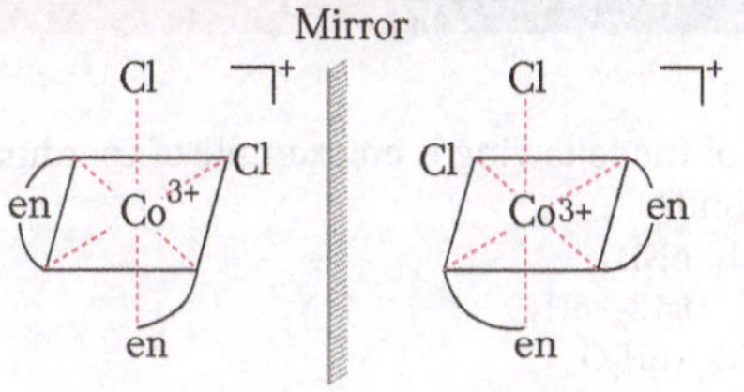

Enantiomorphic pair *d* and *l* of
cis-dichlorido*bis*(ethane-1,2-diamine)cobalt(III) ion-violet

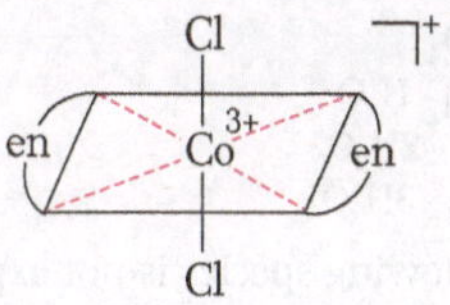

(Symmetrical) *trans*—(no optical isomer possible)-green

- Complex with formula $M(AA)_3$ also show optical isomerism, e.g. $[Co(en)_3]^{3+}$.

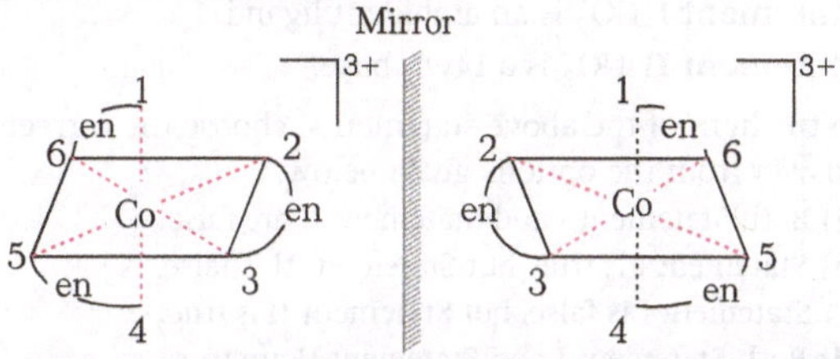

Concept ladder

Complex with three bidentate ligands are always optically active due to the absence of plane of symmetry while complex with two bidentate ligand can form *cis* or *trans* complex. In which *cis*- form is always optically active but *trans*-form may be optically active or not.

- Complexes with formula MA_3B_3 can exist in facial and meridional forms but both the isomers are optically inactive.
- Complexes with formula $MA_2B_2C_2$ are optically active. e.g. $[Pt(Cl_2)(NH_3)_2(py)_2]^{2+}$ can exist in five geometrical isomers but only three of them are isolated. These isomers are optically active in their *cis*-form.

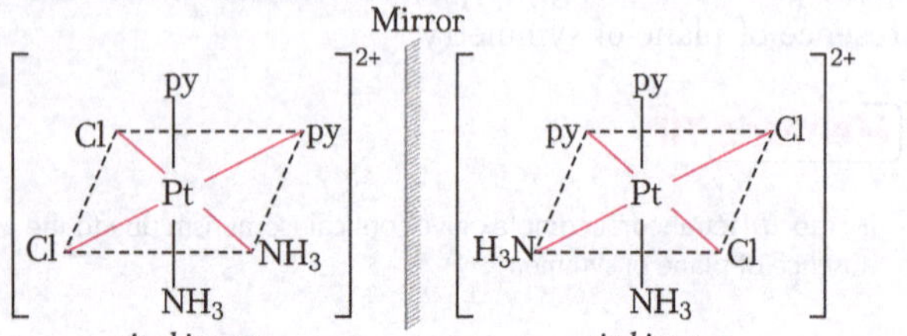

cis-d-isomer *cis-l*-isomer

- Complexes with formula *MABCDEF* exist in 15 geometrical isomers and each isomer is optically active. Thus, there are 30 optical isomers possible. e.g. $[Pt(Br)(Cl)(I)(NO_2)(NH_3)(py)]$.
- Complexes with formula $M(AA)_3$ (where, '*AA*' is symmetrical bidentate ligand) exist as *d*- and *l*-forms. e.g. $[Co(en)_3]^{3+}$ in its *cis*-form shows optical isomerism.

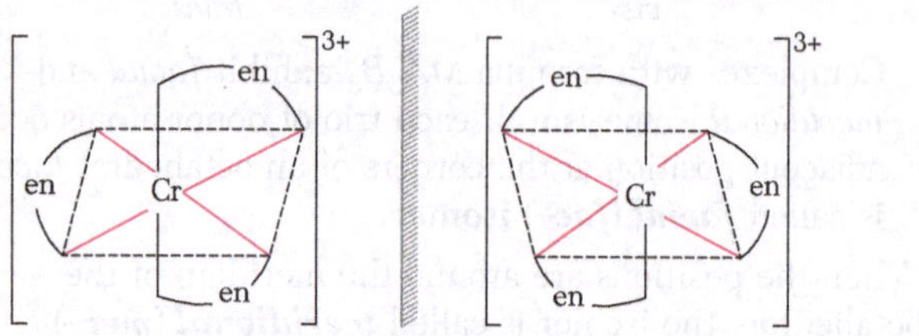

STEP UP Practice 1

1 Which of the following is an example of coordination compound?
(a) $CoCl_3 \cdot 6NH_3$
(b) $KCl \cdot MgCl_2 \cdot 6H_2O$
(c) $FeSO_4 \cdot 6H_2O$
(d) $FeSO_4 \cdot (NH_4)_2SO_4 \cdot 6H_2O$

2 $CuSO_4 \cdot 5H_2O$ is like a complex represented as
(a) $[Cu(H_2O)_5] \cdot SO_4$
(b) $[Cu(H_2O)_4]SO_4 \cdot H_2O$
(c) $[Cu(H_2O)_3]SO_4 \cdot 2H_2O$
(d) $[Cu(H_2O)_2]SO_4 \cdot 3H_2O$

3 Which of the following species is not expected to be a ligand?
(a) NO (b) NH_4^+
(c) $NH_2CH_2CH_2NH_2$ (d) CO

4 Consider the following statements.
Statement I NO_2^- is an ambident ligand.
Statement II NO_2^- is a Lewis base.
In the light of the above statements, choose the correct answer from the options given below.
(a) Both Statement I and Statement II are false.
(b) Statement I is true, but Statement II is false.
(c) Statement I is false, but Statement II is true.
(d) Both Statement I and Statement II are true.

5 The coordination number of a central metal atom in a complex is determined by
(a) the number of ligands around a metal ion bonded by sigma bonds
(b) the number of ligands around a metal ion bonded by pi-bonds except organometallic compounds
(c) the number of ligands around a metal ion bonded by sigma and pi-bonds both except metal carbonyls
(d) the number of only anionic ligands bonded to metal ion

6 Consider the following statements.
Statement I A stable complex is formed when ethylenediamine(en) is added to $[Ni(H_2O)_4]^{2+}$.
Statement II (en) being a strong ligand replaces weak ligand H_2O and thus, chelates is formed.
In the light of the above statements, choose the correct answer from the options given below.
(a) Both Statement I and Statement II are false.
(b) Statement I is true, but Statement II is false.
(c) Statement I is false, but Statement II is true.
(d) Both Statement I and Statement II are true.

7 Which of the following complexes is a homoleptic complex?
(a) $[Co(en)_2Cl_2]$
(b) $[Co(NH_3)_4Cl_2]^+$
(c) $[Pt(NH_3)_2Cl_2]$
(d) $[Fe(CN)_6]^{4-}$

8 Choose the incorrect match from the following with respect to oxidation state of Co.
(a) $[Co(NCS)(NH_3)_5](SO_3) \longrightarrow +3$
(b) $[Co(NH_3)_4Cl_2]SO_4 \longrightarrow +4$
(c) $Na_4[Co(S_2O_3)_3] \longrightarrow +2$
(d) $[Co_2(CO)_8] \longrightarrow 1$

9 The coordination number and oxidation number of Pt in $[Pt(O_2)(en)_2(Br)]^{2+}$ is respectively.
(a) 6 and +4 (b) 4 and +6
(c) 3 and +4 (d) 4 and +3

10 In which of of the following complexes, the oxidation state of central metal is zero?
(a) $[Cr(CO)_6]$
(b) $[Cr(en)_2Cl_2]$
(c) $[Cr(NH_3)_3Cl_3]$
(d) $[Cr(en)_2Cl_2]$

11 The IUPAC name of the complex $[Ag(NH_3)_2][Ag(CN)_2]$ is
(a) diammine silver(II) dicyanidoargentate(II)
(b) diamminesilver(I) dicyanidoargentate(I)
(c) silver diammine(I) dicyanidoargentate(I)
(d) diammine silver(I) dicyanidoargentate(II)

12 The IUPAC name of $K_3[Al(C_2O_4)_3]$ is
(a) trioxalatopotassium(II)
(b) potassium trioxalato aluminate(I)
(c) potassium oxalato aluminium(III)
(d) potassium tris(oxalato) aluminate(III)

13 Match Column I with Column II.

Column I (Complex)	Column II (Type of isomerisation)
A. $[Co(NO_3)(NH_3)_5]SO_4$	1. Linkage isomerism
B. $[Fe(NO_2)(NH_3)_5]Br_2$	2. Ionisation isomerism
C. $[Co(en)_2(H_2O)_2]Cl_3 \cdot H_2O$	3. Coordination isomerism
D. $[Pt(NH_3)_4][PtCl_4]$	4. Hydrate isomerism

Codes
(a) A-1, B-2, C-4, D-3
(b) A-2, B-1, C-4, D-3
(c) A-3, B-4, C-2, D-1
(d) A-2, B-4, C-1, D-3

14 Consider the coordination compounds given below.
I. $[Cu(NH_3)_4][PtCl_4]$ and $[Pt(NH_3)_4][CuCl_4]$
II. $[Pd(PPh_3)_2(NCS)_2]$ and $[Pd(PPh_3)_2(SCN)_2]$
III. $[Co(NH_3)_5NO_3]SO_4$ and $[Co(NH_3)_5SO_4]NO_3$
IV. $[PtCl_2(NH_3)_4]Br$ and $[PtBr_2(NH_3)_4]Cl_2$
V. $[Cr(NH_3)_6][Co(CN)_6]$
How many of the above compounds represent(s) linkage isomerism?
(a) 2 (b) 1
(c) 5 (d) 4

15 Coordination isomerism is caused by the interchange of ligands between the
(a) *cis* and *trans*-form
(b) low oxidation to high oxidation state
(c) complex cation and complex anion
(d) inner sphere and outer sphere

16 Which of the following square planar complexes will show two geometrical isomers?
(a) MA_4 (b) MA_3B
(c) MAB_3 (d) MA_2B_2

17 The number of possible isomers for the square planar complex, $K_2[PdClBr_2SCN]$ is
(a) 1 (b) 2
(c) 3 (d) 4

18 Which of the following is an incorrectly matched pair?
(a) *trans*- $[CoCl_2(en)_2]^+$ — optically inactive.
(b) $[Pt(en)_2Cl_2]^{2+}$ — shows *cis* and *trans* isomerism.
(c) $[Cr(en)_3]^{3+}$ — 1 : 1 molar ratio of racemic mixture.
(d) $[Co(en)_3]^{3+}$ — one optically active isomer.

19 Which of the following coordination number is possible for the coordination compound to show geometrical isomerism?
(a) 6 (b) 4 (Tetrahedral)
(c) 2 (d) 3

Module 2

Bonding in Coordination Compounds (Part-I)

- Werner's Theory
- Valence Bond Theory (VBT)

Bonding in Coordination Compound

Some theories were put forward to explain the pattern of bonding in coordination compounds, which are discussed below.

Werner's Theory

In 1892, Alfred Werner proposed a theory about the structures of coordination compounds. He prepared and characterised a large number of coordination compounds and studied their physical and chemical behaviours by simple experimental techniques.

He prepared and isolated many different compounds from $CoCl_3$ and NH_3 such as

- $CoCl_3 \cdot 6NH_3$ $[Co(NH_3)_6]Cl_3$ Orange-yellow
- $CoCl_3 \cdot 5NH_3$ $[Co(NH_3)_5Cl]Cl_2$ Violet
- $CoCl_3 \cdot 4NH_3$ $[Co(NH_3)_4Cl_2]Cl$ Violet
- $CoCl_3 \cdot 3NH_3$ $[Co(NH_3)_3Cl_3]$ Green

Postulates of Werner's Theory

The main postulates of Werner's theory are as follows

- Each metal ion shows two types of valencies (linkages); primary and secondary valency.
- **Primary valency** are ionisable and it corresponds to **oxidation number** of the central metal atom/ion. It is satisfied by anions and are non-directional in nature.
- **Secondary valency** are non-ionisable and corresponds to **coordination number** of the central metal atom/ion. It is satisfied by neutral or anionic ligands and are directional in nature.
- Metal ion should satisfy both primary and secondary valencies. Some negative ions may satisfy primary as well as secondary valencies and hence have dual nature. e.g. In the complex $[Co(NH_3)_6]Cl_3$, primary valency of Co is three and secondary valency is six.
- The ions/groups bound by the secondary linkages to the metal have characteristic spatial arrangements corresponding to different coordination numbers.

Werner's Representation

Consider the case of $\overset{III}{Co}Cl_3 \cdot xNH_3$ where maximum value of x = C.N. (coordination number) of Co(III) = 6 and minimum value of x = coordination number (C.N.) − (O.N) oxidation number = 6 − 3 = 3.

Various structures are summarised below.

Werner's complex	Modern notation	Ionisation	Secondary valency satisfied by	Primary valency satisfied by
(A) $CoCl_3 \cdot 6NH_3$	$[Co(NH_3)_6]Cl_3$	$[Co(NH_3)_6]^{3+} + 3Cl^-$	Six (NH_3)	Three (Cl^-)
(B) $CoCl_3 \cdot 5NH_3$	$[Co(NH_3)_5Cl]Cl_2$	$[Co(NH_3)_5Cl]^{2+} + 2Cl^-$	Five (NH_3) and one (Cl^-)	Three (Cl^-) [including one (Cl^-) with **dual nature**]
(C) $CoCl_3 \cdot 4NH_3$	$[Co(NH_3)_4Cl_2]Cl$	$[Co(NH_3)_4Cl_2]^+ + Cl^-$	Four (NH_3) and two (Cl^-)	Three (Cl^-) [including two (Cl^-) with **dual nature**]
(D) $CoCl_3 \cdot 3NH_3$	$[Co(NH_3)_3Cl_3]$	$[Co(NH_3)_3Cl_3]$ (single species)	Three (NH_3) and three (Cl^-)	Three (Cl^-) [all with **dual nature**]

Limitations

Werner's theory was unable to account for the following points.

- Definite geometry of coordination compounds.
- Presence of magnetic and optical properties of coordination compounds.

To overcome the limitations of Werner's theory, various theories were put forward such as valence bond theory and crystal field theory.

Valence Bond Theory (VBT)

This theory was proposed by L. Pauling in 1930's. According to this, transition metal ions have incompletely filled *d*-orbitals. These orbitals contain unpaired electrons which couple as fully as possible before bond formation takes place.

- Thus, some $(n-1)\,d$-orbitals becomes vacant and therefore, central metal ion provides number of empty orbitals equal to its coordination number for formation of complex.
- Thus, atomic orbitals present on central metal ion hybridise to form hybrid orbitals. There is interaction of hybrid orbitals of metal ion and orbitals of ligands.
- Ligands donate its lone pairs of electrons, to form bond with metal ion. It describes the geometric structure of complex ion.
- If $(n-1)\,d$-orbitals are involved in hybridisation, then *inner orbital* or *low spin* or *spin paired complex* are formed while involvement of *nd*-orbitals results in *outer orbital* or *high spin* or *spin free complex*.
- Octahedral, square planar and tetrahedral complexes are formed as a result of d^2sp^3 (or sp^3d^2), dsp^2 and sp^3 hybridisation respectively of the central metal atom or ion. It helps to predict the geometry, hybridisation, magnetic properties of a complex.

Number of Orbitals and Types of Hybridisations

Coordination number	Hybridisation	Geometry
4	sp^3	Tetrahedral
4	dsp^2	Square planar
5	sp^3d	Trigonal bipyramidal
6	sp^3d^2 or d^2sp^3	Octahedral

Mentor's Tip

The hybrid orbitals do not actually exist. In fact, hybridisation is a mathematical manipulation of wave equation for the atomic orbitals involved.

Applications of VBT

Some applications of valence bond theory are as follows

In Formation of Complex with Coordination Number 4

Coordination compounds which have C.N. = 4 can have tetrahedral or square planar geometry. It depends upon the orbitals available for hybridisation.

1. In Tetrahedral Complexes

Complexes whose central metal atoms/ions involve one *s* and three *p*-orbitals for bonding, i.e. sp^3, are said to be tetrahedral complexes.

e.g. $[NiCl_4]^{2-}$, $[Ni(CO)_4]$, $[CuCl_4]^{2-}$, $[Zn(NH_3)_4]^{2+}$ etc.

- $[NiCl_4]^{2-}$

  Electronic configuration of Ni$(Z = 28) = [Ar]\,3d^8\,4s^2$.

  Due to presence of 4 Cl^-, oxidation state of Ni is +2.

  Therefore, electronic configuration of Ni^{2+} is $[Ar]\,3d^8\,4s^0$.

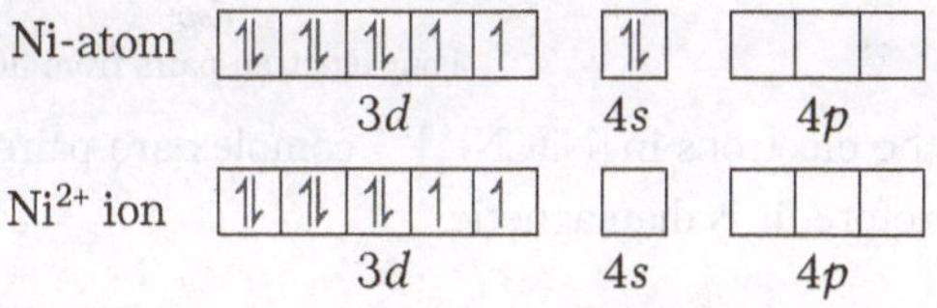

  Each Cl^- ion donate a pair of electrons.

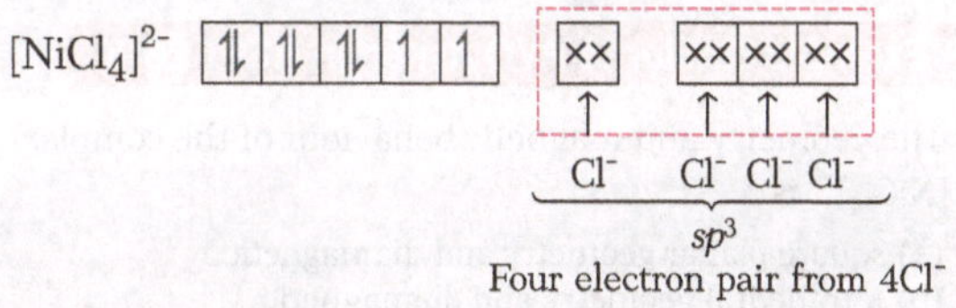

  Due to presence of two unpaired electrons, $[NiCl_4]^{2-}$ is paramagnetic in nature.

- $[Ni(CO)_4]$

  Since, CO is neutral ligand thus, Ni has zero oxidation state.

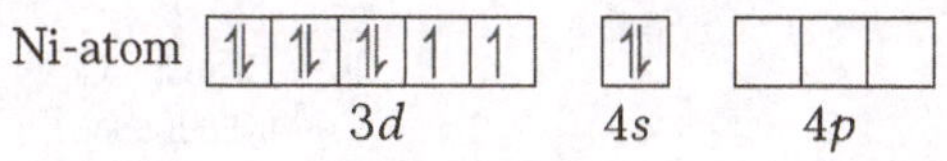

  CO is a strong field ligand, it can pair up the unpaired electrons of Ni.

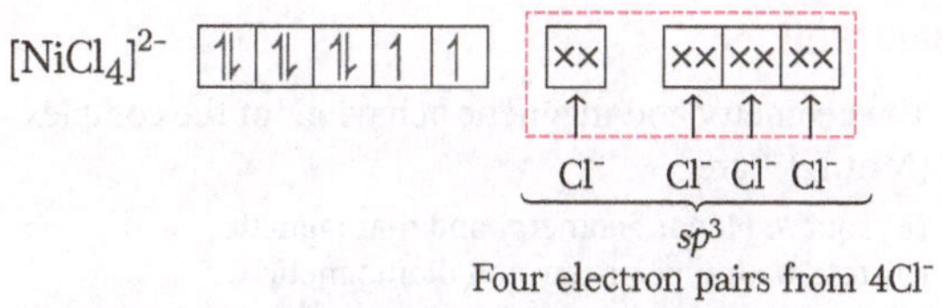

  There is no unpaired electron, hence, $[Ni(CO)_4]$ is diamagnetic in nature.

2. In Square Planar Complexes

Complexes which involves one d, one s and two p-orbitals for bonding, i.e. $dsp^2 d_{x^2-y^2}$ are said to be square planar complexes.

e.g. $[Ni(CN)_4]^{2-}$, $[Pt(CN)_4]^{2-}$, $[Cu(NH_3)_4]^{2+}$ etc.

- $[Ni(CN)_4]^{2-}$]

Ni is present in +2 oxidation state due to four CN^- ligands.

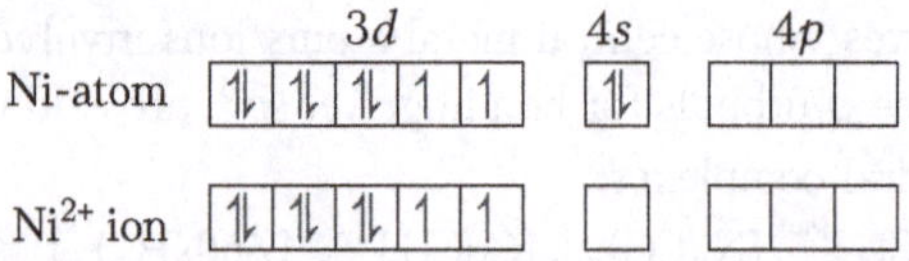

Since, CN^- is a strong field ligand, it pair-ups the electrons of Ni^{2+} ion. Thus, one $(n-1)d$ orbital is vacant.

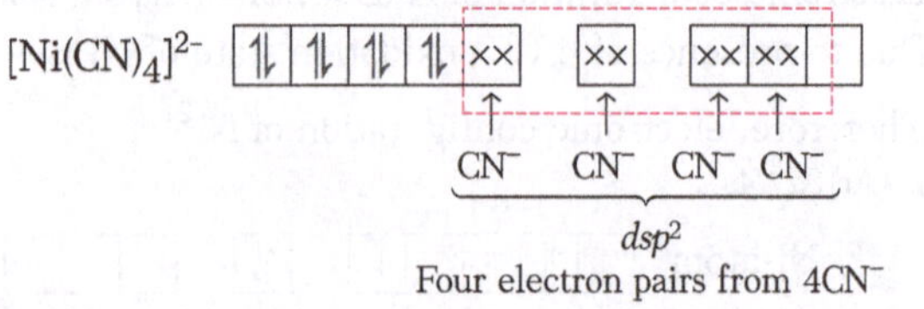

All the electrons in $[Ni(CN)_4]^{2-}$ complex are paired. Therefore, it is diamagnetic.

NEET Close-up

Example Similar to PYQ Asked in NEET 2018

The geometry and magnetic behaviour of the complex $[NiCl_4]^{-2}$ is

(a) square planar geometry and diamagnetic
(b) tetrahedral geometry and diamagnetic
(c) square planar geometry and paramagnetic
(d) tetrahedral geometry and paramagnetic

Sol. (d) $Ni^{+2} = 3d^8 4s^0$

Each Cl^- donate a pair of electrons.

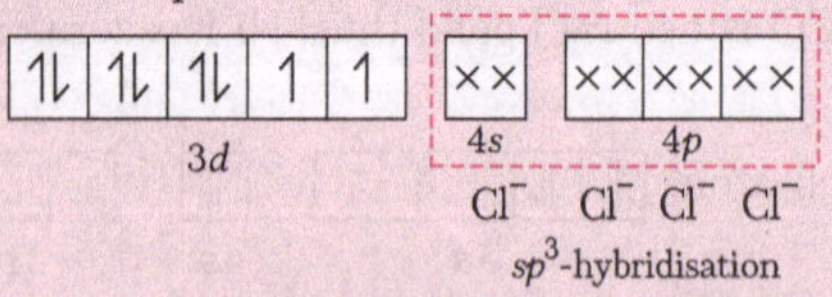

Thus, the complex is sp^3-hybridised with tetrahedral geometry and paramagnetic in nature.

Skill Builder

The geometry and magnetic behaviour of the complex $[MnCl_4]^{-2}$ are

(a) square planar geometry and diamagnetic
(b) tetrahedral geometry and diamagnetic
(c) square planar geometry and paramagnetic
(d) tetrahedral geometry and paramagnetic

For more practice Refer to Q. 12 of Step up Practice 2.

In Formation of Complex with Coordination Number 6

Complex which have CN = 6, can form inner orbital complex (d^2sp^3-hybridisation) or outer orbital complex (sp^3d^2-hybridisation). These complexes have octahedral geometry.

Some of the examples of octahedral complex are given below.

1. Inner Orbital Complex

These complexes involve two inner d-orbitals, ($d_{x^2-y^2}$, dz^2) one s and three p-orbitals for bonding. These are formed by strong field ligands hence are low spin complex. e.g.

$[Co(NH_3)_6]^{3+}$, $[Fe(CN)_6]^{4-}$, $[Cr(NH_3)_6]^{3+}$, $[Fe(CN)_6]^{3-}$ $[Co(ox)_3]^{3-}$ etc.

- $[Co(NH_3)_6]^{3+}$

Since, NH_3 is a neutral ligand, thus, oxidation state of Co is +3.

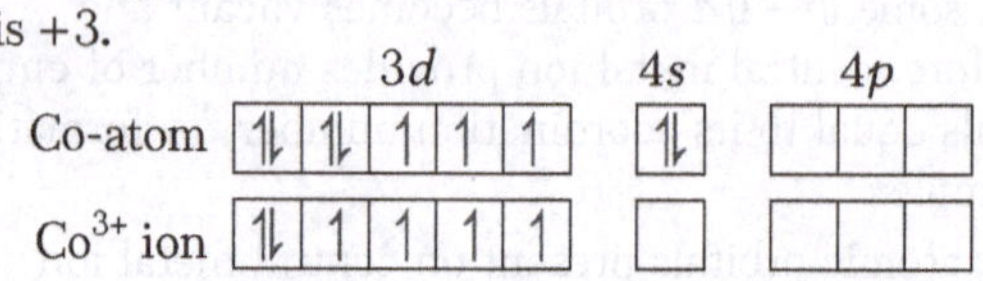

Six pairs of electrons one from each NH_3 molecule, occupy the six hybrid orbitals.

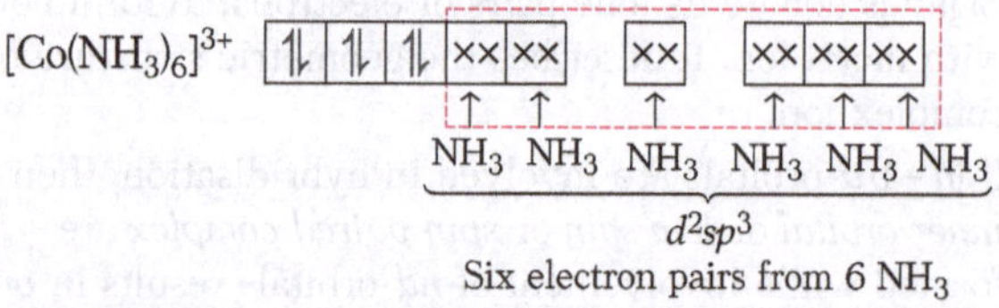

Hence, hybridisation of Co(III) in $[Co(NH_3)_6]^{3+}$ is d^2sp^3 and is diamagnetic due to absence of unpaired electrons.

2. Outer Orbital Complex

These complex involves one s, three p and two outer d-orbitals ($d_{x^2-y^2}$, d_{z^2}) for bonding. These are formed by weak field ligands Hence, are high spin complex,

e.g. $[CoF_6]^{3-}$, $[Fe(H_2O)_6]^{3+}$, $[Co(H_2O)_6]^{2+}$ etc.

- $[CoF_6]^{3-}$

Oxidation state of Co is +3 due to presence of $6F^-$ ligands.

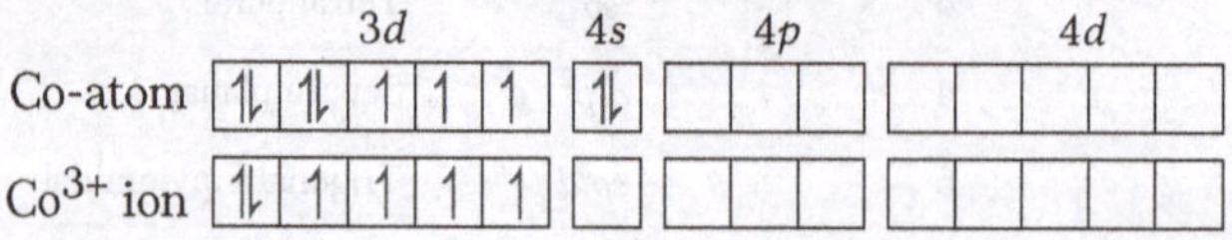

Six pairs of electrons one from each F^- occupy the six hybrid orbitals.

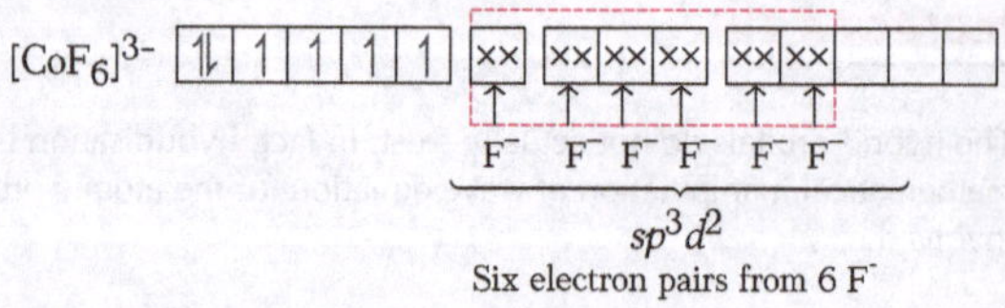

Hence, hybridisation of Co(III) in $[CoF_6]^{3-}$ is sp^3d^2 and is paramagnetic due to presence of unpaired electrons.

NEET Close-up

Example Similar to PYQ Asked in NEET 2024

Direction *(Q. Similar and Skill Builder)* In the light of the statements given below, choose the most appropriate answer from the options given below

(a) Both Statement I and Statement II are false.
(b) Statement I is true, but Statement II is false.
(c) Statement I is false, but Statement II is true.
(d) Both Statement I and Statement II are true.

Statement I Both $[Fe(CN)_6]^{3-}$ and $[Co(C_2O_4)_3]^{3-}$ complexes are octahedral but differ in their magnetic behaviour.

Statement II $[Fe(CN)_6]^{3-}$ is diamagnetic whereas $[Co(C_2O_4)_3]^{3-}$ is paramagnetic.

Sol. (*b*) Statement I is true but Statement II is false. Its correct form is : Hence, $[Fe(CN)_6]^{3-}$ is paramagnetic while $[Co(C_2O_4)_3]^{3-}$ is diamagnetic.

Skill Builder

Statement I Both $[Mn(CN)_6]^{3-}$ and $[MnCl_6]^{3-}$ complexes are octahedral and have same magnetic bahaviour.

Statement II $[Mn(CN)_6]^{3-}$ and $[MnCl_6]^{3-}$ both are paramagnetic.

For more practice Refer to Q. 12 and Q. 13 of Step up Practice 2.

Limitations

VBT was unable to account for the following points

- It does not provide insight into the origin of characteristic colour of the complex ions.
- It does not distinguish between weak and strong ligands.
- It does not give quantitative interpretation of the thermodynamic or kinetic stabilities of coordination compounds.
- There is no quantitative interpretation of magnetic data.
- It does not explain why some complexes are inner orbital and some complexes are outer orbital.
- It fails to give a satisfactory explanation for the formation of some complexes like $[Cu(NH_3)_4]^{2+}$.

Valence bond theory gives no explanation for exciting an electron from 3*d* to 4*p*-orbital which is not energetically favoured.

$[Cu(NH_3)_4]^{2+}$ ion

Expected configuration of $[Cu(NH_3)_4]^{2+}$ ion

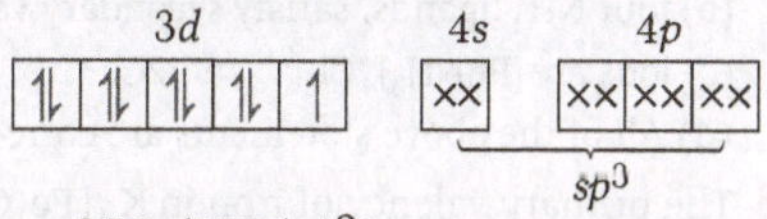

Actual configuration of $[Cu(NH_3)_4]^{2+}$ ion

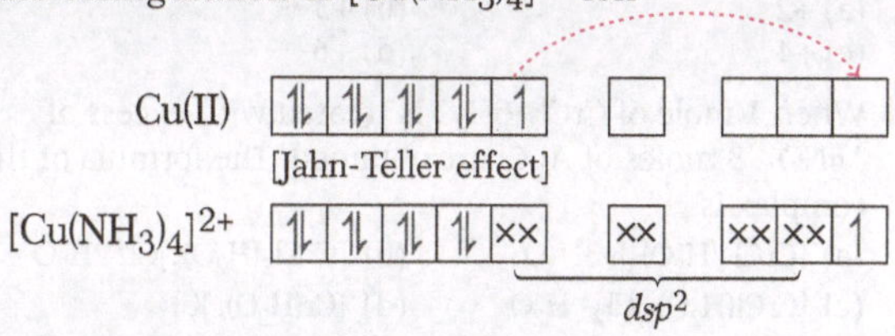

Therefore, the complex is square planar and paramagnetic.

Concept ladder

In octahedral complex, two types of hybridisation is possible, i.e. d^2sp^3 and sp^3d^2.

In d^2sp^3 hybrids, the principal quantum number of *d*-orbitals is one less than the principal quantum number of the *s* and *p*-orbitals. While in sp^3d^2 hybridisation all the hybrids, i.e. *s*, *p* and *d* have same value of principal quantum number.

STEP UP Practice 2

1 The complex

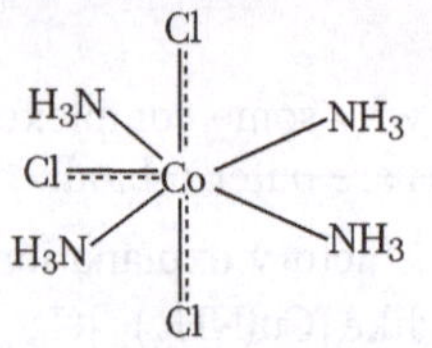

(a) is the molecular complex
(b) has four ions in the aqueous solution
(c) primary valency of cobalt is six
(d) All of the above are correct

2 For the complex $PtCl_4 \cdot 4NH_3$
(a) two Cl^- ligands satisfy primary as well secondary valencies
(b) four NH_3 ligands, satisfy secondary valency
(c) ions are $[Pt(NH_3)_4Cl_2]^{2+}$ and $2Cl^-$
(d) All of the above statements are correct

3 The primary valency of iron in $K_4[Fe(CN)_6]$ is
(a) +2 (b) +3
(c) +4 (d) +6

4 When 1 mole of $CrCl_3 \cdot 6H_2O$ is treated with excess of $AgNO_3$, 3 moles of AgCl are obtained. The formula of the complex is
(a) $[CrCl_3(H_2O)_3] \cdot 3H_2O$ (b) $[CrCl_2(H_2O)_4]Cl \cdot 2H_2O$
(c) $[CrCl(H_2O)_5]Cl_2 \cdot H_2O$ (d) $[Cr(H_2O)_6]Cl_3$

5 One mole of the complex $CoCl_3 \cdot 6H_2O$ on reaction with excess of $AgNO_3$ gives two moles of white precipitate. Thus, complex is
(a) $[Co(H_2O)_6]Cl_3$ (b) $[Co(H_2O)_5Cl]Cl_2 \cdot H_2O$
(c) $[Co(H_2O)_4Cl_2]Cl \cdot 2H_2O$ (d) $[Co(H_2O)_3Cl_3] \cdot 3H_2O$

6 Choose the incorrect match from the following with respect to number of unpaired electrons in the complex ion.
(a) $[Cr(H_2O)_6]^{3+} \longrightarrow 3$ (b) $[Co(CN)_4]^{2-} \longrightarrow 1$
(c) $[Ni(NH_3)_6]^{2+} \longrightarrow 4$ (d) $[MnF_6]^{4-} \longrightarrow 5$

7 In compound $Fe(CO)_5$ the hybridisation of iron is
(a) dsp^3 (b) sp^3d
(c) sp^3d^2 (d) d^2sp^3

8 Choose the incorrect match from the following.
(a) $Ni(CO)_4 \longrightarrow sp^3$ (b) $[Ni(CN)_4]^{2-} \longrightarrow dsp^2$
(c) $[Fe(CN)_6]^{4-} \longrightarrow d^2sp^3$ (d) $[MnF_6]^{4-} \longrightarrow dsp^3$

9 Among the given complexes which of them is an outer orbital complex.
(a) $[Ni(NH_3)_6]^{2+}$ (b) $[Mn(CN)_6]^{4-}$
(c) $[Co(NH_3)_6]^{3+}$ (d) $[Fe(CN)_6]^{4-}$

10 Consider the following complexes :
$[Mn(CN)_6]^{3-}$, $[Fe(CN)_6]^{3-}$, $[Co(H_2O)_6]^{2+}$, $[Co(C_2O_4)_3]^{3-}$, $[CoF_6]^{3-}$
The number of high spin complexe(s) is
(a) 1 (b) 2
(c) 3 (d) 5

11 When excess of ammonia is added to $CuSO_4$ solution, then deep blue coloured complex is formed. Then the geometry and magnetic nature of the complex is
(a) tetrahedral, paramagnetic (b) tetrahedral, diamagnetic
(c) square planar, diamagnetic (d) square planar, paramagnetic

12 The geometry and magnetic behaviour of the complex $[PtCl_4]^{2-}$ is
(a) square planar and paramagnetic respectively
(b) square planar and diamagnetic respectively
(c) tetrahedral and paramagnetic respectively
(d) tetrahedral and diamagnetic respectively

13 Consider the following statements.
Statement I $[Fe(CN)_6]^{3-}$ ion shows magnetic moment corresponding to two unpaired electrons.
Statement II $[Fe(CN)_6]^{3-}$ is paramagnetic in nature.
In the light of the above statements, choose the correct answer from the options given below.
(a) Both Statement I and Statement II are false.
(b) Statement I is true, but Statement II is false.
(c) Statement I is false, but Statement II is true.
(d) Both Statement I and Statement II are true.

14 Choose the incorrect statement about the complex $[Cr(NH_3)_6]Cl_3$.
(a) The complex involves d^2sp^3 hybridisation and is octahedral in shape.
(b) The complex is paramagnetic.
(c) The complex is an outer orbital complex.
(d) The complex gives white precipitate with silver nitrate solution.

15 On the basis of VBT, find which is an inner orbital complex with zero magnetic moment?
(a) $[Mn(CN)_6]^{3-}$ (b) $[Co(NH_3)_6]^{3+}$
(c) $[Cr(H_2O)_6]^{3+}$ (d) $[FeCl_6]^{4-}$

16 Among $[Fe(H_2O)_6]^{3+}$, $[Fe(CN)_6]^{3-}$, $[Fe(Cl)_6]^{3-}$ species, the hybridisation states of the Fe atoms are, respectively.
(a) d^2sp^3, d^2sp^3, sp^3d^2 (b) sp^3d^2, d^2sp^3, d^2sp^3
(c) sp^3d^2, d^2sp^3, sp^3d^2 (d) d^2sp^3, sp^2d^2, sp^3d^2

17 Among the following ions, which one has the highest unpaired electrons?
(a) $[Cr(H_2O)_6]^{3+}$ (b) $[Zn(H_2O)_6]^{2+}$
(c) $[Fe(H_2O)_6]^{2+}$ (d) $[Fe(H_2O)_6]^{3+}$

18 $[Pt(NH_3)_4]Cl_2$ is
(a) pyramidal (b) pentagonal
(c) tetrahedral (d) square planar

19 The geometry of $Ni(CO)_4$ and $Ni(PPh_3)_2Cl_2$ are
(a) square planar and tetrahedral respectively
(b) both tetrahedral
(c) tetrahedral and square planar respectively
(d) both square planar

20 Match Column I with Column II.

Column I (Complex ion)		Column II (No. of unpaired electron(s))
A. $[Cr(H_2O)_6]^{3+}$	1.	1
B. $[Co(CN)_4]^{2-}$	2.	5
C. $[Ni(NH_3)_6]^{2+}$	3.	3
D. $[MnF_6]^{4-}$	4.	2

Codes

(a) A-3 B-2, C-1, D-3 (b) A-2 B-1, C-3, D-4
(c) A-3, B-1, C-4, D-2 (d) A-3 B-2, C-1, D-4

21 Which of the following is incorrect statement regarding limitation of VBT ?

(a) It does not given quantitative intepretation of magnetic data.
(b) It does not explain colour exhibited by coordination compound.
(c) It distinguishes between weak and strong ligands.
(d) It does not give a quantitative interpretation of thermodynamic or kinetic stabilities of coordination compounds..

Module 3

Bonding in Coordination Compounds (Part-II) Metal Carbonyls, Importance of Coordination Compounds

- Crystal Field Theory (CFT)
- Magnetic Properties of Coordination Compounds
- Importance of Coordination Compounds
- Colour in Coordination Compounds
- Organometallic Compounds

Crystal Field Theory (CFT)

This theory was proposed to overcome the shortcomings of valence bond theory. This theory is based on electrostatic or ionic model. It describes the splitting of degenerate *d*-orbitals in presence of ligands.

Some assumptions of crystal field theory are as follows

- Ligands are considered as point charges in case of anions or point dipoles in case of neutral molecules.
- The interaction between metal ion and ligand is purely electrostatic. Therefore, metal ion and ligands do not mix their orbitals, i.e. no overlap of orbitals occur.
- The *d*-orbitals present in metal ion are degenerate. This degeneracy is lost in presence of ligands as the field produced by ligands is not symmetrical.
- Due to this loss in degeneracy, *d*-orbitals are splitted into t_{2g} and e_g sets of orbitals.
- t_{2g} orbitals (d_{xy}, d_{yz}, d_{xz}) are triply degenerate while e_g orbitals ($d_{x^2-y^2}$ and d_{z^2}) are doubly degenerate.

Crystal Field Splitting in Octahedral Coordination Entities

Complex with C.N. = 6 forms octahedral complex. When a ligand approaches to a metal ion, it distorts the spherically symmetrical cloud of electrons in metal ion and repulsions occur between the electrons of *d*-orbitals of metal ion and electrons of ligands.

The $d_{x^2-y^2}$ and d_{z^2} orbital (i.e. e_g orbitals) which point towards the axes along the direction of the ligand will experience more repulsion and will be raised in energy. However, the d_{xy}, d_{zx}, d_{yz} orbitals (i.e. t_{2g} orbitals) which are directed between the axes will be lowered in energy relative to the average energy in the spherical crystal field.

This splitting of degenerate orbitals into two sets is known as **crystals field splitting** and the difference of energy between the two sets of degenerate orbitals as a result of this splitting is known as **crystal field stabilisation energy** (CFSE). It is represented by Δ_o (the subscript *o* is for octahedral.

Mentor's TIP

The 'g' subscript is used for the octahedral and square planar complexes which have centre of symmetry. Tetrahedral complexes lack symmetry. So, 'g' subscript is not used with energy levels.

Hence, the energy of two e_g orbitals will be increased by value of $\frac{3}{5}\Delta_o$ and energy of three t_{2g} orbitals will be decreased by $\frac{2}{5}\Delta_o$.

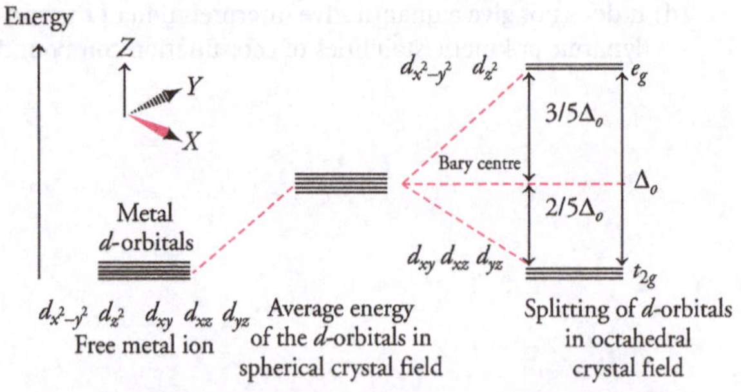

d-orbital splitting in an octahedral crystal field

The value of Δ_o depends on the nature of ligand. Some ligands produce strong fields in which splitting will be larger while some have weak field strength in which splitting will be smaller.

Concept ladder

Electron occupying t_{2g} orbital lowers the energy by $0.40\Delta_o$ and electron occupying e_g orbital increases the energy by $0.60\ \Delta_o$.

Therefore, magnitude of CFSE is given by the relation,

$$CFSE = (-0.40x + 0.60y)\Delta_o + P$$

where, x = number of electrons in t_{2g} orbitals

y = number of electrons in e_g orbitals

P = pairing energy

Therefore, on the basis of field strength, ligands are arranged in series, called **spectrochemical series.**

$I^- < Br^- < SCN^- < Cl^- < S^{2-} < F^- < OH^- < C_2O_4^{2-} < H_2O < NH_3 < en < NO_2^- < CN^- < CO$

If the metal ion has d^1, d^2 or d^3 configuration, the electron occupies t_{2g} orbitals according to Hund's rule (i.e. each orbital is first singly filled.)

For d^4 configuration, the fourth electron can either occupy t_{2g} or e_g orbital. It depends upon the magnitude of pairing energy, P. The two possibilities are

- If $\Delta_o > P$, the fourth electron will pair up and occupies the t_{2g} orbital, thus, forms low spin complex and ligands are known as strong field ligand.
- If $\Delta_o < P$, the fourth electron will not be able to pair-up then it occupy e_g orbital, thus, forms high spin complex and ligand are known as weak field ligands.

e.g. In $[Co(NH_3)_6]^{3+}$, NH_3 is a strong field ligand thus, it has ability to pair the electrons, i.e. $\Delta_o > P$. Hence, it will form low spin complex.

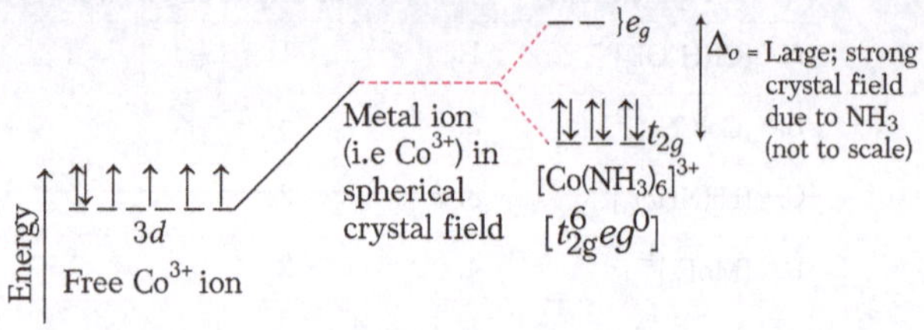

In $[CoF_6]^{3-}$, F^- is a weak field ligand, thus it cannot pair the electrons, i.e. $\Delta_o < P$. Hence, it will form high spin complex.

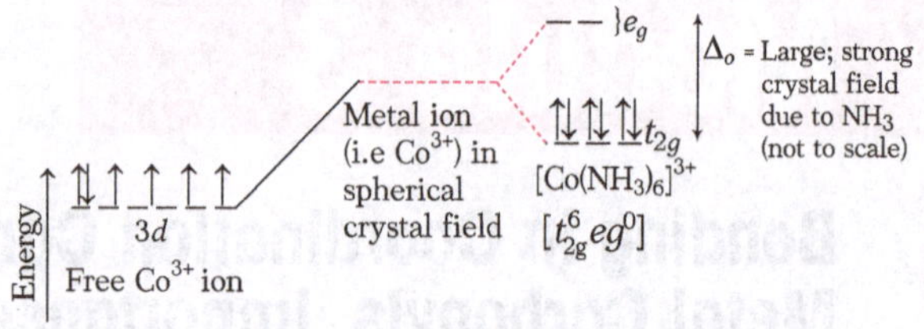

Crystal Field Splitting in Tetrahedral Coordination Entities

Complex with C.N. = 4 forms tetrahedral complex.

In tetrahedral complex formation, the *d*-orbital splitting is inverted and smaller as compared to the octahedral field splitting.

The magnitude of energy separation in tetrahedral complex (Δ_t) is considerably less than in octahedral. This is because of the following two reasons

- These are only four ligands (instead of six), therefore the ligand field is only $\frac{2}{3}$ to the size.

  Hence, the ligand field splitting is also $\frac{2}{3}$ the size.
- The directions of the orbitals does not coincide with the direction of the ligand due to which crystal field splitting again reduces to 2/3.

That's why the tetrahedral crystal field splitting Δ_t is $= \frac{2}{3} \times \frac{2}{3}$ of octahedral crystal field splitting (Δ_o)

The relation can be represented as

$$\Delta_t = \frac{4}{9}\Delta_o$$

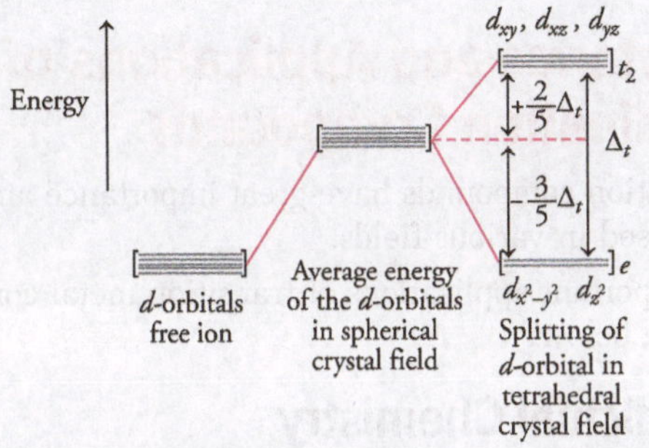

d-orbital splitting in a tetrahedral crystal field

> **Concept ladder**
> In case of tetrahedral complex, low spin configuration is rarely observed.
> CFSE of tetrahedral complexes = $[-0.6y + 0.4x]\Delta_t$
> where, x = number of electrons in t_2 orbitals
> y = number of electrons in e orbitals

Limitations of CFT

Limitations of CFT are as follows

- It is assumed that ligands are point charges and anionic ligands should exert the greatest splitting effect. But, anionic ligands are placed at the low end of spectrochemical series.
- It could not explain the covalent character of bonding between the ligand and central metal ion. Short comings of crystal field theory was explained by **ligand field theory** (LFT). It is considered as the extention of CFT. LFT is a qualitative approach used for octahedral metal complexes.

Colour in Coordination Compounds

A substance appears coloured because it absorbs light that corresponds to wavelength in the visible region and reflects other wavelength. Most transition metal complexes are coloured. In these complexes, *d*-orbitals are not degenerate and split into two sets t_{2g} and e_g which are separated by energies equal to Δ_o.

Energy difference between these two sets is small. Therefore, excitation of electron is quite easy.

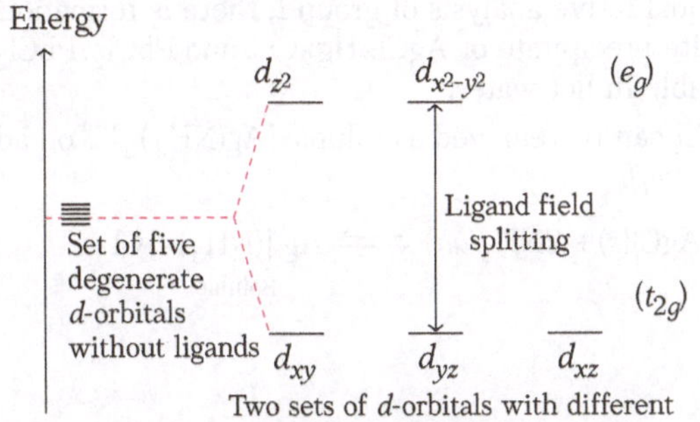

Two sets of *d*-orbitals with different energies in an octahedral complex. (with ligands)

Hence, transition metal complex absorbs visible light which excites the electron from lower t_{2g} energy level to higher e_g level. This transition is called ***d* – *d* transition.**

These complexes reflect the complementary colour of the colour absorbed. Wavelength associated with different colours are given below.

Wavelength absorbed (Å)	**Spectral colour** (Colour absorbed)	**Complementary colour** (Colour observed)
4100	violet	lemon yellow
4300	indigo	yellow
4800	blue	orange
5000	blue-green	red
5300	green	purple
5600	lemon yellow	violet
5800	yellow	indigo
6100	orange	blue
6800	red	blue-green

In absence of ligand, crystal field splitting does not occur and therefore, the metal complexes appear colourless.

e.g. Anhydrous copper sulphate is white while copper sulphate pentahydrates (i.e. $CuSO_4 \cdot 5H_2O$) is blue coloured solution.

> **Concept ladder**
> Some complexes like CrO_4^{2-}, $Cr_2O_7^{2-}$, MnO_4^- etc., have d° configuration of metal ion but have intense colour. Here, colour is due to charge transfer spectra and not due to *d-d* transition.

Magnetic Properties of Coordination Compounds

Transition metal complexes exhibit magnetic properties. The magnetic nature depends on the number of unpaired electrons present. On this basis, these complexes can be paramagnetic (having unpaired electrons) or diamagnetic (having paired electrons) in nature.

The magnetic moment of coordination compounds can be measured by the magnetic susceptibility experiments. The results can be used to obtain information about the number of unpaired electrons and hence structures adopted by metal complexes.

Magnetic nature or magnetic moment can be determined by the relation, $\mu = \sqrt{n(n+2)}$ BM where, n is the number of unpaired electrons. Presence of unpaired electrons can be explained with the help of crystal field theory.

For instance, $[Fe(H_2O)_6]^{2+}$ is paramagnetic but $[Fe(CN)_6]^{4-}$ is diamagnetic in nature.

This can be explained as, since, H_2O is a weak field ligand, it does not pair up the electrons and forms high spin complex ($\Delta_o < P$). While CN^- is a strong field ligand, pairs the electrons and forms low spin complex ($\Delta_o > P$).

Mentor's TIP

Complexes having d^0 or d^{10} configuration of metal ion are always diamagnetic.

Organometallic Compounds

These are the compounds which contain metal-carbon bonds. The first organometallic compound of *d*-block elements was prepared by W.C. Zeise.

Some examples of organometallic compounds are $K[Pt(C_2H_4)Cl_3]$ (Zeise's salt), $Ni(CO)_4$, $[Fe(C_5H_5)_2]$ (also known as **ferrocene**).

Bonding in Metal Carbonyls

The homoleptic carbonyls, i.e. the compounds containing carbonyl ligands (CO) only, are formed by most of the transition metals. These carbonyls have simple and well defined structures.

In these compounds CO acts as donor ligand and donates lone pairs of electrons of carbonyl carbon into vacant orbital of metal forming σ-bond.

It also behaves as an acceptor ligands and forms π-bond by back donation of electrons from filled *d*-orbital of metal to vacant antibonding (π^*)-orbital of CO.

This back-bonding stabilises the metal-ligands interaction. It is also called **synergic bonding.**

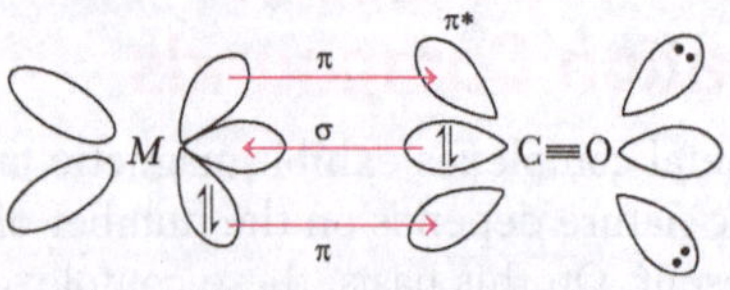

Example of synergic bonding interactions in a carbonyl complex.

Mentor's TIP

Synergic back-bonding increases with increasing electron density on central metal atom/ion.

Structures of some representative homoleptic metal carbonyls are given below.

e.g. Tetracarbonyl nickel (0) is tetrahedral, hexacarbonyl chromium (0) is octahedral etc.

Importance and Applications of Coordination Compounds

Coordination compounds have great importance and widely used in various fields.

Some important applications of transition metal complexes are given below.

In Medicinal Chemistry

- The platinum complex, *cis*-$[Pt(NH_3)_2Cl_2]$ commonly known as ***cis*-platin** is used in the treatment of cancer. It has ability to block the uncontrolled division of cancerous cells that results in growth of tumours.
- EDTA complex of calcium, $[Ca(EDTA)]^{2-}$ is used to treat a person suffering from lead poisoning.

$$Pb^{2+} + [Ca(EDTA)]^{2-} \longrightarrow [Pb(EDTA)]^{2-} + Ca^{2+}$$

EDTA complex of lead is more stable than $[Ca(EDTA)]^{2-}$ complex. Thus, lead complex is excreted from the body and Ca^{2+} remains as the body nutrient.

In Quantitative and Qualitative Analysis

- Traces of Ni^{2+} salt can be detected by dimethyl glyoxime when cherry red precipitate of nickel-dimethyl glyoximate (chelate) is formed.

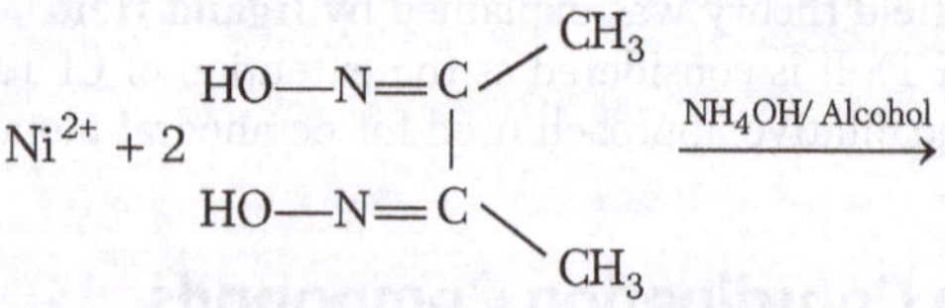

Dimethyl glyoxime

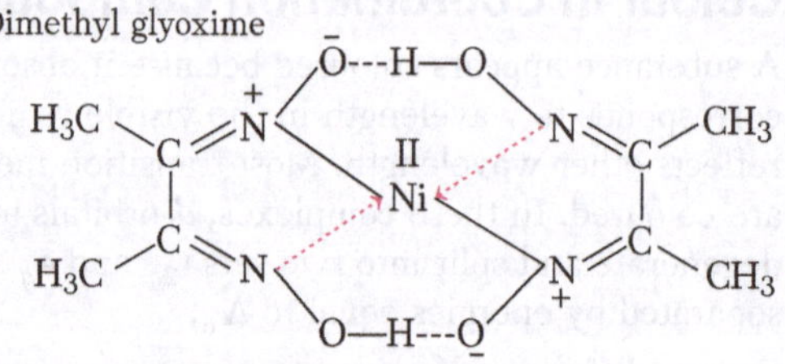

Nickel-dimethyl glyoximate (chelate) (red ppt.)

- In qualitative analysis of group I, there is formation of white precipitate of AgCl, Hg_2Cl_2, and $PbCl_2$. $PbCl_2$ is soluble in hot water.

AgCl can be removed as soluble $[Ag(NH_3)_2]Cl$ on adding $NH_3(aq)$.

$$AgCl(s) + 2NH_3(aq) \rightleftharpoons \underset{\text{Soluble}}{Ag[(NH_3)_2]Cl}$$

- In group II, Cd^{2+} can be precipitated as CdS in presence of Cu^{2+}.
- By treating the solution of Cu^{2+} and Cd^{2+} with an excess of CN^-, Cu^{2+} forms a stable complex in a redox reaction.

$$2Cu^{2+} + 10CN^- \longrightarrow 2\underset{\text{Stable}}{\overset{\text{I}}{[Cu(CN)_4]^{3-}}} + \underset{\text{Cyanogen gas}}{(CN)_2} \uparrow$$

while Cd^{2+} forms less stable complex

$$Cd^{2+} + 4CN^- \rightleftharpoons \underset{\text{Unstable}}{[Cd(CN)_4]^{2-}}$$

When H_2S gas is passed, $[Cd(CN)_4]^{2-}$ is precipitated as CdS without affecting $[Cu(CN)_4]^{3-}$ complex.

In Extraction of Metals

- Nickel can be extracted by Mond's process which involves formation of carbonyl complex of nickel.

$$Ni(s) + 4CO(g) \longrightarrow Ni(CO)_4(g)$$

- Silver (Ag) and gold (Au) can be extracted by formation of cyanide complex.

$$\underset{\text{(Impure or crude)}}{4Au(s)} + 8CN^-(aq) + O_2(g) + 2H_2O(l) \longrightarrow 4OH^-(aq) + 4\overset{\text{I}}{[Au(CN)_2]^-}(aq)$$

$$\underset{\text{(Impure or cruide)}}{2[Au(CN)_2]^-(aq)} + Zn(s) \longrightarrow \overset{\text{II}}{[Zn(CN)_4]^{2-}}(aq) + \underset{\text{(Pure)}}{2Au(s)}$$

In Purification of Water

Purification of water can be done through complex formation. It involves chelation with sodium salt of EDTA. The formation constant of $[Ca(EDTA)]^{2-}$ and $[Mg(EDTA)]^{2-}$ are very large.

Hence, on treating water with sodium salt of EDTA, concentration of Ca^{2+} and Mg^{2+} can be reduced to the point that these ions will not precipitate with soap or detergent.

$$Ca^{2+} + (EDTA)^{4-} \rightleftharpoons [Ca(EDTA)]^{2-}$$

$$Mg^{2+} + (EDTA)^{4-} \rightleftharpoons [Mg(EDTA)]^{2-}$$

In Photography

The photographic "fixing" process removes unreacted AgBr which forms soluble complex with sodium thiosulphate.

$$AgBr(s) + 2S_2O_3^{2-} \longrightarrow \underset{\text{Soluble}}{\overset{\text{I}}{[Ag(S_2O_3)_2]^{3-}}} + Br^-$$

In Biological Processes

Many important biological substances are coordination compounds, e.g.

- Haemoglobin is a protein that carries O_2 and CO_2 in blood.
  It contains iron (II) ions bound to large porphyrin rings.
- Chlorophyll is necessary for photosynthesis in plants. It contains magnesium ions (II) bound to porphyrin rings.
- Vitamin B_{12} is a large complex of cobalt (III).

In Purification of Metals

It can be achieved through formation and subsequent decomposition of their coordination compounds.

e.g. Impure nickel is converted to $[Ni(CO)_4]$ which is decomposed to yield pure nickel.

In Industries as Catalysts

They are used as catalysts for many industrial processes.

e.g. Rh complex, $[(Ph_3P)_3\overset{\text{I}}{Rh}Cl]$ a Wilkinson catalyst is used for hydrogenation of C=C in vegetable oils.

In Electroplating

Articles (using as cathode) can be electroplated with pure Ag and Au (using as anode) much more smoothly and evenly from solutions of the complexes, (with less stable coordination sphere) $[Ag(CN)_2]^-$ and $[Au(CN)_2]^-$ than from a solution of simple metal ions.

STEP UP Practice 3

1 If the crystal field splitting energy for octahedral complexes is Δ_o and for tetrahedral complexes is Δt, the two are related as

(a) $\Delta_t = \frac{4}{9}\Delta_o$ (b) $\Delta_t = \frac{3}{4}\Delta_o$

(c) $\Delta_t = \frac{1}{2}\Delta_o$ (d) $\Delta_o = \frac{4}{9}\Delta_t$

2 In which of the following octahedral complexes of Co (atomic number 27), will the magnitude of Δ_o be the highest?

(a) $[Co(CN)_6]^{3-}$ (b) $[Co(C_2O_4)_3]^{3-}$

(c) $[Co(H_2O)_6]^{3+}$ (d) $[Co(en)_3]^{3+}$

3 In the complex ion ML_6^{n+}, M^{n+} has five *d*-electrons and L is a weak field ligand. According to crystal field theory, the magnetic properties of the complex ion correspond to the number of unpaired electrons is

(a) 1 (b) 5

(c) 4 (d) 2

4 Among the given options which system has maximum number of unpaired electrons?

(a) d^5 (octahedral), high spin

(b) d^9 (octahedral), high spin

(c) d^7 (octahedral), low spin

(d) d^6 (octahedral), low spin

5 Which is the strongest field ligand?

(a) NO_2^- (b) CN^-

(c) Cl^- (d) SCN^-

6 The correct increasing order of Δ_o of the following complex is

(a) $[Cr(NH_3)_6]^{3+} < [Cr(H_2O)_6]^{3+} < [Cr(NO_2)_6]^{3-}$

(b) $[Cr(NO_2)_6]^{3-} < [Cr(NH_3)_6]^{3+} < [Cr(H_2O)_6]^{3+}$

(c) $[Cr(H_2O)_6]^{3+} < [Cr(NH_3)_6]^{3+} < [Cr(NO_2)_6]^{3-}$

(d) $[Cr(NH_3)_6]^{3+} < [Cr(NO_2)_6]^{3-} < [Cr(H_2O)_6]^{3+}$

7 Which of the following ion will produce a small crystal field splitting (a weak ligand field)?

(a) I^- (b) Cl^-

(c) F^- (d) All of these

8 Among the ligands NH_3, en, CN^- and CO, the correct order of their increasing field strength, is

(a) $CO < NH_3 < en < CN^-$ (b) $NH_3 < en < CN^- < CO$

(c) $CN^- < NH_3 < CO < en$ (d) $CN^- < en < NH_3 < CO$

9 The number of unpaired electrons in $[Mn(H_2O)_6]^{2+}$, if H_2O is considered as weak field ligand will be

(a) 3 (b) 1

(c) 5 (d) 4

10 The value of magnetic moment (μ) for the system $t_{2g}^6 e_g^2$ is

(a) 2.83 BM (b) 1.73 BM

(c) 3.87 BM (d) 4.92 BM

11 Which of the following is incorrect match regarding the colour of light absorbed at this respective wavelength?

(a) $[CoCl(NH_3)_5]^{2+} \longrightarrow$ Yellow (535 nm)

(b) $[Co(NH_3)_6]^{3+} \longrightarrow$ Blue (475 nm)

(c) $[Cu(H_2O)_4]^{2+} \longrightarrow$ Red (600 nm)

(d) $[Ti(H_2O)_6]^{3+} \longrightarrow$ Violet (498 nm)

12 Choose the incorrect statement regarding CFT.

(a) It successfully explains the formation of colour in coordination compounds.

(b) It assumes that ligand are point charges.

(c) The cationic ligands are found at the row of spectrochemical series.

(d) It does not take into account the covalent character of bonding between ligand and the central atoms.

13 Consider the following compounds.

$Ni(CO)_4$, $Fe(CO)_5$, $[Co_2(CO)_8]$, $Cr(CO)_6$, $[Mn_2(CO)_{10}]$

The number of homoleptic metal carbonyls is

(a) 1 (b) 2

(c) 4 (d) 5

14 Choose the incorrect match.

(a) Chlorophyll → Magnesium

(b) Cyanocobalamine → Cobalt

(c) Haemoglobin → Iron

(d) Wilkinson catalyst → Platinum

NEET Exclusive EXTRA BYTES

- During naming of ligands, when organic free radicals acts as ligands, the ligands are named as usual, e.g. CH_3 as methyl, C_2H_5 as ethyl etc.
- Square planar complexes of the type $[M(AA)_2]$, MA_4, MA_3B and MAB_3 do not show stereo-isomerism since, all possible arrangements for any of these complexes are identical.

Effective Atomic Number (EAN) Rule

- Sidgwick proposed effective atomic number (EAN) to explain the stability of metal in a complex. EAN is defined as the total number of electrons on the metal atom or ion after the complex formation which should be equal to that of the next higher noble gas.
- If Z is the atomic number, (O.N.) is the oxidation number and (C.N.) is the coordination number of the central metal atom or ion in the complex then

$$\text{EAN} = Z - (\text{O.N.}) + 2 \times (\text{C.N})$$

Assume that each ligand is unidentate.

- A stable complex is formed if the EAN is equal to the atomic number of the next noble gas. EAN rule is mainly applicable to metal carbonyls.

Complex	EAN
$[Cr(CO)_6]$	$36\ [24 - 0 + 2 \times 6]$
$Ni(CO)_4$	$36\ [(28 - 0) + 2 \times 4]$

- **Chelate effect** Stability of a complex depends on the formation of chelate rings. Chelating ligands form more stable complex than monodentate ligands. This effect, called chelation effect is maximum for five and six membered rings. All bidentate and polydentate ligands are chelating ligands.
- If a multidentate ligands happens to be cyclic without any steric effect, a further increase in stability occurs. This is called **macrocyclic effect.**
- $K_3[Co(NO_2)_6]$, i.e. potassium hexanitrito-N-cobaltate(III) is called Fischer's salt. Its common name is potassium cobalt nitrite.
- Ferrocene $[Fe(\eta^5 - C_5H_5)_2]$ and dibenzene chromium $[Cr(\eta^6 - C_6H_6)_2]$ are called Sandwiched compounds (π-bonded organometallic compounds).

GEARING UP FOR NEET

1 An addition compound is 100% ionised into constituent ions. Then the compound is
(a) double salt (b) complex salt
(c) acid salt (d) normal salt

2 What is the value of coordination number and oxidation number of central atom in $[Co(en)_2Cl_2]Cl$ respectively?
(a) 4, +3 (b) 6, +3 (c) 6, +2 (d) 4 +2

3 The coordination number of Pt in the complex ion $[Pt(en)_2Cl_2]^{2+}$ is
(a) 3 (b) 4 (c) 5 (d) 6

4 A chelating ligand has two or more than two donor atoms to bind to a single metal ion. Which of the following is not a chelating ligand?
(a) Thiosulphato (b) Oxalato
(c) Glycinato (d) Ethane-1, 2-diamine

5 The IUPAC name of the coordination compound ion, $[CoCl_2(en)_2]^+$ is
(a) *bis*chlorododi(ethane-1,2-diamine cobalt(II)) ion
(b) dichlorido*bis*(ethane-1,2-diamine)cobalt (III) ion
(c) dichlorodi(ethane-1,2-diamine)cobalt(III) ion
(d) *bis*(ethane-1,2-diamine)dichlorocobaltate(III) ion

6 The IUPAC name of the complex $K[SbCl_5C_6H_5]$ is
(a) potassium pentachlorido(phenyl)antimonate(V)
(b) dutero antimonate(IV)
(c) potassium benzalantimony(III)chlorido
(d) potassium phenylchloroantimonate(V)

7 The IUPAC name of the given complex, $[Ru(NH_3)_5N_2]Cl_2$ is
(a) pentaammine(azido)ruthenium(II)dichloride
(b) rutheniumpentammine(III)dichlorodinitrogen
(c) pentamine(nitrogen)ruthenium(II) chloride
(d) pentaammine(dinitrogen)ruthenium(II) chloride

8 The formula of the given coordination compound potassium tetrahydroxidozincate(II) is
(a) $K[Zn(OH)_4]$ (b) $K_3[Zn(OH)_4]$
(c) $K_2[Zn(OH)_4]$ (d) $K_2[Zn_2(OH)_4]$

9 The IUPAC name for $[Al(OH_2)_5(OH)]^{+2}$ is
(a) aquametaaluminate ion
(b) pentahydroaluminium hydroxo
(c) pentaaquahydroxidoaluminium(III) ion
(d) pentaaquaaluminate(III) hydroxide

10 Linkage isomerism is shown by which of the following pair of compounds?
(a) $[Co(en)_3][Cr(CN)_6]$ and $[Cr(en)_3][Co(CN)_6]$
(b) $[Mn(CO)_5(SCN)]$ and $[Mn(CO)_5(NCS)]$
(c) $[Co(NH_3)_5(NO_3)]SO_4$ and $[Co(NH_3)_5(SO_4)]NO_3$
(d) $[Co(NH_3)_4(H_2O)Cl]Cl_2$ and $[Co(NH_3)_4Cl_2]Cl\cdot H_2O$

11 The number of structural isomers possible for a complex consisting of Co^{3+} as the central metal ion, two en molecules, two Cl^- ions and one NO_2^- ion is
(a) four (b) three
(c) five (d) two

12 Which type of isomerism is shown by $[Cr(H_2O)_6]Cl_3$, $[Cr(H_2O)_5Cl]Cl_2\cdot H_2O$ and $[Cr(H_2O)_4Cl_2]Cl\cdot 2H_2O$?
(a) Hydrate isomerism
(b) Ionisation isomerism
(c) Linkage isomerism
(d) Coordination isomerism

13 The compound $[Co(NH_3)_6][Cr(CN)_6]$ and $[Cr(NH_3)_6][Co(CN)_6]$ exhibit
(a) Linkage isomerism
(b) Polymerisation isomerism
(c) Coordination isomerism
(d) Ionisation isomerism

14 What is the value of x (with sign) in the compound $[Ni(CN)_4]^x$?
(a) +2 (b) −2
(c) 0 (d) +4

15 Among the given compounds which one is an outer orbital complex as well as diamagnetic in nature?
(a) $[Zn(NH_3)_6]^{2+}$ (b) $[Cr(NH_3)_6]^{3+}$
(c) $[Co(NH_3)_6]^{3+}$ (d) $[Ni(NH_3)_6]^{2+}$

16 Among the compounds given below, which one of the following aqua complexes will exhibit the maximum paramagnetic behaviour? (Atomic number Cr = 24, Mn = 25, Fe = 26, Ni = 28)
(a) $[Ni(H_2O)_6]^{2+}$ (b) $[Cr(H_2O)_6]^{2+}$
(c) $[Mn(H_2O)_6]^{2+}$ (d) $[Fe(H_2O)_6]^{2+}$

17 Which of the following compounds shows a magnetic moment of 1.73 BM ?
(a) $[Ni(CN)_4]^{2-}$ (b) $TiCl_4$
(c) $[CoCl_6]^{4-}$ (d) $[Cu(NH_3)_4]^{2+}$

18 $[Cr(H_2O)_6]Cl_2$ (Atomic number of Cr = 24) has a magnetic moment of 3.83 B.M. Then which of the following configuration is correct distribution of 3*d* electrons in the chromium of the complex?
(a) $(e_g)^3(t_{2g})^0$ (b) $(t_{2g})^2(e_g)^1$
(c) $(e_g)^1(t_{2g})^2$ (d) $(t_{2g})^3(e_g)^0$

19 Which of the following is π complex?
(a) Trimethyl aluminium (b) Ferrocene
(c) Diethyl zinc (d) Nickel carbonyl

20 Which of the following statements is incorrect with respect to importance of coordination compound in biological system?
(a) Carboxypeptidase A is an enzyme and contains zinc.
(b) Haemoglobin is the red pigment of blood and contains iron.
(c) Cyanocobalamin in B_{12} and contains cobalt.
(d) Chlorophyll is green pigments in plants and contains calcium.

Assertion-Reason

Direction (Q. Nos. 21 to 27) Given below are two statements, one is labelled as Assertion (A) and the other is labelled as Reason (R).
(a) Both A and R are true and R is the correct explanation of A.
(b) Both A and R are true but R is not the correct explanation of A.
(c) A is true but R is false.
(d) A is false but R is true.

21 **Assertion** (A) In the complex $[Co(NH_3)_3Cl_3]$, chloride ions does not satisfy the primary valencies as well as the secondary valencies of cobalt metal.
Reason (R) $[Co(NH_3)_3Cl_3]$ shows geometrical isomerism only.

22 **Assertion** (A) In $[Co(Cl_2)(en)_2]$ coordination number of Co is 4 and this compound has a square planar geometry.
Reason (R) The coordination number of a central metal atom in a complex is determined by the number of σ-bonds around a metal ion except organometallic compounds.

23 **Assertion** (A) $[Fe(CN)_6]^{3-}$ ion shows magnetic moment corresponding to two unpaired electrons.
Reason (R) It has d^2sp^3 hybridisation of Fe(III).

24 **Assertion** (A) All the octahedral complexes of Ni^{2+} are outer orbital complexes, when $\Delta_o < P$.
Reason (R) Generally outer orbital octahedral complexes are given by weak field ligands.

25 **Assertion** (A) Among the complexes, $[Fe(CN)_6]^{3-}$, $[Fe(H_2O)_6]^{2+}$ and $[Fe(en)_3]^{3+}$, the most stable ion is $[Fe(en)_3]^{3+}$ because of macrocyclic effect.
Reason (R) Ethylenediamine is a weak field ligand and form stable complexes.

26 **Assertion** (A) The theoretical value of magnetic moment (μ) is 1.73 B.M when CN^- ligands join Fe^{3+} ion to yield the complex, $[Fe(CN)_6]^{3-}$
Reason (R) In complex $[Fe(CN)_6]^{3-}$, the central metal ion has two unpaired electrons.

27 **Assertion** (A) $[CoCl(NH_3)_5]^{2+}$ absorbs greater energy at lower wavelength of light in comparison to $[Co(NH_3)_5(H_2O)]^{3+}$.
Reason (R) Wavelength of the light absorbed depends on the oxidation state of the metal ion also.

Statement Type Questions

Direction (Q. Nos. 28 to 34) In the light of the statements given below, choose the most appropriate answer from the options given below
(a) Both Statement I and Statement II are false.
(b) Statement I is true, but Statement II is false.
(c) Statement I is false, but Statement II is true.
(d) Both Statement I and Statement II are true.

28 **Statement** The IUPAC name of $K_3[Cr(CN)_6]$ is potassium hexacyanidochromate(III).
Statement II It is an anionic complex.

29 **Statement I** Charge on the complex of ferric ion with EDTA is minus one.
Statement II EDTA is a bidentate ligand.

30 **Statement I** $K_2[Ni(EDTA)]$ is more stable than $K_3[Al(C_2O_4)_3]$.
Statement II Nickel (Ni) is a transition element while aluminium (Al) is a non-transition element.

31 **Statement I** Square planar complex, Ma_2b_2 has two optically active isomers.
Statement II Mirror image of Ma_2b_2 is non-super imposable.

32 **Statement I** Metal attached with EDTA in an octahedral complex, has a denticity of 4.
Statement II $[EDTA]^{4-}$ bind through two nitrogen and four oxygen atoms to a central metal ion.

33 **Statement I** The central metal ions in and $[Co(C_2O_4)_3]^{3-}$ are d^2sp^3-hybridised.
Statement II $[MnCl_6]^{3-}$ and $[FeF_6]^{3-}$ are paramagnetic and have 5 and 4 unpaired electrons respectively.

34 **Statement I** EDTA is used in the treatment of mercury poisoning.
Statement II Excess of copper and iron are removed by the chelating ligands, D-penicillamine and desferrioxime B (DFOB) *via* the formation of coordination compounds.

35 Which of the following statements is (are) incorrect ?

A. The IUPAC name of $Ba[BrF_4]_2$ is barium tetraflouridobromate(III)

B. The formula of pentaamine(nitrito-o) [cobalt (III) sulphate is $[Co(NH_3)_5(ONO)]SO_4$.

C. The ionic species are written as two words with the cation first for the complex like, $[Co(NH_3)_6][Cr(CN)_6]$.

D. While writing the formula of a coordination compound, the ligands are listed first and then central atom is listed in alphabetical order.

E. The charge of the cation is balanced by the charge of the anion.

Choose the correct answer from the options given below.

(a) A, B and C (b) D and E
(c) Only D (d) Only B

36 Select the correct statements from the following.

A. A coordination entity constitutes a central metal atom or ion bonded to variable number of ions or molecules for tetrahedral complex.

B. In compounds $[NiCl_2(H_2O)_4]$, the central atom/ion is a Lewis acid.

C. Oxalate ion can bind with metal ion through two donor atoms.

D. Coordination number of the central atom/ion can be determined by the number of pi bonds formed by ligand with central atom/ion except organometallic compounds.

E. The ionisable groups which are written outside the bracket are called counter ions.

Choose the correct answer from the options given below.

(a) A, C and E (b) B, C and E
(c) D and E (d) B and C

37 Which of the following statements are correct?

A. The secondary valency is equal to the coordination number and fixed for a metal.

B. $CrCl_3$ and $CoCl_2$ have primary valence of 3 and 2 respectively.

C. The primary valency of the metal ion is satisfied by positive ions.

D. The primary valency is always non-ionisable.

E. Neutral molecules satisfy the primary valency in a complex.

Choose the most appropriate answer from the options given below.

(a) B, D and E only (b) A and B only
(c) C and E only (d) A, D and E only

38 Which of the following statements are correct?

A. $[NiCl_4]^{2-}$ is an inner orbital complex.

B. $[Mn(CN)_6]^{4-}$ is an outer orbital complex.

C. The complex $[Co(NH_3)_6]^{3+}$, is a low spin or spin paired complex.

D. The complex $[CoF_6]^{3-}$ uses outer orbitals of Co(III) in hybridisation.

E. Inner orbital complex have less number of unpaired electrons.

Choose the most appropriate answer from the options given below.

(a) A, C and D (b) D and E
(c) A, B and C (d) C, D and E

39 Select the incorrect statements from the following.

A. Ligands are treated as point dipoles in case of anions or point charges in case of neutral molecules.

B. The degeneracy of the *d*-orbitals can be removed by the ligand electron-metal electron repulsions in tetrahedral complex.

C. For octahedral complexes, the energy of the two e_g orbitals will decrease by $3/5\ \Delta_o$.

D. Ligands for which $\Delta_o < P$ are known as weak field ligands.

E. The cyrstal field splitting Δ_o, depends upon the field produced by the ligand and charge on the metal ion.

Choose the correct answer from the options given below.

(a) A, B and C (b) A, D and E
(c) B, D and C (d) C, D and E

40 Which of the following statements are incorrect?

A. The anion is named first in both positively and negatively charged coordination entities while writing the name of compound.

B. The ligands are named in an alphabetical order before the name of the central atom/ion while writing the name of compound.

C. Name of all the cationic ligands ends with -o.

D. If the complex ion is a cation, the name of the metal ends with the suffix -ate.

E. The neutral complex molecule is named similar to that of the complex cation.

Choose the most appropriate answer from the options given below.

(a) A, C and D
(b) B, C and D
(c) C and E
(d) B, D and E

41 Select the correct statements from the following.

A. decacarbonyldimanganese(0) is made up of two square pyramidal $Mn(CO)_5$ units joined by a Mn—Mn bond.

B. Octacarbonyldicobalt(0) has no Co—Co bond bridged.

C. The metal-carbon bond in metal carbonyls possess both σ and π-characters.

D. The ligand to metal bonding creates a synergic effect which weakens the bond between CO and the metal.

E. The homoleptic carbonyls are formed by most of the transition metals.

Choose the correct answer from the options given below.

(a) B, C and D
(b) A, B and E
(c) A, C and E
(d) C, D and E

Species Selection Type Questions

42 Consider the given compounds.

(i) $[Cr(NH_3)_6]^{3+}$ (ii) $[Fe(NH_3)_4Cl_2]^+$
(iii) $[Mn(CN)_6]^{4-}$ (iv) $[MnF_6]^{4-}$
(v) $[Co(en)(NH_3)_2]^{2+}$ (vi) $[Co(NH_3)_3(NO_2)_3]$
(vii) $[Co(NH_3)_6]^{3+}$

The total number of compounds which are heteroleptic in nature is

(a) 3 (b) 4 (c) 5 (d) 2

43 Consider the following compounds.

(i) $[V(H_2O)_6]^{2+}$ (ii) $[Fe(CN)_6]^{3-}$ (iii) $[Ni(NH_3)_6]^{2+}$
(iv) $[Co(H_2O)_6]^{3+}$ (v) $[Co(C_2O_4)_3]^{3-}$

The number of compounds in which the central metal ions have d^2sp^3 hybridisation is

(a) 2 (b) 4 (c) 3 (d) 5

44 Consider the following ligands.

(i) NO_2^- (ii) CO (iii) $C_2O_4^{2-}$ (iv) SCN^-
(v) $H_2NCH_2CH_2NH_2$

The total number of ligand(s), which is (are) ambidentate in nature is

(a) 4 (b) 3 (c) 1 (d) 2

45 Consider the following compounds,

(i) $[FeF_6]^{3-}$ (ii) $[Co(C_2O_4)_3]^{3-}$ (iii) $[Ni(CN)_4]^{2-}$
(iv) $[MnCl_6]^{3-}$ (v) $[PtCl_2(NH_3)(OH_2)]$

The total number of compound(s) that is (are) diamagnetic in nature is

(a) 1 (b) 3 (c) 2 (d) 4

46 Among the following, the total number of inner orbital complexes is

(i) $[Co(NH_3)_6]^{3+}$ (ii) $[CoF_6]^{3-}$ (iii) $[NiCl_4]^{2-}$
(iv) $[Cu(H_2O)_6]^{2+}$ (v) $[Mn(CN)_6]^{4-}$

(a) 3 (b) 1 (c) 4 (d) 2

47 Consider the ligands given below.

$$C_2O_4^{2-}, CN^-, edta^{4-}, OH^-, S^{2-}, SCN^-, NH_3$$

The number of ligands that are arranged before H_2O in increasing order of spectrochemical series.

(a) 7 (b) 5 (c) 4 (d) 3

Match Type Questions

48 Match the following Column I with Column II.

Column I (Compound)	Column II (Oxidation state of Co)
A. $[Co(NCS)(NH_3)_5]SO_3$	1. 0
B. $[Co(NH_3)_4Cl_2]SO_4$	2. +2
C. $Na_4[Co(S_2O_3)_3]$	3. +4
D. $[Co_2(CO)_8]$	4. +3

Codes

(a) A-1, B-3, C-2, D-4 (b) A-3, B-2, C-1, D-4
(c) A-4, B-1, C-2, D-3 (d) A-4, B-3, C-2, D-1

49 Match the following Column I with Column II.

Column I (IUPAC name)	Column II (Compound/ion)
A. dichlorido*bis*(ethane-1,2-diamine)cobalt(III) ion	1. $[Co(NH_3)_5(CO_3)]Cl$
B. triamminetriaquachromium(III) chloride	2. $[CoCl_2(en)_2]Cl$
C. dichlorido*bis*(ethane-1, 2-diamine)cobalt (III) chloride	3. $[Cr(NH_3)_3(H_2O)_3]Cl_3$
D. pentaamminecarbonatocobalt(III) chloride	4. $[CoCl_2(en)_2]^+$

Codes

(a) A-2, B-4, C-1, D-3 (b) A-4, B-3, C-1, D-2
(c) A-4, B-2, C-3, D-1 (d) A-4, B-3, C-2, D-1

50 Match the following Column I with Column II.

Column I (Complex)	Column II (Isomerism)
A. $K[Cr(H_2O)_2(C_2O_4)_2]$	1. Ionisation
B. $[Co(en)_3]Cl_3$	2. Linkage
C. $[Co(NH_3)_5(NO_2)](NO_3)_2$	3. Geometrical
D. $[Co(SO_4)(NH_3)_5]Br$ and $[CoBr(NH_3)_5]SO_4$	4. Optical

Codes

(a) A-2, B-1, C-4, D-3 (b) A-3, B-4, C-2, D-1
(c) A-2, B-3, C-1, D-4 (d) A-3, B-4, C-1, D-2

51 Match the following Column I with Column II.

Column I (Coordination Compound)	Column II (Properties)
A. $[Cr(NH_3)_4Cl_2]Cl$	1. Paramagnetic and exhibits ionisation isomerism
B. $[Ti(H_2O)_5Cl](NO_3)_2$	2. Diamagnetic and exhibits *cis-trans* isomerism
C. $[Pt(en)(NH_3)Cl]NO_3$	3. Paramagnetic and exhibits *cis-trans* isomerism
D. $[Co(NH_3)_4(NO_3)_2]NO_3$	4. Diamagnetic and exhibits ionisation isomerism

Codes

(a) A-3, B-4, C-1, D-2 (b) A-4, B-3, C-2, D-1
(c) A-1, B-3, C-4, D-1 (d) A-3, B-1, C-4, D-2

52 Match the following Column I with Column II.

Column I (Coordination number and type of hybridisation of the central atom)	Column II (Distribution of hybrid orbital in space)
A. 4, sp^3	1. Trigonal bipyramidal
B. 4, dsp^2	2. Octahedral
C. 5, sp^3d	3. Tetrahedral
D. 6, d^2sp^3	4. Square planar

Codes

(a) A-2, B-1, C-4, D-3 (b) A-1, B-4, C-3, D-2
(c) A-3, B-4, C-1, D-2 (d) A-4, B-3, C-2, D-1

Final Check Through PYQs

Module-I Addition Compounds, Important Terms Related to Coordination Compounds, Nomenclature and Isomerism

1 Given below are two statements. *[NCERT (New) Pg. 122, NEET 2024]*

Statement I $[Co(NH_3)_6]^{3+}$ is a homoleptic complex. whereas $[Co(NH_3)_4Cl_2]^+$ is a heteroleptic complex.

Statement II Complex $[Co(NH_3)_6]^{3+}$ has only one kind of ligands but $[Co(NH_3)_4Cl_2]^+$ has more than one kind of ligands.

In the light of the above statements, choose the correct answer from the options given below.

(a) Both Statement I and Statement II are false.
(b) Statement I is true, but Statement II is false.
(c) Statement I is false, but Statement II is true.
(d) Both Statement I and Statement II are true.

2 Match Column I with Column II. *[NCERT (New) Pg. 127, NEET 2024]*

Column I (Complex)	Column II (Type of isomerism)
A. $[Co(NH_3)_5(NO_2)]Cl_2$	1. Solvate isomerism
B. $[Co(NH_3)_5(SO_4)]Br$	2. Linkage isomerism
C. $[Co(NH_3)_6][Cr(CN)_6]$	3. Ionisation isomerism
D. $[Co(H_2O)_6]Cl_3$	4. Coordination isomerism

Codes

(a) A-2, B-3, C-4, D-1
(b) A-1, B-3, C-4, D-2
(c) A-1, B-4, C-3, D-2
(d) A-2, B-4, C-3, D-1

3 Homoleptic complex from the following complexes is *[NEET 2023]*

(a) diamminechloridonitrito-N-platinum (II)
(b) pentaamminecarbonatocobalt (III) chloride
(c) triamminetriaquachromium (III) chloride
(d) potassium trioxalatoaluminate (III)

4 The IUPAC name of the complex $[Ag(H_2O)_2][Ag(CN)_2]$ is *[NCERT (New) Pg. 124, NEET 2022]*

(a) diaquasilver (II) dicyanidoargentate (II)
(b) dicyanidosilver (I) diaquaargentate (I)
(c) diaquasilver (l) dicyanidoargentate (I)
(d) dicyanidosilver (II) diaquaargentate (ll)

5 Ethylene diaminetetraacetate (EDTA) ion is *[NCERT (New) Pg. 121, NEET 2021]*

(a) hexadentate ligand with four O and two N donor atoms
(b) unidentate ligand
(c) bidentate ligand with two N donor atoms
(d) tridentate ligand with three N donor atoms

6 The type of isomerism shown by the complex $[CoCl_2(en)_2]$ is *[NCERT (New) Pg. 125, NEET 2018]*

(a) ionisation isomerism
(b) coordination isomerism
(c) geometrical isomerism
(d) linkage isomerism

7 The sum of coordination number and oxidation number of the metal *M* in the complex $[M(en)_2(C_2O_4)]Cl$ (where, en is ethylenediamine) is *[NCERT (New) Pg. 122, AIPMT 2015]*

(a) 9
(b) 6
(c) 7
(d) 8

8 The name of complex ion, $[Fe(CN)_6]^{3-}$ is *[NCERT Pg. 124, AIPMT 2015]*

(a) hexacyanoiron (III) ion
(b) hexacyanitoferrate (III) ion
(c) tricyanoferrate (III) ion
(d) hexacyanidoferrate (III)ion

9 The correct order of the stoichiometrics of AgCl formed when $AgNO_3$ in excess is treated with the complexes: $CoCl_3 \cdot 6NH_3$, $CoCl_3 \cdot 5NH_3$, $CoCl_3 \cdot 4NH_3$ respectively is *[NCERT (New) Pg. 119, NEET 2017]*

(a) AgCl, 3 AgCl, 2 AgCl
(b) 3 AgCl, AgCl, 2 AgCl
(c) 3 AgCl, 2 AgCl, AgCl
(d) 2 AgCl, 3 AgCl, AgCl

10 Number of possible isomers for the complex $[Co(en)_2Cl_2]Cl$ will be (en = ethylenediamine) *[NCERT (New) Pg. 126, AIPMT 2015]*

(a) 2
(b) 1
(c) 3
(d) 4

11 Cobalt (III) chloride forms several octahedral complexes with ammonia. Which of the following will not give test for chloride ions with silver nitrate at 25°C ? *[NCERT (New) Pg. 119, AIPMT 2015]*

(a) $CoCl_3 \cdot 3NH_3$
(b) $CoCl_3 \cdot 4NH_3$
(c) $CoCl_3 \cdot 5NH_3$
(d) $CoCl_3 \cdot 6NH_3$

Module-II Bonding in Coordination Compounds

12 Given below are two statements : *[NEET 2024]*

Statement I Both $[Co(NH_3)_6]^{3+}$ and $[CoF_6]^{3-}$ complexes are octahedral but differ in their magnetic behaviour.

Statement II $[Co(NH_3)_6]^{3+}$ is diamagnetic whereas $[CoF_6]^{3-}$ is paramagnetic.

In the light of the above statements, choose the correct answer from the options given below.

(a) Both Statement I and Statement II are false.
(b) Statement I is true, but Statement II is false.
(c) Statement I is false, but Statement II is true.
(d) Both Statement I and Statement II are true.

13 Which complex compound is most stable? *[NEET 2023]*

(a) $[Co(NH_3)_3(NO_3)_3]$ (b) $[CoCl_2(en)_2]NO_3$
(c) $[Co(NH_3)_6]_2(SO_4)_3$ (d) $[Co(NH_3)_4(H_2O)Br](NO_3)_2$

14 Aluminium chloride in acidified aqueous solution forms a complex '*A*', in which hybridisation state of Al is '*B*'. What are '*A*' and '*B*', respectively? *[NEET (Odisha) 2019]*

(a) $[Al(H_2O)_6]^{3+}$, sp^3d^2 (b) $[Al(H_2O)_4]^{3+}$, sp^3
(c) $[Al(H_2O)_4]^{3+}$, dsp^2 (d) $[Al(H_2O)_6]^{3+}$, d^2sp^3

15 The geometry and magnetic behaviour of the complex $[Ni(CO)_4]$ are *[NCERT (New) Pg. 129, NEET 2018]*

(a) square planar geometry and paramagnetic
(b) tetrahedral geometry and diamagnetic
(c) square planar geometry and diamagnetic
(d) tetrahedral geometry and paramagnetic

16 Pick out the correct statement with respect to $[Mn(CN)_6]^{3-}$. *[NCERT (New) Pg. 129, NEET 2017]*

(a) It is sp^3d^2 hybridised and tetrahedral.
(b) It is d^2sp^3 hybridised and octahedral.
(c) It is dsp^2 hybridised and square planar.
(d) It is sp^3d^2 hybridised and octahedral.

17 The hybridisation involved in complex $[Ni(CN)_4]^{2-}$ is (Atomic number of Ni = 28) *[NCERT (New) Pg. 130, AIPMT 2015]*

(a) dsp^2 (b) sp^3 (c) d^2sp^2 (d) d^2sp^3

Module-III Bonding in Coordination Compound (Part-II) Metal Carbonyls, Importance of Coordination Compounds

18 The order of energy absorbed which is responsible for the colour of complexes

(A) $[Ni(H_2O)_2(en)_2]^{2+}$
(B) $[Ni(H_2O)_4(en)]^{2+}$ and
(C) $[Ni(en)_3]^{2+}$ is *[NCERT (New) Pg. 133, NEET 2022]*

(a) (C) > (B) > (A) (b) (C) > (A) > (B)
(c) (B) > (A) > (C) (d) (A) > (B) > (C)

19 Match Column I with Column II. *[NCERT (New) Pg. 131, NEET 2021]*

Column I	Column II
A. $[Fe(CN)_6]^{3-}$	1. 5.92 BM
B. $[Fe(H_2O)_6]^{3+}$	2. 0 BM
C. $[Fe(CN)_6]^{4-}$	3. 4.90 BM
D. $[Fe(H_2O)_6]^{2+}$	4. 1.73 BM

Codes

	A	B	C	D
(a)	4	2	1	3
(b)	2	4	3	1
(c)	1	3	4	2
(d)	4	1	2	3

20 Which of the following is the correct order of increasing field strength of ligands to form coordination compounds? *[NCERT (New) Pg. 132, NEET (Sep.) 2020]*

(a) $SCN^- < F^- < CN^- < C_2O_4^{2-}$
(b) $F^- < SCN^- < C_2O_4^{2-} < CN^-$
(c) $CN^- < C_2O_4^{2-} < SCN^- < F^-$
(d) $SCN^- < F^- < C_2O_4^{2-} < CN^-$

21 The crystal field stabilisation energy (CFSE) for $[CoCl_6]^{4-}$ is 18000 cm^{-1}. The CFSE for $[CoCl_4]^{2-}$ will be *[NCERT (New) Pg. 131, NEET (Odisha) 2019]*

(a) 6000 cm^{-1} (b) 16000 cm^{-1}
(c) 18000 cm^{-1} (d) 8000 cm^{-1}

22 What is the correct electronic configuration of the central atom in $K_4[Fe(CN)_6]$ based on crystal field theory? *[NCERT (New) Pg. 131, NEET (National) 2019]*

(a) $t_{2g}^6 e_g^0$ (b) $e^3 t_2^3$ (c) $e^4 t_2^2$ (d) $t_{2g}^4 e_g^2$

23 Match the metal ions given in Column I with the spin magnetic moments of the ions given in Column II and assign the correct code. *[NCERT (New) Pg. 133, NEET 2018]*

Column I	Column II
A. Co^{3+}	1. $\sqrt{8}$ BM
B. Cr^{3+}	2. $\sqrt{35}$ BM
C. Fe^{3+}	3. $\sqrt{3}$ BM
D. Ni^{2+}	4. $\sqrt{24}$ BM
	5. $\sqrt{15}$ BM

Codes

	A	B	C	D
(a)	4	5	2	1
(b)	1	2	3	4
(c)	3	5	1	2
(d)	4	1	2	3

24 Correct increasing order for the wavelengths of absorption in the visible region for the complexes of Co^{3+} is *[NEET 2017]*

(a) $[Co(en)_3]^{3+}$, $[Co(NH_3)_6]^{3+}$, $[Co(H_2O)_6]^{3+}$
(b) $[Co(H_2O)_6]^{3+}$, $[Co(en)_3]^{3+}$, $[Co(NH_3)_6]^{3+}$
(c) $[Co(H_2O)_6]^{3+}$, $[Co(NH_3)_6]^{3+}$, $[Co(en)_3]^{3+}$
(d) $[Co(NH_3)_6]^{3+}$, $[Co(en)_3]^{3+}$, $[Co(H_2O)_6]^{3+}$

25 An example of a sigma bonded organometallic compound is *[NEET 2017]*

(a) Grignard's reagent (b) ferrocene
(c) cobaltocene (d) ruthenocene

26 Which of the following has longest C—O bond length? (Free C—O bond length in CO is 1.128 Å) *[NEET 2016]*

(a) $[Ni(CO)_4]$ (b) $[Co(CO)_4]^-$
(c) $[Fe(CO)_4]^{2-}$ (d) $[Mn(CO)_6]^+$

27 The correct increasing order of trans-effect of the following species is *[NEET 2016, Phase II]*

(a) $NH_3 > CN^- > Br^- > C_6H_5^-$
(b) $CN^- > C_6H_5^- > Br^- > NH_3$
(c) $Br^- > CN^- > NH_3 > C_6H_5^-$
(d) $CN^- > Br^- > C_6H_5^- > NH_3$

28 Jahn-Teller effect is not observed in high spin complexes of *[NEET 2016, Phase II]*

(a) d^7 (b) d^8 (c) d^4 (d) d^9

29 Which of these statements about $[Co(CN)_6]^{3-}$ is true? *[AIPMT 2015]*

(a) $[Co(CN)_6]^{3-}$ has no unpaired electrons and will be in a low-spin configuration.
(b) $[Co(CN)_6]^{3-}$ has four unpaired electrons and will be in a low-spin configuration.
(c) $[Co(CN)_6]^{3-}$ has four unpaired electrons and will be in a high-spin configuration.
(d) $[Co(CN)_6]^{3-}$ has no unpaired electrons and will be in a high-spin configuration.

30 Among the following complexes, the one which shows zero crystal field stabilisation energy (CFSE) is *[NCERT (New) Pg. 131, AIPMT 2014]*

(a) $[Mn(H_2O)_6]^{3+}$ (b) $[Fe(H_2O)_6]^{3+}$
(c) $[Co(H_2O)_6]^{2+}$ (d) $[Co(H_2O)_6]^{3+}$

31 Which of the following complexes is used to be as an anticancer agent? *[AIPMT 2014]*

(a) *mer*- $[Co(NH_3)_3Cl_3]$ (b) *cis*- $[PtCl_2(NH_3)_2]$
(c) *cis*- $K_2[PtCl_2Br_2]$ (d) Na_2CoCl_4

Answers

Step up Practice 1

1 (a)	2 (b)	3 (b)	4 (d)	5 (a)	6 (d)	7 (d)	8 (d)	9 (a)	10 (a)
11 (b)	12 (d)	13 (b)	14 (b)	15 (c)	16 (d)	17 (d)	18 (d)	19 (a)	

Step up Practice 2

1 (a)	2 (d)	3 (a)	4 (d)	5 (b)	6 (c)	7 (a)	8 (d)	9 (a)	10 (b)
11 (d)	12 (b)	13 (c)	14 (c)	15 (b)	16 (c)	17 (d)	18 (d)	19 (c)	20 (c)
21 (c)									

Step up Practice 3

1 (a)	2 (a)	3 (b)	4 (a)	5 (b)	6 (c)	7 (d)	8 (b)	9 (c)	10 (a)
11 (d)	12 (c)	13 (d)	14 (d)						

Gearing up for NEET

1 (a)	2 (b)	3 (d)	4 (a)	5 (b)	6 (a)	7 (d)	8 (c)	9 (c)	10 (b)
11 (b)	12 (a)	13 (c)	14 (a)	15 (a)	16 (c)	17 (d)	18 (d)	19 (b)	20 (d)
21 (d)	22 (d)	23 (d)	24 (a)	25 (c)	26 (c)	27 (a)	28 (d)	29 (b)	30 (d)
31 (a)	32 (c)	33 (b)	34 (c)	35 (c)	36 (b)	37 (b)	38 (d)	39 (a)	40 (a)
41 (c)	42 (a)	43 (b)	44 (d)	45 (b)	46 (d)	47 (c)	48 (d)	49 (d)	50 (b)
51 (d)	52 (c)								

Final Check through PYQs : Module-I

1 (d)	2 (a)	3 (d)	4 (c)	5 (a)	6 (c)	7 (a)	8 (d)	9 (c)	10 (c)
11 (a)									

Final Check through PYQs : Module-II

12 (d)	13 (b)	14 (a)	15 (b)	16 (b)	17 (a)

Final Check through PYQs : Module-III

18 (b)	19 (d)	20 (d)	21 (d)	22 (a)	23 (a)	24 (a)	25 (a)	26 (c)	27 (b)
28 (b)	29 (a)	30 (b)	31 (b)						

Hints and Solutions

Step up Practice 1

1. (a) $CoCl_3 \cdot 6NH_3$ exists as $[Co(NH_3)_6]Cl_3$ in which six NH_3 ligands are coordinated to cobalt.

2. (b) $CuSO_4 \cdot 5H_2O$ is a monohydrate salt with four H_2O ligands coordinated to Cu^{2+}.

$$[Cu(H_2O)_4]SO_4 \cdot H_2O$$

Fifth H_2O is joined to SO_4^{2-} by H-bonding.

3. (b) Ligand must donate a pair of electron or loosely held electron pair to metal and form a *M*—*L* bond.

e.g. $:\ddot{N}{=}O$, $N\ddot{H}_2CH_2CH_2\ddot{N}H_2$, $:CO$,

Among the given species NH_4^+ does not have any pair of electron.

Hence, NH_4^+ is not a ligand.

4. (d) NO_2^- is an ambidentate ligand and act as Lewis base. It has two binding donor atoms and can coordinate either through nitrogen or through oxygen to a central metal atom or ion. Thus, both Statement I and Statement II are true.

5. (a) The number of central metal atom in a complex is determined by number of sigma bonds.

6. (d) Both Statement I and Statement II are true.

7. (d) Among the given complexes $[Fe(CN)_6]^{4-}$ is a homoleptic complex, as it consists of only one kind of ligand.

8. (d) Among the following the incorrect match is given in (d).

Oxidation state of central metal ion can be calculated by considering the oxidation state of whole molecule is equal to charge present on coordination sphere.

(a) $[Co(NCS)(NH_3)_5]SO_3$

Let the oxidation state of Co be *x*.

$$x - 1 + 5 \times 0 = +2$$
$$x = +2 + 1 \Rightarrow +3$$

(b) $[Co(NH_3)_4Cl_2]SO_4$

Let the oxidation state of Co = *x*

$$\Rightarrow \quad x + 4 \times 0 + 2 \times (-1) = +2$$
$$\Rightarrow \quad x - 2 = +2 \Rightarrow x = +4$$

(c) $Na_4[Co(S_2O_3)_3]$

Let the oxidation state of Co = *x*

$$x + 3 \times (-2) = -4$$
$$x - 6 = -4$$
$$x = -4 + 6 \Rightarrow +2$$

(d) $[Co_2(CO)_8]$

Let the oxidation state of Co = *x*

$$2x - 8 \times 0 = 0 \Rightarrow x = 0$$

9. (a) O_2^- (superoxide) — monodentate

en — bidentate

Br^- — monodentate

Thus, coordination number of Pt is 6.

$$[Pt(O_2)(en)_2(Br)]^{2+}$$
$$\downarrow \quad \downarrow \quad \downarrow \quad \downarrow$$
$$x - 1 + 0 - 1 = 2$$
$$\therefore \quad x = +4$$

Thus, oxidation number of Pt = +4.

10. (a) The oxidation state of central metal is zero in metal carbonyls.

11. (b) The IUPAC name of the given complex is diammine silver(I) dicyanidoargentate(I).

12. (d) The IUPAC name of the given compound is potassium tris(oxalato)aluminate(III).

13. (b) The correct match is A-2, B-1, C-4, D-3.

14. (b) Among the given compounds only $[Pd(PPh_3)_2(NCS)_2]$ and $[Pd(PPh_3)_2(SCN)_2]$ show linkage isomerism due to presence of ambidentate ligands.

15. (c) Coordination isomerism is caused by exchange of ligands between complex cation and complex anion.

16. (d) Among the given square planar complexes, MA_2B_2 complex will show two geometrical isomer.

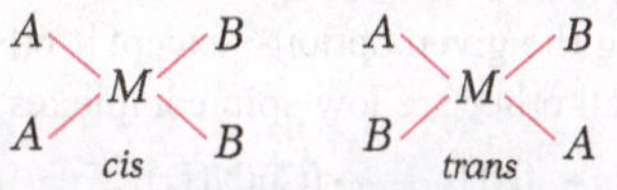

17. (d) Total four isomers are possible which are geometrical, i.e. *cis* and *trans* and linkage isomers (—SCN and —NCS).

18. (d) $[Co(en)_3]^{3+}$ shows two optically active isomers, i.e. *d* and *l* forms.

19. (a) Geometrical isomerism is found in compound having coordination number 4 (square planar but not tetrahedral shaped) as well as coordination number 6.

Step up Practice 2

1. (a) $[Co(NH_3)_3Cl_3]$ is molecular complex and no ionisation occur.

Primary valency is three thus only (a) is correct.

========= Indicates primary and secondary valencies

———— Indicates secondary valencies

--------- Indicates primary valencies

2. (d) $[Pt(NH_3)_4Cl_2]Cl_2 \rightleftharpoons [Pt(NH_3)_4Cl_2]^+ + 2Cl^-$

Two Cl^- ligands are also in coordination sphere thus, they satisfy primary as well as secondary valencies. Four NH_3 ligands satisfy secondary valencies.

3. (*a*) Primary valency or oxidation state of Fe in $K_4[Fe(CN)_6]$ is

$$4(+1) + x + 6(-1) = 0 \Rightarrow x = +2$$

4. (*d*) 1 mole of $AgNO_3$ precipitates one free chloride ion (Cl^-).
Here, 3 moles of AgCl are precipitated by excess of $AgNO_3$. Hence, there must be three free Cl^- ions.
So, the formula of the complex is $[Cr(H_2O)_6]Cl_3$.

5. (*b*) $\underset{1\text{ mol}}{CoCl_3 \cdot 6H_2O} + AgNO_3 \longrightarrow 2\text{ mol AgCl}$
Thus, two Cl atoms are outside the coordination sphere.
C.N. of Co = 6
Thus, $[Co(H_2O)_5Cl]\,Cl_2 \cdot H_2O$.

6. (*c*) The number of unpaired electrons in $[Ni(NH_3)_6]^{2+}$ is 2 and not 4.

7. (*a*) The oxidation number of iron in $[Fe(CO)_5]$ is 0.
Since, CO is a strong field ligand, pairing occurs to rearrange the electrons in 3*d* subshell.

Fe in $[Fe(CO)_5]$	3d					4s	4p		
	⇅	⇅	⇅	⇅	××	××	××	××	××

Five dsp^3 bond to ligands

8. (*d*) Among the given options incorrect match is given in option (d). Its correct hybridisation is sp^3d^2.

9. (*a*) Ni in $[Ni(NH_3)_6]^{2+}$ has sp^3d^2-hybridisation which is an outer complex, having octahedral geometry.

10. (*b*) Among the given options, except $[Co(H_2O)_6]^{2+}$ and $[CoF_6]^{3-}$ all other are low spin complexes.

11. (*d*) $CuSO_4 + 4NH_3 \longrightarrow [Cu(NH_3)_4]^{2-}$
Thus, the compound is square planar and paramagnetic.

12. (*b*) The geometry and magnetic behaviour of given complex is square planar and diamagnetic respectively.

13. (*c*) Statement II is true.
According to VBT, molecular orbital electronic configuration of Fe^{3+} in $[Fe(CN)_6]^{3-}$ is

$[_{18}Ar]$	3d					4s	4p		
	⇅	⇅	1	××	××	××	××	××	××
				CN^-	CN^-	CN^-	CN^-	CN^-	CN^-

Hybridisation [Fe(III)] = d^2sp^3, Number of unpaired electrons (n) = 1
Hence, correct form of Statement I is :
$[Fe(CN)_6]^{3-}$ ion shows magnetic moment corresponding to one unpaired electron.
i.e. $\mu = \sqrt{n(n+2)} = \sqrt{1(1+2)}$
$= \sqrt{3} = 1.73$ BM
Thus, Statement I is false but Statement II is true.

14. (*c*) The incorrect statement is given in option (c). Its correct form is that, the complex is an inner orbital complex, i.e. d^2sp^3, of Cr(III).

15. (*b*) (a) $[Mn(CN)_6]^{3-}$ $Mn^{3+} = 3d^4$

1	1	1	1	

$[Mn(CN)_6]^{3-}$ =	3d					4s	4p		
	⇅	1	1	××	××	××	××	××	××
				CN^-	CN^-	CN^-	CN^-	CN^-	CN^-

d^2sp^3-hybridisation

(i) d^2sp^3-hybridisation of Mn(III).
(ii) Inner orbital complex because $(n-1)\,d$-orbitals are used.
(iii) Paramagnetic, as two unpaired electrons are present.
(iv) Spin only magnetic moment
$(\mu) = \sqrt{2\,(2+2)} = \sqrt{8} = 2.82$ BM

(b) $[Co(NH_3)_6]^{3+}$
$Co^{3+} = 3d^6\,4s^0$

$3d^6$				
⇅	1	1	1	1

$[Co(NH_3)_6]^{3+}$ =	3d					4s	4p		
	⇅	⇅	⇅	××	××	××	××	××	××

d^2sp^3

(NH_3 pair up the unpaired 3*d* electrons.)
(i) d^2sp^3-hybridisation of Co(III)
(ii) Inner orbital complex because of the involvement of $(n-1)$ *d*-orbitals in bonding.
(iii) Diamagnetic, as no unpaired electron is present.
(iv) $\mu = \sqrt{n\,(n+2)}$
$= \sqrt{0\,(0+2)} = 0$ (zero)

(c) $[Cr(H_2O)_6]^{3+}$

$Cr^{3+} = 3d^3\,4s^0$ =	$3d^3$					$4s^0$
	1	1	1			

$[Cr(H_2O)_6]^{3+}$ =	3d					4s	4p		
	1	1	1	××	××	××	××	××	××

d^2sp^3

(i) d^2sp^3-hybridisation of Cr(III).
(ii) Inner orbital complex [as $(n-1)\,d$-orbitals take part.]
(iii) Paramagnetic (as three unpaired electrons are present.)
(iv) $\mu = \sqrt{n\,(n+2)}$
$= \sqrt{3\,(3+2)} = \sqrt{15} = 3.87$ BM

(d) $[Fe(Cl)_6]^{4-}$

$Fe^{2+} = 3d^6$

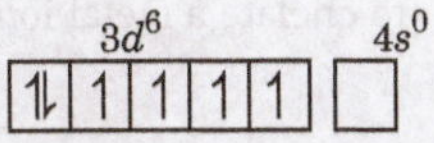

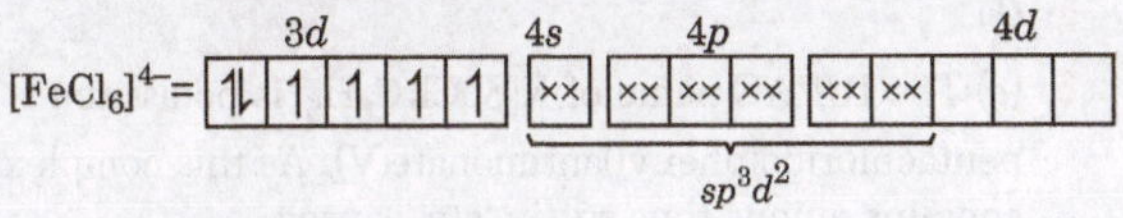

(i) sp^3d^2-hybridisation of Fe(II).

(ii) Outer orbital complex because *nd*-orbitals are involved in hybridisation.

(iii) Paramagnetic (because of the presence of four unpaired electrons).

(iv) $\mu = \sqrt{n(n+2)} = \sqrt{4(4+2)} = \sqrt{24} = 4.9$ BM

16. (*c*)

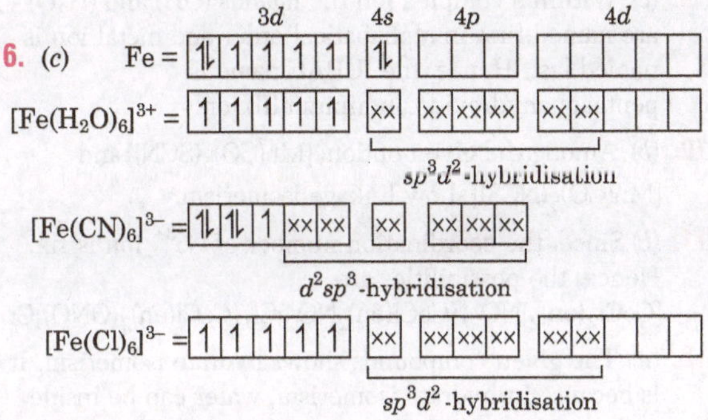

17. (*d*) $[Fe(H_2O)_6]^{3+}$ has five unpaired electrons.

18. (*d*) Since, hybridisation of $[Pt(NH_3)_4]Cl_2$ is dsp^2 so, it is square planar.

19. (*c*) $Ni(CO)_4$ has sp^3 hybridisation of Ni(0), so it geometry would be tetrahedral whereas $Ni(PPh_3)_2Cl_2$ has dsp^2 hybridisation of Ni(II) so its would be square planar.

20. (*c*) [A-3, B-1, C-4, D-2]

A. $[Cr(H_2O)_6]^{3+}$

MOEC (Molecular orbital electronic configuration) of Cr^{3+} in $[Cr(H_2O)_6]^{3+}$ is

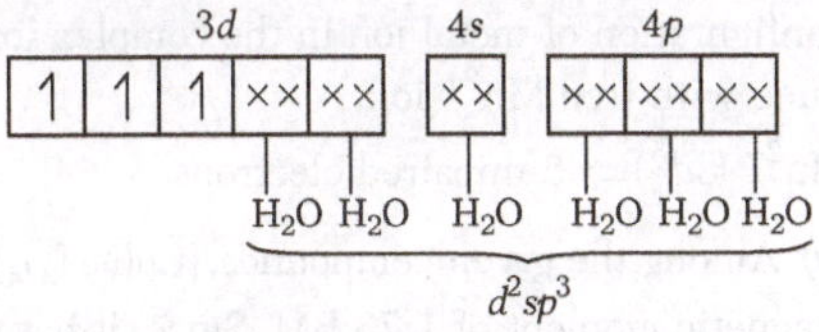

$\Rightarrow$ n (number of unpaired electrons) = 3

B. $[Co(CN)_4]^{2-}$

MOEC of Co^{2+} in $[Co(CN)_4]^{2-}$ is

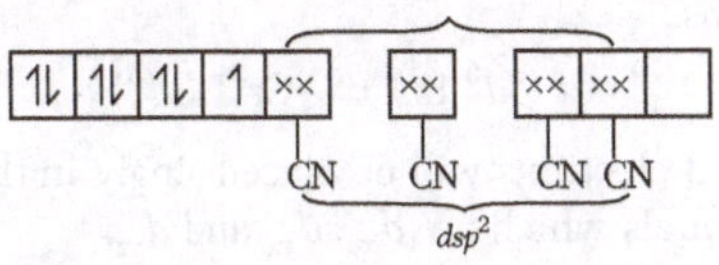

$\Rightarrow n = 1$

C. $[Ni(NH_3)_6]^{2+}$

MOEC of Ni^{2+} in $[Ni(NH_3)_6]^{2+}$ is

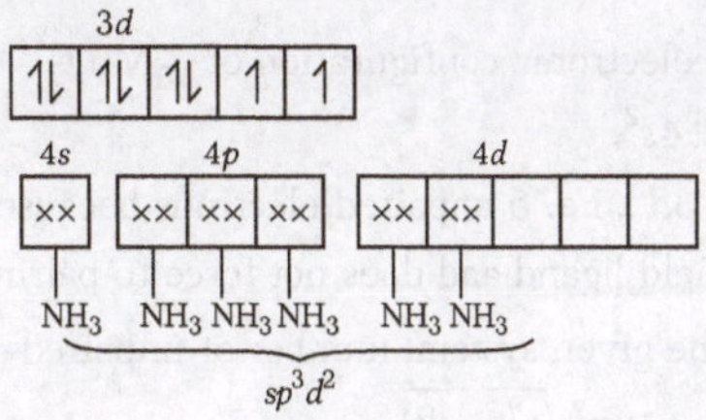

$\Rightarrow n = 2$

D. $[MnF_6]^{4-}$

MOEC of Mn^{2+} in $[MnF_6]^{4-}$ is

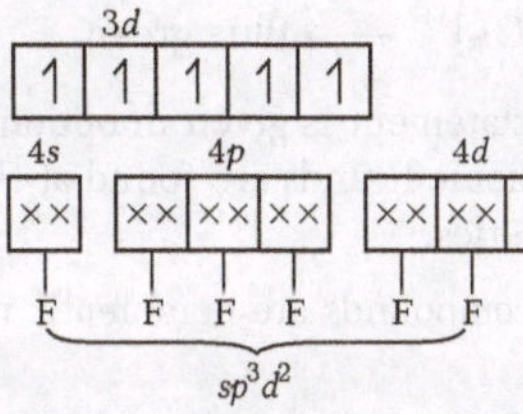

$\Rightarrow n = 5$

21. (*c*) Incorrect statement is given in option (c). Its correct form is :
It does not distinguish between weak and strong ligands.

Step up Practice 3

1. (*a*) In case of CFSE, for octahedral and tetrahedral, the relation is $\Delta_t = \frac{4}{9}\Delta_o$.

2. (*a*) Among the given options $[Co(CN)_6]^{3-}$ will have highest Δ_o value as CN^- is a very strong ligand.

3. (*b*) M^{n+} has five *d* electrons and *L* is a weak ligand, then it cannot force electrons to be paired up. Hence, the number of unpaired electrons will be 5.

4. (*a*) Among the given options, d^5 (octahedral) complex, high spin has maximum number of unpaired electrons.

5. (*b*) Among the given options, the strongest field ligand is CN^-.

6. (*c*) The correct order is

$[Cr(H_2O)_6]^{3+} < [Cr(NH_3)_6]^{3+} < Cr(NO_2)_6]^{3+}$.

It is because for same cation, stronger the ligand, higher will be the Δ_o.

7. (*d*) Strong field ligand produces more crystal field splitting while weak field ligand produces small crystal field splitting. Among the given options all are weak field ligand, so small crystal field splitting is there.

8. (*b*) Based on spectrochemical series, ligands arranged in increasing order of crystal field strength are as follows

$$NH_3 < en < CN^- < CO$$

9. (*c*) The electronic configuration of $_{25}Mn$ is $[Ar]\,3d^5 4s^2$.
Mn^{2+} : $3d^5$, i.e. 5 unpaired electrons because H_2O is weak field ligand and does not force to pairing.

10. (*a*) In the given system, number of unpaired $e^- = 2$

So, $\mu = \sqrt{n(n+2)}$

$= \sqrt{2\,(2+2)} = 2.83$ BM

11. (*d*) The incorrect match is given in option (d) and its correct form is

$$[Ti(H_2O)_6]^{3+} \longrightarrow \text{Blue green.}$$

12. (*c*) The incorrect statement is given in option (c). Its correct form is anionic ligands are found at the row of spectrochemical series.

13. (*d*) All the given compounds are homoleptic metal carbonyls.

14. (*d*) The Wilkinson catalyst contains rhodium.

Gearing up for NEET

1. (*a*) The given feature is a major differentiating point in between complex and double salt and is a characteristic of double salt.

2. (*b*) The oxidation number is $[Co(en)_2Cl_2]Cl$

$$x + 2(0) + (-2) = +1$$
$$x = +3$$

and since the compound contains 4 donor sites of two (en) molecules and 2 donor sites of Cl^- ions. Hence, coordination number is 6.

3. (*d*) The coordination number of Pt in the complex ion is 6. It is because (en) is a bidentate ligand and Cl^- is monodentate.

4. (*a*) A chelating ligand has two or more binding donor atoms attached to a single metal ion.
e.g.

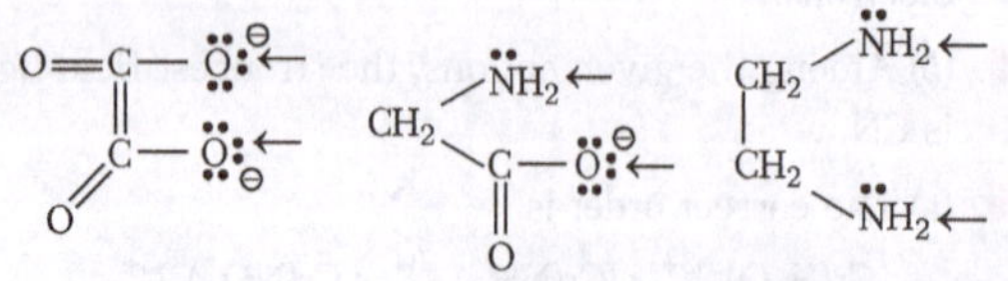

Oxalato Glycinato Ethane-1, 2-diamine

Here, (←) denotes binding site.

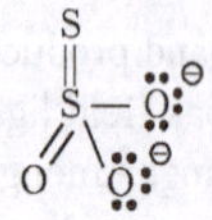

Among the given ligands, thiosulphato ($S_2O_3^{2-}$) is not a chelating ligand because geometrically it is not favourable for $S_2O_3^{2-}$ to chelate a metal ion. It is a monodentate ligand.

5. (*b*)

6. (*a*) The IUPAC name of $K[SbCl_5C_6H_5]$ is potassium pentachlorido(phenyl)antimonate(V). As this complex contains anions thus suffix 'ate' is used.

7. (*d*) The IUPAC name of the given compound is pentaammine(dinitrogen)ruthenium(II) chloride. As cations are named before anions.

8. (*c*) The formula of potassium tetrahydroxidozincate (II) is $K_2[Zn(OH)_4]$.

9. (*c*) Within a complex ion the ligands (OH) and (H_2O) are named first in alphabetical order and metal ion is named last. Hence, the IUPAC name is pentaaquahydroxidoaluminium(III) ion.

10. (*b*) Among the given option, $[Mn(CO)_5(SCN)]$ and $[Mn(CO)_5(NCS)]$ show linkage isomerism.

11. (*b*) Since, the coordination number of Co^{3+} ion is six. Hence, the possibilities are $[CoCl_2(en)_2]NO_2$, $[CoCl(en)_2NO_2]Cl$, $[CoCl(en)_2(ONO)]Cl$

12. (*a*) The given compounds shows hydrate isomerism. It is because in hydrate isomerism, water can be inside and outside the coordination sphere.

13. (*c*) The given compounds shows coordination isomerism because of interchange of ligands between the cations and anion takes place.

14. (*b*) $2 + 4(-1) = x$

$\Rightarrow \quad x = -2$

15. (*a*) Among the given compounds $[Zn(NH_3)_6]^{2+}$ is an outer orbital complex as well as diamagnetic in behaviour with sp^3d^2 hybridisation of Zn(II).

16. (*c*) Since, water (H_2O) is a weak field ligand, there is no change in electronic configuration. Thus, electronic configuration of metal ion in the complex ion is the same with free Mn^{2+} ion.

$Mn^{2+}\ (3d^5) \Rightarrow$ 5 unpaired electrons.

17. (*d*) Among the given compounds, $[Cu(NH_3)_4]^{2+}$ shows magnetic moment of 1.73 BM. Since, it has one unpaired electron.

18. (*d*) Given that, magnetic moment is 3.83 BM, which lies between 3 and 4, so, there are three unpaired electrons.

$$Cr\ (3d^5 4s^1) \Rightarrow Cr^{3+}\ (3d^3)$$

All the 3 electrons will be placed singly in the t_{2g} set of *d*-orbitals which are d_{xy}, d_{yx} and d_{xz}.

19. (*b*) Examples of π-bonded organometallic compound.
Zeise's salt : $K[PtCl_3(\eta^2 - C_2H_4)]$
Ferrocene : $[Fe(\eta^5 - C_5H_5)_2]$
Dibenzene chromium : $[Cr(\eta^2 - C_6H_6)_2]$

20. (*d*) Incorrect statement is given in option (d). It is because chlorophyll contains magnesium.

21. (*d*) A is false but R is true. The correct form of A is : In the complex $[Co(NH_3)_3Cl_3]$ chlorides ions satisfy the primary valency as well as the secondary valency of cobalt (III).

22. (*d*) A is false but R is true.
The correct form of A is :
In $[Co(Cl_2)(en)_2]$ coordination number of Co is 6 and this compound has an octahedral geometry.

23. (*d*) A is false but R is true.
The correct form of A is $[Fe(CN)_6]^{3-}$ ion shows magnetic moment corresponding to one unpaired electron.

24. (*a*) Both A and R are true but R is the correct explanation of A.

25. (*c*) A is true but R is false. The correct form of R is :
Ethylenediamine is a strong field ligand and form stable complexes.

26. (*c*) A is true but R is false. The correct form of R is :
In complex $[Fe(CN)_6]^{3-}$, the central metal ion has one unpaired electron.

27. (*a*) Both A and R are true and R is the correct explanation of A.

28. (*d*) Both Statement I and Statement II are true.

29. (*b*) Statement I is true but Statement II is false. Its correct form is EDTA is a hexadentate ligand.

30. (*d*) Both Statement I and Statement II are true.

31. (*a*) Both Statement I and Statement II are false. Their Reason is square planar complex has a plane of symmetry, hence they are not optically active.

32. (*c*) Statement I is false but Statement II is true.
The correct form of Statement I is :
The denticity of metal attached with EDTA in an octahedral complex is 6.

33. (*b*) Statement I is true but Statement II is false.
The correct form of Statement II is :
$[MnCl_6]^{3-}$ and $[FeF_6]^{3-}$ are paramagnetic and have 4 and 5 unpaired electrons respectively.

34. (*c*) Statement I is false but Statement II is true. The correct form of Statement I is EDTA is used in the treatment of lead poisoning.

35. (*c*) Statement D is incorrect. Its correct form is while writing the formula of the compound, the central atom is listed first followed by ligands in alphabetical order.

36. (*b*) Among the given statements, only B, C and E are correct while the other statements A and D are incorrect.
Their correct forms are :
- A coordination entity constitutes a central metal atom or ion bonded to fixed number of ions or molecules for tetrahedral complex.
- Coordination number of the central atom/ion can be determined only by the number of sigma bonds formed by the ligand with the central atom/ion, except organometallic compounds.

37. (*b*) Among the given statements, A and B are correct while the statements C, D and E are incorrect.
Their corrected forms are :
- The primary valency of the metal ion is satisfied by negative ions.
- The primary valency is normally ionisable.
- Neutral molecules satisfy the secondary valency in a complex.

38. (*d*) Among the given statements, only C, D and E are correct while the statements A and B are incorrect.
Their corrected forms are :
- The complex $[NiCl_4]^{2-}$ is an outer orbital complex.
- The complex $[Mn(CN)_6]^{4-}$ is an inner orbital complex.

39. (*a*) Among the given statements, only A, B and C are incorrect while the statements D and E are correct.
The corrected forms of A, B and C are :
- Ligands are treated as point charges in case of anions or point dipoles in case of neutral molecules.
- The degeneracy of the *d*-orbitals can be removed by the ligand electron-metal electron repulsions in the octahedral complex.
- For octahedral complexes, the energy of the two e_g orbitals will increase by $\frac{3}{5}\Delta_o$.

40. (*a*) Among the given statements, only A, C and D are incorrect while the statements B and E are correct.
The corrected forms of A, C and D are :
- The cation is named first in both positively and negatively charged coordination entities.
- Name of all the anionic ligands ends with -o.

If the complex ion is an anion, the name of the metal ends with the suffix -ate.

41. (c) Among the given statements only A, C and E are correct while the other statements B and D are incorrect. Their corrected forms are :
  - Octacarbonyldicobalt(0) has a Co—Co bond bridged by two CO molecules.
  - The metal to ligand bonding creates a synergic effect which strengthens the bond between CO and the metal.

42. (a) Among the given compounds, only three compounds, i.e. $[Fe(NH_3)_4Cl_2]^+$, $[Co(en)(NH_3)_2]^{2+}$ and $[Co(NH_3)_3(NO_2)_3]$ are heteroleptic in nature.

43. (b) Among the given compounds, only four, i.e. $[V(H_2O)_6]^{2+}$, $[Fe(CN)_6]^{3-}$, $[Co(H_2O)_6]^{3+}$ and $[Co(C_2O_4)_3]^{3-}$ have d^2sp^3-hybridisation of the central metal ions.

44. (d) Among the given ligands, only two ligands NO_2^- and SCN^- are ambidentate in nature.

45. (b) Among the given compounds only three i.e. $[Co(C_2O_4)_3]^{3-}$, $[Ni(CN)_4]^{2-}$ and $[PtCl_2(NH_3)(OH_2)]$ are diamagnetic in nature.

46. (d) Among the given compounds, only two compounds $[Co(NH_3)_6]^{3+}$ and $[Mn(CN)_6]^{4-}$ are inner orbital complexes.

47. (c) Among the given ligands only four, i.e. $C_2O_4^{2-}$, OH^-, S^{2-} and SCN^- are placed before H_2O in spectrochemical series.

48. (d) The correct match is A-4, B-3, C-2, D-1.

49. (d) The correct match is A-4, B-3, C-2, D-1.

50. (b) The correct match is A-3, B-4, C-2, D-1.

51. (d) The correct match is A-3, B-1, C-4, D-2.

52. (c) The correct match is A-3, B-4, C-1, D-2.

Final Check through PYQs

1. (d) Both Statement I and Statement II are true.

2. (a) The correct match is A-2, B-3, C-4, D-1.
  - $[Co(NH_3)_5(NO_2)]Cl_2$ is an example of linkage isomerism. It arises in a compound containing ambidentate ligand.
  - $[Co(NH_3)_5(SO_4)]Br$ is an example of ionisation isomerism. This form of isomerism arises when the counter ion in a complex salt is itself a potential ligand and can displace a ligand which can become counter ion.
  - $[Co(NH_3)_6][Cr(CN)_6]$ is an example of coordination isomerism. It arises from interchange of ligands between cationic and anionic entities of different metal ions present in a complex.
  - $[Co(H_2O)_6]Cl_2$ is an example of solvate isomerism, in this isomerism water is involved as a solvent.

3. (d) Among the given option potassium trioxalatoaluminate (III) is an example of homoleptic complex while all other are examples of hetroleptic complexes.

Complexes in which a metal is bound to only one kind of donor groups are known as **homoleptic complexes.**

While the complexes in which a metal is bonded to more than one kind of donor groups are known as heteroleptic complexes.

4. (c) The complex $[Ag(H_2O)_2][Ag(CN)_2]$ has coordination number 2 and oxidation state of Ag^+ is +1 in both cationic and anionic parts.

Hence, its IUPAC name is diaquasilver (I) dicyanidoargentate (I).

5. (a) Ethylene diaminetetraacetate $(EDTA)^{2-}$ ion.

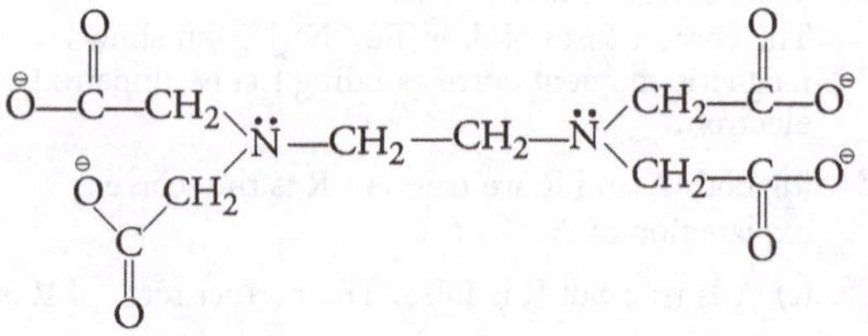

$(EDTA)^{2-}$ is a hexadentate ligand with four 'O' and two 'N' donor atoms.

6. (c) Isomers in which the atoms or ligands occupy different positions around central metal/ion are called geometrical isomers.

In $[CoCl_2(en)_2]$, coordination number of Co is 6 with octahedral geometry.

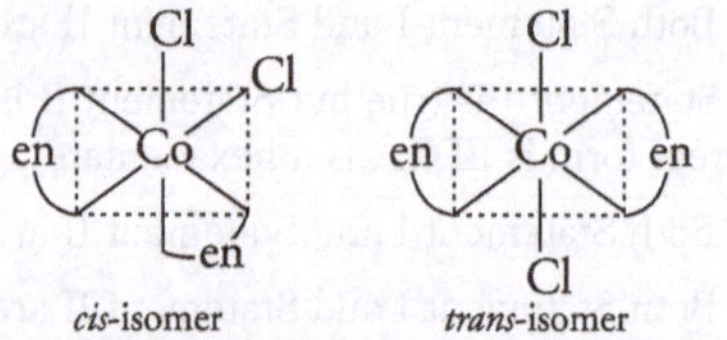

cis-isomer (Optically active) | *trans*-isomer (Optically inactive)

Thus, $[CoCl_2(en)_2]$ shows geometrical isomerism.

7. (a) Given complex compound is $[M(en)_2(C_2O_4)]Cl$.

Let oxidation number of M is x.

$\therefore \quad x + 2\times 0 + 1\times(-2) = +1$

or $\quad x = +3$

Now, as coordination number is defined as the total number of binding sites attached to the metal.

Hence, in the given complex coordination number is 6.

So, the sum of coordination number and oxidation number of the M in the given complex is 9.

8. (d) $[Fe(CN)_6]^{3-}$ = Hexacyanidoferrate (III) ion.

9. (*c*) According to Werner's theory,

$$CoCl_3 \cdot 6NH_3 \longrightarrow [Co(NH_3)_6]^{3+} 3Cl^-$$

$$CoCl_3 \cdot 5NH_3 \longrightarrow [Co(NH_3)_5Cl]^{2+} 2Cl^-$$

$$CoCl_3 \cdot 4NH_3 \longrightarrow [Co(NH_3)_4Cl_2]^+ Cl^-$$

When $AgNO_3$ in excess is treated with these complexes then following reactions takes place :

$$\Rightarrow [Co(NH_3)_6]^{3+} 3Cl^- + \underset{(Excess)}{AgNO_3} \longrightarrow 3AgCl + [Co(NH_3)_6]^{3+}$$

$$\Rightarrow [Co(NH_3)_5Cl]^{2+} 2Cl^- + \underset{(Excess)}{AgNO_3} \longrightarrow 2AgCl + [Co(NH_3)_5Cl]^{2+}$$

$$\Rightarrow [Co(NH_3)_4Cl_2]^+ Cl^- + \underset{(excess)}{AgNO_3} \longrightarrow AgCl + [Co(NH_3)_4Cl_2]^+$$

10. (*c*) $[Co(en)_2Cl_2]Cl$

Possible isomers are

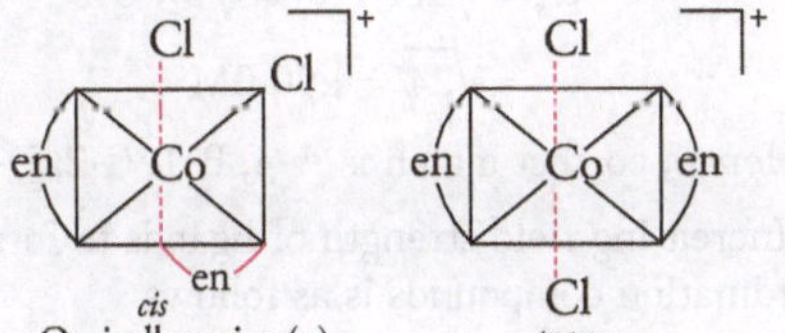

cis Optically active (±) Stereoisomers =2   *trans* Optically inactive Stereoisomers =1

Hence, total number of stereoisomers = 2 + 1 = 3.

11. (*a*) $[Co(NH_3)_6]Cl_3 \longrightarrow [Co(NH_3)_6]^{3+} + 3Cl^-$

$[Co(NH_3)_3Cl_3] \longrightarrow [Co(NH_3)_3Cl_3]$ (non-electrolyte)

$[Co(NH_3)_4Cl_2]\,Cl \longrightarrow [Co(NH_3)_4Cl_2]^+ + Cl^-$

$[Co(NH_3)_5Cl]Cl_2 \longrightarrow [Co(NH_3)_5Cl]^{2+} + 2Cl^-$

So, $[Co(NH_3)_3Cl_3]$ does not ionise so does not give test for chloride ions.

12. (*d*) Both Statement I and Statement II are true.

13. (*b*) Among the given complex $[Co(Cl_2)(en)_2]NO_3$ is most stable because it is a chelating complex.

Ligands en coordinate with central metal atom to form two rings. Due to this reason, there is more force of attraction between the central metal ion and the chelating agent. Therefore, it is thermodynamically more stable.

14. (*a*) Aluminium chloride in an acidified aqueous solution forms an octahedral complex.

An octahedral complex, '*A*' which is $[Al(H_2O)_6]^{3+}$ is formed.

$$Al(13) = 1s^2, 2s^2, 2p^6, 3s^2, 3p^1$$

$$Al^{3+} = 1s^2, 2s^2, 2p^6.$$

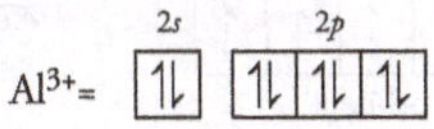

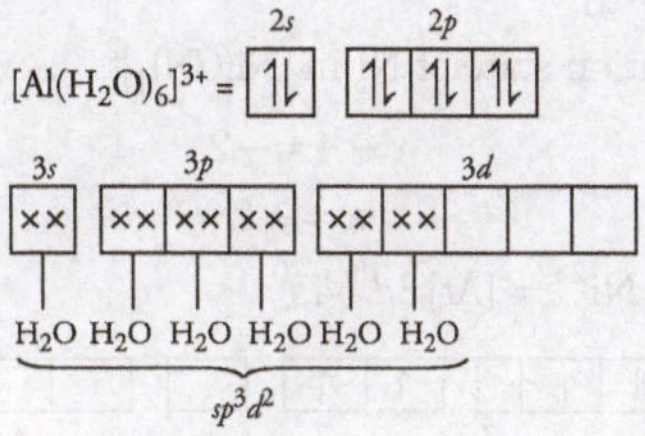

Thus, the hybridisation state of Al(III) in $[Al(H_2O)_6]^{3+}$ is sp^3d^2.

15. (*b*) Electronic configuration of Ni $(Z = 28)$ is $[Ar]_{18}\, 3d^8 4s^2$.

Due to presence of CO (neutral ligand), oxidation state of Ni in $[Ni(CO)_4]$ is 0.

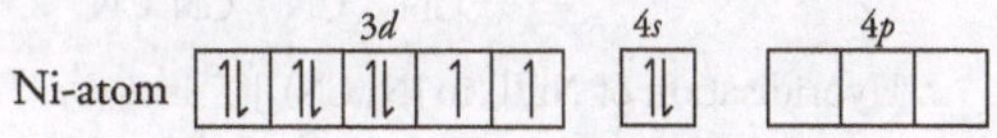

Since, CO is a strong field ligand, it pairs up the unpaired electrons of Ni.

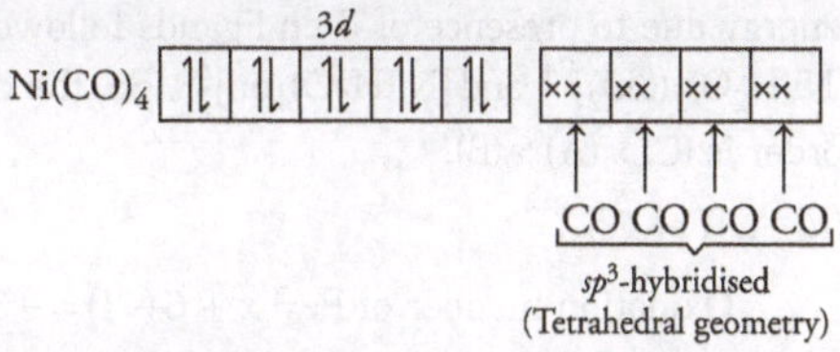

There is no unpaired electron, hence $Ni(CO)_4$ is diamagnetic with tetrahedral geometry.

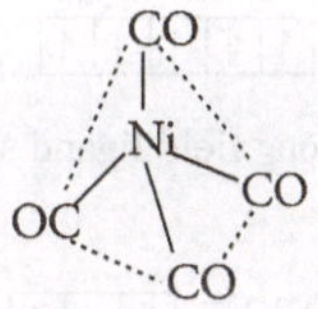

16. (*b*) In the complex $[Mn(CN)_6]^{3-}$, oxidation state of Mn is + 3.

E.C. of $Mn^{+3} \rightarrow 3d^4$

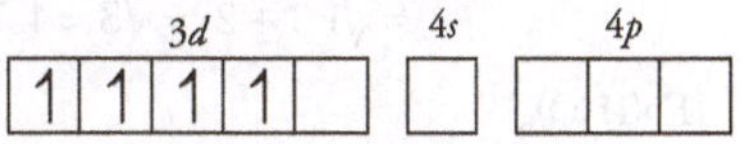

The presence of a strong field ligand CN^- causes pairing of unpaired electrons.

As, coordination number of Mn = 6, so it will form an octahedral complex.

$\therefore [Mn(CN)_6]^{3-} =$

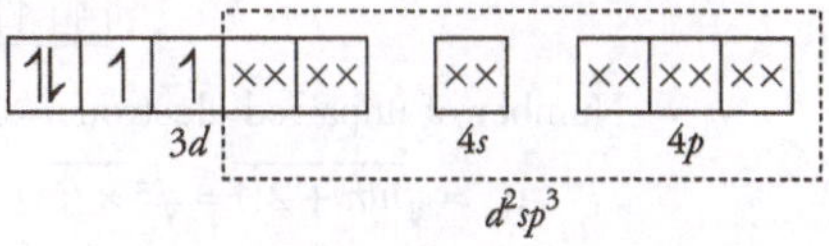

17. (*a*) $[Ni(CN)_4]^{2-}$

Let oxidation state of Ni in $[Ni(CN)_4]^{2-}$ is x.

$\therefore \quad x - 4 = -2$

or $\quad x = +2$

Now, $\quad Ni^{2+} = [Ar]\,3d^8\,4s^0$

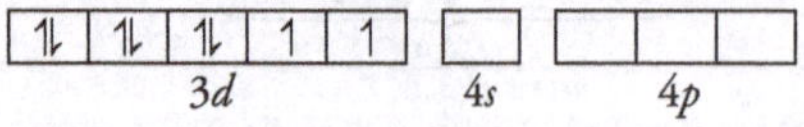

$\because$ CN^- is a strong field ligand. Hence, all unpaired electrons are paired up.

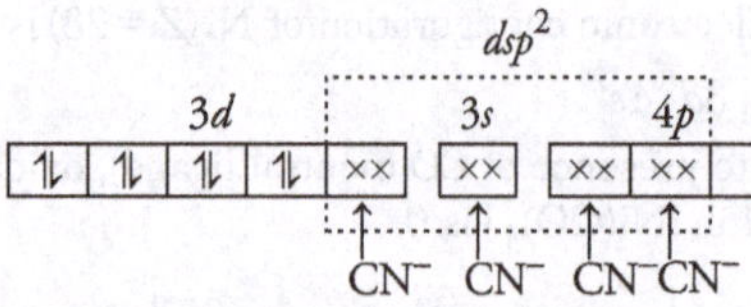

$\therefore$ Hybridisation of Ni(II) in $[Ni(CN)_4]^{2-}$ is dsp^2.

18. (*b*) en is a strong field ligand. As the number of en (strong field ligand) increases, splitting also increases. So, Δ_o increases. Hence, $[Ni(en)_3]^{2+}$ will have highest energy due to presence of 3 en ligands followed by $[Ni(H_2O)_2(en)_2]^{2+}$ and $[Ni(H_2O)_4en]^{2+}$. So, the correct order is (C) > (A) > (B).

19. (*d*) A. $[Fe(CN)_6]^{3-}$

Oxidation number of Fe $= x + 6(-1) = -3$

$x - 6 = -3 \Rightarrow x = +3$

Electronic configuration of $Fe^{3+} \rightarrow [Ar]\,3d^5\,4s^0$

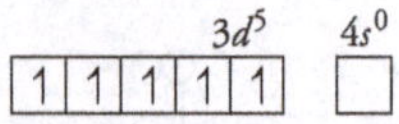

CN^- is a strong field ligand so, pairing of electrons occurs.

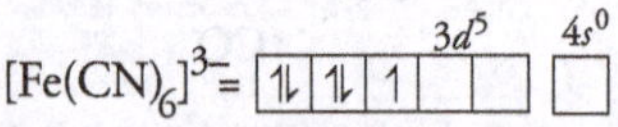

Number of unpaired electrons = 1

$\mu_s = \sqrt{n(n+1)}$

$= \sqrt{1(1+2)} = \sqrt{3} = 1.73$ BM

B. $[Fe(H_2O)_6]^{3+}$

Oxidation state of Fe is +3.

Water is weak field ligand, so pairing of electron does not take place.

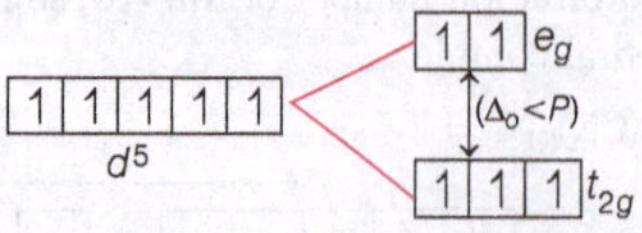

Number of unpaired electrons = 5.

$\mu_s = \sqrt{n(n+2)} = \sqrt{5 \times (5+2)}$

$= \sqrt{5 \times 7} = \sqrt{35} = 5.92$ B.M

C. $[Fe(CN)_6]^{2+}$

Oxidation state of Fe is +2.

Electronic configuration of $Fe^{2+} = [Ar]\,3d^6\,4s^0$

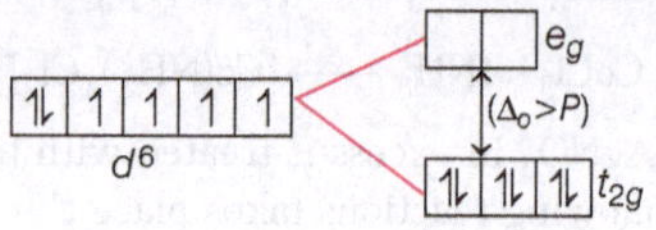

Number of unpaired electrons = 0

$\mu_s = \sqrt{0(0+1)} = 0$ BM

D. $[Fe(H_2O)_6]^{2+}$

Oxidation state of Fe is + 2 $(3d^6)$.

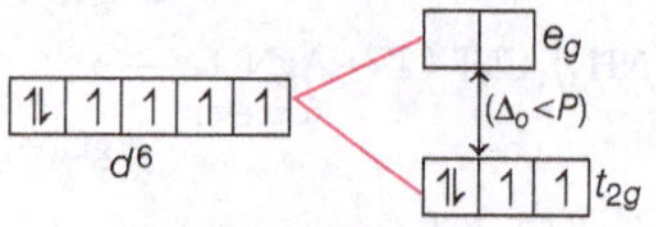

Number of unpaired electrons = 4

$\mu_s = \sqrt{4(4+2)} = \sqrt{4 \times 6}$

$= \sqrt{24} = 4.90$ BM

Hence, correct match is A-4, B-1, C-2, D-3.

20. (*d*) Increasing field strength of ligands to form coordination compounds is as follows

$I^- < Br^- < SCN^- < Cl^- < S^{2-} < F^- < OH^- < C_2O_4^{2-} < H_2O < NCS^- < edta^{4-} < NH_3 < en < CN^- < CO$

So, the order given in option (d) is correct.

$SCN^- < F^- < C_2O_4^{2-} < CN^-$

21. (*d*) $[CoCl_6]^{4-}$ is an octahedral while $[CoCl_4]^{2-}$ is a tetrahedral complex.

$\Delta_{octahedral} = 18000\ cm^{-1}$

We know that,

$\Delta_{tetrahedral} = \frac{4}{9}\Delta_{octahedral} = \frac{4}{9} \times 18000\ cm^{-1} = 8000\ cm^{-1}$

22. (*a*) In $K_4[Fe(CN)_6]$

$Fe^{2+} = [Ar]\,3d^6\,4s^0$.

CN^- is a strong field ligand and as it approaches the metal ion, the electrons must pair up.

The splitting of the *d*-orbitals in two sets orbitals in an octahedral complex, $K_4[Fe(CN)_6]$ may be represented as

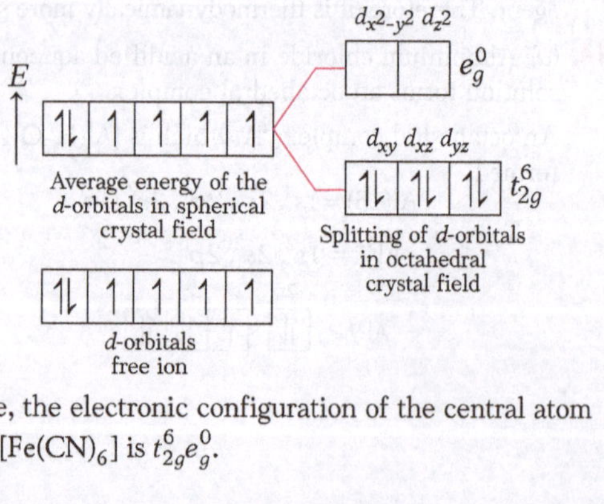

Hence, the electronic configuration of the central atom in $K_4[Fe(CN)_6]$ is $t_{2g}^6 e_g^0$.

23. (*a*) [A-4, B-5, C-2, D-1]

$Co^{3+} = [Ar]\,3d^6$, unpaired $e^-(n) = 4$

Spin magnetic moment

$$\mu = \sqrt{4\,(4+2)} = \sqrt{24} \text{ BM}$$

$Cr^{3+} = [Ar]\,3d^3$, unpaired $e^-(n) = 3$

$$\mu = \sqrt{3\,(3+2)} = \sqrt{15} \text{ BM}$$

$Fe^{3+} = [Ar]\,3d^5$, unpaired $e^-(n) = 5$

$$\mu = \sqrt{5\,(5+2)} = \sqrt{35} \text{ BM}$$

$Ni^{2+} = [Ar]\,3d^8$, unpaired $e^-(n) = 2$

$$\mu = \sqrt{2\,(2+2)} = \sqrt{8} \text{ BM}$$

Thus, option (a) is correct.

24. (*a*) According to spectrochemical series.

$I^- < Br^- < SCN^- < Cl^- < S^{2-} < F^- < OH^- < C_2O_4^{2-} <$
$H_2O < NCS^- < edta^{4-} < NH_3 < en < CN^- < CO$

Weak field ligands → Increasing order of Δ_o → Strong field ligands

The CFSE of ligands attached with Co^{3+} ion is in the order, en > NH_3 > H_2O (From spectrochemical series)

∵ Wavelength of absorbed light $(\lambda) \propto \frac{1}{\Delta_o}$

∴ For ligand the order of wavelength of absorption in the visible region will be : en < NH_3 < H_2O

or, $[Co(en)_3]^{3+} < [Co(NH_3)_6]^{3+} < [Co(H_2O)_6]^{3+}$

25. (*a*) Grignard's reagent is a σ-bonded organometallic compound ($R \overset{\sigma}{—} Mg \underset{(sp)}{\overset{\sigma}{—}} X$)

26. (*c*) $[Fe(CO)_4]^{2-}$

Since metal atom is carrying maximum –ve charge therefore, it would show maximum synergic bonding as a result, C—O bond length would be maximum.

27. (*b*) *trans*-effect is the effect of a coordinated group upon the rate of substitution at the position *trans* to itself in a square or octahedral complex.

As the rate of substitution of the *trans* ligand increases, the intensity of *trans* effect also increases.

Thus, correct order is, $CN^- > C_6H_5^- > Br^- > NH_3$

28. (*b*)

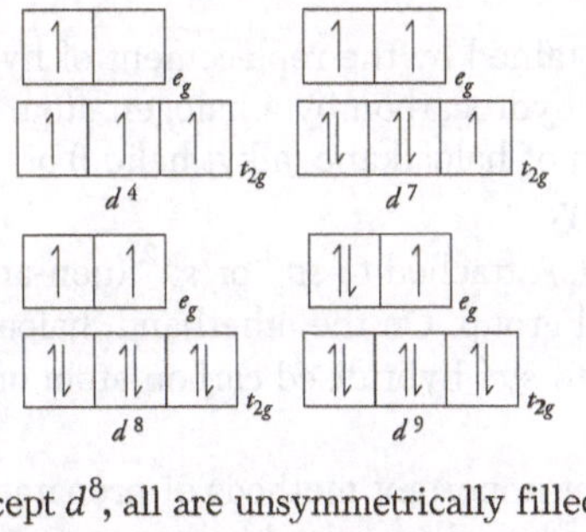

Except d^8, all are unsymmetrically filled, thus d^8 complex will not show Jahn-Teller distortion.

29. (*a*) $[Co(CN)_6]^{3-}$

$Co^{3+} = 1s^2\,2s^2\,2p^6\,3s^2\,3p^6\,3d^6$

CN^- is a strong field ligand and as it approaches the metal ion, the electrons must pair up.

The splitting of the *d*-orbitals into two sets of orbitals in an octahedral $[Co(CN)_6]^{3-}$ may be represented as

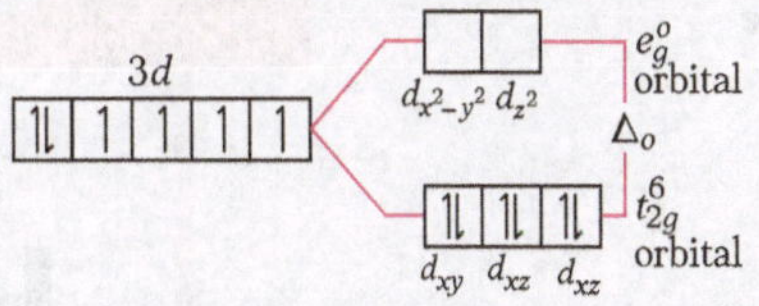

Here, for d^6 ions, three electrons first enter orbitals with parallel spin then the remaining may pair up in t_{2g} orbital giving rise to low spin complex (strong ligand) field.

∴ $[Co(CN)_6]^{3-}$ has no unpaired electron and will be in a low spin configuration.

30. (*b*) The CFSE for octahedral complex is given by

$CFSE = [-0.4\,t_{2g}e^- + 0.6\,e_g e^-] \times \Delta_0$

- For Mn^{3+}, $[3d^4] \rightarrow t_{2g}^3 e_g^1$

  ∴ $CFSE = [(-0.4 \times 3) + (0.6 \times 1)]\Delta_0 = -0.6\Delta_0$

- For Fe^{3+}, $[3d^5] \rightarrow t_{2g}^3 e_g^2$

  ∴ $CFSE = [-(0.4 \times 3) + (0.6 \times 2)]\Delta_0 = 0$

- For Co^{2+}, $[3d^7] \rightarrow t_{2g}^5 e_g^2$

  ∴ $CFSE = [(-0.4 \times 5) + (2 \times 0.6)]\Delta_0 = -0.8\Delta_0$

- For Co^{3+}, $[3d^6] \rightarrow t_{2g}^4 e_g^2$

  ∴ $CFSE = [(-0.4 \times 4) + (2 \times 0.6)]\Delta_0 = -0.4\Delta_0$

31. (*b*) *cis*-platin is known as anti-cancer agent. The formula of *cis*-platin is *cis*-$[PtCl_2(NH_3)_2]$. Here, the word *cis* refers to *cis* geometrical isomer of $[PtCl_2(NH_3)_2]$. It is used as an anti-tumour (anti-cancer) agent.

Skill Builder

- **Sol. of Skill Builder Pg. 250**

(*c*) The IUPAC name of the given complex is hexa-amminocobalt (III) diamminotetrachlorochromate (II).

- **Sol. of Skill Builder Pg. 251**

(*d*) A-4, B-1, C-2, D-3.

- **Sol. of Skill Builder Pg. 258**

(*d*) $Mn^{2+} = 3d^5\,4s^0$

Each Cl^- donate a pair of electrons

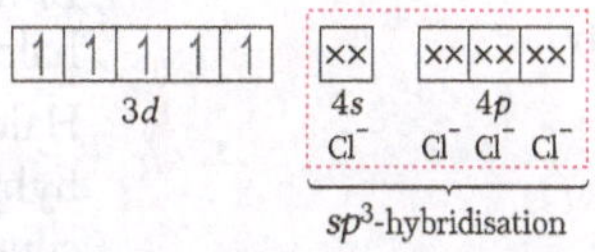

Thus, the complex is sp^3 hybridised with tetrahedral geometry and paramagnetic in nature.

- **Sol. of Skill Builder Pg. 259**

(*d*) Both statement I and Statement II are true.

For deeper insight
Scan the QR Code

Chapter 7

Haloalkanes and Haloarenes

Learning Objectives

Module-I

- Classification
- Nomenclature
- Nature of C—*X* bond
- Methods of Preparation of Haloalkanes
- Physical Properties of Haloalkanes

Module-II

- Nucleophilic Substitution Reactions
- Elimination Reactions
- Reaction with Metals

Module-III

- Method of Preparation of Haloarenes
- Physical Properties of Haloarenes
- Chemical Properties of Haloarenes
- Nucleophilic Substitution Reaction
- Electrophilic Substitution Reaction
- Reaction with Metals

Module-IV

- Dichloromethane
- Trichloromethane
- Triiodomethane
- Tetrachloromethane
- Freons
- DDT

Chapter Overview with NEET Connection

This chapter aims to provide a comprehensive overview of haloalkanes and haloarenes and guide you through the learning process effectively. Stereochemistry is used as a tool for understanding the reaction mechanism. It also highlights the environmental effect of polyhalogen compounds.

Without gripping this chapter, it will be difficult to learn and understand chapters like alcohols, phenols and ethers, amines, biomolecules etc., as the basics of certain mechanism has been discussed in this particular chapter.

Special format questions can be easily framed on the following topics of this chapter.

- Preparation of alkyl halides by alcohol.
- Reaction of phosphorus halides.
- Nucleophilic substitution reaction with stereochemistry.
- Elimination reaction
- Finkelstein reaction
- Wurtz reaction
- Swarts reaction

For better understanding of this chapter a grip over optical isomerism, rearrangement of carbocation, reaction mechanism are required.

Introduction

Haloalkanes and haloarenes are obtained by the replacement of hydrogen atom(s) of an aliphatic or aromatic hydrocarbon by a halogen atom (F, Cl, Br and I) resulting in the formation of haloalkane (alkyl halide) or haloarene (aryl halide), respectively.

Haloalkane contains halogen atom(s) attached to sp^3 or sp^2 (non-aryl) hybridised carbon atom of an alkyl group. On the otherhand, haloarenes contains halogen atom(s) attached to sp^2 hybridised carbon atom of an aryl group.

In this chapter, we will study about important methods of preparation, physical and chemical properties of haloalkanes and haloarenes and of polyhalogen compounds.

Module 1

Classification, Preparation and Physical Properties of Haloalkanes

- Classification
- Nomenclature
- Nature of C—X bond
- Methods of Preparation of Haloalkanes
- Physical Properties of Haloalkanes

Classification

Haloalkanes and haloarenes may be classified as follows

On the Basis of Number of Halogen Atoms

The halogen derivatives of hydrocarbons may be classified as mono, di, or polyhalogen (tri, tetra etc.) compounds depending upon whether they contain one, two or more halogen atoms in their structures. For examples,

Monohalo compounds

CH_3CH_2Br
Bromoethane
(Ethyl bromide)

CH_3CH_2Cl
Chloroethane
(Ethyl chloride)

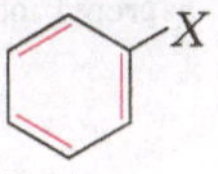

Monohalobenzene

Dihalo compounds

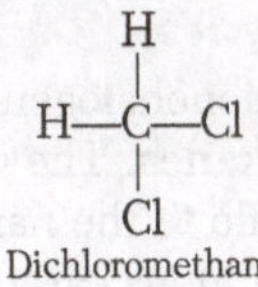

Dichloromethane

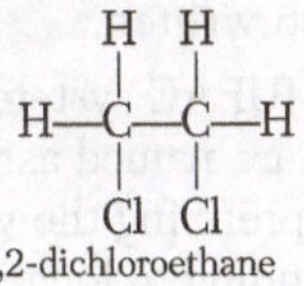

1,2-dichloroethane

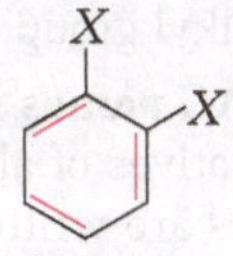

Dihalobenzene

Trihalo compounds

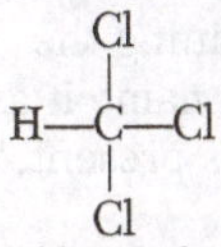

Trichloromethane
(Chloroform)

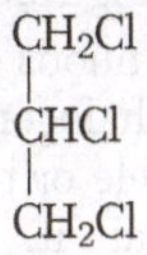

1,2,3-trichloropropane

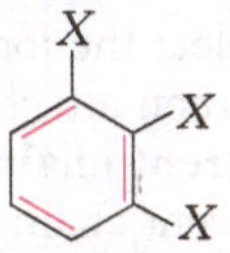

Trihalobenzene

Tetrahalo compounds

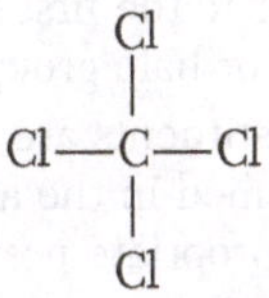

Tetrachloromethane
(Carbon tetrachloride)

On the Basis of Types of Hybridisation

The monohalo compounds may be further classified according to the type of hybridisation of the carbon atom bonded to the halogen atom.

Compounds Containing sp^3 C—X Bond (X = F, Cl, Br, I)

Compounds containing sp^3 C–X bond may be primary (1°), secondary (2°) or tertiary (3°).

These are of following types

(i) **Alkyl halides or haloalkanes** ($R - X$) In alkyl halides, the halogen atom is bonded to an alkyl group (R). They form a homologous series represented by $C_nH_{2n+1}X$. (where, X = F, Cl, Br, I)

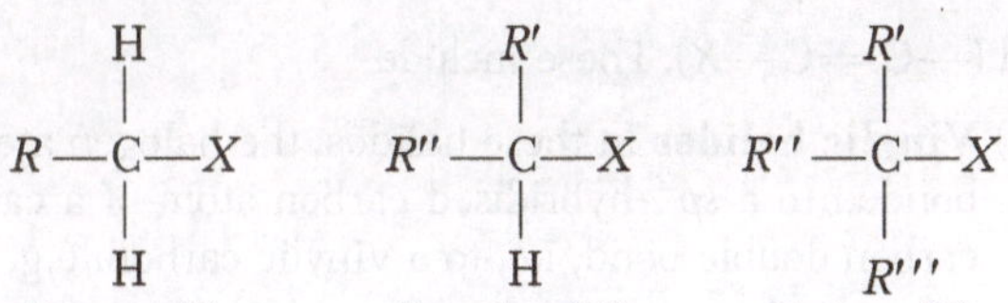

Primary (1°) Secondary (2°) Tertiary (3°)

(ii) **Allylic halides** In these compounds the halogen atom is bonded to a sp^3-hybridised carbon atom adjacent to carbon-carbon double bond (C═C), i.e. to an allylic carbon.

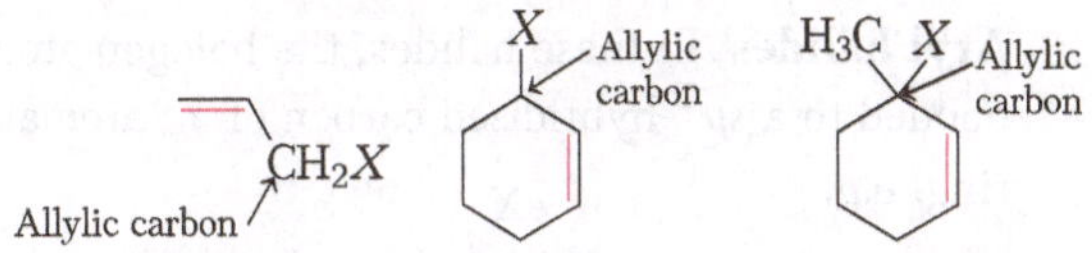

Allyl halide (1°) Allyl halide (2°) Allyl halide (3°)

(iii) **Benzylic halide** In these compounds the halogen atom is bonded to a sp^3-hybridised carbon atom attached to an aromatic ring.

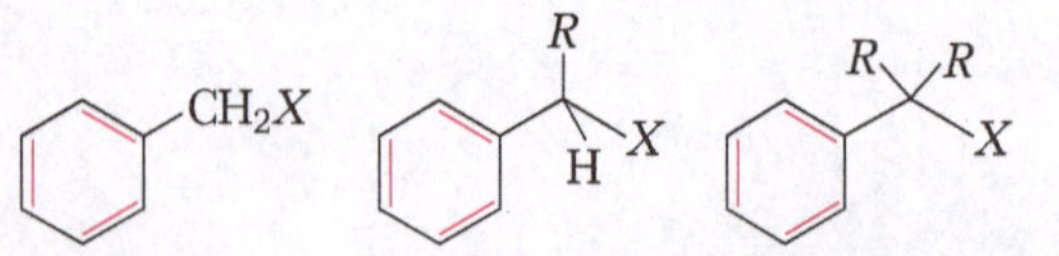

(1°) Benzyl halide | (2°) Benzyl halide | (3°) Benzyl halide [R = Alkyl group]

Concept ladder

Haloalkanes and haloarenes can also be classified as

Compounds containing *sp* C—*X* Bond

- The halogen derivatives of hydrocarbons contain *sp*-hybridised carbon. In these halogen derivatives, halogen is directly bonded to one of the carbon atoms of a triple bond ($—C\equiv C—X$).

e.g. $HC\equiv C—Cl$ (Chloroethyne) $\quad \overset{3}{C}H_3—\overset{2}{C}\equiv \overset{1}{C}—Cl$ (1-chloropropyne)

- On the basis of types of halogen present, these halogen derivative can also be classified as fluoro, chloro, bromo or iodo compounds.

NEET Close-up

Example Similar to PYQ Asked in NEET 2023

The given compound, $CH_2{=}CH-CH_2-X$ is an example of

(a) alkyl halide (b) vinyl halide
(c) aryl halide (d) allylic halide

Sol. (*d*) The given compound, $CH_2{=}CH-CH_2-X$ is an example of allylic halide, as in this the halogen is bonded to the sp^3-hybridised carbon atom next to the carbon-carbon double bond.

Skill Builder

The compound, 1, 1-dichloromethyl benzene is an example of

(a) aryl halide (b) benzylic halide
(c) vinylic halide (d) allylic halide

For more practice Refer to Q. 1 of Step up Practice 1 and Q. 1 of Gearing up for NEET.

Compounds Containing sp^2 C—*X* Bond

These halogen derivatives of hydrocarbon contains sp^2-hybridised carbon. In these compounds, halogen is directly bonded to one of the carbon atoms of a double bond ($—\overset{|}{C}{=}\overset{|}{C}—X$). These include

(i) **Vinylic halides** In these halides, the halogen atom is bonded to a sp^2-hybridised carbon atom of a carbon carbon double bond, i.e. to a vinylic carbon. e.g.

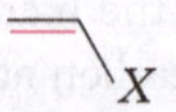

Haloethene (Vinyl halide)

$CH_2{=}\overset{\overset{H}{|}}{C}—Cl$

Chloroethene (Vinyl chloride)

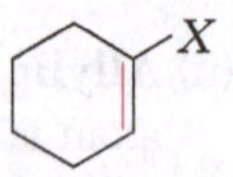

1-halocyclohex-1-ene

(ii) **Aryl halides** In these halides, the halogen atom is bonded to a sp^2-hybridised carbon of an aromatic ring. e.g.

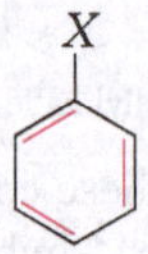

Halobenzene

These aromatic halogen compounds are also called haloarenes.

Nomenclature

Now, let us learn about the common names and IUPAC system of nomenclature for halosubstituted hydrocarbons for haloalkanes and haloarenes and polyhalogen compounds one by one.

Haloalkanes (or Alkyl Halides)

In the **common** or **trivial system** the monohalogen derivatives of alkanes are called **alkyl halides.** These are named by naming the alkyl group attached to halogen and adding the name of the halide.

e.g. CH_3Cl (Methyl chloride) $\quad CH_3CH_2Br$ (Ethyl bromide)

$CH_3CH_2CH_2I$ (*n*-propyl iodide) $\quad CH_3—\underset{\underset{CH_3}{|}}{CH}—CH_2Cl$ (*iso*-butyl chloride)

The names of the alkyl halide is always written as two separate words. The prefixes *n*-, *iso*-, *sec*-, *tert*-, etc., for the alkyl group are also written.

IUPAC names In the IUPAC system, the monohalogen derivatives of alkanes are named as **haloalkanes.** The names are written by prefixing the word halo to the name of the alkane corresponding to longest continuous carbon chain containing the halogen atom. In case of branched chain alkanes, the following rules are followed

- Select the longest continuous chain containing the carbon attached to the halogen group and name it as the **parent chain.** If a double or triple bond is present, the parent chain must contain it.
- Number the carbon atoms of the parent chain, beginning from the end nearer to the first substituent, regardless of whether it is alkyl or halo group.
- If two or more substituents are present on the parent chain, these are named in the alphabetical order alongwith their appropriate positions.

It may be noted that di, tri, tetra etc., are not considered while comparing the substituents for alphabetising purpose.

e.g. 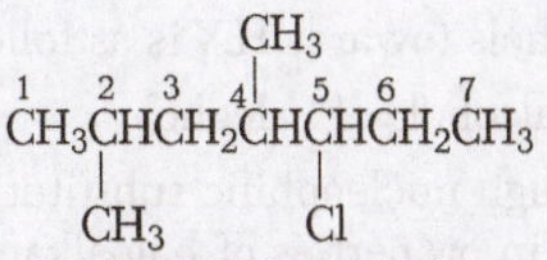
5-chloro-2, 4-dimethylheptane

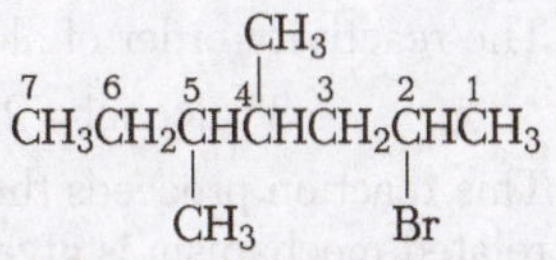
2-bromo-4, 5-dimethylheptane

The dihalo derivatives have special common names depending upon whether the halogen atoms are present on the same or different carbon atoms. These are commonly named according to IUPAC system.

- When both the halogen atoms are attached to the same C-atom, these are called ***geminal* halides** or ***gem*-dihalides**. These are also called alkylidene dihalides or simply alkylidene halides.

e.g. 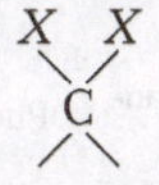

CH_3CHCl_2
Ethylidene chloride
(*gem*-dihalide)
IUPAC name 1, 1-dichloroethane

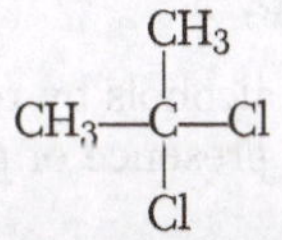
Iso-propylidene dichloride
IUPAC name 2, 2-dichloropropane

$CH_3CH_2CHCl_2$
Propylidene chloride
IUPAC name 1, 1-dichloropropane

- When the two halogen atoms are attached in adjacent C-atoms, they are called ***vicinal* dihalides** or simply ***vic*-dihalides**. These are named as the dihalide of alkene from which they may be prepared by the addition of halogen atoms, i.e. alkylene dihalide.

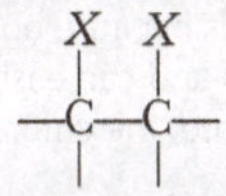
Vicinal dihalide

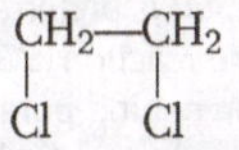
Ethylene dichloride
(*vic*-dihalide)
IUPAC name 1,2-dichloroethane

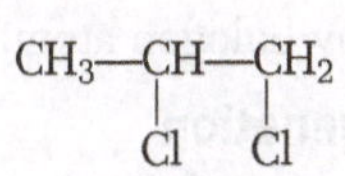
Propylene dichloride
IUPAC name 1,2-dichloropropane

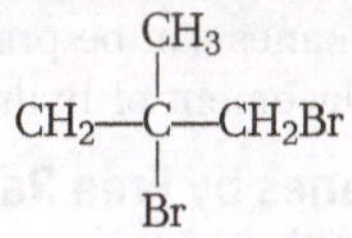
iso-butylene dibromide
IUPAC name 1,2-dibromo-2-methylpropane

Polyhalogen derivatives are named according to IUPAC system. Trihalomethanes and tetrahalomethanes are named as haloforms and carbon tetrahalides respectively.

$CHCl_3$
Chloroform
IUPAC name Trichloromethane

CHI_3
Iodoform
IUPAC name Triiodomethane

CCl_4
Carbon tetrachloride
IUPAC name Tetrachloromethane

Haloarenes (or Aryl Halide)

Haloarenes or aryl halides are named by adding the prefix halo (fluoro, chloro, bromo, iodo) before the name of the aromatic hydrocarbon.

In case of disubstituted compounds, the relative positions of the substituents 1, 2; 1, 3 and 1, 4 are indicated by the prefixes *ortho* (*o*), *meta* (*m*) and *para* (*p*) respectively. e.g.

(i) **For monohaloarene**

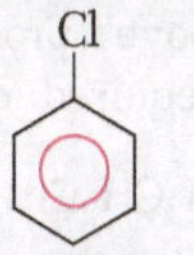
Chlorobenzene

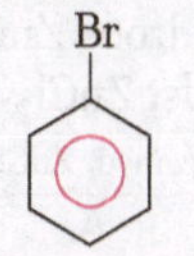
Bromobenzene

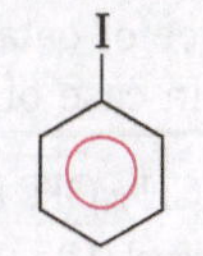
Iodobenzene

(ii) **For dihaloarene**

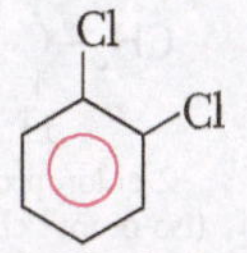
1,2-dichlorobenzene
(*o*-dichlorobenzene)

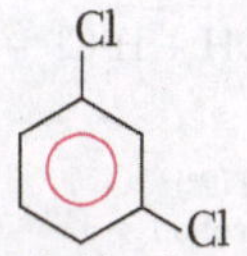
1,3-dichlorobenzene
(*m*-dichlorobenzene)

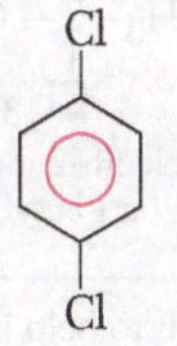
1,4-dichlorobenzene
(*p*-dichlorobenzene)

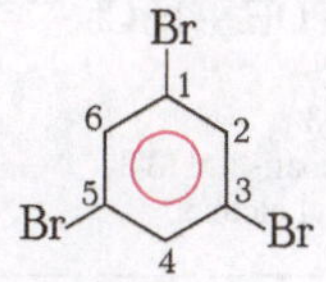
1,3,5-tribromobenzene
(*sym*-tribromobenzene)

Nature of C—*X* Bond

Carbon-halogen bond of alkyl halide is polarised, due to higher electronegativity of halogen than that of carbon. A partial positive charge is present on carbon atom and a partial negative charge is present on halogen atom.

The size of halogen atom increases on moving down the group. Consequently the carbon halogen bond length also increases from C—F to C—I.

The sequence of bond enthalpy of C—*X* bond is $CH_3-F > CH_3-Cl > CH_3-Br > CH_3-I$.

Bond enthalpy is inversely proportional to bond length. In other words, higher the bond length lower will be the bond enthalpy.

Methods of Preparation of Haloalkanes

Various methods of preparation of alkyl halides are discussed below

From Alcohols

Alkyl halides can be prepared from alcohols by reaction with HX, phosphorus halides and thionyl chloride.

By the Reaction of HX

When alcohols react with HX then alkyl halides are formed

$$R\text{—OH} + HX \longrightarrow R\text{—}X + H_2O$$

1° and 2° alcohols react with concentrated HCl in the presence of catalyst, anhydrous $ZnCl_2$ (Groove's process) while in case of 3° alcohols, $ZnCl_2$ is not required. e.g.

$$\underset{\substack{\text{Ethanol (1°)}\\\text{(Ethyl alcohol)}}}{CH_3CH_2\,OH + H\,Cl} \xrightarrow[\Delta]{\text{Anhyd. } ZnCl_2} \underset{\substack{\text{Chloroethane}\\\text{(Ethyl chloride)}}}{CH_3CH_2Cl} + H_2O$$

$$\underset{\substack{\text{Propan-2-ol (2°)}\\\text{(iso-propyl alcohol)}}}{CH_3\text{—}\overset{\overset{CH_3}{|}}{\underset{\underset{H}{|}}{C}}\text{—}OH + H\,Cl} \xrightarrow[\Delta]{\text{Anhyd. } ZnCl_2} \underset{\substack{\text{2-chloropropane}\\\text{(iso-propyl chloride)}}}{CH_3\text{—}\overset{\overset{CH_3}{|}}{\underset{\underset{H}{|}}{C}}\text{—}Cl} + H_2O$$

$$\underset{\substack{\text{2-methylproan-2-ol (3°)}\\\text{(tert-butyl alcohol)}}}{CH_3\text{—}\overset{\overset{CH_3}{|}}{\underset{\underset{CH_3}{|}}{C}}\text{—}OH + H\,Cl} \xrightarrow{\text{Room temp.}} \underset{\substack{\text{2-chloro-2-methylpropane}\\\text{(tert-butyl chloride)}}}{CH_3\text{—}\overset{\overset{CH_3}{|}}{\underset{\underset{CH_3}{|}}{C}}\text{—}Cl} + H_2O$$

Concept ladder

The purpose of anhydrous $ZnCl_2$, is to help in the cleavage of the C—O bond. Anhydrous $ZnCl_2$, is a Lewis acid and therefore, it readily coordinates with the oxygen atom of the alcohols. As a result, the C—O bond weakens and finally breaks to form carbocation. The carbocation, then readily reacts with chloride ion to form chloroalkanes.

Alcohols react with HBr (48%) in the presence of conc. H_2SO_4 and form bromoalkanes.

HBr can also be generated by the action of conc. H_2SO_4 on NaBr or KBr.

$$\underset{\substack{\text{Ethanol}\\\text{(Ethyl alcohol)}}}{CH_3CH_2\,OH + Na\,Br} \xrightarrow[\text{Heat}]{\text{Conc. } H_2SO_4} \underset{\substack{\text{Bromoethane}\\\text{(Ethyl bromide)}}}{CH_3CH_2Br}$$

$$\underset{\text{Ethanol}}{CH_3CH_2OH} + KBr \xrightarrow[\text{Heat}]{\text{Conc. } H_2SO_4} \underset{\text{Bromoethane}}{CH_3CH_2Br} + KHSO_4 + H_2O$$

Alcohols react with HI and form iodoalkanes. HI can also be generated by the action of 95% phosphoric acid on KI.

$$CH_3CH_2\,OH + H\,I \xrightarrow{\text{Reflux}} \underset{\text{Iodoethane}}{CH_3CH_2I} + H_2O$$

$$CH_3CH_2OH + KI + \underset{\text{Phosphoric acid}}{H_3PO_4} \xrightarrow{\text{Heat}} \underset{\text{Iodoethane}}{CH_3CH_2I} + \underset{\substack{\text{Potassium dihydrogen}\\\text{phosphate}}}{KH_2PO_4} + H_2O$$

The reactivity order of HX towards alcohols is as follows

$$HCl < HBr < HI$$

The reactivity order of alcohols towards HX is as follows

$$3° \text{ alcohol} > 2° \text{ alcohol} > 1° \text{ alcohol}$$

This reaction proceeds through nucleophilic substitution related mechanism is given in properties of haloalkanes.

By the Reaction of Phosphorus Halides

Alcohols react with phosphorus halides like PCl_5, PCl_3, PBr_3 or PI_3 and form alkyl halides. PBr_3 and PI_3 are unstable so these are prepared *in situ* by the action of red phosphorus on Br_2 or I_2.

$$\underset{\text{Alcohol}}{R\text{—OH}} + \underset{\substack{\text{Phosphorus}\\\text{pentachloride}}}{PCl_5} \longrightarrow \underset{\text{Chloroalkane}}{RCl} + \underset{\substack{\text{Phosphorus}\\\text{oxychloride}}}{POCl_3} + HCl$$

$$\underset{\text{Alcohol}}{3R\text{—OH}} + \underset{\substack{\text{Phosphorus}\\\text{trichloride}}}{PCl_3} \longrightarrow \underset{\text{Chloroalkane}}{3RCl} + \underset{\text{Phosphorus acid}}{H_3PO_3}$$

By the Reaction of Thionyl Chloride

Chloroalkanes can be prepared from alcohols by refluxing alcohols with thionyl chloride in the presence of pyridine (C_6H_5N).

$$R\text{—OH} + \underset{\substack{\text{Thionyl}\\\text{chloride}}}{SOCl_2} \xrightarrow[\Delta]{\text{Pyridine}} R\text{—Cl} + SO_2\uparrow + HCl\uparrow$$

This process is called as **Darzen's process.**

Mentor's TiP

Darzen's method is preferred than other methods because both the products of the reaction (SO_2 and HCl) are gases and can easily escape leaving behind pure alkyl halide. Therefore, the chloro compounds can be purified easily.

From Hydrocarbons

The haloalkanes can be prepared from alkanes and alkenes by the replacement of hydrogen atom by halogen atom.

From Alkanes by Free Radical Halogenation (Substitution)

Halogens (Cl_2 and Br_2) react with alkanes in the presence of ultraviolet light to form haloalkanes.

$$\underset{\text{Propane}}{CH_3CH_2CH_3} \xrightarrow[\text{Heat}]{Cl_2(\text{1 eqv})/\text{UV light}} \underset{\text{1-chloropropane}}{CH_3CH_2CH_2Cl} + \underset{\text{2-chloropropane}}{CH_3\underset{\underset{Cl}{|}}{C}HCH_3}$$

Similarly,

$$\underset{\text{Butane}}{CH_3CH_2CH_2CH_3} \xrightarrow[\text{or Heat}]{Cl_2(\text{1 eqv})/\text{UV light}} \underset{\text{1-chlorobutane}}{CH_3CH_2CH_2CH_2Cl} + \underset{\text{2-chlorobutane}}{CH_3CH_2\underset{\underset{Cl}{|}}{C}HCH_3}$$

The relative amounts of these isomeric haloalkanes depends upon the nature of the halogen (Cl_2 or Br_2) and the number and type of hydrogen (1°, 2° or 3°) being substituted. In general, the ease of substitution of various hydrogen follows the sequence

$$3° > 2° > 1°$$

However, their relative rates vary with the nature of halogen. Although, it is difficult to separate these complex isomeric mixture as pure compounds. Consequently the yield of any single compound is low.

Iodination is reversible and endothermic but it may be carried out in the presence of an oxidising agent such as HIO_3, HNO_3, etc. The oxidising agent destroys the HI formed and thus drives the reaction towards the forward direction.

$$CH_4 + I_2 \rightleftharpoons CH_3I + HI$$

$$5HI + HIO_3 \rightleftharpoons 3I_2 + 3H_2O$$

Concept ladder

- **Allylic bromination** (allylic free radical substitution) may be carried out by treating alkene with N-bromo succinimide (NBS) or Br_2.
- When propene is treated with NBS in the presence of light and peroxide as initiator, bromination occurs at the methyl group forming a good yield of 3-bromoprop-1-ene (allyl bromide).

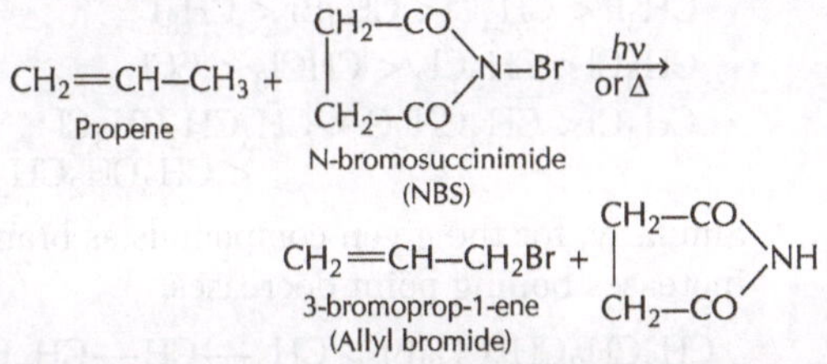

From Alkenes

When alkenes react with hydrogen halides or halogens then haloalkanes will be formed.

(i) **Addition of hydrogen halides** Haloalkanes can be prepared by the electrophilic addition of halogen acids (HBr, HCl or HI) to alkenes.

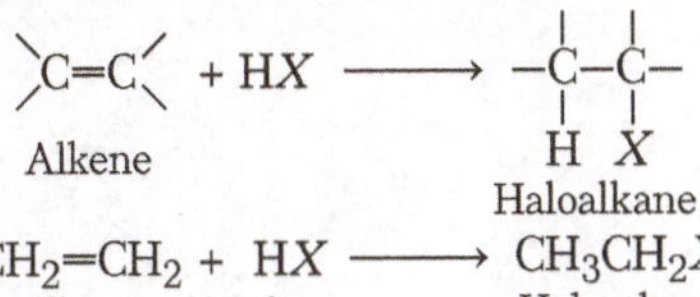

$$\underset{\text{Alkene}}{CH_2{=}CH_2} + \underset{\text{Hydrogen halides}}{HX} \longrightarrow \underset{\substack{\text{Haloethane} \\ (X = Cl, Br, I)}}{CH_3CH_2X}$$

It may be noted that in case of addition to symmetrical alkenes (—HC=CH—), the carbon atoms joined by the double bond are equivalent and, therefore, only one addition product is formed. e.g.

$$\underset{\text{But-2-ene}}{CH_2{-}CH{=}CH{-}CH_3} + \underset{\text{Hydrogen bromide}}{HBr} \longrightarrow \underset{\text{2-bromobutane}}{CH_3CH_2{-}\underset{|\atop Br}{CH}{-}CH_3}$$

During the addition of halogen acids/hydrogen halides to unsymmetrical alkenes, Markovnikov rule is followed. According to this rule, during the addition across unsymmetrical double bond, the negative part of the attacking reagent attaches itself to the carbon atom carrying lesser number of hydrogen atoms while the positive part goes to the carbon atom with more number of hydrogen atoms.

For example, in the case of propene, 2-bromopropane is the major product.

$$\underset{\text{Propene}}{CH_3{-}CH{=}CH_2} + HBr \longrightarrow \underset{\text{2-bromopropane (90\%)}}{CH_3{-}\underset{|\atop Br}{CH}{-}CH_3} + \underset{\text{1-bromopropane (10\%)}}{CH_3{-}CH_2{-}\underset{|\atop Br}{CH_2}}$$

If HBr is added in the presence of organic peroxide to unsymmetrical alkenes then Br will go to the carbon atom which has more number of hydrogen atom. This is known as peroxide effect or Kharasch effect.

$$\underset{\text{Propene}}{CH_3{-}CH{=}CH_2} + HBr \xrightarrow{\text{Peroxide}} \underset{\text{1-bromopropane}}{CH_3{-}CH_2{-}CH_2{-}Br}$$

This addition takes place *via* free radical addition mechanism.

(ii) **Addition of halogens** Reaction of alkene with Br_2 in the presence of CCl_4 gives *vic*-dibromides which are colourless. In the laboratory, addition of bromine in CCl_4 to an alkene resulting in discharge of reddish brown colour of bromine constitutes an important method for the detection of double bond (C=C) in a molecule.

e.g. $$CH_2{=}CH_2 + \underset{\text{(red)}}{Br_2} \xrightarrow{CCl_4} \underset{\substack{vic\text{-dibromide} \\ \text{(colourless)}}}{\underset{|\atop Br}{CH_2}{-}\underset{|\atop Br}{CH_2}}$$

Halogen Exchange

Alkyl iodide and alkyl fluoride are often prepared by this method.

- The iodoalkanes are obtained by heating chloro or bromoalkanes with a concentrated solution of sodium iodide in dry acetone. This reaction is known as **Finkelstein reaction.**

$$R{-}X + NaI \xrightarrow{\text{Dry acetone}} R{-}I + NaX\downarrow \quad (X = Cl, Br)$$

$$CH_3CH_2Br + NaI \xrightarrow{\text{Dry acetone}} \underset{\text{iodoethane}}{CH_3CH_2I} + NaBr\downarrow$$

$$CH_3CH_2Cl + NaI \xrightarrow{\text{Dry acetone}} \underset{\text{iodoethane}}{CH_3CH_2I} + NaCl\downarrow$$

NaCl or NaBr is precipitated in dry acetone. It facilitates the forward reaction according to Le-Chatelier's principle.

- Fluoro alkanes are difficult to prepare directly. These are prepared by treating alkyl chloride or bromide with salts such as mercurous fluoride (Hg_2F_2), silver fluoride (AgF), cobalt fluoride (CoF_2) or antimony trifluoride (SbF_3). This reaction is known as **Swarts reaction.**

$$2CH_3CH_2Cl + \underset{\text{Mercurous fluoride}}{Hg_2F_2} \longrightarrow \underset{\text{fluoroethane}}{2CH_3CH_2F} + Hg_2Cl_2$$

$$CH_3Br + \underset{\text{Silver fluoride}}{AgF} \longrightarrow \underset{\text{fluoromethane}}{CH_3F} + AgBr$$

NEET Close-up

Example Similar to PYQ Asked in NEET 2024

The products A and B in the following reaction, respectively are

$$R{-}OH + NaBr + H_2SO_4 \longrightarrow RBr + H_2O + A$$

$$ROH + SOCl_2 \longrightarrow R{-}Cl + SO_2 + B$$

(a) $NaHSO_4$ and $POCl_3$ (b) $NaHSO_4$ and HCl
(c) HCl and $NaHSO_4$ (d) $POCl_3$ and $NaHSO_4$

Sol. (*b*) In th given question A and B respectively are $NaHSO_4$ and HCl.

Skill Builder

The reactants P and Q in the following reaction, respectively are

$$R{-}OH + P \xrightarrow{ZnCl_2} R{-}Cl + H_2O$$

$$R{-}OH + Q \longrightarrow R{-}Cl + POCl_3 + HCl$$

(a) SCl_2 and H_3PO_3 (b) PCl_5 and HCl
(c) HCl and PCl_5 (d) H_3PO_3 and HCl

For more practice Refer to Q.9 of Step up Practice 1.

Physical Properties of Haloalkanes

Various physical properties of haloalkanes are as follows

(i) **Physical state** Chloride, bromide, fluoride of methane and chloride of ethane are gases at room temperature, rest alkyl halides upto C_{18} are colourless liquids and beyond it are colourless solids.

(ii) **Odour** Many volatile halogen compounds have sweet smell.

(iii) **Solubility** Haloalkanes have polar nature but are insoluble in polar solvents like water because they have no ability to form H-bonds with water.

However, these are soluble in organic solvents like ether, benzene etc.

(iv) **Density** The density of alkyl halide increases with increase in size of alkyl group or increase in molecular weight of X i.e.

$$RF < RCl < RBr < RI$$

(v) **Melting and boiling points** Alkyl halides have higher boiling point than corresponding alkanes. Boiling points depends upon van der Waals' forces of attraction.

Boiling point $\propto$ van der Waals' forces of attraction

$$\propto \text{Molecular weight} \propto \frac{1}{\text{Branching}}$$

e.g. In the given compounds as molecular weight increases, boiling point also increases.

- $CH_3F < CH_3Cl < CH_3Br < CH_3I$
- $CH_3Cl < CH_2Cl_2 < CHCl_3 < CCl_4$
- $CH_3Cl < CH_3CH_2Cl < CH_3CH_2CH_3Cl < CH_3CH_2CH_2CH_2Cl$

Similarly, for the given compounds as branching increases boiling point decreases.

$$CH_3CH_2CH_2CH_2Br > CH_3{-}\underset{\underset{CH_3}{|}}{CH}{-}CH_2Br > CH_3{-}\overset{\overset{CH_3}{|}}{\underset{\underset{CH_3}{|}}{C}}{-}Br$$

STEP UP Practice 1

1 Which of the following is an allylic halide?
(a) 3-bromo-2-methylprop-2-ene
(b) 3-bromobut-1-ene
(c) 3-bromopent-2-ene
(d) 4-bromobut-1-ene

2 Ethylidene chloride is a/an
(a) *vic*-dihalide (b) *gem*-dihalide
(c) allylic halide (d) vinylic halide

3 Consider the following halides.
(i) $C_6H_5CH_2Br$ (ii) $C_6H_5CH_2CH_2Br$
(iii) $C_6H_5C(Br)(CH_3)_2$ (iv) $C_6H_5CH_2{=}CH-CH_2-Br$
(v) C_6H_5Br
How many halide(s), are the example of benzylic halide(s)?
(a) 4 (b) 1 (c) 3 (d) 2

4 Which of the following is incorrectly matched with its common name?
(a) $(CH_3)_3CBr \longrightarrow$ *tert*-butyl bromide
(b) $CH_2{=}CHCl \longrightarrow$ Vinyl chloride
(c) $CHBr_3 \longrightarrow$ Bromoform
(d) $CH_3CH_2CH_2F \longrightarrow$ 1-fluoropropane

5 What should be the correct IUPAC name for diethylbromomethane?
(a) 1-bromo-1, 1-diethylmethane (b) 3-bromopentane
(c) 1-bromo-1-ethylpropane (d) 1-bromopentane

6 Which is the correct IUPAC name for

$CH_3-\underset{\displaystyle C_2H_5}{\underset{|}{C}H}-CH_2-Br$?

(a) 1-bromo-2-ethylpropane
(b) 1-bromo-2-ethyl-2-methylethane
(c) 1-bromo-2-methylbutane
(d) 2-methyl-1-bromobutane

7 Choose the incorrect match.

(a) 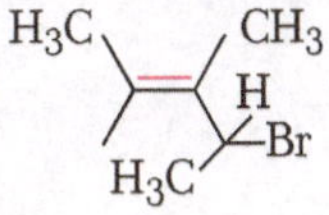 $\longrightarrow$ 4-bromo-2, 3-dimethylpent-2-ene

(b) 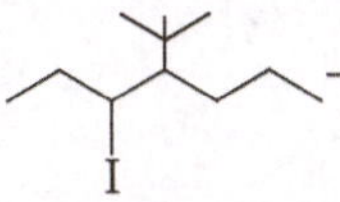 $\longrightarrow$ 4-*tert*-butyl-5-iodoheptane

(c) 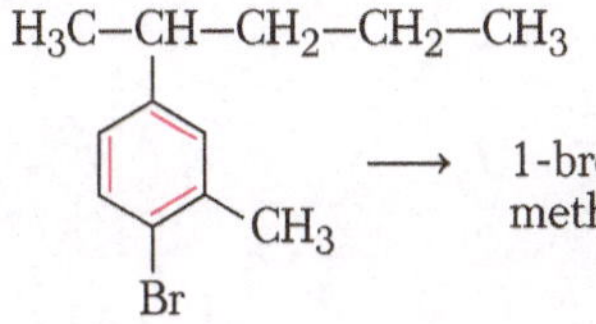 $\longrightarrow$ 1-bromo-4-pentyl-2-methylbenzene

(d) 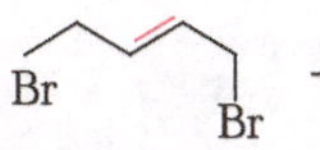 $\longrightarrow$ 1, 4-dibromobut-2-ene

8 Select the correct statement from the following regarding the preparation of haloalkanes?
(a) The hydroxyl group of an alcohol is replaced by halogen on reaction with dil. halogen acids, phosphorus halides or thionyl chloride.
(b) The order of reactivity of alcohols with a given haloacid is $3° > 1° > 2°$.
(c) The reaction of primary alcohol is conducted by simply shaking the alcohol with concentrated HCl at room temperature.
(d) The reactions of secondary alcohols with HCl require the presence of a catalyst, $ZnCl_2$ (anhydrous).

9 Identify the reactant *Y* in the following reaction.

$$CH_3CH_2OH + KI + Y \xrightarrow{\Delta} CH_3CH_2I + KH_2PO_4 + H_2O$$

(a) H_3PO_4 (b) H_2SO_4
(c) HCl (d) HI

10 Which of the following is a halogen exchange reaction?
(a) $RX + NaI \longrightarrow RI + NaX$
(b) $-C{=}C- + HX \longrightarrow -\underset{H}{\underset{|}{C}}-\underset{X}{\underset{|}{C}}-$
(c) $R-OH + HX \xrightarrow{ZnCl_2} R-X + H_2O$
(d) 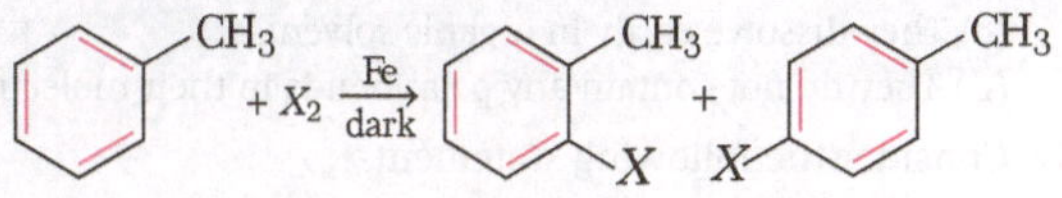

11 Which reagent will carry out the following reaction?
$CH_3CH_2CH_2CH_3 \longrightarrow CH_3CH_2CH_2CH_2Cl + CH_3CH_2CHClCH_3$
(a) Cl_2/UV light
(b) $NaCl + H_2SO_4$
(c) Cl_2 gas in dark.
(d) Cl_2 gas in the presence of iron in dark.

12 $CH_2{=}CHCH_2CH{=}CH_2 \xrightarrow{NBS} A$ (major product). *A* is
(a) $CH_2{=}CH\underset{Br}{\underset{|}{C}H}CH{=}CH_2$
(b) $CH_2{=}CHCH{=}CHCH_2Br$
(c) $CH_2{=}CHCH_2CH{=}CHBr$
(d) $CH_2{=}CHCH_2\underset{Br}{\underset{|}{C}}{=}CH_2$

13 What is the final product of the following reaction?

$$CH_3CH{=}CH_2 + NBS \longrightarrow \xrightarrow{AgCN} \text{(major)}$$

(a) $CH_3CH{=}CHCN$ (b) $CH_3CH{=}CHNC$
(c) $CH_2{=}CHCH_2CN$ (d) $CH_2{=}CHCH_2NC$

14 Which of the following is the best method for the synthesis of alkyl fluorides ?
(a) Free radical fluorination (b) Sandmeyer's reaction
(c) Finkelstein reaction (d) Swarts reaction

15 Identify the reagent(s) 'A' and condition(s) for the chemical reaction given below

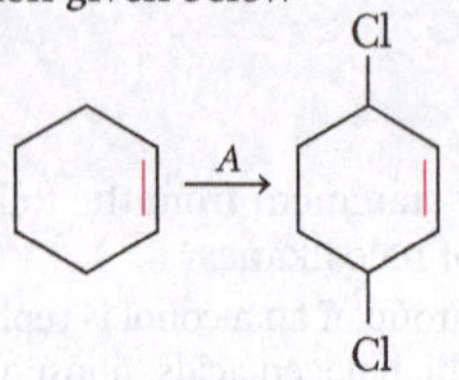

(a) $A = HCl$; anhydrous $FeCl_3$
(b) $A = HCl, ZnCl_2$
(c) $A = Cl_2$; UV light
(d) $A = Cl_2$; dark, anhydrous $AlCl_3$

16 Which is the correct increasing order of boiling points of the following compounds?
1-iodobutane, 1-bromobutane, 1-chlorobutane, butane
(a) Butane < 1-chlorobutane < 1-bromobutane < 1-iodobutane
(b) 1-iodobutane < 1-bromobutane < 1-chlorobutane < Butane
(c) Butane < 1-iodobutane < 1-bromobutane < 1-chlorobutane
(d) Butane < 1-chlorobutane < 1-iodobutane < 1-bromobutane

17 Which of the following statement is correct about alkyl halides?
(a) They dissolve in water quickly.
(b) They are associated with each other by H-bonds.
(c) They dissolve easily in organic solvents.
(d) They do not contain any polar bonds in their molecules.

18 Consider the following statements.
Statement I The boiling points of chlorides, bromides and iodides are considerably higher than those of the hydrocarbons of comparable molecular mass.
Statement II Greater polarity of C—X bond as well as higher molecular mass (as compared to the parent hydrocarbon) results in the stronger intermolecular forces of attraction in the halogen derivatives.
In the light of the above statements, choose the most appropriate answer from the options given below.
(a) Both Statement I and Statement II are false.
(b) Statement I is true, but Statement II is false.
(c) Statement I is false, but Statement II is true.
(d) Both Statement I and Statement II are true.

19 Which of the following statements is incorrect?
(a) Alkyl bromides and iodides develop colour when exposed to light.
(b) For the same alkyl group, the boiling points of alkyl halides increases in the order : $RI < RCl < RBr < RF$.
(c) The boiling point of isomeric haloalkanes decrease with increase in branching.
(d) Bromo, iodo and polychloro derivatives of hydrocarbons are heavier than water.

20 Which of the following alkyl halide is incorrectly matched with their bond-length/pm?
(a) $H_3C—F \longrightarrow 139$ pm
(b) $H_3C—Cl \longrightarrow 135$ pm
(c) $H_3C—Br \longrightarrow 193$ pm
(d) $H_3C—I \longrightarrow 214$ pm

21 Arrange the following compounds in the increasing order of their densities.

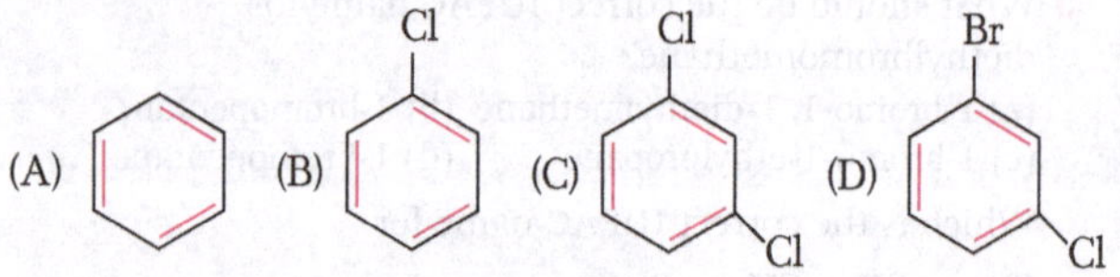

(a) (A) < (B) < (C) < (D)
(b) (A) < (C) < (D) < (B)
(c) (D) < (C) < (B) < (A)
(d) (B) < (D) < (C) < (A)

Module 2

Chemical Reactions of Haloalkanes

• Nucleophilic Substitution Reactions • Elimination Reactions • Reaction with Metals

Chemical Reactions of Haloalkanes

The carbon-halogen bond of haloalkane is polar. As a result the two atoms do not share their bonding electrons equally. This causes the haloalkanes to undergo substitution and elimination reactions.

Nucleophilic Substitution Reactions

These reactions involve substitution that begins with nucleophilic attack at that part of the substrate molecule which is electron deficient. The atom which departs with its bonding pair of electrons is called leaving group.

$$R—\underset{\substack{\uparrow \\ \text{Leaving group}}}{X} + Nu^- \longrightarrow R—Nu + X^-$$

For a nucleophilic substitution reaction to occur, the carbon atom attached to the leaving group must be a partial positive charge because this is the site where the nucleophile will attack. Most heteroatoms are more electronegative than carbon, so they tend to withdraw electron density from the bond shared with the carbon atom, creating the electrophilic centre.

When a nucleophile is present, it can react with the electrophilic carbon atom and substitution occurs.

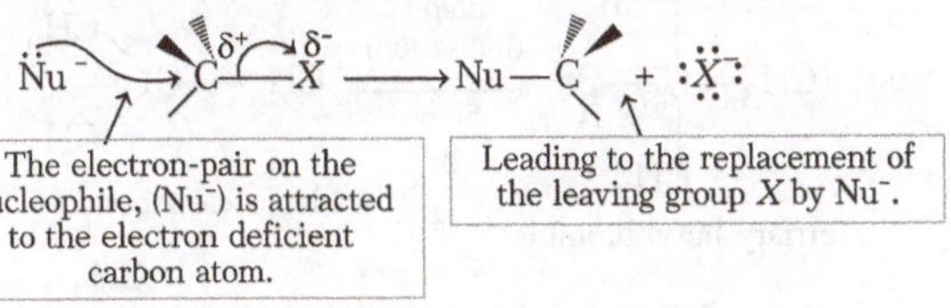

The halide ions are particularly good leaving groups, thus an alkyl halide is the most common substrate for nucleophilic (electron rich species) substitution reactions. The leaving group ability of halide ions follows the order,

$$I^- > Br^- > Cl^- > F^-$$

Iodide ion has the larger size than all the others halides and can accomodate the negative charge easily, thus behaves as the best leaving group.

Groups like cyanides and nitrites possess two nucleophilic centres and are called ambident nucleophiles.

Types of Nucleophilic Substitution Reactions

There are mainly two types of nucleophilic substitution reactions. i.e.

(i) Substitution nucleophilic bimolecular (S_N2)

(ii) Substitution nucleophilic unimolecular (S_N1)

Substitution Nucleophilic Bimolecular (S_N2)

The term bimolecular means that rate of a reaction depends upon the concentration of two molecules, i.e. on substrate and nucleophile. It follows second order kinetics. These reactions are commonly seen in primary alkyl halides and alcohols and takes place in one step.

$$\text{Rate} \propto \underset{\substack{\downarrow \\ RX}}{[A]}\ \underset{\substack{\downarrow \\ Nu^-}}{[B]}$$

Mechanism

These reactions take place through a transition state.

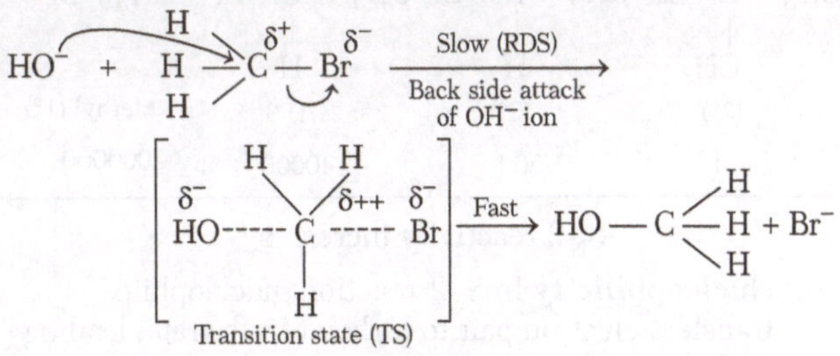

As the hydroxide ion approaches the molecule from the back side, an effective collision takes place. The —OH bond is formed and the —Br bond is broken simultaneously with the liberation of bromide ion.

As the reaction progresses and the bond between the incoming nucleophile and the carbon atom start forming and the bond between carbon atom and leaving group weakens. As this happens, the three carbon-hydrogen bonds of the substrate start moving away from the attacking nucleophile.

In transition state all the 3C—H bonds are in same plane and the attacking and leaving nucleophiles are partially attached to the carbon (penta-coordinated sp^2- carbon in TS).

As the attacking nucleophile approaches closer to the carbon, C—H bonds still keep on moving in the same direction till the attacking nucleophile attaches to carbon and leaving group leaves the carbon. In the transition state, carbon is simultaneously bonded to five atoms, thus structures are unstable and cannot be isolated.

The relative order of alkyl halides towards S_N2 reaction is

Methyl halides > primary halides > secondary halides > tertiary halides

Factors Affecting S_N2 Reactions

Various factors affecting S_N2 reactions are as follows

(i) **Steric effects** The presence of bulky substituents on or near the C-atom bonded to halogen tends to hinder the approach of the nucleophile to that C-atom and makes the reaction difficult. Amongst all the 1° alkyl halides are reactive towards S_N2 as they are sterically less hindered and has only 3H-atoms on the α-carbon for $CH_3—X$.
While tertiary alkyl halides with three bulky alkyl groups are least reactive followed by secondary halides (with two bulky alkyl group) and primary halides (with one bulky alkyl group). Thus, the reactivity order of alkyl halides towards S_N2 reactions is as follows

Primary halide > Secondary halide > Tertiary halide

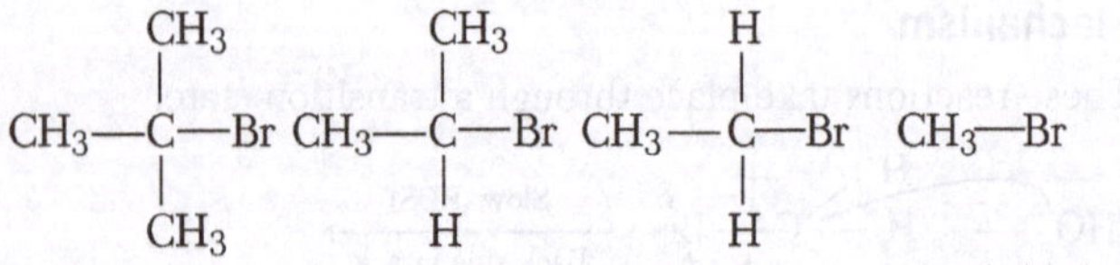

(3°) (2°) (1°) Methyl (1°)

(< 1) 500 40000 2000000

S_N2 reactivity increases →

(ii) **Nucleophilicity** In S_N2 reaction, nucleophile transfers electron pair to carbon of substrate, leading to the formation of transition state.
Hence, a stronger nucleophile will react with substrate at a faster rate. e.g. R_3P, $I^{\ominus}$, $HS^{\ominus}$, $RS^{\ominus}$ are very good nucleophile while *R*COOH is a weak nucleophile.
Weak nucleophile fails to promote the S_N2 reaction, therefore reaction with weak nucleophile often proceed by S_N1 mechanism if the substrate is secondary or tertiary.

(iii) **Leaving group ability** More the ability of leaving group, faster is the reaction by S_N2 mechanism, e.g. leaving group reactivity for S_N2 reaction given by halides are as follows

F^-	Cl^-	Br^-	I^-
1	200	10000	20000

Relative reactivity ⟶ Increases

(iv) **Effect of solvent** S_N2 mechanism is favoured by polar, aprotic solvents such as DMSO (dimethyl-sulphoxide) and DMF. (N, N-methyl formamide)

NEET Snapshot

Aprotic solvent such as N, N-dimethyl formamide (DMF) increases the reactivity rate. ***[NEET 2016]***

Aprotic solvents are the solvents that lacks an acidic proton and is polar. They dissolves ionic reagents chiefly through their bonding to the cation. They leave the anion free and hence are highly reactive.

Polar, aprotic solvents increase the reactivity of nucleophiles in S_N2 reactions.

Substitution Nucleophilic Unimolecular (S_N1)

The term unimolecular means that rate of nucleophilic substitution reaction depends upon the concentration of the substrate only and not on the nucleophile. It follows first order kinetics. This reaction takes place in two steps.

$$\text{Rate} \propto [\text{Substrate}] \downarrow RX$$

Mechanism

***Step* I** The polarised *R*—*X* bond undergoes slow cleavage to produce a carbocation and a halide ion.

$$R—X \underset{\text{Step}}{\overset{\text{Slowest}}{\rightleftharpoons}} R^+ + X^-$$

***Step* II** The carbocation thus formed is then attacked by nucleophile.

$$R^+ + \underset{\text{(Nucleophile)}}{OH^-} \xrightarrow{\text{Fast}} R—OH$$

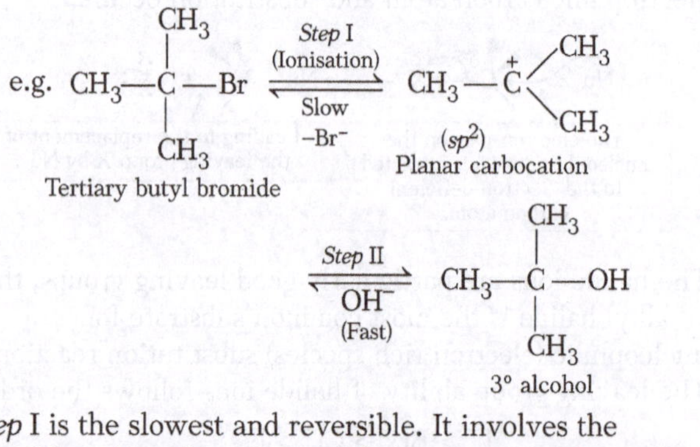

Step I is the slowest and reversible. It involves the *R*—*X* bond breaking for which the energy is obtained through solvation of halide ion with the proton of protic solvent. Since, the rate of reaction depends upon the slowest step, the rate of reaction depends only on the concentration of alkyl halide.

- **Relative reactivity of haloalkanes towards S_N1 reactions** The order of reactivity will be tertiary alkyl halide > secondary alkyl halide > primary alkyl halide > methyl halide.

Factors Affecting S_N1 Reactions

Various factor affecting S_N1 reactions are as follows

(i) **Structure of alkyl halide** The order of reactivity depends upon the stability of carbocation which are intermediates in the first step. Greater the stability of the carbocation, greater will be its ease of formation from alkyl halide and hence faster will be the rate of the reaction. As we know, 3° carbocation is most stable, therefore, the *tert*-alkyl halides will undergo S_N1 reaction very fast.

Since, the stability of carbocation decreases in the order.

Benzyl carbocation > Allyl carbocation > 3° carbocation (except Me_3C^+) > 2° carbocation > 1° carbocation

Allyl and benzyl carbocations are more stable due to resonance.

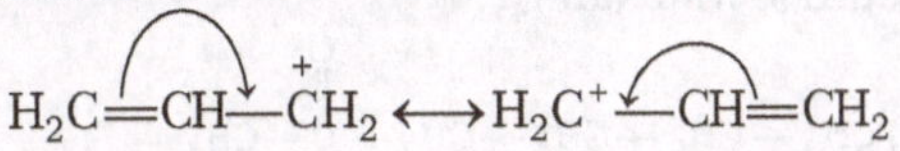

Allyl carbocation (1°)

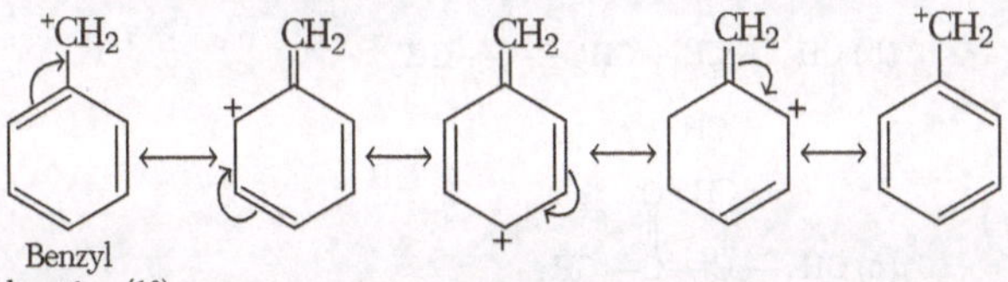

Benzyl carbocation (1°)

Thus, reactivity of haloalkanes towards S_N1 reactions decrease in the same order.

Benzylic halide > allylic halides > 3° alkyl halide > 2° alkyl halide > 1° alkyl halide.

For example, it has been observed that the reaction of $(CH_3)_3CBr$ with OH^- ion to give 2-methyl-2-propanol is about 1 million times as fast as the corresponding reaction of the methyl bromide to give methanol.

> **Concept ladder** During the S_N1 reaction, carbocation is formed so there may be possibility of rearrangement in the product, i.e. major product will be formed from possibly most stable carbocation.

(ii) **Nucleophilicity** S_N1 reactions do not depend on the concentration of nucleophile. Therefore, these reactions are not affected by concentration of nucleophile.

Here, weaker nucleophile is preferred.

(iii) **Leaving group ability** Good leaving groups such as $Cl^{\ominus}$, $Br^{\ominus}$, $I^{\ominus}$ help in proceeding the S_N1 reactions faster.

(iv) **Solvent effect** Reaction by S_N1 is favoured by solvents of high ionising power, i.e. by polar protic solvents (like water, alcohol, acetic acid) that help to pull the leaving group out of the molecule and stabilises the carbocation intermediate as well.

Difference between S_N1 and S_N2 Reaction

S_N1	S_N2
• $R-X + Nu^- \longrightarrow R-Nu$	• $R-X + Nu^- \longrightarrow R-Nu$
Mechanism $R-X \underset{\text{R.D.S}}{\overset{\text{Slow step}}{\rightleftharpoons}} \underset{\text{Carbocation}}{R^{\oplus}} + X^-$ $R^{\oplus} \xrightarrow[\text{Fast step}]{X^-} R-X$	**Mechanism** $R-X + \bar{N}u$ → Rate determining step (RDS), Slow step → $\left[\overset{\delta-}{Nu} \cdots \overset{\delta++}{R} \cdots \overset{\delta-}{X}\right]$ Transition state $\xrightarrow{\text{Fast}}$ $R-Nu + X^-$
• Unimolecular nucleophilic substitution reaction	• Bimolecular nucleophilic substitution reaction
• Order of reaction = 1	• Order of reaction = 2
• Molecularity = 1	• Molecularity = 2
• Two or multi step process	• One step process
• Carbocations are formed.	• No carbocation is formed.
• Rate = k [Alkyl halide]	• Rate = k [Alkyl halide] [Nu^-]
• Polar protic solvents favours S_N1 reactions.	• Polar aprotic solvents like DMF, DMSO favours S_N2 reaction.
• Partial racemisation is observed [when the carbon bearing the LG is asymmetric]	• Walden inversion occurs.
• Nucleophiles are weak base.	• Nucleophile are strong base.
• The order of reactivity follows the sequence 3° > 2° > 1° > CH_3-X alkyl halides	• The order of reactivity follows the sequence CH_3-X > 1° > 2° > 3° alkyl halides

Some of the nucleophilic substitution reactions of alkyl halides are as follows

$R-X$:
- $\xrightarrow{Aq.\ KOH}$ $R-OH + KX$
- $\xrightarrow{H_2O}$ $ROH + HX$
- $\xrightarrow{KCN}$ $R-CN$ (major) + KX
- $\xrightarrow{AgCN}$ $R-NC$ (major) + AgX
- $\xrightarrow{NaNO_2}$ $R-O-N=O$ (major) + NaX (Alkyl nitrile)
- $\xrightarrow{AgNO_2}$ $R-NO_2$ (major) + AgX (Nitroalkane)

Stereochemical Aspects of Nucleophilic Substitution Reactions

Some basic stereochemical principles and notations are as follows

(i) **Optical activity** Plane of plane polarised light is rotated when it is passed through the solutions of certain compounds. Such compounds are called optically active compounds. If compound rotates the light towards right (clockwise), it is called dextrorotatory or *d*-form or (+). If the light is rotated towards left (anti-clockwise) it is said to be laevorotatory or *l*-form or (–).

(ii) **Molecular asymmetry, chirality and enantiomers**

If all the substituents attached to tetrahedral carbon are different, the mirror image of the molecule is not superimposed on the molecule, such a carbon is called asymmetric carbon or stereocentre. The resulting molecule would lack symmetry and is referred to as asymmetric molecule.

The objects which are non-superimposable on their mirror image are called **chiral** and this property is known as **chirality.**

The stereoisomers related to each other as non-superimposable mirror images are called **enantiomers.**

(iii) **Retention, inversion and racemisation** When a chemical reaction involves bond cleavage or bond formation at an asymmetric carbon atom, three different products may be formed.

For example, during the substitution of a group *X* by *Y* in the following reaction, the three possible products may be shown below:

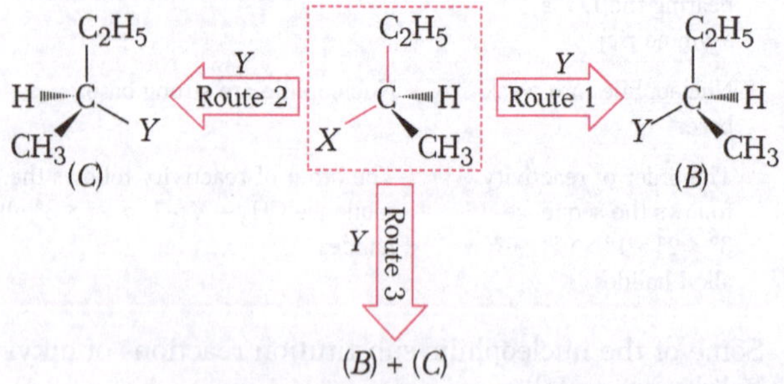

- If *B* is the only product, the process is called **retention** of configuration because *B* has the same configuration as the starting reactant.
- If *C* is the only product, the process is called **inversion** of configuration because *C* has the configuration opposite to the starting reactant *A*.
- If an equimolar mixture of *B* and *C* (i.e. a 50 : 50 mixture) is formed, then the process is called **racemisation** and the product is **optically inactive** because one isomer will rotate light in the direction opposite to another.

NEET Close-up

Example Similar to PYQ Asked in NEET 2014

Which of the following compounds will undergo racemisation under solution of KOH hydrolysis?

(a) $C_6H_5—C(=O)—CH(CH_3)—CH_2—CH_3$

(b) $CH_3CH_2CH_2Cl$

(c) $CH_3—CH(CH_3)—CH_2Br$

(d) $CH_3—CH_2—CH(CH_3)—CH_2—CH_3$

Sol. (*a*) Due to chirality $\left[C_6H_5—C(=O)—CH(CH_3)—CH_2—CH_3\right]$ only compound (a) will undergo racemisation.

Skill Builder

Which of the following will not give a racemic mixture on reduction with $NaBH_4$.

(a) $CH_3—CH_2—CH_2—CH_2—C(=O)—CH_3$

(b) $CH_3—CH(CH_3)—CH_2—C(=O)—CH_3$

(c) $CH_3—C(CH_3)_2—C(=O)—CH_3$

(d) $CH_3CH_2—C(=O)—CH_2CH_3$

For more practice Refer to Q. 11 and Q.17 of Gearing up for NEET.

A. Stereochemical Aspects of S_N2 Reaction

In S_N2 mechanism, the attack of nucleophile, OH^- occurs at the rear side of the molecule relative to the halogen atom.

In other words, OH group has not taken the position previously occupied by the halogen atom but on the side opposite to one where the halogen atom is present.

As a result S_N2 reactions are always accompanied by inversion of configuration in much the same way as an umbrella is turned inside out in a strong wind. This process is called **inversion of configuration** or **Walden inversion.**

Thus, in case of optically active alkyl halide, the product obtained has an inversion of configuration, i.e. there is change in sign of rotation from (+) to (–) and *vice-versa.* For example, (–)-2-bromooctane on treatment with aqueous KOH solution gives (+)-octan-2-ol as the product.

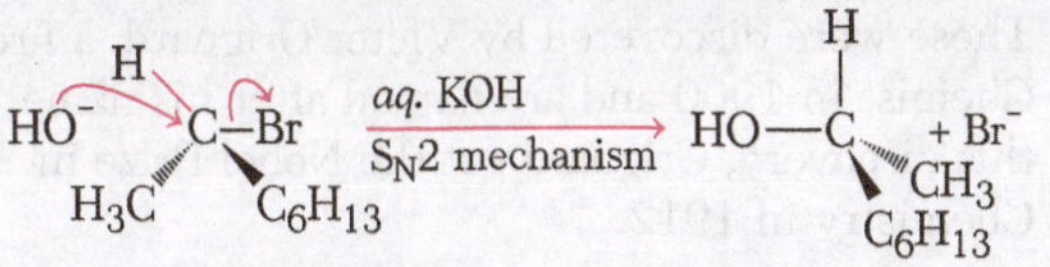

(+)-octan-2-ol

Thus, S_N2 reactions of optically active alkyl halides are accompanied by inversion of configuration.

B. Stereochemical Aspects of S_N1 Reaction

In case of optically active alkyl halide, the product obtained during S_N1 reaction is a racemic mixture. This is because the intermediate carbocation formed in the slow step is planar (achiral) species (carbocation).

Therefore, the attack of the nucleophile, OH^- ion can take place with equal ease from both the faces (front and rear) forming a mixture of two enantiomers. In one enantiomer, the nucleophile occupies the same position as originally occupied by the halogen atom while in the other enantiomer the nucleophile occupies the position opposite to that of the halogen atom.

As a result, mixture of molar ratio, $x : x$ of the two enantiomers (*laevo* and *dextro*) is formed. Therefore, the product formed is a racemic mixture (±) which is optically inactive ($2x$%) and ($100 - 2x$)% of excess. Inversion-excess will make the mixture of products optically active, where $40 < x < 50$.

Thus, S_N1 reactions of optically active alkyl halides are accompanied by racemisation, to an extent of 80 to <100%.

For example, hydrolysis of optically active 2-bromobutane results in the formation of racemic mixture (±)-butan-2-ol (major).

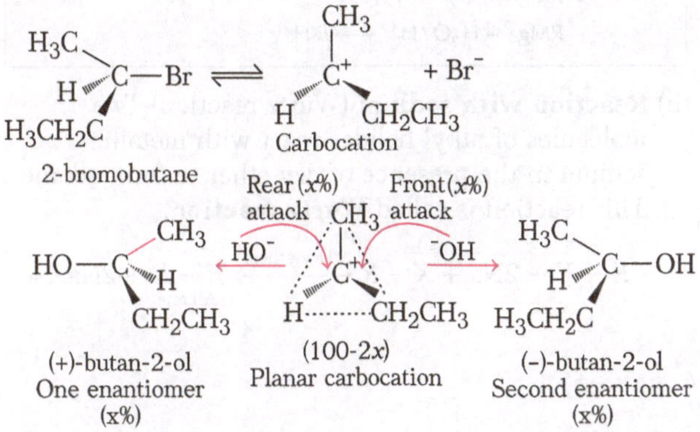

⇒ So, % inversion > % retention
($100 - x$) (x)

Where, $40 < x < 50$

NEET Snapshot

In an S_N1 reaction on chiral centres, there is more inversion than retention, which leads to partial racemisation. *[NEET 2015]*

The leaving group, in most cases, remains weakly attracted to the carbocation due to electrostatic forces, so it occupies the front side of the carbocation and as a result, backside attack becomes less sterically hindered than front side attack and polar solvent molecules also block two faces of the trigonal planar carbocation intermediate.

Elimination Reactions

When alkyl halides with β-hydrogen are heated in presence of alcoholic KOH, a molecule of HX is eliminated and alkene is formed, this reaction is known as **dehydrohalogenation.**

In this reaction hydrogen of alkyl halide is eliminated from β-carbon and halogen from α-carbon. This reaction is also known as **β-elimination** or **1, 2-elimination reaction.**

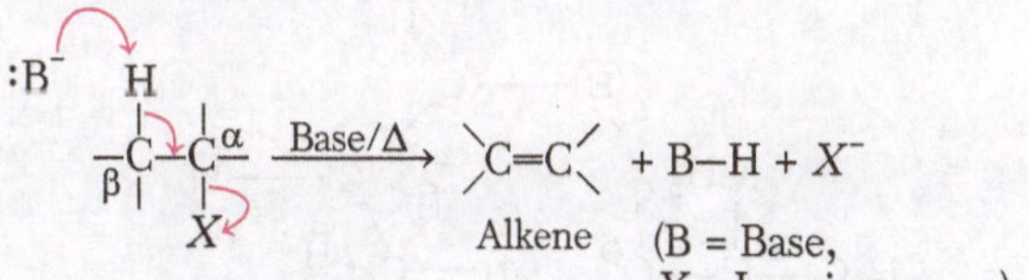

(C_α—X and C_β—H are anti to each other)

If more than one β-hydrogen are present then β-elimination takes place according to Saytzeff's rule, According to this rule, in dehydrohalogenation reactions, more substituted alkene will be formed as the major product. e.g.

$$\overset{\beta}{CH_3}-\overset{\beta}{CH_2}-\underset{Br}{\overset{\alpha}{CH}}-\overset{\beta}{CH_3} \xrightarrow[-KBr,\ -H_2O]{\text{Alc. KOH, }\Delta} \underset{\text{But-2-ene (80\%)}}{CH_3-CH=CH-CH_3} + \underset{\text{But-1-ene (20\%)}}{CH_3-CH_2-CH=CH_2}$$

Concept ladder

In presence of bulky base, e.g. $(CH_3)_3C\bar{O}\overset{+}{K}$, elimination proceeds *via* Hofmann's rule.

Here, least substituted alkene is obtained because a bulky base suffers steric hinderance in abstracting a proton from more substituted β-carbon.

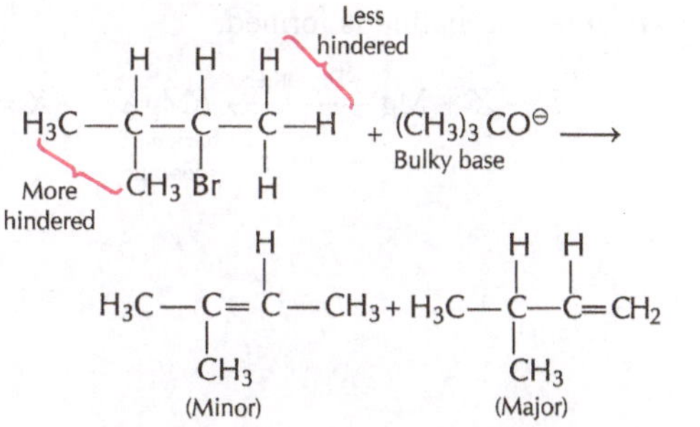

Elimination *versus* Substitution

An alkyl halide with β-hydrogen atoms, when reacted with a base or a nucleophile has two competing routes. These are

(i) Substitution (S_N1 and S_N2)

(ii) Elimination (E1 and E2)

It depends upon the nature of alkyl halide, strength and size of base/nucleophile and reaction conditions.

Thus, a bulkier nucleophile will prefer to act as a base and abstracts a proton rather than approach towards a tetravalent carbon atom (steric reasons) and *vice-versa*. Similarly, a 1° alkyl halide will prefer a S_N2 reaction, a 2° halide-S_N2 or elimination depending upon the strength of base/nucleophile and 3° halide elimination than S_N1 depending upon the stability of carbocation or the more substituted alkene.

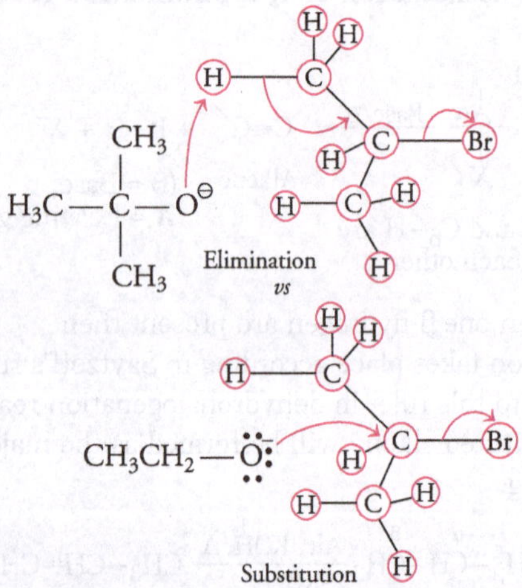

Reaction with Metals

Active metals like sodium, magnesium, lithium, etc. readily combine with alkyl chlorides, bromides and iodides to give compounds containing carbon-metal bond. Such compounds are called **organometallic compounds.**

(i) **Reaction with magnesium** (Formation of Grignard reagent) When a solution of an alkyl halide in dry ether is treated with magensium, an alkyl magnesium halide is formed.

$$R-X + \text{Mg} \xrightarrow{\text{Dry ether}} \underset{\text{Grignard reagent}}{R\text{MgX}} \quad (X = \text{Cl, Br, I})$$

Mentor's TIP

Reactivity of *R*I, *R*Br, *R*Cl with Mg to form Grignard reagent is in order *R*I > *R*Br > *R*Cl.

For a given halide, reactivity order of '*R*' is 1° > 2° > 3°.

These were discovered by Victor Grignard, a French Chemist in 1900 and are named after his name. For this discovery, Grignard got the Nobel Prize in Chemistry in 1912.

In the Grignard reagent, the carbon-magnesium bond is covalent but highly polar with carbon pulling electrons from electropositive magnesium. This is because of large electronegativity difference between carbon (2.5) and magnesium (1.2).

The magnesium-halogen bond is essentially ionic. Thus, Grignard reagent may be represented as

$$\overset{\delta-}{R}-\overset{\delta+}{\text{Mg}}\overset{\delta-}{X} \rightleftharpoons \overset{\ominus}{R} + \overset{\oplus}{MgX}$$

These Grignard reagents are very reactive compounds. They react with any source of proton (Bronsted acid) to form hydrocarbon.

$$R\text{Mg}X + \underset{\text{Source of proton}}{Z\text{H}} \longrightarrow \underset{\text{Hydrocarbon}}{R\text{H}} + Z\text{Mg}X$$

where, *Z* may be OH, *R*O, NH_2, RNH_2, $RC\equiv H$, etc.

It is therefore necessary to avoid even traces of moisture from a Grignard reagent. That is why reaction is carried out in dry ether.

Concept ladder

Compounds of Grignard reagent are the compounds through which almost all the category can be produced. Some of its important reactions are

- $RMgX + CuX + R'CN \longrightarrow R-CO-R'$
- $R'_3SnCl + RMgX \longrightarrow R'_3Sn—R$
- $RMgX + CO_2 \longrightarrow RCO_2H$
- $RMgX + O_2 \longrightarrow ROH$
- $RMgX + H_2O/H^+ \longrightarrow R'H$

(ii) **Reaction with sodium** (Wurtz reaction) Two molecules of alkyl halides react with metallic sodium in the presence of dry ether to form alkanes. This reaction is called **Wurtz reaction.**

$$R-X + 2\text{Na} + X-R \xrightarrow{\text{Dry ether}} \underset{\text{Alkane}}{R-R} + 2\text{Na}X\downarrow$$

STEP UP Practice 2

1 Reaction of ethyl bromide with aqueous sodium hydroxide involves
(a) racemisation (b) S_N1 mechanism
(c) retention of configuration (d) S_N2 mechanism

2 Which of the following structures is enantiomeric with the molecule (A) given below?

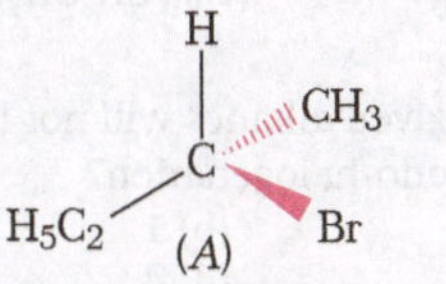

(a)
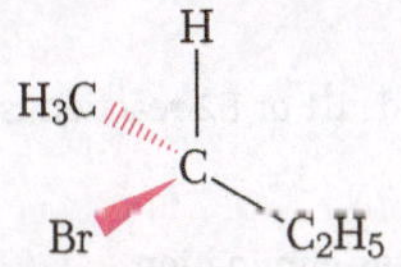

(b)
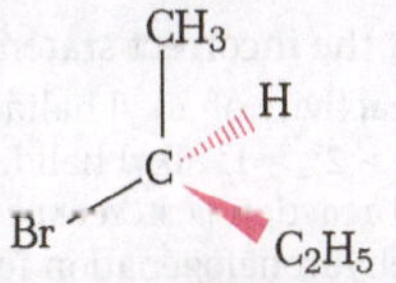

(c)
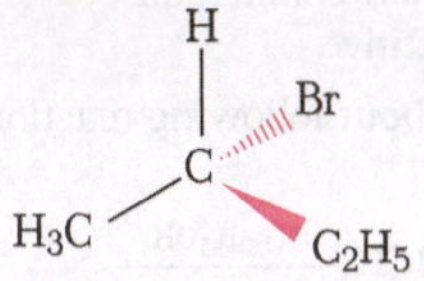

(d)
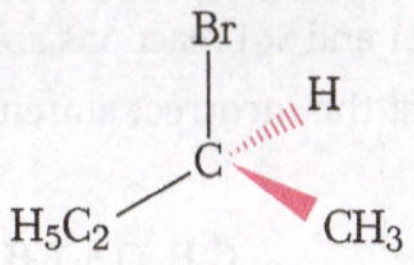

3 Molecule whose mirror image is non-superimposable over them are known as chiral. Which of the following molecules is chiral in nature?
(a) 2-bromobutane (b) 1-bromobutane
(c) 2-bromopropane (d) 2-bromopropan-2-ol

4 The major product formed in the following reaction is

$$CH_3-\underset{\underset{Cl}{|}}{CH}-CH_2-CH_2-OH \xrightarrow{Aq.\ KOH}$$

(a) $CH_3CH{=}CHCH_2OH$
(b) $CH_2{=}CH-CH_2-CH_2OH$
(c) $CH_3-CH-CH_2$ (with CH and CH_2 joined through $O-CH_2$ ring)
(d) $CH_3-\underset{\underset{OH}{|}}{CH}-CH_2-CH_2OH$

5 Select the incorrect statement about the *neo*-pentyl bromide from the following.
(a) The primary carbon atom that bears the leaving (bromide) group is hindered by the *tert*-butyl group, so backside approach of a nucleophile is prevented, making this a poor S_N2 substrate.
(b) It reacts with H_2O by S_N1 reaction forming *neo*-pentyl alcohol.
(c) It cannot react by S_N1 reaction because a highly unstable primary carbocation would be formed.
(d) By suitable conditions, it can be made to react by S_N1 reaction, then a rearrangement leads to the formation of a most stable tertiary carbocation.

6 Identify Z, in the following series.

$$C_2H_5I \xrightarrow{Alc.\ KOH} X \xrightarrow{Br_2} Y \xrightarrow{KCN} Z$$

(a) CH_3CH_2CN (b) $NCCH_2-CH_2CN$
(c) $BrCH_2-CH_2CN$ (d) $BrCH{=}CHCN$

7 Chloromethane on treatment with excess of ammonia yields mainly
(a) N, N-dimethylmethanamine $\left[CH_3-N\begin{matrix}CH_3\\ CH_3\end{matrix}\right]$
(b) N-methylmethanamine $(CH_3-NH-CH_3)$
(c) methanamine (CH_3NH_2)
(d) mixture containing all these in equal proportion

8 Consider the following statements.
Statement I *neo*-pentyl halides react slowly in substitution process.
Statement II *neo*-pentyl halides being primary in nature react *via* S_N2 mechanism, under S_N2 condition.
In the light of the above statements, choose the most appropriate answer from the options given below.
(a) Both Statement I and Statement II are false.
(b) Statement I is true, but Statement II is false.
(c) Statement I is false, but Statement II is true.
(d) Both Statement I and Statement II are true.

9 Following reactions take place in presence of
I. $2CH_3CH_2Br + 2Na \longrightarrow$ *n*-butane
II. $CH_3\underset{\underset{Cl}{|}}{CH}CH_3 + CH_3CH_2\bar{O} \longrightarrow$ Prop-1-ene
(a) KOH, $AlCl_3$ (b) Dry ether, CH_3CH_2OH
(c) OH^-, *RMgX* (d) CH_3CH_2OH, HCl

10 Which compound undergoes nucleophilic substitution (S_N2) with NaCN at the fastest rate?

(a)
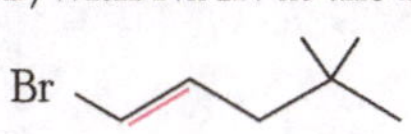

(b)
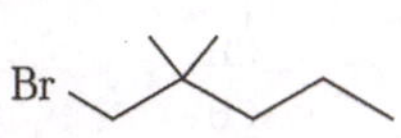

(c)
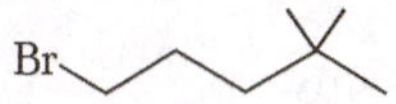

(d)
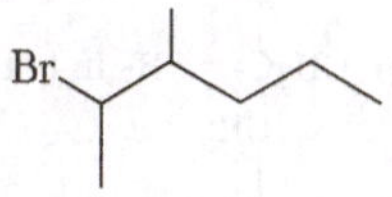

11 Consider the following statements.
Statement I Configuration is only retained in the product of S_N1 reaction.
Statement II Intermediate of an S_N1 reaction is a carbocation and nucleophilic attacks the available side of it.
In the light of the above statements, choose the most appropriate answer from the options given below.
(a) Both Statement I and Statement II are false.
(b) Statement I is true but Statement II is false.
(c) Statement I is false but Statement II is true.
(d) Both Statement I and Statement II are true.

12 Which of the following is most reactive towards HCl?
(a) $CH_2=CHCH_2OH$
(b) $CH_3CH_2CH_2OH$
(c) $CH_3\underset{OH}{CH}CH_3$
(d) $CH_2=CHOH$

13 Alkyl halides can be converted into Grignard reagents by
(a) boiling them with Mg ribbon in alcoholic solution
(b) refluxing them with magnesium powder in dry ether
(c) refluxing them with $MgCl_2$ solution
(d) warming them with $MgCl_2$

14 Consider the following compounds

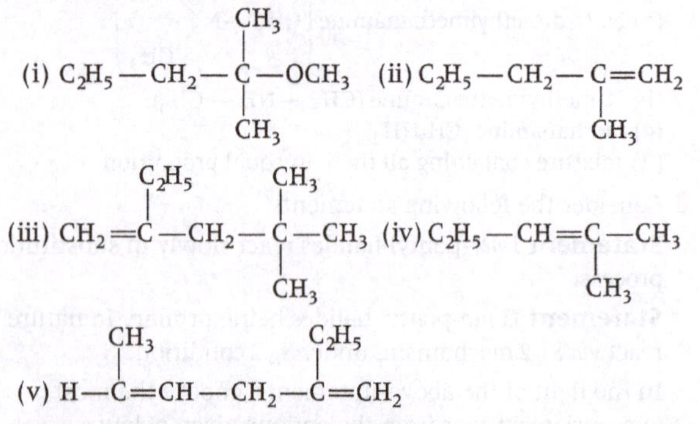

When 2-chloro-2-methyl pentane reacts with sodium methoxide in methanol then how many of the above compounds will be formed one of the products?
(a) 4 (b) 2
(c) 3 (d) 1

15 Consider the following reaction.

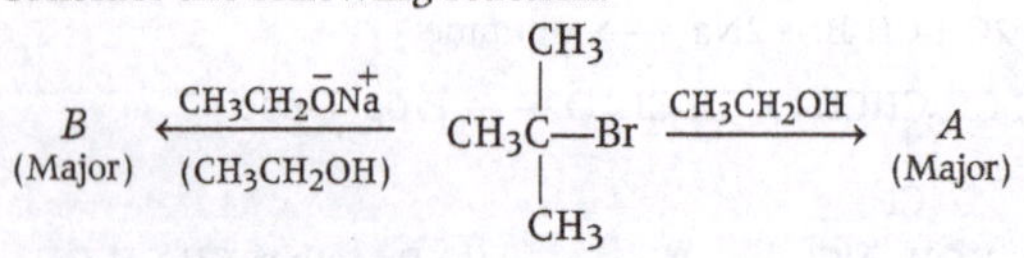

A and B are respectively,
(a) $CH_3\underset{CH_3}{\overset{CH_3}{C}}-OCH_2CH_3$ in both cases
(b) $CH_3\overset{CH_3}{C}=CH_2$ in both cases
(c) $CH_3\underset{CH_3}{\overset{CH_3}{C}}-OCH_2CH_3$ and $CH_3-\underset{CH_2}{\overset{CH_3}{C}}$
(d) $CH_3-\underset{CH_2}{\overset{CH_2}{C}}$ and $CH_3\underset{CH_3}{\overset{CH_3}{C}}-OCH_2CH_3$

16 Consider the following addition reaction,
$CH_3\underset{CH_3}{CH}CH=CH_2 + HBr \longrightarrow$

Select the incorrect statement about this reaction.
(a) It follows electrophilic addition mechanism.
(b) Most stable intermediate is the carbocation, i.e. $CH_3\underset{CH_3}{C}H\overset{\oplus}{C}HCH_3$.
(c) Final product is $(CH_3)_2\underset{Br}{C}CH_2CH_3$.
(d) In presence of benzoyl peroxide, final product is $(CH_3)_2CHCH_2CH_2Br$.

17 Consider the following alkanes.
(i) $(CH_3)_3CH$ (ii) $(CH_3)_2CHCH_2CH(CH_3)_2$
(iii) $CH_3CH_2CH_2CH_3$ (iv) $(CH_3CH_2)_4C$
(v) $(CH_3CH_2CH_2)_4C$
How many of the given alkanes will not form racemic mixture as a product on mono-halogenation?
(a) 3 (b) 1
(c) 2 (d) 4

18 Select the incorrect statement.
(a) Reactivity of alkyl halides towards E1 or E2 reaction is $3° > 2° > 1°$ alkyl halide.
(b) E1 reaction is stereospecific.
(c) Dehydrohalogenation follows *trans*-elimination.
(d) E1 and S_N1 reactions are competitive.

19 Select the incorrect statements about following reaction,
$$C_2H_5\bar{O} + CH_3CH_2\underset{}{\overset{Br}{C}}HCH_3 \xrightarrow{C_2H_5OH}$$
(a) It is termed as β-elimination reaction.
(b) C_2H_5O is a Bronsted-base.
(c) Products are but-1-ene and but-2-ene.
(d) This reaction involves two step mechanism.

20 What is the decreasing stability order (most stable → least stable) of the following carbocations?

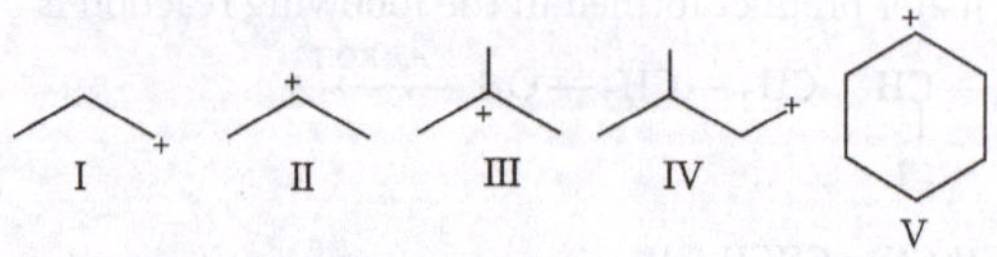

(a) I > II > I > IV > V
(b) I ≈ IV > II ≈ V > III
(c) III > II ≈ V > I ≈ IV
(d) III > I ≈ IV > II ≈ V

21 Which of the following reactions is incorrectly matched with their mechanism?

(a) 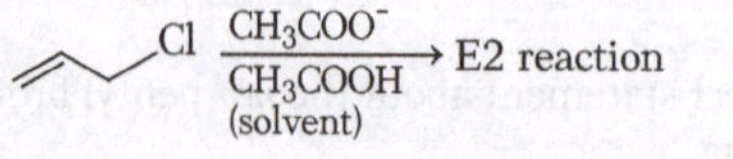

(b) 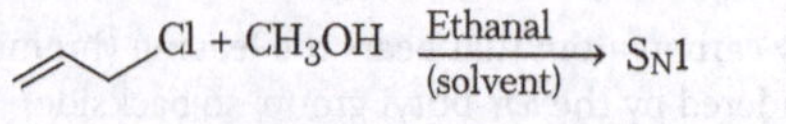

(c) 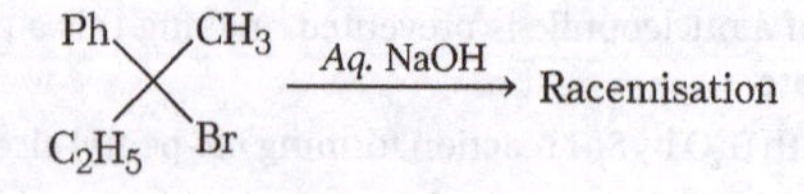

(d) $H_3C-\underset{I}{\overset{H}{C}}-CH_3 \xrightarrow[CH_3CC_2H_5OH]{C_2H_5ONa}$ Elimination

22 From each of the following pairs select the compound that will react faster with sodium iodide in acetone.

I. 2-chloropropane II. 2-bromopropane
III. 1-bromobutane IV. 2-bromobutane

(a) Both I and III (b) Both I and IV
(c) Both II and III (d) Both II and IV

23 Consider the following statements.

Statement I When *neo*-pentyl bromide is subjected to Wurtz reaction, the product formed is 2,2,5,5-tetramethyl hexane.

Statement II Ethyl bromide and *n*-propyl bromide is allowed to react with sodium, in dry ether they produce mixture of four alkanes.

In the light of the above statements, choose the most appropriate answer from the options given below

(a) Both Statement I and Statement II are false.
(b) Statement I is true but Statement II is false.
(c) Statement I is false but Statement II is true.
(d) Both Statement I and Statement II are true.

24 CH_3CH_2Cl by Wurtz reaction forms

(a) ethane, ethene and butane
(b) ethene and butane
(c) only butane
(d) only ethane

Module 3

Preparation, Physical and Chemical Properties of Haloarenes

- Methods of Preparation of Haloarenes
- Physical Properties of Haloarenes
- Chemical Properties of Haloarenes
- Nucleophilic Substitution Reaction
- Electrophilic Substitution Reaction
- Reaction with Metals

Methods of Preparation of Haloarenes

Following are the methods of preparation of haloarenes

From Hydrocarbons by Electrophilic Substitution

Haloarenes (aryl chlorides and bromides) can be prepared by electrophilic substitution of arenes with halogens (X = Cl, Br) in the presence of Lewis acid catalysts like iron or iron (III) chloride.

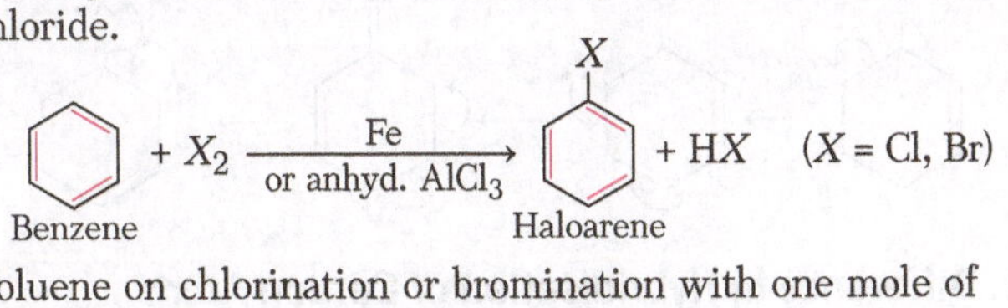

Toluene on chlorination or bromination with one mole of chlorine in the presence of Fe in dark, forms *o*- and *p*-haloderivatives.

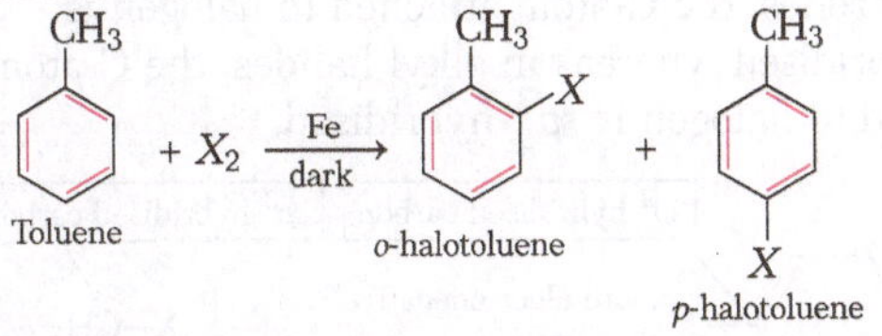

The *ortho* and *para*-isomers can be easily separated due to large difference in their melting points.

Reactions with iodine are reversible in nature and require the presence of an oxidising agent (HNO_3, HIO_4) to oxidise the HI formed during iodination. Fluoro compounds are not prepared by this method due to high reactivity of fluorine.

Mentor's TIP

Toluene reacts with halogen in the presence of sunlight (UV) results into side chain benzylic halogenation.

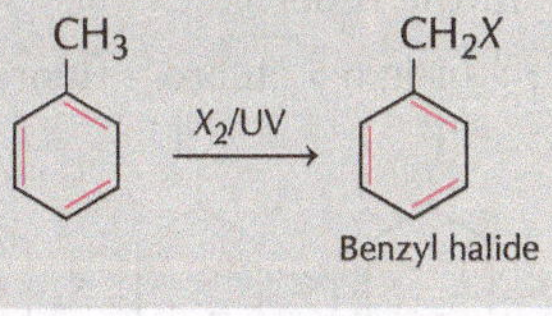

From Amines by Sandmeyer's Reaction

When a primary aromatic amine, dissolved or suspended in cold aqueous mineral acids followed by treatment with sodium nitrite then diazonium salt is formed. This freshly prepared benzene diazonium salt is treated with cuprous chloride or cuprous bromide results in the replacement of the diazonium group by —Cl or —Br. This reaction is called **Sandmeyer's reaction**.

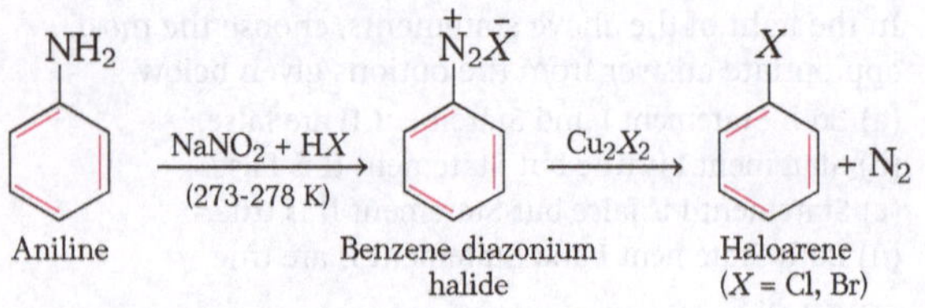

Replacement of the diazonium group by iodine does not require the presence of cuprous halide and is done simply by shaking the diazonium salt with potassium iodide.

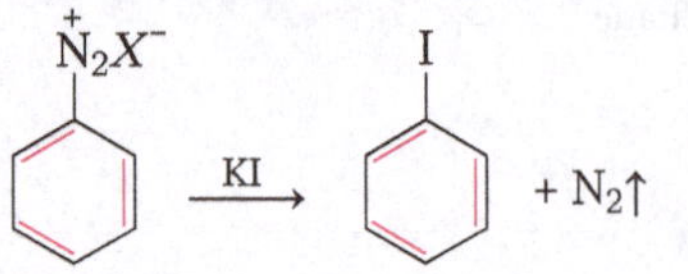

Concept ladder

Balz-Schiemann reaction can also be used to prepare fluoride by reaction of diazonium salt with HBF_4 and heating it. The reaction involved is as follows

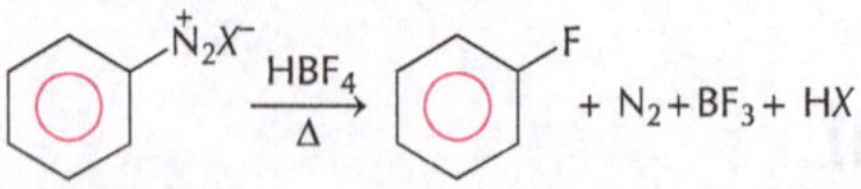

Physical Properties of Haloarenes

The important physical properties of haloarenes or aryl halides are

(i) **Physical state** These are generally colourless liquids or crystalline solids.

(ii) **Solubility** The aryl halides are heavier than water. These are insoluble in water but soluble in organic solvents.

(iii) **Melting and boiling points** The melting and boiling points of aryl halides are nearly the same as those of alkyl halides containing the same number of carbon atoms.

The boiling points of monohalogen derivatives of benzene are in the order:

iodo > bromo > chloro > fluoro

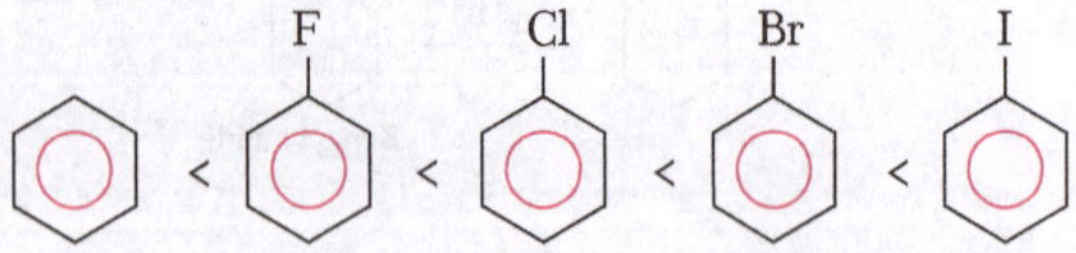

b.p. (K) 353 < 358 < 405 < 429 < 462

This trend is same as for alkyl halides.

For the same halogen atom, the melting and boiling points increases as the size of the aryl group increases.

The boiling points of isomeric dihaloarenes are nearly the same but their melting points are quite different as shown below :

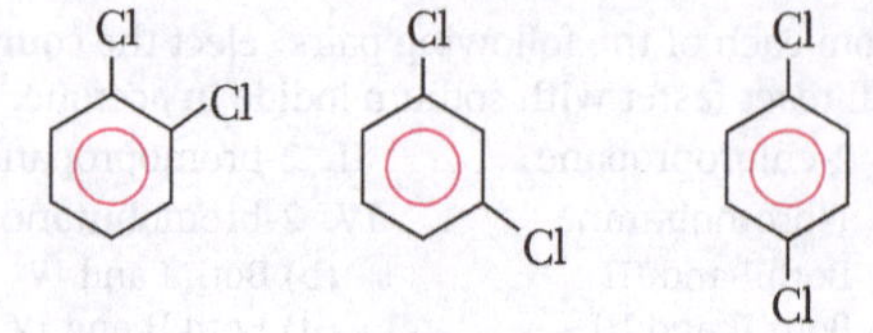

	ortho		*meta*		*para*
b.p.	453 K	>>	446 K	<	448 K
m.p.	256 K	>	249 K	<<	323 K

Generally, the melting point of *para* isomer is quite higher than that of *ortho* or *meta* isomers. This is due to the fact that it has symmetrical structure and therefore, its molecules can closely pack in the crystal lattices. As a result, intermolecular forces of attraction are stronger and therefore, greater energy is required to break its lattice and it melts at higher temperature.

(iv) **Dipole moment** Fluorobenzene, chlorobenzene and bromobenzene have lower dipole moments than the corresponding methyl halides.

Chemical Properties of Haloarenes

Haloarenes gives various types of chemical reactions. This is due to the presence of C—*X* bond in aryl halides that have double bond character due to conjugation between lone pair (+*R* or +*M*) of halogen and benzene ring.

Nucleophilic Substitution Reactions

Aryl halides are less reactive than alkyl halides towards nucleophilic substitution reactions due to following reasons.

1. Resonance Effect

The C—*X* bond of aryl halide is stronger and acquires a partial double bond character due to resonance. The lone pairs of halogen atom are delocalised in the benzene ring and following resonating structures are possible.

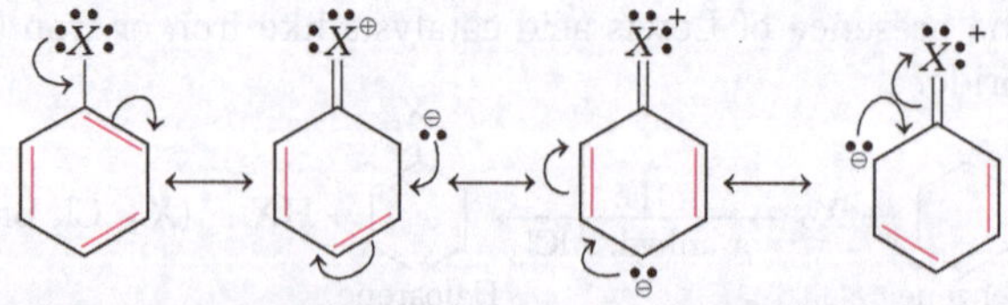

2. Difference in Hybridisation of Carbon Atom in C—*X* Bond

In haloarenes, the C-atom attached to halogen is sp^2-hybridised whereas in alkyl halides, the C-atom attached to halogen is sp^3-hybridised.

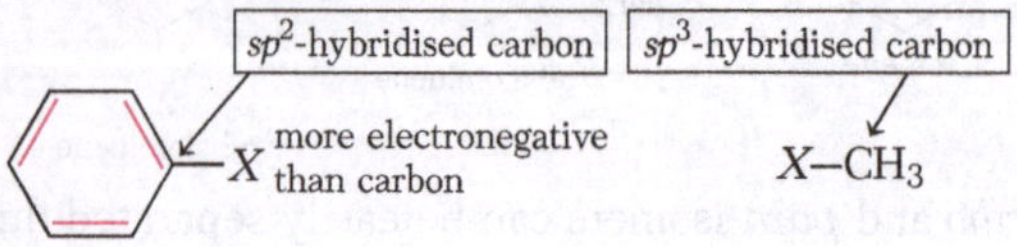

R—*X*	Carbon atom of (C—*X*)	*s*-character
Aryl halide	sp^2	33.3%
Alkyl halide	sp^3	25.0%

Greater the *s*-character, greater is the electronegativity of carbon and thus, bonding pair of (C—*X*) is held tightly and bond length is shortened.

Since, it is difficult to break a shorter bond than a longer bond, therefore, haloarenes are less reactive than haloalkanes towards S_N reaction.

3. Polarity of Carbon-Halogen Bond

The sp^2 hybridised carbon atom involved in C—*X* bond of haloarene molecule is more electronegative than the sp^3 hybrid carbon atom of alkyl halide. Therefore, this sp^2 hybridised carbon has less tendency to release electrons to the Cl-atom and the C—Cl bond of aryl halides is less polar than that of alkyl halides. This is supported by the fact that the dipole moment of chlorobenzene is 1.73 D while the dipole moment of chloroethane is 2.05 D. Thus, lesser the polarity of C—Cl bond, lesser is the reactivity.

4. Instability of Phenyl Cation

In case of haloarenes, the phenyl cation formed as a result of self ionisation will not be stabilised by resonance because the sp^2 hybridised orbital of carbon having positive charge is perpendicular to the *p*-orbital of the phenyl ring.

Therefore, phenyl cation is not formed and therefore, S_N1 mechanism cannot occur.

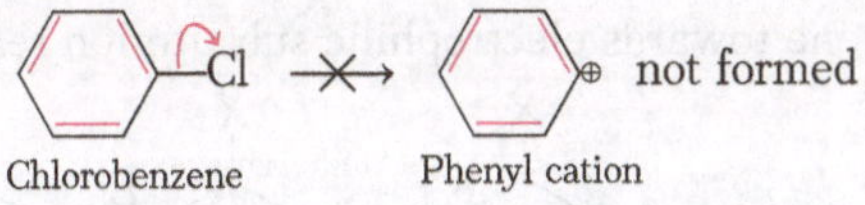

5. Repulsion between the Electron rich Attacking Nucleophiles and Electron Rich Arenes

Because of electron rich arenes, electron rich nucleophile will not approach closely for the attack due to repulsion.

Thus, haloarenes are less reactive towards the substitution reactions than haloalkanes.

However, under drastic conditions, aryl halides undergo substitution reactions as discussed below.

On heating aryl halides with aqueous solution of sodium hydroxide at 623 K and under pressure (300 atm), the halogen atom is replaced by hydroxyl group forming phenol.

In the first step, sodium phenoxide is formed which on acidification gives phenol.

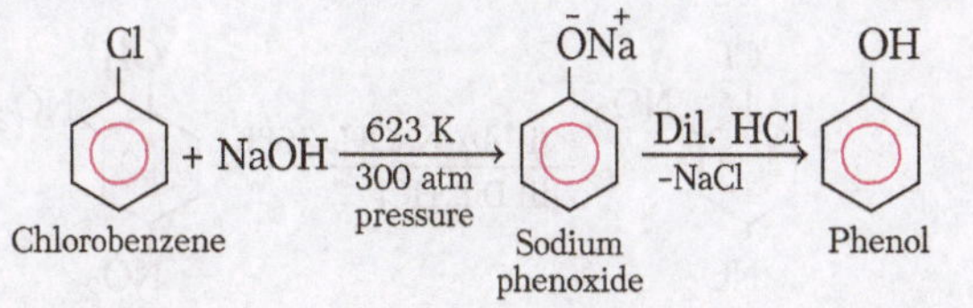

This reaction forms the basis of **Dow's process** for the manufacture of phenol.

NEET Close-up

Example Similar to PYQ Asked in NEET 2020

Which of the following compounds undergoes nucleophilic substitution exclusively by S_N1 mechanism?

(a) Benzyl bromide (b) Ethyl bromide
(c) Bromobenzene (d) *Iso*-propyl bromide

Sol. (*a*) In benzyl bromide, the carbocation formed during S_N1 mechanism is resonance stabilised hence it will undergoes nucleophilic substitution exclusively by S_N1 reaction.

Skill Builder

Arrange the following halides in the increasing order of S_N1 reactivity.

(I) $CH_3CH_2CH_2Cl$ (II) $CH_2{=}CHCH(Cl)CH_3$
(III) $CH_3CH_2CH(Cl)CH_3$

(a) III < II < I (b) I < III < II (c) III < I < II (d) I < II < III

For more practice Refer to Q. 20 of Gearing up for NEET.

Effects of Substituents on Reactivity of Haloarenes (Aryl Halides)

The presence of certain groups at certain positions of the ring markedly affects the reactivity of haloarenes. It has been observed that the presence of electron withdrawing groups such as $—NO_2$, —CN, —COOH, etc., at *o*-and *p*-positions to the halogen atom greatly activates the halogen towards nucleophilic substitution reactions. For example, chlorobenzene is converted into phenol by heating in 6-8% aqueous NaOH only at temperatures above 623 K whereas *p*-chloronitrobenzene is converted into nitrophenol by aqueous NaOH at 443 K.

As the number of *ortho* and *para* nitro groups on the ring is increased, the reactivity increases.

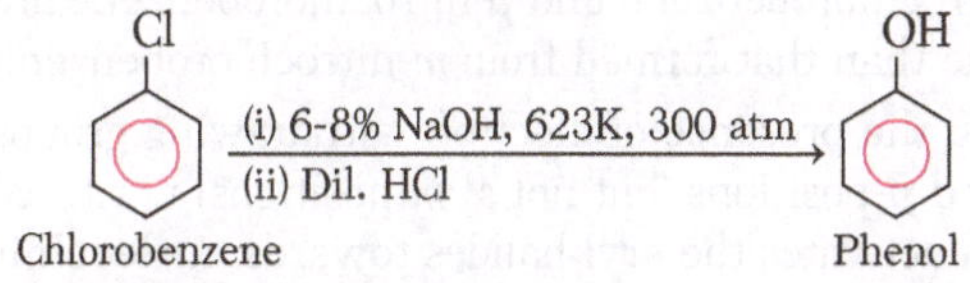

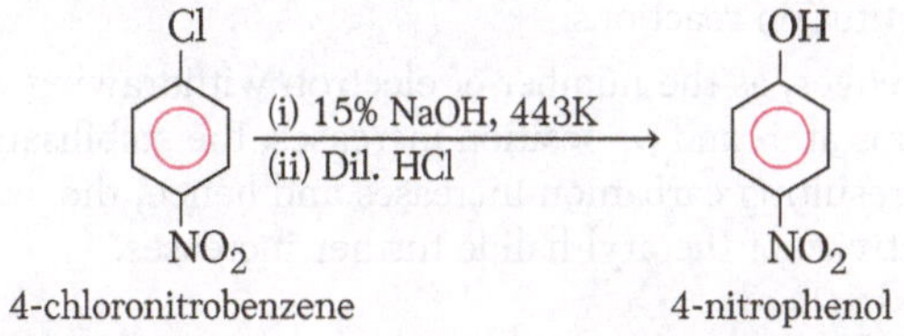

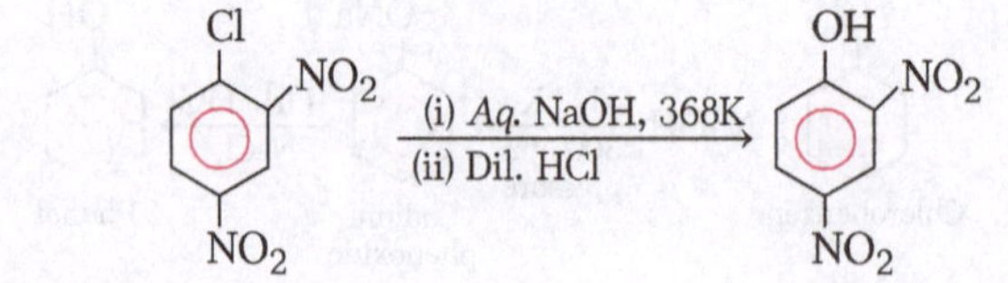

2, 4-dinitrochlorobenzene 2, 4-dinitrophenol

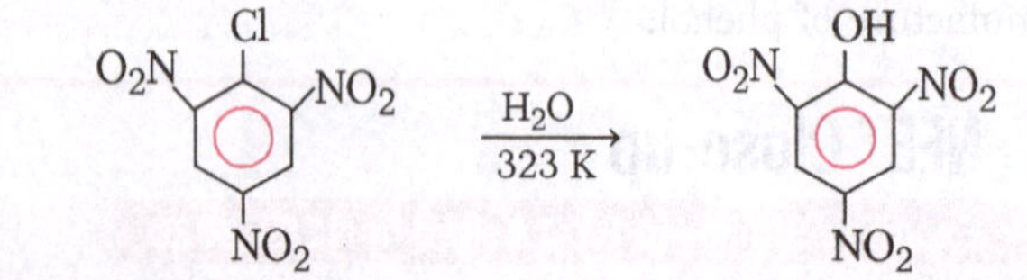

2, 4, 6-trinitrochlorobenzene 2, 4, 6-trinitrophenol

Explanation for Effect of —NO_2 Group

The presence of —NO_2 groups at *ortho* and *para*-positions withdraws electrons density from the benzene ring and therefore, facilitates the attack of the nucleophile on haloarenes.

The carbanion, thus formed is stabilised through resonance.

- In case of *o*- and *p*- chlorobenzenes, one of the resonating structures bears a negative charge on the carbon atom bearing the $-NO_2$ group. Therefore, these carbanions are stabilised by the $-NO_2$ group as well as π-electrons of the benzene ring.

For *para*-position For *ortho*-position

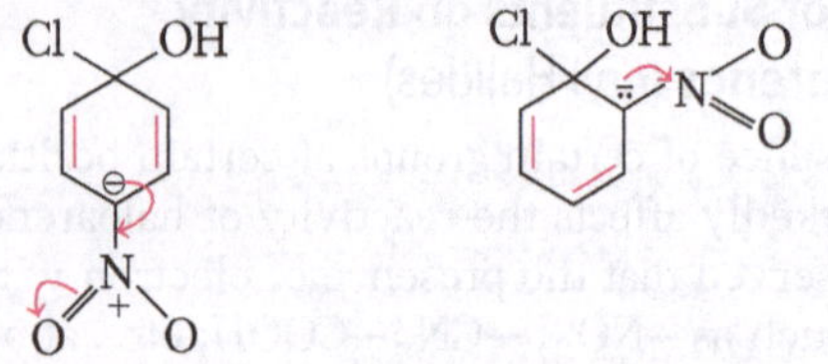

- However, in case of *m*-nitrochlorobenzene, none of the resonating structures bear the negative charge on carbon atom bearing the $-NO_2$ group. Therefore, the nitro group at *meta*-position does not stabilise the negative charge but the carbanion is stabilised only by the π-electrons of the benzene ring.
- In other words, the carbanions formed from *o*-nitrochlorobenzene and *p*-nitrochlorobenzene are most stable than that formed from *m*-nitrochlorobenzene.
- Thus, the presence of electron withdrawing groups at *o*- and *p*-positions (but not at *m*-positions) w.r.t. halogen atom activates the aryl halides towards nucleophilic substitution reactions.
- Moreover, as the number of electron withdrawing groups at *o*- and *p*- position increases, the stabilisation of the resulting carbanion increases and hence, the reactivity of the aryl halide further increases.
- It may be noted that although the presence of $-NO_2$ group (electron withdrawing group) at *m*-position w.r.t. the halogen does not stabilise the carbanion by resonance effect, it does stabilise it somewhat by the inductive effect (*–I*) as compared to the carbanion resulting from chlorobenzene itself.

Therefore, *m*-nitrochlorobenzene is more reactive than chlorobenzene towards nucleophilic substitution reactions.

Concept ladder

Halobenzene in the presence of strong base ($\overset{\ominus}{N}H_2$) react with ammonia and form aniline. Such type of reaction can be explained by elimination-addition or by benzyne mechanism.

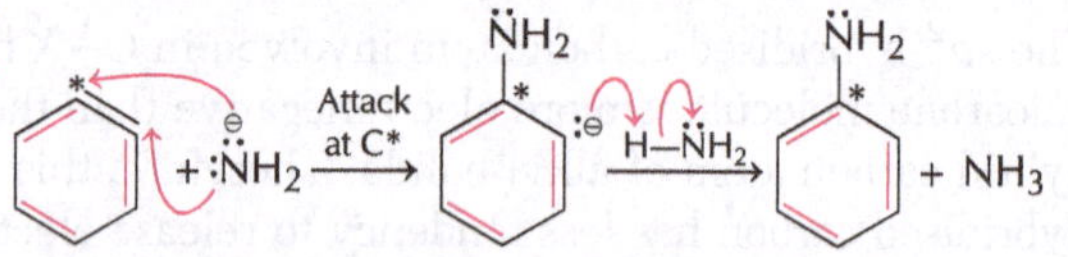

Substitution at the carbon (*) that was attached to the leaving group is called direct (ipso) substitution. Substitution at the adjacent carbon is called cine substitution.

Electrophilic Substitution Reactions

The aromatic ring to which halogen is attached can undergo the typical electrophilic aromatic substitution reactions such as nitration, sulphonation, halogenation, Friedel-Crafts alkylation. Like any other substituent, halogen also affects the reactivity and orientation in these reactions.

Here, halogen is unusual in being deactivating (due to *–I*-effect) yet *ortho* and *para*-directing (electron density is high). Due to this reaction, haloarenes are less reactive than benzene towards electrophilic substitution reactions.

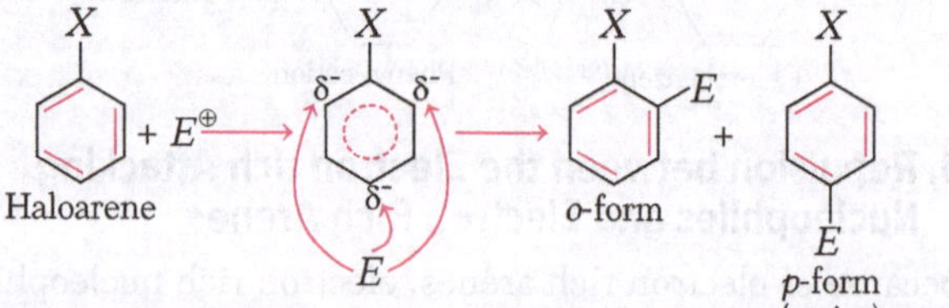

Haloarene o-form p-form (major)

Some important reactions of chlorobenzene are given below

(i) **Halogenation** It takes place by reacting haloarenes in the presence of ferric salt as catalyst.

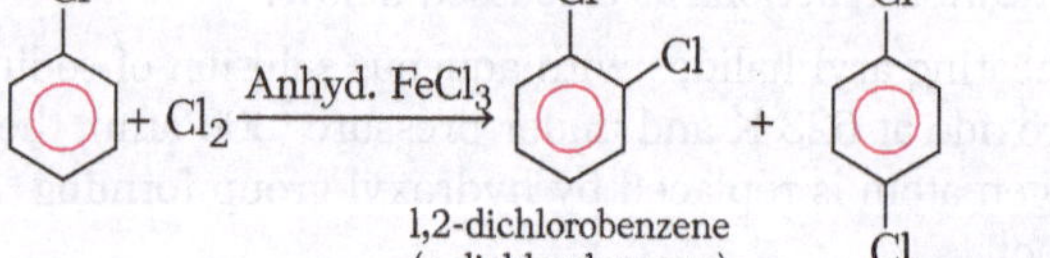

1,2-dichlorobenzene (*o*-dichlorobenzene) (minor)

1, 4-dichlorobenzene (*p*-dichlorobenzene) (major)

(ii) **Nitration** It is carried out by heating haloarene with conc. HNO_3 in the presence of conc. H_2SO_4.

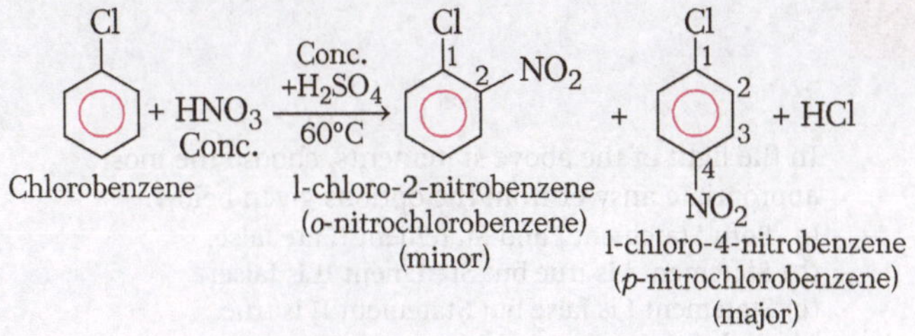

(iii) **Sulphonation** It is carried out by heating haloarene with concentrated H_2SO_4.

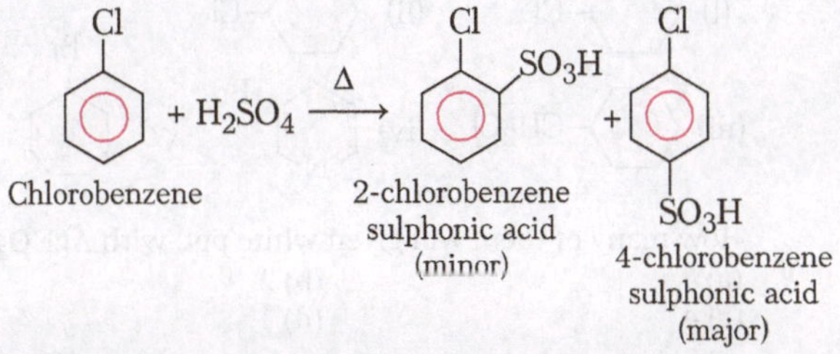

(iv) **Alkylation and acylation** (or alkanoylation) The reaction, known as Friedel-Crafts reaction, is carried by treating haloarene with alkyl chloride or aryl chloride in the presence of anhydrous aluminium chloride acting as catalyst. e.g.

(a) **Friedel-Craft alkylation**

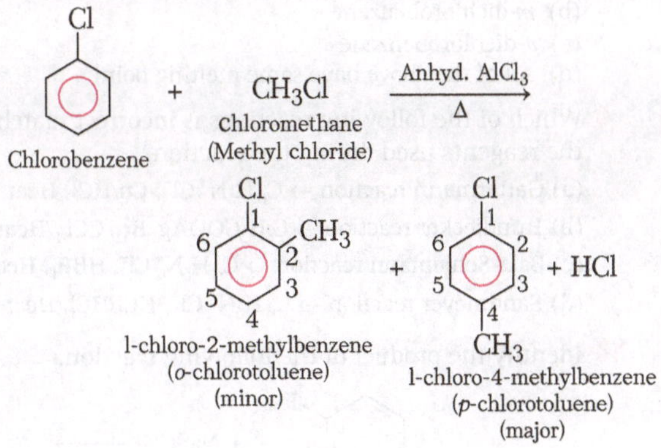

(b) **Friedel-Craft acylation**

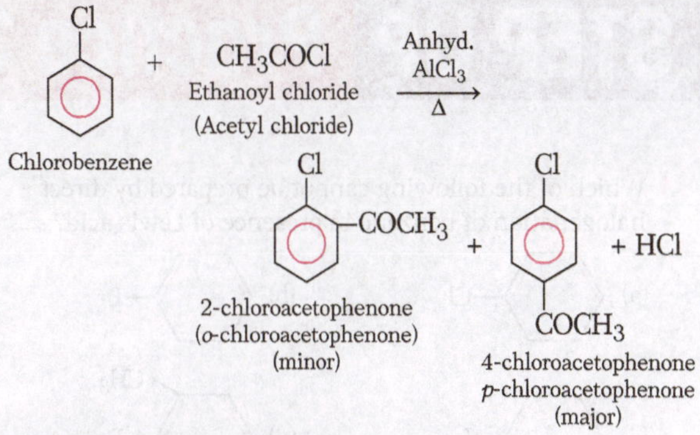

Reaction with Metals

Various types of reactions of haloarenes with metals are discussed below.

Wurtz-Fittig reaction

Reaction of aryl halide and alkyl halide with sodium metal in the presence of dry ether is called Wurtz-Fittig reaction.

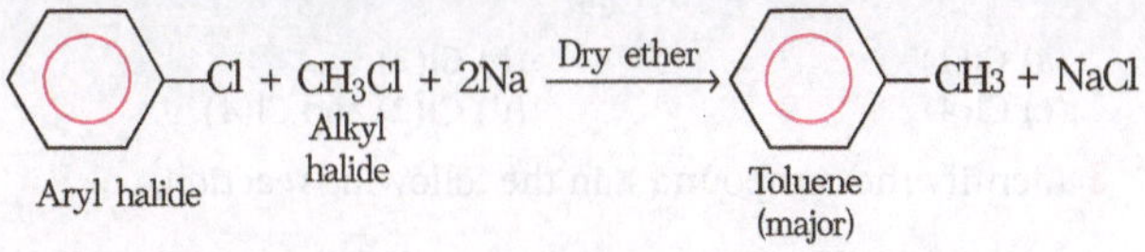

Fittig Reaction

Reaction of aryl halides with sodium metal in the presence of dry ether to form biphenyl is called Fittig reaction.

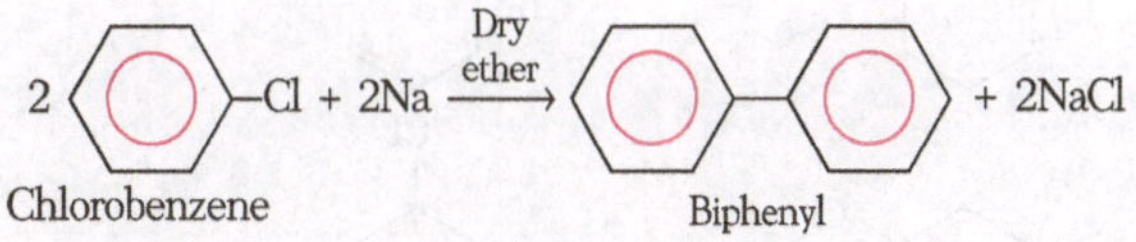

Concept ladder

Reaction of iodoarene with copper powder in a sealed tube to form diaryl is called **Ullmann diaryl synthesis.**

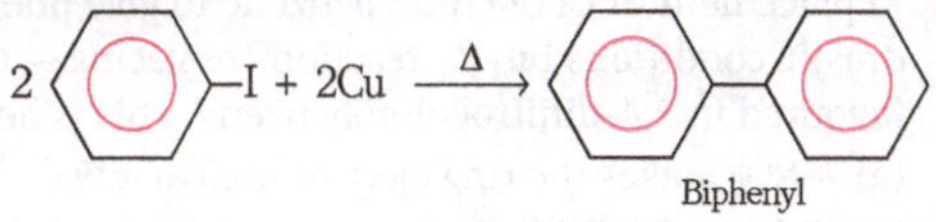

STEP UP Practice 3

1 Which of the following cannot be prepared by direct halogenation of benzene in presence of Lewis acid?

(a) 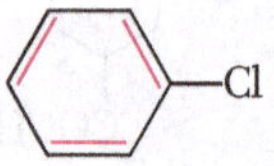

(b) 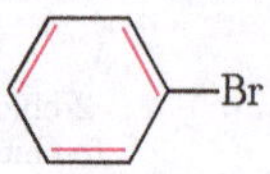

(c) 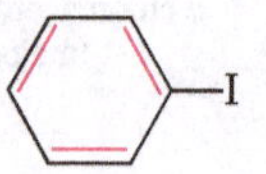

(d) 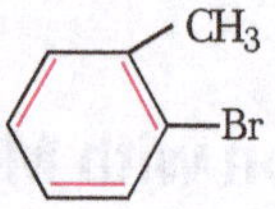

2 Which Cl is most easily replaced *via* S_N reaction?

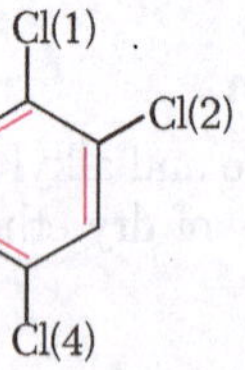

(a) Cl(1) (b) Cl(2)
(c) Cl(4) (d) Cl(2) and Cl(4)

3 Identify the compound *Y* in the following reaction.

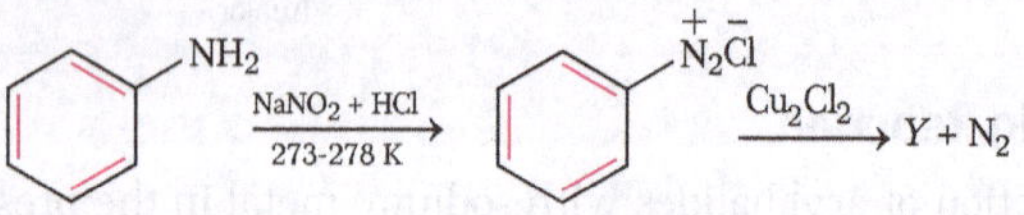

(a) 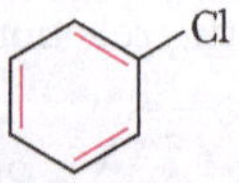

(b) 

(c) 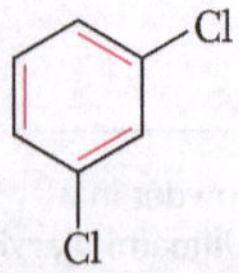

(d) 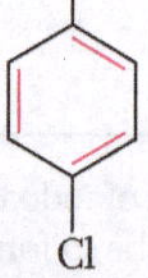

4 Replacement of Cl of chlorobenzene to give phenol requires drastic conditions but S_N reaction (replacing —Cl) is favoured in 2,4-dinitrochlorobenzene. This is because

(a) —NO_2 makes the ring electron-rich at *ortho* and *para*-position
(b) —NO_2 withdraws electrons from *meta*-positions
(c) —NO_2 donates electron at *meta*-position
(d) —NO_2 withdraws electron from *ortho/para*-positions

5 Consider the following statements.

Statement I Reactivity in chlorobenzene is controlled by stronger inductive effect and orientation is controlled by resonance effect.

Statement II The resonance effect tends to oppose the inductive effect for the attack at *o*-and *p*-positions.

In the light of the above statements, choose the most appropriate answer from the options given below.

(a) Both Statement I and Statement II are false.
(b) Statement I is true but Statement II is false.
(c) Statement I is false but Statement II is true.
(d) Both Statement I and Statement II are true.

6 Consider the following compounds.

(i) 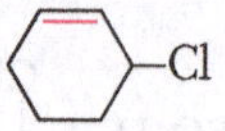

(ii) 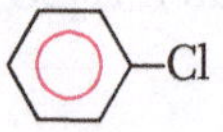

(iii) 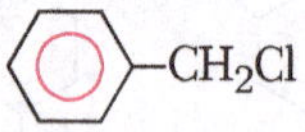

(iv) 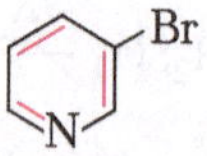

(v) 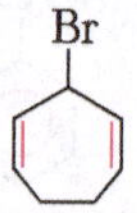

How many of them will given white ppt. with $AgNO_3$?

(a) 3 (b) 2
(c) 4 (d) 1

7 $\underset{(A)}{C_6H_4Cl_2} \xrightarrow{Cl_2/Fe} \underset{(B)}{C_6H_3Cl_3}$

Only one type of product *B* is formed, when *A* is

(a) *o*-dichlorobenzene (b) *m*-dichlorobenzene
(c) *p*-dichlorobenzene (d) *o*-, *p*-dichlorobenzene

8 Which of the following possesses highest melting point?

(a) *o*- dichlorobenzene
(b) *m*-dichlorobenzene
(c) *p*-dichlorobenzene
(d) All of the above have same melting point

9 Which of the following reactions is incorrect match with the reagents used during the reaction?

(a) Gattermann reaction → $C_6H_5N_2^+Cl^-$, Cu/HCl, Heat
(b) Hundiecker reaction → C_6H_5COOAg, Br_2, CCl_4/Heat
(c) Balz-Schiemann reaction → $C_6H_5N_2^+Cl^-$, HBF_4, Heat
(d) Sandmeyer reaction → $C_6H_5N_2^+Cl^-$, KCl/HCl, Heat

10 Identify the product of the following reaction.

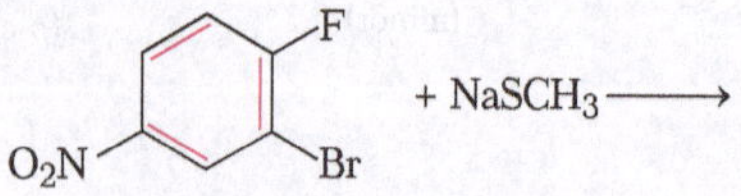

(a) 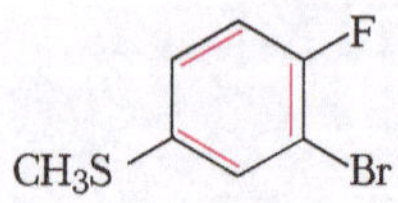

(b) 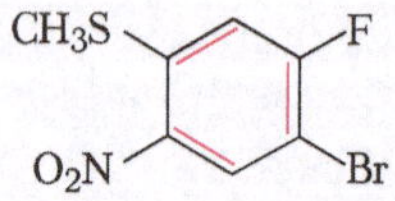

(c) 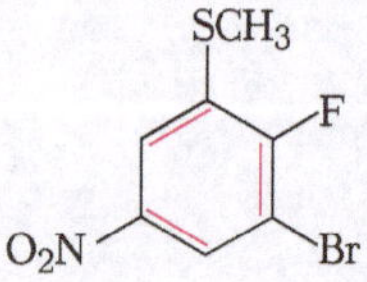

(d) 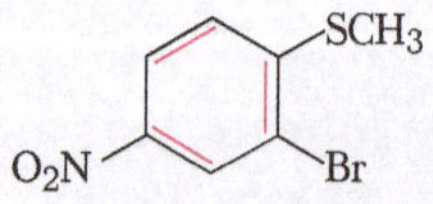

11 Consider the following statements.

Statement I Aryl iodides can be prepared by reaction of arenes with iodine in the presence of an oxidising agent.

Statement II Oxidising agent oxidises I_2 into HI.

In the light of the above statements, choose the most appropriate answer from the options given below.
(a) Both Statement I and Statement II are false.
(b) Statement I is true but Statement II is false.
(c) Statement I is false but Statement II is true.
(d) Both Statement I and Statement II are true.

12 Toluene is nitrated and the resulting product is reduced with tin and hydrochloric acid. The product so obtained is diazotised and then heated with cuprous bromide. The reaction mixture so formed contains
(a) mixture of *o*-and-*p*-bromotoluenes
(b) mixture of *o*-and-*p*-dibromobenzenes
(c) mixture of *o*-and-*p*-bromoanilines
(d) mixture of *o*-and-*m*-bromotoluenes

13 Chlorobenzene is formed by reaction of chlorine with benzene in the presence of $AlCl_3$. Which of the following species attacks the benzene ring in this reaction?
(a) Cl^- (b) Cl^+
(c) $AlCl_3$ (d) $[AlCl_4]^-$

14 Which of the following products is correctly matched regarding Wurtz-Fittig reaction?
(a) $C_6H_5I + 2Na + CH_3I \longrightarrow C_6H_5CH_3 + 2NaI$
(b) $2C_6H_5I + 2Na \longrightarrow C_6H_5C_6H_5 + 2NaI$
(c) $2CH_3CH_2I + 2Na \longrightarrow CH_3CH_2CH_2CH_3 + 2NaI$
(d) $CH_3Br + AgF \longrightarrow CH_3F + AgBr$

15 What is the end product of the following reaction?

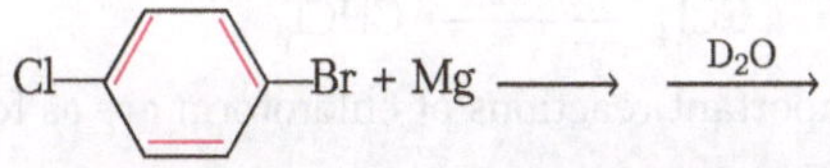

(a) 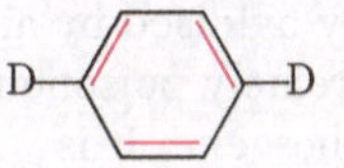

(b) 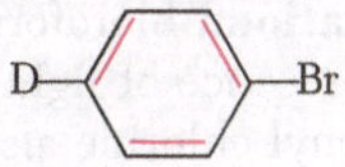

(c) 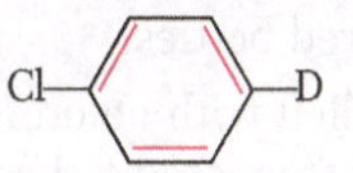

(d) 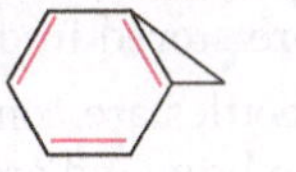

16 Consider the following statements.

Statement I In monohaloarenes, further electrophilic substitution occurs at *ortho*-and *para*-position.

Statement II Halogen atom is a ring deactivator.

In the light of the above statements, choose the most appropriate answer from the options given below.
(a) Both Statement I and Statement II are false.
(b) Statement I is true, but Statement II is false.
(c) Statement I is false, but Statement II is true.
(d) Both Statement I and Statement II are true.

17 $X \xrightarrow[\text{Boiling}]{Cl_2}$ Benzotrichloride $\xrightarrow[\Delta]{H_3O^+} Y$

X and *Y* are
(a) benzene, benzaldehyde (b) toluene, benzaldehyde
(c) toluene, benzoic acid (d) benzene, benzoic acid

18 When 2, 4-dinitrochlorobenzene reacts with methylamine, the major product is

(a) 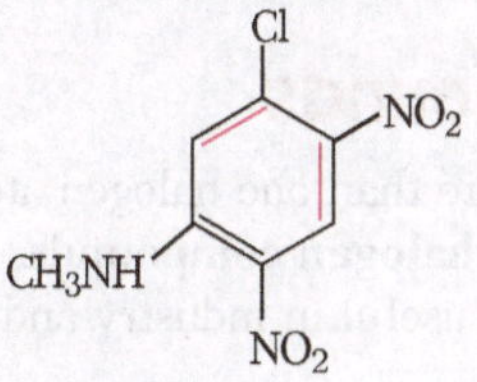

(b) 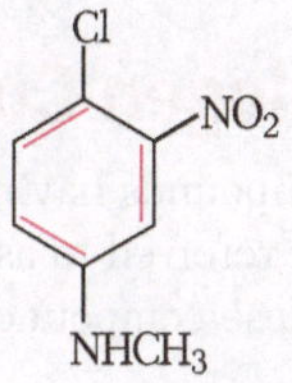

(c) 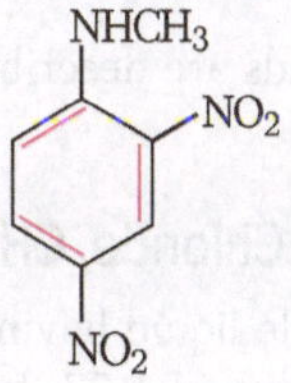

(d) 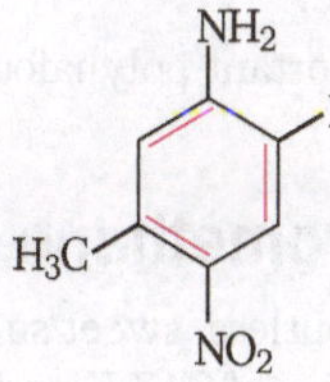

19 In the ArS_E2 of haloarene, incorrect intermediate is

(a) 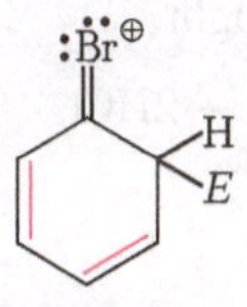

(b) 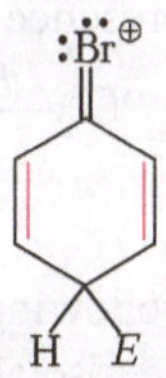

(c) 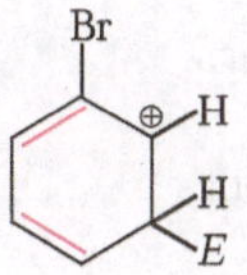

(d) 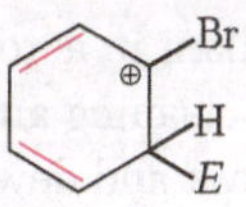

20 Consider the following compounds.
(i) Adjacent trimethyl benzene
(ii) Unsymmetrical trimethyl benzene
(iii) *o*-bromotoluene
(iv) Symmetrical tribromobenzene
(v) Chlorobenzene

How many of them give(s) one isomer on reaction with $Cl_2/FeCl_3$?
(a) 1 (b) 2 (c) 3 (d) 4

Module 4

Polyhalogen Compounds

• Dichloromethane • Trichloromethane • Triiodomethane • Tetrachloromethane
• Freons • DDT

Polyhalogen Compounds

Carbon compounds having more than one halogen atom are usually referred to as **polyhalogen compounds.** Many of these compounds are useful in industry and agriculture.

Some important polyhalogen compounds are described as follows

Dichloromethane (Methylene Chloride, CH_2Cl_2)

It is a colourless, sweet smelling, volatile liquid having low boiling point of 313 K and specific gravity of 1.37. It is prepared industrially by the direct chlorination of methane in the presence of diffused sunlight.

$$\underset{\text{Methane}}{CH_4} + 2Cl_2 \xrightarrow{h\nu} \underset{\text{Methylene chloride}}{CH_2Cl_2} + 2HCl$$

Uses

It is used in the following ways

- as a solvent and also as a paint remover.
- as a propellant in aerosols.
- as a metal cleaning and finishing solvent.
- as refrigerant and dewaxing agents.
- as a process solvent in the manufacture of drugs.

Harmful Effects (Physiological Effects)

Some of the important harmful effects of methylene chloride are as follows

- It affects the human central nervous system.
- Exposure to low levels of methylene chloride in air can lead to slightly impaired hearing and vision.
- Exposure to high levels of methylene chloride can cause dizziness, nausea, tingling and numbness in the fingers and toes.
- Direct contact with skin in humans causes intense burning and mild redness of the skin.
- Direct contact with eyes can burn the cornea.

Trichloromethane (Chloroform, $CHCl_3$)

It is commonly known as chloroform. It is a colourless liquid with sweet odour. It is non-flammable but its vapour burns with green flame. In industry, $CHCl_3$ is produced by heating a mixture of chlorine and either chloromethane or methane.

CH_3CH_2OH on reaction with moist bleaching powder is converted into $CHCl_3$ (Haloform reaction)

(i) $$CaOCl_2 + H_2O \longrightarrow Ca(OH)_2 + Cl_2$$

$$Cl_2 + H_2O \longrightarrow 2HCl + \underset{\text{(Oxidising agent)}}{[O]}$$

(ii) $$CH_3CH_2OH + [O] \longrightarrow CH_3CHO + H_2O$$

(iii) $$CH_3CHO + 3Cl_2 \longrightarrow \underset{\text{Chloral}}{CCl_3CHO} + 3HCl$$

(iv) $$\underset{\text{Chloral}}{2CCl_3CHO} + Ca(OH)_2 \longrightarrow \underset{\text{Chloroform}}{2CHCl_3} + (HCOO)_2Ca$$

It can also be prepared by the partial reduction of carbon tetrachloride.

$$CCl_4 \xrightarrow{Fe/H_2O} CHCl_3$$

Some of the important reactions of chloroform are as follows

(i) **Oxidation** Chloroform is slowly oxidised by air in the presence of light to an extremely poisonous gas carbonyl chloride also called phosgene. It is therefore stored in dark coloured bottles.

These bottles are completely filled with chloroform upto the brim and are properly stoppered to keep air out.

$$\underset{\text{Chloroform}}{2CHCl_3} + O_2 \xrightarrow{\text{Sunlight}} \underset{\text{Phosgene}}{2COCl_2} + 2HCl$$

> **Concept ladder**
> 1% ethanol is added to phosgene gas to convert it into diethyl carbonate which is non-volatile and non-toxic.
> $$\underset{\text{Phosgene}}{COCl_2} + \underset{\text{Ethanol}}{2C_2H_5OH} \longrightarrow \underset{\text{Diethyl carbonate}}{(C_2H_5)_2CO_3} + 2HCl$$

Uses

It is used in following ways

- as a solvent for fats, alkaloids, iodine and other substances.
- as a laboratory reagent.
- In the preparation of chloropicrin, chloretone, etc.

- In medicines.
- In the production of freon refrigerant, *R*-22 ($CHClF_2$).
- As an anaesthetic in surgery but now it has been replaced by other anaesthetics such as ether.

Harmful Effects

Harmful effects of chloroform are as follows

- Chloroform affects the central nervous system. Inhaling it, 900 ppm (in air), for a short time can cause dizziness, fatigue and headache.
- Chronic exposure to chloroform damages liver and kidney due to the formation of phosgene gas inside the body.
- Skin develops sore if immersed directly into the chloroform.

Triiodomethane (Iodoform, CHI_3)

It is yellow coloured crystalline solid with characteristic unpleasant odour.

Uses

It is used in following ways.

- As an antiseptic due to the liberation of free iodine.

$$\underset{\text{Triiodomethane}}{CHI_3} \xrightarrow[\text{heat}]{\text{Air, moisture}} \underset{\text{Iodine}}{I_2} \uparrow + CO_2 + H_2O$$

  But due to its unpleasant smell, it has been replaced by other formulations containing iodine.
- In the pharmaceutical industry.

Concept ladder Iodoform test is used to detect the presence of $CH_3—\overset{O}{\overset{\|}{C}}—$ groups, i.e. methyl ketones. The compound is heated with iodine and potassium hydroxide. The formation of a yellow precipitate confirms the presence of methyl ketones.

Tetrachloromethane

(Carbon Tetrachloride, CCl_4)

It is a colourless oily liquid with sweet smell. Its boiling point is 350 K. It is formed from chloroform as follows

$$CHCl_3 + Cl_2 \xrightarrow{h\nu} CCl_4 + HCl$$

Uses

It is used in following ways

- In large quantities, in the manufacture of refrigerants and propellants for aerosol cans.
- As a feed stock in the synthesis of chlorofluorocarbons (freons) and other chemicals pharmaceutical manufacturing and general solvent use.
- As a cleaning fluid, as a degreasing agent and as a spot remover.
- As fire extinguisher, under the name of pyrene.

Harmful Effects (Physiological Effects)

Its harmful effects are as follows

- Exposure to CCl_4 causes liver cancer in humans.
- The most common effects are dizziness, light headedness, nausea and vomiting which can cause permanent damage to nerve cells. In several cases, these effects can lead to stupor coma, unconsciousness or even death.
- Exposure of CCl_4 vapours can make heartbeat irregular or even can stop it. When brought in contact with eyes, it may cause irritation in eyes.
- It is also harmful to environment. When it is released in air, it rises in the atmosphere and depletes the ozone layer.
- Depletion of ozone layer increases the human exposure to UV rays which causes skin cancer, eye diseases and disorders and possible disruption of the immune system.

Freons

Chlorofluorocarbon compounds (CFC) of methane and ethane are collectively known as freons.

They are extremely stable, unreactive, non-toxic, non-corrosive and easily liquefiable gases.

Freon-12 (dichlorodifluoromethane, CCl_2F_2) is one of the most common freons in industrial use. It is manufactured from tetrachloromethane by **Swarts reaction.**

Concept ladder The reaction involved in the formation of freon-12 by Swarts reaction is as follows

$$3CCl_4 + 2SbF_3 \longrightarrow 2SbCl_3 + \underset{\text{Freon}}{3CCl_2F_2}$$

Uses

It is used in following ways

- As refrigerant in refrigerators and air conditioners.
- As propellant for aerosols and foams to spray out deodorants, cleansers, shaving creams, hair sprays and insecticides.

Harmful Effects

Most freon makes its way into the atmosphere where it undergoes photochemical decomposition and initiates radical chain reactions (by Cl^-) for depletion of the ozone layer (stratosphere).

Therefore, the use of freons as propellants and refrigerants has been drastically discouraged.

DDT (*p,p'*-Dichloro Diphenyl Trichloroethane)

DDT, the first chlorinated organic insecticides, was originally prepared in 1873. **Paul Muller** was awarded the Nobel prize in medicine and physiology in 1948 for this discovery.

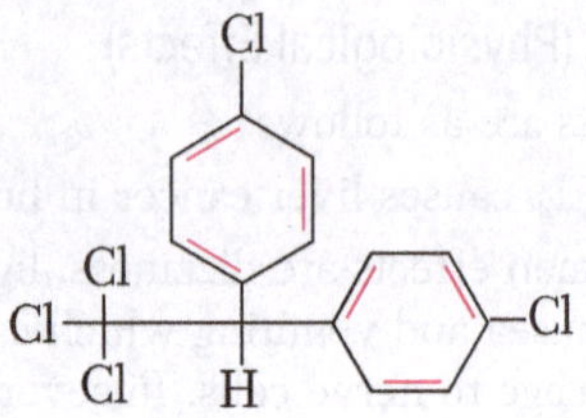

(DDT)

It is formed, when chlorobenzene reacts with CCl_3CHO (chloral) in presence of conc. H_2PO_4.

It is a white powder, insoluble in water but soluble in oil.

Uses

- DDT is a cheap but powerful insecticide.
- It is popularly very effective against anopheles mosquitoes (causes malaria) and lices which carry typhus.

Harmful Effects

DDT is non-biodegradable and extremely stable compound which acts as water pollutant and kills aquatic animals thus imbalancing the water ecosystem. When higher animals (including humans) feed on dead fishes killed by DDT, it enters in their food chains.

DDT gets stored in fat tissues of animal and increases in amount over the time. Researches have shown that such deposition in long run may cause cancer and other harmful diseases. Hence, DDT has been banned in many countries.

STEP UP Practice 4

1 Which of the following is an anaesthetic?
(a) C_2H_4 (b) $CHCl_3$ (c) CH_3Cl (d) C_2H_5OH

2 Phosgene is a common name for
(a) phosphoryl chloride (b) thionyl chloride
(c) carbon dioxide and phosphine (d) carbonyl chloride

3 Which of the following is incorrect for chloroform?
(a) It is rapidly oxidised by air in the presence of light.
(b) Its vapour causes unconsciousness when inhaled.
(c) It is immiscible with water.
(d) It is readily soluble in alcohol and ether.

4 Consider the following statements.
Statement I Chloroform on reaction with HNO_3 form chloropicrin, which is used as an anaesthetic.
Statement II Chloroform condenses with acetone in presence of KOH to form chloretone.
In the light of the above statements, choose the correct answer from the options given below.
(a) Both Statement I and Statement II are false.
(b) Statement I is true but Statement II is false.
(c) Statement I is false but Statement II is true.
(d) Both Statement I and Statement II are true.

5 Consider the following compounds.
(i) Freon refrigerant, *R*-22 (ii) Freon-12
(iii) Carbonyl chloride (iv) Methylene chloride
(v) Phosgene
How many of them can be prepared from trichloromethane?
(a) 4 (b) 3 (c) 2 (d) 1

6 Which of the following is incorrect regarding dichloromethane?
(a) It is used as a solvent and also a paint remover.
(b) It has very high boiling point.
(c) It is also known as methylene chloride.
(d) It is used as a process solvent in the manufacture of drugs.

7 Which of the following is a liquid at room temperature?
(a) CH_3I (b) CH_3Br
(c) C_2H_5Cl (d) CH_3F

8 Consider the following statements.
Statement I CCl_4 and $CHCl_3$ can be distinguished by the action of RNH_2 + alc. KOH.
Statement II When CCl_4 is boiled with KOH, the carbon dioxide is formed as a product.
In the light of the above statements, choose the correct answer from the options given below.
(a) Both Statement I and Statement II are false.
(b) Statement I is true, but Statement II is false.
(c) Statement I is false, but Statement II is true.
(d) Both Statement I and Statement II are true.

9 Which of the following statements is not correct about freons?
(a) Freon-14 is CF_4, Freon-13 is CF_3Cl.
(b) They are chlorofluorocarbons.
(c) They are used as refrigerants.
(d) Freon-12 is CF_2Cl_2 and freon-11 is $CFCl_3$.

10 Which of the following polyhalogen compounds is not correctly matched with their uses?
(a) Dichloromethane ⟶ Metal cleaning
(b) Triiodomethane ⟶ Antiseptic
(c) Tetrachloromethane ⟶ Manufacture of refrigerants
(d) Freon ⟶ Insecticides

11 DDT is a/an
(a) insecticide (b) bleaching agent
(c) hypnotic (d) oxidising agent

12 The compound formed on heating chlorobenzene with chloral in presence of conc. H_2SO_4 is
(a) hexachloroethane (b) DDT
(c) freon (d) gammexane

NEET Exclusive EXTRA BYTES

- Primary alkyl halides on oxidation with dimethyl sulphoxide (DMSO) give aldehydes and secondary alkyl halides give ketones.
- The presence of halogen in an organic compounds can be tested by **Beilstein test** ($X \neq F$) and **Lassaigne's test** ($X \neq F$).
- Depending upon the types of linkages, halogen compounds are ionic halogens (benzene diazonium halides and quaternary ammonium halides), Labile halogens (alkyl, allyl and benzyl halide) and inert halogens (vinyl and aryl halide). A distinction between these types of halogens is carried out on the basis of $AgNO_3$ test.
  (i) **$AgNO_3$ test in the cold** The appearance of a white or yellow precipitate indicates ionic halogens.
  (ii) **$AgNO_3$ test in the hot** The appearance of a white or yellow ppt. indicates labile halogen.
  (iii) If both the above tests are negative, the presence of inert halogens is indicated.
- When silver salts of carboxylic acid are heated with bromine, the corresponding alkyl bromides are formed. The reaction is called **Hunsdiecker reaction.**

$$R\text{—}\overset{\overset{\displaystyle O}{\|}}{C}\text{—}OAg + Br_2 \xrightarrow[CCl_4]{\Delta} R\text{—}Br + AgBr + CO_2$$

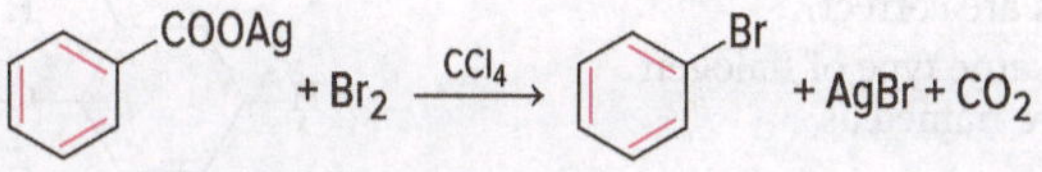

The important characteristic of the reactions are as follows
(i) The reaction proceeds through free radical mechanism.
(ii) The length of carbon chain is reduced by one carbon atom.
(iii) The yield in case of chlorides is very low, while iodine under such conditions give esters. (Birnbaum-Simonini reaction).

$$2R\text{—}\overset{\overset{\displaystyle O}{\|}}{C}\text{—}OAg + I_2 \longrightarrow R\text{—}\overset{\overset{\displaystyle O}{\|}}{C}\text{—}OR + 2AgI + CO_2$$

(iv) Aryl bromides and chlorides may be prepared conveniently.
- Fluorination of benzene diazonium chloride by using fluoroboric acid (HBF_4) is called Balz-Schiemann reaction. This method is more convenient than direct halogenation as followed by heating.

GEARING UP FOR NEET

1 Which of the following is vinyl halide?
(a) 3-chloro-4-methyl hexane
(b) 4-bromo-4-methyl pent-2-ene
(c) 1-bromo-2-(1-methyl propyl) benzene
(d) 3-chloro-5-methyl hex-2-ene

2 The IUPAC name of tertiary butyl iodide is
(a) 4-iodobutane
(b) 2-iodobutane
(c) 1-iodo-3-methylpropane
(d) 2-iodo-2-methylpropane

3 Which of the following statements are correct?
A. The dihaloalkanes having the same type of halogen atoms on same carbon atom are named as alkylidene or *gem*-dihalides.
B. The compound $(CH_3)_3CBr$ has the 2-bromo-2-2 di-methylpropane as its IUPAC name.
C. In common name system, *gem*-dihalides are named as alkylene dihalides.
D. The common names of alkyl halides are derived by naming the alkyl group followed by the name of halide.
E. When both halogen atoms are present on the adjacent (α, β) carbon atoms of the chain, the compound is called *vic*-dihalide.

Choose the correct answer from the options given below.
(a) A, C and E (b) B and C only
(c) A, D and E (d) C and E only

4 Bond dipole moments increase in the order
(a) $C—F < C—Cl < C—Br < C—I$
(b) $C—F < C—Cl < C—I < C—Br$
(c) $C—I < C—Br < C—F < C—Cl$
(d) $C—I < C—Br < C—Cl < C—F$

5 When 3-methyl-2-butanol reacts with $HCl/ZnCl_2$, most stable intermediate formed is
(a) $(CH_3)_2CH\overset{\oplus}{C}HCH_3$ (b) $(CH_3)_2\overset{\oplus}{C}CH_2CH_3$
(c) $(CH_3)_2CHCH_2\overset{\oplus}{C}H_2$ (d) $CH_3CHCH_2CH_3$ with $\oplus CH_2$ on C-2

6 The reaction of $SOCl_2$ on alkanols to form alkyl chlorides gives good yields because
(a) alkyl chlorides are immiscible with $SOCl_2$
(b) the reaction does not occur *via*. intermediate formation of an alkyl chlorosulphite
(c) alcohol and $SOCl_2$ are soluble in water
(d) the other products of the reaction are gaseous and escape out

7 $(CH_3)_3C—CH=CH_2 \xleftarrow{\text{II}} (CH_3)_3CCH(Cl)CH_3 \xrightarrow{\text{I}} (CH_3)_2C=C(CH_3)_2$

In this reaction
(a) I is E1, II is E2 (b) I is E2, II is E1
(c) Both are E1 (d) Both are E2

8 Which hydrogen is abstracted most easily by bromination in the following compound?

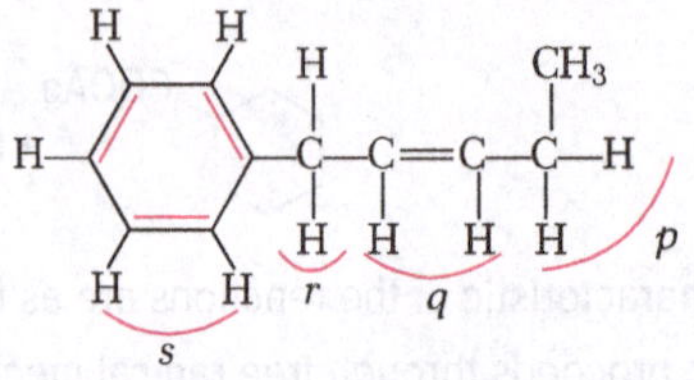

(a) *p* (b) *q* (c) *r* (d) *s*

9 What is the main product of the reaction between 2-methyl propene with HBr?
(a) 1-bromo butane
(b) 1-bromo-2-methyl propane
(c) 2-bromo butane
(d) 2-bromo-2-methyl propane

10 In the preparation of ethyl chloride by the reaction,

$$CH_3CH_2OH + HCl \xrightarrow[ZnCl_2]{\text{Anhy.}} CH_3CH_2Cl + H_2O$$

The major reason for using anhydrous $ZnCl_2$ as a catalyst is that
(a) it assists in forming the nucleophile Cl^- from HCl.
(b) it absorbs water formed in the reaction and drives the equilibrium to the right.
(c) it co-ordinates with oxygen of ethyl alcohol and increases the leaving group ability of the —OH group.
(d) it co-ordinates with the product CH_3CH_2Cl and drives the reaction to the right.

11 For which of the following alkanes, a racemic mixture is formed due to mono-halogenation of 2°-carbon atom?
(a) $(CH_3)_4C$ (b) $(CH_3)_2CHCH_2CH(CH_3)_2$
(c) $CH_3CH_2CH_2CH_3$ (d) $(CH_3CH_2)_4C$

12 How many monohalogenation products are possible in the following reaction? (Do not consider stereoisomers)

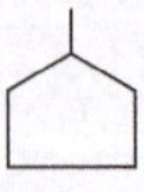 $+ Cl_2 \xrightarrow{\text{Light}}$ Monohalogenation products

(a) 2 (b) 3 (c) 4 (d) 5

13 The species shown in the box represents ...... of the reaction between isopropyl alcohol and hydrogen bromide.

$$\overset{\delta+}{(CH_3)_2CH}\cdots\overset{\delta+}{OH_2}$$

(a) the alkyloxonium ion intermediate
(b) the transition state of the biomolecular proton transfer step
(c) the transition state of the capture of the carbocation by a nucleophile
(d) the transition state of the unimolecular dissociation step

14 Which of the following organic compounds will give a mixture of 1-chlorobutane and 2-chlorobutane on chlorination?

(a) $H_3C-CH(CH_3)-CH=CH_2$ (b) $HC\equiv C-CH=CH_2$
(c) $H_2C=CH-CH=CH_2$ (d) $CH_2=CH-CH_2-CH_3$

15 Which of the carbon atoms present in the molecule given below are asymmetric?

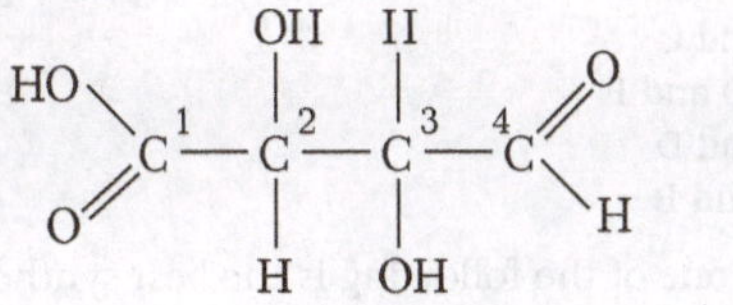

(a) 1, 2, 3 and 4 (b) 2 and 3
(c) 1 and 4 (d) 1, 2 and 3

16 Arrange the following isomeric compounds in increasing order of their boiling points.

(i) $(CH_3)_2CH-CH_2Br$ (ii) $CH_3CH_2CH_2CH_2Br$

(iii) $H_3C-C(CH_3)(Br)-CH_3$

(a) (ii) < (i) < (iii) (b) (i) < (ii) < (iii)
(c) (iii) < (i) < (ii) (d) (iii) < (ii) < (i)

17 Which of the following compounds will give racemic mixture on nucleophilic substitution by OH ion?

(i) $CH_3-CH(C_2H_5)-Br$ (ii) $CH_3-C(Br)(C_2H_5)-CH_3$

(iii) $CH_3-CH(C_2H_5)-CH_2Br$

(a) Only (i) (b) (i), (ii) and (iii)
(c) Both (ii) and (iii) (d) Both (i) and (iii)

18 Which of the following compounds does not undergo nucleophilic substitution reactions?

(a) Ethyl bromide (b) Vinyl chloride
(c) Isopropyl chloride (d) Benzyl chloride

19 Aryl halide is less reactive than alkyl halide towards nucleophilic substitution because

(a) less stable carbonium ion
(b) due to large C—Cl bond energy
(c) inductive effect
(d) resonance stabilisation and sp^2-hybridisation of 'C' attached to halide.

20 In the following pairs of halogen compounds which compound undergoes faster S_N1 reaction?

(a) (i) 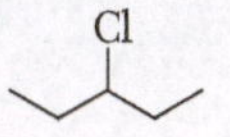 (ii) 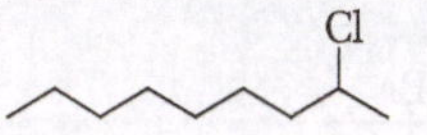

(b) (i) 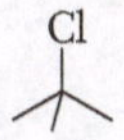 (ii) 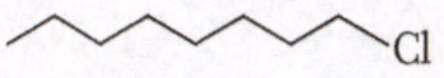

(c) (i) 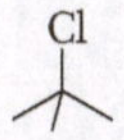 (ii) 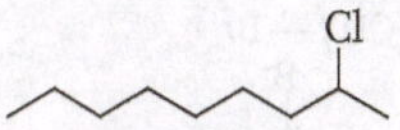

(d) (i) 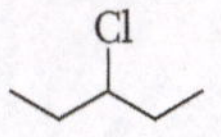 (ii) 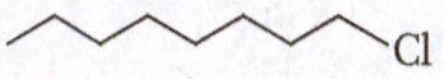

21 $\underset{(A)}{C_3H_6Cl_2} \xrightarrow[\text{(ii) } H_3O^+ \text{ (iii) } \Delta]{\text{(i) KCN}} CH_3CHCOOH$ (with CH_3 on the CH). Hence, *A* is

(a) 1,1-dichloropropane (b) 1,2-dichloropropane
(c) 2,2-dichloropropane (d) 1,3-dichloropropane

22 Which one of the following compounds is most rapidly hydrolysed by $S_N1$mechanism?

(a) $CH_3CH=CHCl$ (b) $ClCH_2CH=CH_2$
(c) 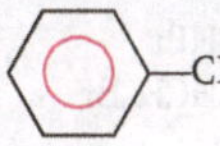$-CH_2Cl$ (d) $(C_6H_5)_3CCl$

23 CH_3-CH_2-Br on treatment with $LiAlH_4$ (in ether medium) gives ethane gas while $(CH_3)_3C-Br$ on same treatment gives H_2 gas because

(a) the former is S_N2 and later is E2 reaction
(b) the former is E2 and later is S_N2 reaction
(c) the former is $S_N1$and later is E2 reaction
(d) the former is E2 and later is $S_N1$reaction

24 When *neo*-pentyl chloride is heated at 300°C with anhy. $AlCl_3$, it gives,

(a) 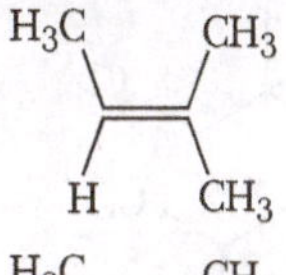 (b) 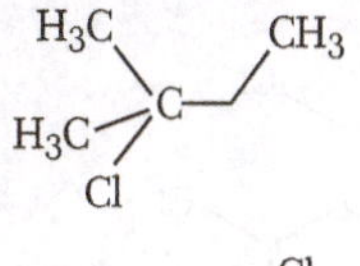

(c) 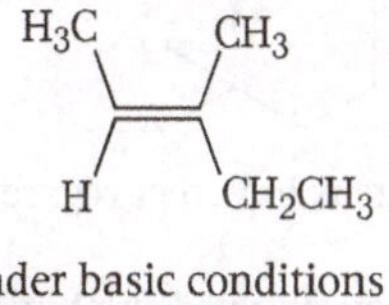 (d) 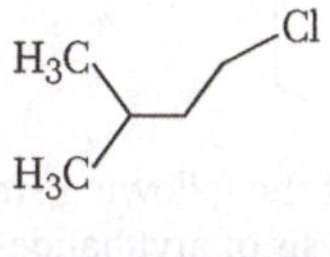

25 Under basic conditions which one suffers elimination the most?

(a) $(CH_3)_3CCl$ (b) $(H_3C)_2CHCH_2Cl$
(c) $CH_3CH_2CH(Cl)CH_3$ (d) $CH_3CH_2CH_2CH_2Cl$

26 Which of the following is the best method to prepare fluoroethane is ?

(a) $C_2H_5OH \xrightarrow{HF/H_2SO_4, \Delta}$

(b) $C_2H_5OH \xrightarrow{HF}$

(c) $C_2H_5Cl \xrightarrow{Hg_2F_2/\Delta}$

(d) $C_2H_6 \xrightarrow{F_2, h\nu}$

27 Which of the following will be most reactive for E1 reaction?

(a) 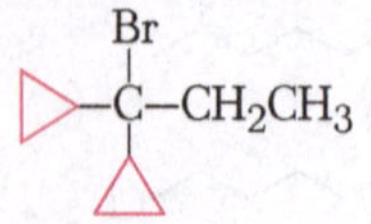

(b) $C_6H_5-CH_2-Br$

(c) $CH_2=CH-CH(Br)-CH_3$

(d) $CH_2=CH-C(Br)(CH_3)-CH_3$

28 Maximum yield of following alkyl bromides is formed by Borodine-Hunsdiecker reaction.

(a) CH_3CH_2Br (b) $(CH_3)_2CHBr$
(c) $(CH_3)_3CBr$ (d) C_6H_5Br

29 Which of the following compounds cannot form Grignard reagent?

(a) CH_3CH_2Br (b) $CH_2=CHBr$
(c) $HC\equiv CCH_2Br$ (d) $CH_2=CHCH_2Br$

30 Which of the following products is incorrect matched with the given reaction?

(a) $C_2H_5Br + KNO_2 \longrightarrow C_2H_5-O-N=O$ (major) + KBr

(b) $C_2H_5Br + AgNO_2 \longrightarrow C_2H_5NO_2$ (major) + AgBr

(c) $C_2H_5Br + AgCN \longrightarrow C_2H_5NC$ (major) + AgBr

(d) $C_2H_5Br + KCN \longrightarrow C_2H_5NC$ (major) + KBr

31 Which of the following species is most reactive towards S_N2 reaction?

(a) 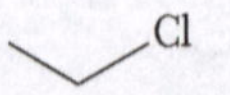 (b) 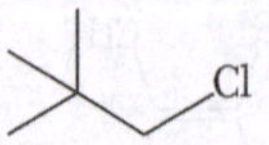

(c) 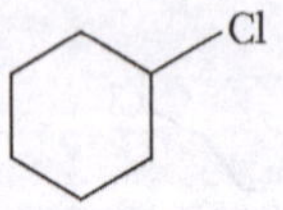 (d) 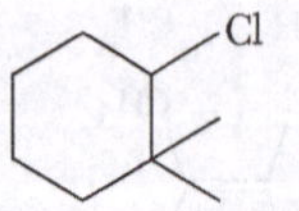

32 Which of the following statements is incorrect regarding the analysis of aryl halides?

(a) Aryl halide are soluble in cold concentrated sulphuric acid.

(b) Inertness toward bromine in carbon tetrachloride and toward permanganate solution.

(c) Formation of orange to red colours when treated with chloroform and aluminium chloride.

(d) Dissolution in cold fuming sulphuric acid but at a slower rate than that of benzene.

33 Which of the following statements are incorrect regarding the given reaction?

$$C_7H_8 \xrightarrow{3Cl_2/\Delta} A \xrightarrow{Br_2/Fe} B \xrightarrow{Zn/HCl} C$$

A. The product 'A' is *meta*-directing in nature.

B. The product 'C' is 3-bromo-2,4,6-trichlorotoluene.

C. The product 'B' contains the 10 total number of carbon and hydrogen atoms.

D. The product A, B and C are the derivatives of benzene ring.

E. The product 'C'and reactant are similar except the presence of bromine atom.

Choose the correct answer from the options given below.

(a) B and C
(b) A, D and E
(c) A and D
(d) A and B

34 Which one of the following is the best synthesis of 2-chloro-4-nitrobenzoic acid?

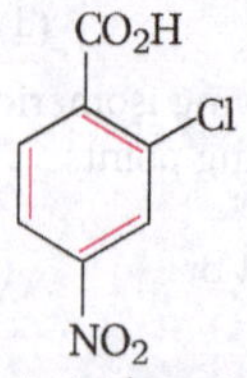

2-chloro-4-nitrobenzoic acid

(a) 1. Heat benzoic acid with conc. HNO_3, conc. H_2SO_4 at 50°C
2. 1 eqv. Cl_2,$FeCl_3$

(b) 1. Treat toluene with Conc. HNO_3, conc. H_2SO_4 at 50°C
2. $K_2Cr_2O_7$, H_2O, H_2SO_4,heat
3. 1 eqv. Cl_2, $FeCl_3$

(c) 1. Treat toluene with conc. HNO_3, conc. H_2SO_4 at 50°C
2. 1 eqv. Cl_2, $FeCl_3$
3. $K_2Cr_2O_7$, H_2O, H_2SO_4, heat

(d) 1. Treat nitrobenzene with 1 eqv. Cl_2, $FeCl_3$,
2. CH_3Cl, $AlCl_3$
3. $K_2Cr_2O_7$, H_2O, H_2SO_4, heat

35 $C_6H_5CH_2-C(CH_3)(Br)-CH_2-CH_3 \xrightarrow[C_2H_5OH]{C_2H_5ONa}$ 'A'

Major product (A) is

(a) 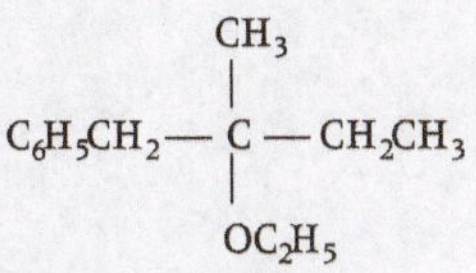

(b) 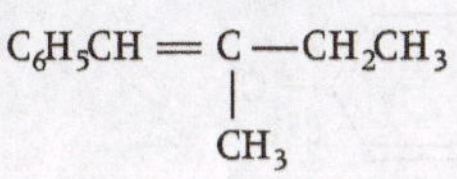

(c) 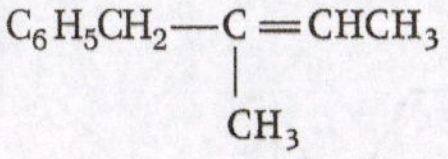

(d) 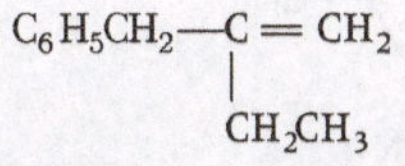

36 *m*-bromotoluene is prepared by
(a) bromination of toluene
(b) Friedel-Craft's reaction of bromobenzene with CH_3Cl.
(c) bromination of nitrobenzene and subsequent replacement of $—NO_2$ group with methyl group
(d) bromination of aceto-*p*-toluidine followed by hydrolysis and deamination

37 Which of the following is correctly matched with the isomers formed when one more substituent is introduced (directly or indirectly)?

(a) 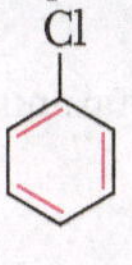 ⟶ 2 isomeric product

(b) 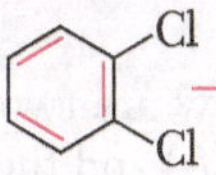 ⟶ 3 isomeric product

(c) 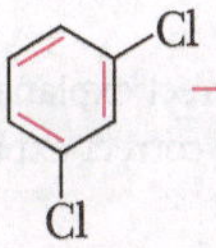 ⟶ 3 isomeric product

(d) 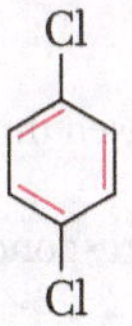 ⟶ 2 isomeric product

38 For the reaction,

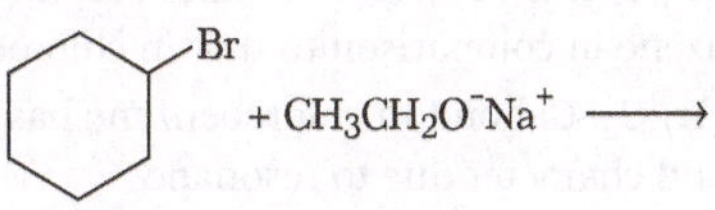

The major product is formed by
(a) an S_N1 reaction (b) an E1 reaction
(c) an S_N2 reaction (d) an E2 reaction

39 The reaction,

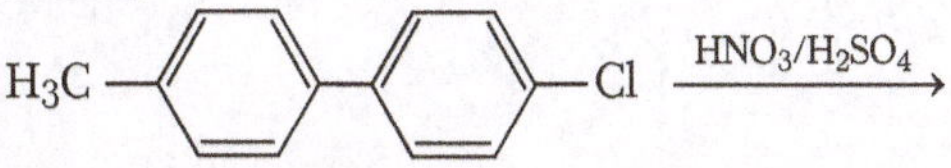

gives the major product as

(a) 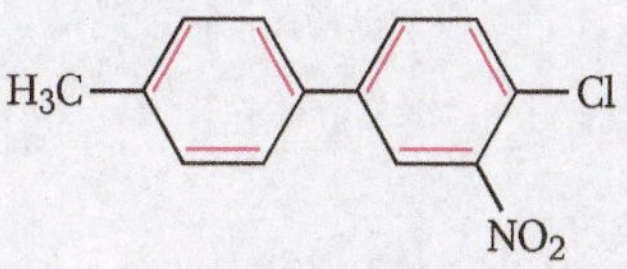

(b) 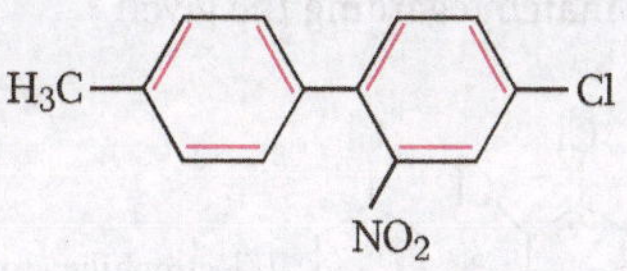

(c) 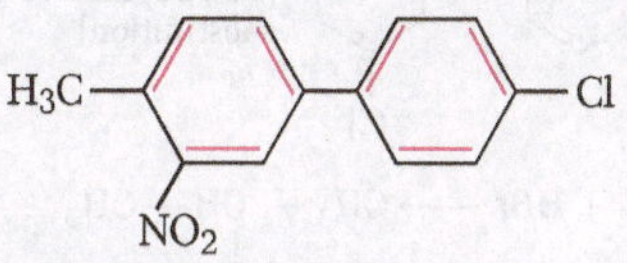

(d) 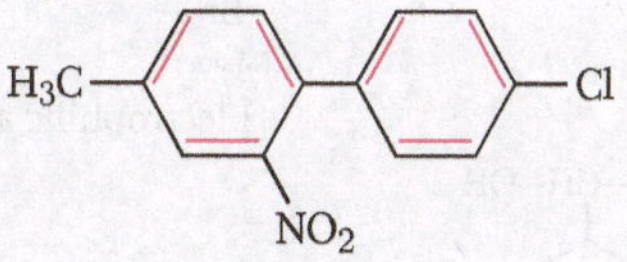

40 Which of the following product is the correct match with the given reaction?

(a) 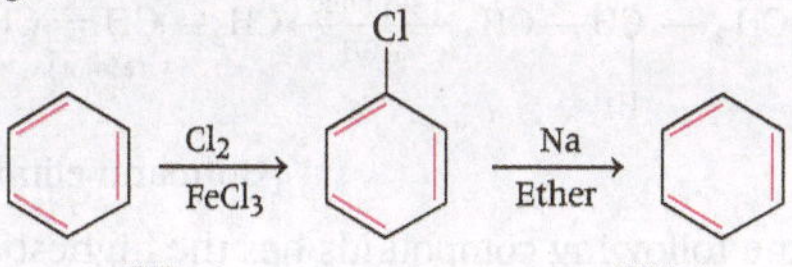

(b) 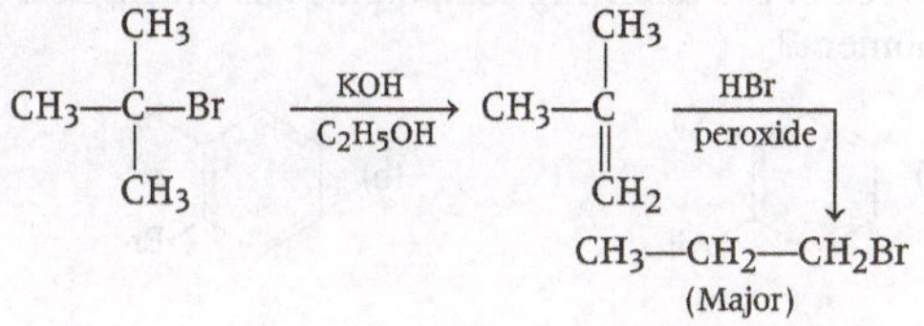

(c) 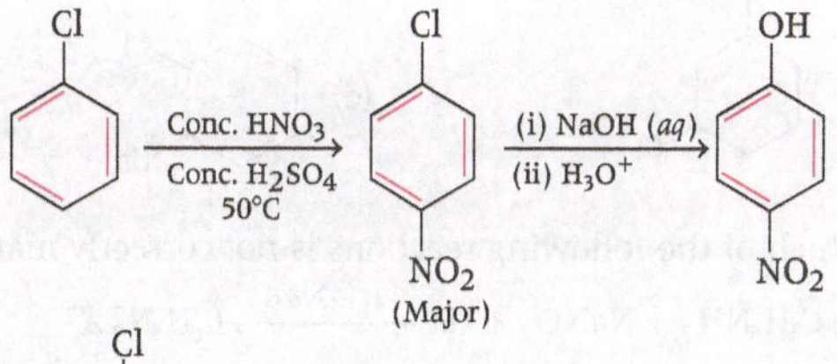

(d) 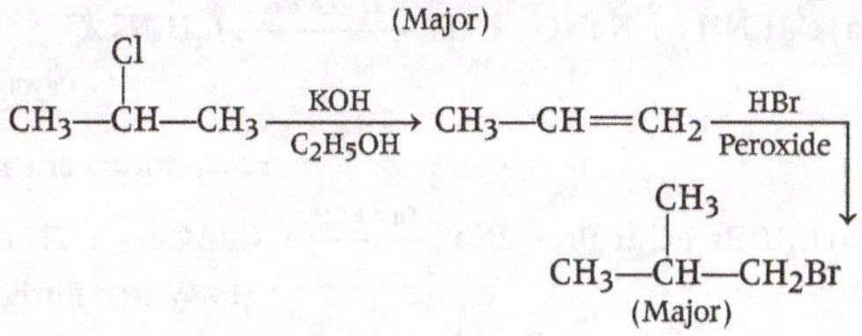

41 Arrange the following in increasing order of reactivity in aromatic nucleophilic substitution.

I. 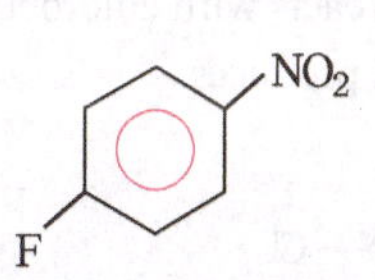

II. 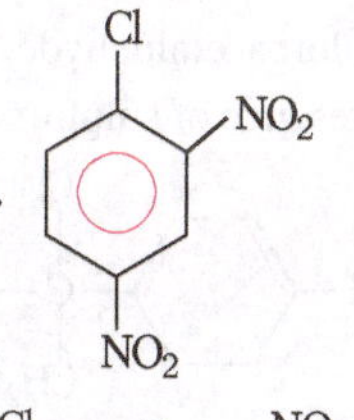

III. 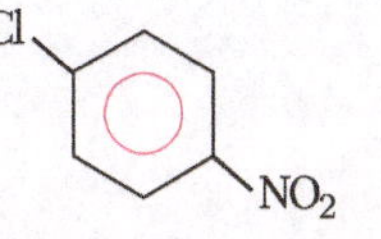

IV. 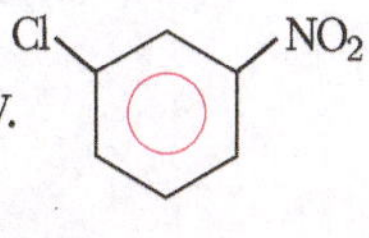

(a) I < IV < III < II
(b) IV < III < I < II
(c) I < IV < II < III
(d) IV < I < II < III

42 Select the incorrect match regarding the given reactions.

(a) 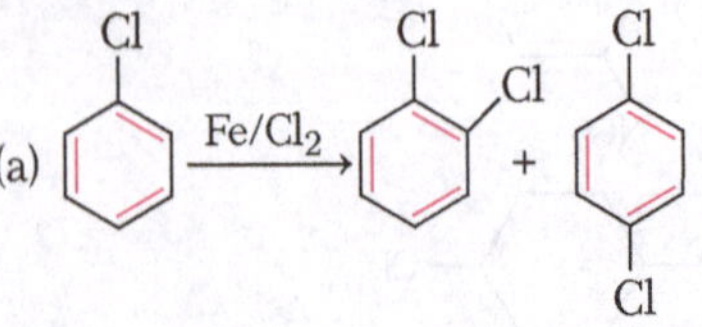 [Electrophilic aromatic substitution]

(b) $CH_3—CH{=}CH_2 + HBr \longrightarrow CH_3—\underset{Br}{CH}—CH_3$ (Major) [Electrophilic addition]

(c) 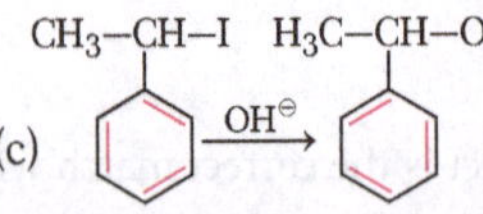 [Nucleophilic substitution (S_N1)]

(d) $CH_3—CH_2—\underset{Br}{CH}—CH_3 \xrightarrow[KOH]{Alcoholic} CH_3—CH{=}CHCH_3$ (Major) [Hofmann elimination]

43 Which of the following compounds has the highest dipole moment?

(a) 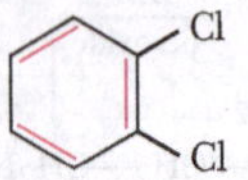 (b) 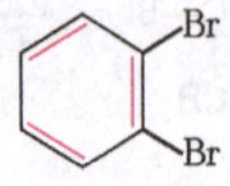

(c) 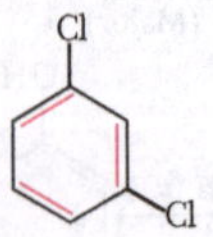 (d) 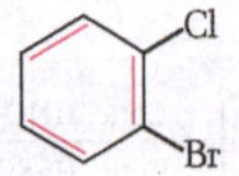

44 Which of the following reactions is not correctly matched?

(a) $C_6H_5NH_2 + NaNO_2 + HX \xrightarrow{273-278\ K} C_6H_5N_2^+X^- \xrightarrow{Cu_2Cl_2} C_6H_5Cl$
$\Rightarrow$ Sandmeyer's reaction

(b) $C_6H_5Br + C_2H_5Br + 2Na \xrightarrow{Dry\ ether} C_6H_5C_2H_5 + 2NaBr$
$\Rightarrow$ Wurtz-Fittig reaction

(c) $2C_2H_5Br + 2Na \xrightarrow{Dry\ ether} C_4H_{10} + 2NaBr \Rightarrow$ Wurtz reaction

(d) $CH_3Br + AgF \longrightarrow CH_3F + AgBr \Rightarrow$ Etard reaction

45 Trichloroacetaldehyde, CCl_3CHO reacts with chlorobenzene in presence of sulphuric acid and produces.

(a) 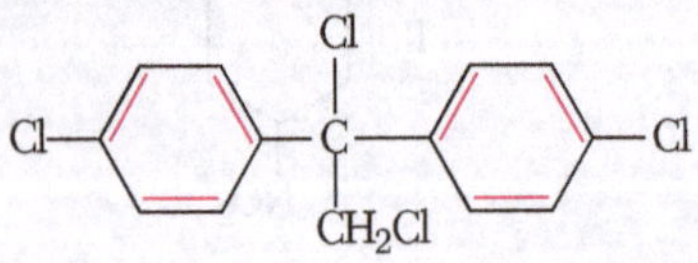

(b) 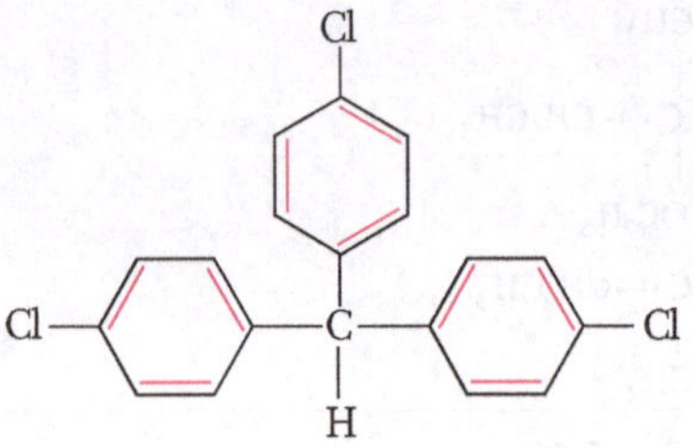

(c) 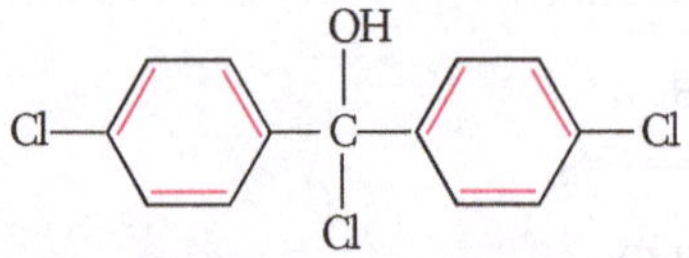

(d) 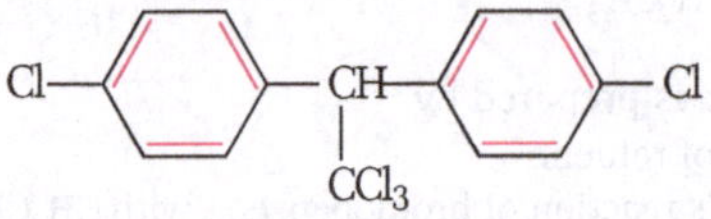

46 An organic compound on heating with CuO produces CO_2 but no water. The organic compound may be
(a) chloroform (b) methane
(c) ethyl iodide (d) carbon tetrachloride

47 Which of the following polyhalogen compounds is incorrect match with their uses?
(a) Dichloromethane $\longrightarrow$ Paint remover
(b) Triiodomethane $\longrightarrow$ Antiseptic
(c) Tetrachloromethane $\longrightarrow$ Manufacturing of paints
(d) Freons $\longrightarrow$ Aerosol propellants

Assertion-Reason

Directions (Q.Nos. 48 to 54) Given below are two statements, one is labelled as Assertion (A) and the other is labelled as Reason (R).
(a) Both A and R are true and R is the correct explanation of A.
(b) Both A and R are true but R is not the correct explanation of A.
(c) A is true but R is false.
(d) A is false but R is true.

48 **Assertion** (A) Conc. sulphuric acid is not used during the reaction of alcohol with KI.
Reason (R) Conc. H_2SO_4 converts KI to corresponding acid HI which is then oxidised by H_2SO_4 to I_2.

49 **Assertion** (A) It is difficult to replace chlorine by —OH in chlorobenzene in comparison to that in chloroethane.
Reason (R) C—Cl bond in chlorobenzene has a partial double bond character due to resonance.

50 **Assertion** (A) During debromination of *meso*-2,3-di bromobutane, the major compound formed is *trans* 1-butene.
Reason (R) Debromination is a *trans*-elimination reaction.

51 **Assertion** (A) Bromobenzene upon reaction with Br_2/Fe gives 1,4-dibromobenzene as the major product.

Reason (R) In bromobenzene, the inductive effect of the bromo group is more dominant than the mesomeric effet in directing the incoming electrophile.

52 **Assertion** (A) The compound 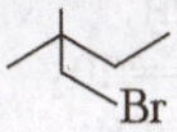 will give product under E2 reaction.

Reason (R) In the given compounds, β-hydrogen is absent.

53 **Assertion** (A) A solution of 1-chloro-1-phenyl ethane in toluene racemises slowly in the presence of a small amount of $SbCl_5$, due to the formation of carbocation.

Reason (R) The carbocation is a planar species, so it can be attacked by $SbCl_6^-$ ethers from the front or back side of the carbocation with equal ease.

54 **Assertion** (A) Chloroform is stored in dark coloured bottles.

Reason (R) Chronic chloroform exposure may cause damage to the liver and kidney.

Statement Type Questions

Directions (Q.Nos. 55 to 60) In the light of the statements given below choose the correct answer from the options given.

(a) Both Statement I and Statement II are false.
(b) Statement I is true but Statement II is false.
(c) Statement I is false but Statement II is true.
(d) Both Statement I and Statement II are true.

55 **Statement I** Reaction between alcohols and *HX* follows S_N1 mechanism.

Statement II In S_N1 mechanism no intermediate formation takes place.

56 **Statement I** In the following reaction,
$CHCl_3 + C_6H_5NH_2 + 3NaOH \longrightarrow A + 3B + 3C$, the product *A* is phenyl cyanide.

Statement II Strong reducing agent converts $CHCl_3$ into C_2H_4.

57 **Statement I** 2-bromo-3-methylbutane changes to 2-ethoxy-2-methylbutane as a major product on reaction with CH_3CH_2OH.

Statement II 2° carbocation undergoes rearrangement that results in the formation of more stable 3° carbocation.

58 **Statement I** *n*-propyl bromide on treatment with ethanolic potassium hydroxide produces propene.

Statement II Dehydrohalogenation of *n*-PrBr into propene can be done only by strong base like $NaNH_2$.

59 **Statement I** In the reaction,

$$PhN_2Cl \xrightarrow[H_2O]{\text{Boil}} (A) \xrightarrow{BrO_3^- + Br^- + H^+} (B) \xrightarrow[\text{dust}]{\text{Zn}} (C)$$

the product *B* is 2,3,5-tribromophenol.

Statement II Dipole moment of product *B* is less than product *C* in the above reaction.

60 **Statement I** Haloarenes are less reactive than haloalkanes towards nucleophilic substitution reaction.

Statement II The C—Cl bond length in haloalkanes is shorter than the bond length of haloarenes.

61 Select the incorrect statements from the following.

A. Carbon-halogen bond length increases from C—F to C—I.
B. Due to more electronegativity of carbon atoms than halogen, C—*X* bond of alkyl halide is polarised.
C. Carbon-halogen, i.e. C—*X* bond enthalpies increase from C—F to C—I.
D. The C—*X* bond in haloarenes are more polar than in haloalkanes.
E. Due to resonance, the C—*X* bond acquires partial double bond character, therefore cleavage of C—*X* bond becomes difficult in haloarenes.

Choose the correct answer from the options given below.

(a) A, C and D (b) B, C and D
(c) D and E (d) B and D

62 Which of the following statements are correct?

A. Bromides and iodides do not develop any colour, when exposed to light.
B. Methyl chloride and methyl bromide are gases at room temperature.
C. Due to greater polarity as well as higher molecular mass as compared to the parent hydrocarbon, the intramolecular forces of attraction are weaker in the halogen derivatives.
D. For the same alkyl group, the boiling point of alkyl halides decreases in the order : $RI > RBr > RCl > RF$.
E. 2-bromo-2-methyl propane has the low boiling point than the 1-bromobutane.

Choose the correct answer from the options given below.

(a) A and D only (b) C and D only
(c) B and C only (d) B, D and E only

63 Which of the following statements are incorrect?

A. Ethylbromide reacts with sodium in ether to give hydrocarbons containing same the number of carbon atoms present in the halide.
B. Grignard reagents are highly reactive and react with any source of proton to give hydrocarbons.
C. 2-bromopentane is heated with potassium ethoxide in ethanol to give *cis*-pent-2-ene.
D. The reaction of ethyl bromide and silver cyanide results in the formation of ethyl isocyanide, as the major product.
E. 3-bromohexane reacts with Na to form 4,5-diethyl octane.

Choose the correct answer from the options given below.

(a) B and D only (b) A and B only

(c) A, D and E only (d) A and C only

64 Select the correct statements from the following.

A. All alkyl halides can be prepared by Swarts reaction except alkyl fluorides.

B. In Sandmeyer's reaction, solution of freshly prepared diazonium salt with cuprous bromide, replaces diazonium group by F.

C. Aryl fluorides can be prepared by electrophilic substitution of arenes.

D. *p*-dichlorobenzene has higher melting point than *o*-dichlorobenzene.

E. $C_6H_5CHClC_6H_5$ is more easily hydrolysed by *aq.* KOH than $C_6H_5CH_2Cl$.

Choose the correct answer from the options given below.

(a) B and C (b) D and E

(c) A and B (d) B and D

65 Which of the following statements are correct?

A. The *ortho* and *para*-isomers of halotoluene (X=Cl) can be easily separated due to large difference in their melting points.

B. Reaction of toluene with iodine in the presence of an oxidising agent is irreversible in nature.

C. Due to high reactivity of fluorine, fluoro compounds are not prepared by electrophilic substitution of arenes with fluorine.

D. Benzene on reaction with Cl_2 in the presence of UV light gives benzene hexachloride.

E. Grignard reagents are highly reactive and react with any source of proton to give hydrocarbons.

Choose the correct answer from the options given below.

(a) B, C and D (b) A, C, D and E

(c) A, D and E (d) A, B and C

66 Which of the following statements are incorrect?

A. In nitrite ion, the linkage through oxygen results in nitroalkanes while through nitrogen it leads to alkyl halides.

B. The reaction between CH_3Cl and hydroxide ion to yield methanol and chloride ion follows a second order kinetics.

C. Tertiary halides react most rapidly in S_N2 reactions.

D. S_N1 reactions are generally carried out in polar aprotic solvents.

E. The reaction between *tert*-butyl bromide and hydroxide ion yield *tert*-butyl alcohol and follows the first order kinetics.

Choose the correct answer from the options given below.

(a) B and E (b) A, C and D

(c) B, C and D (d) D and E

Species Selection Type Questions

67 Consider the following halides.

(i) *iso*-propyl chloride (ii) Bromopropane

(iii) *iso*-butyl chloride (iv) 2-propyl chloride

(v) *n*-propyl chloride (vi) *n*-butyl chloride

(vii) 2-butyl bromide

The total number of 2° halides are

(a) 3 (b) 4 (c) 2 (d) 5

68 Consider the following compounds.

(i) $Cl-CH=CH_2$ (ii) $H_2N-CH=CH_2$

(iii) $CH_3O-CH=CH_2$ (iv) $F_3C-CH=CH_2$

(v) $CH_3-CH=CH_2$

How many of them will favour majorly when treated with HCl and yield(s) an anti of Markovnikov's product?

(a) 2 (b) 4 (c) 3 (d) 1

69 Consider the following reagents.

(i) HCl and anhydrous $ZnCl_2$

(ii) NaCl

(iii) PF_3

(iv) $SOCl_2$

(v) NaCl and H_2SO_4

How many of them is/are used for preparation of alkyl chloride from alcohol?

(a) 4 (b) 3 (c) 1 (d) 2

70 Consider the following compounds.

(i) $(CH_3)_3CCl$ (ii) $CH_3CH_2-CH(Cl)-CH_3$

(iii) $CH_3CH_2CH_2-Cl$ (iv) $(H_3C)_2CH-CH_2-Cl$

(v) H_3C-CH_2-Cl

How many of them will favour elimination reaction over substitution?

(a) 3 (b) 4

(c) 2 (d) 1

71 Consider the following compounds,

(i) 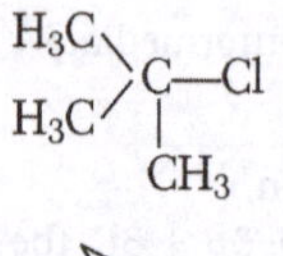 (ii) 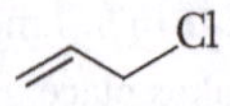

(iii) 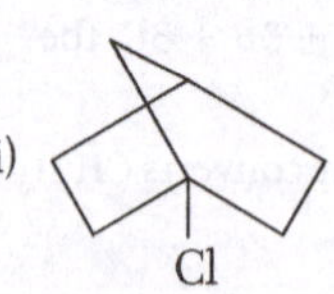 (iv) 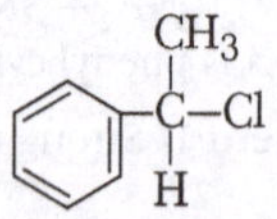

(v) 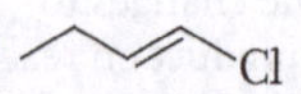

How many of them are inactive towards S_N1 reaction?

(a) 2 (b) 3 (c) 1 (d) 4

72 Consider the following compounds.

(i) Vinyl chloride (ii) Ethyl bromide

(iii) *iso*-propyl chloride (iv) 3-chloro-1-propene

(v) Benzyl chloride

How many of them does not undergo nucleophilic substitution reaction?

(a) 1 (b) 4

(c) 2 (d) 3

73 Consider the following compounds.

(i) 

(ii) $CH_3—CH_2Br$

(iii) CH_3CH_2Br

(iv) $CH_3—CH_2—\underset{}{\overset{OH}{|}}CH—CH_3$

(v) 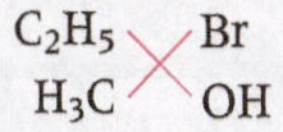

The number of compound(s) that will undergo elimination reaction with $C_2H_5O^-Na^+$ is

(a) 3 (b) 2 (c) 4 (d) 1

74 Consider the following compounds.

(i) *m*-chlorotoluene
(ii) *m*-cyanobenzaldehyde
(iii) Unsymmetrical trimethylbenzene
(iv) Mesitylene
(v) *m*-dibromobenzene

How many of them do not give 3 isomers on nitration?

(a) 3 (b) 2 (c) 4 (d) 1

75 Consider the following compounds.

(i) Benzene (ii) Benzoic acid
(iii) Phenol (iv) Benzene chloride
(v) *iso*-propyl benzene

How many of them will be formed when chlorobenzene fused with solid NaOH?

(a) 3 (b) 4 (c) 2 (d) 1

Match Type Questions

76 Match the structures of compounds given in Column I with the classes of compounds given in Column II.

Column I	Column II
A. $CH_3—\underset{X}{\underset{|}{CH}}—CH_3$	1. Aryl halide
B. $CH_2=CH—CH_2—X$	2. Alkyl halide
C. 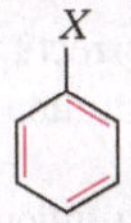	3. Vinyl halide
D. $CH_2=CH—X$	4. Allyl halide

Codes

	A	B	C	D		A	B	C	D
(a)	2	4	1	3	(b)	1	4	2	4
(c)	3	4	2	1	(d)	1	2	3	4

77 Match Column I with Column II.

Column I (Halides)	Column II (Classification)
A. 1-iodo-2,2-dimethyl butane	1. 4°
B. 2-chloro-3-methyl butane	2. 3°
C. 2-bromo-2-methylpropane	3. 2°
D. tetraethyl ammonium bromide	4. 1°

Codes

	A	B	C	D		A	B	C	D
(a)	3	4	1	2	(b)	4	3	2	1
(c)	2	3	4	1	(d)	3	4	1	2

78 Match Column I with Column II.

Column I (Halides)	Column II (IUPAC name)
A. $BrCH_2—CH=CH_2$	1. 2-chloro-2-methyl -3-phenyl pentane
B. 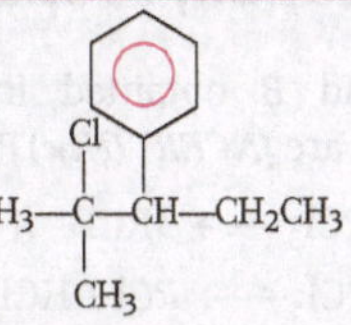	2. 2-chloro-2- methyl propane
C. $(CH_3)_3CCl$	3. 4-bromo-3-methyl but-1-ene
D. $CH_2=CH—\overset{CH_3}{\overset{|}{CH}}—CH_2Br$	4. 3-bromopropene

Codes

	A	B	C	D		A	B	C	D
(a)	3	2	4	1	(b)	4	3	1	2
(c)	3	1	2	4	(d)	4	1	2	3

79 Match the Column I with Column II.

Column I (Reaction)	Column II (Name)
A. Benzene diazonium salt $+ Cu_2X_2$	1 Wurtz-Fittig reaction
B. Ethyl chloride + NaI $\xrightarrow[\text{Acetone}]{\text{Dry}}$	2. Fittig reaction
C. Chlorobenzene+ 2Na (Excess) $\xrightarrow[\text{Ether}]{\text{Dry}}$	3. Finkelstein reaction
D. Bromobenzene + Chloromethane $\xrightarrow[\text{Ether}]{\text{Dry}}$	4. Sandmeyer reaction

Codes

	A	B	C	D		A	B	C	D
(a)	2	4	3	1	(b)	4	3	2	1
(c)	2	3	4	1	(d)	3	1	4	2

80 Match the species in Column I with corresponding reactants in Column II and choose the correct option.

Column I	Column II
A. Gattermann reaction	1. $C_6H_5COOAg \cdot Br_2$ CCl_4 / Heat
B Hunsdiecker reaction	2. Hg_2F_2/Δ
C. Swarts reaction	3. $C_6H_5N_2^+Cl^-$, CuCl / HCl, Heat
D. Sandmeyer reaction	4. $C_6H_5N_2^+Cl^-$, Cu / HCl, Heat

Codes

	A	B	C	D		A	B	C	D
(a)	1	2	3	4	(b)	4	1	2	3
(c)	4	3	2	1	(d)	1	2	4	3

Final Check Through PYQs

Module-I Classification, Preparation and Physical Properties of Haloalkanes

1 The products *A* and *B* obtained in the following reactions, respectively are *[NCERT (New) Pg. 164, NEET 2024]*

$$3ROH + PCl_3 \longrightarrow 3RCl + A$$

$$ROH + PCl_5 \longrightarrow RCl + HCl + B$$

(a) $POCl_3$ and H_3PO_3
(b) $POCl_3$ and H_3PO_4
(c) H_3PO_4 and $POCl_3$
(d) H_3PO_3 and $POCl_3$

2 The given compound

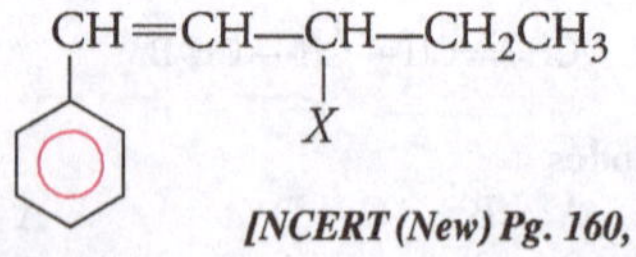

[NCERT (New) Pg. 160, NEET 2023]

is an example of

(a) aryl halide
(b) allylic halide
(c) vinylic halide
(d) benzylic halide

3 The correct sequence of bond enthalpy of C—*X* bond is *[NCERT (New) Pg. 163, NEET 2024]*

(a) $CH_3—Cl > CH_3—F > CH_3—Br > CH_3—I$
(b) $CH_3—F < CH_3—Cl < CH_3—Br < H_3—I$
(c) $CH_3—F > CH_3—Cl > CH_3—Br > CH_3—I$
(d) $CH_3—F < CH_2Cl > CH_3—Br > CH_3—I$

Module-II Chemical Reactions of Haloalkanes

4 The compound that will undergo S_N1 reaction with the fastest rate is *[NEET 2024]*

(a) 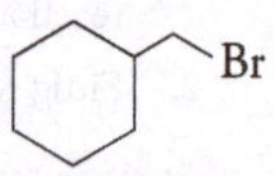

(b) 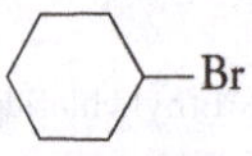

(c) 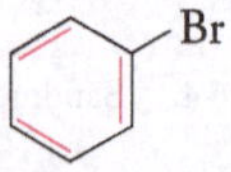

(d) 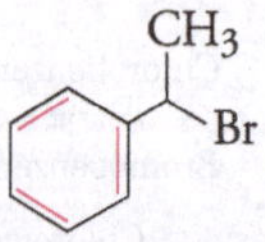

5 The incorrect statement regarding chirality is *[NCERT (New) Pg. 179, NEET 2022]*

(a) S_N1 reaction yields 1 : 1 mixture of both enantiomers.
(b) the product obtained in S_N2 reaction of haloalkane having chirality at the reactive site shows inversion of configuration.
(c) enantiomers are superimposable mirror images of each other.
(d) a racemic mixture shows zero optical rotation.

6 Consider the reaction

$$CH_3CH_2CH_2Br + NaCN \longrightarrow CH_3CH_2CH_2CN + NaBr$$

This reaction will be fastest in *[NEET 2016, Phase-II]*

(a) ethanol
(b) methanol
(c) N, N-dimethylformamide (DMF)
(d) water

7 For the following reactions, *[NEET 2016, Phase I]*

(i) $CH_3CH_2CH_2Br + KOH \longrightarrow CH_3CH{=}CH_2 + KBr + H_2O$

(ii) 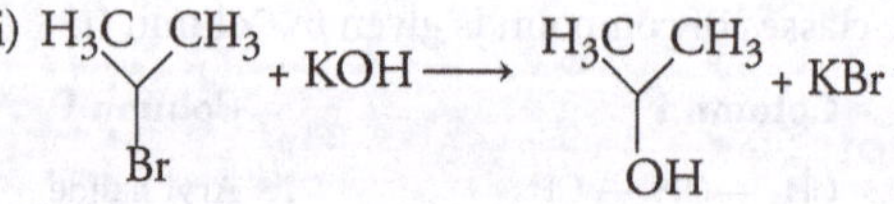

(iii) 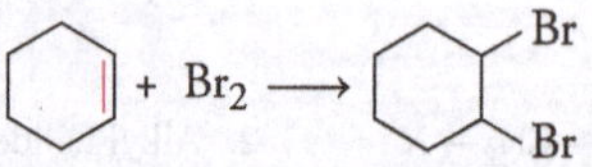

Which of the following statements is correct?

(a) (i) is elimination reaction, (ii) is substitution and (iii) is addition reaction.
(b) (i) is elimination, (ii) and (iii) are substitution reactions.
(c) (i) is substitution, (ii) and (iii) are addition reactions.
(d) (i) and (ii) are elimination reactions and (iii) is addition reaction.

8 In an S_N1 reaction on chiral centre, there is *[NCERT (New) Pg. 178, 179, NEET 2025]*

(a) inversion more than retention leading to partial racemisation
(b) 100% retention
(c) 100% inversion
(d) 100% racemisation

9 Which of the following compounds will undergo racemisation when solution of KOH hydrolysis? ***[AIPMT 2014]***

(i) 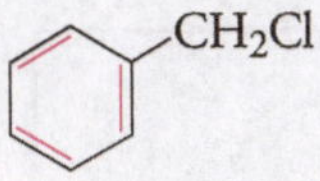 (ii) $CH_2CH_2CH_2Cl$

(iii) $H_3C—\underset{|}{\overset{CH_3}{CH}}—CH_2Cl$ (iv) 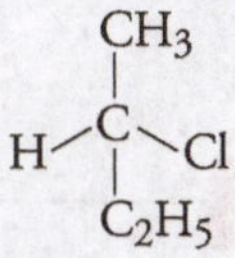

(a) (i) and (ii) (b) (ii) and (iv)
(c) (iii) and (iv) (d) only (iv)

Module-III Preparation, Physical and Chemical Properties of Haloarenes

10 Which of the following sequence of reactions is suitable to synthesise chlorobenzene? ***[NEET 2022]***

(a) Phenol, $NaNO_2$, HCl, CuCl

(b) 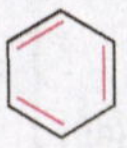 , HCl

(c) 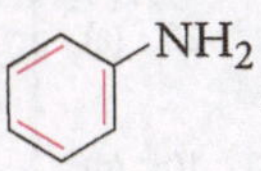 , HCl, Heating

(d) Benzene, Cl_2, anhydrous $FeCl_3$

11 Which of the following will not undergo S_N1 reaction with OH^-? ***[NCERT (New) Pg. 173, 174, NEET 2024]***

(a) $CH_2=CH—CH_2Cl$ (b) $(CH_3)_3CCl$

(c) 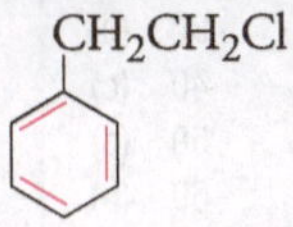 (d) 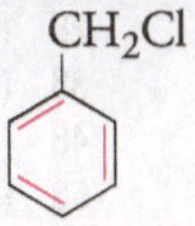

12 The hydrolysis reaction that takes place at the slowest rate, among the following is ***[NEET (Odisha) 2019]***

(a) 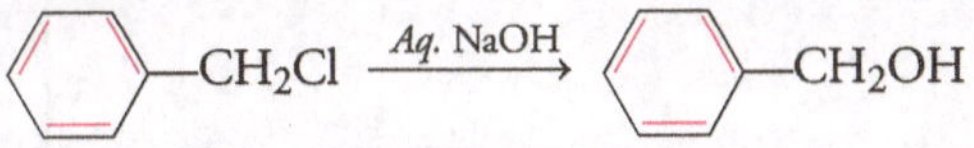

(b) 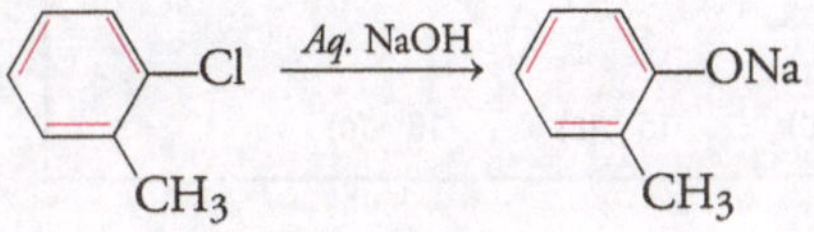

(c) $H_3C—CH_2—Cl \xrightarrow{NaOH} H_3C—CH_2—OH$

(d) $H_2C=CH—CH_2Cl \xrightarrow{\text{Dil. NaOH}} H_2C=CH_2—CH_2OH$

13 Which chloro derivative of benzene among the following would undergo hydrolysis most readily with aqueous sodium hydroxide to furnish the corresponding hydroxy derivative? ***[NEET 2017]***

(a) 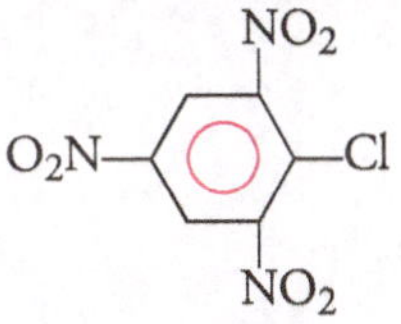 (b) 

(c) 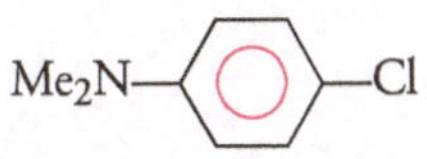 (d) C_6H_5Cl

14 Which of the following can be used as the halide component for Friedel-Crafts reaction? ***[NCERT (New) Pg. 185, NEET 2016, Phase II]***

(a) Chlorobenzene (b) Bromobenzene
(c) Chloroethene (d) *iso*-propyl chloride

15 The reaction of $C_6H_5CH=CHCH_3$ with HBr produces ***[AIPMT 2015]***

(a) $C_6H_5\underset{\underset{Br}{|}}{C}HCH_2CH_3$ (b) $C_6H_5CH_2\underset{\underset{Br}{|}}{C}HCH_3$

(c) $C_6H_5CH_2CH_2CH_2Br$ (d) 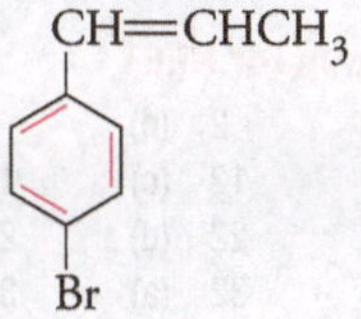

16 What products are formed when the following compound is treated with Br_2 in the presence of $FeBr_3$? ***[AIPMT 2014]***

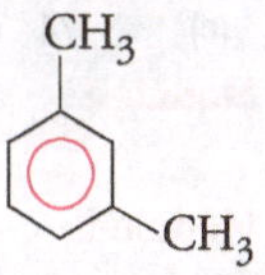

(a) 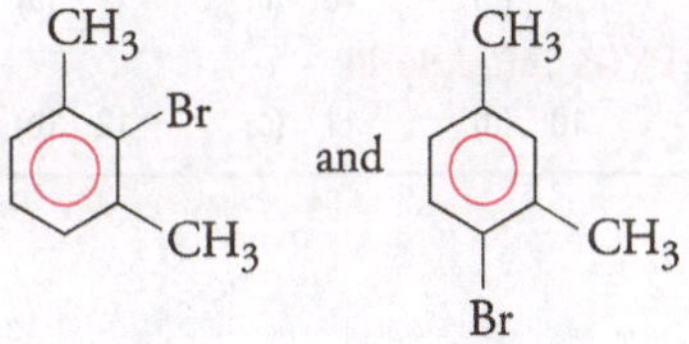

(b) 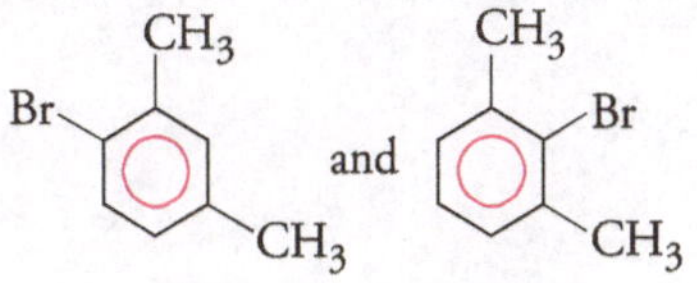

(c) 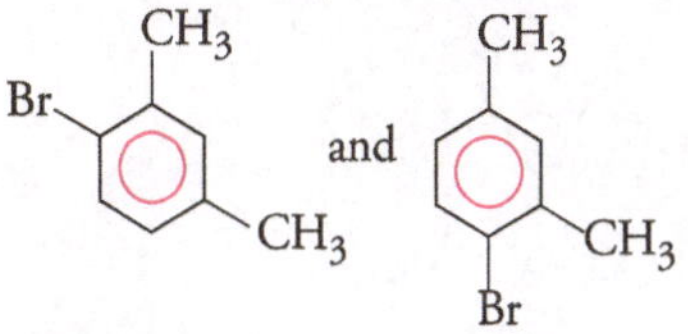

(d) 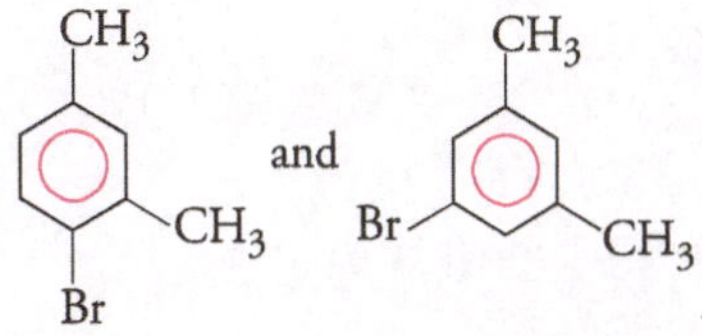

Answers

Step up Practice 1

1 (b)	2 (b)	3 (d)	4 (d)	5 (b)	6 (c)	7 (b)	8 (d)	9 (a)	10 (a)
11 (a)	12 (a)	13 (d)	14 (d)	15 (c)	16 (a)	17 (c)	18 (d)	19 (b)	20 (b)
21 (a)									

Step up Practice 2

1 (d)	2 (a)	3 (a)	4 (d)	5 (b)	6 (b)	7 (c)	8 (d)	9 (b)	10 (c)
11 (c)	12 (a)	13 (b)	14 (c)	15 (c)	16 (b)	17 (b)	18 (b)	19 (d)	20 (c)
21 (a)	22 (d)	23 (b)	24 (a)						

Step up Practice 3

1 (c)	2 (d)	3 (a)	4 (d)	5 (d)	6 (a)	7 (c)	8 (c)	9 (d)	10 (d)
11 (b)	12 (a)	13 (b)	14 (a)	15 (c)	16 (d)	17 (c)	18 (c)	19 (c)	20 (a)

Step up Practice 4

1 (b)	2 (d)	3 (a)	4 (c)	5 (b)	6 (b)	7 (a)	8 (d)	9 (d)	10 (d)
11 (a)	12 (b)								

Gearing up for NEET

1 (d)	2 (d)	3 (c)	4 (c)	5 (b)	6 (d)	7 (a)	8 (c)	9 (d)	10 (c)
11 (c)	12 (c)	13 (d)	14 (d)	15 (b)	16 (c)	17 (a)	18 (b)	19 (d)	20 (c)
21 (c)	22 (d)	23 (a)	24 (b)	25 (a)	26 (c)	27 (a)	28 (a)	29 (c)	30 (d)
31 (a)	32 (a)	33 (b)	34 (c)	35 (b)	36 (d)	37 (c)	38 (d)	39 (c)	40 (c)
41 (b)	42 (d)	43 (a)	44 (d)	45 (d)	46 (d)	47 (c)	48 (a)	49 (a)	50 (d)
51 (c)	52 (d)	53 (a)	54 (b)	55 (b)	56 (a)	57 (a)	58 (d)	59 (a)	60 (b)
61 (b)	62 (d)	63 (d)	64 (b)	65 (b)	66 (b)	67 (b)	68 (d)	69 (b)	70 (c)
71 (a)	72 (a)	73 (c)	74 (d)	75 (d)	76 (a)	77 (b)	78 (d)	79 (b)	80 (b)

Final Check through PYQs : Module-I

1 (d)	2 (b)

Final Check through PYQs : Module-II

3 (c)	4 (d)	5 (c)	6 (c)	7 (a)

Final Check through PYQs : Module-III

8 (a)	9 (d)	10 (d)	11 (c)	12 (b)	13 (a)	14 (d)	15 (a)	16 (c)

Hints and Solutions

Step up Practice 1

1. (*b*) 3-bromobut-1-ene is an allylic halides.

$$H_2C{=}CH{-}\underset{\substack{|\\ Br}}{CH}{-}CH_3$$

because the halogen atom is bonded to sp^3-hybridised carbon atom next to carbon-carbon double bond.

2. (*b*) In ethylidene chloride ($H_3C-CHCl_2$) both halogen atoms are present on same carbon atom, so it is *gem*-dihalide.

3. (*d*) Among the given halides, only two i.e. (i) and (iii) are benzylic halides while others, i.e.
   - $C_6H_5CH_2CH_2Br \longrightarrow$ Alkyl halide
   - $C_6H_5-CH_2=CH-CH_2-Br \longrightarrow$ Allyl halide
   - $C_6H_5Br \longrightarrow$ Aryl halide

4. (*d*) Among the given match, (d) is incorrect match with its common name.
   Its correct match is :
   $$CH_3CH_2CH_2F \longrightarrow n\text{-propyl fluoride}$$

5. (*b*) The correct IUPAC name for diethyl bromomethane is

$$\underset{5}{H_3C}-\underset{4}{CH_2}-\overset{\substack{Br\\ |}}{\underset{\substack{|\,3\\ H}}{C}}-\underset{2}{CH_2}-\underset{1}{CH_3}$$

3-bromopentane

6. (*c*) The IUPAC name of the given compound,

$$H_3C-\overset{2}{\underset{\substack{|\\ \underset{3}{CH_2}-\underset{4}{CH_3}}}{CH}}-\overset{1}{CH_2}-Br$$ is 1-bromo-2-methylbutane.

7. (*b*) Among the given compounds, (b) is incorrect match.
   Its correct match is

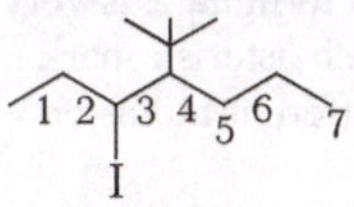

$\longrightarrow$ 4-*tert*-butyl-3-iodoheptane

8. (*d*) Among the given statements, statement (d) is correct while other are incorrect. Their correct form are as given
   - The hydroxyl group of an alcohol is replaced by halogen on reaction with concentrated halogen acids, phosphorus halides or thionyl chloride.
   - The order of reactivity of alcohols with a given haloacid is 3° > 2° > 1°.
   - The reaction of tertiary alcohols is conducted by simply shaking the alcohol with concentrated HCl at room temperature.

9. (*a*) The reactant *Y* in the given reaction is H_3PO_4.

10. (*a*) Among the given reactions, reaction (a) is halogen exchange reaction because in this reaction both the reactants (organic and inorganic halides) exchange their halogens to form the product.

11. (*a*) The given reaction is a free radical substitution reaction. It involve the replacement of 1° and 2° hydrogen of alkanes by chlorine. It occurs in the presence of ultraviolet light or at high temperature. The chlorination does not occur at room temperature (in absence of light). In this reaction, light is absorbed by chlorine molecule and activated chlorine initiates the reaction as follows

Step 1 $Cl-Cl \xrightarrow[\text{light}]{UV} 2\dot{Cl}$

$\dot{Cl} + CH_3-CH_2-CH_2-CH_3 \longrightarrow CH_3CH_2CH_2-\dot{C}H_2 + HCl$

Step 2 $CH_3-CH_2-CH_2-\dot{C}H_2 + Cl_2 \longrightarrow CH_3-CH_2-CH_2-CH_2Cl + \dot{Cl}$

Step 3 $CH_3-CH_2-CH_2-\dot{C}H_2 + \dot{Cl} \longrightarrow CH_3CH_2CH_2CH_2Cl$

Similarly, second product is formed.
So, option (a) is the correct.

12. (*a*) The reaction proceeds as follows

$$\underset{\text{2°-allylic free radical substitution occurs}}{H_2C{=}CH-CH_2-CH{=}CH_2} \xrightarrow{NBS} H_2C{=}CH-\underset{\substack{|\\ Br}}{CH}-CH{=}CH_2$$

13. (*d*) $\underset{\text{Propene}}{CH_2{=}CHCH_3} \xrightarrow[\text{Allylic position in affected}]{NBS} CH_2{=}CHCH_2Br \xrightarrow[\text{(more covalent in nature)}]{AgCN} \underset{\text{(Major)}}{CH_2{=}CHCH_2NC}$

14. (*d*) Alkyl fluorides can be prepared by action of mercurous fluoride or antimony trifluorides (inorganic fluorides) on corresponding alkyl halide (X = Cl, Br). This reaction is known as Swarts reaction.

$$CH_3Br + AgF \longrightarrow \underset{\text{Methyl fluoride}}{CH_3F} + AgBr$$

15. (*c*)

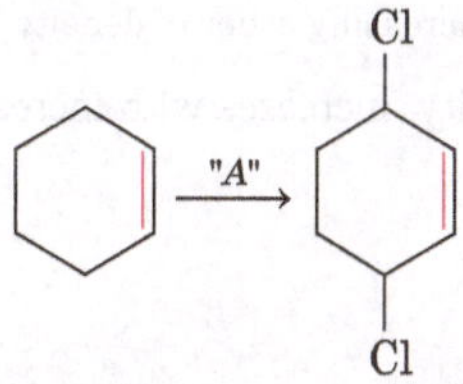

For substitution at allylic position in the given compound, the reagent used is Cl_2/UV light.

The reaction is free radical halogenation.

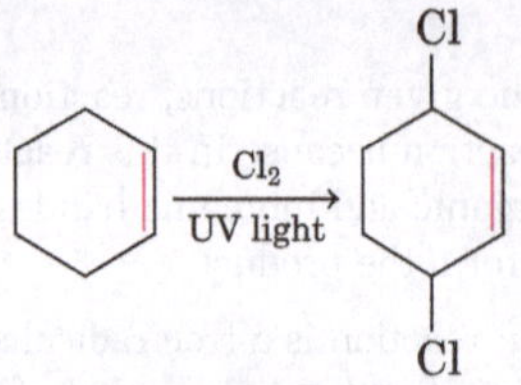

16. (*a*) Higher the molecular mass of the molecule, greater will be its boiling point. Thus, correct order is butane < 1-chlorobutane < 1-bromobutane < 1-iodobutane.

17. (*c*) Among the given statements, (c) is correct while other are incorrect about alkyl halides.

Their correct forms are

- Alkyl halides do not dissolve in water quickly.
- Alkyl halides are not associated with each other by H-bonds, although hydrogen bonding is possible only if H-atom is attached to electronegative N, O or F atom (N < O < F).
- Carbon-halogen bond is polar due to the electronegativity difference between carbon and halogen.

18. (*d*) Both Statement I and Statement II are true.

19. (*b*) Among the given statements, (b) is incorrect while other are correct.

Its correct form is :

For the same alkyl group, the boiling points of alkyl halides increase in the order : $RF < RCl < RBr < RI$.

20. (*b*) Among the given alkyl halides, (b) is incorrect match.

Its correct match is :

- $H_3C—Cl \longrightarrow 178$ pm
- As we know the bond length of alkyl halides increase down the group from C—F to C—I.

So, the value of bond length $H_3C—Cl$ will be high than the value of $H_3C—F$.

21. (*a*) Increasing order of the density of the compounds are

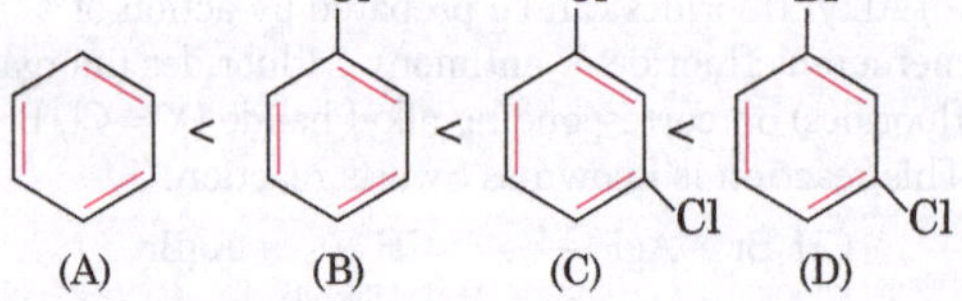

(A) (B) (C) (D)

Increasing order of density

Because density increases with increase in mass (molar mass) or size.

Step up Practice 2

1. (*d*) The reaction of ethyl bromide with aqueous sodium hydroxide involves S_N2 mechanism.

The reaction proceeds as follows

$$CH_3CH_2Br \xrightarrow{Aq.\ NaOH} CH_3CH_2OH + NaBr$$

Since, the reaction rate depends upon the concentration of both reactant and nucleophile, it is a S_N2 reaction. It involves inversion of configuration.

2. (*a*) The stereoisomers related to each other as non-superimposable mirror images are called enantiomers. Enantiomers possess identical physical properties.

They only differ with respect to the rotation of plane polarised light. If one of the enantiomer is dextrorotatory, the other will be laevorotatory. Here, the enantiomer of molecule (*A*) is shown below.

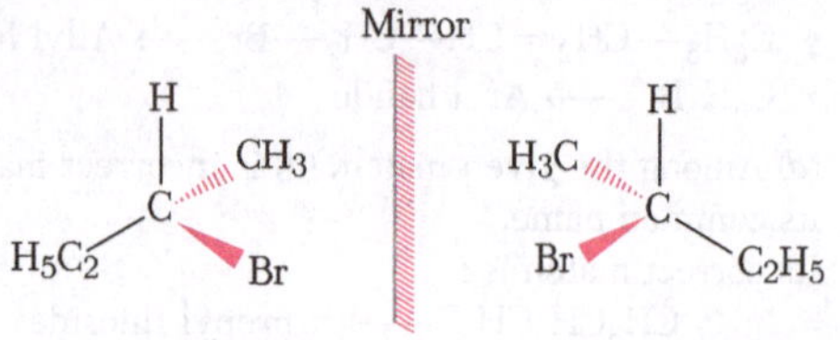

Hence, option (a) is correct.

3. (*a*) Chiral/asymmetric carbon is that carbon in which carbon has formed four bonds with four different groups. The structural formula of the given compounds are

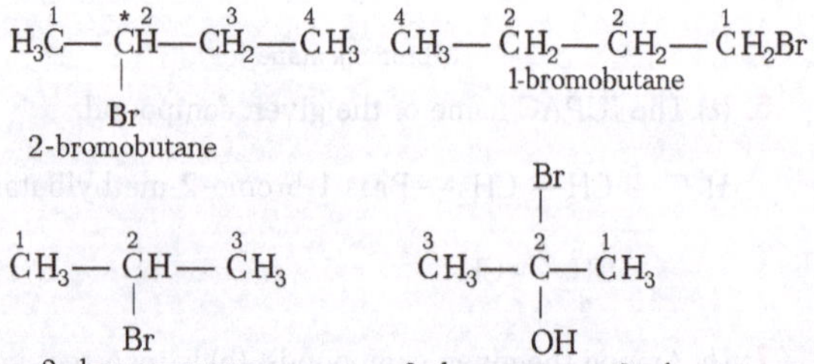

2-bromobutane, 1-bromobutane, 2 - bromopropane, 2 - bromopropan - 2 - ol

With the help of these structural formula it is very clear that 2-bromobutane in which asterisk mark carbon atom is bonded to four different atoms or groups.

So, this molecule is chiral in nature. Other molecules do not contain four different atom in groups.

4. (*d*) The reaction proceeds as

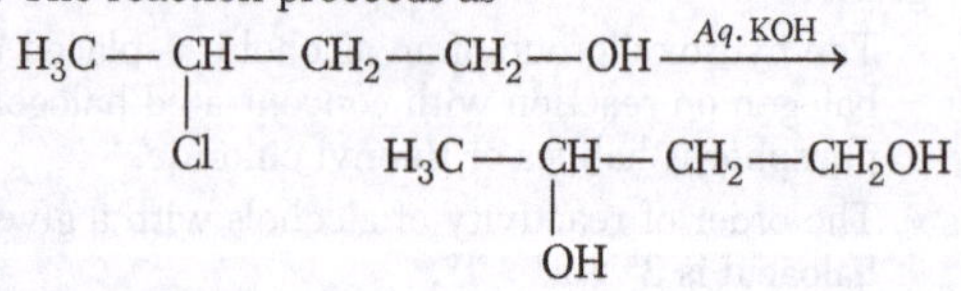

The given reaction proceeds through S_N2 mechanism.

5. (b) Among the given statements, statement (b) is incorrect about *neo*-pentyl bromide.

Its correct form is :

neo-pentyl bromide (i.e. 1° alkyl bromide) through S_N2 path forms *neo*-pentyl alcohol.

6. (b) The reaction proceed as

$$C_2H_5I \xrightarrow[-HI]{\text{Alc. KOH}} \underset{(X)}{CH_2{=}CH_2} \xrightarrow{Br_2} \underset{(Y)}{BrCH_2{-}CH_2{-}Br} \xrightarrow{KCN} \underset{(Z)}{NCCH_2{-}CH_2CN}$$

7. (c) Chloromethane on treatment with excess of ammonia yields mainly methanamine (CH_3NH_2).

The reaction is proceed as

$$CH_3Cl \xrightarrow{\text{Excess of } NH_3} \underset{\text{(Methanamine)}}{CH_3{-}NH_2} \xrightarrow{CH_3Cl} CH_3{-}NH{-}CH_3 \xrightarrow{CH_3Cl} CH_3{-}\underset{\substack{|\\CH_3}}{N}{-}CH_3$$

If the two reactants are present in equimolar amount, a mixture of primary, secondary and tertiary amine is obtained.

8. (d) Both Statement I and Statement II are true.

9. (b) The reaction is proceed as

$$2CH_3CH_2Br + 2Na \xrightarrow[\text{ether}]{\text{Dry}} CH_3CH_2CH_2CH_3 + 2NaBr$$

This reaction is called **Wurtz reaction.**

- $$CH_3\underset{\substack{|\\Cl}}{C}HCH_3 + CH_3CH_2\bar{O} \xrightarrow{CH_3CH_2OH} CH_3{-}CH{=}CH_2 + HCl$$

β-elimination

the reaction is proceed *via* mechanism.

10. (c) The compound 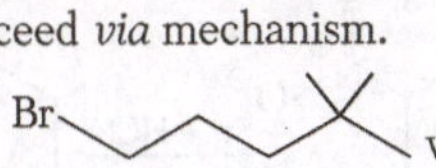 will undergo S_N2 nucleophilic substitution reaction with NaCN at the fastest rate because CN^- is a strong base and in compound (c), Br is attached with least crowded (at β and γ carbon 1°-carbons) and easy to break with NaCN.

11. (c) Statement I is false but Statement II is true.

The correct form of Statement I is :

A mixture of retention and inversion is observed in the product of S_N1 reaction.

12. (a) Among the given compounds, (a) is most reactive towards HCl because the intermediate (i.e. the carbocation) formed is resonance stabilised (allyl 1° carbocation).

13. (b) Alkyl halides can be converted into Grignard reagents by refluxing them with magnesium powder in dry ether.

14. (c) When 2-chloro-2-methyl pentane reacts with sodium methoxide in methanol then only (i), (ii) and (iv) will be obtained as products.

15. (c) The reaction proceeds as

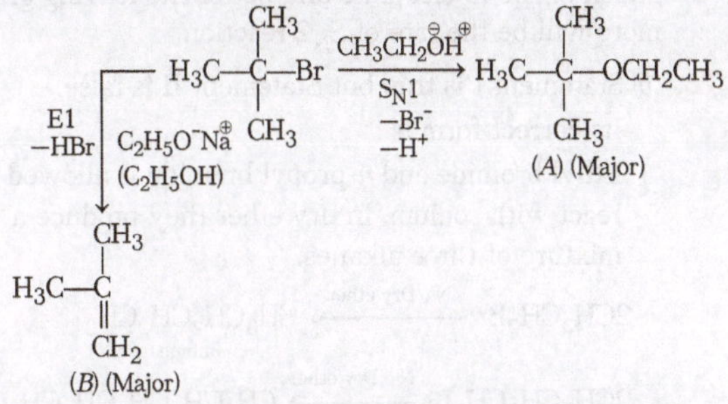

Product *A* is formed *via* S_N1 reaction while the product *B* is formed through elimination reaction (E1).

16. (b)

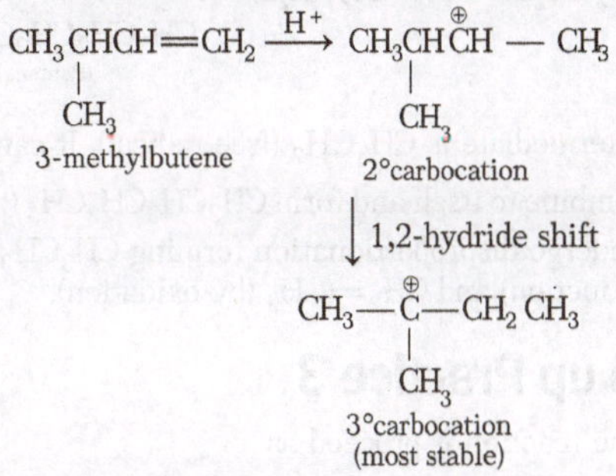

17. (b) Among the given alkanes, only one, i.e. (i) will not form racemic mixture on monohalogenation.

18. (b) E1 reactions are stereoselective reactions and this selectivity can be explained by simply comparing the stability of alkenes.

19. (d) Among the given statements, statement (d) is incorrect while the other statements are correct about the given reaction.

Its correct form is :

The given reaction involves one step E2 mechanism in which β-hydrogen and halogen are removed to form a double bond.

20. (c) The correct decreasing stability order of the given carbocation is

$$\underbrace{III}_{3^\circ} > \underbrace{II \approx V}_{2^\circ} > \underbrace{I \approx IV}_{1^\circ}$$

21. (a) Among the given match, (a) is incorrectly matched with the given mechanism.

Its corrected match is :

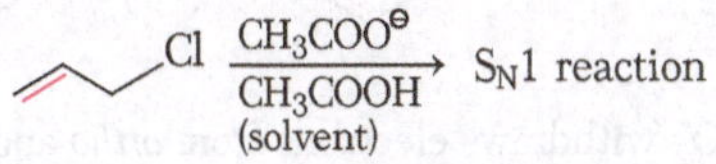

22. (d) Both II and IV, i.e. 2-bromopropane and 2-bromobutane will react faster with sodium iodide in acetone.

As, NaI in polar aprotic solvent (acetone) it favours S_N2 reaction mechanism.

The reaction works the best with methyl and primary halides because bulky alkyl groups block the backside attack of the nucleophile and better the leaving group more will be the rate of S_N2 reaction.

23. (*b*) Statement I is true but Statement II is false.

Its correct form is :

Ethyl bromide and *n*-propyl bromide is allowed to react with sodium, in dry ether they produce a mixture of three alkanes.

- $2CH_3CH_2Br \xrightarrow{\text{Na/Dry ether}} \underset{\text{Butane}}{CH_3CH_2CH_2CH_3}$
- $2CH_3CH_2CH_2Br \xrightarrow{\text{Na/Dry ether}} \underset{\text{Hexane}}{CH_3CH_2CH_2CH_2CH_2CH_3}$
- $CH_3CH_2Br + CH_3CH_2CH_2Br \xrightarrow{\text{Na/Dry ether}} \underset{\text{(Pentane)}}{CH_3CH_2CH_2CH_2CH_3}$

24. (*a*) Intermediate is $CH_3\dot{C}H_2$ (free radical). It can

(i) combine to itself and form $CH_3CH_2CH_2CH_3$ (butane).

(ii) undergo disproportionation forming CH_3CH_3 (by reduction) and $CH_2{=}CH_2$ (by oxidation).

Step up Practice 3

1. (*c*) The reaction is proceed as

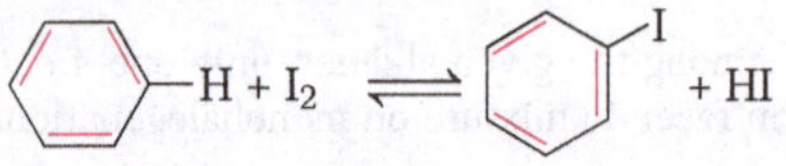

Due to the formation of HI in the above reaction, aryl iodide are reduced back to the aromatic hydrocarbon by HI as it is a good reducing agent.

2. (*d*) Due to the presence of electron withdrawing (–*I*) group (i.e. Cl) the Cl at 2 and 4 positions (cannot show +*R* to each other as they are *m*-to each other) will be easily replaced *via* S_N reaction.

3. (*a*) When a primary aromatic amine, dissolved or suspended in cold aqueous mineral acid and treated with sodium nitrite, a diazonium salt is formed. When this freshly prepared diazonium salt is mixed with cuprous chloride, then diazonium group is replaced by — Cl. Then chlorobenzene is formed which is *Y* in this reaction.

The reaction is proceed as follows

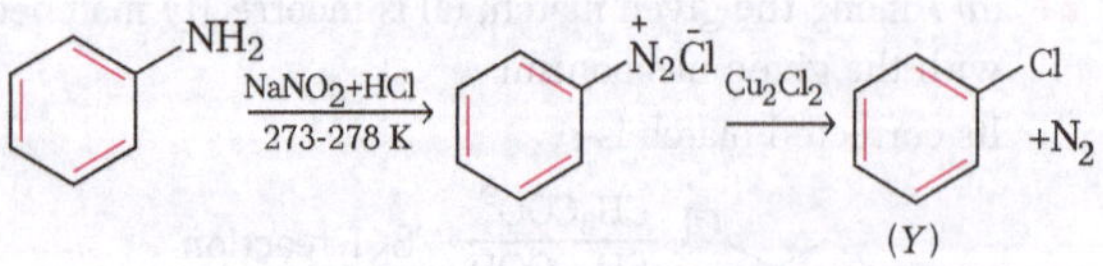

4. (*d*) $-NO_2$ withdraws electrons from *ortho* and *para* positions. $-NO_2$ group shows –*M* effect due to which electrons are withdrawn from *ortho* and *para*- position which makes the benzene ring more excite to electrophilic substitution reaction and hence replacement of Cl can be done easily.

5. (*d*) Both Statement I and Statement II are true.

6. (*a*) Among the given compounds, only three, i.e. (i), (iii) and (v) will give white ppt. with $AgNO_3$. The compounds which form the stable carbocation will give white ppt. with $AgNO_3$.

7. (*c*) The reaction proceeds as

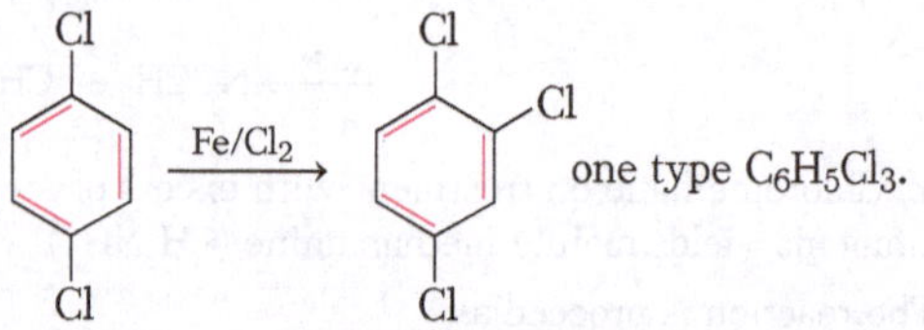

8. (*c*) Due to symmetry, *para*- isomers fit in crystal lattice better as compared to *ortho* and *meta*-isomers.

9. (*d*) Among the given reactions, (d) is incorrectly matched with the reagents used during the reaction. Its correct match is :

Sandmeyer reaction → $C_6H_5N_2^+Cl^-$, CuCl/HCl, heat.

10. (*d*) The reaction proceeds as follow

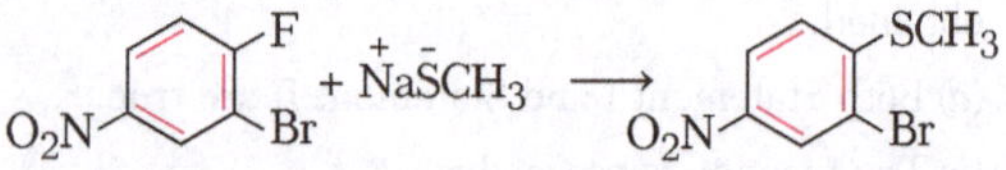

Due to *para*-effect (–*R*) of $-NO_2$ group, S_N reaction replaces F-atom rather than Br-atom.

11. (*b*) Statement I is true but Statement II is false.

The corrected form of Statement II is :

Oxidising agent oxidises HI into I_2 to prevent the possibility of backward reaction.

12. (*a*) The reaction is proceed as

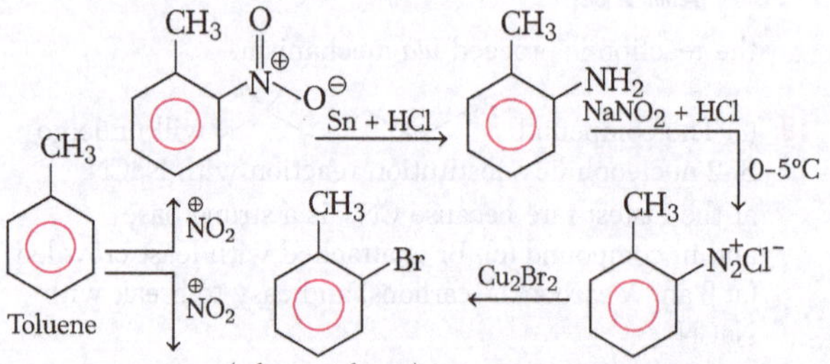

(*o*-bromotoluene)

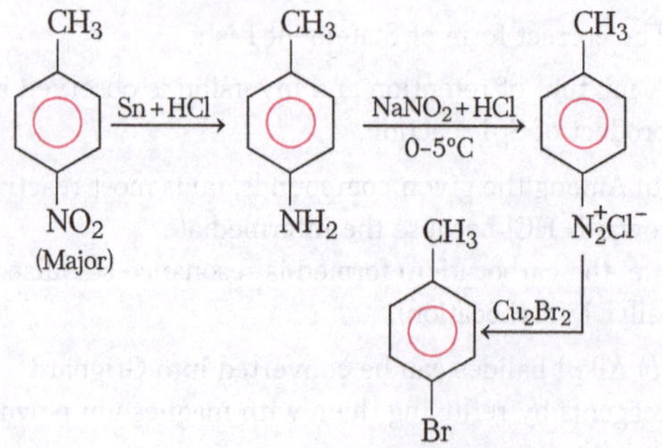

(*p*-bromotoluene)

13. (*b*) In this reaction, $AlCl_3$ acts as a catalyst which activates the chlorine molecule to show heterolytic cleavage.

$AlCl_3$ is an electron deficient molecule and form $AlCl_4^-$ and Cl^+ when reacts with Cl_2.

This Cl^+ electrophile attacks on electron rich benzene ring to form chlorobenzene.

$$AlCl_3 + Cl_2 \longrightarrow [AlCl_4]^- + Cl^+$$

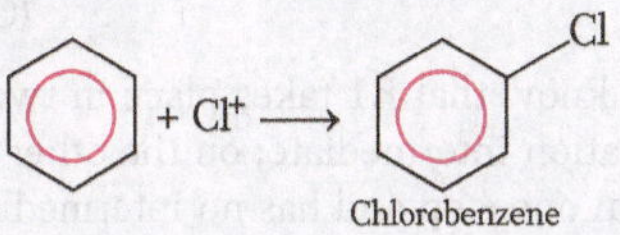

Chlorobenzene

14. (*a*) Among the given reactions, (a) is correctly matched regarding Wurtz-Fittig reaction because this is the reaction of an aryl halide with an alkyl halide and sodium metal to give substituted aromatic compound.

15. (*c*) The reaction is proceed as

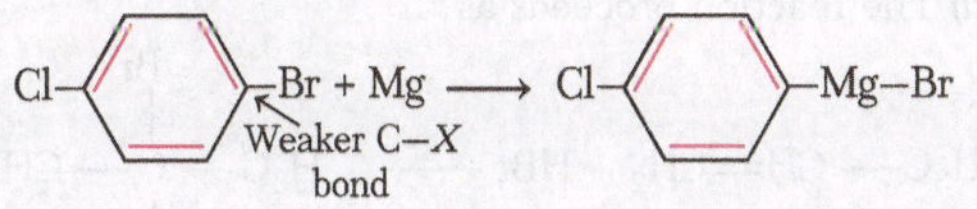

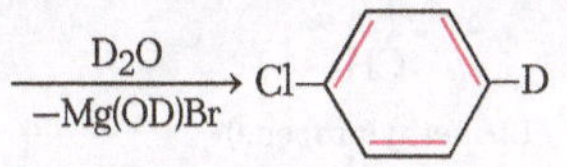

Thus, the end product of the given reaction is,

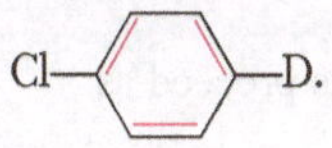

16. (*d*) Both Statement I and Statement II are true.

17. (*c*) The reaction proceeds as

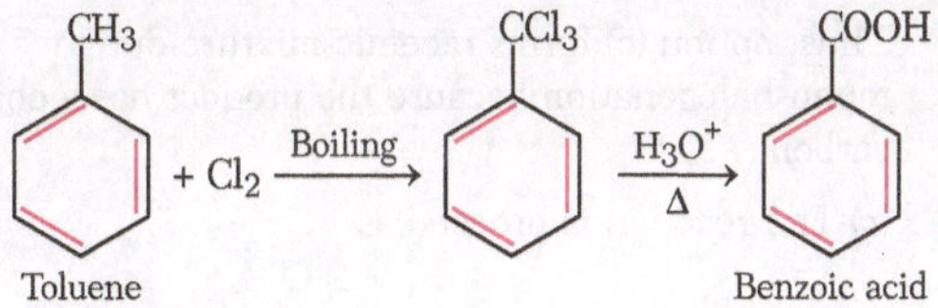

Toluene (*X*) Benzoic acid (*Y*)

Thus, the products *X* and *Y* are toluene and benzoic acid respectively.

18. (*c*) The reaction proceeds as

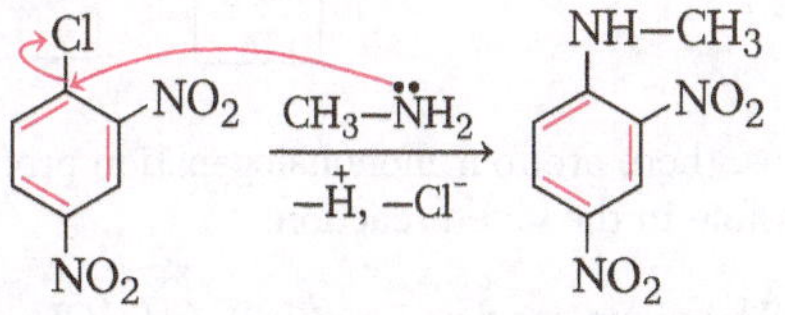

19. (*c*) Among the given intermediates, (c) is incorrect in the ArS_E2 of haloarene due to *meta*-attack.

20. (*a*) Among the given compounds, only one, i.e. (iv) give one isomer on reaction with $Cl_2/FeCl_3$.

Step up Practice 4

1. (*b*) Inhalation of $CHCl_3$ vapours produces loss of consciousness and is therefore, used as a general anaesthetic agent in surgery.

2. (*d*) Phosgene is a common name for carbonyl chloride, i.e. $COCl_2$.

3. (*a*) Among the given statements, (a) is incorrect for chloroform.

Its correct form is :

It is slowly oxidised by air in the presence of light.

4. (*c*) Statement I is false but Statement II is true.

The correct form of Statement I is :

Chloroform on reaction with HNO_3 forms chloropicrin, $Cl_3(C-NO_2)$ which is used as an insecticide.

5. (*b*) Among the given compounds, only three, i.e. (i), (iii) and (v) can be prepared from trichloromethane.

6. (*b*) Among the given statements, (b) is incorrect regarding dichloromethane.

Its corrected form is :

Dichloromethane has low boiling point of 313 K.

7. (*a*) CH_3I is a liquid at room temperature and solidifies at -66.5°C. Others CH_3F, CH_3Cl, CH_3Br and C_2H_5Cl are gases at room temperature.

8. (*d*) Both Statement I and Statement II are true.

9. (*d*) Among the given statements, (d) is incorrect about freons. Its corrected form is :

Freon-12 is CF_2Cl_2 and freon-11 is $CFCl_3$.

10. (*d*) Among the given match, (d) is not correctly match with its use. Its correct match is :

Freon ⟶ Aerosol propellants

11. (*a*) DDT is a non-biodegradable insecticide.

12. (*b*) The reaction is proceed as follow

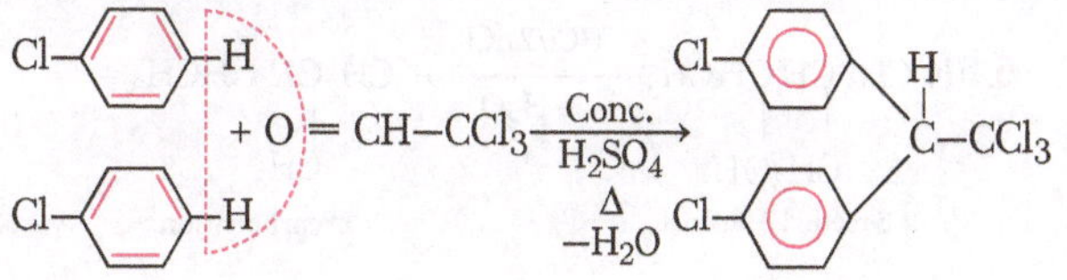

(DDT)

Gearing up for NEET

1. (*d*) Among the given compounds, 3-chloro-5-methyl hex-2-ene is vinyl halide

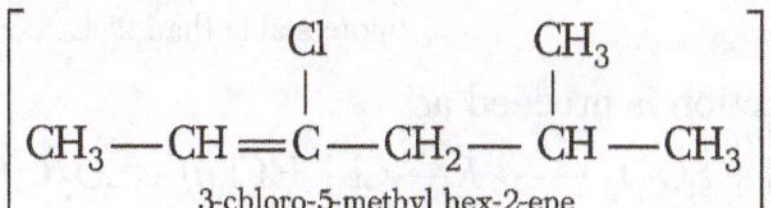

3-chloro-5-methyl hex-2-ene

while other compounds, i.e.

- $CH_3-CH_2-CH(Cl)-CH(CH_3)-C_2H_5$

3-chloro-4-methyl hexane → alkyl halide

- $CH_3CH=CH-C(Br)(CH_3)-CH_3$

4-bromo-4-methyl pent-2-ene → allyl halide

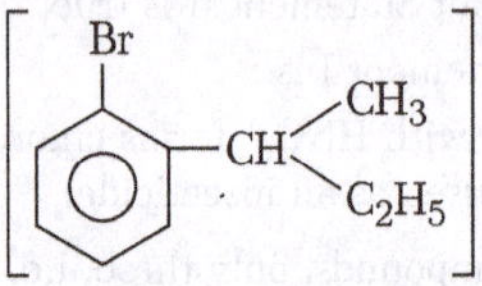

1-bromo-2-(1-methyl propyl) benzene → aryl halide are different from vinyl halide in nature.

2. (*d*) The IUPAC name of tertiary butyl iodide is

$$\overset{1}{H_3C}-\overset{2}{C}(CH_3)(I)-\overset{3}{CH_3}$$

(2-iodo-2-methylpropane)

3. (*c*) Among the given statements, only A, D and E are correct while the statements B, and C are incorrect.

Their correct form are as follows

- The IUPAC name of the compound $(CH_3)_3CBr$ is 2-bromo-2-methyl propane.
- In common name system, *gem*-dihalides are named as alkylidene halides.

4. (*c*) The correct increasing order is

C—I < C—Br < C—F < C—Cl.

5. (*b*) $\underset{\text{3-methyl-2-butanol}}{CH_3CH(CH_3)CH(OH)CH_3} \xrightarrow[-H_2O]{HCl/ZnCl_2} \underset{2^\circ\text{carbocation}}{CH_3CH(CH_3)\overset{\oplus}{C}HCH_3}$

$\xrightarrow{\text{1,2-hydride shift | Rearrangement}} CH_3-\overset{\oplus}{C}(CH_3)-CH_2CH_3$

3° carbocation (more stable than 2° carbocation)

6. (*d*) The reaction is proceed as

$$R-OH + SOCl_2 \longrightarrow R-Cl + HCl(g) + SO_2(g)$$

The gaseous by -products escape out on its own continuously, driving the reaction in forward reaction.

7. (*a*) The reaction is proceed as

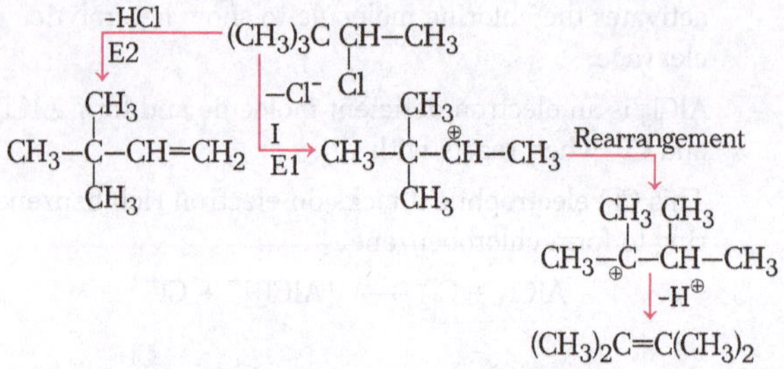

As we know that E1 takes place in two steps and has a carbocation intermediate; on the other hand E2 takes place in one step and has no intermediate.

So, reaction I proceeds *via* E1 and reaction II proceeds *via* E2 mechanisms.

8. (*c*) Because the H-atom at the *r* position is allylic as well as benzylic hence, abstracted most easily by bromination.

9. (*d*) The reaction proceeds as

$$\underset{\text{(2-methylpropene)}}{H_3C-C(CH_3)=CH_2} + HBr \longrightarrow \underset{\substack{\text{2-bromo-2-methyl propane}\\ \text{(Major)}}}{H_3C-C(Br)(CH_3)-CH_3}$$

10. (*c*)

11. (*c*) The reaction is proceed as

$$CH_3\overset{2^\circ}{C}H_2\overset{2^\circ}{C}H_2CH_3 \xrightarrow[-HX]{X_2} CH_3\overset{*}{C}H(X)-CH_2CH_3$$

Thus, option (c) forms racemic mixture due to mono-halogenation because the product has a chiral carbon.

12. (*c*) The reaction is proceed as

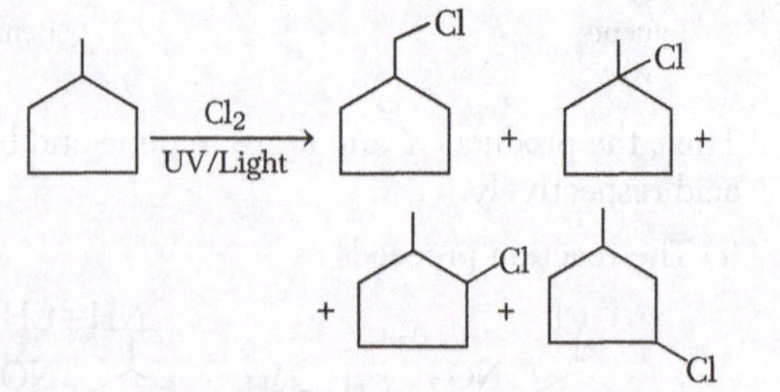

Thus, there are four monohalogenation products are possible in the given reaction.

13. (*d*) The given species, i.e. $(CH_3)_2\overset{\delta+}{CH}..\overset{\delta+}{OH_2}$ represents the transition state of the unimolecular dissociation step.

14. (*d*) Among the given compounds, $CH_2=CH-CH_2-CH_3$ will give a mixture of 1-chlorobutane and 2-chlorobutane on chlorination.

The reaction proceeds as

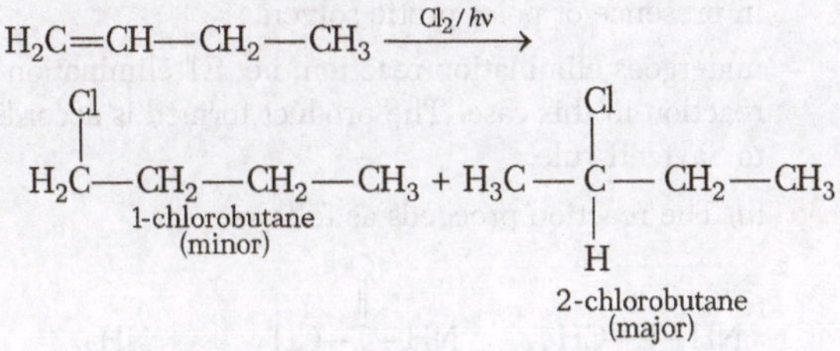

15. (*b*) In the given molecule carbon at C-2 and C-3 are asymmetric (i.e. have four different group) in nature.

16. (*c*) Boiling point of a compound depends upon the surface area. Higher the surface area, higher will be the boiling point of a compound.

Surface area decreases with increase in branching. If the compound has branching then its boiling point will be minimum.

Thus, the increasing order of their boiling points is

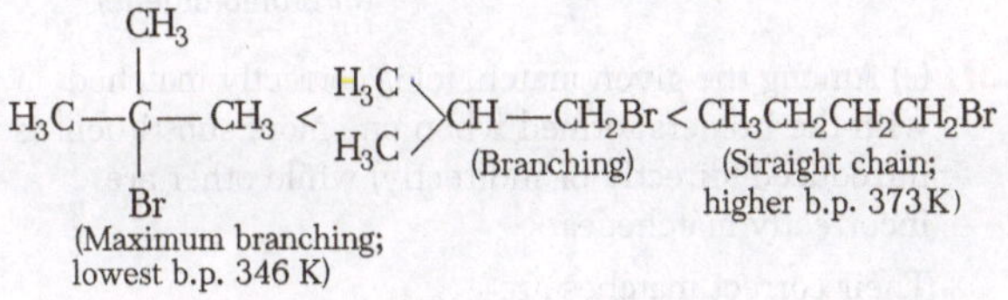

17. (*a*) A mixture containing two enantiomers in equimolar amount have zero optical rotation, as the rotation due to one isomer is cancelled by the rotation due to other isomer. Such a mixture is known as racemic mixture.

All those compounds which follow S_N1 mechanism during nucleophilic substitution reaction form racemic mixture.

Order of reactivity of alkyl halides towards S_N1 reaction follows as

Tertiary halide > secondary halide > primary halide > CH_3X.

Thus, $CH_3-\overset{*}{C}H(C_2H_5)-Br$ contains a chiral carbon and gives a racemic product.

Hence, option (a) is correct.

18. (*b*) As a result of resonance in vinyl chloride, the carbon-chloride bond acquires some double bond character. Hence, vinyl chloride does not undergo nucleophilic substitution reactions.

19. (*d*) Aryl halide is less reactive than alkyl halide towards nucleophile substitution because resonance stabilisation and sp^2-hybridisation of 'C' attached to halide.

20. (*c*) As, in S_N1 reaction the rate depends upon the intermediate (i.e. carbocation) stability.

Hence, option (c) is correct because in (i) compound 3° carbocation and in (ii) compound 2° carbocation are formed.

21. (*c*) The reaction proceeds as

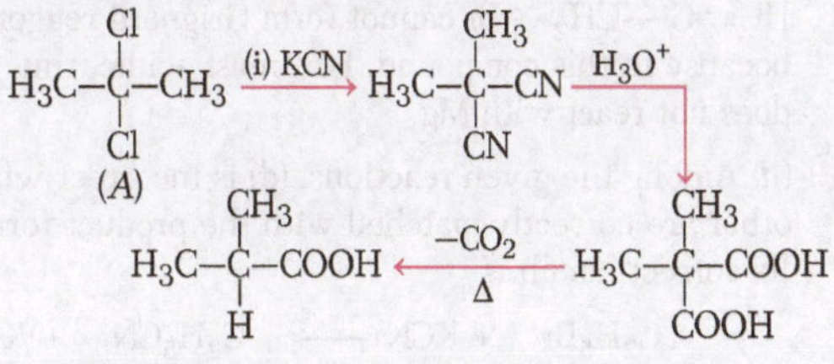

Thus, the reactant (*A*) is 2,2-dichloropropane.

22. (*d*) As S_N1 reaction proceed through formation of a stable carbocation as an intermediate hence compound (d) which has 3° benzyl carbocation as an intermediate is most rapidly hydrolysed by S_N1 mechanism.

23. (*a*) The reaction is proceed *via* S_N2 mechanism

$$H_3C-CH_2-Br \xrightarrow[\text{(LAH)}]{H^{\ominus}} CH_3-CH_3 + HBr \quad \text{(Ethane)}$$

while the reaction,

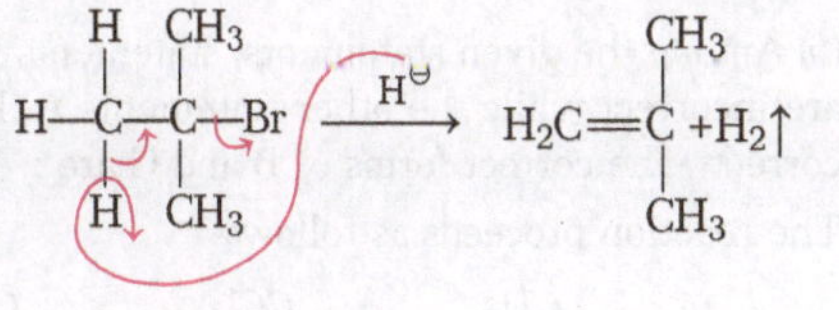

proceed *via.* E2 mechanism.

24. (*b*) The reaction (isomerisation) proceeds as follows

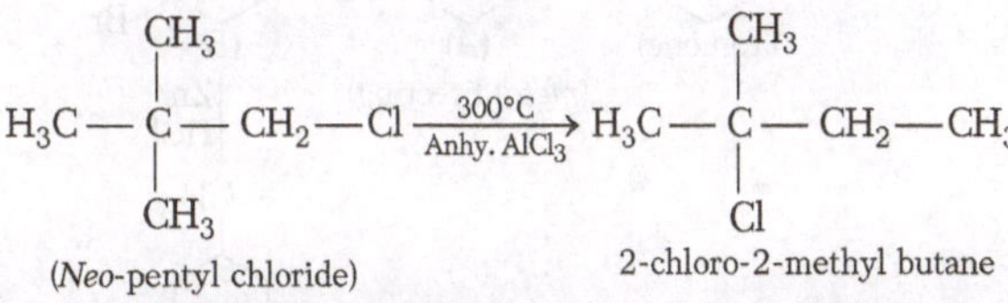

25. (*a*) Tertiary alkyl halide produces most stable 3° carbocation as an intermediate hence suffers elimination the most.

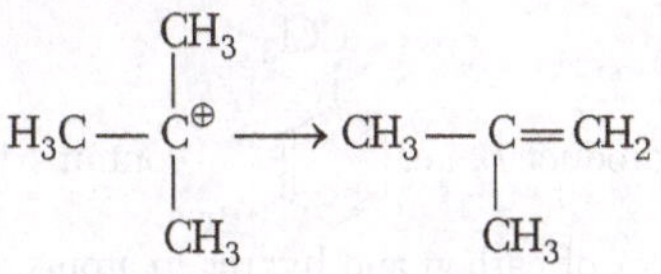

26. (*c*) The reaction is proceed as

$$H_3C-CH_2-Cl \xrightarrow{Hg_2F_2/\Delta} H_3C-CH_2-F \quad \text{(Fluoroethane)}$$

The given reaction is called **Swarts reaction.**

27. (*a*) Among the given compounds, (a) will be most reactive for E1 reaction due to the formation of most stable carbocation in this compound.

28. (*a*) Hunsdiecker reaction is the reaction of a silver carboxylate with a halogen to form an alkyl halide. The yield of alkyl halide follows the order 1° > 2° > 3° hence CH_3CH_2Br formed in maximum yield by Borodine-Hunsdiecker reaction.

29. (c) Among the given compounds, (c), i.e. $HC \equiv C—CH_2—Br$ cannot form Grignard reagent because in this compound, H is most acidic, thus C—Br does not react with Mg.

30. (d) Among the given reactions, (d) is incorrect while other are correctly matched with the product formed. Its correct match is

$$\underset{\text{(Bromoethane)}}{C_2H_5Br} + KCN \longrightarrow \underset{\text{(Ethane nitrile) (Major)}}{C_2H_5CN} + KBr$$

31. (a) Among the given species, (a), i.e.  is most reactive towards S_N2 reaction because S_N2 reactions occur when alkyl halide is sterically least hindered, 1°-carbon.

32. (a) Among the given statements, (a) is incorrect regarding the analysis of aryl halides. Its correct form is :

Aryl halides are insoluble in cold concentrated sulphuric acid.

33. (b) Among the given statements, statements B and C are incorrect while the other statements A, D and E are correct. The correct forms of B and C are :

The reaction proceeds as follows

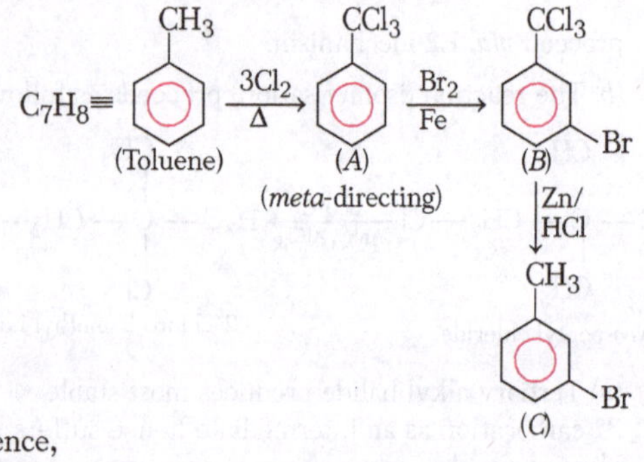

Hence,

- The product '*C*' is *m*-bromotoluene.
- The product *B*, i.e. 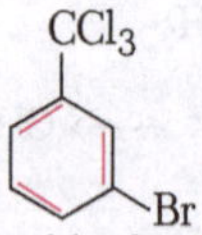 contains 11 total number of carbon and hydrogen atoms.

34. (c) The reaction is proceed as follow

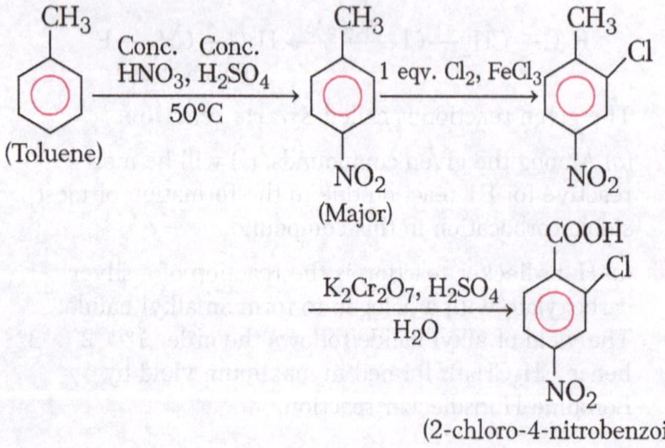

35. (b) Strong nucleophile, on reacting with 3° alkyl halide in presence of polar protic solvent undergoes elimination reaction, i.e. E1 elimination reaction in this case. The product formed is according to Saytzeff rule.

36. (d) The reaction proceeds as follows

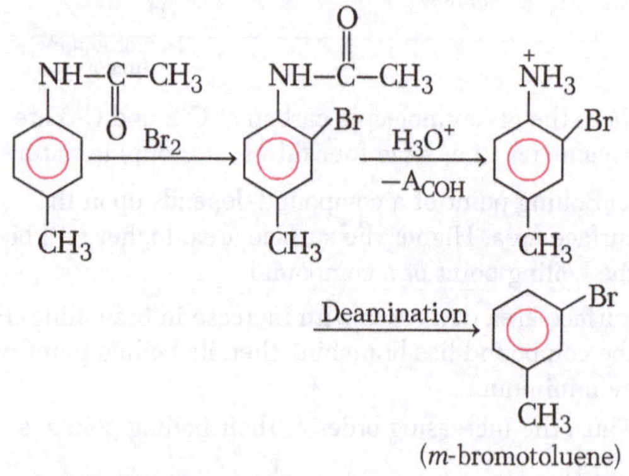

37. (c) Among the given match, (c) is correctly matched with the isomers formed when one more substituent is introduced (directly or indirectly) while other are incorrectly matchedes.

Their correct matches are

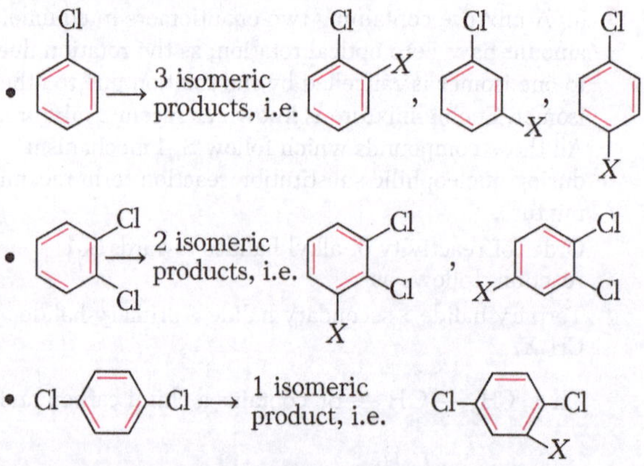

38. (d) The given reaction proceeds *via* E2 reaction because the leaving group and hydrogen atom are anti-periplanar to each other.

The reaction proceeds as follow

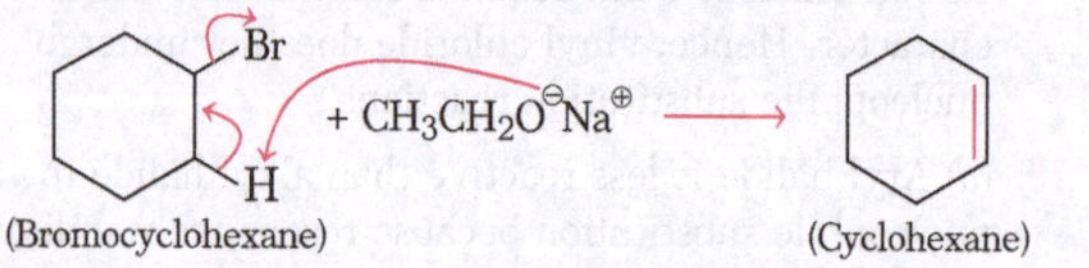

39. (c) The reaction is proceed as follow

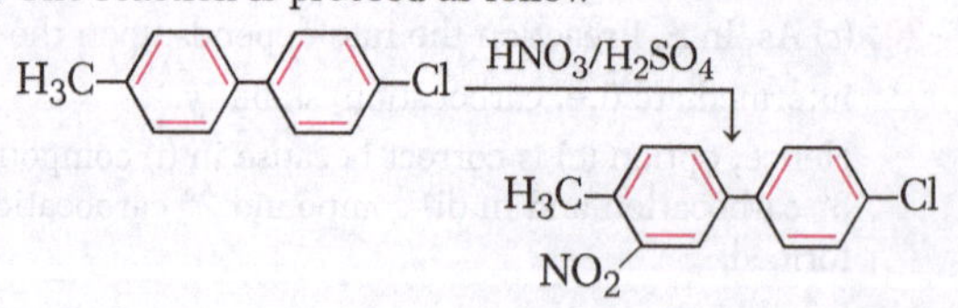

40. (*c*) Among the given matches, (c) is the correct match while the other products are incorrect matches with the given reaction.

Their correct matches are,

- 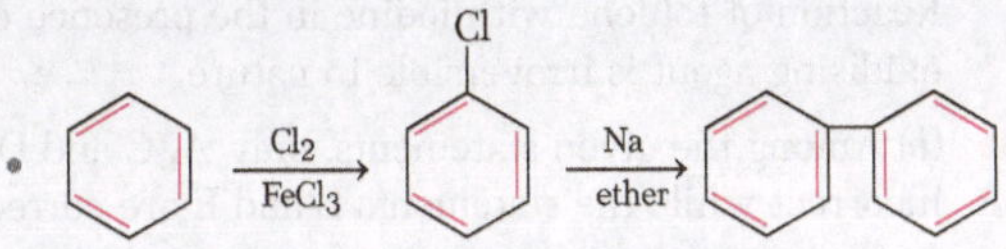
- 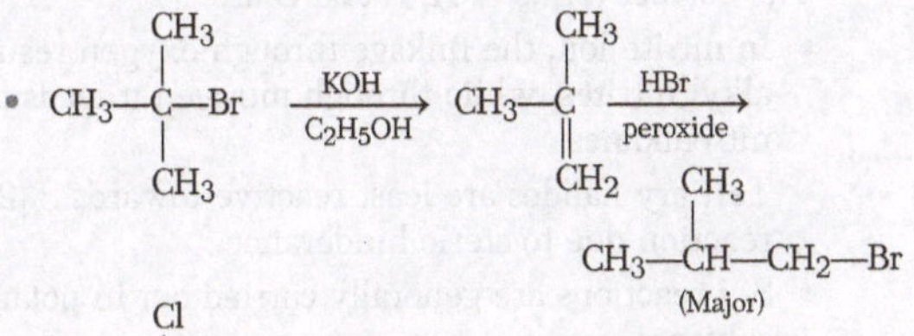
- $CH_3-\underset{|}{\overset{Cl}{CH}}-CH_3 \xrightarrow[C_2H_5OH]{KOH} CH_3-CH=CH_2 \xrightarrow[peroxide]{HBr} \underset{(Major)}{CH_3-CH_2-CH_2-Br}$

41. (*b*) II is most reactive due to two $-NO_2$ at *o* and *p*-positions. IV is least reactive due to each of resonance activation by nitro group present at *meta*-position. I is more reactive than III due to less steric hindrance and greater electrophilicity at α-carbon of *p*-fluoronitrobenzene.

42. (*d*) Its correct match is

$$CH_3-CH_2-\underset{Br}{\underset{|}{CH}}-CH_3 \xrightarrow[KOH]{Alcoholic} CH_3-CH=CHCH_3$$

[Saytzeff elimination]

43. (*a*) Due to large size of Br atoms, repulsion increases and dipole moment decreases.

Also, dipole moment follow the order $p < m < o$.

Hence, the compound, 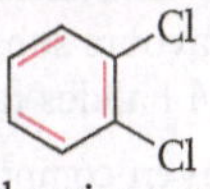 has the highest dipole moment among the given compounds.

44. (*d*) Among the given reactions, (d) is not correctly matched.

Its correct match is :

$CH_3Br + AgF \longrightarrow CH_3F + AgBr$ (Swarts reaction.)

45. (*d*) The reaction proceeds as follows

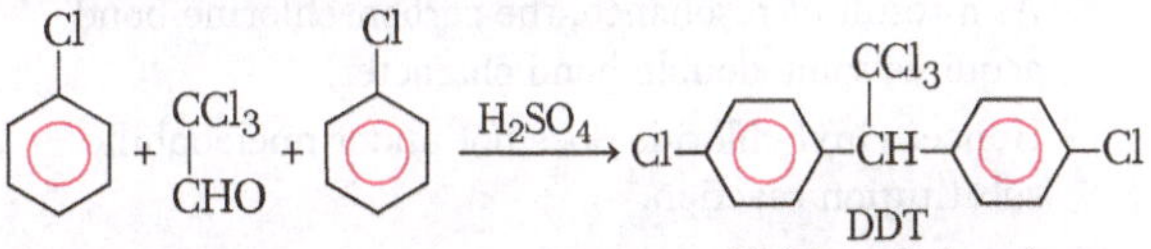

DDT
(dichloro diphenyl-trichloroethane)

46. (*d*) Since, the compound on heating produces only CO_2 but no water, thus the compound does not cotnain any hydrogen, hence, it is CCl_4.

47. (*c*) Among the given match, (c) is the incorrect match with the given uses.

Its correct match is :

Tetrachloromethane → Manufacturing of refrigerants.

48. (*a*) Both A and R are true and is R is the correct explanation of A.

49. (*a*) Both A and R are true and is R is the correct explanation of A.

50. (*d*) A ia false but R is true.

The correct form of A is :

During debromination of *meso*-2,3-dibromobutane the major product formed is *trans*-2-butene.

51. (*c*) A is true but R is false.

The correct form of R is :

In bromobenzene, directing nature of incoming electrophile controlled by its mesomeric effect (+*M*) and it also gives stabilisation to the arenium ion.

52. (*d*) A is false but R is true.

The correct form of A is :

The given compound, 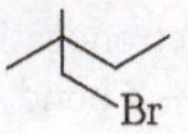 will not give product under E2 reaction because there is no β-hydrogen is present.

53. (*a*) Both A and R are true and is R is the correct explanation of A.

54. (*b*) Both A and R are true but R is not the correct explanation of A.

The correct explanation of A is :

Chloroform is stored in dark coloured bottles because it gets oxidised by air in sunlight to poisonous phoesgene gas.

55. (*b*) Statement I is true but Statement II is false.

Its correct form is :

In S_N1 mechanism, carbocation is formed as an intermediate.

56. (*a*) Both Statement I and Statement II are false.

Their correct forms are,

- In the given reaciton
$$CHCl_3 + C_6H_5NH_2 + 3NaOH \longrightarrow \underset{(A)}{C_6H_5NC} + \underset{(B)}{3NaCl} + \underset{(C)}{3H_2O}$$
the product '*A*' is phenyl isocyanide.
- Strong reducing agent converts $CHCl_3$ into CH_4.

57. (*a*) Both Statement I and Statement II are false. Their correct forms are,

- 2-bromo-3-methylbutane changes to 2-methyl but-2-ene as a major product on reaction with CH_3CH_2OH.
- The given reaction proceeds *via.* elimination instead of substitution mechanism.

58. (*d*) Both Statement I and Statement II are true.

59. (*a*) Both Statement I and Statements II are false. The correct form of Statements I is :

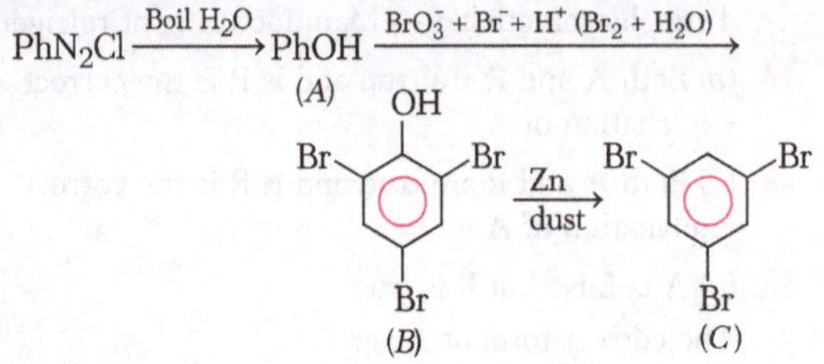

The product '*B*' is 2,4,6-tribromophenol.

$\Rightarrow \mu_B \neq 0$, but $\mu_C = 0$

60. (*b*) Statement I is true but Statement II is false.

The correct form of Statement II is :

The C—Cl bond length in haloalkanes is longer than haloarenes.

61. (*b*) Among the given statements, B, C and D are incorrect while the statements A and E are correct.

The correct forms of B, C and D are

- Due to more electronegativity of halogen atoms than carbon atoms, C—*X* bond of alkyl halide is polarised.
- C—*X* bond enthalpies decrease from C–F to C–I. The bond enthalpies order of alkyl halide is

  C—F > C—Cl > C—Br > C—I.
- The C—*X* bond in haloalkanes are more polar than in haloarenes.

62. (*d*) Among the given statements, only B, D and E are correct while the statements A and C are incorrect.

The correct forms of A and C are,

- Bromides and iodides develop colour when they exposed to light.
- Due to greater polarity as well as higher molecular mass as compared to the parent hydrocarbon, the intermolecualr forces of attraction are stronger in the halogen derivatives.

63. (*d*) Among the given statements, only A and C are incorrect while the statements B, D and E are correct.

The correct form of A and C are,

- Ethylbromide react with sodium in dry ether to give hydrocarbons containing double the number of carbon atoms present in the halide.
- 2-bromopentane is heated with potassium ethoxide in ethanol give *trans*-pent-2-ene.

64. (*b*) Among the given statements, only D and E are correct while other statements A, B and C are incorrect.

The correct forms of A, B and C are

- The synthesis of alkyl fluorides is best accomplished by Swarts reaction.
- In Sandmeyer's reaction, solution of freshly prepared diazonium salt with cuprous bromide, replaces diazonium group by Br.
- Aryl chlorides and bromides can be easily prepared by electrophilic substitution of arenes.

65. (*b*) Among the given statements, only 'B' statement is not correct. Its correct form is :

Reaction of toluene with iodine in the presence of an oxidising agent is irreversible in nature.

66. (*b*) Among the given statements, only A, C and D are incorrect while the statements B and E are correct.

The correct forms of A, C and D are

- In nitrite ion, the linkage through oxygen results in alkyl nitrites, while through nitrogen it leads to the nitroalkanes.
- Tertiary halides are least reactive towards S_N2 reaction due to steric hinderance.
- S_N1 reactions are generally carried out in polar protic solvents.

67. (*b*) Among the given halides, only four, i.e. (i), (ii), (iv), (vii) are 2° halides.

68. (*d*) Among the given compounds, only one, i.e. (iv) will favour majorly when treated with HCl and yields an anti of Markovnikov's product.

Because, attachment of electron-withdrawing group (—*R* or —*I*) will follow anti-Markovnikov's pathway (even in absence of organic peroxide which favours free radical addition) through electrophilic addition pathway.

$$(-I)\ F_3C \leftarrow CH{=}CH_2 \xrightarrow[\text{Slow}]{\overset{\delta+}{H}\text{—}\overset{\delta-}{Cl}} F_3C\text{—}CH_2\text{—}\overset{\oplus}{C}H_2 \xrightarrow{Cl^{\ominus}} F_3C\text{—}CH_2CH_2Cl$$

69. (*b*) Among the given reagents, only three, i.e. (i), (iv) and (v) reagents are used for the preparation of alkyl chloride from alcohol.

70. (*c*) Among the given compounds, only two, i.e. (i) and (ii) will favours elimination over substitution because 1° alkyl halide favours substitution whereas secondary and tertiary alkyl halides favour elimination.

71. (*a*) Among the given compounds, only two, i.e. (iii) and (v) are inactive towards S_N1 reaction because in (iii) compound, the carbocation is on bridge head carbon of the bicyclo system which is not stable and in (v) compound, the carbocation formed is not stable.

72. (*a*) Among the given compounds, only one, i.e. (i) does not undergo nucleophilic substitution reaction.

As a result of resonance, the carbon-chlorine bond acquires some double bond character.

Hence, vinyl chloride does not under nucleophilic substitution reaction.

73. (*c*) Among the given compounds only four compounds i.e. (i), (ii), (iii) and (v) will undergo elimination reaction to give alkene. There is an atom elimination of hydrogen from β-carbon and a halogen atoms from the α-carbon atom and compound (iv) [(v) also in Ist step] undergoes acid-base reaction.

74. (*d*) Among the given compounds, only one, i.e. (iv) does not give 3 isomers on nitration.

75. (*d*) Among the given compounds, only one, i.e. (iii) is formed when chlorobenzene fused with solid NaOH.

The reaction proceeds as follow

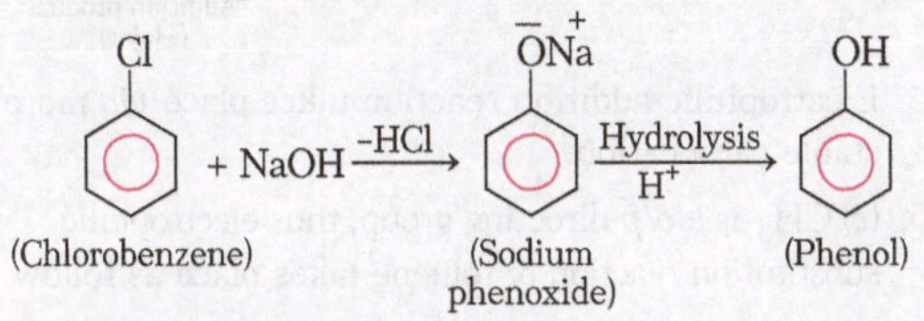

76. (*a*) The correct match is A-2, B-4, C-1, D-3.

77. (*b*) The correct match is A-4, B-3, C-2, D-1.

78. (*d*) The correct order is A-4, B-1, C-2, D-3.

79. (*b*) The correct match is A-4, B-3, C-2, D-1.

80. (*b*) The correct match is A-4, B-1, C-2, D-3.

Final Check through PYQs

1. (*d*) The reactions involved are

$$3R—OH + PCl_3 \longrightarrow 3RCl + H_3PO_3$$

$$R—OH + PCl_5 \longrightarrow R—Cl + HCl + POCl_3$$

Hence, products *A* and *B* are,

$$A = H_3PO_3 \text{ and } B = POCl_3$$

2. (*b*) The given compound

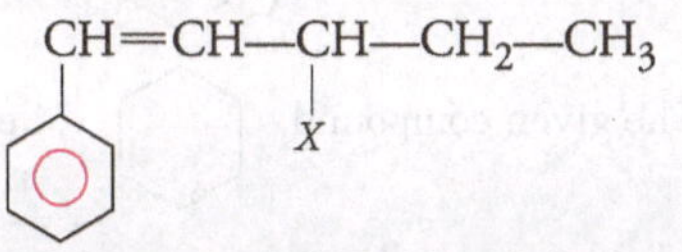

is an example of allylic halides. As in this, the halogen is bonded to the sp^3-hybridised carbon atom next to the carbon-carbon double bond, which is called as allylic halides.

Benzylic halides In these halides, the halogen atom is bonded to the sp^3-hybridised carbon atom next to an aromatic ring.

Vinylic halide In these halides, the halogen atom is bonded to the sp^2-hybridised carbon of one of the carbon atoms of a double bond.

Aryl halide In these halides, the halogen atom is bonded to the sp^2-hybridised carbon atom of an aromatic ring.

3. (*c*) As the size of halide increases, bond length increases and bond enthalpy decreases. Thus, the correct order of bond enthalpy is

$$CH_3—F > CH_3—Cl > CH_3—Br > CH_3—I.$$

4. (*d*) Reactivity toward $S_N1 \propto$ stability of carbocation, and stability of carbocation depends upon the number of α-hydrogen (hyperconjugations) and resonance.

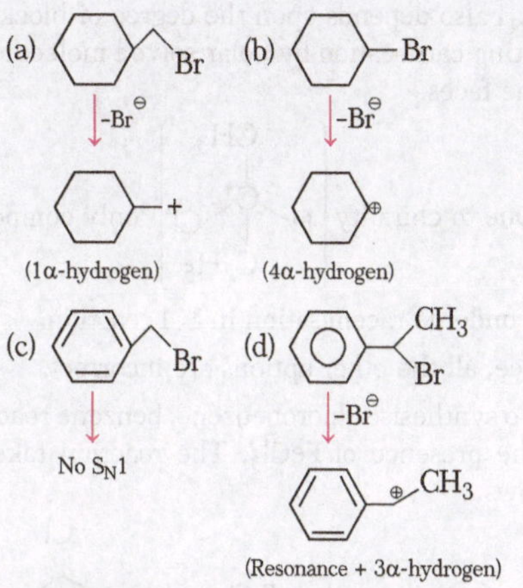

5. (*c*) Enantiomers are non-superimposable mirror images of each other. They have identical physical properties, i.e. melting point, boiling point, refracive index etc. and differ only with respect to the rotation of plane polarised light. If one of the enantiomer is dextrorotatory, then the other will be laevorotatory.

6. (*c*) The reaction

$$\underset{\text{Bromopropane}}{CH_3CH_2CH_2Br} + \underset{\text{Sodium cyanide}}{NaCN} \longrightarrow \underset{\substack{\text{Butyl cyanide} \\ \text{(Major)}}}{CH_3CH_2CH_2CN} + NaBr$$

follows S_N2 mechanism and thus favoured by polar aprotic solvent, i.e. N, N-dimethylformamide (DMF).

$$H—\overset{\overset{\large O}{\|}}{C}—N(CH_3)_2$$

7. (*a*) Reaction (i) is an elimination reaction, (ii) is a substitution reaction and (iii) is an addition reaction.

(i) $\underset{\beta\text{-elimination reaction}}{CH_3CH_2CH_2Br + KOH} \longrightarrow CH_3CH{=}CH_2 + KBr + H_2O$

(ii)

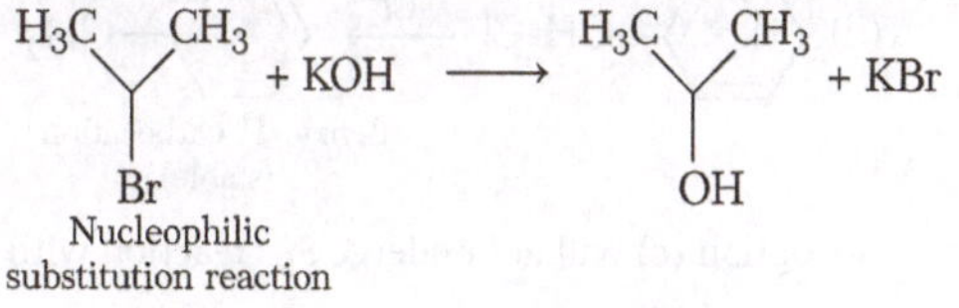

(iii)

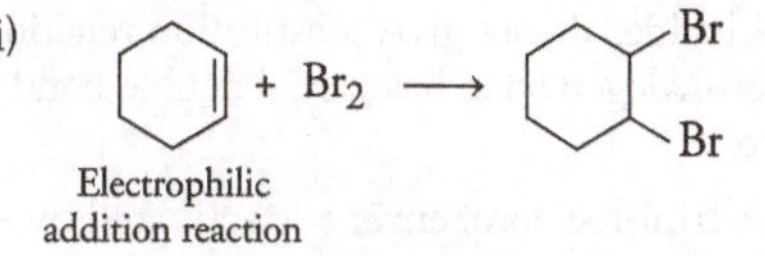

8. (*a*) In optically active alkyl halides, S_N1 reaction is accompanied by a racemisation. The carbocation formed in the slow step is sp^2-hybridised in planar structure and attack of nucleophile may take place from either side resulting in a mixture of products, one with the same configuration and other with inverted configuration. The isomer corresponding to inversion of configuration is present in slight excess as S_N1 also depends upon the degree of blocking of reacting carbocation by polar solved molecules in both of the faces.

9. (*d*) Due to chirality $\left[H-\overset{CH_3}{\underset{C_2H_5}{C^*}}-Cl\right]$ only compound (iv) will undergo racemisation in S_N1 reaction.

Hence, all the other options are incorrect.

10. (*d*) To synthesise chlorobenzene, benzene reacts with Cl_2 in the presence of $FeCl_3$. The reaction takes place as follows,

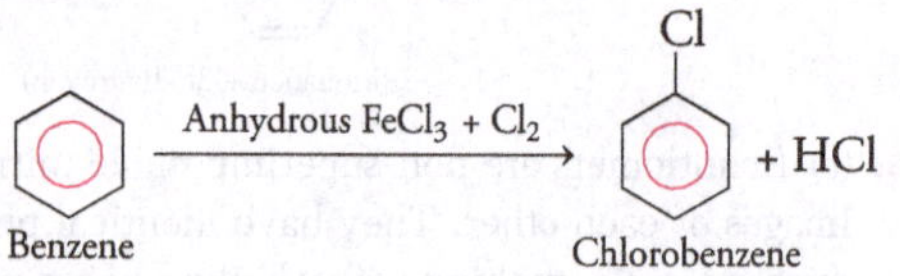

11. (*c*) An S_N1 reaction proceeds through formation of a stable carbocation as an intermediate. Here,

(a) $CH_2{=}CH{-}CH_2Cl \xrightarrow{-Cl^-} CH_2{=}CH{-}\overset{\oplus}{C}H_2$

Allyl-1°-carbocation (stable)

(b) $(CH_3)_3CCl \xrightarrow{-Cl^-} CH_3-\overset{\oplus}{\underset{CH_3}{C}}-CH_3$

tert-butyl carbocation (stable) (9 hyperconjugations)

(c) 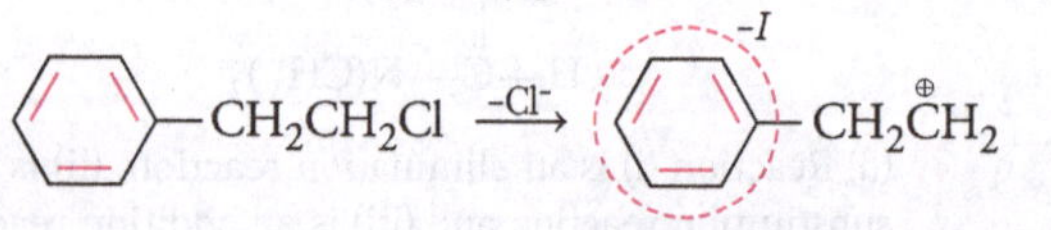

1° carbocation (less stable due to –*I* effect of the phenyl group)

(d) 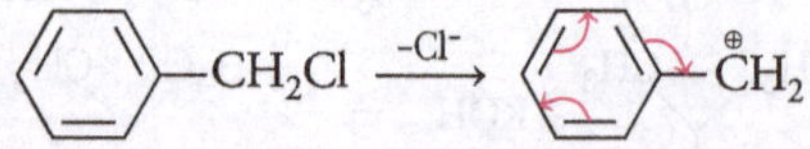

Benzyl-1° carbocation (stable)

So, option (c) will not undergo S_N1 reaction with OH^-.

12. (*b*) Aryl halides do not give substitution reactions as carbon-halogen bond has partial double bond character.

13. (*a*) 2,4,6-trinitrochlorobenzene is activated by –*R* effect by three NO_2 groups at *o*- and *p*-positions on nucleophilic substitution (ArS_N2) reaction.

Hence, it undergoes hydrolysis with *aq.* NaOH most readily.

14. (*d*) *iso*-propyl chloride can be used as the halide component (alkyl halide) for Friedel-Craft reaction.

15. (*a*) $C_6H_5CH{=}CHCH_3 + H^+ \xrightarrow{\text{Slow}} C_6H_5-\overset{+}{C}H-CH_2-CH_3$

Stable carbocation (Benzyl)

$C_6H_5\overset{+}{C}HCH_2CH_3 + Br^- \xrightarrow{\text{Fast}} C_6H_5-\underset{Br}{CH}-CH_2CH_3$

Addition product (Major)

Electrophilic addition reaction takes place *via* more stable carbocation.

16. (*c*) CH_3 is a *o*/*p*-directing group, thus electrophilic substitution reaction of toluene takes place as follow

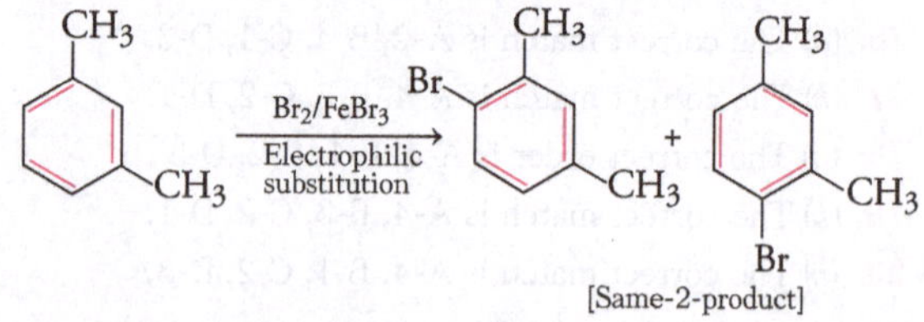

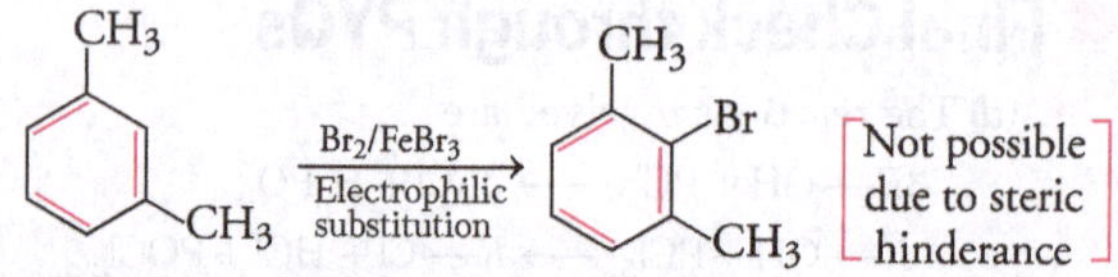

Skill Builders

- **Sol. of Skill Builder Pg. 286**

(*b*) The given compound 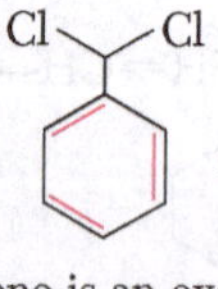 , i.e.

1,1-dichloromethylbenzene is an example of benzylic halide.

- **Sol. of Skill Builder Pg. 290**

(*c*) In the given question *P* and *Q* are respectively HCl and PCl_5.

- **Sol. of Skill Builder Pg. 296**

(*d*) $CH_3-CH_2-\underset{\|\atop O}{C}-CH_2CH_3 \xrightarrow[\text{(ii) } H_2O]{\text{(i) } NaBH_4\text{, THF}} CH_3CH_2-\overset{H}{\underset{OH}{C}}-CH_2CH_3$

It is an achiral molecule, i.e. no racemisation will occur.

- **Sol. of Skill Builder Pg. 303**

(*b*) Order of reactivity of alkyl halides towards S_N1 reaction is 1° < 2° < 3° < allylic.

Hence, the correct increasing order is I < III < II.

For deeper insight
Scan the QR Code

Chapter 8

Alcohols, Phenols and Ethers

Learning Objectives

Module-I

- Classification
- Structure
- Nomenclature
- Isomerism
- Methods of Preparation
- Physical Properties

Module-II

- Reactions Involving O—H bond Cleavage
- Reactions Involving C—O bond Cleavage
- Distinction between 1°, 2° and 3° Alcohols
- Some Commercially Important Alcohol

Module-III

- Classification
- Structure
- Nomenclature
- Isomerism
- Methods of Preparation
- Physical Properties
- Chemical Properties

Module-IV

- Classification
- Structure
- Nomenclature
- Isomerism
- Methods of Preparation
- Physical Properties
- Chemical Properties

Chapter Overview with *NEET Connection*

This chapter is useful for the learning of preparation and chemical properties of alcohols, phenols and ethers. Without gripping this chapter, it will be difficult to learn and understand, the preparation of carbonyl and carboxylic compounds and their interconversion reactions.

Special format questions can be easily framed on the following topics of this chapter.

- Acidity of alcohols and phenols
- Preparation of phenol from cumene
- Oxidation reaction of alcohol
- Reaction of ether with HI

For better understanding of this chapter a grip over chemical properties of hydrocarbons and alkyl halides and aryl halides are required especially nucleophilic substitution and elimination reactions of alkyl halides provide a solid foundation to grip this chapter.

Introduction

The compound obtained by replacing one hydrogen atom from aliphatic hydrocarbons by hydroxyl group are **alcohols** whereas those obtained by replacing hydrogen atom of aromatic hydrocarbons are **phenols.**

The substitution of a hydrogen atom in a hydrocarbon by an alkoxy (*R*O) or aryloxy (ArO) group gives another class of compounds known as **ethers.**

In this chapter, we will study in detail about the chemistry of these compounds, namely alcohols, phenols and ethers.

Module 1

Alcohols (Part I)

- Classification
- Isomerism
- Structure
- Methods of Preparation
- Nomenclature
- Physical Properties

Classification

On the basis of number of —OH groups present in the molecule, these are classified as mono-, di-, tri or polyhydric compounds. Depending on whether they contain one, two, three or more hydroxyl groups respectively. Their structures are as follows.

e.g CH_3OH , (Monohydric); CH_2OH—CH_2OH (Dihydric), CH_2OH—CHOH—CH_2OH (Trihydric)

Monohydric alcohols can be further classified according to the hybridisation of the carbon atom to which the hydroxyl group is attached.

Compounds Containing sp^3 C—OH Bond

In this class of alcohols, the –OH group is attached to a sp^3 hybridised carbon atom of an alkyl group. They are further classified as primary, secondary and tertiary. In these three types of alcohols, the –OH group is attached to primary, secondary and tertiary carbon atom, respectively.

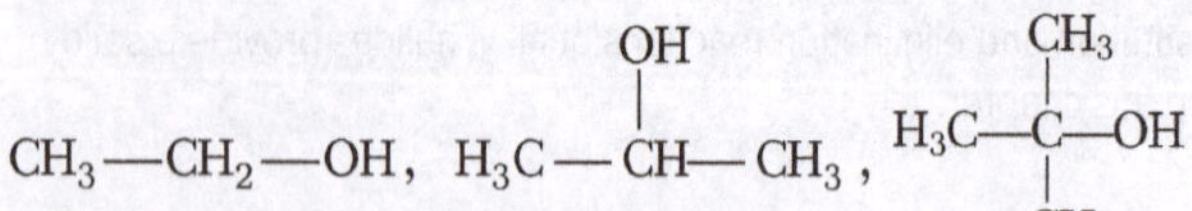

Primary (1°) alcohol Secondary (2°) alcohol Tertiary (3°) alcohol

Allylic Alcohols

These are the compounds in which the –OH group is bonded to a sp^3 hybridised carbon atom next to carbon-carbon double bond.

CH_2=CH—CH_2—OH, Primary (1°)

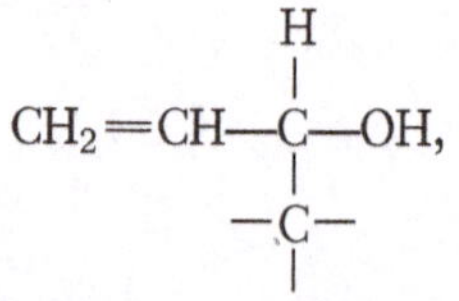

Secondary (2°)

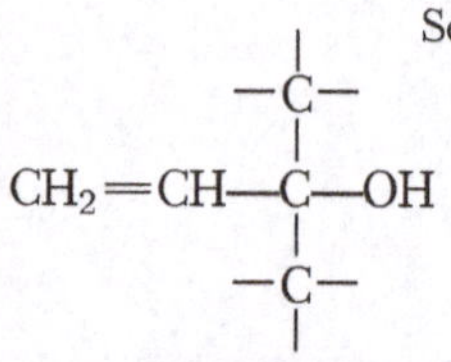

Tertiary (3°)

Benzylic Alcohols

These are the compounds in which the –OH group is bonded to a sp^3 hybridised carbon atom next to an aromatic ring.

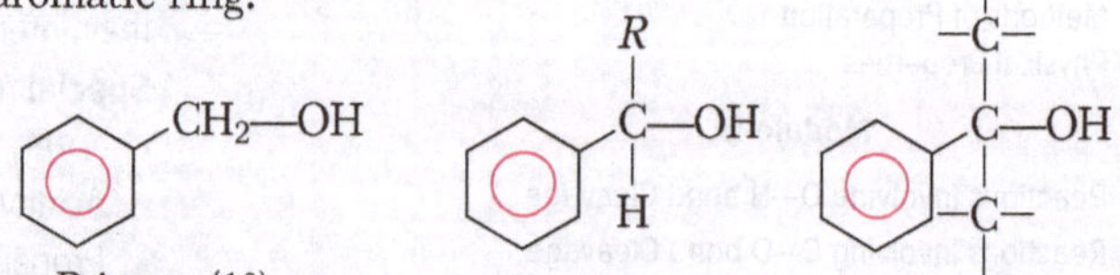

Primary (1°) Secondary (2°) Tertiary (3°)

Mentor's TIP

Compounds in which a hydroxyl group is bonded to an unsaturated carbon atom of a double bond (i.e. C=C—OH) are called **enols.**

Compounds Containing sp^2 C—OH Bond

Vinylic Alcohols

These are the compounds in which the –OH group is bonded to an sp^2 hybridised carbon atom of a carbon-carbon double bond.

H_2C=CH—OH

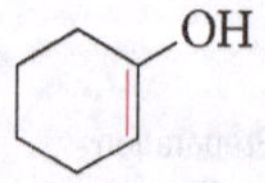

Structure

The structure of an alcohol resembles the structure of water with an alkyl group replacing one of the hydrogen atoms of water. Both have sp^3-hybridised oxygen atoms but the C—O—H bond angle in methanol (108.9°) is considerably larger than the H—O—H bond angle in water (104.5°) because the methyl group is much larger than a hydrogen atom but slightly less than the tetrahedral angle (109°28′) due to repulsion between the unshared electron pairs of oxygen.

The bulky methyl group counter acts the bond angle compression caused by non-bonding (lone) electron pairs of oxygen. The O—H bond lengths are about the same in water and methanol (0.96 Å) but the C—O bond is considerably longer (1.41 Å), reflecting the larger covalent radius of carbon compared to hydrogen.

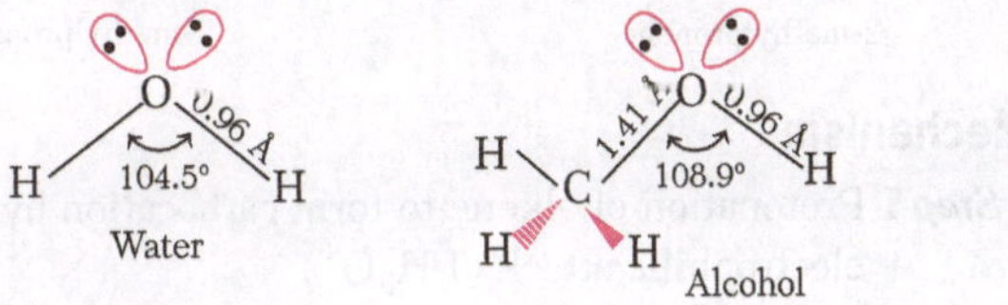

Water Alcohol

Nomenclature

For the simpler alcohols, the common names are most often used. A common name consists of the name of the alkyl group followed by the word 'alcohol'.

e.g. CH_3CH_2OH Ethyl alcohol (1°); $CH_3CH(OH)CH_3$ *iso*-propyl alcohol (2°); $(CH_3)_3C-OH$ *tert*-butyl alcohol (3°)

IUPAC System

IUPAC system is the most versatile system. The rules for nomenclature of alcohol are as follows

- Select the longest continuous carbon chain that contains the —OH group as the parent chain.
- Each name is derived by replacing the terminal '–e' of the corresponding alkane name by '–ol'.
- Indicate the position of —OH group by a number in the parent chain, generally using the lowest possible number for this purpose.
- Indicate the position of other groups by the number in the parent chain.
- For naming of polyhydric alcohol 'e' is retained and the ending 'ol' is added.

CH_3OH Methanol; $CH_3CH_2CH_2OH$ Propanol

$CH_3CH(OH)CH_2Br$ 1-bromopropan-2-ol; $CH_2(OH)—CH_2(OH)$ Ethane-1, 2-diol

- Cyclic alcohols are named by using the prefix cyclo and considering the —OH group attached to C-1.

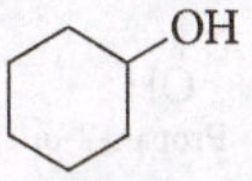

Cyclohexanol

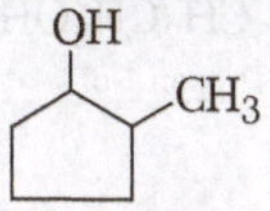

2-methylcyclopentanol

NEET Close-up

Example Similar to PYQ Asked in NEET 2021

What is the IUPAC name of the organic compound '*A*' formed in the following chemical reaction?

$$CH_3CH{=}CHCO_2CH_3 \xrightarrow{LiAlH_4} 'A' + \text{Methanol}$$

(a) 4-methyl heptan-4-ol (b) But-2-en-1-ol
(c) 4-methyl heptan-3-ol (d) Pent-3-en-1-ol

Sol. (*b*) $LiAlH_4$ reagent is used for the reduction of –CHO, $—\overset{O}{\overset{\|}{C}}—OCH_3$. It does not reduce double bonds.

The given reaction proceeds as follows

$$CH_3—CH{=}CH—\overset{O}{\overset{\|}{C}}—OCH_3 \xrightarrow{LiAlH_4} \underset{\text{(But-2-en-1-ol)}}{CH_3—CH{=}CHCH_2OH} + \underset{\text{(Methanol)}}{CH_3OH}$$

Skill Builder

What is the IUPAC name of the compound '*X*' in the following chemical reaction?

$$CH_3—\underset{CH_3}{\overset{CH_3}{C}}—CH{=}CH_2 \xrightarrow{BH_3,\,THF} \xrightarrow{H_2O_2/OH^-} X$$

(a) 3,3-dimethylbutane (b) 3,3-dimethylbutanol
(c) 2,3-dimethylbutanol (d) 2-methyl-but-3-ol

For more practice Refer to Q. 14 of step up Practice-1.

Isomerism

Alcohols exhibit following types of isomerism

(i) **Chain isomerism** Alcohols with four or more carbon atoms exhibit this type of isomerism in which compounds have similar molecular formula but the carbon skeleton is different.

$$CH_3—CH_2—CH_2—CH_2OH \qquad CH_3—CH(CH_3)—CH_2OH$$

Butan-1-ol — 2-methylpropan-1-ol

(ii) **Position isomerism** Alcohols with three or more carbon atoms can exhibit position isomerism. In this type of isomerism, the position of the functional group, i.e. — OH group varies.

$$CH_3CH_2CH_2OH \qquad CH_3CH(OH)—CH_3$$

Propan-1-ol — Propan-2-ol

(iii) **Functional isomerism** Alcohols with two or more carbon atoms can exhibit functional isomerism with ethers.

Thus, ethers and alcohols have same molecular formula but have different functional groups, hence they are called functional isomers.

$$CH_3CH_2CH_2CH_2OH \qquad CH_3CH_2OCH_2CH_3$$

Butan-1-ol — Ethoxyethane

(iv) **Optical isomerism** Alcohols containing chiral centres shows optical isomerism. These optical isomers can rotate the plane of polarised light in different directions.

$$CH_3—\overset{*}{C}H(OH)—CH_2—CH_3, \quad CH_3—CH_2—CH_2—\overset{*}{C}H(OH)—CH_3$$

Butan-2-ol — Pentan-2-ol

$$CH_3—CH(CH_3)—\overset{*}{C}H(OH)—CH_3$$

3-methylbutan 2-ol

Preparation of Alcohols

The important methods of preparation of alcohols are

From Alkenes

Alkenes can be converted into alcohols by the following methods

(i) By Acid Catalysed Hydration

Alkenes react with water in the presence of an acid as catalyst to form an alcohol, this process is called hydration. In case of unsymmetrical alkenes, the addition of water takes place according to Markovnikov's rule.

$$>C=C< + H_2O \overset{H^+}{\rightleftharpoons} —C(H)—C(OH)—$$

Alkene — Alcohol

e.g. $$CH_2=CH_2 + H_2O \xrightarrow{\text{Dil.}H_2SO_4} CH_3CH_2OH$$

Alkene — Ethanol (1°)

$$CH_3CH=CH_2 + H_2O \xrightarrow{\text{Dil.}H_2SO_4} CH_3—CH(OH)—CH_3$$

Propene — Propan-2-ol (2°)

$$CH_3C(CH_3)=CH_2 + H_2O \xrightarrow{\text{Dil.}H_2SO_4} CH_3—C(CH_3)_2—OH$$

2-methylpropene — 2-methylpropan-2-ol (3°)

Mechanism

***Step* I** Protonation of alkene to form carbocation by electrophilic attack of H_3O^+.

$$H_2O + H^+ \longrightarrow H_3O^+$$

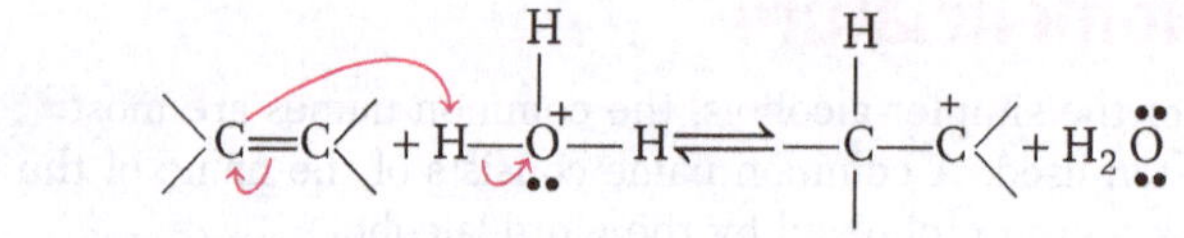

***Step* II** Nucleophilic attack of water on carbocation.

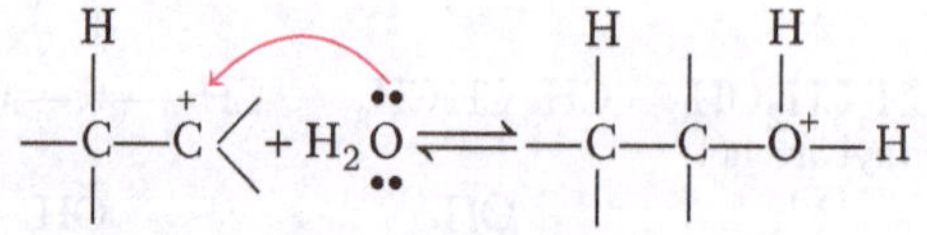

***Step* III** Deprotonation to form an alcohol.

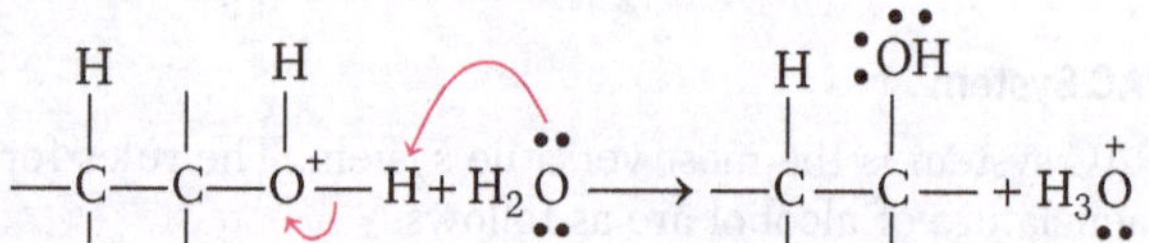

Mentor's TIP

Many alkenes do not easily undergo hydration in dilute aqueous acid because they are nearly insoluble in water. In such case concentrated sulphuric acid is used, in which alkenes are soluble forming alkyl hydrogen sulphate which on boiling with water changes to alcohol.

$$\underset{\text{Ethene}}{CH_2=CH_2} + \underset{\text{Conc. sulphuric acid}}{HOSO_3H} \longrightarrow \underset{\text{Ethyl hydrogen sulphate}}{CH_3CH_2—OSO_3H} \xrightarrow{\text{Boiling }H_2O} \underset{\text{Ethanol}}{CH_3CH_2OH} + H_2SO_4$$

(ii) By Hydroboration-Oxidation

Alkenes react with diborane (B_2H_6) in the presence of THF to form trialkylboranes which on oxidation gives alcohol. In this reaction, addition of water takes place according to anti-Markovnikov's rule.

$$\underset{\text{Propene}}{CH_3CH=CH_2} \xrightarrow{(BH_3)_2 \text{ in THF}} CH_3-\underset{\underset{H}{|}}{CH}-\underset{\underset{BH_2}{|}}{CH_2}$$

$$\xrightarrow{CH_3-CH=CH_2} (CH_3-CH_2-CH_2)_2BH \xrightarrow{CH_3-CH=CH_2}$$

$$(CH_3-CH_2-CH_2)_3B \xrightarrow[H_2O]{3H_2O_2,\bar{O}H} \underset{\text{Propan-1-ol}}{3CH_3-CH_2-CH_2-OH} + \underset{\text{Boric acid}}{B(OH)_3}$$

This mechanism proceeds *via* transition state hence, no rearrangement takes place as seen in the hydration of alkenes.

> **Concept ladder**
> Alcohols are also prepared by oxymercuration -demercuration reaction. In this reaction, mercury (II) acetate reacts with alkene in presence of water to give β-hydroxy alkyl mercury (II) acetate. This step is called **oxymercuration** and is carried out in a mixture of H_2O and THF as solvent, which is treated directly with $NaBH_4$ to form alcohol and this step is called **demercuration**. The product formation takes place according to Markovnikov's rule without any rearrangement.

From Carbonyl Compounds

Alcohols can be prepared from carbonyl compounds by the following methods.

(i) By Reduction of Aldehydes and Ketones

Carbonyl compounds (aldehyde and ketones) can be reduced to alcohols either by catalytic hydrogenation or by hydride transfer reducing agent like lithium aluminium hydride ($LiAlH_4$) and sodium borohydride ($NaBH_4$). During reduction aldehydes gives primary alcohols while ketones give secondary alcohols.

e.g.

$$\underset{\text{Aldehyde}}{RCHO} \xrightarrow[LiAlH_4 \text{ or } NaBH_4]{H_2 \text{ (Ni or Pd or Pt)}} \underset{\text{Primary alcohol}}{RCH_2OH}$$

$$\underset{\text{Ketone}}{R_2C=O} \xrightarrow[LiAlH_4 \text{ or } NaBH_4]{H_2 \text{ (Ni or Pt or Pd)}} \underset{\text{Secondary alcohol}}{R_2C(OH)H}$$

(ii) By Reduction of Carboxylic Acids and Esters

Carboxylic acids and its derivatives (acid halides, ester and anhydride) are reduced to primary alcohols in the presence of strong reducing agent ($LiAlH_4$).

$$\underset{\text{Carboxylic acid}}{RCOOH} \xrightarrow[\text{(ii) } H_2O/H^+]{\text{(i) } LiAlH_4} \underset{\text{Primary alcohol}}{RCH_2OH}$$

$$\underset{\text{Ester}}{R-\overset{\overset{O}{||}}{C}-OR'} \xrightarrow[\text{(ii) } H_2O/H^+]{\text{(i) } LiAlH_4} \underset{\text{Mixture of alcohols}}{RCH_2OH + R'OH}$$

$LiAlH_4$ can reduce carboxylic acids, esters, aldehydes, ketones, acid halides, anhydride, amides, alkyl halides and nitriles while $NaBH_4$ can reduce ketones, aldehydes and acid halides only.

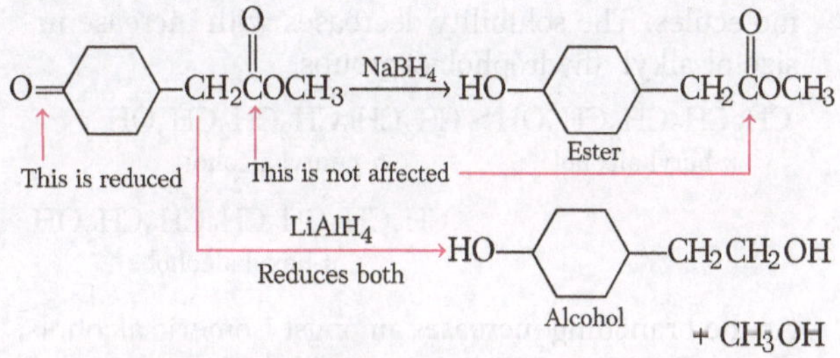

From Grignard Reagents

Aldehydes and ketones reacts with Grignard reagent to give the corresponding alcohol. The first step is the nucleophilic addition of Grignard reagent to the carbonyl group to form an adduct. Hydrolysis of adduct yields an alcohol.

$$>C=O + \underset{\text{Grignard reagent}}{\overset{\delta- \ \delta+}{RMgX}} \xrightarrow{\text{Dry ether}} \underset{\text{Adduct}}{\left[>C\begin{matrix}\bar{O}\overset{+}{M}gX \\ R\end{matrix}\right]} \xrightarrow{H_2O/H^+} >C\begin{matrix}OH \\ R\end{matrix} + Mg(OH)X$$

All aldehydes (other than formaldehyde) give secondary alcohols while ketones gives tertiary alcohols.

$$\underset{\text{Methanal}}{HCHO} \xrightarrow[\text{(ii) } H_2O/H^+]{\text{(i) } CH_3MgX} \underset{\text{Ethanol}}{\underset{(1°)}{CH_3CH_2OH}} + Mg(OH)X$$

$$\underset{\text{Ethanal}}{CH_3CHO} \xrightarrow[\text{(ii) } H_2O/H^+]{\text{(i) } CH_3MgX} \underset{\underset{(2°)}{\text{Propan-2-ol}}}{CH_3\underset{\underset{CH_3}{|}}{CH}OH} + Mg(OH)X$$

$$\underset{\text{Propan-2-one}}{CH_3-\underset{\underset{CH_3}{|}}{C}=O} \xrightarrow[\text{(ii) } H_2O/H^+]{\text{(i) } CH_3MgX} \underset{\underset{\textit{Tert}\text{-butyl alcohol}}{(3°)}}{CH_3-\overset{\overset{CH_3}{|}}{\underset{\underset{CH_3}{|}}{C}}-OH} + Mg(OH)X$$

Physical Properties

The properties of alcohols are chiefly due to —OH group. The nature of alkyl groups simply modify these properties. Various physical properties shown by alcohol are discussed below

(i) **Physical state** Lower alcohols are colourless liquids with characteristic smell while higher alcohols are colourless, odourless waxy solids.

(ii) **Solubility** Solubility of alcohols in water is due to their ability to form hydrogen bonds with water molecules. The solubility decreases with increase in size of alkyl (hydrophobic) groups.

$$\underset{n\text{-butyl alcohol}}{CH_3CH_2CH_2CH_2OH} > \underset{n\text{-pentyl alcohol}}{CH_3CH_2CH_2CH_2CH_2OH} > \underset{n\text{-hexyl alcohol}}{CH_3CH_2CH_2CH_2CH_2CH_2OH}$$

As the branching increases amongst isomeric alcohols, the surface area of the non-polar hydrocarbon part decreases and the solubility increases.

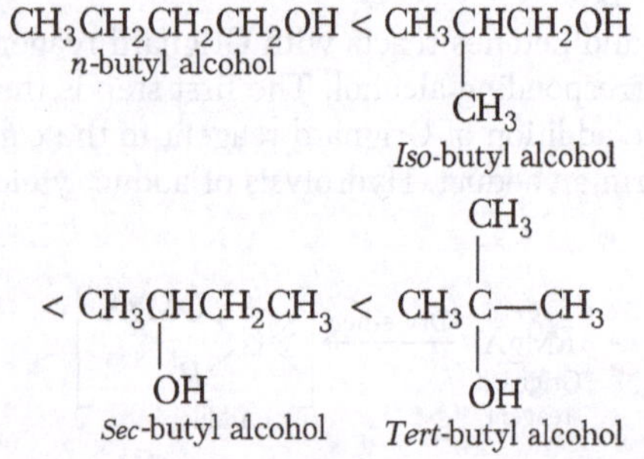

Concept ladder The solubility of alcohols in water gradually decreases as the hydrocarbon position of the molecule lengthens, long chain, alcohols are more 'alkane-like' and are therefore less like water.

(iii) **Boiling point** Boiling point of alcohols are higher than that of hydrocarbons, ethers, haloalkanes and haloarenes of comparable molecular masses. This is because of the presence of intermolecular hydrogen bonding in alcohols.

e.g. The boiling point of ethyl alcohol, dimethyl ether and propane are

Compound	Molecular weight	Boiling point
Ethyl alcohol	46	351 K
Dimethyl ether	46	248 K
Propane	44	231 K

The boiling points of alcohols increase with increase in the number of carbon atoms due to increase in van der Waals' forces.

The boiling points decrease with increase of branching in carbon chain due to decrease in van der Waals' forces with decrease in surface area.

Compound	$CH_3CH_2CH_2CH_2OH$ Butan-1-ol	$CH_3CH_2CH(OH)CH_3$ Butan-2-ol	$(CH_3)_3COH$ 3-methyl propan-2-ol
Boiling point	391 K	373 K	356 K

STEP UP Practice 1

1. The IUPAC nomenclature for the compound (*A*) is

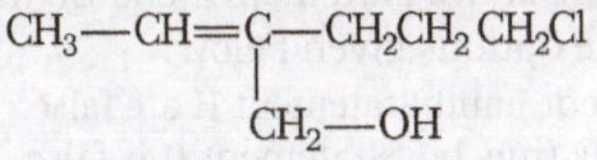

(*A*)

(a) 1-chloro-4-(hydroxy methyl) hex-4-ene
(b) 2-(chloropropyl) but-2-en-1-ol
(c) 2-(3-chloropropyl) but-2-en-1-ol
(d) (3-propyl chloro) but-2-en-1-ol

2. Which of the following is not correctly match with the given IUPAC name?
(a) $CH_3CH(OH)CH_2Br \longrightarrow$ 1-bromo propan-2-ol
(b) $CH_3CH_2CH(CH_3)CH_2OH \longrightarrow$ 3-methyl butan-1-ol
(c) $CH_3CH(OH)CH(CH_3)_2 \longrightarrow$ 3-methyl butan-2-ol
(d) $CH_2(OH)CH_2(OH) \longrightarrow$ Ethane-1, 2-diol

3. Consider the following compounds.
(i) Benzyl alcohol (ii) Vinyl alcohol
(iii) 2, 2-dimethyl propan-1-ol (iv) Prop-1-en-1-ol
(v) *Tert*-butyl alcohol
How many of them have sp^3-hybridisation of carbon atom to which —OH group is attached?
(a) 2 (b) 1 (c) 4 (d) 3

4. Total number of structural isomers shown by $C_4H_{10}O$ are
(a) 3 (b) 5 (c) 7 (d) 6

5. Consider the following compounds.
(i) Butan-1-ol (ii) Ethoxy ethane
(iii) 2-methyl propan-1-ol (iv) Butan-2-ol
(v) 3-methyl butan-2-ol
How many of them are chain isomers of each other?
(a) 4 (b) 1 (c) 3 (d) 2

6. In the following reaction,

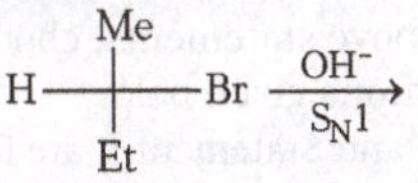

product formed will
(a) retain it's configuration (b) invert it's configuration
(c) be a racemic mixture (d) be a *meso*-compound

7. 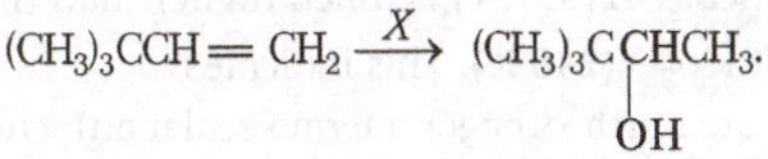

In the given reaction *X* can be
(a) $BH_3 \cdot THF / H_2O_2 \cdot OH^-$ (b) H_3O^+
(c) $Hg(OAc)_2 / NaBH_4, NaOH$ (d) MnO_2

8. Formation of alcohol by oxymercuration-demercuration of alkene
(a) involves carbocations and rearrangement
(b) involves carbanions and rearrangement
(c) is stereospecific
(d) does not involve rearrangement

9. Consider the following reaction.

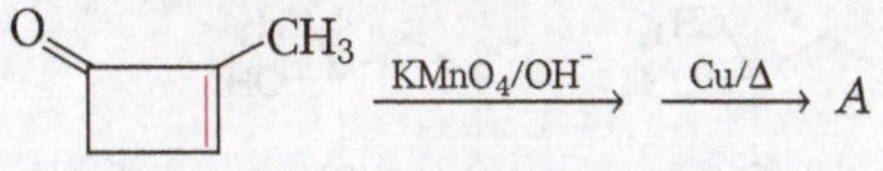

A formed is

(a) 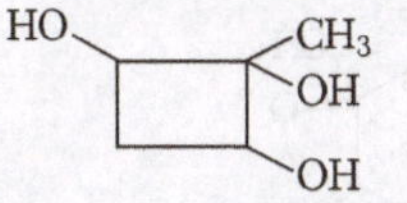 (b) 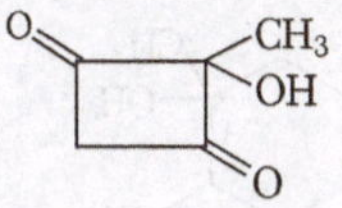

(c) 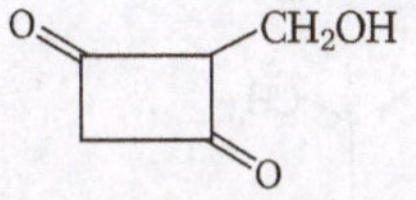 (d) 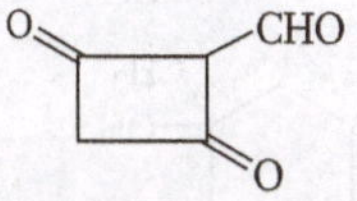

10. Select the incorrect statement about hydroboration-oxidation.
(a) Addition is against Markovnikov's rule.
(b) Intermediate is a carbocation.
(c) It does not involve rearrangement.
(d) Addition of boron and hydrogen to double bond is a *syn*-addition.

11. Which of the following reagents would carry out the following transformation? ($D = {}^2H$, the mass-2 isotope of hydrogen)

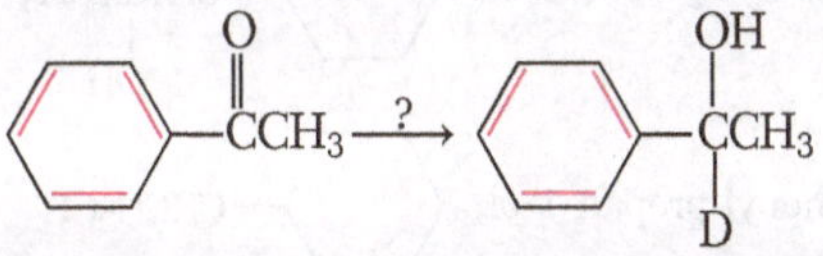

(a) $NaBD_4$ in CH_3OH (b) $NaBD_4$ in CH_3OD
(c) $LiAlH_4$ then D_2O (d) $LiAlD_4$ then D_2O

12 Which of the following reagent is the correct match with the given reaction?

(a) 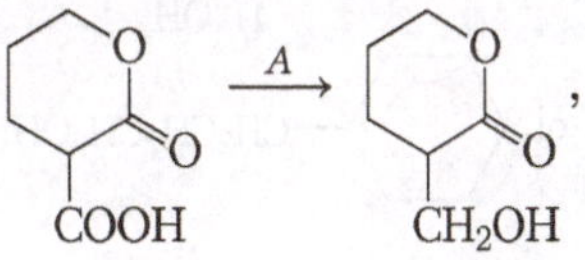 , $A = B_2H_6/H_2O$

(b) 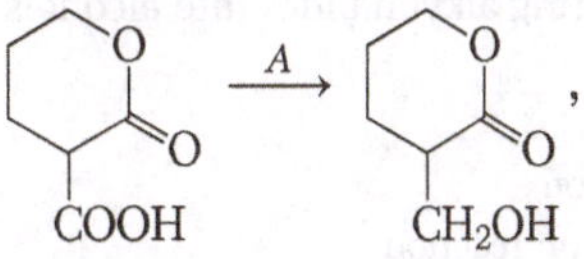 , $A = LiAlH_4$

(c) 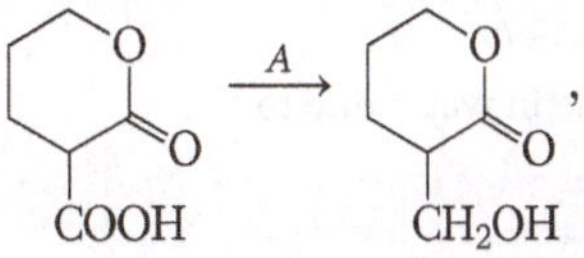 , $A = CH_3OH/Na$

(d) 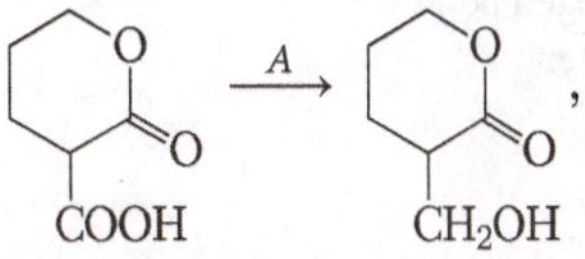 , $A = H_2/Pt$

13. 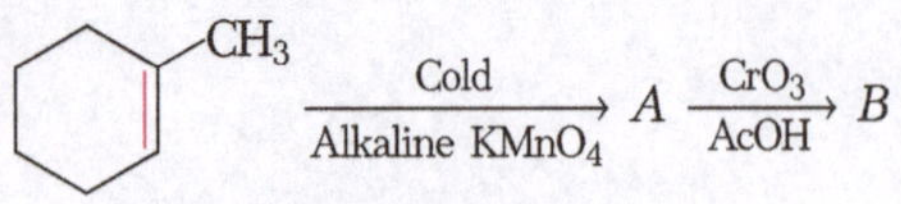

A and *B* respectively are

(a) 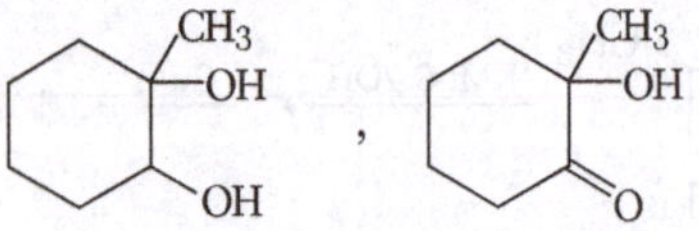

(b) 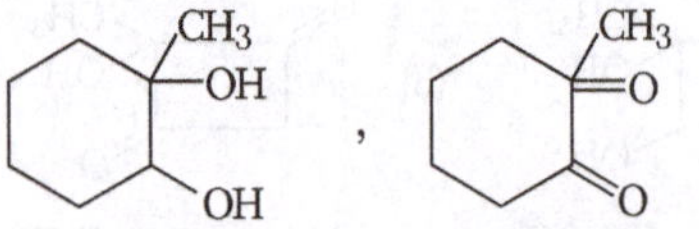

(c) 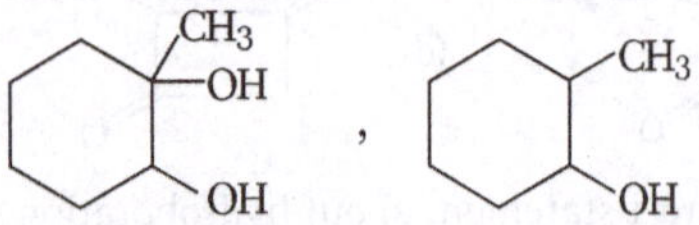

(d) no formation of *A* and *B* takes place

14. Write the IUPAC name and the product '*A*' of the following reaction.

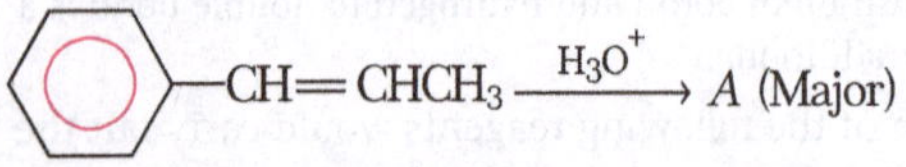

(a) 3-phenyl-propan-2-ol, 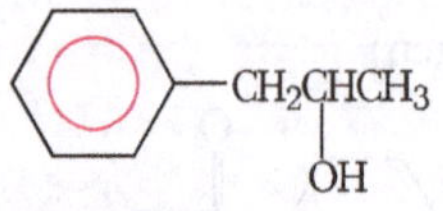

(b) 1-phenyl propan-1-ol, 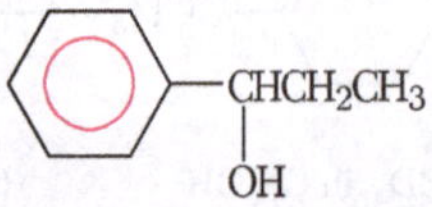

(c) 3-phenyl-propan-2-ol, 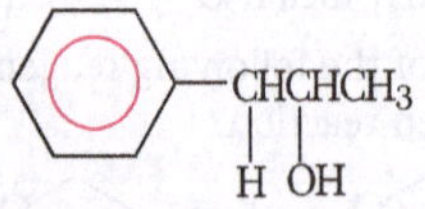

(d) 3-phenyl propan-1-ol, 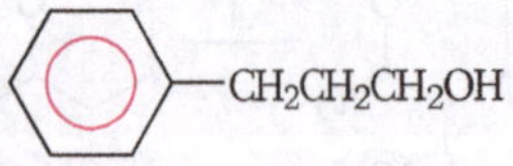

15. The process of converting alkyl halides into alcohols involves ……… .
(a) addition reaction
(b) substitution reaction
(c) dehydrohalogenation reaction
(d) rearrangement reaction

16. Ethyl alcohol is soluble in water due to
(a) acidic nature
(b) basic nature
(c) formation of hydrogen bond
(d) dissociation in water

17. Consider the following statements.

Statement I CF_3OH is more acidic than CH_3OH.

Statement II Strong electron withdrawing effect of the three fluorine atoms in CF_3 group delocalise the negative charge on oxygen.

In the light of the above statements, choose the correct answer from the options given below.
(a) Both Statement I and Statement II are false.
(b) Statement I is true, but Statement II is false.
(c) Statement I is false, but Statement II is true.
(d) Both Statement I and Statement II are true.

18. Which of the following is correctly match?
(a) Solubility of alcohol in water $\rightarrow$ hydrophobic —*R* group
(b) Solubility of alcohol in water $\rightarrow$ hydrophilic —OH group
(c) Solubility of alcohol in water $\rightarrow$ hydrophilic —*R* group
(d) Solubility of alcohol in water $\rightarrow$ hydrophobic —OH group

19. Dipole moment of $CH_3CH_2CH_3$ (I), CH_3CH_2OH (II) and CH_3CH_2F (III) is in order
(a) I < II < III (b) I > II > III (c) I > II > III (d) III < I < II

20. Arrange the following compounds in increasing order of boiling point.
Propan-1-ol, butan-1-ol, butan-2-ol, pentan-1-ol
(a) Propan-1-ol, butan-2-ol, butan-1-ol, pentan-1-ol
(b) Propan-1-ol, butan-1-ol, butan-2-ol, pentan-1-ol
(c) Propan-1-ol, butan-2-ol, pentan-1-ol, butan-1-ol
(d) Propan-1-ol, pentan-1-ol, butan-2-ol, butan-1-ol

21. Which has maximum pK_a value?

(a)  (b) 

(c) 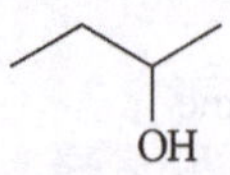 (d) 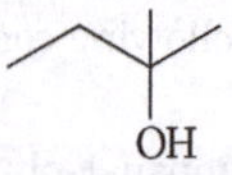

22. Consider the following statements.

Statement I Alcohols are soluble in water.

Statement II Intermolecular hydrogen bonding increases the boiling point of alcohols.

In the light of the above statements, choose the correct answer from the options given below.
(a) Both Statement I and Statement II are false.
(b) Statement I is true, but Statement II is false.
(c) Statement I is false, but Statement II is true.
(d) Both Statement I and Statement II are true.

23. Boiling point of CH_3CH_2OH (351 K) is much higher than that of isomeric ether. $(CH_3)_2O$ (248 K). This indicates
(a) hydrogen bonds are much stronger intermolecular attractions than dipole-dipole attractions
(b) dipole-dipole attractions are much stronger than hydrogen bonds
(c) $(CH_3)_2O$ has two hydrophobic groups while CH_3CH_2OH has one
(d) $(CH_3)_2O$ has two hydrophilic groups while CH_3CH_2OH has one

Module 2

Alcohols (Part-II) Chemical Reactions of Alcohols

- Reactions Involving O—H Bond Cleavage
- Distinction between 1°, 2° and 3° Alcohols
- Reactions Involving C—O Bond Cleavage
- Some Commercially Important Alcohols

Chemical Reactions

Alcohols react both as nucleophiles and electrophiles. The bond between O—H is broken where alcohols react as nucleophiles. The bond between C—O is broken when they react as electrophiles.

On the basis of cleavage of different bonds, the reactions of alcohols may be divided into following types

Reactions Involving O—H Bond Cleavage

Following reactions can be studied in O—H bond cleavage.

Acidity of Alcohols

Alcohols are acidic due to polar nature of O—H bond. An electron donating group ($—CH_3, —C_2H_5$) increases the electron density on oxygen, thus, decrease the polarity of —OH bond. Therefore, acidic nature decreases.

The order of acidic strength of alcohols are as follows

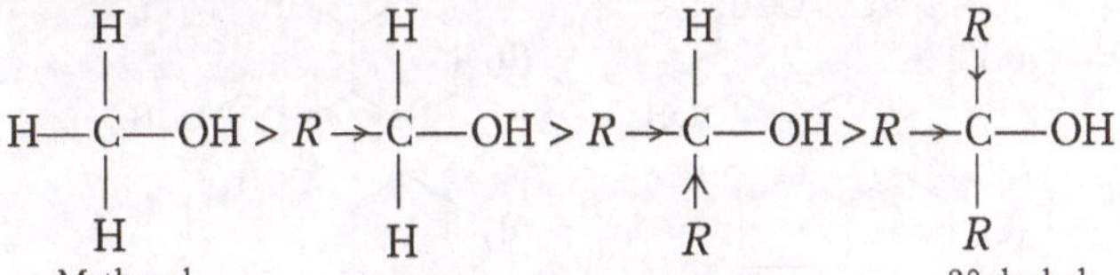

Methanol > 1° alcohol > 2° alcohol > 3° alcohol

However, alcohols are weaker acids than water

$$R—\ddot{\underset{\cdot\cdot}{O}}:^{-} + H—\ddot{\underset{\cdot\cdot}{O}}—H \longrightarrow \underset{\text{Conjugate acid}}{R—O—H} + \underset{\text{Conjugate base}}{\overset{-}{\ddot{O}}H}$$

(Base) (Acid)

Alcohols act as Bronsted bases as well. It is due to the presence of unshared electron pairs on oxygen, which makes them proton acceptors.

Reaction with Metals

Alcohols react with metals to produce alkoxide and hydrogen gas. This reaction shows the acidic nature of alcohols.

$$\underset{\text{Alcohol}}{ROH} + \underset{\text{Metal}}{M} \longrightarrow \underset{\text{Alkoxide}}{RO^{-}M^{+}} + \frac{1}{2}H_2\uparrow$$

(M = Na, K, Mg, Al etc.)

Reactivity of alcohols with metal is in the following order

$$CH_3OH > 1° > 2° > 3°$$

This reaction shows that alcohols act as Bronsted acids i.e. they can donate a proton to a stronger base ($:\bar{B}$).

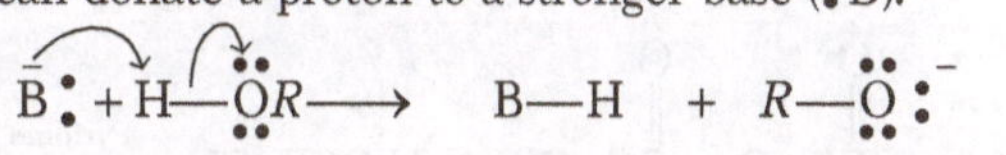

Base + Acid ⟶ Conjugate acid + Conjugate base

Concept ladder

Alkoxide (RO^{-}) is a conjugate base of alcohol. It is a stronger base than the hydroxide ion ($\bar{O}H$). Alkoxide are used as an important synthetic reagents. For example sodium and potassium alkoxide are often used as bases in organic synthesis like dehydrohalogenation.

Esterification

Alcohols react with carboxylic acids in the presence of a few drops of conc. H_2SO_4 or HCl as a catalyst to form esters.

$$\underset{\text{Acid}}{RCOOH} + \underset{\text{Alcohol}}{HOR'} \xrightleftharpoons{\text{Conc. } H_2SO_4} \underset{\text{Ester}}{RCOOR'} + H_2O$$

The equilibrium can be shifted towards ester formation by removing water as soon as it is formed. It can be done by adding benzene as a co-solvent and distilling the azeotropic mixture of benzene and water. (The benzene-water azeotrope contains 9% water and boils at 342 K).

The presence of bulky groups near the site of reaction, whether in the alcohol or in the acid, slows down esterification (and reverse hydrolysis) process.

Thus, reactivity of alcohols for given acid is in order

$$CH_3OH > 1° > 2° > 3°$$

and those of acids for given alcohol is in order

$$HCOOH > CH_3COOH > RCH_2COOH > R_2CHCOOH > R_3CCOOH$$

> **Concept ladder**
>
> It is important to note that esterification involves the cleavage of O—H bond of alcohol. This has been proved through esterification by isotopic tracer technique when an alcohol with heavy oxygen (O^{18}) undergoes esterification then the resulting ester contains this isotope of oxygen as shown below.
>
> 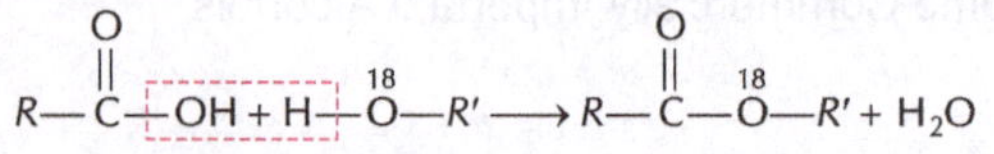
>
>
> So, technically, it is not any acid-base reaction, rather it is a nucleophilic-addition elimination.

Alcohols are treated with acid chloride in the presence of bases like pyridine or acid anhydride.

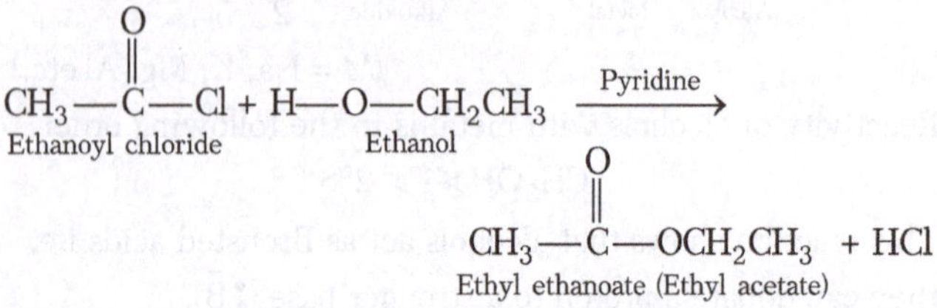

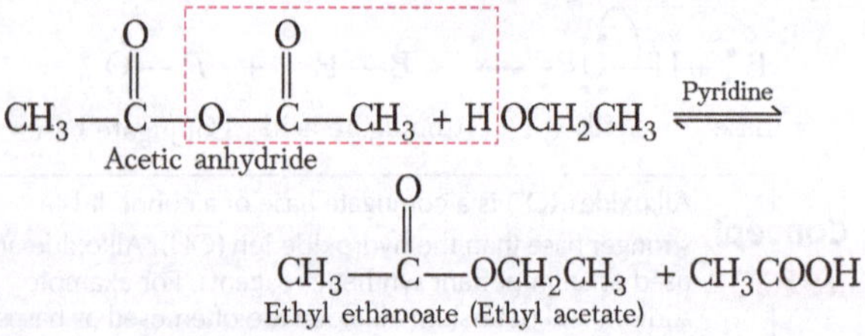

- Here, esterification reaction is called acylation reaction. If the acid halide or anhydride used are acetyl chloride and acetic anhydride, the reaction is usually called acetylation.
- The order of reactivity of alcohols in reaction involving O–H cleavage is primary > secondary > tertiary.

Reactions Involving C—O Bond Cleavage

Following reactions can be studied in C–O bond cleavage.

Reaction with Hydrogen Halides

Alcohols react readily with hydrogen halides to yield alkyl halides and water.

$$\underset{\text{Alcohol}}{R\text{—}OH} + HX \xrightarrow{ZnCl_2} \underset{\text{Alkyl halide}}{R\text{—}X} + H_2O$$

e.g.

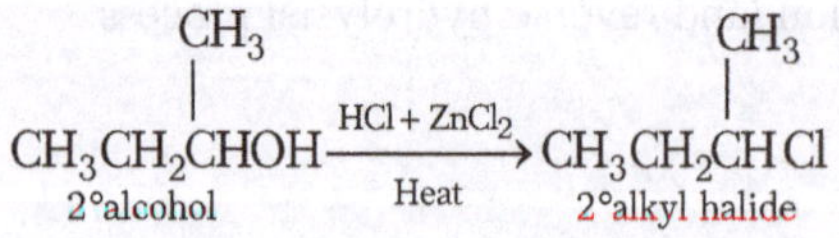

Here, mixture of conc. HCl and anhyd. $ZnCl_2$ is called **Lucas reagent.** Reactivity order for HX

$$HI > HBr > HCl$$

NEET Close-up

Example Similar to PYQ Asked in NEET 2023

Consider the following reaction and identify the product 'A'

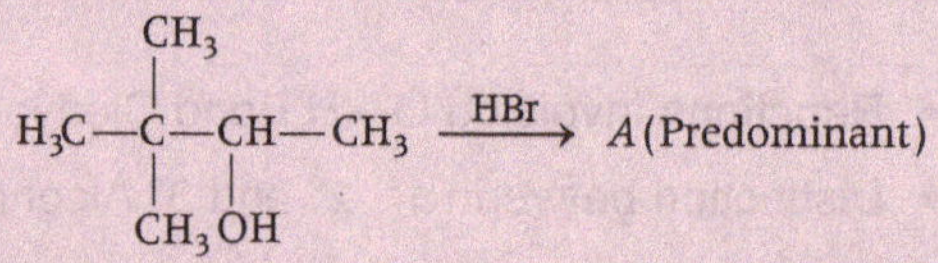

A is

(a) $(CH_3)_3C(Br)CHCH_3$ (b) $(CH_3)_2$—$CHC(Br)(CH_3)_3$
(c) $(CH_3)_2C(Br)CH(CH_3)_2$ (d) $CH_2(Br)CH_2CH(CH_3)_2$

Sol. (c) The reaction proceeds as follows

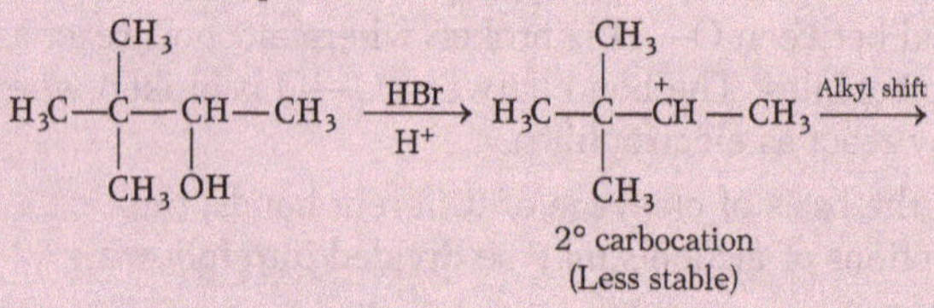

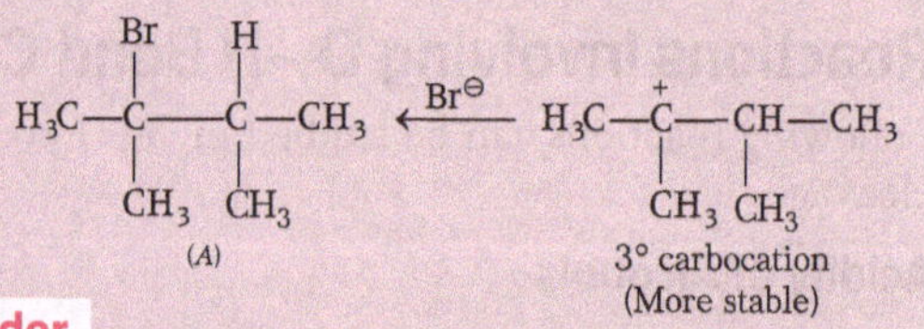

Skill Builder

Major product of the following reaction is

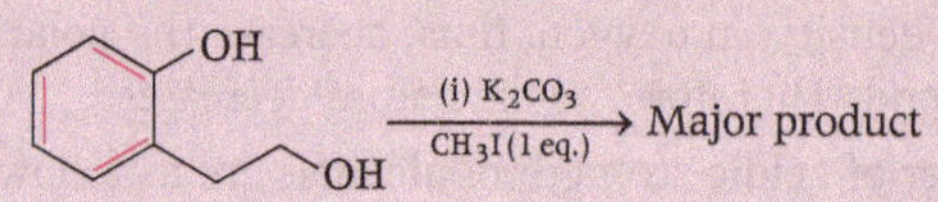

(a) 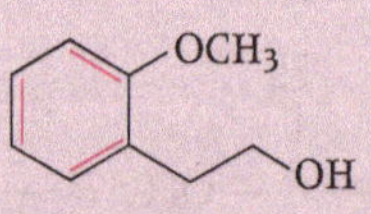

(b) 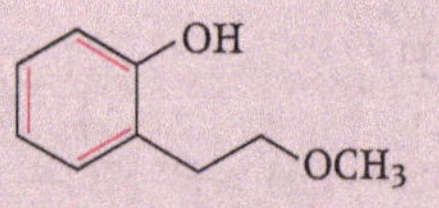

(c) 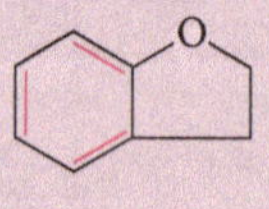

(d) 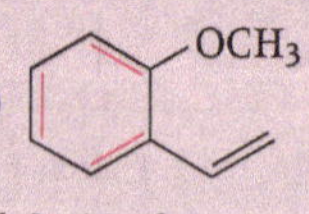

For more practice Refer to Q. 9 and Q. 11 of step up practice 2.

Reaction with Phosphorus Halides

Phosphorus halides such as PCl_5, PCl_3, PBr_3 ($P + Br_2$) or PI_3 ($P + I_2$) react with alcohols to form corresponding haloalkanes.

$$\underset{\text{Alcohol}}{R\text{—}OH} + PCl_5 \longrightarrow \underset{\text{Alkyl halide}}{R\text{—}Cl} + \underset{\text{Phosphorus oxychloride}}{POCl_3} + HCl$$

$$\underset{\text{Alcohol}}{3R\text{—}OH} + PX_3 \longrightarrow \underset{\text{Alkyl halide}}{3R\text{—}X} + \underset{\text{Phosphorus acid}}{H_3PO_3}$$

(X = Cl, Br or I)

Reaction with Thionyl Chloride

Alcohol react with thionyl chloride to give alkyl halide

$$ROH + SOCl_2 \longrightarrow R—Cl + SO_2\uparrow + HCl\uparrow$$

Mentor's TiP

Reaction of alcohol (with aryl group) with $SOCl_2$ takes place *via* S_N1 mechanism but if the reaction takes place in the presence of pyridine then S_N2 mechanism is followed.

Dehydration

Alcohols undergo dehydration to form alkenes on treating with a protic acid, e.g. concentrated H_2SO_4 or H_3PO_4 or catalysts such as anhydrous zinc chloride or alumina.

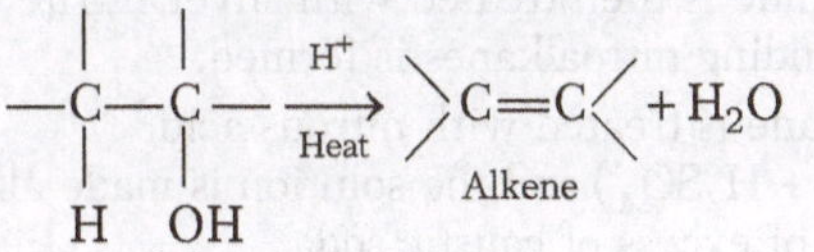

Relative ease of dehydration of alcohols follows the following order

Tertiary > Secondary > Primary

Mechanism

The mechanism follows the following three steps

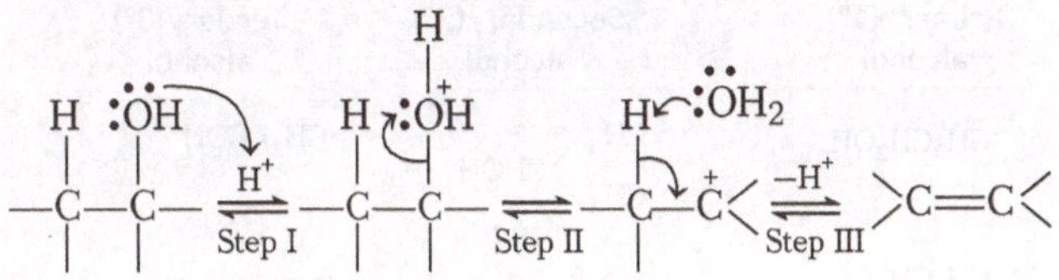

***Step* I** Formation of protonated alcohol.

***Step* II** Formation of carbocation. It is slowest step and hence, the rate determining step of the reaction.

***Step* III** Formation of ethene by elimination of a proton. In practice, alkene boils at lower temperature than the alcohol.

Mentor's TiP

The acid used in step I is released in step III. To drive the equilibrium to the right, ethene is removed as it is formed.

The dehydration of 2° and 3° alcohols always occurs in accordance with **Saytzeff's rule.** According to this rule, the more highly substituted alkene is always the major product. e.g.

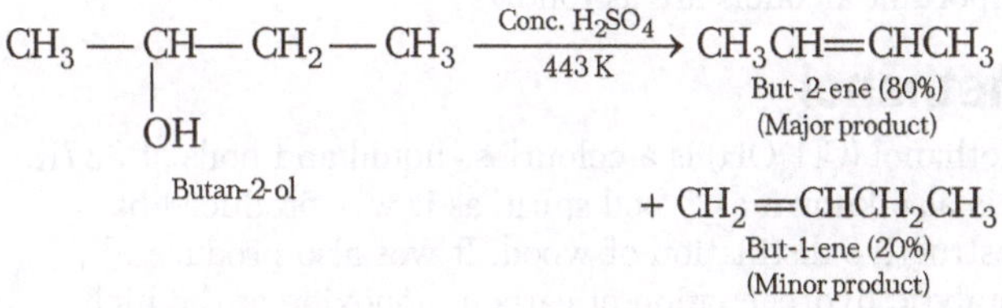

During the reaction carbocation is form as the intermediate so, if possible then rearrangement should take place.

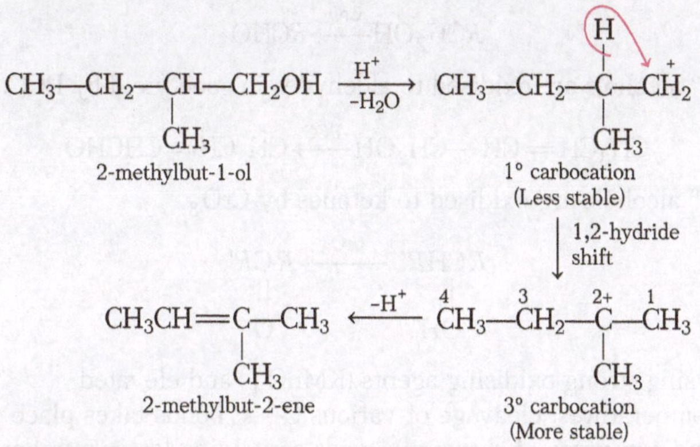

Oxidation

Oxidation of alcohols involves the formation of a carbon-oxygen double bond with cleavage of an O—H and C—H bonds.

Such a cleavage and formation of bonds occur in oxidation reactions. These are also known as dehydrogenation reaction.

The oxidation of alcohols can be carried out by a number of reagents such as aqueous, alkaline or acidified $KMnO_4$, acidified $K_2Cr_2O_7$, nitric acid, chromic acid etc. These reagent are strong oxidising agents. 1° alcohol undergoes oxidation reaction to form first an aldehyde and then carboxylic acid, 2° alcohol form ketone in the presence of strong oxidising agents.

$$\underset{\text{1° alcohol}}{RCH_2OH} \xrightarrow{[O]} \underset{\text{Aldehyde}}{RCHO} \xrightarrow{[O]} \underset{\text{Carboxylic acid}}{RCOOH}$$

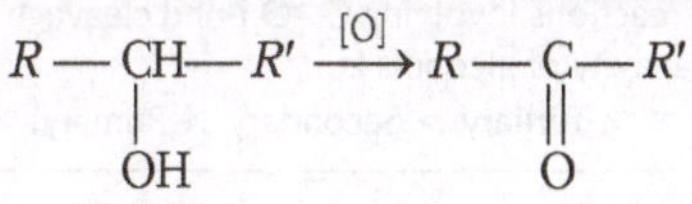

Tertiary alcohols can be oxidised under vigorous conditions only. Using conc. HNO_3, they get dehydrated to alkenes.

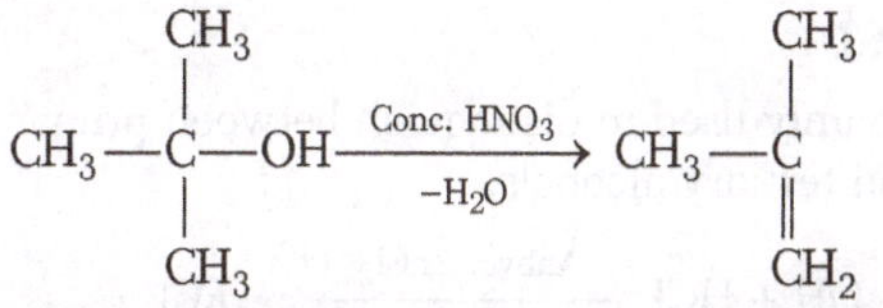

Alcohols undergoes oxidation reaction in the presence of weak oxidising agents like pyridinium chlorochromate (PCC), Collin's reagent (CrO_3 + pyridine + CH_2Cl_2) and Cu/300°C to form carbonyl compounds.

CrO_3 in anhydrous medium is used as the oxidising agent for the isolation of aldehydes from 1° alcohol.

$$RCH_2OH \xrightarrow{CrO_3} RCHO$$

1° alcohols are oxidised to aldehydes in good yield by PCC.

$$CH_3CH{=}CH{-}CH_2OH \xrightarrow{PCC} CH_3CH{=}CHCHO$$

2° alcohols are oxidised to ketones by CrO_3.

$$RCH(OH)R' \xrightarrow{CrO_3} RC(=O)R'$$

Using strong oxidising agents ($KMnO_4$) and elevated temperatures, cleavage of various C—C bonds takes place and a mixture of carboxylic acids containing lesser number of carbon atoms is formed.

3° alcohols do not oxidise by weak oxidising agents but in the presence of Cu/300°C it undergo dehydration.

$$R{-}CH_2OH \xrightarrow[300°C]{Cu} R{-}CHO$$

$$R{-}CH(OH){-}R' \xrightarrow[300°C]{Cu} R{-}C(=O){-}R'$$

$$R{-}C(R)(CH_3){-}OH \xrightarrow[300°C]{Cu} R{-}C(R){=}CH_2$$

Concept ladder

- PCC is a complex of chromium trioxide with pyridine and HCl.
- MnO_2 oxidises the —OH group of allylic and benzylic 1° or 2° alcohols to aldehydes and ketones respectively. In reactions involving C—O bond cleavage the order of reactivity of alcohols is

  Tertiary > Secondary > Primary.

Distinction Between 1°, 2° and 3° Alcohols

Distinction among 1°, 2° and 3° alcohols can be made by following methods

Lucas Test

This test is mainly used to distinguish between primary, secondary and tertiary alcohols.

$$\underset{(1°,\ 2°,\ 3°)}{R{-}OH} + HCl \xrightarrow[+\ HCl]{Anhyd.\ ZnCl_2} \underset{(Turbidity)}{RCl}$$

3° alcohols – Immediate turbidity

2° alcohol – 5 mins

1° alcohol – No turbidity at room temperature

On heating – 30 mins

NEET Snapshot

$CH_3{-}C(CH_3)_2OH$ reacts immediately with Lucas ragent. *[NEET 2024]*

Lucas reagent is used to distinguish between primary, secondary and tertiary alcohol an the basis of rate at which they turn the solution turbid when alcohols react with it.

The tertiary alcohols react immediately due to formation of the stable tertiary carbocation.

Victor Meyer's Test

In this test, the following steps are involved.

- Alcohol is reacted with conc. HI or red phosphorus and iodine to form corresponding alkyl iodide.
- Alkyl iodide is then treated with silver nitrite when corresponding nitroalkanes is formed.
- Nitroalkane is treated with nitrous acid ($NaNO_2 + H_2SO_4$) and the solution is made alkaline by addition of excess of caustic soda.

Observation

If blood red colouration appears, it indicates a primary alcohol. If blue colouration appears, it indicates a secondary alcohol and if the solution remains colourless, it indicates a tertiary alcohol.

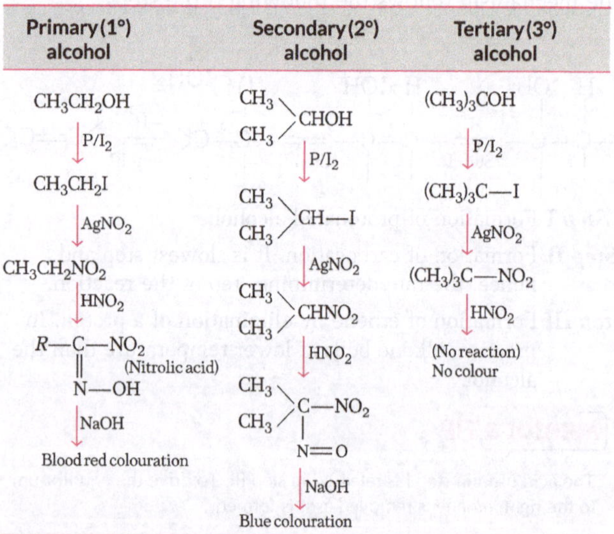

Some Commercially Important Alcohols

Important properties and uses of some commercially important alcohols are as follows

Methanol

Methanol (CH_3OH) is a colourless liquid and boils at 337K. It is also known as 'wood spirit' as it was produced by destructive distillation of wood. It was also produced by catalytic hydrogenation of carbon monoxide at the high temperature and pressures and in the presence of $ZnO\text{-}Cr_2O_3$ catalyst.

$$CO + 2H_2 \xrightarrow[\substack{200\text{-}300\text{ atm} \\ 573\text{-}676\text{ K}}]{ZnO\text{-}Cr_2O_3} CH_3OH$$

It is highly poisonous in nature. Ingestion of even small quantities of methanol is hazardous and large quantities can cause even death. It is used as a solvent in paints, varnishes and for manufacturing formaldehyde, dyes, medicines and perfumes.

Ethanol

Ethanol (C_2H_5OH) is a colourless liquid with boiling point 351K. It is used in alcoholic beverages, produced by fermentation of sugars by yeast. The sugar in molasses, sugarcane or fruits is converted to glucose and fructose in the presence of an enzyme, invertase. Glucose and fructose undergo fermentation in the presence of enzyme, zymase, which is found in yeast.

$$C_{12}H_{22}O_{11} + H_2O \xrightarrow{\text{Invertase}} \underset{\text{Glucose}}{C_6H_{12}O_6} + \underset{\text{Fructose}}{C_6H_{12}O_6}$$

$$C_6H_{12}O_6 \xrightarrow{\text{Zymase}} 2C_2H_5OH + 2CO_2$$

It is used as a solvent in paint industry.

It is also a good industrial solvent, hence it is made unfit for drinkable purposes, by addition of a denaturant like CH_3OH (which is poisonous) some copper sulphate (to give it a colour) and pyridine (a foul smelling liquid).

It gives carbon dioxide and water on burning. Thus, it is used as a fuel. It is safe and can be used to dissolve many organic compounds, which are insoluble in water.

Ethanol is used for medical purposes as a Central Nervous System (CNS) depressant.

STEP UP Practice 2

1. What is the correct order of reactivity of alcohols in the following reaction?

$$R—OH + HCl \xrightarrow{ZnCl_2} R—Cl + H_2O$$

(a) 1°> 2°> 3° (b) 1°< 2°> 3°
(c) 3°> 2°> 1° (d) 3°> 1°> 2°

2. When sodium is added to ethanol
(a) no action occurs
(b) H_2O is formed
(c) $Na^+O^-C_2H_5$ and O_2 are formed
(d) $Na^+O^-C_2H_5$ and H_2 are formed

3. 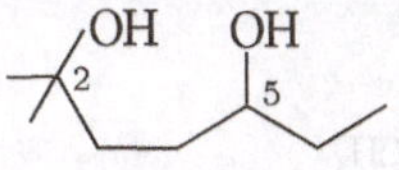

In this diol
(a) —OH at C_2 is more nucleophilic than that of at C_5
(b) —OH at C_2 is more acidic than at C_5
(c) both behave as a base
(d) both behave as an acid

4. Which of the following is hydrated to a maximum extent?
(a) $CH_3—C(CH_3)_2—CH=CH_2$ (b) $CH_3—CH=CH_2$
(c) $CH_2=CH_2$ (d) $CH\equiv CH$

5. Which one of the following reactions is not correctly match with the given product, when heated with copper at 300°C?
(a) Secondary alcohol ⟶ Ketone
(b) Tertiary alcohol ⟶ Olefin
(c) Phenol ⟶ Benzyl alcohol
(d) Primary alcohol ⟶ Aldehyde

6. Which of the following compounds give most stable carbocation (intermediate) on dehydration?
(a) $CH_3C(CH_3)_2—OH$ (b) $CH_3CH(CH_3)CH_2CH_2OH$
(c) $CH_3CH(OH)CH_2CH_3$ (d) $CH_3CH_2CH_2CH_2OH$

7. Consider the following reagents.
(i) $SOCl_2$ (ii) TsCl (iii) PCl_5
(iv) Br_2 (v) $(CH_3)_3CO^-$
How many of them can convert R—OH, into R—Cl with inversion of the configuration on chiral carbon?
(a) 3 (b) 4 (c) 2 (d) 1

8. In the following reaction most stable intermediate formed is

$$CH_3CH(CH_3)CH=CH_2 + H_2O \xrightarrow{H^+}$$

(a) $CH_3CH(CH_3)CH_2\overset{\oplus}{C}H_2$ (b) $CH_3CH(CH_3)\underset{\oplus}{C}HCH_3$
(c) $CH_3\underset{\oplus}{C}(CH_3)CH_2CH_3$ (d) $CH_3CH(CH_3)CH_2\overset{\oplus}{C}H_2$

9. $CH_3C(CH_3)_2—CH(OH)CH_3 \xrightarrow{\text{Conc. } H_2SO_4} A$ (predominant).

'A' is

(a) $(CH_3)_3CCH=CH_2$ (b) $(CH_3)_2C=C(CH_3)_2$

(c) $CH_2=C(CH_3)CH_2CH_2CH_3$ (d) $(CH_2)_3CH_2(CH)=CH_2$

10. For the following reaction, select the statement that best describes the situation

$$RCH_2OH + PCC\ [C_5H_5NH^+ ClCrO_3^-] \longrightarrow$$

(a) the alcohol is oxidised to an acid and the Cr(VI) is reduced

(b) the alcohol is oxidised to an aldehyde and the Cr(VI) is reduced

(c) the alcohol is reduced to an aldehyde and the Cr(III) is oxidised

(d) the alcohol is oxidised to a ketone and the Cr(VI) is reduced

11. $C_2H_5OH \xrightarrow[443\text{ K}]{\text{Conc. } H_2SO_4} Z$

In the above reaction Z is identified as

(a) $C_2H_5—O—C_2H_5$ (b) C_2H_5CHO

(c) $CH_2=CH_2$ (d) $C_2H_5OSO_4$

12. Which of the following product is correctly match with the given reaction?

(a) 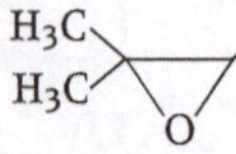 $\xrightarrow{LiAlH_4}$ $CH_3CH(CH_3)CH_2CH_2OH$

(b) 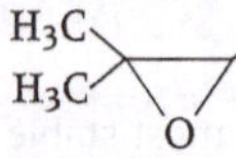 $\xrightarrow{LiAlH_4}$ $CH_3CH_2CH_2CH_2CH_2OH$

(c) 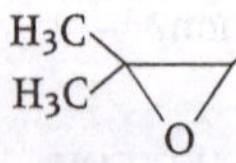 $\xrightarrow{LiAlH_4}$ $CH_3—C(CH_3)(OH)—CH_2CH_3$

(d) 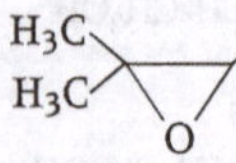 $\xrightarrow{LiAlH_4}$ No reaction

13. Alcohols given below follow which of the following mechanism with conc. HCl/anhydrous $ZnCl_2$

CH_3OH (I), CH_3CH_2OH (II), $CH_3CH(OH)CH_3$ (III)

(a) S_N1, S_N2, S_N2 (b) S_N2, S_N2, S_N1

(c) S_N2, S_N1, S_N1 (d) S_N1, S_N1, S_N2

14. CH_3CH_2OH can be converted into CH_3CHO by … .

(a) catalytic hydrogenation

(b) treatment with $LiAlH_4$

(c) treatment with pyridinium chlorochromate

(d) treatment with $KMnO_4$

15. Consider the following statements.

Statement I Addition reaction of water to but-1-ene in acidic medium yields butan-2-ol as major product.

Statement II The addition of alkene with water in acidic medium proceeds through the formation of transition state.

In the light of the above statements, choose the correct answer from the options given below.

(a) Both Statement I and Statement II are false.

(b) Statement I is true but Statement II is false.

(c) Statement I is false but Statement II is true.

(d) Both Statement I and Statement II are true.

16. Consider oxidation of following alcohols.

I. $CH_2=CHCH_2OH \xrightarrow{A} CH_2=CHCHO$

II. $(CH_3)_3COH \xrightarrow{B} CH_3C(CH_3)=CH_2$

III. $CH_3CH_2OH \xrightarrow{C} CH_3CO_2H$

IV. $CH_3CH=CHCH_3 \xrightarrow{D} CH_3CO_2H$

A, B, C and D are oxidising agents which are respectively.

	A	B	C	D
(a)	MnO_2	Cu/Δ	H_2CrO_4	$KMnO_4$/Δ
(b)	Cu/Δ	MnO_2	H_2CrO_4	$KMnO_4$/Δ
(c)	MnO_2	Cu/Δ	$KMnO_4$/Δ	H_2CrO_4
(d)	MnO_2	H_2CrO_4	Cu/Δ	$KMnO_4$

17. Consider the following reactions,

I. $CH_3CH_2CH(OH)CH_3 \xrightarrow{H^+} A$ (Major)

II. $CH_3C(CH_3)_2—CH(OH)CH_3 \xrightarrow{H^+} B$ (Major)

Products A and B (both alkenes) are respectively

(a) $CH_3CH=CHCH_3$, $CH_3C(CH_3)_2CH=CH_2$

(b) $CH_3CH_2CH=CH_2$, $CH_3C(CH_3)_2CH=CH_2$

(c) $CH_3CH=CHCH_3$, $CH_3C(CH_3)=C(CH_3)CH_3$

(d) $CH_3CH_2CH=CH_2$, $CH_3C(CH_3)=C(CH_3)CH_3$

18. Dehydration of alcohols takes place more rapidly with $POCl_3$ than with H_2SO_4. Select incorrect statement(s) about the following dehydration reaction.

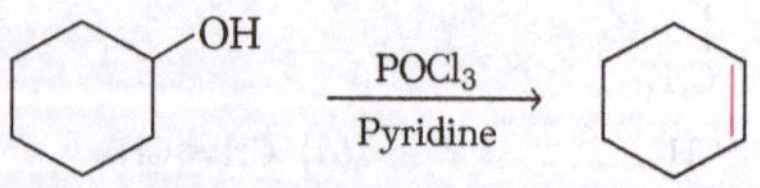

(a) It does not involve carbocation formation.

(b) It involves the formation of $R—OPOCl_2$ with $—OPOCl_2$ as a better leaving group.

(c) It involves E2 mechanism as pyridine base abstracts proton from the adjacent carbon at the same time at which —$OPOCl_2$ is leaving.

(d) It is E1 reaction without formation of carbocation.

19. Consider the following compounds.

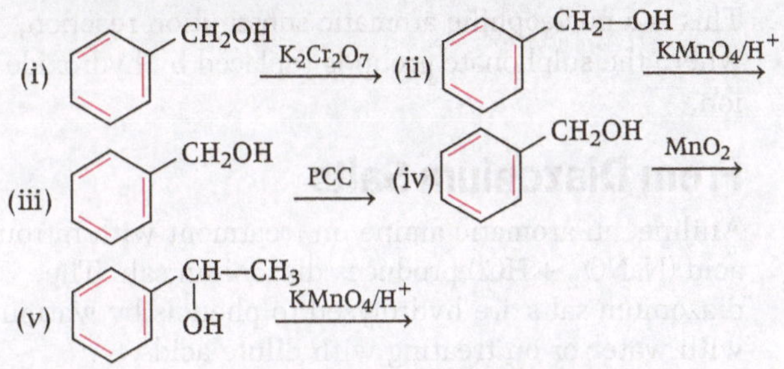

How many of them are formed benzoic acid?

(a) 1 (b) 2

(c) 3 (d) 4

20 Consider the following statements.

Statement I The reaction of alcohol with acid chloride is carried out in the presence of an acid.

Statement II Addition reaction of water to but-1-ene in acidic medium yields butan-2-ol as major product.

In the light of the above statements, choose the correct answer from the options given below.

(a) Both Statement I and Statement II are false.

(b) Statement I is true but Statement II is false.

(c) Statement I is false but Statement II is true.

(d) Both Statement I and Statement II are true.

Module 3

Phenols

- Classification
- Structure
- Nomenclature
- Isomerism
- Methods of Preparation
- Physical Properties
- Chemical Properties

Classification

On the basis of number of —OH groups present these are classified as mono-, di-, tri- or polyhydric compounds depending on whether they contains one, two, three or more hydroxyl group respectively. Their structures are as follows

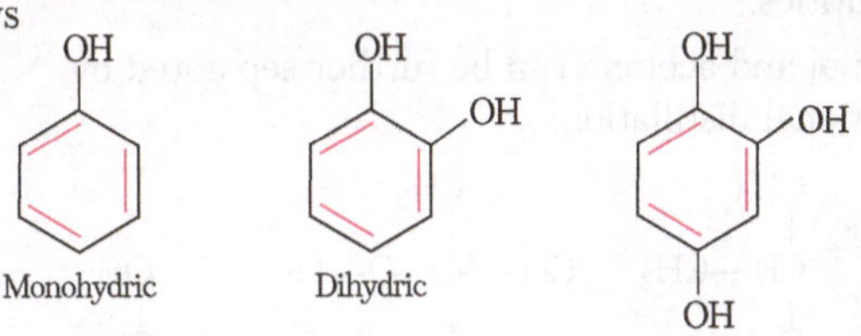

Monohydric Dihydric Trihydric

Structure

In phenols, the oxygen of —OH group is attached to sp^2-hybridised carbon of benzene ring.

The carbon oxygen bond length is slightly less than that of aliphatic alcohol due to presence of partial double bond character between carbon and oxygen and sp^2-hybridised state of carbon to which oxygen is attached.

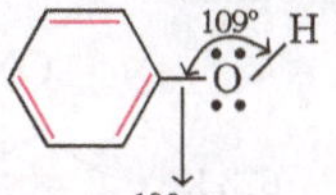

Phenol

Nomenclature

Phenol is an accepted IUPAC as well as common name. In these substituted phenols the positions of the substituents are indicated by the prefix 1,2 (*ortho*), 1,3 (*meta*) and 1,4 (*para*). e.g.

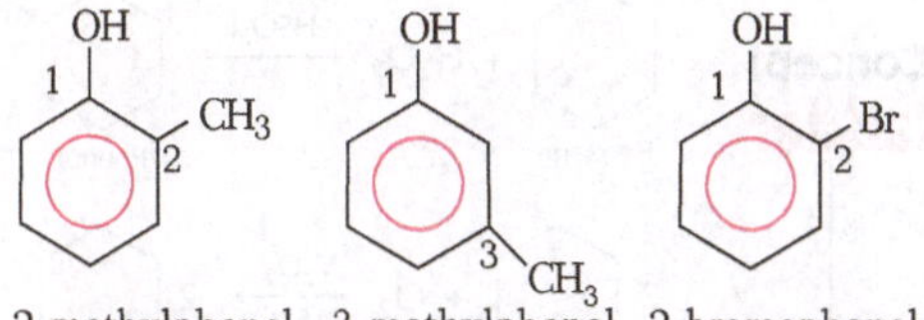

IUPAC name	2-methylphenol	3-methylphenol	2-bromophenol
Common name	*o*-cresol	*m*-cresol	*o*-bromophenol

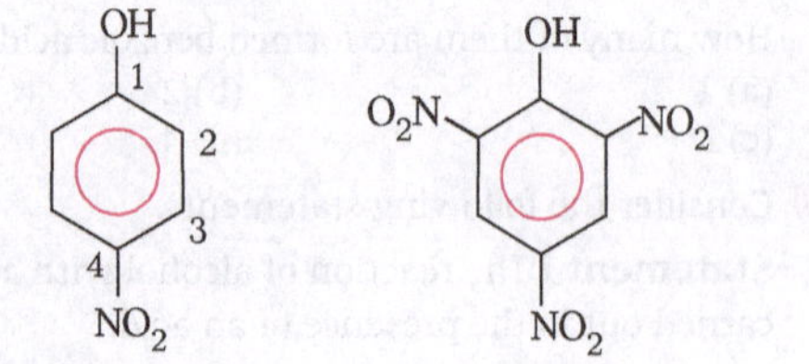

IUPAC name	4-nitrophenol	Picric acid
Common name	*p*-nitrophenol	2, 4, 6-trinitrophenol

Isomerism

Substituted derivatives of phenols show positional isomerism. In this type of isomerism, the difference lies in the position of substituent group or atom in the same chain. e.g.

Positional Isomers of Cresols

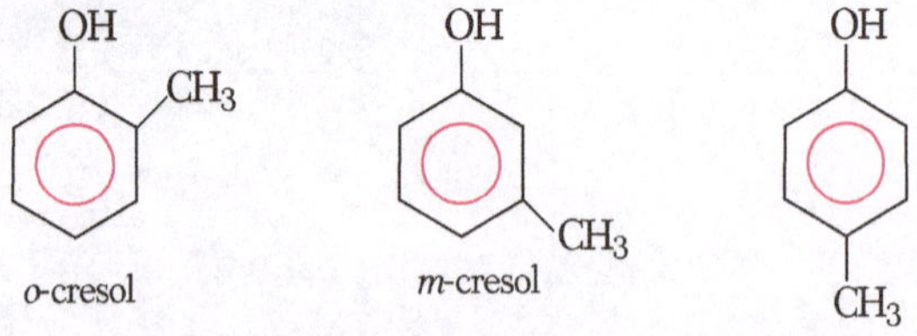

o-cresol, *m*-cresol, *p*-cresol

Preparation of Phenols

Phenol (carbolic acid) was 1st isolated from coal tar. Now-a-days, phenol is commercially produced synthetically. In laboratory, phenols can be prepared from benzene derivatives by any of the following methods.

From Haloarenes

Chlorobenzene is fused with NaOH at 623 K and 320 atmospheric pressure. Phenol is obtained by acidification of sodium phenoxide so produced.

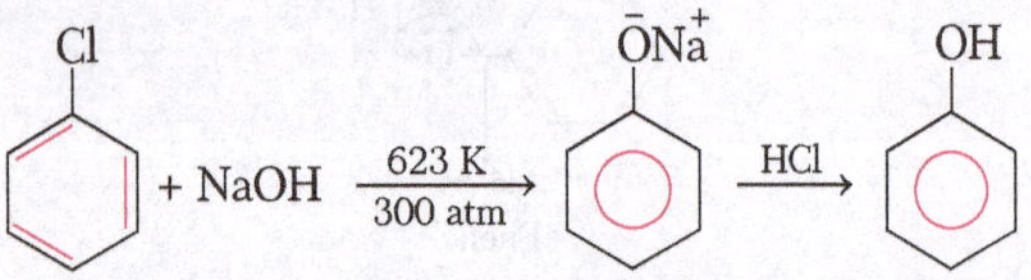

Sodium phenoxide

Concept ladder

Phenol can also be prepared by direct hydroxylation of benzene. Or by oxidation of benzene with V_2O_5 at 315°C. The reaction involved in both the processes are respectively as follows

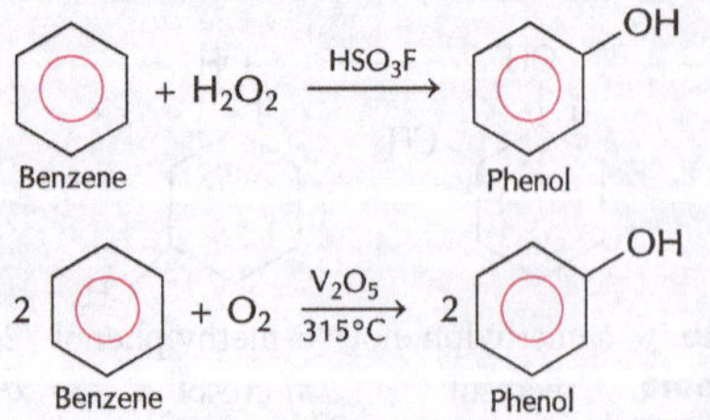

From Benzene Sulphonic Acid

Sodium salt of benzene sulphonic acid is fused with NaOH to form sodium phenoxide. This on treatment with dilute acid yields phenol.

This is a nucleophilic aromatic substitution reaction, where the sulphonate group is replaced by hydroxide ion.

From Diazonium Salts

Aniline, an aromatic amine on treatment with nitrous acid ($NaNO_2 + HCl$) produces diazonium salt. The diazonium salts are hydrolysed to phenols by warming with water or on treating with dilute acids.

***Step* I** Formation of diazonium salt

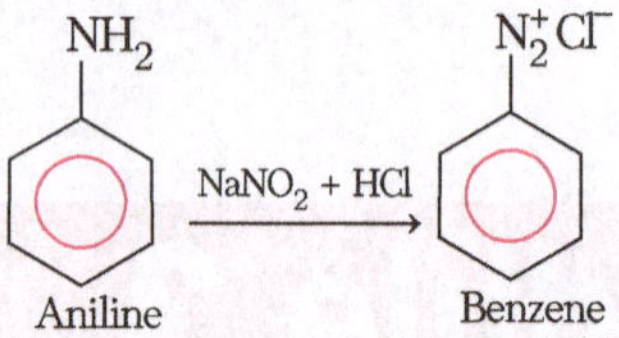

Aniline — Benzene diazonium chloride

***Step* II** Hydrolysis of benzene diazonium chloride

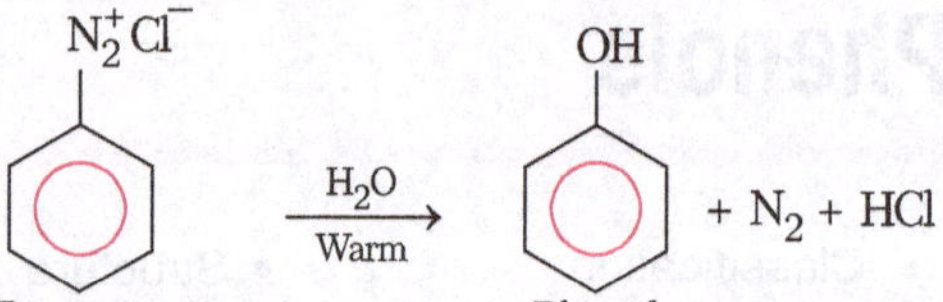

Benzene diazonium chloride — Phenol

From Cumene

The oxidation of cumene (*iso*-propyl benzene) results in the formation of cumene hydroperoxide, which on hydrolysis in acidic medium produces phenol and acetone.The reaction is carried out at 150°C in presence of catalyst.

The reaction produces acetone as a byproduct in large quantities.

Phenol and acetone can be further separated by fractional distillation.

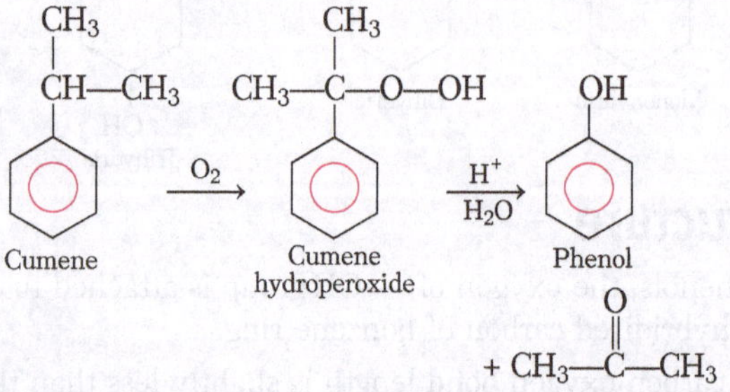

NEET Close-up

Example Similar to PYQ Asked in NEET 2019

The structure of intermediate *A* in the following reaction is

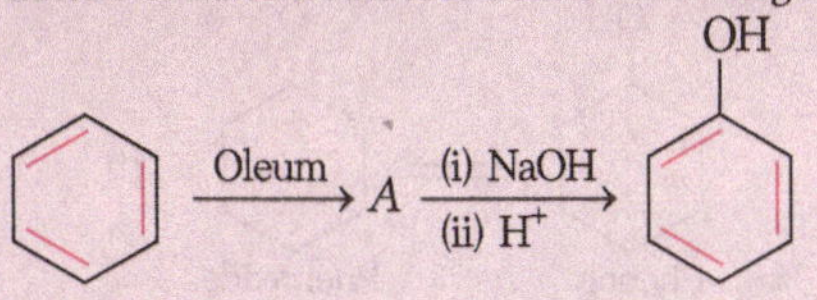

(a) 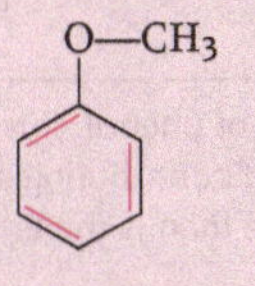

(b) 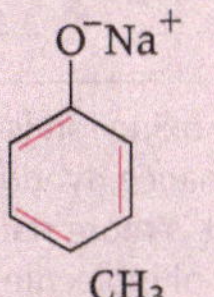

(c) 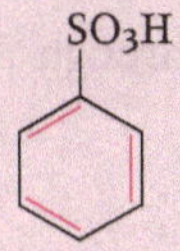

(d) 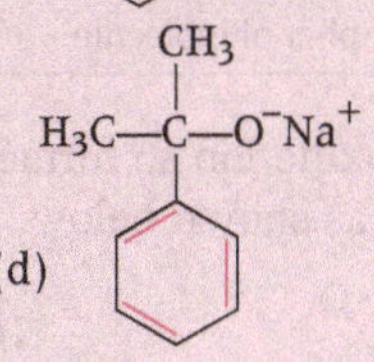

Sol. (*c*) The given reaction proceeds as follows

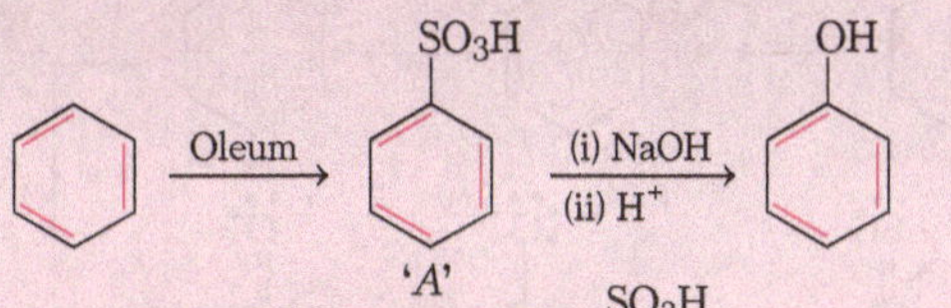

Thus, the intermediate '*A*' is 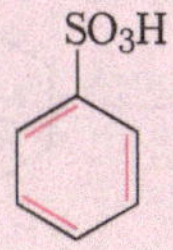

Skill Builder

Choose the correct structure of intermediate '*X*' in the following reaction is

$$\text{Chlorobenzene} + \text{NaOH} \xrightarrow[300\ \text{atm}]{623\ \text{K}} \text{'}X\text{'} \xrightarrow{\text{HCl}} \text{Phenol}$$

(a) 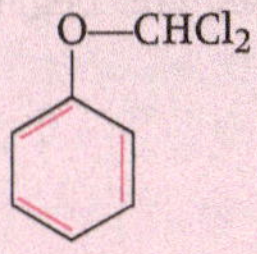

(b) 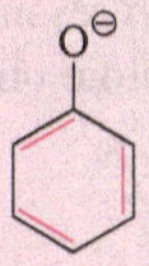

(c) 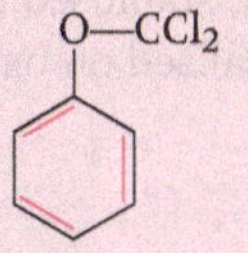

(d) 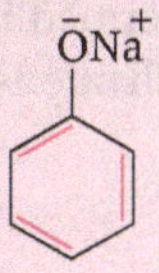

For more practice Refer to Q. 7 of step up Practice-3.

Physical Properties

Like alcohols, properties of phenols is due to —OH group while nature of aryl groups simply modify these properties.

Various physical properties shown by phenol are as follows

(i) **Physical state** It is a colourless, crystalline, deliquescent solid. It attains pink colour on exposure to air and light. It has a characteristic carbolic odour and a strong corrosive action on skin.

(ii) It is sparingly soluble in water but readily soluble in organic solvents such as alcohol, benzene and ether.

Solubility The solubility decreases with increase in size of aryl groups.

(iii) **Boiling points** They are capable of forming intermolecular H-bonding. Thus, they have high boiling point.

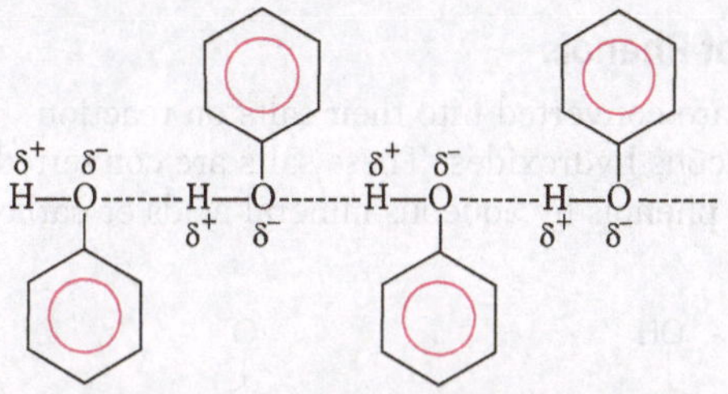

(intermolecular H-bonding among phenol molecules)

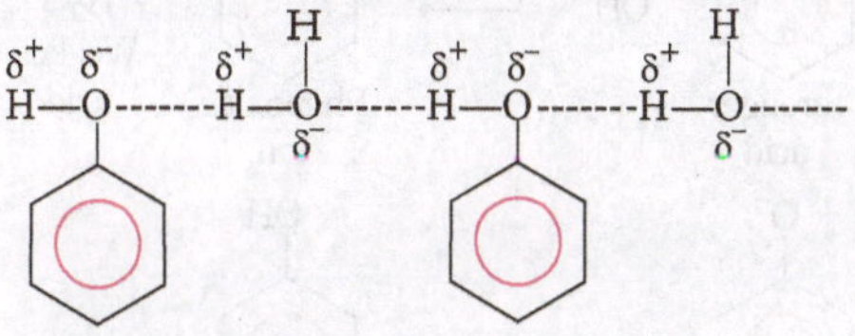

(crossed intermolecular H-bonding between water and phenol molecules).

Due to intramolecular hydrogen bonding, derivatives of phenol, i.e. *o*-nitrophenol has lower solubility in water and lower boiling point. Due to this, association with different molecules decreases hence, they are comparatively volatile in nature.

On the other hand, *m* and *p*- isomer have intermolecular hydrogen bonding. Thus, they have an appreciable value of boiling point and are soluble in water.

This may be represented as follows

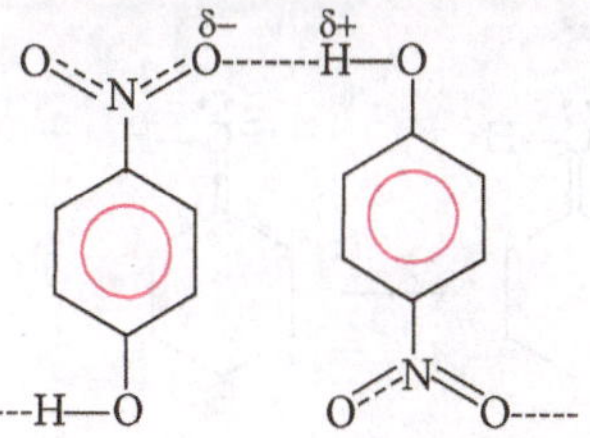

Intermolecular hydrogen bonding in *p*-nitrophenol molecules

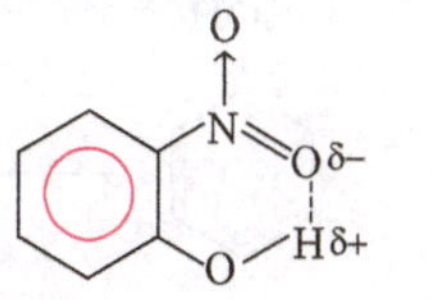

Intramolecular hydrogen bonding in *o*-nitrophenol (chelation)

Comparison of Properties of Nitrophenols

Isomer	Boiling point at 760 mm	Solubility g/100g H_2O	Reaction with steam
o-nitrophenol	373 K	0.2	volatile in steam
p-nitrophenol	552 K	1.69	non-volatile in steam
m-nitrophenol	467 K	1.35	non-volatile in steam

Chemical Properties

Various chemical properties of phenols are as follows

Reaction Involving Cleavage of O—H Bond

Following reactions can be studied in O—H bond cleavage.

Acidity of Phenols

Phenols are converted into their salts on reaction with aqueous hydroxides. These salts are converted into free phenols by aqueous mineral acids or carboxylic acids.

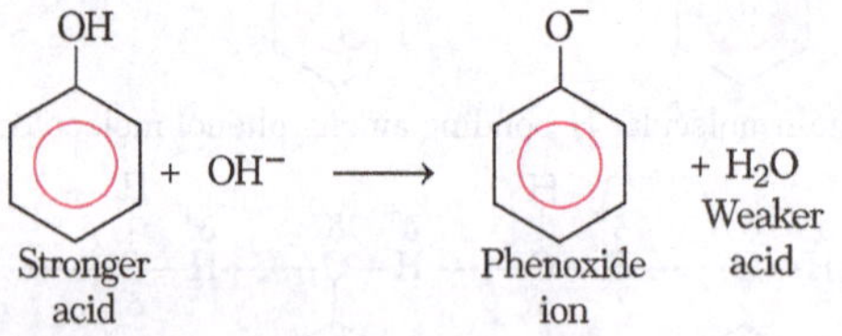

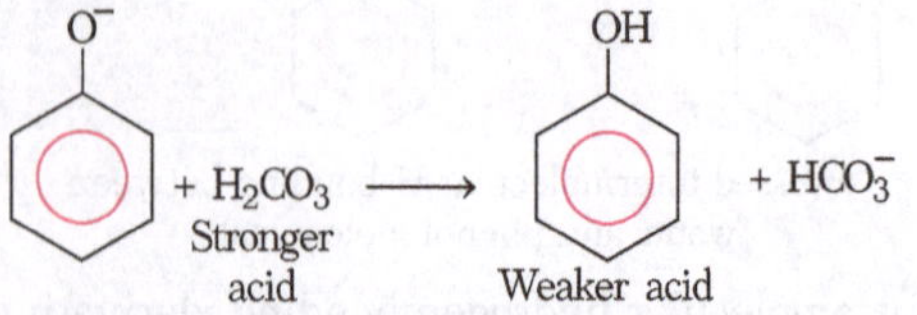

Phenols react with active metal to give hydrogen and also turn blue litmus red.

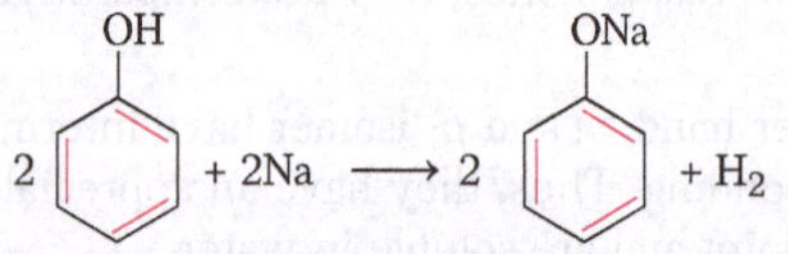

The acidic nature of phenols can be explained by the following resonating structures.

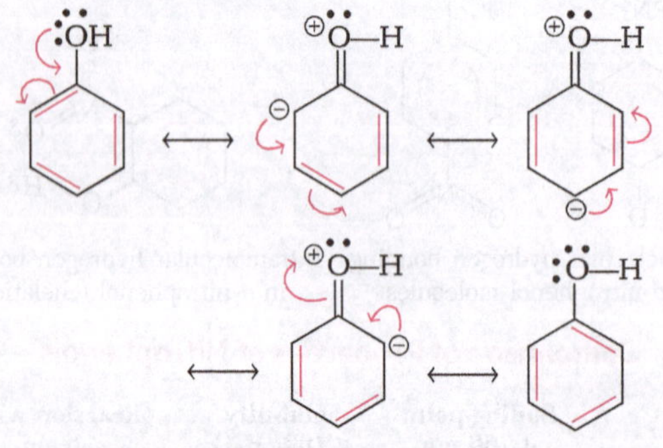

The hydroxyl group in phenol is directly attached to the sp^2-hybridised carbon of benzene ring which acts as an electron withdrawing group.

As a result of resonance, the oxygen atom acquires a partial positive charge and partial double bond character with sp^2-hybridised carbon of the ring. It weakens the O—H bond and thus, the release of proton is facilitated.

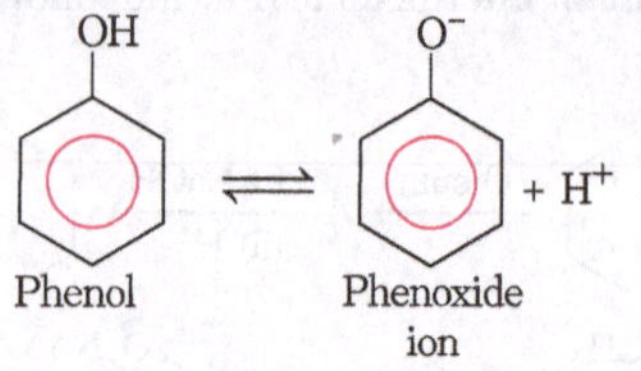

Concept ladder Phenoxide ion is the conjugate base of phenol. It is also a resonance hybrid of equal number of contributing structures but it is more stabilised by resonance than is the unionized phenol molecule.

The phenoxide ion so formed is stabilised through resonance as shown below.

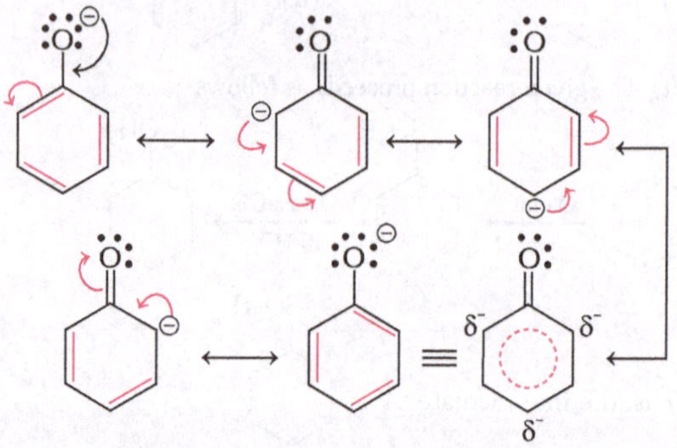

Here, phenoxide ion is better resonance stabilised than phenol. This extra stabilisation of phenoxide ion shifts the equilibrium in the forward direction. Thus, phenol is considerably stronger acid than alcohols but weaker acid than carboxylic acid. This is because the alkoxide ion formed is not stabilised through resonance. The negative charge is localised on oxygen atom only.

e.g.

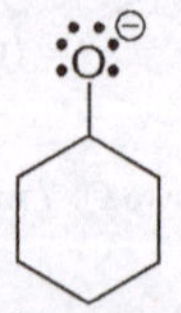

Cyclohexanoate ion

Effect of Substituents on Acidity of Phenols

Acidity of phenols is attributed to the resonance stabilisation of phenoxide ion relative to phenol. Therefore, if a substituent stabilises the phenoxide ion by dispersal of negative charge, it increases the acidity of phenols. Electron withdrawing groups (EWG) such as NO_2,—CN,

—CHO, —X (halogens) increases the acidity of phenols, whereas electron donating groups (EDG) such as —NH_2, —OR (alkoxy) —R (alkyl) decreases the acidity of phenols.

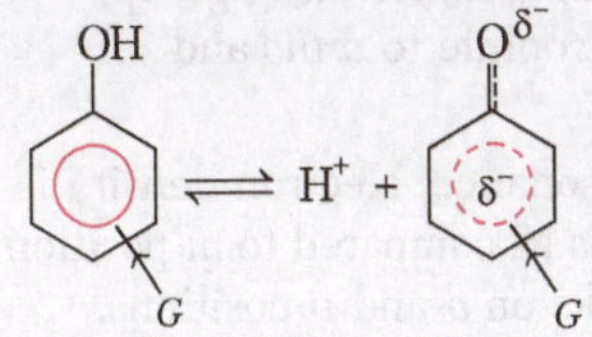

***G* releases electrons,** intensifies the negative charge, destabilises ion, decreases acidity.

$G = —CH_3, —C_2H_5$

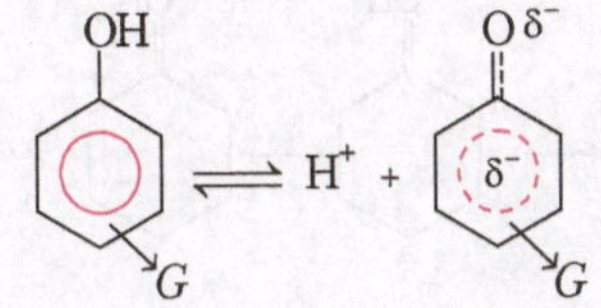

***G* withdraws electrons,** disperses negative charge, stabilises ion, increases acidity.

$G = —NO_2, —CN, X, —\overset{\oplus}{N}R_3, —CHO, —COX, —COOR$

Comparison of Acidic Strength

(i) **In nitrophenols** The acidic strength of nitrophenols is in the order as follows

p-nitrophenol > *o*-nitrophenol > *m*-nitrophenol.

A nitro group at *o*-and *p*-positions, withdraw electrons of O—H bond by –*R* effect, which increases the acidity of *o*-and *p*-nitrophenol.

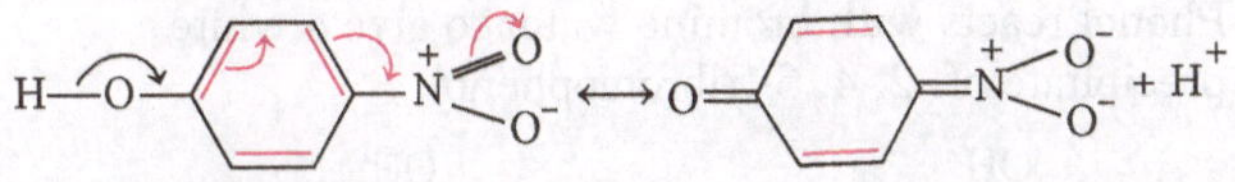

p-nitrophenol

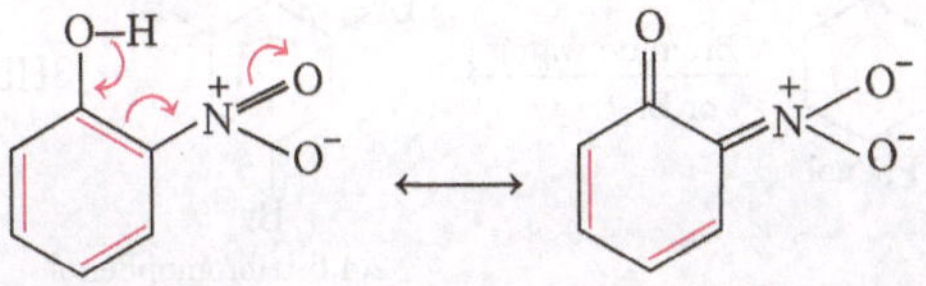

o-nitrophenol

o-nitrophenol is less acidic than *p*-nitrophenol due to presence of intramolecular H-bonding which makes removal of proton difficult. Lower acidity in case of *meta*-isomer is explained by the fact that *m*-nitro phenoxide ion is stabilised by inductive effect only and no resonance effect is observed in —NO_2. More the number of nitro groups attached to *o*-and *p*-positions, more is the acidity of nitrophenols.

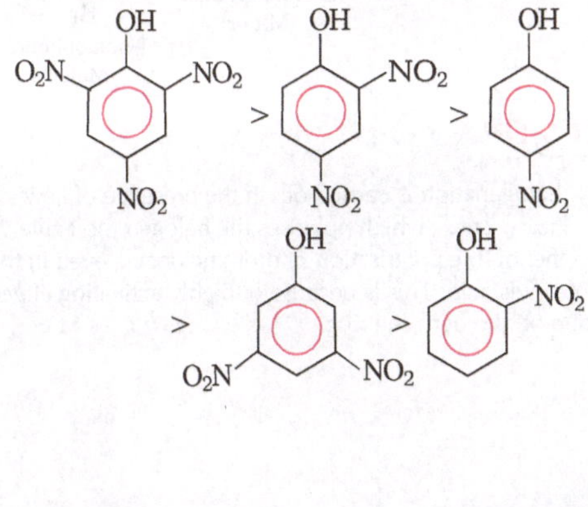

(ii) **In halophenols** All halophenols are more acidic than phenols due to –*I* effect of halogen. –*I* effect decreases with increase in distance. Therefore, order of acidity in halophenols is as follows

o-halophenol > *m*-halophenol > *p*-halophenol

Among different *o*-halophenols, order of acidity is as *o*-chlorophenol > *o*-bromophenol > *o*-iodophenol > *o*-fluorophenol.

Concept ladder

o-fluorophenol is the weakest acid due to strong intramolecular H-bonding.

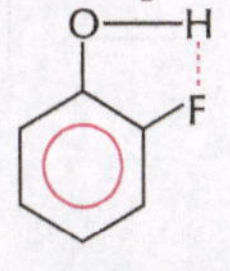

(iii) **In isomeric cresols** Acidic strength of cresols decreases in the order

phenol > *m*-cresol > *p*-cresol > *o*-cresol.

m-cresol is stronger acid than *o*-and *p*-cresols because electron donating groups such as —$CH_3(R)$, destabilises the phenoxide ion and decreases the acidity. Due to stronger +*I*-effect of —CH_3 group at *o*-and *p*-position, *m*-cresol is stronger acid.

NEET Close-up

Example Similar to PYQ Asked in NEET 2020

Which of the following substituted phenol is most acidic?

(a) 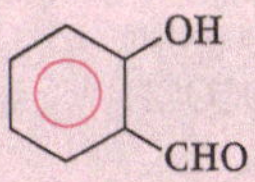

(b) 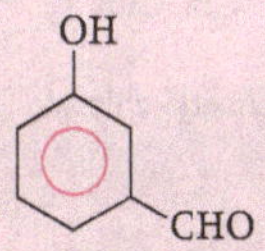

(c) 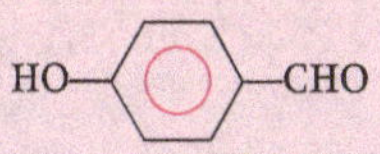

(d) 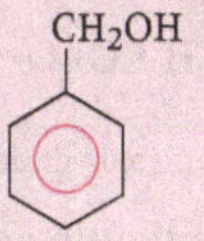

Sol. (*c*) The phenoxide ion from *o*-hydroxybenzaldehyde and *p*-hydroxybenzaldehyde are stabilised by –*I* and *R* effect of –CHO group but due to the chelation in *o*-isomer it is difficult to remove the H-atom. Hence, *p*-hydroxybenzaldehyde is the strongest acid.

Skill Builder

Choose the correct order of decreasing acidic strength of the following compounds.

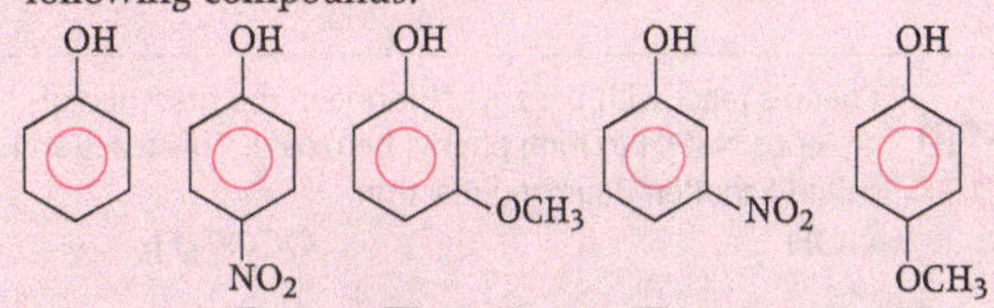

I II III IV V

(a) IV > V > III > II > I
(b) V > IV > III > II > I
(c) V > IV > II > I > III
(d) II > IV > I > III > V

For more practice Refer to Q. 12 and Q. 14 of step up Practice-3.

Reaction with $FeCl_3$

Neutral ferric chloride solution, when treated with phenol gives violet colouration due to formation of coloured complex of iron. It is a characteristic reaction to the existence of keto-enol tautomerism in phenols predominantly in enolic form.

This reaction is used as a qualitative detection of phenolic functional group.

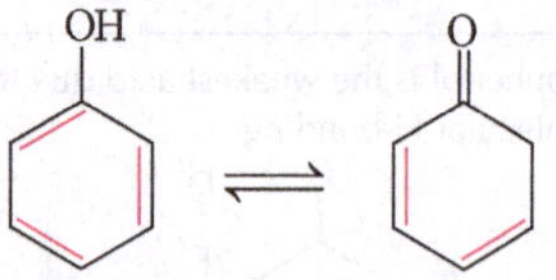

Enol Keto

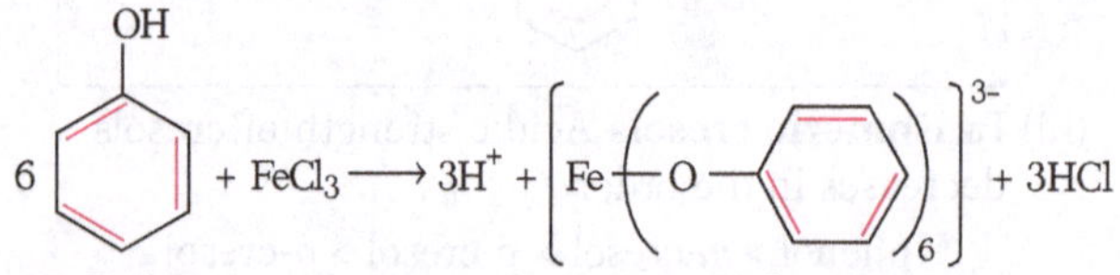

Enol Violet colour

Esterification

When phenol is treated with acetyl chloride or acetic anhydride in the presence of pyridine it forms ester. This reaction is reversible in nature. The pyridine (base) removes HCl formed and it also shifts the equilibrium to the right hand side.

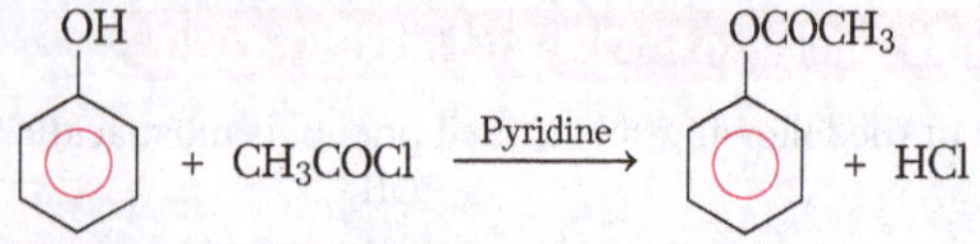

Phenol Acetyl chloride Phenyl acetate

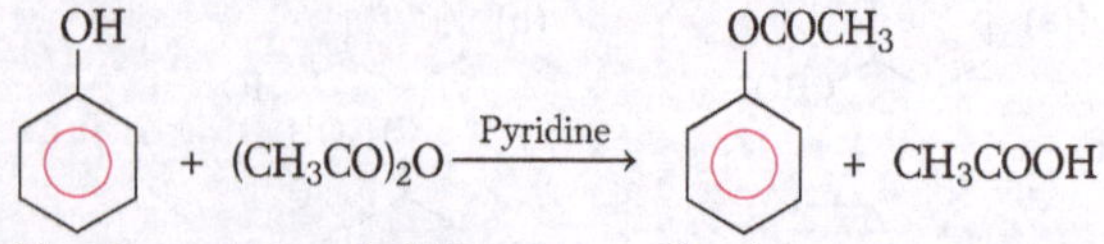

Phenol Acetic anhydride Phenyl acetate

Acetylation of salicylic acid produces, aspirin, which has analgesic, anti-inflammatory and anti-pyretic properties.

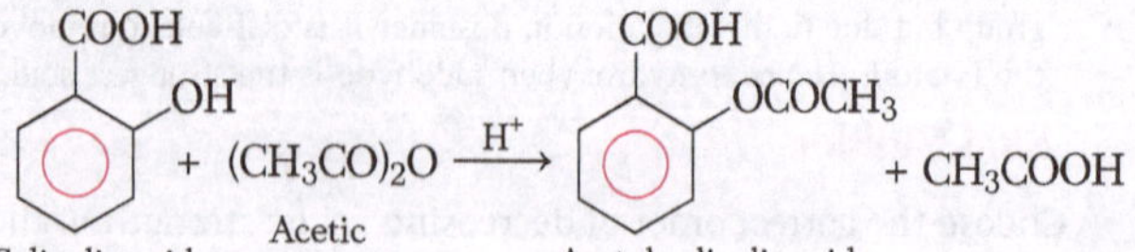

Salicylic acid Acetic anhydride Acetyl salicylic acid (Aspirin)

Concept ladder

Phenols react with benzoyl chloride in the presence of aqueous NaOH to form phenyl benzoate. This reaction is called Schotten Baumann reaction.

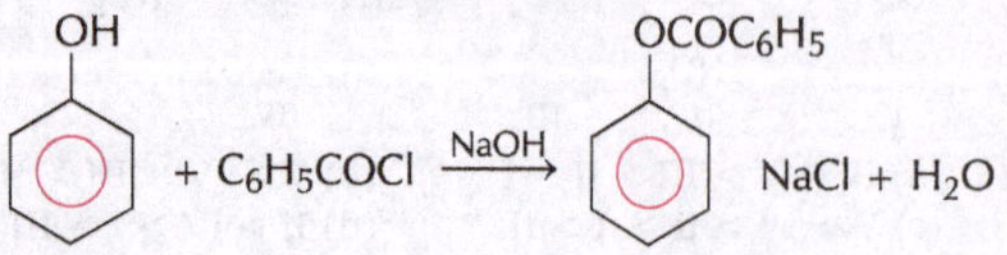

Phenol Benzoyl chloride Phenyl benzoate

Electrophilic Aromatic Substitution

Phenols undergo electrophilic substitution reactions due to presence of —OH group (an activating group) which directs incoming electrophile to *ortho* and *para*-positions.

It is observed that, due to resonance, electron density is increased at *o*-and *p*-positions as compared to *m*-position. Therefore, electrophile attacks on *o*-and *p*-positions.

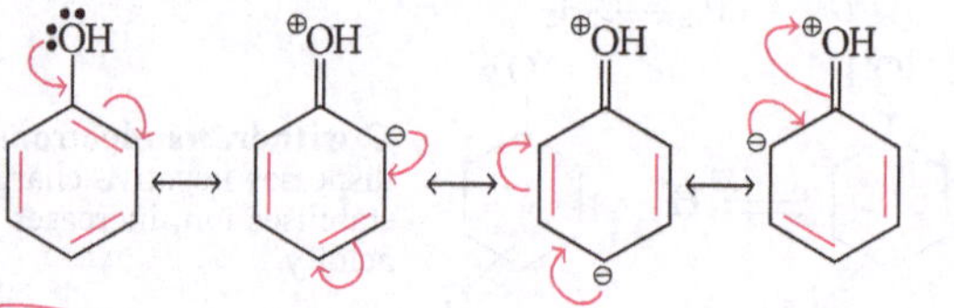

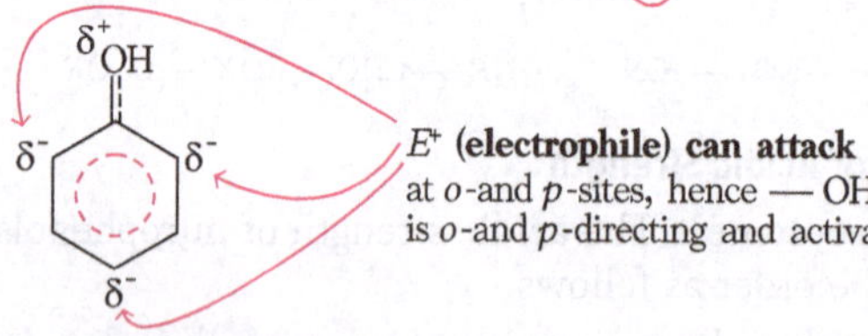

E^+ (electrophile) can attack at *o*-and *p*-sites, hence — OH group is *o*-and *p*-directing and activating group.

Some of electrophilic substitution reactions of phenols are as follows

Halogenation

Phenol reacts with bromine water to give a white precipitate of 2, 4, 6-tribromophenol.

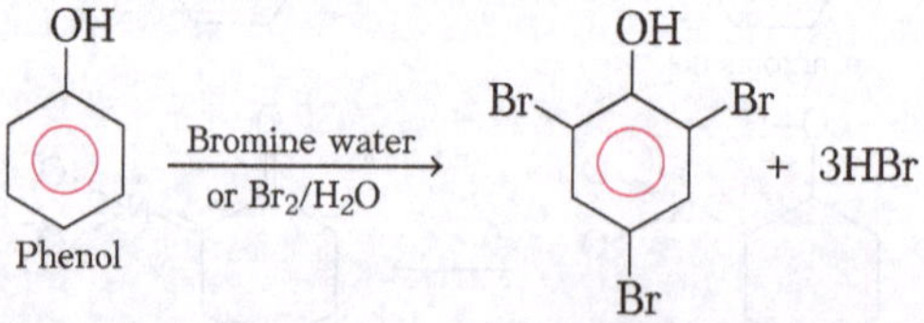

Phenol 2,4,6-tribromophenol (White ppt.)

However, if the reaction is carried out in solvents of low polarity such as CS_2 or CCl_4, at a low temperature, a mixture of *ortho* and *para* bromophenol is obtained.

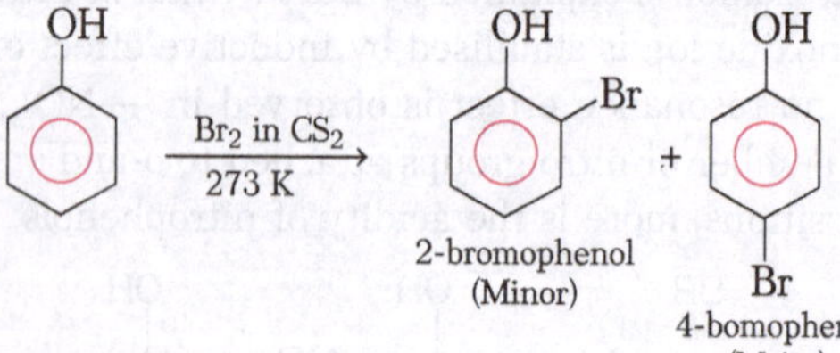

2-bromophenol (Minor) 4-bomophenol (Major)

Mentor's TIP

Generally, halogenation is carried out in the presence of Lewis acid like $FeBr_3$, $AlBr_3$, $ZnCl_2$ which polarises the halogen molecule. While in case of phenol, the polarisation of bromine occurs even in the absence of Lewis acid. This is because of highly activating effect of —OH group on the benzene ring.

Nitration

When phenol is treated with conc. HNO_3 and conc. H_2SO_4, it form 2, 4, 6-trinitrophenol (picric acid). The yield of nitro product is low because of the oxidation of ring by conc. HNO_3.

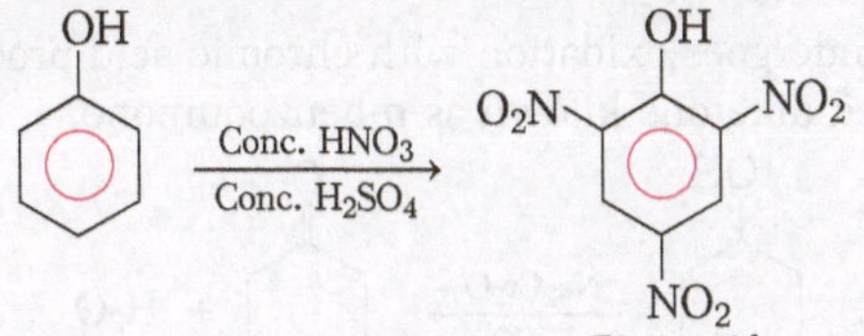

Picric acid

Picric acid is prepared by treating phenol first with conc. sulphuric acid which converts it to phenol-2, 4-disulphonic acid and then with concentrated nitric acid to get 2,4,6-trinitrophenol.

However, if the reaction is carried out in the presence of dilute nitric acid at low temperature (298 K) it give a mixture of *ortho* and *para*-nitrophenols.

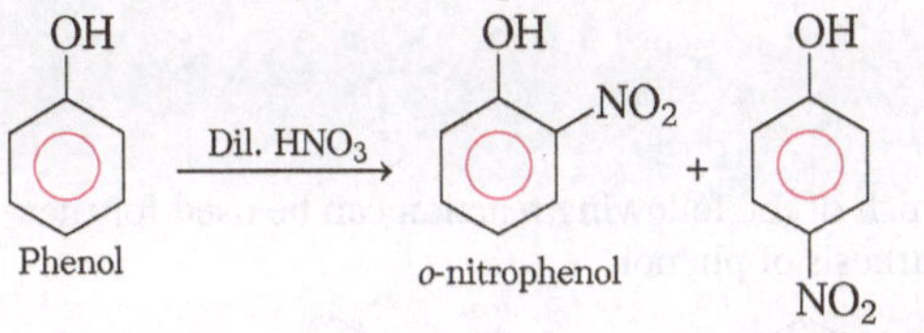

The *o*-and *p*-isomers can be separated by steam distillation *o*-nitrophenol is steam volatile due to intramolecular H-bonding while *p*-nitrophenol is less volatile due to intermolecular H-bonding.

Sulphonation

The replacement of a hydrogen atom by a sulphonic acid group in a ring is called sulphonation. Phenol reacts with concentrated H_2SO_4 or oleum to form a mixture of *o*-and *p*-hydroxy benzene sulphonic acids.

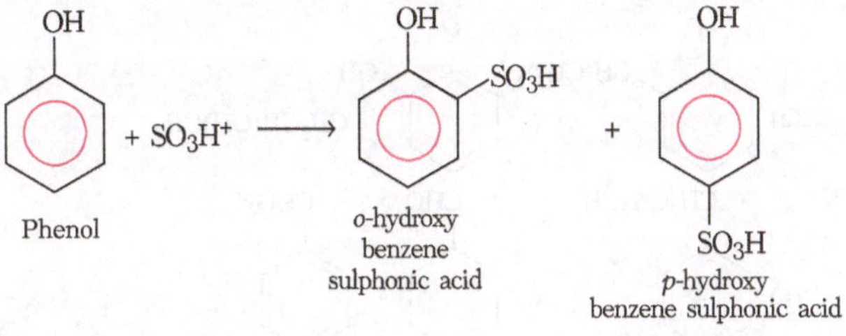

At low temperature, *ortho*-isomer is the major product and at high temperature (373 K), *para*-isomer is favoured.

Reimer-Tiemann Reaction

Phenol reacts with chloroform in presence of alkaline solution at 330 K followed by acid hydrolysis to give salicylaldehyde as the major product. This reaction is known as Reimer-Tiemann reaction.

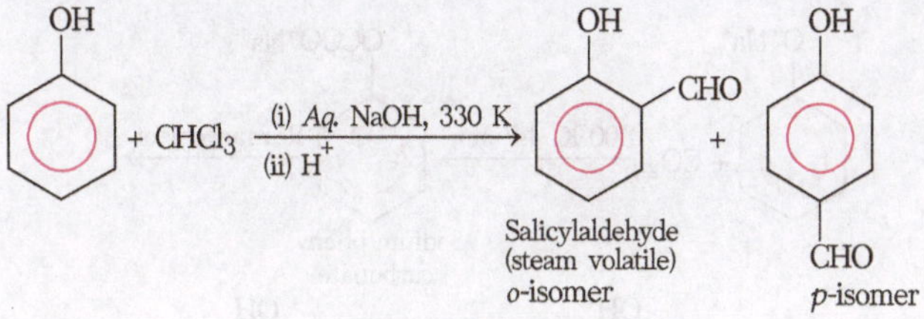

Ortho-isomer is stabilised by intramolecular H-bonding. In this reaction electrophile is dichlorocarbene ($:CCl_2$).

NEET Snapshot

Phenol on reaction with $CHCl_3$ and NaOH involves dichlorocarbene electrophile. ***[NEET 2018]***

The electrophile dichlorocarbene ($:CCl_2$) is generated from chloroform by the action of base NaOH. Although $:CCl_2$ is electrically neutral but it is strongly electrophilic as it contains a carbon atom with only six electrons (a sextet).

Mechanism

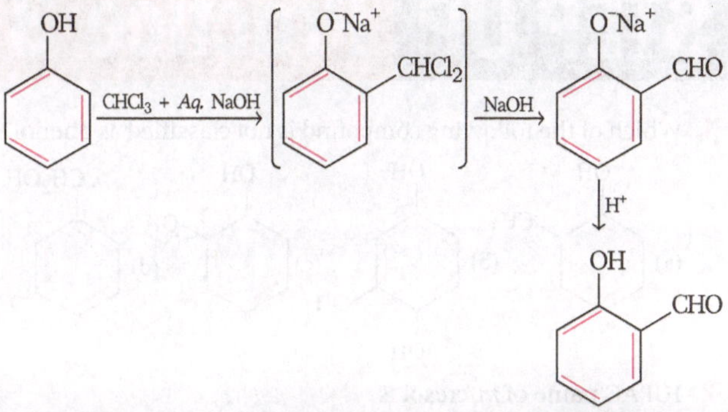

Salicylaldehyde

The intermediate substituted benzal chloride is hydrolysed in the presence of alkali to produce salicylaldehyde.

If carbon tetrachloride (CCl_4) is used instead of $CHCl_3$, salicylic acid is formed as a major product.

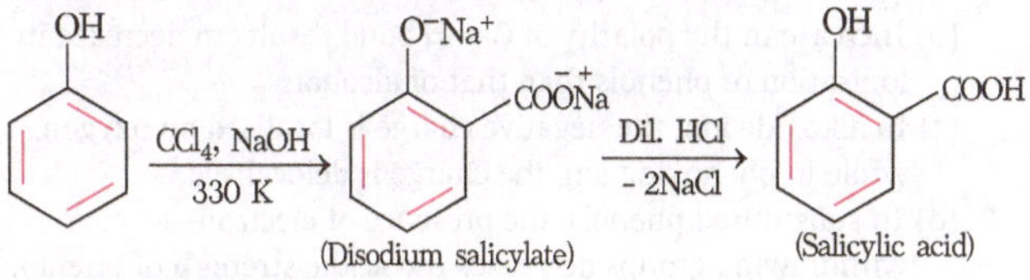

Kolbe's Reaction

Sodium phenoxide (formed by action of base on phenol) reacts with carbon dioxide at 120-140°C, high pressure followed by acid hydrolysis to produce salicylic acid. This reaction is known as **Kolbe-Schmidt reaction.**

This is an example of electrophilic substitution reaction where CO_2 acts as an electrophile. It is used for the conversion of phenol into hydroxy carboxylic acid.

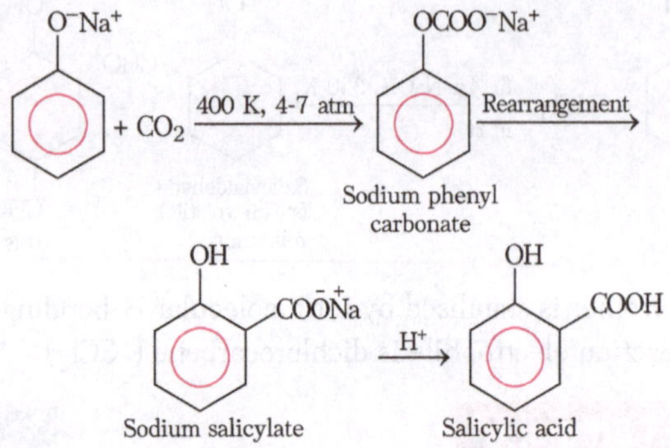

Reaction of Phenol with Zinc Dust

Benzene can be obtained by distillation of phenol with zinc dust.

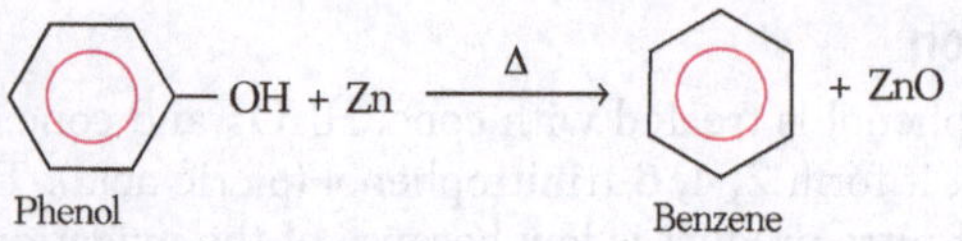

Oxidation

Phenol undergoes oxidation with chromic acid produces a conjugated diketone known as *p*-benzoquinone.

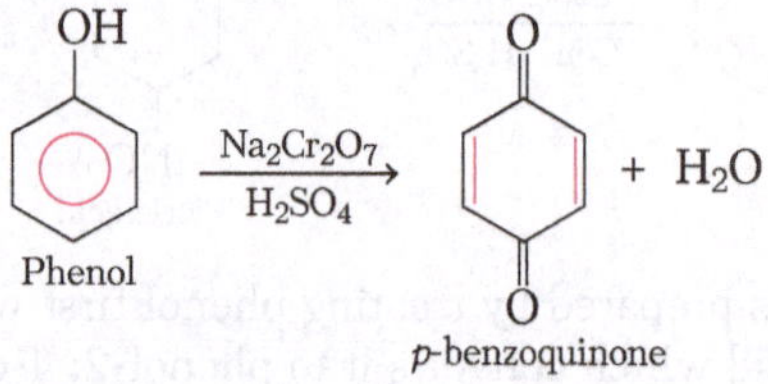

In the presence of air, phenols are slowly oxidised to dark coloured mixtures containing quinones.

STEP UP Practice 3

1. Which of the following compound is not classified as phenol?

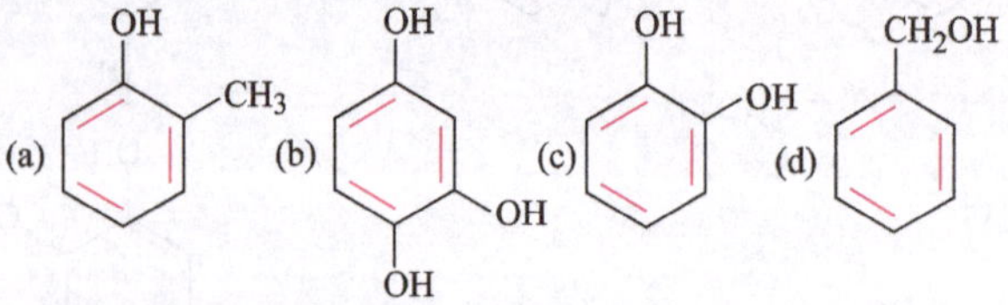

2. IUPAC name of *m*-cresol is

(a) 3-methylphenol (b) 3-chlorophenol

(c) 3-methoxyphenol (d) benzene-1,3-diol

3. Which of the following statements is correct regarding phenol?

(a) The electron density increases on oxygen due to higher electronegativity of sp^2-hybridised carbon atom of phenol.

(b) Increase in the polarity of O—H bond results in decrease in ionisation of phenols than that of alcohols.

(c) In alkoxide ion, the negative charge is localised on oxygen, while in phenoxide ion, the charge is delocalised.

(d) In substituted phenols, the presence of electron withdrawing groups decreases the acidic strength of phenol.

4. In addition to phenol, one important solvent acetone is the side product when source is

(a) cumene (b) benzene (c) benzoquinone (d) octane

5. Main source of phenolic compounds is

(a) 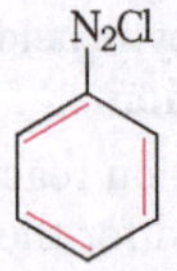

(b) 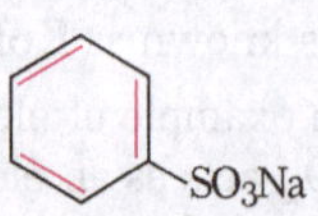

(c) middle oil (d) heavy oil

6. Which of the following reaction can be used for the synthesis of phenol.

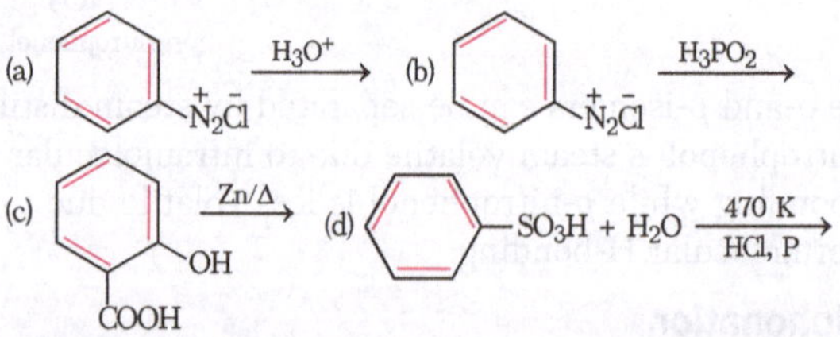

7. Identify the major products *P*, *Q* and *R* in the following sequence of reactions :

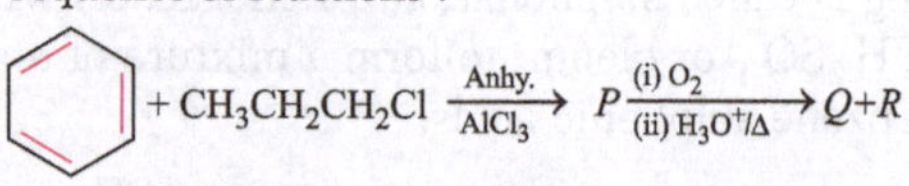

P *Q* *R*

(a) 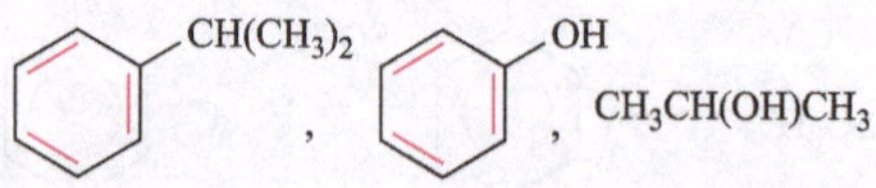

(b) 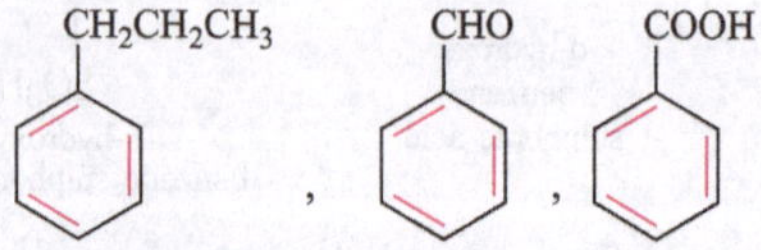

(c) 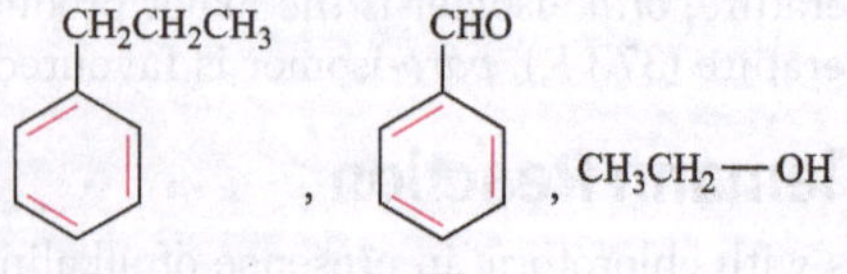

(d) 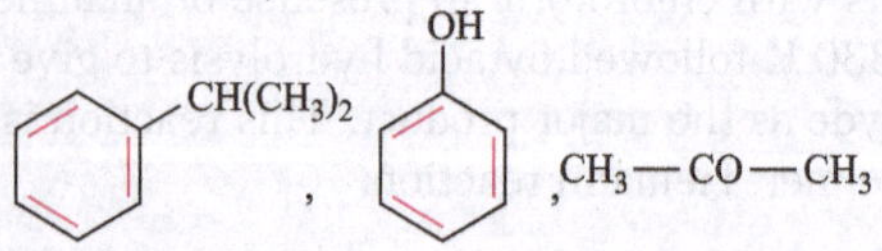

8. Which of the following is correctly match?
(a) Cumene hydroperoxide $\xrightarrow[H_2O]{H^+}$ Phenol
(b) Cumene $\xrightarrow{O_2}$ Phenol
(c) Benzene sulphonic acid $\xrightarrow[\text{(ii) } H^+]{\text{(i) NaOH}}$ Benzene + Phenol
(d) Benzene diazonium chloride $\xrightarrow[\text{(ii) Warm}]{\text{(i) } H_2O}$ Phenol + N_2O + H_2

9. Consider the following statements.
Statement I Ethanol is a weaker acid than phenol.
Statement II Phenol is more stable than phenoxide.
In the light of the above statements, choose the correct answer from the options given below.
(a) Both Statement I and Statement II are false.
(b) Statement I is true but Statement II is false.
(c) Statement I is false but Statement II is true.
(d) Both Statement I and Statement II are true.

10. Which of the following statements is correct?
(a) NO_2 group in nitrophenol will decrease the acidity of phenol.
(b) Phenol is less acidic than ethanol.
(c) Phenol is more acidic than ethanol.
(d) Phenol is more acidic than acetic acid.

11. Mark the correct increasing order of reactivity of the following compounds with HBr/HCl.

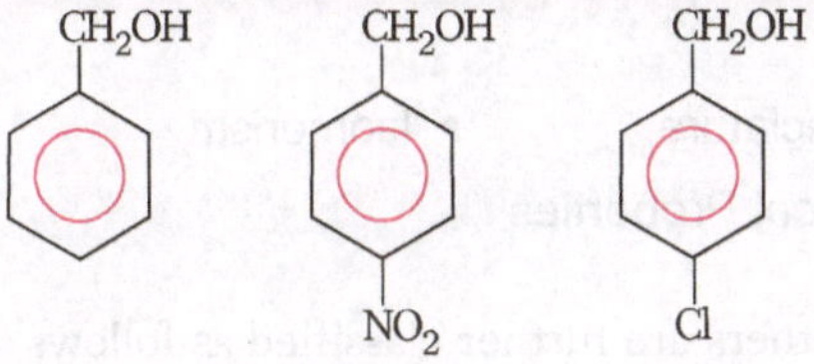

(I) (II) (III)

(a) I < II < III (b) II < I < III
(c) II < III < I (d) III < II < I

12. Which of the following option is the correct order of increasing acidity for the given compounds?

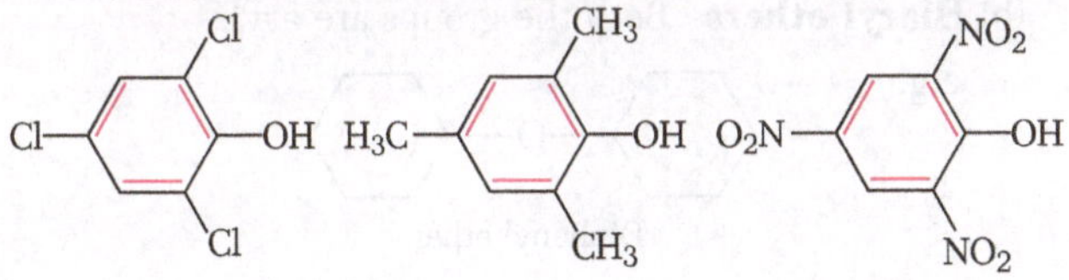

I II III

(a) II < III > I (b) III > I > II (c) III > II < I (d) II < I < III

13. Consider the following statements.
Statement I *p*-nitrophenol is more acidic than phenol.
Statement II Nitro group helps in the stabilisation of the phenoxide ion by dispersal of negative charge due to resonance.
In the light of the above statements, choose the correct answer from the options given below.
(a) Both Statement I and Statement II are false.
(b) Statement I is true, but Statement II is false.
(c) Statement I is false, but Statement II is true.
(d) Both Statement I and Statement II are true.

14. Which of the following is most acidic?
(a) Benzyl alcohol (b) Cyclohexanol
(c) Phenol (d) *m*-chlorophenol

15. 

Which is true about C—O bond lengths?
(a) $x = y$ (b) $x > y$
(c) $x < y$ (d) is not predictable

16. The ionisation constant of phenol is higher than that of ethanol because
(a) phenoxide ion is bulkier than ethoxide ion
(b) phenoxide ion is stronger base than ethoxide ion
(c) phenoxide ion is stabilised through delocalisation
(d) phenoxide ion is less stable than ethoxide ion

17. In the following reaction,

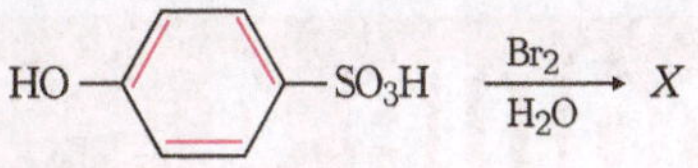

X is identified as
(a) 2,4,6-tribromophenol
(b) 2-bromo-4-hydroxybenzene sulphonic acid
(c) 3,5-dibromo-4-hydroxybenzene sulphonic acid
(d) 2-bromophenol

18. Which of the following product is formed between the reaction of phenol with CO_2 and NaOH followed by hydrolysis?

(a) 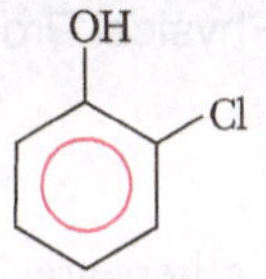
(b) 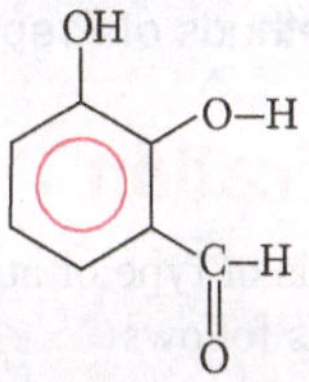
(c) 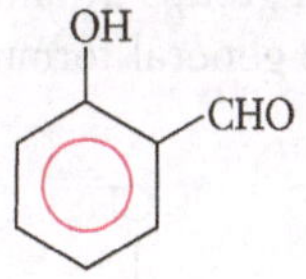
(d) 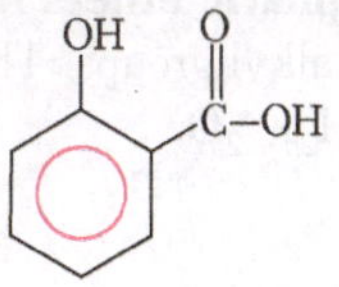

19. 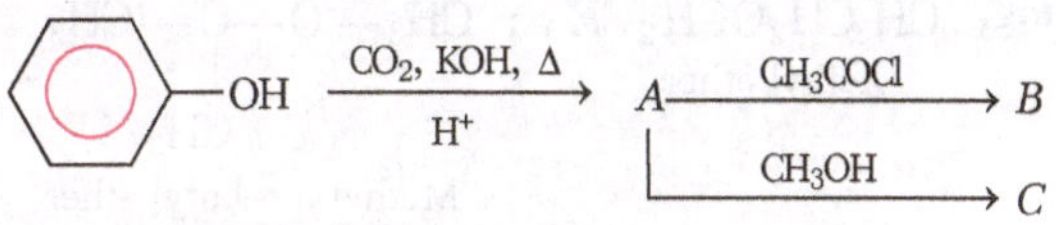

A, B, C respectively are
(a) salicylic acid, aspirin and oil of winter-green
(b) aspirin, salicylic acid and oil of winter-green
(c) salicylic acid, oil of winter-green, and aspirin
(d) None of the above is correct

20. What is the major product in the following series of reaction?

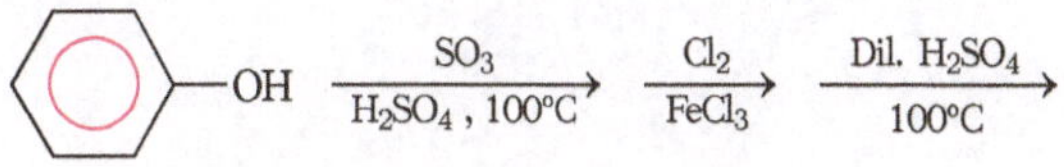

(a)  (b) 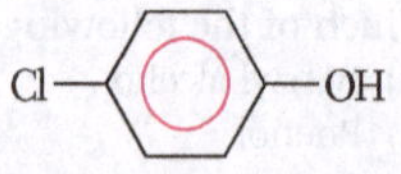

(c) 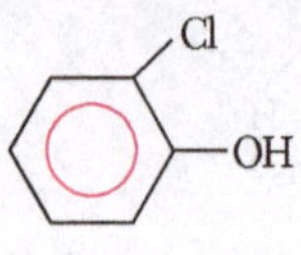 (d) 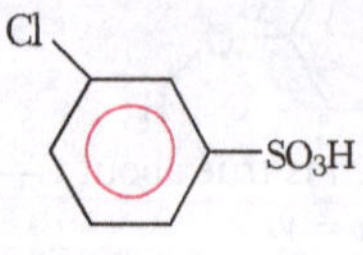

21. The conversion of *m*-nitrophenol to resorcinol involves
(a) hydrolysis, diazotisation and reduction
(b) diazotisation, reduction and hydrolysis
(c) hydrolysis, reduction and diazotisation
(d) reduction, diazotisation and hydrolysis

22. 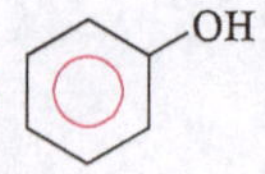 $\xrightarrow{K_2S_2O_8 + KOH}$?

The major product is
(a) *p*-benzoquinone (b) *p*-benzenediol
(c) benzene sulphonic acid (d) diphenyl ether

23 Consider the following reagents.
(i) hot conc. HCl (ii) PhCl, *aq*. NaOH
(iii) $SOCl_2$ (iv) $(CH_3)_2C{=}CH_2, H_2SO_4$
(v) Br_2 in CS_2

How many of the given compounds will not react with phenol?
(a) 4 (b) 2 (c) 3 (d) 1

Module 4

Ethers

- Classification
- Structure
- Nomenclature
- Isomerism
- Methods of Preparation
- Physical Properties
- Chemical Properties

Classification

On the basis of type of attached groups, ethers are classified as follows

(i) **Aliphatic ethers** Both attached groups (*R* and *R′*) are alkyl groups. They have the general formula as $C_nH_{2n+2}O$.

e.g. $CH_3CH_2OCH_2CH_3$; $CH_3—O—C(CH_3)_2—CH_3$

Diethyl ether ; Methyl *tert*-butyl ether

(ii) **Aromatic ethers** Either one or both the attached groups (*R* and *R′*) is/are aryl groups.

e.g. 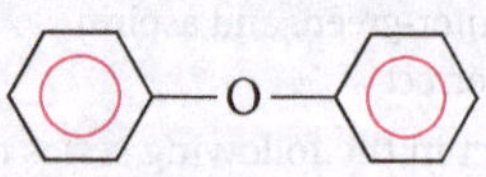 ; 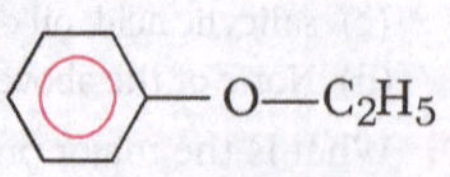

Diphenyl ether ; Ethyl phenyl ether

Aromatic ethers are further classified as follows

(a) **Phenolic ethers** One of the group is aryl and other is alkyl.

e.g. $CH_3—O—C_6H_5$
Phenolic ether

(b) **Diaryl ethers** Both the groups are aryl.

e.g. 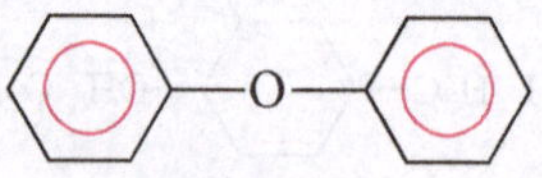

Diphenyl ether

On the basis of symmetry, ethers are classified as follows

(i) **Simple or symmetrical ethers** Here, both alkyl or aryl groups bonded to O-atom are same.

e.g. $CH_3—O—CH_3$; 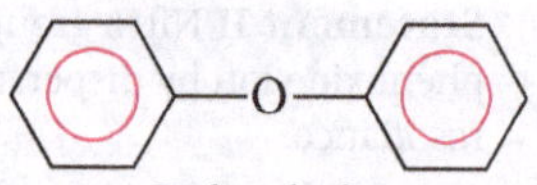

Dimethyl ether ; Diphenyl ether

(ii) **Mixed or unsymmetrical ethers** Here, both alkyl or aryl groups bonded to O-atom are different.

e.g. $CH_3—O—CH_2CH_3$ (Ethyl methyl ether) ; $C_6H_5—O—CH_2C_6H_5$ (Benzyl phenyl ether)

Structure

Ethers are bent molecules with bond angle $\angle ROR'$ is approx 110° and O-atom is sp^3-hybridised. In ethers, the repulsion between the bulkier alkyl groups almost counter balance the effect of lone pair-lone pair interactions and hence tetrahedral angle (109.5°) is almost retained.

The C—O bond length (141 pm) is almost the same as in alcohols.

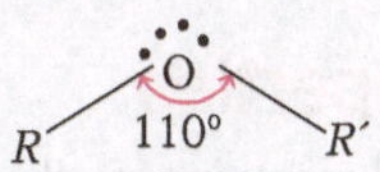

Ethers

Nomenclature

In IUPAC system, ethers are called as alkoxyalkanes. Here, ethereal oxygen is taken alongwith smaller alkyl group, which is regarded as substituent on large alkyl group as parent hydrocarbon.

e.g. $CH_3—O—\overset{2}{C}H(\overset{1}{C}H_3)\overset{3}{C}H_3$; $CH_3—O—\overset{2}{C}(\overset{1}{C}H_3)(\overset{3}{C}H_3)—CH_3$

Common name	Methyl *iso*-propyl ether	*tert*-butyl methyl ether
IUPAC name	2-methoxypropane	2-methoxy-2-methylpropane

IUPAC names of a few typical ethers are as follows

$CH_3O—\overset{1}{C}H(OCH_3)—\overset{2}{C}H_3$ (1, 1-dimethoxyethane)

$\overset{1}{C}H_3—\overset{2}{C}H(OH)—\overset{3}{C}H_2\overset{4}{C}H_2OCH_3$ (4-methoxybutan-2-ol)

Isomerism

Following types of isomerisms are shown by ethers

(i) **Functional isomerism** Both —O— and —OH are the possible functional groups with general molecular formula, $C_nH_{2n+2}O$.

e.g. $CH_3—O—CH_3$ (Dimethylether) and CH_3CH_2OH (Ethanol (or ethyl alcohol))

Functional isomers of oxiranes are aldehydes and ketones. e.g.

$CH_3—CH—CH_2$ (with O bridging the two carbons), CH_3CH_2CHO, $CH_3—CO—CH_3$

(ii) **Metamerism** Ethers having the same molecular formula but different alkyl groups on either side of the divalent atom like oxygen are called metamers. The phenomenon is called metamerism. Two pairs of metamers are possible with molecular formula $C_4H_{10}O$.

(a) $CH_3—O—CH_2CH_2CH_3$ (Methyl propylether) and $CH_3CH_2OCH_2CH_3$ (Diethylether)

(b) $CH_3O—\overset{2}{C}H(\overset{3}{C}H_3)—\overset{1}{C}H_3$ (2-methoxypropane) and $CH_3CH_2OCH_2CH_3$ (Diethylether)

Preparation of Ethers

Ethers are generally prepared by the following methods

By Dehydration of Alcohols

Symmetrical ethers are prepared by heating alcohols at 413 K with sulphuric acid. While heating alcohols at 443 K with H_2SO_4 will give alkene.Here, the temperature plays an important role in deciding the product.

$$2CH_3CH_2OH \text{ (Ethanol)} \xrightarrow[413K]{\Delta,\ H_2SO_4} CH_3CH_2OCH_2CH_3 \text{ (Diethyl ether)} + H_2O$$

$$2CH_3CH_2OH \text{ (Ethanol)} \xrightarrow[\Delta,\ 443K]{H_2SO_4} 2CH_2{=}CH_2 \text{ (Ethene)} + 2H_2O$$

Thus, by controlling the temperature, nature of the product can be changed. This reaction is an example of nucleophilic substitution (S_N) reaction in which protonated alcohol is the substrate and second molecule of alcohol acts as a nucleophile.

Mechanism

(i) $CH_3CH_2\ddot{O}H + H^+ \longrightarrow CH_3CH_2—\overset{+}{\ddot{O}}(H)—H$

(ii) $CH_3CH_2—\ddot{O}(H): + CH_3—CH_2—\overset{+}{O}(H)H \longrightarrow CH_3CH_2—\overset{+}{O}(H)—CH_2CH_3 + H_2O$

(iii) $CH_3CH_2—\overset{+}{O}(H)—CH_2CH_3 \longrightarrow CH_3CH_2—O—CH_2CH_3 + H^+$

This method is suitable for the preparation of ethers having 1° alkyl groups only.

The reaction can follow S_N1 mechanism if alcohol is 2° or 3° while S_N2 mechanism will be followed if alcohol is 1°.

Mentor's TIP

2° or 3° alcohols do not form ether with conc. H_2SO_4 as it undergoes elimination reaction and form alkene.

Williamson Synthesis

This is one of the best method for the preparation of symmetrical and unsymmetrical ethers. In this method, sodium or potassium alkoxide is heated with an alkyl halide to form an ether. The reaction involves nucleophilic substitution (S_N2) attack of an alkoxide ion on primary alkyl halide.

$$\underset{\text{Alkoxide}}{R\bar{O}Na^+} + \underset{\text{Alkyl halide}}{R'—X} \xrightarrow{S_N2} \underset{\text{Ether}}{R—O—R'} + NaX$$

2° or 3° alkyl halide does not give Williamson synthesis as in the presence of alkoxide it undergo elimination reaction.

e.g. $CH_3—CH_2—Cl + C_2H_5O^-Na^+ \longrightarrow \underset{\text{Diethyl ether}}{C_2H_5OC_2H_5} + NaCl$

$$\underset{\text{Methyl chloride}}{CH_3—Cl} + \underset{\text{Sodium } tert\text{-butoxide}}{(CH_3)_3CO^-Na^+} \longrightarrow \underset{tert\text{-butyl ethyl ether}}{CH_3—C(CH_3)_2—O—CH_3}$$

Concept ladder The *tert*-butyl ethyl ether cannot be prepared by treating sodium ethoxide with *tert*-butyl chloride or bromide as under these conditions $C_2H_5O^-$ (ethoxide ion) will cause the elimination of alkyl halide to form an alkene as the main product.

Similarly, alkyl aryl ethers (phenolic ethers) can be easily prepared by treating phenoxide with a suitable alkyl halide.

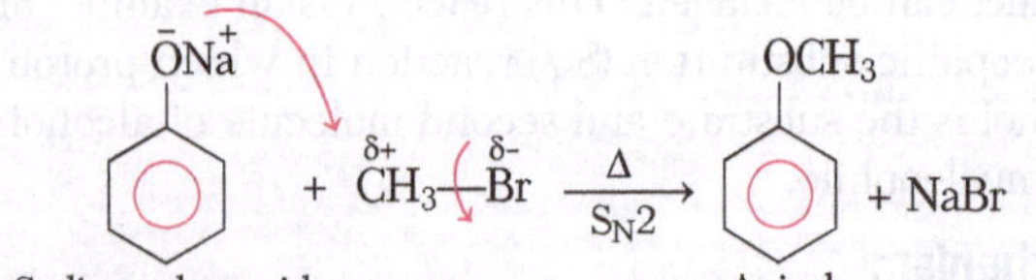

Sodium phenoxide — Anisole

Physical Properties

Various physical properties of ether are as follows

(i) **Physical state** Both dimethyl ether and ethyl methyl ether are gases. All other ethers are colourless liquids with characteristic odour called ethereal smell.

(ii) **Dipole moment** Although ethers lack the polar hydroxyl group of alcohols, they are still significantly polar compounds. The dipole moment of ether is the sum of two polar C—O bonds, with a substantial contribution from the two lone pair of electrons.

(iii) **Boiling point** The small polarity of ethers however, does not affect their boiling points appreciably which are much the same as that of alkanes of comparable molecular weights. Ethers have lower boiling points than the isomeric alcohols since ethers cannot form hydrogen bonds due to absence of –OH groups.

However, ethers form hydrogen bonds with the other compounds that have O—H or N—H groups.

(iv) **Solubility** Ethers, upto three carbon atoms, are soluble in water due to the formation of intermolecular H-bonds between water and ethereal oxygen.

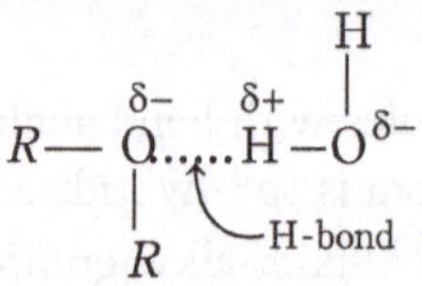

As the molecular mass increases, the solubility of ethers in water decreases due to a corresponding increase in the hydrocarbon portion of the molecule, which is hydrophobic.

Chemical Properties

Some of the chemical reactions of ethers are as follows

Cleavage of C—O Bond in Ethers

Ethers are readily cleaved by halogen acids at 373K to form an alcohol and an alkyl halide.

$$\underset{\text{Ether}}{R—O—R'} + \underset{\text{1 eq.}}{HX} \xrightarrow{373K} \underset{\text{Alcohol}}{R—OH} + \underset{\text{Alkyl halide}}{R'—X}\ ;\ [X = \text{Br or I}]$$

e.g. $\underset{\text{Dimethyl ether}}{CH_3—O—CH_3} + \underset{\text{1 eq.}}{HI} \xrightarrow{373K} \underset{\text{Methanol}}{CH_3OH} + \underset{\text{Methyl iodide}}{CH_3I}$

If excess of acid is used then only alkyl halide is formed because the alcohol formed reacts further with halogen acid to form the corresponding alkyl halide.

$$\underset{\text{Simple ether}}{R—O—R} + \underset{\text{Excess}}{2HI} \xrightarrow{373K} \underset{\text{Alkyl iodide}}{2R—I} + H_2O$$

e.g. $\underset{\text{Diethylether}}{CH_3CH_2—O—CH_2CH_3} + \underset{\text{Excess}}{2HI} \xrightarrow{373K} \underset{\text{Ethyl iodide}}{2\,CH_3CH_2I} + H_2O$

In case of unsymmetrical ethers, halogen goes preferentially with smaller alkyl group or more stable carbocation.

e.g. $\underset{\text{Methoxy ethane}}{CH_3—O—C_2H_5} + HI \longrightarrow \underset{\text{Methyl iodide}}{CH_3I} + \underset{\text{Ethanol}}{C_2H_5OH}$

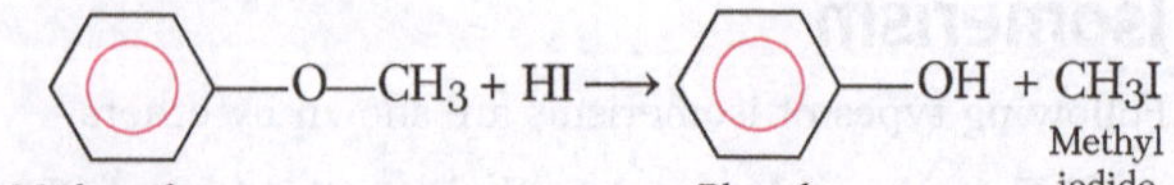

Methoxy benzene — Phenol

Mechanism

***Step* I** Formation of oxonium ions.

$$CH_3—\ddot{O}—C_2H_5 + \overset{+}{H}—\overset{-}{I} \rightleftharpoons \underset{\text{Oxonium ion}}{CH_3—\overset{+}{O}(H)—C_2H_5} + I^-$$

The reaction takes place with HBr or HI because Br^- or I^- are good nucleophiles. Hence, the order of reactivity of HX is HI > HBr > HCl.

***Step* II** Attack by iodide ion [or a nucleophile] on oxonium ion. Cleavage involves nucleophilic attack by halide ion on the protonated ether with displacement of the weakly basic alcohol molecule.

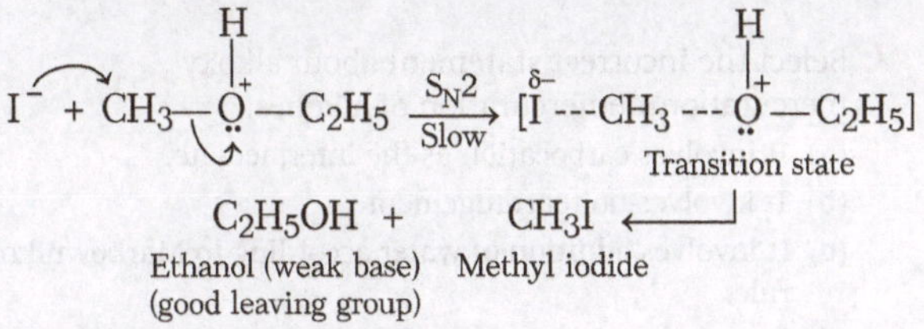

In the following reaction,

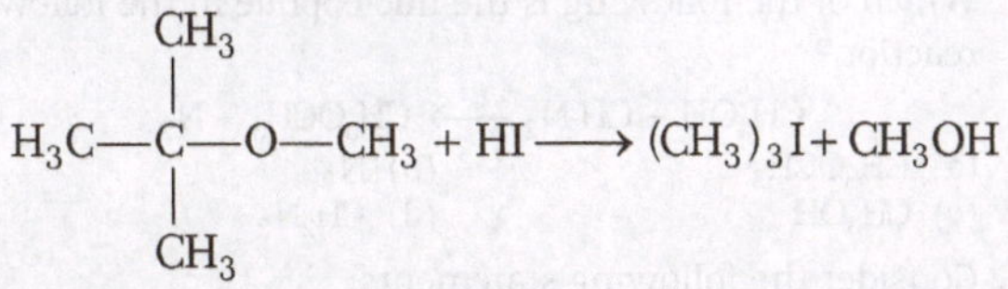

S_N1 mechanism is followed as $(CH_3)_3C^{\oplus}$ is most stable carbocation and I^- is attached to it.

NEET Close-up

Example Similar to PYQ Asked in NEET 2020

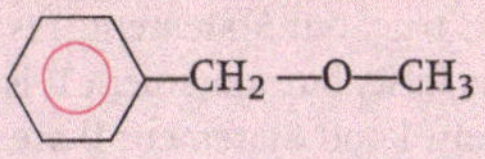

The ether shown above on cleavage with HI gives which of the following products?

(a) 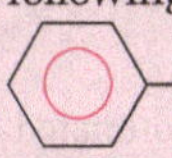 CH_2OH, CH_3I (b) 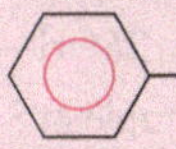 CH_2I, CH_3OH

(c) 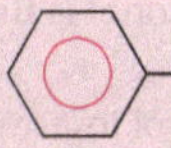 CH_2I, CH_3I (d) 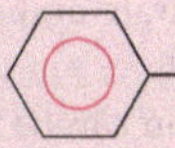 CH_2OH, CH_3OH

Sol. (*b*) The reaction proceeds as follows

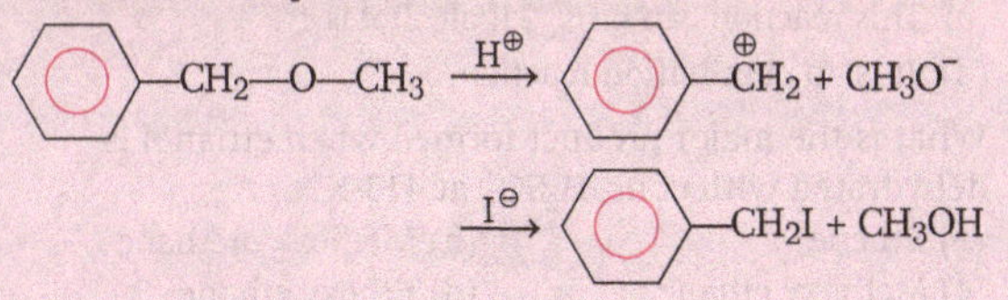

Thus, the products are 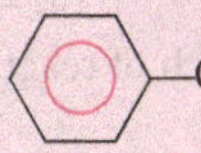 $CH_2I + CH_3OH$

Skill Builder

Acetic anhydride reacts with diethyl ether in the presence of anhydrous $AlCl_3$ to give

(a) CH_3COOH (b) $CH_3CH_2COOCH_3$
(c) $CH_3COOCH_2CH_3$ (d) CH_3CH_2OH

For more practice Refer Q.18 for step up Practice-4.

Electrophilic Substitution Reactions of Aryl Ethers

Due to +*R*-effect of alkoxy group (—O*R*) electron density in the benzene ring increases at two *ortho* and one *para* position as compared to *m*-position.

Thus, the benzene ring is activated towards electrophilic substitution reactions at *o* and *p*-positions mainly.

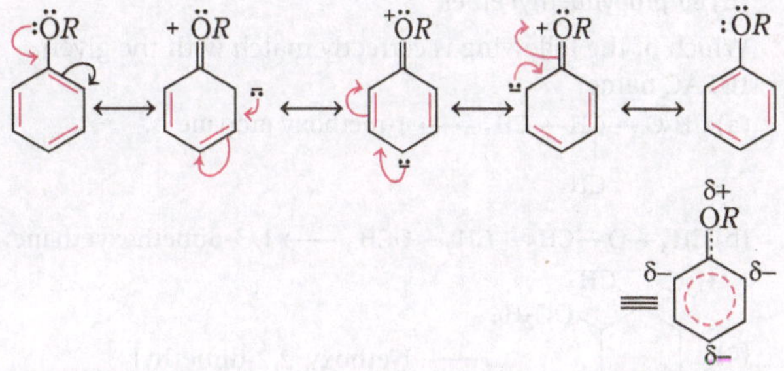

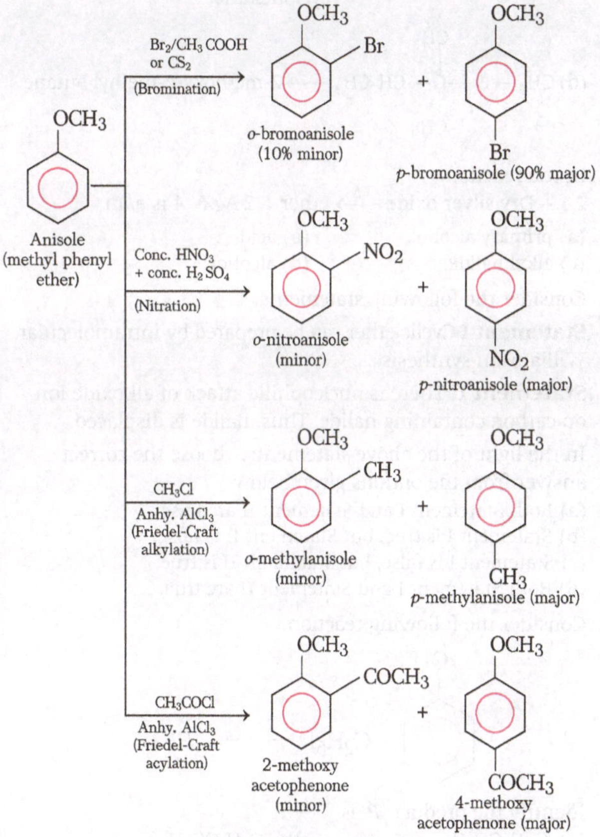

STEP UP Practice 4

1. IUPAC name of the compound $CH_3—\underset{\displaystyle CH_3}{\underset{|}{CH}}—OCH_3$ is
   (a) 1-methoxy-1-methylethane
   (b) 2-methoxy-2-methylethane
   (c) 2-methoxypropane
   (d) *iso*-propylmethyl ether

2. Which of the following is correctly match with the given IUPAC name?
   (a) $CH_3O—\underset{\displaystyle CH_3}{\underset{|}{CH}}—CH_3 \longrightarrow$ 1-methoxy propane
   (b) $CH_3—O—CH_2—CH_2—OCH_3 \longrightarrow$ 1, 3-dimethoxyethane
   (c) 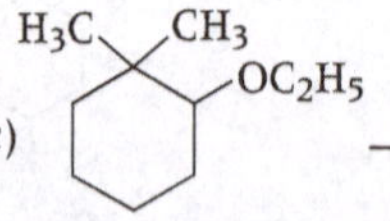
   $\longrightarrow$ 1-ethoxy, 2,2-dimethyl cyclohexane
   (d) $CH_3—O—\overset{\displaystyle CH_3}{\overset{|}{\underset{\displaystyle CH_3}{\underset{|}{C}}}}—CH_2CH_3 \longrightarrow$ 2-methoxy-2-methyl butane

3. In the reaction,
   $2A$ + Dry silver oxide $\xrightarrow{\Delta}$ ether + 2 AgX, A is a/an
   (a) primary alcohol (b) acid
   (c) alkyl halide (d) alcohol

4. Consider the following statements.
   Statement I Cyclic ether can be prepared by intramolecular Williamson synthesis.
   Statement II There is nucleophilic attack of alkoxide ion on carbon containing halide. Thus, halide is displaced.
   In the light of the above statements, choose the correct answer from the options given below.
   (a) Both Statement I and Statement II are false.
   (b) Statement I is true, but Statement II is false.
   (c) Statement I is false, but Statement II is true.
   (d) Both Statement I and Statement II are true.

5. Consider the following reaction.
   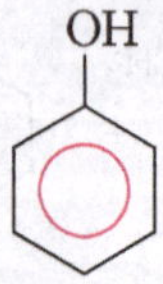
   $+ C_2H_5I \longrightarrow$ '*P*'
   Identify the product '*P*' is
   (a) $C_6H_5OC_2H_5$ (b) $C_2H_5OC_2H_5$
   (c) $C_6H_5OC_6H_5$ (d) C_6H_5I

6. Choose the incorrect match.
   (a) $PhCH_2Cl$ + Sodium methoxide $\longrightarrow$ Ether
   (b) $CH_2{=}CHCH_2Cl$ + Sodium methoxide $\longrightarrow$ Ether
   (c) $CH_2{=}CHCl$ + Sodium methoxide $\longrightarrow$ Ether
   (d) $CH_3CH_2CH_2Cl$ + Sodium methoxide $\longrightarrow$ Ether

7. Select the incorrect statement about alkoxy mercuration-demercuration of alkenes.
   (a) It involves carbocation as the intermediate.
   (b) It involves no rearrangement.
   (c) It involves addition of water according to Markownikoff's rule.
   (d) Identical regiochemistry is seen in product.

8. Which of the following is the nucleophile in the following reaction?
   $$CH_3OH + CH_2N_2 \longrightarrow CH_3OCH_3 + N_2$$
   (a) CH_3OCH_3 (b) N_2
   (c) CH_3OH (d) CH_2N_2

9. Consider the following statements.
   Statements I *t*-butyl methyl ether is not prepared by the reaction of *t*-butyl bormide with sodium ethoxide.
   Statement II Sodium methoxide is a strong nucleophile.
   In the light of the above statements, choose the correct answer from the options given below.
   (a) Both Statement I and Statement II are false.
   (b) Statement I is true, but Statement II is false.
   (c) Statement I is false, but Statement II is true.
   (d) Both Statement I and Statement II are true.

10. Select the incorrect statement(s) about following reaction.
    $$2ROH \xrightarrow{H^+} ROR + H_2O$$
    (a) It is an example of S_N reaction in which protonated alcohol is the substrate and second molecule of alcohol is the nucleophile.
    (b) This reaction can be S_N1 if protonated alcohol loses water before attack of second molecule.
    (c) This reaction can be S_N2 if alcohol is 1°.
    (d) It is an elimination reaction.

11. What is the major product formed when ethanol is dehydrated with conc. H_2SO_4 at 413 K?
    (a) Ethene (b) Methoxy methane
    (c) Methoxy ethane (d) Ethoxy ethane

12. Choose the correct match of reactants regarding the given products.
    (a) 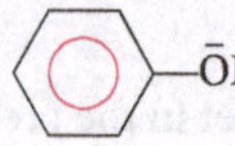 $\bar{O}Na^+ + C_2H_5I \longrightarrow$ Phenol
    (b) 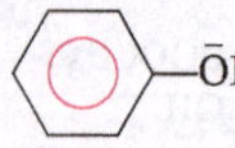 $\bar{O}Na^+ + C_2H_5I \longrightarrow$ Ethyl phenyl alcohol
    (c) 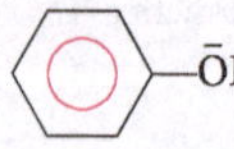 $\bar{O}Na^+ + C_2H_5I \longrightarrow$ Phenetole
    (d)  $\bar{O}Na^+ + C_2H_5I \longrightarrow$ Anisole

13. Select the incorrect statement about the following reaction of ether synthesis.

$$RX + R'ONa \longrightarrow ROR' + NaX$$

(a) It follows S_N2 mechanism.
(b) Alkyl halide (RX) should be 2° or 3° while alkoxide ($RO^- Na^+$) should be 1°.
(c) Alkyl halide should be 1° while alkoxide should be 2° or 3°.
(d) 2° and 3° alkyl halides may undergo E2 elimination in the presence of a strong base to form alkenes.

14. Consider the following compounds.
(i) C_2H_5ONa (ii) KI
(iii) KCl (iv) $(CH_3CO)_2O$
(v) CH_3CH_2Cl
How many of them are added to ether to test its purity?
(a) 1 (b) 4
(c) 2 (d) 3

15. When ethyl hydrogen sulphate is heated with excess of ethyl alcohol at 410 K, the product obtained is
(a) ethane
(b) ethylene
(c) diethylether
(d) diethyl sulphate

16. Consider the following reactions.

(i) $(CH_3)_2CH\text{—}CH_2Br \xrightarrow{C_2H_5OH} (CH_3)_2CH\text{—}CH_2OC_2H_5 + HBr$

(ii) $CH_3\text{—}C(CH_3)_2\text{—}ONa + CH_3Br \longrightarrow CH_3\text{—}O\text{—}C(CH_3)_2\text{—}CH_3 + NaBr$

The mechanisms of reactions (i) and (ii) are respectively
(a) S_N1 and S_N2 (b) S_N1 and S_N1
(c) S_N2 and S_N2 (d) S_N2 and S_N1

17. An ether is more volatile than an alcohol having the same molecular formula. This is due to
(a) dipolar character of ethers
(b) alcohols having resonance structure
(c) intermolecular hydrogen bonding in ethers
(d) intermolecular hydrogen bonding in alcohols

18. In the following reaction, final product *P* is

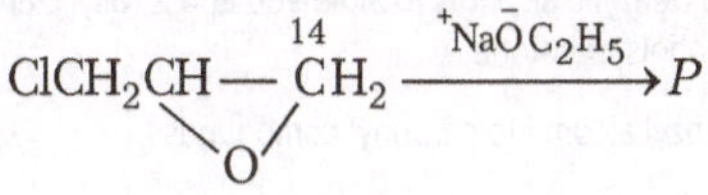

(a) $ClCH_2\overset{14}{C}HCH_2OC_2H_5$ (with OH on the labelled carbon)
(b) $ClCH_2CH\overset{14}{C}H_2ONa$ (with OC_2H_5 on CH)
(c) 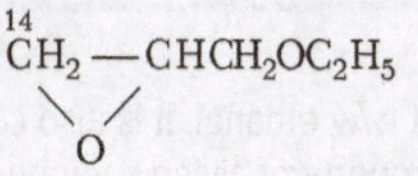
(d) 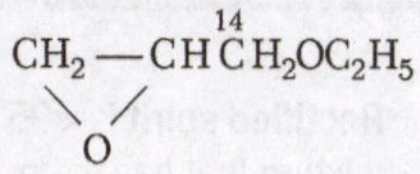

19. What are the products of the reaction given below?

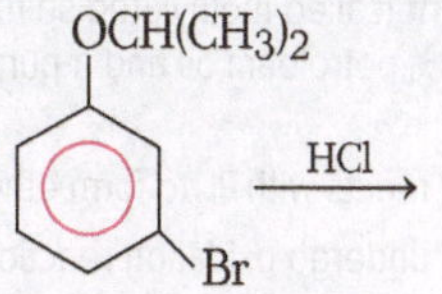

(a) $(CH_3)_2CHCl$ and *m*-bromophenol
(b) $(CH_3)_2CHCl$ and *m*-bromochlorobenzene
(c) $(CH_3)_2CHOH$ and *m*-bromophenol
(d) $(CH_3)_2CHOH$ and *m*-bromochlorobenzene

20. Consider the following compounds.
(i) 1-methoxy butane
(ii) 1-methoxy-2-methylpropane
(iii) 2-methoxy-2-methylpropane
(iv) Methoxybenzene
(v) Di-*tert*-butyl ether
How many of them yields methanol as one of the products on reaction with cold hydroidic acid?
(a) 4 (b) 2
(c) 3 (d) 1

21. Which of the following reaction is corretly match with the given product?

(a) Ethylene glycol 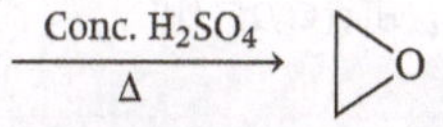

(b) Ethylene glycol 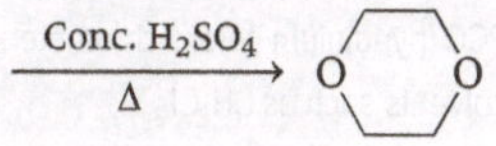

(c) Ethylene glycol $\xrightarrow[\Delta]{\text{Conc. } H_2SO_4}$ CHO—CHO

(d) Ethylene glycol $\xrightarrow[\Delta]{\text{Conc. } H_2SO_4} HOCH_2CH_2OCH_2CH_2OH$

22. Ether is a good solvent for Grignard reagent. Which property makes it a good solvent?
(a) It acts as a base towards acidic magnesium.
(b) It makes H-bonding with Grignard reagent.
(c) It acts as an acid towards basic magnesium.
(d) It is an electron rich species.

NEET Exclusive EXTRA BYTES

- **Rectified spirit** is ≈95 per cent *w/w* ethanol. It is also called **95% alcohol.** It is a mixture of 95% alcohol and 5% water (bp 351.15 K). A liquid mixture that has the peculiar property of giving a vapour of the same composition is called an **azeotrope** or a **constant-boiling mixture.** Thus, rectified spirit contains two components and is a **binary azeotrope.**
- **Denatured spirit** (called methylated spirit) is 95% rectified spirit and 5% methanol. Mineralised methylated spirit is 90% rectified spirit, 9% methanol and 1% petroleum oil and a purple dye (for distinction). 100% ethyl alcohol is called absolute alcohol and is obtained from rectified spirit.
- Ethylene glycol reacts with PI_3 to form ethylene. While it undergoes dehydration in the presence of anhyd. $ZnCl_2$ to form acetaldehyde.
- Ethylene glycol undergo oxidation reaction in the presence of dil. HNO_3 to form oxalic acid while in the presence of $KMnO_4/H^+$ or $K_2Cr_2O_7/H^+$ to form formic acid.
- When a pinacol such as 2,3-dimethyl butane-2, 3-diol is heated with conc. H_2SO_4, it undergoes dehydration with migration of methyl group to the adjacent carbon to form *tert*-butyl methyl ketone called the pinacolone.

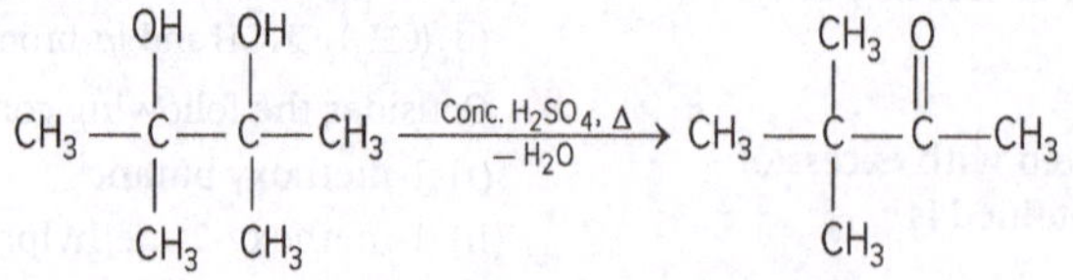

Pinacol Pinacolone

It is called pinacol-pinacolone rearrangement.

Different Oxidising Agents

S. No.	Oxidising agents	Conversion
1.	Cu at 570 K	1° alcohol to aldehyde; 2° alcohol to ketone, 3° alcohol to alkene
2.	MnO_4^- / H^+ or $Cr_2O_7^{2-} / H^+$	1° alcohol to carboxylic acid 2° alcohol to ketone 2° alcohol is also oxidised to ketone by CrO_3 in acetic acid
3.	PCC (pyridinium chloro chromate : $C_5H_5\overset{\oplus}{N}HCrO_3^{\ominus}$) PCC is soluble in non-polar solvents such as CH_2Cl_2	1° alcohol to aldehyde and 2° alcohol to ketone
4.	PDC (pyridinium dichromate $(C_5H_5NH)_2^{2+}\ Cr_2O_7^{2-}$	1° alcohol to aldehyde 2° alcohol to ketone
5.	H_2CrO_4 (chromic acid)	1° alcohol to carboxylic acid
6.	$CrO_3 \cdot H_2SO_4$/acetone	2° alcohol to ketone
7.	Jones reagent (chromic acid in aqueous acetone solution)	1° alcohol to carboxylic acid and 2° alcohol to ketone without affecting (C $=$C) bond
8.	MnO_2	1° allylic and benzylic alcohols to aldehyde and 2° allylic and benzylic alcohols to ketone
9.	N_2O_4 in $CHCl_3$ (Field's method)	1° and 2° benzyl alcohol to carbonyl compounds
10.	Collin's reagent (CrO_3 in pyridine) neutral $KMnO_4$, 71% HNO_3	1° alcohol to carboxylic acid and 2° alcohol to ketone

GEARING UP FOR NEET

1. Which of the following alkyl halide is hydrolysed to alcohol to a maximum extent?
(a) CH_3F (b) CH_3Cl (c) CH_3I (d) CH_3Br

2. In the hydration of an alkene carbocation is formed from
(a) carbanion (b) oxonium ion
(c) hydroxide ion (d) hydride ion

3. In the following reaction,

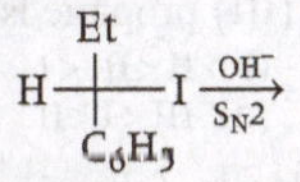

(a) retains configuration (b) inverts configuration
(c) is a racemic mixture (d) is a *meso*-compound

4. Which of the following statement is correct for hydration of alkene?
(a) It follows S_N1 mechanism.
(b) It is an irreversible process.
(c) It takes place through carbocation mechanism.
(d) It follows all of the above.

5. Which of the following has lowest boiling point?
(a) *p*-nitrophenol (b) *m*-nitrophenol
(c) *o*-nitrophenol (d) Phenol

6. Phenol reacts with excess of bromine water to produce
(a) *o*-bromophenol
(b) *p*-bromophenol
(c) 2,4,6-tribromophenol
(d) mixture of *o*- and *p*-bromophenol

7. Phenol $\xrightarrow{NaNO_2/H_2SO_4} B \xrightarrow{H_2O} C \xrightarrow{NaOH} D.$

Name of the reaction is
(a) Liebermann's reaction (b) Phthalein fusion test
(c) Reimer-Tiemann reaction
(d) Schotten-Baumann reaction

8. Addition of methanol to 2-methylpropene in the presence of conc. H_2SO_4 gives
(a) *tert*-butyl alcohol (b) *tert*-butyl methyl ether
(c) di-*tert*-butyl ether (d) dimethyl ether

9. Which of the following phenols has the largest pK_a value (i.e. least acidic)?

(a) 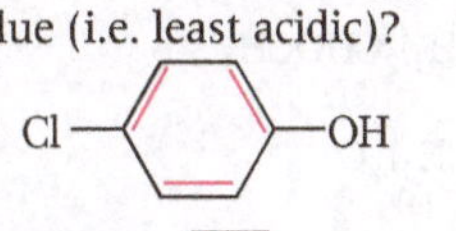 (b) 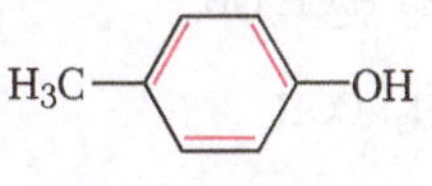

(c) 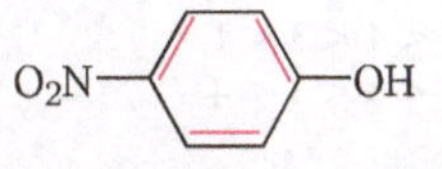 (d) 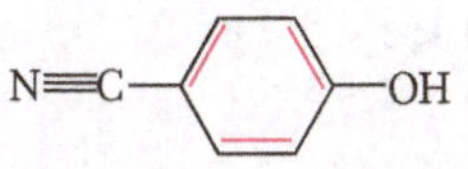

10. In the following reaction, (X) is

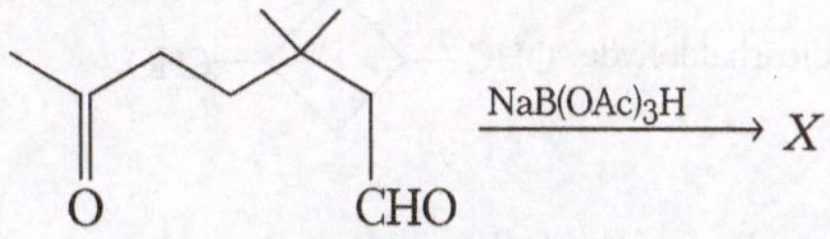

(a) 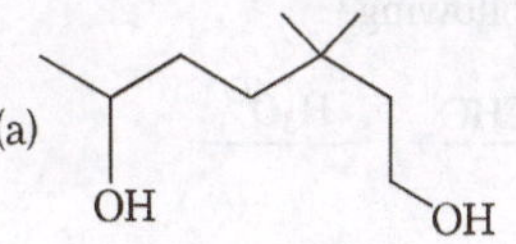 (b) 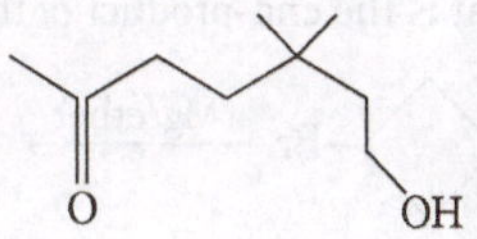

(c) 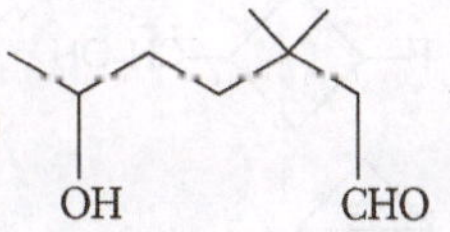 (d) 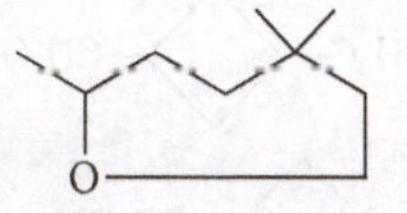

11. 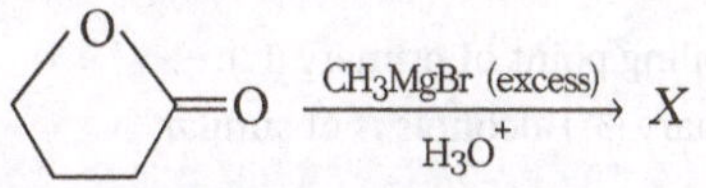

X is

(a) 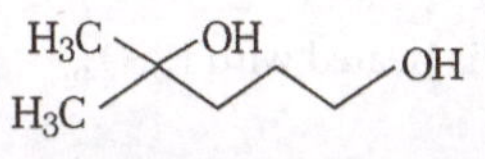 (b) 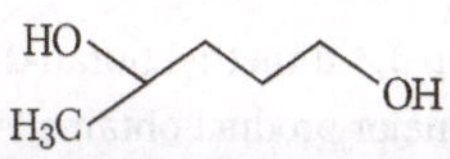

(c) 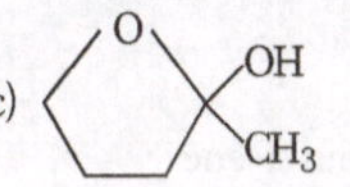 (d) 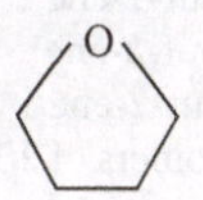

12. 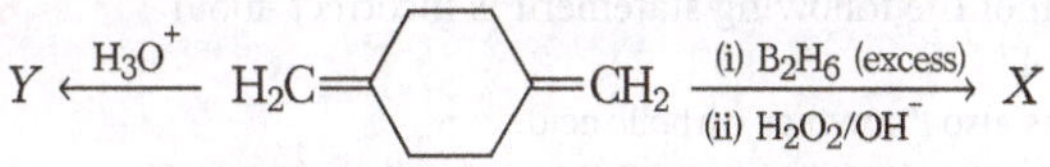

X and Y respectively in the above reaction are

(a) 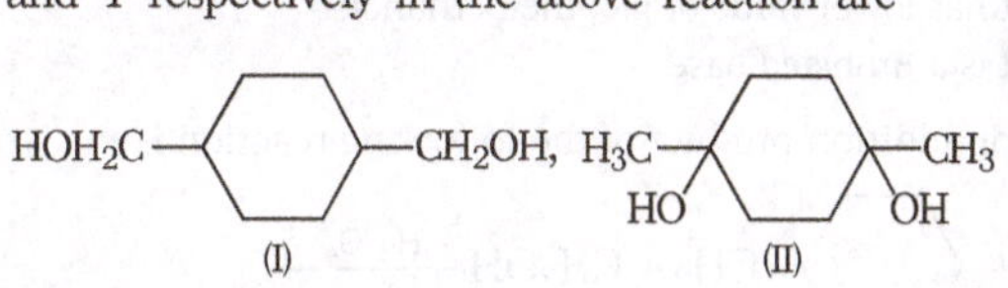

(b) II and I
(c) I in both case
(d) II in both case

13. Identify the product 'A' with its IUPAC name formed in the following reaction.

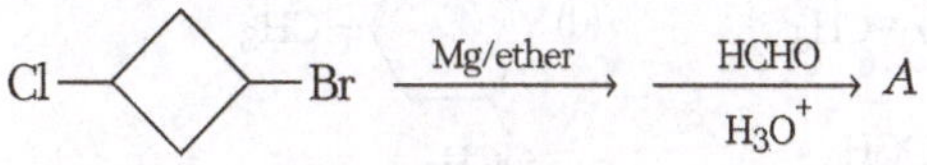

(a) (3-bromocyclobutyl) methanol, 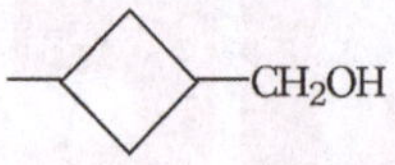

(b) (3-chlorocyclobutyl) methanol, 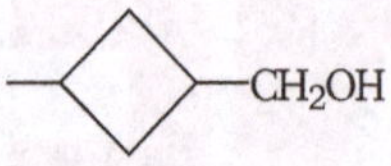

(c) 1,3-cyclobutane dimethanol 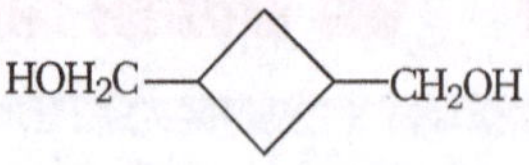

(d) Cyclobutyl-1,4-dicarbaldehyde, 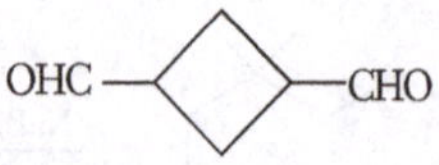

14. What is the end-product of the following?

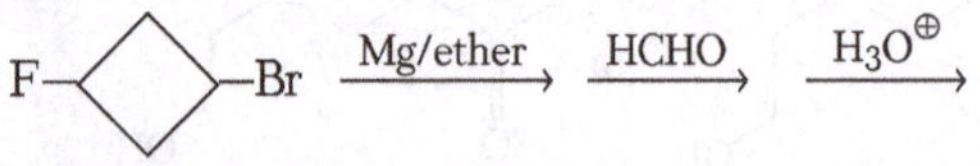

(a) 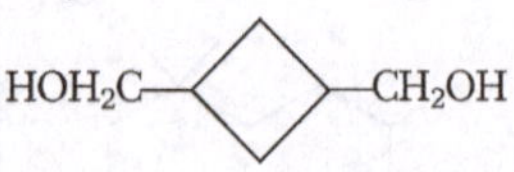 (b) 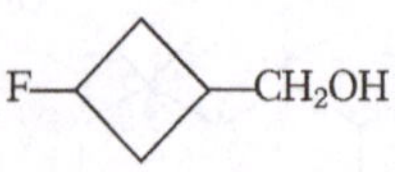

(c) 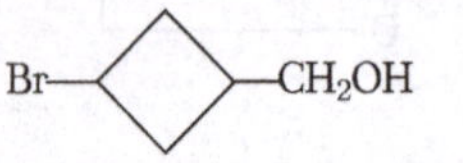 (d) 

15. The correct order of boiling point of primary (1°), secondary (2°) and tertiary (3°) alcohols is of similar molecular mass.

(a) 1° > 2° > 3° (b) 2° > 1° > 3°
(c) 2° > 3° > 1° (d) 3° > 2° > 1°

16. When 3,3-dimethyl butan-2-ol is heated with H_2SO_4, the major product obtained is

(a) 3,3-dimethyl but-1-ene
(b) 3,3-dimethyl but-2-ene
(c) 2,3-dimethyl but-2-ene
(d) *cis* and *trans*-isomers of 2,3-dimethyl but-1-ene

17. Which of the following statement is incorrect about phenol?

(a) It is also known as carbolic acid.
(b) It can be obtained by acidification of sodium phenoxide.
(c) It has lower value of pK_a then ethanol.
(d) It is a Bronsted base.

18. Major addition product of the following reaction is

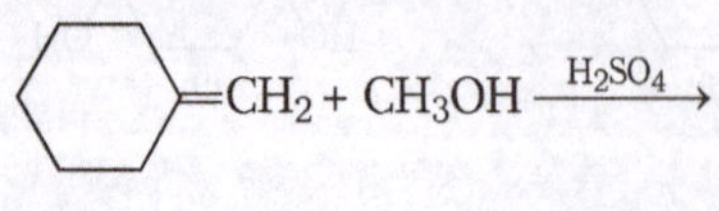

(a) 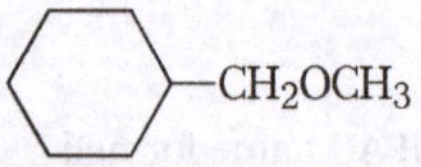 (b) 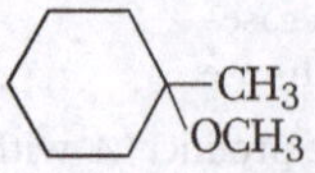

(c) 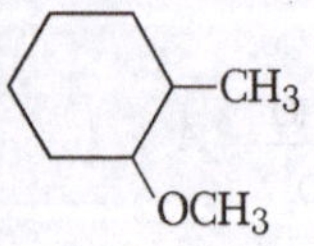 (d) 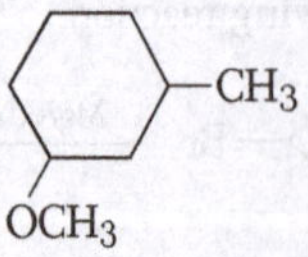

19. Ethanethiol (CH_3CH_2SH) is a gas at room temperature but ethanol is a liquid. The reason for this is

(a) the C—S—H bonds in ethanethiol are linear
(b) the C—O—H bonds in ethanol are linear
(c) ethanethiol has a higher boiling point
(d) it does not form intermolecular H-bond

20. Consider the following reactions.

$$(CH_3)_2CHOH \xrightarrow[I]{PBr_3} (CH_3)_2CHBr$$
$$(CH_3)_2CHOH \xrightarrow[II]{HBr + ZnCl_2} (CH_3)_2CHBr$$

These reactions are of the type

	I	II		I	II
(a)	S_N1	S_N2	(b)	S_N2	S_N1
(c)	S_N2	S_N2	(d)	S_N1	S_N1

21. Increasing order of dipole-moments of (I) ethanol, (II) methoxymethane and (III) propane is

(a) I < II < III (b) II < III < I
(c) III < II < I (d) III < I < II

22. Which product is obtained by the following esterification?

$$C_6H_5CH_2\overset{O}{\overset{\|}{C}}OH + CH_3CH_2\overset{18}{O}H \xrightarrow[Heat]{H^+} ?$$

(a) $C_6H_5CH_2\overset{O}{\overset{\|}{C}}OCH_2CH_3$

(b) $C_6H_5CH_2\overset{O}{\overset{\|}{C}}-\overset{18}{O}CH_2CH_3$

(c) $C_6H_5CH_2\overset{^{18}O}{\overset{\|}{C}}-\overset{18}{O}CH_2CH_3$

(d) $CH_3CH_2\overset{^{18}O}{\overset{\|}{C}}OCH_2C_6H_5$

23. $CH_2{=}CH\underset{OH}{\underset{|}{C}}HCH_2CH_2OH \xrightarrow{MnO_2} A$. The product A is

(a) $CH_2{=}CH\underset{O}{\underset{\|}{C}}CH_2CH_2OH$ (b) $CH_2{=}CH\underset{OH}{\underset{|}{C}}HCH_2CHO$

(c) $CH_2{=}CH\underset{O}{\underset{\|}{C}}CH_2CHO$ (d) $CH_2{=}CH\underset{O}{\underset{\|}{C}}CH_2\overset{O}{\overset{\|}{C}}OH$

24. The correct increasing order of boiling point of the given substance are the following substances in order of increasing boiling point.

$\underset{(1)}{CH_3CH_2CH_2CH_2OH}$, $\underset{(2)}{(CH_3)_2CHOCH_3}$

$\underset{(3)}{(CH_3)_3COH}$, $\underset{(4)}{(CH_3)_4C}$

(a) 1 < 3 < 2 < 4 (b) 2 < 4 < 3 < 1
(c) 4 < 2 < 3 < 1 (d) 2 < 3 < 1 < 4

25. In the following reaction which bonds are cleaved?

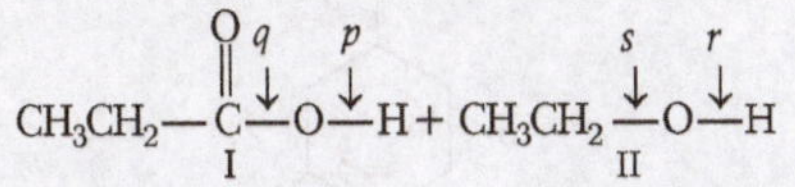

(a) bond p of I and s of II (b) bond q of I and r of II
(c) bond p of I and r of II (d) bond q of I and s of II

26. What is the major product 'Z' in the following sequence of reactions?

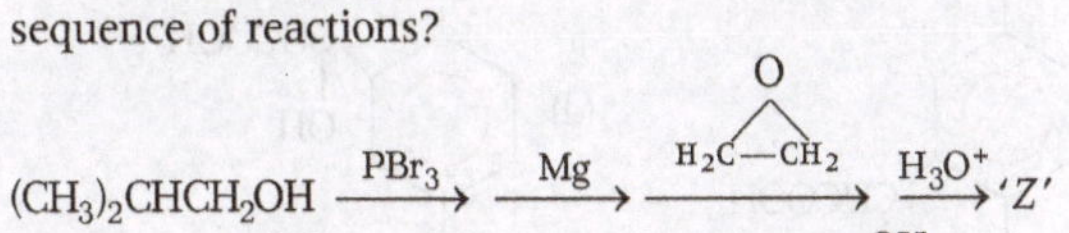

(a) $(CH_3)_2CH\underset{}{C}H(OH)\,CH_2CH_3$ (b) $(CH_3)_2CHCH_2\,CH(OH)\,CH_3$
(c) $(CH_3)_2CHCH_2CH_2OH$ (d) $(CH_3)_2CHCH_2CH_2CH_2OH$

27. 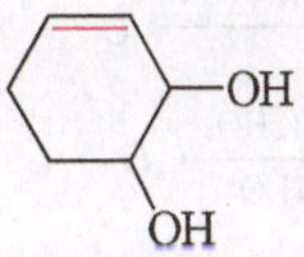

A. Identify product

A, in the given reaction.

(a) 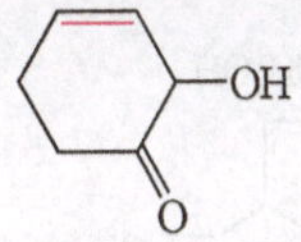

(b) 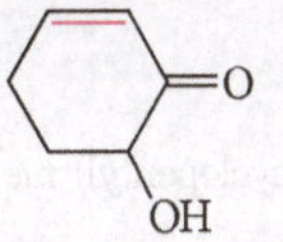

(c) 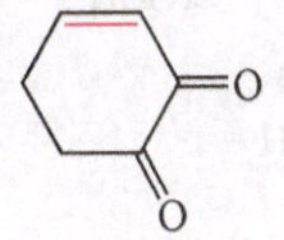

(d) 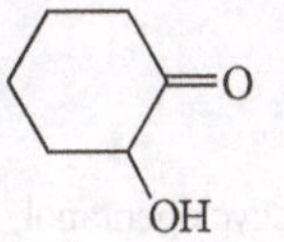

28. The correct order of dehydration of alcohols will be

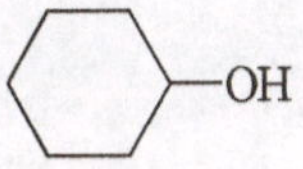

(I)

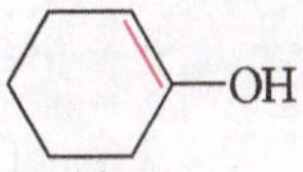

(II)

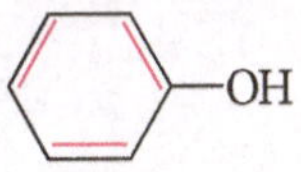

(III)

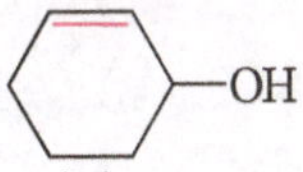

(IV)

(a) I < II < III < IV (b) I > II > III > IV
(c) III < II < I < IV (d) II < III < IV < I

29. Ester $A(C_4H_8O_2)$ + CH_3MgBr (2 parts) $\xrightarrow{H_3O^+}$ $C_4H_{10}O$ (Alcohol B)

Alcohol B reacts fastest with Lucas reagent. Hence, A and B are

(a) $CH_3COC_2H_5$, $(CH_3)_3COH$ (b) $HCOC_3H_7$, $(CH_3)_2CHOH$
(c) $CH_3COC_2H_5$, $(CH_3)_2CHOH$ (d) $HCOC_3H_7$, $(CH_3)_3COH$

30. The major product of the following reaction is

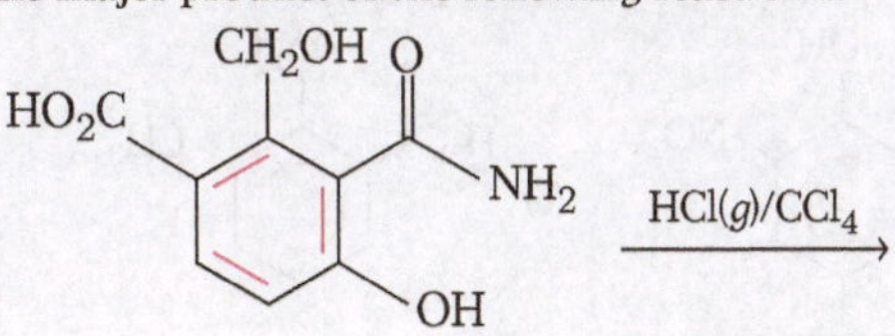

(a) 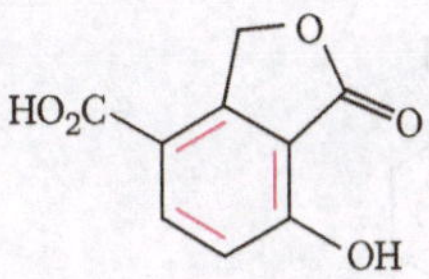

(b) 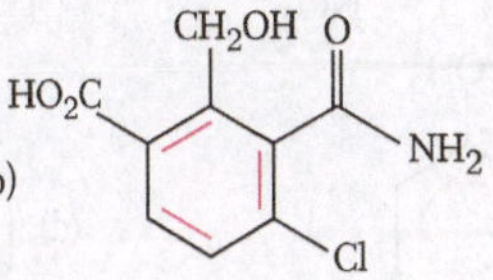

(c) 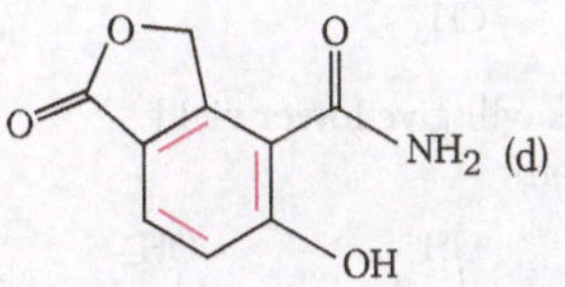

(d) 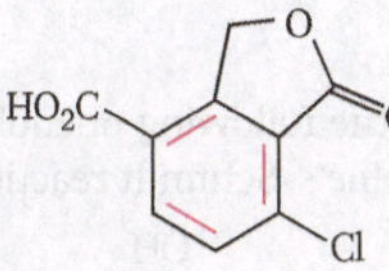

31 The structure of intermediate 'P' and product 'R' respectively, in the following reaction, are

Aniline $\xrightarrow[HCl]{NaNO_2}$ 'P' $\xrightarrow[Warm]{H_2O}$ Phenol + R + HCl

(a) 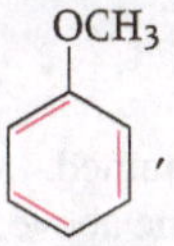

, N_2
(b) 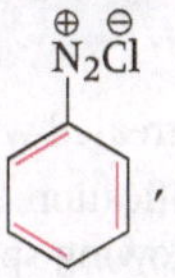

, N_2
(c) 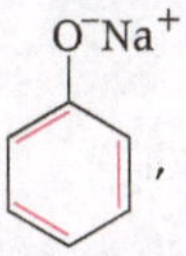

, H_2
(d) 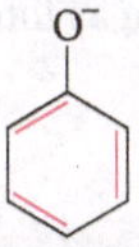

, H_2

32. Which of the following compound has maximum ionisation constant K_a?

(a) 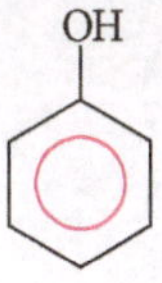

(b) 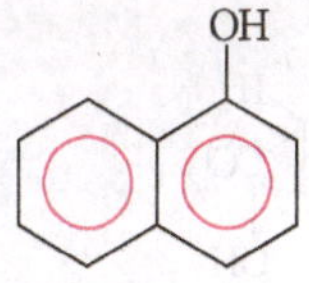

(c) 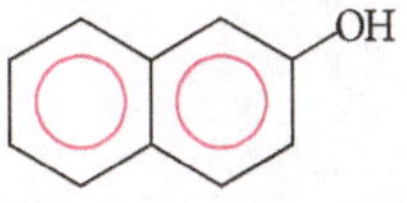

(d) 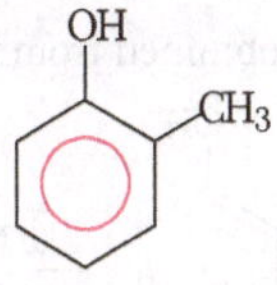

33. Which of the following has highest dipole moment?

(a) 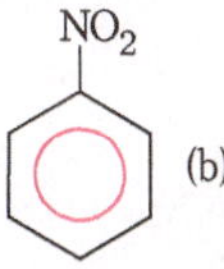

(b) 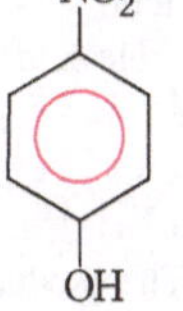

(c) 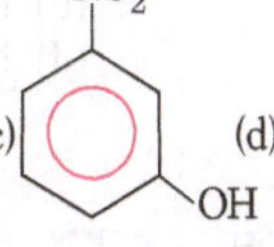

(d) 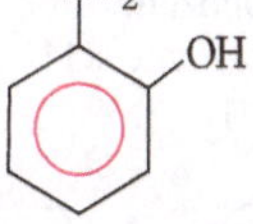

34. Which has maximum pK_a value in phenols?

(a) 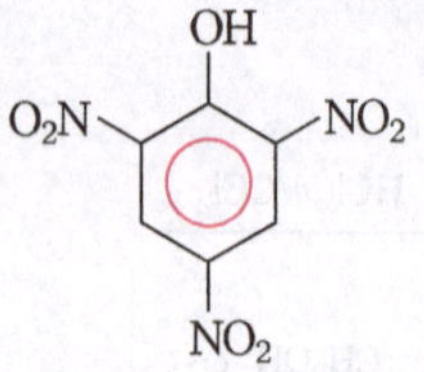 (b) 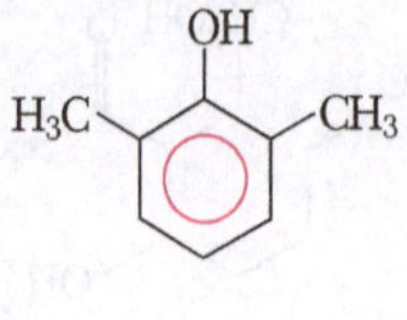

(c)  (d) 

35. Which of the following phenols will give lower yield during Kolbe's-Schmidt reaction?

(a)  (b)  (c)  (d) 

36. When phenol is treated with $CHCl_3$ and NaOH followed by acidification, salicylaldehyde is obtained. Which of the following species is involved in the above mentioned reaction as intermediates?

(a) 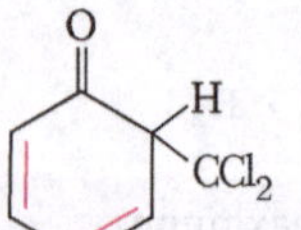 (b) 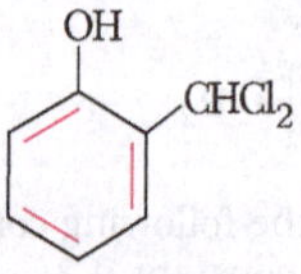

(c) 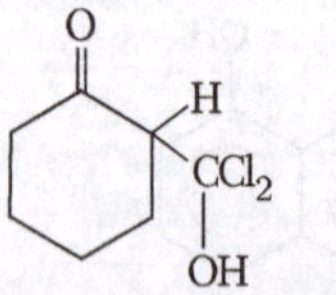 (d) 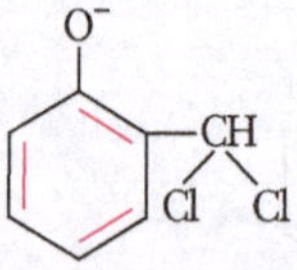

37. The product obtained from the following reaction is

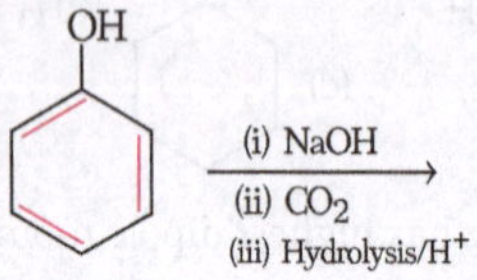

(a) benzene (b) toluene
(c) salicylic acid (d) benzoic acid

38. 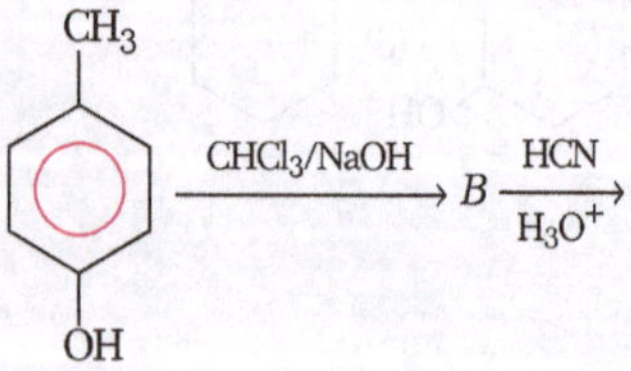 The product *C* is

A

(a) 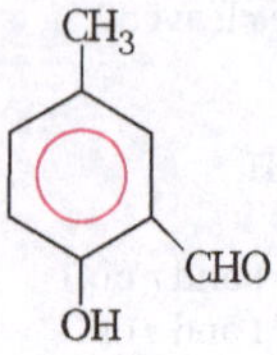 (b) 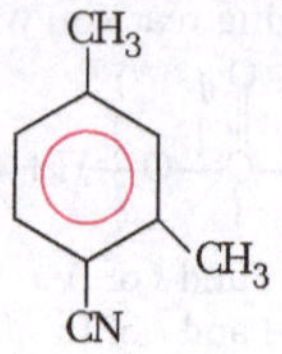

(c) 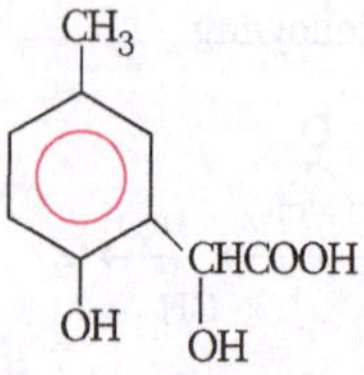 (d) 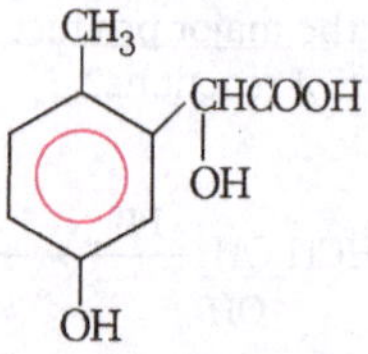

39. Write the IUPAC name and identify product '*D*' of the following reaction.

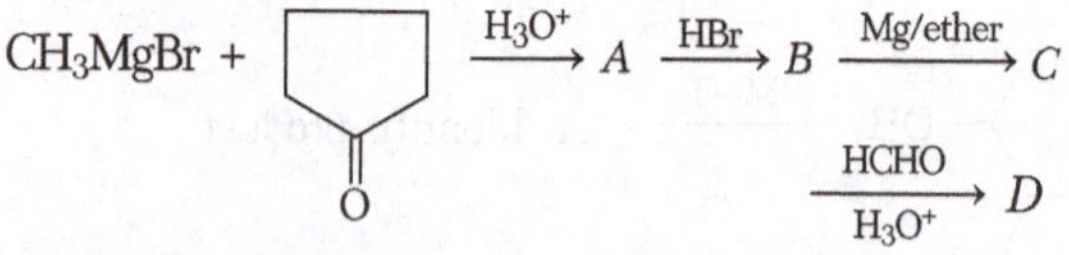

(a) (1-methylcyclopentyl) methanol 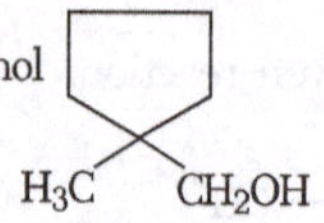

(b) (3-methylcyclopentyl) methanol 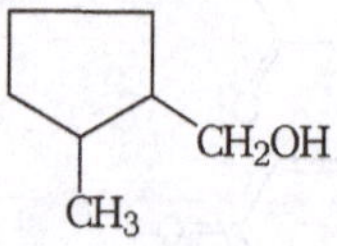

(c) 2,3-methylcyclopentanol, 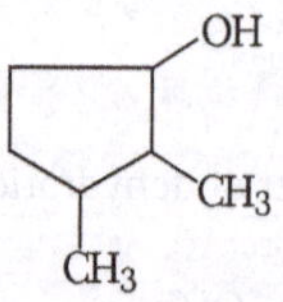

(d) Cyclohexylmethanol, 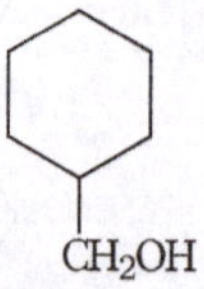

40. When phenol reacts with chloroform and with an alkali like NaOH, the compound formed is salicylaldehyde. If we use pyrene instead of chloroform, the product obtained is
(a) salicylic acid
(b) cyclohexanol
(c) phenolphthalein
(d) salicylaldehyde

41. 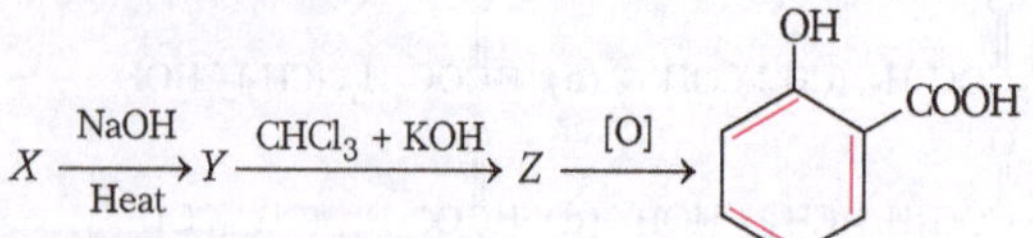

In the above reaction *X* is
(a) phenol (b) benzoic acid
(c) salicylaldehyde (d) carbonic acid

42. Which of the following is obtained on treating phenol with conc. HNO_3/H_2SO_4 mixture?

(a) 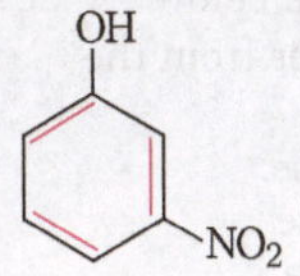 (b) 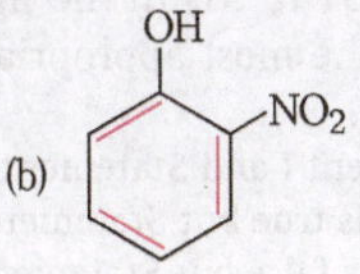

(c) 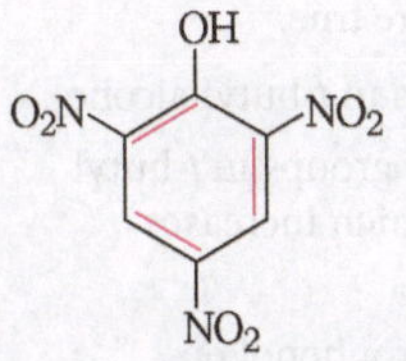 (d) 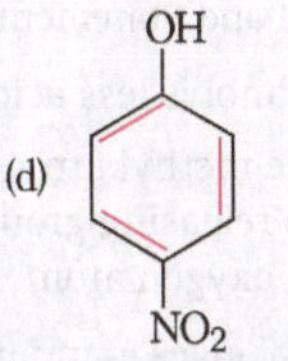

43. Oxiranes are cleaved under acidic and basic conditions because of

(a) decrease in bond-angle to 61.5° from normal tetrahedral angle of sp^3-hybridisation, i.e. 109.5°.

(b) strong, H^+ and OH^-

(c) formation of oxonium ion

(d) formation of carbocation

44. 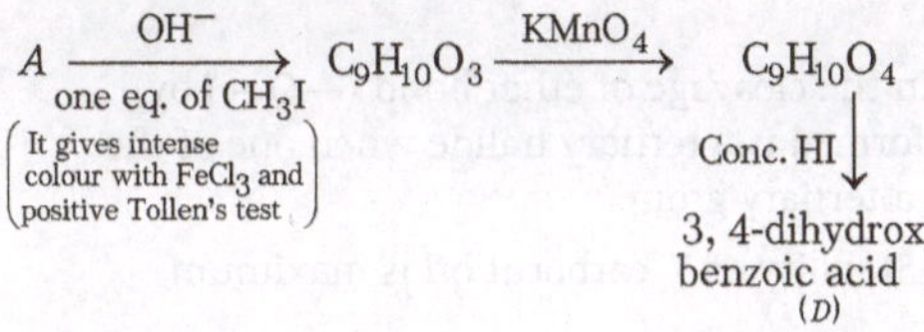

Here, *A* is

(a) 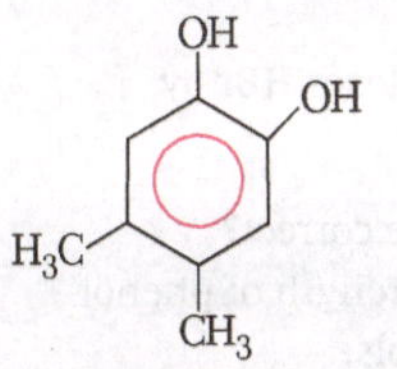 (b) 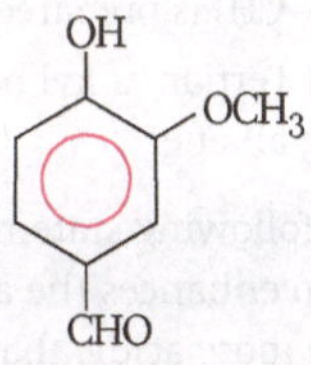

(c) 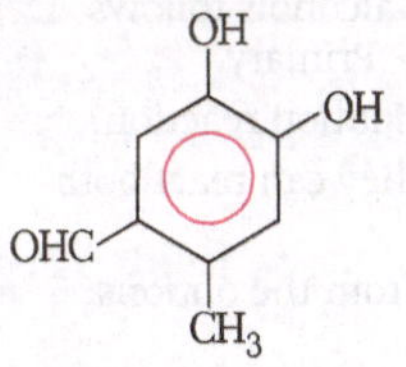 (d) 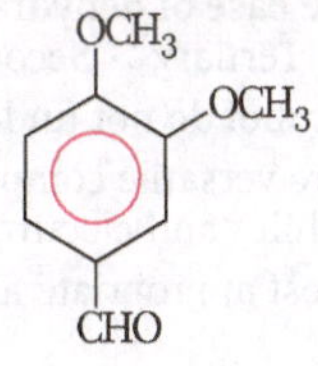

45. *n*-propyl alcohol and isopropyl alcohol can be distinguishes by

(a) PCl_5

(b) redcution

(c) oxidation with potassium dichromte

(d) ozonolysis

46. Phenol is heated with phthalic anhydride in the presence of conc.H_2SO_4. The product gives pink colour with alkali. The product is

(a) phenolphthalein

(b) bakelite

(c) salicylic acid

(d) fluorescein

47. Which one of the following ethers is the most unreactive towards cleavage with HBr?

(a) $C_6H_5OCH_2C_6H_5$

(b) $H_2C{=}CHCH_2OCH_2CH{=}CH_2$

(c) $C_6H_5OC_6H_5$

(d) $(CH_3)_3COC(CH_3)_3$

48. What is the product of the following reaction?

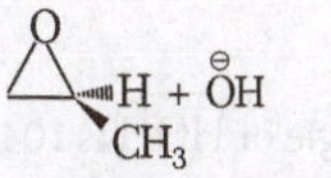

(a) A pure enantiomer of propan-1,2 diol

(b) Racemic mixture of propan-1,2-diol

(c) Unequal amount of enantiomers of propane-1, 2-diol

(d) Formation of propane-1,3-diol

49. Which of the following is the correct statement about the following reaction?

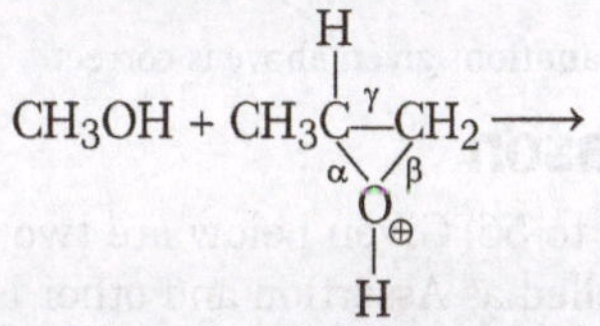

(a) α-bond is cleaved when product formed is $CH_3CH(OH)—CH_2OCH_3$

(b) β-bond is cleaved when product formed is $CH_3CH(OCH_3)—CH_2OH$

(c) α-bond is cleaved when product formed is $CH_3CH(OCH_3)—CH_2OH$

(d) β-bond is cleaved when product formed is $CH_3CH(OH)—CH_2OCH_3$

50. Select the incorrect statement from the following.

(a) Ethers are weakly polar compounds.

(b) Ethers have lower boiling points than the isomeric alcohols.

(c) Dipole moment of ether is the sum of the two polar C—O bonds with a substantial contribution from the two lone pairs of electrons.

(d) The cleavage of ethers take place with concentrated HI or HBr at low temperature.

51. Which of the following statements are incorrect?

A. The solubility of alcohols and phenols increases with increase in size of alkyl/aryl group.

B. Alcohols are versatile compounds.

C. Propanol and methoxymethane have comparable molecular mass but boiling point of propanol is less than methoxymethane.

D. The —OH group in alcohols and phenols is involved in intermolecular hydrogen bonding.

E. The boiling point of alcohols and phenols are higher in comparison to ethers of comparable molecular masses.

Choose the correct answer from the options given below.

(a) B, C, D and E
(b) A and C
(c) A, C, D and E
(d) B, C and D

52. In H_2O, there is bond-angle of $\widehat{HOH}$ is 104.5° due to repulsion, but in ether bond-angle $\widehat{ROR}$ is 110°. It is due to

(a) H is polar while *R* is non-polar
(b) H is non-polar while *R* is polar
(c) repulsion between the bulkier alkyl groups that almost counterbalances the effect of lone pair-lone pair interactions
(d) None of the explanations given above is correct

Assertion-Reason

Directions (Q.Nos. 53 to 56) Given below are two statements: one is labelled as Assertion and other is labelled as Reason.

(a) Both A and R are true R is the correct explanation of A.
(b) Both A and R are true but R is not the correct explanation of A.
(c) A is true but R is false.
(d) A is false but R is true.

53. **Assertion** (A) Sulphuric acid is used during the reaction of alcohols with KI in the conversion of an alcohol to the alkyl iodide.

Reason (R) H_2SO_4 being an oxidising agent, oxidises KI to I_2 before it is able to react with alcohols to form alkyl iodides.

54. **Assertion** (A) 2, 4, 6-trinitrophenol does not undergo substitution of the —OH group like butanol.

Reason (R) The C—O bond in 2,4,6-trinitrophenol have single bond character hence cannot be easily cleaved by a nucleophile.

55. **Assertion** (A) Methoxymethane and ethyl alcohol has comparable molecular weight but boiling point of ethyl alcohol is more than dimethyl ether.

Reason (R) Ethyl alcohol forms intermolecular H-bonding while methoxymethane forms intramolecular H-bonding.

56. **Assertion** (A) *o*-nitrophenol is less soluble in water than the *m* and *p*-isomers of nitrophenol.

Reason (R) *m*- and *p*-nitrophenols exist as associated molecules.

Statement Type Questions

Direction (Q. Nos. 57 to 61) In the light of the below statements, choose the most appropriate answer from the options given below.

(a) Both Statement I and Statement II are false.
(b) Statement I is true but Statement II is false.
(c) Statement I is false but Statement II is true.
(d) Both Statement I and Statement II are true.

57. **Statement I** Methanol is less acidic than *t*-butyl alcohol.

Statement II Three methyl attracting groups in *t*-butyl alcohol are electron releasing group which increases electron-density on oxygen atom.

58. **Statement I** Phenol gives *o*-and *p*-nitrophenol on nitration with conc. HNO_3 and H_2SO_4 mixture.

Statement II —OH group in phenol is *o*-and *p*-directing.

59. **Statement I** Phenol forms 2, 4, 6-tribromophenol on treatment with Br_2 in carbon disuplhide at 273 K.

Statement II In case of phenol the polarisation of bromine molecule takes place even in the presence of Lewis acid.

60. **Statement I** In the cleavage of ether bond (—O—) by HI, the halide formed is a tertiary halide when one of the alkyl groups is a tertiary group.

Statement II Stability of 3° carbocation is maximum.

61. **Statement I** Starting with $(CH_3)_3CBr$ and $CH_3\bar{O}\overset{+}{Na}$, $(CH_3)_3C—O—CH_3$ is prepared.

Statement II Tertiary alkyl bromide loses HBr by CH_3O^- forming alkene.

62. Which of the following statements are correct?

A. Nitro group enhances the acidic strength of phenol.
B. Cresols are more acidic than phenols.
C. The relative ease of dehydration of alcohols follows the order : Tertiary > Secondary > Primary
D. Tertiary alcohol do not undergo oxidation reaction.
E. Alcohols are versatile compound, they can react both as nucleophiles and electrophiles.

Choose the most appropriate answer from the options given below.

(a) A, C, D and E (b) B, C, D and E
(c) A, D and E (d) B, C and E

63. Which of the following statements are correct?

A. Among pentan-2-ol, 2-methyl butanol and 1-pentanol, pentan-2-ol gives the best yield of dialkyl ether when heated with trace of sulphuric acid.
B. Williamson synthesis used for the preparation of dimethyl ether follows S_N1 mechanism.
C. Anisole can be prepared by the action of methyl iodide and sodium phenoxide.

D. Ether is obtained from ethyl alcohol in presence of H_2SO_4 at 113 K.

E. In continuous etherification process, the intermediate is ethyl hydrogen sulphite.

Choose the most appropriate answer from the options given below.

(a) B and D (b) C and E
(c) A and C (d) A and D

64. Select the correct statements from the following.

A. Ethers form peroxides by free radical oxidation.
B. Ethers are used as industrial solvents for oils, resins guns etc.
C. An oxygen of ether group can only be found within an acyclic carbon chain.
D. The higher ethers are highly volatile and flammable.
E. The miscibility of ethers with water resembles those of alcohols having the same molecular mass.

Choose the correct answer from the options given below.

(a) A, B and D (b) B, C and E
(c) A, B and E (d) B, D and E

65. Which of the following statements are not correct?

A. Aldehydes and ketones on catalytic reduction by dehydrogenation give primary and secondary alcohol respectively.
B. Alkyl halides on reaction with alcoholic potash gives alcohol.
C. Aldehydes on reaction with Grignard's reagent gives primary or secondary alcohol.
D. Alkenes reacts with water in presence of acid as catalyst to form alcohols.
E. Acetone reacts with sodium borohydride to produce 1° alcohol.

Choose the most appropriate answer from the options given below.

(a) A, C and E (b) A, B and D
(c) B and D (d) B and E

Species Selection Type Questions

66. Consider the following species.

(i) B_2H_6 (ii) H_2O (iii) OH^- (iv) $NaBH_4$
(v) $LiAlH_4$ (vi) H_2O_2 (vii) $Hg(OAc)_2$

Total number of species that will be used to convert propene to 1-propanol are

(a) 3 (b) 4
(c) 5 (d) 2

67. Consider the following compounds,

(i) 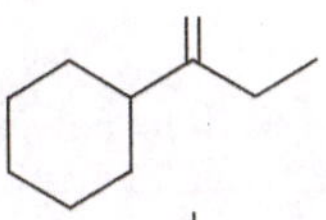
(ii) 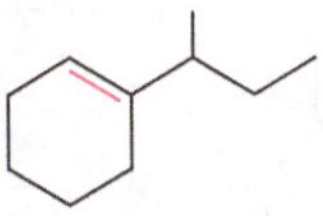
(iii) 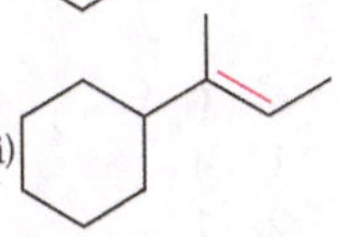
(iv) 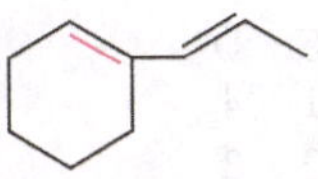
(v) 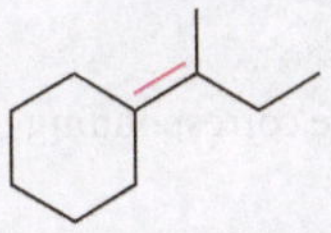
(vi) 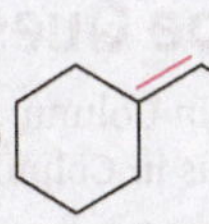
(vii) 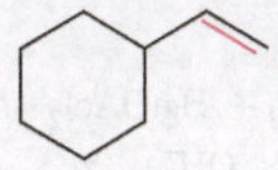

How many of them will be formed as a product by dehydration of

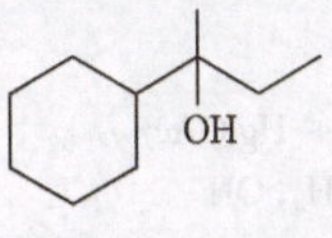 is

(a) 4 (b) 2 (c) 3 (d) 5

68. Consider the following reagents,

(i) $KMnO_4$ (ii) NaOH
(iii) $K_2Cr_2O_7$ (iv) H_2SO_4
(v) MnO_2

How many of them are suitable for converting benzyl alcohol into benzaldehyde?

(a) 2 (b) 3 (c) 1 (d) 4

69. Consider the following compounds.

(i) 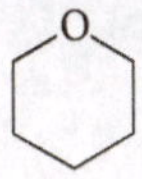
(ii) 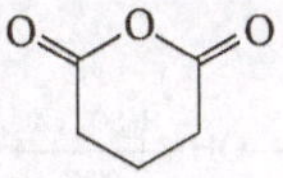
(iii) 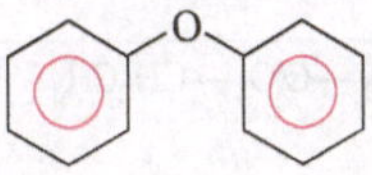
(iv) 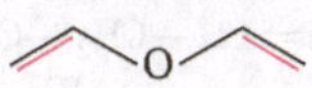
(v) 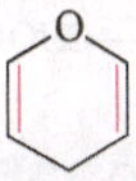
(vi) 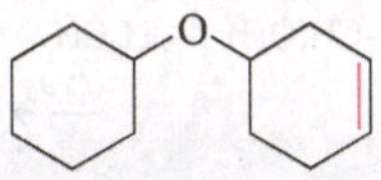
(vii) 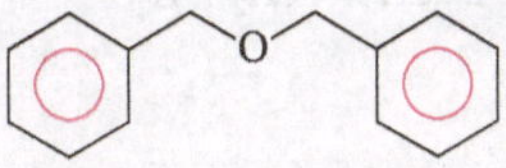

How many of them represent the structure of an ether?

(a) 4 (b) 6 (c) 5 (d) 3

70. Consider the following compounds.

(i) 2,2-dimethylpropan-1-ol
(ii) 2-methoxy propane
(iii) 2-methyl propan-1-ol
(iv) 2-methyl propan-2-ol
(v) 1-methoxy propane

How many of them are the isomer of diethyl ether?

(a) 1 (b) 4 (c) 2 (d) 3

71. Consider the following compounds.

(i) Bromobenzene (ii) Ethyl alcohol
(iii) Phenol (iv) Ethyl bromide
(v) Ethane

How many of them are formed when ethyl phenyl ether boiled with conc. hydrobromic acid?

(a) 1 (b) 3 (c) 2 (d) 4

Matching Type Questions

72. Match the species in Column I with the corresponding method of synthesis in Column II.

Column I	Column II
A. $(CH_3)_3CCH(OH)CH_3$	1. $(CH_3)_3CCH{=}CH_2 + Hg(OAc)_2 \cdot THF \cdot H_2O/NaBH_4, OH^-$
B. $(CH_3)_2CHC(OH)(CH_3)_2$	2. $(CH_3)_3CCH{=}CH_2 + H_3O^+$
C. $(CH_3)_3CCH_2CH_2OH$	3. $(CH_3)_3CCH{=}CH_2 + Hg(OAc)_2 \cdot THF \cdot CH_3OH/NaBH_4, OH^-$
D. $(CH_3)_3CCH(OCH_3)CH_3$	4. $(CH_3)_3CCH{=}CH_2 + BH_3 \cdot THF / H_2O_2, OH^-$

Codes

	A	B	C	D		A	B	C	D
(a)	4	1	2	3	(b)	1	2	4	3
(c)	3	4	1	2	(d)	4	3	2	1

73 Match the reaction in Column I with the product given in Column II.

Column I	Column II
A. $CH_3—CH_2—OH \xrightarrow[443K]{H_2SO_4, \Delta}$	1. CH_3CHO
B. $CH_3—CH{=}CH—CH_2—OH \xrightarrow{PCC}$	2. $CH_3—C(O)—CH_2CH_3$
C. $CH_3—CH(OH)—CH_2CH_3 \xrightarrow{CrO_3}$	3. $CH_3—CH{=}CH—CHO$
D. $CH_3—CH_2—OH \xrightarrow[573 K]{Cu}$	4. $CH_2{=}CH_2 + H_2O$

Codes

	A	B	C	D		A	B	C	D
(a)	2	1	4	3	(b)	3	4	1	2
(c)	4	1	2	3	(d)	4	3	2	1

74. Match the mixtures (in Column I) with the suitable reagents properties (in Column II) to distinguish.

Column I	Column II
A. 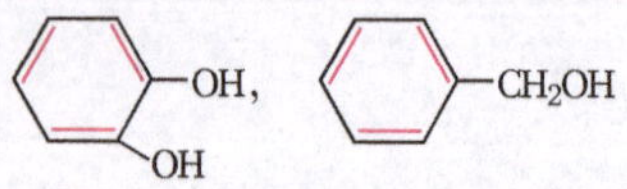	1. Boiling points
B. 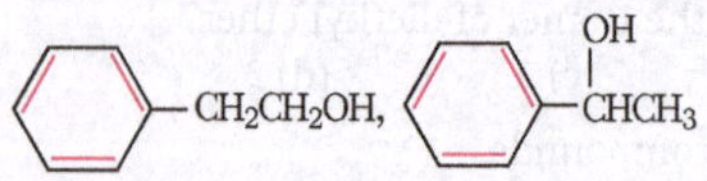	2. Neutral $FeCl_3$
C. 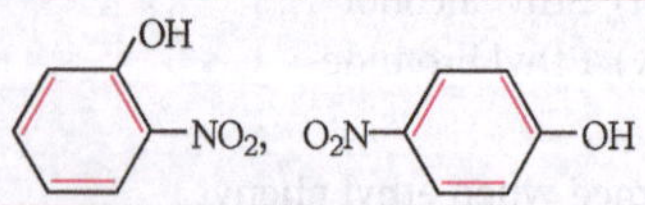	3. Iodoform test
D. 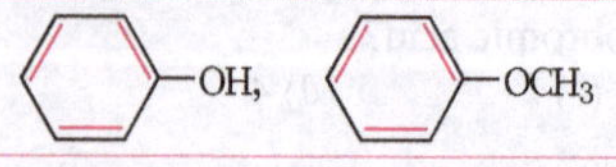	4. Oxidation by $KMnO_4$

Codes

	A	B	C	D
(a)	4	3	2	1
(b)	4	3	1	2
(c)	2	3	1	4
(d)	3	2	4	1

75. Match the reacting species with phenol (in Column I) with the name of reaction (in Column II) and choose the correct option.

Column I	Column II
A. Phenol + $CHCl_3$ + KOH $\longrightarrow$	1. Friedel-Craft's reaction
B. Phenol + NaOH + $CO_2 \longrightarrow$	2. Phthalein test
C. Phenol + Phthalic anhydride $\xrightarrow{Conc.\ H_2SO_4}$	3. Kolbe's reaction
D. Phenol + NaOH $\xrightarrow{CH_3Cl/AlCl_3}$	4. Reimer-Tiemann reaction

Codes

	A	B	C	D
(a)	1	2	3	4
(b)	2	1	3	4
(c)	4	3	2	1
(d)	3	4	1	2

76. Match the structures of the compounds given in Column I with the name of the compounds given in Column II.

Column I	Column II
A. 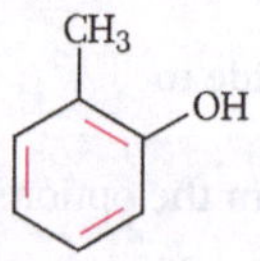	1. Hydroquinone
B. 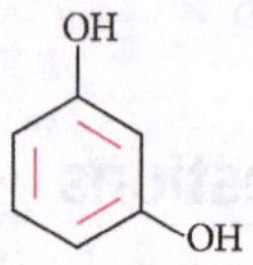	2. *o*-cresol
C. 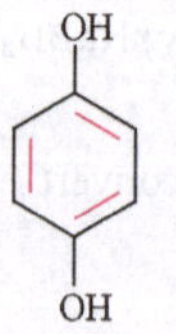	3. Resorcinol
D. 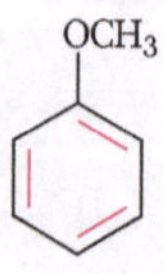	4. Anisole

Codes

	A	B	C	D		A	B	C	D
(a)	2	3	1	4	(b)	3	2	1	4
(c)	4	1	2	3	(d)	3	4	2	1

77. Match the species given in Column I with the corresponding properties given in Column II.

Column I	Column II
A. CH_3OH	1. Gives ketone on reaction with Cu
B. CH_3CH_2OH	2. Gives white ppt. with Lucas reagent immediately
C. $(CH_3)_2CHOH$	3. Cannot be synthesised using Grignard's reagent
D. $(CH_3)_3COH$	4. Gives iodoform test

Codes

	A	B	C	D
(a)	3	4	1	2
(b)	2	3	4	1
(c)	4	1	2	3
(d)	3	1	4	2

78 Match the starting materials given in Column-I with the products formed by these (Column II) in the reaction with HI and choose the correct answer using the code given below :

Column I	Column II
A. $CH_3—O—CH_3$	1. 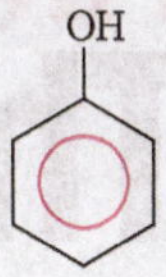 $+ CH_3I$
B. 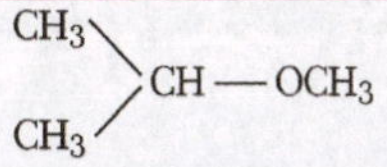	2. 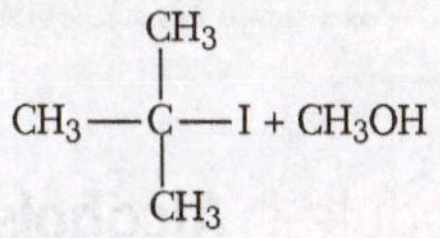
C. 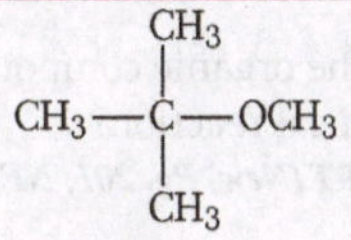	3. 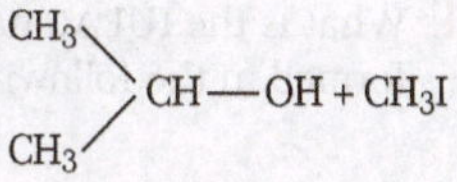
D. 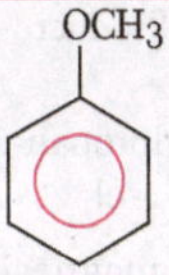	4. $CH_3OH + CH_3I$

Codes

	A	B	C	D
(a)	4	3	2	1
(b)	3	4	1	2
(c)	3	4	2	1
(d)	4	3	1	2

Final Check Through PYQs

Module-I Alcohols (Part I)

1. What is the IUPAC name of the organic compound formed in the following chemical reaction?
[NCERT (New) Pg. 201, NEET 2021]

$$\text{Acetone} \xrightarrow[\text{(ii) } H_2O,\ H^+]{\text{(i) } C_2H_5MgBr,\ \text{dry ether}} \text{Product}$$

(a) 2-methylbutan-2-ol (b) 2-methylpropan-2-ol
(c) pentan-2-ol (d) pentan-3-ol

2. Reaction between acetone and methyl magnesium chloride followed by hydrolysis will give
[NCERT (New) Pg. 201, NEET 2020]

(a) *iso*-propyl alcohol (b) *sec*-butyl alcohol
(c) *tert*-butyl alcohol (d) *iso*-butyl alcohol

3. $CH_3CH_2CH{=}CH_2 \xrightarrow[H_2O,H_2O_2,OH^-]{B_2H_6} Z$

What is Z? **[NCERT (New) Pg. 200, NEET (Oct.) 2020]**

(a) $CH_3CH_2CH_2CH_2OH$ (b) $CH_3CH_2\underset{\displaystyle OH}{\underset{|}{C}}HCH_3$
(c) $CH_3CH_2CH_2CHO$ (d) $CH_3CH_2CH_2CH_3$

Module-II Alcohols (Part II) Chemical Reactions of Alcohols

4. Which one of the following alcohols reacts instantaneously with Lucas reagent? **[NEET 2024]**

(a) $CH_3{-}CH_2{-}CH_2{-}CH_2OH$
(b) $CH_3{-}CH_2{-}\underset{\displaystyle CH_3}{\underset{|}{CH}}{-}OH$
(c) $CH_3{-}\underset{\displaystyle CH_3}{\underset{|}{CH}}{-}CH_2OH$
(d) $CH_3{-}\underset{\displaystyle CH_3}{\overset{\displaystyle CH_3}{\overset{|}{\underset{|}{C}}}}{-}OH$

5. Major products A and B formed in the following reaction sequence, are **[NEET 2024]**

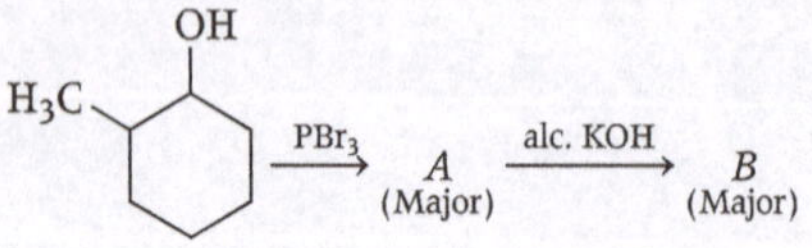

(a) $A =$ 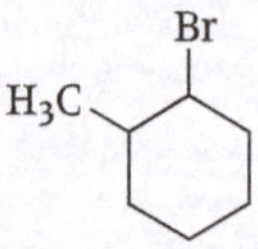 $: B =$ 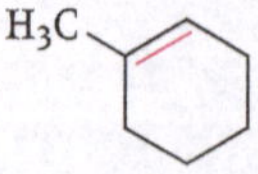

(b) $A =$ 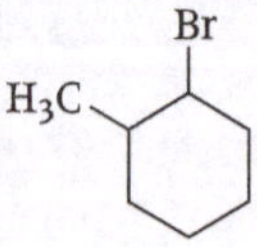 $: B =$ 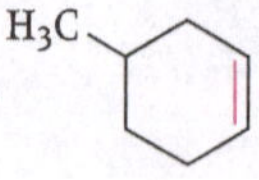

(c) $A =$ 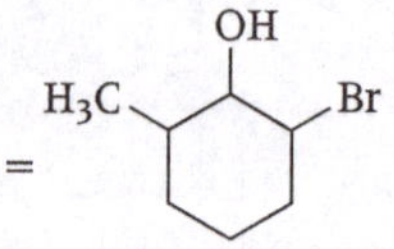 $: B =$ 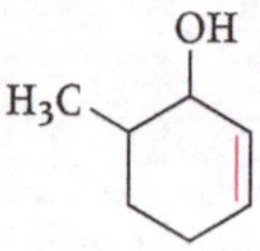

(d) $A =$ 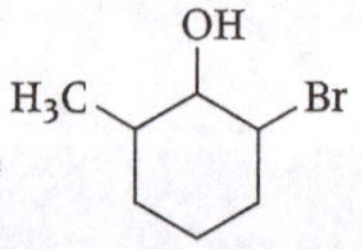 $: B =$ 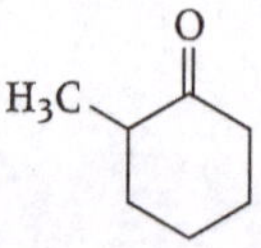

6. Consider the following reaction and identify the product (P).

$$CH_3{-}\underset{\displaystyle CH_3}{\underset{|}{CH}}{-}\underset{\displaystyle OH}{\underset{|}{CH}}{-}CH_3 \xrightarrow{HBr} \text{Product } (P)$$

3-methylbutan-2-ol

[NEET 2023]

(a) $CH_3CH{=}CH{-}CH_3$ (b) $CH_3{-}\underset{\displaystyle CH_3}{\underset{|}{CH}}{-}\underset{\displaystyle Br}{\underset{|}{CH}}{-}CH_3$
(c) $CH_3{-}\underset{\displaystyle CH_3}{\overset{\displaystyle CH_3}{\overset{|}{\underset{|}{C}}}}{-}CH_2Br$ (d) $CH_3{-}\underset{\displaystyle CH_3}{\overset{\displaystyle Br}{\overset{|}{\underset{|}{C}}}}{-}CH_2{-}CH_3$

7. Which amongst the following will be most readily dehydrated under acidic conditions?
[NCERT (New) Pg. 209, NEET 2023]

(a) 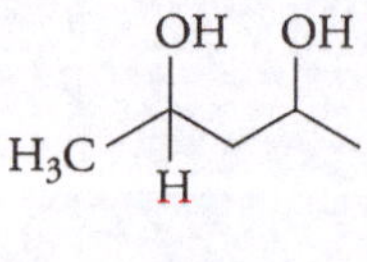 (b) 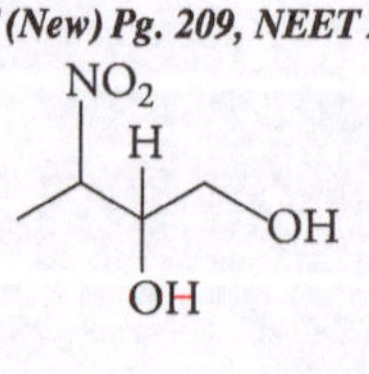

(c) 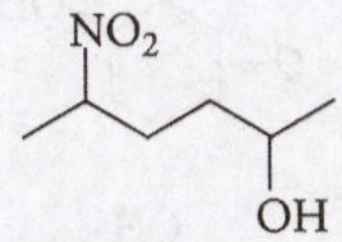

(d) 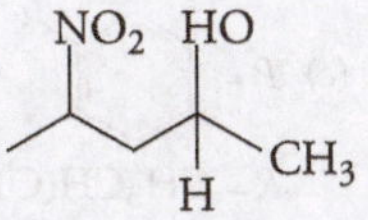

8. Given below are two statements.

Statement I In Lucas test, primary, secondary and tertiary alcohols are distinguished on the basis of their reactivity with conc. HCl + $ZnCl_2$, known as Lucas reagent.

Statement II Primary alcohols are most reactive and immediately produce turbidity at room temperature on reaction with Lucas reagent.

In the light of the above statements, choose the most appropriate answer from the options given below.

[NCERT (New) Pg. 208, NEET 2022]

(a) Both Statement I and Statement II are false.
(b) Statement I is true but Statement II is false.
(c) Statement I is false but Statement II is true.
(d) Both statement I and Statement II are true.

9. When vapours of a secondary alcohol is passed over heated copper at 573 K, the product formed is *[NCERT (New) Pg. 210, NEET (Odisha) 2019]*

(a) a carboxylic acid (b) an aldehyde
(c) a ketone (d) an alkene

10. The reaction that does not give benzoic acid as the major product is *[NEET (Odisha) 2019]*

(a) 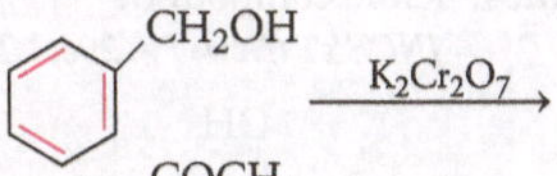

(b) 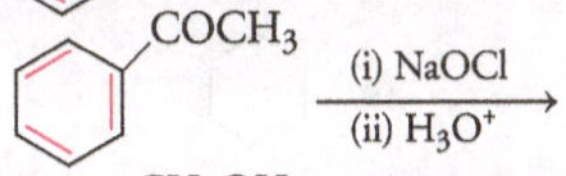

(c) 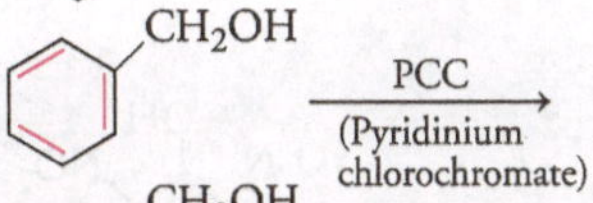

(d) 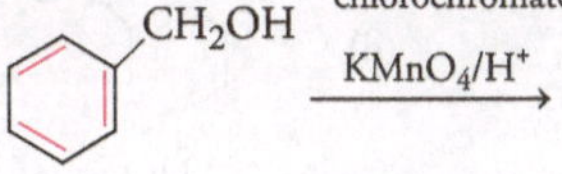

11. The compound *A* on treatment with Na gives *B*, and with PCl_5 gives *C*. *B* and *C* react together to give diethyl ether. *A*, *B* and *C* are in the order *[NCERT (New) Pg. 205, NEET 2018]*

(a) $C_2H_5Cl, C_2H_6, C_2H_5OH$
(b) $C_2H_5OH, C_2H_5Cl, C_2H_5ONa$
(c) $C_2H_5OH, C_2H_6, C_2H_5Cl$
(d) $C_2H_5OH, C_2H_5ONa, C_2H_5Cl$

12. Which of the following reagents would distinguish *cis*-cyclopenta-1, 2-diol from the *trans*-isomer? *[NEET 2016, Phase II]*

(a) Ozone
(b) MnO_2
(c) Aluminium isopropoxide
(d) Acetone

13. Which of the following reaction(s) can be used for the preparation of alkyl halides? *[AIPMT 2015]*

I. $CH_3CH_2OH + HCl \xrightarrow{\text{Anhyd.}ZnCl_2}$
II. $CH_3CH_2OH + HCl \longrightarrow$
III. $(CH_3)_3COH + HCl \longrightarrow$
IV. $(CH_3)_2CHOH + HCl \xrightarrow{\text{Anhyd.}ZnCl_2}$

(a) I, III and IV
(b) I and II
(c) Only IV
(d) III and IV

14. Which of the following is not the product of dehydration of

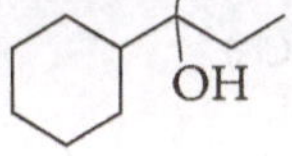

[NCERT (New) Pg. 209, AIPMT 2015]

(a) 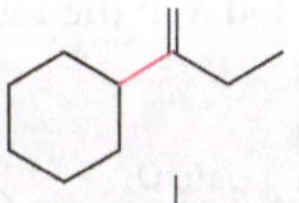

(b) 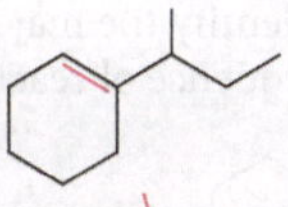

(c) 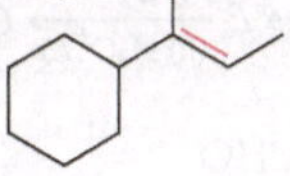

(d) 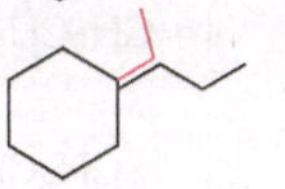

Module-III **Phenols**

15. Which of the following substituted phenols is the strongest acid? *[NCERT (New) Pg. 206, NEET (Oct.) 2020]*

(a) 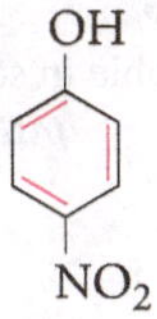

(b) 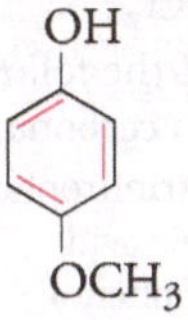

(c) 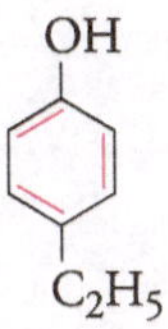

(d) 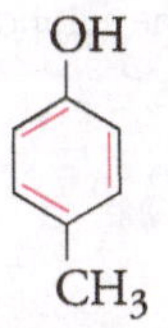

16. The structure of intermediate *A* in the following reaction, is *[NCERT (New) Pg. 202, NEET (National) 2019]*

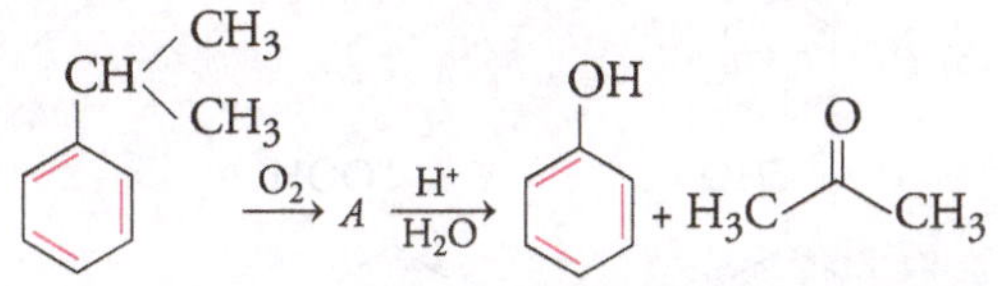

(a) 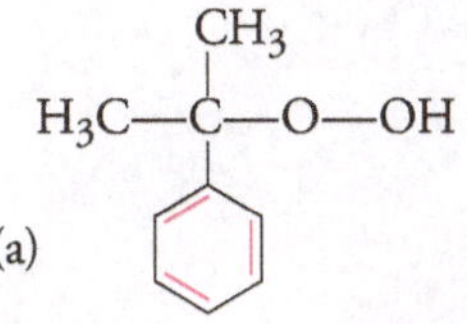

(b) 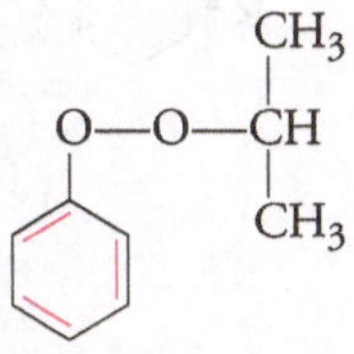

(c) 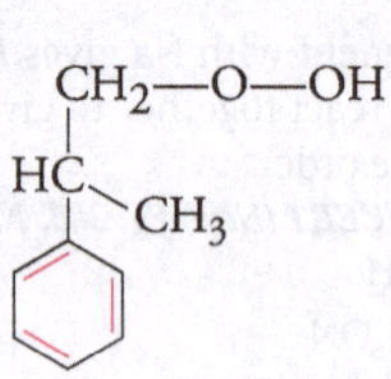

(d) 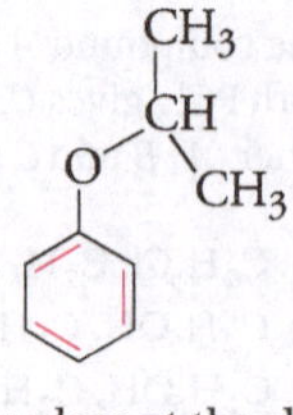

17. The hydrolysis reaction that takes place at the slowest rate, among the following is **[NEET (Odisha) 2019]**

(a) 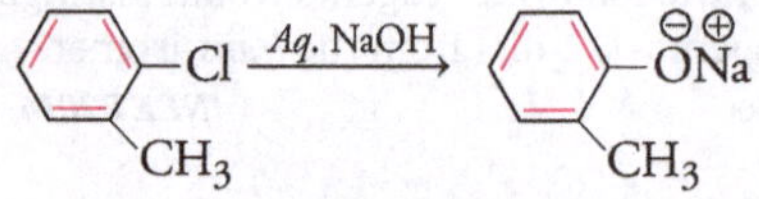

(b) $H_3C—CH_2—Cl \xrightarrow{Aq.\ NaOH} H_3C—CH_2—OH$

(c) $H_2C{=}CH—CH_2Cl \xrightarrow{Aq.\ NaOH} CH_2{=}CH—CH_2—OH$

(d) 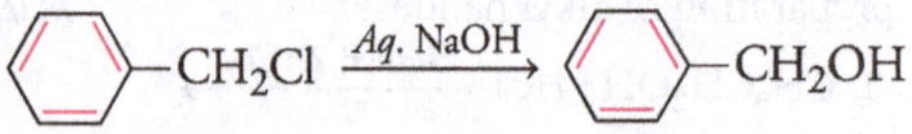

18. In the reaction,

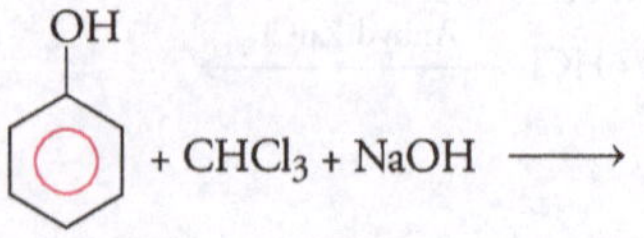

the electrophile involved is

[NCERT (New) Pg. 213, NEET 2018]

(a) dichloromethyl cation ($\overset{+}{C}HCl_2$)

(b) formyl cation ($\overset{+}{C}HO$)

(c) dichloromethyl anion ($\overset{-}{C}HCl_2$)

(d) dichlorocarbene ($:CCl_2$)

19. Identify the major product *P*, *Q* and *R* in the following sequence of reactions

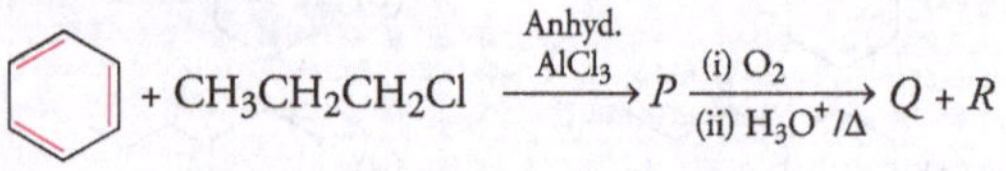

(a) $P =$ 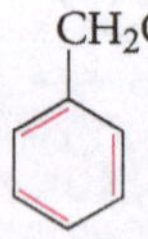

, $Q =$ 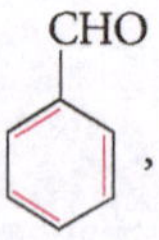

,

$R = CH_3CH_2—OH$

(b) $P =$ 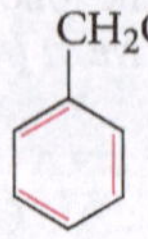

,

$Q =$ 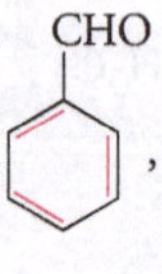

, $R =$ 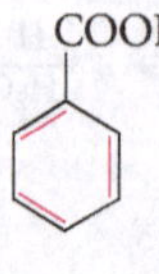

(c) $P =$ 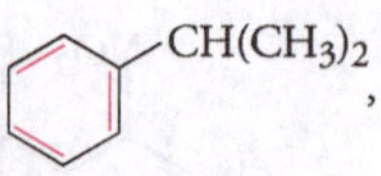

, $Q =$ 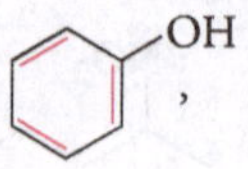

,

$R = CH_3CH(OH)CH_3$

(d) $P =$ 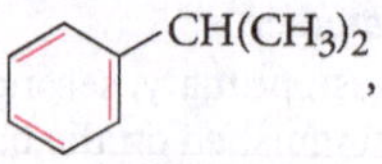

, $Q =$ 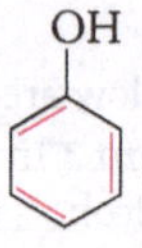

,

$R = CH_3—CO—CH_3$

20. Compound *A*, $C_8H_{10}O$, is found to react with NaOI (produced by reacting *Y* with NaOH) and yields a yellow precipitate with characteristic smell. *A* and *Y* are respectively. **[NEET 2018]**

(a) 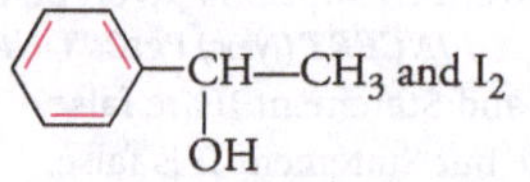

(b) 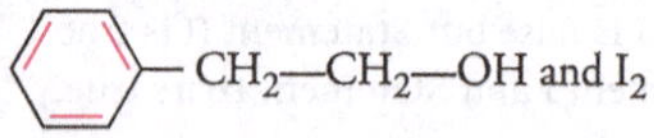

(c) 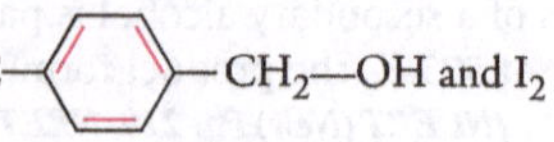

(d) 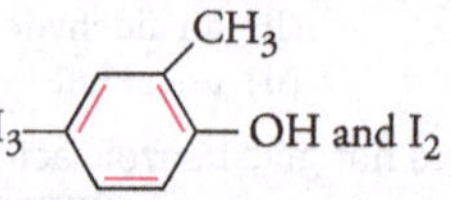

21. Which one is the most acidic compound?

[NCERT (New) Pg. 206, NEET 2017]

(a) 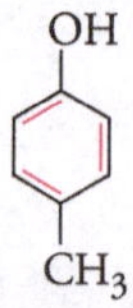

(b) 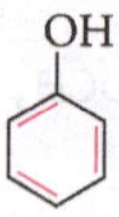

(c) 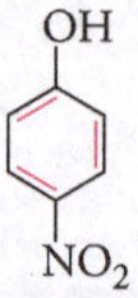

(d) 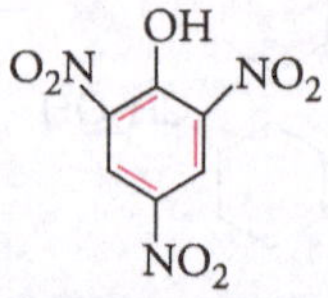

22. Reaction of phenol with chloroform in the presence of dilute sodium hydroxide finally introduces, which one of the following functional group?

[NCERT (New) Pg. 213, AIPMT 2015]

(a) $—CH_2Cl$ (b) —COOH

(c) $—CHCl_2$ (d) —CHO

23. Which of the following will not be soluble in sodium hydrogen carbonate? **[AIPMT 2014]**

(a) 2,4,6-trinitrophenol

(b) Benzoic acid

(c) *o*-nitrophenol

(d) Benzene sulphonic acid

Final Check

Module-IV Ethers

24. Anisole on cleavage with HI gives
[NCERT (New) Pg. 218, NEET (Sep.) 2020]

(a) 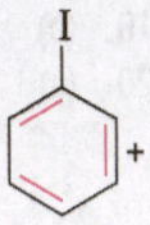 + CH_3OH (b) 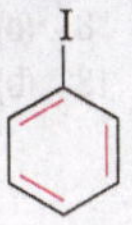 + C_2H_5I

(c) 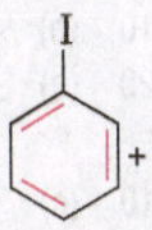 + C_2H_5OH (d) 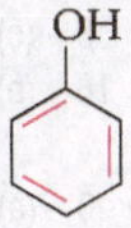 + CH_3I

25. The major products *C* and *D* formed in the following reactions respectively are
[NCERT (New) Pg. 218, NEET (Odisha) 2019]

$$H_3C-CH_2-CH_2-OC(CH_3)_3 \xrightarrow[\Delta]{\text{Excess HI}} C + D$$

(a) $H_3C-CH_2-CH_2-I$ and $I-C(CH_3)_3$
(b) $H_3C-CH_2-CH_2-OH$ and $I-C(CH_3)_3$
(c) $H_3C-CH_2-CH_2-I$ and $HO-C(CH_3)_3$
(d) $H_3C-CH_2-CH_2-OH$ and $HO-C(CH_3)_3$

26. The compound that is most difficult to protonate is *[NEET 2019]*

(a) Ph–O–H (b) H–O–H
(c) H_3C–O–H (d) H_3C–O–CH_3

27. The heating of phenyl-methyl ethers with HI produces. *[NEET 2017]*
(a) ethyl chlorides (b) iodobenzene
(c) phenol (d) benzene

28. The reaction

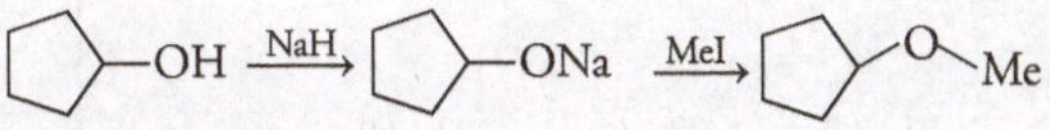

can be classified as
[NCERT (New) Pg. 215, 216, NEET 2016, Phase I]

(a) Alcohol formation reaction
(b) Dehydration reaction
(c) Williamson alcohol synthesis reaction
(d) Williamson ether synthesis reaction

29. The reaction, $CH_3-\underset{CH_3}{\overset{CH_3}{C}}-ONa + CH_3CH_2Cl \xrightarrow{-NaCl} CH_3-\underset{CH_3}{\overset{CH_3}{C}}-OCH_2CH_3$

is called *[NCERT (New) Pg. 216, AIPMT 2015]*
(a) Williamson synthesis
(b) Williamson continuous etherification process
(c) Etard reaction
(d) Gatterman-Koch reaction

30. Identity *Z* in the sequence of reactions,
[NCERT (New) Pg. 215, AIPMT 2014]

$$CH_3CH_2CH=CH_2 \xrightarrow{HBr/H_2O_2} Y \xrightarrow{C_2H_5ONa} Z$$

(a) $CH_3-(CH_2)_3-O-CH_2CH_3$
(b) $(CH_3)_2CH_2-O-CH_2CH_3$
(c) $CH_3(CH_2)_4-O-CH_3$
(d) $CH_3CH_2-CH(CH_3)-O-CH_2CH_3$

31. Among the following sets of reactants which one produces anisole? *[NCERT (New) Pg. 213, AIPMT 2014]*
(a) CH_3CHO, $RMgX$
(b) C_6H_5OH, NaOH, CH_3I
(c) C_6H_5OH, neutral $FeCl_3$
(d) $C_6H_5-CH_3$, CH_3COCl, $AlCl_3$

Answers

Step up Practice 1

1 (c)	2 (b)	3 (d)	4 (c)	5 (d)	6 (c)	7 (c)	8 (d)	9 (b)	10 (b)
11 (a)	12 (a)	13 (a)	14 (b)	15 (b)	16 (c)	17 (d)	18 (b)	19 (a)	20 (a)
21 (d)	22 (d)	23 (a)							

Step up Practice 2

1 (c)	2 (d)	3 (a)	4 (a)	5 (c)	6 (a)	7 (a)	8 (c)	9 (b)	10 (b)
11 (c)	12 (c)	13 (b)	14 (c)	15 (b)	16 (a)	17 (c)	18 (b)	19 (b)	20 (c)

Step up Practice 3

1 (d)	2 (a)	3 (c)	4 (a)	5 (c)	6 (a)	7 (d)	8 (a)	9 (b)	10 (c)
11 (c)	12 (d)	13 (d)	14 (d)	15 (c)	16 (c)	17 (c)	18 (d)	19 (a)	20 (c)
21 (d)	22 (b)	23 (c)							

Step up Practice 4

1 (c)	2 (d)	3 (c)	4 (d)	5 (a)	6 (c)	7 (a)	8 (c)	9 (d)	10 (d)
11 (d)	12 (c)	13 (b)	14 (a)	15 (c)	16 (c)	17 (d)	18 (d)	19 (a)	20 (d)
21 (b)	22 (a)								

Gearing up for NEET

1 (c)	2 (b)	3 (b)	4 (c)	5 (c)	6 (c)	7 (a)	8 (b)	9 (b)	10 (b)
11 (a)	12 (a)	13 (b)	14 (b)	15 (a)	16 (c)	17 (d)	18 (b)	19 (d)	20 (b)
21 (c)	22 (b)	23 (a)	24 (c)	25 (b)	26 (d)	27 (b)	28 (c)	29 (a)	30 (a)
31 (b)	32 (b)	33 (d)	34 (b)	35 (b)	36 (d)	37 (c)	38 (c)	39 (d)	40 (a)
41 (a)	42 (c)	43 (a)	44 (b)	45 (c)	46 (a)	47 (c)	48 (a)	49 (d)	50 (d)
51 (b)	52 (c)	53 (d)	54 (c)	55 (c)	56 (b)	57 (c)	58 (d)	59 (a)	60 (d)
61 (c)	62 (a)	63 (c)	64 (c)	65 (d)	66 (a)	67 (c)	68 (c)	69 (b)	70 (b)
71 (c)	72 (b)	73 (d)	74 (b)	75 (c)	76 (a)	77 (a)	78 (a)		

Final Check through PYQs : Module-I

1 (a)	2 (c)	3 (a)

Final Check through PYQs : Module-II

4 (d)	5 (a)	6 (d)	7 (a)	8 (b)	9 (c)	10 (c)	11 (d)	12 (d)	13 (a)
14 (b)									

Final Check through PYQs : Module-III

15 (a)	16 (a)	17 (a)	18 (d)	19 (d)	20 (a)	21 (d)	22 (d)	23 (c)

Final Check through PYQs : Module-IV

24 (d)	25 (a)	26 (a)	27 (c)	28 (d)	29 (a)	30 (a)	31 (b)

Hints and Solutions

Step up Practice 1

1. (c) $\overset{4}{CH_3}—\overset{3}{CH}=\overset{2}{C}(\overset{1}{CH_2OH})— CH_2CH_2CH_2Cl$ (A)

The IUPAC nomenclature for the given compound (A) is 2-(3-chloropropyl) but-2-en-1-ol.

2. (b) Among the given match, (b) is not correctly matched with the given IUPAC name.

The corrected match is :

- $\overset{4}{CH_3}—\overset{3}{CH_2}—\overset{2}{CH}(CH_3)—\overset{1}{CH_2OH} \longrightarrow$ 2-methyl butan-1-ol.

3. (d) Among the given compounds, only three, i.e.

(i), 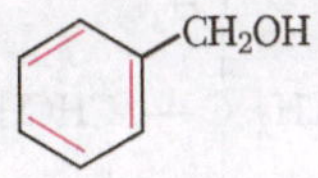 (iii) $H_3C—C(CH_3)(CH_3)—CH_2(OH)$ and

(v) $CH_3—C(CH_3)(CH_3)—OH$ have sp^3-hybridisation of carbon atom to which –OH group is attached.

4. (c) In $C_4H_{10}O$, degree of unsaturation = 0

There are four structural isomers of alcohol and 3 isomers of ether and one is optically active.

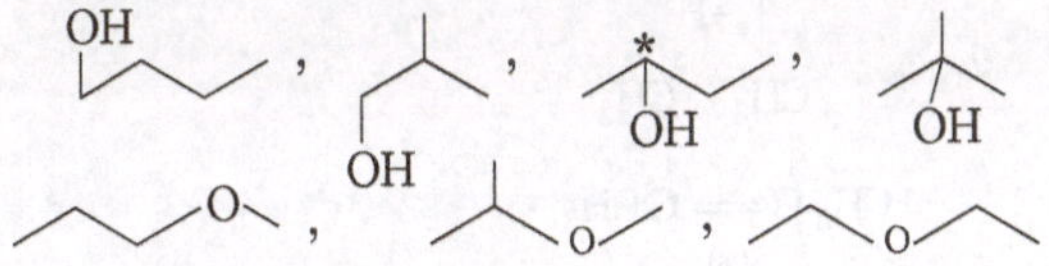

So, there are total 7 isomers.

5. (d) Among the given compounds, only compound and (iii) is chain isomer with each other.

- $CH_3—CH_2—CH_2—CH_2—OH$, Butan-1-ol

$CH_3—CH(CH_3)—CH_2—OH$, 2-methyl propan-1-ol

$CH_3CH_2—OCH_2CH_3$ Ethoxy ethane (it shows functional isomerism with butan-1-ol)

- $CH_3—CH(OH)—CH_2—CH_3$, Butan-2-ol. It is positional isomer of butan-1-ol

$CH_3—CH(CH_3)—CH(OH)—CH_3$ 3-methyl butan-2-ol (Does have not same molecular formula with any one)

6. (c) The given reaction will follow S_N1 mechanism and thus the product formed will be a racemic mixture.

7. (c) Here, X is $Hg(OAc)_2/NaBH_4$, NaOH

$Hg(CH_3COO)_2 / NaBH_4, OH^-$ - gives alcohol by Markovnikov's rule without rearrangement as no carbocation intermediate.

$BH_3 \cdot HF/H_2O_2/OH^-$ gives alcohol by anti-Markovnikov's rule

H_3O^+ (hydration) - gives alcohol by Markovnikov's rule and carbocation intermediate can undergo rearrangement.

MnO_2 is a reagent that converts allylic alcohol to allylic carboxyl.

8. (d)

9. (b)

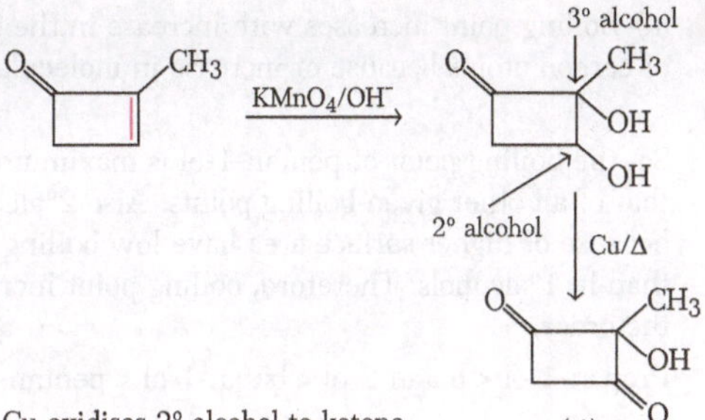

Cu oxidises 2° alcohol to ketone. (A)

10. (b) No intermediate is formed in hydroboration oxidation but addition of BH_3 leads to the formation of a transition state.

11. (a) $NaBD_4$ in CH_3OH helps in reductions of given ketone to alcohol.

12. (a) Among the given match, (a) is correctly matched with the given reaction.

13. (a)

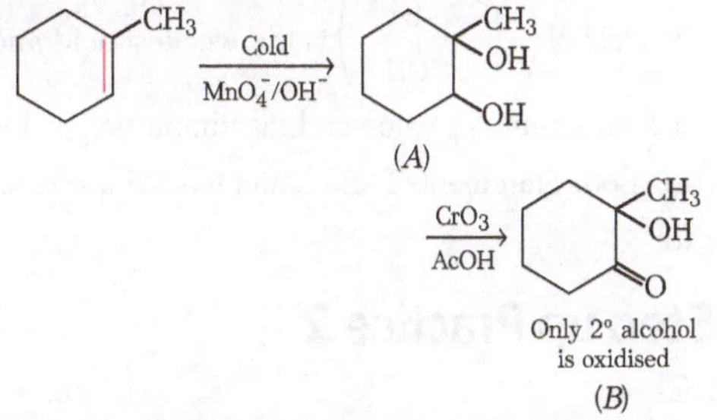

14. (b)

15. (b) An addition reaction is a reaction where two or more molecules combine to form a larger one. These reactions occur to change the unsaturated compound to saturated compound. In dehydrohalogenation reaction, alkyl halides give alkenes.

Rearrangement gives the structural isomers of the reactant while in substitution reaction one of the groups or atoms is replaced by other group. Therefore, the process of converting alkyl halides into alcohol involves substitution reaction.

$$\underset{\text{Alkyl halide}}{R\text{—}X} \xrightarrow{OH^-} \underset{\text{Alcohol}}{R\text{—}OH}$$

Reaction of alkyl halides

Primary alkyl halides - S_N2

Secondary alkyl halides - S_N1

Tertiary alkyl halides - S_N1

16. (c)
17. (d) Both Statement I and Statement II are true.
18. (b) Solubility of alcohol in water is due to hydrophilic —OH group.
19. (a) The correct order of dipole moment is

$$\underset{\text{(I)}}{CH_3CH_2CH_3} < \underset{\text{(II)}}{CH_3CH_2OH} < \underset{\text{(III)}}{CH_3CH_2F}.$$

20. (a) Boiling point increases with increase in the number of carbon atoms because of increase in molecular mass.

So, the boiling point of pentan-1-ol is maximum than that of all other given boiling points. Also 2°alcohols because of higher surface area have low boiling point than in 1°alcohols. Therefore, boiling point increases in the order.

Propan-1-ol < butan-2-ol < butan-1-ol < pentan-1-ol

Here, the correct option is (a).

21. (d) $pK_a = -\log K_a$

Acidic character $\propto K_a \propto \dfrac{1}{pK_a}$

1° alcohol () is the strongest acid thus has maximum K_a value and minimum pK_a value

3° alcohol (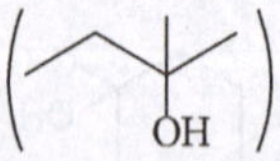) is the weakest acid and thus has minimum K_a value and maximum pK_a value.

22. (d) Both Statements I and Statements II are true.
23. (a)

Step up Practice 2

1. (c)
2. (d)
3. (a) Basic nature of alcohols is in order 3° > 2° > 1° which is the order for nucleophilicity.

Thus, alcohol at $C_2(3°)$ is more nucleophilic than at $C_5(2°)$.

4. (a)
5. (c) Among the given match, (c) is not correctly matched with the given product because the oxidation of phenol gives benzoquinone and not benzyl alcohol.
6. (a) $CH_3—C(CH_3)_2—OH$ compound on dehydration formed the most stable carbocation, i.e. 3° carbocation.
7. (a) Among the given reagent only three, i.e. (i), (ii) and (iii) are convert R—OH into R—Cl with inversion of the configuration on chiral carbon.
8. (c) $CH_3—CH(CH_3)—CH{=}CH_2 + H_2O \xrightarrow{H^+}$

$$CH_3—CH(CH_3)—\overset{+}{C}H—CH_3 \xrightarrow{\text{Rearangement}} CH_3—\overset{+}{C}(CH_3)—CH_2CH_3$$

9. (b) $\underset{\text{3, 3-dimethyl butan-2-ol}}{CH_3C(CH_3)_2—CH(OH)CH_3} \xrightarrow{H^+} CH_3C(CH_3)_2—CH(\overset{\oplus}{O}H_2)CH_3$

$\downarrow -H_2O$

$$\underset{\substack{\text{3° carbocation}\\ \text{(more stable than 2° carbocation)}}}{CH_3\overset{\oplus}{C}(CH_3)—CH(CH_3)CH_3} \xleftarrow[\text{Rearrangement}]{\text{(1, 2 methyl shift)}} \underset{\text{2° carbocation}}{CH_3C(CH_3)_2—\overset{\oplus}{C}HCH_3}$$

$\downarrow -H^{\oplus}$

$$\underset{\substack{(A)\\ \text{2, 3-dimethylbut-2-ene}}}{CH_3(CH_3)C{=}C(CH_3)CH_3}$$

10. (b) $RCH_2OH + Cr(VI) \longrightarrow RCHO + Cr(III)$ (In PCC)
11. (c) The reaction can be written as

$$CH_3CH_2OH \xrightarrow[443\ K]{\text{Conc. } H_2SO_4} CH_3\overset{\oplus}{C}H_2 \longrightarrow \underset{(Z)}{CH_2{=}CH_2}$$

12. (c) Among the given match, (c) is correctly matched with the given product.
13. (b) 1° alcohol follow S_N2

2°, 3° alcohol follow S_N1

$$\underset{\text{(1° alcohol)}}{CH_3OH}\quad \underset{\text{(1°) alcohol}}{CH_3CH_2OH}\quad \underset{\text{2° alcohol}}{CH_3CH(OH)CH_3}$$

14. (*c*) Ethanal (CH_3CHO) is an oxidised product of ethanol. Pyridinium chlorochromate ($C_5H_5\overset{+}{N}HCl\overset{-}{Cr}O_3$) oxidises primary alcohols to aldehydes. Strong oxidising agents such as $KMnO_4$ are used for converting alcohols to carboxylic acid.

The oxidation process can be stopped at the aldehyde stage if Cr(VI) reagents such as Collin's reagent ($CrO_3 \cdot 2C_5H_5N$), Corey's reagent or pyridinium chlorochromate and pyridinium dichromate [$(C_5H_5NH)_2^{2+} Cr_2O_7^{2-}$] in anhydrous medium are used as the oxidising agent. So, the correct option is (c).

$$\underset{\text{Ethanol}}{CH_3CH_2OH} \xrightarrow{PCC} \underset{\text{Ethanal}}{CH_3CHO}$$

15. (*b*) Statement I is true and Statement II is false.

Correct statement II Addition of water to alkene in acidic medium proceeds through the formation of carbocation.

16. (*a*)

17. (*c*)

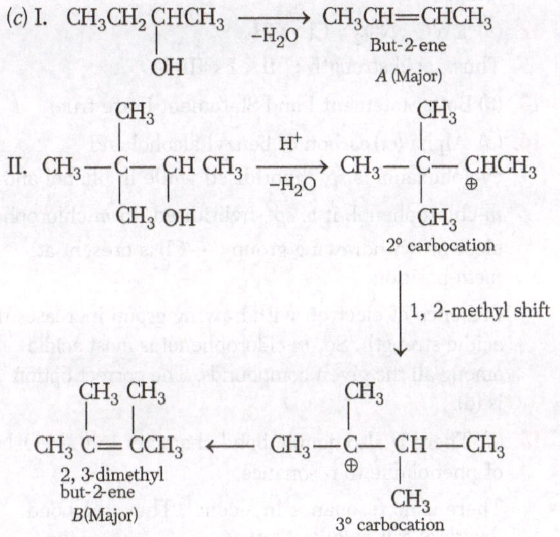

18. (*b*) Mechanism for dehydration of alcohol using $POCl_3$ with pyridine is as follows

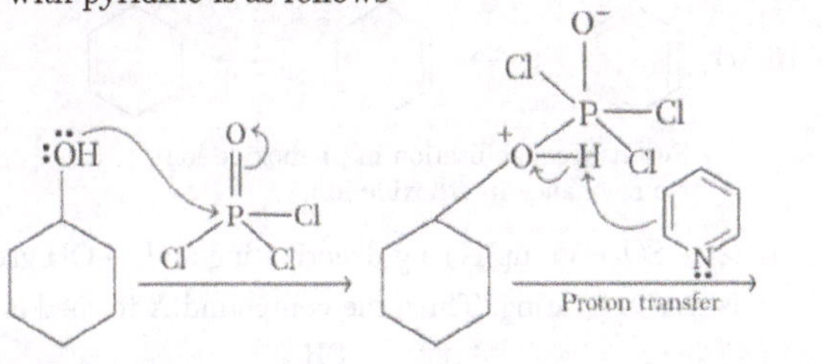

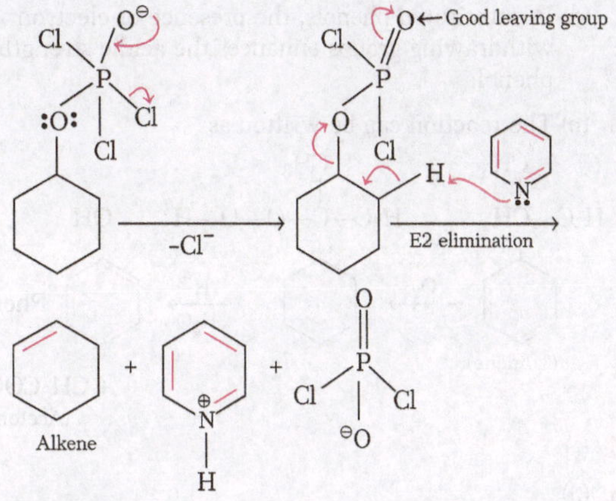

19. (*b*) Among the given reactions, only (i), (ii) formed benzoic acid.

20. (*c*) Statement I is false but Statement II is true.

Its corrected form is :

The reaction of alcohol with acid chloride is carried out in the presence of a base (pyridine) to neutralise HCl.

Step up Practice 3

1. (*d*) $C_6H_5CH_2OH$ is not classified as phenols because in this molecule –OH group is directly attached to alkyl group not with aryl group.

Options (a), (b) and (c) are phenols.

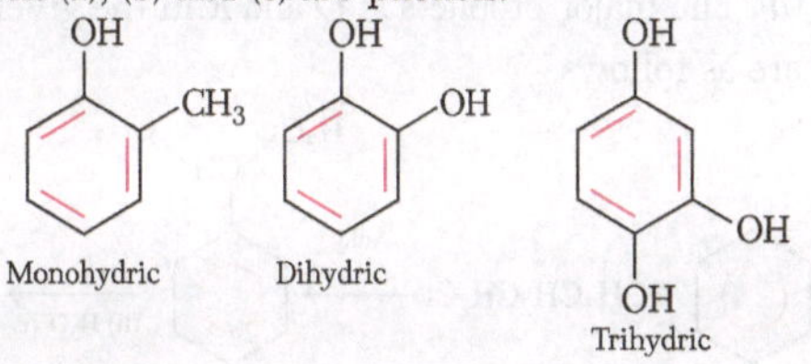

2. (*a*)

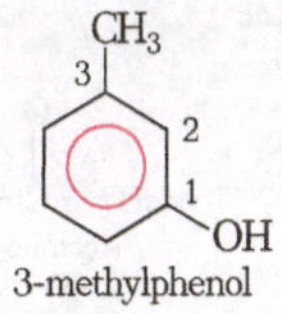

3. (*c*) Statement (c) is correct, regarding phenol whereas other statements (a, b and d) are incorrect.

Corrected statements are as follows :

(a) The electron density decreases on oxygen due to the higher electronegativity of sp^2-hybridised carbon of phenol.

(b) Increase in the polarity of O—H bond results in an increase in ionisation of phenols than that of alcohols.

(d) In substituted phenols, the presence of electron withdrawing groups enhances the acidic strength of phenol.

4. (*a*) The reaction can be written as

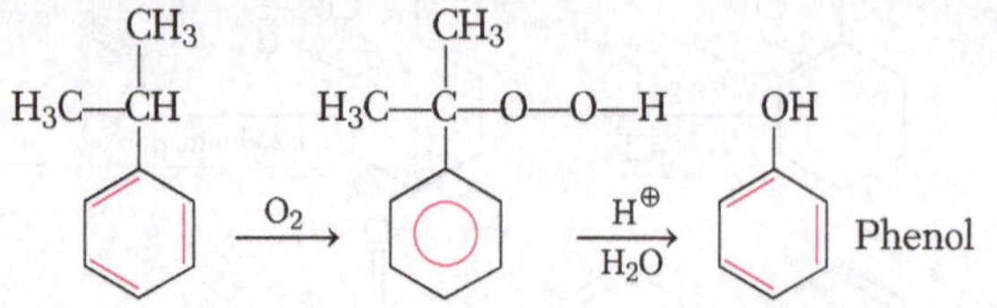

(Cumene) Phenol + CH_3COCH_3 (Acetone)

5. (*c*)

6. (*a*)

(a) (b) (c) (d)

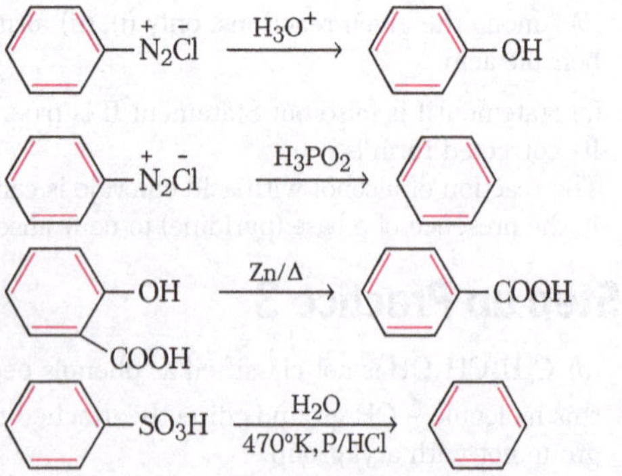

7. (*d*) The major products *P*, *Q* and *R* in the given reaction are as follows

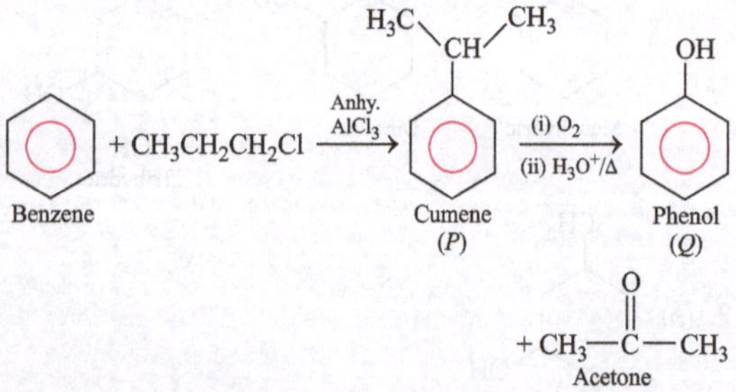

Benzene, Cumene (*P*), Phenol (*Q*), Acetone (*R*)

8. (*a*) Among the given match, (a) is correct while other are incorrect. Their correct matched are

- Cumene $\xrightarrow{O_2}$ Cumene hydroperoxide
- Benzene sulphonic acid $\xrightarrow[\text{(ii) } H^+]{\text{(i) NaOH}}$ Phenol
- Benzene diazonium chloride $\xrightarrow[\text{Warm}]{\text{(i) } H_2O}$ Phenol $+ N_2 + HCl$

9. (*b*) Statement I is true but Statement II is false.
Its corrected form is :
Phenoxide is more stable than phenol as the negative charge on oxygen in it is delocalised over the benzene ring.

10. (*c*) Phenol is more acidic than ethanol because after losing a proton phenols forms phenoxide ion which is stabilised by resonance whereas ethoxide ion is not.

11. (*c*) Reaction of the given compounds with HBr/HCl is a nucleophilic substitution reaction. It follows S_N1 mechanism. S_N1 mechanism depends upon the stability of carbocation.

Presence of electron withdrawing group decreases the stability of carbocation. In compound (II) and (III), EWG is present at *para*-position.
Since, —NO_2 group is a stronger EWG than —Cl.
So, $NO_2—C_6H_5—\overset{+}{C}H_2$ carbocation will be less stable than $Cl—C_6H_5—\overset{+}{C}H_2$ carbocation.
Thus, the order of stability of carbocation is

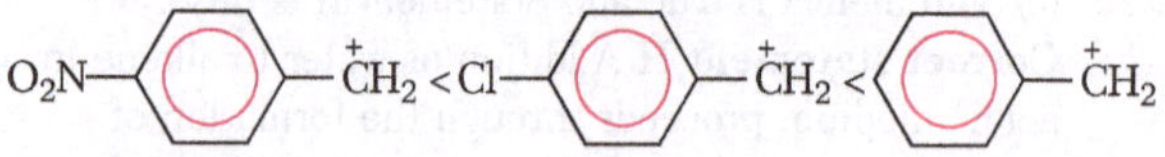

(II) (III) (I)

Therefore, compound (II) is least reactive and correct option is (c).

12. (*d*) EWG : $NO_2 > Cl > CH_3$.
Thus, acid strength : II < I < III

13. (*d*) Both Statement I and Statement II are true.

14. (*d*) Alpha (α) carbon of benzyl alcohol and cyclohexanol is sp^3-hybridised while in phenol and *m*-chlorophenol, it is sp^2-hybridised. In *m*-chlorophenol electron withdrawing group (— Cl) is present at *meta*-position.

Presence of electron withdrawing group increases the acidic strength. So, *m*-chlorophenol is most acidic among all the given compounds. The correct option is (d).

15. (*c*) There is also double bond character in (C—O) bond of phenol due to resonance.
There is no resonance in alcohol. Thus, the bond length of *x* is smaller than *y*.

16. (*c*)

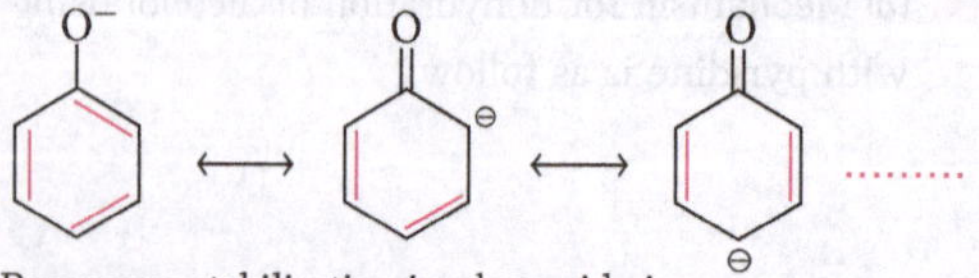

Resonance stabilisation in phenoxide ion
No resonance in ethoxide ion.

17. (*c*) $—SO_3H$ group is ring deactivating and —OH group is ring activating. Thus, the compound *X* formed is

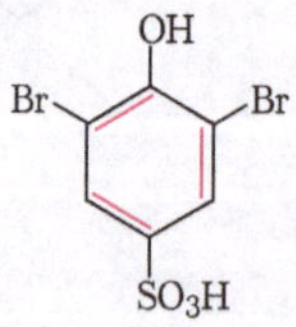

18. (*d*)

19. (*a*) The reaction is proceed as

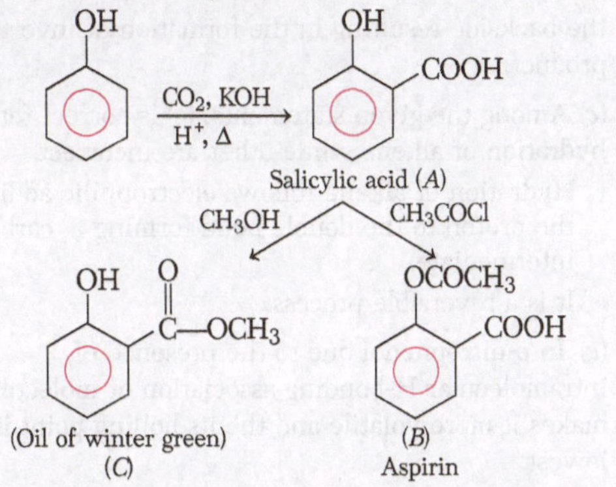

20. (*c*) Sulphonation blocks *p*-position and chlorination gives *o*-isomer w.r.t. —OH group. In last stage desulphonation gives final product.

21. (*d*)

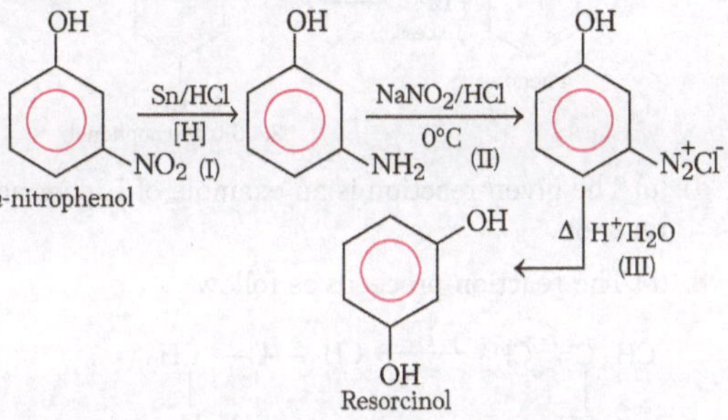

In the above reaction step I is the reduction, step II is diazotisation and III is hydrolysis in acidic medium.

22. (*b*) The reaction will takes place as follow

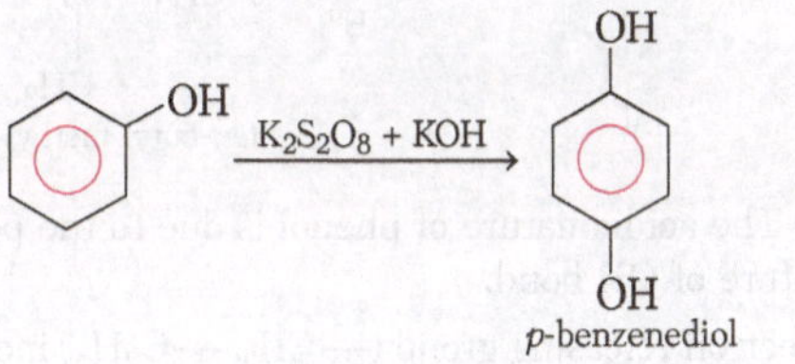

23. (*c*) Among the given reagents, phenol does not react with (i) and (iii) because the C—O bond of phenol is strong on account of double bond character due to resonance. No reaction with (ii) as aryl halides (unless activated) are inert toward nucleophilic displacements.

Step up Practice 4

1. (*c*)

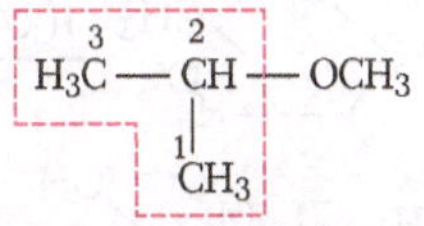

IUPAC name of the above compound is 2-methoxypropane and correct option is (c).

2. (*d*) Among the given match, only (d) is correctly match while other are incorrect.

Their correct match is

- $CH_3OCH—CH_3$ (with CH_3 on CH) ⟶ 2-methoxy propane
- $CH_3—O—CH_2—CH_2—OCH_3$ ⟶ 1, 2-dimethyloxyethane
- 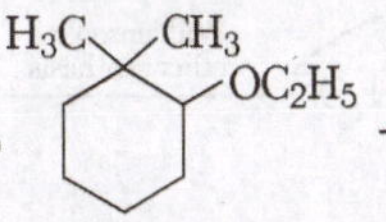

⟶ 2-ethoxy-1,1-dimethyl cyclohexane

3. (*c*) An alkyl halide on heating with dry silver oxide gives ether.

$$\underset{(A)}{2R—X} + Ag_2O \xrightarrow[\text{Dry ether}]{\Delta} R—O—R + 2AgX$$

4. (*d*) Both Statements I and II are true.

5. (*a*) The compound '*P*' is

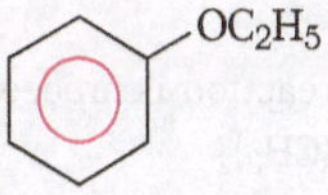

6. (*c*) As, vinyl chloride is least reactive towards nucleophilic displacement with sodium methoxide as its C—Cl bond is quite strong on account of double bond character due to resonance.

$$\underset{\text{(Vinyl chloride)}}{CH_2{=}\underset{|}{C}H\text{ (Cl)}} + NaOCH_3 \longrightarrow \text{No reaction}$$

7. (*a*) It involves mercurinium ion as the intermediate.

8. (*c*) In the given reaction, CH_3OH acts as a nucleophile.

9. (*d*) Both Statement I and Statement II are true.

10. (*d*)

11. (*d*) $\underset{\text{Ethanol}}{CH_3CH_2OH} \xrightarrow[\Delta]{\text{Conc.}H_2SO_4} \underset{\text{Ethoxyethane}}{CH_3CH_2OCH_2CH_3}$

12. (*c*) Among the given match, (c) is correctly match with the given product.

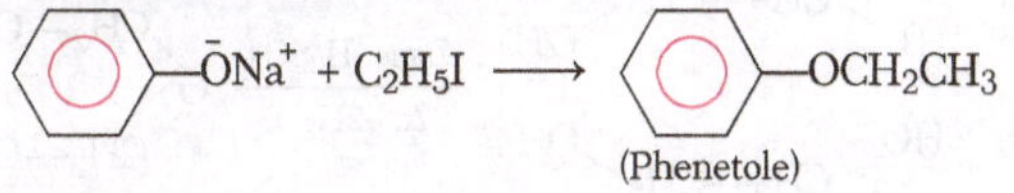

13. (*b*) If *RX* is 2° or 3°, *R*ONa will cause elimination. Thus, (b) is incorrect statement.

14. (*a*) Among the given compounds, only one, i.e. (ii) is added to the ether to test its purity. KI is added to ether to test its purity because ether generally has peroxide as impurity. On adding KI, ether peroxide, oxidises KI into I_2 and itself gets reduced to ether.

$$2I^- \longrightarrow I_2 + 2e^-$$

$$\text{Ether peroxide} + 2e^- \longrightarrow \text{Ether} + O_2$$

15. (*c*) The reaction is proceed as

$$CH_3CH_2OSO_3H + CH_3CH_2OH \xrightarrow{410\text{ K}} \underset{\text{Diethyl ether}}{CH_3CH_2OCH_2CH_3} + H_2SO_4$$

16. (c) Both the given reactions, proceed through S_N2 mechanisms.

17. (d) Alcohols have stronger intermolecular H-bonding and ethers have weaker intermolecular H-bonding therefore ethers are more volatile than alcohols.

18. (d)

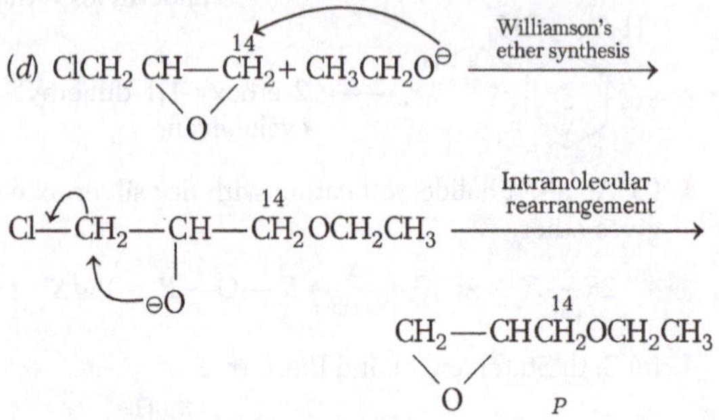

19. (a) The reaction is proceed as

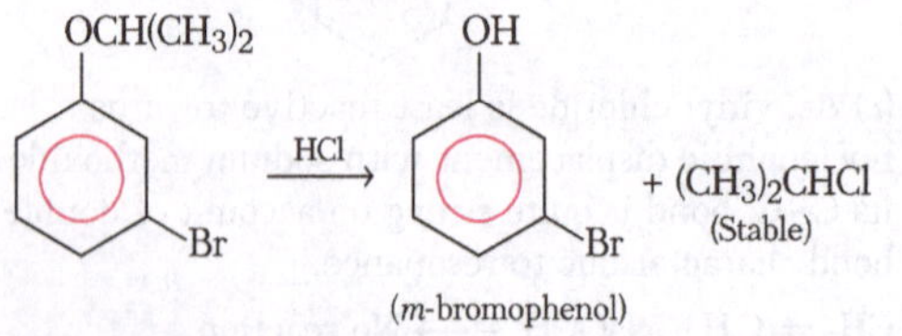

20. (d) Among the given compounds, only one, i.e. (iii) will give methanol as one of the products on reaction with cold hydroiodic acid.

According to Zeisel method, when an ether reacts with cold HI, alkyl iodide and alcohol are formed. In case of unsymmetrical ether, the alkyl halide is always formed from the smaller alkyl group provided no tertiary (3°) alkyl group is present and if any 3° alkyl group is present, the halogen gets attached with it.

21. (b) Among the given match, only (b) is correctly match with the given product.

The reaction is proceed as

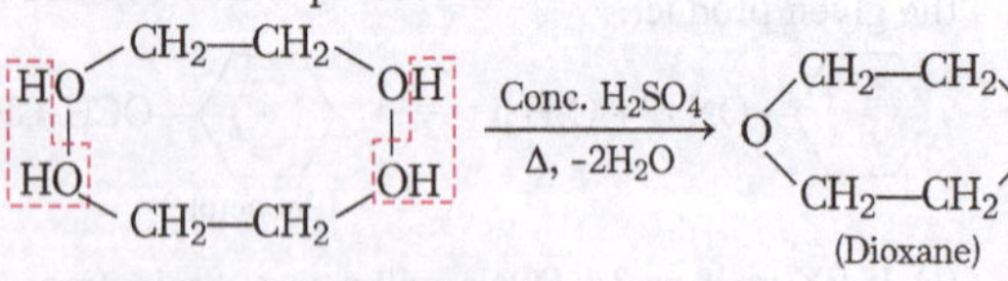

22. (a)

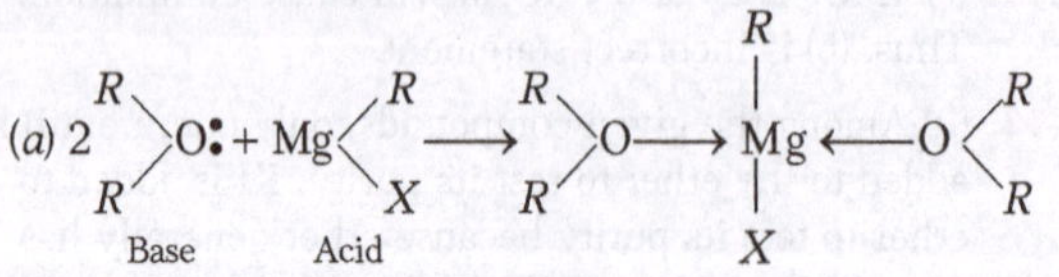

Gearing Up for NEET

1. (c) Among the given options, CH_3I will be hydrolysed to alcohol to a maximum extent because the bond formed between carbon and iodine is the weakest bond. In other words, iodine is a better leaving group.

2. (b)

3. (b) S_N2 reaction takes place by nucleophilic attack on the backside resulting in the formation of inverted product.

4. (c) Among the given statements, (c) is correct for hydration of alkene while other are incorrect.
   - Hydration of alkene follows electrophilic addition of the proton to the double bond forming a carbocation intermediate.
   - It is a reversible process.

5. (c) In o-nitrophenol due to the presence of intramolecular H-bonding association of molecule makes it more volatile and the its boiling point is lowest.

6. (c)

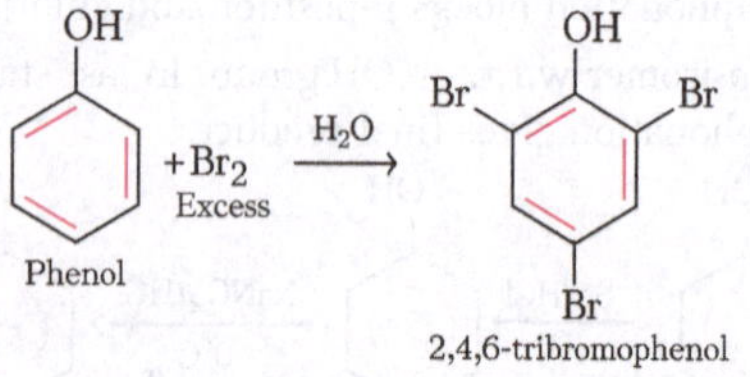

7. (a) The given reaction is an example of Liebermann's reaction.

8. (b) The reaction proceeds as follow

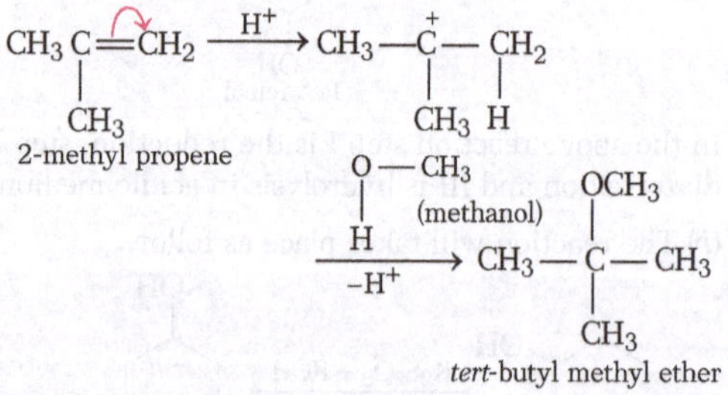

9. (b) The acidic nature of phenol is due to the polar nature of OH bond.

Electron releasing group ($-CH_3$, $-C_2H_5$) increase electron density on oxygen decreasing the polarity of O—H bond.

10. (b) Only —CHO group is reduced by $NaB(OAc)_3H$ as it is a selective reagent for the reduction of carbonyl group.

11. (a) The reaction is proceed as

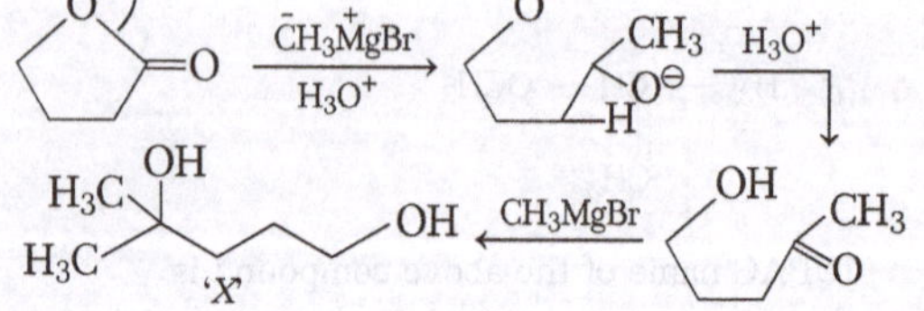

12. (a)

13. (*b*)

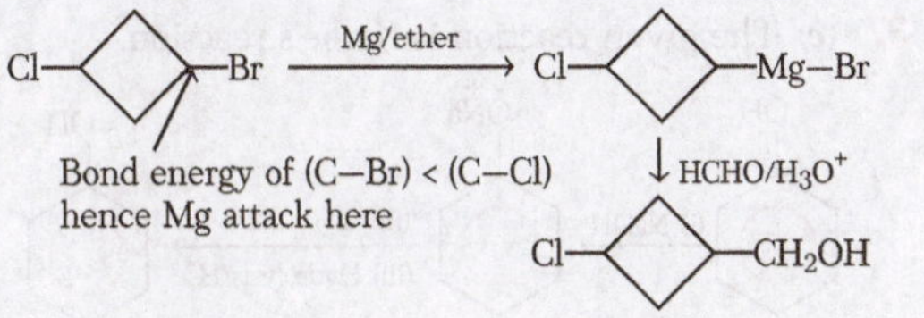

(*A*)
(3-chlorocyclobutyl)methanol

14. (*b*)

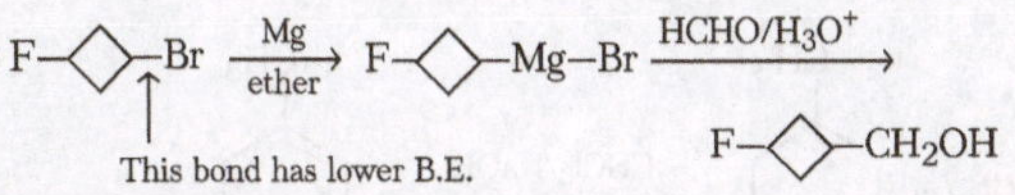

15. (*a*) In alcohols, the boiling points decrease with increase in branching of carbon chain. So, the correct order for boiling point is $1° > 2° > 3°$.

16. (*c*) The reaction proceeds as follow

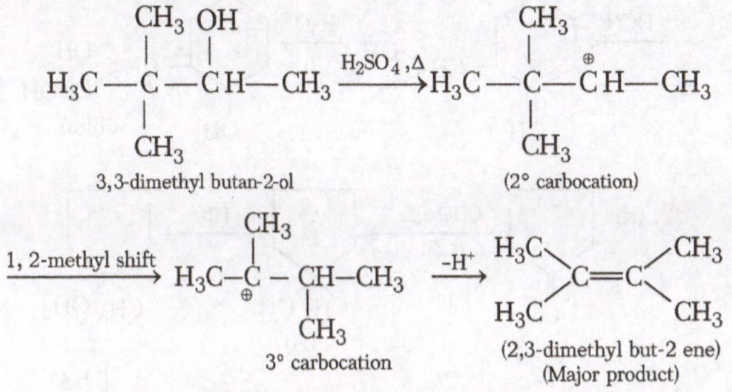

17. (*d*) Phenols are Bronsted acids, i.e. they can donate a proton to a stronger base forming phenoxide while resonance stabilised.

18. (*b*) The reaction will proceed as

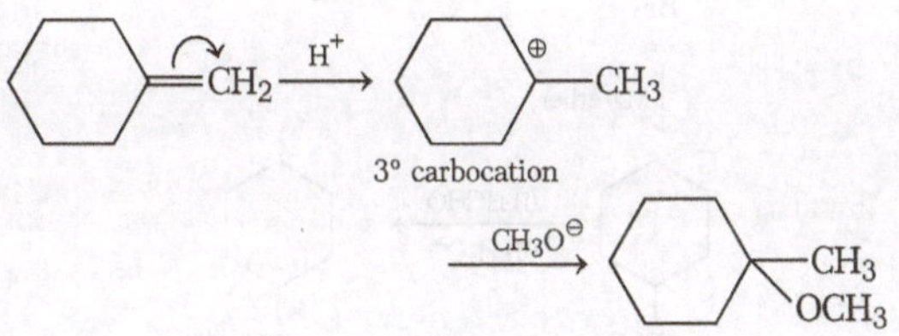

19. (*d*)

20. (*b*) The compound $(CH_3)_2CHOH$ with PBr_3 follows S_N2 mechanism and with $HBr + ZnCl_2$ follows S_N1 mechanism due to formation of carbocation.

21. (*c*) The correct order of dipole moment is propane < methoxymethane < ethanol.

22. (*b*) During esterification the cleavage of O—H bond from alcohols takes place and not O—H bond of carboxylic acid.

$$C_6H_5CH_2\overset{O}{\overset{\|}{C}}OH + CH_3CH_2\overset{18}{O}H \xrightarrow[\Delta]{H^+} C_6H_5—CH_2—\overset{O}{\overset{\|}{C}}—\overset{18}{O}—CH_2CH_3$$

23. (*a*) There is oxidation of alcohol at allylic or benzylic position by MnO_2. So, product *A* is

$$CH_2=CH—\overset{O}{\overset{\|}{C}}—CH_2CH_2OH$$

24. (*c*) The correct order of boiling point is $(CH_3)_4C < (CH_3)_2CHOCH_3 < (CH_3)_3COH < CH_3CH_2CH_2CH_2OH$.

Alcohols have high boiling point than thus parent hydrocarbon due to the presence of H-bonding. Among different classes of alcohols, 1° alcohol will have maximum boiling point due to less branching.

25. (*b*)

$$\underset{(I)}{CH_3CH_2—\overset{O}{\overset{\|}{C}}\overset{q}{\vdots}O\overset{p}{\vdots}H} + \underset{(II)}{CH_3CH_2\overset{s}{\vdots}\overset{18}{O}\overset{r}{\vdots}H} \rightleftharpoons CH_3CH_2\overset{O}{\overset{\|}{C}}—\overset{18}{O}—CH_2CH_3 + H_2O$$

During esterification the cleavage of O—H bond from alcohols takes place and not O—H bond of carboxylic acid which indicate the cleavage of bond *q* of I and *r* of II.

26. (*d*) The reaction is proceeds as follow

$$(CH_3)_2CHCH_2OH \xrightarrow{PBr_3} (CH_3)_2CHCH_2Br \xrightarrow{Mg} (CH_3)_2CHCH_2MgBr \xrightarrow{H_2\overset{O}{C}—CH_2}$$

$$(CH_3)_2CHCH_2CH_2CH_2OMgBr \xrightarrow{H_3O^⊕} \underset{(Z)}{(CH_3)_2CHCH_2CH_2CH_2OH}$$

27. (*b*) MnO_2 oxidised allylic alcohol to ketone over 2° alcohol.

Thus, the reaction is proceed as

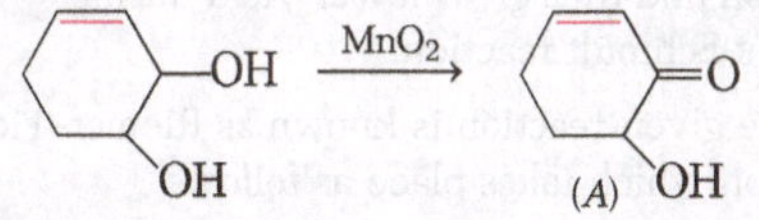

28. (*c*) Greater the conjugation, greater the stability and thus, greater is the dehydration. Thus, correct order for dehydration of alcohols is III < II < I < IV.

29. (*a*) Alcohol *B* is 3° as it reacts fastest with Lucas reagent.

$$\underset{(A)}{CH_3\overset{O}{\overset{\|}{C}}OC_2H_5} \xrightarrow{CH_3MgBr} CH_3\overset{O}{\overset{\|}{C}}CH_3 \xrightarrow[H_3O^+]{CH_3MgBr} \underset{(B)}{(CH_3)_3COH}$$

30. (a)

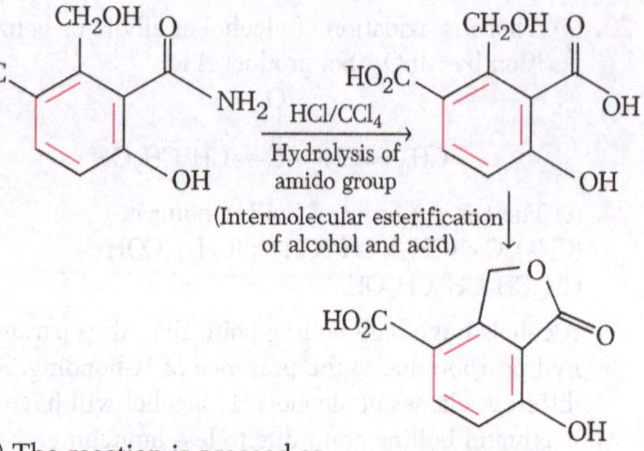

31. (b) The reaction is proceed as

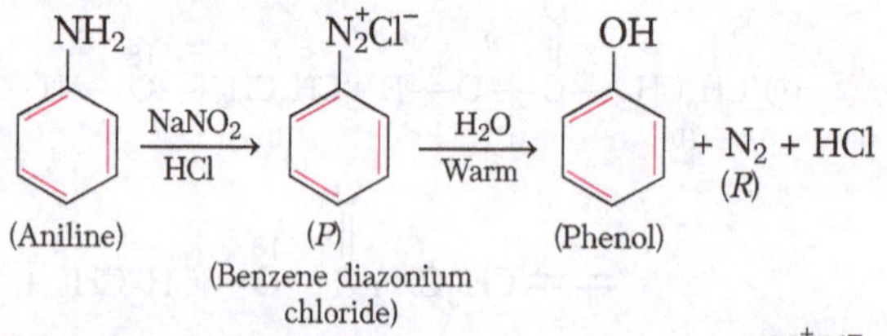

Thus, the intermediate '*P*' and product '*R*' are 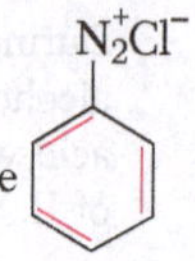 and N_2 respectively in the given reaction.

32. (b) Greater stability of conjugate base, more is the acidic strength and more is the value of K_a. Among the given options, (b) has the more stable conjugate base during resonance thus will have maximum K_a value.

33. (d) *o*-isomer has maximum dipole moment.

34. (b) Maximum pK_a value means least acidic (maximum basic).

—NO_2 : (EWG) increases acidic strength.
—CH_3 : (ERG) decreases acidic strength.
Thus, (b) will have lower maximum pK_a.

35. (b) —NO_2 deactivates benzene ring for electrophilic reaction and thus gives lower yield during Kolbe's-Schmidt reaction.

36. (d) The given reaction is known as Riemer-Tiemann reaction which takes place as follows

$$CHCl_3 + \overset{-}{O}H \rightleftharpoons H_2O + \overset{-}{C}Cl_3$$

$$\overset{-}{C}Cl_3 \xrightarrow{-Cl} :CCl_2$$

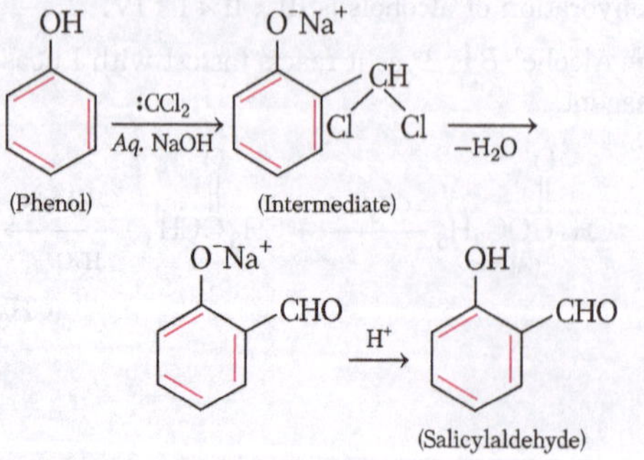

37. (c) The given reaction is Kolbe's reaction.

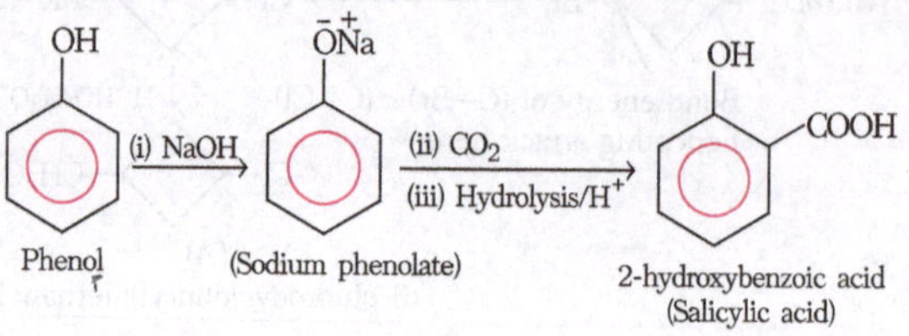

38. (c)

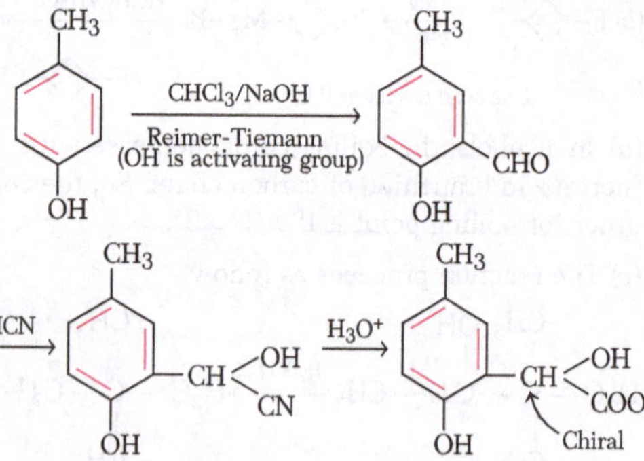

39. (d)

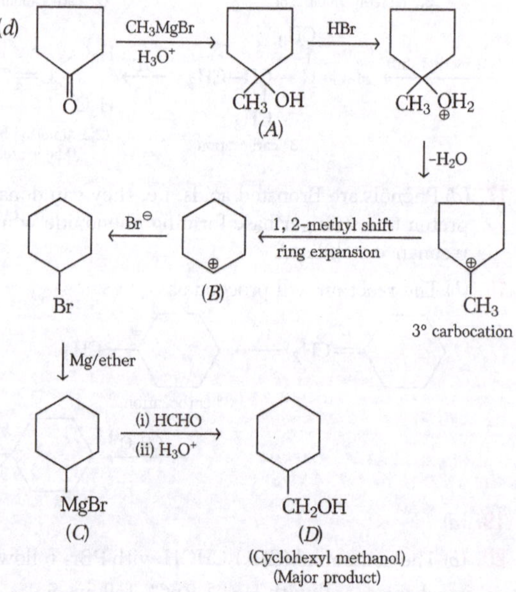

40. (a) Pyrene is CCl_4, thus by Reimer-Tiemann reaction, –COOH group is introduced into phenol and the product obtained is salicylic acid.

The reaction will proceed as

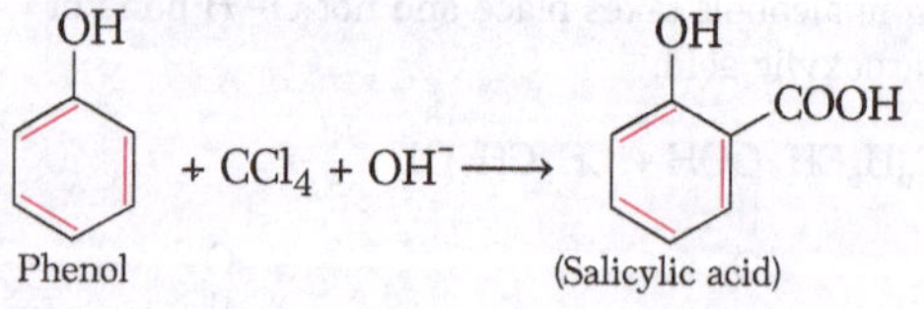

41. (*a*) The reaction proceeds as follows

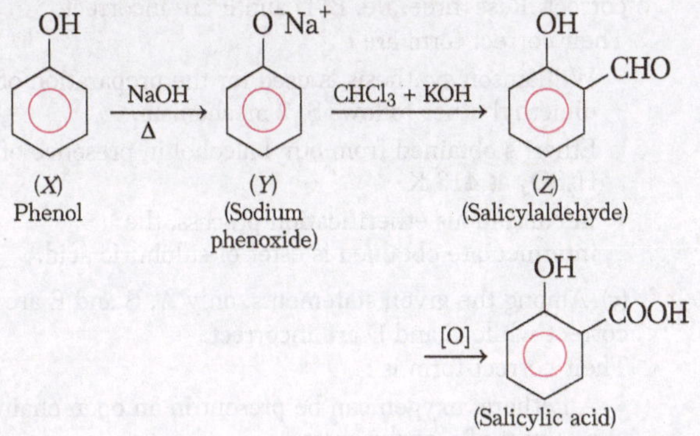

42. (*c*)

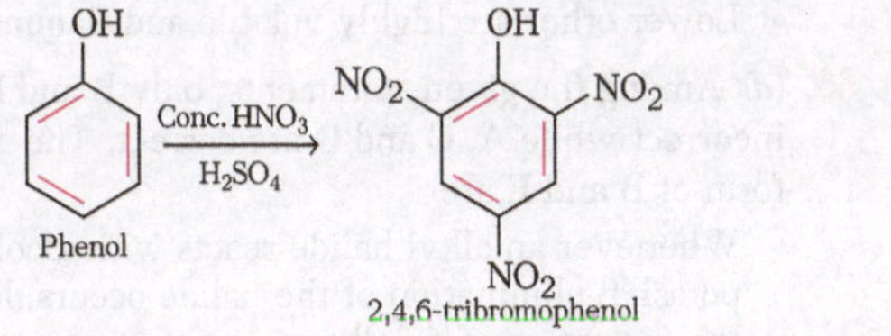

43. (*a*)

44. (*b*) The reaction will proceed as

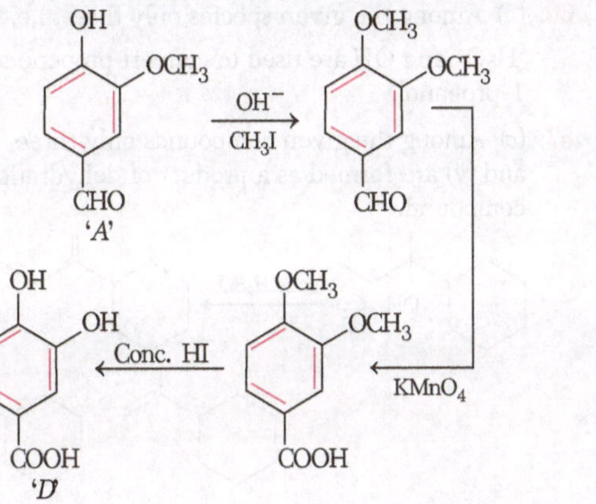

As '*A*' gives intense purple colour with $FeCl_3$ this means *A* has phenolic group. It also gives Tollen's test, thus —CHO group is also present.

45. (*c*) Both the alcohols can be distinguish by potassium dichromate.

$$\underset{(n\text{-propyl alcohol})}{CH_3CH_2CH_2OH} + K_2Cr_2O_7 + H^+ \longrightarrow \underset{(\text{Propanol})}{CH_3CH_2CHO}$$

$$\underset{(Iso\text{-propyl alcohol})}{CH_3-\underset{OH}{\underset{|}{CH}}-CH_3} + K_2Cr_2O_7 + H^+ \longrightarrow \underset{(\text{Acetone})}{CH_3-\underset{O}{\underset{\|}{C}}-CH_3}$$

46. (*a*) The reaction will proceed as

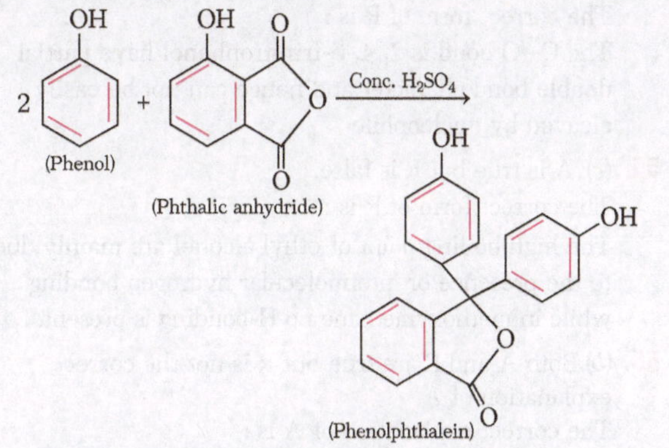

47. (*c*) Due to the delocalisation of lone pair of electrons of O-atom with phenyl ring in both side makes it very stable. Thus, it is most unreactive towards the cleavage with HBr.

48. (*a*)

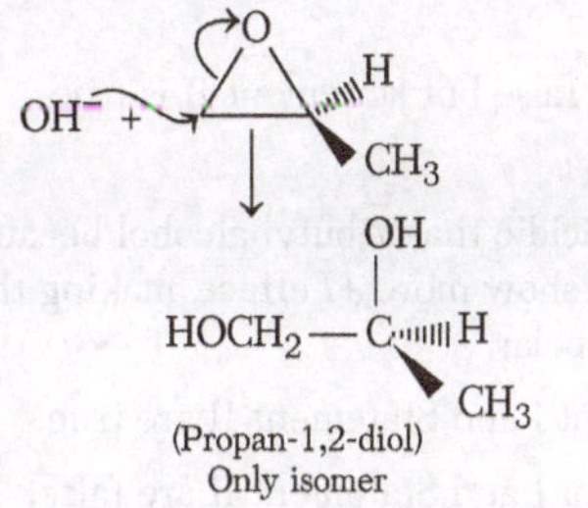

49. (*d*) Attacks at least substituted site and thus β-bond is cleaved.

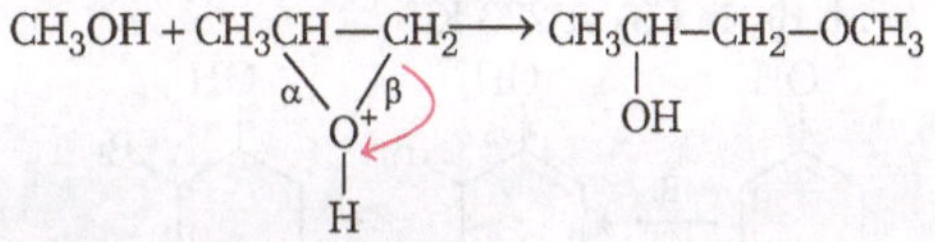

50. (*d*) Its correct form is :

The cleavage of ethers take place with concentrated HI or HBr at high temperature.

51. (*b*) Among the given statements, only A and C are incorect while all other statements are correct.

The correct form of A and C are

- The solubility of alcohols and phenols decreases with increase in size of alkyl/aryl group.
- Propanol and methoxy methane have comparable molecular mass but boiling point of propanol is higher than methoxymethane.

52. (*c*)

53. (*d*) A is false but R is true.

The correct form of A is :

Sulphuric acid is not used during the reaction of alcohols with KI in the conversion of an alcohol to the alkyl iodide. Instead, a non-oxidising acid such as H_3PO_4 is used.

54. (c) A is true but R is false.
The correct form of R is :
The C—O bond is 2, 4, 6-trinitrophenol have partial double bond character and hence can not be easily cleaved by nucleophile.

55. (c) A is true but R is false.
The correct form of R is :
The high boiling point of ethyl alcohol are mainly due to the presence of intermolecular hydrogen bonding while in methoxymethane no H-bonding is present.

56. (b) Both A and R are true but R is not the correct explanation of A.
The correct explanation of A is :
Due to the presence of intramolecular hydrogen bonding, *o*-nitrophenol does not form hydrogen bonds with H_2O but *meta* and *para*-nitrophenol form hydrogen bonds with water. Thus it is less soluble in water.

57. (c) Statement I is false but statement II is true.
It correct form is :
CH_3OH is more acidic than *t*-butyl alcohol because the tert butyl groups show more $+I$ effect, making the O—H bond less polar.

58. (d) Both Statement I and Statement II are true.

59. (a) Both Statement I and Statement II are false.
Their correct form are
- Phenol forms monobromophenols on treatment with Br_2 in CS_2 at 273 K.

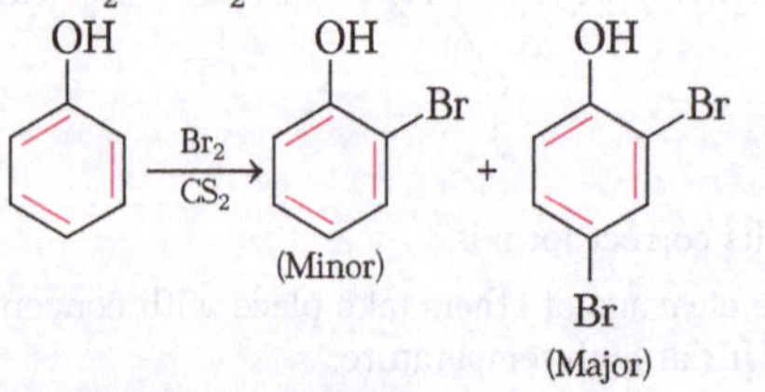

- In phenol, the polarisation of bromine molecule takes place even in the absence of Lewis acid.

60. (d) Both Statement I and Statement II are true.

61. (c) Statement I is false but Statement II is true.
Its correct form is :
As, $(CH_3)_3CBr$ is a tertiary halide and $CH_3O^-Na^+$ is a nucleophile as well as base.
In the compound, i.e. $(CH_3)_3CBr$ substitution is not possible due to steric hinderence hence elimination take place, so alkene, i.e. $(CH_3—\overset{\overset{\large CH_3}{|}}{C}=CH_2)$ is the major product not an ether.

62. (a) Among the given statements A, C, D and E are correct while B is incorrect. The correct form of statement B is : Cresols are less acidic than phenol.

63. (c) Among the given statement, only A and C are correct. Rest three, i.e. B, D and E are incorrect.
Their correct form are :
- Williamson synthesis is used for the preparation of dimethyl ether follows S_N2 mechanism.
- Ether is obtained from ethyl alcohol in presence of H_2SO_4 at 413 K.
- In continuous etherification process, the intermediate obtained is ester of sulphuric acid.

64. (c) Among the given statements, only A, B and E are correct while C and D are incorrect.
Their correct form is :
- An etheral oxygen can be present in an open chain as a part of a cyclic system.
- Lower ether are highly volatile and flammable.

65. (d) Among the given statements, only B and E are incorrect while A, C and D are correct. The correct form of B and E are
- Whenever an alkyl halide reacts with alcoholic potash β-elimination of the halide occurs, leading to the formation of an alkene.
- Acetone reacts with sodium borohydride to produce 2° alcohol.

66. (a) Among the given species only three, i.e. B_2H_6, H_2O_2 and $\bar{O}H$ are used to convert propene to 1-propanol.

67. (c) Among the given compounds only three, i.e, (i), (iii) and (v) are formed as a product of dehydration of given compound.

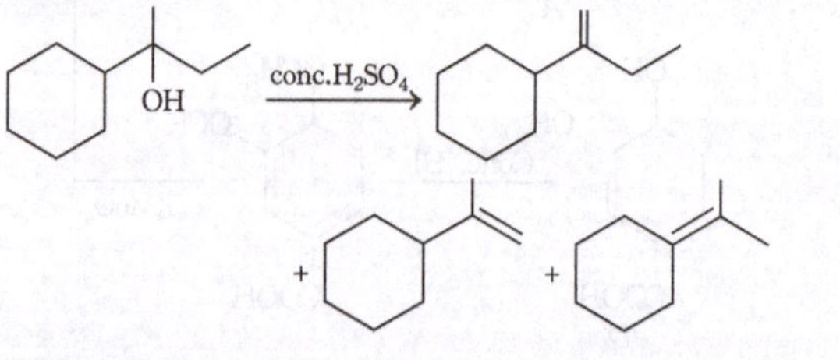

68. (c) Among the given reagent, the suitable reagent for converting benzyl alcohol into benzaldehyde is MnO_2.

69. (b) Among the given compounds, all are ether except (ii) because this compound is a cyclic anhydride.

70. (b) Among the given compounds, only four, i.e. (ii), (iii), (iv) and (v) are the isomer of diethyl ether.

71. (c) Among the given compounds, only two, i.e. (iii) and (iv) are formed when ethyl phenyl ether boiled with conc. hydrobromic acid.
The reaction can be written as

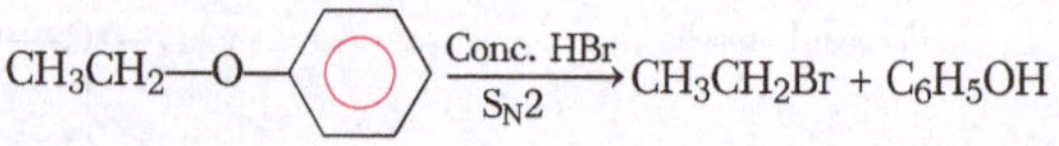

72. (b) The correct match is A-1, B-2, C-4, D-3.

73. (d) The correct match is A-4, B-3, C-2, D-1.

74. (*b*) The correct match is A-4, B-3, C-1, D-2.

75. (*c*) The correct match is A-4, B-3, C-2, D-1.

- 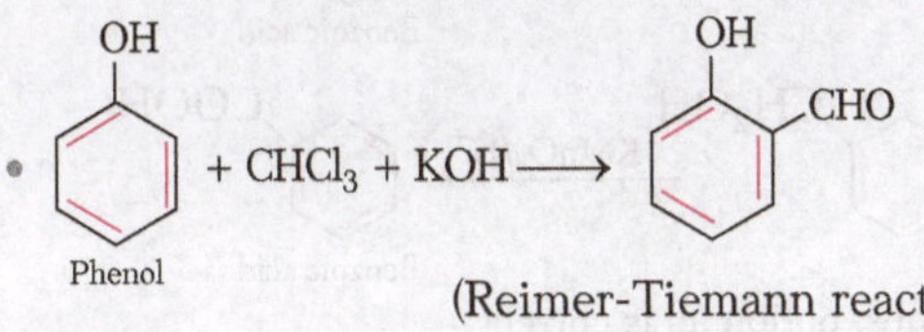

(Reimer-Tiemann reaction)

- 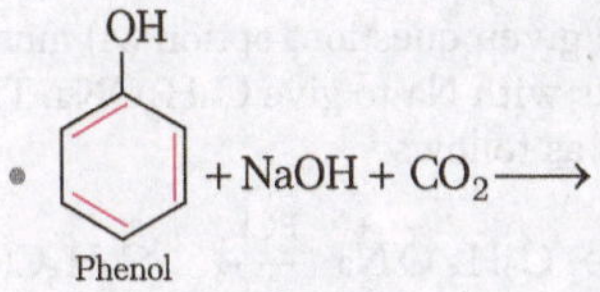

(by Kolbe's reaction)

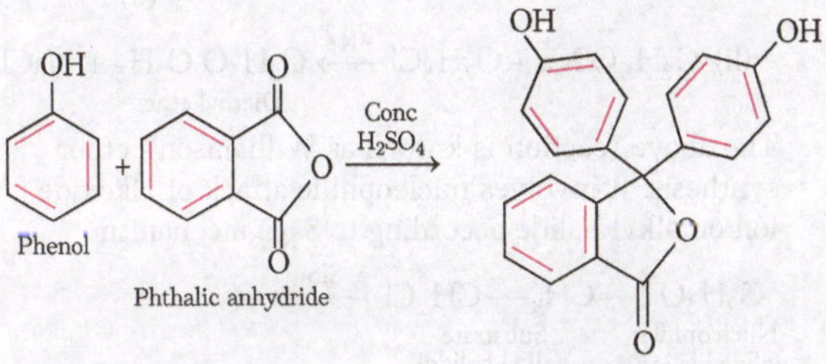

Phenolphthalein (Phthalein test)

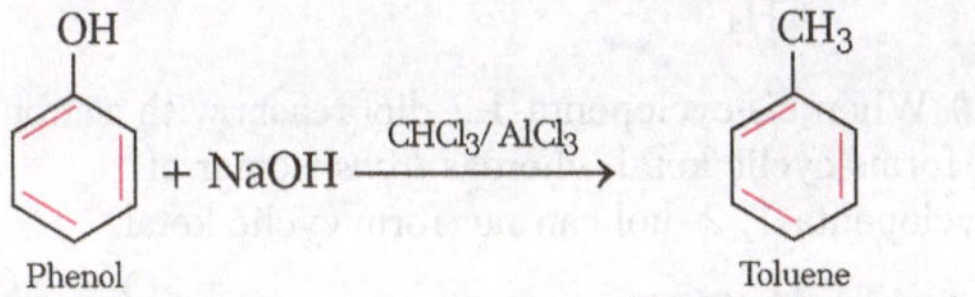

Toluene (Friedel-Crafts reaction)

76. (*a*) The correct match is A-2, B-3, C-1, D-4.

77. (*a*) The correct match is A-3, B-4, C-1, D-2.

78. (*a*) The correct match is A-4, B-3, C-2, D-1.

Final Check Through PYQs

1. (*a*)

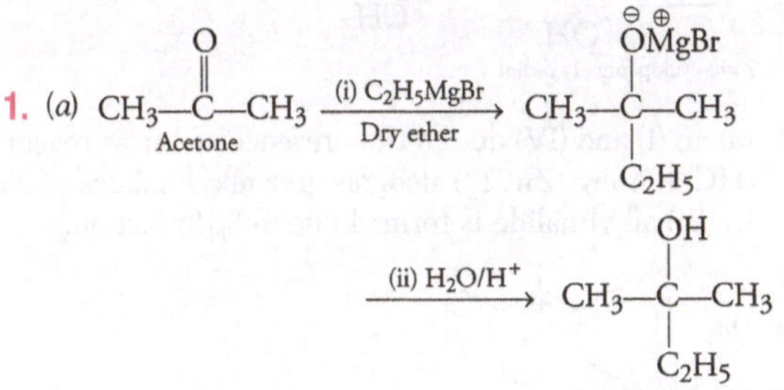

2-methyl butan-2-ol

2. (*c*) The given equation is represented as

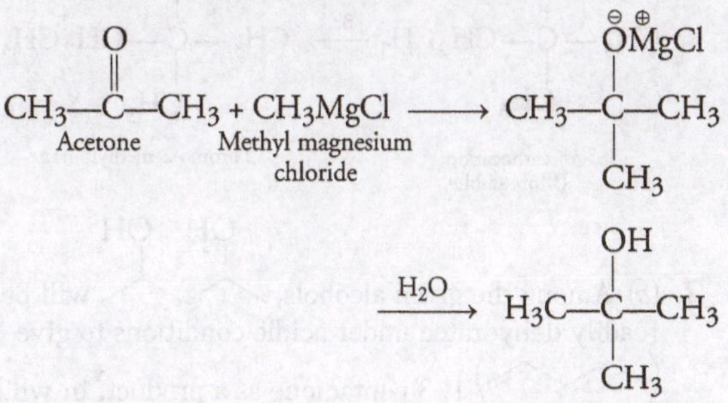

tert-butyl alcohol

3. (*a*)

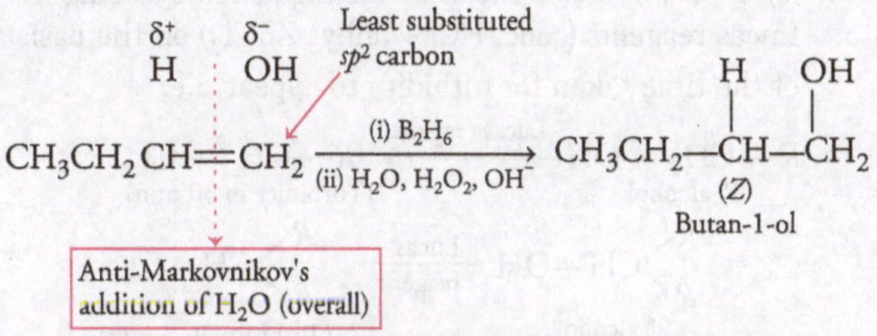

It is hydroboration-oxidation (HBO) reaction of an alkene which undergoes hydration to give an alcohol.

4. (*d*) The reactivity order of alcohols toward Lucas reagent 3° alcohol > 2° alcohol > 1° alcohol

$CH_3-CH_2-CH_2-CH_2-OH$ = 1° alcohol

$CH_3-CH_2-CH(CH_3)-OH$ = 2° alcohol

$CH_3-CH(CH_3)-CH_2-OH$ = 1° alcohol

$CH_3-C(CH_3)_2-OH$ = 3° alcohol

5. (*a*) The complete reaction is as follows

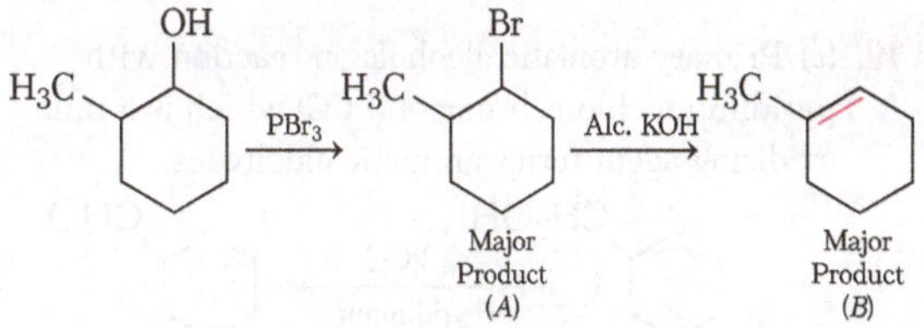

6. (*d*)

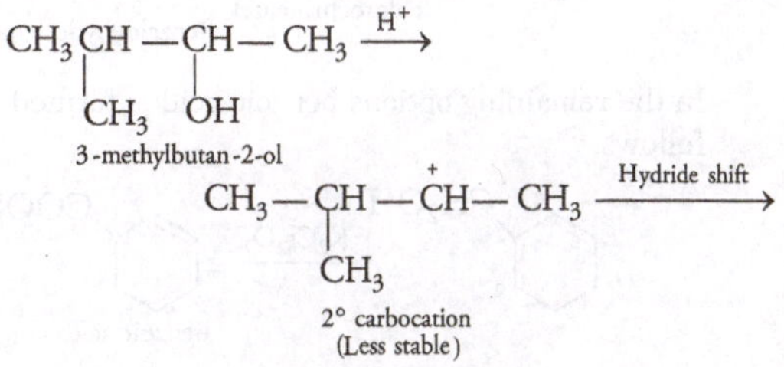

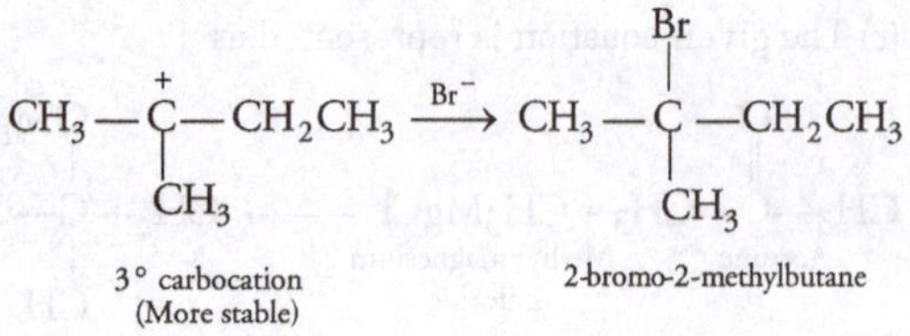

7. (*a*) Among the given alcohols, 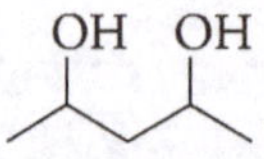 will be most readily dehydrated under acidic conditions to give 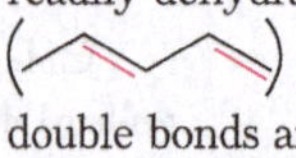 1, 3 pentadiene as a product, in which double bonds are present in conjugation.

8. (*b*) 1°, 2°, 3° alcohols can be distinguished by using Lucas reagents (conc. HCl + anhy. $ZnCl_2$) on the basis of the time taken for turbidity to appear, i.e.

$$\underset{1^\circ \text{ alcohol}}{R—CH_2—OH} \xrightarrow{\text{Lucas reagent}} \underset{\text{(Turbidity in 30 min)}}{R—CH_2—Cl}$$

$$\underset{2^\circ \text{ alcohol}}{R_2CH—OH} \xrightarrow{\text{Lucas reagent}} \underset{\text{(Turbidity in 5 min)}}{R_2CH—Cl}$$

$$\underset{3^\circ \text{ alcohol}}{R_3C—OH} \xrightarrow{\text{Lucas reagent}} \underset{\text{(Turbidity appears immediately)}}{R_3C—Cl}$$

Hence the order of reactivity of alcohol towards Lucas reagent is in the order 3° > 2° > 1°.
So, Statement I is true but Statement II is false.

9. (*c*) When vapours of alcohols are passed over heated copper at 573 K, primary and secondary alcohols undergo dehydrogenation to give aldehydes and ketones, respectively. While tertiary alcohols undergo dehydration to give alkenes.

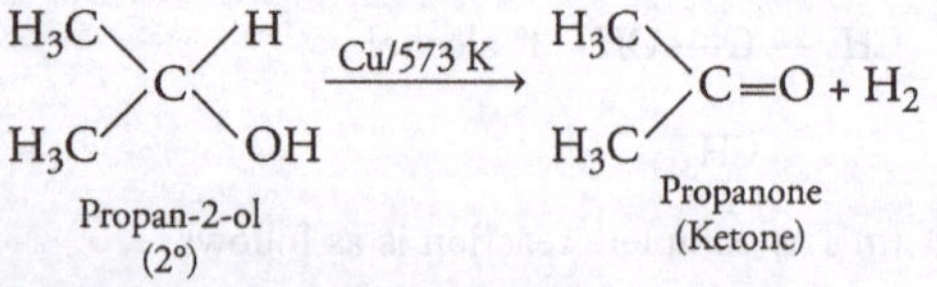

10. (*c*) Primary aromatic alcohols on reaction with pyridinium chlorochromate (PCC) which is a mild oxidising agent forms aromatic aldehydes.

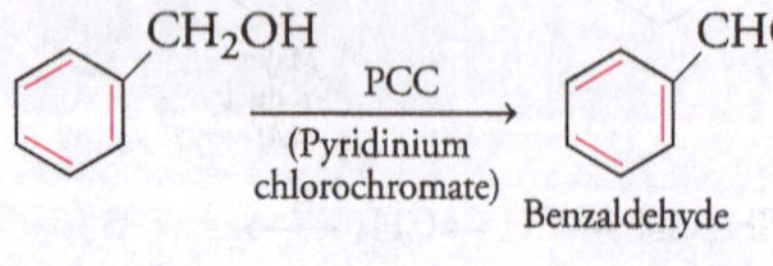

In the remaining options benzoic acid is formed as follows

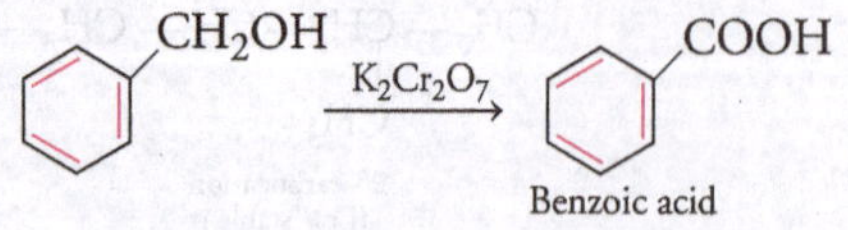

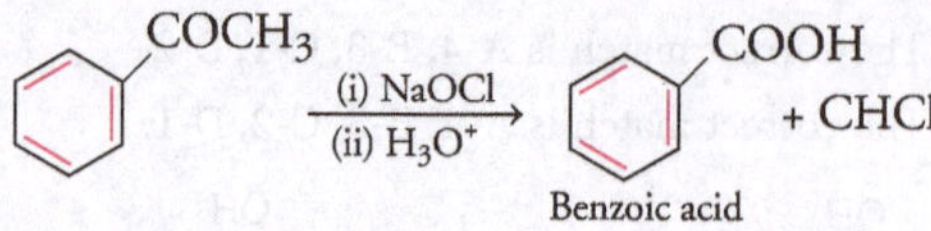

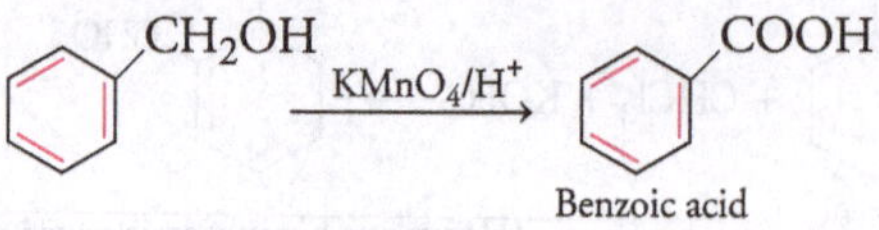

Thus, option (c) is correct.

11. (*d*) According to the given question, option (*A*) must be C_2H_5OH, as it reacts with Na to give C_2H_5ONa. The reaction sequence is as follows

(i) $$\underset{\substack{\text{Ethanol}\\(A)}}{C_2H_5OH} \xrightarrow{Na} \underset{\substack{\text{Sodium ethoxide}\\(B)}}{C_2H_5\overset{-}{O}\overset{+}{Na}} \xrightarrow{PCl_5} \underset{\substack{\text{Ethyl chloride}\\(C)}}{C_2H_5Cl}$$

(ii) $$C_2H_5\overset{-}{O}\overset{+}{Na} + C_2H_5Cl \xrightarrow{S_N2} \underset{\text{Diethyl ether}}{C_2H_5O\,C_2H_5} + NaCl$$

The above reaction is known as Williamson's ether synthesis. It involves nucleophilic attack of alkoxide ion on alkyl halide according to S_N2 mechanism.

$$\underset{\substack{\text{Nucleophile}\\\text{(alkoxide ion)}}}{C_2H_5O^-} + \underset{\substack{\text{Substrate}\\\text{(alkyl halide)}}}{CH_3—CH_2Cl} \xrightarrow{\text{Slow}}$$

$$C_2H_5O...\overset{+}{\underset{|\;CH_3}{C}}H_2...Cl^- \xrightarrow{\text{Fast}} C_2H_5—O—C_2H_5 + Cl^-$$

12. (*d*) When *cis*-cyclopenta-1,2-diol reacts with acetone, it forms cyclic ketal whereas *trans*-isomer of cyclopenta-1, 2-diol can not form cyclic ketal.

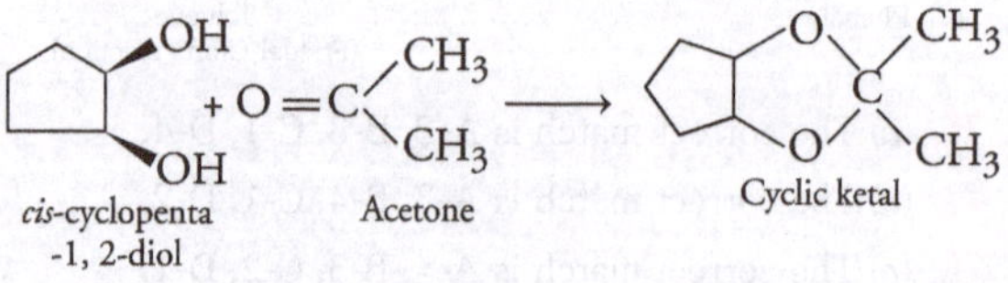

But,

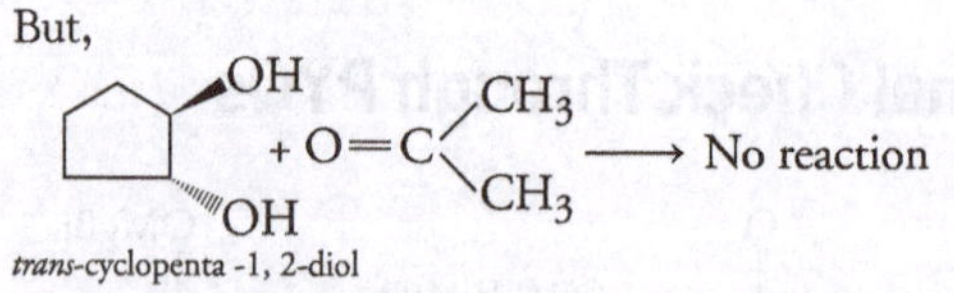

13. (*a*) In (I) and (IV) due to the presence of Lucas reagent (HCl + Anhy. $ZnCl_2$) alcohols give alkyl halides while in (III) alkyl halide is formed due to S_N1 reaction.

14. (*b*)

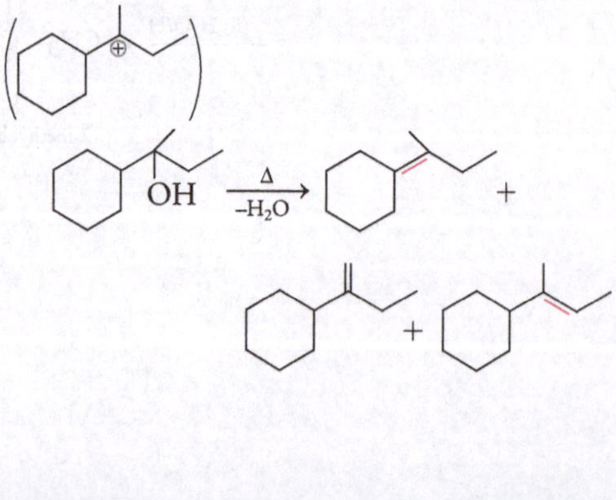

15. (*a*) EDG (+ *R*, + *I*) decreases acidity and EWG (– *R*, – *I*) increases acidity of phenol.

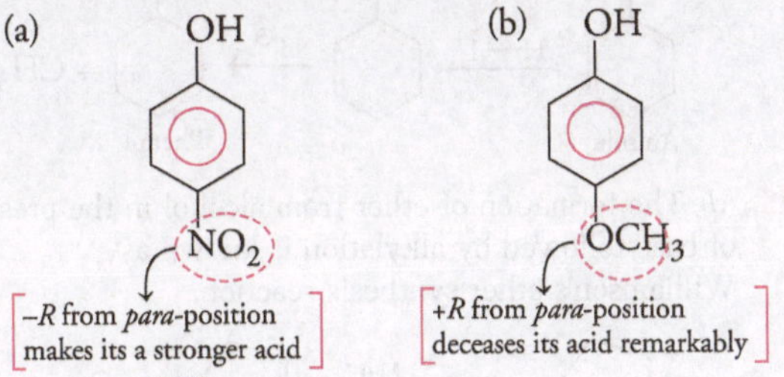

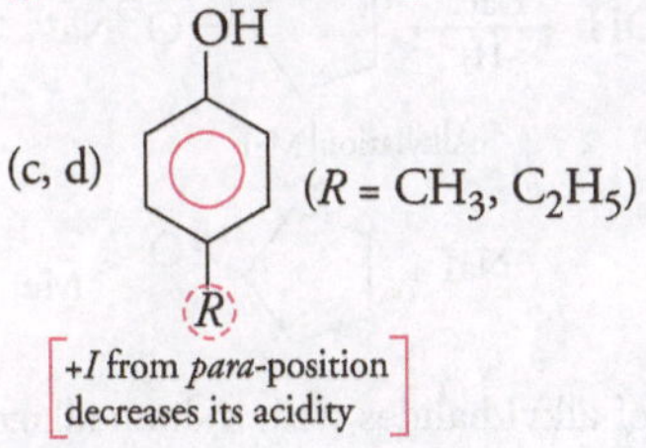

Thus, option (a) is correct.

16. (*a*) The given reaction is of phenol production starting with cumene and intermediate (*A*) is cumene hydroperoxide.

In the process, cumene (isopropylbenzene) is oxidised in the presence of air to cumene hydroperoxide. It is then converted to phenol and acetone by treating with dilute acid. Acetone, a by-product of this reaction is also obtained in large quantities by this method. The reaction takes place as follows

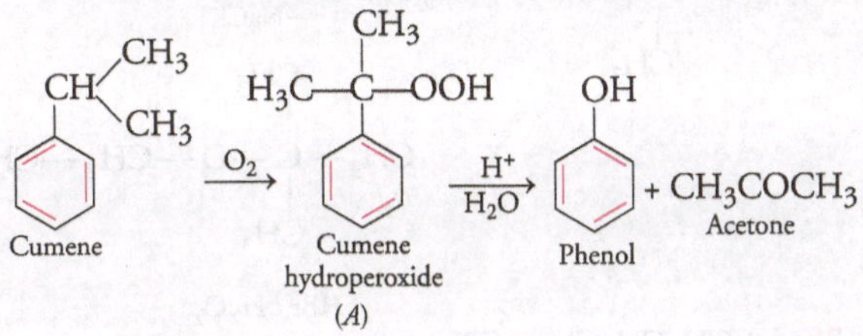

17. (*a*) 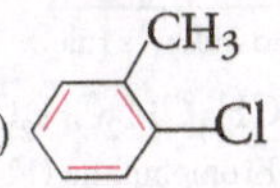 is a benzylic halide. Thus, there is a partial double bond character between sp^3-hybridised C atom next to an aromatic ring and Cl. It is most difficult to break this bond and hence it undergoes hydrolysis reaction with slowest rate.

18. (*d*) It is Reimer-Tiemann reaction. The electrophile formed is dichlorocarbene ($:CCl_2$). The mechanism is as follows

$$CHCl_3 + OH^- \rightleftharpoons \bar{C}Cl_3 + H_2O$$

$$\downarrow -Cl^-(\alpha\text{-elimination})$$

$$:CCl_2$$

Dichlorocarbene (electrophile)

19. (*d*) $CH_3—CH_2—CH_2—Cl + AlCl_3 \longrightarrow$

$$\underset{(1° \text{ carbocation})}{CH_3CH_2\overset{+}{C}H_2AlCl_4} \xrightarrow[-AlCl_4]{1,2\text{-}H^+ \text{ shift}} \underset{(2° \text{ carbocation})}{CH_3\overset{+}{C}HCH_3}$$

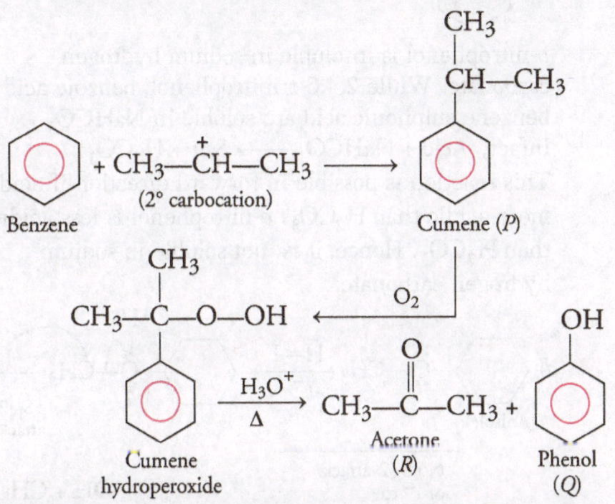

20. (*a*) Iodoform reaction with sodium hypoiodite is used for the detection of CH_3CO group. Also compounds containing $CH_3CH(OH)$ group shows positive iodoform test as it produces CH_3CO group on oxidation. Since, among the compounds, $CH_3CH(OH)$ group is given only in the substrate of option (a) hence, it is correct. The reaction of compound *A* with NaOI is given as follows

$$2NaOH + I_2 \longrightarrow NaOI + NaI + H_2O$$

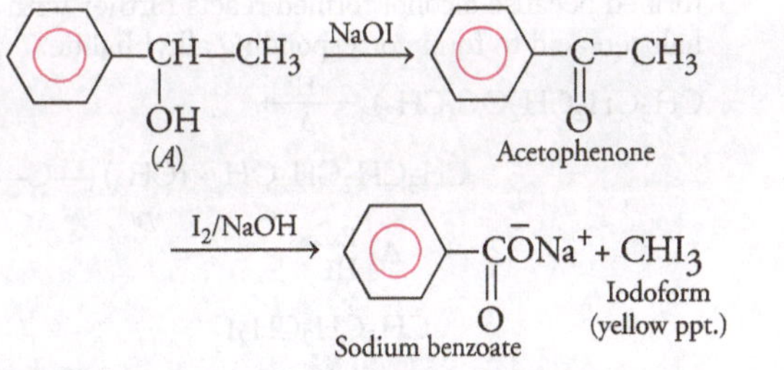

21. (*d*) Picric acid (2, 4, 6-trinitrophenol) is extremely more acidic than given compounds because its pK_a value is close to zero also due to the presence of three strong electron withdrawing group (—NO_2group) at *ortho* and *para*-positions, picric is more acidic compound.

↑ pK_a value ↓ the acidic character.

22. (*d*) 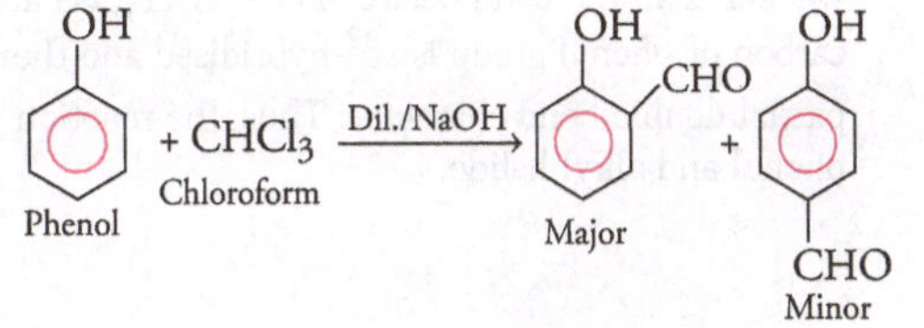

This is Reimer-Tiemann reaction. So, —CHO group is introduced at *o*- and *p*-position forming *o*-substituted product as a major product.

23. (*c*)

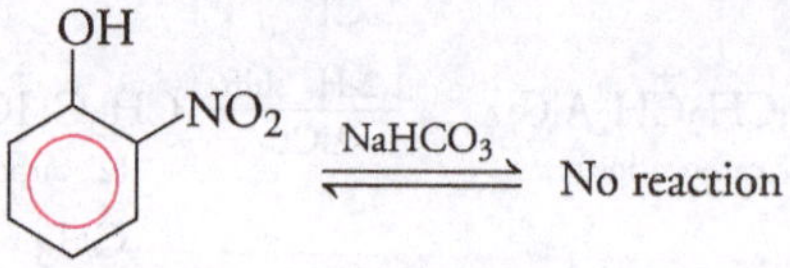

o-nitrophenol is insoluble in sodium hydrogen carbonate. While 2,4,6-trinitrophenol, benzoic acid and benzene sulphonic acid are soluble in $NaHCO_3$.

Infact, Acid + $NaHCO_3 \longrightarrow$ Salt + H_2CO_3

This reaction is possible in forward direction if acid is more acidic than H_2CO_3. *o*-nitrophenol is less acidic than H_2CO_3. Hence, it is not soluble in sodium hydrogen carbonate.

24. (*d*)

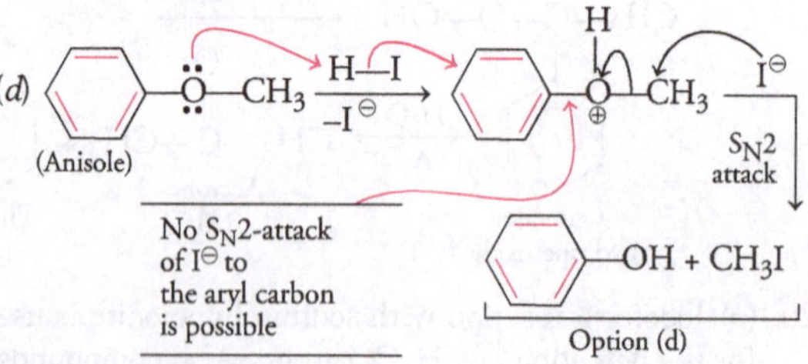

So, even with excess of HI, anisole will give phenol and methyl iodide (as in option-d).

25. (*a*) Ethers are readily cleaved by heating in presence of halogen acids to form alcohol and an alkyl halide. In case of unsymmetrical ethers, halogen goes preferentially with smaller alkyl group or more stable carbocation. If excess of acid is used then only alkyl halide is formed because alcohol formed reacts further with halogen acid to form corresponding alkyl halide.

$$CH_3CH_2CH_2OC(CH_3)_3 \xrightarrow[\Delta]{HI} CH_3CH_2CH_2OH + \underset{'D'}{(CH_3)_3—C—I}$$

$$CH_3CH_2CH_2OH \xrightarrow[\Delta]{\text{Excess HI}} \underset{'C'}{CH_3CH_2CH_2I}$$

26. (*a*) In $Ph — \ddot{\underset{..}{O}} — H$, the lone pair of oxygen is in conjugation with phenyl group. Thus, it is least basic among the given compounds and is most difficult to protonate.

27. (*c*) In anisole, methyl phenyl oxonium ion is formed by protonation of ether. The bond between O —CH_3 is weaker than the bond between O—C_6H_5, because the carbon of phenyl group is sp^2-hybridised and there is a partial double bond character. Thus, the reaction yields phenol and alkyl halide.

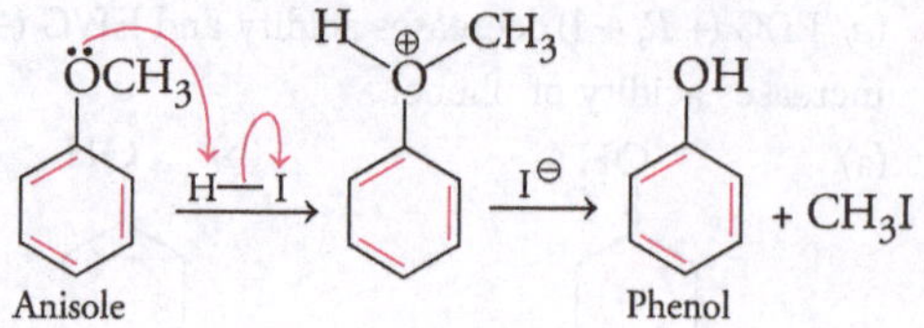

28. (*d*) The formation of ether from alcohol in the presence of base followed by alkylation is known as Williamson's ether synthesis reaction.

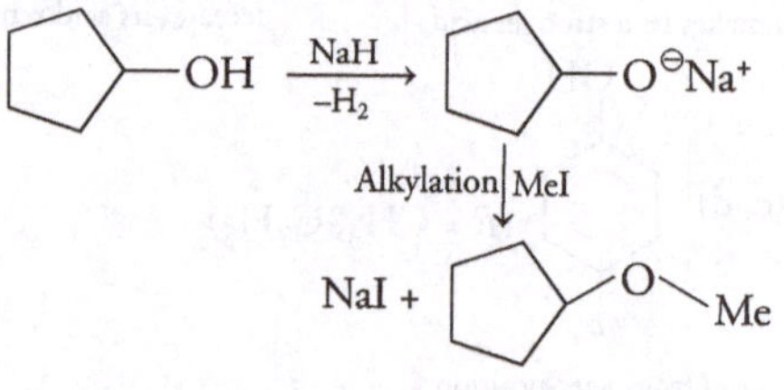

29. (*a*) The reaction of alkyl halides with sodium alkoxide or sodium phenoxide to form ethers is called Williamson synthesis.

Here, in this reaction alkyl halide should be primary and alkoxide, should be bulkier as shown below.

$$\underset{\text{Alkyl halide}}{R—X} + \underset{\text{Sodium alkoxide}}{R'—ONa} \longrightarrow \underset{\text{Ether}}{R—O—R'} + NaX$$

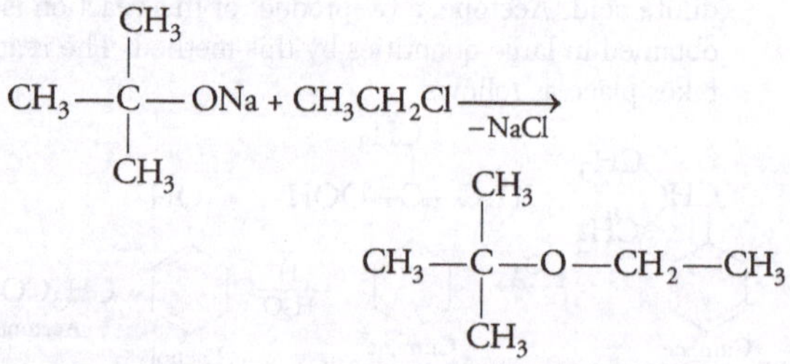

30. (*a*) $CH_3CH_2CH{=}CH_2 \xrightarrow[\text{Anti-Markovnikov's rule}]{HBr / H_2O_2} \underset{\text{Bromobutane (1° product) (Y)}}{CH_3CH_2CH_2CH_2Br}$

$$CH_3CH_2CH_2CH_2Br \xrightarrow[S_N2\text{ reaction}]{C_2H_5ONa} \underset{\text{Ethoxy-butane (Z)}}{CH_3CH_2CH_2CH_2OC_2H_5}$$

31. (*b*) Williamson's synthesis

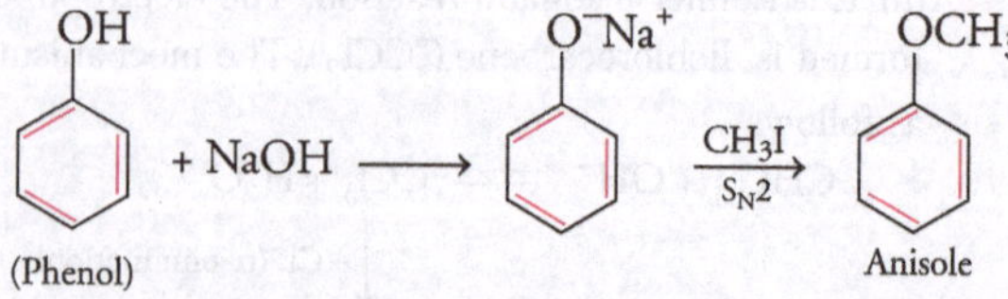

Skill Builder

- **Sol. of Skill Builder Pg. 337**

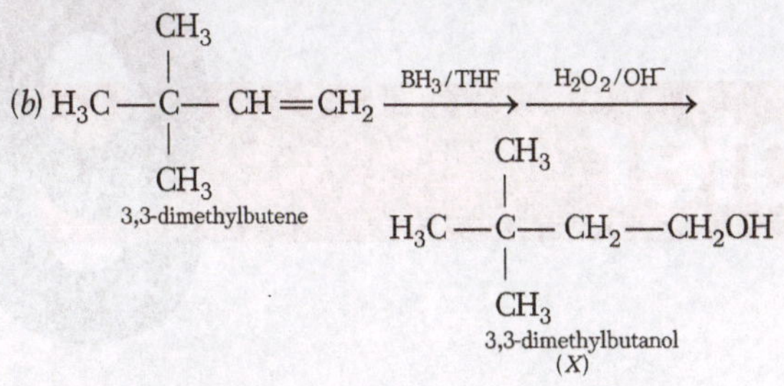

Thus,, the IUPAC name of the compound X is 3,3-dimethylbutanol.

- **Sol. of Skill Builder Pg. 344**

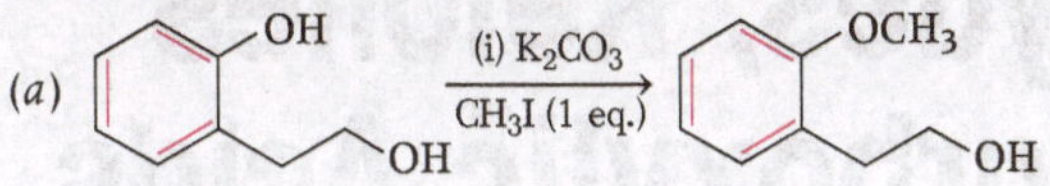

- **Sol. of Skill Builder Pg. 351**

(*d*) The given reaction is proceed as

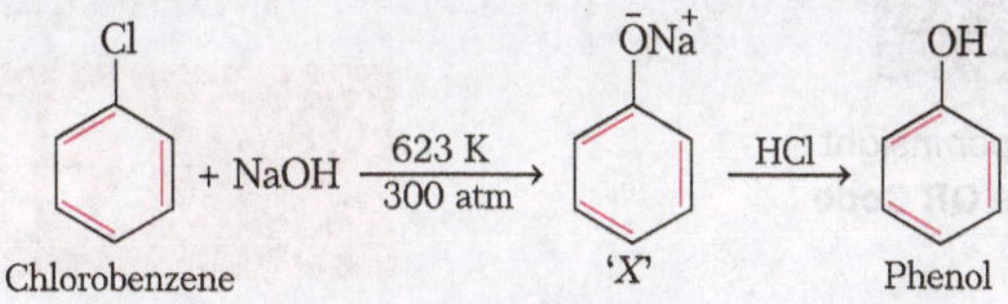

- **Sol. of Skill Builder Pg. 353**

(*d*) Electron withdrawing group increases the acidity while electron donating group decreases the acidity of phenol.

- **Sol. of Skill Builder Pg. 361**

(*c*) $\underset{\text{Acetic anhydride}}{(CH_3CO)_2O} + \underset{\text{Diethyl ether}}{(C_2H_5)_2O} \xrightarrow{AlCl_3} 2CH_3COOC_2H_5$

For deeper insight
Scan the QR Code

Chapter 9

Aldehydes, Ketones and Carboxylic Acids

Learning Objectives

Module-I

- Nomenclature and Isomerism
- Structure
- Methods of Preparation of Aldehydes and Ketones
- Methods of Preparation of Aldehydes Only
- Methods of Preparation of Ketones Only
- Physical Properties

Module-II

- Chemical Reactions of Carbonyl Compounds
- Nucleophilic Addition Reaction
- Nucleophilic Addition Elimination Reaction
- Oxidation Reaction
- Reduction Reaction
- Aldols, Cannizzaro Reaction
- Electrophilic Substitution Reaction

Module-III

- Classification
- Nomenclature
- Isomerism
- Methods of Preparation of Carboxylic Acids
- Chemical Properties of Carboxylic Acids
- Method of Preparation of Aromatic Carboxylic Acids
- Physical Properties of Aromatic Carboxylic Acids
- Chemical Properties of Aromatic Carboxylic Acids

Chapter Overview with *NEET Connection*

This chapter is useful for the learning of preparation and chemical properties of aldehydes, ketones and carboxylic acids. Without gripping this chapter, it will be difficult to learn and understand the interconversion of organic reactions. Chapters like amines and biomolecules can be better understood only after studying this chapter.

Special format questions can be easily framed on the following topics of this chapter.

- Oxidation reaction of aldehyde and ketone
- Haloform reaction
- Aldol condensation
- Cannizzaro reaction
- Acidity of carboxylic acids

For better understanding of this chapter a proper grip over chemical properties of hydrocarbons, alkyl halides, aryl halides, alcohols, phenols and ethers is required.

Introduction

The class of organic compounds which contains $—\overset{O}{\overset{\|}{C}}—$ functional groups are called carbonyl compounds. These compounds are classified into aldehydes and ketones. In aldehyde, the carbonyl group is bonded to a carbon and hydrogen while in the ketones it is bonded to two carbon atoms. The carbonyl compounds in which carbon of carbonyl group is bonded to oxygen of hydroxy moiety (–OH) are known as carboxylic acids. Carbonyl and carboxylic compounds may be aliphatic or aromatic in nature.

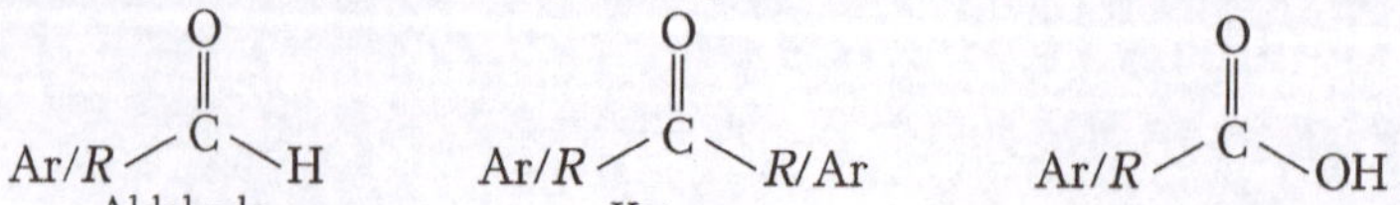

Aldehyde Ketone Carboxylic acid

Module 1

Aldehyde and Ketones : Introduction & Methods of Preparation

- Nomenclature and Isomerism • Structure • Methods of Preparation of Aldehydes and Ketones
- Methods of Preparation of Aldehydes Only • Methods of Preparation of Ketones Only • Physical Properties

Aldehydes and ketones are the simplest and most important carbonyl compounds.

Nomenclature

There are two systems of nomenclature of aldehydes and ketones.

Common Names

The common names of most aldehydes are derived from the common names of the corresponding carboxylic acids by replacing the ending '–ic' acid with aldehyde.

CH_3CHO
Acetaldehyde

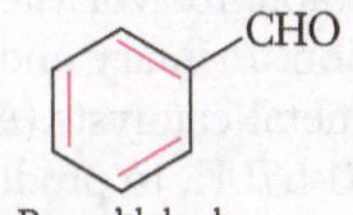

Benzaldehyde

The common names of ketones are derived by naming two alkyl or aryl groups bonded to the carbonyl group.

$$CH_3-\overset{O}{\overset{\|}{C}}-CH_3$$

Acetone (Dimethyl ketone)

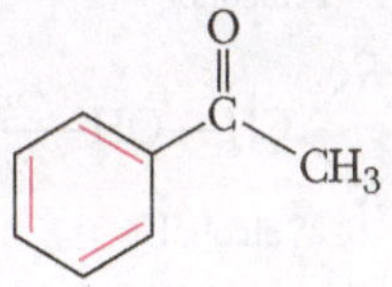

Acetophenone

IUPAC Names

In IUPAC system, naming of aldehyde is done by replacing the terminal 'e' of the alkanes with suffix 'al' while ketones with suffix 'one'. Position of carbonyl carbon in aldehydes is always C-1 while in ketones, it gets lowest possible number.

e.g. $H-\overset{O}{\overset{\|}{C}}-H$; $CH_3-\overset{O}{\overset{\|}{C}}-H$; $\overset{3}{CH_3}-\underset{CH_3}{\underset{|}{\overset{2}{CH}}}-\overset{1}{CHO}$;

Methanal; Ethanal; 2 - methylpropanal

$CH_3-\overset{O}{\overset{\|}{C}}-CH_3$; $\overset{5}{CH_3}\overset{4}{CH_2}\overset{3}{CH_2}\underset{2}{\overset{O}{\overset{\|}{C}}}\underset{1}{CH_3}$

Propan-2-one; Pentan-2-one

Isomerism

Carbonyl compounds show following types of isomerism

(i) **Chain isomerism** Aldehydes those have atleast four carbon atoms and ketones having atleast five carbon atoms, show chain isomerism.

These isomers have same molecular formula but different structural formula. e.g. C_4H_8O.

$\overset{4}{CH_3}\overset{3}{CH_2}\overset{2}{CH_2}\overset{1}{CHO}$, Butan - 1 - al

$CH_3-\underset{CH_3}{\underset{|}{CH}}-CHO$ 2 - methylpropanal

(ii) **Metamerism** In this isomerism, the difference lies in nature of alkyl groups attached to a polyvalent functional group. These isomers are called metamers.

$CH_3CH_2-\overset{O}{\overset{\|}{C}}-CH_2CH_3$; $CH_3\overset{O}{\overset{\|}{C}}-CH_2CH_2CH_3$

Pentan - 3 - one; Pentan - 2 - one

(iii) **Functional isomerism** These isomers have same molecular formula but different functional groups. It is shown by both ketones and aldehyde.

e.g. $CH_3-\overset{O}{\overset{\|}{C}}-CH_3$; $CH_3-CH_2-\overset{O}{\overset{\|}{C}}-H$

Propan-2-one; Propanal

Mentor's TIP

If two molecules contain same functional group (polyvalent) then never write chain or position isomerism, it will always be metamerism.

Structure

Carbonyl carbon atom in aldehydes and ketones are sp^2-hybridised. It is attached to three atoms which lie in same plane while the π-electron cloud lies above and below the plane. The bond angle formed between the bond pairs is about 120° as expected of a trigonal coplanar.

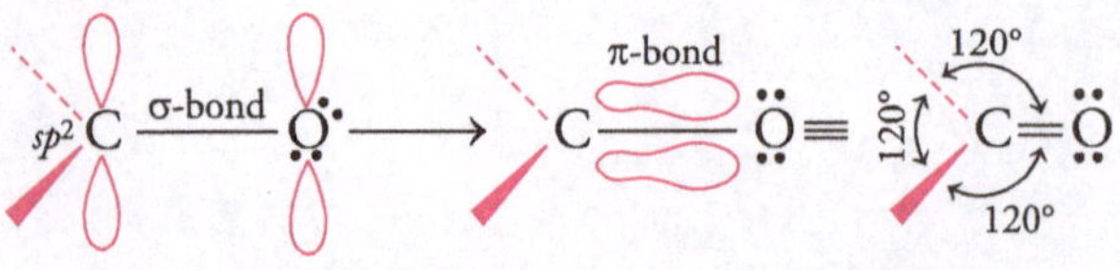

Orbital diagram for the formation of carbonyl group

The double bond between carbon and oxygen is similar to alkene double bond but it is shorter and stronger than double bond of alkene (C=C).

The carbon-oxygen double bond is polar in nature because oxygen is more electronegative than carbon. Hence, the carbonyl carbon is an electrophilic (Lewis acid) and carbonyl oxygen is a nucleophilic (Lewis base) centre.

Thus, π-electron cloud is displaced towards oxygen. Due to this, carbon bears partial positive charge while oxygen bears partially negative charge.

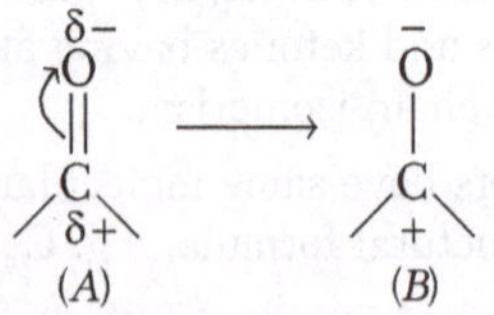

Preparation of Aldehydes and Ketones

Some of the important methods for the preparation of aldehydes and ketones are given below

By Oxidation of Alcohols

Alcohols undergo controlled oxidation to give aldehydes and ketones. Primary alcohols are easily oxidised to carboxylic acids with oxidants such as $KMnO_4$ (in neutral, acidic or alkaline medium), CrO_3 and $K_2Cr_2O_7$ in acidic medium.

$$\underset{1° \text{ alcohol}}{R-CH_2-OH} \xrightarrow[H_2SO_4]{K_2Cr_2O_7} \underset{\text{Acid}}{R-\overset{O}{\overset{\|}{C}}-OH} + H_2O$$

$$\underset{2° \text{ alcohol}}{R_2CH-OH} \xrightarrow[H_2SO_4]{K_2Cr_2O_7} \underset{\text{Ketone}}{R_2C=O} + H_2O$$

$$CH_3(CH_2)_6CH_2OH \xrightarrow[\text{Jones reagent}]{CrO_3/H_2SO_4} CH_3(CH_2)_6COOH$$

Carbonyl compounds formed in the above reaction is easily oxidised to carboxylic acids. So, to prevent further oxidation, carbonyl compound should be removed from reaction mixture.

Pyridinium chlorochromate (PCC) in anhydrous medium like CH_2Cl_2 are better oxidising agents than acidified $K_2Cr_2O_7$ or alkaline $KMnO_4$ for converting 1° alcohols to aldehydes and 2° alcohols to ketones.

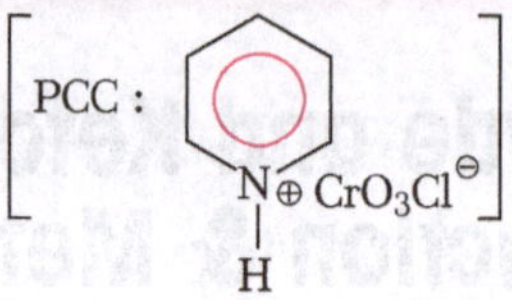

$$\underset{1° \text{ alcohol}}{RCH_2OH} \xrightarrow[CH_2Cl_2]{\text{PDC or PCC}} \underset{\text{Aldehyde}}{R\overset{O}{\overset{\|}{C}}H} \longrightarrow \text{No further reaction}$$

$$\underset{2° \text{ alcohol}}{RCH(OH)R'} \xrightarrow[CH_2Cl_2]{\text{PCC}} \underset{\text{Ketone}}{R\overset{O}{\overset{\|}{C}}R'} + H_2O \longrightarrow \text{No further reaction}$$

> **Concept ladder**
> - Sarett and Collin's reagents are also used for converting 1° alcohols to aldehydes and 2° alcohols to ketones.
> - **Sarett reagent** is a 1 : 2 complex of chromium trioxide in pyridine as solvent (i.e. $CrO_3 \cdot 2C_5H_5N$).
> - **Collin's reagent** is a modification of Sarett reagent. In this, CH_2Cl_2 is taken as a solvent.

By Dehydrogenation of Alcohols

This method is suitable for volatile alcohols and is of industrial application. Primary and secondary alcohols react with heavy metal catalysts (Ag or Cu) at a temperature of 520-570K, to produce aldehydes and ketones respectively.

$$\underset{1° \text{ alcohol}}{RCH_2OH} \xrightarrow[520-570K]{Cu,\Delta} \underset{\text{Aldehyde}}{RCHO} + H_2$$

$$\underset{2° \text{ alcohol}}{R_2CH-OH} \xrightarrow[520K]{Cu,\Delta} \underset{\text{Ketone}}{R_2C=O} + H_2$$

On the other hand, 3° alcohols undergo dehydration to give alkenes as product.

$$\underset{3° \text{ alcohol}}{H_3C-C(CH_3)_2-OH} \xrightarrow[520\text{ K}]{Cu,\Delta} \underset{\text{Alkene}}{CH_3-C(=CH_2)-CH_3} + H_2O$$

From Hydrocarbons

Alkenes and alkynes undergoes reductive ozonolysis to give carbonyl compounds.

(i) Ozonolysis of Alkene

Reaction of alkenes with ozone followed by subsequent hydrolysis in presence of Zn forms aldehydes and ketones. In this reaction, ozonide is formed as an intermediate.

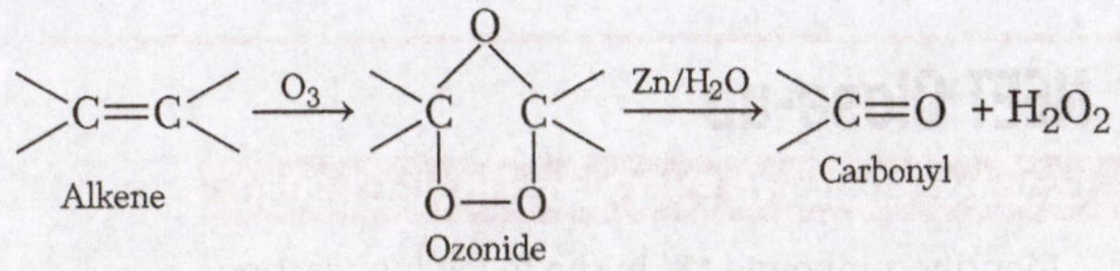

Here, Zn dust removes H_2O_2 as shown in reaction

$$Zn + H_2O_2 \longrightarrow ZnO + H_2O$$

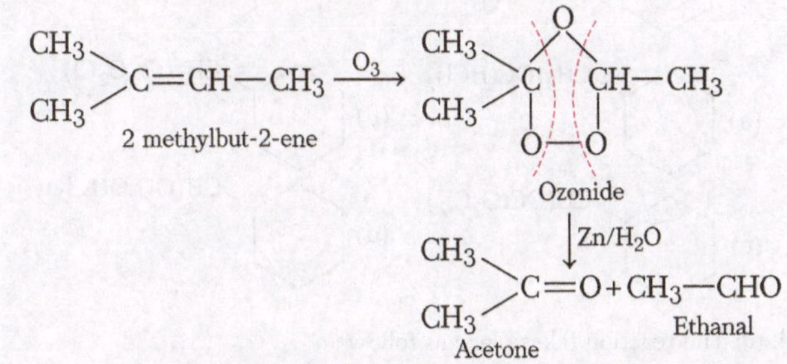

Easiest method to derive products by ozonolysis of alkenes is to

(a) break (C=C) bond (b) place O-atoms at breaking point

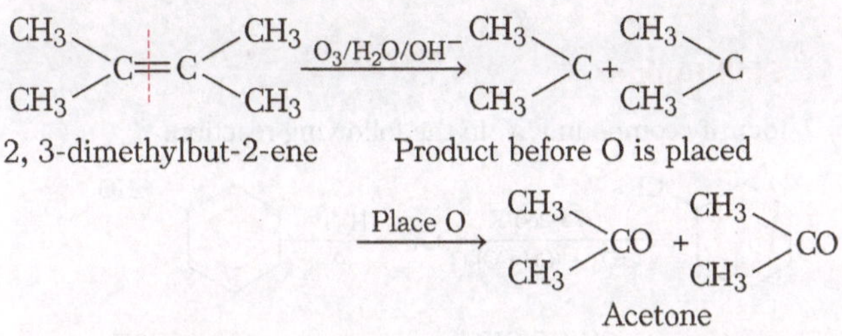

Mentor's TIP

By using the products obtained one can identify the alkene used as a reactant. Simply place the products of ozonolysis in such a way that O- atoms are face to face. Then replace O-atoms by (=) bond.

(ii) From Hydration of Alkynes

Alkynes in presence of dilute H_2SO_4 and $HgSO_4$ undergo hydration to give aldehydes or ketones. Enol is formed as an intermediate which tautomerises to its keto form.

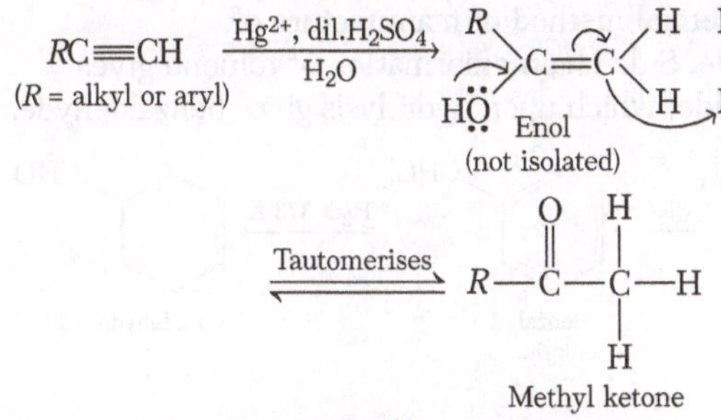

$$\underset{\text{Ethyne}}{CH \equiv CH} \xrightarrow[HgSO_4]{H_2O/\ H^+} \underset{\text{Ethanal}}{CH_3CHO}$$

$$\underset{\text{Propyne}}{CH_3C \equiv CH} \xrightarrow[HgSO_4]{H_2O/H^+} \underset{\text{Propanone}}{CH_3COCH_3}$$

Methods of Preparation of Aldehydes Only

Some of the methods for the preparation of aldehydes only are as follows

From Acyl Chlorides (Acid Chloride)

Acid chlorides on reaction with H_2 in presence of Pd and $BaSO_4$ poisoned by traces of sulphur or quinoline (i.e. Lindlar's catalyst) produces aldehyde. This reaction is known as **Rosenmund reduction.**

e.g. 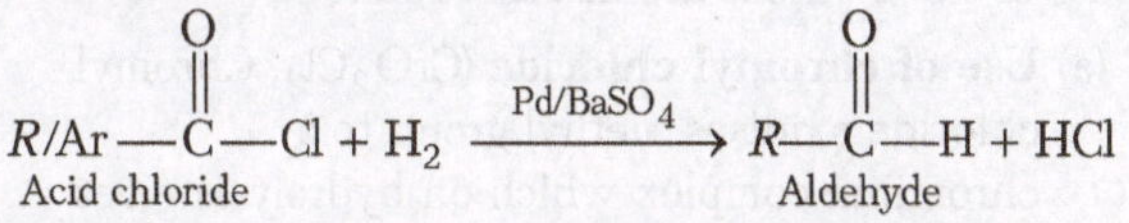

Acid chlorides can also be reduced into aldehydes by using lithium tri-*t*-butoxy aluminium hydride $[LiAlH(O\text{-}t\text{-}C_4H_9)_3]$.

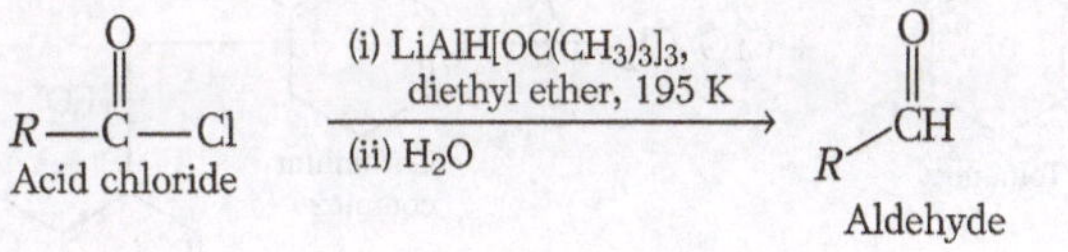

In this reaction, reduction occurs by transfer of hydride ion from aluminium atom to carbonyl carbon of acyl chloride.

From Esters

Esters can be reduced to aldehydes selectively using diisobutyl aluminium hydride (DIBAL-H).

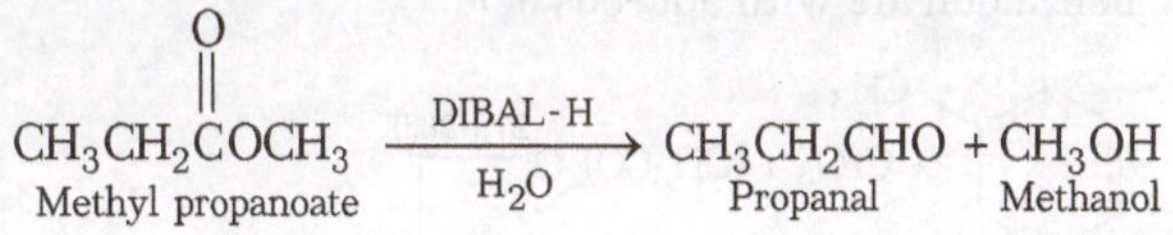

From Nitriles

Alkyl cyanides react with $SnCl_2$/HCl to give imines followed by hydrolysis to give corresponding aldehydes. This method is known as **Stephen reduction.**

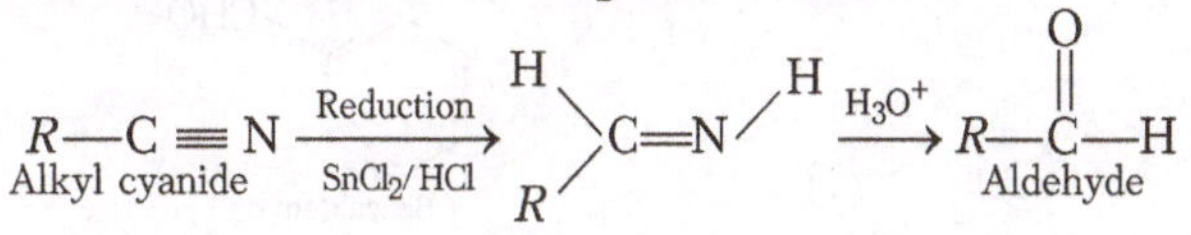

DIBAL-H is also used to reduce nitriles into aldehydes.

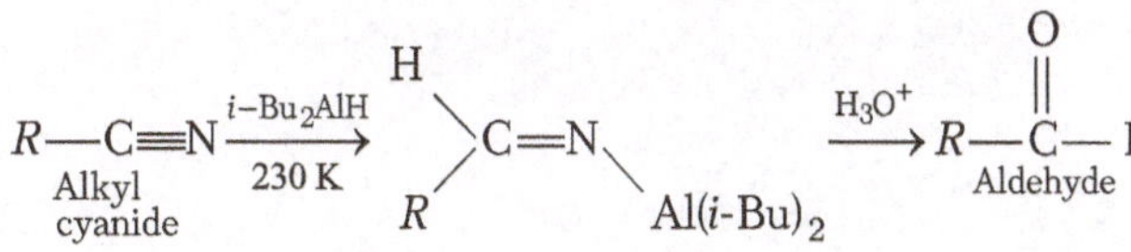

From Aromatic Hydrocarbons

By using following methods aromatic aldehydes can be prepared from aromatic hydrocarbons.

(i) By Oxidation of Methylbenzene

Strong oxidising agents oxidises toluene and its derivatives to benzoic acids.

However, it is possible to stop the oxidation at the aldehyde stage with suitable reagents that convert the methyl group to an intermediate that is difficult to oxidise further.

Some of the methods are discussed below

(a) **Use of chromyl chloride** (CrO_2Cl_2, Chromyl chloride oxidises methyl group to a chromium complex which on hydrolysis gives benzaldehyde. This reaction is called as **Etard reaction.**

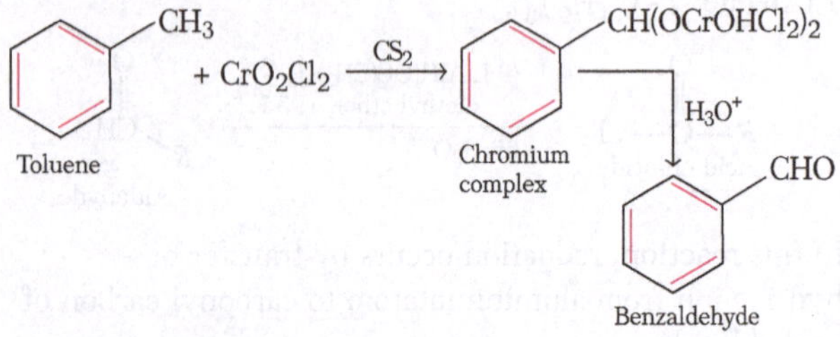

(b) **Use of chromic oxide** (CrO_3) Reaction of chromic oxide in acetic anhydride with toluene or substituted toluene gives benzylidene diacetate. This benzylidene diacetate is hydrolysed to corresponding benzaldehyde with aqueous acid.

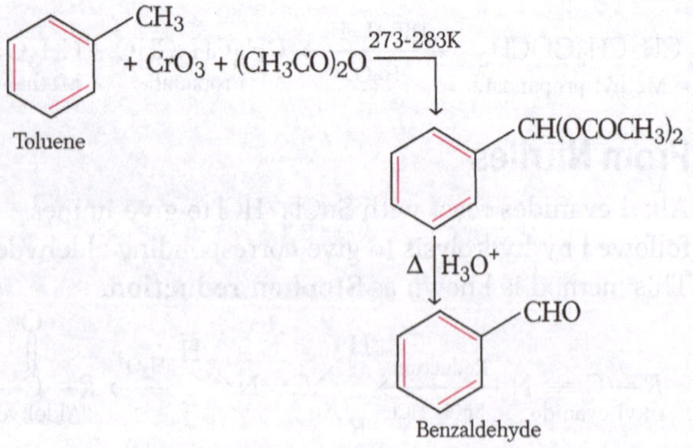

NEET Close-up

Example Similar to PYQ Asked in NEET 2020

Identify compound '*X*' in the following reaction.

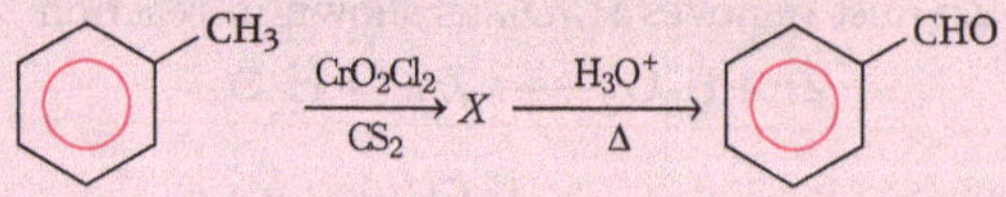

(a) 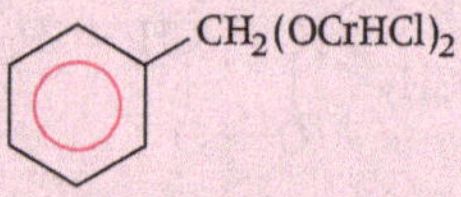

(b) 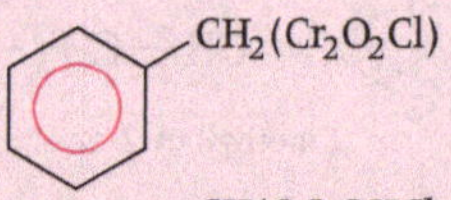

(c) 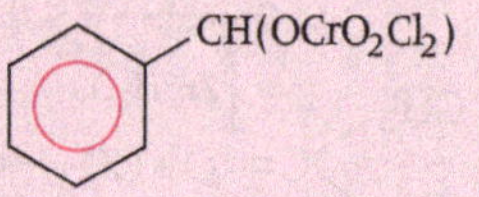

(d) 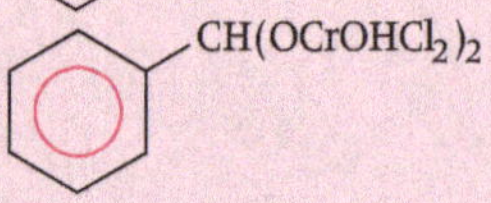

Sol. (*d*) The reaction takes place as follows

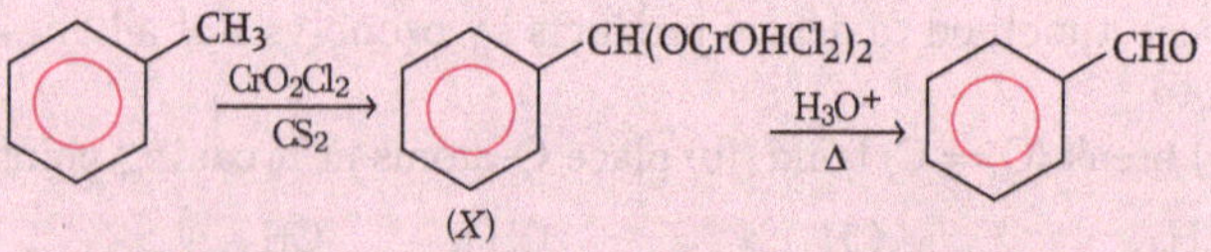

Skill Builder

Identify compound '*X*' in the following reaction.

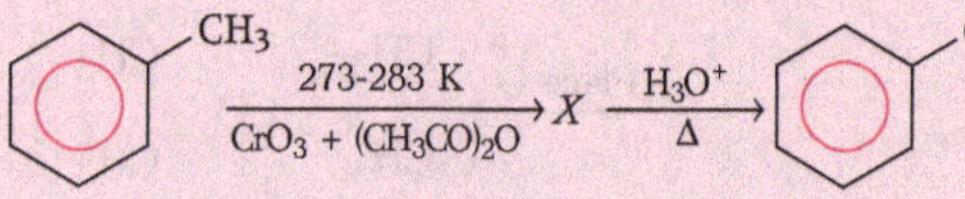

(a) 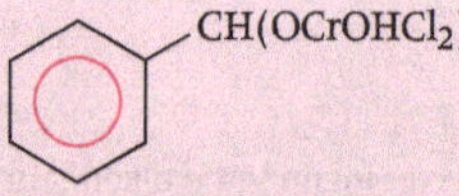

(b) 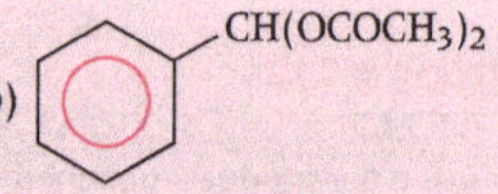

(c) 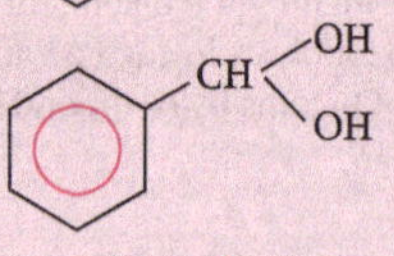

(d) 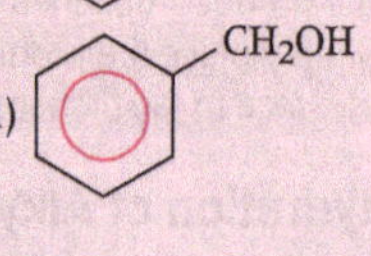

For more practice Refer to Q.22 of Step up practice 1.

(ii) By Side Chain Chlorination followed by Hydrolysis

It is a commercial method of manufacture of benzaldehyde. Side chain chlorination of toluene gives benzal chloride, which upon hydrolysis gives benzaldehyde.

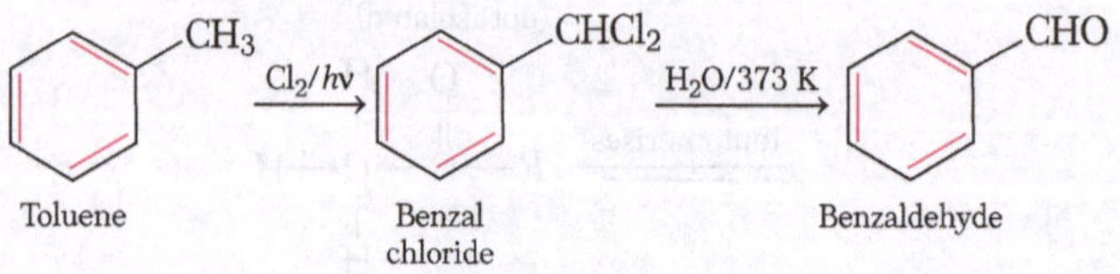

(iii) By Gattermann-Koch Reaction

Treatment of benzene or its derivative with carbon monoxide and hydrogen chloride in the presence of anhy. $AlCl_3$ or CuCl gives benzaldehyde or substituted benzaldehyde.

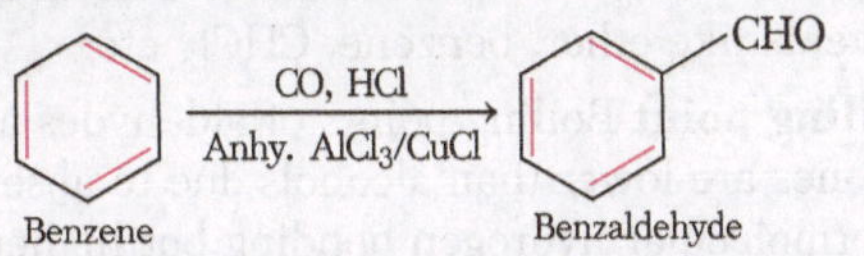

Benzene　　Benzaldehyde

The above reaction is called as **Gattermann-Koch reaction.**

NEET Close-up

Example Similar to PYQ Asked in NEET 2020

Identify compound (*A*) in the following reaction.

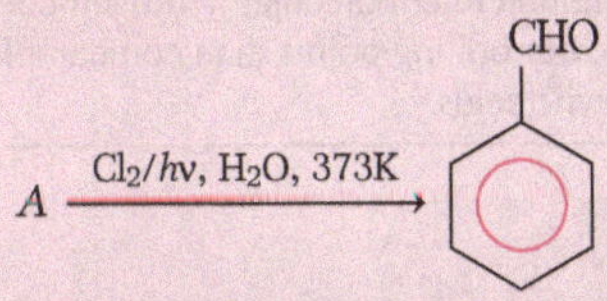

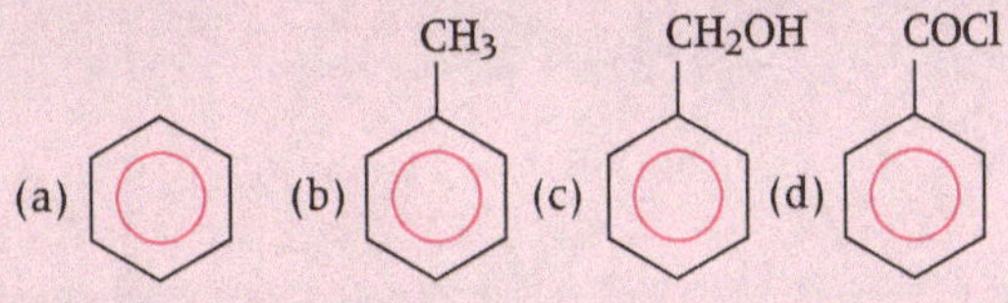

Sol. (*b*) The reaction takes place as follows

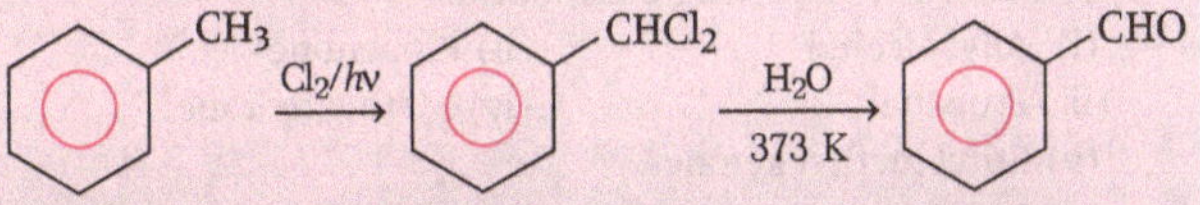

Toluene (*A*)　　Benzyl chloride　　Benzyl aldehyde

Skill Builder

Identify compound (*A*) in the following reactions,

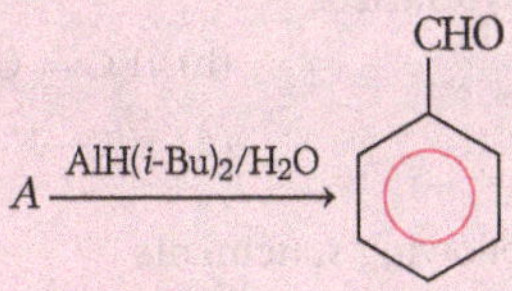

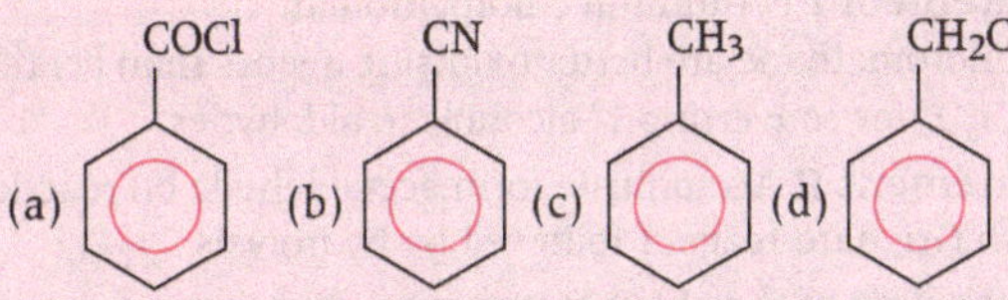

For more practice Refer to Q.16 of Step up practice 1.

Methods of Preparation of Ketones

Some of the methods for the preparation of ketones only are

From Acyl Chloride

Ketones can be easily prepared by the action of a suitable dialkyl cadmium (prepared by the reaction of cadmium chloride with Grignard's reagent) on an acyl chloride.

$$2RMgX + CdCl_2 \longrightarrow R-Cd-R + MgCl_2 + MgX_2$$

$$R-Cd-R + 2R'COCl \longrightarrow 2RCOR' + CdCl_2$$

Lithium salts of carboxylic acids and acid chloride can also be converted into corresponding ketones by the help of lithium salts.

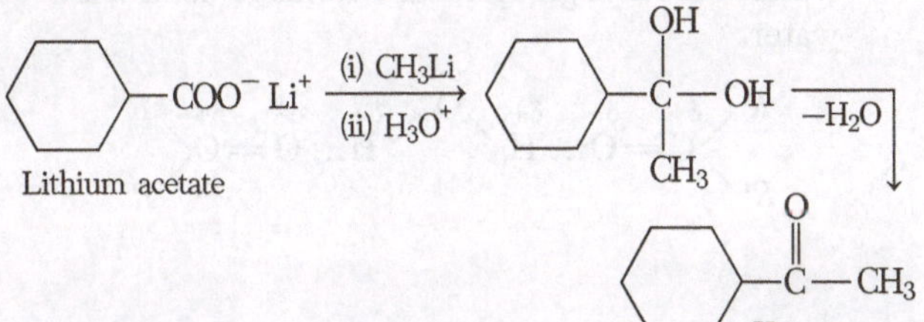

Lithium acetate　　Ketone

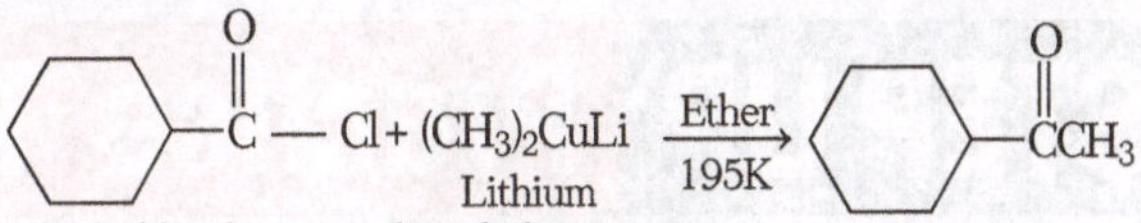

Acid chloride　　Lithium dimethyl cuprate (Gilmann reagent)　　Ketone

> **Concept ladder** Lithium dialkyl cuprate is a weak organometallic reagent which is used to stop the reaction at ketone stage. It reacts faster with acid chloride or esters.

From Nitriles

Reaction of nitriles with Grignard reagent followed by hydrolysis gives ketone.

$$CH_3-CH_2-C\equiv N + C_6H_5MgBr \xrightarrow{\text{Ether}}$$

$$CH_3CH_2-C(=NMgBr)-C_6H_5 \xrightarrow{H_3O^+} C_2H_5-C(=O)-C_6H_5$$

1-phenyl propanone

From Benzene or Substituted Benzenes

When benzene or substituted benzene is treated with acid chloride in the presence of anhydrous $AlCl_3$, then it gives corresponding ketone. This reaction is called as **Friedel-Crafts acylation reaction.**

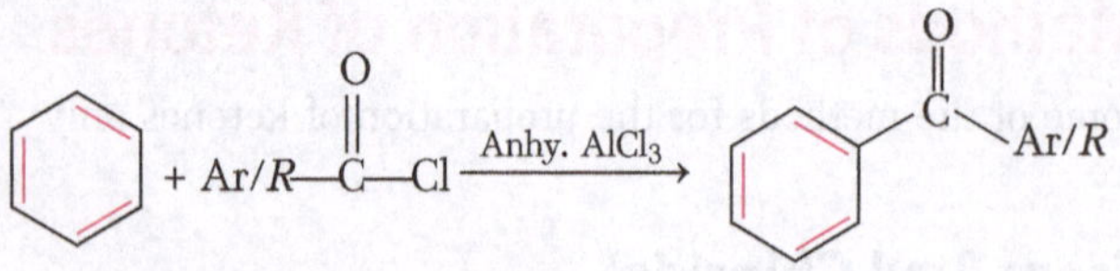

Physical Properties

(i) **Physical state** Methanal is a pungent smelling gas while ethanal is a volatile liquid. Rest of the aldehydes and ketones containing upto eleven carbon atoms are colourless liquids and higher members are solids.

(ii) **Solubility** Aldehydes and ketones are soluble in water. Carbonyl group readily forms H-bond with water.

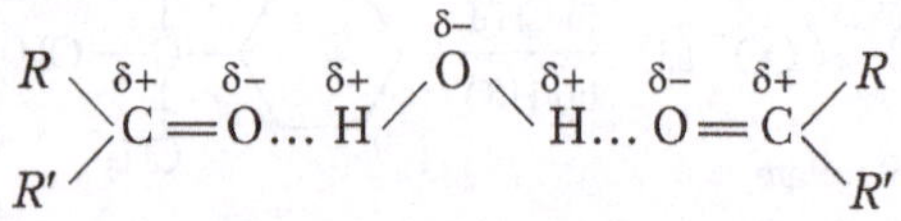

Solubility decreases with increase in length of alkyl chain. Therefore, carbonyl compounds upto four carbon atoms are soluble and higher members are insoluble.

Higher carbonyl compounds are soluble in organic solvents like ether, benzene, $CHCl_3$ etc.

(iii) **Boiling point** Boiling points of aldehydes and ketones are lower than alcohols due to absence of intermolecular hydrogen bonding but higher than non-polar compounds such as hydrocarbons due to dipole-dipole interaction. Ketones have slightly higher boiling point than aldehydes because of presence of two electron-donating groups around carbonyl carbon.

Concept ladder Both aldehydes and ketones (by themselves) are not capable of exhibiting intermolecular hydrogen bonds. Thus, they have lower boiling points than comparable alcohol or carboxylic acids.

STEP UP Practice 1

1 The IUPAC name of the compound is

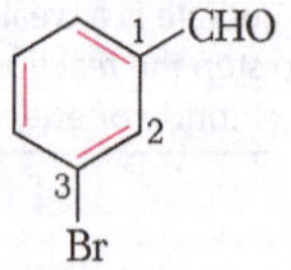

(a) *m*-bromobenzaldehyde (b) 3-bromobenzene carbaldehyde
(c) 4-bromobenzaldehyde (d) 2-bromobenzaldehye

2 IUPAC name of which of the following compound is 4-nitrobenzaldehyde ?

(a) $CH_3COCH_2CH_2CH_3$
(b) $(CH_3)_2\,CHCHO$
(c) $CH_3—CH_2—CO—CH_2—NO_2$
(d) $CHO(C_6H_4)\,NO_2$

3 Which of the following compounds is commonly known as phthaldehyde?

(a) 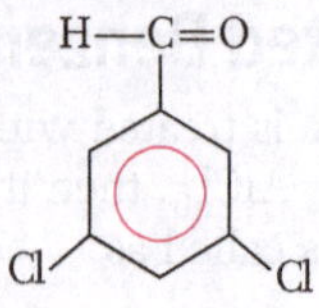
(b) 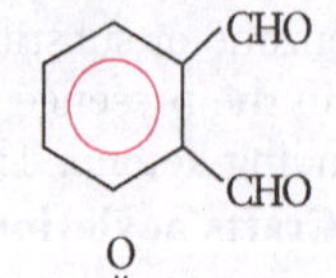
(c) 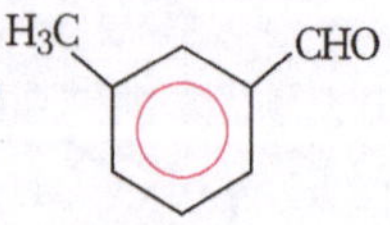
(d) 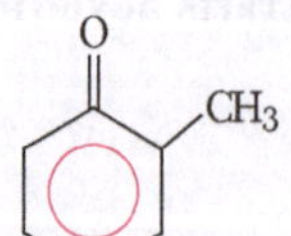

4 Consider the following compounds

(i) Allyl alcohol (ii) Propanone
(iii) Propanal (iv) Methyl oxirane
(v) Ethyl methyl ketone

The number of compounds that are functional isomers of molecular formula $C_nH_{2n}O$.

(a) 2 (b) 3
(c) 4 (d) 1

5 In which of the following compound the carbon bonded to oxygen is sp^2-hybridised?

(a) $H_2C=O$ (b) $H_2C=C=O$
(c) $H_3C—\ddot{\underset{\cdot\cdot}{O}}—CH_3$ (d) $H_3C—N=O$

6 Consider the following statements

Statement I Pyridinium chlorochromate in dichloromethane are better oxidising agents than acidified $K_2Cr_2O_7$ for converting 1° alcohols to aldehydes.

Statement II Acetonitrile form acetaldehyde on reaction with Grignard reagent followed by hydrolysis.

In the light of the above statements, choose the most appropriate answer from the options given below.

(a) Both Statement I and Statement II are false.
(b) Statement I is true but Statement II is false.
(c) Statement I is false but Statement II is true.
(d) Both Statement I and Statement II are true.

7 Select the incorrect statement.
(a) PCC oxidises 1° alcohol to aldehyde and 2° alcohol to ketone.
(b) Cu dehydrates 3° alcohol to alkene.
(c) 1° alcohol react with copper at 530 K to give aldehyde.
(d) Pentene upon ozonolysis produces propanal.

8 Which of the following is the incorrect match regarding the product formed ?
(a) 3° alcohol $\xrightarrow[520\text{ K}]{\text{Cu, }\Delta}$ Alkene
(b) 2° alcohol $\xrightarrow[520\text{ K}]{\text{Cu, }\Delta}$ Ketone
(c) 2 butene $\xrightarrow[H_2O/Zn]{O_3}$ Ethanal
(d) Acid chloride $\xrightarrow[H_2,\text{ Xylene}]{Pd/BaSO_4}$ Alcohol

9 Pure propanone can be prepared by ozonolysis of
(a) 1,2-dimethyl-2-butene (b) 1-pentene
(c) 2-methyl-2-butene (d) 2,3-dimethyl-2-butene

10 An olefin on ozonolysis yields a mixture of acetone and methyl ethyl ketone. The possible structure of the olefin is
(a) $CH_3\overset{CH_3}{C}{=}\overset{CH_3}{C}CH_3$ (b) $C_2H_5\overset{C_2H_5}{C}{=}CH_2$
(c) $CH_3\overset{CH_3}{C}{=}\overset{CH_3}{C}CH_2CH_3$ (d) $CH_3CH{=}CHCH_3$

11 Consider the following statements.
Statement I Addition of water to ethyne in the presence of H_2SO_4 and $HgSO_4$ gives acetone.
Statement II Nitriles in the presence of hydrochloric acid and stannous chloride on hyrolysis give aldehyde.
In the light of the above statements, choose the most appropriate answer from the options given below
(a) Both Statement I and Statement II are false.
(b) Statement I is true but Statement II is false.
(c) Statement I is false but Statement II is true.
(d) Both Statement I and Statement II are true.

12 Which of the following products will be formed on addition of water to but-1-yne in the presence of $HgSO_4$ and dil. H_2SO_4?
(a) $CH_3-CH_2-CH_2-\overset{O}{\overset{\|}{C}}-H$
(b) $CH_3-CH_2-\overset{O}{\overset{\|}{C}}-CH_3$
(c) $CH_3-CH_2-\overset{O}{\overset{\|}{C}}-OH + CO_2$
(d) $CH_3-\overset{O}{\overset{\|}{C}}-OH + H-\overset{O}{\overset{\|}{C}}-H$

13 An acid chloride on reaction with $H_2/Pd\text{-}BaSO_4$ changes to $(CH_3)_2CHCHO$. This acid chloride on reaction with CH_3MgBr/H_3O^+ gives
(a) $(CH_3)_3COH$ (b) $(CH_3)_2CHOH$
(c) $(CH_3)_2CHCOCH_3$ (d) $(CH_3)_2CHCHO$

14 Which does not produce aldehyde in the following reactions?
(a) $RCN \xrightarrow{\text{Reduction}/H_3O^+}$ (b) $RCN \xrightarrow{SnCl_2/H_3O^+}$
(c) $RCN \xrightarrow[H_3O^+]{CH_3MgBr}$ (d) $HCN \xrightarrow[H_3O^+]{CH_3MgBr}$

15 Which of the following nitriles will form aldehyde on reaction with Grignard reagent?
(a) HCN (b) CH_3CN (c) $(CH_3)_2CHCN$ (d) $CH_2{=}CHCN$

16 Identify compound (*A*) in the following reaction.

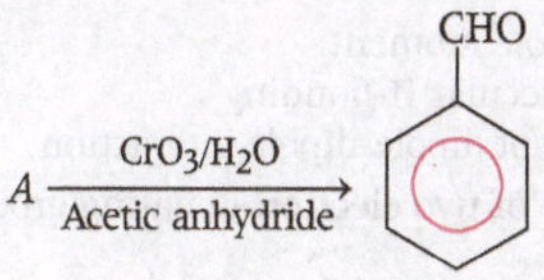

(a) 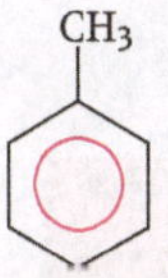

(b) 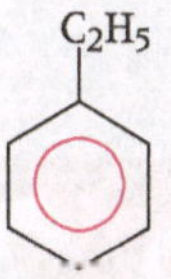

(c) 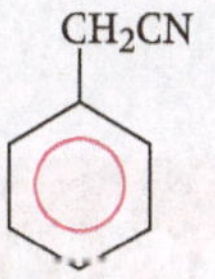

(d) 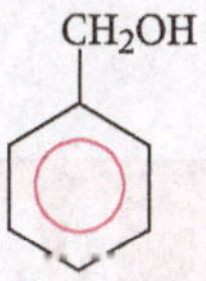

17 Which of the following is not correctly matched regarding the product formed ?
(a) Benzoyl chloride $\xrightarrow[H_2]{Pd\text{-}BaSO_4}$ Benzoic acid
(b) Alkyl nitrile $\xrightarrow[H_2O]{AlH(i\text{-}Bu)_2}$ Aldehyde
(c) $CH_3(CH_2)_9-\overset{O}{\overset{\|}{C}}-OC_2H_5 \xrightarrow[H_2O]{\text{DIBAL-H}} CH_3(CH_2)_9-\overset{O}{\overset{\|}{C}}-H$
(d) Acid chloride $\xrightarrow[\text{diethyl ether, 195 K}\atop H_2O]{LiAlH[OC(CH_3)_3]_3}$ Aldehyde

18 Consider the following reaction sequence :
(i) $R-C{\equiv}N \xrightarrow[230\text{ K}]{\text{DIBAL-H}}$
(ii) $CH_3CH_2CN \xrightarrow[\text{ether, }H_3O^+]{C_6H_5MgBr}$
(iii) $\begin{matrix}CH_3\\CH_3\end{matrix}\!\!>C{=}CH-CH_3 \xrightarrow[Zn/H_2O]{O_3}$
(iv) $(CH_3)_3C-OH \xrightarrow[520\text{ K}]{\text{Cu, }\Delta}$
(v) $R-\overset{OH}{\overset{|}{CH}}-R' \xrightarrow[CH_2Cl_2]{PCC}$
The number of reactions that will produce ketone only.
(a) 3 (b) 2
(c) 4 (d) 1

19 Grignard reagent can convert the following into carbonyl compound expect in
(a) $CH_3\overset{O}{\overset{\|}{C}}Cl$ (b) $H\overset{O}{\overset{\|}{C}}OCH_3$
(c) $CH_3C{\equiv}N$ (d) CH_3CH_2OH

20 Which of the following is incorrect statement ?
(a) Methanal is a pungent smelling gas, while ethanol is a volatile.
(b) Aldehydes and ketones containing upto eleven carbon atoms are colourless liquid.
(c) Carbonyl compounds upto four carbon atoms are soluble in water.
(d) Boiling points of aldehydes and ketones are higher than alcohols.

21 Ketones have higher boiling points than aldehydes because of
(a) high dipole moment
(b) intermolecular H-bonding
(c) presence of dipole-dipole interaction
(d) presence of two electron-donating groups

22 Identify compound *X* in the following sequence of reaction.

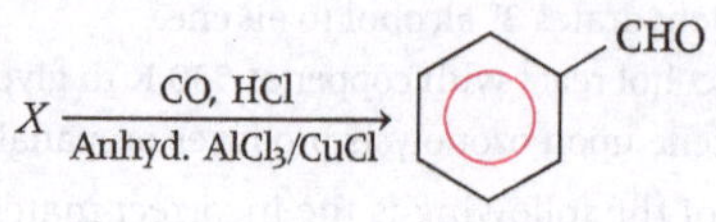

(a) 

(b) 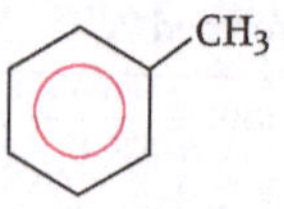

(c) 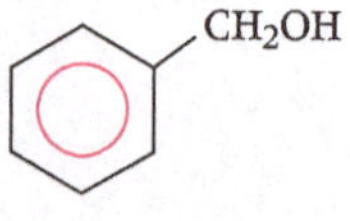

(d) 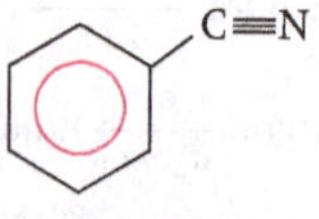

Module 2

Aldehydes and Ketones : Chemical Reactions and Uses

- Chemical Reactions of Carbonyl Compounds
- Nucleophilic Addition Reactions
- Nucleophilic Addition-Elimination Reactions
- Oxidation Reactions
- Reduction Reactions
- Aldol's Reactions
- Cannizzaro's Reaction
- Electrophilic Substitution Reactions

Chemical Reactions of Carbonyl Compounds

Carbonyl compounds give chemical reactions due to carbonyl group and α-hydrogens. The chemical reactions of carbonyl can be discussed below.

Nucleophilic Addition Reactions

Aldehydes and ketones undergo nucleophilic addition reaction due to polar nature of carbonyl carbon.

The hybridisation of carbon changes from sp^2 to sp^3 in this process and a tetrahedral alkoxide intermediate is produced.

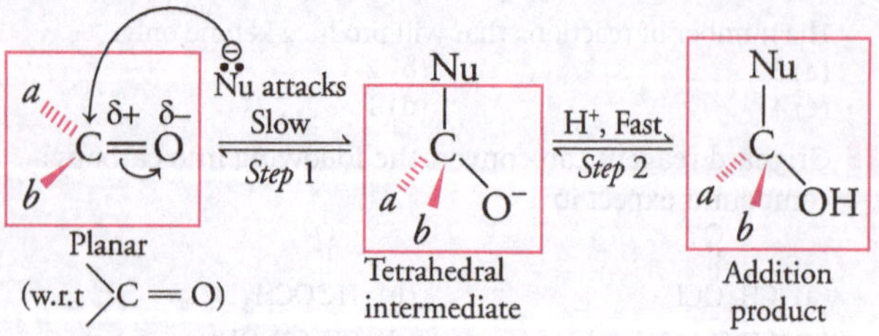

Nucleophilic Attack on Carbonyl Carbon

Protonation of carbonyl group increases electrophilic nature.

Aldehydes are more reactive than ketones due to following reasons.

- Alkyl groups of ketones show +*I* effect, which decreases positive charge on the carbonyl carbon. Therefore, tendency of nucleophilic attack decreases.
- More the number of alkyl (or aryl) groups, more will be the steric hinderance and due to this, tendency of nucleophilic attack decreases.

Thus, sequence of reactivity towards nucleophilic attack is

$$H—CHO > CH_3—CHO > CH_3—\overset{O}{\overset{\|}{C}}—CH_3$$

Electron withdrawing substituents ($—CF_3$, $—CCl_3$) cause the carbonyl carbon to be more positive and thus the addition reaction is made more favourable.

Various nucleophilic addition and nucleophilic addition elimination reactions given by carbonyl compounds is discussed below.

Addition of Hydrogen Cyanide

Aldehydes and ketones react with hydrogen cyanide to form cyanohydrins which are useful synthetic intermediates.

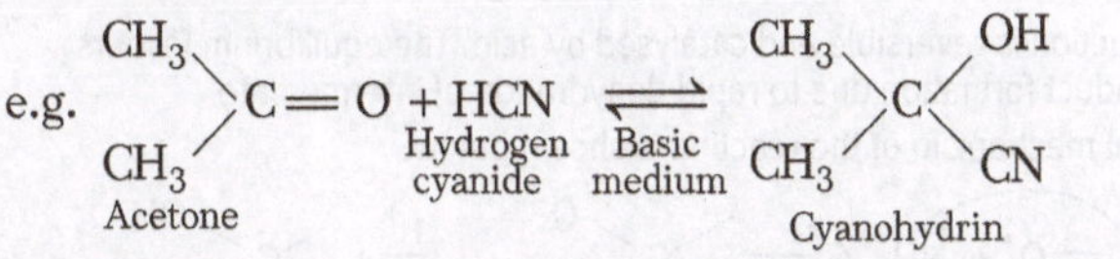

HCN is a toxic gas. So, it is obtained from reaction of NaCN and HCl.

Mechanism

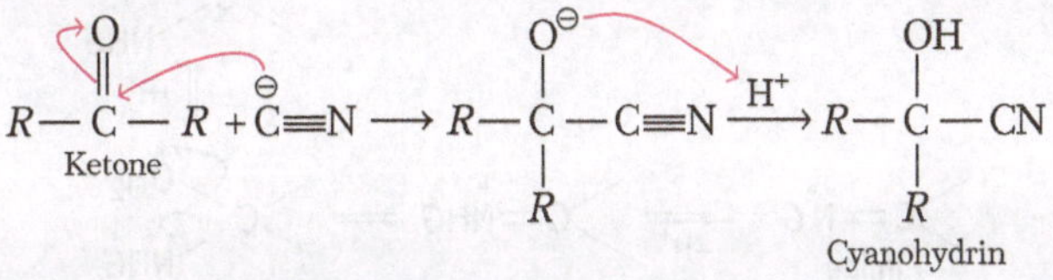

It is a nucleophilic addition reaction and the addition of cyanide ion is a rate determining step.

Mentor's TIP

- In basic medium, cyano group is eliminated because oxygen atom have partial negative charge. Thus, cyanohydrins are converted back into carbonyl compounds.
- While in acidic medium, cyanide group is hydrolysed to carboxylic group to give α-hydroxy carboxylic acid.

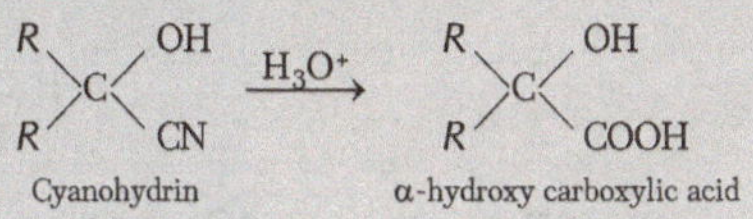

- All aldehydes form cyanohydrin but in ketones, only acetone, butanone, pentan-3-one and pinacolone form cyanohydrin.

Addition of Sodium Hydrogen Sulphite

Carbonyl compounds react with sodium bisulphite to give white crystalline addition product, i.e. hydroxy sulphonic acid salt.

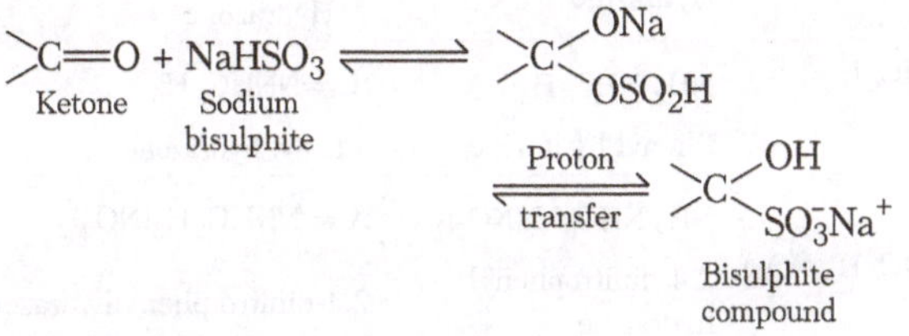

The position of the equilibrium lies largely to the right hand side for most aldehydes and to the left for most ketones due to steric reasons.

The bisulphite compounds are soluble in water. These compounds are converted back into carbonyl compounds on heating with acid or sodium carbonate solution. This reaction is used to distinguish carbonyl compounds with others which does not form bisulphite compounds.

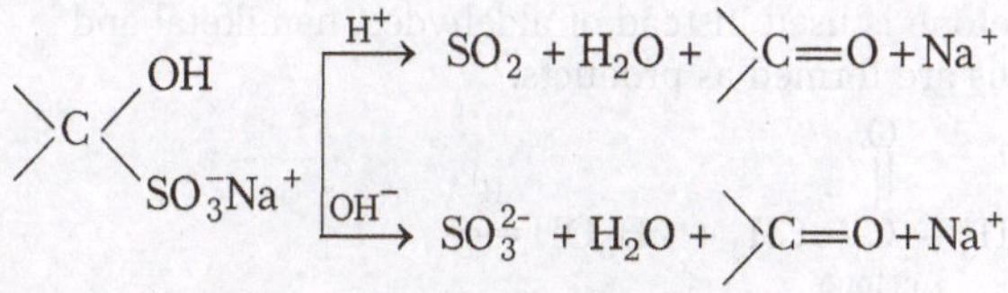

Only methyl ketones undergo addition reaction with $NaHSO_3$. Higher ketones (as acetophenone) do not react due to steric hindrance.

Addition of Grignard Reagents

Carbonyl compounds react with Grignard reagent to give alcohols. Aldehydes form secondary alcohols [except formaldehyde which forms primary alcohol] and ketones form tertiary alcohols.

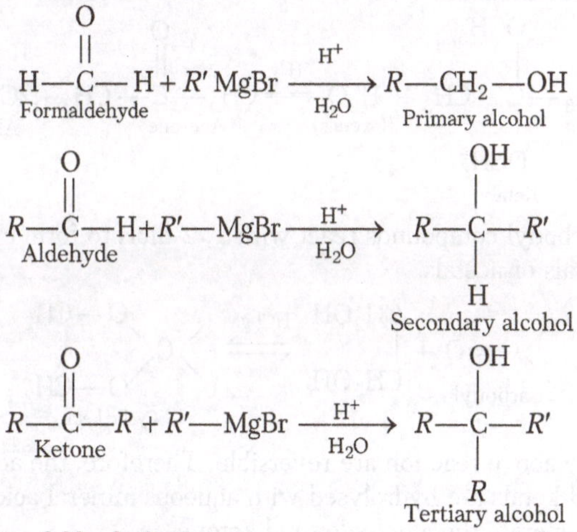

Addition of Alcohols

Aldehydes react with alcohols to give addition product. When aldehydes react with one equivalent of a monohydric alcohol, alkoxy alcohol intermediate, known as **'hemiacetals'** are formed as product.

The intermediate reacts with second equivalent of alcohol to give 'acetals'. The reaction is catalysed by an acid as alcohol is a poor nucleophile.

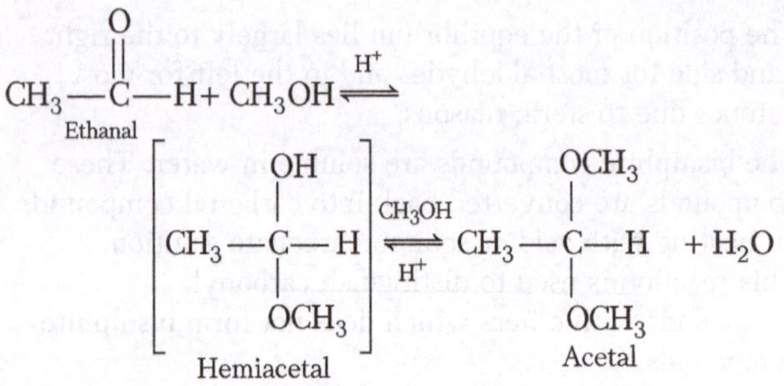

If ketone is used instead of aldehydes, hemiketal and ketals are formed as products.

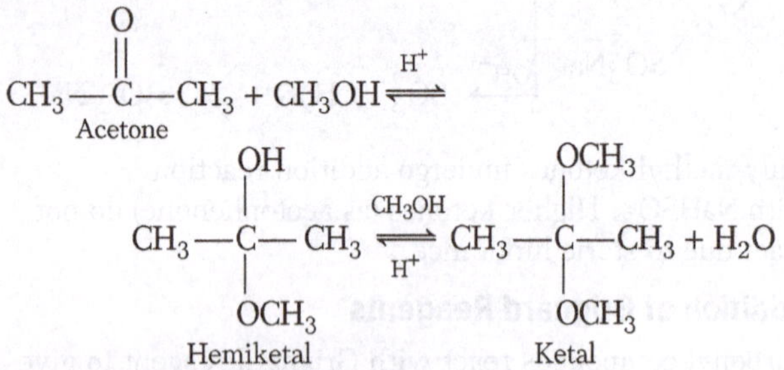

Acetal or ketal formation is a reversible reaction and can be converted back into carbonyl compounds in aqueous acidic medium.

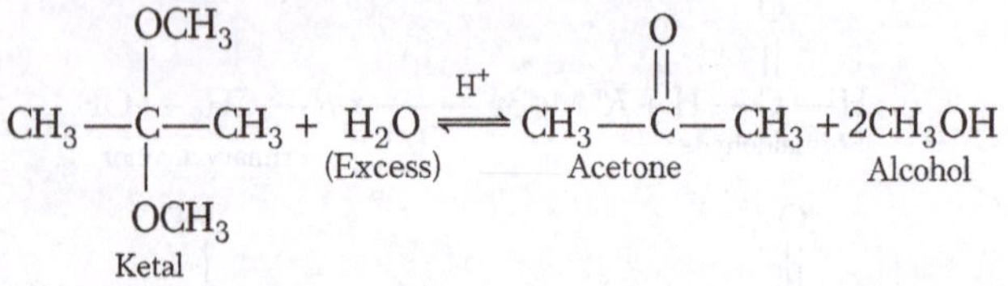

Carbonyl compounds react with 1, 2-diols to form cyclic ketals or acetals.

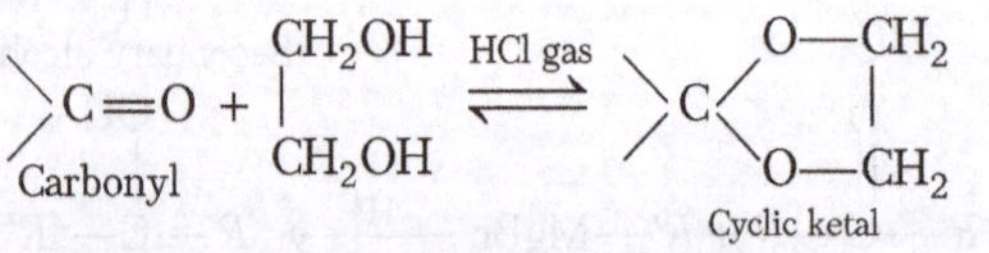

The above reaction are reversible. Therefore, the acetals and ketals are hydrolysed with aqueous mineral acids to regenerate the aldehydes and ketones.

Nucleophilic Addition-Elimination Reactions

Some important example of nucleophilic addition-elimination reactions are

Addition of Ammonia and its Derivatives

When carbonyl compounds react with ammonia and its derivatives (primary amine), it undergoes nucleophilic addition-elimination reactions. This results in the formation of compounds containing carbon-nitrogen double bond called **imines**. These are formed due to elimination of water and also called **Schiff bases**.

NEET Snapshot

Schiff's base will be formed when aldehyde reacts with primary amine. ***[NEET 2016]***

Yes, its true. The reaction proceeds as

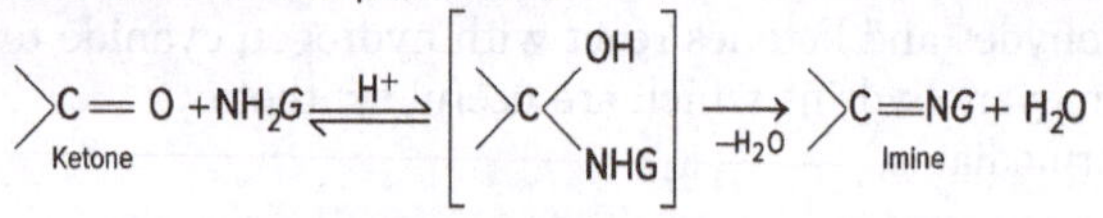

The reaction is reversible and catalysed by acid. The equilibrium favours the product formation due to rapid dehydration of intermediate.

General mechanism of the reaction is shown below.

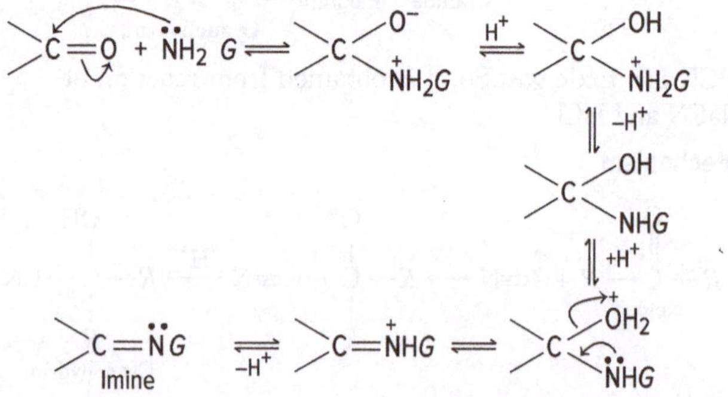

Schiff's base is pink in colour. This can be decolourised by passing SO_2 gas. The solution obtained after passing SO_2 into Schiff's base is known as Schiff's reagent.

Some of these reaction are discussed below in table given below.

Group G	Reagent name	Carbonyl derivative
—H	NH_2—H Ammonia	>C=NH, CH_3CH=NH Imine Aldimine $(H_3C)_2$C=NH Ketimine
—OH	NH_2 OH Hydroxylamine	>C=NOH Oxime
—*R*	NH_2—*R* Aliphatic amine	>C=N*R* Azomethine (Schiff base)
—NH_2	NH_2 NH_2 Hydrazine	>C=N—NH_2 Hydrazone
—NHC_6H_5	NH_2 NHC_6H_5 Phenyl hydrazine	>C=$NNHC_6H_5$ Phenyl hydrazone
—$NHC_6H_3(NO_2)_2$	NH_2 $NHC_6H_3(NO_2)_2$ 2,4-dinitrophenyl hydrazine (2, 4-DNP)	>C=$NNHC_6H_3(NO_2)_2$ 2,4-dinitro phenylhydrazone
—$NHCONH_2$	NH_2 $NHCONH_2$ Semicarbazide	>C=$NNHCONH_2$ Semicarbazone

Oxidation Reactions

Oxidation product of carbonyl compound depends upon nature of oxidising agents.

Oxidation by Strong Oxidisng Agents

Strong oxidising agents like HNO_3, $KMnO_4$, $K_2Cr_2O_7$ etc., oxidises aldehydes to carboxylic acids.

$$\underset{\text{Aldehyde}}{R-\overset{\overset{\large O}{\|}}{C}-H} \xrightarrow{[O]} \underset{\text{Carboxylic acid}}{R-\overset{\overset{\large O}{\|}}{C}-OH}$$

Ketones do not undergo oxidation reactions readily. However, under vigorous conditions, i.e. strong oxidising agents and at elevated temperatures they undergo oxidation. Their oxidation involves breaking of carbon bond to form a mixture of carboxylic acids having carbon atoms lesser than the parent ketone. e.g.

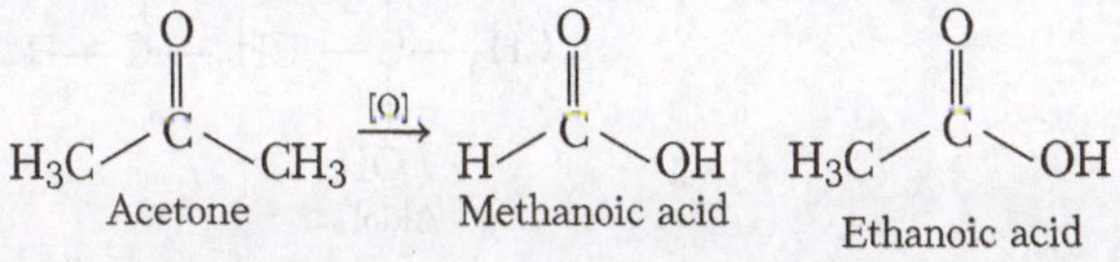

In case of unsymmetrical ketones, CO group goes with alkyl group possessing maximum number of α-H with respect to carbonyl group. This is known as Popoff's rule.

$$CH_3-CH_2-\overset{\overset{\large O}{\|}}{C}-CH_3 \xrightarrow{[O]} CH_3-CH_2-COOH + \underset{\text{Acetic acid}}{CH_3-COOH}$$

Mentor's Tip

It number of α-H are same then CO group goes with the alkyl group that posses minimum number of carbon atom.

Oxidation by Mild Oxidising Agents

Mild oxidising agents oxidises only aldehyde into carboxylic acid. They do not oxidise ketones. Main mild oxidising agents are

(i) **Tollen's reagent** Aldehydes reduce Tollen's reagent to Ag and appears in the form of silver mirror. This reaction is used to distinguish aldehydes from ketones and called **silver-mirror test.** It is given by all aldehydes and reducing sugars.

Tollen's reagent is an ammoniacal solution of silver nitrate in the form of $[Ag(NH_3)_2]^+ OH^-$.

$$\underset{\text{Aldehyde}}{RCHO} + \underset{\substack{\text{Tollen's reagent}\\\text{(Colourless solution)}}}{2[Ag(NH_3)_2]^+} + 3OH^- \xrightarrow{\Delta} RCOO^- + \underset{\substack{\text{Silver}\\\text{mirror}}}{2Ag\downarrow} + 4NH_3 + 2H_2O$$

Ketones do not reduce Tollen's reagent. (except α-hydroxy ketones such as fructose.)

(ii) **Fehling's solution** Aldehydes reduce Fehling's solution (alkaline solution of cupric ion complexed with tartarate ion). In this reaction, Cu^{2+} is reduced to Cu^+ (red precipitate).

$$\underset{\text{Aldehyde}}{RCHO} + \underset{\text{Fehling solution}}{2Cu^{2+}} + 5OH^- \xrightarrow{\Delta} RCOO^- + \underset{\substack{\text{Red brown}\\\text{ppt.}}}{Cu_2O\downarrow} + 3H_2O$$

Ketones and aromatic aldehydes do not give this reaction.

NEET Snapshot

Fehling's solution *A* is aqueous solution of copper sulphate. ***[NEET 2024]***

Fehling reagent is used to distinguish between aldehydes and ketones. It is formed by the mixing of two solutions.

- **Fehling solution *A*** (aqueous copper sulphate)
- **Fehling solution *B*** (alkaline sodium potassium tartarate, Rochelle salt).

These two solutions are mixed in equal proportions before the test.

(iii) **Benedict's solution** Aldehydes reduce Benedict's solution (alkaline solution of cupric citrate) to Cu^+. Red precipitate of Cu_2O is formed.

$$\underset{\text{Aldehyde}}{RCHO} + 2Cu^{2+} + 5OH^- \longrightarrow RCOO^- + \underset{\text{Red ppt.}}{Cu_2O\downarrow} + 3H_2O$$

(iv) **Oxidation of methyl ketones by Haloform reaction** Carbonyl compounds having $CH_3-\overset{\overset{\large O}{\|}}{C}-$ group, on treatment with an excess of halogen in the presence of dil. NaOH gives haloform ($CHCl_3$, $CHBr_3$, CHI_3) and the salt of a carboxylic acid having one carbon atom less than the original carbonyl compounds. This reaction is known as **haloform reaction.** This oxidation does not affect a carbon-carbon double bond, if present in the molecule. e.g.

$$\underset{\text{Acetaldehyde}}{CH_3CHO} \xrightarrow{X_2/OH^-} HCOO^- + \underset{\text{Haloform}}{CHX_3}$$

$(X = Cl, Br, I)$

$$\underset{\text{Acetone}}{CH_3-\overset{\overset{\large O}{\|}}{C}-CH_3} \xrightarrow{X_2/OH^-} CH_3COO^- + \underset{\text{Haloform}}{CHX_3}$$

> **Concept ladder**
> When I_2 is used as the halogen in the above reaction, yellow ppt. iodoform are formed and the test is called iodoform test.
> - Iodoform reaction is carried out with sodium hypoiodite which is used for detection of CH_3CO group or $CH_3CH(OH)$ group which produces CH_3CO group on oxidation.

Reduction Reactions

Some examples of reduction reactions are as follows

(a) Reduction to Alcohols

Catalytic reduction with Ni|Pt|Pd-H_2 or chemical reduction with $LiAlH_4$ or $NaBH_4$ of aldehydes and ketones gives 1° and 2° alcohols, respectively.

$$R{-}CHO \xrightarrow[\text{Or } NaBH_4,\ H_3O^+]{LiAlH_4,\ H_3O^+} R{-}CH_2OH$$

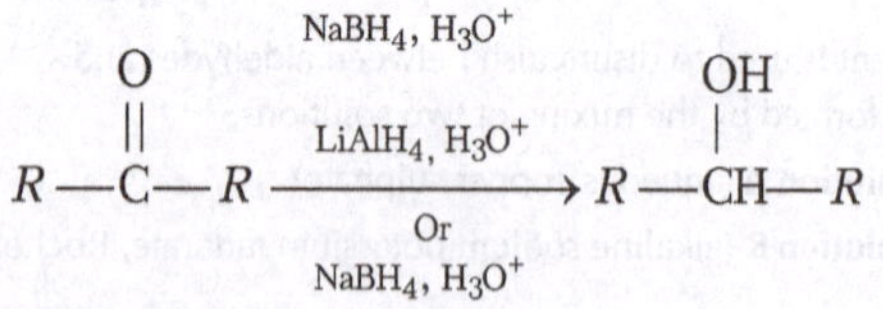

$LiAlH_4$ is a much more powerful reducing agent than $NaBH_4$. It not only reduces aldehydes and ketones but also reduces acids, esters, amides and nitriles, even double bond of α, β-unsaturated aldehydes and ketones.

$NaBH_4$ is used for selective reduction. It reduces carbonyl group but doesn't reduce ester, acid chloride and double bonds. Therefore, it is regioselective in nature.

(b) Reduction to Hydrocarbons

Reduction of aldehydes and ketones to hydrocarbons occurs with (i) Zn-Hg/HCl **Clemmensen reduction,** (ii) NH_2NH_2/KOH in ethylene glycol-**Wolff-Kishner reduction.**

$$>C{=}O \xrightarrow[HCl]{Zn\text{-}Hg} >CH_2 + H_2O$$

(Clemmensen reduction)

$$>C{=}O \xrightarrow[-H_2O]{NH_2NH_2} >C{=}NNH_2 \xrightarrow[\Delta]{KOH/\text{ Ethylene glycol}} >CH_2 + N_2$$

(Wolff-Kishner reduction)

> **Concept ladder**
> Clemmensen reduction is used for selective reduction of ketones which contain phenolic or carboxylic groups as these groups are sensitive to base. While Wolff-Kishner reduction is preferred for compounds sensitive to acid.

Reactions Due to α-Hydrogen

The acidity of α—H atoms of carbonyl compounds is due to the strong electron withdrawing effect of the carbonyl group and resonance stabilisation of the conjugate base.

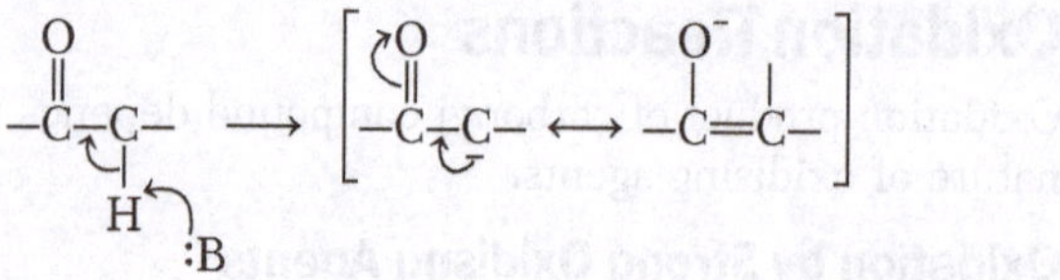

Aldol Condensation

Two molecules of an aldehyde or ketone may combine in presence of dilute base to form β-hydroxy aldehyde (aldol) or β-hydroxy ketone (ketol), respectively.

Presence of α-hydrogen in atleast one type of molecules is necessity of reaction. This is known as **aldol reaction.**

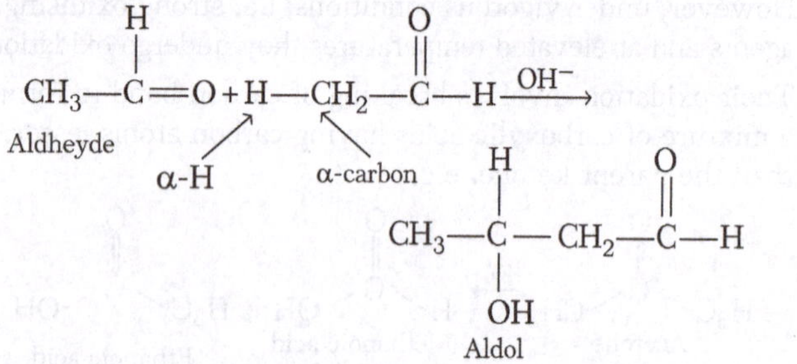

On heating, aldol loses water and form α, β-unsaturated compounds. This is called aldol condensation.

e.g.

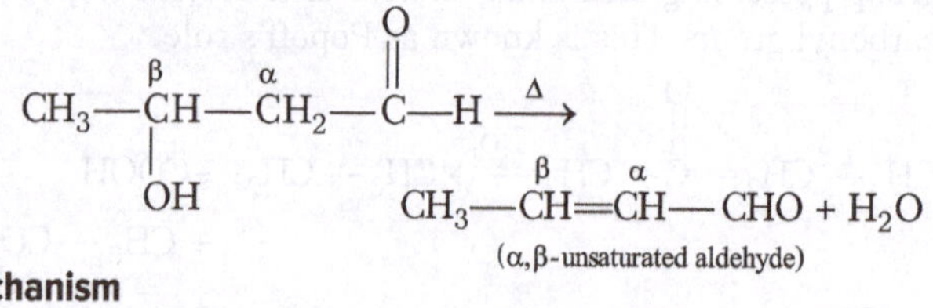

Mechanism

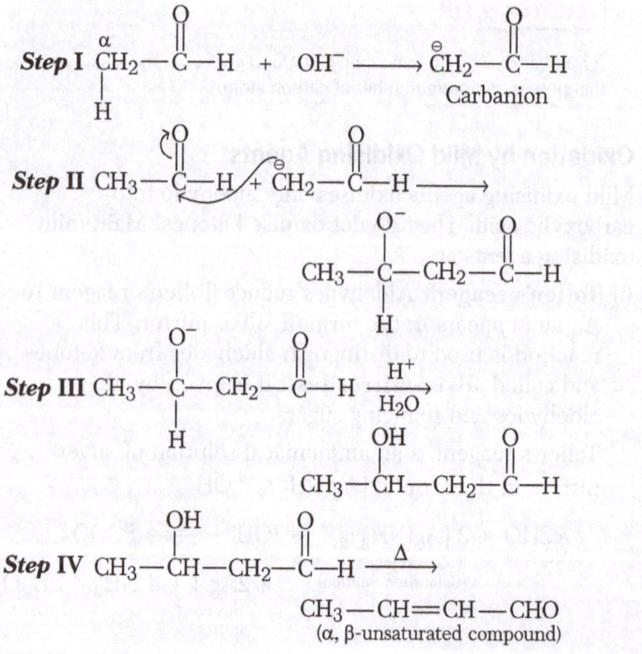

Similarly,

$$2CH_3COCH_3 \underset{}{\overset{Ba(OH)_2}{\rightleftharpoons}} CH_3-\underset{OH}{\overset{CH_3}{\overset{|}{\underset{|}{C}}}}-CH_2CO-CH_3$$

Propanone — 4-hydroxy-4-methyl pentan-2-one (Ketol)

$$\xrightarrow[\Delta]{-H_2O} CH_3-\overset{CH_3}{\overset{|}{C}}=CH-CO-CH_3$$

4-methylpent-3-en-2-one (Aldol condensation product)

Cross Aldol Condensation

Different carbonyl compounds having acidic hydrogen at α-position are condensed to give α, β-unsaturated compounds. Then, reaction is called cross-aldol condensation.

$$\underset{\text{Acetaldehyde}}{CH_3-\overset{H}{\overset{|}{C}}=O} + \underset{\text{Acetone}}{HCH_2-\overset{O}{\overset{\|}{C}}-CH_3} \xrightarrow{OH^-} CH_3-\underset{OH}{\underset{|}{\overset{H}{\overset{|}{C}}}}-CH_2-\overset{O}{\overset{\|}{C}}-CH_3$$

There are four products possible by cross-aldol condensation if both the reactants have α-hydrogen.

e.g.

$$CH_3CHO + CH_3CH_2CHO \xrightarrow[\Delta]{NaOH}$$

$$\underset{\text{But-2-enal}}{CH_3-CH=CH-CHO} + \underset{\text{2-methylpent-2-enal}}{CH_3CH_2CH=\underset{CH_3}{\underset{|}{C}}CHO}$$

But-2-enal (From two molecules of ethanal); 2-methylpent-2-enal (From two molecules of propanal)

Simple or self aldol products

$$+\ \underset{\text{2-methylbut-2-enal}}{CH_3-CH=\underset{CH_3}{\underset{|}{C}}-CHO} + \underset{\text{Pent-2-enal}}{CH_3CH_2CH=CHCHO}$$

(From one molecule of ethanal and one molecule of proponal)

Cross aldol products

Ketones can also be used as one component in cross aldol reactions.

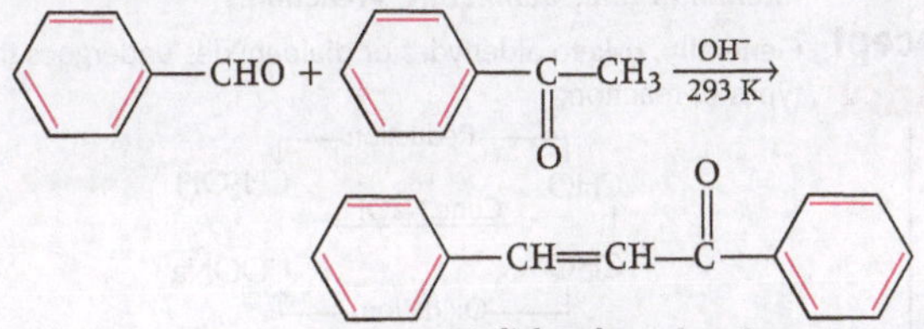

1,3-diphenylprop-2-en-1-one (Benzalacetophenone) (Major product)

Concept ladder

If two or more carbonyl groups are present in the molecule, there can be **intramolecular aldol reaction** thus formation of rings is preferred as

Six membered > Five membered > Four membered

e.g.

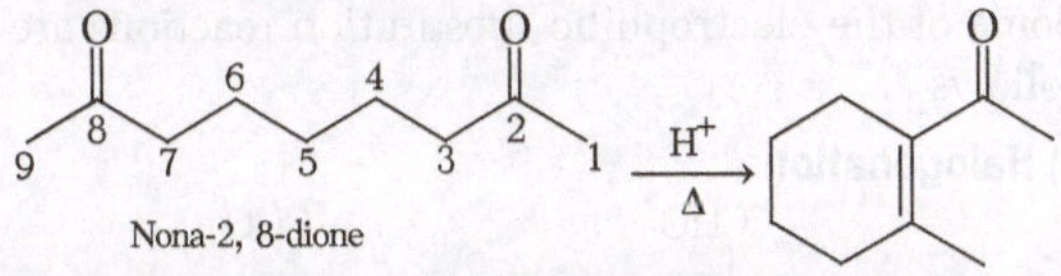

Nona-2, 8-dione

Other Reactions

Apart from nucleophilic addition reaction reduction, oxidation and reactions due to α-hydrogen. These are some other reactions which are as follows

Cannizzaro's Reaction

Aldehydes which do not have hydrogen at α-carbon, undergo Cannizzaro's reaction in presence of 50% aqueous or ethanolic alkali solution. In this reaction, one molecule is reduced to alcohol and other is oxidised to salt of corresponding acid.

$$2HCHO + \underset{(50\%)}{NaOH} \xrightarrow{\Delta} CH_3OH + HCO\bar{O}\overset{+}{N}a$$

Reduction (HCHO → CH_3OH); Oxidation (HCHO → $HCOONa$)

Crossed-Cannizzaro Reaction

In such reactions, it is formaldehyde which is always oxidised.

$$\underset{\text{Formaldehyde}}{HCHO} + \underset{\text{Benzaldehyde}}{C_6H_5CHO} \xrightarrow{OH^-} HCOO^- + C_6H_5CH_2OH$$

In this case HCHO is a better reducing agent than C_6H_5CHO thus HCHO is oxidised and C_6H_5CHO is reduced.

Concept ladder

Reaction in which half part is oxidised and other half part is reduced (of the same molecule) are also called **internal** or **interamolecular Cannizzaro's reaction.**

Generally, α-keto aldehydes or dialdehydes undergoes this types of reaction.

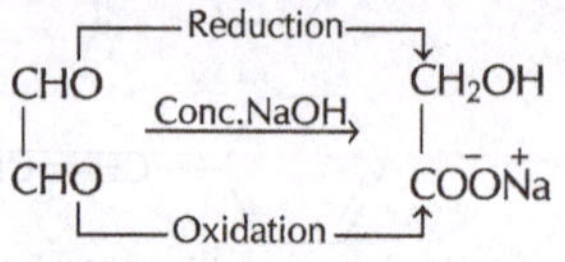

Electrophilic Substitution Reactions

Aromatic aldehydes undergo electrophilic substitution reactions at *m*-position, due to presence of —CHO group.

—CHO group is deactivating group and directs incoming electrophile at *m*-position.

Some of the electrophilic substitution reactions are as follows

(i) Halogenation

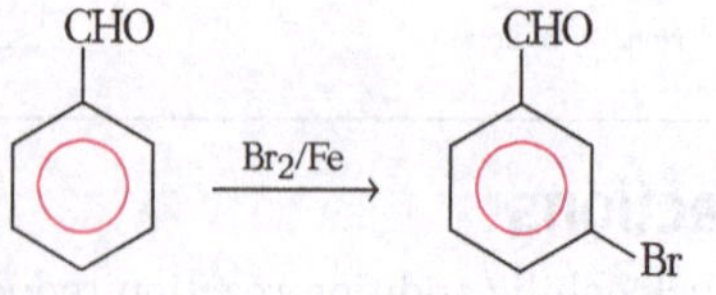

m-bromobenzaldehyde

(ii) Nitration

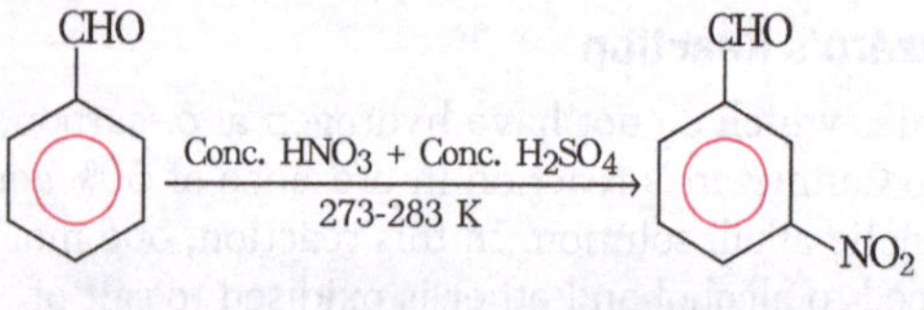

m-nitrobenzaldehyde

(iii) Sulphonation

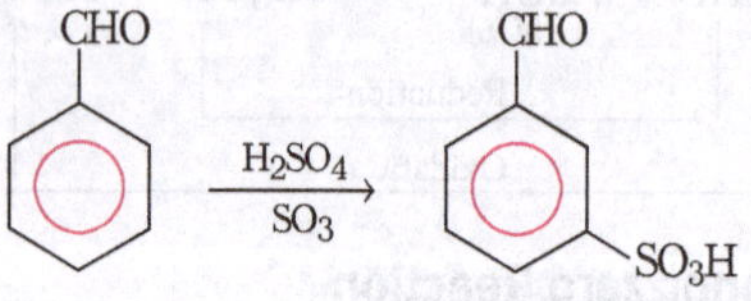

m-benzaldehyde sulphonic acid

NEET Close-up

Example Similar to PYQ Asked in NEET 2021

What is the IUPAC name of the organic compound formed in the following chemical reaction ?

$$\text{Benzaldehyde} \xrightarrow[273\text{-}283\ K]{HNO_3 \mid H_2SO_4} \text{Product}$$

(a) *m*-nitrobenzoic acid (b) 2,4,6-trinitrobenzaldehyde
(c) *m*-nitrobenzaldehyde (d) *p*-nitrobenzaldehyde

Sol. (*c*) Benzaldehyde undergo electrophilic substitution at the ring in the presence of HNO_3/H_2SO_4 at 273-283 K temperature.

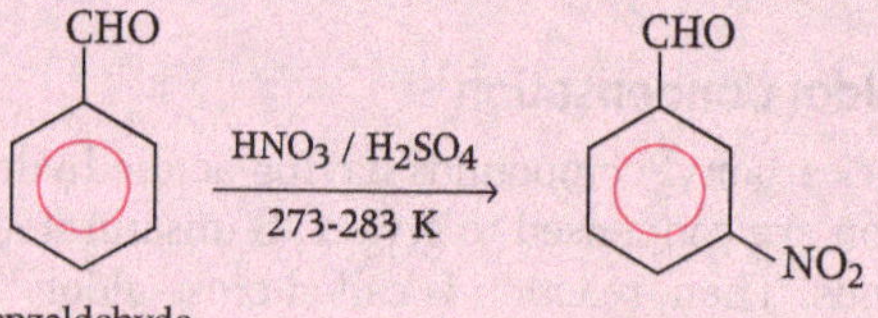

Benzaldehyde *m*-nitrobenzaldehyde

Skill Builder

What is the IUPAC name of the organic compound formed in the following chemical reaction ?

$$\text{Acetone} \xrightarrow[\text{KOH/ethylene glycol}]{NH_2{-}NH_2,\ \Delta} \text{Product}$$

(a) Propanal (b) Propanol (c) Propane (d) Propan-2-ol

For more practice Refer to Q.25 and Q.26 of Step up practice 2.

Uses

- Aldehydes and ketones are used in industries as solvents, reagents for synthesising the other products.
- Propanone (acetone) is used in nail paint remover. It is used as a solvent in industries and laboratories.
- Many aldehydes and ketones are known for their odours and flavours. e.g. Vanillin, camphor etc.
- Formaldehyde is used as a disinfectant. 40% of aqueous HCHO (known as formalin) is used in preserving biological specimens.
- Formaldehyde is used in manufacture of polymers like bakelite, when treated with phenol.
- Ethanal is used for silvering of mirrors.
- Benzaldehyde is used in perfume industry as a flavouring agent.

STEP UP Practice 2

1 Which of the following compounds is most reactive towards nucleophilic addition reactions?

(a) $CH_3-\overset{O}{\overset{\|}{C}}-H$ (b) $CH_3-\overset{O}{\overset{\|}{C}}-CH_3$

(c) 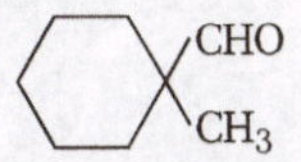 (d) 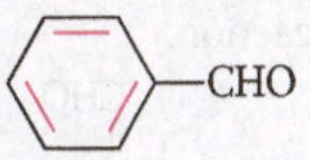

2 Order of reactivity towards nucleophilic addition

(a) $CH_3CHO > CH_3COCH_3 > HCHO$

(b) $CH_3COCH_3 > HCHO > CH_3CHO$

(c) $HCHO > CH_3CHO > CH_3COCH_3$

(d) $CH_3CHO > HCHO > CH_3COCH_3$

3 Consider the following statements.

Statement I The α-hydrogen atom in carbonyl compounds is less acidic in nature.

Statement II The anion formed after the loss of α-hydrogen atom is resonance stabilised.

In the light of the above statements, choose the correct answer from the options given below.

(a) Both Statement I and Statement II are false.
(b) Statement I is true but Statement II is false.
(c) Statement I is false but Statement II is true.
(d) Both Statement I and Statement II are true.

4 Consider the following reaction.

$$(CH_3)_2C{=}O + HCN \rightleftharpoons \text{'}A\text{'} \xrightarrow{H_3O^+} \text{'}B\text{'}$$

Product of the given reaction

(a) $(CH_3)_2C(CN)(CN)$ (b) $(CH_3)_2C(OH)(CN)$

(c) $(CH_3)_2C(COOH)(CN)$ (d) $(CH_3)_2C(OH)(COOH)$

5 Consider the following reactions,

$$CH_3\overset{O}{\overset{\|}{C}}CH_2CH_2\overset{O}{\overset{\|}{C}}OCH_2CH_3 \xrightarrow[\text{(ii) } H_3O^+]{\text{(i) } CH_3MgBr \text{ (one mole)}} A,$$

A formed in this reaction is

(a) $CH_3\overset{OH}{\overset{|}{\underset{CH_3}{\underset{|}{C}}}}CH_2CH_2\overset{O}{\overset{\|}{C}}OCH_2CH_3$ (b) $CH_3\overset{O}{\overset{\|}{C}}CH_2CH_2\overset{O}{\overset{\|}{C}}CH_3$

(c) 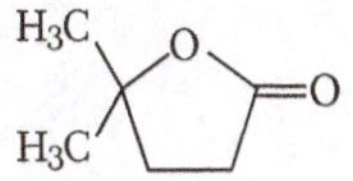 (d) $CH_3\overset{CH_3}{\overset{|}{\underset{OH}{\underset{|}{C}}}}CH_2CH_2\overset{CH_3}{\overset{|}{\underset{OH}{\underset{|}{C}}}}CH_3$

6 Consider the following reaction,

$$CH_3\underset{O}{\underset{\|}{C}}CH_2CH_2CH_2Cl \xrightarrow[\text{(ii) } H_3O^+]{\text{(i) } CH_3MgBr} A. \text{ Here is}$$

(a) $CH_3\overset{CH_3}{\overset{|}{\underset{OH}{\underset{|}{C}}}}CH_2CH_2CH_2Cl$ (b) $CH_3\underset{O}{\underset{\|}{C}}CH_2CH_2CH_2CH_3$

(c) 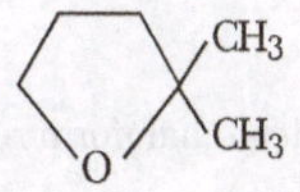 (d) 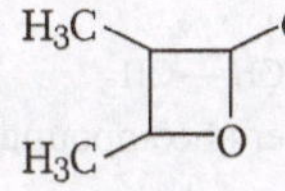

7 Acetone and methyl magnesium bromide react to produce a product which on hydrolysis gives

(a) *n*-butyl alcohol (b) secondary butyl alcohol
(c) tertiary butyl alcohol (d) None of these

8 Which of the following is correct regarding an acetal?

(a) It is the condensation product from 2 molecules of aldehyde.
(b) It is the condensation product from 2 molecules of ketone.
(c) It is the condensation product from 2 molecules of alcohol.
(d) It is a diether.

9 The product formed when acetone react with 1, 2-diols in the presence of HCl is

(a) $CH_3-\overset{OH}{\overset{|}{C}H}-CH_2-CHO$ (b) 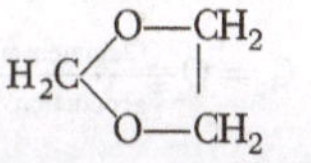

(c) $CH_3-CH=CH-CHO$ (d) 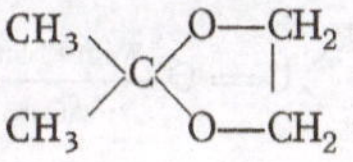

10 Consider the following reaction,

$$CH_3CH_2\overset{O}{\overset{\|}{C}}CH_3 \xrightarrow[H_2SO_4]{K_2Cr_2O_7} P$$

The product *P* is

(a) $CH_3-CH_2-\overset{O}{\overset{\|}{C}}-COOH$ (b) CH_3-CH_2-CHO
(c) CH_3CHO (d) CH_3COOH

11 Consider the following statements.

Statement I Aldehydes and ketones both react with Tollen's reagent to form silver mirror.

Statement II Aldehydes and ketones both react with N_2H_4/KOH to form hydrocarbons.

In the light of the above statements, choose the correct answer from the options given below.

(a) Both Statement I and Statement II are false.
(b) Statement I is true, but Statement II is false.
(c) Statement I is false, but Statement II is true.
(d) Both Statement I and Statement II are true.

12 When acetaldehyde is heated with Fehling's solution, it gives a precipitate of

(a) Cu_2O (b) $Cu + Cu_2O + CuO$
(c) Cu (d) CuO

13 Identify correct product of the following oxidation reaction

$$CH_3CH_2COCH_3 \xrightarrow{SeO_2}$$

(a) CH_3CH_2COCHO (b) $CH_3CO\cdot COCH_3$
(c) CH_3COCH_2CHO (d) CH_3CH_2COOH

14 Consider the following compounds :

I. $CH_3CH{=}C(CH_3){-}C(CH_3){=}O$ II. $CH_3{-}\overset{O}{\overset{\|}{C}}{-}CH_3$

III. CH_3CH_2CHO IV. C_6H_5CHO

V. $CH_3{-}CH(OH){-}CH_3$

The number of compounds that will undergo haloform reaction

(a) 4 (b) 2
(c) 3 (d) 1

15 Which pair can be distinguished by using Tollen's reagent?

(a) Ethanol and propanol
(b) Ethanoic acid and propanone
(c) Ethanoic acid and propanal
(d) Methanol and methanoic acid

16 Which of the following is the incorrect match ?

(a) $R{-}COCH_3$ Tollen's reagent, 2 Ag ↓, silver mirror
(b) $R{-}CHO$ and Fehling's solution, Cu_2O ↓, red colour
(c) $R{-}CHO$ and Benedict's solution, Cu_2O ↓, red colour
(d) $R{-}CHO$ and Schiff's reagent, magenta colour

17 Which one of the following pair is not correctly matched ?

(a) $\begin{matrix}R\\R'\end{matrix}\!\!>C{=}O \xrightarrow[\text{reduction}]{\text{Clemmensen}} R{-}CH_2{-}R'$

(b) $\begin{matrix}R\\R'\end{matrix}\!\!>C{=}O \xrightarrow[\text{reduction}]{\text{Wolff-Kishner}} R{-}CH(OH){-}R'$

(c) $R{-}CHO \xrightarrow{NaBH_4} R{-}CH_2OH$

(d) $R{-}\overset{O}{\overset{\|}{C}}{-}R' \xrightarrow[H_3O^+]{LiAlH_4} R{-}CH(OH)R'$

18 Consider the following reaction.

$$CH_3CHO + LiAlH_4 \longrightarrow CH_3CH_2OH$$

Nucleophile added in this reaction is

(a) AlH_4^- (b) Li^+ (c) H^+ (d) H^-

19 The reagent A in the following reaction is

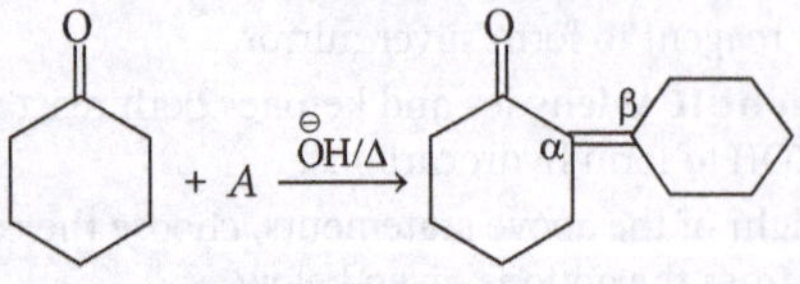

(a) 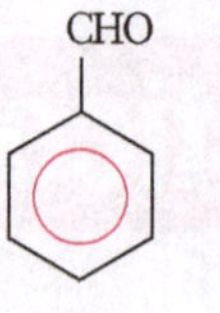
(b) 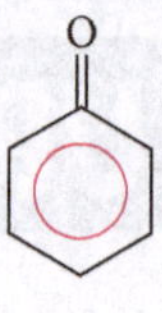
(c) 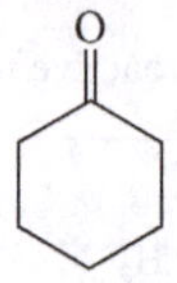
(d) 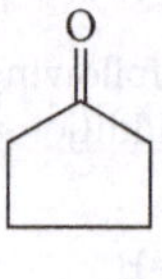

20 In the reaction,

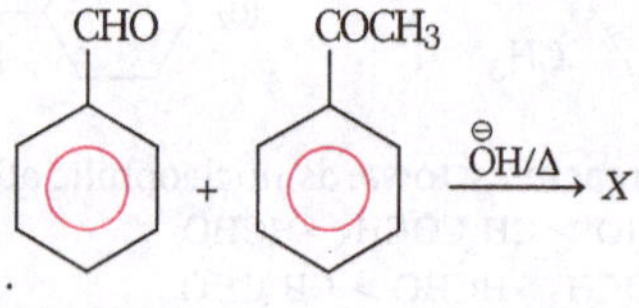

The product X is

(a) 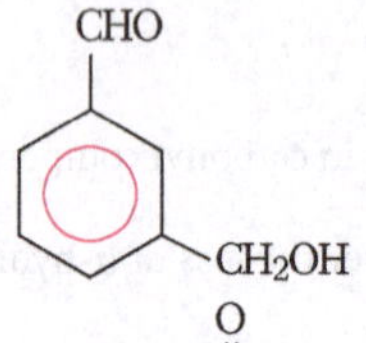
(b) 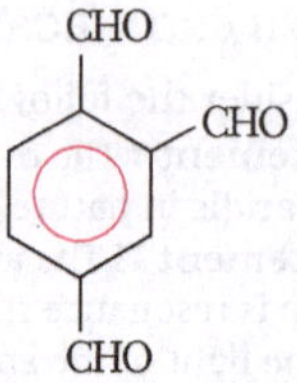
(c) 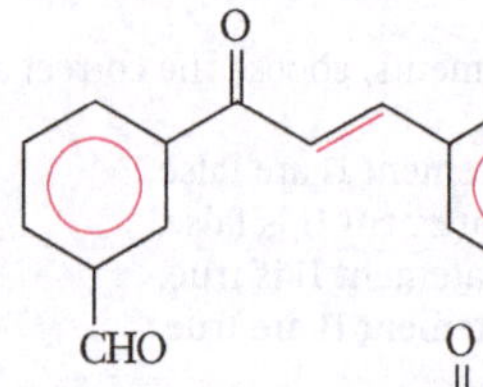
(d) 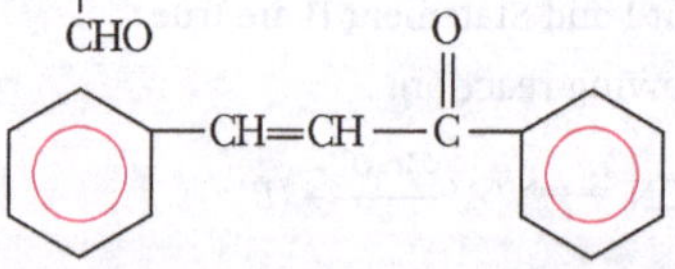

21 Predict the correct intermediate and product in the following reaction.

$$2CH_3{-}CHO \underset{}{\overset{\text{Dil. NaOH}}{\rightleftharpoons}} \underset{(A)}{\text{Intermediate}} \xrightarrow{\Delta} \underset{(B)}{\text{Product}}$$

(a) $A = CH_3CH_2CH_2OH$; $B = CH_3CH(CHO){-}CH{=}CH$

(b) $A = CH_3{-}CH(OH){-}CH_2{-}CHO$; $B = CH_3{-}CH{=}CH{-}CHO$

(c) $A = CH_3{-}CH(OH){-}CH_2{-}CHO$; $B = CH_3{-}C(OH){=}CH_2$

(d) $A = CH_3{-}CH_2{-}CH(OH){-}CHO$; $B = CH_3{-}CH{=}CH{-}CHO$

22 Consider the following reaction :

$$CH_3CHO + CH_3CH_2CHO \xrightarrow[\Delta]{NaOH} CH_3CH = CH{-}CHO$$
$$+ CH_3CH_2{-}CH{=}\underset{\underset{CH_3}{|}}{C}{-}CHO + CH_3{-}CH{=}\underset{\underset{CH_3}{|}}{C}{-}CHO + X$$

The product X is

(a) $CH_3CH = CH{-}CH_3$

(b) $CH_3{-}\overset{\overset{OH}{|}}{CH}{-}CH{-}CHO$

(c) $CH_3{-}C{=}CH{-}CH_2{-}CHO$

(d) $CH_3CH_2{-}CH{=}CH{-}CHO$

23 Consider the following compounds

I. $(CH_3)_3CCHO$ II. $(CH_3)_2CH\ CHO$

III. $C_6H_5\ CHO$ IV. $(CH_2OH)_3C{\cdot}CHO$

V. $CH_3CH_2CH{=}\underset{\underset{CH_3}{|}}{C}{-}CHO$

The number of compounds that will undergo Cannizzaro reaction.

(a) 3 (b) 2

(c) 4 (d) 1

24 Which one of the following is not formed when acetaldehyde react with propanal in the presence of NaOH followed by heating ?

(a) $CH_3{-}CH = CH{-}CHO$

(b) $CH_3CH_2{-}CH{=}\overset{\overset{CH_3}{|}}{C}{-}CHO$

(c) $CH_3{-}CH{=}\underset{\underset{CH_3}{|}}{C}{-}CHO$

(d) $CH_3{-}CH_2{-}CH_2{-}\underset{\underset{OH}{|}}{CH}{-}CHO$

25 What is the IUPAC name of the organic compound formed in the following chemical reaction ?

$$\text{Propanone} \underset{\Delta}{\overset{Ba(OH)_2}{\rightleftharpoons}} \text{product}$$

(a) 2-methylpent-2-en-4-one (b) 4-methylpent-3-en-2-one

(c) 3-methylpent-3-en-2-one (d) 4-methyl but-2-enal

26 What is the IUPAC name of the organic compound formed in the following chemical reaction?

$$\text{Acetophenone} \xrightarrow[\overset{\ominus}{O}H,\ 293\ K]{C_6H_5CHO} \text{Product}$$

(a) 1,4-diphenylprop-2-en-1-one

(b) pent-2-enal

(c) 1,2-diphenyl prop-2-en-1-one

(d) 1,3-diphenylprop-2-en-1-one

27 Which of the following is the incorrect statement ?

(a) Benzaldehye is a colourless liquid and steam volatile.

(b) Acetophenone is sparingly soluble in water but dissolves readily in diethyl ether

(c) 40% of formaldehyde solution is used to preserve biological specimens.

(d) Formaldehyde is used as a starting material in the manufacture of ethyl acetate and drugs.

Module 3

Carboxylic Acid

- Classification
- Nomenclature
- Isomerism
- Methods of Preparation of Carboxylic Acids
- Chemical Properties of Carboxylic Acids
- Method of Preparation of Aromatic Carboxylic Acids
- Physical Properties of Aromatic Carboxylic Acids
- Chemical Properties of Aromatic Carboxylic Acids

The carbonyl compounds in which carbonyl group is bonded to hydroxyl group are known as **carboxylic acids.** The general formula of aliphatic carboxylic acids is C_nH_{2n+1} COOH (aliphatic class).

Classification

Depending upon the number of carboxylic groups present in molecules, these are classified as monocarboxylic acid, dicarboxylic acid or tricarboxylic acids.

Monocarboxylic acids

HCOOH ; CH_3COOH ;

Formic acid; Acetic acid

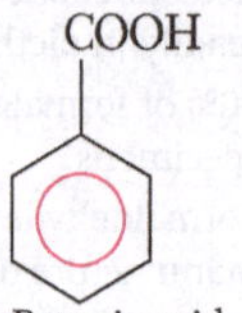

Benzoic acid

Dicarboxylic acid

COOH–COOH ; $CH_2(COOH)_2$;

Oxalic acid; Malonic acid

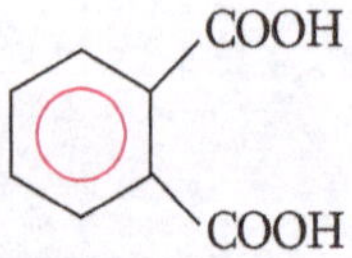

Phthalic acid

Nomenclature

There are two systems of naming carboxylic acids.

Common Names

The common names of carboxylic acid end with suffix-ic acid and has been derived from Latin or Greek names of their natural sources. For example, formic acid was obtained from red ants (Latin: formica means ant), acetic acid from vinegar (Latin : acetum, means vinegar).

IUPAC Names

In IUPAC system, carboxylic acids are named by replacing suffix 'e' of the alkanes with 'oic acid'. Select longest carbon chain containing carboxyl group as parent chain. The position of a substituent is designated by a number. The carboxyl group is always the C-1 carbon. If more than one carboxyl groups are present, prefixes di, tri etc., are used.

Names of Some Carboxylic Acids with their Common and IUPAC Name

Molecular formulae	Common name	IUPAC name
HCOOH	Formic acid	Methanoic acid
CH_3COOH	Acetic acid	Ethanoic acid
$(CH_3)_2CHCH_2COOH$	Isovaleric acid	3-methylbutanoic acid
$(CH_3)_3CCOOH$	Pivalic acid	2,2-dimethylpropanoic acid
$CH_3(CH_2)_4COOH$	Caproic acid	Hexanoic acid
$CH_3(CH_2)_8COOH$	Capric acid	Decanoic acid
$H_2C(COOH)_2$	Malonic acid	Propanedioic acid
CH_2COOH–CH_2COOH	Succinic acid	Butanedioic acid
CHCOOH=CHCOOH	Maleic acid	But-2-enedioic acid
CH_2COOH–CHCOOH–CH_2COOH	–	Propane-1,2,3-tri carboxylic acid

Isomerism

Carboxylic acids show functional isomers. The compounds having same molecular formula but different structures due to difference in functional groups attached. e.g.

- Hydroxy carbonyl compound (aldehyde or ketone)
- Hydroxy oxirane
- Esters

e.g. Functional isomers of acetic acid are

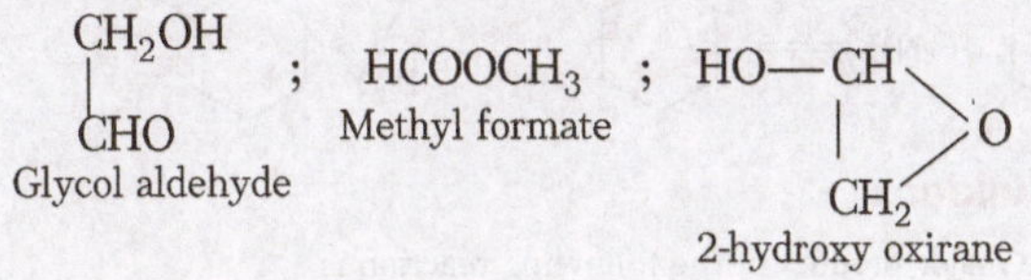

Functional isomers of phenyl acetic acid are

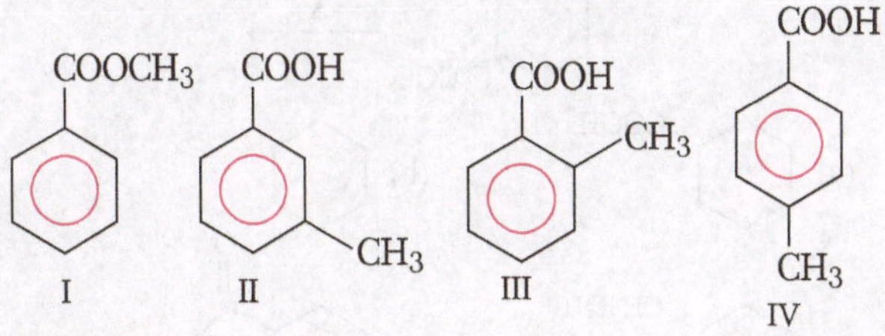

Structure

In carboxylic acids, the bonds to the carboxyl carbon lie in one plane. The entire molecule is planar with sp^2-hybridised carbon atom and trigonal planar geometry.

e.g. Structure of formic acid is shown below.

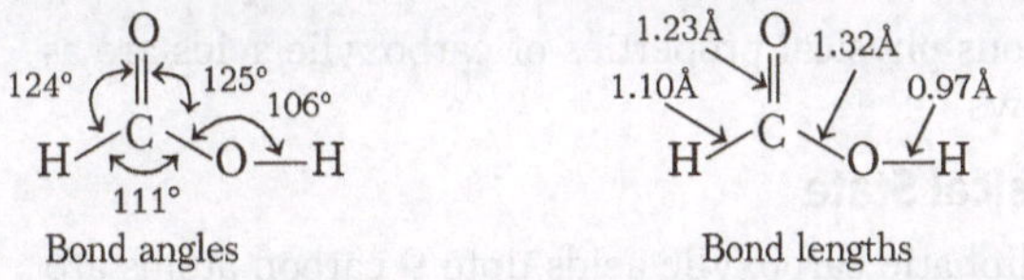

The carboxylic carbon is less electrophilic than carbonyl carbon because of the possible resonance structure shown below :

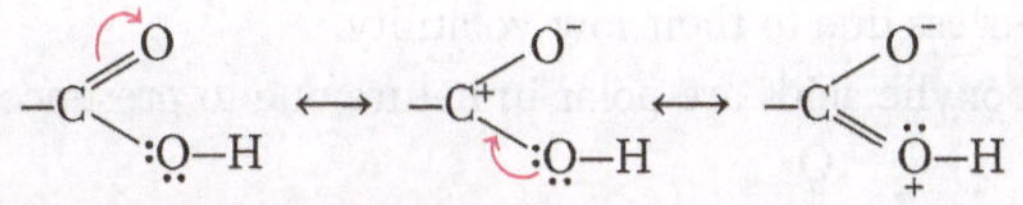

Methods of Preparation of Carboxylic Acids

Following methods are used for the preparation of carboxylic acids.

From Grignard Reagent

Grignard reagent ($RMgX$) reacts with solid carbon dioxide (i.e. dry ice) in presence of dry ether, followed by acidic hydrolysis yields carboxylic acids.

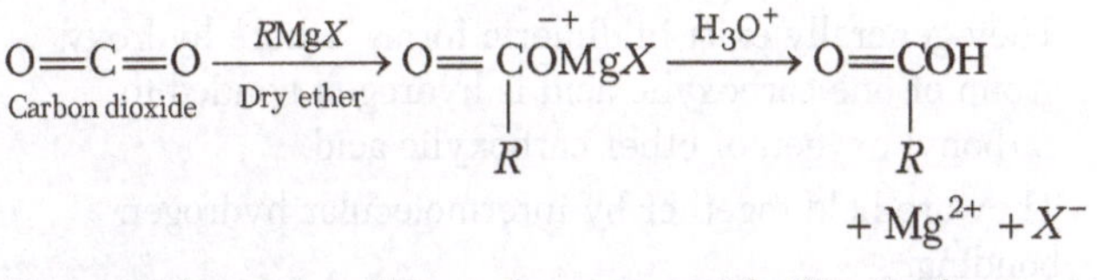

Process of reacting Grignard reagent with CO_2 is also known as **carbonation of organometallic reagents.**

Mentor's TIP

This method gives carboxylic acids with one carbon atom more than starting compound. Thus, HCOOH cannot be prepared by this method.

From Primary Alcohols and Aldehydes

Primary alcohols are easily oxidised to carboxylic acids with oxidants such as $KMnO_4$ (in neutral, acidic or alkaline medium), CrO_3 and $K_2Cr_2O_7$ in acidic medium. (Jones reagent).

e.g. $$RCH_2OH \xrightarrow[H_3O^+]{\text{Alk. } KMnO_4} RCOOH$$

or $$CH_3(CH_2)_6CH_2OH \xrightarrow[\text{Jones reagent}]{CrO_3\text{-}H_2SO_4} CH_3(CH_2)_6COOH$$

Secondary alcohols are oxidised to ketones. Tertiary alcohols are not oxidised due to lack of hydrogen at α-carbon.

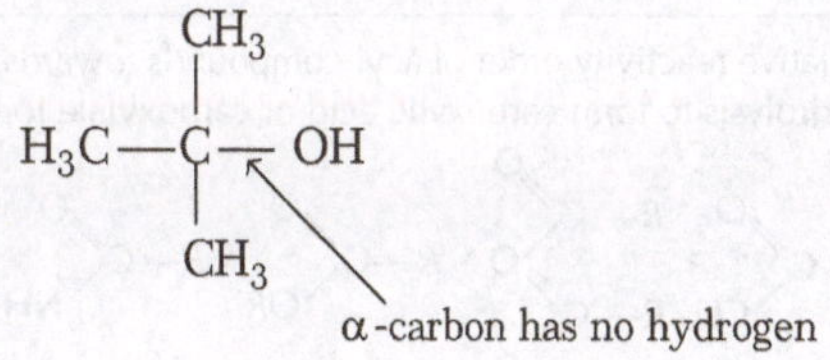

However, strong oxidising agents oxidise secondary and tertiary alcohols to acids of fewer number of carbon atoms with cleavage of C — C bonds.

Carboxylic acids are also prepared from aldehydes by the use of mild oxidising agents.

From Hydrolysis of Acid Derivatives and Nitriles

Esters

Hydrolysis of esters can occur *via* both acidic or basic hydrolysis. Acidic hydrolysis of esters gives directly carboxylic acids while basic hydrolysis gives carboxylate which on acidification give corresponding carboxylic acid. Alkaline hydrolysis of esters is preferred over acidic hydrolysis, because it is irreversible as base is a strong nucleophile which favours hydrolysis and carboxylate ion cannot attack $R'OH$ (nucleophile).

Reaction in acidic medium is given below.

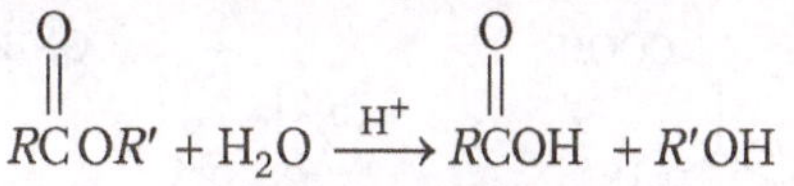

Reaction in basic medium is given below.

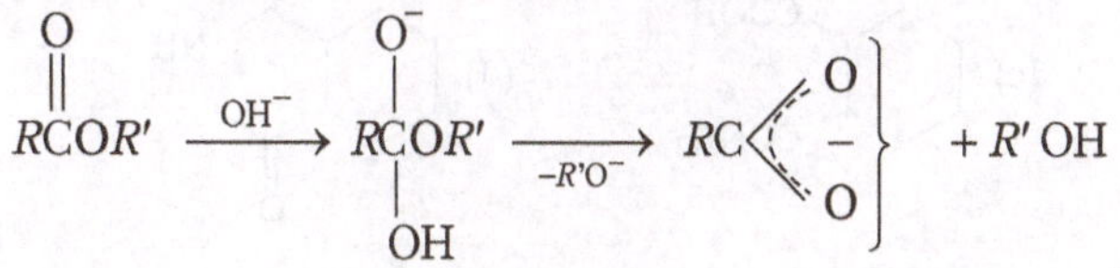

Acid Chlorides

Acid chlorides are hydrolysed with aqueous base to form carboxylate ion which form carboxylic acid on acidification.

$$\underset{\text{Acid chloride}}{R-\overset{O}{\overset{\|}{C}}-Cl} + H_2O \xrightarrow{H^+} \underset{\text{Carboxylic acid}}{R-\overset{O}{\overset{\|}{C}}-OH} + HCl$$

Anhydrides

Acid anhydrides are hydrolysed with aqueous base to form carboxylate ions which form carboxylic acid on acidification.

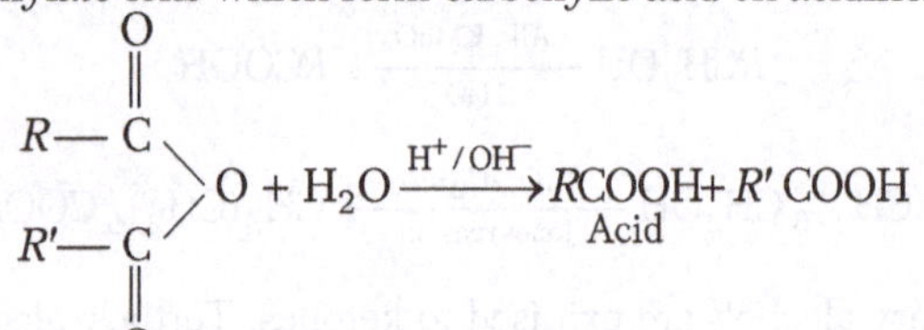

Acid anhydride

Concept ladder

Relative reactivity order of acyl compounds towards hydrolysis to form carboxylic acid or carboxylate ion is

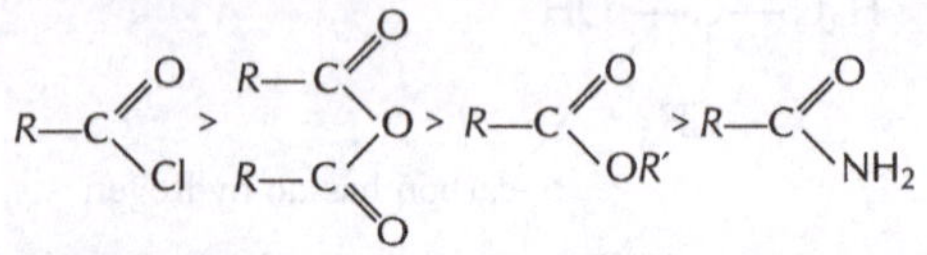

Nitriles and Amides

Nitriles are hydrolysed to amides and then to acids in the presence of H^+ or $\overline{O}H$ as catalyst. Mild reaction conditions are used to stop the reaction at the amide stage.

$$R-CN \xrightarrow[H_2O]{H^+ \text{ or } \overline{O}H} R-\overset{O}{\overset{\|}{C}}-NH_2 \xrightarrow[\Delta]{H^+ \text{ or } \overline{O}H} RCOOH$$

$$\underset{\text{Ethanamide}}{CH_3CONH_2} \xrightarrow[\Delta]{H_3O^+} \underset{\text{Ethanoic acid}}{CH_3COOH} + NH_3$$

NEET Close-up

Example Similar to PYQ Asked in NEET 2019

The major product of the following reaction is

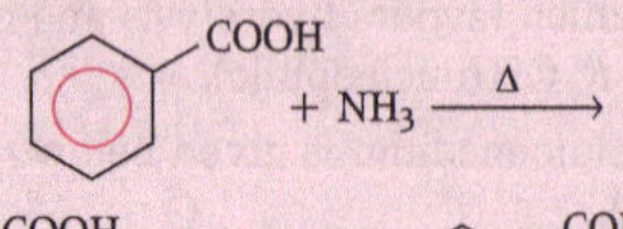

(a) 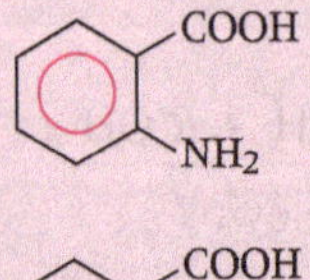

(b) 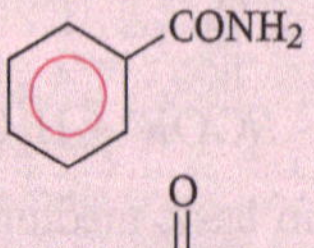

(c) 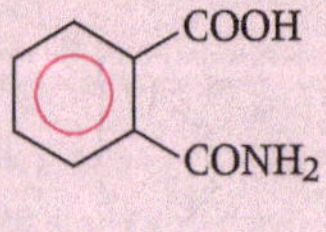

(d) 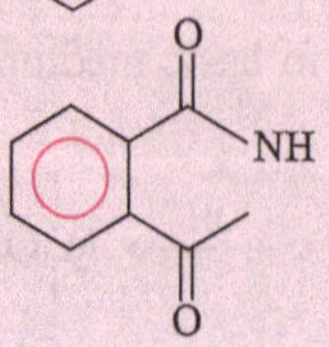

Sol. (*b*) The reaction takes place as follows

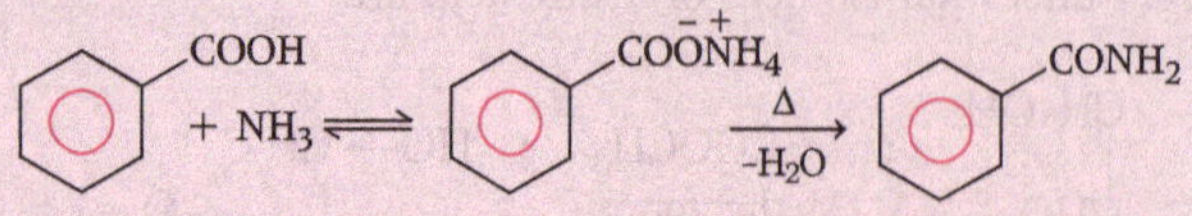

Skill Builder

The major product of the following reaction is

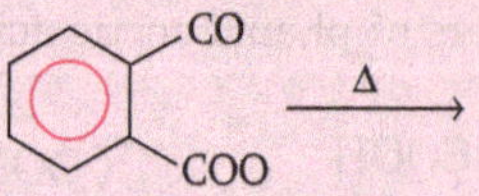

(a) 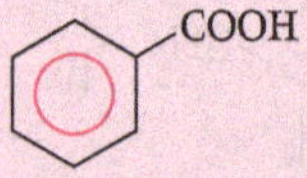

(b) 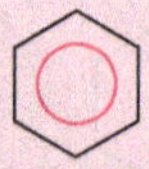

(c) 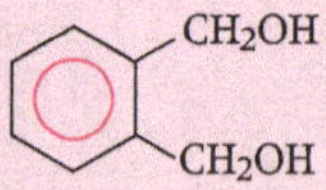

(d) 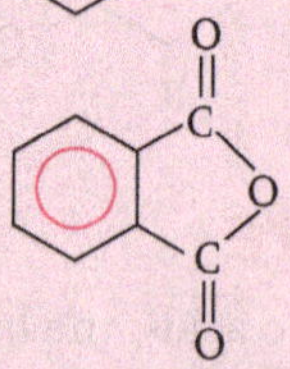

For more practice Refer to Q.17 of Step up practice 3.

Physical Properties of Carboxylic Acids

Various physical properties of carboxylic acids are as follows

Physical State

- Aliphatic carboxylic acids upto 9 carbon atoms are colourless liquids at room temperature with unpleasant odours.
- The higher acids are wax like solids that are practically odourless due to their low volatility.
- Carboxylic acids are polar in nature due to presence of carbonyl ($-\overset{O}{\overset{\|}{C}}-$) and hydroxy (—OH) groups. They have tendency to form H-bonding with each other and also with other polar molecules.

$$R-\underset{\delta+}{\overset{\overset{\delta-}{O}}{\overset{\|}{C}}}-\overset{\delta-}{O}-\overset{\delta+}{H}$$

First four members are miscible with water, carboxylic acid with five carbon is partially soluble and higher ones are insoluble in water.

They generally exist in dimeric forms, where hydroxy group of one carboxylic acid is hydrogen bonded to carbonyl oxygen of other carboxylic acid.

They are held together by intermolecular hydrogen bonding.

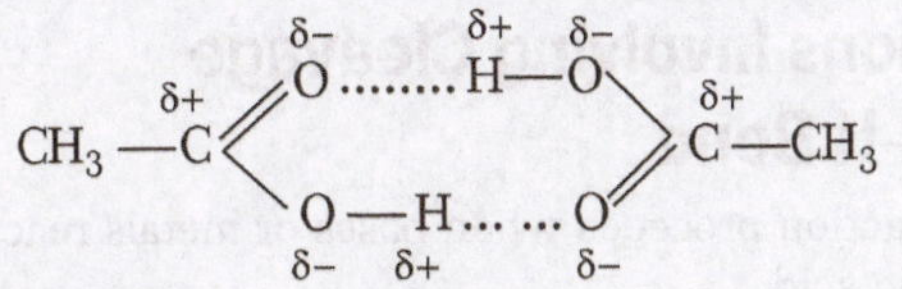

Therefore, they have high melting and boiling points.

Solubility

Carboxylic acids are also soluble in less polar solvents like ether, alcohol, benzene, etc. Most carboxylic acids are quite soluble in relatively non-polar solvents such as $CHCl_3$ because the acid continues to exist in dimeric form in the non-polar solvent.

Chemical Properties of Carboxylic Acids

Acidic nature and some chemical reaction of carboxylic acids are as follows

Acidic Nature of Carboxylic Acids

Carboxylic acids are the most acidic among the organic compounds. These acids ionise in aqueous solution giving carboxylate ion.

$$R-\overset{\overset{\displaystyle O}{\|}}{C}-OH + H_2O \rightleftharpoons \underset{\substack{\text{Carboxylate ion}\\ \text{Conjugate base}}}{R-\overset{\overset{\displaystyle O}{\|}}{C}-O^-} + \underset{\substack{\text{Hydronium}\\ \text{ion}}}{H_3O^+} \quad \text{...(i)}$$

Both carboxylic acid and carboxylate ion are stabilised by resonance but the carboxylate ion is better resonance stabilised because it consists of two equivalent and identical cannonical forms. It is because of this carboxylate ion has greater stability over carboxylic acid.

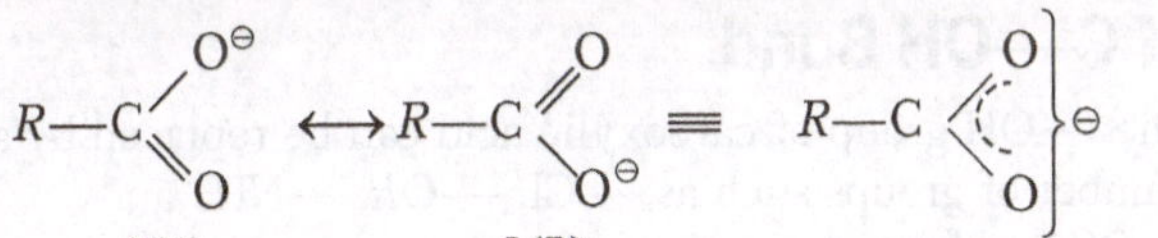

I (A) I (B) I (C)

Mentor's Tip

Acidity of carboxylic acid depends upon stability of carboxylate ion, i.e. as the stability of carboxylate ion increases the acidity of carboxylic acid also increases and *vice-versa*.

Carboxylic acids are more acidic than alcohols. Both, acid and alcohol involves cleavage of O—H bond. Dissociation of acid gives carboxylate ion in which negative charge is distributed equally over two oxygen atoms. Whereas, in alkoxide ion, it is concentrated on one oxygen atom. Therefore, delocalisation of charge makes carboxylate ion more stable than alkoxide ion.

Effect of Substituents on Acidity

Acidity of carboxylic acid depends on the formation of carboxylate ion. Any factor which tends to stabilise the carboxylate ion will increase the acidic strength of carboxylic acid.

At the same time, any factor which tends to destabilise the ion, will decrease the acidic strength of carboxylic acid.

(i) Effect of Electron Withdrawing Substituents

An electron withdrawing group (EWG) stabilises the carboxylate ion by dispersal of negative charge. Thus, increases the acidic character.

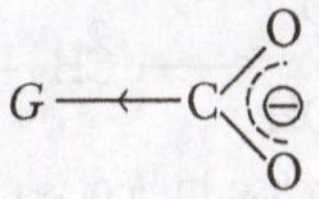

Some trends of compounds containing —COOH group are as follows

- Acidic strength increases with increase in number of electron withdrawing groups.

e.g.

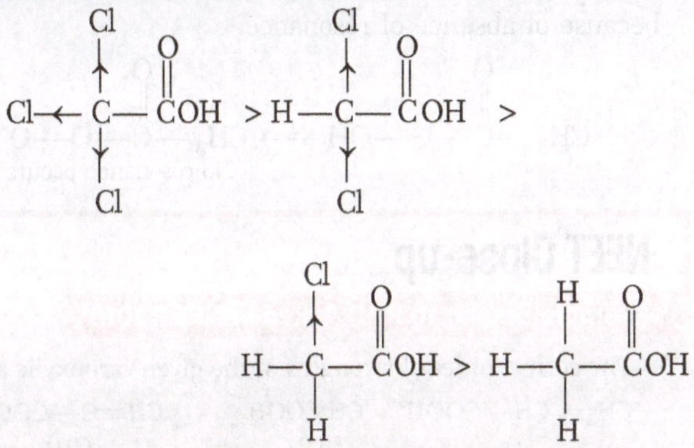

- Position of electron withdrawing groups also affect the acidity of carboxylic acids. As the distance between electron withdrawing group and —COOH group increases, acidic nature decreases.

e.g. $CH_3CH(Cl)COOH > CH_2(Cl)CH_2COOH > CH_3CH_2COOH$

- $-I$-effect of halogens follows the order as

$$F > Cl > Br > I$$

Therefore, sequence for the acidity of halocarboxylic acids is

$$F—CH_2COOH > Cl—CH_2COOH > Br—CH_2COOH > I—CH_2COOH$$

(ii) Effect of Electron Releasing Substituents

An electron donating group (EDG) destabilises the carboxylate ion and thus, decreases the acidic character.

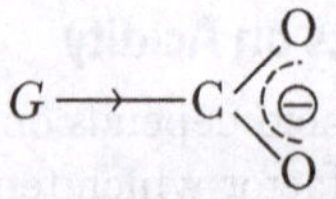

Acidic strength decreases with increase in number of electron donating groups.

$HCOOH > CH_3COOH > CH_3CH_2COOH > (CH_3)_2CHCOOH$

(iii) Effect of Hybridisation on Acidity

- Acidic character increases when acetylinic, vinyl or phenyl groups are directly attached to the carboxylic group. This is because, sp^2-hybridised carbon atom is directly attached to —COOH group.

e.g.

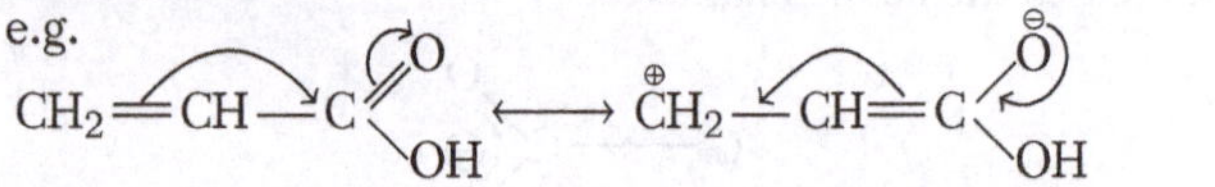

Therefore, with increase in % of *s*-character of α-carbon, acidity of carboxylic acid increases.

e.g. $\underset{sp}{HC\equiv \overset{\alpha}{C}}—COOH > \underset{sp^2}{CH_2=\overset{\alpha}{C}H}—COOH > \underset{sp^3}{\overset{\alpha}{C}H_3}COOH$

- Peroxy acids are weaker acids than carboxylic acids because of absence of resonance.

$$CH_3—\overset{O}{\overset{\|}{C}}—O—OH \longrightarrow \underset{\text{No resonance occurs}}{CH_3—\overset{O}{\overset{\|}{C}}—O—O^{\ominus}}$$

NEET Close-up

Example Similar to PYQ Asked in NEET 2016

The correct order of strengths of the given carboxylic acids.

$CH_2=CH—COOH$	CH_3COOH	$CH\equiv C—COOH$
(I)	(II)	(III)

(a) III < I < II (b) II < I < III
(c) I < II < III (d) II < III < I

Sol. (*b*) Increase in % *s*-character of α-carbon, increases the acidity of carboxylic acid.

$CH_3COOH < CH_2=CH–COOH < CH\equiv C—COOH$

Skill Builder

The correct order of strengths of the carboxylic acids.

$CH_3\underset{Cl}{\underset{\vert}{C}H}COOH$	CH_3CH_2COOH	$\underset{Cl}{\underset{\vert}{C}H_2}—CH_2COOH$
(I)	(II)	(III)

(a) I > III > II (b) I > II > III (c) II > III > I (d) III > II > I

For more practice Refer to Q.12 & Q.13 of Step up practice 3.

Reactions Involving Cleavage of O—H Bond

These reaction proceeds when bases or metals react with carboxylic acid.

(i) Reaction with Bases

Carboxylic acids react with bases to form ionic salts which are soluble in water. This reaction shows their acidic character.

$$R—\overset{O}{\overset{\|}{C}}—OH + NaHCO_3 \longrightarrow R\overset{O}{\overset{\|}{C}}—\overset{-}{O}\overset{+}{Na} + CO_2 + H_2O$$

$$R—\overset{O}{\overset{\|}{C}}—OH + NaOH \longrightarrow R—\overset{O}{\overset{\|}{C}}—\overset{-}{O}\overset{+}{Na} + H_2O$$

Concept ladder The reaction of carboxylic with $NaHCO_3$ is used as a qualitative test for detection of carboxylic of carboxyl functional group in an organic compound.

(ii) Reaction with Metals

Carboxylic acids also react with metal like Na or Zn to produce metallic salts with liberation of hydrogen.

$$2R—\overset{O}{\overset{\|}{C}}—OH + 2Na \longrightarrow 2R\overset{O}{\overset{\|}{C}}—\overset{-}{O}\overset{+}{Na} + H_2\uparrow$$

$$2R—\overset{O}{\overset{\|}{C}}—OH + Zn \longrightarrow (RCOO)_2Zn + H_2\uparrow$$

Reactions Involving Cleavage of C—OH Bond

The —OH group of carboxylic acid can be replaced by a number of groups such as —Cl, —*OR*, —NH_2 and —OC*R* to form derivatives of carboxylic acids.

(i) Esterification

Carboxylic acids react with alcohols to form esters in presence of conc. H_2SO_4.

$$R—\overset{O}{\overset{\|}{C}}—OH + H—OR' \underset{H_2SO_4}{\overset{\text{Conc.}}{\rightleftharpoons}} \underset{\text{Ester}}{R—\overset{O}{\overset{\|}{C}}—OR'} + H_2O$$

Mechanisms

The reaction proceeds *via* addition elimination mechanism and it involves the following steps :

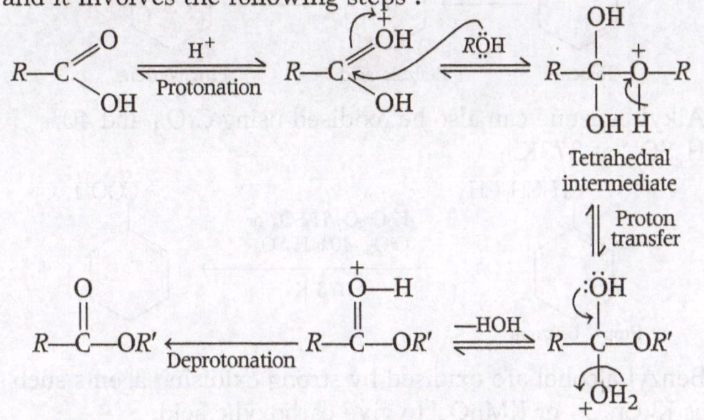

The order of reactivity of carboxylic acid is follows as

$HCOOH > CH_3COOH > (CH_3)_2CCOOH > (CH_3)_3CCOOH$

(ii) Reaction with Phosphorus Halides

Carboxylic acid reacts with PCl_3 and PCl_5 to produce acyl halide.

$$3RCOOH + PCl_3 \longrightarrow \underset{\text{Acyl halide}}{3RCOCl} + H_3PO_3$$

$$RCOOH + PCl_5 \longrightarrow RCOCl + POCl_3 + HCl\uparrow$$

(iii) Reaction with Thionyl Chloride

Carboxylic acid reacts with $SOCl_2$ to produce acyl halide.

$$RCOOH + SOCl_2 \longrightarrow RCOCl + SO_2\uparrow + HCl\uparrow$$

$SOCl_2$ is preferred over phosphorus halides as it produces gaseous SO_2 and HCl as byproducts which escape the reaction mixture and makes the purification of product easier.

(iv) Reaction with Ammonia

The reaction of carboxylic acids with ammonia forms ammonium salt of carboxylic acid, which on heating undergoes elimination to produce amide.

The nitrogen of ammonia and its derivatives are better nucleophiles. So, it captures the proton from — OH group of carboxylic acid to form ammonium carboxylate salt.

$$\textit{Step I}\ R{-}\overset{O}{\overset{\|}{C}}{-}OH + NH_3 \longrightarrow R{-}\overset{O}{\overset{\|}{C}}{-}\bar{O}\overset{+}{N}H_4$$

$$\textit{Step II}\ R{-}\overset{O}{\overset{\|}{C}}{-}\bar{O}\overset{+}{N}H_4 \xrightarrow{\Delta} \underset{\text{Amide}}{R{-}\overset{O}{\overset{\|}{C}}{-}NH_2} + H_2O$$

(v) Formation of Anhydride

Carboxylic acids undergo dehydration, on reaction with phosphorus pentoxide (P_2O_5) or H_2SO_4 to produce acid anhydride.

$$\underset{\text{Acid}}{R{-}\overset{O}{\overset{\|}{C}}{-}OH} + HO{-}\overset{O}{\overset{\|}{C}}{-}R \xrightarrow[-H_2O]{P_2O_5,\Delta} \underset{\text{Acid anhydride}}{R{-}\overset{O}{\overset{\|}{C}}{-}O{-}\overset{O}{\overset{\|}{C}}{-}R}$$

(vi) Reaction with Diazomethane

Carboxylic acids, on reaction with diazomethane give high yields of methyl esters at room temperature.

e.g. $$\underset{\text{Propanoic acid}}{CH_3CH_2COOH} + \underset{\text{Diazomethane}}{CH_2N_2} \longrightarrow \underset{\text{Methyl propionate}}{CH_3CH_2COOCH_3} + N_2\uparrow$$

Reactions Involving —COOH Group

Carboxylic acids give following reactions due to the presence of carboxylic group.

(i) Decarboxylation

On heating sodium or potassium salts of carboxylic acid with sodalime (NaOH + CaO) in the ratio of 3 : 1 decarboxylation occurs which gives alkane as a final product. The reaction is used to degrade the carbon chain as the product contains one carbon less than parent acid.

$$\underset{\text{Sodium salt of carboxylic acid}}{R{-}\overset{O}{\overset{\|}{C}}{-}\overset{-\ +}{ONa}} + NaOH \xrightarrow[\Delta]{CaO} R{-}H + Na_2CO_3$$

Mentor's Tip

If there is a keto group at β-position or (—C = C—) bond between β and γ-position then decarboxylation occurs by simple heating.

$$\overset{\gamma}{C}H_2{=}\overset{\beta}{C}H\overset{\alpha}{C}H_2COOH \xrightarrow{\Delta} CH_2{=}CH - CH_3 + CO_2\uparrow$$

Decarboxylation can also occur by the electrolysis of aqueous solution of sodium or potassium salts of carboxylic acids to give alkanes. This process is known as **Kolbe's electrolysis.**

$$2CH_3COO^-K^+ \longrightarrow 2CH_3COO^- + 2K^+$$

At anode,

$$2CH_3COO^- \xrightarrow[-2e^-]{} \underset{\text{Unstable}}{2CH_3COO} \xrightarrow{\Delta} CH_3{-}CH_3 + CO_2$$

At cathode, $2K^+ \xrightarrow{+2e^-} 2K \xrightarrow{+2H_2O} 2KOH + H_2$

(ii) Reduction

Carboxylic acids undergo reduction to form alkanes, alcohols and carboxyl compounds with different reagents.

$$\underset{\text{Carboxylic acid}}{R{-}COOH} \xrightarrow[\Delta]{\text{Red P/HI}} \underset{\text{Alkane}}{R{-}CH_3} + 2H_2O + 3I_2$$

$$R{-}COOH \xrightarrow[\text{Ether, } H_3O^+]{LiAlH_4} \underset{\text{Alcohol}}{R{-}CH_2OH}$$

$$R{-}COOH \xrightarrow[\Delta]{\text{Or } B_2H_6\text{/ether}} \underset{\text{Alcohol}}{R{-}OH}$$

Reaction due to α-Hydrogen

The reaction in which α-hydrogen of the carboxylic acid is replaced by halogen atom on reaction with red phosphorus in presence of Cl_2 or Br_2 gives α-halo carboxylic acids. This reaction is known as **Hell-Volhard Zelinsky** (HVZ) **reaction.**

$$R{-}CH_2{-}COOH \xrightarrow[\text{(ii) } H_2O]{\text{(i) } X_2\text{/Red phosphorus}} R{-}\underset{\displaystyle X}{\underset{|}{CH}}{-}COOH$$

(where, X = Cl, Br)

If no α-hydrogen is present in carboxylic acid, then no reaction occurs.

$$\text{e.g.}\quad CH_3\overset{\displaystyle CH_3}{\overset{|}{\underset{\displaystyle CH_3}{\underset{|}{C}}}}COOH + Br_2 \xrightarrow{\text{Red P}} \text{No reaction}$$

α-halogenated acids are good starting material for the preparation of substituted carboxylic acids.

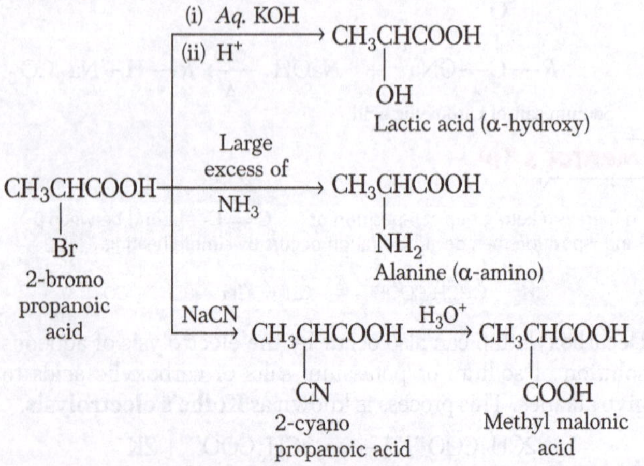

Method of Preparation of Aromatic Carboxylic Acids

Organic compounds in which carboxyl group (—COOH) is directly attached to an aromatic ring are known as aromatic carboxylic acids.

Aromatic carboxylic acids are generally prepared by following methods.

(i) Oxidation of Alkyl Benzene

Alkyl benzene on reaction with alkaline $KMnO_4$ gives aromatic acid. In this reaction, benzene ring does not undergo oxidation but alkyl group gets oxidised and produces benzoic acid (whatever the length of side chain, oxidation product is benzoic acid).

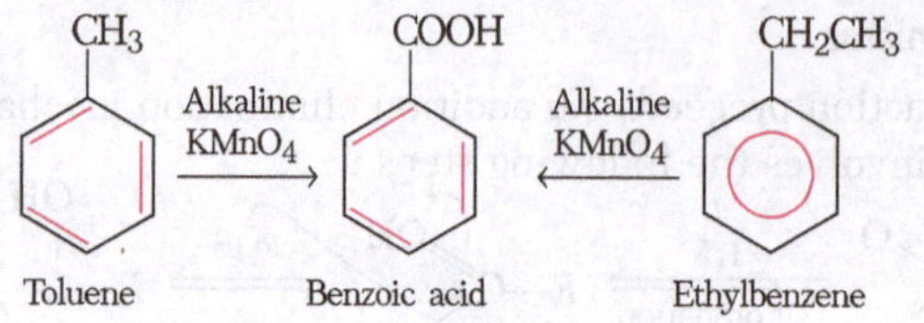

Alkyl benzene can also be oxidised using CrO_3 and 40% H_2SO_4 at 373K.

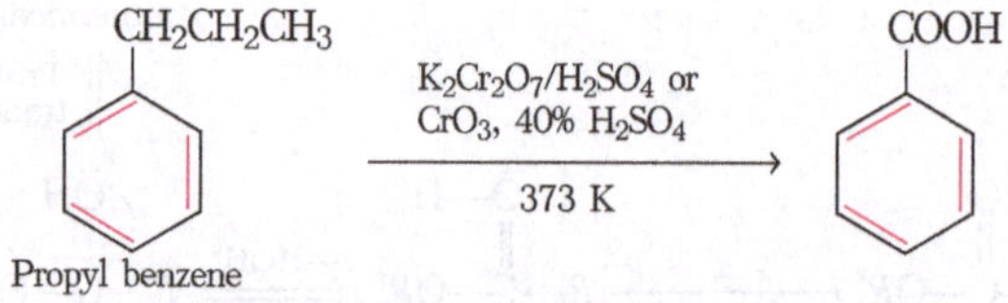

Benzyl alcohol are oxidised by strong oxidising agents such as $K_2Cr_2O_7$ or $KMnO_4$ to give carboxylic acid.

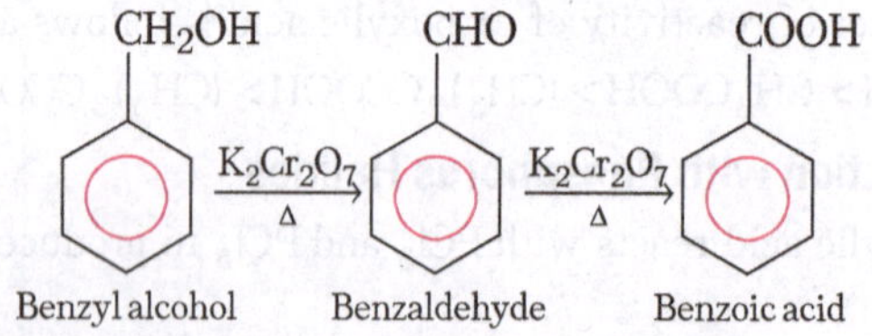

(ii) Hydrolysis of Acid Derivatives and Nitriles

Aromatic acid derivatives on hydrolysis gives benzoic acid. Similarly, benzonitrile on hydrolysis also gives benzoic acid.

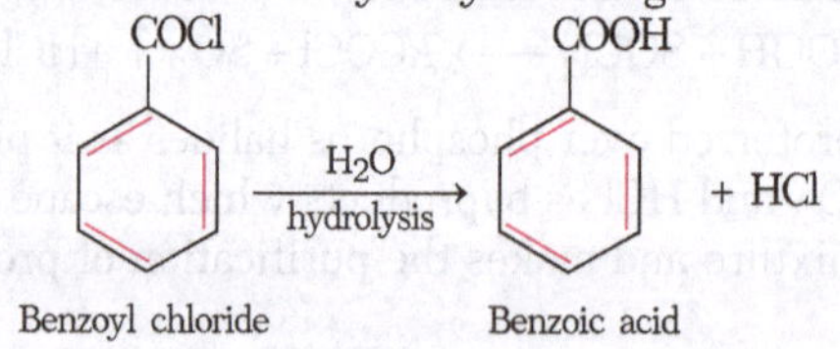

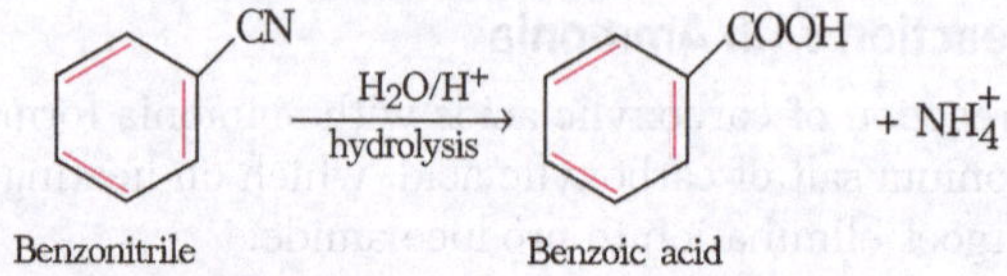

Physical Properties of Aromatic Carboxylic Acids

The aromatic carboxylic acids exhibit polarity due to presence of polar carbonyl and hydroxyl group. In general, carboxylic acids exist in the *dimer form* due to intermolecular hydrogen bonding. The aromatic carboxylic acids are generally crystalline solids with high melting point.

However, the substituted carboxylic acids may form intramolecular hydrogen bonding as in case of 2-hydroxy benzoic acid (salicylic acid).

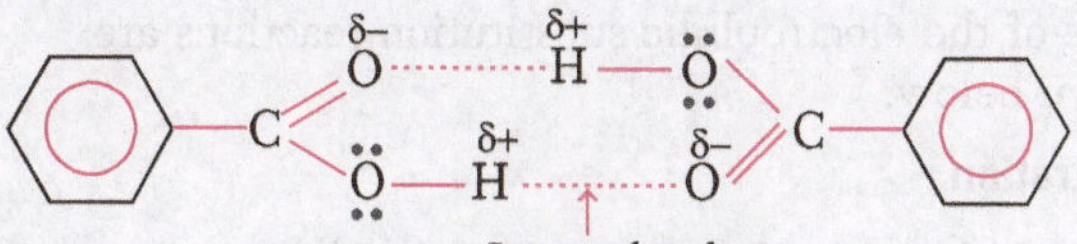

Intermolecular hydrogen bonding in benzoic acid

Intramolecular hydrogen bonding

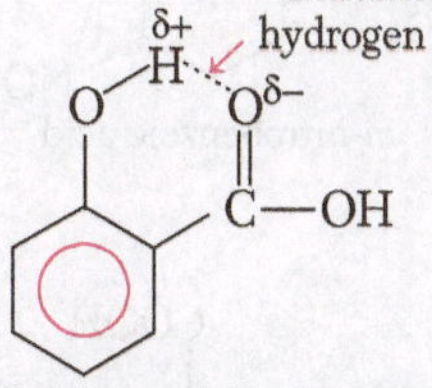

Salicylic acid (or 2-hydroxybenzoic acid)

Chemical Properties of Aromatic Carboxylic Acids

Aromatic carboxylic acids show chemical reactions similar to aliphatic carboxylic acids, like reaction with bases, phosphorus halide, thionyl chloride etc.

They also give electrophilic substitution reactions. Acidic nature and electrophilic substitution reactions of aromatic carboxlic acids are as follows

Acidity of Aromatic Acids

In aromatic carboxylic acids, carbonyl carbon is sp^2-hybridised and stabilises the charge in carboxylate ion through resonance. Thus, increases the acidity.

Resonance in aromatic carboxylic ion is shown below.

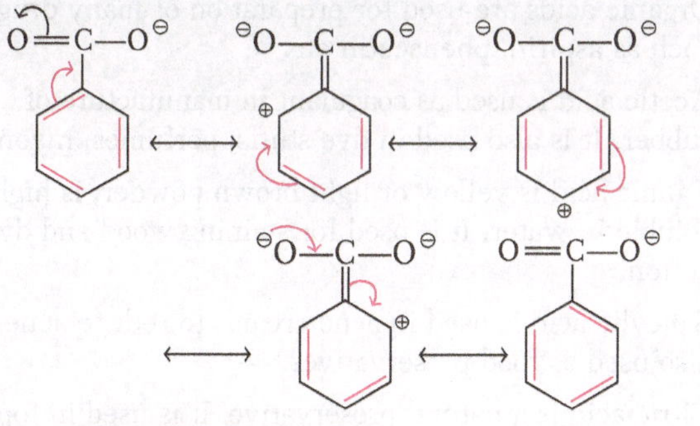

Effect of Substituents on Acidity

- Electron withdrawing groups stabilise the anion by dispersal of negative charge thus, increases the acidity.
- Electron donating groups destabilise the anion by increasing electron density thus, decreases the acidity.

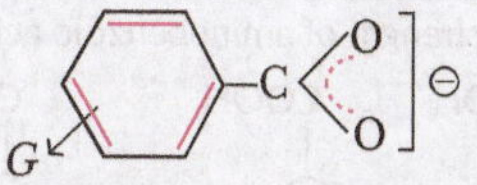

G withdraws electrons, stabilises anion, strengthen acid

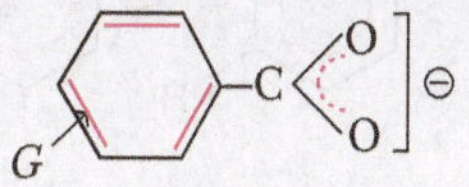

G releases electrons, destabilises anion, weakens acid

Concept ladder Both the acid strengthening and weakening effect are more pronounced at the *para*-positions than at the *meta*-positions because of the resonating structure of benzoic acid.

Ortho-effect

o-substituted benzoic acids are stronger acids than benzoic acid. This is known as ***ortho*-effect**. This is due to steric and electronic factors. It does not matter whether the substituent is electron releasing or electron withdrawing.

Various trends due to *ortho*-effect are as follows

- Acidity order for methyl benzoic acid.

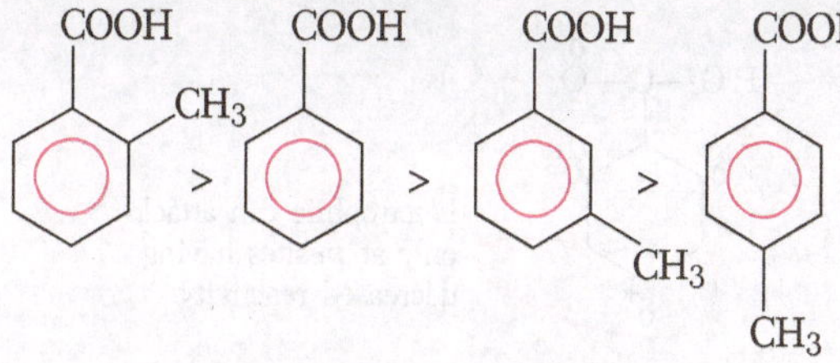

- Acidity order for isomers of nitrobenzoic acids.

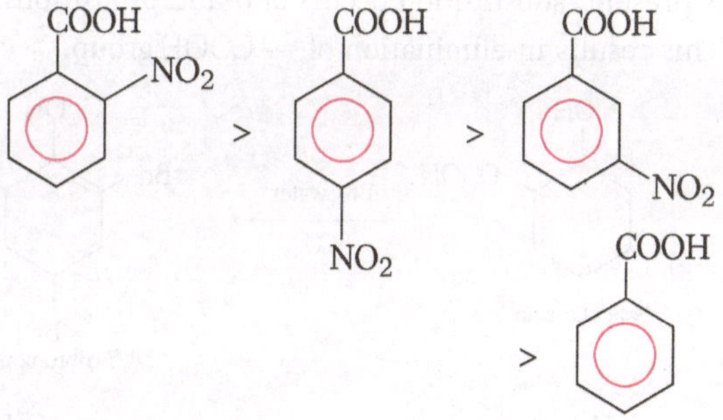

- Acidic strength for isomers of methoxy benzoic acids.

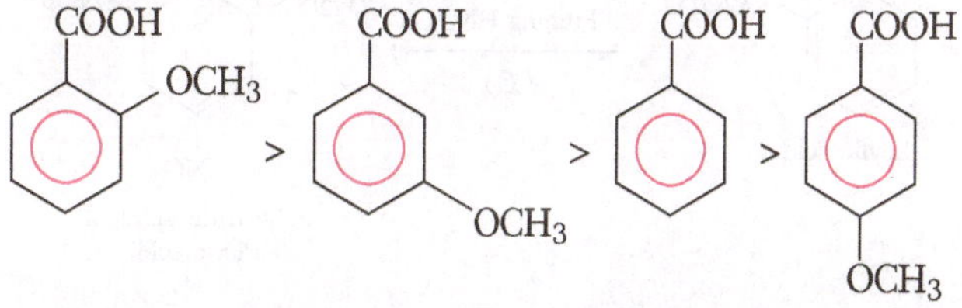

Concept ladder

Acidic strength of aminobenzoic acids.

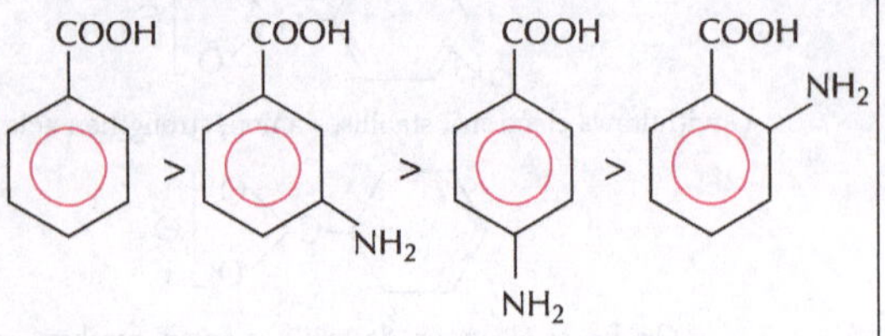

Explanation *o*-aminobenzoic acid is less acidic as compared to carboxylic acid due to formation of Zwitter ion *via* H-bonding.

Electrophilic Substitution Reactions

Aromatic carboxylic acids undergo electrophilic substitution reaction at *m*-position due to presence of electron withdrawing group, i.e. —COOH group. This can be represented by following resonating structures. Due to delocalisation of π-electrons, electron density is decreased at *o*-and *p*-positions. Thus, electrophile attacks at *m*-position.

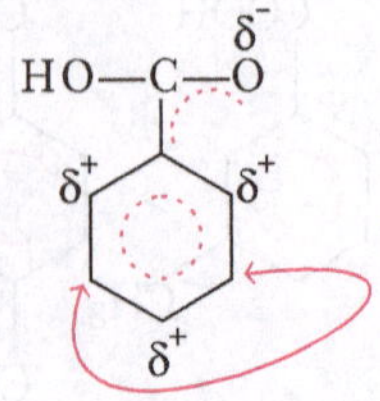

Electrophile can attack only at *m*-sites having decreased reactivity.

If electron donating group (such as —OH in salicylic acid) is present, substitution occurs at *o*-and *p*-positions. This results in elimination of —COOH group.

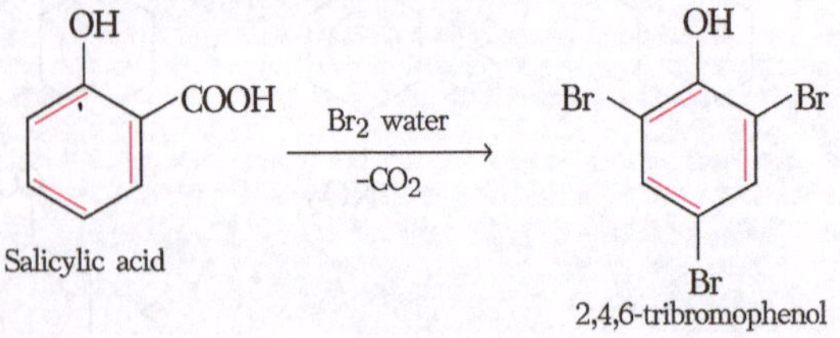

Salicylic acid → 2,4,6-tribromophenol

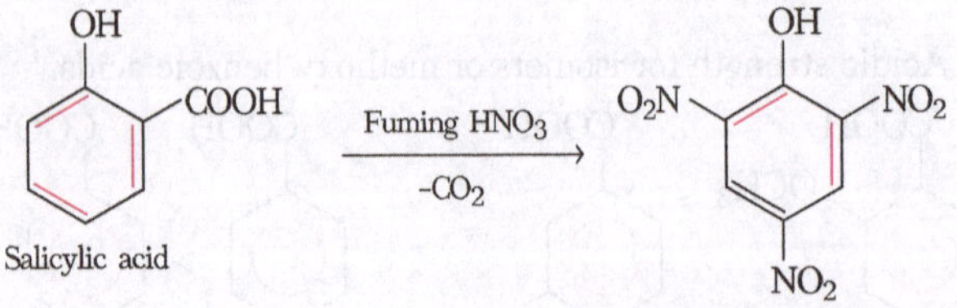

Salicylic acid → 2,4,6-trinitrophenol (Picric acid)

Some of the electrophilic substitution reactions are shown below.

(i) Nitration

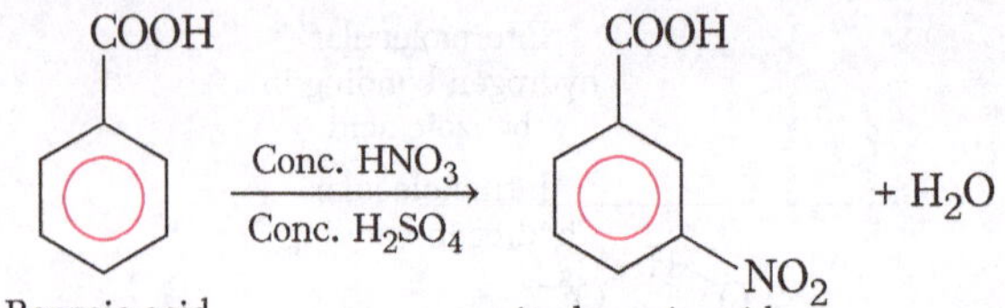

Benzoic acid → *m*-nitrobenzoic acid

(ii) Sulphonation

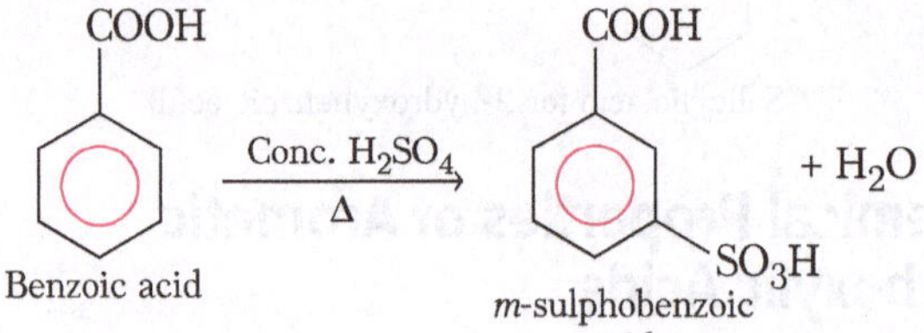

Benzoic acid → *m*-sulphobenzoic acid

(iii) Halogenation

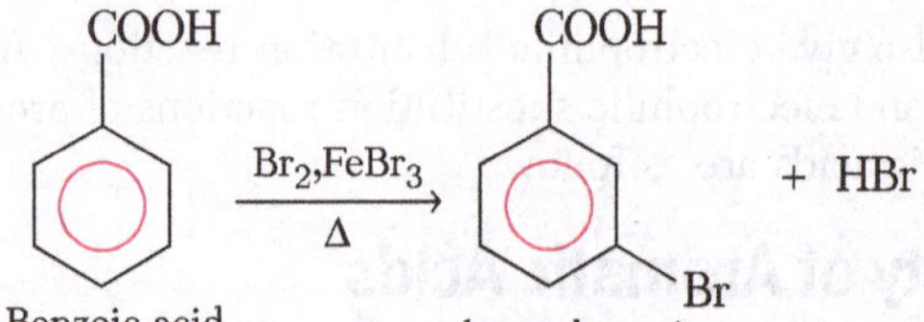

Benzoic acid → *m*-bromobenzoic acid

Uses

- Higher fatty acids are used in manufacture of soaps.
- Organic acids are used for preparation of many drugs such as aspirin, phenacetin etc.
- Acetic acid is used as coagulant in manufacture of rubber. It is also used in dye stuffs, perfumes, rayon etc.
- Tannic acid is yellow or light brown powder, is highly soluble in water. It is used for staining wood and dyeing cotton.
- Salicylic acid is used in acne creams to reduce acne. It is also used as food preservatives.
- Citric acid is a natural preservative. It is used in foods and soft drinks.
- Oxalic acid is used in bleaching and cleansing solutions.
- Acetic acid is used in foods such as 2-3% solution of CH_3COOH in water known as vinegar.

STEP UP Practice 3

1 Which of the following is not a dicarboxylic acid ?
(a) Glutaric acid (b) Malonic acid
(c) Phthalic acid (d) Caproic acid

2 Which of the following is not correctly matched with their common names ?
(a) $H_2C\begin{matrix} /COOH \\ \backslash COOH \end{matrix} \longrightarrow$ Malonic acid
(b) $\begin{matrix} CHCOOH \\ \| \\ CHCOOH \end{matrix} \longrightarrow$ Maleic acid
(c) $\begin{matrix} CH_2CH_2COOH \\ | \\ CH_2CH_2COOH \end{matrix} \longrightarrow$ Glutaric acid
(d) $\begin{matrix} CH_2COOH \\ | \\ CH_2COOH \end{matrix} \longrightarrow$ Succinic acid

3 What is the IUPAC name of the acrylic acid ?
(a) Prop-2-enoic acid (b) Octadecanoic acid
(c) Hexanoic acid (d) Ethanedioic acid

4 The IUPAC name of caproic acid is
(a) 3-methylbutanoic acid
(b) hexanoic acid
(c) but-2-enoic acid
(d) but-2-enediaic acid

5 $CH_3CH_2CH_2CH_2OH \xrightarrow[\text{(in excess)}]{Cr_2O_7^{2-}/H_3O^+} X$

The product X is
(a) CH_3CHO (b) CH_3COOH
(c) $CH_3CH_2CH_2COOH$ (d) CH_3CH_2CHO

6 $CO_2 \xrightarrow[\text{Dry ether}]{C_2H_5MgBr} X \xrightarrow{H_3O^+} Y$?

The prodcut Y is
(a) pentanoic acid
(b) butanoic acid
(c) propanoic acid
(d) 2-methyl propanoic acid

7 The organic product formed in the reaction.

$$C_6H_5COOCH_3 \xrightarrow{H_3O^+} ?$$

(a) C_6H_5COOH (b) HCHO
(c) C_6H_5CHO (d) $C_6H_5CH_2OH$

8 Consider the following reaction sequence.

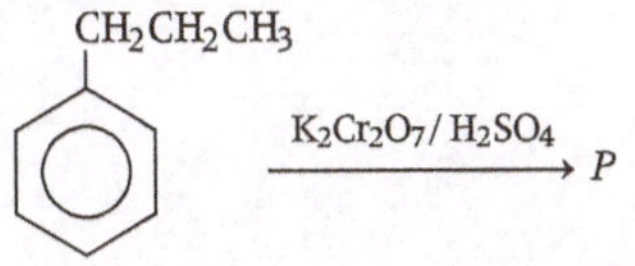

The product P is

(a) 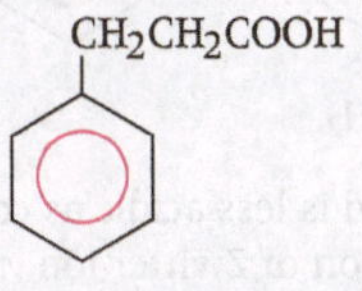 (b) 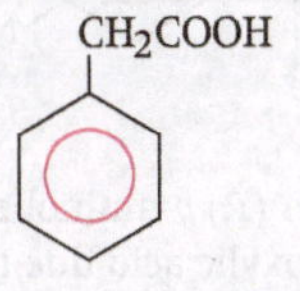

(c) 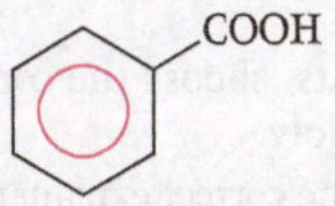 (d) 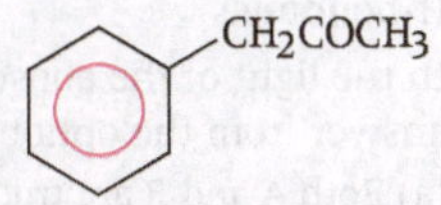

9 Acid anhydride when hydrolysed with aqueous base and further on acidification to form
(a) RCOOH (b) R—CH_2OH
(c) R—CHO (d) R—COOR'

10 Which of the following is the incorrect statement ?
(a) Carboxylic acids have tendency to undergo H-bonding with each other.
(b) First four members of carboxylic acid are miscible with water.
(c) Carboxylic acids are held together by intramolecular hydrogen bonding.
(d) Carboxylic acids are less soluble in less polar solvents.

11 Which of the following is incorrect statements?
(a) Carboxylic acids have high melting and boiling points.
(b) Aliphatic carboxylic acids upto nine carbon atom are colourless liquid with unpleasant odours.
(c) Higher acids are odourless due to their low volatility.
(d) Solubility of carboxylic acids increases with increase in number of carbon atom.

12 The correct acidity order of the following is

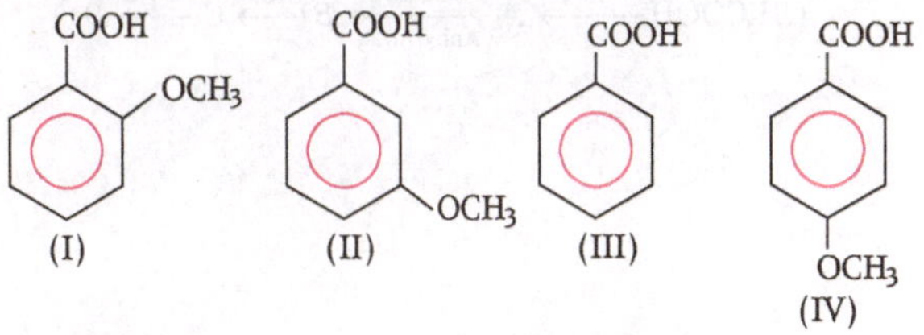

(a) I ≈ II > III > IV (b) I ≈ III > IV > I
(c) II > I > III > IV (d) III > IV > II > I

13 The correct order of increasing acids strength of the compounds :
I. CH_3COOH II. CH_3OCH_2COOH
III. CF_3COOH IV. $\begin{matrix} CH_3 \\ C_2H_5 \end{matrix}\!\!>\!CH—COOH$

(a) I < II < IV < III (b) III < IV < I < II
(c) II < IV < I < III (d) IV < I < II < III

14 Given below are two statements, one is labelled as Assertion (A) and the other is labelled as Reason (R).

Assertion (A) The correct order of acidic strength of aminobenzoic acid is

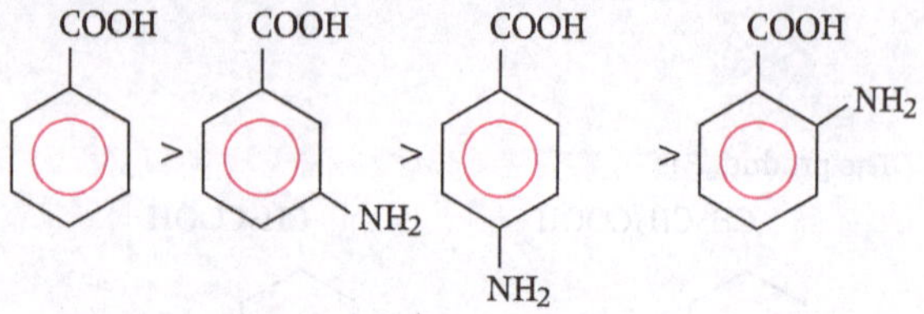

Reason (R) *o*-aminobenzoic acid is less acidic as compared to carboxylic acid due to formation of Zwitter ion *via* H-bonding.s

In the light of the above statements, choose the correct answer from the options given below.

(a) Both A and R are true and R is the correct explanation of A.
(b) Both A and R are true but R is not the correct explanation of A.
(c) A is true but R is false.
(d) A is false but R is true.

15 When propionic acid is treated with aqueous sodium bicarbonate, CO_2 is liberated. The CO_2 comes from

(a) CH_3 group
(b) COOH group
(c) CH_2 group
(d) sodium bicarbonate

16 In the reaction

$$CH_3CH_2COOH \xrightarrow[\text{Conc. } H_2SO_4]{R\text{—}OH} B$$

The product *B* is,

(a) CH_3CH_2COOR (b) CH_3CH_2COOH with OH below
(c) $CH_3CH=CH\text{—}COOH$ (d) $CH_3CH=CH\text{—}COOR$

17 Consider the following reaction sequence.

$$CH_3COOH \xrightarrow{SOCl_2} A \xrightarrow[\text{Anhy. AlCl}_3]{\text{Benzene}} B \xrightarrow{HCN} C \xrightarrow{H_2O} D$$

The product *D* is

(a) 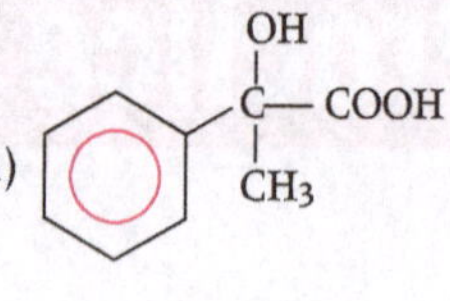 (b) 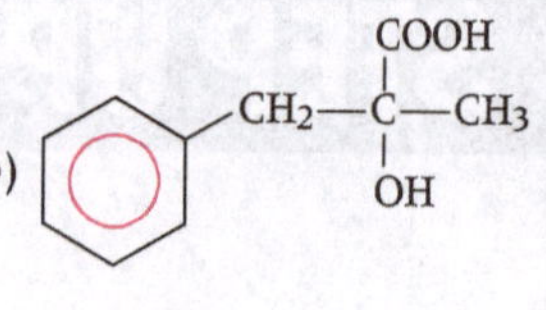

(c) 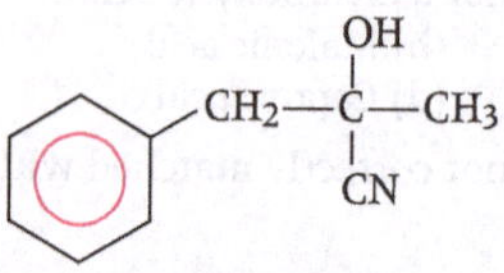 (d) 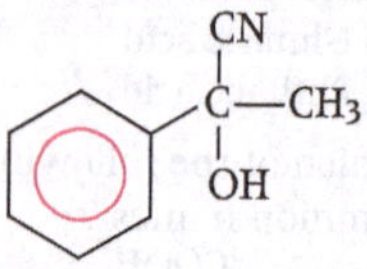

18 Consider the following reaction sequence.

(i) $2CH_3COOK \xrightarrow{\text{Electrolysis}}$ (ii) $CH_3CH_2COOH \xrightarrow{LiAlH_4}$

(iii) $CH_3CH_2CH_2COOH \xrightarrow[\Delta]{\text{Red P/HI}}$ (iv) $R\text{—}CH_2COOH \xrightarrow[\text{HBr}]{Br_2, \text{ Red P}}$

(v) $R\text{—}COOH \xrightarrow{P_2O_5, \Delta}$

The number of reactions that will give alkane as a product.

(a) 3 (b) 1 (c) 4 (d) 2

19 Consider the following statements.

Statement I Aromatic carboxylic acids undergo electrophilic substitution reaction at *o*/*p*-position due to the presence of electron withdrawing group.

Statement II Electron density is increased at *o*-and *p*-positions due to delocalisation of π-electrons.

In the light of the above statements, choose the correct answer from the options given below.

(a) Both Statement I and Statement II are false.
(b) Statement I is true but Statement II is false.
(c) Statement I is false but Statement II is true.
(d) Both Statement I and Statement II are true.

20 Benzoic acid reacts with conc. HNO_3 and conc. H_2SO_4 to give

(a) 3-nitrobenzoic acid (b) 2-nitrobenzoic acid
(c) 2,3-dinitrobenzoic acid (d) 2, 4-dinitrobenzoic acid

NEET Exclusive EXTRA BYTES

Distinguish Tests

(i) Aldehyde and Ketone

S. No.	Test	*R*CHO	*R*CO*R*
1.	Schiff's reagent	Magenta colour is restored by *R* CHO	No reaction
2.	Tollen's reagent	Reduced by *R* CHO	Not reduced
3.	Fehling's solution	Reduced by *R* CHO (except C_6H_5CHO)	Not reduced; α-hydroxy ketones reduce Tollen's reagent and Fehling's solution (—$\overset{\alpha}{C}$H(OH)—CO—)
4.	$K_2Cr_2O_7 + H_2SO_4$	Oxidised to *R*COOH	Alkyl group adjacent to keto group and with smaller number of H-atoms is oxidised (denoted by *) $CH_3CO\overset{*}{C}H_2CH_3 \xrightarrow{[O]} 2CH_3COOH$
5.	Iodoform test (Haloform test)	Only CH_3CHO gives this test	$R—\overset{O}{\overset{\Vert}{C}}—CH_3$ (all ketones containing acetyl group CH_3CO) gives this test
6.	Peroxy acid (Caro's acid, peroxy benzoic acid) Baeyer-Villiger oxidation	Acid is formed $RCHO \xrightarrow{[O]} RCOOH$	Ester is formed $R—\overset{O}{\overset{\Vert}{C}}—R' \xrightarrow{O} R—\overset{O}{\overset{\Vert}{C}}—O—R'$
7.	Acetal with alcohol	Formed	Not formed

(ii) Formaldehyde and Acetaldehyde

S. No.	Reaction/Test	HCHO	CH_3CHO
1.	Cannizzaro	Yes (with no α-H)	No
2.	Aldol	No	Yes (with at least one α-H)
3.	Haloform	No	Yes
4.	With conc. NaOH solution	Cannizzaro reaction	resinous product
5.	With NH_3	Urotropine	$CH_3CH{=}NH$ (aldimine)that undergoes trimer formation 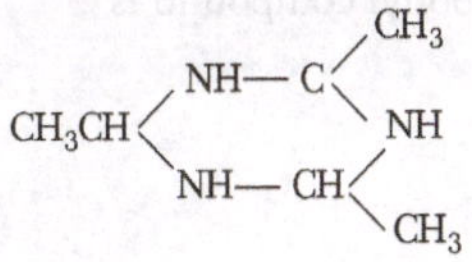

(iii) Acetaldehyde and Acetone

S. No.	Reaction/Test	CH_3CHO	CH_3COCH_3
1.	Tollen's reagent	Reduced	No effect
2.	Fehling's solution	Reduced	No effect
4.	With alcohol	Acetal is formed	No reaction

(iv) Benzaldehyde and Acetaldehyde

S. No.	Reaction/Test	C_6H_5CHO	CH_3CHO
1.	Fehling solution	is not reduced	is reduced (giving red ppt.)
2.	Cannizzaro	yes (with no α—H)	No
3.	Aldol	No	Yes
4.	Iodoform test	No	Yellow ppt.

GEARING UP FOR NEET

1 The correct IUPAC name for the following compound is

$$\overset{5}{CH_3}—\overset{4}{CH_2}—\underset{3}{\overset{O}{\overset{\|}{C}}}—\overset{2}{CH_2}\overset{1}{CHO}$$

(a) 3-oxopentanal (b) 3-oxopentanol
(c) 3-pentan-1-ol (d) oxopentanone

2 The IUPAC name of the compound is

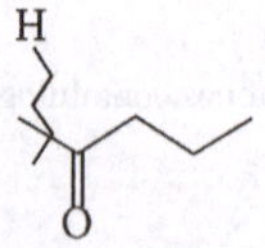

(a) 3, 3-dimethylheptan-4-one
(b) 5, 5-dimethylheptan-4-one
(c) 5-ethyl-5-methylhexan-4-one
(d) 2-ethyl-2-methylhexan-3-one

3 Which of the following is incorrect match with their common name?
(a) $CH_2{=}CHCHO \longrightarrow$ Acrolein
(b) $(CH_3)_2CHCHO \longrightarrow$ *Iso*-butyraldehyde
(c) $CH_3CH_2CH_2CH_2CHO \longrightarrow$ Valeraldehyde
(d) 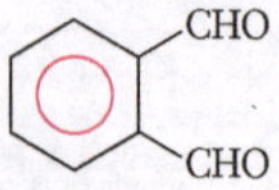

$\longrightarrow$ Mesityl oxide

4 In Clemmensen reduction, carbonyl compound is treated with ....
(a) zinc amalgam + HCl
(b) sodium amalgam + HCl
(c) zinc amalgam + nitric acid
(d) sodium amalgam + HNO_3

5 Which of the following compounds will give butanone on oxidation with alkaline $KMnO_4$ solution?
(a) Butan-2-ol (b) Butan-1-ol
(c) Pentan-2-ol (d) Pentan-1-ol

6 Acetaldehye does not respond to
(a) Tollen's test (b) Benedict's test
(c) Lucas test (d) Iodoform test

7 Which is the most suitable reagent for the following conversion?

$$CH_3—CH{=}CH—CH_2—\overset{O}{\overset{\|}{C}}—CH_3 \longrightarrow CH_3—CH{=}CH—CH_2—\overset{O}{\overset{\|}{C}}—OH$$

(a) Tollen's reagent (b) Benzoyl peroxide
(c) I_2 and NaOH solution (d) Sn and NaOH solution

8 The carboxyl functional group (—COOH) is present in
(a) acrolein (b) picric acid
(c) aspirin (d) barbituric acid

9 For the following transformation

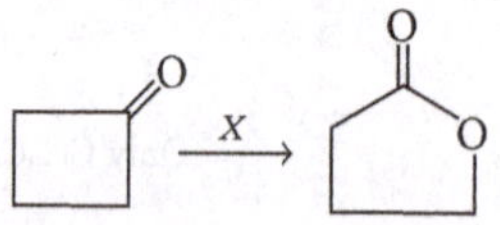

reagent *X* used is
(a) SeO_2 (b) $C_6H_5CO_3H$ (c) ClO^- (d) Se

10 Which of the following is incorrectly matched with its IUPAC name ?
(a) Glutaric acid $\longrightarrow$ Pentanedioic acid
(b) Succinic acid $\longrightarrow$ Butanedioic acid
(c) Malonic acid $\longrightarrow$ Propanedioic acid
(d) Isobutyric acid $\longrightarrow$ Butanoic acid

11 In the following reduction reaction, reducing agent used is

$$CH_3\overset{O}{\overset{\|}{C}}OCH(CH_3)_2 \longrightarrow CH_3CHO + (CH_3)_2CHOH$$

(a) DIBAL-H (b) $LiAlH_4$
(c) $NaAlH_4$ (d) H_2/Pd-$BaSO_4$

12 Consider the following reaction,

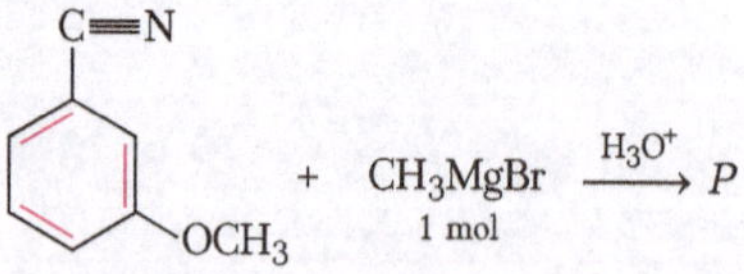

The product *P* in this reaction is

(a) 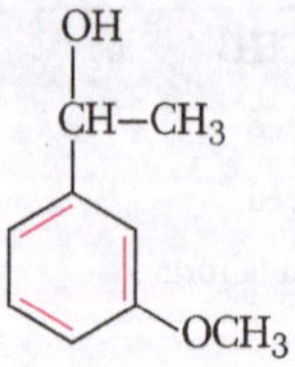

(b) 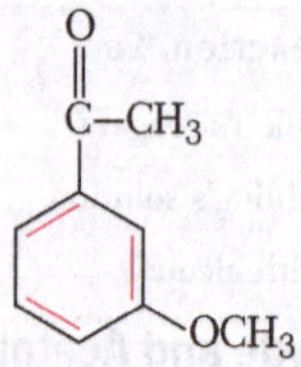

(c) 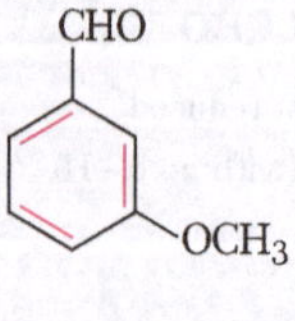

(d) 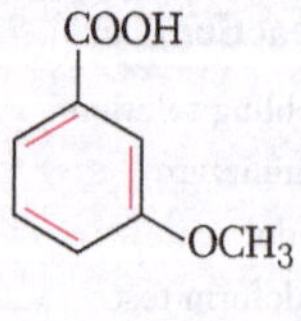

13 Which of the following reactant is the incorrect match with the given reagent for the preparation of benzaldehyde ?
(a) Benzene $\longrightarrow$ Co, HCl and anhy. $AlCl_3$
(b) Benzonitrile $\longrightarrow$ HCl, $SnCl_2$, H_3O^+
(c) Benzoyl chloride $\longrightarrow$ HCN and H_3O^+
(d) Toluene $\longrightarrow Cl_2 / h\nu, H_2O$

14 Cyanohydrin of which of the following compounds forms lactic acid?
(a) HCHO (b) CH_3CHO
(c) CH_3CH_2CHO (d) CH_3COCH_3

15 When acetaldehyde is heated with Fehling's solution, it gives a precipitate of
(a) Cu_2O
(b) $Cu + Cu_2O + CuO$
(c) Cu
(d) CuO

16

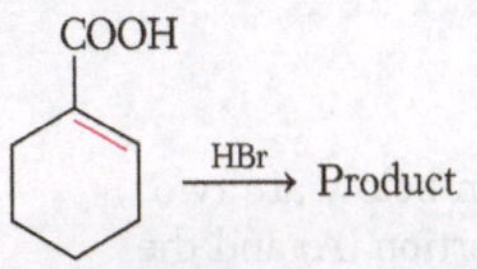

The product of the above reaction is

(a) 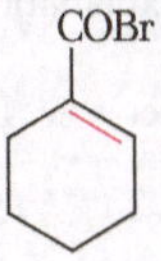 (b) 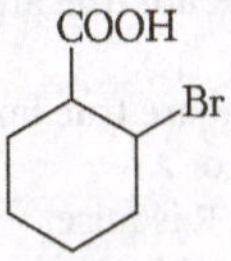

(c) 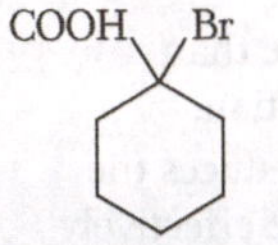 (d) 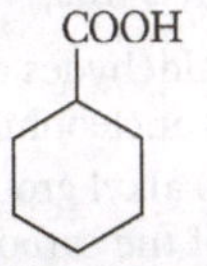

17 Which of the following acids is isomeric with phthalic acid ?
(a) Succinic acid
(b) Salicylic acid
(c) 1-4-benzene dicarboxylic acid
(d) Palmitic acid

18 Increasing order of boiling points of the following compounds is

CH_3CHO, (I) CH_3CH_2OH, (II)
CH_3OCH_3, (III) $CH_3CH_2CH_3$ (IV)

(a) I < II < III < IV
(b) IV < III < II < I
(c) IV < III < I < II
(d) II < I < III < IV

19 Consider the following reaction.

$$CH_3MgBr + CH_2{=}CH-\overset{O}{\overset{\|}{C}}-H \xrightarrow{H_3O^+} \text{Product}$$

The product formed in the above reaction is

(a) $CH_2{=}CH-C(OH)(CH_3)-H$ (b) $CH_2(OH)CH{=}CH-CH_3$

(c) $CH_3CH_2CH_2CHO$ (d) $CH_3-CH_2{=}CH-\overset{O}{\overset{\|}{C}}-H$

20 Which of the following is the incorrect statement about carbonyl compounds?
(a) Aldol condensation of acetaldehyde gives $CH_3\underset{}{\overset{OH}{\overset{|}{C}H}}-CH_2-CHO$.
(b) Aromatic aldehyde and formaldehyde undergo Cannizzaro reaction.
(c) Protonation of a carbonyl compound decreases electrophilic nature and, thus nucleophilic attack is retarded.
(d) H_2/Pd $BaSO_4$ is used to reduce CH_3COCl and CH_3CHO.

21 Which of the following is incorrect statement ?
(a) Aldehydes are generally more reactive than ketones in nucleophilic addition reaction.
(b) Cannizzaro reaction involves oxidation as well as reduction of aldehydes having lack of α – H atom.
(c) Benzaldehyde forms addition product with ammonia.
(d) Benzaldehyde on reaction with HNO_3/H_2SO_4 at 273-283 K gives *m*-nitrobenzaldehyde.

22 Consider the following reaction,

$$CH_3CHO \xrightarrow[\text{(ii) } H_2O]{\text{(i) } CH_3MgBr} (A) \xrightarrow{H_2SO_4,\,\Delta} (B) \xrightarrow[\text{oxidation}]{\text{Hydroboration}} (C)$$

Compounds *A* and *C* in the above reaction are ....
(a) identical (b) positional isomers
(c) functional isomers (d) optical isomers

23 What is the final product of the following cross aldol condensation?

$$CH_3\overset{O}{\overset{\|}{C}}H + CH_3CH_2\overset{O}{\overset{\|}{C}}CH_3 \xrightarrow{OH^-} \xrightarrow{\Delta}$$

(a) $CH_3CH{=}CHCH_2\overset{O}{\overset{\|}{C}}CH_3$ (b) $CH_3CH_2\underset{CH_3}{\underset{|}{C}}{=}CHCH_3$

(c) $CH_3CH{=}\underset{CH_3}{\underset{|}{C}}\overset{O}{\overset{\|}{C}}CH_3$ (d) $CH_3CH{=}CHCH{=}CHCH_3$

24 Which one of the following product is formed, when calcium salt of adipic acid is heated?

(a) 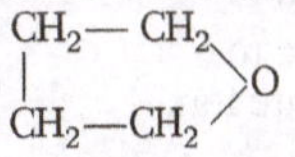 (b) 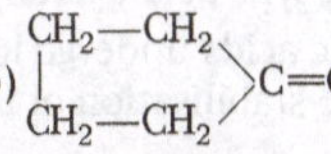

(c) 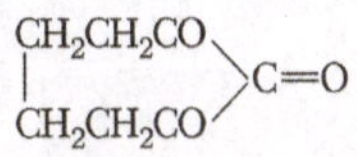 (d) $\begin{matrix} CH_2CH_2COOH \\ | \\ CH_2CH_2COOH \end{matrix}$

25 The major product in the following reaction is

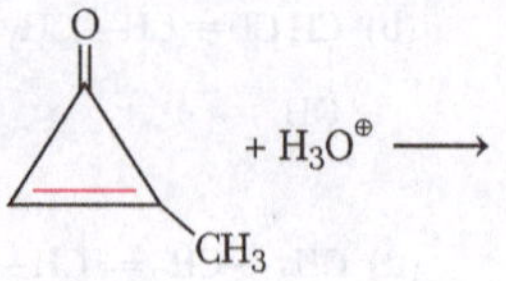

(a) 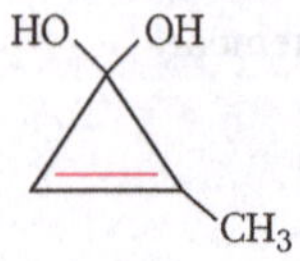 (b) 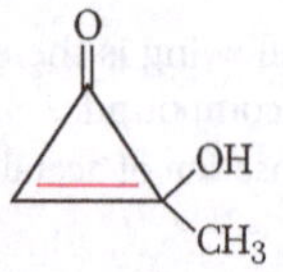

(c) 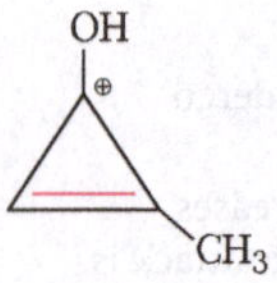 (d) 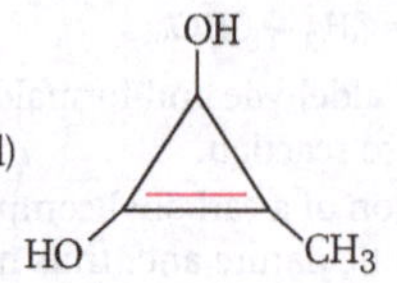

26 Select the incorrect statement.
(a) Carbonyl compounds are attacked by nucleophiles.
(b) An aldehyde has a greater partial positive charge on its carbonyl carbon.
(c) Protonation of a carbonyl compound decreases electrophilic nature and thus, nucleophilic attack is retarded.
(d) Hydration of CCl_3CHO is more than that of CH_3CHO.

27 Which of the following species is the conjugate acid of the hemiacetal formed by reaction of benzaldehyde with methanol containing a traces of an acid?

(a) $C_6H_5HC\langle^{OH}_{OCH_3}$ (b) $C_6H_5CH{=}\overset{+}{O}CH_3$

(c) $C_6H_5HC\langle^{OH}_{\overset{+}{O}(H)CH_3}$ (d) $C_6H_5HC\langle^{OH}_{\overset{+}{O}H_2}$

28 Which of the following statements are correct?
A. Carboxylic acids are weaker acid than mineral acids.
B. The conjugate base of carboxylic acid is stabilized by two equivalent resonance structure.
C. Electron donating groups increase the acidity of carboxylic acids by inductive effect.
D. Carboxylic acids reacts with sodium metal liberates H_2 gas.
E. Carboxylic acids dissociate in water to give hydronium ion and carboxylate anion.

Choose the correct answer from the options given below.
(a) A, B and D (b) B and D
(c) B, C and D (d) A, B, D and E

29 Select the incorrect statements from the following.
A. Carbolic acid does not liberate CO_2 on treatment with aqueous sodium bicarbonate solution.
B. Acetyl salicylic acid is known as aspirin.
C. Carboxylic acids undergo ionisation due to resonance stabilisation of the carboxylate ion.
D. Sulphonation of benzoic acid produces mainly *o*-and *p*-sulphobenzoic acid.
E. Lactic acid on oxidation by alkaline potassium permanganate gives cinnamic acid.

Choose the correct answer from the options given below.
(a) B and C (b) D and E (c) A and B (d) C and D

30 Which of the following statement is incorrect?
(a) Acetone and acetophenone can be distringuished by saturated solution of $NaHSO_3$.
(b) Acetaldehyde and benzaldehyde can be distinguished by iodoform test.
(c) $Ph{-}O{-}\overset{O}{\overset{\|}{C}}{-}Ph$ can be prepared by the reaction of phenol and benzoyl chloride in the presence of pyridine.
(d) The compound CH_3CH_2CHO undergo benzoin condensation.

Assertion-Reason

Directions (Q. Nos. 31 to 35) Given below are two statements : One is labelled as Assertion (A) and the other is labelled as Reason (R).
(a) Both A and R are true and R is the correct explanation of A.
(b) Both A and R are true but R is not the correct explanation of A.
(c) A is true but R is false.
(d) A is false but R is true.

31 **Assertion** (A) Aldehydes are more reactive than ketones towards nucleophilic addition reaction.
Reason (R) Two alkyl groups in ketones reduces the electrophilicity of the carbonyl carbon more effectively than in aldehyde.

32 **Assertion** (A) Ketones react with ethylene glycol in the presence of dry HCl to form ethylene glycol ketals.
Reason (R) Dry HCl protonates the oxygen of carbonyl compound and decreases the electrophilicity of the carbonyl carbon.

33 **Assertion** (A) Carboxylic acids have higher boiling points than aldehydes and ketones.
Reason (R) Carboxylic acid has more extensive association of molecules through intermolecular H-bonding.

34 **Assertion** (A) Benzoic acid has higher molecular weight in benzene and less in water.
Reason (R) Benzoic acid dissociates in water and associates in benzene.

35 **Assertion** (A) The solubility of carboxylic acids increases by increasing the number of carbon atoms.
Reason (R) Higher carboxylic acid has more hydrophobic interaction of hydrocarbon part with water.

Statement Type Questions

Directons (Q. Nos. 39 to 42) In the light of the statements given below, choose the correct answer from the options given below.

(a) Both Statement I and Statement II are false.
(b) Statement I is true but Statement II is false.
(c) Statement I is false but Statement II is true.
(d) Both Statement I and Statement II are true.

36 **Statement I** Chromyl chloride oxidises methyl group to a chromium complex, which on hydrolysis gives corresponding benzaldehyde.
Statement II Benzylidene diacetate can be hydrolysed to benzaldehyde with aqueous acid.

37 **Statement I** Nitriles are selectively reduced by di-*iso*-butyl aluminium hydride to imines followed by hydrolysis to aldehydes.
Statement II Addition of water to ethyne in the presence of H_2SO_4 and $HgSO_4$ gives benzaldehyde.

38 **Statement I** Formaldehyde is a planar molecule.
Statement II It contains sp^2-hybridised carbon atom.

39 **Statement I** The α-H atom in carbonyl compounds is less acidic.
Statement II The anion formed after the loss of α-hydrogen atom is resonance stabilised.

40 **Statement I** Cannizzaro reaction converts HCHO into HCOONa and CH_3OH.
Statement II Cannizzaro reaction is a proton hydride transfer reaction.

41 **Statement I** Treating an alkyl nitrile with phenyl magnesium bromide followed by hydrolysis yield a aldehyde.
Statement II Substituted benzene is treated with acid chloride in the presence of anhydrous aluminium chloride to give corresponding ketone.

42 **Statement I** Carboxylic acids on heating with H_2SO_4 or P_2O_5 give carboxylate anions and hydronium ion.
Statement II Aromatic carboxylic acids in electrophilic substitution reactions acts as a deactivating and *meta*-directing group.

43 Which of the following statements are incorrect?
A. Phenyl ethanal does not undergo benzoin condensation.
B. PCC in CH_2Cl_2 is used for converting 1° and 2° alcohol to aldehyde and ketone respectively.
C. 3° alcohol react with copper at 530 K to produce aldehyde.
D. Boiling point of aldehyde and ketones are higher than alcohols of similar molecular mass.
E. Carbonyl compounds react with sodium bisulphite to give white crystalline adduct, which is insoluble in water.

Choose the correct answer from the options given below.
(a) C and D (b) B and E
(c) A and B (d) B and D

44 Which of the following statements are incorrect?
A. Aldehydes and ketones react with hydrogen cyanide to yield cyanoalcohol.
B. Butan-2-ol on oxidation with alkaline $KMnO_4$ solution give butanone.
C. Pent-3-en-2-ol is converted into pent-3-en-2-one by using chromic anhydride in presence of glacial of toluene acid.
D. Oxidation of methyl ketones by haloform also affects carbon-carbon double bond, if present in the molecule.
E. Fehling's solution does not react with benzaldehyde.

Choose the correct answer from the options given below.
(a) A and D (b) Only E
(c) B and C (d) A and B

Species Selection Type Questions

45 Consider the following reagents.
(i) $LiAlH_4$ (ii) $H_2/Pd-BaSO_4$
(iii) DIBAL-H (iv) $SnCl_2/HCl$
(v) $AlH(i-Bu)_2/H_2O$

How many number of reagents that can be used to reduce CH_3COCl into CH_3CHO?
(a) 2 (b) 1
(c) 3 (d) 4

46 Consider the following compounds.
(i) CH_3CHO (ii) $C_6H_5COCH_3$
(iii) C_6H_5CHO (iv) CH_3COCH_3
(v) $CH_3-CH(OH)-CH_2CH_3$

The number of compounds that will give positive iodoform test are
(a) 1 (b) 3
(c) 2 (d) 4

47 Consider the following compounds.

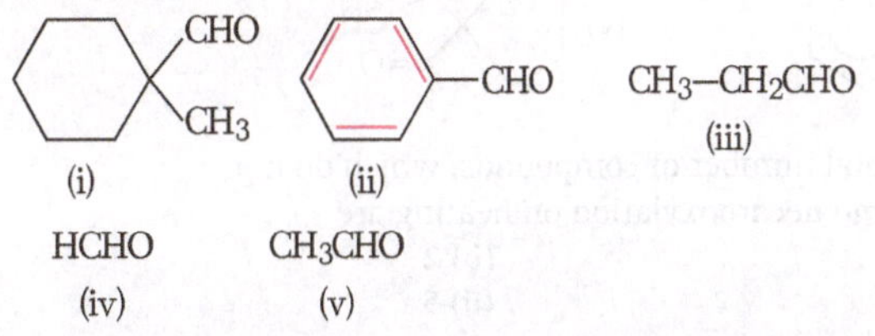

How many number of compounds that will undergo Cannizzaro's reaction?
(a) 3 (b) 2
(c) 1 (d) 4

48 Consider the following compounds.

(i) $(CH_3)_3CCHO$ (ii) CCl_3CHO

(iii) 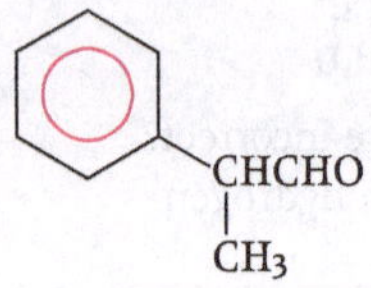 (iv) 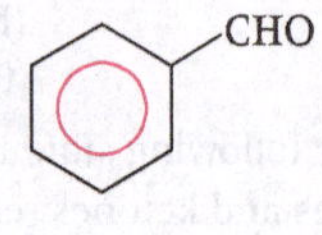

(v) 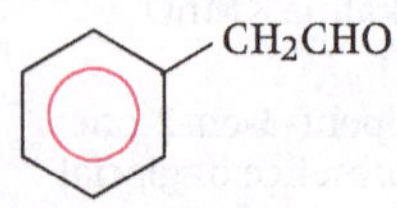 (vi) $CH_3CH_2CH_2—CHO$

(vii) 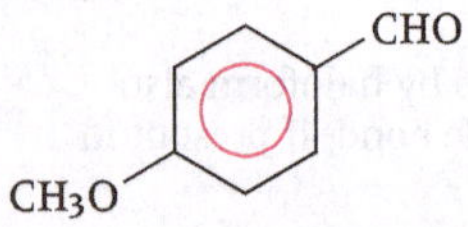

The number of compounds that will give aldol condensation reaction are

(a) 2 (b) 4
(c) 3 (d) 5

49 Consider the following reactions,

(i) $CH_3CH_2COCH_3 \xrightarrow{SeO_2}$

(ii) $CH_3CH_2CHO \xrightarrow{LiAlH_4}$

(iii) 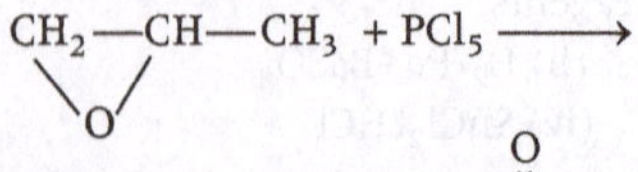

(iv) $CH_3—CH=CH—CH_2—\overset{O}{\overset{\|}{C}}—CH_3 \xrightarrow[NaOH]{I_2}$

(v) $CH_3CH_2COCH_3 \xrightarrow[H_3O^+]{C_6H_5CO_3H}$

The number of reactions that will produce carboxylic acid are

(a) 4 (b) 2
(c) 3 (d) 1

50 Consider the following compounds,

(i) 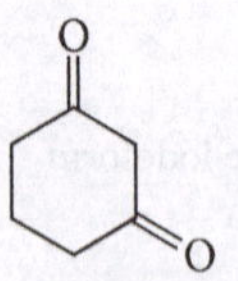 (ii) 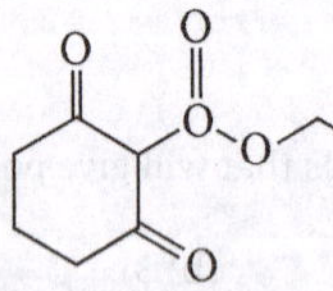 (iii) 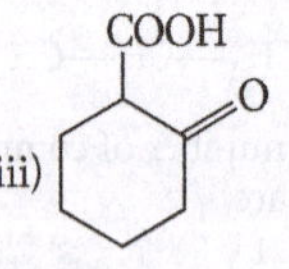

(iv) 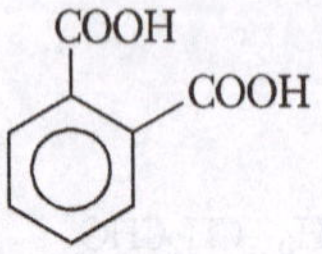 (v) 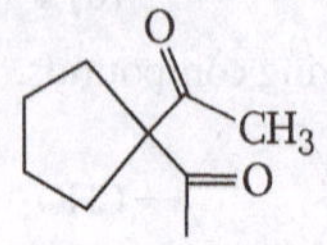

The total number of compounds, which do not undergo decarboxylation on heating are

(a) 3 (b) 2
(c) 4 (d) 5

Matching Type Questions

51 Match the reactions given in Column I with the suitable reagents given in Column II.

Column I (Reactions)	Column II (Reagents)
A. Benzophenone → Diphenylmethane	1. $LiAlH_4$
B. Benzaldehyde → 1-phenylethanol	2. DIBAL-H
C. Cyclohexanone → Cyclohexanol	3. Zn(Hg)/Conc. HCl
D. Phenyl benzoate → Benzaldehyde	4. CH_3MgBr

Codes

	A	B	C	D		A	B	C	D
(a)	3	4	1	2	(b)	4	3	1	2
(c)	3	4	2	1	(d)	4	3	2	1

52 Match the reactions given in Column I with their names given in Column II.

Column I	Column II
A. 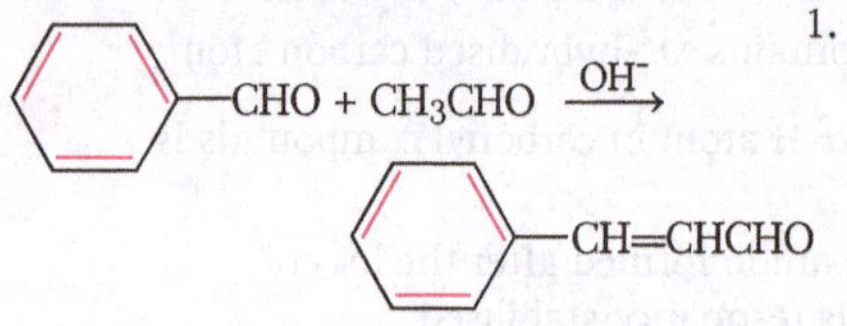	1. Perkin
B. 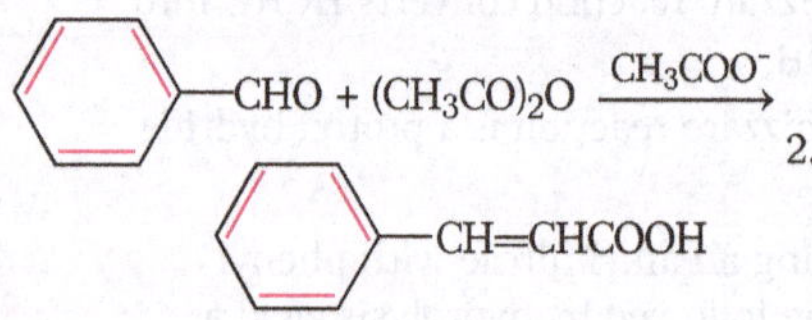	2. Friedal-Crafts acylation reaction
C. 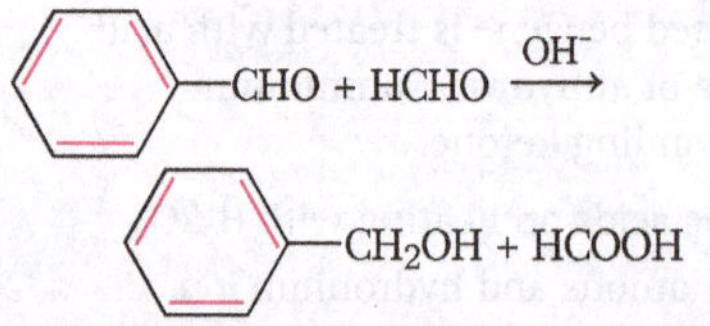	3. Claisen Schmidt
D. 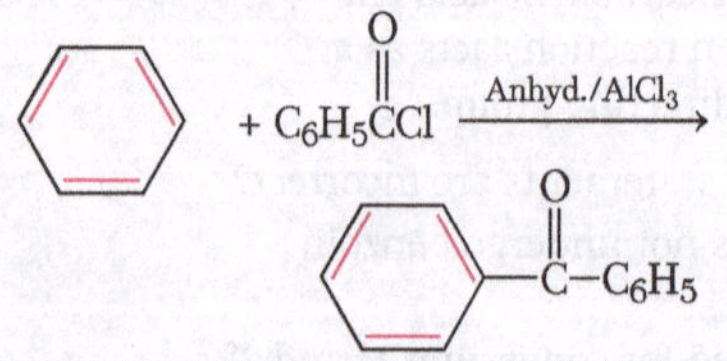	4. Crossed Cannizzaro

Codes

	A	B	C	D		A	B	C	D
(a)	3	1	4	2	(b)	3	1	2	4
(c)	1	3	2	4	(d)	1	3	4	2

53 Match the reactions given in Column I with the suitable reagents given in Column II.

Column I	Column II
A. $C_6H_5COCH_3 \longrightarrow C_6H_5CH_2CH_3$	1. (i) $SnCl_2/HCl$ (ii) H_3O^+
B. $C_6H_5COCH_3 \longrightarrow C_6H_5CH(OH)CH_3$	2. Zn - Hg / HCl
C. $C_6H_5CH_3 \longrightarrow C_6H_5CHO$	3. $NaBH_4$
D. $CH_3CN \longrightarrow CH_3CHO$	4. (i) CrO_2Cl_2/CS_2 (ii) H_3O^+

Codes

	A	B	C	D
(a)	2	3	4	1
(b)	2	1	4	3
(c)	2	1	3	4
(d)	3	2	4	1

54 Match the reactant given in Column I with the name of reaction given in Column II.

Column I (Reactant/Product)	Column II (Reaction)
A. $CH_3CN \xrightarrow[\text{(ii) } H_2O/H^+]{\text{(i) } SnCl_2/HCl} CH_3CHO$	1. Etard reaction
B. $CH_3CH_2COOH \xrightarrow[\text{(ii) } H_2O]{\text{(i) } Cl_2/\text{Red P}} CH_3CH(Cl)COOH$	2. Rosenmund reduction
C. $CH_3-\overset{O}{\overset{\Vert}{C}}-Cl + H_2 \xrightarrow[BaSO_4]{Pd\text{-}Cl} CH_3-\overset{O}{\overset{\Vert}{C}}-H$	3. Stephen reaction
D. 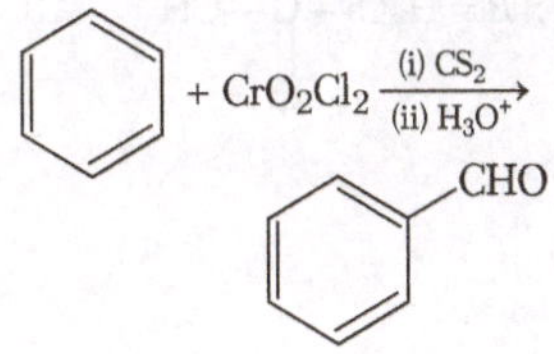	4. Hell-Volhard Zelinsky reaction.

Codes

	A	B	C	D
(a)	2	1	4	3
(b)	2	1	3	4
(c)	3	4	2	1
(d)	4	3	2	1

55 Match the acid given in Column I with their uses given in Column II.

Column I (Acids)	Column II (Uses)
A. Methanoic acid	1. Vinegar in food industry
B. Ethanoic acid	2. Perfumes
C. Hexanedioic acid	3. Electroplating industries
D. Esters of benzoic acid	4. Nylon-6,6.

Codes

	A	B	C	D
(a)	2	3	4	1
(b)	3	1	4	2
(c)	3	4	2	1
(d)	4	2	1	3

56 Match the reaction given in Column I with the name of reaction given in Column II.

Column I	Column II
A. $2CH_3CHO \xrightarrow[\Delta]{\overline{OH}} CH_3CH{=}CHCHO$	1. Gattermann-Koch
B. $2HCHO \xrightarrow{\overline{OH}} HCOO^- + CH_3OH$	2. Benzoin
C. $C_6H_5CHO \xrightarrow[KCN]{\text{Alcoholic}} C_6H_5-\overset{O}{\overset{\Vert}{C}}-\underset{OH}{\underset{\vert}{C}}HC_6H_5$	3. Cannizzaro
D. $C_6H_5 + CO + HCl \xrightarrow{\text{Anhy. } AlCl_3} C_6H_5CHO$	4. Aldol

Codes

	A	B	C	D
(a)	4	3	2	1
(b)	4	2	3	1
(c)	4	1	2	3
(d)	2	3	4	1

Final Check Through PYQs

Module-I Carbonyl Compounds (Aldehydes and Ketones)

1 What is the IUPAC name of the organic compound formed in the following chemical reaction?

[NCERT (New) Pg. 237, NEET 2021]

$$\text{Acetone} \xrightarrow[\text{(ii) } H_2O,\ H^+]{\text{(i) } C_2H_5MgBr,\ \text{Dry ether}} \text{Product}$$

(a) 2-methyl propan 2-ol
(b) pentan-2-ol
(c) pentan-3-ol
(d) 2-methyl butan-2-ol

2 Identify compound X in the following sequence of reactions.

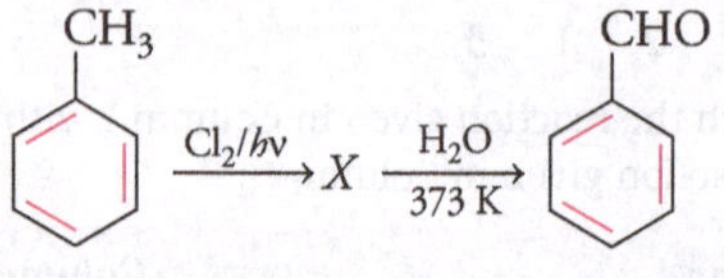

[NCERT (New) Pg. 233, NEET (Sept.) 2020]

(a) 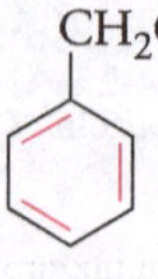
(b) 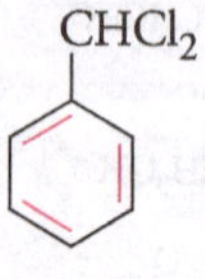
(c) 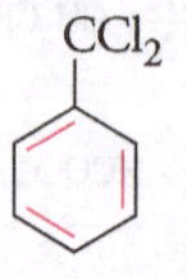
(d) 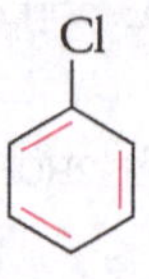

3 Identify compound (A) in the following reaction.

[NCERT (New) Pg. 232, NEET (Oct.) 2020]

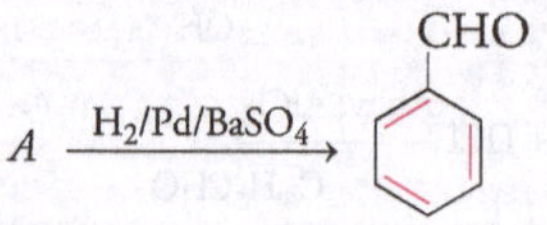

(a) Benzoyl chloride
(b) Toluene
(c) Acetophenone
(d) Benzoic acid

4 The reaction that does not give benzoic acid as the major product is *[NCERT (New) Pg. 252, 253, Odisha NEET 2019]*

(a) 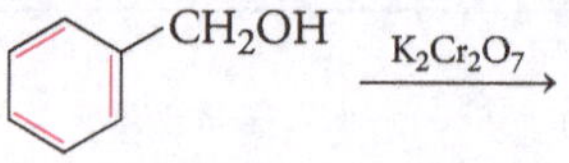

(b) 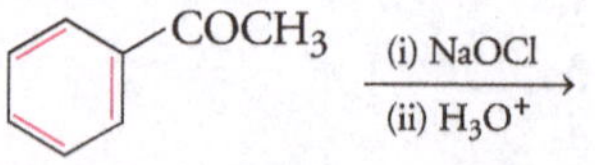

(c) 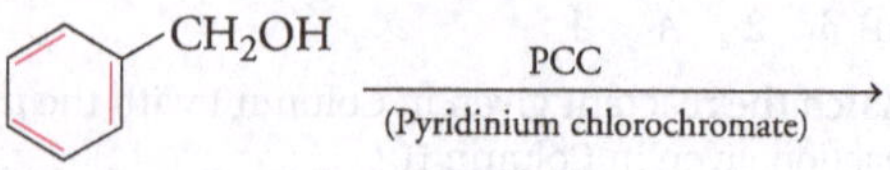

(d) 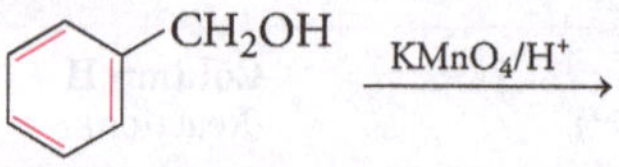

5 Predict the correct intermediate and product in the following reaction. *[NEET 2017]*

$$H_3C{-}C\equiv CH \xrightarrow[HgSO_4]{H_2O,\ H_2SO_4} \underset{(A)}{\text{Intermediate}} \longrightarrow \underset{(B)}{\text{Product}}$$

(a) $A = H_3C{-}\underset{\underset{SO_4}{|}}{C}{=}CH_2$; $B = H_3C{-}\underset{\underset{O}{\|}}{C}{-}CH_3$

(b) $A = H_3C{-}\underset{\underset{OH}{|}}{C}{=}CH_2$; $B = H_3C{-}\underset{\underset{SO_4}{|}}{C}{=}CH_2$

(c) $A = H_3C{-}\underset{\underset{O}{\|}}{C}{-}CH_3$; $B = H_3C{-}C\equiv CH$

(d) $A = H_3C{-}\underset{\underset{OH}{|}}{C}{=}CH_2$; $B = H_3C{-}\underset{\underset{O}{\|}}{C}{-}CH_3$

Module-II Chemical Properties and Uses of Aldehydes and Ketone

6 Fehling's solution "A" is *[NCERT (New) Pg. 239, NEET 2024]*

(a) aqueous copper sulphate
(b) alkaline copper sulphate
(c) alkaline solution of sodium potassium tartrate (rochelle's salt)
(d) aqueous sodium citrate

7 Identify product (*A*) in the following reaction.

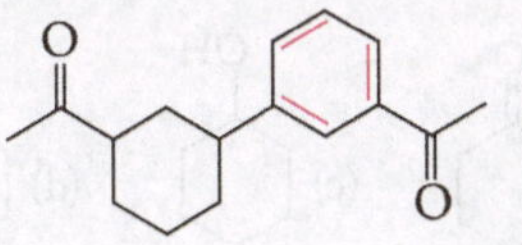

$\xrightarrow[\text{Conc.HCl}]{\text{Zn-Hg}}$ (*A*) + $2H_2O$

[NCERT (New) Pg. 239, NEET 2023]

(a) 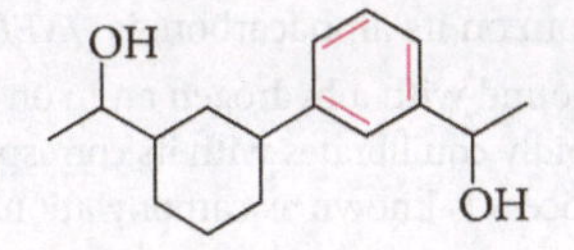

(b) 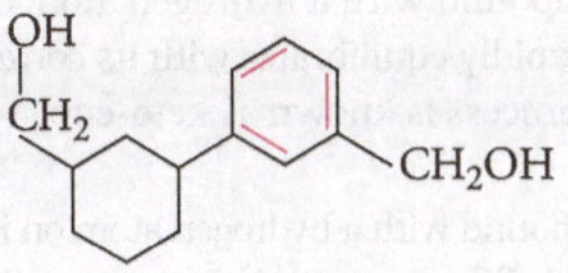

(c) 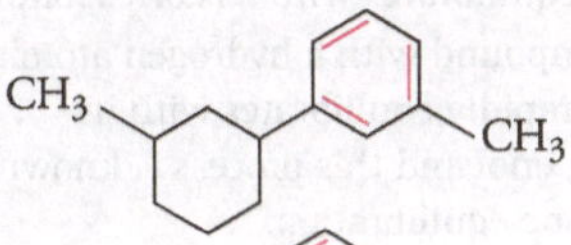

(d) 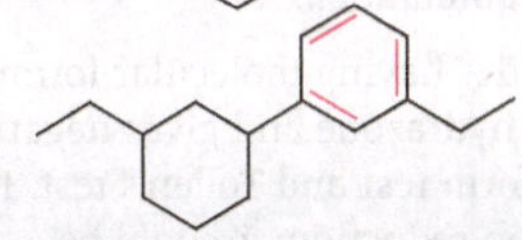

8 Identify the major product obtained in the following reaction *[NCERT (New) Pg. 239, NEET 2023]*

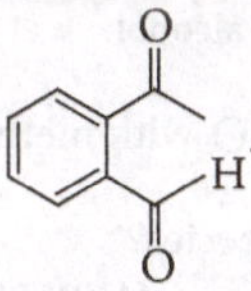

$+ 2[Ag(NH_3)_2]^+ + 3OH^- \xrightarrow{\Delta}$ Major product

(a) 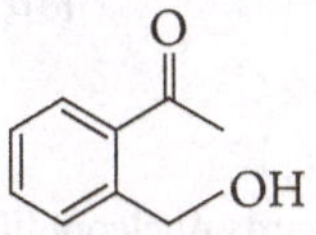
(b) 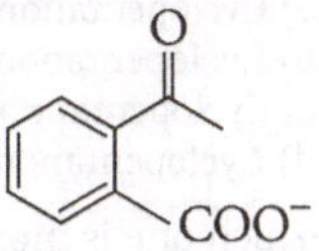
(c) 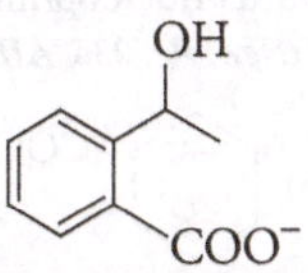
(d) 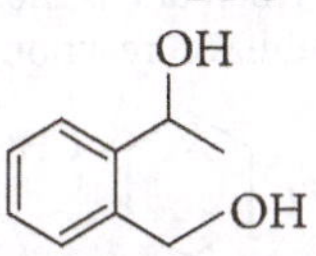

9 Which one of the following is not formed when acetone reacts with 2-pentanone in the presence of dilute NaOH followed by heating? *[NCERT (New) Pg. 241, NEET 2022]*

(a) 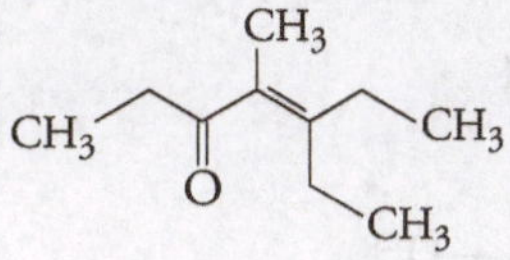
(c) 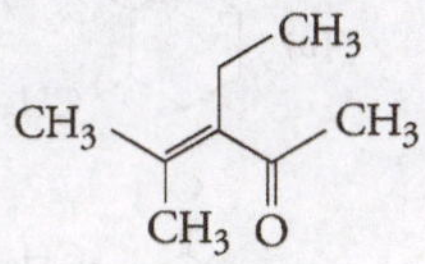
(b) 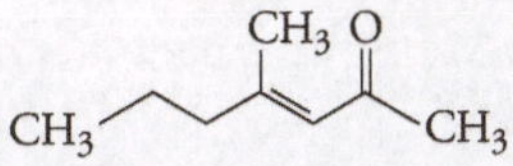
(d) 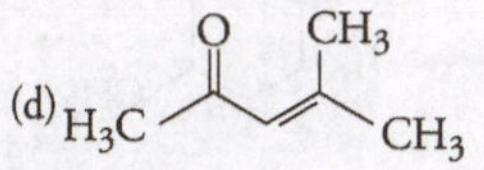

10 Given below are two statements.

Statement I The boiling points of aldehydes and ketones are higher than hydrocarbons of comparable molecular masses because of weak molecular association in aldehydes and ketones due to dipole-dipole interactions.

Statement II The boiling points of aldehydes and ketones are lower than the alcohols of similar molecular masses due to the absence of H-bonding.

In the light of the above statements, choose the correct answer from the options given below.

[NCERT (New) Pg. 231, NEET 2022]

(a) Both Statement I and Statement II are false.
(b) Statement I is true, but Statement II is false.
(c) Statement I is false, but Statement II is true.
(d) Both Statement I and Statement II are true.

11 Match Column I with Column II.

	Column I (Products formed)		Column II (Reaction of carbonyl compound with)
A.	Cyanohydrin	1.	NH_2OH
B.	Acetal	2.	RNH_2
C.	Schiff's base	3.	Alcohol
D.	Oxime	4.	HCN

[NEET 2022]

Codes

	A	B	C	D		A	B	C	D
(a)	2	3	4	1	(b)	1	3	2	4
(c)	4	3	2	1	(d)	3	4	2	1

12 The product formed in the following thermal reaction is

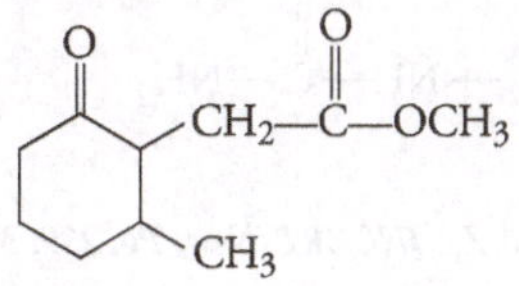

$\xrightarrow[C_2H_5OH]{NaBH_4}$? *[NEET 2021]*

(a) 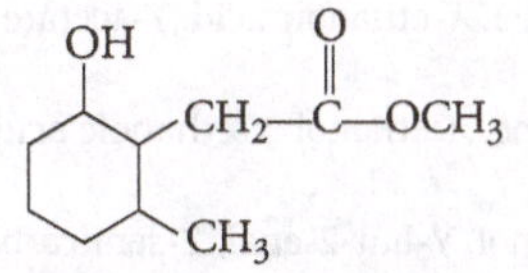

(b) 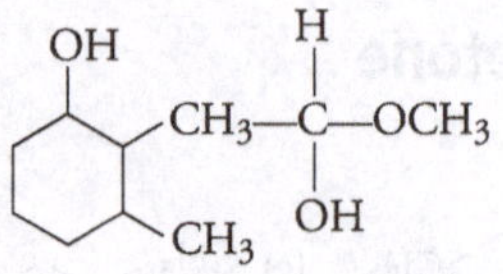

(c) 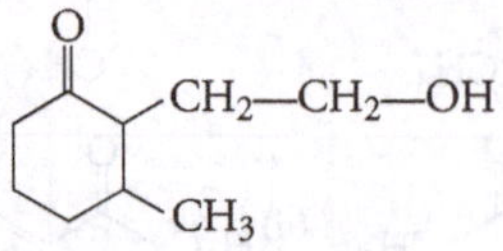

(d) 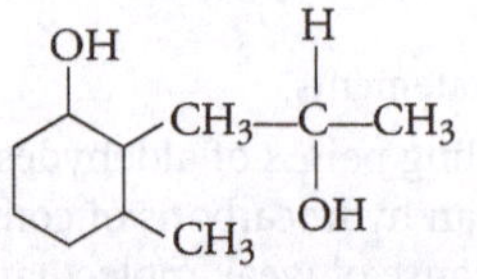

13 Reaction between benzaldehyde and acetophenone in presence of dilute NaOH is known as *[NCERT (New) Pg. 242, NEET (Sept.) 2020]*
(a) Cannizzaro's reaction
(b) Cross Cannizzaro's reaction
(c) Cross aldol condensation
(d) Aldol condensation

14 Reaction between acetone and methyl-magnesium bromide followed by hydrolysis will give *[NEET 2020]*
(a) *sec*-butyl alcohol (b) *tert*-butyl alcohol
(c) *iso*-butyl alcohol (d) *iso*-propyl alcohol

15 Which of the following product is formed when cyclohexanone undergoes aldol condensation followed by heating? *[NCERT (New) Pg. 241, NEET 2017]*

(a) 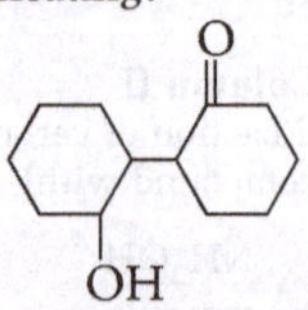 (b) 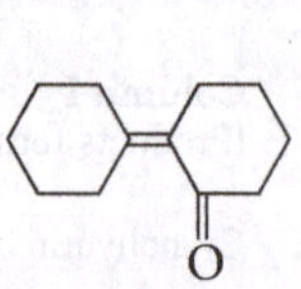

(c) 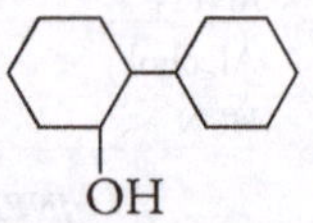 (d) 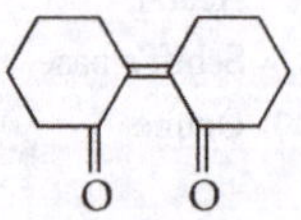

16 Consider the reactions,

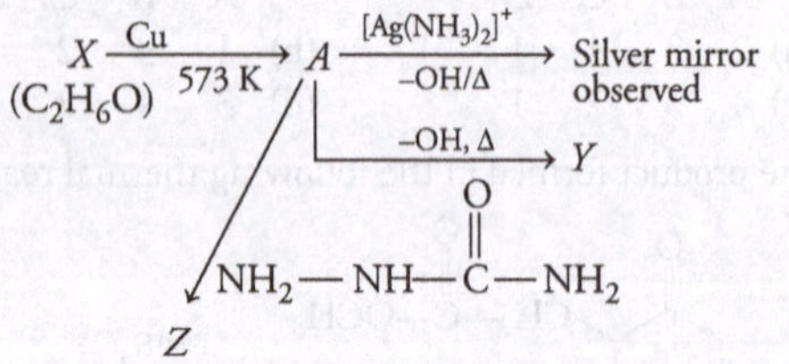

Identify *A*, *X*, *Y* and *Z*. *[NCERT (New) Pg. 239, NEET 2017]*
(a) *A*-methoxymethane, *X*-ethanoic acid, *Y*-acetate ion, *Z*-hydrazine
(b) *A*-methoxymethane, *X*-ethanol, *Y*-ethanoic acid, *Z*-semicarbazide
(c) *A*-ethanal, *X*-ethanol, Y-but-2-enal, *Z*-semicarbazone
(d) *A*-ethanol, *X*-acetaldehyde, *Y*-butanone, *Z*-hydrazone

17 The product formed by the reaction of an aldehyde with a primary amine is *[NEET 2016, Phase I]*
(a) ketone (b) carboxylic acid
(c) aromatic acid (d) Schiff's base

18 The correct structure of the product *A* formed in the reaction *[NCERT (New) Pg. 232, NEET 2016, Phase II]*

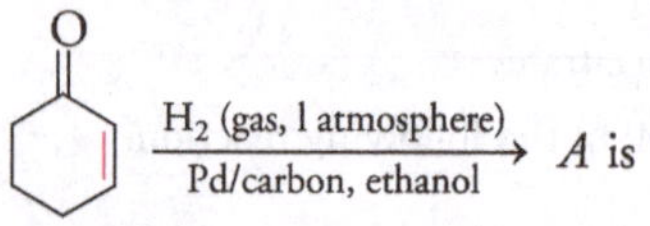

(a) 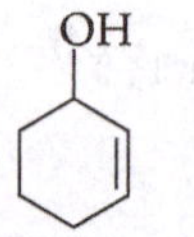 (b) 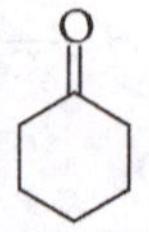 (c) 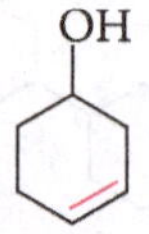 (d) 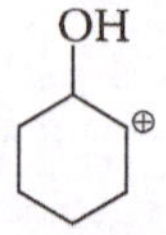

19 The correct statement regarding a carbonyl compound with a hydrogen atom on its alphacarbon, is *[NEET 2016]*
(a) a carbonyl compound with a hydrogen atom on its alpha-carbon rapidly equilibrates with its corresponding enol and this process is known as carbonylation.
(b) a carbonyl compound with a hydrogen atom on its alpha-carbon rapidly equilibrates with its corresponding enol and this process is known as keto-enol tautomerism.
(c) a carbonyl compound with a hydrogen atom on its alpha-carbon never equilibrates with its corresponding enol.
(d) a carbonyl compound with a hydrogen atom on its alpha-carbon rapidly equilibrates with its corresponding enol and this process is known as aldehyde-ketone equilibration.

20 An organic compound *X* having molecular formula $C_5H_{10}O$ yields phenyl hydrazone and gives negative response to the iodoform test and Tollen's test. It produces *n*-pentane on reduction. *X* could be *[NCERT (New) Pg. 239, AIPMT 2015]*
(a) pentanal (b) 2-pentanone
(c) 3-pentanone (d) *n*-amyl alcohol

21 Treatment of cyclopentanone 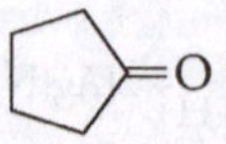 with methyl lithium gives which of the following species? *[AIPMT 2015]*
(a) Cyclopentanonyl anion
(b) Cyclopentanonyl cation
(c) Cyclopentanonyl radical
(d) Cyclopentanonyl biradical

22 Which one is most reactive towards nucleophilic addition reaction? *[NCERT (New) Pg. 236, AIPMT 2014]*

(a) 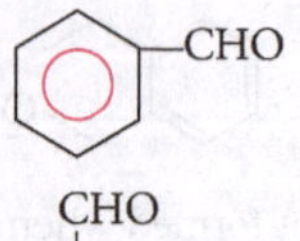 (b) 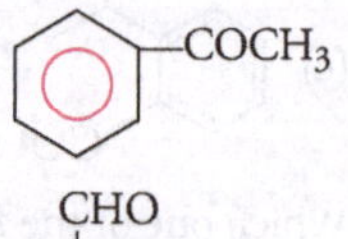

(c) 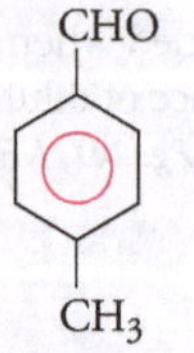 (d) 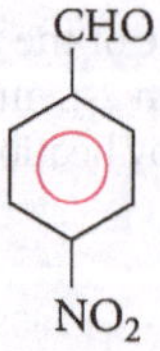

Module-III Carboxylic Acids

23 Match Column I with Column II.

Column I (Reactions)	Column II (Condition)
A. 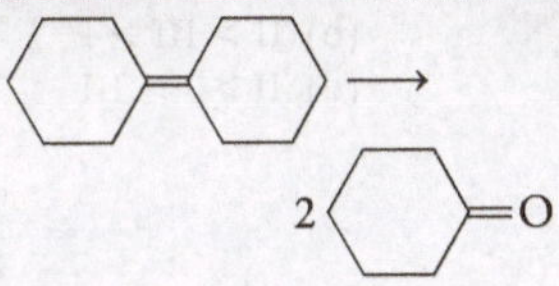	1. 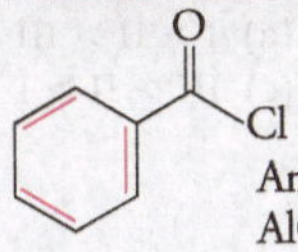 Anhyd. $AlCl_3$
B. 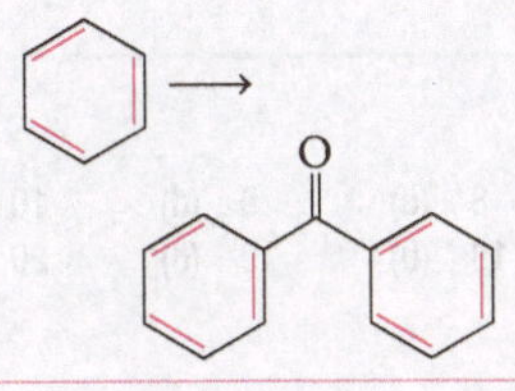	2. CrO_3
C. 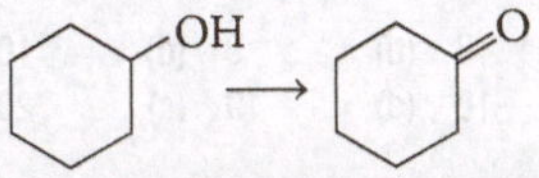	3. $KMnO_4/KOH, \Delta$
D. 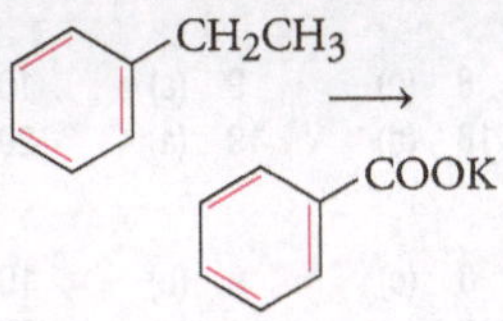	4. (i) O_2 (ii) $Zn - H_2O$

Codes

	A	B	C	D
(a)	4	1	3	2
(b)	3	1	2	4
(c)	4	1	2	3
(d)	1	4	2	3

24 Complete the following reaction.

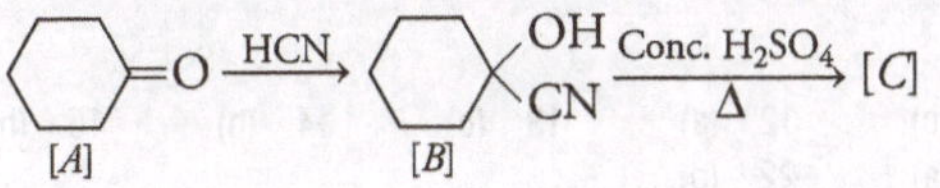

is .... *[NCERT (New) Pg. 237, NEET 2023]*

(a) 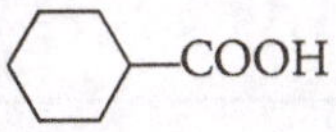 (b) 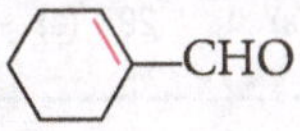

(c) 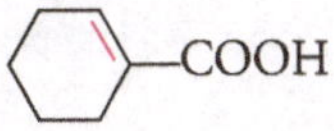 (d) 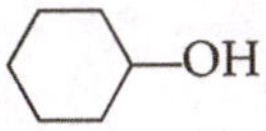

25 $RMgX + CO_2 \xrightarrow[\text{Ether}]{\text{Dry}} Y \xrightarrow{H_3O^+} RCOOH$

What is Y in the above reaction?

[NCERT (New) Pg. 246, NEET 2022]

(a) $RCOO^-Mg^+X$ (b) $R_3CO^-Mg^+X$

(c) $RCOO^-X^+$ (d) $(RCOO)_2Mg$

26 Match Column I with Column II.

Column-I	Column-II
A. 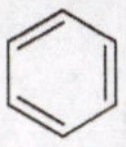 $\xrightarrow[\text{Anhyd. } AlCl_3/CuCl]{CO, HCl}$	1. Hell-Volhard-Zelinsky reaction
B. $R-\overset{O}{\overset{\parallel}{C}}-CH_3 + NaOX \rightarrow$	2. Gattermann-Koch reaction
C. $R-CH_2-OH + R'COOH \xrightarrow{\text{Conc. } H_2SO_4}$	3. Haloform reaction
D. $R-CH_2-COOH \xrightarrow[\text{(ii) } H_2O]{\text{(i) } X_2/\text{Red P}}$	4. Esterification

Codes *[NEET 2021]*

	A	B	C	D
(a)	4	1	2	3
(b)	3	2	1	4
(c)	1	4	3	2
(d)	2	3	4	1

27 Which of the following acid will form an (i) anhydride on heating and (ii) acid imide on strong heating with ammonia? *[NCERT (New) Pg. 252, 253, NEET (Oct.) 2020]*

(a) 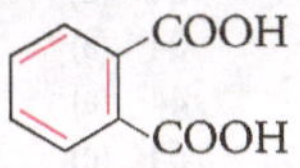 (b) 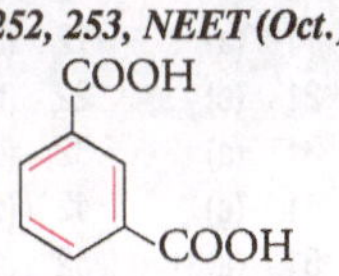

(c) 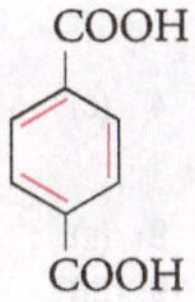 (d) 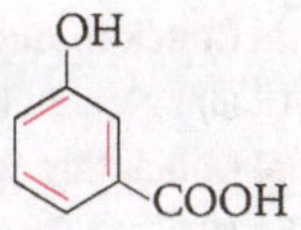

28 The major product of the following reaction is :

[NCERT (New) Pg. 253, NEET (National) 2019]

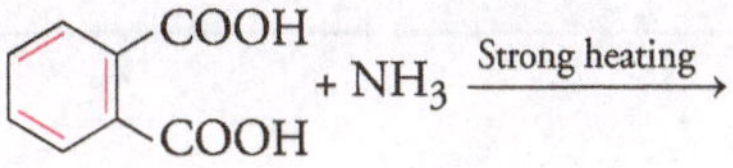

(a) 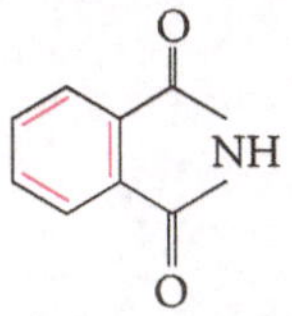 (b) 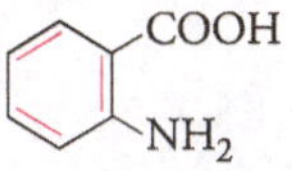

(c) 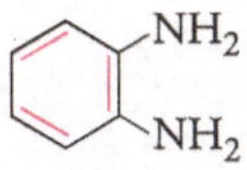 (d) 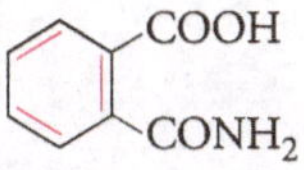

29 Carboxylic acids have higher boiling points than aldehydes, ketones and even alcohols of comparable molecular mass. It is due to their *[NCERT (New) Pg. 249, NEET 2018]*

(a) more extensive association of carboxylic acid *via* van der Waals' force of attraction
(b) formation of carboxylate ion
(c) formation of intramolecular H-bonding
(d) formation of intermolecular H-bonding

30 The correct order of strengths of the carboxylic acids *[NCERT (New) Pg. 250, NEET 2016, Phase II]*

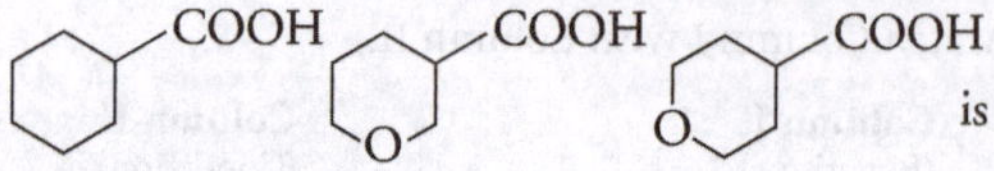

I II III is

(a) I > II > III (b) II > III > I
(c) III > II > I (d) II > I > III

Answers

Step up Practice 1

1 (b)	2 (d)	3 (b)	4 (c)	5 (a)	6 (b)	7 (d)	8 (d)	9 (d)	10 (c)
11 (c)	12 (b)	13 (c)	14 (c)	15 (a)	16 (a)	17 (a)	18 (b)	19 (d)	20 (d)
21 (d)	22. (a)								

Step up Practice 2

1 (a)	2 (c)	3 (c)	4 (d)	5 (c)	6 (c)	7 (c)	8 (d)	9 (d)	10 (d)
11 (a)	12 (a)	13 (a)	14 (c)	15 (c)	16 (a)	17 (b)	18 (d)	19 (c)	20 (d)
21 (b)	22 (d)	23 (c)	24 (d)	25 (b)	26 (d)	27 (d)			

Step up Practice 3

1 (d)	2 (c)	3 (a)	4 (b)	5 (c)	6 (c)	7 (a)	8 (c)	9 (a)	10 (c)
11 (d)	12 (a)	13 (d)	14 (a)	15 (d)	16 (a)	17 (a)	18 (d)	19 (a)	20 (a)

Gearing up for NEET

1 (a)	2 (a)	3 (d)	4 (a)	5 (a)	6 (c)	7 (c)	8 (c)	9 (b)	10 (d)
11 (a)	12 (b)	13 (c)	14 (b)	15 (a)	16 (b)	17 (c)	18 (c)	19 (a)	20 (c)
21 (c)	22 (b)	23 (c)	24 (b)	25 (c)	26 (c)	27 (c)	28 (d)	29 (b)	30 (d)
31 (a)	32 (c)	33 (a)	34 (a)	35 (d)	36 (d)	37 (b)	38 (d)	39 (c)	40 (d)
41 (c)	42 (c)	43 (a)	44 (a)	45 (b)	46 (d)	47 (a)	48 (c)	49 (d)	50 (a)
51 (a)	52 (a)	53 (a)	54 (c)	55 (b)	56 (a)				

Final Check through PYQs : Module-I

1 (d)	2 (b)	3 (a)	4 (c)	5 (d)

Final Check through PYQs : Module-II

6 (a)	7 (d)	8 (b)	9 (a)	10 (d)	11 (c)	12 (a)	13 (c)	14 (b)	15 (b)
16 (c)	17 (d)	18 (b)	19 (b)	20 (c)	21 (a)	22 (d)			

Final Check through PYQs : Module-III

23 (c)	24 (c)	25 (a)	26 (d)	27 (a)	28 (a)	29 (d)	30 (b)

Hints and Solutions

Step up Practice 1

1. (*b*) The correct IUPAC name of the given compound

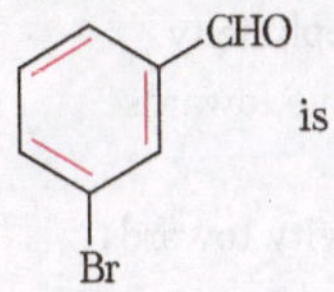

is 3-bromobenzene carbaldehyde.

2. (*d*) The compound (d) has two IUPAC name

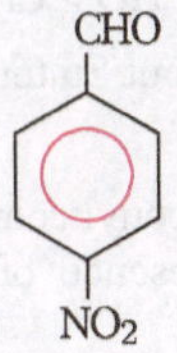

4-nitrobenzene carbaldehyde
or
4-nitrobenzaldehyde

3. (*b*) 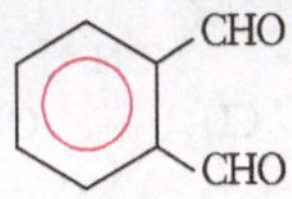 is known as phthaldehyde.

4. (*c*) Among the given compounds only (i), (ii), (iii) and (iv) are functional isomer with molecular formula C_3H_6O.

$CH_2=CHCH_2OH$ (Allyl alcohol) $\quad CH_3COCH_3$ (Propanone) $\quad CH_3CH_2CHO$ (Propanal)

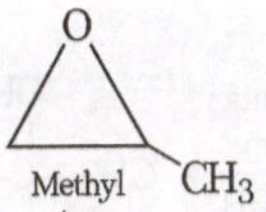

Methyl oxirane

$C_2H_5COCH_3$ Ethyl methyl ketone

5. (*a*)

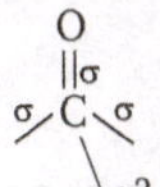

sp^2-hybridised

Thus, option (a) is the correct answer.

6. (*b*) Statement I is true but Statement II is false.

Acetonitrile form acetone on reaction with Grignard reagent followed by hydrolysis.

$$CH_3C\equiv N \xrightarrow[H_3O^+]{CH_3-MgBr} CH_3-\overset{O}{\overset{\|}{C}}-CH_3$$

7. (*d*) Pentene upon ozonolysis produces butanal and methanal.

$$\underset{\text{Pentene}}{C_5H_{10}} \xrightarrow{O_3/H_2O} CH_3-CH_2-CH_2-\underset{\underset{O}{\|}}{CH}+H-\underset{\underset{O}{\|}}{CH}$$

8. (*d*) The incorrect match is (d).

Acid chlorides on reaction with H_2 in presence of xylene, Pd and $BaSO_4$ produces aldehyde.

$$\underset{\text{Acid chloride}}{R-\overset{O}{\overset{\|}{C}}-Cl}+H_2 \xrightarrow{Pd/BaSO_4,\ \text{Xylene}} \underset{\text{Aldehyde}}{R-\overset{O}{\overset{\|}{C}}-H}+HCl$$

9. (*d*) Propanone can be prepared by ozonolysis of 2,3-dimethyl-2-butene.

$$H_3C-\overset{CH_3}{\overset{|}{C}}=\overset{CH_3}{\overset{|}{C}}-CH_3 \xrightarrow{O_3/H_2O} \begin{matrix}CH_3\\CH_3\end{matrix}\!\!>C=O$$

10. (*c*) 2,3-dimethylpent-2-ene on ozonolysis yields a mixture of acetone and ethyl methyl ketone.

$$H_3C-\overset{CH_3}{\overset{|}{C}}=\overset{CH_3}{\overset{|}{C}}-CH_2CH_3 \xrightarrow{O_3/Zn} \begin{matrix}CH_3\\CH_3\end{matrix}\!\!>C=O+\begin{matrix}CH_3\\C_2H_5\end{matrix}\!\!>C=O$$

11. (*c*) Statement I is false but Statement II is true.

Addition of water to ethyne in the presence of H_2SO_4 and $HgSO_4$ gives acetaldehyde.

$$\underset{\text{Ethyne}}{CH\equiv CH} \xrightarrow[HgSO_4]{H_2O/H^+} \underset{\text{Acetaldehyde}}{CH_3CHO}$$

12. (*b*) But-1-yne in the presence of dil. H_2SO_4 and $HgSO_4$ undergo hydrolysis to give butanone.

$$\underset{\text{But-1-yne}}{CH_3-CH_2-C\equiv CH} \xrightarrow[HgSO_4]{H_2O/H^+} \underset{\text{Butanone}}{CH_3-CH_2-\overset{O}{\overset{\|}{C}}-CH_3}$$

13. (*c*) $R\overset{O}{\overset{\|}{C}}Cl \xrightarrow{H_2/Pd\text{-}BaSO_4} RCHO$

Thus, $RCOCl$ is

$$(CH_3)_2CH\overset{O}{\overset{\|}{C}}-Cl \xrightarrow{H_2/Pd/BaSO_4} (CH_3)_2CHCHO$$

$$(CH_3)_2CH\overset{O}{\overset{\|}{C}}-Cl \xrightarrow[H_3O^+]{CH_3MgBr} (CH_3)_2CH\overset{O}{\overset{\|}{C}}-CH_3$$

Hence, the acid chloride $(CH_3)_2CHCOCl$ on reaction with CH_3MgBr/H_3O^+ gives $(CH_3)_2CH-\overset{O}{\overset{\|}{C}}-CH_3$.

14. (c) Alkyl nitrile treated with Grignard reagent followed by hydrolysis gives a ketone.

$$R-CN \xrightarrow[H_3O^+]{CH_3MgBr} R-\overset{O}{\overset{\|}{C}}-CH_3$$

15. (a) HCN react with Grignard reagent to form aldehyde.

$$HCN + CH_3MgBr \longrightarrow \underset{\text{Ethanal}}{CH_3\overset{\|}{\underset{O}{C}}H}$$

16. (a) The reaction takes place as follows

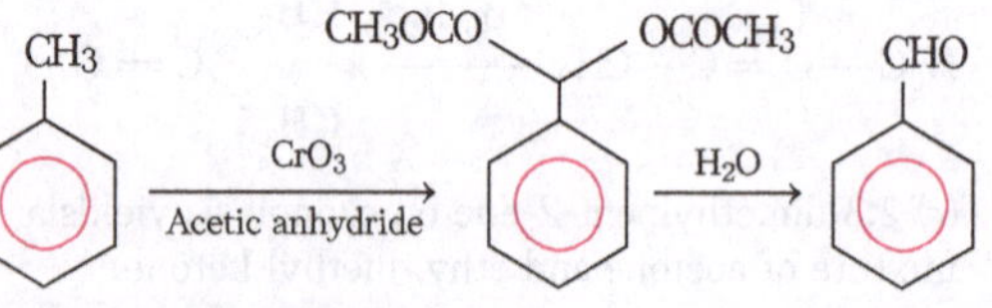

(A)

17. (a) The incorrect match is option (a).

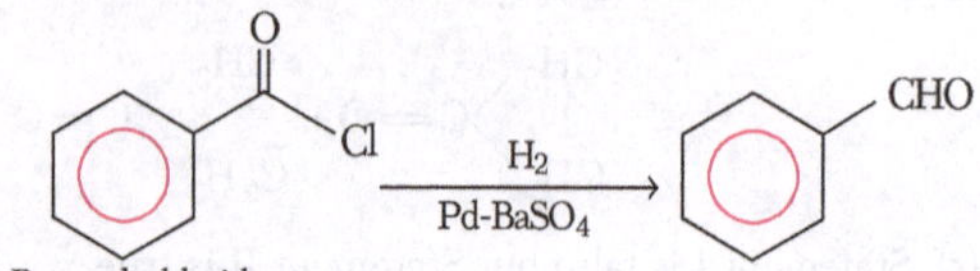

Benzoyl chloride (Benzaldehyde)

18. (b) Among the given reactions only two, i.e. (ii) and (v) will produce only ketone.

$$CH_3-CH_2CN \xrightarrow[\text{ether, } H_3O^+]{C_6H_5MgBr} C_2H_5-\overset{O}{\overset{\|}{C}}-C_6H_5$$

$$R-\overset{OH}{\overset{|}{CH}}-R' \xrightarrow[CH_2Cl_2]{PCC} R-\overset{O}{\overset{\|}{C}}-R'$$

19. (d) Grignard reagent convert alcohol into alkane.

$$CH_3CH_2OH + RMgBr \longrightarrow \underset{\text{(Alkane)}}{RH}$$

20. (d) Boiling points of aldehydes and ketones are lower than alcohols due to absence of intermolecular hydrogen bonding.

21. (d) Due to the presence of two electron donating groups in ketone, it has higher boiling point than aldehydes.

22. (a) The reaction takes place as follows

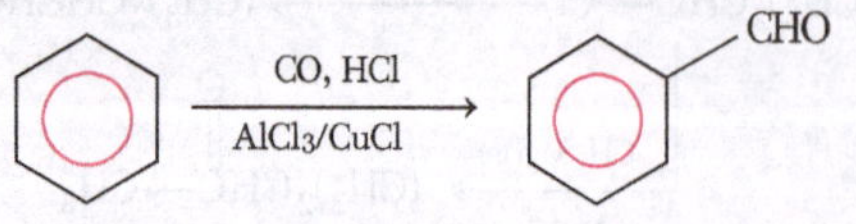

(X)

Step up Practice 2

1. (a) Reactivity of carbonyl compounds can be decided by two factors

(i) **Steric factor** Lesser the steric hindrance, greater will be its reactivity.

(ii) **Electronic factor** Greater the number of alkyl groups lesser will be its electrophilicity.

Hence, CH_3CHO is most reactive towards nucleophilic addition reaction.

2. (c) The correct sequence of reactivity towards nucleophilic attack is

$$HCHO > CH_3CHO > CH_3COCH_3$$

3. (c) Statement I is false but Statement II is true.

Its correct form is :

The α—H atom in carbonyl compound is more acidic in nature due to the presence of electron withdrawing carbonyl group.

4. (d) The reaction is as follows

$$(CH_3)_2C{=}O + HCN \rightleftharpoons (CH_3)_2C(OH)(CN) \xrightarrow{H_3O^+} (CH_3)_2C(OH)(COOH)$$

5. (c) Keto group is more reactive than ester group for the addition of Grignard reagent.

$$CH_3\overset{O}{\overset{\|}{C}}CH_2CH_2\overset{O}{\overset{\|}{C}}OCH_2CH_3 \xrightarrow[\text{(ii) } H_3O^{\oplus}]{\text{(i) } CH_3MgBr \text{ (one mole)}}$$

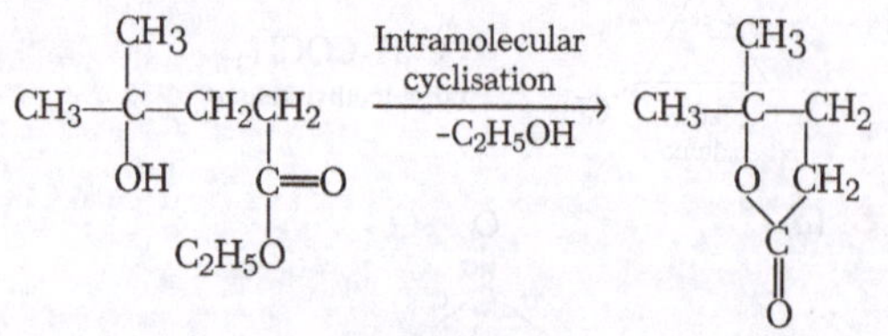

6. (c) $CH_3\underset{\underset{O}{\|}}{C}CH_2CH_2CH_2Cl \xrightarrow[\text{(ii) } H_3O^+]{\text{(i) } CH_3MgBr}$

$$CH_3-\overset{CH_3}{\overset{|}{\underset{OH}{\underset{|}{C}}}}-CH_2CH_2CH_2Cl$$

Intramolecular cyclisation

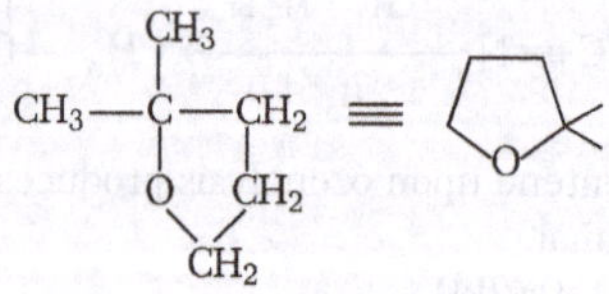

7. (c) The reaction can takes place as follows

$$(CH_3)_2C{=}O + CH_3MgBr \longrightarrow (CH_3)_2C(OMgBr)(CH_3)$$

$$\xrightarrow{H_2O} Mg(Br)OH + CH_3{-}\underset{CH_3}{\overset{CH_3}{\underset{|}{\overset{|}{C}}}}{-}OH$$

Thus, option (c) is the correct answer.

8. (d) Acetal is a diether. Acetal is formed by the reaction of aldehyde with alcohol.

9. (d) Acetone react with 1,2-diols in the presence of HCl to give cyclic ketal.

$$(CH_3)_2C{=}O + \begin{array}{l} CH_2{-}OH \\ | \\ CH_2{-}OH \end{array} \xrightarrow{HCl} (CH_3)_2C\begin{array}{l} O{-}CH_2 \\ \quad\;\; | \\ O{-}CH_2 \end{array}$$

10. (d) The reaction takes place as follows

$$CH_3{-}CH_2{-}\overset{O}{\overset{\|}{C}}{-}CH_3 \xrightarrow[H_2SO_4]{K_2Cr_2O_7} 2CH_3COOH$$

11. (a) Both Statement I and Statement II are false.

12. (a) Acetaldehyde is heated with Fehling's solution, a reddish brown precipitate of Cu_2O is obtained.

$$R{-}CHO + 2Cu^{2+} + 5\overset{-}{O}H \longrightarrow RCOO^- + Cu_2O + 3H_2O$$

13. (a) The reaction takes place as follows

$$CH_3CH_2COCH_3 \xrightarrow{SeO_2} CH_3\,CH_2\overset{O}{\overset{\|}{C}}{-}CHO + H_2O + Se$$

Aldehyde or ketone with a methyl or methylene group adjacent to carbonyl group are oxidised by SeO_2.

14. (c) Among the given compounds only three, i.e. I, II and V on treatment with an excess of halogen in the presence of dil. NaOH to give haloform and the salt of a carboxylic acid having one carbon atom less than the original compound.

The compounds that have CH_3CO group or $CH_3CH(OH)$ group undergo haloform reaction.

15. (c) Ethanoic acid and propanal can be distinguished by using Tollen's reagent.

16. (a) Ketones do not reduce Tollen's reagent. Hence, option (a) is the incorrect match.

17. (b) The incorrect match is option (b).

$$\begin{array}{l} R \\ R' \end{array}\!\!>C{=}O \xrightarrow[\text{reduction}]{\text{Wolff-Kishner}} R{-}CH_2{-}R'$$

18. (d) In this reaction H^- acts as a nucleophile.

$$LiAlH_4 \rightleftharpoons Li^+ + (AlH_4^-) \rightleftharpoons \underset{\text{Nucleophile}}{H^-}$$

19. (c) The reaction takes place as follows

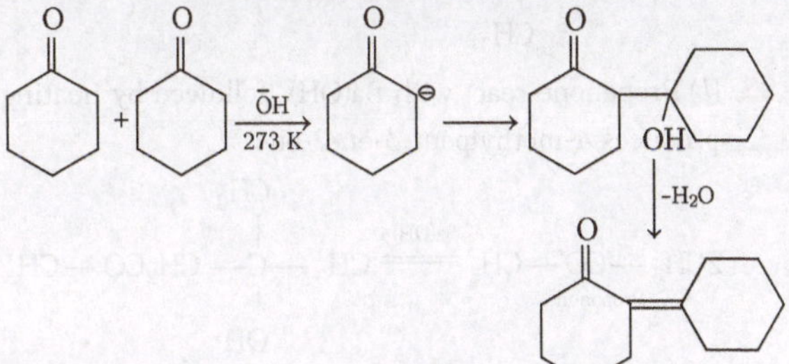

Thus, the reagent '*A*' is

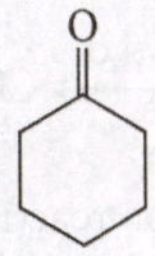

20. (d) The reaction takes place as follows

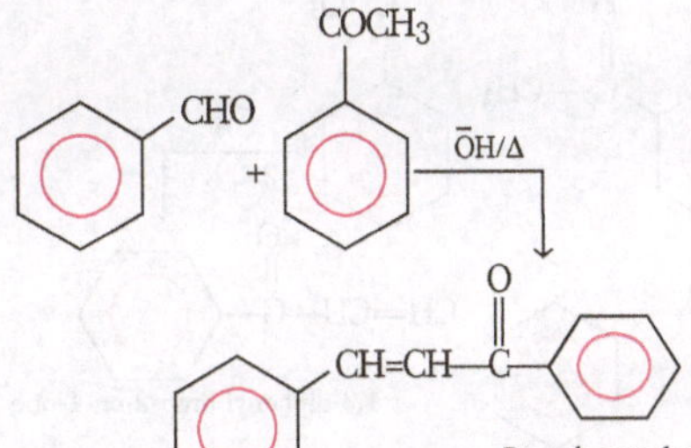

Benzalacetophenone

21. (b) The reaction takes place as follows

$$2CH_3CHO \underset{}{\overset{\text{Dil. NaOH}}{\rightleftharpoons}} \underset{(A)}{CH_3{-}\underset{OH}{\underset{|}{CH}}{-}CH_2{-}CHO} \xrightarrow[-H_2O]{\Delta}$$

$$\underset{(B)}{CH_3{-}CH{=}CH{-}CHO}$$

22. (d) The product X is $CH_3CH_2{-}CH{=}CH{-}CHO$.

23. (c) Aldehydes which do not have an α-hydrogen atom, undergo self oxidation and reduction reaction on heating with concentrated alkali.

Among the given compounds only four, i.e. I, III, IV and V will undergo Cannizzaro reaction.

24. (d) When acetaldehyde reacts with propanal in the presence of NaOH followed by heating, then the products will be formed according to cross-aldol condensation.

$$CH_3CHO + CH_3CH_2CHO \xrightarrow[\Delta]{NaOH}$$

$$CH_3{-}CH{=}CH{-}CHO +$$

$$CH_3CH_2—CH{=}\underset{}{\overset{CH_3}{\overset{|}{C}}}—CHO +$$
$$CH_3—CH{=}\underset{\underset{CH_3}{|}}{C}—CHO + CH_3CH_2—CH{=}CHCHO$$

25. (*b*) Propanone react with $Ba(OH)_2$ followed by heating produces 4-methylpent-3-en-2-one.

$$\underset{\text{Propanone}}{2CH_3—CO—CH_3} \xrightleftharpoons{Ba(OH)_2} CH_3—\underset{\underset{OH}{|}}{\overset{\overset{CH_3}{|}}{C}}—CH_2CO—CH_3$$

$$\xrightarrow{\Delta,-H_2O} \underset{\text{4-methylpent-3-en-2-one}}{CH_3—\overset{\overset{CH_3}{|}}{C}{=}CH—CO—CH_3}$$

26. (*d*) Acetophenone on reaction with benzaldehyde in basic medium gives 1,3-diphenylprop-2-en-1-one.

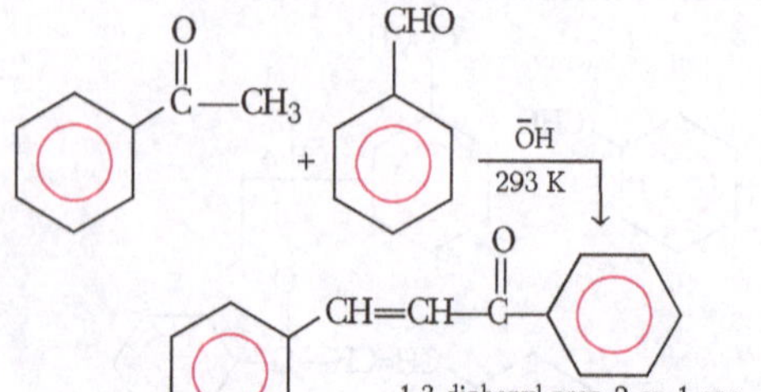

1,3-diphenyl prop-2-en-1-one

27. (*d*) Acetaldehyde is used primarily as a starting material in the manufacture of ethyl acetate, vinyl acetate polymers and drugs.

Step up Practice 3

1. (*d*) Caproic acid is a monocarboxylic acid with molecular formula $CH_3(CH_2)_4COOH$.

2. (*c*) The incorrect match is given in option (c)

It correct match is-

$$\begin{matrix} CH_2—CH_2—COOH \\ | \\ CH_2—CH_2—COOH \end{matrix}$$ is an adipic acid.

3. (*a*) IUPAC name of the acrylic acid is prop-2-enoic acid.

4. (*b*) The IUPAC name of caproic acid $[CH_3(CH_2)_4COOH]$ is hexanoic acid.

5. (*c*) The reaction takes place as follows

$$CH_3CH_2CH_2CH_2OH \xrightarrow{Cr_2O_7^{2-}/H_3O^+} CH_3CH_2CH_2CHO$$
$$\xrightarrow{Cr_2O_7^{2-}/H_3O^+} \underset{(X)}{CH_3CH_2CH_2COOH}$$

6. (*c*) The reaction takes place as follows

$$O{=}C{=}O \xrightarrow[\text{dry ether}]{C_2H_5MgBr} O{=}\underset{\underset{C_2H_5}{|}}{C}OMgX$$
$$\xrightarrow{H_3O^+} O{=}\overset{\overset{OH}{|}}{C}—C_2H_5$$

7. (*a*) The reaction takes place as follows

$$C_6H_5\overset{\overset{O}{\|}}{C}—OCH_3 \xrightarrow[H^+]{H_2O} C_6H_5COOH + CH_3OH$$

8. (*c*) The reaction takes place as follows :

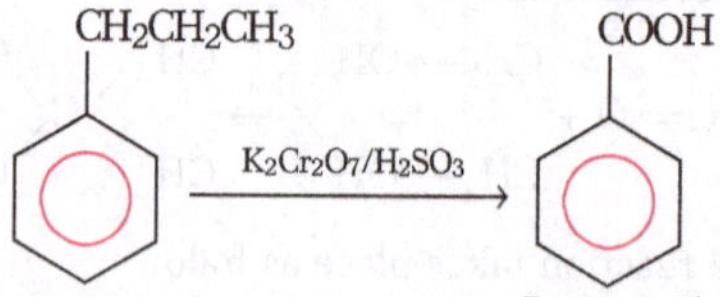

Benzoic acid

9. (*a*) Acid anhydrides are hydrolysed with aq. base to form carboxylate ions which form carboxylic acid on acidification.

$$\begin{matrix} R—\overset{\overset{O}{\|}}{C} \\ \quad\quad >O \\ R'—\underset{\underset{O}{\|}}{C} \end{matrix} + H_2O \xrightarrow{H^+|\bar{O}H} RCOOH + R'COOH$$

10. (*c*) Carboxylic acids are held together by intermolecular hydrogen bonding.

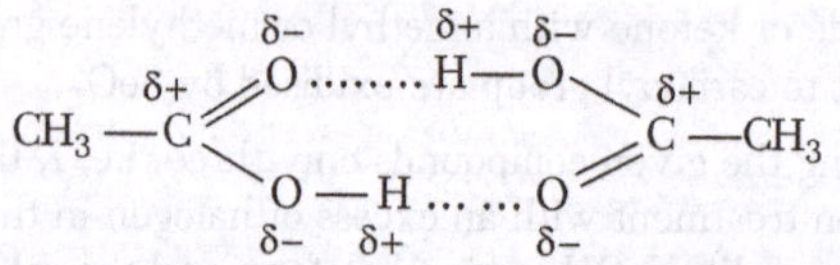

11. (*d*) The solubility of carboxylic acid decreases with increasing number of carbon atoms.

12. (*a*) The correct order of acidity is as I ≈ II > III > IV. *ortho*-substituted benzoic acids are stronger acids than *para*/*meta* substituted and benzoic acid.

13. (*d*) The correct increasing order of acid strength is as follow

$$IV < I < II < III$$

Acidic strength decreases with increase in number of electron donating group and increases with increase in number of electron withdrawing group.

14. (*a*) Both A and R are true and R is the correct explanation of A.

15. (*d*) Propionic acid reacts with aqueous sodium bicarbonate to form ionic salts and liberate CO_2 gas. The CO_2 comes from sodium bicarbonate.

16. (*a*) The reaction takes place as follows

$$CH_3CH_2COOH + R—OH \xrightarrow[H_2SO_4]{Conc.} CH_3CH_2—\overset{O}{\overset{||}{C}}— OR + H_2O$$

'*B*'

Thus, the product '*B*' is CH_3CH_2COOR.

17. (*a*) The reaction takes place as follows

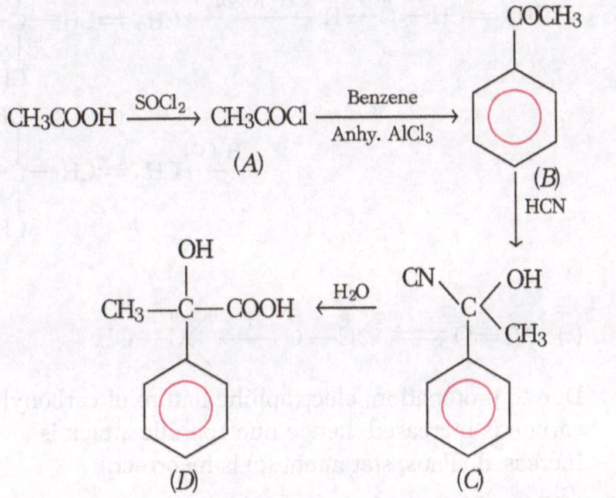

18. (*d*) Among the given reactions only two, i.e. (i) and (iii) will give alkane as a product.

(i) $2CH_3COOK \xrightarrow{Electrolysis} CH_3—CH_3$

(ii) $CH_3CH_2CH_2COOH \xrightarrow[\Delta]{Red\ P/HI} CH_3CH_2CH_2CH_3 + 2H_2O + 3\ I_2$

19. (*a*) Both Statement I and Statement II are false.

Aromatic carboxylic acids undergo electrophilic substitution reaction at *m*-position due to presence of electron withdrawing group.

Due to delocalisation of π-electrons, electron density is decreased at *o*-and *p*-positions.

20. (*a*) Nitration of benzoic acid gives *m*-nitrobenzoic acid.

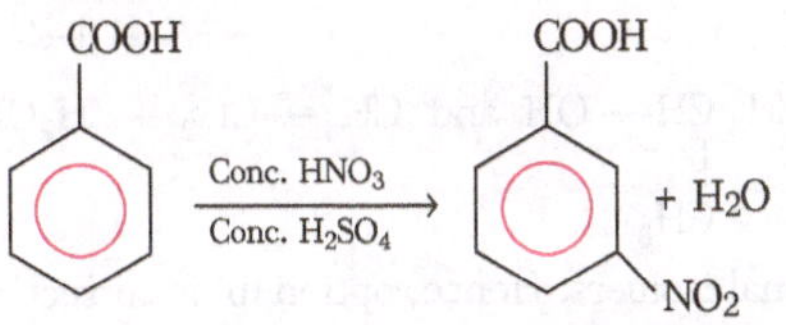

(3-nitrobenzoic acid)

Gearing up for NEET

1. (*a*) The correct IUPAC name of the given compound

$$CH_3—CH_2—\overset{O}{\overset{||}{C}}— CH_2CHO$$ is 3-oxopentanal.

2. (*a*) The IUPAC name of the compound is

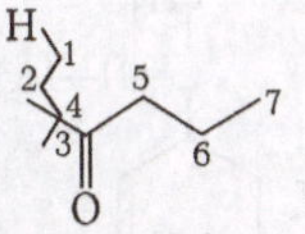

3,3-dimethylheptan-4-one

3. (*d*) The incorrect match is (d) with their common name. It is correct common name is

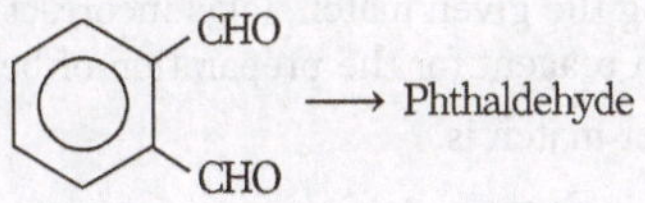

4. (*a*) In Clemmensen reduction, carbonyl compound is treated with zinc amalgam and HCl to give alkane.

5. (*a*) Butan-2-ol gives butanone on oxidation with alkaline $KMnO_4$ solution.

$$\underset{\text{Butan-2-ol}}{CH_3CH_2\underset{OH}{\underset{|}{C}H}CH_3} \xrightarrow{KMnO_4\ (alk.)} \underset{\text{Butanone}}{CH_3—CH_2—\underset{O}{\underset{||}{C}}—CH_3}$$

6. (*c*) Acetaldehyde does not respond to Lucas test. This test is used to distinguish different type of alcohols.

7. (*c*) Iodoform test is used to detect the presence of $—COCH_3$ group which is converted into $—COOH$ group by $NaOX$ ($NaOH + X_2$).

The reaction is shown as,

$$\underset{\text{Hex-4-ene-2-one}}{CH_3—CH{=}CH—CH_2—\overset{O}{\overset{||}{C}}—CH_3} \xrightarrow[\text{(Iodoform reaction)}]{I_2/NaOH\ solution} \underset{\text{Pent-3-ene-1-oic acid}}{CH_3—CH{=}CH—CH_2—\overset{O}{\overset{||}{C}}—OH}$$

8. (*c*) In aspirin —COOH functional group is present.

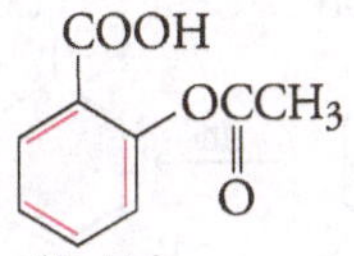

(Aspirin)

9. (*b*) *X* is $C_6H_5CO_3H$ (peroxy benzoic acid) which oxidises ketone into ester. This reaction is known as Beayer-Villiger oxidation.

10. (*d*) The incorrect match is option (d).
IUPAC name of isobutyric acid is 2-methyl propanoic acid.

11. (*a*) In the mentioned reduction reaction, DIBAL-H is used as a reducing agent.

12. (*b*) The reaction takes place as follows

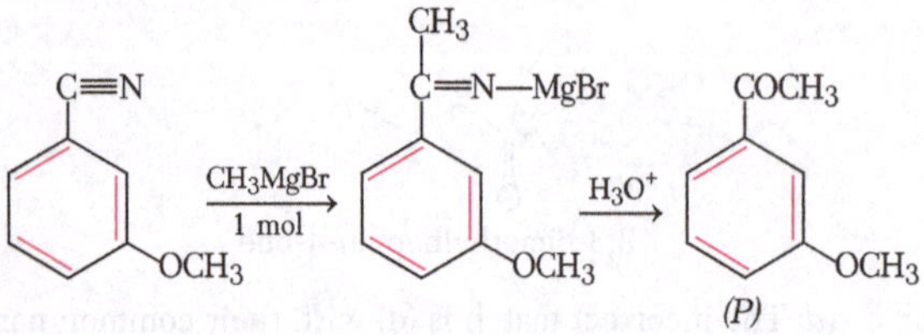

(*P*)

13. (*c*) Among the given match, (c) is incorrect match with the given reagent for the preparation of benzaldehyde.
Its correct match is

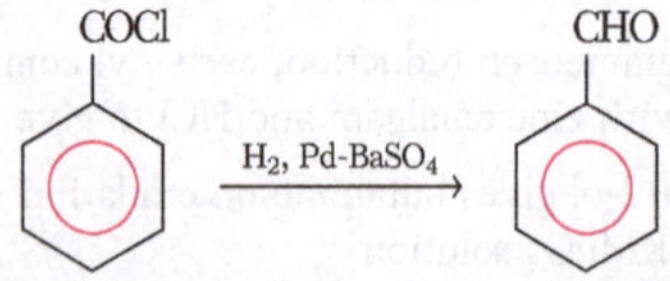

Benzoyl chloride → Benzaldehyde

14. (*b*) Cyanohydrin of ethanal forms lactic acid.

$$\underset{\text{Ethanal}}{CH_3CHO} \xrightarrow{HCN} \underset{\text{Cyanohydrin}}{CH_3CH(OH)CN} \xrightarrow{H_3O^+} \underset{\text{Lactic acid}}{CH_3CH(OH)COOH}$$

15. (*a*) Acetaldehyde when is heated with Fehling's solution it gives a red precipitate of Cu_2O.

16. (*b*) The addition of HBr to α, β-unsaturated acids follows anti to Markownikoff rule.
The reaction will proceed as

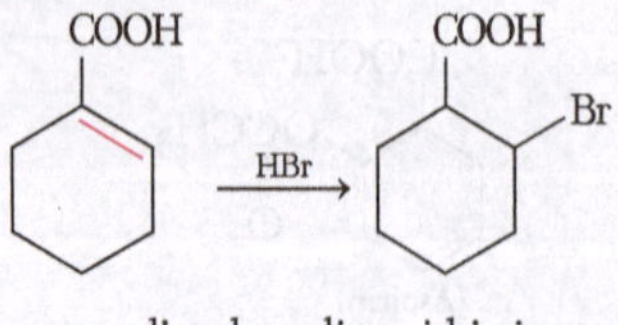

17. (*c*) 1,4-benzene dicarboxylic acid is isomeric with phthalic acid.

18. (*c*) The correct increasing order of boiling points of the given compounds are as follow

$$IV < III < I < II$$

Alcohol > Aldehyde > Ether > Hydrocarbon
Alcohols has maximum boiling point because of the hydrogen bonds.
Between aldehydes and ether, aldehydes has higher boiling point as it is more polar.

19. (*a*) The reaction proceeds as follows

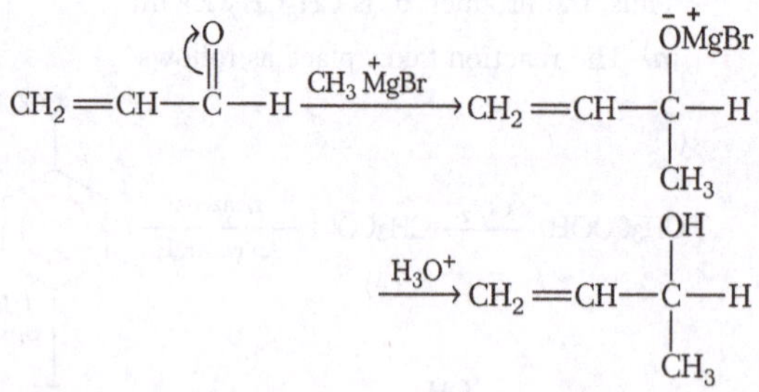

20. (*c*) $\rangle C=O \rightleftharpoons \rangle \overset{\oplus}{C}-\overset{\ominus}{O} \xrightarrow{H^+} \rangle \overset{\oplus}{C}-OH$

Due to protonation, electrophilic nature of carbonyl carbon is increased, hence nucleophilic attack is increased. Thus, statement (c) is incorrect.

21. (*c*) Benzaldehyde does not yield a simple addition product with ammonia, it forms a complex product.

22. (*b*) Chemical reaction can be shown as

$$\underset{\text{Ethanal}}{CH_3CHO} \xrightarrow[\text{(ii) } H_2O]{\text{(i) } CH_3MgBr} \underset{\substack{(A)\\ \text{Propan-2-ol}}}{CH_3-CH(CH_3)-OH} \xrightarrow[\text{Dehydration}]{H_2SO_4,\,\Delta}$$

$$\underset{\substack{(B)\\ \text{Propene}}}{CH_3-CH=CH_2} \xrightarrow[\text{(Hydroboration oxidation)}]{\text{(i) } BH_3 \text{ (ii) } H_2O_2/OH^{\ominus}} \underset{\substack{(C)\\ \text{Propan-1-ol}}}{CH_3-CH_2-CH_2OH}$$

Thus, $CH_3CH(CH_3)-OH$ and $CH_3-CH_2-CH_2OH$ are positional isomers. Hence, option (b) is correct.

23. (*c*) The reaction proceeds as follows

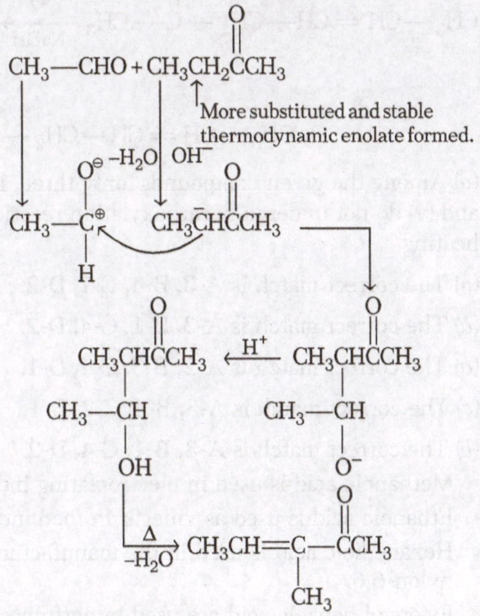

24. (*b*) The reaction will proceed as follow

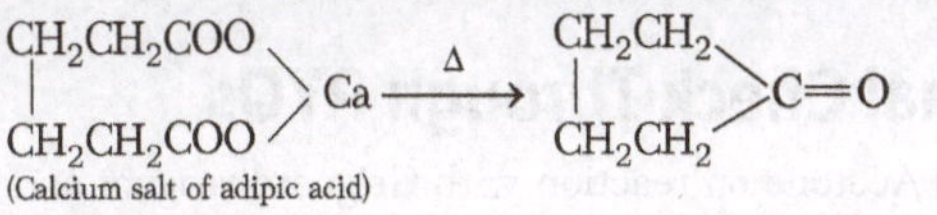

25. (*c*) The reaction will take place as

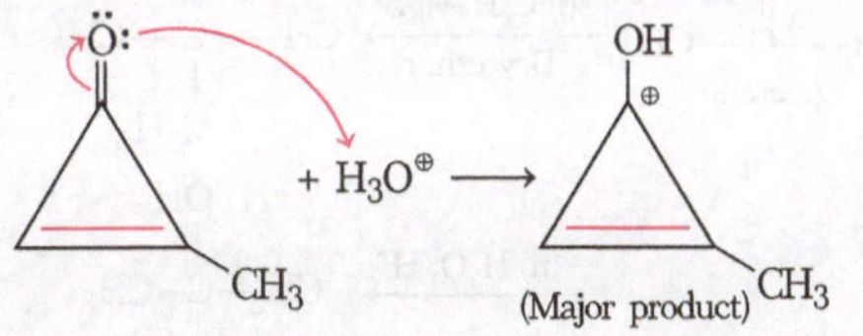

26. (*c*)

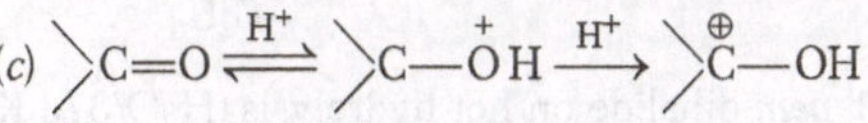

Due to protonation, electrophilic nature of carbonyl carbon is increased, hence nucleophilic attack is increased. Thus, statement (c) is incorrect.

27. (*c*)

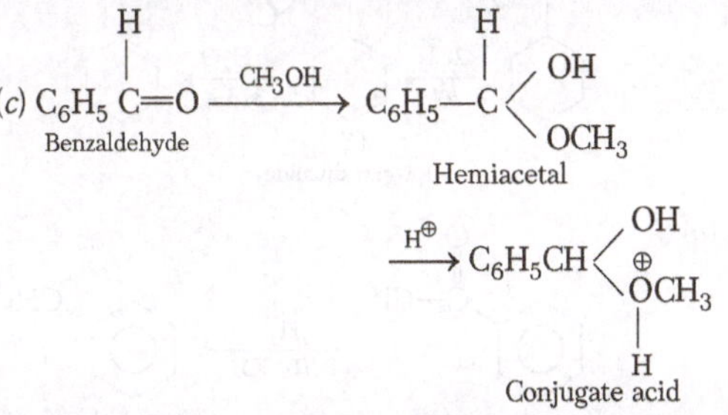

28. (*d*) Among the given statements only C is incorrect.

The correct form of statement C is

Electron withdrawing groups increase the acidity of the carboxylic acids by stabilising the conjugate base through delocalisation of the negative charge by inductive effect or resonance effect.

29. (*b*) Among the given statements only D and E are incorrect. The correct form of these statements are as

- Sulphonation of benzoic acid produces mainly *m*-sulphobenzoic acid.
- Lactic acid on oxidation by alkaline potassium permanganate gives pyruvic acid.

30. (*d*) Aliphatic aldehydes like CH_3CH_2CHO do not give benzoin condensation.

31. (*a*) Both A and R are true and R is the correct explanation of A.

32. (*c*) A is true but R is false.

The correct form of R is :

Dry HCl protonates the oxygen of carbonyl compound and increases the electrophilicity of the carbonyl carbon.

33. (*a*) Both A and R are true and R is the correct explanation of A.

34. (*a*) Both A and R are true and R is the correct explanation of A.

In water,

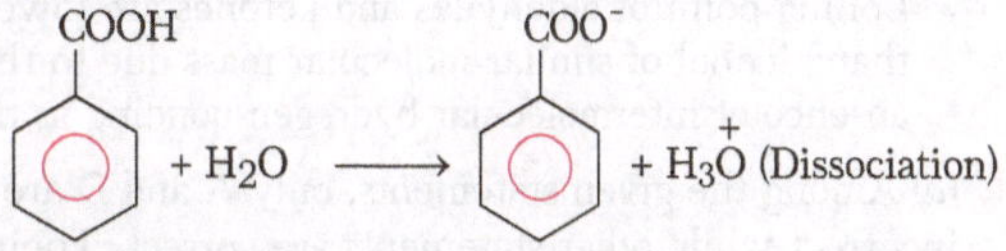

In benzene solution,

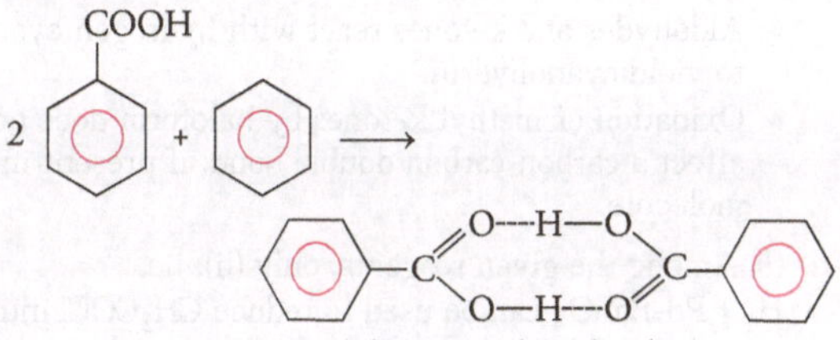

35. (*d*) A is false but R is true.

The solubility of carboxylic acids decreases by increasing the number of carbon atoms.

36. (*d*) Both Statement I and Statement II are true.

37. (*b*) Statement I is true but Statement II is false.

Its correct form is :

Addition of water to ethyne in the presence of H_2SO_4 and $HgSO_4$ gives acetaldehyde.

38. (*d*) Both Statement I and Statement II are true.

39. (*c*) Statement I is false but Statement II is true. The α-hydrogen atom in carbonyl compounds is more acidic.

40. (*d*) Both statement I and Statement II are true.

41. (*c*) Statement I is false but Statement II is true.

Treating an alkyl nitrile with phenyl magnesium bromide followed by hydrolysis yield a ketone.

$$CH_3—CH_2—C{\equiv}N + C_6H_5MgBr \xrightarrow{\text{Ether}} CH_3CH_2—C(=NMgBr)—C_6H_5 \xrightarrow{H_3O^+} \underset{\text{Propiophenone}}{C_2H_5—\overset{O}{\overset{\|}{C}}—C_6H_5}$$

42. (c) Statement I is false but Statement II is true.

Its correct form is :

Carboxylic acids on heating with mineral acids (H_2SO_4 or P_2O_5) give corresponding anhydride.

43. (a) Among the given statements only statement C and D are incorrect. The correct form of these statements are as follow

- 3° alcohols undergo dehydration to give alkenes as a product with Cu at 530 K.

$$\underset{\text{3° alcohol}}{CH_3—C(CH_3)_2—OH} \xrightarrow[530\ K]{Cu,\ \Delta} \underset{\text{Alkene}}{CH_3—C(=CH_2)—CH_3} + H_2O$$

- Boiling point of aldehydes and ketones are lower than alcohol of similar molecular mass due to the absence of intermolecular hydrogen bonding in them.

44. (a) Among the given statements, only A and D are incorrect while other statements are correct. Their correct form are

- Aldehydes and ketones react with hydrogen cyanide to yield cyanohydrin.
- Oxidation of methyl ketones by haloform does not affect a carbon-carbon double bond, if present in the molecule.

45. (b) Among the given reagents, only (ii), i.e. H_2 | Pd-$BaSO_4$ can be used to reduce CH_3COCl into CH_3CHO. This reaction is called Rosenmund reduction.

46. (d) Among the given compounds, only four i.e., (i), (ii), (iv) and (v) will give positive iodoform test. Iodoform reaction with sodium hypoiodite is used for detection of CH_3CO group or $CH_3CH(OH)$ group.

47. (a) Among the given compounds, only three i.e, (i), (ii) and (iv) will undergo Cannizzaro's reaction. Necessary condition for Cannizzaro reaction is absence of α-hydrogen atom.

48. (c) Among the given compounds only three i.e. (iii), (v) and (vi) will give aldol condensation reaction.

Aldol condensation reaction given by those compounds that have atleast one α-hydrogen atom.

49. (d) Among the given reactions only one i.e, (iv) will produce carboxylic acid.

$$CH_3—CH{=}CH—CH_2—\overset{O}{\overset{\|}{C}}—CH_3 \xrightarrow[NaOH]{I_2} CH_3—CH{=}CH—CH_2—\overset{O}{\overset{\|}{C}}—OH$$

50. (a) Among the given compounds, only three, i.e. (i), (ii) and (v) do not undergo decarboxylation reaction on heating.

51. (a) The correct match is A-3, B-4, C-1, D-2.

52. (a) The correct match is A-3, B-1, C-4, D-2.

53. (a) The correct match is A-2, B-3, C-4, D-1.

54. (c) The correct match is A-3, B-4, C-2, D-1.

55. (b) The correct match is A-3, B-1, C-4, D-2.

- Methanoic acid is used in electroplating industry.
- Ethanoic acid is used as vinegar in food industry.
- Hexanedioic acid is used in the manufacture of nylon-6,6.
- Esters of benzoic acid are used in perfumes.

56. (a) The correct match is A-4, B-3, C-2, D-1.

Final Check Through PYQs

1. (d) Acetone on reaction with Grignard reagent and on further hydrolysis given 2-methylbutan-2-ol.

$$\underset{\text{Acetone}}{CH_3—\overset{O}{\overset{\|}{C}}—CH_3} \xrightarrow[\text{Dry ether}]{\text{(i) } C_2H_5MgBr} CH_3—\overset{\overset{-\ +}{OMgBr}}{\overset{|}{C}}—CH_3 \ (\text{with } C_2H_5) \xrightarrow{\text{(ii) } H_2O,\ H^+} CH_3—\overset{OH}{\overset{|}{C}}—CH_3 \ (\text{with } C_2H_5)$$

2. (b) 1,1-*gem*-dihalide on hot hydrolysis (H_2O/373 K) can produce an aldehyde.

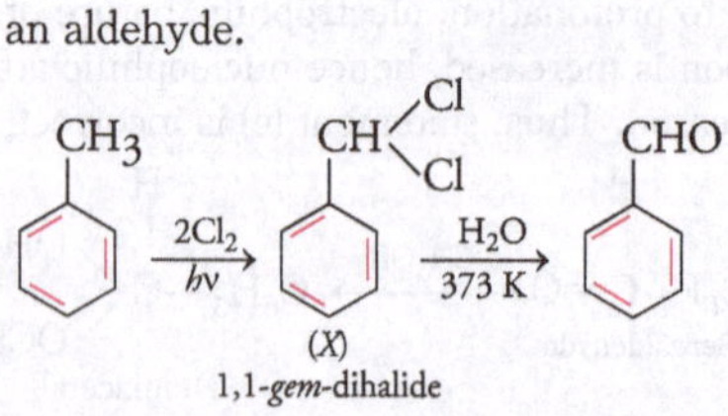

3. (a)

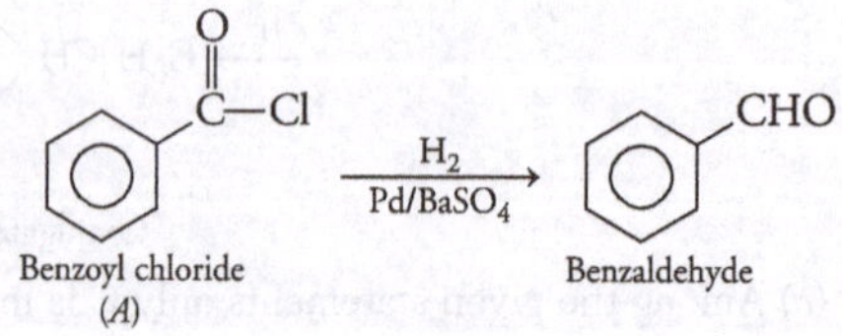

It is Rosenmund reaction, in which an acid chloride gets converted into an aldehyde by using H_2/Pd/$BaSO_4$ as a reagent.

4. (*c*) PCC (Pyridinium chlorochromate) is used to convert alcohols to aldehydes. Thereby preventing its further oxidation to benzoic acid.

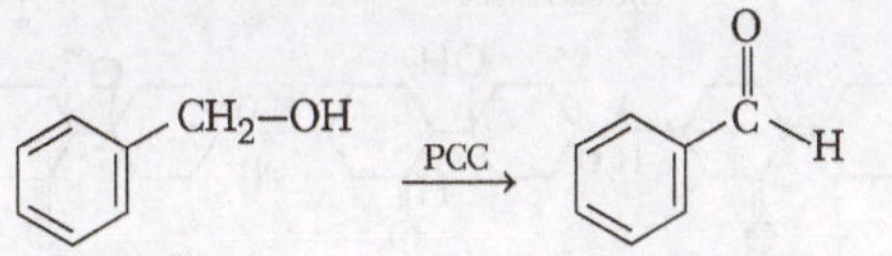

(Benzyl alcohol) (Benzaldehyde)

5. (*d*)

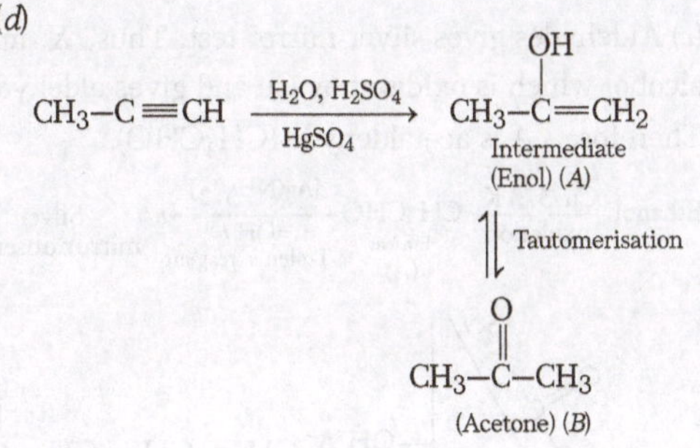

Therefore,

$$A = CH_3—\overset{OH}{\overset{|}{C}}=CH_2;\ B = CH_3—\overset{O}{\overset{\|}{C}}—CH_3$$

6. (*a*) Fehling reagent comprises of two solutions Fehling *A* ⟶ aqueous solution of $CuSO_4$.

Fehling *B* ⟶ alk. sodium potassium tartarate (Rochelle salt).

7. (*d*) The reaction is as follows

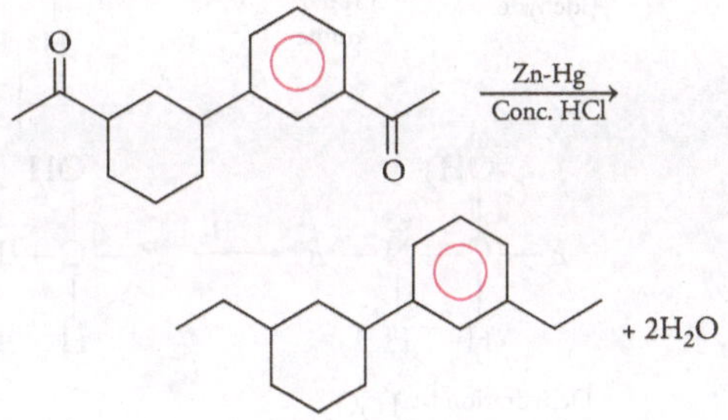

(*A*)

This reaction is an example of Clemmensen reduction reaction.

8. (*b*) The reaction can be written as follows

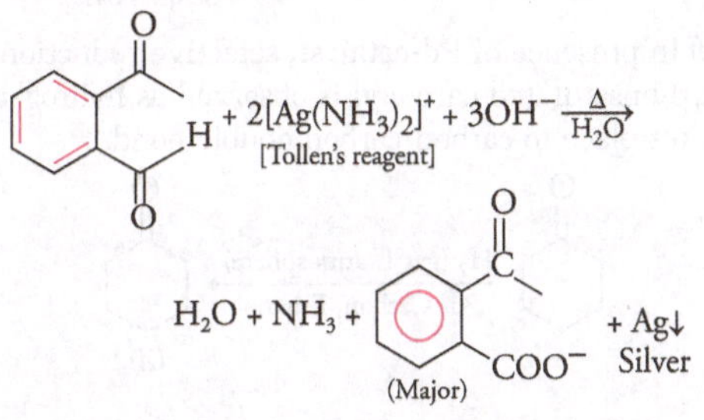

Tollen's reagent oxidises only the aldehyde group in the above reaction and not the ketonic group.

9. (*a*) When acetone reacts with 2-pentanone in presence of dilute NaOH followed by heating then the products will be formed according to cross aldol condensation.

Self aldol

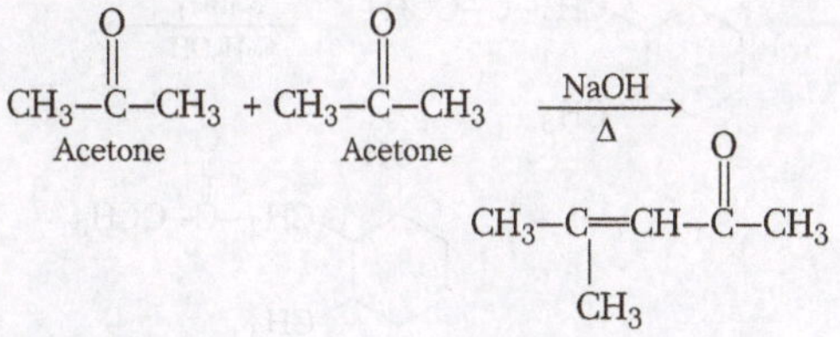

Cross aldol

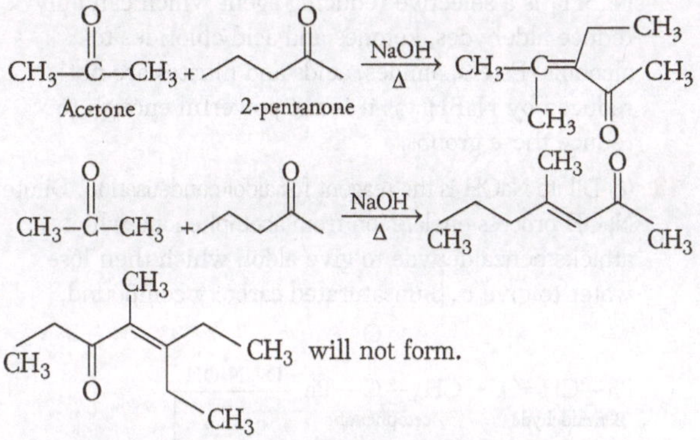

Hence, (a) is the correct option.

10. (*d*) Boiling point of comparable molecular mass molecules is as follows

R—OH > aldehyde-ketone > alkane.

Hence, both statement I and statement II are true. So, the correct option is (d).

11. (*c*) The correct match is option (c), i.e.

(A)-(4), (B)-(3), (C)-(2), (D)-(1).

Products formed	Reaction of carbonyl compound with
Cyanohydrin	HCN
Acetal	Alcohol
Schiff's base	RNH_2
Oxime	NH_2OH

The reactions involved are as follows

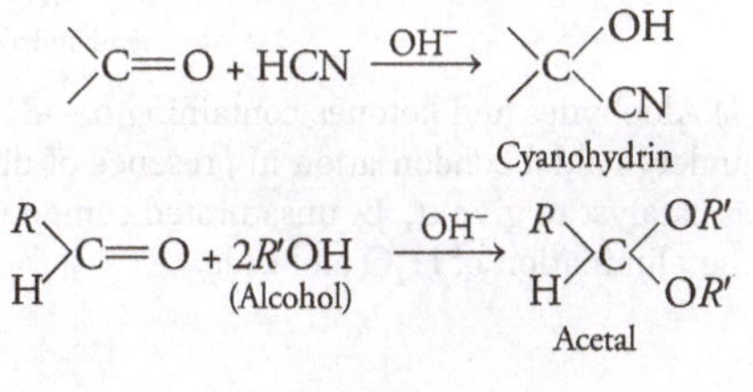

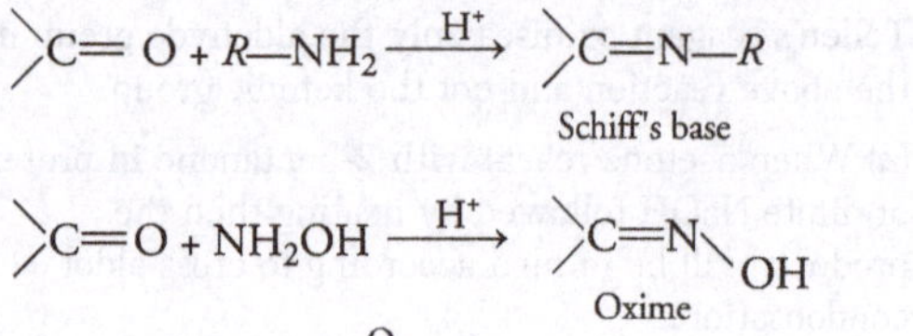

12. (a)

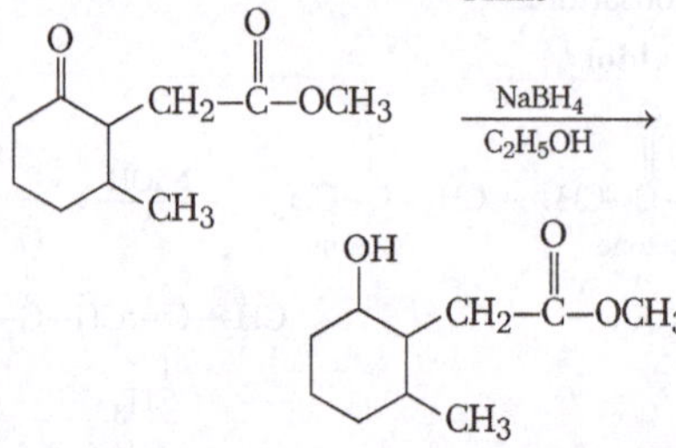

$NaBH_4$ is a selective reducing agent which can only reduce aldehydes, ketones and acid chlorides to alcohols. Esters, amides, acids and nitrites are not reduced by $NaBH_4$ as it is not powerful enough to reduce these groups.

13. (c) Dilute NaOH is the reagent for aldol condensation. Dilute NaOH process enolate ion from acetophenone which attacks benzaldehyde to give aldol, which then lose water to give α, β-unsaturated carboxy compound.

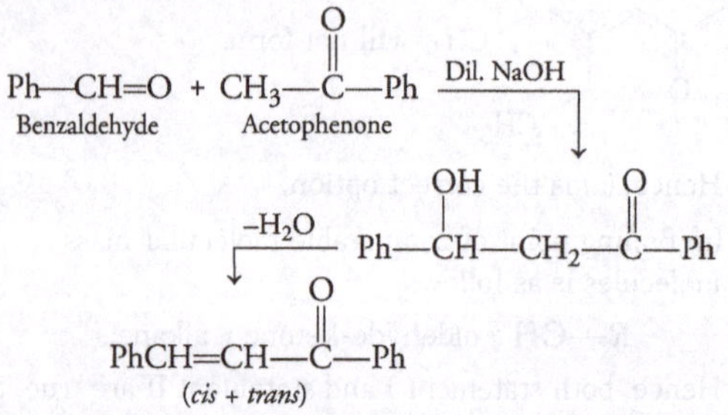

It is cross aldol condensation or Claisen-Schmidt reaction or Claisen reaction.

14. (b)

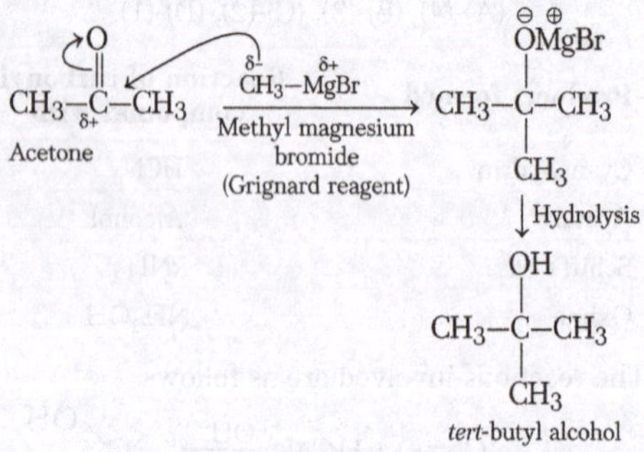

15. (b) Aldehydes and ketones containing α—H atoms undergo aldol condensation in presence of dilute alkali as catalyst to give α, β- unsaturated compound with the elimination of H_2O molecule.

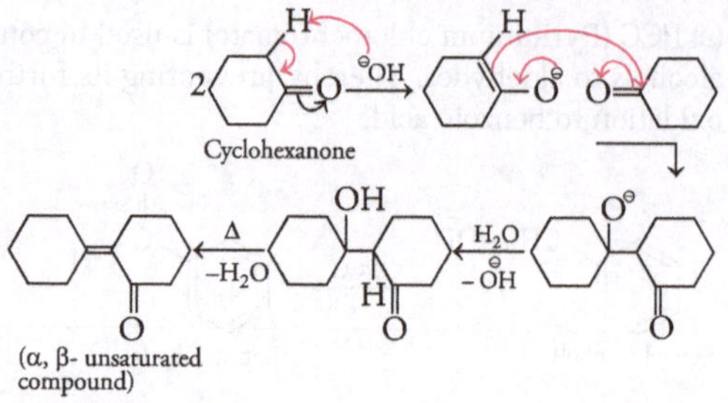

16. (c) Aldehydes gives silver mirror test. Thus, 'X' may be alcohol which is oxidised by Cu and gives aldehydes. Therefore, A is acetaldehyde (CH_3CHO).

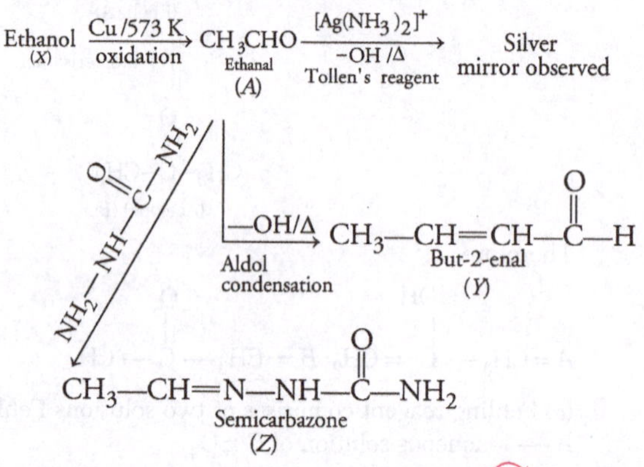

17. (d)

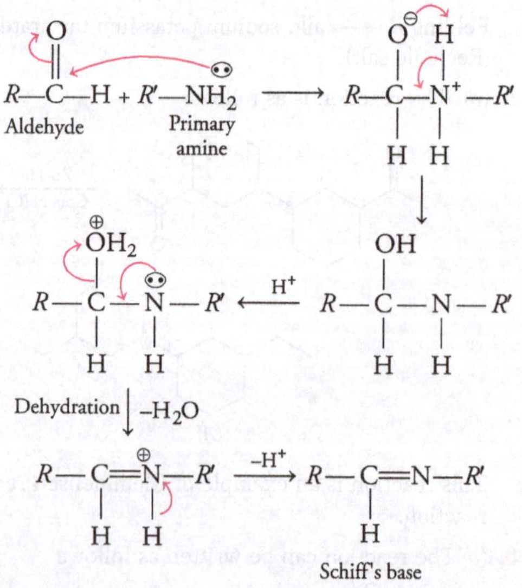

18. (b) In presence of Pd-catalyst, selective reduction of α, β-unsaturated carbonyl is observed as hydrogenation takes place to carbon-carbon double bond.

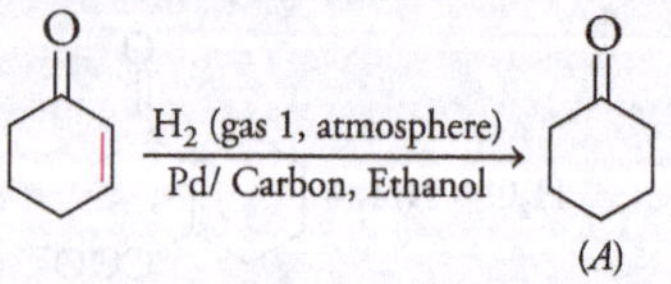

19. (*b*) Keto-enol tautomerism is represented as

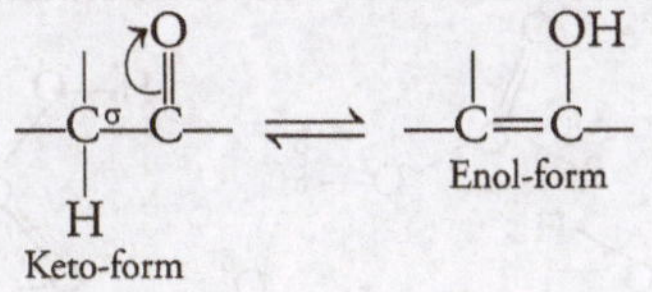

20. (*c*) Since, the compound *X* yields phenyl hydrazone and gives negative response to the iodoform test and Tollen's test, it must contain a C=O group but is neither a methyl ketone nor an aldehyde.

The structure of *X* having molecular formula $C_5H_{10}O$. could be

$$CH_3-CH_2-\overset{O}{\overset{\|}{C}}-CH_2-CH_3$$

3-pentanone

21. (*a*)

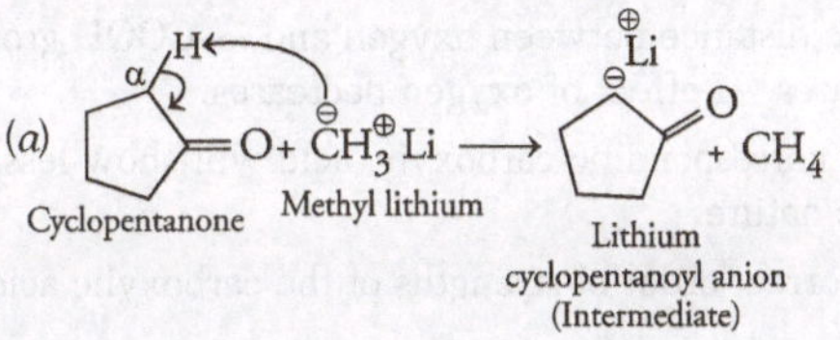

Here, CH_3Li abstract an active proton from cyclo pentanone forming methane leaving behind an intermediate lithium cyclopentanoyl anion.

22. (*d*) The reactivity towards nucleophilic addition reaction is enhanced by electron withdrawing group ($-NO_2$) and reduced by electron donating group ($-CH_3$).

Between aldehydes and ketones, aldehdyes are more reactive towards nucleophilic addition reaction.

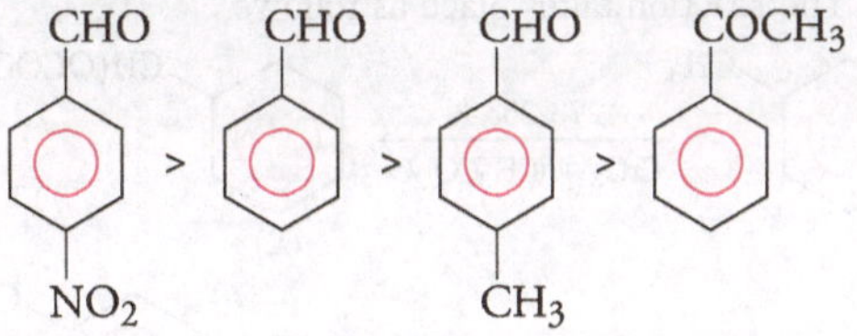

23. (*c*) The correct match is A-4, B-1, C-2, D-3.

A. 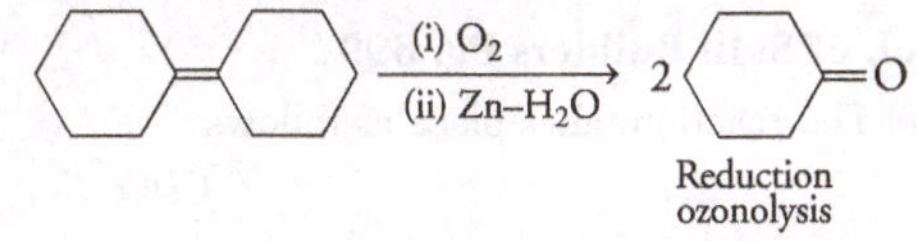

B. 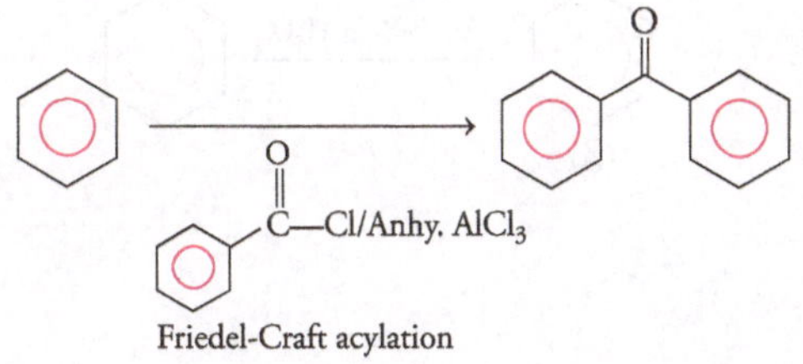

C. 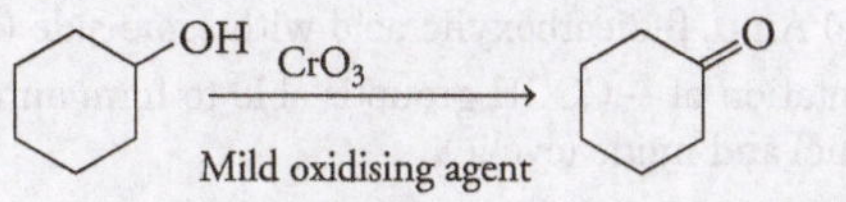

D. 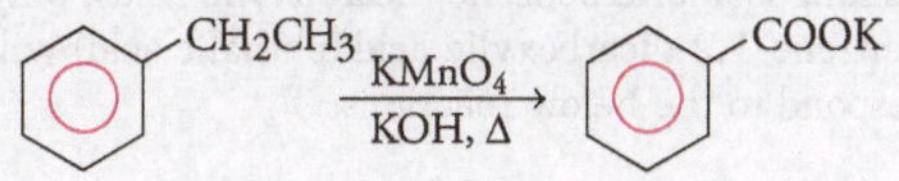

24. (*c*)

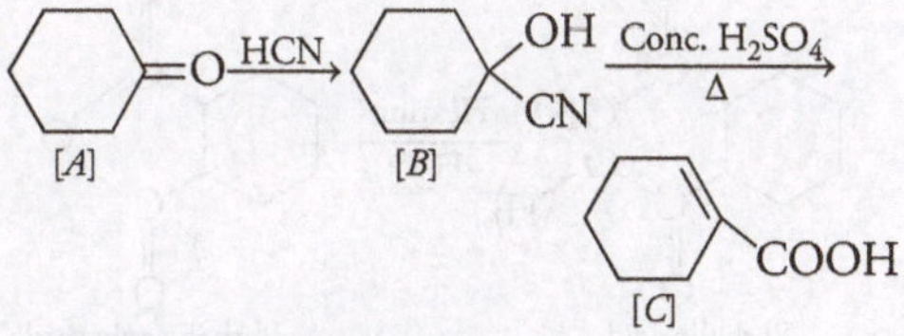

25. (*a*)

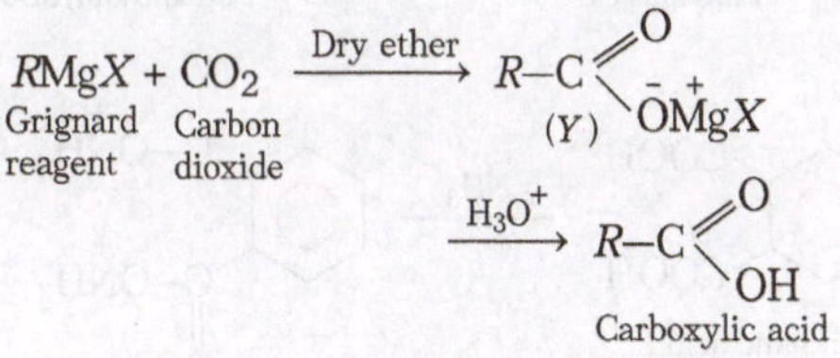

26. (*d*)

A. **Gattermann-Koch reaction** Benzene or its derivatives are treated with CO and HCl in presence of anhydrous $AlCl_3$ / CuCl to give benzaldehyde.

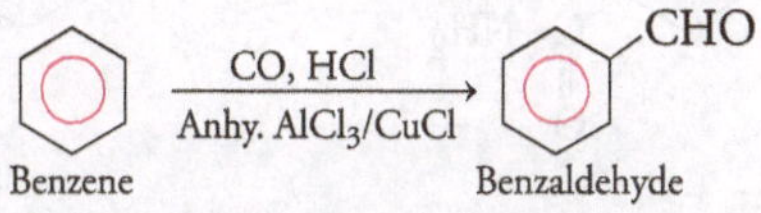

B. **Haloform reaction** Treatment of carbonyl compound having atleast one methyl group attached to the C=O with X_2 / NaOH or NaO*X* to give sodium salt of carboxylic acid and haloform.

$$\underset{\text{Aldehyde}}{R-\overset{O}{\overset{\|}{C}}-CH_3} + NaOX \longrightarrow R-\overset{O}{\overset{\|}{C}}-O^{\ominus}Na^{\oplus} + CHX_3$$

C. **Esterification** Carboxylic acid reacts with an alcohol in acidic medium to give ester.

$$\underset{\text{Alcohol}}{R-CH_2-OH} + \underset{\text{Acid}}{R'COOH} \xrightarrow{\text{Conc. } H_2SO_4} \underset{\text{Ester}}{R-CH_2-O-\overset{O}{\overset{\|}{C}}-R'}$$

D. **Hell-Volhard Zelinsky reaction** Treatment of carboxylic acid having α-hydrogen with PX_3 or X_2/ Red P to produce α-halocarboxylic acid.

$$\underset{\text{Carboxylic acid}}{R-CH_2-\overset{O}{\overset{\|}{C}}-OH} \xrightarrow[\text{(ii) } H_2O]{\text{(i) } X_2\text{/Red P}} \underset{\alpha\text{-halocarboxylic acid}}{R-\underset{X}{\underset{|}{CH}}-\overset{O}{\overset{\|}{C}}-OH}$$

Hence, correct match is A-2, B-3, C-4, D-1.

27. (*a*) (a) An α, β-dicarboxylic acid with same-side (*syn*) orientation of −COOH group is able to form anhydride (cyclic) and imide (cyclic).

Among isomeric benzene dicarboxylic acids, only benzene-1,2-dicarboxylic acid (phthalic acid) will respond to the below reactions.

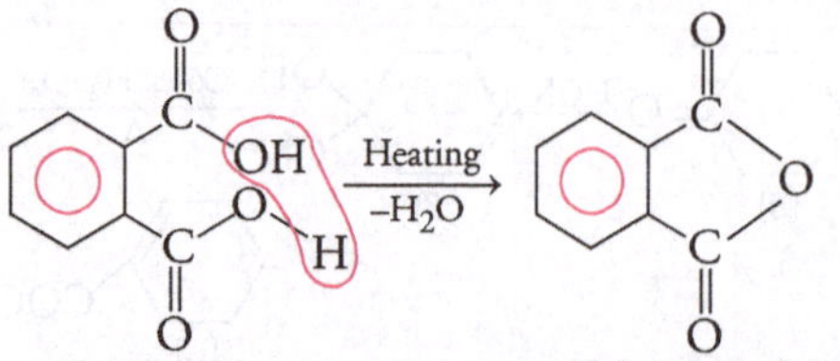

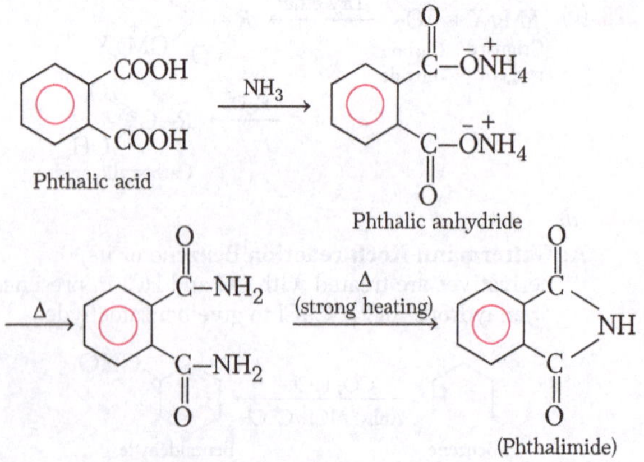

28. (*a*) Phthalic acid reacts with ammonia to give ammonium phthalate salt which on further heating at high temperature gives phthalamide.

Further on heating removes ammonia is phthalimide is formed.

The reaction takes place as follows

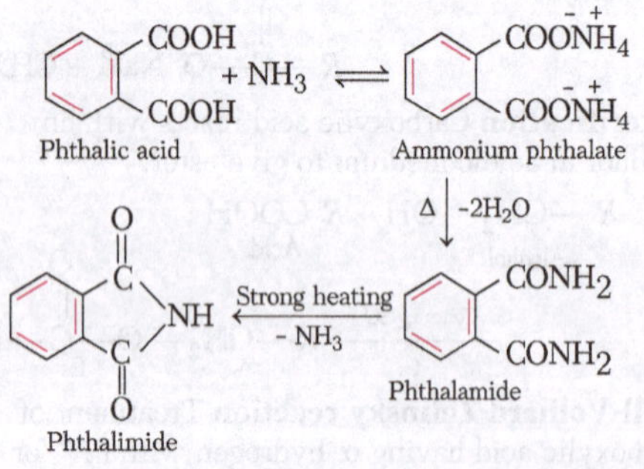

29. (*d*) Carboxylic acids have higher boiling points than aldehyde, ketones and even alcohols of comparable molecular mass because of the extent of intermolecular-hydrogen bonding with water, due to which they exist as associated molecules.

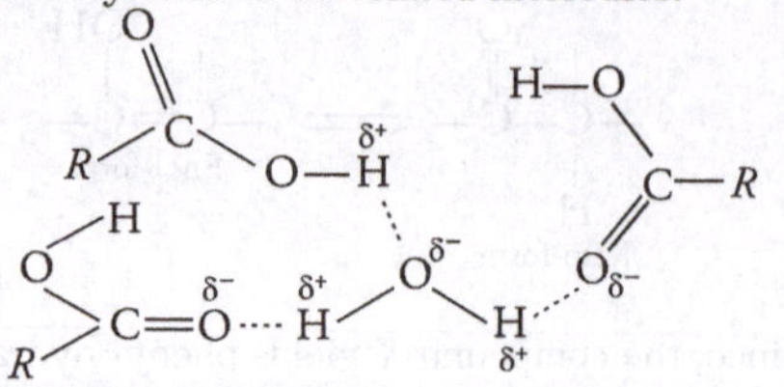

The hydrogen bonds are not completely broken in the vapour state. In fact mostly carboxylic acids exist as dimer in the vapour state or aprotic solvent.

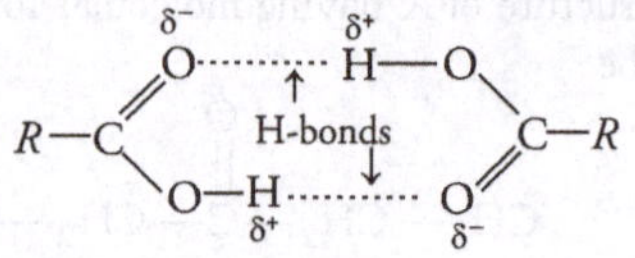

30. (*b*) The oxygen atom present in the ring shows *I*-effect. As the distance between oxygen and —COOH group increases, −*I*-effect of oxygen decreases.

Thus, corresponding carboxylic acid will show less acidic nature.

The correct order of strengths of the carboxylic acids is

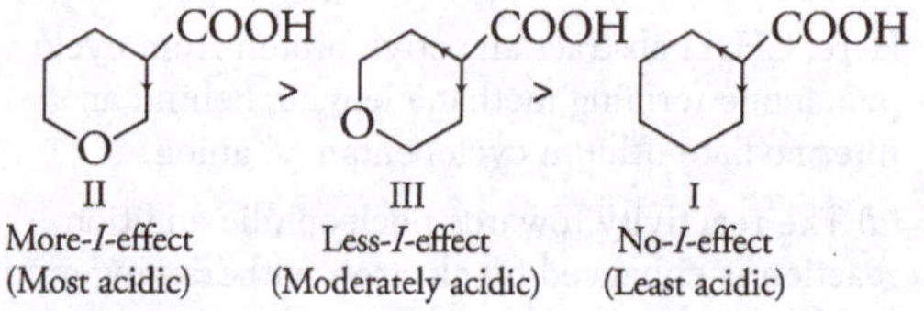

Skill Builder

- **Sol. of Skill Builders Pg. 398**

(*b*) The reaction takes place as follows

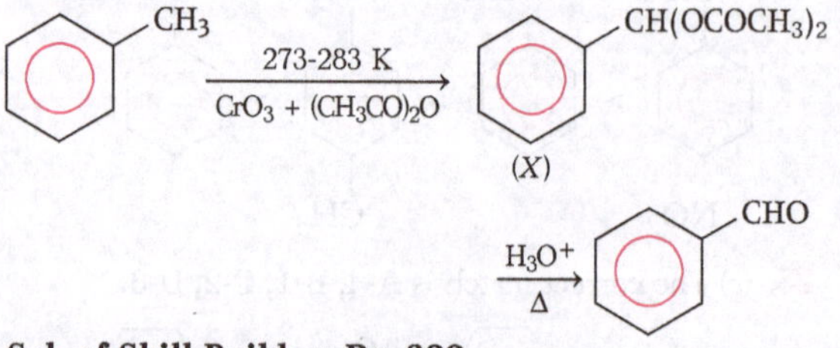

- **Sol. of Skill Builders Pg. 399**

(*b*) The reaction takes place as follows

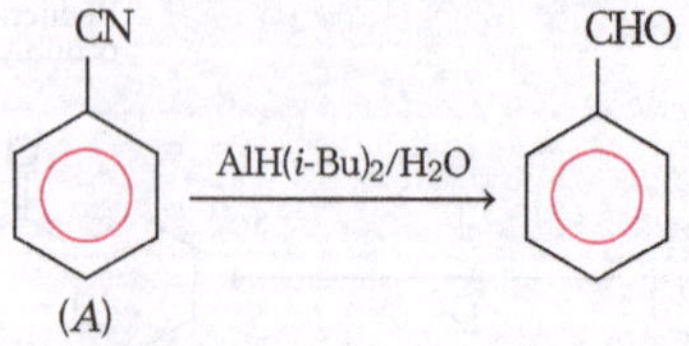

- **Sol. of Skill Builders Pg. 408**

  (*c*) Acetone on reaction with hydrazine followed by heating with potassium hydroxide in high boiling solvent such as ethylene glycol gives propane.

$$(CH_3)_2C{=}O \xrightarrow[-H_2O]{NH_2{-}NH_2} (CH_3)_2C{=}NNH_2 \xrightarrow[\text{Ethylene glycol}]{KOH,\ \Delta} \underset{\text{Propane}}{CH_3CH_2CH_3} + N_2$$

- **Sol. of Skill Builders Pg. 414**

  (*d*) The reaction takes place as follows

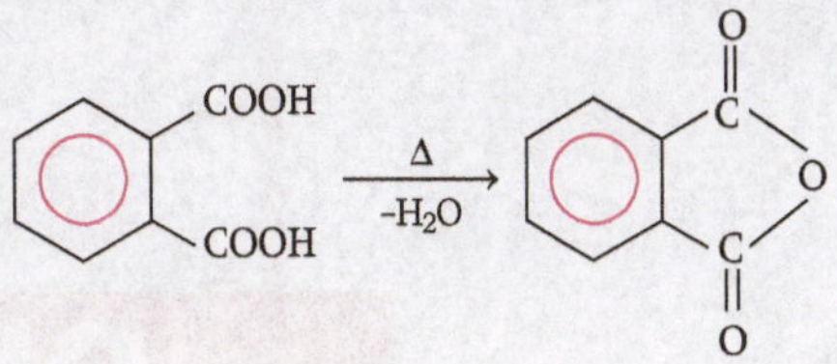

- **Sol. of Skill Builders Pg. 416**

  (*a*) As the distance between electron withdrawing group and —COOH group increases, acidic nature increases.

  Thus, the correct order of strength of carboxylic acids are as follows

$$I > III > II$$

For deeper insight
Scan the QR Code

Chapter 10

Amines

Learning Objectives

Module-I

- Classification
- Structure
- Nomenclature
- Isomerism
- Methods of Preparation
- Physical Properties
- Chemical Properties

Module-II

- Classification
- Nomenclature and Isomerism
- Methods of Preparation
- Physical Properties
- Chemical Properties

Module-III

- Methods of Preparation
- Physical Properties
- Chemical Properties

Chapter Overview with NEET Connection

This chapter is useful for the learning of preparation, basicity and diazotisation of amines. It will be difficult to learn and understand chapter like biomolecules specially proteins without gripping this chapter.

Special format questions can be easily framed on the following topics of this chapter.

- Hoffmann bromamide degradation reactions
- Gabriel phthalimide synthesis.
- Basicity of amines
- Coupling reaction of benzene diazonium salt.

For better understanding of this chapter a grip over inductive effect, resonance Lewis acid, Lewis base, nomenclature etc., is required.

As the foundation of basicity of amines is related to their structure, hence along with understanding of Lewis concept a prerequisite of structures of compounds is also required.

Introduction

Amines constitute an important class of organic compounds. These are derived by replacing one or more hydrogen atom(s) of ammonia molecule by alkyl or aryl group(s). That's why, these are also known as **derivatives of ammonia**. Amines are the most important organic compounds as they occur among proteins, vitamins, alkaloids and hormones.

Further, these are other important nitrogen containing organic compounds like diazonium salts, cyanides etc.

They are the most reactive derivatives of aromatic primary amines. In this chapter, we will study about each of them in a sequential manner.

Module 1

Aliphatic Amines

- Classification
- Structure
- Nomenclature
- Isomerism
- Methods of Preparation
- Physical Properties
- Chemical Properties

Classification

Aliphatic amines are called **alkyl derivatives of ammonia.** These are further classified as primary (RNH_2 or 1°) , secondary (R_2NH or 2°) and tertiary (R_3N or 3°) depending upon the number of hydrogen atoms replaced by alkyl groups in ammonia molecule.

Amines are said to be simple when all the alkyl or aryl groups are same and mixed when they are different. If the number of H-atoms attached to N-atom is *n*, then degree of amine is $(3-n)°$. Degree and functional group of various amines are shown below.

- R—N(H)—H; $n = 2$, 1° (primary), $—NH_2$ (amino-group)
- R_2NH ; $n = 1$, 2° (secondary), —NH— (imino-group)
- R—N(R)—R; $n = 0$, 3° (tertiary), —N< (tertiary nitrogen atom)

Structure

The nitrogen atom in amines is sp^3-hybridised. The three alkyl groups are at the corners of a tetrahedron and their shape is trigonal pyramidal.

The bond angle becomes lesser than 109.5° due to the bond pair-lone pair repulsion (e.g. bond angle for trimethylamine is 108°).

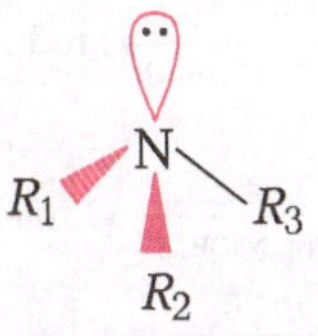

Pyramidal shape

Nomenclature

In common system, aliphatic amines are named as **alkylamines** as one word.

But in systematic IUPAC nomenclature, they are named as alkanamines by adding the suffix "amine" to the name of the chain to which NH_2 group is attached with replacement of the final '–e'.

In case, more than one amino group is present at different positions in the parent chains, their positions are specified by giving numbers to the carbon atoms bearing $—NH_2$ groups and suitable prefix such as di, tri etc., is attached to the amine. To name 2° and 3° amines. Locant N is used to designate substituent attached to N-atom.

e.g.

	$CH_3CH_2NH_2$	$CH_3CH_2CH_2N(CH_2CH_3)—CH_3$
Common name	Ethylamine	Ethylmethylpropylamine
IUPAC name	Ethanamine	N-ethyl-N-methyl-1-propanamine

$NH_2—CH_2—CH_2—NH_2$

Common name	Ethylenediamine
IUPAC name	Ethane-1,2-diamine

In the IUPAC system, the substituent $—NH_2$ is called the **amino group.**

e.g. $H_2NCH_2CH_2OH$ (2-aminoethanol) $H_2NCH_2CH_2C(=O)—OH$ (3-aminopropanoic acid)

Isomerism

Amines show chain, position and functional isomerism as well as they show metamerism too.

Metamerism is present in those molecules that have same molecular formula but differ with respect to the alkyl groups on either sides of the nitrogen atom.

e.g. $C_2H_5NHC_2H_5$ (N-ethylethanamine) $CH_3—NHCH(CH_3)_2$ (N-methylpropan-2-amine)

Concept ladder

- When alkyl groups of a tertiary amine are different, then amine will be chiral. There should be two enantiomeric forms of the tertiary amine. These enantiomers are impossible to resolute as they interconvert rapidly. The barrier of interconversion is 25 kJ mol^{-1} only. This interconversion is called as **pyramidal or nitrogen inversion.**

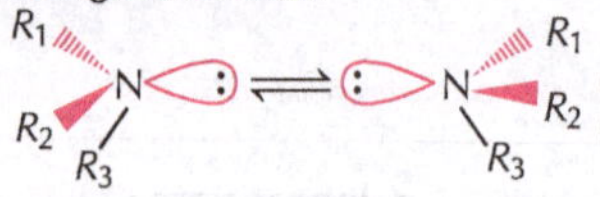

(cannot be resolved due to rapid interconversion)

- However, ammonium salts cannot undergo inversion because they do not have an unshared pair of electrons. Therefore, these quaternary NH_4^+ salts with four different groups are chiral and can be resolved into separate enantiomers.

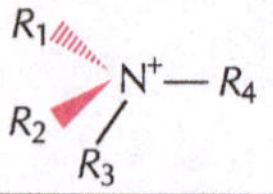

(can be resolved, chiral)

Methods of Preparation

Amines are generally prepared by the following methods.

Ammonolysis of Alkyl Halides

Alkyl halide on reaction with an ethanolic solution of ammonia undergoes nucleophilic substitution reaction by S_N2 mechanism in which the halogen atom is replaced by an amino ($—NH_2$) group. In this process cleavage of the C—X bond by ammonia molecule is known as **ammonolysis.**

The reaction is carried out in a sealed tube at 373 K. The primary amine thus obtained behaves as a nucleophile and can further react with alkyl halide to form secondary and tertiary amines and eventually quaternary ammonium salt.

$$R—Cl + NH_3 \xrightarrow{C_2H_5OH} R—\ddot{N}H_2$$

$$\underset{(1°)}{R\ddot{N}H_2} \xrightarrow[-HX]{RX} \underset{(2°)}{R_2\ddot{N}H} \xrightarrow[-HX]{RX} \underset{(3°)}{R_3\ddot{N}} \xrightarrow{RX} \underset{\text{Quaternary ammonium salt}}{R_4\overset{+}{N}X^-}$$

This reaction involves nucleophilic attack of NH_3 molecule (through lone pair) on alkyl halide by S_N2 mechanism. The free amine can be obtained from ammonium salt by treatment with a strong base.

$$R—\overset{+}{N}H_3X^- + NaOH \longrightarrow R—NH_2 + H_2O + \overset{+}{N}aX^-$$

The order of reactivity of halides with amines is

$$RI > RBr > RCl.$$

It should be noted that ammonolysis gives the highest yield with primary halides (where substitution predominates) and is of no use with tertiary alkyl halides (where elimination predominates).

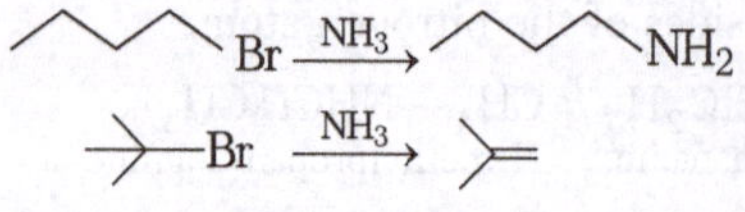

(substitution)

(elimination)

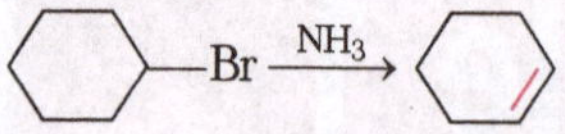

(elimination)

Ammonolysis has the disadvantage of yielding a mixture of 1°, 2° and 3° amines and also a quaternary ammonium salt. Due to which it is difficult to separate them. Moreover this method does not allow the preparation of aniline and other aromatic amine.

NEET Close-up

Example Similar to PYQ Asked in NEET 2023

Which of the following reactions will not give primary amine as the product?

(a) $CH_3—CH_2—Cl \xrightarrow[\text{(ii) Reduction}]{\text{(i) Ethanolic NaCN}}$ Products

(b) $CH_3—CN \xrightarrow[\text{(ii) Na(Hg)/}C_2H_5OH]{\text{(i) }H_2/Ni}$ Products

(c) $CH_3—\overset{O}{\overset{\|}{C}}—NH_2 \xrightarrow{Br_2/NaOH}$ Products

(d) $CH_3—CH_2—Cl \xrightarrow[\text{(ii) }C_2H_5Cl\text{ (1 mole)}]{\text{(i) }NH_3}$ Product

Sol. (*d*) Among the given reactions, only (d) will not give primary amine as the product.

- $CH_3—CH_2Cl \xrightarrow[\text{NaCN}]{\text{(i) Ethanolic}} CH_3—CH_2—CN \xrightarrow{\text{Reduction}} \underset{(1° \text{ amine})}{CH_3—CH_2—CH_2—NH_2}$

- $CH_3—CN \xrightarrow[\text{(ii) Na(Hg)/}C_2H_5OH]{\text{(i) }H_2/Ni} \underset{(1° \text{ amine})}{CH_3—CH_2—NH_2}$

- $CH_3—\overset{O}{\overset{\|}{C}}—NH_2 \xrightarrow{Br_2/NaOH} \underset{(1° \text{ amine})}{CH_3—NH_2}$

- $CH_3—CH_2—Cl \xrightarrow{\text{(i) }NH_3} C_2H_5—NH_2 \xrightarrow{C_2H_5—Cl} \underset{(2° \text{ amine})}{C_2H_5—\overset{H}{\overset{|}{N}}—C_2H_5}$

Skill Builder

Which of the following reactions will not give primary amine as the product?

(a) $C_2H_5—CH_2—Br \xrightarrow[\text{(ii) Reduction}]{\text{(i) Ethanolic NaCN}}$ Product

(b) $C_2H_5—CN \xrightarrow[\text{(ii) Na(Hg)/}C_2H_5OH]{\text{(i) }H_2/Ni}$ Product

(c) $C_2H_5—\overset{O}{\overset{\|}{C}}—NH_2 \xrightarrow[\text{(ii) NaOH, }\Delta]{\text{(i) }Br_2}$ Product

(d) $C_2H_5—CH_2—Br \xrightarrow[\text{(ii) }C_2H_5Br\text{ (1 mole)}]{\text{(i) }NH_3}$ Product

For more practice Refer to Q.7 and Q. 11 of step up practice 1.

Reduction of Nitriles

Reduction of nitriles with lithium aluminium hydride ($LiAlH_4$) or catalytic dehydrogenation gives primary amines. Generally, it is carried out in the presence of reagents like H_2 and Ni.

$$CH_3C\equiv N \xrightarrow[\text{or } LiAlH_4/\text{ether} \\ \text{or } Na(Hg)/C_2H_5OH]{H_2/Ni} CH_3CH_2NH_2$$

This is an excellent method for ascent of amine series, i.e., for preparation of amines containing one carbon atom more than the starting amine. This is a step-up synthesis.

Concept ladder Reduction of nitriles to primary amines by using Na and alcohol is called as **Mendius reaction.**

Reduction of Nitro Compounds

Nitro alkanes react with hydrogen in the presence of Ni or finely divided Pt or Pd to give primary amines. This type of reduction is called **catalytic reduction.**

$$R{-}NO_2 + 3H_2 \xrightarrow[\text{Ethanol}]{Ni/Pt} R{-}NH_2 + 2H_2O$$

Reduction of nitroalkanes can also occur with active metals like Fe, Sn, Zn in presence of conc. HCl.

$$CH_3CH_2NO_2 + 6[H] \xrightarrow{Sn/\text{conc. HCl}} CH_3CH_2NH_2 + 2H_2O$$

This reaction is preferred in aromatic amines.

Mentor's TIP

If a compound contains some easily hydrogenated group such as carbon-carbon multiple bond ($>C=C<$ or $-C\equiv C-$) then this method of reduction is not used.

Reduction of Amides

The amides can easily be reduced to primary amines by using Na/C_2H_5OH or $LiAlH_4$ in presence of dry ether.

$$\underset{\text{Acetamide}}{CH_3{-}\overset{O}{\overset{\|}{C}}{-}NH_2} \xrightarrow[Na/C_2H_5OH]{LiAlH_4/\text{Dry ether}} \underset{\text{Ethanamine}}{CH_3CH_2NH_2} + H_2O$$

Hoffmann Bromamide Degradation Reaction

Primary acid amides react with an aqueous or ethanolic solution of NaOH or KOH and Br_2 to give primary amines. This method yields amine that contains one carbon atom less than the reactant (amide).

$$\underset{\text{Amide}}{R{-}\overset{O}{\overset{\|}{C}}{-}NH_2} + Br_2 + 4NaOH \xrightarrow{\Delta} \underset{1^\circ \text{ amine}}{RNH_2} + 2NaBr + Na_2CO_3 + 2H_2O$$

e.g. $$\underset{\text{Propanamide}}{C_2H_5{-}\overset{O}{\overset{\|}{C}}{-}NH_2} + Br_2 + NaOH \xrightarrow{\Delta} \underset{\text{Ethylamine}}{C_2H_5NH_2} + 2NaBr + Na_2CO_3 + 2H_2O$$

NEET Snapshot

Propanamide reacts with ethanolic sodium hydroxide and bromine to give ethylamine. ***[NEET 2020]***

In the given degradation reaction, the migration of an alkyl or aryl group takes place from carbonyl carbon of the amide to the nitrogen and involves intermolecular rearrangement to give final product.

Gabriel Phthalimide Synthesis

This method is used for the preparation of aliphatic as well as aromatic primary amines (having electron withdrawing group at *o*-and *p*-positions).

Phthalic anhydride is converted into phthalimide thus, blocking two H-atoms of NH_3 for further reaction with *RX*.

Then this, phthalimide on treatment with *alc.* KOH forms potassium salt of phthalimide which on heating with suitable alkyl halide forms N-substituted phthalimides. These on alkaline or acid hydrolysis produces the corresponding 1° amine and phthalic acid as by product.

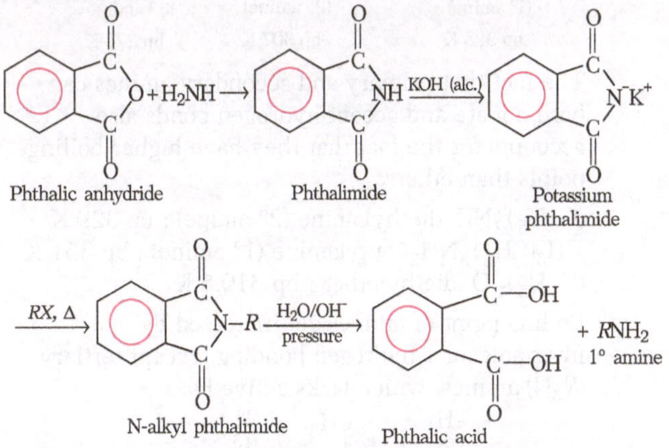

1° aromatic amine cannot be synthesised by this method. This is because aryl halides do not undergo nucleophilic substitution reaction with anion formed by phthalimide.

Concept ladder

Acid chloride react with sodium azide in the presence of basic medium (NaOH) to form primary amine. This reaction is known as **Curtius degradation method.**

$$\underset{\text{Acyl chloride}}{R-\overset{O}{\overset{\|}{C}}-Cl} \xrightarrow{NaN_3} \underset{\text{Acyl azide}}{R-\overset{O}{\overset{\|}{C}}-N_3} \xrightarrow[-N_2]{} \underset{\text{Alkyl isocyanate}}{R-N=C=O}$$

$$\xrightarrow[\Delta]{2NaOH} RNH_2 + Na_2CO_3$$

In this reaction intramolecular alkyl shift is very similar to that of Hofmann bromamide degradation.

Physical Properties

Some important physical properties of amines are discussed below.

(i) **Physical state** Lower amines are gases or low-boiling liquids, with a characteristic ammonia like smell. Higher amines are liquids and have fishy odour.

(ii) **Boiling point** Amines are more polar than alkanes but less polar than alcohols. For similarly constituted compounds, boiling points and dipole moments of alkyl amines are higher than those of alkanes but lower than those of alcohols.
e.g.

Compound	Boiling point	Dipole moment
$CH_3CH_2CH_3$	231 K	0 D
$CH_3CH_2NH_2$	290 K	1.2 D
CH_3CH_2OH	351 K	1.7 D

- Among isomeric amines, primary amines have the highest boiling points and tertiary amines have the lowest.

$$\underset{\substack{(1^\circ\text{ amine})\\ \text{bp 323 K}}}{CH_3CH_2CH_2NH_2} > \underset{\substack{(2^\circ\text{ amine})\\ \text{bp 307 K}}}{CH_3CH_2NHCH_3} > \underset{\substack{(3^\circ\text{ amine})\\ \text{bp 276 K}}}{(CH_3)_3N}$$

- The fact that primary and secondary amines can both donate and accept hydrogen bonds also accounts for the fact that they have higher boiling points than ethers.
  $(C_2H_5)_2NH$ diethylamine (2° amine) : bp 329 K
  $CH_3(CH_2)_3NH_2$ butylamine (1° amine) : bp 351 K
  $(C_2H_5)_2O$ diethylether : bp 310.5 K
- Boiling point of amines get increased by intermolecular hydrogen bonding [except tertiary (R_3N) amines, which lacks active H].

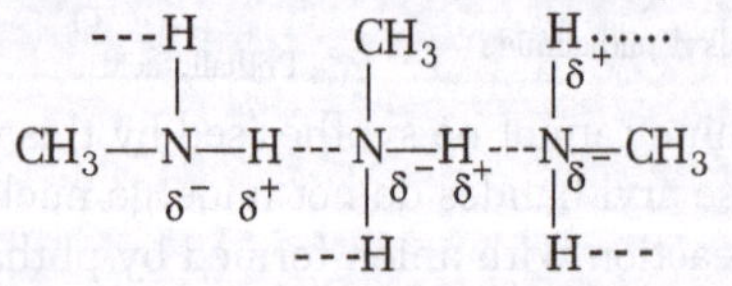

Primary amines have two, secondary amines have one while tertiary amines have no hydrogen linked to nitrogen. Thus, among isomeric amines, primary amines have the highest while tertiary amines have the lowest boiling point.

(iii) **Solubility** All three types of amines (1°, 2° and 3°) having low molecular weight (gases) are highly soluble in water and other organic solvents like alcohols due to intermolecular H-bonding. But solubility decreases with increase in number of carbon atoms (molecular weights).

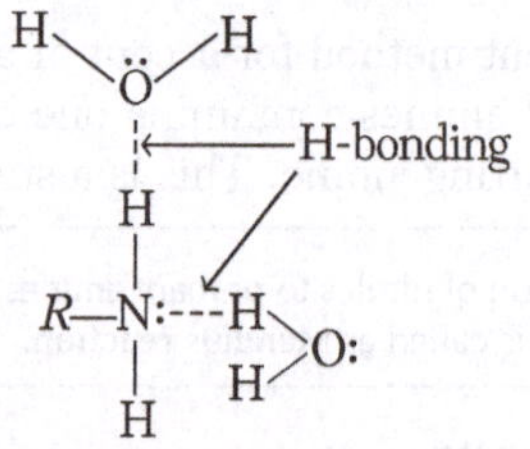

Chemical Reactions

Difference in electronegativity between nitrogen and hydrogen atoms and the presence of unshared pair of electrons over the nitrogen atom makes amines reactive. Morever amines behave as nucleophiles due to presence of unshared electron pair.

Some of the chemical reactions (properties) of amines are described below

Basic Character

Amines react with mineral acid (or in water) to form ammonium salts which shows that they are basic in nature. They behave as Lewis base due to presence of unshared pair of electrons on nitrogen atom.

$$R\ddot{N}H_2 + H_2O \rightleftharpoons RNH_3^+ + OH^-$$

$$K_b = \frac{[R-\overset{+}{N}H_3][\overset{-}{O}H]}{[R-\ddot{N}H_2]}$$

Here, K_b is called dissociation constant for base. Greater the value of K_b, stronger will be the base. Basic character of amines, can also be expressed in terms of pK_b values.

$$pK_b = -\log K_b$$

Smaller the pK_b values, stronger is the base.

Alkylamine *versus* Ammonia

Basicity of amines is related to their structure. Basic character of amine depends upon the ease of formation of the cation by accepting a proton from the acid. The more stable the cation is relative to amine, more basic is amine.

$$R-\underset{H}{\underset{|}{\overset{H}{\overset{|}{N}}}}\!: + H^+ \rightleftharpoons R-\underset{H}{\underset{|}{\overset{H}{\overset{|}{N^+}}}}-H$$

The order of basicity of alkyl amines and ammonia in gaseous and aqueous phase follows different order, are discussed below.

Case I. **Basicity in gaseous phase**

Here, the electron releasing nature of alkyl group (R) pushes the electrons toward nitrogen and makes the unshared pair more available for sharing with the proton of the acid.

Also, the substituted ammonium ion formed from the amine gets stabilised due to the dispersal of positive charge by +*I*-effect of '*R*' groups. Hence, alkyl amines are stronger bases than ammonia.

We can conclude that the basic nature of aliphatic amines should increase with increase in the number of alkyl groups.

Therefore, order of basicity in gaseous phase is as follows : 3° amine > 2° amine > 1° amine > NH_3

But the trend is not the same in aqueous state.

Case II. **Basicity in aqueous phase**

The substituted ammonium cation is stabilised by the following factors.

- Electron releasing effect of the alkyl group (+*I*).
- Solvation effect (greater the size of the ion lesser will be the solvation and the less stabilised is the ion).
- Steric hinderance.

Order of stability of solvated ions

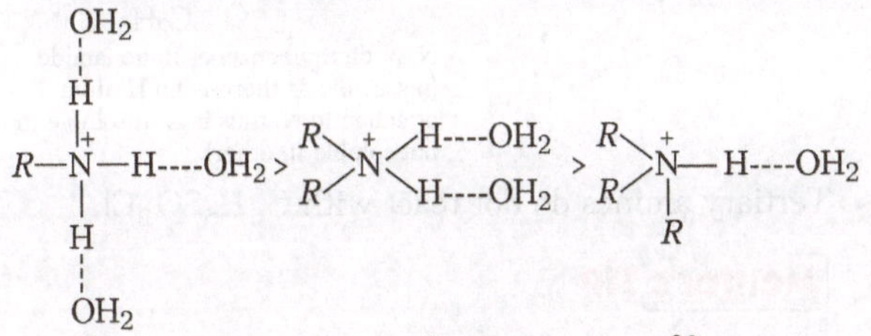

1° 2° 3°

Greater is the stability of the substituted ammonium cation, stronger will be the corresponding amine as a base. Thus, the order of basicity of aliphatic amines should be 1° > 2° > 3°.

Secondly, when alkyl group is small (such as $—CH_3$ group) there is no steric hindrance to H-bonding but when the alkyl group is bigger then there will be steric hinderance to H-bonding. Therefore, the order of basic strength is different when different alkyl groups ($—CH_3$ or $—C_2H_5$) are attached. The order are given below

- In case of methyl substituted amines.

$$\underset{(2°)}{(CH_3)_2NH} > \underset{(1°)}{CH_3NH_2} > \underset{(3°)}{(CH_3)_3N} > NH_3$$

- In case of ethyl substituted amines.

$$\underset{(2°)}{(C_2H_5)_2NH} > \underset{(3°)}{(C_2H_5)_3N} > \underset{(1°)}{C_2H_5NH_2} > NH_3$$

Concept ladder
Basicity is controlled by the availability of the lone pair (on the N-atom) for protonation. Due to +*I* effect of alkyl group the lone pair becomes more available in amines. This increase the basicity of the amines relative to NH_3.

Alkylation

Aliphatic amines undergo alkylation on reaction with alkyl halides.

$$CH_3NH_2 \xrightarrow{CH_3X} (CH_3)_2NH \xrightarrow{CH_3X} (CH_3)_3N \xrightarrow{CH_3X} [(CH_3)_4]N^+X^-$$

Acylation

Aliphatic amines react with acid chlorides or anhydrides or esters by nucleophilic substitution reaction. This reaction is known as acylation to give respective amides. This reaction is carried out in the presence of a base, stronger than the amine like pyridine, which removes HCl so formed and shifts the equilibrium to the right hand side.

e.g. $$\underset{\text{Ethanamine}}{C_2H_5NH_2} + \underset{\text{Ethanoyl chloride}}{CH_3COCl} \xrightarrow{\text{Base}} \underset{\text{N-ethylethanamide}}{C_2H_5NH\overset{O}{\overset{\|}{C}}CH_3} + HCl$$

$$C_2H_5NH_2 + \underset{\text{Ethanoic anhydride}}{CH_3\underset{O}{\underset{\|}{C}}—O—\underset{O}{\underset{\|}{C}}CH_3} \xrightarrow{\text{Base}} \underset{\text{N-ethyl ethanamide}}{C_2H_5—\underset{H}{\underset{|}{\ddot{N}}}—\underset{O}{\underset{\|}{C}}CH_3} + CH_3COOH$$

Benzoylation

Aliphatic amines react with benzoyl chloride to form benzamide.

e.g. $$\underset{\text{Methanamine}}{CH_3NH_2} + \underset{\text{Benzoyl chloride}}{C_6H_5COCl} \longrightarrow \underset{\text{N-methylbenzamide}}{CH_3NHCOC_6H_5} + HCl$$

Carbylamine Reaction

Aliphatic amines on heating with chloroform and alcoholic KOH forms isocyanides or carbylamines which are foul smelling substances. Secondary and tertiary amines do not show this reaction.

e.g. $\underset{1^\circ \text{ amine}}{CH_3NH_2} + CHCl_3 + \underset{\text{Alcoholic}}{3KOH} \xrightarrow{\Delta} \underset{\substack{\text{Isocyanide} \\ \text{(carbylamines)}}}{CH_3NC} + 3KCl + 3H_2O$

This reaction is used to test 1°amines (both aromatic and aliphatic) are called carbylamine or isocyanide reaction.

Reaction with Nitrous Acid

Three classes of amines react differently with nitrous acid which is prepared *in situ* from a mineral acid and sodium nitrite. Aliphatic primary amines reacts with nitrous acid to form aliphatic diazonium salt which is unstable, thus liberate nitrogen gas.

$$\underset{1^\circ \text{amine}}{R{-}NH_2} + HONO \xrightarrow{NaNO_2 + HCl} [R{-}\overset{+}{N_2}\overset{-}{Cl}] \xrightarrow{H_2O} \underset{\text{Alcohol}}{ROH} + N_2\uparrow + HCl$$

RNH_2 is converted into ROH by HNO_2. Intermediate is a carbocation which may undergo rearrangement to give various products.

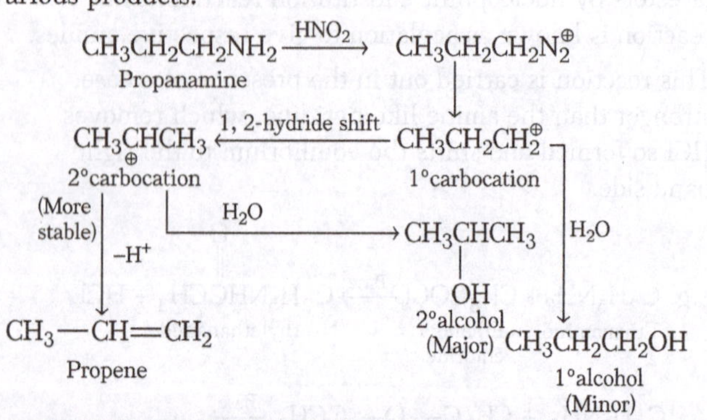

Concept ladder

Secondary aliphatic amines react with nitrous acid to form N-nitrosoamine which is yellow oily insoluble liquid.

Tertiary aliphatic amines reacts with nitrous acid to form trialkylammonium nitrite ($R_3\overset{+}{N}HNO_2^-$), that is soluble in water.

Reaction with Aryl Sulphonyl Chloride

Benzenesulphonyl chloride (Hinsberg's reagent) reacts with primary and secondary amines to form sulphonamide. This reaction is used to distinguish 1°, 2° and 3° amines.

- Primary amines react with benzene sulphonyl chloride to yield N-alkyl benzene sulphonamide.

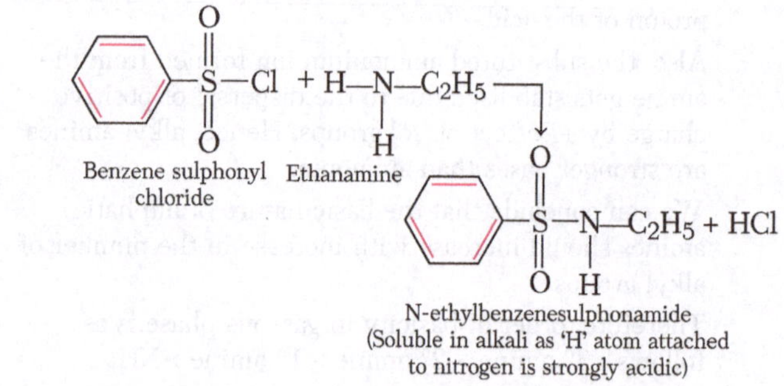

- Secondary amines react with $C_6H_5SO_2Cl$ to yield N, N-dialkylbenzenesulphonamide.

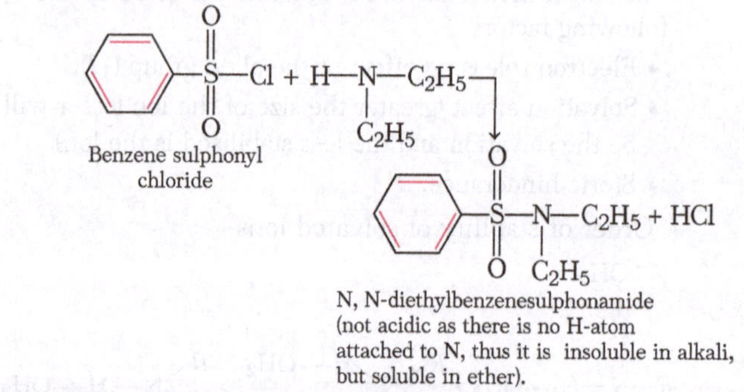

- Tertiary amines do not react with $C_6H_5SO_2Cl$.

Mentor's Tip

These days benzene sulphonyl chloride is replaced by sulphonyl chloride.

STEP UP Practice 1

1 Among the following compounds, which one is heterocyclic tertiary aromatic amine?
(a) Piperidine (b) N,N-dimethyl aniline
(c) *o*-toluidine (d) Pyridine

2 Consider the following statements.
Statement I Amines are pyramidal in shape.
Statement II N-atom is sp^3-hybridised in amines.
In the light of the above statements, choose the most appropriate answer from the options given below
(a) Both Statement I and Statement II are false.
(b) Statement I is true but Statement II is false.
(c) Statement I is false but Statement II is true.
(d) Both Statement I and Statement II are true.

3 The IUPAC nomenclature for the given compound is

$$CH_3CH_2CH_2—\underset{}{\overset{CH_2CH_3}{\overset{|}{N}}}—CH_3$$

(a) Ethylmethyl propylamine
(b) N-ethyl-N-methyl-1-propanamine
(c) N-methyl-N-ethyl-1-propanamine
(d) N-methyl ethanamine

4 Which of the following category of amine will show metamerism?
(a) Secondary amine (b) Primary amine
(c) Tertiary amine (d) Quaternary amine

5 Consider the following compounds,

(i) $CH_3CH_2—\overset{CH_3}{\overset{|}{N}}—CH_2CH_3$ (ii) $CH_3CH_2NHCH_2CH_3$

(iii) $CH_3CH_2CH_2—\overset{CH_3}{\overset{|}{N}}—CH_2CH_3$ (iv) $CH_3CH_2—\overset{NH_2}{\overset{|}{CH}}—CH_3$

(v) $CH_3—\overset{CH_2CH_3}{\overset{|}{N}}—CH_3$

How many compounds possesses a chiral nitrogen atom?
(a) 3 (b) 1 (c) 2 (d) 4

6 C_3H_9N cannot represent
(a) primary amine (b) secondary amine
(c) tertiary amine (d) quaternary ammonium salt

7 Which of the following is the best method of preparation of 1° aliphatic amines from alkyl halide
(a) Hofmann bromamide reaction (b) reaction with NH_3
(c) Gabriel phthalimide reaction (d) Sandmeyer reaction

8 A primary amine is formed from an amide by the treatment with bromine and alkali. The primary amine has
(a) 1 carbon atom less than amide
(b) 1 carbon atom more than amide
(c) 1 hydrogen atom less than amide
(d) 1 hydrogen atom more than amide

9 Which of the following reaction is correctly matched with the product?
(a) $CH_3CN + H_3O^+ \longrightarrow CH_3CH_2NH_2$
(b) $CH_3CN + LiAlH_4 \longrightarrow CH_3CH_2NH_2$
(c) $CH_3CN + DIBAL\text{-}H/H_3O^+ \longrightarrow CH_3CH_2NH_2$
(d) $CH_3CN + CH_3MgBr/H_3O^+ \longrightarrow CH_3CH_2NH_2$

10 An isocyanide on hydrolysis gives
(a) N-substituted amide
(b) 1° amine and formic acid
(c) carboxylic acid and ammonia
(d) an amide

11 Which of the following is not the best method for preparation of only 1° amine?
(a) $CH_3Cl + NH_3 \xrightarrow{3CH_3Cl}$
(b) $CH_3Cl \xrightarrow{KCN} \xrightarrow{Sn/HCl}$
(c) $CH_3NH_2 \xrightarrow[\Delta]{CHCl_3/KOH} \xrightarrow{Sn/HCl}$
(d) $CH_3CN \xrightarrow{H_2/Ni}$

12 Among the following which one does not act as an intermediate in Hofmann rearrangement?
(a) $RNCO$ (b) $R\overset{O}{\overset{||}{C}}NH_2$
(c) $RCONHBr$ (d) None of these

13 Consider the following statements.
Statement I Hoffmann's bromamide reaction is given by primary amines.
Statement II Primary amines are more basic than secondary amines.
In the light of the above statements, choose the most appropriate answer from the options given below.
(a) Both Statement I and Statement II are false.
(b) Statement I is true but Statement II is false.
(c) Statement I is false but Statement II is true.
(d) Both Statement I and Statement II are true.

14 Which of the following reaction is incorrectly matched with the name for the given reactions?
(a) $RCONH_2 \xrightarrow{Br_2/NaOH, \Delta} RNH_2$ (Hofmann's bromamide)
(b) $RCOOH \xrightarrow{N_3H, \Delta} RNH_2$ (Schmidt)
(c) $RCOCl \xrightarrow[H_3O^+]{NaN_3} RNH_2$ (Ritter)
(d) $RCl \xrightarrow[NaOH]{KOH, Phthalimide} RNH_2$ (Gabriel's phthalimide)

15 Consider the following reaction.

$$RCOOH \xrightarrow{N_3H, \Delta} \text{Product 'P'}$$

Product P and name of reaction is

(a) RNH_2, Schmidt reaction (b) $RCONH_2$, Schmidt reaction
(c) $RCONH_2$, Hofmann reaction (d) NRH_2, Hofmann reaction

16 Ethylcyanide (A) can be converted to ethylamine (B) by

(a) $A \xrightarrow{Sn/HCl} B$ (b) $A \xrightarrow{H_3O^+} \xrightarrow[\Delta]{NH_3} \xrightarrow[\Delta]{Br_2/NaOH} B$

(c) $A \xrightarrow{LiAlH_4} B$ (d) $A \xrightarrow{Br_2/NaOH} B$

17 Select the incorrect statement about the following reaction.

$$R-Br + NaN_3 \xrightarrow{\text{Step I}} RN_3 \xrightarrow{\text{Step II}} R-NH_2$$

(a) Step I is an S_N2 reaction
(b) R—Br should be 1° or 2° alkyl bromide
(c) Step II uses $NaBH_4$ / H_2O or $LiAlH_4$
(d) Step I and Step II both represent an S_N2 reaction.

18 CH_3NHCH_3 by reductive amination using CH_2O changes to $(CH_3)_3N$ through which of the following intermediate?

(a) Carbinolamine $CH_3-\underset{\underset{CH_2OH}{|}}{N}-CH_3$
(b) Imine $CH_3N=CH_2$
(c) Formyldimethylamine $CH_3-\underset{\underset{CHO}{|}}{N}-CH_3$
(d) Amine $CH_3CH_2NH_2$

19 Select the correct statement.

(a) Methyl cyanide is reduced to ethylamine by $LiAlH_4$ / H^+.
(b) Methyl isocyanide is hydrolysed to ethylamine.
(c) Homologated 1° amide is obtained in the given process.

$$R-Br \xrightarrow{NaCN} \xrightarrow{LiAlH_4}$$

(d) Acetamide is reduced to methyl amine by $LiAlH_4$.

20 Consider the following statements.

Statement I Amines are polar compounds.
Statement II Amines possess electronegativity difference between nitrogen and carbon.

In the light of the above statements, choose the most appropriate answer from the options given below

(a) Both Statement I and Statement II are false.
(b) Statement I is true but Statement II is false.
(c) Statement I is false but Statement II is true.
(d) Both Statement I and Statement II are true.

21 Which of the following is most volatile?

(a) $CH_3CH_2CH_2NH_2$ (b) $(CH_3)_3N$
(c) $\begin{matrix} CH_3CH_2 \\ CH_3 \end{matrix}\rangle NH$ (d) $CH_3CH_2NH_2$

22 Boiling points are normally highest for

(a) tertiary amines (b) secondary amines
(c) primary amines (d) quaternary amines

23 The correct decreasing order of basic strength of given species H_2O, NH_3, OH^-, NH_2^- is .... .

(a) $NH_2^- > OH^- > NH_3 > H_2O$ (b) $OH^- > NH_2^- > H_2O > NH_3$
(c) $NH_3 > H_2O > NH_2^- > OH^-$ (d) $H_2O > NH_3 > OH^- > NH_2^-$

24 Amongst the following, the strongest base in aqueous medium is ....

(a) CH_3NH_2 (b) $NCCH_2NH_2$ (c) $(CH_3)_2NH$ (d) $C_6H_5NHCH_3$

25 Acid anhydrides on reaction with primary amines give ....

(a) amide (b) imide
(c) secondary amine (d) imine

26 Consider the following reaction.

$$CH_3\underset{\underset{CH_3}{|}}{C}H\overset{\overset{NH_2}{|}}{C}HCH_3 + O{=}N-OH \xrightarrow{H_2O/\bar{O}H}$$

Major product formed in above reaction is

(a) $CH_3\underset{\underset{CH_3}{|}}{C}H\overset{\overset{N=NOH}{|}}{C}HCH_3$ (b) $CH_3\underset{\underset{CH_3}{|}}{\overset{\overset{OH}{|}}{C}}CH_2CH_3$

(c) $CH_3\underset{\underset{CH_3}{|}}{C}H\overset{\overset{OH}{|}}{C}HCH_3$ (d) $CH_3\underset{\underset{CH_3}{|}}{C}HCH_2CH_3$

27 Consider the following reaction, $CH_3\underset{\underset{\oplus N(CH_3)_3OH^{\ominus}}{|}}{C}HCH_2CH_3 \xrightarrow{\Delta}$

Major alkene formed in above reaction is

(a) $CH_3CH{=}CHCH_3$ (b) $CH_2{=}CHCH_2CH_3$
(c) $(CH_3)_2C{=}CH_2$ (d) $(CH_3)_2C{=}C(CH_3)_2$

28 Primary amine reacts with carbon disulphide in the presence of excess of mercuric chloride and produce isothiocyanate. This reaction is known as

(a) Hoffmann's bromamide reaction
(b) Hoffmann mustard oil reaction
(c) Carbylamine reaction
(d) Mercuration-demercuration reaction

29 Consider the following gases,

(i) NH_3 (ii) N_2 (iii) H_2 (iv) C_2H_6 (v) CH_4

How many of them evolved when methylamine reacts with nitrous acid?

(a) 3 (b) 4 (c) 2 (d) 1

30 $RCH_2CH_2NH_2$ does not undergo E2 elimination. It is attributed that

(a) formation of unstable alkene
(b) $NH_2^{\ominus}$ is a very poor leaving group
(c) $NH_2^{\ominus}$ is a very good leaving group
(d) maximum basic nature

31 $\underset{(X)}{C_4H_{11}N} + HNO_2 \longrightarrow C_4H_{10}O$ (3° alcohol) hence, X will be

(a) $CH_3\overset{\overset{CH_3}{|}}{C}H-CH_2NH_2$
(b) $CH_3-CH_2-CH_2-CH_2-NH_2$
(c) $CH_2{=}\underset{\underset{CH_3}{|}}{C}-CH_2-NH_2$
(d) $(CH_3)_3CNH_2$

Module 2

Aromatic Amines

- Classification
- Nomenclature and Isomerism
- Methods of Preparation
- Physical Properties
- Chemical Properties

Classification

Aromatic amines are also classified as 1°, 2° and 3° depending upon the number of hydrogen atoms replaced by aryl groups from ammonia molecule.

Nomenclature

In common system of nomenclature, they are named as derivatives of aniline while in IUPAC system, the names are obtained by replacing the terminal 'e' from the name of the corresponding arene by the suffix 'amine'.

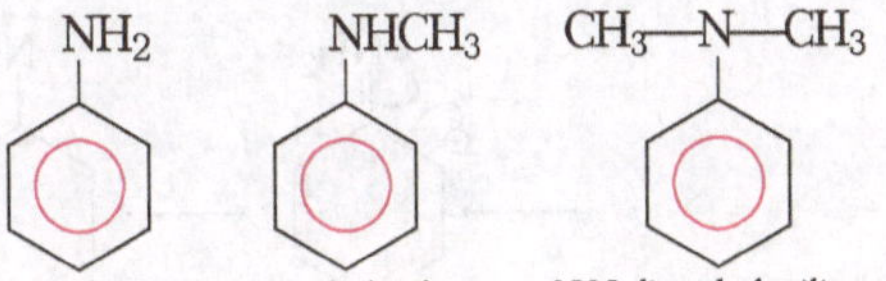

Common name	Aniline	N-methylaniline	N,N-dimethylaniline
IUPAC name	Benzenamine	N-methylbenzenamine	N,N-dimethylbenzenamine

Isomerism

Aromatic amines show position isomerism due to the presence of group at *o*, *m* and *p*-position on benzene ring.

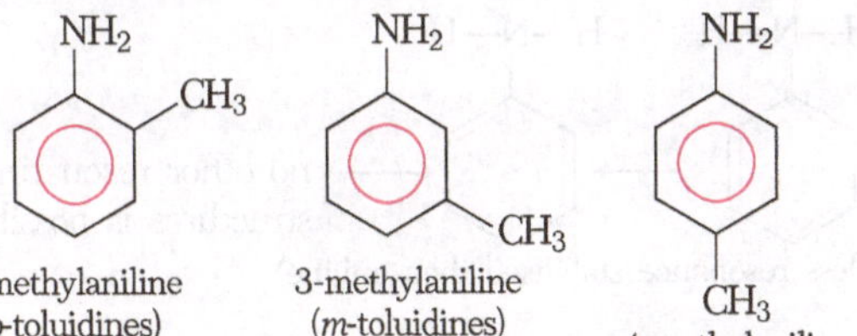

2-methylaniline (*o*-toluidines) 3-methylaniline (*m*-toluidines) 4-methylaniline (*p*-toluidines)

Methods of Preparation

Some of the important methods for the preparation of aniline are given below.

Reduction of Nitro Compounds

Nitro arenes can be reduced to amines by passing hydrogen gas in the presence of finely divided Ni, Pd or Pt and also by reduction with metals in acidic medium.

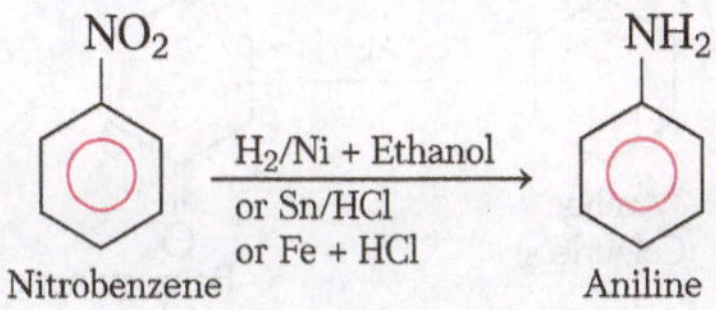

Reduction with iron scrap and hydrochloric acid is preferred because $FeCl_2$ formed gets hydrolysed to release HCl during the reaction. Thus, only a small amount of HCl is required to initiate the reaction.

Mentor's TiP

- If nitrobenzene undergoes reduction reaction in the presence of $CH_3ONa/CH_3OH/\Delta$ then it converts into azoxybenzene ($C_6H_5-N{=}N(\rightarrow O)-C_6H_5$).
- On the other hand, if it undergoes reduction in the presence of $LiAlH_4$ then it is converted into azobenzene ($C_6H_5-N{=}N-C_6H_5$).

Hoffmann's Bromamide Degradation Reaction

Aromatic amides react with an aqueous solution of KOH and Br_2 to give aromatic amine.

$$Ar-\overset{O}{\overset{\|}{C}}-NH_2 \xrightarrow{Br_2 + KOH} Ar-NH_2 + CO_2\uparrow$$

This reaction involves intramolecular phenyl migration, the rate of which is increased by the presence of electron releasing substituent.

Ammonolysis of Aryl Chlorides

Aryl chlorides react with ammonia to form aromatic amines.

e.g.

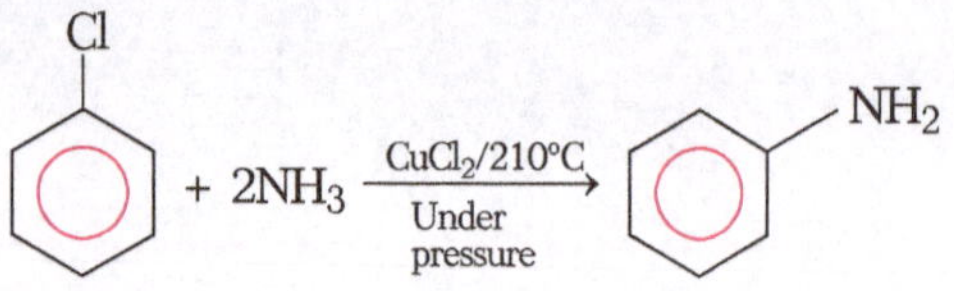

Chlorobenzene Aniline

This method can be carried out conveniently under ordinary conditions if a strong electron withdrawing group (e.g. NO_2) is present at *ortho* or *para*-position to —Cl.

Physical Properties

(i) **Physical state** They are colourless liquids or solids, but due to air oxidation, they turn brown.

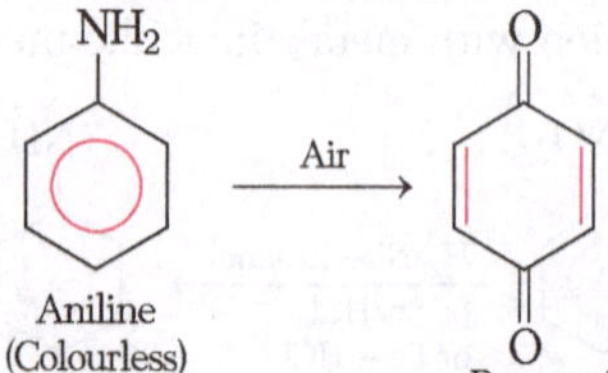

Aniline (Colourless) Benzoquinone

(ii) **Solubility** They are slightly soluble or insoluble in water (polar solvent) having larger hydrocarbon part which decreases their ability form H-bonds with water. But highly soluble in benzene and other organic solvents.

(iii) **Boiling point** They have high boiling point due to intermolecular H-bonding. N,N-dimethyl aniline has lower boiling point due to lack of H-bonding but molecular weight is also an important factor that affects boiling point. *para*-substituted aniline, being the most symmetric, has the highest melting point. Thus, *p*-toluidine is solid at room temperature while *o*-and *m*-toluidines are liquids.

Mentor's Tip

- Pyridine is more basic than aniline, it does not use lone-pair of N-atom in delocalisation. That's why electron lone pair of N in pyridine are shown outside the ring.

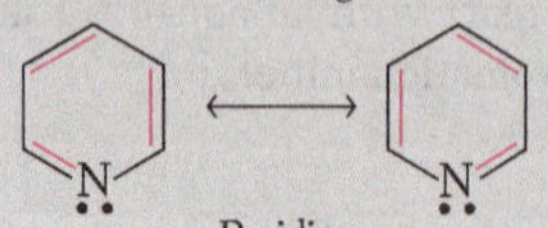

Pyridine

- Pyrrole uses lone-pair on N-atom in delocalisation, hence, less electrons are available for protonation. As a result, it is less basic than pyridine.

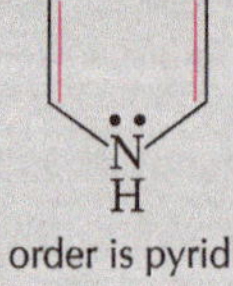

The decreasing basicity order is pyridine > aniline > pyrrole.

Chemical Properties

Basic character and important chemical reactions of aromatic amines are described below.

Basic Character of Aromatic Amines

Factors that increase the ability of nitrogen atom in an amine to share its electron pair, increases the basicity of amine and *vice-versa*.

Generally, aromatic amines are less basic than ammonia and aliphatic amines. It is because; in arylamines, the $—NH_2$ group is attached directly to the benzene ring. The unshared electron pair on nitrogen atom is in conjugation with benzene ring and thus making it less available for protonation.

Also, anilinium ion is less resonance stabilised than aniline.

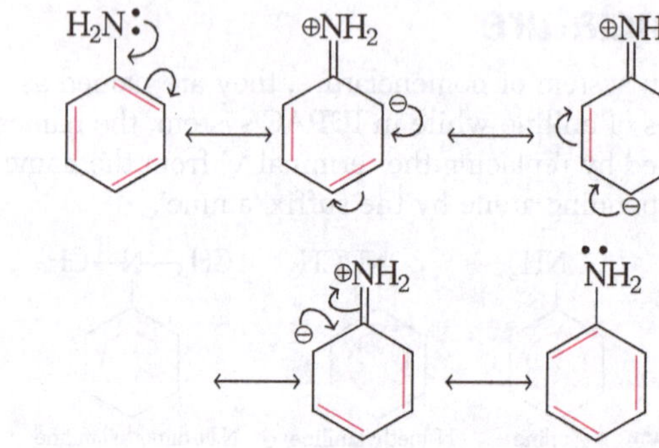

(resonance stabilised aniline decreases basic character compared to aliphatic amines)

On the other hand, anilinium ion obtained by accepting a proton can have only two resonating structures (Kekule).

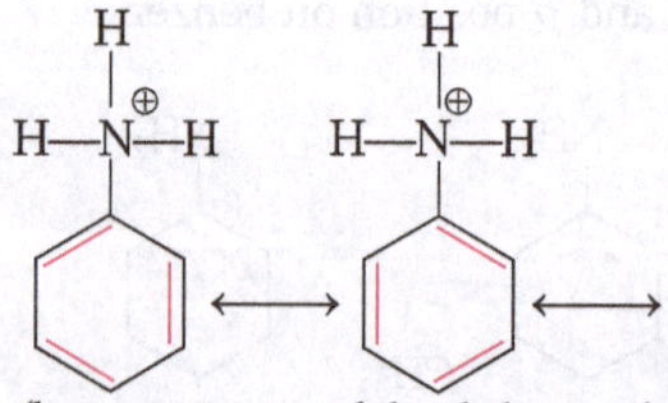

no other resonating structures is possible.

(less resonance stabilised than aniline)

Greater the number of resonating structures, greater is the stability. Thus, aniline is more stable than anilinium ion. Hence, the proton acceptability or the basic nature of aniline or other aromatic amines would be less than that of ammonia.

Effect of Substituent Group on Basicity of Aromatic Amines

- Electron-releasing groups like ($—NH_2$, $—OCH_3$, $—CH_3$) increase basic nature of aromatic amines.

- Electron-withdrawing groups like ($-NO_2$, $-SO_3H$, $-COOH$, $-X$) decrease basic nature of aromatic amines.

NEET Snapshot

The correct increasing order of basic strength for the given compounds is

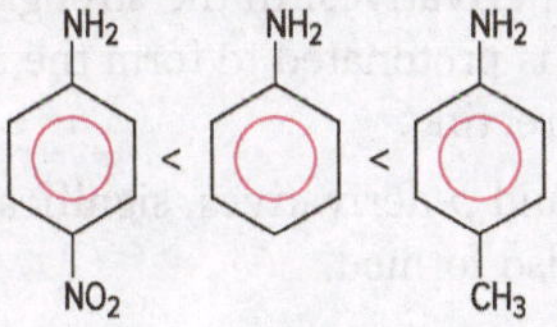

[NEET 2017]

The presence of electron withdrawing groups (NO_2) at *ortho* and *para* position decreases electron density over the ring by $-M$ effect while electron donating group (CH_3) increases the electron density over the benzene ring by $+I$ effect. So, aniline is less basic than *p*-toluidene and more basic than *p*-nitroaniline.

Alkylation

Aromatic amines react with alkyl halide to give respective secondary and tertiary amines. e.g.

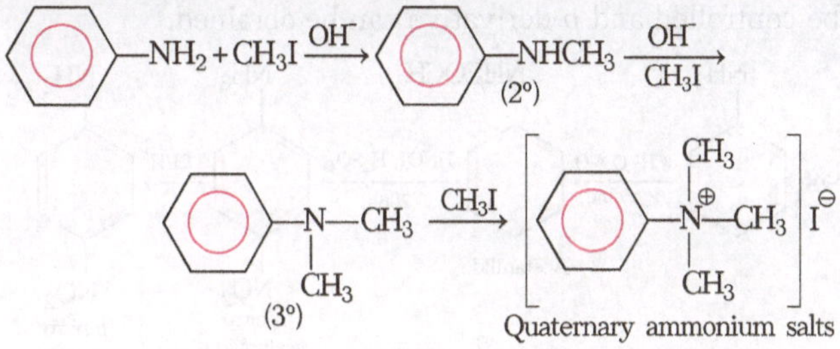

The process of conversion of 1° amines into quaternary ammonium salt is called **Hofmann exhaustive alkylation.** Quaternary ammonium salt is not affected by hydroxide ion because ammonium ion has no proton to give.

Acylation

Aromatic amine reacts with acetyl chloride in the presence of pyridine to form N-phenyl ethanamide.

e.g.

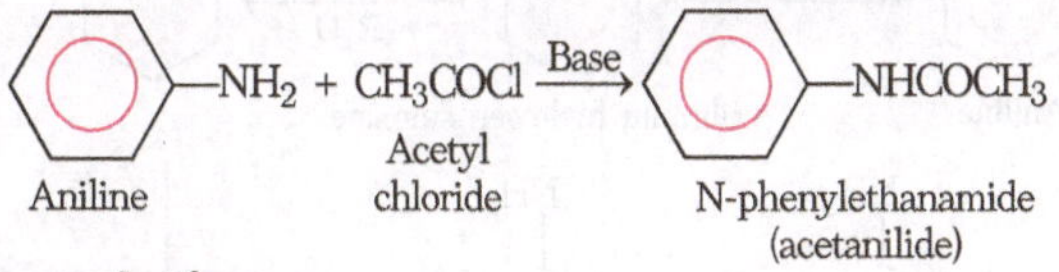

Benzoylation

Aromatic amine reacts with benzoyl chloride in presence of *aq.* NaOH to give N-phenyl benzamide.

e.g.

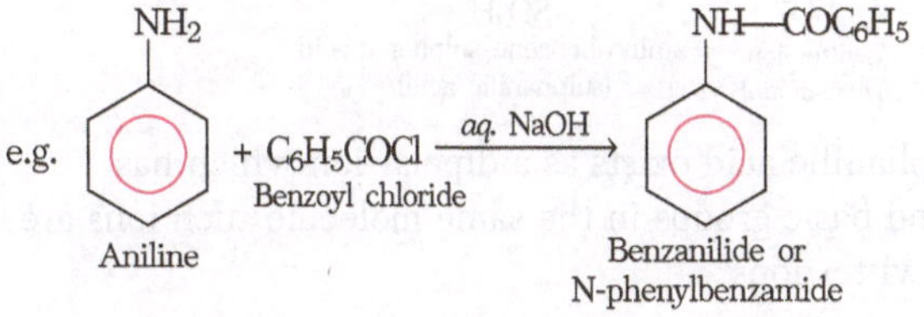

Carbylamine Reaction

Only 1° amines give this reaction when unpleasant smell of isocyanide is obtained on heating a mixture of alcoholic KOH, $CHCl_3$ and 1° amine.

e.g.

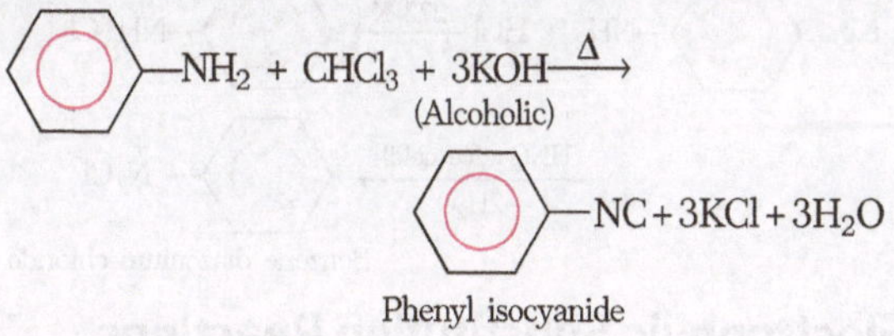

NEET Close-up

Example Similar to PYQ Asked in NEET 2020

Which of the following amine will give the carbylamine test?

(a) $C_6H_5-C(NH_2)(H)-CH_3$ (b) $C_6H_5N(CH_3)_2$

(c) $(C_6H_5)_3N$ (d) $C_6H_5NHCH_2CH_3$

Sol. (a) Among the given compounds, only (a) will give the carbylamine test because this test is given by primary amine (aliphatic or aromatic) only.

Skill Builder

Which of the following will not give the carbylamine test?

(a) N,N-diethylaniline (b) 4,4′-methylenedianiline

(c) *p*-nitroaniline (d) *o*-methylaniline

For more Practice Refer to Q. 6 of step up practice-2.

Reaction with Aryl Sulphonyl Chloride (Sulphonylation)

Aromatic amine reacts with benzene sulphonyl chloride to give N-phenyl benzene sulphonamide.

e.g.

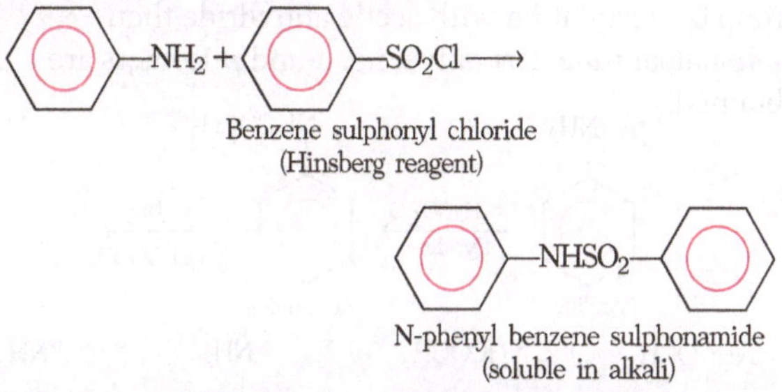

2° amine also reacts with this reagent but the product formed is insoluble in alkali. This provides a method (called Hinsberg method) for the separation of mixture of 1°, 2° and 3° amines.

Diazotisation Reaction

Primary aromatic amines react with HNO_2 under ice cold conditions to form benzene diazonium chloride. The reaction is called **diazotisation reaction.**

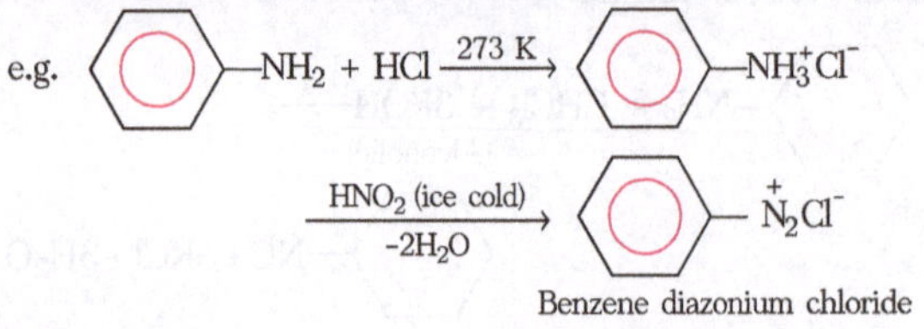

Electrophilic Substitution Reactions

—NH_2 group is *o*- and *p*-directing activating group and become centres of high electron density. The ring undergoes electrophilic substitution easily even under mild conditions.

(i) Bromination

On bromination in aqueous medium, aniline gives a *tri*-substituted product.

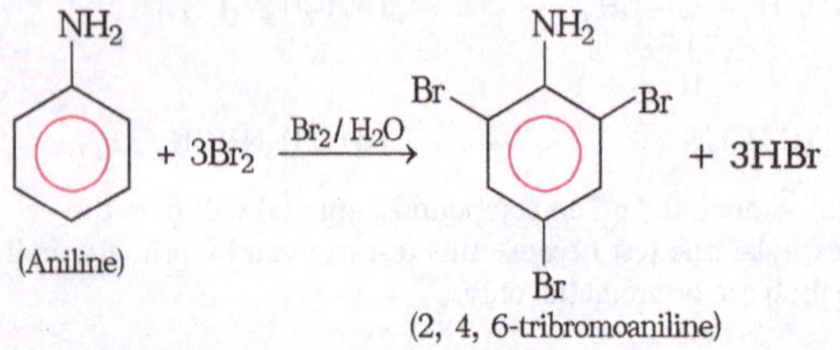

Concept ladder

- Aniline does not undergo Friedel-Craft reaction (alkylation and acetylation) because of the salt formation with aluminium chloride (Lewis acid) which is used as a catalyst.
- Nitrogen of aniline acquires positive charge and hence act as a strong electron withdrawing group for further reaction.

Hence, the lone pair of electrons on nitrogen is less available for donation to benzene ring by resonance. Therefore, activating effect of —$NHCOCH_3$ group is less than that of amino group. —NH_2 group is greatly activating group hence, reaction takes place rapidly.

However, if ring is deactivated by protecting the —NH_2 group by acetylation with acetic anhydride then monohaloaniline derivative, i.e. *o*-and *p*-isomers are obtained.

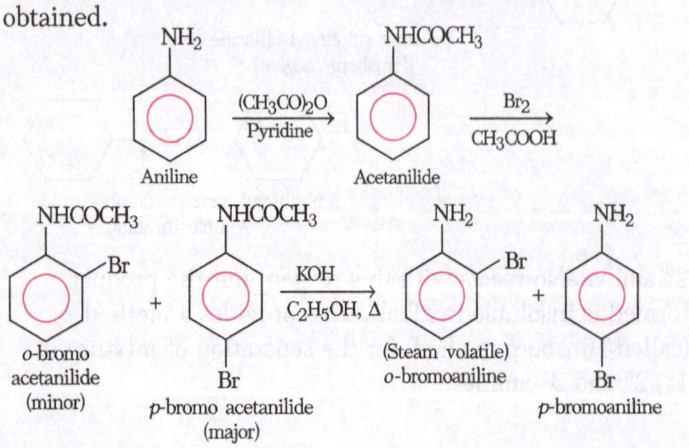

The lone pair of electrons on nitrogen of acetanilide on nitrogen of acetanilide interacts with O-atom due to resonance.

(ii) Nitration

Nitration of aniline yields tarry oxidation products in addition to nitro derivatives. In the strongly acidic medium, aniline is protonated to form the anilinium ion which is *meta*-directing.

Thus, besides *o*-and *p*-derivatives, significant amount of *m*-derivative is also formed.

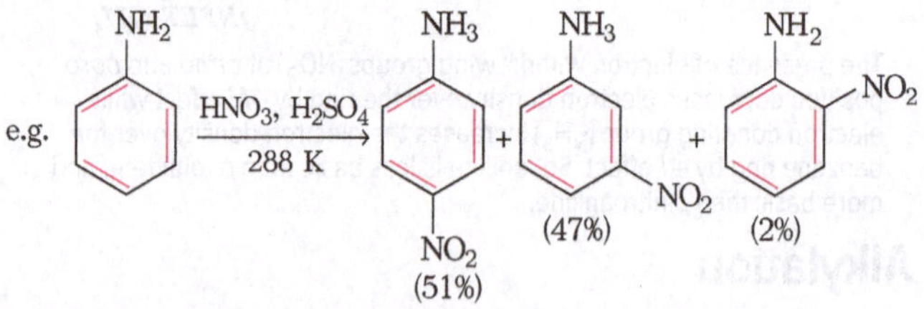

However, by protecting the —NH_2 group by acetylation reaction with acetic anhydride, the nitration reaction can be controlled and *p*-derivative can be obtained.

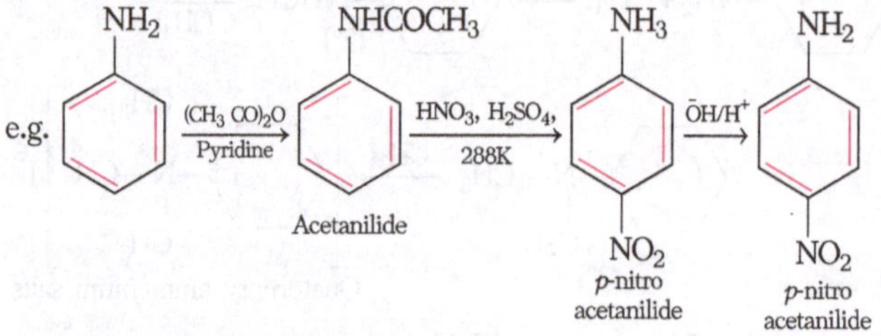

(ii) Sulphonation

Aniline when treated with conc. H_2SO_4 forms anilinium hydrogen sulphate which on heating at 453-473 K gives sulphanilic acid.

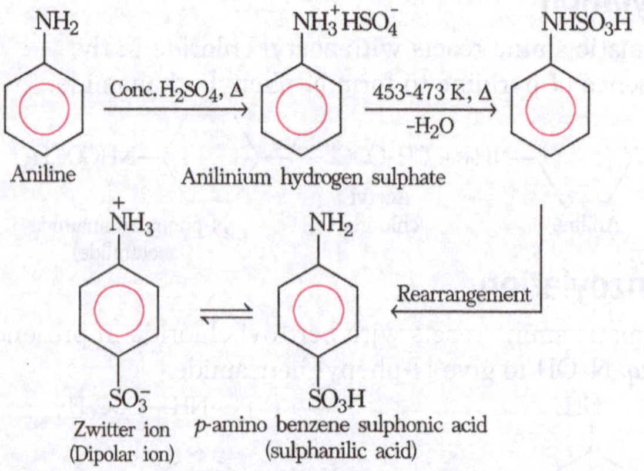

The sulphanilic acid exists as a dipolar ion which has acidic and basic groups in the same molecule such ions are called Zwitter ions.

NEET Close-up

Example Similar to PYQ Asked in NEET 2024

Direction *(Q. Similar and Skill Builder)* In the light of the statements given below, choose the most appropriate answer from the options given below

(a) Both Statement I and Statement II are false.
(b) Statement I is true but Statement II is false.
(c) Statement I is false but Statement II is true.
(d) Both Statement I and Statement II are true.

Statement I Aniline reacts with nitrous acid at low temperature to form diazonium salts.

Statement II Aniline can be prepared by reduction of nitro compounds.

Skill Builder

Statement I Aromatic primary amines can be prepared by Gabriel pthalimide synthesis because they can undergo nucleophilic substitution with anion formed by pthalimide.

Statement II Primary aliphatic amines react with nitrous acid to form aliphatic diazonium salts which being unstable, liberate nitrogen gas quantitatively and alcohol.

For more practice Refer to Q. 23 of step up practice-2.

Distinction and Separation of 1°, 2° and 3° Amines

S.No.	Test	1° amine	2° amine	3° amine
1.	**Carbylamine test** (reaction with chloroform and alcoholic KOH)	Unpleasant smell of alkyl isocyanide is obtained $RNH_2 + CHCl_3 + 3KOH \xrightarrow{\Delta} RNC + 3KCl + H_2O$	2° amine does not give this reaction	3° amine does not give this reaction
2.	**Reaction with HNO_2**	N_2 is evolved $R\text{—}NH_2 + HNO_2 \xrightarrow[\text{(ii) } H_2O]{\text{(i) } NaNO_2 + HCl} ROH + N_2\uparrow + HCl$	Oily nitrosamine is formed $R_2NH + HNO_2 \longrightarrow \underset{\text{(oily)}}{R_2NNO} + H_2O$	Only dissolves, forming $R_3NH^+ NO_2^-$
3.	**Hinsberg's test** [with benzene sulphonyl chloride i.e. $C_6H_5SO_2Cl$]	N-alkyl benzene sulphonamide is formed. It is soluble in alkali. 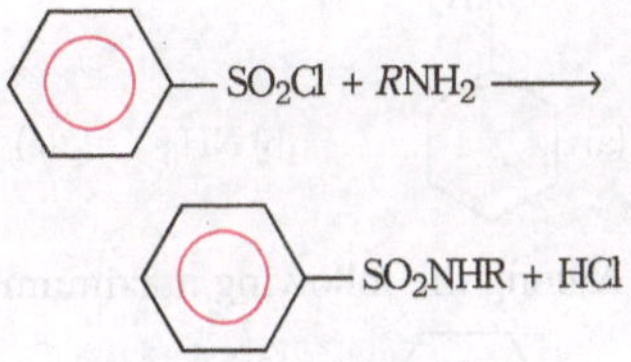 N-alkyl benzenesulphonamide (soluble in NaOH)	N,N-dialkyl benzenesulphonamide is formed. It is insoluble in alkali 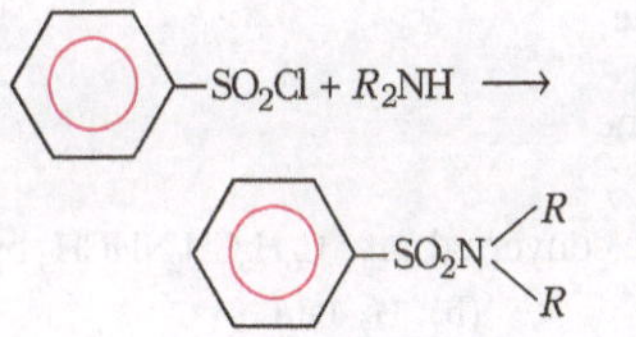 N,N-dialkyl benzenesulphonamide (insoluble in NaOH)	No reaction 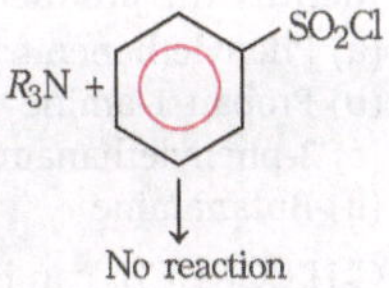 No reaction
4.	**Hoffmann mustard oil reaction** (reaction with CS_2 followed by $HgCl_2$)	$RNH_2 + CS_2 \longrightarrow S{=}C\begin{smallmatrix} NHR \\ SH \end{smallmatrix}$ $\xrightarrow{HgCl_2} \underset{\text{Black ppt.}}{HgS} + RNCS + 2HCl$	$R_2NH + CS_2 \longrightarrow S{=}C\begin{smallmatrix} NR_2 \\ SH \end{smallmatrix}$ $\downarrow HgCl_2$ No ppt.	$R_3N + CS_2 \longrightarrow$ No reaction

STEP UP Practice 2

1 The IUPAC name of the given compound $C_6H_5—CH_2—N(CH_3)_2$ is
(a) N,N-dimethylaniline
(b) N,N-dimethyl phenylmethanamine
(c) N,N-dimethylmethananiline
(d) N,N-dimethylphenylamine

2 Which of the following is correctly matched with their IUPAC name?

(a) 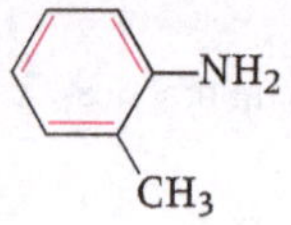 ⟶ 2-methylamine

(b) 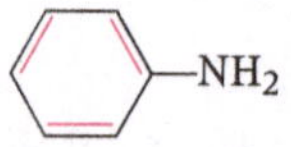 ⟶ Benzenaniline

(c) 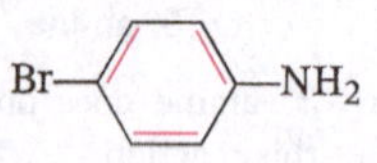 ⟶ *p*-bromoaniline

(d) 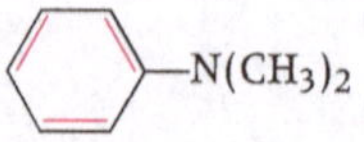 ⟶ N,N-dimethylbenzenamine

3 In the given reaction,

$$C_6H_5—CH_2—Cl \xrightarrow[\text{NaCN}]{\text{Ethanolic}} A \xrightarrow[H_2/Ni]{} B$$

Identify the product '*B*'.
(a) Phenylethanenitrile
(b) Propan-1-amine
(c) 2-phenylethanamine
(d) Butanamine

4 $C_6H_5CONHCH_3$ can be converted into $C_6H_5CH_2NHCH_3$ by
(a) $NaBH_4$ (b) H_2-Pd/C
(c) $LiAlH_4/H_2O$ (d) Zn-Hg/HCl

5 Consider the following statements.
Statement I Chlorobenzene reacts with $NaNH_2$ forming aniline.
Statement II (C—Cl) bond is stabilised due to delocalisation of π-electrons by resonance.
In the light of the above statements, choose the most appropriate answer from the options given below
(a) Both Statement I and Statement II are false.
(b) Statement I is true but Statement II is false.
(c) Statement I is false but Statement II is true.
(d) Both Statement I and Statement II are true.

6 Carbylamine test is performed in alc. KOH by heating a mixture of
(a) an alkyl halide and a primary amine
(b) an alkyl cyanide and a secondary amine
(c) chloroform and copper powder
(d) trihalogenated methane and a primary amine

7 Consider the following statements.
Statement I Acylation of amines give a monosubstituted product whereas alkylation of amines give a polysubstituted product.
Statement II Acyl group sterically hinders the approach of further acyl groups.
In the light of the above statements, choose the most appropriate answer from the options given below
(a) Both Statement I and Statement II are false.
(b) Statement I is true but Statement II is false.
(c) Statement I is false but Statement II is true.
(d) Both Statement I and Statement II are true.

8 Which reducing agent is used for the reduction of nitro compound to phenyl amine?
(a) $LiAlH_4$ (b) Sn/HCl
(c) Na/Alcohol (d) H_2/Ni

9 Choose the one with the lowest boiling point.

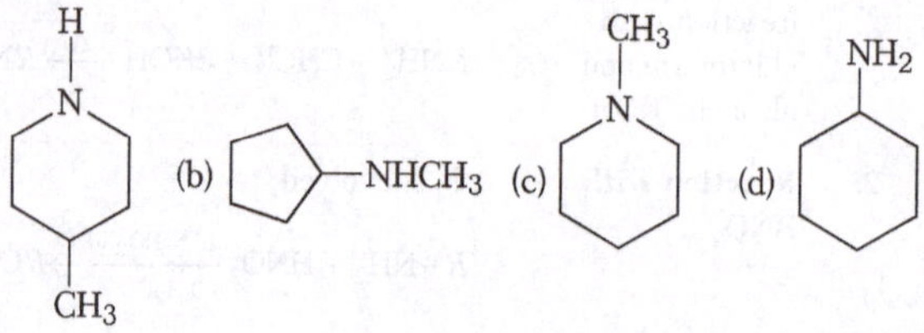

10 Among the following amines, the strongest Bronsted base is ……… .

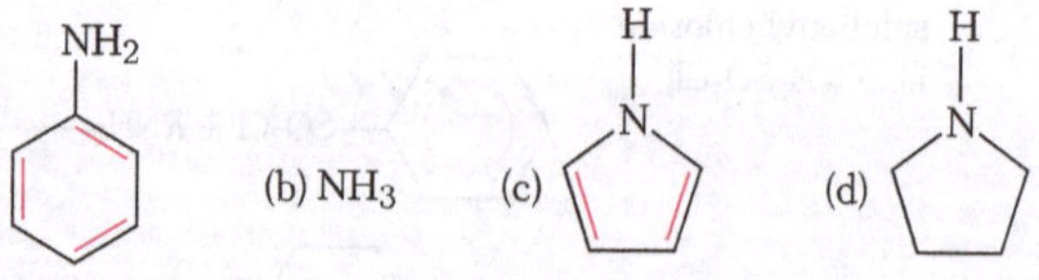

11 Among the following maximum pK_b value is of

(a) 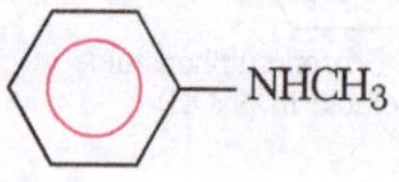 (b) $(CH_3CH_2)_2NH$

(c) $(CH_3)_2NH$ (d) 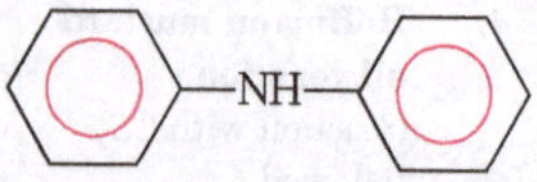

12 Consider the following comparison of basic nature of amines.

I. 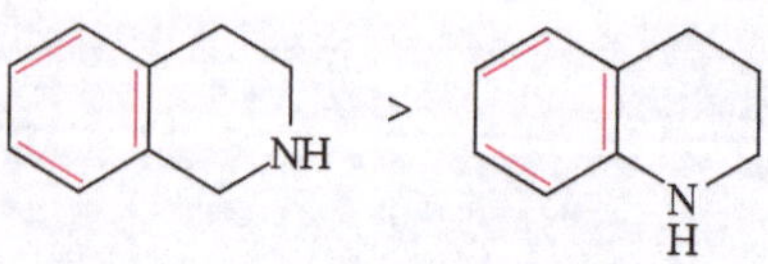

II. 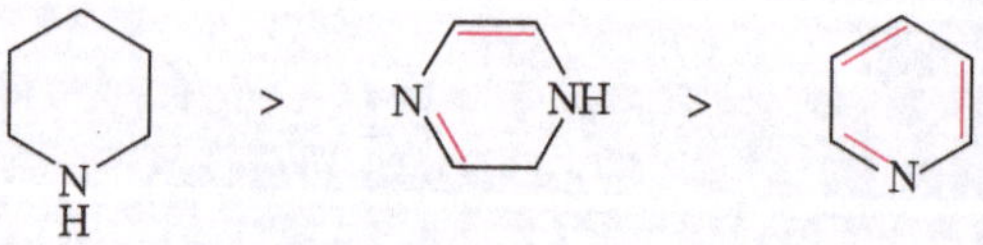

III. 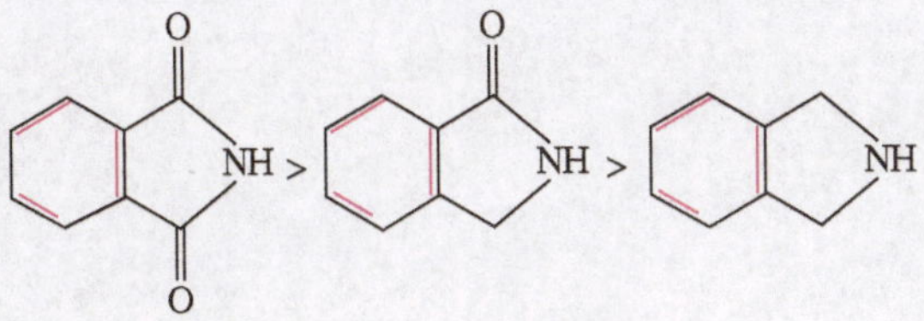

Correct comparisons are

(a) I, II and III
(b) Both I and II
(c) Both II and III
(d) Both I and III

13 Thermal decomposition of

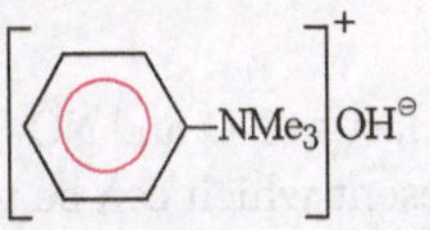 give

(a) 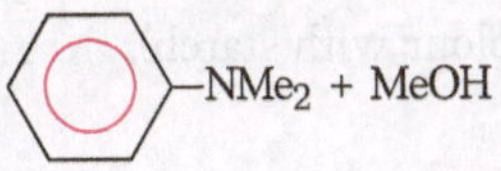
(b) 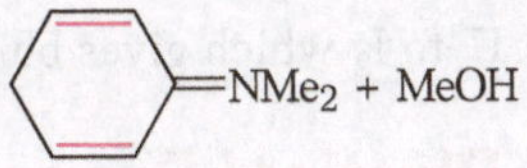
(c) 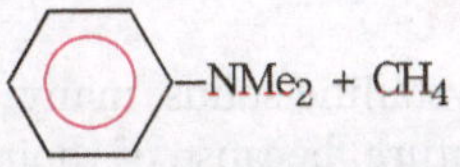
(d) No reaction

14 In the nitration of benzene using a mixture of conc. H_2SO_4 and conc. HNO_3, the species which initiates the reaction is ....

(a) NO_2 (b) NO^+ (c) NO_2^+ (d) NO_2^-

15 Pyridine is less basic than triethylamine because

(a) pyridine has aromatic character
(b) nitrogen in pyridine is sp^2-hybridised
(c) pyridine is a cyclic system
(d) in pyridine, lone pair of nitrogen is delocalised

16 Which of the following reaction is not correctly matched with their product?

(a) 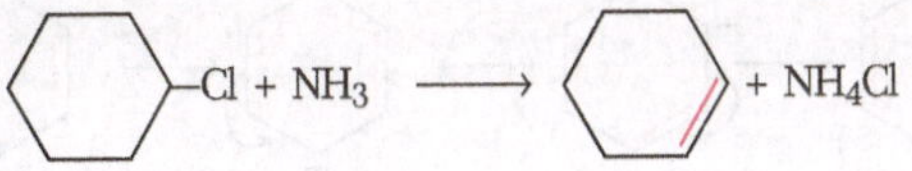

(b) 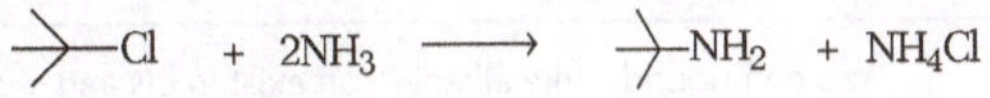

(c) 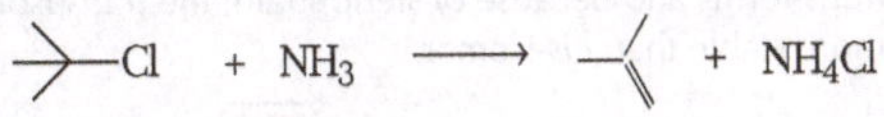

(d) 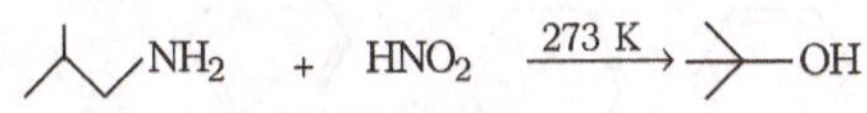

17 $—NH_2$ in benzene nucleus is protected before any S_E reaction as $—NH_2$ group is

(a) greatly activating; *o*, *p*-directing
(b) deactivating; *o*, *p*-directing
(c) activating; *m*-directing
(d) deactivating ; *m*-directing

18 Consider the following reaction,

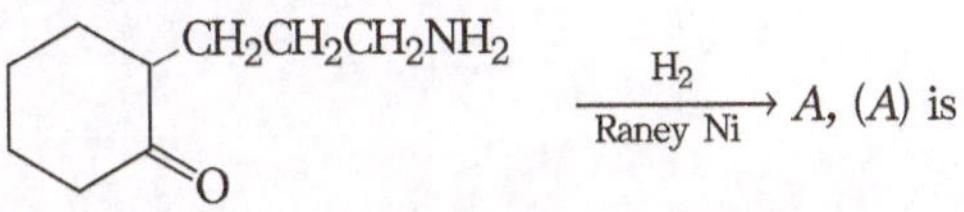

(a) 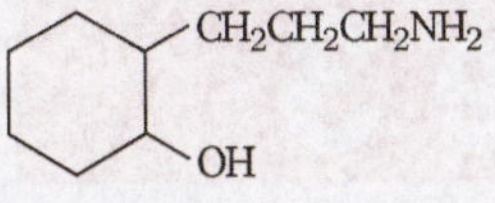
(b) 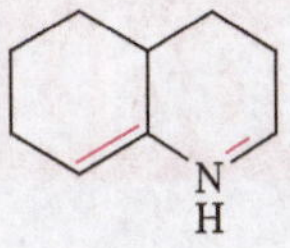
(c) 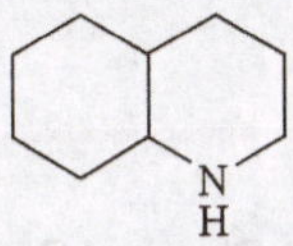
(d) 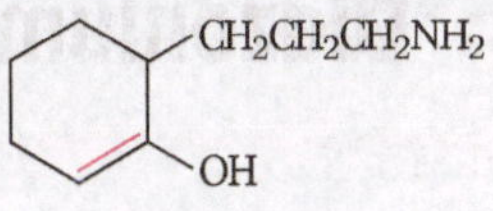

19 Which of the following reaction is correctly matched?

(a) Reaction of 1° amine with $CHCl_3$ $\longrightarrow$ Hofmann mustard oil reaction
(b) Reaction of 1° amine with $CHCl_3$ + KOH $\longrightarrow$ Hofmann mustard oil reaction
(c) Reaction of 1° amine with CS_2 + $HgCl_2$ $\longrightarrow$ Hofmann mustard oil reaction
(d) Reaction of aromatic amine with iodoform $\longrightarrow$ Hofmann mustard oil reaction

20 Consider the following reaction,

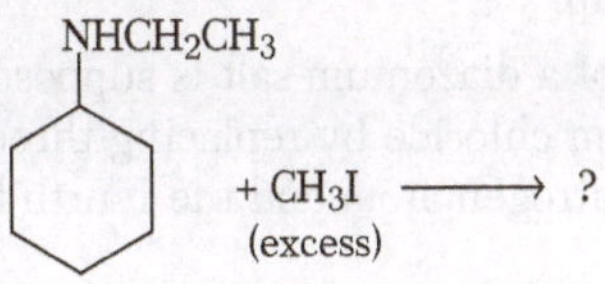

Final product formed in above reaction is

(a) a primary amine
(b) a secondary amine
(c) a tertiary amine
(d) a quaternary ammonium salt

21 Reduction of aromatic nitro compounds using Fe and HCl gives ....

(a) aromatic oxime
(b) aromatic hydrocarbon
(c) aromatic primary amine
(d) aromatic amide

22 Consider the following compounds.

(i) Methylamine
(ii) Phosgene
(iii) Phosphine
(iv) Dimethylamine
(v) Acetamide

How many of them are used to manufacture methyl isocyanide that caused "Bhopal tragedy"?

(a) 3
(b) 1
(c) 4
(d) 2

23 Given below are two statements.

Statement I In Hofmann bromamide degradation reaction migration of an aryl group takes place from carbonyl carbon of the amide to the nitrogen atom.

Statement II Aromatic primary amines on heating with chloroform and ethanolic potassium hydroxide form isocyanide or carbylamines.

In the light of the above statements, choose the correct answer from the options given below.

(a) Both Statement I and Statement II are false.
(b) Statement I is true, but Statement II is false.
(c) Statement I is false, but Statement II is true.
(d) Both Statement I and Statement II are true.

Module 3

Diazonium Salts

• Methods of Preparation • Physical Properties • Chemical Properties

Diazonium Salts

The general formula of diazonium salts is $R\overset{+}{N}_2X^-$ where, R stands for an aryl group and X^- may be Cl^-, Br^- etc.

They are named by suffix diazonium to the name of the parent hydrocarbon from which they are formed followed by the name of the anion. The $N_2^{\oplus}$ group is called diazonium group.

The structure of a diazonium salt is supposed to be derived from ammonium chloride by replacing three hydrogen atoms with a nitrogen atom and the fourth by a phenyl group.

$$\left[\begin{array}{c} H \\ | \\ H-\overset{+}{N}-H \\ | \\ H \end{array}\right]Cl^- \qquad [C_6H_5-N\equiv N]Cl^-$$

Ammonium chloride — Benzene diazonium chloride

Methods of Preparation

Diazonium salts can be prepared by **diazotisation** of aniline. In this reaction, ice-cold solution of HNO_2 ($NaNO_2$ + HCl or $NaNO_2 + H_2SO_4$) is added to ice-cold solution of primary aromatic amine dissolved in acid to form diazonium salt.

Due to its instability, the diazonium salt is not generally stored and is used immediately after its preparation.

$$NaNO_2 + HCl \longrightarrow HNO_2 + NaCl$$

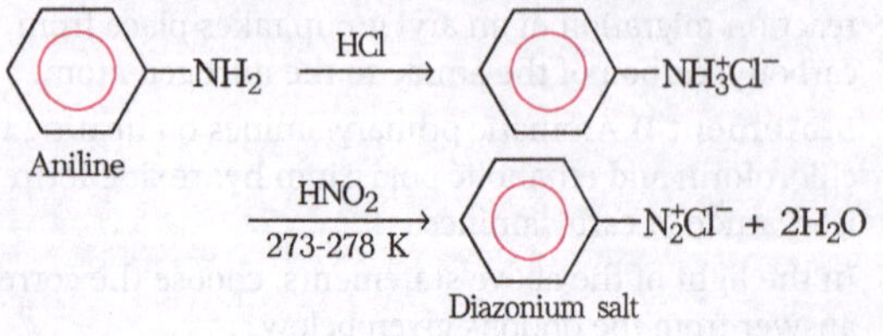

Here, some HNO_2 is lost as NO and NO_2. So, excess of $NaNO_2$ should be present which can be tested by KI-starch paper when blue colour appears. (HNO_2 oxidises I^- to I_2 which gives blue colour with starch).

Physical Properties

- Dry diazonium salts are crystalline solids, many of them are explosive in nature, because of their unstability they are seldom isolated and are used in solution (*in situ*).
- They are water soluble due to their ionic nature.
- In aqueous solution, they are good conductors of electricity.
- Aromatic diazonium salts are more stable than aliphatic diazonium salts ($R\overset{+}{N}_2$) and the stability is attributed to resonance.

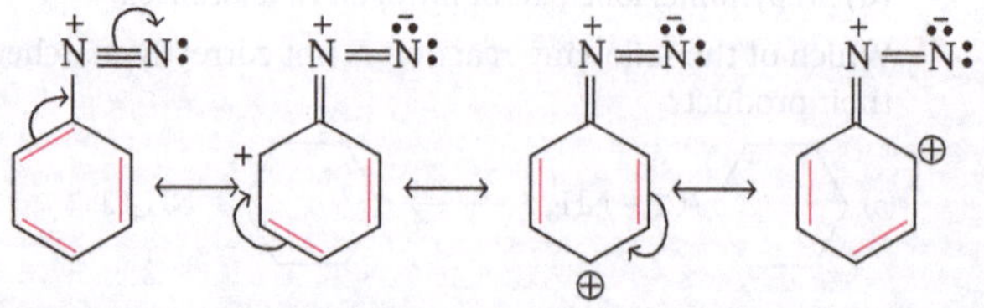

Concept ladder

Azo compounds, like alkenes can exist in *cis* and *trans*-forms and because of steric strain, the *trans*-isomer is more stable than *cis*-isomer.

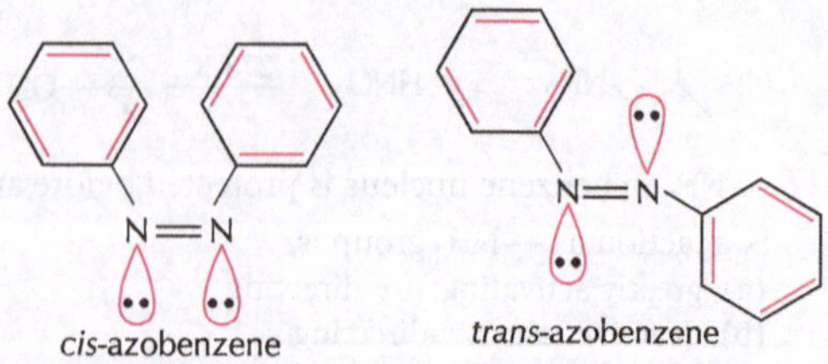

cis-azobenzene — *trans*-azobenzene

Chemical Properties

The reactions of diazonium salts can be broadly divided into following two categories.

I. Reactions Involving Displacement of Nitrogen

Diazonium group can be easily substituted by other group such as Cl^-, I^-, CN^- etc., which can displace nitrogen from the aromatic ring as it is very good leaving group. The nitrogen so formed escapes from the reaction mixture as a gas.

(i) Replacement by Halide or Cyanide Ion

In the presence of Cu(I) ion, the halide (Cl^- and Br^-) and cyanide (CN^-) nucleophiles can be introduced in benzene ring. This reaction is called as **Sandmeyer reaction.**

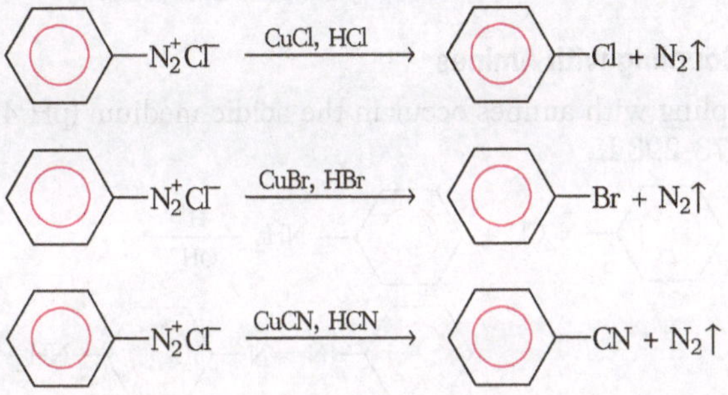

Alternatively, nucleophiles such as Cl^- or Br^- can also be introduced in the benzene ring by treating the diazonium salt solution with corresponding halogen acid in the presence of copper powder. This reaction is known as **Gattermann reaction.**

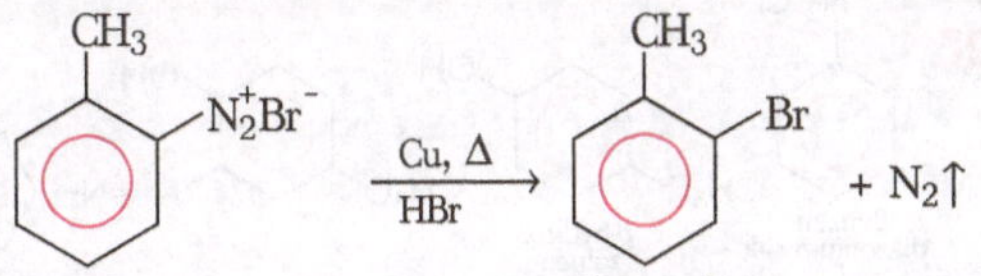

Bromotoluene

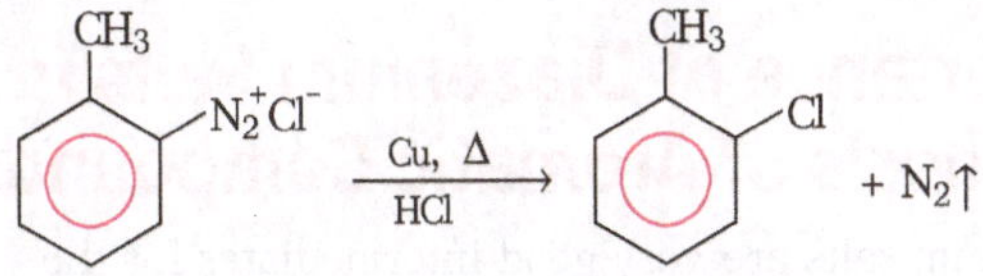

Chlorotoluene

(ii) Replacement by Iodide Ion

Iodine is not easily introduced into the benzene ring directly but when the diazonium salt solution is treated with potassium iodide, iodobenzene is formed.

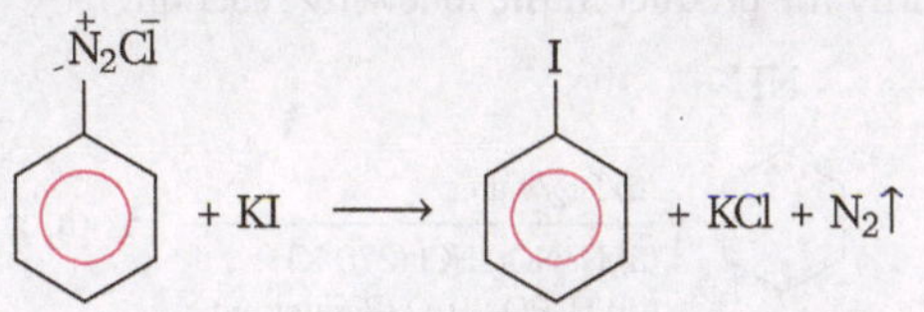

Iodobenzene

(iii) Replacement by Fluoride Ion

When arenediazonium chloride is treated with fluoroboric acid, arenediazonium fluoroborate is precipitated which on heating decomposes to yield aryl fluoride or fluorobenzene.

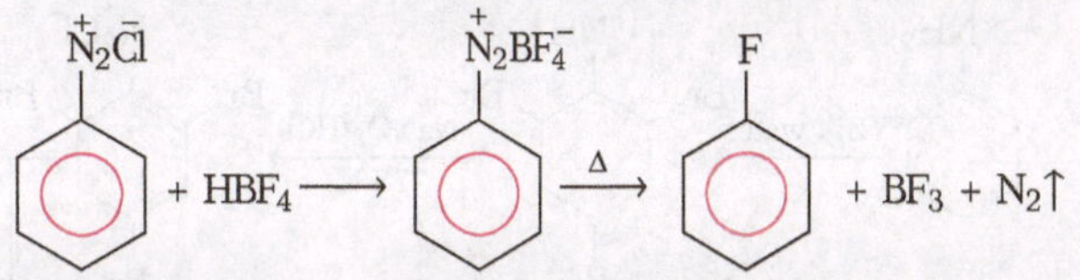

Diazonium salt Fluorobenzene

(iv) Replacement by Hydrogen

Certain mild reducing agents like hypophosphorus acid (phosphinic acid) or ethanol reduces diazonium salts to arenes and themselves get oxidised to phosphorus acid and ethanal, respectively.

$$Ar\overset{+}{N}_2\,Cl^- + H_3PO_2 + H_2O \longrightarrow ArH + N_2 + H_3PO_3 + HCl$$

(v) Replacement by Hydroxyl Group

If the temperature of the diazonium salt solution is raised to 283 K, then the salt gets hydrolysed to phenol.

$$ArN_2^+Cl^- + H_2O \longrightarrow ArOH + N_2 + HCl$$

(vi) Replacement by —NO_2 Group

When diazonium fluoroborate is heated with aqueous sodium nitrite solution in the presence of copper then nitrobenzene is formed.

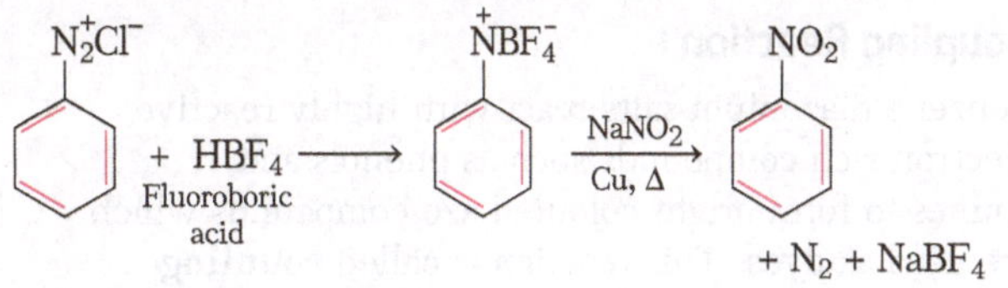

NEET Close-up

Example Similar to PYQ Asked in NEET 2023

Identify the product in the following reaction,

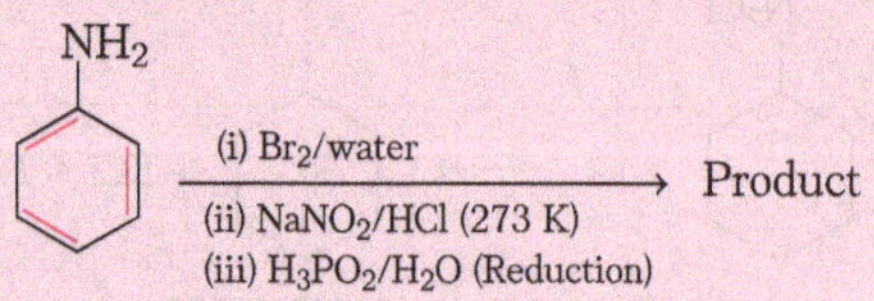

(a) 1,3,5-tribromobenzene
(b) Bromobenzene
(c) Bromophosphobenzene
(d) Bromonitrobenzene

Sol. (*a*) The reaction proceeds as follows

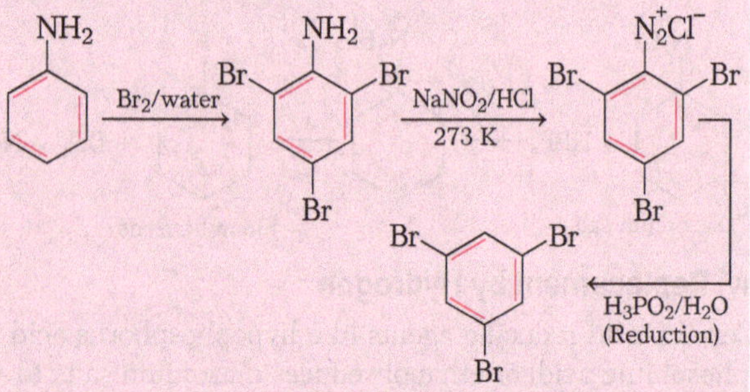

Skill Builder

Identify *Y* in the reaction,

$$C_6H_5NH_2 \xrightarrow[273\ K]{NaNO_2/HCl} X \xrightarrow[Dil.\ H_2SO_4]{H_2O} Y$$

(a) $C_6H_5N_2Cl$ (b) C_6H_5OH
(c) C_6H_5NHOH (d) C_6H_6

For more practice Refer to Q. 7 of Step up practice-3 and Q. 36 and Q.37 of Gearing up for NEET.

II. Reactions Involving Retention of Diazo Group

Coupling Reaction

Benzene diazonium salts react with highly reactive electron rich compounds such as phenols and amines to form bright coloured azo compounds which are used as dyes. This reaction is called **coupling reaction.**

The azo products obtained have an extended conjugate system having both the aromatic rings joined. In general, through the —N = N—bond.

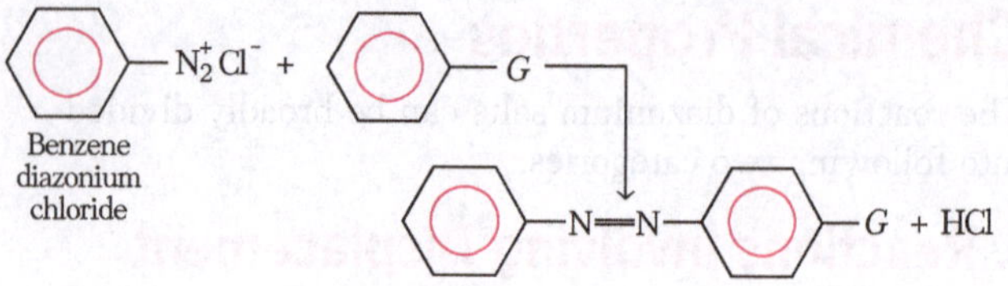

(*G* is strong electron-releasing group: —OH, —NR_2, —NH*R*, — NH_2 etc.)

(a) Coupling with Phenols

Coupling with phenols occurs in the basic medium (pH 9-10) at 273-298 K.

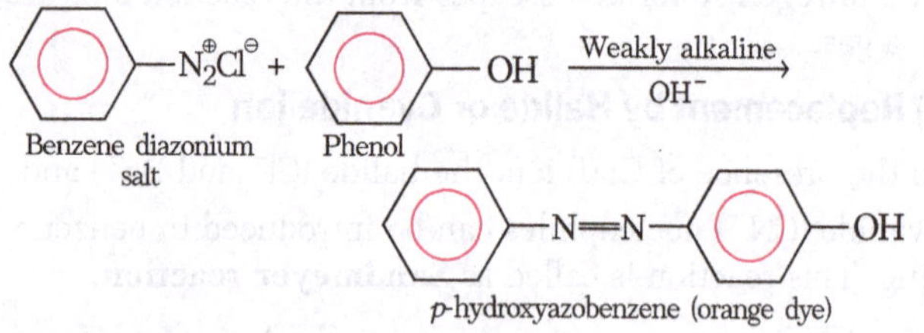

(b) Coupling with Amines

Coupling with amines occur in the acidic medium (pH 4.5) at 273-298 K.

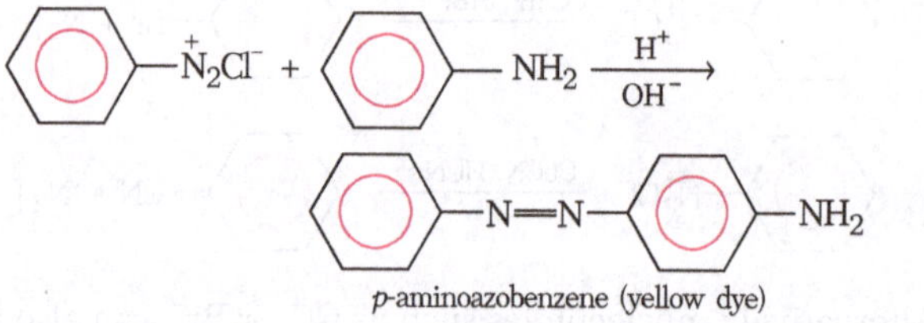

Concept ladder

Coupling with benzene substrates occur preferentially at the less sterically hindered *p*-position to the hydroxy or amino group but if this position is blocked, then *o*-coupling occurs.

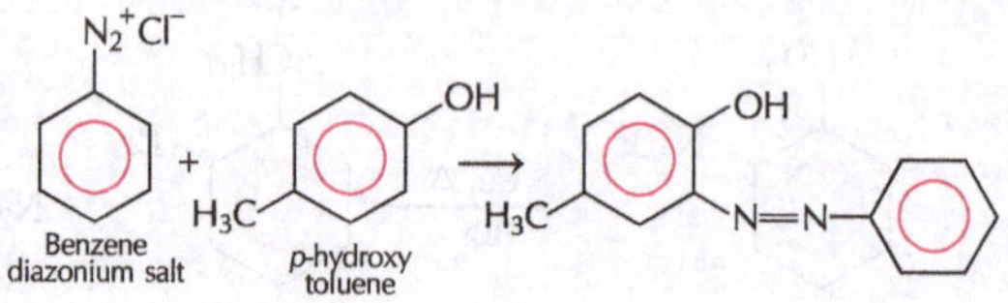

Importance of Diazonium Salts in Synthesis of Aromatic Compounds

Diazonium salts are very good intermediates for the introduction of —F, —Cl, —Br, —I, —CN, —OH, —NO_2 groups into the aromatic ring. The replacement of diazo group by other groups is helpful in preparing those substituted aromatic compounds which cannot be prepared by direct substitution in benzene or substituted benzene.

STEP UP Practice 3

1 Benzene diazonium chloride reacts with hypophosphorus acid to produce
(a) phenol
(b) benzene
(c) *p*-hydroxyazobenzene
(d) benzonitrile

2 Sodium sulphite reacts with benzene diazonium chloride forming
(a) phenyl hydrazine
(b) aniline
(c) benzene
(d) benzonitrile

3 Select the incorrect statement(s).
(a) CH_3CN is named as methane nitrile.
(b) Urea is an amide of carbamic acid.
(c) Urea is excreted in the urine as the end product of protein metabolism.
(d) Urea is a diamide.

4 Given below are two statements.
Statement I Azo dye is prepared by the coupling of phenol and *o*-nitroaniline.
Statement II *p*-Hydroxyazobenzene is an orange dye.
In the light of the above statements, choose the most appropriate answer from the options given below.
(a) Both Statement I and Statement II are false.
(b) Statement I is true but Statement II is false.
(c) Statement I is false but Statement II is true.
(d) Both Statement I and Statement II are true.

5 In the following compounds I and II, which positions are activated for coupling reactions?

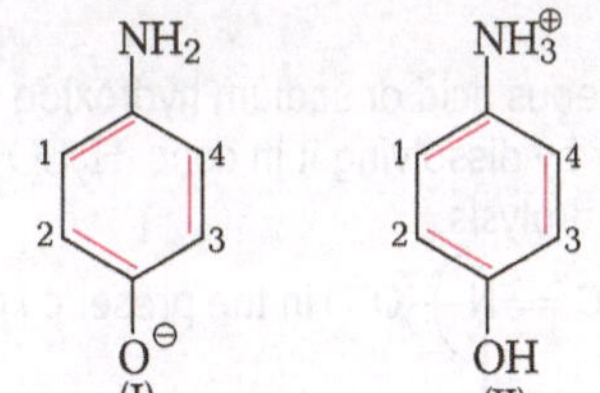
(I) (II)

(a) 2 or 3 in (I) and 1 and 4 in (II)
(b) 1 or 4 in (I) and 2 and 3 in (II)
(c) 1 or 4 in (I) and (II)
(d) 2 or 3 in (I) and (II)

6 Which of the following product is incorrectly matched with the given reaction?

(a) $R—NC \xrightarrow{H_2O + H^{\oplus}} RNH_2 + HCOOH$

(b) $R—NC \xrightarrow{LiAlH_4} R—\underset{\displaystyle H}{\underset{|}{N}}—CH_3$

(c) $RNC \xrightarrow{O_2/NiCl_2} R—N{=}C{=}O$

(d) $R—N{\equiv}C + Cl_2 \longrightarrow RNHCHCl_2$

7 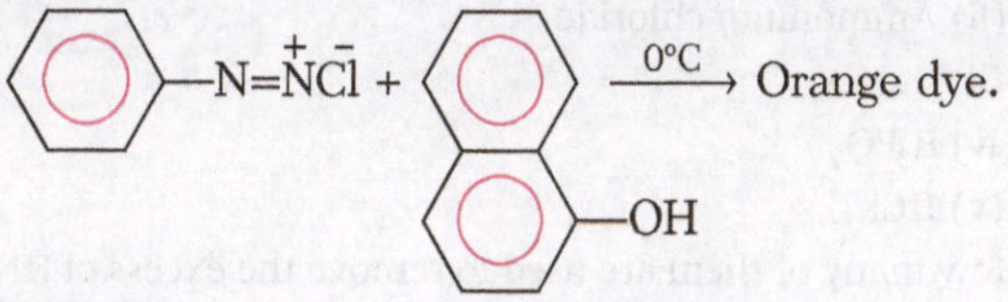

It will be

(a) 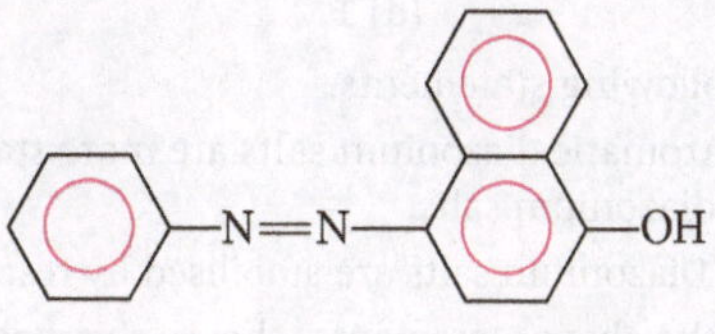

(b) 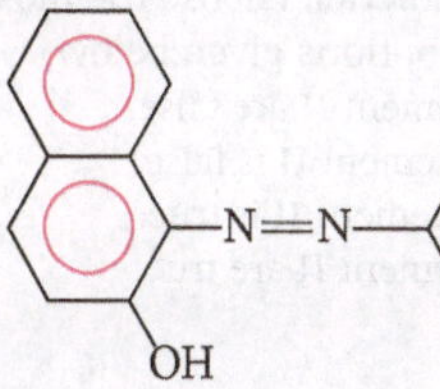

(c) 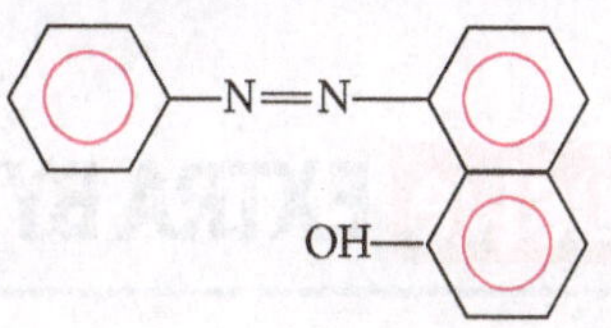

(d) 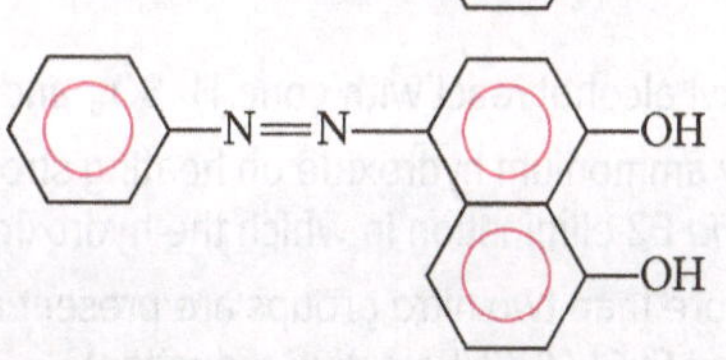

8 Given below are two statements.
Statement I Benzene diazonium chloride give test for nitrogen.
Statement II Loss of N_2 gas takes place during heating.
In the light of the above statements, choose the most appropriate answer from the options given below
(a) Both Statement I and Statement II are false.
(b) Statement I is true but Statement II is false.
(c) Statement I is false but Statement II is true.
(d) Both Statement I and Statement II are true.

9 Select the correct statement about arene diazonium ions.
(a) They act as strong electrophiles in S_E reaction.
(b) They react only with strongly activated ring (as phenol).
(c) They do not decomposes easily in the dry state.
(d) They are coloured crystalline solid.

10 Aromatic diazonium group can be replaced by various groups/atoms. In this context, choose the incorrect match of reagent-reaction types.
(a) $H_3PO_2 \longrightarrow$ Hydrogen (b) Sandmeyer $\longrightarrow$ Chlorine
(c) $H_2O/\Delta \longrightarrow$ Hydroxyl group (d) $HBF_4/\Delta \longrightarrow BF_3$ group

11 Diazotisation of aniline is done by HNO_3.

Consider the following reagents.

(i) Urea
(ii) Ammonium chloride
(iii) $NaNO_2$
(iv) H_3PO_2
(v) HCl

How many of them are used to remove the excess of HNO_3?

(a) 3 (b) 2
(c) 4 (d) 1

12 Consider the following statements.

Statement I Aromatic diazonium salts are more stable than aliphatic diazonium salts.

Statement II Diazonium salts are stabilised by resonance.

In the light of the above statements, choose the most appropriate answer from the options given below.

(a) Both Statement I and Statement II are false.
(b) Statement I is true but Statement II is false.
(c) Statement I is false but Statement II is true.
(d) Both Statement I and Statement II are true.

13 The colour of *p*-amino azobenzene is

(a) yellow
(b) congo red
(c) brown
(d) violet

14 What is the known name of the given reaction?

$$C_6H_5\overset{+}{N_2}Cl^- \xrightarrow[\text{HCl}]{\text{Cu}} C_6H_5X + N_2$$

(a) Gattermann reaction
(b) Sandmeyer reaction
(c) Dehydrogenation reaction
(d) Esterification reaction

15 Which of the following statement is correct about the reaction of diazonium salts?

(a) Their reactions involved the displacement of nitrogen and inversion of diazo group.
(b) The yield of Gattermann reaction is found to be better than Sandmeyer reaction.
(c) Their solution is treated with potassium iodide in the presence of copper powder, iodobenzene is formed.
(d) Certain mild reducing agents like phosphinic acid or ethanol reduce diazonium salts to arenes.

NEET Exclusive EXTRA BYTES

- Tertiary alkyl alcohol react with conc. H_2SO_4 and HCN to form 1° amine and the reaction is known as **Ritter reaction**
- Quaternary ammonium hydroxide on heating strongly decomposes to yield water, a tertiary amine and alkene. This method proceeds *via* E2 elimination in which the hydroxide ion functions as the base.
- If two or more than two nitro groups are present at *meta*-positions then one of them gets reduced to amino group with $(NH_4)_2S$ and $SnCl_2$/HCl (Selective reduction).
- Cyanides get hydrolysed to carboxylic acid, when it is refluxed with strong aqueous acid or sodium hydroxide solution. This type of hydrolysis is known as complete hydrolysis while with cold conc. HCl or by dissolving it in conc. H_2SO_4 followed by pouring it into water gives amide. This type of hydrolysis is known as partial hydrolysis.
- Nitro compounds having alpha-hydrogen convert into aci-nitro derivatives ($—C=\overset{+}{N}(O^-)—O^-$) in the presence of base. This on hydrolysis with conc. H_2SO_4 gives carbonyl compounds. The reaction is known as **Nef reaction**.

Substrate	Reagent	Product
$R—CH_2—NO_2$	(i) Conc. NaOH (ii) Conc. H_2SO_4	$R—CHO$
$R—CH(R)—NO_2$	(i) Conc. NaOH (ii) Conc. H_2SO_4	$R—C(=O)—R$

GEARING UP FOR NEET

1 The IUPAC name for $(CH_3)_2NC(CH_3)_3$ is

(a) N, N-dimethyl-2-methyl-1-butanamine
(b) N, N-dimethyl-2-methyl-2-propanamine
(c) trimethyl *t*-butyl amine
(d) *N*, *N*-trimethyl-4-butanamine

2 Which of the following compound is incorrectly matched with their IUPAC name?

(a) $C_6H_5CH_2NH_2 \longrightarrow$ N-methyl aniline
(b) $C_6H_5NHCH_3 \longrightarrow$ N-methyl benzenamine
(c) $C_6H_5NHC_6H_5 \longrightarrow$ N-phenyl benzenamine
(d) $CH_3CH_2NHCH_3 \longrightarrow$ N-methyl ethanamine

3 The source of nitrogen in Gabriel synthesis of amines is ....

(a) sodium azide, NaN_3
(b) sodium nitrite, $NaNO_2$
(c) potassium cyanide, KCN
(d) potassium phthalimide, $C_6H_4(CO_2)N^-K^+$

4 Consider the following reaction sequence,

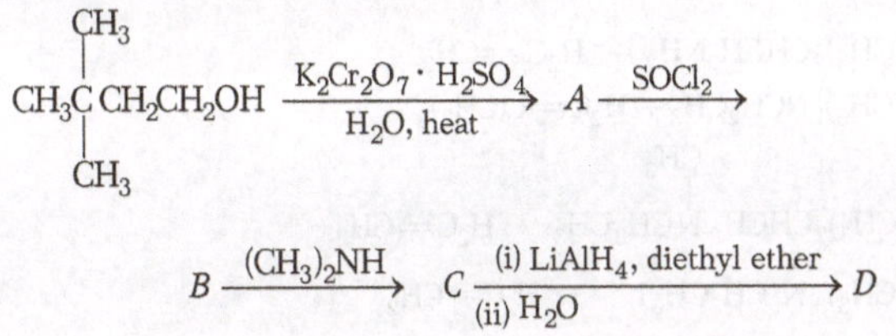

Identify the product *D* formed in above reaction,

(a) 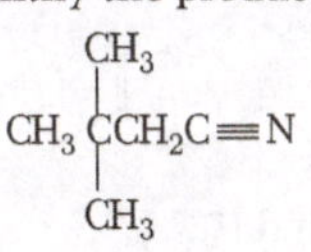
(b) 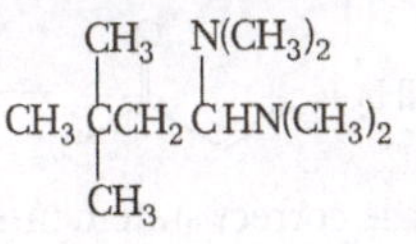
(c) 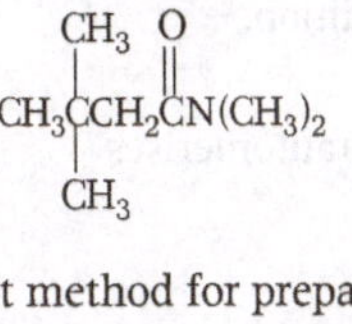
(d) 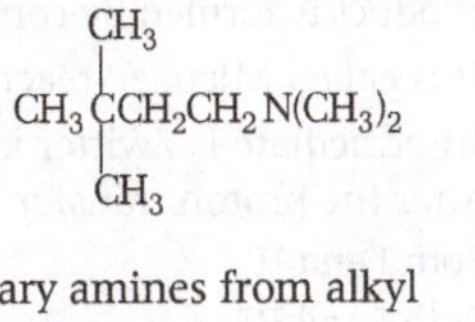

5 Best method for preparing primary amines from alkyl halides without changing the number of carbon atoms in the chain is

(a) Hofmann bromamide reaction
(b) Gabriel phthalimide synthesis
(c) Sandmeyer reaction
(d) Reaction with NH_3

6 Select the incorrect statements from the following facts about Curtius and Hofmann rearrangement

(a) are synthetic methods for preparation of primary amines.
(b) involve intermolecular alkyl/aryl migration.
(c) involve isocyanate as an intermediate.
(d) they take place with complete retention of stereochemical configuration in the migrating alkyl group.

7 Amongst the given set of reactants, the most appropriate for preparing 2° amine is ....

(a) $2°R—Br + NH_3$
(b) $2°R—Br$ + NaCN followed by H_2 / Pt
(c) $1°R—NH_2 + RCHO$ followed by H_2 / Pt
(d) $1°R—Br$(2 mol) +potassium phthalimide followed by H_3O^+ / heat

8 The most reactive amine towards dilute hydrochloric acid is ....

(a) $CH_3—NH_2$
(b) 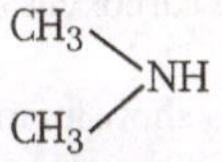
(c) 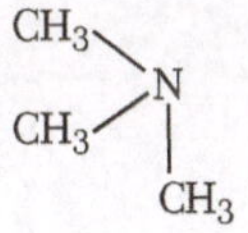
(d) 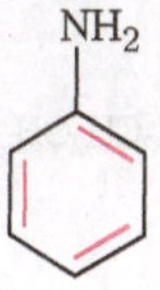

9 Select the incorrect statement from the following.

(a) Methyl amine is more basic than ammonia.
(b) Alkyl amine are stronger bases than ammonia.
(c) The order of basicity of amines in the gaseous phase follows the order $3° > 2° > 1° > NH_3$.
(d) Amines behaves as Lewis acid.

10 Among the following the strongest base is

(a) 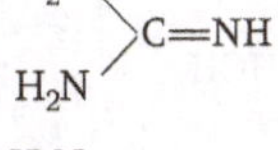
(b) 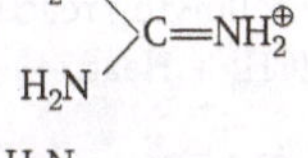
(c) 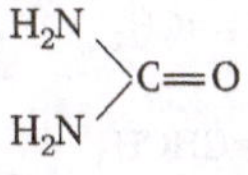
(d) 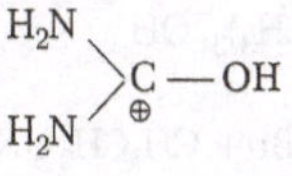

11 Consider the structure.

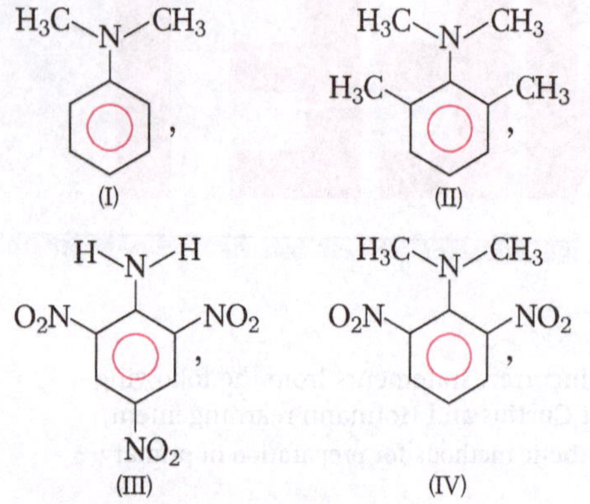

Which of the following statements are correct?

(a) Basic strength of II is greater than IV.
(b) Basic strength of II is less than that of I.
(c) Basic strength of IV is greater than I.
(d) Basic strength of IV is less than III.

12 Among the following, the most basic in gaseous phase is

(a) NH_3 (b) $CH_3CH_2NH_2$
(c) $(CH_3CH_2)_2NH$ (d) $(CH_3CH_2)_3N$

13 Which of the following statement is not correct?

(a) Primary amines show intermolecular hydrogen bonding.
(b) Secondary amines show intermolecular hydrogen bonding.
(c) Amines have lower boiling points as compared to those of alcohols and carboxylic acids of comparable molar masses.
(d) Tertiary amines show intermolecular hydrogen bonding.

14 Dipole moment of

$CH_3CH_2CH_3$, (I) CH_3CH_2OH, (II) $CH_3CH_2NH_2$ (III)

will be in order

(a) I < II < III (b) III < II < I
(c) I < III < II (d) II < III < I

15 Which of the following statements is true?

(a) Triethylamine forms a soluble compound with Hinsberg reagent and KOH.
(b) Dimethylamine reacts with KOH and phenol to form an azo dye.
(c) When diethylamine is oxidised by $KMnO_4$, the product is $(CH_3CH_2)_2N—N(CH_2CH_3)_2$.
(d) Methylamine reacts with PhMgBr to give toluene.

16 Consider the following reaction,

1. $CH_3CH_2CH(\overset{+}{N}(CH_3)_3\,\overset{-}{O}H)CH_3$ + Heat ⟶ $CH_3CH=CHCH_3$ (X) + $CH_3CH_2CH=CH_2$ (Y)

2. $CH_3CH_2CHBr(CH_3)$ + $CH_3CH_2\overset{-}{O}\overset{+}{Na}$ ⟶ $CH_3CH=CHCH_3$ (X) + $CH_3CH_2CH=CH_2$ (Y)

The products $CH_3CH=CHCH_3(X)$ and $CH_3CH_2CH=CH_2(Y)$ can be obtained.
What will be the major product of each of the two reactions shown?

(a) 1 − X, 2 − X (b) 1 − Y, 2 − X
(c) 1 − X, 2 − Y (d) 1 − Y, 2 − Y

17 Following 1° amine has chiral carbon as indicated

$H—\overset{*}{C}(CH_3)(C_2H_5)—NH_2$. This on reaction with ($NaNO_2$ + HCl) forms

(a) 1° alcohol with retention of configuration
(b) 2° alcohol with inverted configuration
(c) racemic mixture of 2° alcohol
(d) racemic mixture of 1° alcohol

18 Select the incorrect statement(s) about the following reaction,

$$[(CH_3)_3N^{\oplus}CH_2CH_3]OH^{\ominus} \xrightarrow{\Delta} (CH_3)_3N + CH_2=CH_2 + H_2O$$

(a) This reaction is called Hofmann elimination.
(b) OH^- ion functions as a base in E2 elimination.
(c) Less substituted alkene is the predominant alkene.
(d) OH^- ion functions as a base in S_N2 reaction.

19 Consider the following sequence of reactions,

$$(CH_3)_2CHCH_2N(CH_2CH_3)_2 \xrightarrow{CH_3I} \xrightarrow[H_2O]{Ag_2O} \xrightarrow{Heat} ?$$

The major end product formed in above reaction are

(a) $(CH_3)_2CHCH_2NH_2 + H_2C=CH_2$
(b) $(CH_3)_2NCH_2CH_3 + H_2C=C(CH_3)_2$
(c) $(CH_3)_2CHCH_2N(CH_3)CH_2CH_3 + H_2C=CH_2$
(d) $(CH_3)_3\overset{+}{N}CH_2CH_3I^- + H_2C=CH_2$

20 CH_3NH_2 reacts with α, β-unsaturated ketone as shown

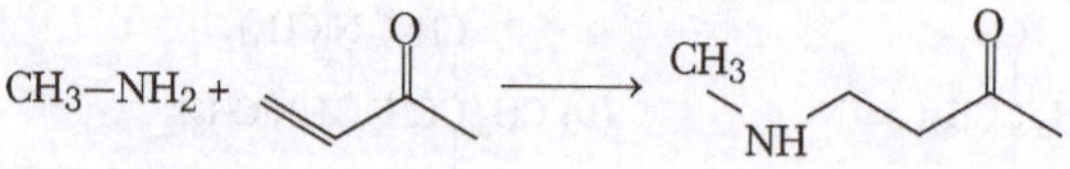

Select the correct statements out of I, II and III.

I. Product is formed by conjugate addition.
II. It is called Michael reaction.
III. Intermediate is Zwitter ion which tautomerises after the proton transfer.

(a) Both I and II
(b) Both I and III
(c) Both II and III
(d) I, II and III

21 Consider the following sequence of reactions.

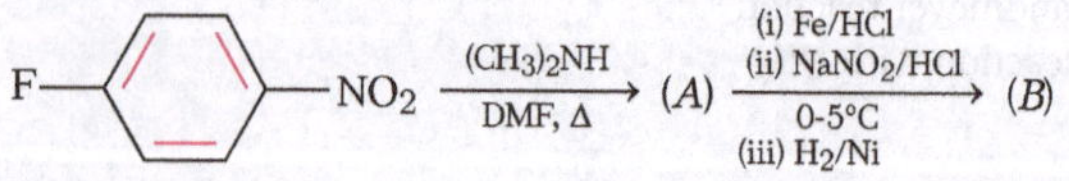

The product (*B*) is

(a) 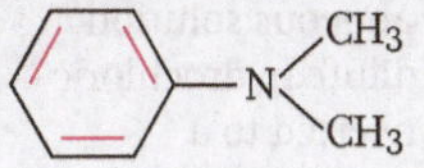

(b) 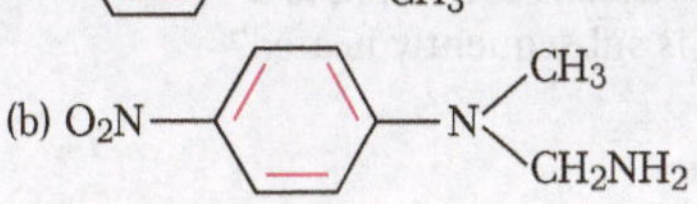

(c) 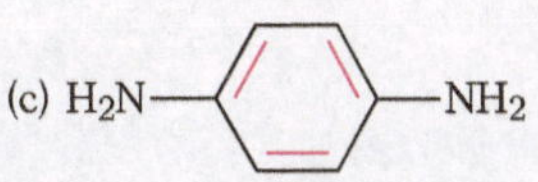

(d) 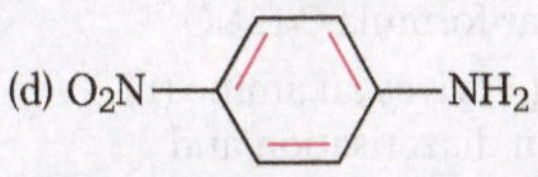

22 The best reagent for converting, 2-phenylpropanamide into 1-phenylethanamine is ....

(a) excess H_2/Pt (b) NaOH / Br_2
(c) $NaBH_4$ /methanol (d) $LiAlH_4$ /H_2O

23 Identify the strongest and weakest bases among the following and choose the correct code that are given below of these compounds.

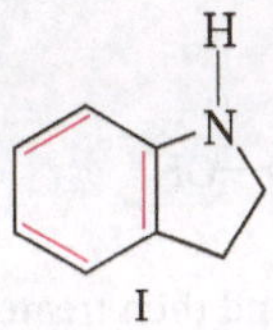
I

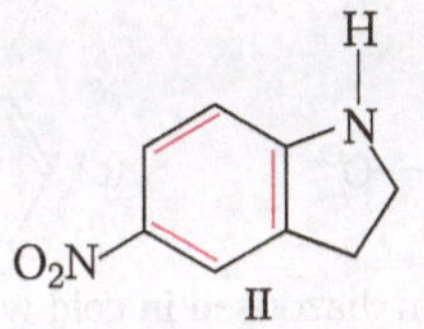
II

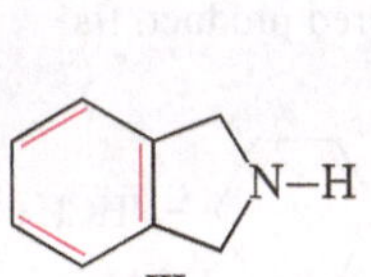
III

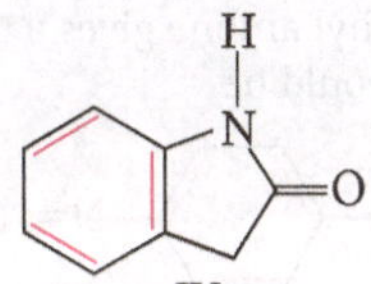
IV

	Strongest	**Weakest**
(a)	IV	I
(b)	IV	II
(c)	I	IV
(d)	III	IV

24 Which of the following is maximum basic in nature?

(a) 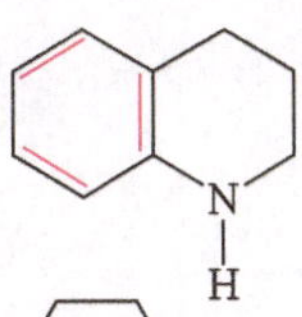

(b) 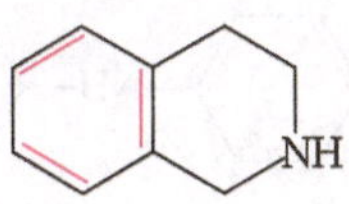

(c) 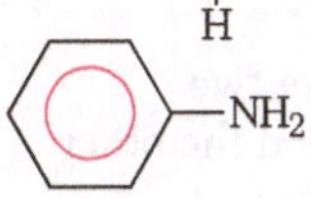

(d) 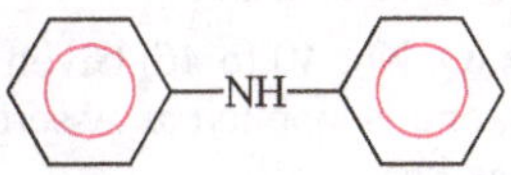

25 Consider the following compounds.

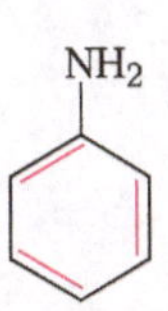
(I)

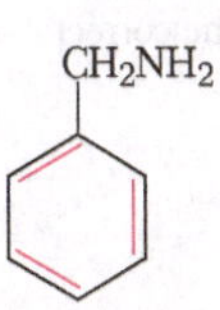
(II)

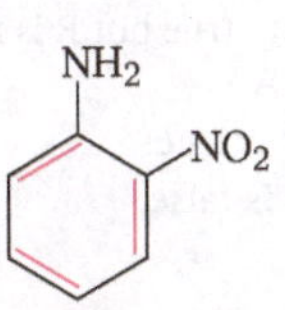
(III)

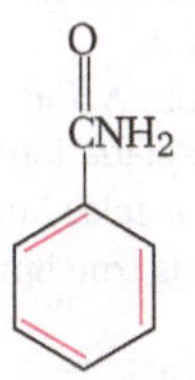
(IV)

Rank the above compounds in order of increasing basicity (weakest to strongest).

(a) IV < II < I < III
(b) IV < I < III < II
(c) IV < III < I < II
(d) II < I < III < IV

26 Which of the following C_8H_9NO isomers is the weakest base?

(a) *o*-aminoacetophenone
(b) *m*-aminoacetophenone
(c) *p*-aminoacetophenone
(d) Acetanilide

27 Which of the following compounds is the weakest Bronsted base?

(a) 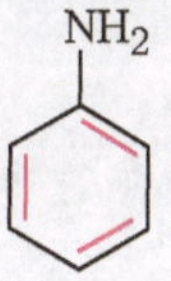
(b) 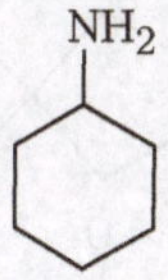
(c) 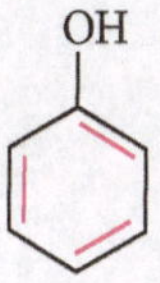
(d) 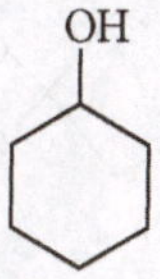

28 Among the following compounds, the increasing order of their basic strength is

I. 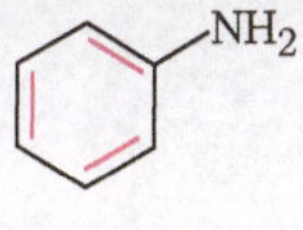
II. 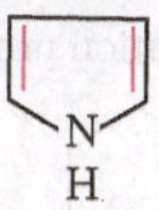
III. 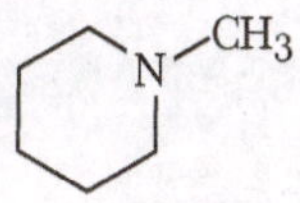
IV. 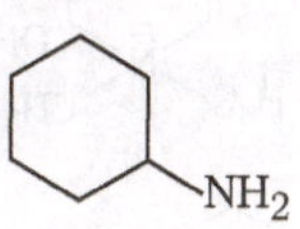

(a) I < II < IV < III
(b) I < II < III < IV
(c) II < I < IV < III
(d) II < I < III < IV

29 Which of the following statement is not correct regarding ethylamine and aniline?

(a) Each has —NH_2 group.
(b) Both dissolve in HCl to form salt as a product.
(c) Each react with a mixture of $CHCl_3$ and KOH to form a bad smelling compound.
(d) Each react with HNO_2 to give a hydroxy compound.

30 Which of the following reagents would not be a good choice for reducing an aryl nitro compound to an amine?

(a) H_2(excess) / Pt (b) $LiAlH_4$ in ether
(c) Fe and HCl (d) Sn and HCl

31 In the following sequence of reactions

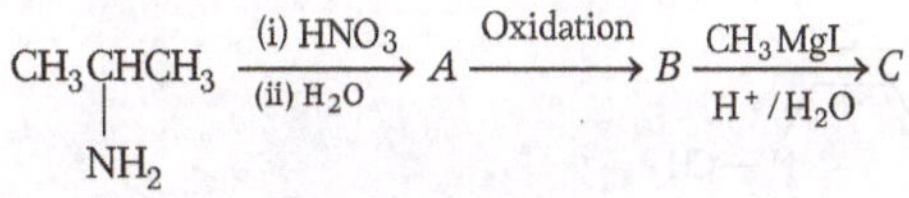

The compound *C* formed would be

(a) 1,1-dimethyl ethanol
(b) 1-butanol
(c) 2-butanol
(d) 2-methyl-propan-2-ol

32 Which of the following statements is incorrect about aniline?

(a) It does not undergo Friedel-Crafts reaction due to salt formation with aluminium chloride.

(b) It reacts with concentrated sulphuric acid to form anilinium hydrogen sulphate.

(c) It reacts with sodium to give hydrogen.

(d) It is soluble in water.

33 Consider the following reaction,

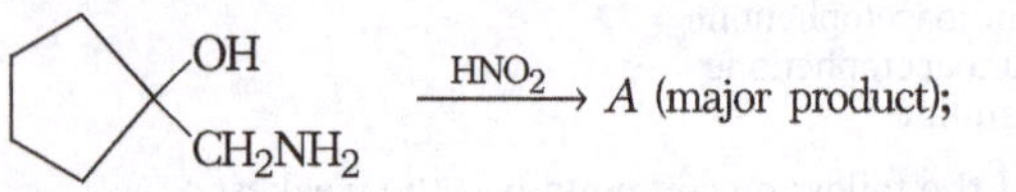

Here, 'A' is

(a) 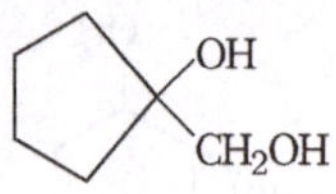

(b) 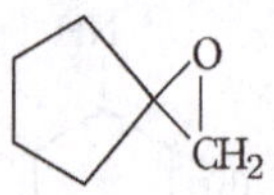

(c) 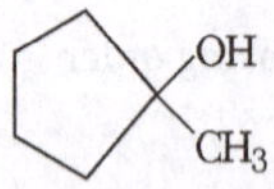

(d) 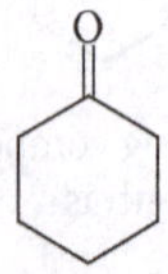

34 Hoffmann elimination product of (A) is

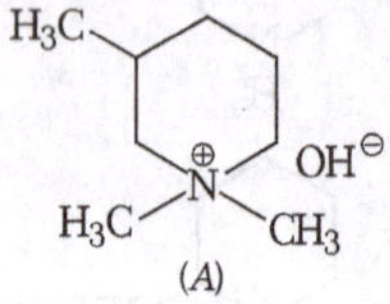

(A)

(a) 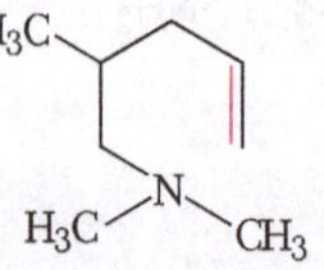

(b) 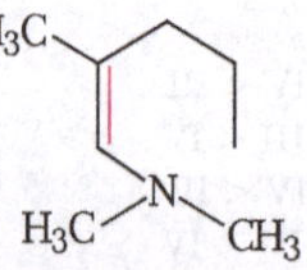

(c) 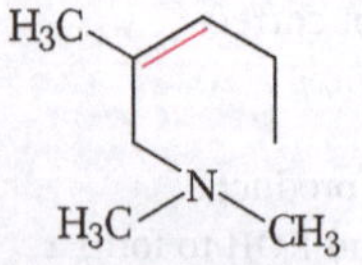

(d) 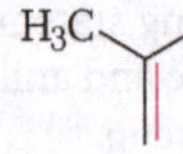

35 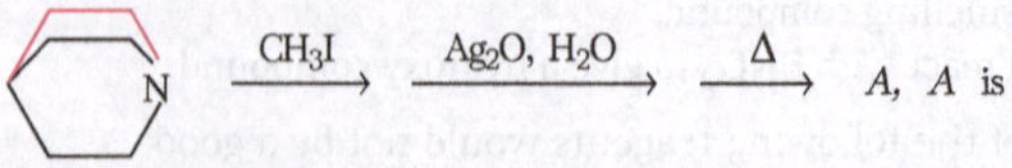

(a) 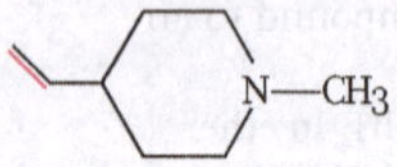

(b) 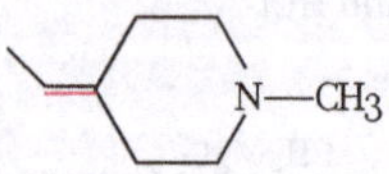

(c) 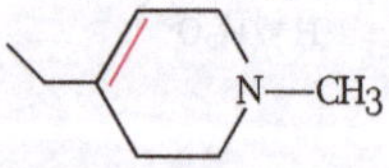

(d) 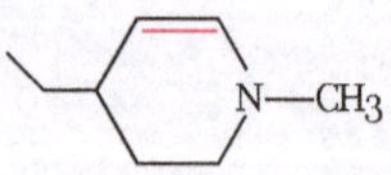

36 Aniline is reacted with bromine water and the resulting product is treated with an aqueous solution of sodium nitrite in the presence of dilute hydrochloric acid. The compound so formed is converted to a tetrafluoroborate, which is subsequently heated? The final product is

(a) 1,3,5-tribromobenzene

(b) *p*-bromofluorobenzene

(c) *p*-bromoaniline

(d) 2,4,6-tribromofluorobenzene

37 A compound (*X*) has the molecular formula C_7H_7NO. On treatment with Br_2 and KOH (*X*) gives an amine (*Y*). (*Y*) gives carbylamine test (*Y*) upon diazotisation and coupling with phenol gives an azo dye (*Z*). *X* is

(a) $PhCONH_2$ (b) $PhCONHCOCH_3$

(c) $PhNO_2$ (d) $PhCOONH_4$

38 Which of the following undergoes coupling reaction at the fastest rate?

(a) 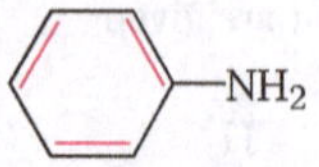

(b) 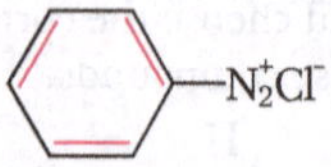

(c) 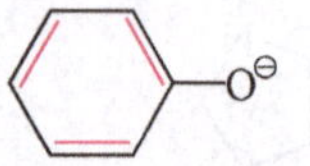

(d) 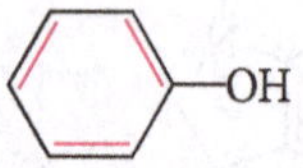

39 Aniline when diazotised in cold water and then treated with dimethyl aniline gives a coloured product. Its structure would be

(a) 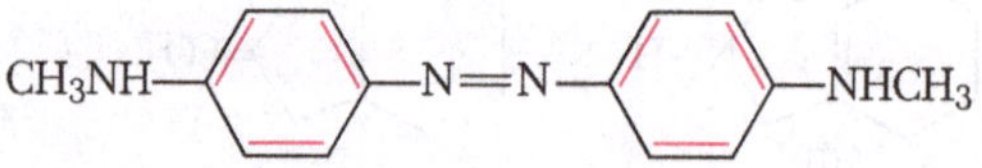

(b) 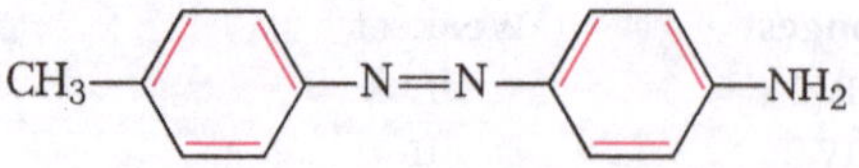

(c) 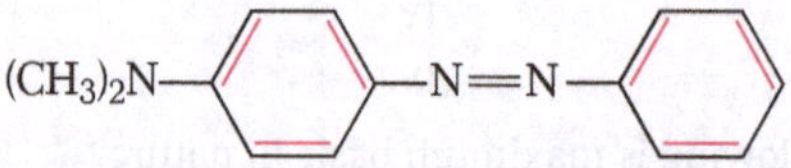

(d) 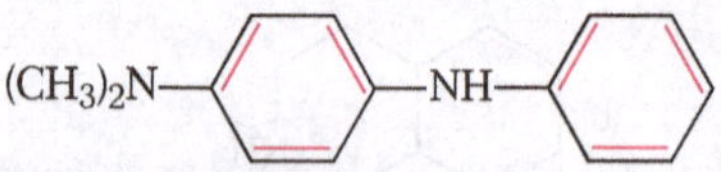

Assertion-Reason

Directions (Q. No. 40 to 46) Given below are two statements, one is labelled as Assertion (A) and the other is labelled as Reason (R).

(a) Both A and R are true and R is the correct explanation of A.

(b) Both A and R are true but R is not the correct explanation of A.

(c) A is false but R is true.

(d) A is true but R is false.

40 **Assertion** (A) Basicity of $CH_3CH_2NH_2$ (I), NH_3 (II) and $C_6H_5NH_2$ (III) is in order III > I > II.

Reason (R) Electron donating group increase the basicity of amines and electron withdrawing groups decrease the basicity of amines.

41 **Assertion** (A) Hoffmann's bromamide reaction is given by primary amines.

Reason (R) Primary amines are less basic than secondary amines.

42 **Assertion** (A) Only a small amount of HCl is required in the reduction of nitro compounds with iron scrap and HCl in the presence of tin.

Reason (R) $FeCl_2$ formed get hydrolysed to release HCl during the reaction.

43 **Assertion** (A) *p*-toluidine is solid at room temperature while *o*- and *m*- isomers are liquids.

Reason (R) Being symmetrical, *p*-isomers have strong intermolecular H-bonding giving solid state of high melting point.

44 **Assertion** (A) N, N-diethylbenzenesulphonamide is insoluble in alkali.

Reason (R) Sulphonyl group attached to nitrogen atom is strong electron withdrawing group.

45 **Assertion** (A) N-ethylbenzenesulphonamide is soluble in alkali.

Reason (R) Hydrogen atom attached to nitrogen in sulphonamide is strongly acidic in nature.

46 **Assertion** (A) Aqueous H_3PO_2 converts benzene diazonium salt into benzene.

Reason (R) H_3PO_2 acts as an oxidising agent.

Statement Type Questions

Directons (Q. Nos. 47 to 53) In the following questions, two statements (I & II) are given. In the light of the given statements, choose the correct option given below.

(a) Both Statement I and Statement II are false.
(b) Statement I is true but Statement II is false.
(c) Statement I is false but Statement II is true.
(d) Both Statement I and Statement II are true.

47 **Statement I** Total possible structural isomers of $C_4H_{11}N$ are 7.

Statement II 1°, 2° and 3° are functional isomers of each other.

48 **Statement I** All the three classes of amines are hydrogen bond donors, while primary and secondary amines are hydrogen bond acceptors.

Statement II Lower aliphatic amines are soluble in water.

49 **Statement I** In carbylamine reaction, —NH_2 group is converted into —NC group.

Statement II Carbylamine reaction involves the reaction between primary amine and chloroform in basic medium.

50 **Statement I** Aromatic amines are generally less basic than alkyl amines.

Statement II The nitrogen lone pair electrons are delocalised by interaction with the aromatic ring π-electron system of the aromatic ring.

51 **Statement I** The reaction of acetamide with bromine in the presence of NaOH formed primary amine.

Statement II Acetamide and ethylamine can be distinguished by reacting with aq. HCl and heat.

52 **Statement I** Sulphanilic acid migrates to anode in basic medium and to cathode in acidic medium.

Statement II Sulphanilic acid is a dipolar ion and exists as cation in acidic medium and as an anion in basic medium.

53 **Statement I** Methanamine on reaction with benzoyl chloride produce N-methylbenzamide.

Statement II Benzamine on reaction with ethanoic anhydride gives acetanilide.

54 Which of the following statements are correct?

A. Nitro compounds are reduced to amines by reduction with metals in basic medium.
B. The process of cleavage of the C—*X* bond by amine group is known as ammonolysis.
C. In ammonolysis, primary amine is obtained as a major product by taking large excess of ammonia.
D. The free amine can be obtained from the ammonium salt by treatment with a weak base.
E. The order of reactivity of halides with amines are *R*I > *R*Br > *R*Cl.

Choose the correct answer from the options given below.

(a) A, B and E
(b) B and D
(c) B, C and D
(d) C and E

55 Select the incorrect statements from the following.

A. Reduction of nitriles with lithium aluminium hydride is used for ascent of amine series.
B. Methyl amide on reduction with lithium aluminium hydride yield ethylamine.
C. Ammonolysis of benzyl chloride yield N, N-dimethyl methanamine with 2 moles of CH_3Cl.
D. Ammonolysis has an advantage of yielding a mixture of primary, secondary and tertiary amines.
E. Propane nitrile on reduction with Na(Hg)/C_2H_5OH formed butan-1-amine.

Choose the correct answer from the options given below.

(a) C, D and E (b) A, D and B
(c) A, B and C (d) B, C and D

56 Select the correct statements from the following.

A. Amines behave as nucleophiles due to the presence of unshared electron pair.

B. Aliphatic amines are stronger bases than ammonia and weaker bases than aromatic amines.

C. Amines salts are insoluble in water but soluble in organic solvents like ether.

D. N-methylmethanamine is strong base than methanamine.

E. Basic character of an amine depends upon the ease of formation of the cation, more stable the cation, more basic is the amine.

Choose the correct answer from the options given below:

(a) B, C and D (b) A, B, C and E
(c) A, D and E (d) A, B and D

57 Select the incorrect statement from the following.

A. Base-weakening substituents are the one that activate an aromatic ring towards electrophilic substitution.

B. Aliphatic amine forms stable diazonium salt with nitrous acid.

C. All amino compounds can be distinguished by using the reagents chloroform and potassium hydroxide.

D. The sulphonamide formed from secondary amine does not form sodium salt and is also insoluble in water.

E. When diazonium fluoroborate is heated with aqueous $NaNO_2$ in the presence of Cu, the diazonium group is replaced by —NO_2 group.

Choose the correct answer from the options given below.

(a) B, C and D (b) A, B and E
(c) C, D and A (d) A, B and C

58 Which of the following statements are incorrect?

A. Aliphatic and aromatic primary and secondary amines react with acid chlorides, anhydrides by electrophilic substitution reaction known as acylation.

B. Acylation reaction are carried out in the presence of a base weaker than the amine.

C. Methanamine reacts with benzoyl chloride gives N-methyl benzamide.

D. The products obtained by acylation reaction are known as amines.

E. The reaction of aliphatic/aromatic amine with C_6H_5COCl known as benzoylation.

Choose the correct answer from the options given below.

(a) B and C (b) C, D and E
(c) A, B and D (d) A, D and E

59 Select the correct statements from the following.

A. Primary aliphatic amines react with nitrous acid to form stable aliphatic diazonium salts and liberate nitrogen gas.

B. Aromatic primary amines react with nitrous acid at high temperature.

C. Benzene sulphonyl chloride reacts with primary and secondary amine to form sulphonamides.

D. Tertiary amines do not react with benzene sulphonyl chloride.

E. These days benzene sulphonyl chloride is replaced by *p*-toluene sulphonyl chloride.

Choose the correct answer from the options given below:

(a) C, D and E (b) B and C
(c) A, B and D (d) A, B and E

60 Which of the following statements are correct?

A. Aniline are usually colourless but get coloured on storage due to atmospheric oxidation.

B. Lower aliphatic amines are insoluble in water.

C. Amines are soluble in organic solvents like alcohol, ether and benzene.

D. Alcohols are more polar than amines and form stronger intramolecular hydrogen bonds than amines.

E. The lower aliphatic amines are gases with fishy odour.

Choose the correct answer from the options given below.

(a) A, C and E (b) B and E
(c) B, C and A (d) D and E

61 Which of the following statements are correct?

A. Aryl fluorides and iodides can not be prepared by direct halogenation.

B. The cyano group cannot be introduced by nucleophilic substitution of chlorine in chlorobenzene.

C. The diazonium salts are not good intermediates for the introduction of —F, —Cl, —Br, —I etc., groups into the aromatic ring.

D. If the temperature of the diazonium salt solution is kept at low, then the salt gets hydrolysed to phenol.

Choose the correct answer from the options given below.

(a) B, C and D (b) C, D and E
(c) A, B and C (d) A, B and C

62 Which of the following statements are incorrect?

A. Direct nitration of aniline yields tarry oxidation products in addition to the nitro derivatives.

B. Due to high reactivity of aromatic amines, electrophilic substitution occurs at *meta*-positions.

C. Aniline reacts with bromine water at room temperature to give a yellow precipitate of 3, 5-dibromoaniline.

D. Activating effect of $-NHCOCH_3$ group is less than that of amino group.

E. In strongly basic medium, aniline formed the anilinium ion which is *meta*-directing.

Choose the correct answer from the options given below:

(a) A and C (b) A and D (c) D and B (d) B, C and E

Species Selection Type Questions

63 Consider the following compounds name,

(i) Methyl aniline
(ii) Propanediamine
(iii) N-pentyl-2-propyl amine
(iv) *m*-xylidine
(v) Isopropyl amine
(vi) *t*-butylamine
(vii) N-phenyl hydroxylamine

How many of them are incorrect?

(a) 4 (b) 5 (c) 3 (d) 2

64 Consider the following compounds,

(i) *tert*-butylamine (ii) *sec*-butylamine
(iii) Isobutylamine (iv) *n*-butylamine
(v) Ethylamine

How many compounds exhibit optical isomerism?

(a) 3 (b) 2 (c) 1 (d) 4

65 Consider the following compounds.

(i) CH_3CH_2CN (ii) $CH_3-CH_2-\overset{O}{\overset{\|}{C}}-NH_2$

(iii) 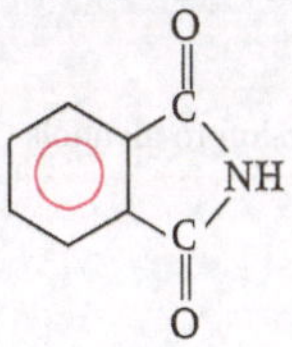 (iv) 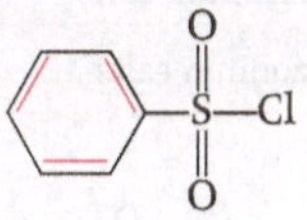

(v) 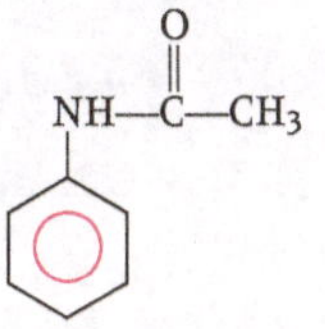

How many compounds will form primary amines upon reduction?

(a) 1 (b) 2 (c) 3 (d) 4

66 Consider the following compounds,

(i) $CH_3-CH=CH-CH_3$
(ii) $CH_3CH_2CH(OH)CH_3$
(iii) $CH_3-CH_2-CH_2-CH_3$
(iv) $CH_2=C(CH_3)-OH$
(v) $CH_3CH_2CH_2CH_2OH$
(vi) $CH_3-CH=CH-CH_2-OH$
(vii) $H_3C-C(CH_3)_2-OH$

How many compounds are formed when butan-1-amine reacts with nitrous acid at 0°C?

(a) 2 (b) 5
(c) 4 (d) 3

67 Consider the following reactions.

(i) $C_6H_5CONH_2 \xrightarrow{NaOBr}$
(ii) $C_6H_5CONH_2 \xrightarrow{LiAlH_4/H_2O}$
(iii) $C_6H_5CN \xrightarrow{LiAlH_4}$
(iv) Potassium phthalimide $\xrightarrow[\text{(b) } Aq.\text{ NaOH}]{\text{(a) } C_6H_5CH_2Br}$
(v) $C_6H_5CH_2Cl \xrightarrow{\text{Ammonia}}$

How many reactions will give benzylamine?

(a) 3 (b) 1
(c) 2 (d) 4

68 In the following reactions,

(i) 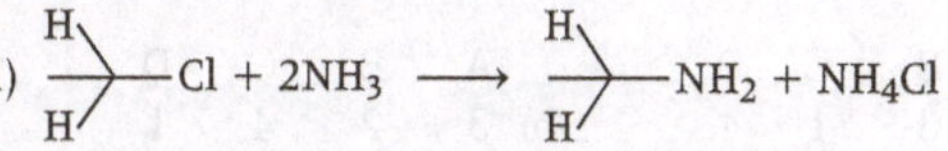

(ii) $R-NH_2 + CHCl_3 + 3KOH \xrightarrow{\Delta} RCONH_2 + 2H_2O$

(iii) 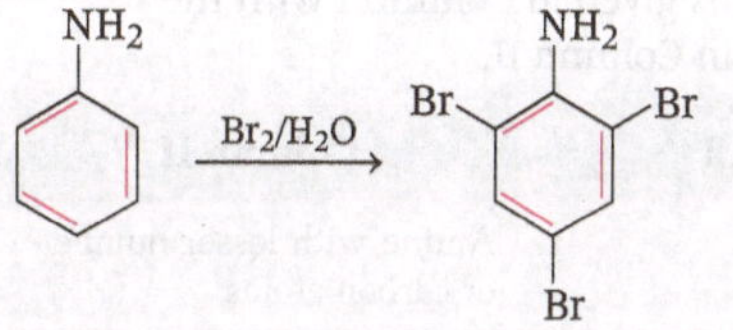

(iv) 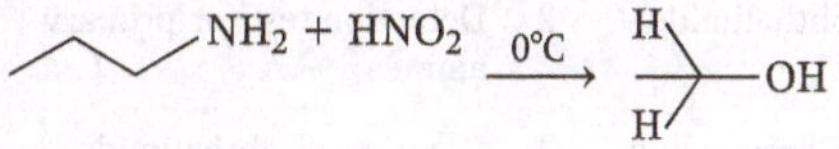

(v) 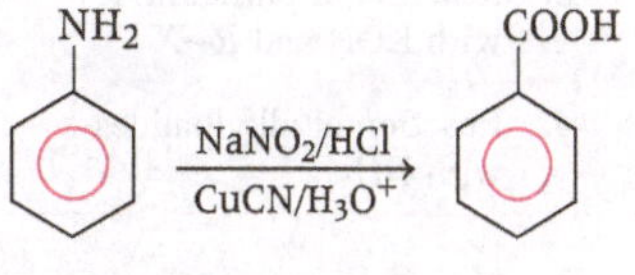

How many reactions are correct?

(a) 2 (b) 3
(c) 4 (d) 5

69 Consider the following compounds,

(i) $(C_6H_5)_3N$ (ii) 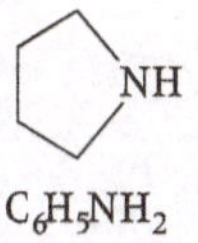

(iii) $C_6H_5NHC_6H_5$ (iv) $C_6H_5NH_2$

(v) 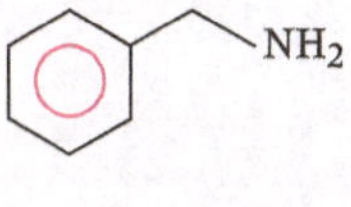

How many compounds, give a product containing a carbon-nitrogen double bond when react with acetone in the presence of NaOH?

(a) 3 (b) 4 (c) 1 (d) 2

70 Consider the following compounds,

(i) Azoxybenzene (ii) Azobenzene

(iii) Hydrazobenzene (iv) Benzyl alcohol

(v) Benzyl amine

How many of them are obtained when $PhNO_2$ is reduced in alkaline medium i.e, Na_3AsO_3 / NaOH, $SnCl_2$ / NaOH, Zn/NaOH

(a) 4 (b) 2 (c) 3 (d) 1

Match the Columns

71 Match the species given in Column I with their degree (1°, 2°, 3°) given in Column II.

	Column I		Column II
A.	$(CH_3)_3C—NH_2$	1.	Tertiary
B.	$(CH_3)_2NH$	2.	Primary
C.	$(CH_3)_3N$	3.	Secondary
D.	$(CH_3)_4\overset{\oplus}{N}\overset{\ominus}{Cl}$	4.	Quaternary

Codes

	A	B	C	D		A	B	C	D
(a)	2	3	1	4	(b)	3	2	4	1
(c)	4	3	2	1	(d)	1	4	2	3

72 Match the reactions given in Column I with the statements given in Column II.

Column I	Column II
A. Ammonolysis	1. Amine with lesser number of carbon atoms
B. Gabriel phthalimide synthesis	2. Detection test for primary amines
C. Hofmann bromamide reaction	3. Reaction of phthalimide with KOH and *R*–*X*
D. Carbylamine reaction	4. Reaction of alkylhalides with NH_3

Codes

	A	B	C	D
(a)	2	3	1	4
(b)	3	1	4	2
(c)	3	4	2	1
(d)	4	3	1	2

73 Match the reaction name given in Column I with the reacting substances given in Column II.

Column I	Column II
A. Schmidt reaction	1. $RCONH_2 \xrightarrow[\Delta]{Br_2/NaOH} RNH_2$
B. Carbylamine reaction	2. $RNH_2 + CS_2 + HgCl_2 \longrightarrow$ Black ppt.
C. Hofmann-bromamide degradation reaction	3. $RCOOH + N_3H \xrightarrow{\Delta} RNH_2$
D. Hofmann-mustard oil reaction	4. $RNH_2 + CHCl_3 + KOH \xrightarrow{\Delta} RNC$

Codes

	A	B	C	D
(a)	2	3	1	4
(b)	3	4	1	2
(c)	2	1	4	3
(d)	4	1	2	3

74 Match the compounds given in Column I with the items given in Column II.

Column I	Column II
A. Benzene sulphonyl chloride	1. Zwitter ion
B. Sulphanilic acid	2. Hinsberg reagent
C. Alkyl diazonium salts	3. Dyes
D. Aryl diazonium salts	4. Conversion to alcohols

Codes

	A	B	C	D
(a)	4	3	2	1
(b)	2	3	4	1
(c)	1	4	3	2
(d)	2	1	4	3

Final Check Through PYQs

Module-I Aliphatic Amines

1 Identify the major product C formed in the following reaction sequence : **[NEET 2024]**

$$CH_3—CH_2—CH_2—I \xrightarrow{NaCN} A \; CH_3—CH_2—CH_2—CN \xrightarrow[\text{Partial hydrolysis}]{OH^-} B \xrightarrow[Br_2]{NaOH} \underset{(\text{Major})}{C}$$

(a) propylamine (b) butylamine
(c) butanamide (d) α-bromobutanoic acid

2 Which of the following reactions will not give primary amine as the product? **[NCERT (New) Pg. 271, NEET 2023]**

(a) $CH_3CN \xrightarrow[\text{(ii) } H_3O^+]{\text{(i) } LiAlH_4}$ Product

(b) $CH_3NC \xrightarrow[\text{(ii) } H_3O^+]{\text{(i) } LiAlH_4}$ Product

(c) $CH_3CONH_2 \xrightarrow[\text{(ii) } H_3O^+]{\text{(i) } LiAlH_4}$ Product

(d) $CH_3CONH_2 \xrightarrow{Br_2/KOH}$ Product

3 Identify the compound that will react with Hinsberg's reagent to give a solid which dissolve in alkali. **[NCERT (New) Pg. 271, NEET 2021]**

(a) $H_3C—CH_2—\ddot{N}(CH_3)—CH_2—CH_3$

(b) $H_3C—CH_2—\ddot{N}O_2$

(c) $H_3C—CH_2—\ddot{N}H—CH_2$

(d) $H_3C—CH_2—\ddot{N}H_2$

4 Reaction of propanamide with ethanolic sodium hydroxide and bromine will give **[NCERT (New) Pg. 264, NEET (Oct.) 2020]**

(a) ethylamine (b) methylamine
(c) propylamine (d) aniline

5 The amine that reacts will Hinsberg's reagent to give an alkali insoluble product is **[NCERT (New) Pg. 271, NEET (Odisha) 2019]**

(a) $CH_3—CH(CH_3)—NH—CH(CH_3)CH_3$

(b) $CH_3—CH_2—N(CH_2CH_3)—CH_2CH_3$

(c) $CH_3—C(NH_2)(CH_3)—CH_2CH_2CH_3$

(d) $CH_3—C(CH_3)_2—CH(CH_3)—NH_2$

6 The correct order of the basic strength of methyl substituted amines in aqueous solution is **[NCERT (New) Pg. 269, NEET (National) 2019]**

(a) $(CH_3)_3N > CH_3NH_2 > (CH_3)_2NH$
(b) $(CH_3)_3N > (CH_3)_2NH > CH_3NH_2$
(c) $CH_3NH_2 > (CH_3)_2NH > (CH_3)_3N$
(d) $(CH_3)_2NH > CH_3NH_2 > (CH_3)_3N$

7 Which of the following reactions is appropriate for converting acetamide to methanamine? **[NEET 2017]**

(a) Carbylamine reaction
(b) Hofmann hypobromamide reaction
(c) Stephen's reaction
(d) Gabriel's phthalimide synthesis

8 The number of structural isomers possible from the molecular formula C_3H_9N is **[AIPMT 2015]**

(a) 4 (b) 5
(c) 2 (d) 3

Module-II Aromatic Amines

9 Consider the following statements..

Statement I Aniline does not undergo Friedel-Crafts alkylation reaction

Statement II Aniline cannot be prepared through Gabriel synthesis. *[NEET 2024]*

In the right of the above statement, choose the correct answer from the options given below.

(a) Both Statement I and Statement II are true
(b) Both Statement I and Statement II are false
(c) Statement I is true but Statement II is false.
(d) Statement I is false but Statement II is true.

10 Which of the following amine will give the carbylamine test? *[NCERT (New) Pg. 271, NEET (Sep.) 2020]*

(a) 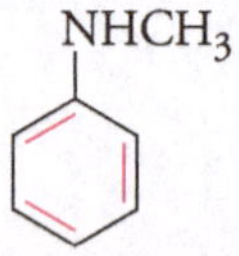
(b) 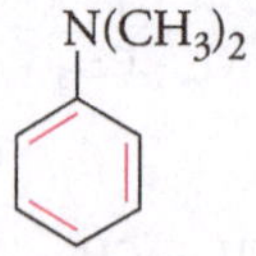
(c) 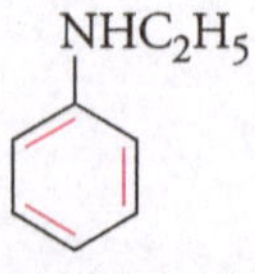
(d) 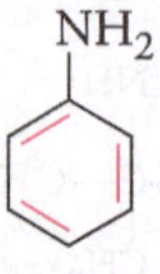

11 Nitration of aniline in strong acidic medium also gives *m*-nitroaniline because *[NCERT (New) Pg. 273, NEET 2018]*

(a) in absence of substituents nitro group always goes to *m*-position
(b) in electrophilic substitution reactions amino group is *m*-directive
(c) in-spite of substituents nitro group always goes to only *m*-position
(d) in acidic (strong) medium aniline is present as anilinium ion

12 The correct increasing order of basic strength for the following compounds is *[NCERT (New) Pg. 269, NEET 2017]*

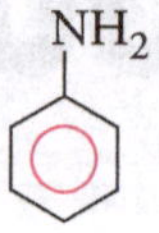
(I)

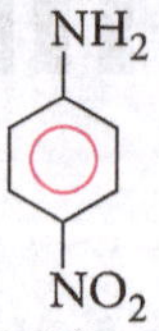
(II)

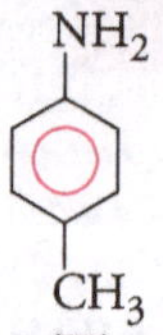
(III)

(a) II < III < I
(b) III < I < II
(c) III < II < I
(d) II < I < III

13 The correct statement regarding the basicity of arylamines is *[NCERT (New) Pg. 269, NEET 2016, Phase I]*

(a) Arylamines are generally more basic than alkylamines because the nitrogen lone-pair electrons are not delocalised by interaction with the aromatic ring π-electron system.
(b) Arylamines are generally more basic than alkylamines because of aryl group.
(c) Arylamines are generally more basic than alkylamines, because the nitrogen atom in arylamines is *sp*-hybridised.
(d) Arylamines are generally less basic than alkylamines because the nitrogen lone-pair electrons are delocalised by interaction with the aromatic ring π-electron system.

14 Consider the nitration of benzene using mixed conc. H_2SO_4 and HNO_3. If a large amount of $KHSO_4$ is added to the mixture, the rate of nitration will be *[NEET 2016, Phase I]*

(a) slower
(b) unchanged
(c) doubled
(d) faster

Module-III Diazonium Salts

15 Identify the product in the following reaction.

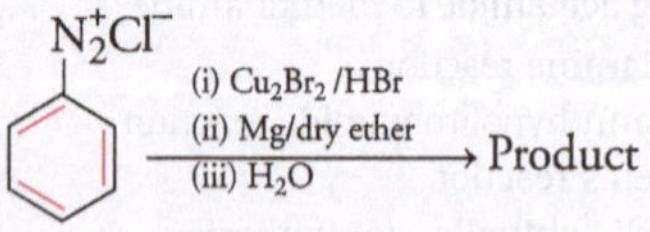

[NEET 2023]

(a) 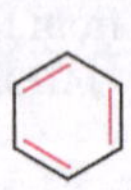
(b) 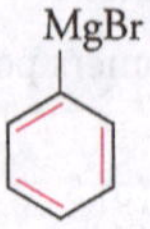
(c) 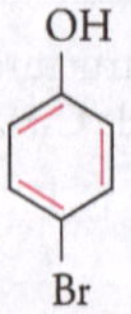
(d) 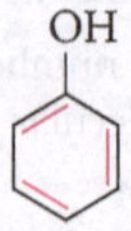

16 Consider the following statements. *[NCERT (New) Pg. 274, NEET 2022]*

Statement I Primary aliphatic amines react with HNO_2 to give unstable diazonium salts.

Statement II Primary aromatic amines react with HNO_2 to form diazonium salts which are stable even above 300 K.

In the light of the above statements, choose the most appropriate answer from the options given below.

(a) Both Statement I and Statement II are false.
(b) Statement I is true but Statement II is false.
(c) Statement I is false but Statement II is true.
(d) Both Statement I and Statement II are true.

17 The product formed from the following reaction sequence is *[NEET 2022]*

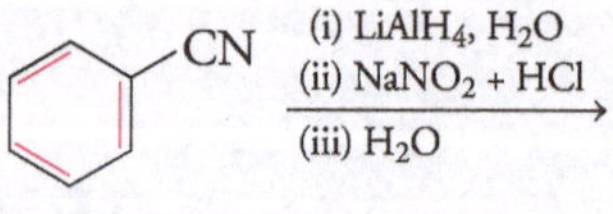

(a) 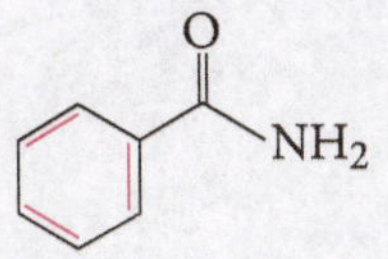
(b) 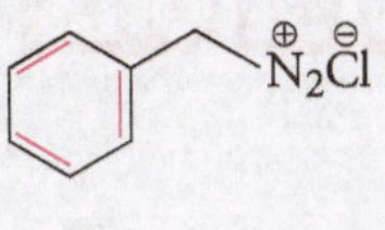
(c) 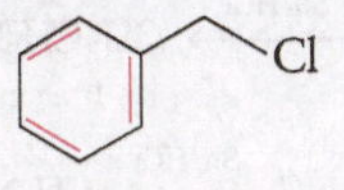
(d) 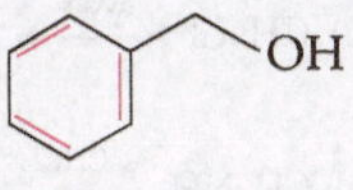

18 The reagent '*R*' in the given sequence of chemical reaction is **[NCERT (New) Pg. 276, NEET 2021]**

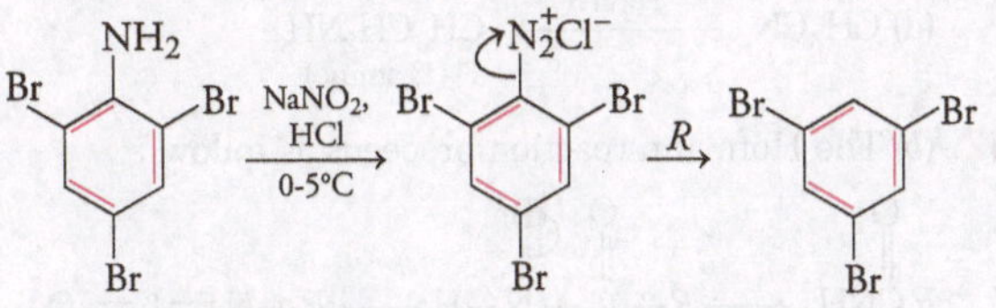

(a) CuCN/KCN
(b) H_2O
(c) CH_3CH_2OH
(d) HI

19 A given nitrogen-containing aromatic compound '*A*' reacts with Sn/HCl, followed by HNO_2 to give an unstable compound '*B*', '*B*', on treatment with phenol, forms a beautiful coloured compound '*C*' with the molecular formula $C_{12}H_{10}N_2O$. The structure of compound '*A*' is **[NCERT (New) Pg. 276, NEET 2016]**

(a) 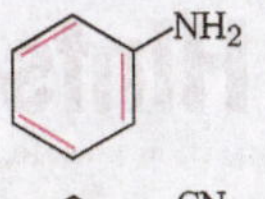
(b) 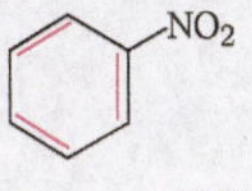
(c) 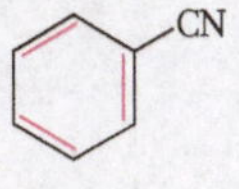
(d) 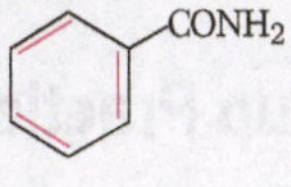

20 In the following reaction, the product (*A*) is

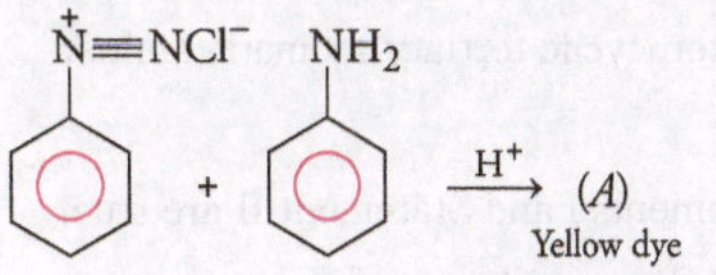

[NCERT (New) Pg. 276, AIPMT 2014]

(a) 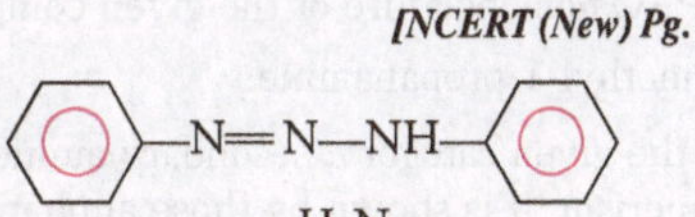
(b) 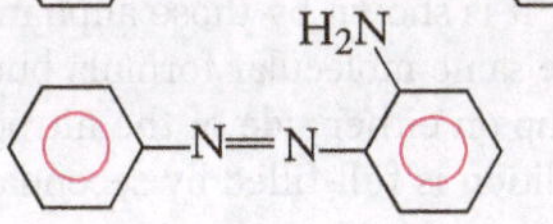
(c) 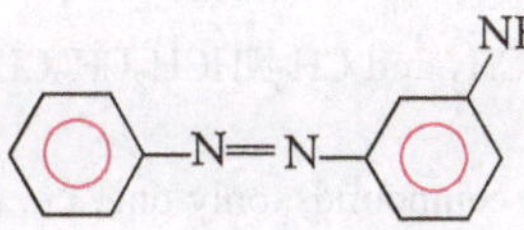
(d) 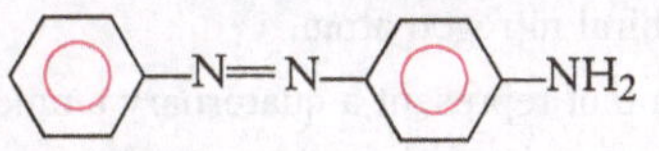

Answers

Step up Practice 1

1 (d)	2 (d)	3 (b)	4 (a)	5 (b)	6 (d)	7 (c)	8 (a)	9 (b)	10 (b)
11 (c)	12 (b)	13 (a)	14 (c)	15 (a)	16 (b)	17 (d)	18 (a)	19 (a)	20 (d)
21 (b)	22 (c)	23 (a)	24 (c)	25 (a)	26 (b)	27 (b)	28 (b)	29 (d)	30 (b)
31 (d)									

Step up Practice 2

1 (b)	2 (d)	3 (c)	4 (c)	5 (d)	6 (d)	7 (b)	8 (b)	9 (c)	10 (d)
11 (d)	12 (b)	13 (a)	14 (c)	15 (b)	16 (b)	17 (a)	18 (c)	19 (c)	20 (d)
21 (c)	22 (d)	23 (d)							

Step up Practice 3

1 (b)	2 (a)	3 (a)	4 (c)	5 (b)	6 (d)	7 (a)	8 (c)	9 (b)	10 (d)
11 (b)	12 (d)	13 (a)	14 (a)	15 (d)					

Gearing up for NEET

1 (b)	2 (a)	3 (d)	4 (d)	5 (b)	6 (b)	7 (c)	8 (b)	9 (d)	10 (a)
11 (a)	12 (d)	13 (d)	14 (c)	15 (c)	16 (b)	17 (c)	18 (d)	19 (c)	20 (d)
21 (a)	22 (b)	23 (d)	24 (b)	25 (c)	26 (d)	27 (c)	28 (a)	29 (d)	30 (b)
31 (d)	32 (d)	33 (d)	34 (a)	35 (a)	36 (d)	37 (a)	38 (b)	39 (c)	40 (c)
41 (c)	42 (a)	43 (a)	44 (b)	45 (a)	46 (d)	47 (c)	48 (c)	49 (d)	50 (d)
51 (b)	52 (d)	53 (d)	54 (d)	55 (a)	56 (c)	57 (d)	58 (c)	59 (a)	60 (a)
61 (d)	62 (d)	63 (a)	64 (c)	65 (b)	66 (d)	67 (d)	68 (b)	69 (d)	70 (c)
71 (a)	72 (d)	73 (b)	74 (d)						

Final Check through PYQs : Module-I

1 (a)	2 (b)	3 (d)	4 (a)	5 (a)	6 (d)	7 (b)	8 (a)

Final Check through PYQs : Module-II

9 (a)	10 (d)	11 (d)	12 (d)	13 (d)	14 (a)

Final Check through PYQs : Module-III

15 (a)	16 (b)	17 (d)	18 (c)	19 (b)	20 (d)

Hints and Solutions

Step up Practice 1

1. (*d*) Among the given compounds, pyridine, i.e.

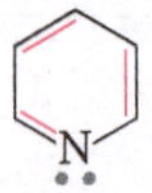

is heterocyclic tertiary aromatic amine.

2. (*d*) Both Statements I and Statement II are true.
3. (*b*) The IUPAC nomenclature of the given compound is N-ethyl-N-methyl-1-propanamine.
4. (*a*) Among the given category, secondary amine will show metamerism. It is shown by those aliphatic amines which have same molecular formula but different alkyl group on either side of the nitrogen atom and this condition is full-filled by secondary amine.

   e.g. $CH_3CH_2NHCH_2CH_3$ and $CH_3NHCH_2CH_2CH_3$ are metamers.
5. (*b*) Among the given compounds, only one, i.e. (iii) possesses a chiral nitrogen atom.
6. (*d*) C_3H_9N cannot represent a quaternary ammonium salt because for a quaternary salt using alkyl group a minimum of four carbons are required.
7. (*c*) Gabriel phthalimide reaction is the best method for the preparation of 1° aliphatic amnes from alkyl halide.
8. (*a*) A primary amine is formed from an amide by the treatment with bromine and alkali. The primary amine has 1 carbon atom less than present in the amide and this reaction is known as Hoffmann bromamide degradation reaction.
9. (*b*) Among the given reactions, only (b) is correctly matched with the product while other are incorrect.

   Their correct match are
   - $CH_3CN + H_3O^+ \longrightarrow CH_3COOH$
   - $CH_3CN + \text{DIBAL-H}/H_3O^+ \longrightarrow CH_3CHO$
   - $CH_3CN + CH_3MgBr/H_3O^+ \longrightarrow (CH_3)_2CO$
10. (*b*) An isocyanide on hydrolysis gives primary amine and formic acid.
11. (*c*) (a) $CH_3Cl \xrightarrow{NH_3} \underset{(1° \text{ amine})}{CH_3NH_2} \xrightarrow{CH_3Cl} \underset{(2° \text{ amine})}{(CH_3)_2NH}$

    $\xrightarrow{CH_3Cl} \underset{(3° \text{ amine})}{(CH_3)_3N} \xrightarrow{CH_3Cl} (CH_3)_4N^{\oplus}Cl^{\ominus}$

    Mixture is formed

    (b) $CH_3Cl \xrightarrow{KCN} CH_3CN \xrightarrow{Sn/HCl} \underset{1° \text{ amine}}{CH_3CH_2NH_2}$

    (c) $CH_3NH_2 \xrightarrow[\Delta]{CHCl_3/KOH} CH_3NC \xrightarrow{Sn/HCl} \underset{2° \text{ amine (pure)}}{CH_3NHCH_3}$

    (d) $CH_3CN \xrightarrow{H_2/Ni} \underset{(1° \text{ amine})}{CH_3CH_2NH_2}$
12. (*b*) The Hofmann reaction proceeds as follow :

    $$R\overset{O}{\overset{\|}{C}}NH_2 \longrightarrow R—\overset{O}{\overset{\|}{C}}—\overset{Br}{N}—H \longrightarrow R—N{=}C{=}O$$
13. (*a*) Both Statements I and Statement II are false..

    Their corrected form are :
    - Hoffmann bromamide reaction is given by amide.
    - Primary amines are less basic than secondary amines.
14. (*c*) Ritter reaction is represent as

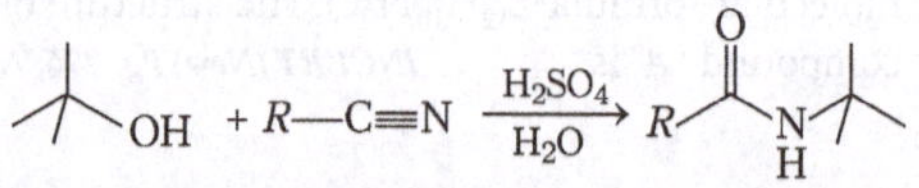

15. (*a*) The reaction proceeds as follow :

    $$RCOOH \xrightarrow[-CO_2,\ -N_2]{N_3H,\ \Delta} \underset{(1° \text{ amine})}{R—NH_2}$$

    and the given reaction is called "Schmidt reaction".
16. (*b*) $\underset{(A)}{CH_3CH_2CN} \longrightarrow \underset{\text{One carbon less}}{\underset{(B)}{CH_3CH_2NH_2}}$

    The reaction proceeds as follow :

    $$\underset{\text{Ethylcyanide } (A)}{CH_3CH_2CN} \xrightarrow[LiAlH_4]{Sn/HCl} \underset{\text{Propyl amine}}{CH_3CH_2CH_2NH_2} \text{ (incorrect)}$$

    $$CH_3CH_2CN \xrightarrow{H_3O^{\oplus}} CH_3CH_2\overset{O}{\overset{\|}{C}}OH \xrightarrow[\Delta]{NH_3} CH_3CH_2\overset{O}{\overset{\|}{C}}NH_2 \xrightarrow[\Delta]{Br_2/NaOH} \underset{\text{Ethylamine } (B)}{CH_3CH_2NH_2}$$

    and Br_2/NaOH react with amide not with cyanide group.

    Thus, option (b) is true.
17. (*d*) Among the given statements, statement (d) is incorrect while other statements are correct.

18. (*a*) The reaction is proceed as

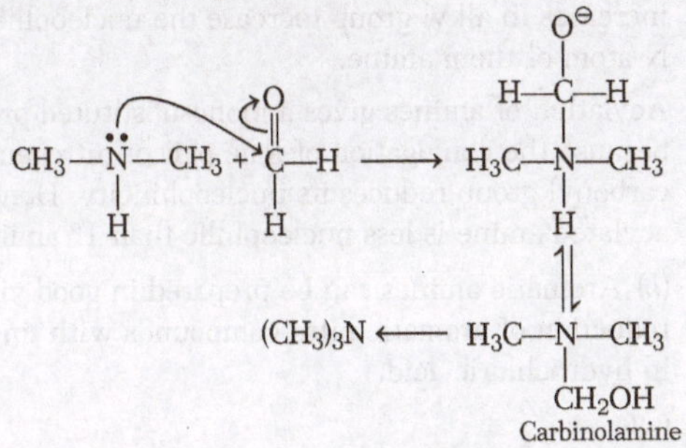

19. (*a*) Among the given statements, (a) is correct, i.e.

$$\underset{\text{Methyl cyanide}}{CH_3CN} \xrightarrow{LiAlH_4} \underset{\text{Ethylamine}}{CH_3CH_2NH_2}$$

while other statements are incorrect.

Their correct form are given as

- Methyl isocyanide is hydrolysed methylamine and formic acid.
- 1° amine is obtained in the given proceses i.e,

$$R\text{—}Br \xrightarrow{NaCN} R\text{—}CN \xrightarrow{LiAlH_4} \underset{(1^\circ \text{ amine})}{RCH_2NH_2}$$

- Acetamide is reduced to ethylamine by $LiAlH_4/H^+$

20. (*d*) Both Statement I and Statement II are true.

21. (*b*) $(CH_3)_3N$ is most volatile due to lack of H-bonding.

22. (*c*) Boiling points are normally highest for primary amines due to intermolecular hydrogen bonding.

23. (*a*)

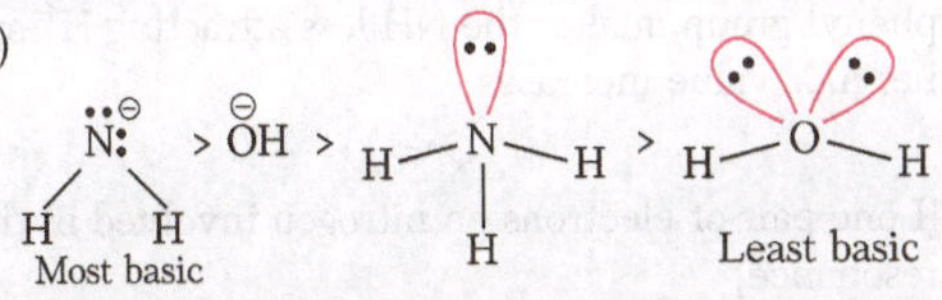

Basic strength of the above species can be explained on the basis of electronegativity of central atom and its proton accepting tendency. Here, amide ion is most basic among given compounds due to presence of negative charge and two pair of electrons on nitrogen atom.

24. (*c*)

	Compound	Factors responsible for basic character are
(a)	$CH_3\text{—}NH_2$	Inductive effect (+ *I*)
(b)	$NC\text{—}CH_2\text{—}NH_2$	Inductive effect (– *I*)
(c)	$(CH_3)_2NH$	Inductive effect (+ *I*) and solvation
(d)	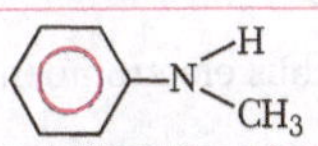	– *I*-effect and resonance

25. (*a*) Acid anhydride on reaction with primary amine produces amide as shown in reaction

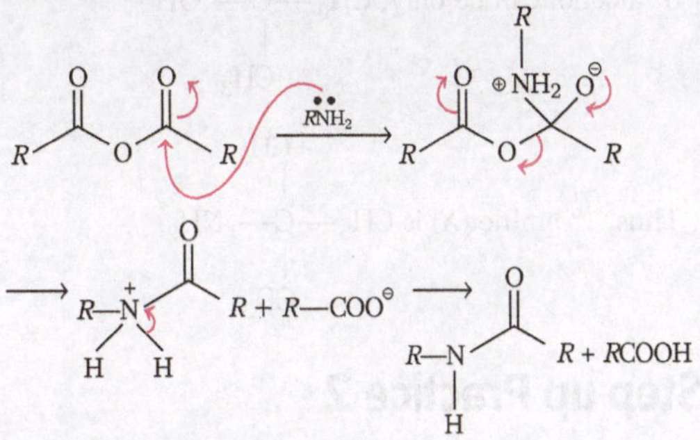

26. (*b*) The reaction is proceed as follow :

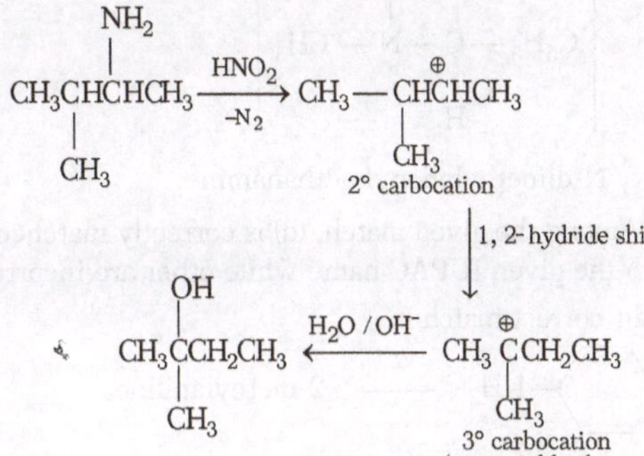

27. (*b*) Least substituted alkene is formed.
Hence, $CH_2{=}CHCH_2CH_3$ is formed.

28. (*b*) The reaction proceeds as follow :

$$\underset{(1^\circ \text{ amine})}{R\text{—}NH_2} + S{=}C{=}S \longrightarrow R\text{—}\underset{\underset{H}{|}}{N}\text{—}\overset{\overset{S}{\|}}{C}\text{—}SH \xrightarrow{HgCl_2}$$

$$\underset{(\text{alkyl } iso\text{-thioacyanate})}{R\text{—}N{=}C{=}S} + HgS + 2HCl$$

29. (*d*) Among the given gases, only one, i.e. (ii) is evolved when methylamine reacts with nitrous acid.

30. (*b*) $RCH_2CH_2NH_2$ does not undergo E2 elimination. It is attributed that $NH_2^{\ominus}$ is a very poor leaving group.

31. (*d*) $\underset{(X)}{C_4H_{11}N} \xrightarrow{HNO_2} C_4H_{10}O$ (3° alcohol)

(*X*) reacts with HNO_2 forming alcohol.
Thus, *X* is 1° amine.
$C_4H_{10}O$ is 3° alcohol formed from 1° amine.

3° alcohol can be only, $CH_3—C(CH_3)_2— OH$

Thus, 1° amine (*X*) is $CH_3—C(CH_3)_2— NH_2$.

Step up Practice 2

1. (*b*) The IUPAC name of the given compound, i.e.

$$C_6H_5—\underset{H}{\overset{H}{C}}—\overset{CH_3}{N}— CH_3$$

is N, N-dimethylphenylmethanamine.

2. (*d*) Among the given match, (d) is correctly matched with the given IUPAC name while other are incorrect. Their correct match is

- 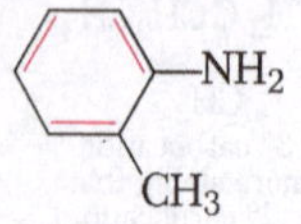 $\longrightarrow$ 2-methylaniline
- 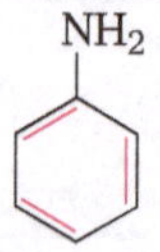 $\longrightarrow$ Benzenamine
- 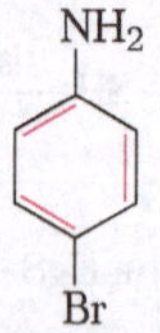 $\longrightarrow$ 4-bromoaniline

3. (*c*) The reaction proceeds as follow

$$\underset{\text{(Benzyl chloride)}}{C_6H_5CH_2—Cl} \xrightarrow[\text{NaCN}]{\text{Ethanolic}} C_6H_5—CH_2—C\equiv N \xrightarrow{H_2/Ni} \underset{\text{(2-phenyl ethanamine)}}{C_6H_5—CH_2—CH_2—NH_2}$$

4. (*c*) The reaction proceeds as follow :

$$C_6H_5—\overset{O}{\overset{\|}{C}}—NHCH_3 \xrightarrow[\text{(ii) } H_2O]{\text{(i) } LiAlH_4} C_6H_5—CH_2—NH—CH_3$$

5. (*d*) Both Statements I and Statement II are true.

6. (*d*) Carbylamine test is performed by heating a mixture of trihalogenated methane ($CHCl_3$) and a primary aromatic amine with ethanolic potassium hydroxide.

7. (*b*) Alkylation gives polysubstituted products because increases in alkyl group increase the nucleophilicity of N-atom of them amine.
Acylation of amines gives a monosubstituted product because the conjugation of lone pair of nitrogen with carbonyl group reduces its nucleophilicity. Hence, acylated amine is less nucleophilic than 1° amines.

8. (*b*) Aromatic amines can be prepared in good yields by reduction of aromatic nitro compounds with tin metal in hydrochloric acid.
e.g.

$$C_6H_5NO_2 + 6H^+ \xrightarrow{Sn+HCl} \underset{\text{(Aniline)}}{C_6H_5—NH_2} + 2H_2O$$

9. (*c*) Among the given compounds, (c) has lowest boiling point due to lack of H-atom at N-atom (3° amine) hence, there is no H-bonding. Thus, has least boiling point.

10. (*d*) Aniline is a weaker base than NH_3 due to delocalisation of lone pair of electrons of the N-atom over the benzene ring. Pyrrole is not more basic because the lone pair of electrons on the N-atom is donated towards aromatic sextet formation.
Therefore, pyrrolidine is strongest base as lone pair of nitrogen does not involved in resonance and also due to presence of two alkyl ring residue, basic strength becomes high among the four given compounds.

11. (*d*) pK_b is log inverse of K_b, so it is maximum for the weakest base, presence of two electron withdrawing phenyl group, makes the NH less attracting H^+ species, i.e. pK_b value increases

Or

[Lone pair of electrons on nitrogen involved in the resonance]

12 (*b*) I. 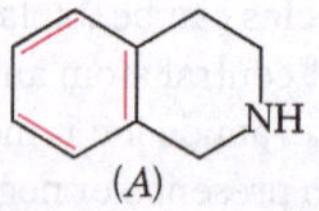 2° amine

(*A*)

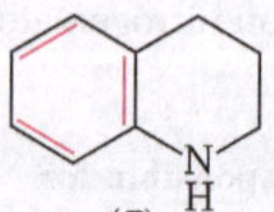 2° amine; lone-pair on N is used in delocalisation of π-electrons.

(*B*)

Thus, (*A*) is more basic than (*B*).

II. 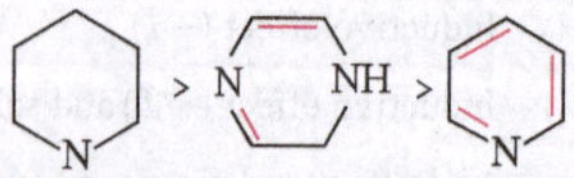

III. Carbonyl group is (EWG), thus electron density is decreased.
Hence, first is least basic, last one is maximum basic, thus incorrect comparsion. Hence, I and II are true.

13 (*a*) The reaction proceeds as follow

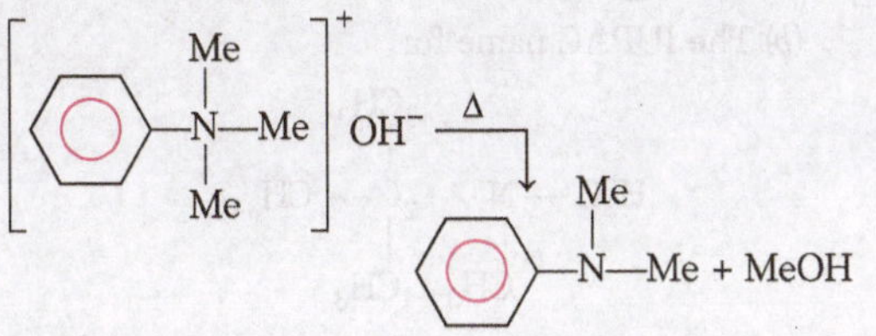

14 (*c*) Nitration of benzene using a mixture of conc. H_2SO_4 and conc. HNO_3 proceeds as

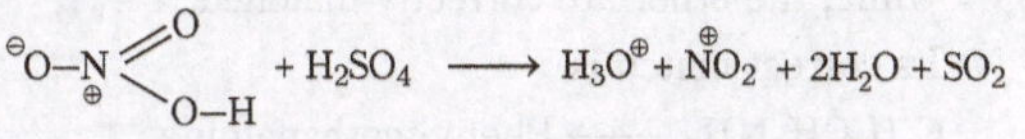

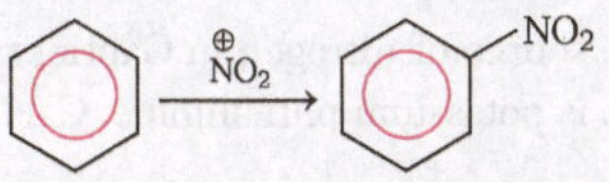

This reaction is an example electrophilic substitution reaction.

15. (*b*) Pyridine is less basic than triethylamine because nitrogen in pyridine is sp^2-hybridised.

16. (*b*) Among the given reaction, (b) is not correctly matched with the given product. As, NH_3 (a strong nucleophile) causes elimination from 3° alkyl halide, thus it is incorrect.

17. (*a*) As —NH_2 group is greatly activating; *o-p*-directing, so, —NH_2 group in benzene nucleus is protected before any S_E reaction.

18. (*c*) The reaction proceeds as follow

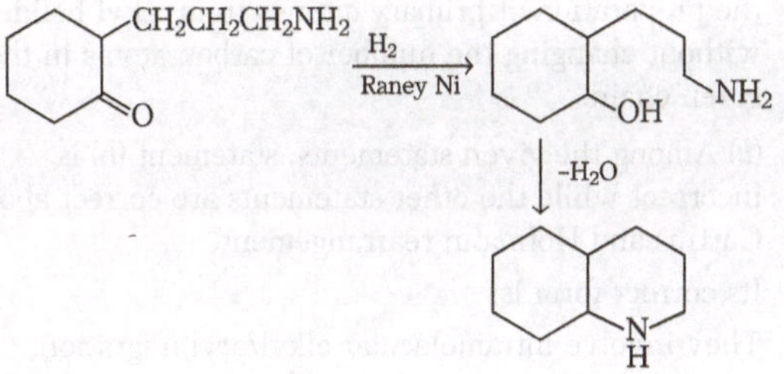

19. (*c*) Among the given match, only (c) is correctly matched regarding Hofmann mustard oil-reaction.

e.g.

$$Ar/R{-}NH_2 + S{=}C{=}S \longrightarrow Ar/R{-}\overset{H}{N}{-}\overset{S}{\overset{\|}{C}}{-}SH \xrightarrow{HgCl_2} Ar/R{-}N{=}C{=}S + HgS + 2HCl$$

(Alkyl isothiocyanate)

20 (*d*) The reaction proceeds as follow :

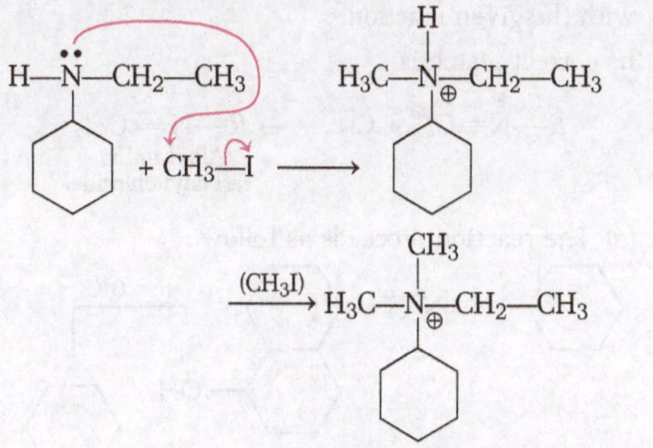

(a quaternary ammonium salt)

21. (*c*) Reduction of aromatic nitro compounds using Fe and HCl gives aromatic primary amine.

22. (*d*) Among the given compounds, only two, i.e. (i) and (ii) are used to manufacture methyl isocyanide that caused "Bhopal tragedy".

23. (*d*) Both Statement I and Statement II are true.

Step up Practice 3

1. (*b*) $H_3PO_2 + H_2O \longrightarrow H_3PO_3 + 2H$

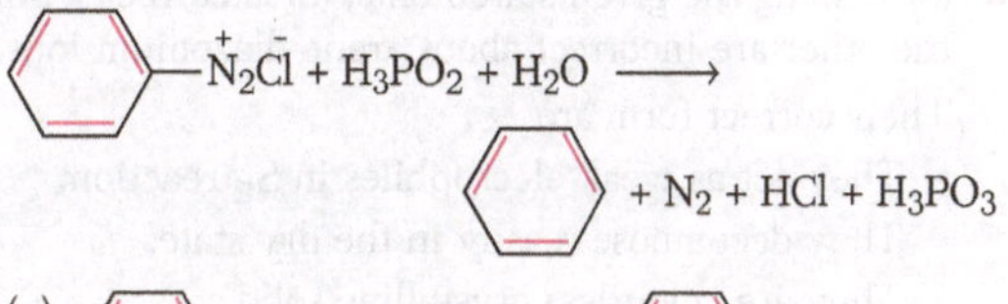

2. (*a*)

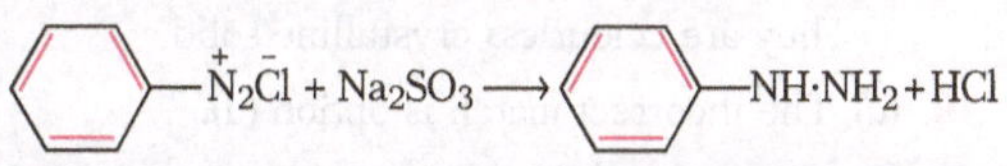

Phenyl hydrazine

3. (*a*) Among the given statements, (a) is incorrect while other are correct. Its corrected form is:

CH_3CN is named as methyl cyanide.

4. (*c*) Statement I is false while the statement II is true.

The correct form of Statement I is Azo dye is prepared by the coupling of phenol and diazonium chloride.

5. (*b*) Among the given compounds, the position 1 or 4 and the position 2 and 3 are activated for coupling reactions in compounds I and II respectively.

- On comparing O^- and NH_2, O^- group has a greater effect than NH_2, therefore 1 or 4 in (I) will be more activated for coupling reactions.
- The —OH group is the electron releasing group whereas, —$\overset{\oplus}{NH_3}$ is an electron withdrawing in nature, therefore, 2 and 3 in (II) is more activated for coupling reactions.

6. (d) Among the given match, (d) is incorrectly matched with the given reaction.

Its correct match is

$$R{-}\overset{\oplus}{N}{\equiv}\overset{\ominus}{C}{:} + Cl_2 \longrightarrow \underset{\text{(Alkyl imino carbonyl chloride)}}{R{-}N{=}CCl_2}$$

7. (a) The reaction proceeds as follow :

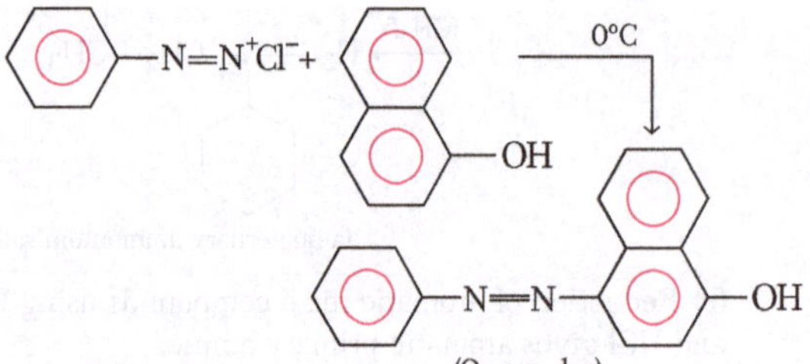

(Orange dye)

8. (c) Statement I is false but Statement II is true.

The correct form of Statement I is:

Benzene diazonium chloride does not give test for nitrogen, if nitrogen is lost, then NaCN will not be formed and hence the compound will not give positive test for nitrogen.

9. (b) Among the given statements, (b) is correct while the other are incorrect about arene diazonium ions.

Their correct form are

- They act as weak elecrophiles in S_E reaction.
- They decomposes easily in the dry state.
- They are colourless crystalline solid.

10. (d) The incorrect match is option (d).

Its correct match is:

$HBF_4/\Delta \longrightarrow$ Fluoride ion, i.e.

$$ArN_2^+Cl^- \; HBF_4 \longrightarrow ArN_2^+BF_4^- \xrightarrow{\Delta} Ar{-}F + BF_3 + N_2$$

11. (b) Among the given compounds, only two, i.e. (i) and (ii) are used to remove the excess of HNO_3.

12. (d) Both Statement I and Statement II are true.

13. (a) The colour of *p*-amino azobenzene, i.e.

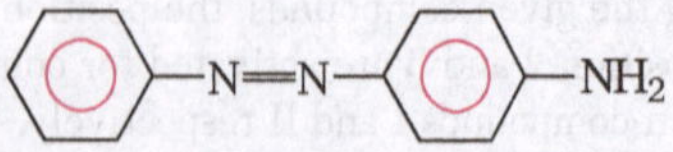

is yellow.

14. (a) The given reaction is known as "Gattermann reaction".

15. (d) Among the given statements, (d) is correct while others are incorrect.

Their correct form are

- The reaction of diazonium salts involving displacement of nitrogen and retention of diazo group.
- The yield of Sandmeyer reaction is found to be better than Gattermann reaction.
- Diazonium salt solution, formed iodobenzene when it is treated with potassium iodide.

Gearing up for NEET

1. (b) The IUPAC name for,

$$H_3C{-}\underset{\underset{CH_3}{|}}{N}{-}\,{}_2\overset{\overset{{}_3CH_3}{|}}{\underset{\underset{{}_1CH_3}{|}}{C}}{-}CH_3$$

N, N-dimethyl-2-methyl-2-propanamine.

2. (a) Among the given match, (a) is incorrectly matched while, the other are correctly matched.

Its correct match is

$C_6H_5CH_2NH_2 \longrightarrow$ Phenylmethanamine

3. (d) The source of nitrogen in Gabriel synthesis of amines is potassium phthalimide, $C_6H_4(CO_2)N^-K^+$.

4. (d) $RCH_2OH \xrightarrow{Cr_2O_7^{2-}/H^+} \underset{(A)}{R\overset{O}{\overset{\|}{C}}OH} \xrightarrow{SOCl_2} \underset{(B)}{R\overset{O}{\overset{\|}{C}}OCl}$

$\xrightarrow{(CH_3)_2NH} \underset{(C)}{R\overset{O}{\overset{\|}{C}}{-}N(CH_3)_2} \xrightarrow[H_2O]{LiAlH_4} \underset{(D)}{RCH_2N(CH_3)_2}$

Thus, $CH_3{-}\overset{\overset{CH_3}{|}}{\underset{\underset{CH_3}{|}}{C}}{-}CH_2CH_2N(CH_3)_2$

5. (b) Gabriel phthalimide synthesis is the best method for the preparation of primary amines from alkyl halides without changing the number of carbon atoms in the given chain.

6. (b) Among the given statements, statement (b) is incorrect while the other statements are correct about Curtius and Hofmann rearrangement.

Its correct form is:

They involve intramolecular alkyl/aryl migration.

7. (c) Chemical transformation can be shown as

$$R{-}NH_2 + RCHO \longrightarrow [R{-}N{=}\underset{\underset{H}{|}}{C}{-}R] \xrightarrow{H_2/Pt} \underset{\text{2° amine}}{R{-}\underset{\underset{H}{|}}{N}{-}\overset{\overset{H}{|}}{\underset{\underset{H}{|}}{C}}{-}R}$$

While other given set of reactants give primary amine only.

8. (b) Greater the strength of base, greater will be its reactivity towards dilute HCl. Hence, $(CH_3)_2NH$ has highest basic strength as it has highest reactivity.

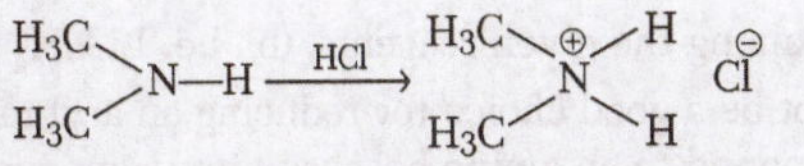

9. (*d*) Amines have an unshared paired of electrons on nitrogen atom due to which they behave as Lewis base.

10. (*a*) Among the given compounds, (a) is the strongest base because 'N' has more donor ability of lone pair than oxygen 'O'.

11. (*a*) Statement (a) is correct because electron donating group increase the electron density on N-atom and increase its basic strength.

12. (*d*) The basicity order of amines in gaseous phase is $3° > 2° > 1° >$ ammonia.

13. (*d*) Among the given statements, (d) is not correct.

Its correct form is

In a tertiary amine, there is no polarised hydrogen because all the hydrogens are replaced by alkyl or aryl groups.

So, tertiary amines can not show hydrogen bonding.

14. (c) The correct order of dipole moment is I < III < II.

15. (*c*) Among the given statements, only (c) is correct while other are incorrect.

Their correct form are

- Triethylamine does not react with Hinsberg's reagent and KOH because it is a 3° amine.
- Azo dyes are not formed by secondary amines, i.e. dimethyl amine.
- Methylamine reacts with PhMgBr to give benzene.

16. (*b*) In (1) major product is least substituted alkene, i.e. *Y* and in (2) major product is more substituted alkene, i.e. *X*. Thus, for reaction (1) major product is *Y* and for reaction (2) major product is *X*.

17. (*c*) The reaction proceeds as follow :

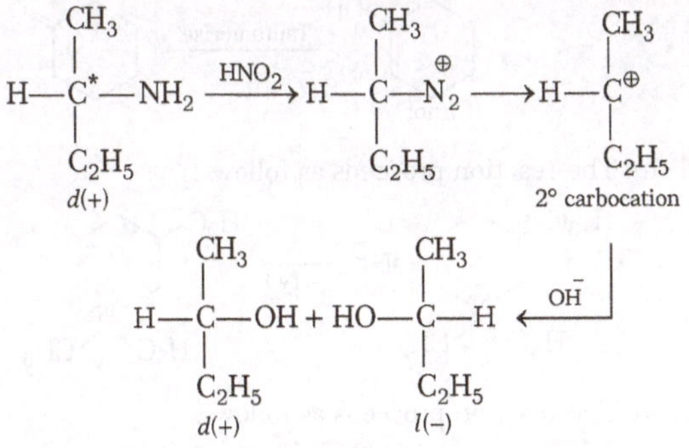

d(+) and *l*(−) 2° alcohols are formed in equal amounts thus, mixture is racemic.

18. (*d*) Among the given statements, only (d) is incorrect while other are correct about the given reaction.

19. (*c*)

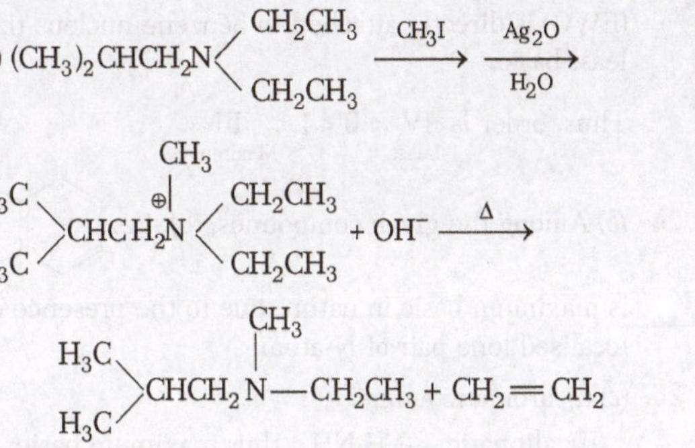

20. (*d*) All the given statements are correct about the given reaction.

The reaction proceeds as follow :

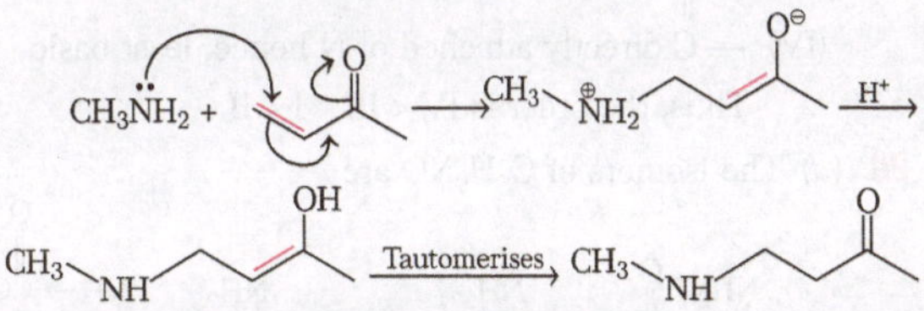

21. (*a*) The reaction proceeds as follow :

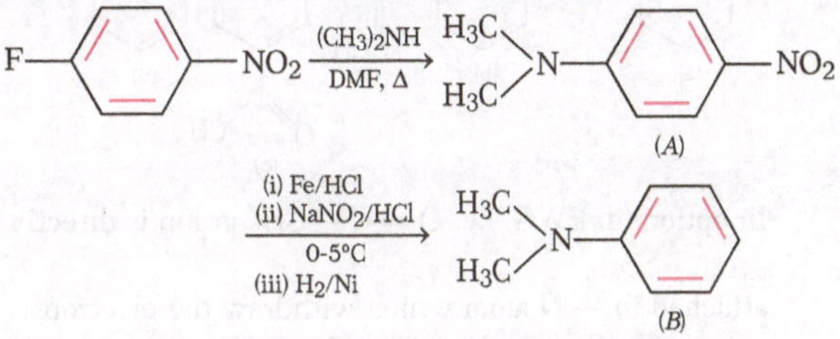

22. (*b*) The best reagent for converting 2-phenylpropanamide into 1-phenylethanamine is by NaOH / Br_2 and chemical transformation can be done as

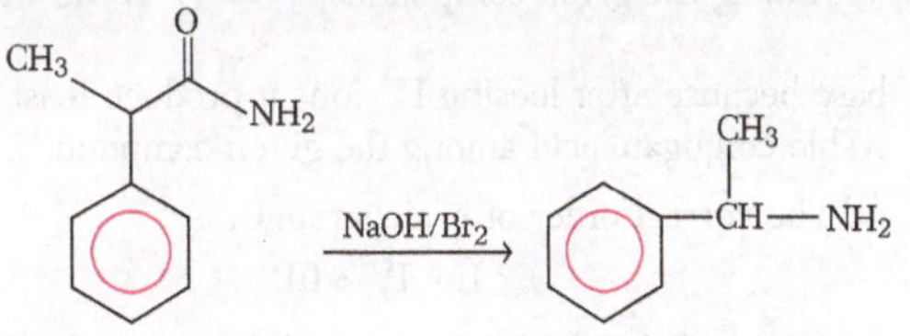

2-phenylpropanamide 1-phenylethanamine

This occurs due to intramolecular migration of alkyl group. It is an example of Hofmann bromamide reaction.

23. (*d*) I. 2° aromatic

II. 2° aromatic but less basic than (I) due to $—NO_2$ (EWG)

III. 2° aliphatic

IV. 2° aromatic but less basic than (I) and (III) both due to adjacent carbonyl group.

(EWG) is directly attached to benzene nucleus thus, least basic.

Thus, order is IV < II < I < III
(Least) (Maximum)

24. *(b)* Among the given compounds, (b), i.e. 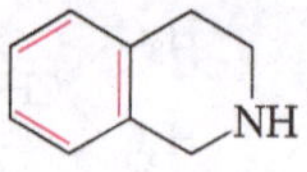 is maximum basic in nature due to the presence of localised lone pair of N-atom.

25. *(c)* (I) aromatic amine.

(II) aliphatic $—CH_2NH_2$, thus maximum basic.

(III) aromatic but $-NO_2$ group is (EWG) decreasing electron density at N-atom.

(IV) —C(=O) directly attached of N hence, least basic

Thus, the order is IV < III < I < II.

26. *(d)* The isomers of C_8H_9NO are

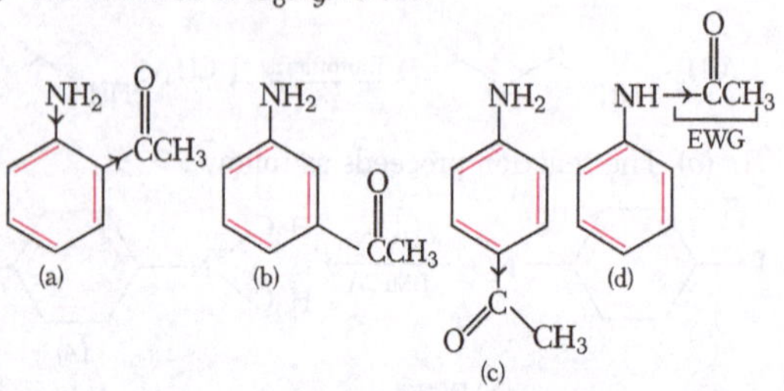

In option (d) EWG, i.e. O=C—CH_3 group is directly attached to —N atom which withdraw the electron pair and reduce the basicity at N-atom.

27. *(c)* Among the given compounds, 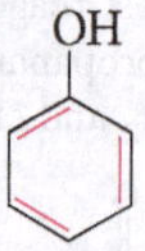 is the weakest base because after loosing H^+ ions it produce least stable conjugate acid among the given compounds.

28. *(a)* The correct order of basic strength is

I < II < IV < III.

29. *(d)* Among the given statements, (d) is not correct regarding ethylamine and aniline.

Its correct form is

Ethylamine, when reacts with HNO_2 give hydroxy compound

$$C_2H_5—NH_2 + HNO_2 \longrightarrow C_2H_5—OH + N_2 + H_2O$$

while the aniline forms diazonium salt instead of hydroxy compound as shown below.

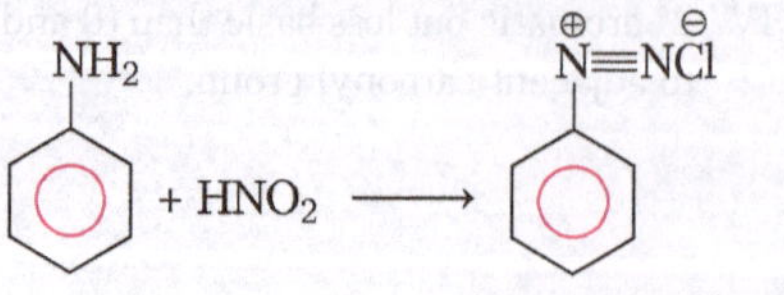

(Diazonium salt)

30. *(b)* Among the given reagents, (b), i.e. $LiAlH_4$ in ether is not be a good choice for reducing an aryl nitro compound to an amine because nitro compound reduced with metal in acidic medium to amine.

31. *(d)* The reaction proceeds as follow

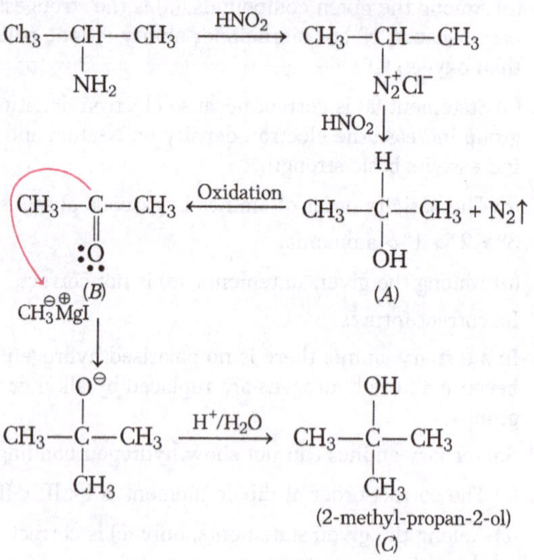

32. *(d)* Aniline is insoluble in water because its $—NH_2$ group can not form H-bond with water due to bulky phenyl group.

33. *(d)* The reaction proceeds as follow

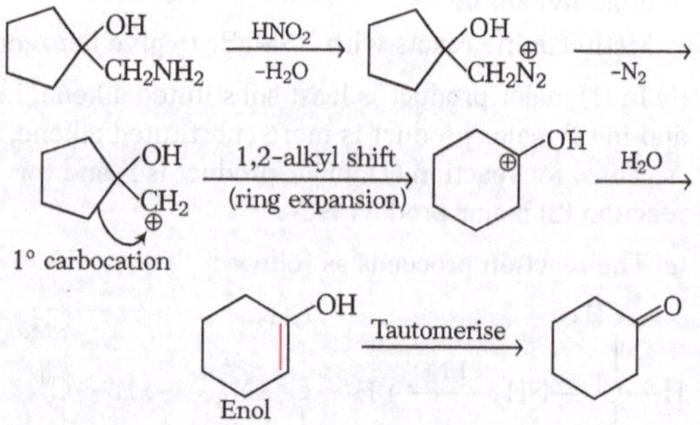

34. *(a)* The reaction proceeds as follow :

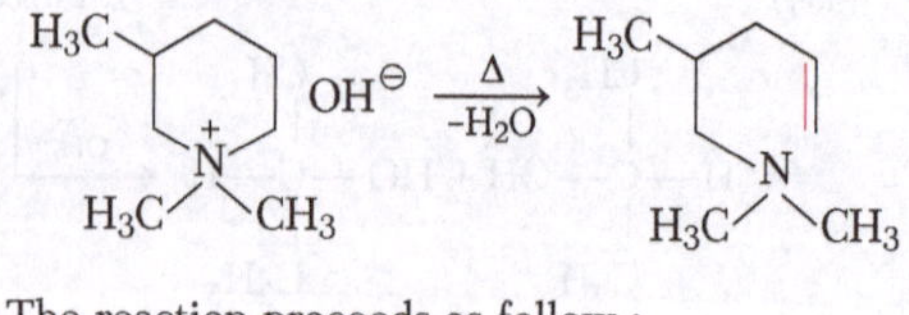

35. *(a)* The reaction proceeds as follow :

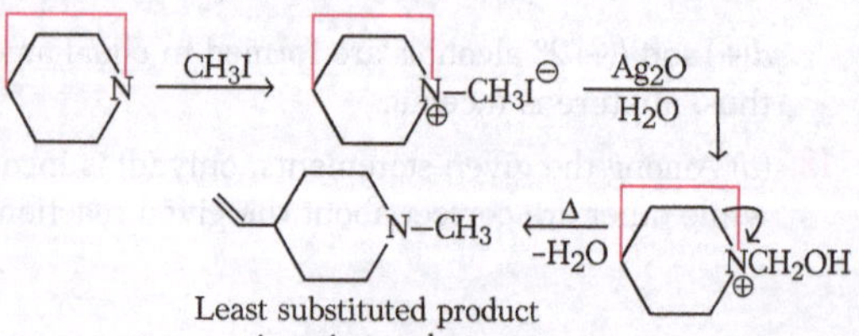

Least substituted product is major product

(A)

36. (*d*)

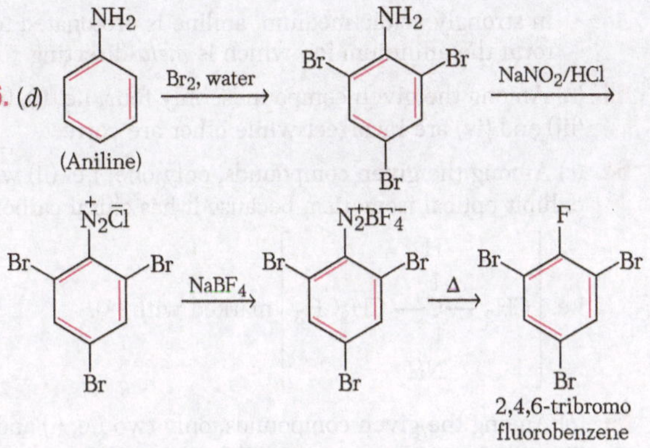

37. (*a*) The reaction proceeds as follow :

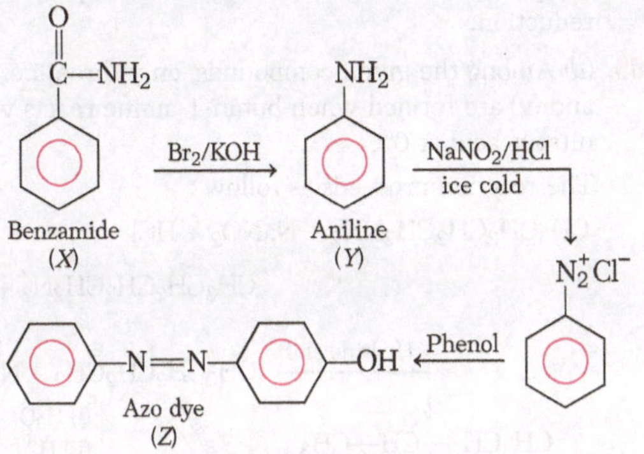

Thus, the compound *X* is $C_6H_5CONH_2$.

As, *Y* gives carbylamine test because it is a primary aromatic amine.

38. (*b*) Benzene diazonium salt is a weak electrophile and undergoes coupling reactions with activating group.

39. (*c*) The reaction is proceed as

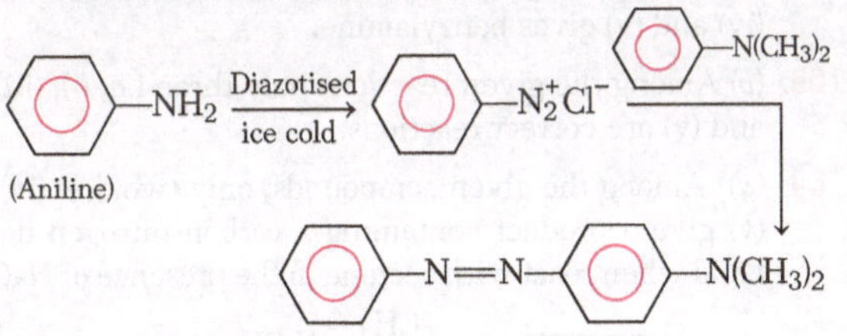

40. (*c*) A is false but R is true.

The correct form of A is :

Basicity of $CH_3CH_2NH_2$ (I), NH_3 (II) and $C_6H_5NH_2$ (III) is in order I > II > III.

41. (*c*) A is false but R is true.

The correct form of A is:

Hoffmann's bromamide reaction is given by amides not by amines.

42. (*a*) Both A and R are true and R is the correct explanation of A.

43. (*a*) Both A and R are true and R is the correct explanation of A.

44. (*b*) Both A and R are true and R is not the correct explanation of A.

N, N-diethylbenzenesulphonamide is insoluble in alkali due to absence of acidic H-atom attached to nitrogen.

45. (*a*) Both A and R are true and R is the correct explanation of A.

46. (*d*) A is true but R is false.

The corrected form of R is:

H_3PO_2 acts as a reducing agent.

47. (*c*) Statement I is false but Statement II is true.

Its correct form is:

Total possible structure of $C_4H_{11}N$ are 8.

48. (*c*) Statement I is false but Statement II is true.

Its corrected form is:

Primary and secondary amines are both hydrogen bond donors and acceptors, but tertiary amines function only as hydrogen bond acceptors.

49. (*d*) Both Statements I and Statement II are true.

50. (*d*) Both Statements I and Statement II are true.

51. (*b*) Statement I is true but Statement II is false. The correct form of Statement II is:

Acetamide and ethylamine can be distinguished by reacting with *aq.* NaOH and heat.

Because acetamide in the presence of NaOH and heat librates NH_3 but ethylamine does not.

52. (*d*) Both Statements I and Statement II are true.

53. (*d*) Both Statements I and Statement II are true.

54. (*d*) Among the given statements, only C and E are correct while the other statements A, B and D are incorrect.

This correct form are

- Nitro compounds are reduced to amines by reduction with metal in acidic medium.
- The process of cleavage of the C—*X* bond by ammonia molecule is known as ammonolysis.
- The free amine can be obtained from the ammonium salt by treatment with a strong base.

55. (*a*) Among the given statements, only C, D and E are incorrect while the statements A and B are correct.

The correct form of C, D and E are as follows

- Ammonolysis of benzyl chloride yield N,N-dimethyl phenyl methanamine with 2 moles of CH_3Cl.
- Ammonolysis has the disadvantage of yielding a mixture of primary, secondary and tertiary amines and also a quaternary ammonium salt.
- Propane nitrile on reduction with $Na(Hg)/C_2H_5OH$ formed propan-1-amine.

56. (*c*) Among the given statements, A, D and E are correct while the other statements B and C are incorrect.

Their correct form are as follows

- Aliphatic amines are stronger bases than ammonia and aromatic amines.
- Amine salts are soluble in water but insoluble in organic solvents like ether.

57. (*d*) Among the given statement, A, B and C are incorrect while D and E are correct.

Their correct form are

- Base-weakening substituents are the one that deactivate an aromatic ring towards electrophilic substitution.
- Aliphatic amine form unstable diazonium salt which decompose to give nitrogen and aliphatic alcohols.
- Only primary amine can be distinguished as it produces carbylamine having most offensive smell.

58. (*c*) Among the given statements, A, B and D are incorrect while the other C and E are correct.

The corrected form of A, B and D are

- Aliphatic and aromatic primary and secondary amines react with acid chlorides, anhydrides by nucleophilic substitution reaction, known as acylation.
- Acylation reaction are carried out in the presence of a base stronger than the amine.
- The products obtained by acylation reaction are known as amide.

59. (*a*) Among the given statements C, D and E are correct while other statements A and B are incorrect.

Their correct form are

- Primary aliphatic amines react with nitrous acid to form unstable aliphatic diazonium salts and liberate nitrous gas.
- Aromatic primary amines react with nitrous acid at low temperature (273-278 K).

60. (*a*) Among the given statements, only A, C and E are correct while other B and D are incorrect.

Their correct form are:

- Lower aliphatic amines are soluble in water.
- Alcohols are more polar than amines and form stronger intermolecular hydrogen bonds than amines.

61. (*d*) Among the given statements, A, B and C are correct while the statement D is incorrect.

Its correct form is:

If the temperature of the diazonium salt solution is allowed to rise upto 283 K, then the salt gets hydrolysed to phenol.

62. (*d*) Among the given statements, B, C and E are incorrect while the statements A and D are correct.

The corrected form of B, C and E are

- Due to the high reactivity of aromatic amines electrophilic substitution occurs at *ortho* and *para*-position.
- Aniline reacts with bromine water at room temperature to give a white precipitate of 2,4,6-tribromoaniline.
- In strongly acidic medium, aniline is protonated to form the anilinium ion which is *meta*-directing.

63. (*a*) Among the given compounds, only four, i.e. (i), (ii), (iii) and (iv) are incorrect while other are correct.

64. (*c*) Among the given compounds, only one, i.e. (ii) will exhibit optical isomerism because it has chiral carbon,

i.e. 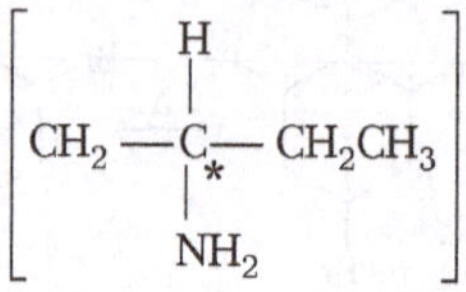

marked with (*).

65. (*b*) Among the given compounds, only two i.e, (i) and (ii) will give primary amines. While the other compounds do not give primary amines upon reduction.

66. (*d*) Among the given compounds, only three, i.e. (i), (ii) and (v) are formed when butan-1-amine reacts with nitrous acid at 0°C.

The reaction proceeds as follow :

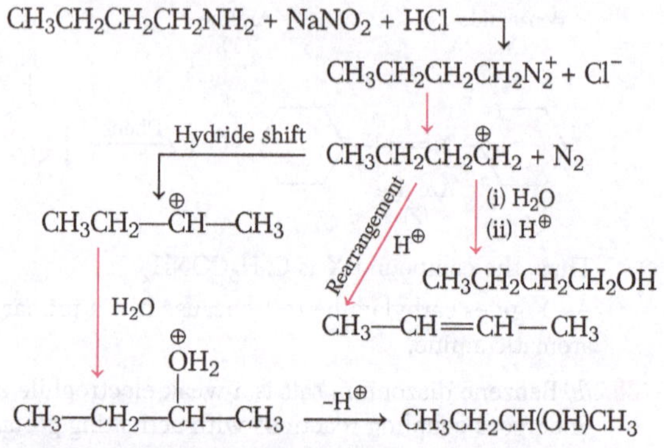

67. (*d*) Among the given reactions only four i.e, (ii), (iii), (iv) and (v) gives benzylamine.

68. (*b*) Among the given reactions only three i.e, (i), (iii) and (v) are correct reactions.

69. (*d*) Among the given compounds, only two, i.e. (iv) and (v) give a product containing a carbon-nitrogen double bond when react with acetone in the presence of NaOH.

e.g. $C_6H_5N\boxed{H_2 + O}{=}C(CH_3)_2 \xrightarrow[-H_2O]{NaOH} C_6H_5N{=}C(CH_3)_2$

70. (*c*) Among the given compounds, only three, i.e. (i), (ii) and (iii) are obtained when $PhNO_2$ is reduced in alkaline medium.

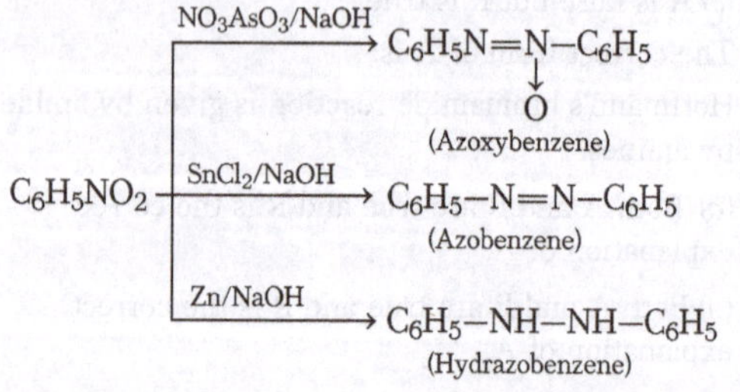

71. (*a*) The correct match is A-2, B-3, C-1, D-4.

72. (*d*) The correct match is A-4, B-3, C-1, D-2.

73. (*b*) The correct match is A-3, B-4, C-1, D-2.

74. (*d*) The correct match is A-2, B-1, C-4, D-3.

Final Check through PYQs

1. (*a*) The complete reaction is as follow :

$$CH_3-CH_2-CH_2-I \xrightarrow[S_N2]{NaCN} \underset{\text{(Product } A)}{CH_3-CH_2-CH_2-CN}$$

$$\xrightarrow[\text{partial hydrolysis}]{\bar{O}H} \underset{\text{(Product } B)}{CH_3-CH_2-CH_2-CONH_2}$$

$$\xrightarrow[Br_2]{NaOH} \underset{(C)}{CH_3-CH_2-CH_2-NH_2}$$

2. (*b*) Among the given reactions, primary amine will not form in case of 2nd reaction.

- $CH_3NC \xrightarrow[\text{(ii) } H_2O]{\text{(i) } LiAlH_4} CH_3-\underset{H}{N}-CH_3$ (2° amine)
- $CH_3-CN \xrightarrow[\text{(ii) } H_2O]{\text{(i) } LiAlH_4} CH_3CH_2NH_2$ (Primary amine)
- $CH_3-\underset{O}{\overset{\|}{C}}NH_2 \xrightarrow[\text{(ii) } H_2O]{\text{(i) } LiAlH_4} CH_2CH_2NH_2$ (Primary amine)
- $CH_3CONH_2 \xrightarrow{Br_2/NaOH} CH_3NH_2$ (Primary amine)

3. (*d*) Benzene sulphonyl chloride ($C_6H_5SO_2Cl$), (also known as Hinsberg's reagent) reacts with primary amines to form sulphonamides. Due to presence of strong electron withdrawing sulphonyl group, the hydrogen attached to N is highly acidic. Hence, it is soluble in alkali.

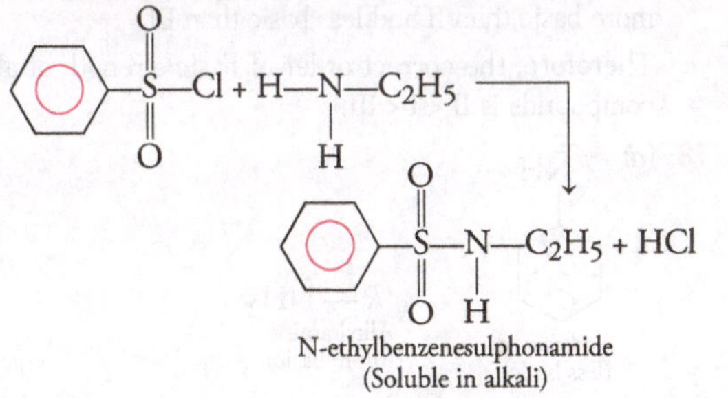

N-ethylbenzenesulphonamide
(Soluble in alkali)

4. (*a*)

$$\underset{\substack{\text{Propanamide} \\ \text{(No. of C-atoms =3)}}}{CH_3CH_2-\overset{O}{\overset{\|}{C}}-NH_2} \xrightarrow[Br_2]{NaOH\text{-}C_2H_5OH} \underset{\substack{\text{Ethylamine (1°-amine)} \\ \text{(No. of C-atoms =2)}}}{CH_3CH_2-NH_2} + Na_2CO_3 + NaBr$$

It is Hofmann bromamide reaction in which an amide degrades into primary (1°) amine with one carbon less than substrate.

5. (*a*) Secondary amines on reaction with Hinsberg's reagent (benzene sulphonyl chloride) forms N,N-dialkyl benzene sulphonamide.

The product formed is not acidic as no H-atom is attached to N. Thus, it is insoluble in alkali.

The reaction of 2° amine given in option (a) takes place as follows

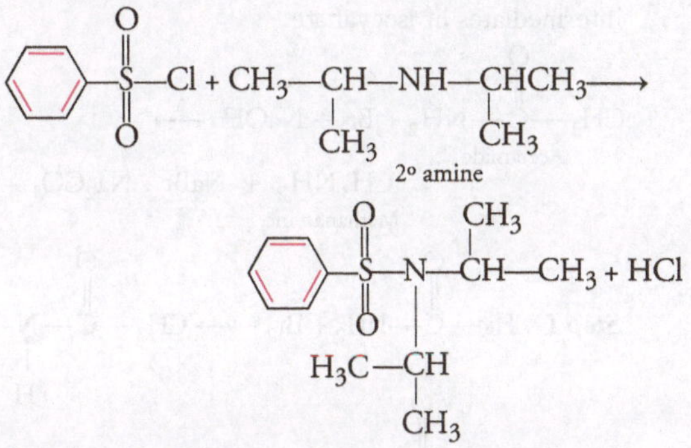

On the other hand, 1° amines react with Hinsberg's reagent to yield N-alkyl benzene sulphonamide which is soluble in alkali and 3° amines do not react with $C_6H_5SO_2Cl$. The remaining options contain 1° and 3° amines. Thus, option (a) is correct.

6. (*d*) Basic strength of methyl substituted amines in aqueous solution depends upon the ease of formation of cation by accepting a proton from the acid.

$$R-\underset{H}{\overset{H}{N}}: + H^+ \rightleftharpoons R-\underset{H}{\overset{H}{\overset{+}{N}}}-H$$

The basic strength can be decided by both inductive effect and solvation effect of alkyl group. In aqueous phase, the substituted $\overset{+}{N}H_4$ cations get stabilised not only by electron releasing effect of alkyl group (+ *I*) but also by solvation with water molecules. Greater the size of ion, lesser will be solvation and less stabilised is the ion. The order is as follows

Inductive effect $(CH_3)_3N > (CH_3)_2(NH) > (CH_3)NH_2$

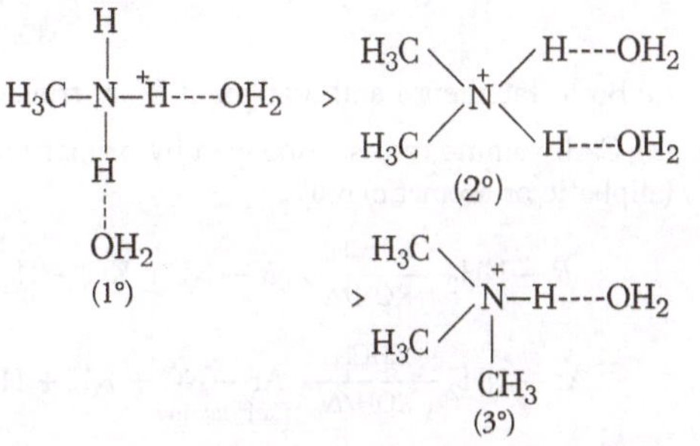

Strong +*I*-effect and hydrogen bonding favours higher basic strength of 2° amine. Thus, the correct order of basic strength in aqueous media will be

$$(CH_3)_2NH > CH_3NH_2 > (CH_3)_3N.$$

7. (*b*) The conversion of amide with no substituent on nitrogen to an amine containing one carbon less by the action of alkaline hypobromide or bromine in presence of NaOH. It involves the migration of alkyl or aryl group with its electron pair to electron deficient N from adjacent carbon. The reaction involves the intermediates of isocyanate.

$$\underset{\text{Acetamide}}{CH_3-\overset{O}{\overset{\|}{C}}-NH_2} + Br_2 + NaOH \xrightarrow{\Delta} \underset{\text{Methanamine}}{CH_3NH_2} + NaBr + Na_2CO_3 + H_2O$$

Step I $CH_3-\overset{O}{\overset{\|}{C}}-NH_2 + Br_2 \longrightarrow CH_3-\overset{O}{\overset{\|}{C}}-\underset{H}{\underset{|}{N}}-Br$

Step II $CH_3-\overset{O}{\overset{\|}{C}}-\underset{H}{\underset{|}{N}}-Br + OH^- \longrightarrow CH_3-\overset{O}{\overset{\|}{C}}-\overset{\ominus}{N}-Br + H_2O$

Step III $CH_3-\overset{O}{\overset{\|}{C}}-\overset{\ominus}{N}-Br \longrightarrow CH_3-\overset{O}{\overset{\|}{C}}-\ddot{N}: + \overset{\ominus}{Br}$

Step IV $CH_3-\overset{O}{\overset{\|}{C}}-\ddot{N}: \xrightarrow[\text{alkyl migration}]{\text{intermolecular}} CH_3NCO$

Step V $CH_3NCO + 2OH^- \xrightarrow{\Delta} CH_3NH_2 + CO_3^{2-}$

8. (*a*) Structural isomers of C_3H_9N are

$$\underbrace{CH_3CH_2CH_2NH_2,\ CH_3-\underset{NH_2}{\underset{|}{C}H}-CH_3}_{1^\circ\text{-amine}}$$

$$\underset{2^\circ\text{-amine}}{CH_3-CH_2-NH-CH_3},\ \underset{3^\circ\text{- amine}}{CH_3-\underset{CH_3}{\underset{|}{N}}-CH_3}$$

9. (*a*) Both statement I and Statement II are true.

10. (*d*) Carbylamine test is responded by primary amine (aliphatic or aromatic) only.

$$R-NH_2 \xrightarrow[KOH/\Delta]{CHCl_3} R-NC + KCl + H_2O$$

$$Ar-NH_2 \xrightarrow[KOH/\Delta]{CHCl_3} \underset{\text{Carbylamine}}{Ar-NC} + KCl + H_2O$$

Thus, it responds to carbylamine test.

11. (*d*) In strongly acidic medium, aniline is protonated to form the anilinium ion.

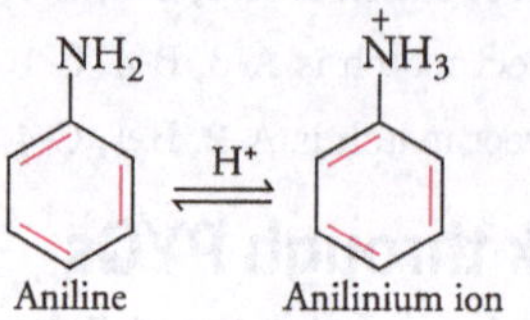

Since, anilinium ion so formed is *meta*-directing, thus besides *ortho* and *para* derivatives, significant amount of *meta*-derivative is also formed.

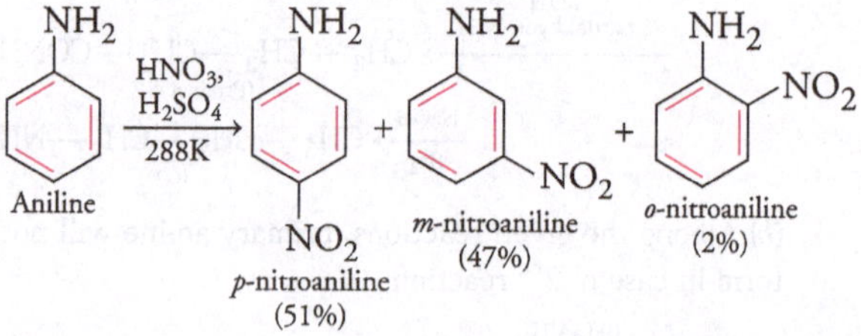

12. (*d*) This type of problem can be solved by application of electron- withdrawing and electron donating group.

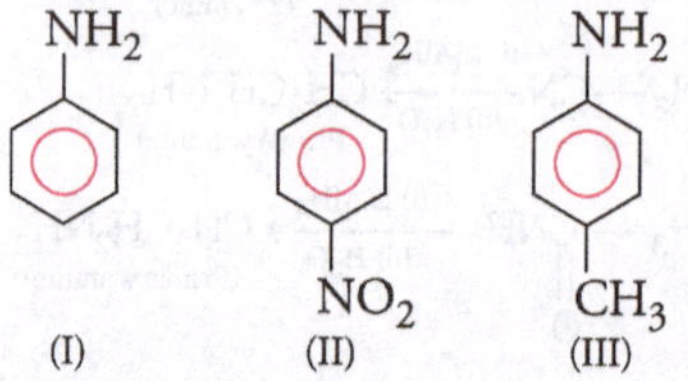

In III, —CH_3 group is an electron donating and *o*/*p*-directing group which increase the electron density on benzene ring at *ortho or para* position.

In II, —NO_2 group is an electron withdrawing group which decrease the electron density on benzene ring. Hence, the III is more basic than II.

In I, there is no substituent attached, due to which I is more basic than II and less basic than III.

Therefore, the correct order of basic strength of above compounds is II < I < III.

13. (*d*)

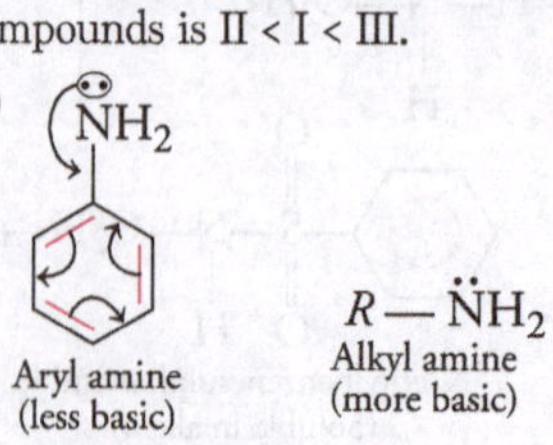

Due to delocalisation of lone pair of electrons of N-atom to the benzene ring, it losses its basicity and becomes less basic than alkyl amine.

On the other hand, alkyl amine has free lone pair of electron as well as +*I*-effect of alkyl group increases electron density on N-atom enhancing its basic nature.

14. (*a*) In the nitration of benzene in the presence of conc. H_2SO_4 and HNO_3, nitrobenzene is formed.

$$HNO_3 + H_2SO_4 \rightleftharpoons \underset{\text{Electrophile}}{NO_2^+} + \underset{\text{Nucleophile}}{HSO_4^-} + H_2O$$

If large amount of $KHSO_4$ is added to this mixture, more HSO_4^- ion furnishes and hence the concentration of NO_2^+, i.e. electrophile decreases.

As concentration of electrophile decreases, rate of electrophilic aromatic reaction also decreases.

15. (*a*)

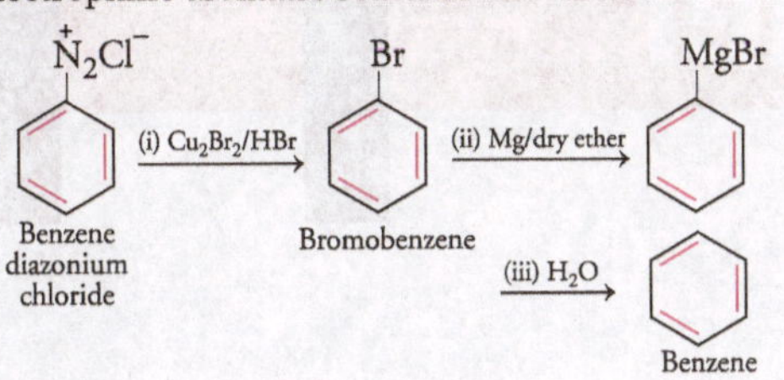

16. (*b*) $\underset{\text{1° aliphatic amines}}{R—NH_2} \xrightarrow{HNO_2} \underset{\text{Alkyl diazonium ion (unstable)}}{R—\overset{\oplus}{N_2}}$

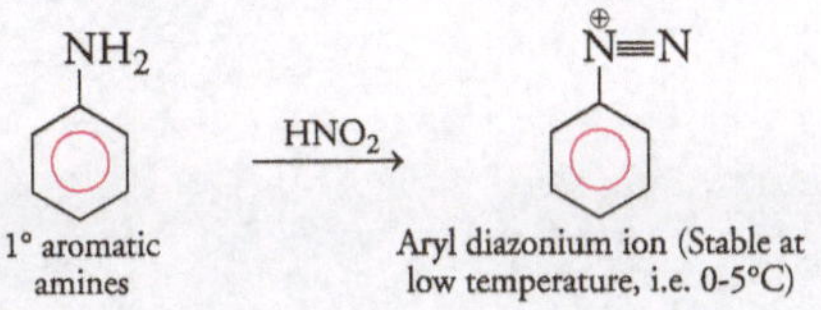

So, Statement I is true but Statement II is false.

17. (*d*) The given reaction is represented as

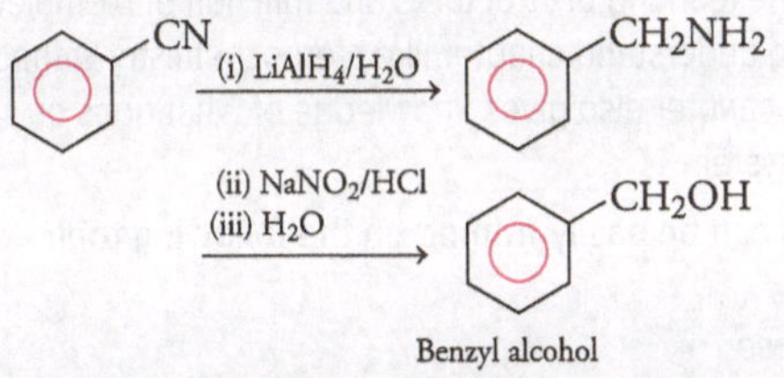

18. (*c*) The given chemical reaction is represented as

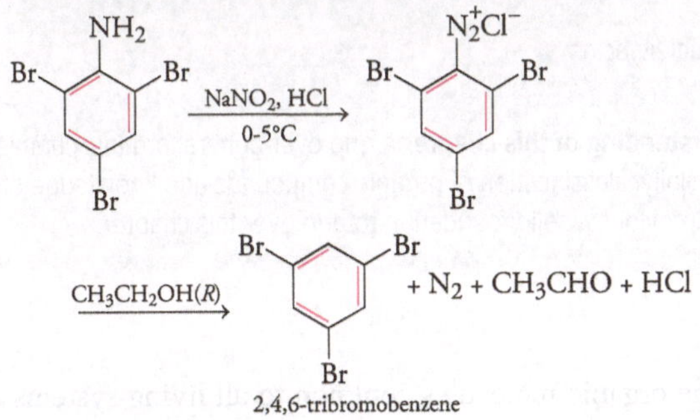

Hence, R is CH_3CH_2OH

19. (*b*)

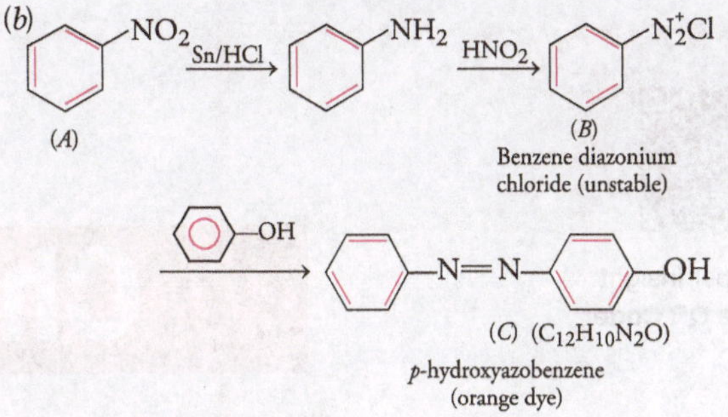

Hence, *A* is nitrobenzene.

20. (*d*) The given reaction is represented as

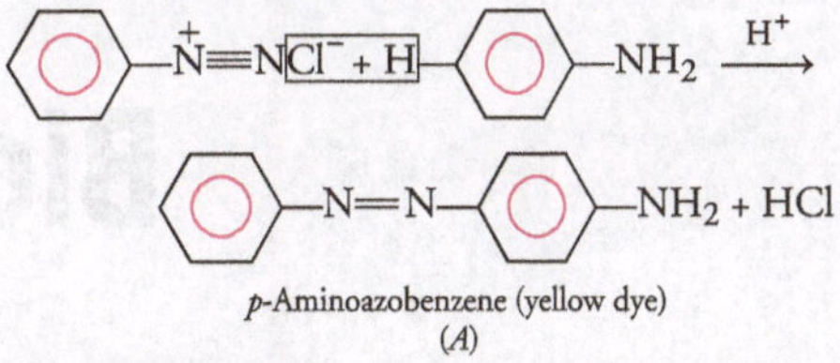

Skill Builder

- **Sol. of Skill Builder Pg. 450**

(*d*) Among the given reactions, only (d) will not give primary amine as the product.

$$C_2H_5—CH_2—Br \xrightarrow{\text{(i) } NH_3} C_2H_5—CH_2—NH_2$$

$$\xrightarrow{C_2H_5—Br} \underset{\text{(2° amine)}}{C_2H_5CH_2—\overset{H}{\overset{|}{N}}—C_2H_5}$$

- **Sol. of Skill Builder Pg. 459**

(*a*) N, N-diethylaniline is 3° amine thus, will not give the carbylamine test.

- **Sol. of Skill Builder Pg. 461**

(*c*) Statement I is false but Statement II is true. The correct form of statement I is : Aromatic primary amines cannot be prepared by Gabriel pthalimide synthesis because aryl halides do not undergo nucleophilic substitution with the anion formed by pthalimide.

- **Sol. of Skill Builder Pg. 466**

(*b*) $C_6H_5—NH_2 \xrightarrow[273\ K]{NaNO_2/HCl} \underset{(X)}{C_6H_5N_2Cl}$

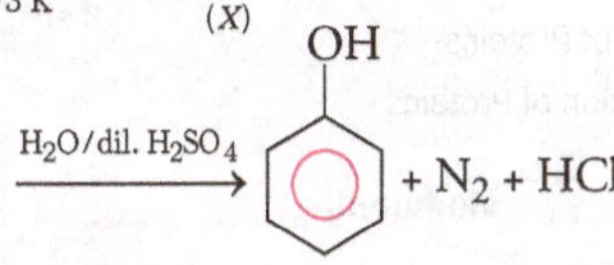

For deeper insight
Scan the QR Code

Chapter 11

Biomolecules

Chapter Overview with
NEET Connection

This chapter is useful for the learning of structures and function of biomolecules. It will be difficult to learn and understand chapter like stereochemistry without gripping this chapter. This chapter also gives knowledge of what goes on chemically within a living system.

Special format questions can be easily framed on the following topics of this chapter.

- Cyclic structure of glucose
- Essential and non-essential amino acids
- Vitamins
- Structure of nucleic acids
- Hormones

For better understanding of this chapter a grip over general organic chemistry is required. Especially, classification of organic compounds and knowledge of functional group provides a solid foundation to grip over this chapter.

Learning Objectives

Module-I

- Classification of Carbohydrates
- Monosaccharides (Glucose and Fructose)
- Disaccharides (Sucrose, Lactose and Maltose)

Module-II

- Amino Acids
- Classification of Amino Acids
- Peptides
- Types of Proteins
- Structure of Proteins
- Denaturation of Proteins

Module-III

- Enzymes
- Hormones
- Vitamins
- Nucleic Acids
- Structure of Nucleic Acids
- DNA Fingerprinting

Introduction

Biomolecules are the organic molecules common to all living systems on earth. These molecules perform several physiological functions and act as building blocks of living body. They include carbohydrates, proteins, enzymes, lipids, hormones, vitamins, nucleic acids etc.

Proteins and carbohydrates are essential constituents of our food. Vitamins and mineral salts play an important role in the various functionings of living organisms.

Module 1

Carbohydrates

- Classification of Carbohydrates
- Disaccharides (Sucrose, Lactose and Maltose)
- Monosaccharides (Glucose and Fructose)

Carbohydrates

Carbohydrates (saccharides) occur naturally in the animal and plant kingdom. Sugars, starch and cellulose are the best known members of this class. Chemical analysis of sugar and other carbohydrates shows that they are composed of only the carbon, hydrogen and oxygen and they appear to be the hydrates of carbon. Their general formula is $C_x(H_2O)_y$.

Glucose $(C_6H_{12}O_6) : C_6 \cdot 6H_2O$

Sucrose $(C_{12}H_{22}O_{11}) : C_{12} \cdot 11H_2O$

But all the compounds which fit into this formula may not be classified as carbohydrates, e.g. Acetic acid (CH_3COOH). Similarly, rhamnose ($C_6H_{12}O_5$) is a carbohydrate but does not fit in the formula.

Chemically, the carbohydrates may be defined as optically active polyhydroxy aldehydes or ketones or the compounds which produce such units on hydrolysis.

Classification of Carbohydrates

I. Depending upon their behaviour on hydrolysis these are classified into three categories.

(i) **Monosaccharides** These are the simplest carbohydrates that cannot be hydrolysed into simpler units (monomers). In other words, it is made up of a single monomer itself. About 20 monosaccharides are known to occur in nature, e.g. glucose, fructose, galactose, etc.

These are further classified as **aldose** (functional group is aldehyde) and **ketose** (functional group is ketone).

(ii) **Oligosaccharides** These carbohydrates produce 2-10 monomer units upon hydrolysis. The ones that produce 2 monomer units are called **disaccharides** (sucrose, lactose, maltose) and the ones that produce 3 monomer units are called **trisaccharides** (raffinose) and so on.

$$\underset{\text{Sucrose}}{C_{12}H_{22}O_{11}} + H_2O \xrightarrow{H^+} \underset{\text{D-(+)-glucose}}{C_6O_{12}O_6} + \underset{\text{D-(-)-fructose}}{C_6H_{12}O_6}$$

(iii) **Polysaccharides** These carbohydrates produce large number of monomer units (at least > 10) upon hydrolysis, e.g. glycogen, starch, cellulose etc.

II. On the basis of sweetness in taste, carbohydrates are divided into two simple types which are as follows

(i) **Sugars** They taste sweet on our tongue. This class includes monosaccharides and disaccharides as mentioned above.

(ii) **Non-sugars** They do not taste sweet and include mainly polysaccharides.

Concept ladder Sugars are water soluble, whereas non-sugars are water insoluble or less soluble than sugars.

III. On the basis of reducing activity, carbohydrate can be classified as follows

(i) **Reducing carbohydrates** They contain free functional group (aldehyde or ketone) and reduce Fehling's solution and Tollen's reagent. These include all the monosaccharides (aldose and ketose).

(ii) **Non-reducing carbohydrates** They have bonded functional groups and cannot reduce Fehling's solution or Tollen's reagent. These include oligosaccharides and polysaccharides.

NEET Close-up

Example Similar to PYQ Asked in NEET 2016

Which of the following is a reducing sugar?

(a) Lactose (b) Raffinose
(c) Sucrose (d) α-D-glucose + β - D-fructose

Sol. (*a*) Among the given options lactose is a reducing sugar because free aldehyde group may be produced at C-1 of glucose unit.

Skill Builder

Out of maltose (I), cellobiose (II), sucrose (III) and lactose (IV), reducing sugars are

(a) I, II and III (b) I, II and IV
(c) II, III and IV (d) Only IV

For more practice Refer to Q. 6 and 7 of step up practice 1 and Q. 10 of Gearing up for NEET.

Monosaccharides

As discussed earlier, monosaccharides are the simplest carbohydrates and also called **simple sugars**. On the basis of functional group present, these are further classified as

(i) **Aldose** They contain aldehyde $(-\overset{\overset{\large O}{\|}}{C}-H)$ group as main functional group alongwith few hydroxyl (—OH) groups. Thus, they can be termed as polyhydroxy aldehydic monosaccharides, e.g. glucose, galactose.

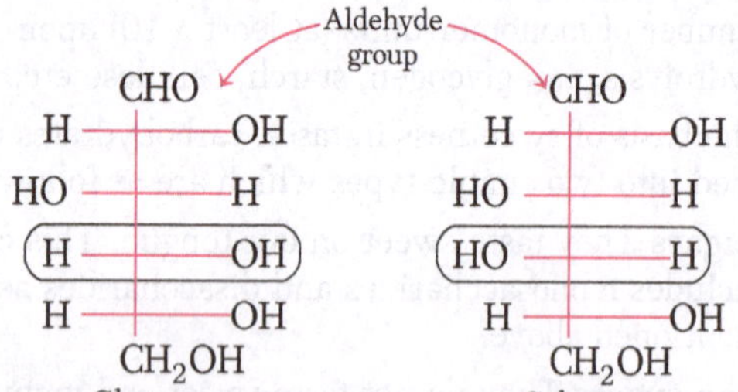

Glucose (aldohexose) Galactose (aldohexose)

(ii) **Ketose** They contain ketone $(-\overset{\overset{\large O}{\|}}{C}-)$ group as main functional group alongwith few hydroxyl (—OH) groups. Thus, they can be termed as polyhydroxy ketonic monosaccharides. e.g. fructose.

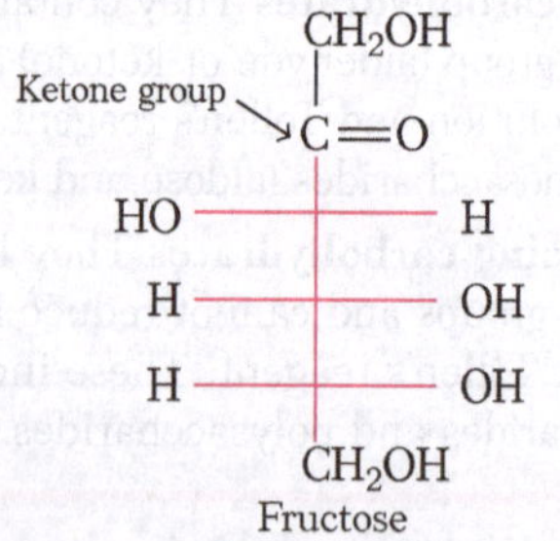

Fructose (Ketohexose)

Glucose

It is an **aldohexose** having molecular formula $C_6H_{12}O_6$ **aldohexose.** Due to the dextrorotatory optical activity of natural glucose, it is also called **dextrose.** It is white powdery solid, soluble in water and has melting point of 423 K. In nature it is found in sweet fruits, flower nectar etc., in free as well as in combined state. It constitutes about 20% of grapes and for this reason it is also known as **grape sugar.**

In our body, it is essentially present to be consumed up by different organs as an energy source. It is a normal constituent of blood and travels through our blood stream to our cells. Hence, it is also termed as **blood sugar.**

Preparation

It can be prepared by hydrolysis of cane sugar or starch in following ways.

(i) **From cane sugar** (sucrose) Cane sugar consists of sucrose which when hydrolysed in acidic medium produces glucose and fructose in equal amounts.

$$\underset{\text{Sucrose}}{C_{12}H_{22}O_{11}} + H_2O \xrightarrow{H^+} \underset{\text{Glucose}}{C_6H_{12}O_6} + \underset{\text{Fructose}}{C_6H_{12}O_6}$$

(ii) **From starch** Commercially glucose is produced from starch, which is derived from potatoes or corns. The hydrolysis takes place by boiling it with dil. H_2SO_4 at 393 K under pressure.

$$\underset{\text{Starch or Cellulose}}{(C_6H_{10}O_5)_n} + nH_2O \xrightarrow[\text{393 K, 2-3 atm}]{H^+} \underset{\text{Glucose}}{nC_6H_{12}O_6}$$

Mentor's TiP

- Glucose and fructose are separated by fractional crystallisation.
- Few disaccharides like lactose (gives glucose and galactose) and maltose (gives 2 units of glucose) are also used as sources of glucose.

Structure

Two types of structure, the open chain structure and cyclic structure, have been suggested for glucose molecule which are discussed below.

1. Open Chain Structure

As discussed above, glucose is an aldohexose, having six carbon atoms including one aldehydic group. Its structure can be represented by using Fischer projection as

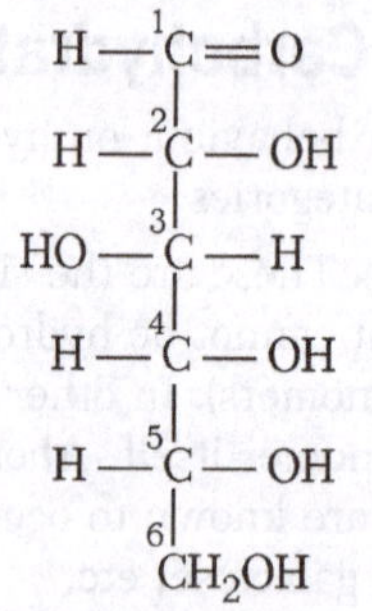

D-glucose
(Specific rotation = 53°)

The following chemical reactions give evidences in favour of open chain structure of glucose.

- On prolonged heating with HI, glucose forms n-hexane which shows that all six carbon atoms are linked in a straight chain.

$$\underset{\text{Glucose}}{CHO-(CHOH)_4-CH_2OH} \xrightarrow{HI/\Delta} \underset{n\text{-hexane}}{CH_3-CH_2-CH_2-CH_2-CH_2-CH_3}$$

- Glucose reacts with hydroxyl amine to form an oxime. This reaction confirms the presence of $>C=O$ group in glucose.

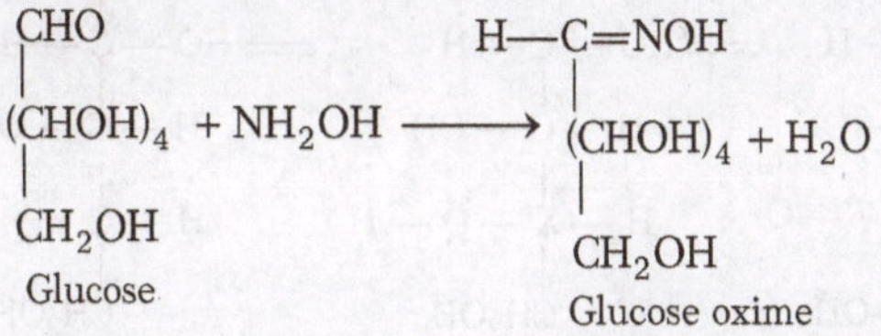

- It forms cyanohydrin on reaction with hydrogen cyanide.

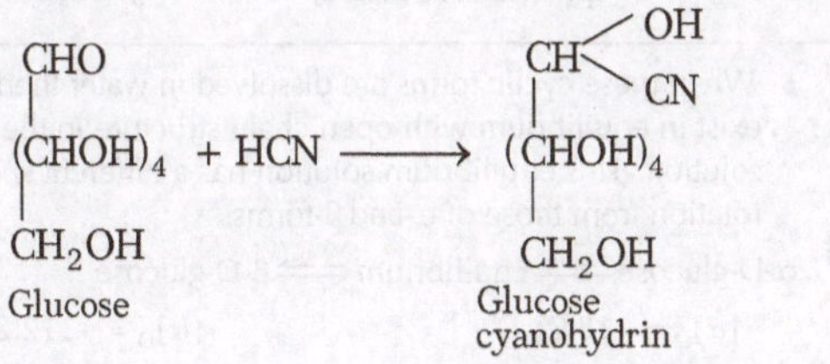

Thus, one new (C—C) bond is formed. This reaction suggest that glucose contains a carbonyl group.

- Oxidation of glucose with Br_2 water (mild oxidising agent) gives gluconic acid. This reaction indicates that the carbonyl group is present as an aldehydic group.

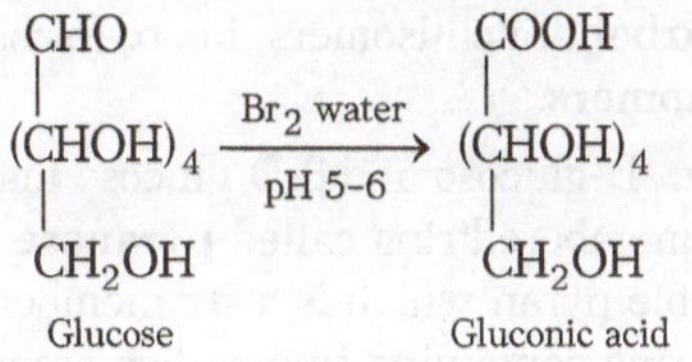

- Reduction of glucose with $NaBH_4$ or $Na(Hg) / H_2O$ forms D-sorbitol (hexahydric alcohol).

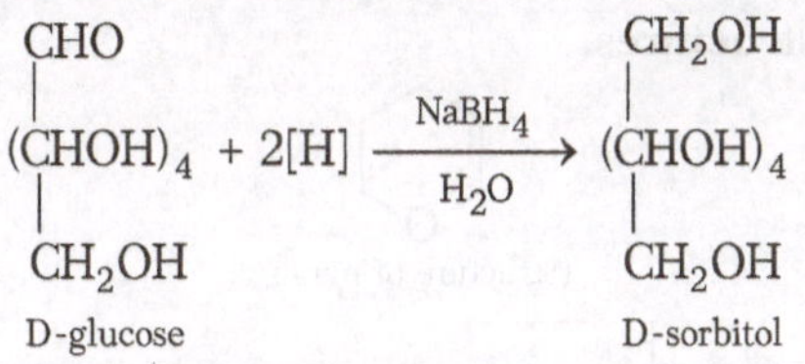

- Acetylation of glucose with acetic anhydride forms penta-acetate derivative, indicating presence of five —OH groups. Since, it exists as a stable compound, 5—OH groups should be attached to different carbon atoms.

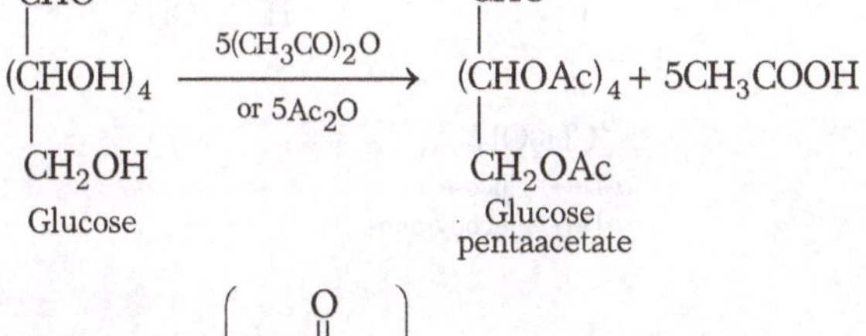

Here, Ac is $\left(CH_3\overset{O}{\overset{\|}{C}}—\right)$.

- Glucose as well as gluconic acid on oxidation with nitric acid yields a dicarboxylic acid, a saccharic acid. This indicates the presence of a primary alcoholic (—OH) group in glucose.

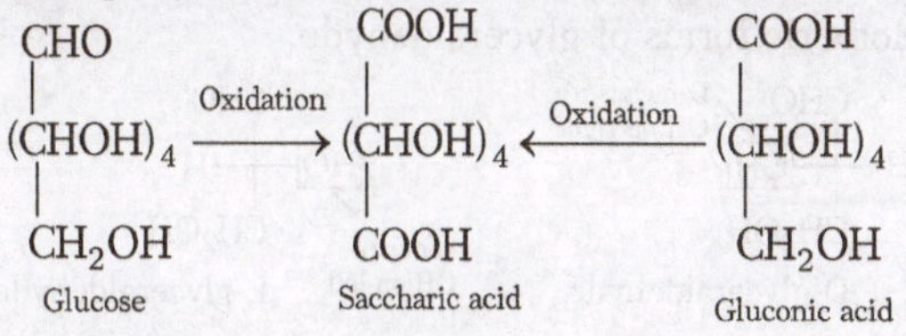

- Glucose reduces both Tollen's reagent and Fehling's solution (a test of reducing sugars).

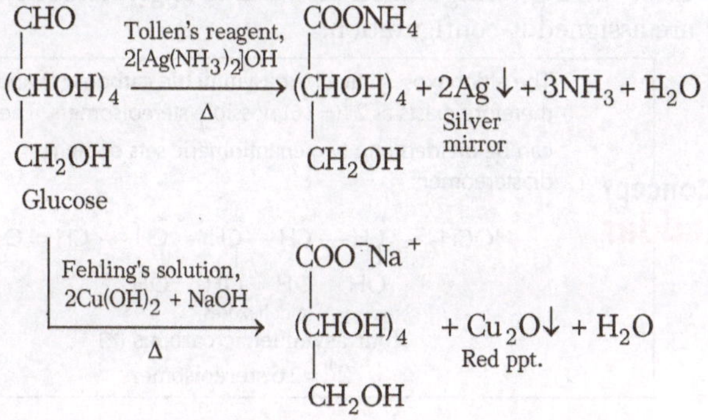

NEET Close-up

Example Similar to PYQ Asked in NEET 2024

The reagents with which glucose react to give the corresponding test/product ?

A. Br_2 water B. HI, Δ
C. Fehling's solution D. $NaBH_4$ E. NH_2OH

Choose the correct options from the given below.

(a) B and C (b) A, B, C, D and E
(c) B and E (d) A, C and D

Sol. (*b*) Glucose reacts with all the given reagents to form products as given below.

A. Glucose $\xrightarrow{Br_2 \text{ water}}$ Gluconic acid
B. Glucose $\xrightarrow{HI, \Delta}$ *n*-hexane
C. Glucose $\xrightarrow{\text{Fehling's solutuion}}$ Red ppt.
D. Glucose $\xrightarrow{NaBH_4}$ D-sorbitol
E. Glucose $\xrightarrow{NH_2OH}$ Glucose oxime

Skill Builder

The reagent with which an aldohexose react to give the corresponding product to be chiral.

A. Sodium borohydride B. Acetic anhydride
C. Hydroxyl amine D. Seliwanoff's reagent
E. Sodium hydrogen sulphite

Choose the correct options from the given below.

(a) A, B and C (b) B and D (c) C and E (d) A, D and E

For more practice Refer to Q. 13 of Step-up practice-1.

D, L-Configuration

Glucose is correctly named as D-(+)-glucose. 'D' or 'L' letter before the name of any compound indicates the relative configuration of particular stereoisomer in relation to two enantiomeric forms of glyceraldehyde.

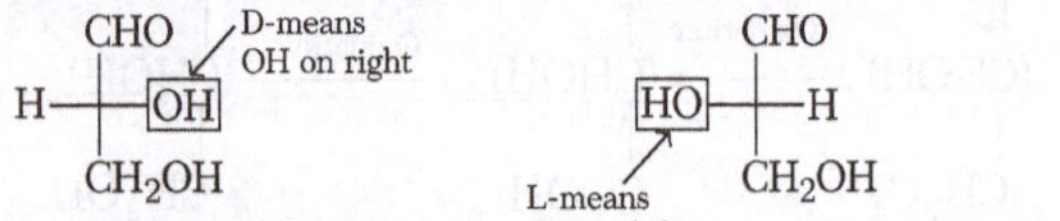

D-glyceraldehyde L-glyceraldehyde

The monosaccharides having configuration identical to D-glyceraldehyde are assigned D-configuration whereas those having configuration identical to L-glyceraldehyde are assigned L-configuration.

> **Concept ladder**
>
> The aldohexoses have four asymmetric carbons (*) and therefore exists as $2^4 (= 16)$ possible stereoisomers. These can be divided into two enantiomeric sets of eight diastereomers.
>
> 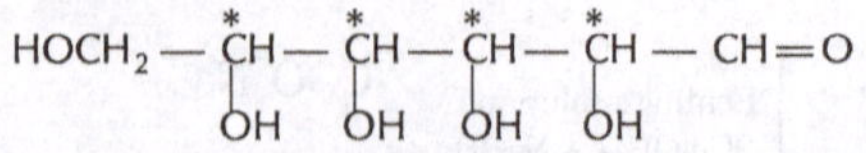
>
> Aldohexoses
>
> four asymmetric carbons (*)
>
> $2^4 = 16$ stereoisomers

2. Cyclic Structure

Glucose, also show following chemical reactions that are against the open chain structure.

- Despite having aldehydic group, glucose does not give 2, 4-DNP test or Schiff's test and does not form hydrogen sulphite addition product with $NaHSO_3$.
- Glucose penta-acetate does not react with hydroxyl-amine indicating the absence of free —CHO groups.
- Glucose exists in two crystalline anomeric forms, i.e. α - D-glucose and β-D-glucose. Thus, they have different melting points and specific rotations $[\alpha]_D$. The α-form is obtained by crystallisation from concentrated solution of glucose at 303 K while the β-form is obtained by crystallisation from hot and saturated aqueous solution at 371 K.

This behaviour could not be explained by open chain structure. It was proposed that in this structure —OH of C - 5 is added to the aldehydic carbon (C-1). Thus, a cyclic hemiacetal structure is formed.

It was found that glucose forms a 6-membered ring in which —OH at C-5 is involved in ring formation.

This cyclic structure explains the absence of —CHO group and the existence of α-and β-forms.

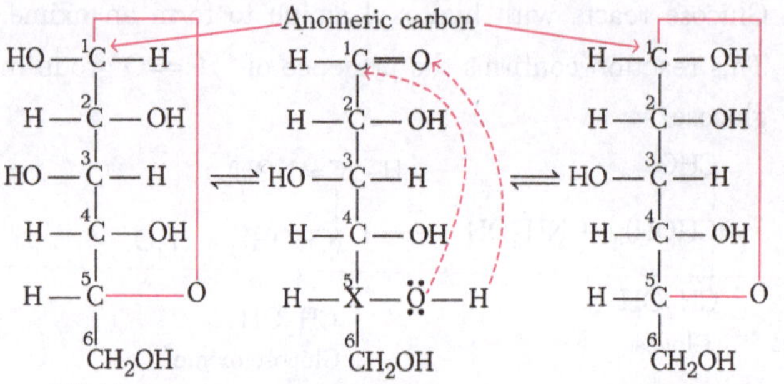

β-D-(+)-glucose [cyclic structure] D-glucose [open chain structure] α-D-(+)-glucose [cyclic structure]

> **Concept ladder**
>
> - When these cyclic forms are dissolved in water then these exist in equilibrium with open chain structure in the solution. This equilibrium solution has a different specific rotation from those of α-and β-forms.
>
> α-D-glucose ⇌ Equilibrium ⇌ β-D-glucose
>
> $[\alpha]_D = +18.7°$ $[\alpha]_D = +112.2°$
>
> m.p = 423 K $[\alpha]_D = +52.6°$ m.p = 419 K
>
> - This spontaneous change in specific rotations of solution of an optically active compound is called **mutarotation.**

The two cyclic hemiacetal forms of glucose differ only in the configuration of hydroxyl group at C-1 called **anomeric carbon**. Such isomers, i.e. α-forms and β-form are called **anomers.**

Structure of α-D-glucose and β-D-glucose may be drawn in a simple six membered ring called **pyranose structures.** These resemble pyran which is a six membered heterocyclic ring containing five carbon atoms and one oxygen atom. These structures were suggested by Haworth and are known as **Haworth projection formulae** or **pyranose structures.**

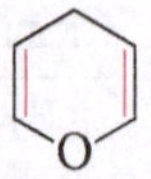

(Structure of pyran)

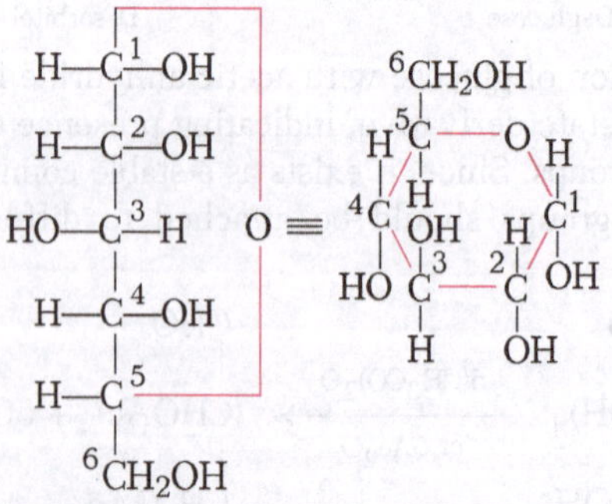

α-D-(+)-glucose

α-D-(+)-glucopyranose

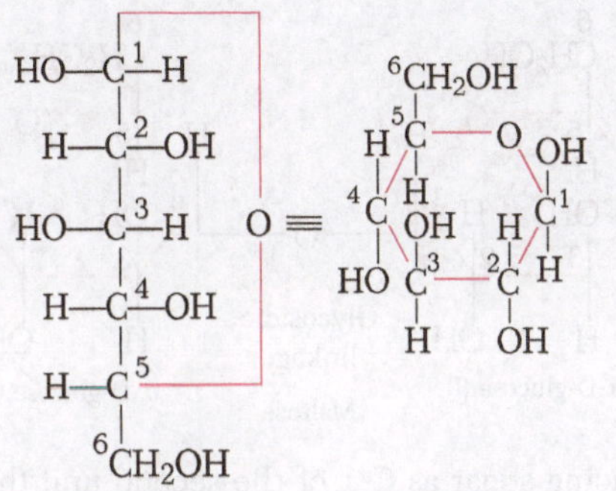

β-D-(+)-glucose
β-D-(+)-glucopyranose

Mentor's TIP

Groups on the right in a Fischer projection are written down in a Haworth projection and groups on the left in a Fischer projection are written up in a Haworth projection.

Fructose

Like glucose, fructose also has the molecular formula $C_6H_{12}O_6$ but belongs to the class ketohexose as it consists of six carbon atoms and a ketonic ($>C{=}O$) group. It is found in most of the fruits, hence is also called as **fruit sugar.** As the natural fructose is laevorotatory, it is called **laevulose.**

Preparation

As discussed earlier fructose can be produced from cane sugar, alongwith glucose.

Structure

On the basis of its reactions, that are shown by fructose, it was found that fructose have a ketonic functional group at C-2 and six membered chain of carbon atoms. It has two primary alcoholic (—CH_2OH) groups and three secondary alcoholic ($>$CHOH) groups. The open chain structure of fructose is shown as

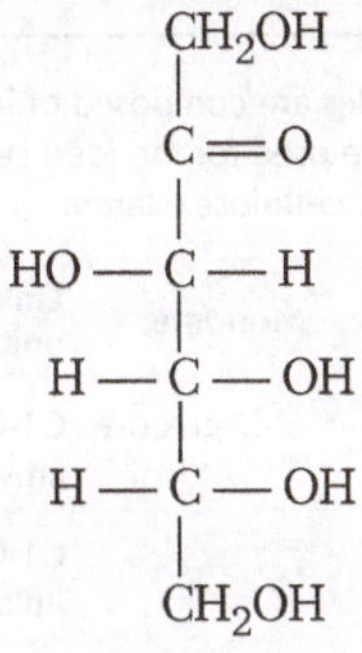

D-fructose

Like glucose, fructose too exists in cyclic forms that include α- and β- anomeric forms as represented below, using the **Fischer projections.**

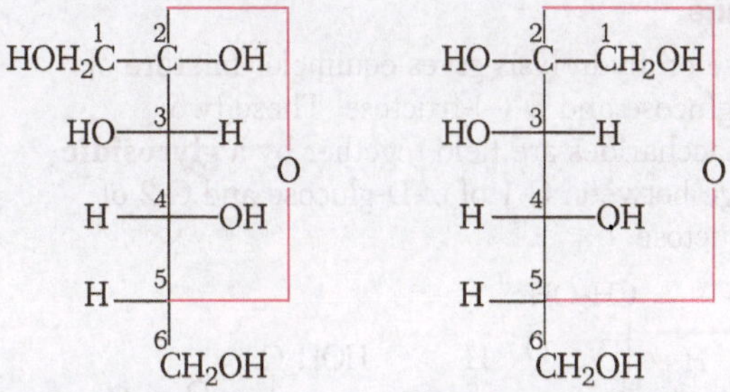

α-D-(—)-fructofuranose β-D-(—)-fructofuranose

The above structures can also be represented using **Haworth's projection** as

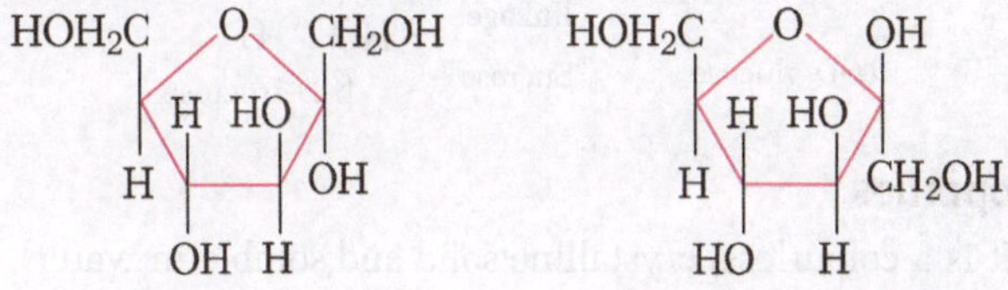

α-D-(-)-fructofuranose β-D-(—)-fructofuranose

Concept ladder

The cyclic fructose is called fructofuranose as it resembles with furan which is a 5-membered cyclic compound with one oxygen and four carbon atoms.

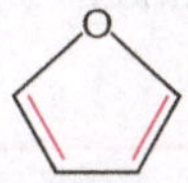

(Furan)

Properties

- Fructose is a colourless crystalline compound having melting point of 375 K.
- It is readily soluble in water but sparingly soluble in alcohols and insoluble in ether and benzene.
- It is sweetest among all known carbohydrates.
- It forms a laevorotatory solution and like glucose it also shows mutarotation.

Disaccharides

These saccharides on hydrolysis with dilute acids or enzymes gives two molecules of monosaccharides. These monosaccharides may be same or different.

These two monomer units are joined together through an **oxide linkage** which is formed by the loss of a water molecule. Such a linkage between two monosaccharide units through an oxygen atom is called as **glycosidic linkage.**

Some important disaccharides are as follow

1. Sucrose

It is actually the common table sugar we use in our daily lives. It is found in all green plants and commercially obtained from sugar cane and sugar beets. The molecular formula of sucrose is $C_{12}H_{22}O_{11}$.

Structure

Sucrose on hydrolysis gives equimolar mixture of D-(+)-glucose and D-(–)-fructose. These two monosaccharides are held together by a **glycosidic linkage** between C-1 of α-D-glucose and C-2 of β-D-fructose.

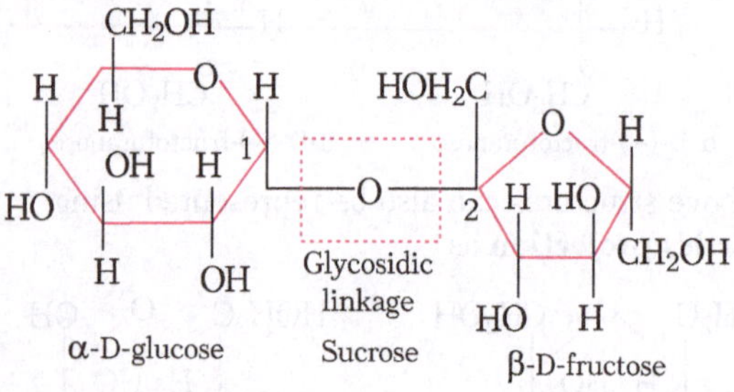

Properties

- It is a colourless, crystalline solid and soluble in water.
- It is dextrorotatory but does not show mutarotation.
- Since, the reducing groups of glucose and fructose are involved in glycosidic bond formation, sucrose is a **non-reducing sugar.** Thus, it does not reduce Tollen's reagent or Fehling's solution.

NEET Snapshot

Sucrose on hydrolysis gives α-D-glucose and β-D-fructose. ***[NEET 2020]***

Sucrose is composed of a molecule of glucose joined to a molecule of fructose by an α-1, β-2 glycosidic linkage.

When sucrose is hydrolysed it forms equimolar quantity of D-glucose and L-fructose. The solution of formed products, is found to be laevorotatory which was dextrorotatory in the beginning.

This change in optical properties of sucrose from *dextro* to *laevo* is called **inversion of cane sugar**. The equimolar product formed (that is D-glucose and L-fructose) is called **invert sugar**.

2. Maltose

It is naturally found in germinating seeds. It can be produced by the partial hydrolysis of starch by the enzymes (amylase or diastase).

$$\underset{\text{Starch}}{2(C_6H_{10}O_5)_n} + nH_2O \xrightarrow{\text{Enzyme}} \underset{\text{Maltose}}{nC_{12}H_{22}O_{11}}$$

Hydrolysis of maltose by the enzyme maltase produces two units of glucose.

$$\underset{\text{(Maltose)}}{C_{12}H_{22}O_{11}} + H_2O \xrightarrow{\text{Maltase}} \underset{\text{(Glucose)}}{2C_6H_{12}O_6}$$

Structure

Maltose is composed of two α -D-glucose units joined by a glycosidic linkage (at C - 1 of one unit with C - 4 of the another unit).

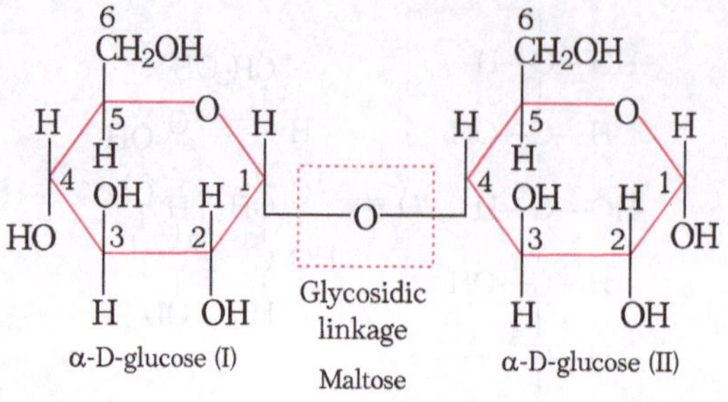

It is a reducing sugar as C-1 of the second unit (having aldehyde group is not involved in the glycosidic linkage.

3. Lactose

It is commonly found in milk and is known as **milk sugar.** Upon hydrolysis, it produces one unit of glucose and one unit of galactose.

$$C_{12}H_{22}O_{11} + H_2O \xrightarrow[\text{(enzyme)}]{\text{Lactose}} \underset{\text{Glucose}}{C_6H_{12}O_6} + \underset{\text{Galactose}}{C_6H_{12}O_6}$$

Structure

The molecule of lactose is composed of β-D-glucose unit and a β-D-galactose unit. The units are joined by the glycosidic linkage (at C-4 of glucose and C-1 of galactose).

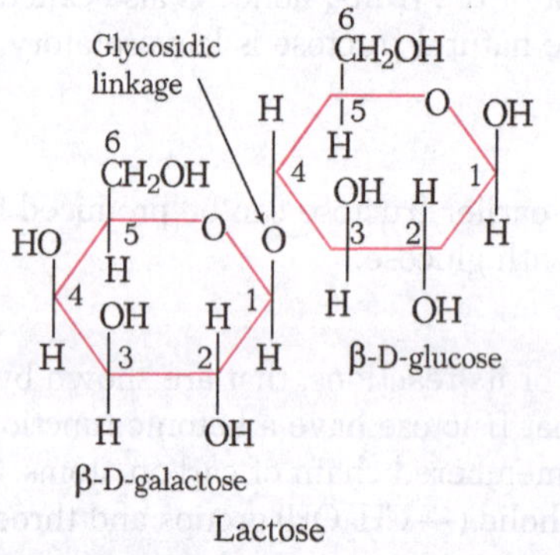

Due to reducing functional group present at C-1 of glucose unit, lactose is a reducing sugar.

Concept ladder

Polysaccharides are composed of large number of monomer units. They are used for the food storage or act as structural materials, e.g. cellulose, starch.

Polysaccharides	Monomer	Linkage between monomer unit
Starch	α-D-glucose	C1-C4 glycosidic linkage in amylose
		C1-C4 or C1-C6 glycosidic linkage in amylopectin
Cellulose	β-D-glucose	C1-C4 glycosidic linkage

STEP UP Practice 1

1 All of the following are common monosaccharides of interest in human biochemistry except

(a) glucose (b) fructose
(c) ribose (d) maltose

2 The bond connecting the two monosaccharides in maltose is a(an) .... linkage.

(a) α-1,4-glycosidic
(b) β-1,4-glycosidic
(c) 1,2-anomeric
(d) α-1,6-glycosidic

3 Consider the following statements.

Statement I Deoxyribose, $C_5H_{10}O_4$ is not a carbohydrate.

Statement II Carbohydrates are hydrates of carbon so all compounds which follow $C_x(H_2O)_y$ formula are carbohydrates.

In the light of the above statements, choose the most appropriate answer from the options given below

(a) Both Statement I and Statement II are false.
(b) Statement I is true, but Statement II is false.
(c) Statement I is false, but Statement II is true.
(d) Both Statement I and Statement II are true.

4 When a monosaccharide forms a cyclic hemiacetal, the carbon atom that contained the carbonyl group is identified as the anomeric carbon atom because

(a) the carbonyl group is drawn to the right
(b) the carbonyl group is drawn to the left
(c) its substituents can assume at α or β-position
(d) it forms bond to an —*OR* and an —*OR*′

5 A sugar is classified as a D-isomer if the hydroxyl group

(a) on the chiral carbon nearest to the carbonyl points to the left
(b) on the chiral carbon nearest to the carbonyl points to the right
(c) on the chiral carbon farthest from the carbonyl points to the left
(d) on the chiral carbon farthest from the carbonyl points to the right

6 Common reducing reactions of monosaccharides are due to

(a) their cyclic structures
(b) the presence of at least one hydroxyl group
(c) the presence of more than one hydroxyl group
(d) the presence of a carbonyl group, usually on C-1 carbon atom

7 Which of the following disaccharides are correctly matched according to their classification?

(a) α-D-glucose + α-D-glucose — Non-reducing sugar
(b) α-D-glucose + β-D-fructose — Reducing sugar
(c) β-D-fructose + β-D-glucose — Non-reducing sugar
(d) β-D-galactose + β-D-glucose — Reducing sugar

8 Consider the following saccharides.

(i) Sucrose (ii) Glycogen
(iii) Maltose (iv) Lactose
(v) Fructose

How many saccharides are not disaccharides?

(a) 4 (b) 2
(c) 3 (d) 1

9 Structure of disaccharide formed by glucose and fructose is given below. Identify anomeric carbon atoms in monosaccharide units.

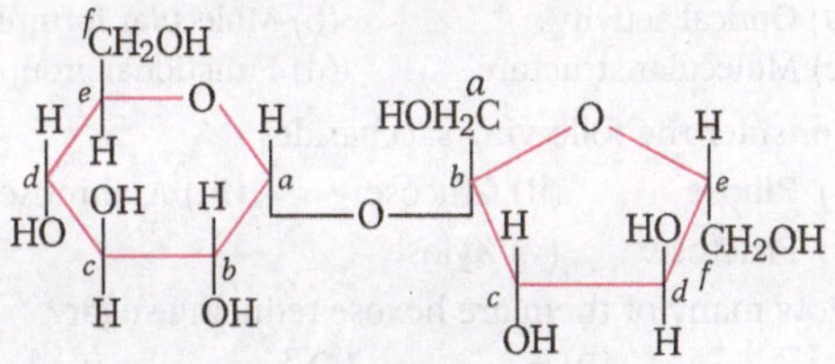

(a) '*a*' carbon of glucose and '*a*' carbon of fructose
(b) '*a*' carbon of glucose and '*e*' carbon of fructose
(c) '*a*' carbon of glucose and '*b*' carbon of fructose
(d) '*f*' carbon of glucose and '*f*' carbon of fructose

10 The option that contains incorrect match with its characteristic is

(a) Starch — Dietary source for human beings
(b) Carbohydrates — Storage of starch in plants
(c) Carbohydrates — Storage of glycogen in human beings
(d) Glycogen — Found in yeast and fungi

11 Choose the correct match according to their classification.

(a) Glycogen — Disaccharides
(b) Allose — Disaccharides
(c) Cellulose — Monosaccharides
(d) Mannose — Monosaccharides

12 Consider the following statements.

Statement I Sucrose is not a reducing sugar.

Statement II Reducing groups of glucose and fructose are involved in glycosidic bond.

In the light of the above statements, choose the most appropriate answer from the options given below.

(a) Both Statement I and Statement II are false.
(b) Statement I is true, but Statement II is false.
(c) Statement I is false, but Statement II is true.
(d) Both Statement I and Statement II are true.

13 Which of the following product is not correctly matched with the given reaction?

(a) Glucose $\xrightarrow{\text{HI + Red P}}$ (*n*-hexane)

(b) Glucose $\xrightarrow{\text{HCN}}$ (Glucocyanohydrin)

(c) Glucose $\xrightarrow{NH_2OH}$ (Glucoxime)

(d) Glucose $\xrightarrow{Br_2/\text{water}}$ Saccharic acid

14 All of the statements concerning monosaccharides are correct except

(a) the number of stereoisomers possible is 2^n, where, n is the number of chiral carbon atoms in the molecule

(b) monosaccharides with 5 or 6 carbon atoms exist in solution in cyclic form

(c) the two different cyclic forms of a particular monosaccharide are called tautomers

(d) a molecule is classified as a D- or L- isomer by the position of the hydroxyl group on the chiral centre farthest from the carbonyl group

15 Which of the following is similar in cases of both glucose and fructose?

(a) Optical activity (b) Molecular formula
(c) Molecular structure (d) Functional group

16 Consider the following saccharides.

(i) Ribose (ii) Glucose (iii) Arabinose
(iv) Fructose (v) Xylose

How many of them are hexose reducing sugar?

(a) 2 (b) 4 (c) 3 (d) 1

17 The cyclic structures of monosaccharides are given below.

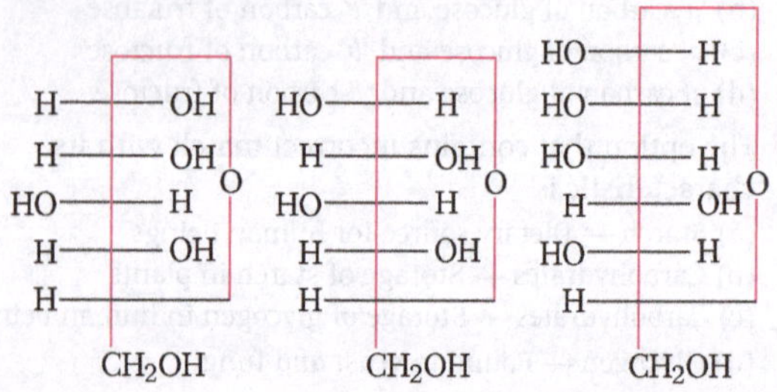

(I) (II) (III)

Which of them are anomers?

(a) Both I and II
(b) Both II and III
(c) Both I and III
(d) III is anomer of I and II

18 Optical rotations of some compounds along with their structures are given below. Which of them have D-configuration ?

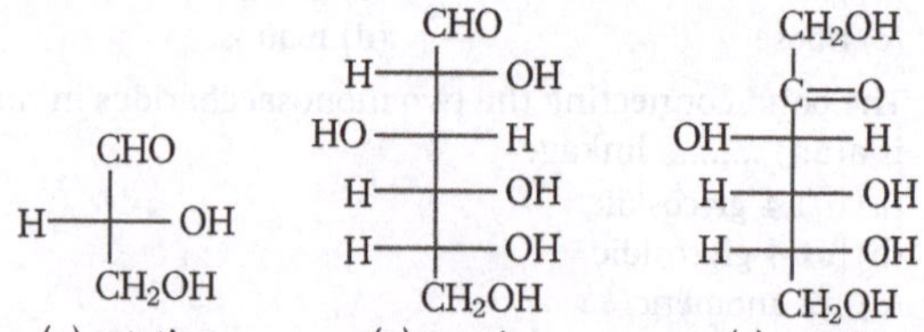

(+) rotation (I) (+) rotation (II) (–) rotation (III)

(a) I, II and III (b) Both II and III
(c) Both I and II (d) Only III

19 Biomolecules can be classified as lipids on the basis of

(a) a common structure consisting of long hydrocarbon chains

(b) the presence of many hydroxyl groups and atleast one carbonyl group

(c) the presence of atleast one hydroxyl group and one carboxylic acid group on each molecule

(d) the physical property as solubility in non-polar organic solvents

20 When a monosaccharide forms a ring by interaction of one of its hydroxyl group with its aldehyde group, the bond is referred to as a (an) .... linkage?

(a) ether (b) ester
(c) acetal (d) hemiacetal

21 The carbon atoms involved in glycosidic linkage of glucose and fructose in sucrose are respectively.

(a) C_1 and C_2 (b) C_1 and C_4
(c) C_1 and C_6 (d) C_2 and C_4

Module 2

Proteins

- Amino Acids
- Classification of Amino Acids
- Peptides
- Types of Proteins
- Structure of Proteins
- Denaturation of Proteins

Proteins

These are large biomolecules that occur in every living organism. Chief sources of proteins are milk, cheese, pulses, peanuts, fish, meat, etc. They are of many different types and have many different biological functions. The word protein is derived from greek word, proteios which means primary.

e.g. The keratin present in skin and fingernails and myosin present in muscles are proteins. Regardless of their appearance or function, all proteins are made up of several amino acid units linked together into a long chain, through **peptide bonds**.

When we hydrolyse the protein, it forms smaller units called **peptides** which on further hydrolysis produce monomer units, which are amino acids.

$$\text{Protein} \xrightarrow{\text{Hydrolysis}} \text{Peptides} \xrightarrow{\text{Hydrolysis}} \text{Amino acids}$$

Thus, protein can be called **polymer of amino acids.**

Amino Acids

As their name implies, amino acids are bifunctional. They contain an acidic carboxyl group (—COOH) and a basic amino group ($—NH_2$). Depending upon the relative position of these two groups, amino acids are classified as α, β, γ, δ etc.

Hydrolysis of proteins gives only α-amino acid. In this type, both — COOH and — NH_2 groups are attached to the same carbon atom as represented below.

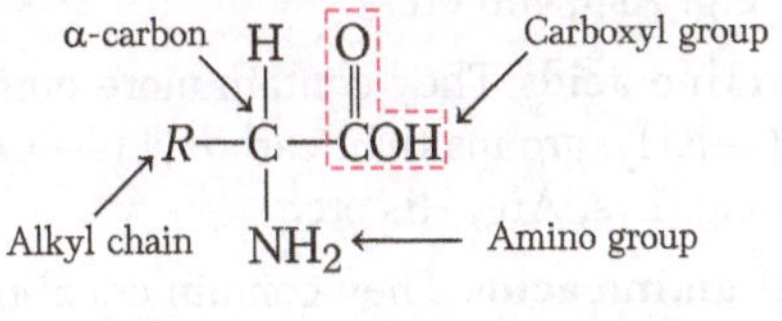

Amino acids are usually colourless, crystalline solids. These are water soluble, high melting solids and behave like salts rather than simple amines or carboxylic acids.

This type of structure where both acidic group (acquiring negative charge) and basic group (acquiring positive charge) are present is called **Zwitter ionic structure.**

Zwitter ion is a cation in acidic medium and migrates toward the cathode on passing electric current. It is an anion in basic medium and migrates towards the anode on passing electric current.

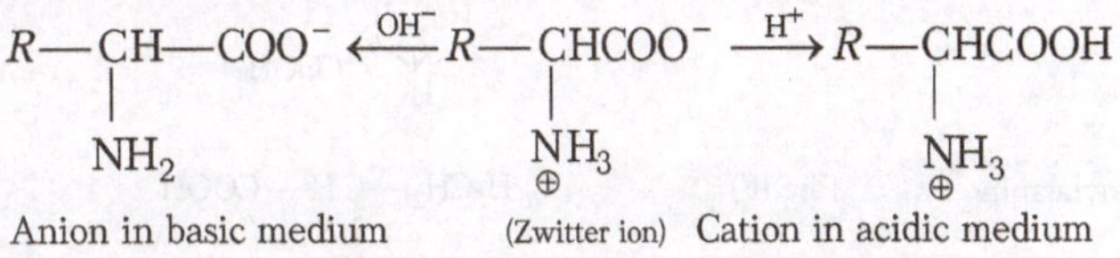

Concept ladder

- An amino acid bears a positive charge in acidic solution (low pH) and a negative charge in basic solution (high pH).
- The **isoelectric point** (PI) of the amino acid is the pH at which a molecule exists as a Zwitter ion (or) dipolar ion and carries no net charge.
- It is the pH at which the amount of negative charge on an amino acid exactly balances the amount of positive charge.

There are about 20 amino acids commonly found in proteins (refer table) and are standard amino acids. All are α-amino acids that means, amino group in each amino acid is a substituent on the α-carbon, i.e. next to the carboxyl carbon. Most of them have primary amino group — NH_2. However, proline is a secondary amine.

Each of the amino acids in table is referred by a three-letter symbol, e.g. gly for glycine, ala for alanine. In addition, a **one-letter symbol** is also used, as shown in parentheses in the table.

Amino Acids, their Symbols and Structures

Name	3-letter symbol (1-letter)	Structure
Neutral		
Glycine	Gly (G)	H_2N-CH_2-COOH
Alanine	Ala (A)	$CH_3-CH(NH_2)-COOH$
Valine*	Val (V)	$CH_3-CH(CH_3)-CH(NH_2)-COOH$
Leucine*	Leu (L)	$CH_3-CH(CH_3)-CH_2-CH(NH_2)-COOH$
Isoleucine*	Ile (I)	$CH_3-CH_2-CH(CH_3)-CH(NH_2)-COOH$
Serine	Ser (S)	$HO-CH_2-CH(NH_2)-COOH$
Proline	Pro (P)	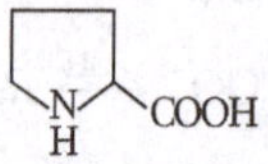
Phenylalanine*	Phe (F)	$C_6H_5CH_2-CH(NH_2)-COOH$
Cysteine	Cys (C)	$HS-CH_2-CH(NH_2)-COOH$
Glutamine	Gln (Q)	$H_2N-C(=O)-CH_2-CH_2-CH(NH_2)-COOH$
Methionine*	Met (M)	$H_3C-S-CH_2-CH_2CH(NH_2)-COOH$
Tryptophan*	Trp (W)	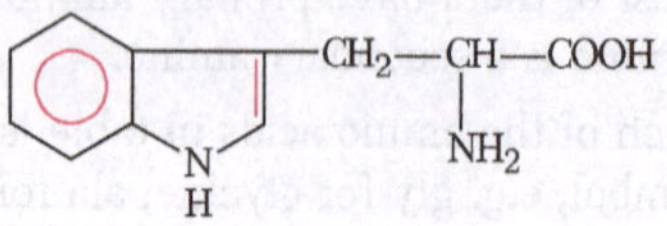
Threonine*	Thr (T)	$H_2N-CH(CH(OH)-CH_3)-COOH$
Tyrosine	Tyr (Y)	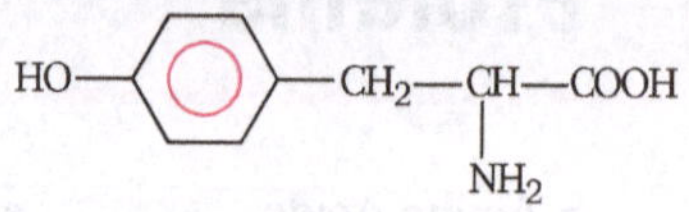
Acidic		
Aspartic acid	Asp (D)	$HOOC-CH_2-CH(NH_2)-COOH$
Glutamic acid	Glu (E)	$HOOC-CH_2-CH_2-CH(NH_2)-COOH$
Asparagine	Asn (N)	$H_2N-C(=O)-CH_2-CH(NH_2)-COOH$
Basic		
Lysine*	Lys (K)	$H_2N-CH_2-(CH_2)_3-CH(NH_2)-COOH$
Arginine*	Arg (R)	$HN=C(NH_2)-NH-(CH_2)_3-CH(NH_2)-COOH$
Histidine*	His (H)	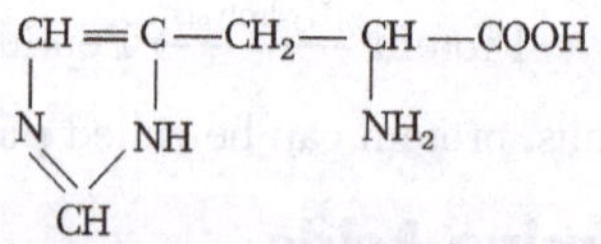

** Essential amino acids defined on next page.*

Classification of Amino Acids

I. On the basis of relative number of amino and carboxyl groups present, amino acids are classified in following three types.

(i) **Acidic amino acids** They contain more number of carboxylic (—COOH) groups than amino (—NH_2) groups. e.g. Asp, Glu etc.

(ii) **Basic amino acids** They contain more number of amino (—NH_2) groups than carboxyl (— COOH) groups. e.g. Lys, Arg, His etc.

(iii) **Neutral amino acids** They contain equal number of amino (—NH_2) groups and carboxyl (—COOH) groups, e.g. Gly, Ala, Val etc.

NEET Close-up

Example Similar to PYQ Asked in NEET 2020

Which of the following is a basic amino acid?

(a) Tyrosine (b) Arginine
(c) Cysteine (d) Proline

Sol. (*b*) Among the given compounds, arginine is a basic amino acid because it contains more number of $—NH_2$ groups as compared to —COOH groups.

Structure of arginine is

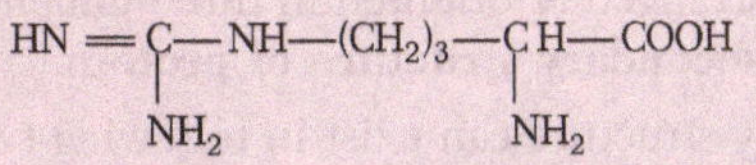

Skill Builder

Which of the following is not a neutral amino acid?

(a) Ser (b) Leu
(c) Met (d) His

For more practice Refer to Q. 5 of step up practice 2 and Q. 44 of Gearing up for NEET.

II. On the basis of requirement in human diet, amino acids are classified into following two types

(i) **Essential amino acids** These are the amino acids that are not synthesised in human body and must be obtained from our diet. e.g. Val, Leu, Lys etc.

(ii) **Non-essential amino acids** These are the amino acids that can be synthesised in our body and hence are not essentially required in our diet, e.g. Gly, Ala, Ser etc.

Concept ladder

Except, glycine, all other naturally occurring α-amino acids are optically active, since the α-carbon atom is asymmetric. These exist in both 'D' and 'L' forms. Most naturally occurring amino acids have L-configuration.

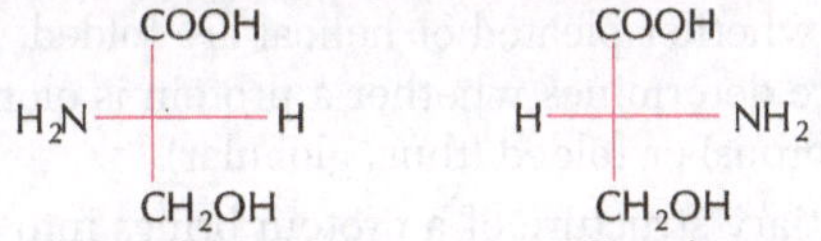

L-serine (*S*) D-serine (*R*)

Fischer projections

Peptides

Amino acids may be joined together by an amide linkage called as **peptide linkage** (—C(=O)NH—) or **peptide bond.** Each amino acid unit in a peptide is called a **residue.** In this linkage, an amino group from one residue forms an amide bond —CONH— with the carboxyl of a second residue; the amino group of the second, forms an amide bond with the carboxyl of a third, and so on.

e.g. Alanylserine is a **dipeptide** that results when an amide bond is formed between the carboxyl group of alanine and the amino group of serine.

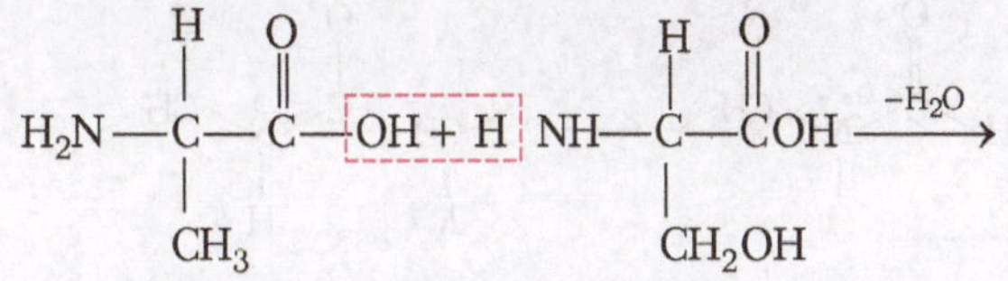

Alanine (Ala) Serine (Ser)

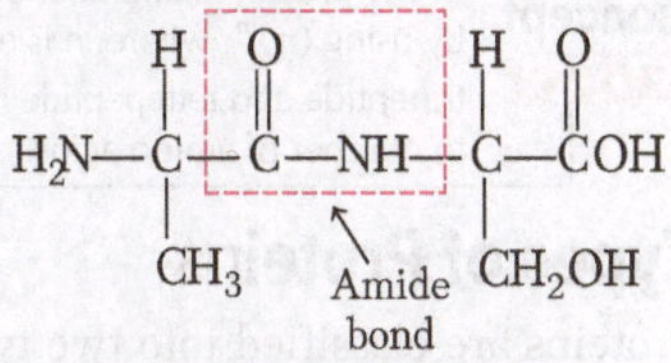

Alanylserine (Ala-Ser)

The term oligopeptide is generally used for the peptides containing about three to ten amino acid residues. The term polypeptide is used if the unit consist of more than 10 amino acids.

A polypeptide with more than hundred amino acid residues, having molecular mass higher than 10,000 u is called protein.

Polypeptides are amphoteric because of the presence of terminal ammonium and carboxylate ions as well as the ionised side chains of amino acid residues. Most of the toxins (poisonous substances) in animal venoms and in plant sources are polypeptides.

Some oligopeptides such as oxytoxin, vasopressin etc.. are effective hormones. Aspartame (a derivative of dipeptide) is an artificial sugar substitute.

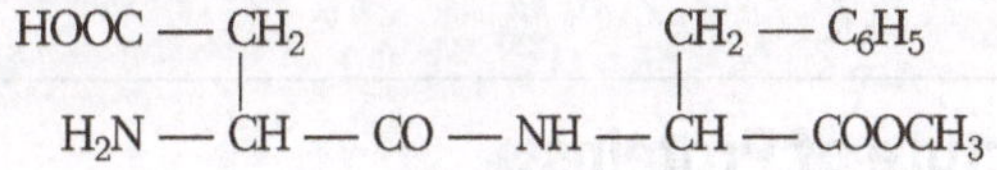

Aspartame

Characteristics of Peptide Bond

- Peptide bond is formed by the linkage of carboxyl (—C(=O)—OH) group of one amino acid with amino $(—NH_2)$ group of another amino acid, with removal of a water molecules.
- A peptide bond has about 40% double-bond character because of resonance.
- Steric hindrance causes the *trans*-configuration to be more stable than the *cis*-configuration, so the α-carbons of adjacent amino acids are *trans* to each other.

- As a consequence of the partial double-bond character of the peptide bond, free rotation is not possible around this bond.

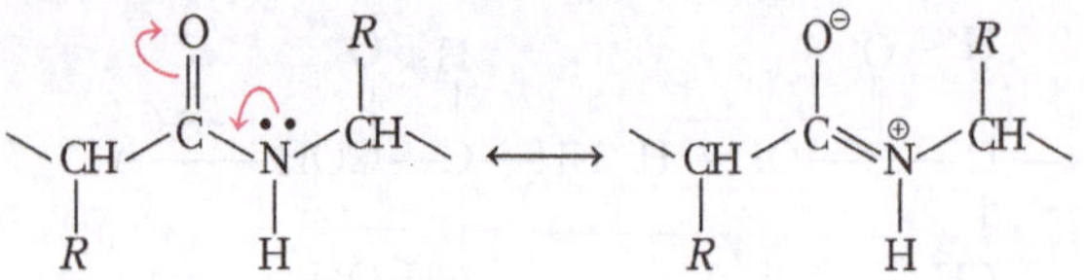

Concept ladder In any protein the number of polypeptides can be calculated by using $(n)^m$, where, n is equal to 2, 3 or 4 for dipeptides, tripeptide and tetrapeptide respectively, where, m is equal to number of amino acids.

Types of Proteins

Proteins are classified into two types of the basis of their molecular shape

(i) **Fibrous proteins** These are elongated thread like molecules held together by hydrogen and disulphide bonds. These proteins are insoluble in water (due to hydrophobic part) and are highly resistant to digestive enzymes. They form protective covering of body. e.g. Keratin, collagen.

(ii) **Globular proteins** These are spherical, having highly coiled chains and are soluble in water. e.g. Myoglobin, albumin, enzymes, antibodies.

Concept ladder
- If a protein on hydrolysis give a non-protein portion (prosthetic group) it is called **conjugated protein,** e.g. nucleoproteins (nucleic acid + protein), phosphoproteins (phosphate group + protein).
- If a smaller protein is formed by partial hydrolysis of larger protein, it is called **derived protein,** e.g. protease, peptones etc.

Structure of Proteins

As we have discussed above, protein is a long peptide chain of amino acids. This long chain further acquire different configurations that results into a complex structure. On the basis of different configuration or conformations, there are mainly four types of structure of protein. These are as follows

1. Primary Structure

The most basic aspect of protein structure is the primary structure a specific sequence in which the α-amino acids are joined together by peptide bonds having one or more polypeptide chains. Primary structure is represented by using the three-letter abbreviations for the α-amino acids.

e.g. If a peptide is formed by three amino acids say glycine, alanine and proline, then it can be represented as gly-ala-pro. Here, each hyphen represent a peptide bond. Primary structure gives an idea about the linkage of amino acid. All the amino acids are arranged in single, linear, polypeptide chain. Primary structure of insulin has two peptide chains held together by two (—S—S—) linkage.

2. Secondary Structure

In a primary structure few bonds are free to rotate while others are not. It can give many conformation. Out of these conformations, the stable one, which is held by many hydrogen bonds, gives rise to the secondary structure of protein.

Thus, the structure that describes, how a peptide chain is arranged or oriented in three-dimensional space, is called **secondary structure of protein.**

Secondary structure can exist in following two forms

(i) **α-helix** It is the spiral chain of peptide. In this structure, a protein chain is coiled about a central axis. It is held in place by hydrogen bonding that occurs by twisting into a right handed screw (helix) between the hydrogens of —NH groups and oxygens of C═O groups that are oriented towards each other on the inside of the helix. e.g. α-keratin, myosine, actin.

(ii) **β-pleated sheet** It resembles the pleated folds of drapery in which two protein chains are lined up parallel to each other running in opposite directions, i.e. the N-terminal of one chain is near the C-terminal of the other. This puts the —NH group of one chain opposite to the C═O group of the other chain, permitting intermolecular hydrogen bonding that holds the sheet together.

e.g. Fibroin, silk fibre, dragline of silk (spider wave).

3. Tertiary Structure

The overall shape of a protein molecule is defined by the tertiary structure. It gives us idea that how the protein chains, whether pleated or helical are folded. The tertiary structure determines whether a protein is elongated (and thus, fibrous) or folded (thus, globular).

The tertiary structure of a protein brings into close proximity of α-amino acids that are very far apart in the primary structure, thereby creating chemical sites. The tertiary structure is held together through a number of chemical interactions as discussed below.

(i) **Hydrogen bond** Present between oxygen atom of —COOH group of one amino acid and hydrogen atom of —NH_2 group of another amino acid, e.g. all types of protein.

(ii) **Electrostatic bond** Present between —COO^- group of one amino acid and —NH_3^+ of another amino acid, e.g. aspartic acid, glutamic acid.

(iii) **Disulphide bond** Formed between the —SH group of sulphur containing amino acid. e.g. Cysteine and methionine.

(iv) **Hydrophobic bond** No true bond formed between hydrophobic alkyl chains of amino acids. e.g. All types of protein.

4. Quaternary Structure

Certain proteins, usually globular proteins organise into aggregates, or assemblies with spatial orientation. These aggregates are described as the quaternary structure of the protein. It is composed of two or more protein.

The binding forces of these peptides are hydrogen bond or electrostatic bond or hydrophobic bond (other than covalent bonds).

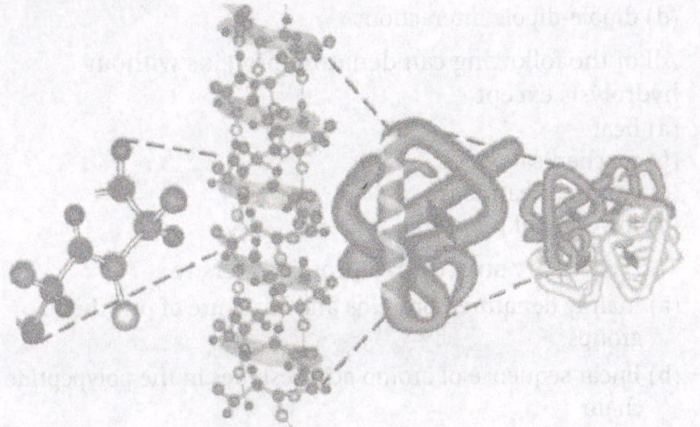

(a) Primary structure (b) Secondary structure (c) Tertiary structure (d) Quaternary structure

Schematic representation of different structure of protein.

Denaturation of Proteins

When a protein in its native form is subjected to physical change like change in temperature or chemical change like change in pH, the hydrogen bonds are disturbed.

The loss in biological activity of proteins due to unfolding of globules and uncoiling of helix is called **denaturation of proteins**. During the denaturation, primary structure remains intact but secondary and tertiary structures are destroyed.

e.g. The coagulation of egg white on boiling, curdling of milk caused by bacteria due to formation of lactic acid etc.

Concept ladder

Proteins can be easily characterised by colour reactions. Their presence can be detected by the following tests.

(i) **Ninhydrin test** Protein when treated with a pyridine solution of ninhydrin, it result in formation of intense purple coloured complex.

(ii) **Biuret test** When an alkaline solution of proteins is treated with a drop of aqueous copper sulphate, it gives reddish-violet colour indicating the presence of peptide linkage.

(iii) **Nitroprusside test** When sodium nitroprusside is added to proteins containing —SH group, a violet colour is observed.

(iv) **Millon's test** Protein with Millon's reagent gives white precipitate that on heating gives red precipitate.

STEP UP Practice 2

1 Members of which class of biomolecules are the building blocks of proteins?

(a) Glycerols (b) Monosaccharides
(c) Fatty acids (d) Amino acids

2 Two functional groups that are present in all amino acids are the .... group and the .... group.

(a) hydroxyl amide (b) carboxyl, amine
(c) carboxyl, phosphate ester (d) acetal, amine

3 Consider the following statements.

Statement I The carbon atom next to the carboxyl group is known as α-carbon in an amino acid.

Statement II The biologically significant amino acids are principally, α-amino acids.

In the light of the above statements, choose the correct answer from the options given below.

(a) Both Statement I and Statement II are false.
(b) Statement I is true, but Statement II is false.
(c) Statement I is false, but Statement II is true.
(d) Both Statement I and Statement II are true.

4 In the tetrapeptide Ala-Cys-Val-Leu, the N-terminal amino acid is

(a) Ala (b) Cys
(c) Val (d) Leu

5 Which of the following is correctly match?

(a) Histidine — Non-essential basic amino acid
(b) Asparagine — Essential basic amino acid
(c) Methionine — Essential basic amino acid
(d) Arginine — Essential basic amino acid

6 Which of the following amino acid is correctly matched with their classification?

(a) Proline — a primary amino acid
(b) Serine — an achiral amino acid
(c) Leucine — a secondary amino acid
(d) Phenylalanine — a neutral and non-polar amino acid

7 Consider the following statements.

Statement I Glycine can be obtained through diet.

Statement II It is an essential amino acid.

In the light of the above statements, choose the correct answer from the options given below.
(a) Both Statement I and Statement II are false.
(b) Statement I is true, but Statement II is false.
(c) Statement I is false, but Statement II is true.
(d) Both Statement I and Statement II are true.

8 The peptide bond joining amino acids into proteins is a specific example of the
(a) amide bond (b) carbonyl bond
(c) ester bond (d) glycosidic bond

9 Which of the following linkages, joins two amino acids?
(a) Ionic linkages
(b) Glycosidic linkages
(c) Amide linkages
(d) Hydrogen

10 The bond present in helical structure of protein is the
(a) dipeptide bonds
(b) hydrogen bonds
(c) ether bonds
(d) peptide bonds

11 The type of bond that is most important in maintaining secondary structure of a protein is
(a) disulphide bridges
(b) hydrogen bonding within the backbone
(c) hydrogen bonding between *R* groups
(d) salt-bridges

12 The amino acid sequence of a protein is known as its
(a) primary structure
(b) secondary structure
(c) tertiary structure
(d) quaternary structure

13 Select the correct match.
(a) Glycoproteins — Simple protein
(b) Myosin — Globular protein
(c) Albumin — Derived protein
(d) Collagen — Fibrous protein

14 All of the following are examples of fibrous proteins except
(a) wool (b) fingernails
(c) skin (d) insulin

15 Each polypeptide in a protein has amino acids linked with each other in a specific sequence. This sequence of amino acids is said to be ....
(a) primary structure of proteins
(b) secondary structure of proteins
(c) tertiary structure of proteins
(d) quaternary structure of proteins

16 Proteins are found to have two different types of secondary structure *viz* α-helix and β-pleated sheet structure. α-helix structure of protein is stabilised by
(a) peptide bonds
(b) van der Waals' forces
(c) hydrogen bonds
(d) dipole-dipole interactions

17 All of the following can denature proteins without hydrolysis except
(a) heat
(b) mechanical stress
(c) enzyme treatment
(d) lowering of pH

18 The secondary structure of protein refers to
(a) mainly denatured proteins and structure of prosthetic groups
(b) linear sequence of amino acid residues in the polypeptide chain
(c) regular folding patterns of continuous portions of the polypeptide chain
(d) three-dimensional structure, specially the bond between amino acid residues that are far apart from each other in polypeptide chain

19 Consider the following examples.
(i) Souring of milk.
(ii) Formation of cheese.
(iii) Using a curling iron on your hair.
(iv) Coagulation of egg white on boiling.
(v) Digestion of a non-proteinaceous.
How many of them are the examples of denaturing?
(a) 3 (b) 4
(c) 2 (d) 1

Module 3

Enzymes, Hormones, Vitamins and Nucleic Acids

• Enzymes • Hormones • Vitamins • Nucleic Acids • Structure of Nucleic Acids • DNA Fingerprinting

Enzymes

These are naturally occurring simple or conjugate proteins acting as specific catalysts in cell processes. These are biocatalysts and some enzymes can be non-protein also. The enzyme facilitates a biochemical reaction by providing alternate path with lower activation energy and thus increasing the rate of reaction. During reactions, enzymes get inactivated and thus, periodically their replacement is necessary.

Enzymes are grouped into six classes according to the kind of reaction they catalyse.

- Hydrolases catalyse hydrolysis reactions.
- Isomerases catalyse isomerisations.
- Ligases catalyse the bonding together of two molecules.
- Lyases catalyse the breaking away of a small molecule such as H_2O from a substrate.
- Oxidoreductases catalyse oxidations and reductions.
- Transferases catalyse the transfer of a group from one substrate to another.

Classification of Enzymes

S. No.	Main class	Some subclasses	Types of reaction catalysed
1.	Hydrolases	Lipases	Hydrolysis of an ester group
		Nucleases	Hydrolysis of a phosphate group
		Proteases	Hydrolysis of an amide group
2.	Isomerases	Epimerases	Isomerisation of stereogenic centre
3.	Ligases	Carboxylases	Addition of CO_2
		Synthetases	Formation of new bond
4.	Lyases	Decarboxylases	Loss of CO_2
		Dehydrases	Loss of H_2O
5.	Oxidoreductases	Dehydrogenases	Introduction of double bond by removal of H_2
		Oxidases	Oxidation
		Reductases	Reduction
6.	Transferases	Kinases	Transfer of a phosphate group
		Transaminases	Transfer of an amino group

All known enzymes are globular proteins. In addition to the protein part, most enzymes also have small non-protein parts called **cofactors**.

The protein part in such enzymes is called an **apoenzyme**, and the combination of apoenzyme plus cofactor is called a **holoenzyme.**

$$\text{Holoenzyme} = \text{Cofactor} + \text{Apoenzyme}$$

Only holoenzyme have biological activity, neither cofactor nor apoenzyme catalyses reactions by themselves.

Cofactors can be either inorganic ions, such as Zn^{2+}, or small organic molecules, called **coenzymes.**

The requirement of many enzymes for inorganic cofactors is the main reason for our dietary need of trace minerals. Iron, zinc, copper, manganese, and numerous other metal ions are all essential minerals that act as enzyme cofactors, though the exact biological role is not known in all cases. A variety of organic molecules act as coenzymes.

Concept ladder

Enzymes are highly specific in nature w.r.t its substrate and active site. In the same way only certain keys fit a lock, like that only certain substrate fit an enzymes active site. This specific fit allows the enzyme to stabilise the molecule so This can be chemically altered. If the substrate is not of the correct shape, then it won't fit into the enzyme and no chemical reaction can occur. Such mechanism of enzyme action is called **lock and key mechanism.**

Hormones

The chemical substances secreted into blood by ductless glands (endocrine glands) are called **hormones.** These molecules act as intercellular messengers. They participate in different specific biochemical reactions and hence control specific physiological processes.

Based on their chemical compositions, hormones are divided into two main classes (i) based on their structure –**steroid hormones** and **non-steroid hormones** (ii) based on activity in the cell. Important hormones, their type, source and functions are listed in table.

Classification and Function of Hormones

Type	Sub-type	Examples	Source	Functions
Steroids	Sex hormones	(i) Male sex hormones (Androgens)	Testis	**Testosterone** is responsible for male characteristics (deep voice, facial hair, physical constitution) during puberty. Synthetic testosterone analogs are used in medicine to promote muscle and tissue growth.
		(ii) Female sex hormones (Estrogens and progesterone)	Ovary	(a) **Estradiol** is responsible for secondary female characteristics and participates in control of menstrual cycle. (b) **Progesterone** is responsible for preparing the uterus for implantation of the fertilised egg and also plays important role as **birth-control agents.**
	Corticosteroids (Adrenal cortical hormones)	(i) Mineralocorticoids	Adrenal cortex	These regulate NaCl in the body and cause excretion of potassium in urine; are made by different cells in adrenal cortex.
		(ii) Glucocorticoids	Adrenal cortex	They modify certain metabolic reactions and have anti-inflammatory effect; are made by adrenal cortex.
Non-steroids	Peptide hormones	Insulin	Pancreas	Insulin has much effect on carbohydrate metabolism. This decreases glucose concentration in blood and is thus known as **hyperglycemic** factor. It promotes anabolic processes and inhibits catabolic ones. Its deficiency causes **diabetes mellitus.** Sanger (Nobelist) determined the structure of insulin.
		Oxytocin	Posterior pituitary	Causes contraction of smooth muscle, including contraction of uterus during child birth. It helps in milk ejection from mammary gland.
		Vasopressin	Posterior pituitary	It inhibits excretion of water from the body in form of urine.
		Glycogen	Pancreas	It hydrolyses glycogen and elevates blood sugar level.
	Amino acid derivatives	Thyroidal hormones	Thyroid	Thyroxin and triiodothyronine affect the general metabolism independent of their nature and specific activity. Thyroid gland is known as pace-setter of the endocrine system.
		Epinephrine (adrenaline)	Adrenal medulla	It increases blood pressure and heart beat. It increases alertness in body including secretion of sweat and dilation of pupil.

NEET Snapshot

Out of thyroxin, insulin, adrenaline and estradiol, only adrenaline is produced under the condition of stress which stimulates glycogenolysis in the liver of human beings. ***[NEET 2014]***

Adrenaline hormone is released from the adrenal glands in a stressful situation. It is commonly known as 3F hormone. The 3F's stand for flight fight and fear, adrenaline takes care of emergency functions, during above mentioned situations.

Glycogenolysis is the process of breakdown of glycogen into the glucose. In particular, it is crucial for controlling blood glucose lends and the fight-or-flight response.

Vitamins

These are the organic molecules which function in trace amounts in the body. They are required for the proper functioning of the cell, normal growth and reproduction and their absence causes specific deficiency diseases. Plants can synthesise all vitamins whereas only a few are synthesised in animals.

Vitamins are generally regarded as organic compounds required in the diet in small amounts to perform specific biological functions for normal maintenance of optimum growth and health of the organism. The term "Vitamine" was coined from the word vital + amine since the earlier identified compounds had amino groups. Later work showed that most of them did not contain amino groups so the letter 'e' was dropped and term vitamin is used these days.

Mentor's TIP

Many though not all, coenzymes are **vitamins**, small organic molecules that must be obtained in the diet and are required in trace amounts for proper growth.

Vitamins are designated by the alphabets, e.g. A, B, C, D, E etc., in order of their discovery. Further any subgroup of individual vitamins is designated by the number subscript, e.g. B_1, B_2, B_6, B_{12}, etc.

Physiological Functions

The daily dose of any vitamin for any individual is not a fixed quantity and varies according to the size, age and rate of metabolism of the individual. A lack of one or more vitamins leads to characteristic deficiency symptoms in human (refer to table). Multiple deficiencies caused by lack of more than one vitamin are common and this condition is known as a **vitaminosis**.

Classification of Vitamins

Depending upon their solubility, all the known vitamins can be classified into following two groups.

(i) **Water-soluble vitamins** These include vitamins B and C. These vitamins must be supplied regularly in diet because they are regularly excreted through urine. Fruits and vegetables are a good source of water soluble vitamins. These vitamins are destroyed by prolonged heating (cooking).

(ii) **Fat-soluble vitamins** These include vitamins A, D, E and K. These vitamins are non-polar, hydrophobic (water insoluble), fairly stable and are not destroyed by heat. These are stored in liver and adipose tissues.

Vitamins, their Enzyme Functions, Sources and Deficiency Symptoms

S. No.	Vitamins	Enzyme function	Source	Deficiency symptom
Water-soluble vitamins				
1.	Ascorbic acid (Vitamin C)	Hydroxylases	Citrus fruits, amla, green vegetables	Bleeding gums, bruising (scurvy)
2.	Thiamine (Vitamin B_1)	Reductases	Yeast, milk, green vegetables, cereals	Fatigue, depression, beri-beri (loss of appetite and retarted growth)
3.	Riboflavin (Vitamin B_2)	Reductases	Yeast, milk, vegetables, egg-white, liver, kidney	Cheilosis (cracked lips,) scaly skin, digestive disorders
4.	Pyridoxine (Vitamin B_6)	Aminotransferases	Cereal , grams, molasses, yeast, egg- yolk and meat	Anaemia, irritability, weakness, convulsions
5.	Niacin (Vitamin B_3)	Reductases	Fresh meat, liver, fish, cereals, milk	Dermatitis, dementia
6.	Cyanocobalamine (Vitamin B_{12})	Isomerases	Liver of ox, sheep, pig, fish, egg, curd	Megaloblastic anaemia, neurodegeneration
7.	Pantothenic acid (Vitamin B_5)	Acyltransferases	Yeast, liver, kidneys, tomatoes	Weight loss, irritability
Fat-soluble vitamins				
8.	Retinol (Vitamin A)	Visual system	Fish oil, rice-polishing, liver, kidney butter, milk, carrots	Night blindness, xerophthalmia, dry skin
9.	Calciferol (Vitamin D)	Calcium metabolism	Sunlight, liver, egg, meat, milk	Rickets (bone deformities in children) and osteomalacia (soft bones and joints pain in adults)
10.	Tocopherol (Vitamin E)	Antioxidant	Wheat germ oil, cotton seed oil and soyabean oil	Hemolysis of red blood cells
11.	Phylloquinone (Vitamin K)	Blood clotting	Cereals, leafy-vegetables	Hemorrhage, delayed blood clotting

NEET Close-up

Example Similar to PYQ Asked in NEET 2021

The cheilosis deficiency is a deficiency disease of

(a) vitamin B_6
(b) vitamin B_3
(c) vitamin B_2
(d) vitamin B_1

Sol. (c) The cheilosis deficiency is a deficiency disease of vitamin B_2, in this disease the fissuring at corners of mouth and lips occur.

Skill Builder

The increased fragility of RBCs is deficiency disease of

(a) vitamin E (b) vitamin B_{12}
(c) vitamin B_2 (d) vitamin K

For more practice Refer to Q. 18 of Step up practice 3 and Q. 33 and Q. 73 of Gearing up for NEET.

Nucleic Acids

The nucleus of a living cell is responsible for the transmission of inherent characters also called heredity. The particles in nucleus of the cell, responsible for heredity are called chromosomes which are made up of proteins and another type of biomolecules called nucleic acids.

The nucleic acids are the chemical carriers of a cell's genetic information. The chemical composition of nucleic acids acts as coded information. This information when expressed, determines the nature of the cell, controls cell growth (and division) and directs biosynthesis of proteins (including enzymes) required for cellular functions.

Nucleic acids are of two types

(i) DNA-Deoxyribonucleic acid

(ii) RNA-Ribonucleic acid

Chemical Composition of Nucleic Acids

Nucleic acids are biopolymers made up of **nucleotides** joined together to form a long chain. Hence, these are also called **polynucleotides**. Each nucleotide is composed of an aldopentose sugar linked to a heterocyclic nitrogenous base and further to a phosphate group. Combined form of sugar and base is called **nucleoside** and that of nucleoside and phosphate group is called **nucleotide**.

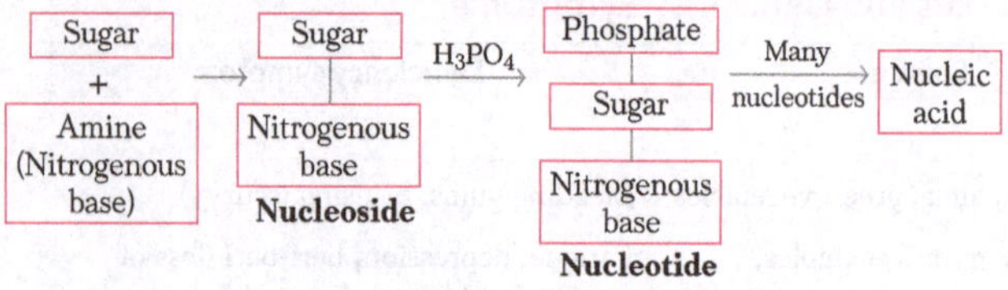

Thus, on complete hydrolysis of nucleic acid, three compounds (pentose sugar, phosphoric acid and nitrogenous base) are formed as discussed below.

(i) **Pentose sugar** The sugar component in RNA is ribose, and the sugar in DNA is 2′-deoxyribose.

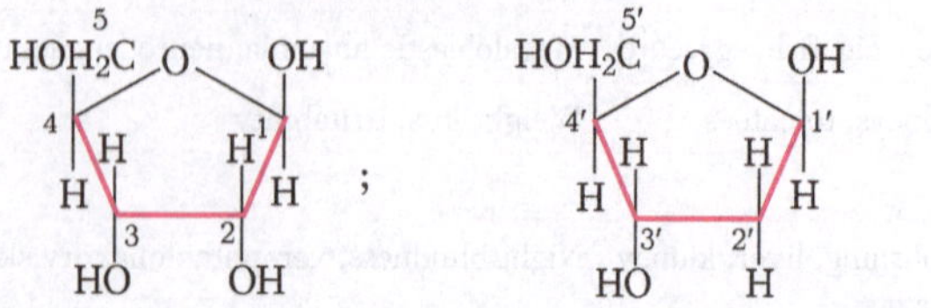

β-D-ribose used in RNA ; β-D-2′-deoxyribose used in DNA

The prefix 2′-deoxy means that oxygen is missing from the 2′ position of ribose.

(ii) **Phosphoric acid** It is present as a phosphate (PO_4^{3-}) group in the nucleotide. It plays an important role of linking two nucleotides. The linkage is called **phosphodiester linkage** (discussed later).

(iii) **Nitrogenous bases** These are the heterocyclic compounds of nitrogen. These are further divided into two groups.

(a) **Purines** These are bicyclic groups containing N-atoms in each of the cycles.

Examples are adenine (A) and guanine (G)

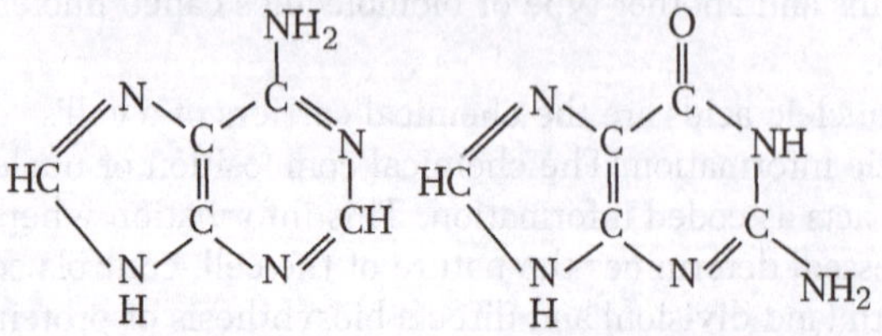

Adenine (A) Guanine (G)

(b) **Pyrimidines** These are single cyclic bases. The examples are cytosine (C), thymine (T) and uracil (U).

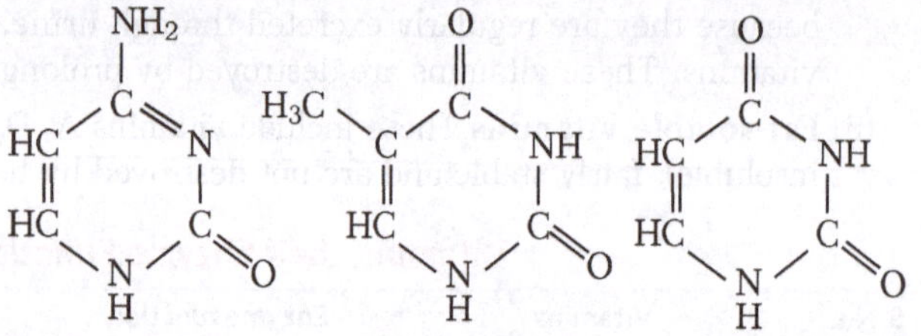

Cytosine (C) Thymine (T) Uracil (U)

- Three bases, A, G and C are common to both DNA and RNA. While the base 'T' is exclusive to DNA and the base 'U' is exclusive to RNA.
- So, there are four bases in each DNA and RNA. i.e. DNA contains bases A, G, C, T while RNA like A, G, C, U.
- Thus, DNA differ from RNA in sugar as well as nitrogenous base.

NEET Snapshot

The central dogma of molecular genetics states that the genetic information flows from DNA to RNA to proteins. ***[NEET 2016]***

The genetic information is copied from one strand of the DNA into *m*RNA and this process is called **transcription**.

Transcription is followed by translation. Translation is the process by which the proetin is synthesised from the information contained in the *m*RNA.

Structure of Nucleic Acids

In both DNA and RNA, the heterocyclic amine base is bonded to C-1′ of the sugar called nucleoside and the phosphoric acid is bonded by a phosphate ester linkage to C-5′ sugar position called nucleotide.

Thus, nucleosides and nucleotides have the general structure as shown below.

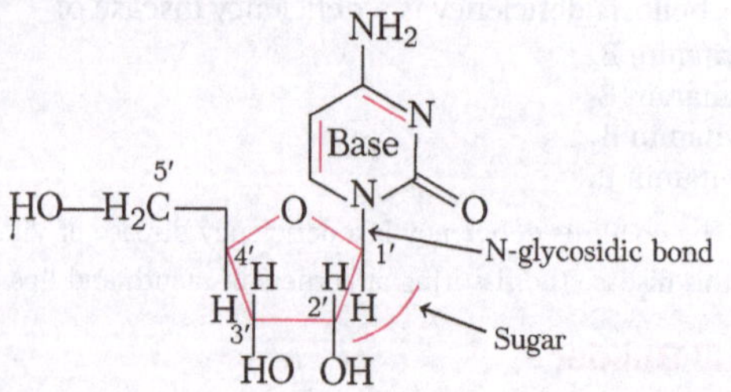

Nucleoside

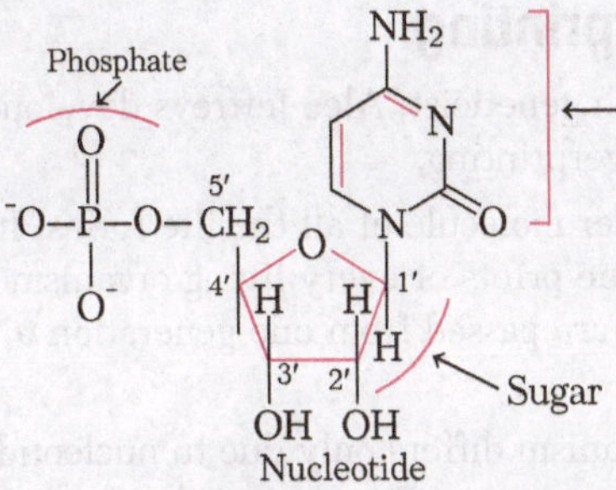

Nucleotide

Structure of nucleic acid

NEET Close-up

Example Similar to PYQ Asked in NEET 2023

Direction *(Q. Similar and Skill Builder)* In the light of the statements given below, choose the most appropriate answer from the options given below

(a) Both Statement I and Statement II are false.

(b) Statement I is true, but Statement II is false.

(c) Statement I is false, but Statement II is true.

(d) Both Statement I and Statement II are true.

Statement I A nucleoside consist of a nitrogenous base and a five carbon sugar.

Statement II Nucleosides can be thought of as a nucleotide without a phosphate group.

Sol. (*d*) Both Statement I and Statement II are true.

Skill Builder

Statement I In nucleoside the anomeric carbon is linked through a glycosidic bond to the N9 of a purine or the N1 of a pyrimidine.

Statement II Nucleotides are the molecular building blocks of the DNA and RNA.

For more practice Refer to Q. 29 of Step up practice 3 and Q. 40 of Gearing up for NEET.

The structure of nucleic acid can be divided into two categories (with special reference to DNA).

(i) **Primary structure** It gives information about the sequence of nucleotides in the chain of nucleic acid.

This structure is formed by the linkage of one nucleotide with other through the **phosphodiester linkage** between 5′ and 3′ carbon atoms of the pentose sugar.

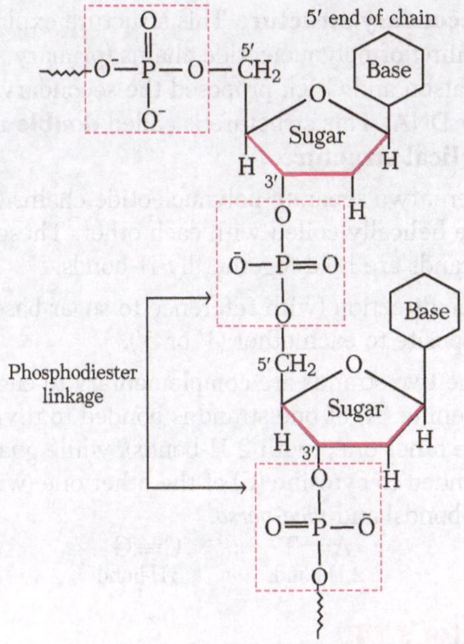

Primary structure of DNA

Information regarding the sequence of nucleotides in the chain of a nucleic acids called its **primary structure.** Phosphodiester linkage, connects a sugar base with other one. The phosphate group in this linkage is attached to C-5′ position of one sugar and the C-3′ position of the other one. One end of the nucleic acid polymer has a free hydroxyl group at C-3′ (the 3′ end) and the other end has a phosphate at C-5′ (the 5′ end).

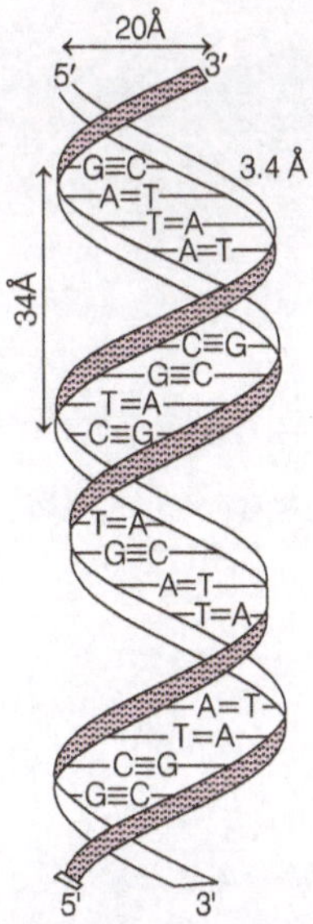

Double helix structure of DNA

(ii) **Secondary structure** This structure explains the coiling of polynucleotide chains (primary structure). Watson and Crick proposed the secondary structure for DNA. This structure is called **double stranded helical structure.**

Here, two separate polynucleotide chains (or strands) are helically coiled with each other. These two strands are held together by H-bonds.

The direction (with reference to sugar base) is opposite to each other (3′ or 5′).

The two strands are complementary to each other as adenine (A) of one strand is bonded to thymine (T) of the other one, (with 2 H-bonds), while guanine (G) is bonded to cytosine (C) of the other one (with 3 H-bonds) and *vice-versa.*

$$\underset{\text{2 H-bonds}}{A{=}T} \quad ; \quad \underset{\text{3 H-bond}}{C{\equiv}G}$$

Mentor's Tip

- RNA molecules are of three types and they perform different functions. They are named as messenger RNA (*m*-RNA), ribosomal RNA (*r*-RNA) and transfer RNA (*t*-RNA).
- *m*-RNA molecules carry the coding sequences for protein synthesis.
- *r*-RNA molecules form the core of a cells ribosome, the structure in which protein synthesis takes place.
- *t*-RNA molecules carry amino acids to the ribosomes during protein synthesis.

DNA Fingerprinting

In 1984, a British geneticist, Alec Jeffreys developed the technique of fingerprinting.

DNA is the master molecule of all the life forms. It constitute the blue prints of every living organism through which character are passed from one generation to other generation.

Every living organism differs only due to nucleotide sequences of chromosome. The nucleotides form codes; this coded genetic information can be profiled to produce most authentic identity card of any organism. This identification at genetic level is called DNA fingerprinting or DNA profiling.

Uses

- In forensic laboratories for identification of criminals.
- To determine paternity of an individual.
- To identify the dead bodies in any accident by comparing the DNA's of parents or children.
- To identify racial groups and to rewrite biological evolution.

Note **Har Gobind Khorana** shared the Nobel Prize for Medicine and Physiology in 1968 with **Marshall Nirenberg** and **Robert Holley** for cracking the genetic code.

STEP UP Practice 3

1 Enzymes are members of which class of biomolecules?
(a) Carbohydrates
(b) Lipids
(c) Nucleic acids
(d) Proteins

2 When substrate molecules occupy all of the active sites in the enzyme available for a particular reaction, the enzyme is said to be
(a) denatured (b) hydrolysed
(c) activated (d) saturated

3 A competitive inhibitor of an enzyme acts by
(a) modifying one of the amino acid residues of the enzyme
(b) modifying structure of the substrate
(c) competing with the substrate to bind to the active site of the enzyme
(d) increasing temperature of the reaction mixture

4 Consider the following statements.

Statement I The non-protein part of an enzyme is called a co-factor.

Statement II These co-factors are basically the additional chemical groups, which appear in those enzymes that are conjugated protein molecules.

In the light of the above statements, choose the correct answer from the options given below.
(a) Both Statement I and Statement II are false.
(b) Statement I is true, but Statement II is false.
(c) Statement I is false, but Statement II is true.
(d) Both Statement I and Statement II are true.

5 The enzyme which hydrolyses triglycerides to fatty acids and glycerol is called
(a) maltase
(b) lipase
(c) zymase
(d) pepsin

6 Consider the following statements.

Statement I Enzymes are highly specific in their action, both with respect to the substrate they act upon and the kind of reaction they catalyse.

Statement II The "lock and key" hypothesis cannot explain the specificity of enzyme-substrate interaction.

In the light of the above statements, choose the correct answer from the options given below.
(a) Both Statement I and Statement II are false.
(b) Statement I is true, but Statement II is false.
(c) Statement I is false, but Statement II is true.
(d) Both Statement I and Statement II are true.

7 Which of the following is a function of enzymes?
(a) Structure and support
(b) Nutritional reserves
(c) Biochemical catalysts
(d) Communication between cells

8 Poisons such as heavy metal ions or insecticides cannot disrupt enzyme function by
(a) competitive inhibition
(b) irreversible inhibition
(c) disruption of tertiary structure
(d) covalent modification

9 Hormones are produced in the .... system.
(a) digestive (b) endocrine
(c) excretory (d) nervous

10 Hormones regulate biochemical reactions by
(a) performing the same role as enzymes in certain reactions
(b) acting rapidly on receptor sites close to the point where the hormone was produced
(c) acting to produce indirect effects on reactions occurring at some distance from the site of hormone production
(d) interacting with substrate to prevent their participation in specific reactions

11 Which one is correctly match?
(a) Epinephrine hormone — Polypeptide
(b) Growth hormone — Polypeptide
(c) Thyroxine hormone — Polypeptide
(d) Estrogen hormone — Polypeptide

12 Which type of hormone actually enters the target cell?
(a) Amino acid derivatives (b) Enzymes
(c) Peptides (d) Steroids

13 Which statement regarding polypeptide hormones is incorrect?
(a) This class of hormones includes all the regulatory hormone produced by the pituitary gland.
(b) Vasopressin is an example.
(c) Insulin is an example.
(d) Sex hormones are included in this category.

14 Consider the following hormones.
(i) Estrogens (ii) Insulin
(iii) Norepinephrine (iv) Androgens
(v) Endrophins

How many of them are steroids in nature?
(a) 2 (b) 1 (c) 3 (d) 4

15 Consider the following statements.

Statement I Vitamin C is easily oxidised in air, especially in presence of Cu^{2+} or Fe^{2+} ions.

Statement II Both the forms of vitamin C are biologically active, due to the conversion of dehydroascorbic acid to ascorbic acid and are found in body fluids.

In the light of the above statements, choose the correct answer from the options given below.
(a) Both Statement I and Statement II are false.
(b) Statement I is true, but Statement II is false.
(c) Statement I is false, but Statement II is true.
(d) Both Statement I and Statement II are true.

16 Which of the following B group vitamins can be stored in our body?
(a) Vitamin B_1
(b) Vitamin B_2
(c) Vitamin B_6
(d) Vitamin B_{12}

17 The vitamin most closely associated with carbohydrate metabolism is
(a) vitamin B_1 (b) vitamin B_2
(c) vitamin D_2 (d) vitamin B_{12}

18 Which of the following vitamin is incorrectly match with the given diseases?
(a) Vitamin B_6 — Convulsions
(b) Vitamin D — Osteomalacia
(c) Vitamin A — Xerophthalmia
(d) Vitamin B_{12} — Beri-Beri

19 Consider the following vitamins.
(i) A (ii) K (iii) D
(iv) C (v) B
How many of them is/are fat soluble vitamins?
(a) 3 (b) 2
(c) 1 (d) 4

20 A vitamin is
(a) a nutrient involving trace metals that is necessary for good health
(b) a polypeptide used to manufacture enzymes
(c) a lipid complex which is an important part of all cells
(d) a small organic molecule obtained from the diet and necessary for good health

21 Select the correct match.
(a) Anti-haemorrhagic factor — Vitamin K
(b) Anti-haemorrhagic factor — Vitamin D_2
(c) Anti-haemorrhagic factor — Vitamin A_2
(d) Anti-haemorrhagic factor — Vitamin B_{12}

22 What is the repeating unit of nucleic acids?
(a) Monosaccharides (b) Amino acids
(c) Nucleotides (d) Nucleosides

23 Nucleic acids are the polymers of
(a) nucleosides (b) nucleotides
(c) bases (d) sugars

24 The backbone of a nucleic acid molecule consists of
(a) alternating sugar and phosphate groups linked by phosphate ester bonds
(b) alternating sugar and nitrogen base groups linked by amide bonds
(c) alternating nitrogen bases and phosphate groups linked by amide bonds and strengthened by hydrogen bonds
(d) sugar molecules bonded from the C-3 of one molecule to the C-5 of the other by glycosidic linkages

25 Which of the following DNA sequence is correctly match with its complementary strand?
(a) T-C-G-A — T-G-C-A (b) T-C-G-A — C-T-A-C
(c) T-C-G-A — A-G-C-T (d) T-C-G-A — G-A-T-C

26 A sequence of how many nucleotides in messenger RNA makes a codon for an amino acid?
(a) Three (b) Four (c) One (d) Two

27 The central dogma of molecular genetics states that
(a) every copy of DNA is an exact replica of the parent molecule
(b) DNA stores genetic information of RNA reads, decodes, and uses that information
(c) in DNA and RNA adenine always pairs with thymine and cytosine always pairs with guanine
(d) each amino acid is coded by a unique set of three base pairs

28 Which of the following bases is not correctly match according to their presence?
(a) Adenine — DNA (b) Guanine — RNA
(c) Uracil — RNA (d) Thymine — RNA

29 Given below are two statements.
Statement I Nucleotides are joined together by glycosidic linkage between 5′ and 3′ carbon atoms of the pentose sugar.
Statement II Information regarding the sequence of nucleotides in the chain of a nucleic acid is called its primary structure.
In the light of the above statements, choose the correct answer from the options given below.
(a) Both Statement I and Statement II are false.
(b) Statement I is true, but Statement II is false.
(c) Statement I is false, but Statement II is true.
(d) Both Statement I and Statement II are true.

NEET Exclusive EXTRA BYTES

- All monosaccharides and disaccharides are sweet in taste. Therefore, they are commonly known as sugars. The degree of sweetness is determined with respect to sucrose. Degree of sweetness of some monosaccharides and disaccharides is given below.

Sugar	Relative sweetness
Glucose	74
Fructose	173
Sucrose	100
Maltose	32
Lactose	16

- Two diastereomers that differ in configuration at only one asymmetric carbon are called epimers. Thus, D-glucose and D-mannose are C-2 epimers, D-glucose and D-galactose are C-4 epimers.
- The reduction of glucose with $NaBH_4$ forms D-sorbitol while that of fructose forms a mixture of D-sorbitol and D-mannitol.
- The isoelectric point of an amino acid that has an ionisable side chain is the average of the pK_a value of the similarly ionising groups.
- Chargaff's rule states that in DNA of any cell, the amount of guanine should be equal to the amount of cytosine and the amount of adenine should be equal to the amount of thymine.
  So, the total amount of purine (i.e. A and G) is equal to the amount of pyridine (C and T).
  $$A + G = C + T$$
- **Denaturation** is generally irreversible, but many examples are known where it has been reversed. This reversal of denaturation is called **renaturation** or **refolding**.
- Although proteins are composed of 12 different amino acids, protein synthesis requires only 20 because proline is converted to hydroxy proline and cystrine is converted to cystine after synthesis of polypeptide chain has taken place.

GEARING UP FOR NEET

1 Apart from aldehydic group, glucose consists of hydroxyl group. The number of primary and secondary hydroxyl groups respectively are
(a) 1 and 4 (b) 2 and 3 (c) 3 and 2 (d) 4 and 1

2 Which of the following compounds is formed when glucose react with Br_2 water at pH 5-6?
(a) Glucaric acid (b) Saccharic acid
(c) Gluconic acid (d) Acetic acid

3 Which of the following is the correct structure of sucrose?
(a) 1-α-D-glucosyl-4-fructose (b) 1-β-D-gucosyl-2-fructose
(c) 1-α-D-glucosyl-2-fructose (d) 1-α-D-fructosyl-4-glucose

4 A hemiacetal linkage consists of a
(a) carbon atom bonded to both —OH and —*OR* groups
(b) carbonyl group that is also bonded to a hydroxyl group
(c) carbonyl group that is also bonded to an ether linkage
(d) carbon atom bonded to two —OH groups`

5 Which of the following pairs represent anomers?

(a)
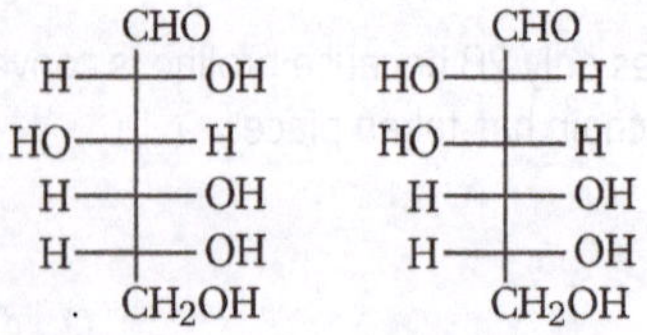

(b)
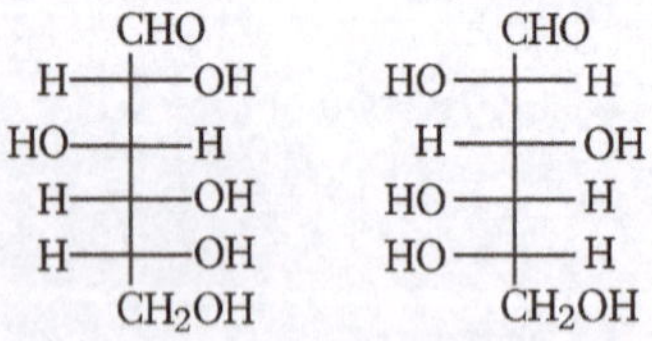

(c)
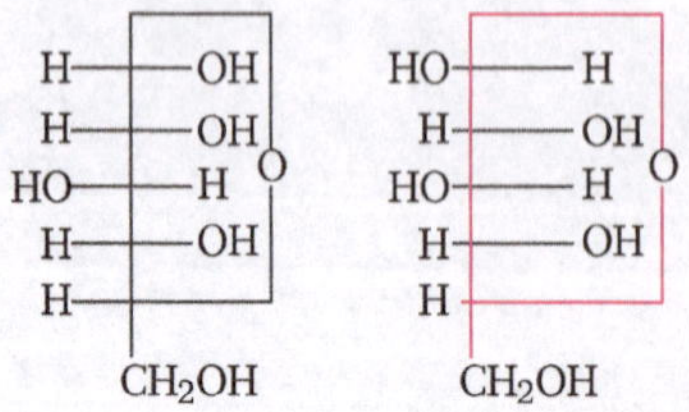

(d)
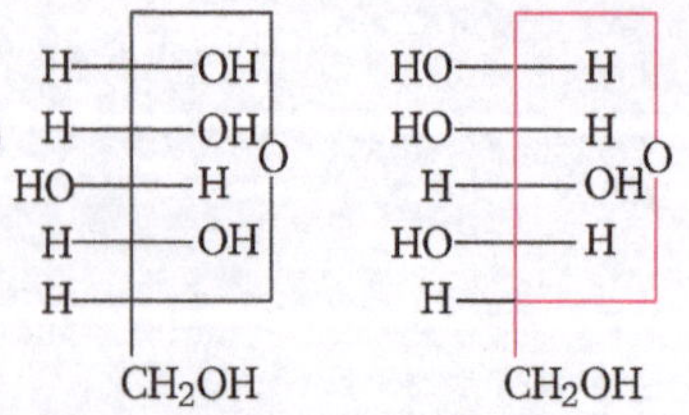

6 Sucrose is not a reducing sugar becuase its
(a) hemiacetal groups cannot be converted to aldehyde groups
(b) disaccharide bond is an α-1,4-linkage
(c) disaccharide bond is a β-1,4-linkage
(d) disaccharide bond is a 1,2-anomeric linkage

7 Sucrose on hydrolysis gives
(a) laevorotatory glucose, dextrorotatory fructose
(b) dextrorotatory glucose, dextrorotatory glucose
(c) laevorotatory fructose, laevorotatory fructose
(d) dextrorotatory glucose, laevorotatory fructose

8 Three structures are given below in which two glucose units are linked. Which of these linkages between glucose units are between C-1 and C-4 and which linkages are between C-1 and C-6?

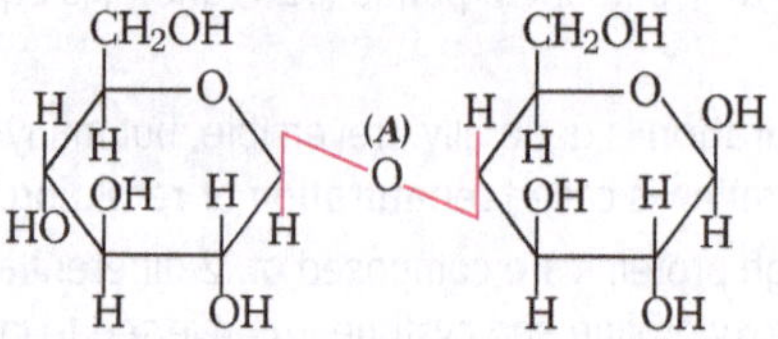

(I)

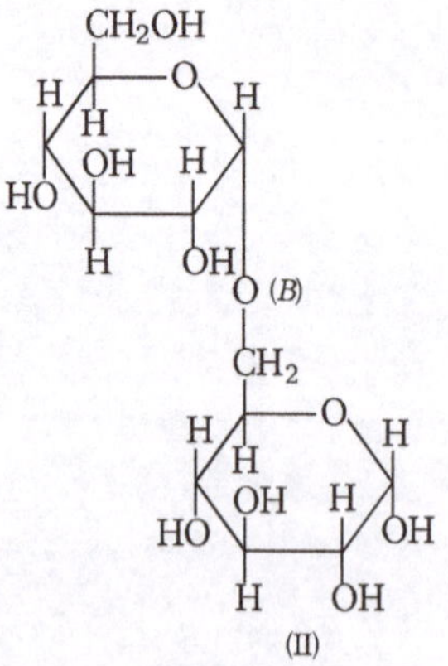

(II)

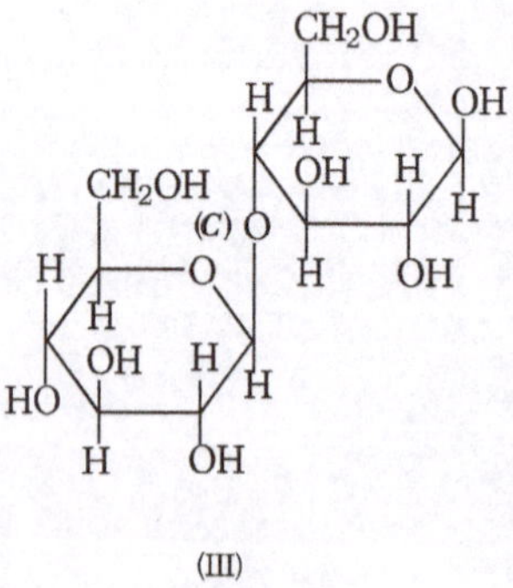

(III)

(a) (*A*) is between C-1 and C-4, (*B*) are between C-1 and C-6
(b) (*A*) and (*B*) are between C-1 and C-4, (*C*) is between C-1 and C-6
(c) (*A*) and (*C*) are between C-1 and C-4, (*B*) is between C-1 and C-6
(d) (*A*) and (*C*) are between C-1 and C-6, (*B*)is between C-1 and C-4

9 Which of the following reactions of glucose can be explained only by its cyclic structure?
(a) Glucose forms pentaacetate.
(b) Glucose reacts with hydroxylamine to form an oxime.
(c) Pentaacetate of glucose does not react with hydroxyl amine.
(d) Glucose is oxidised by nitric acid to gluconic acid.

10 In disaccharides, if the reducing groups of monosaccharides, i.e. aldehydic or ketonic groups are bonded, these are non-reducing sugars. Which of the following disaccharide is a non-reducing sugar?

(a)
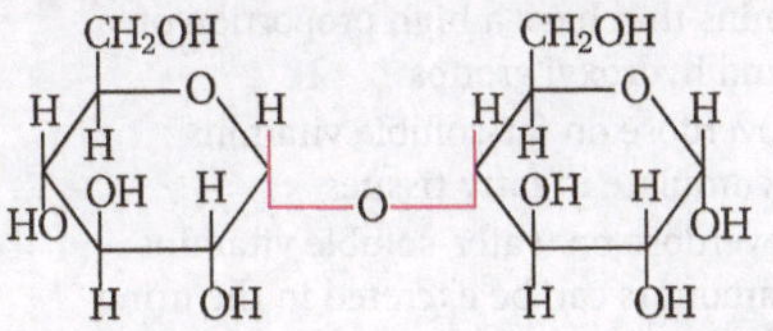

(b)
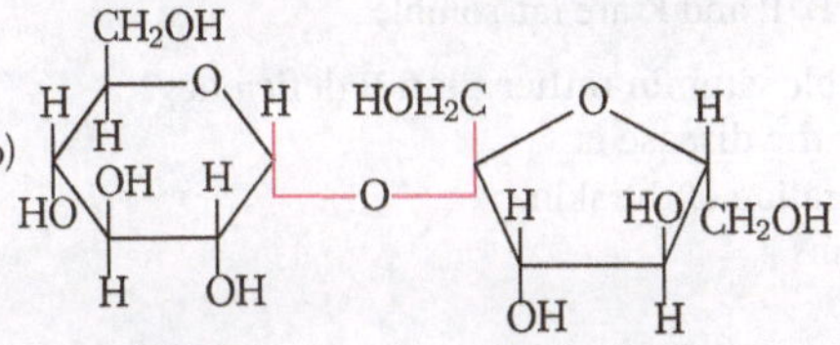

(c)
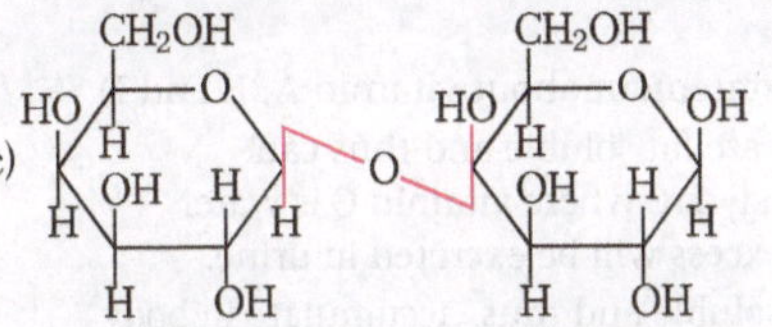

(d)
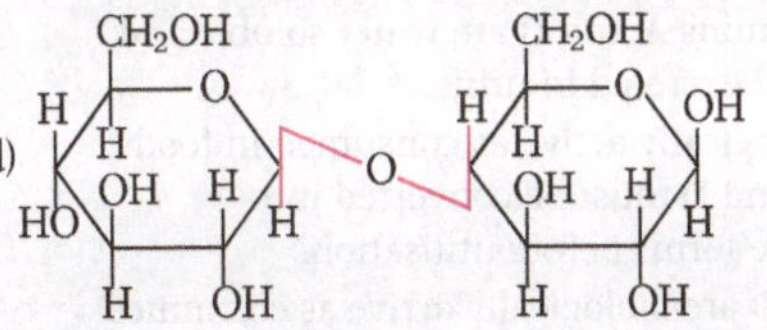

11 Which of the following statements are incorrect about glucose?
A. It is an aldohexose.
B. On heating with HI it forms *n*-hexane.
C. It is present in furanose form.
D. It does not give 2,4-DNP test.
E. The β-form of glucose is obtained from concentrated solution of glucose at 303 K.

Choose the correct answer from the options given below.
(a) B, C and D (b) B and C (c) A and D (d) C and E

12 Choose the correct match.
(a) Serum albumin — Globular protein
(b) Serum albumin — Structural protein
(c) Serum albumin — Transport protein
(d) Serum albumin — Storage protein

13 Which statement is incorrect about peptide bond

$$-\overset{\overset{\displaystyle O}{\|}}{C}-\ddot{N}H-\ ?$$

(a) C—N bond length in proteins is longer than usual bond length of C—H bond.
(b) Spectroscopic analysis show planar structure of $-\overset{\overset{\displaystyle O}{\|}}{C}-NH-$ group.
(c) C—N bond length in proteins is smaller than usual bond length of C—N bond.
(d) In this linkage, an amide formed between —COOH group and $-NH_2$ group.

14 How many different tripeptides can be formed from one molecule each of the amino acids tyrosine, valine and alanine?
(a) 3 (b) 6 (c) 9 (d) 12

15 The isoelectric point of an amino acid is
(a) the pH at which it exists in basic form
(b) the pH at which it exists in acid form
(c) the pH at which it exists in Zwitter ion form
(d) the pH equal to its pK_a

16 The non-protein portion required by some enzymes for proper functioning is called a(an)
(a) zymogen (b) substrate (c) inhibitor (d) cofactor

17 Enzymes have an optimum temperature for their catalytic activity. This is best explained by the balance between the ... number of collisions and the ... rate of denaturation of the enzyme as temperature increase.
(a) increased; increased (b) decreased; increased
(c) increased; decreased (d) decreased; decreased

18 Enzymes functions as catalysts by
(a) changing the value of the free energy change to a more favourable value
(b) changing the value of the equilibrium constant to a more favourable value
(c) lowering the value of the activation energy
(d) increasing the amount of time needed to reach equilibrium

19 The part of an enzyme that is formed of protein is called
(a) apoenzyme (b) holoenzyme
(c) cofactor (d) coenzyme

20 All of the following characteristics correctly describes can enzyme except
(a) dissolve in water (b) have a globular shape
(c) behave as substrates (d) contain an active site

21 Which of the following statements about enzymes are correct?
A. Enzymes lack in nucleophilic groups.
B. Pepsin is proteolytic enzyme.
C. Enzymes catalyse chemical reactions by lowering the activation energy.
D. Enzymes are highly specific both in binding chiral substrates and in catalysing their reactions.
E. Enzymes are needed in large quantity for the progress of a reaction.

Choose the correct answer from the options given below.
(a) A, B and E only (b) A and B only
(c) C and E only (d) B, C and D only

22 Which of the following hormones is incorrectly match with their classification?
(a) Endorphins — Polypeptides
(b) Epinephrine — Polypeptides
(c) Estradiol — Female sex hormone
(d) Insulin — Polypeptides

23 The hormone which controls the processes like burning of fats, proteins and carbohydrates to liberate energy in the body is
(a) cortisone (b) thyroxine (c) adrenalin (d) insulin

24 Androgens are a specific type of steroid whose function is to
(a) maintain pregnancy
(b) promote development of secondary male sex characteristics
(c) promote development of secondary female sex characteristics
(d) regulate the sodium/potassium balance in cellular fluids

25 One example of an amino acid derivative that act as both a hormone and a neurotransmitter is
(a) epinephrine (b) thyroxine
(c) growth hormone (GH) (d) estrogen

26 All of the following types of molecules can be classified as lipids except
(a) triacylglycerols (b) steroids
(c) glycoproteins (d) eicosanoids

27 Steroids are
(a) simple esters of long chain alcohols and fatty acids
(b) esters of glycerol with three predominantly saturated fatty acids
(c) esters of glycerol with three predominantly unsaturated fatty acids
(d) based on a tetracyclic ring system with substituents at various positions

28 The diseases identified as diabetes are primarily associated with a malfunction of the hormone
(a) glucagon (b) insulin
(c) epinephrine (d) cortisone

29 Which of the following statements about hormones is not correct?
(a) Hormones can affect biochemical reactions by inhibiting enzymes.
(b) Hormones are transported in the bloodstream.
(c) Hormones can affect biochemical reactions by activating enzymes.
(d) Hormones are very specific, affecting only chemical reaction.

30 Which of the following description is correct for hormones?
A. Produced by the nervous system.
B. Transported in the blood stream.
C. Interact with any cell having the appropriate receptor.
D. Act within 1 second or less after release.
E. Effects may last several hours or days.

Choose the correct answer from the options given below
(a) A, C and D only
(b) B and C only
(c) B, C and E only
(d) A, D and E only

31 Utilisation of calcium and phosphorus in the formation of bones is dependent on
(a) pyridoxal phosphate (b) carboxybiotin
(c) pantothenic acid (d) vitamin D

32 All of the following statements concerning vitamins are true except
(a) fat-soluble vitamins that have a high proportion of polar carbonyl and hydroxyl groups
(b) it is possible to overdose on fat-soluble vitamins because they accumulate in fatty tissues
(c) it is difficult to overdose on water-soluble vitamins because excess amounts can be excreted in the urine
(d) vitamins A, D, E and K are fat-soluble

33 The water soluble vitamin rather than B deficiency responsible for the disease is
(a) burning sensation of the skin
(b) bleeding gums
(c) convulsions
(d) loss of appetite

34 Choose the correct statement about vitamin A, B and D.
(a) Vitamin A and D are fat soluble and thus can accumulate in body fat, where vitamin C is water soluble and the excess will be excreted in urine.
(b) Vitamin C is fat soluble and thus, accumulate in body fat, whereas vitamins A and D are water soluble and the excess will be excreted in urine.
(c) Vitamin C is biologically active as consumed in foods, but vitamins A and D must be converted into biologically active forms before utilisation.
(d) Vitamins A and D are biologically active as consumed in food, but vitamin C must be converted into biologically active forms before utilisation.

35 The sequence in the structure of nucleic acid is
(a) base + phosphate + pentose
(b) phosphate group + pentose + base
(c) pentose + base + phosphate group
(d) phosphate group + base + pentose

36 In replication of DNA, each new double strand consists of one template strand and one new strand. Therefore, replication is said to be
(a) repetitive
(b) semiconservative
(c) polymeric
(d) catabolic

37 When a new strand of RNA is transcribed from the DNA strand shown, its base sequence will be

Informational strand of DNA : TTACGGAT

Template strand of DNA : AATGCCTA

(a) TTACGGAT (b) AATGCCTA
(c) UUACGGAU (d) AAUGCCUA

38 Which of the following is a major function of nucleic acids?
(a) Storage and transfer of genetic information
(b) Storage and intracellular transfer of energy
(c) Catalysis of virtually all biochemical reactions
(d) Structural support in both plants and animals

39 In DNA, the complementary bases are
(a) adenine and thymine, guanine and cytosine
(b) uracil and adenine, cytosine and guanine
(c) adenine and guanine, thymine and cytosine
(d) adenine and thymine, guanine and uracil

40 Dinucleotide is obtained by joining two nucleotides together by phosphodiester linkage. Between which carbon atoms of pentose sugars of nucleotides are these linkages present?
(a) 5′ and 3′ (b) 1′ and 5′ (c) 5′ and 5′ (d) 3′ and 3′

41 The chemical combination of ribose and one of the five nitrogen bases results in formation of a
(a) nucleotide (b) nucleoside
(c) DNA molecule (d) chromosome

Assertion-Reason

Directions (Q. Nos. 42 to 46) Given below are two statements, one is labelled as Assertion (A) and the other is labelled as Reason (R).
(a) Both A and R are true and R is the correct explanation of A.
(b) Both A and R are true but R is not the correct explanation of A.
(c) A is true but R is false.
(d) A is false but R is true.

42 **Assertion** (A) Glucose give Schiff's test and it forms hydrogen sulphite addition product with $NaHSO_3$.
Reason (R) Glucose have an aldehydic group.

43 **Assertion** (A) Glucose gets oxidised to saccharic acid on reaction with a oxidising agent like bromine water.
Reason (R) In glucose the carbonyl group is present as an aldehydic group.

44 **Assertion** (A) The amino acid 'Asp' is a basic amino acid.
Reason (R) In basic amino acid, the number of amino group is more than the carboxyl group.

45 **Assertion** (A) Nucleotides are phosphate esters of nucleosides.
Reason (R) The various nucleotides in nucleic acids are linked to a heterocyclic nitrogenous base and further to the phosphate group.

46 **Assertion** (A) During denaturation secondary and tertiary structures are destroyed but primary structure remains intact.
Reason (R) Secondary and tertiary structures are held together by strong dipeptide linkage.

Statement Type Questions

Directons (Q. Nos. 47 to 53) In the light of the statements given below choose the correct answer from the options given.
(a) Both Statement I and Statement II are false.
(b) Statement I is true, but Statement II is false.
(c) Statement I is false, but Statement II is true.
(d) Both Statement I and Statement II are true.

47 **Statement I** D-(+)-glucose is dextrorotatory in nature.
Statement II 'D' represent its dextrorotatory nature.

48 **Statement I** β-glycosidic linkage is present in maltose.
Statement II Maltose is composed of two glucose units in which C-1 of one glucose unit is linked to C-4 of another glucose unit.

49 **Statement I** Covalent linkage that maintains a higher order protein structure is the disulphide bond.
Statement II These interactions are weak and easily disrupted by thermal motion.

50 **Statement I** The pH at which amino acids (also proteins) carry no net charge is called its isoelectric point.
Statement II The isoelectric point of glycine is 6.

51 **Statement I** In presence of enzyme, substrate molecule can be attacked by the reagent effectively.
Statement II Inactive sites of enzymes hold the substrate molecule in a suitable position.

52 **Statement I** Epinephrine and norepinephrine mediate responses to external stimuli.
Statement II Thyroxine produced in the thyroid gland is an iodinated derivative of amino acid tryptophan.

53 **Statement I** In secondary structure of RNA, single stranded helics is present which sometimes foldsback on itself.
Statement II RNA molecules are of two types, i.e. *m*-RNA and *t*-RNA.

54 Which of the following statements are incorrect?
A. Glucose can be obtained by hydrolysis of cellulose by boiling it with dilute H_2SO_4 at 393 K under pressure.
B. Pyran is a cyclic organic compound with two oxygen atom and six carbon atom in the ring.
C. When our body needs sucrose, enzymes break the glycogen down to sucrose.
D. Carbohydrates are found in biosystem in combination with many proteins and lipids.
E. D-ribose and 2-deoxy-D-ribose are present in nucleic acids.

Choose the correct answer from the options given below.
(a) A and E only (b) C and E only
(c) B and D only (d) B and C only

55 Select the correct statements from the following.

A. The amino acid, tyrosine was first obtained from cheese.

B. When carboxyl group of glycine combines with the amino group of alanine then formed glycylalanine.

C. When the polypeptide chains run parallel and are held together by hydrogen and disulphide bonds, then spherical like structure is formed.

D. The main forces which stabilise the 2° and 3° structures of proteins are hydrogen bonds and electrostatic forces of attraction.

E. The primary structure of proteins arise due to the regular folding of the backbone of the polypeptide chain.

Choose the correct answer from the options given below.

(a) A, B and D only (b) A, D and E only
(c) C, B and E only (d) B and C only

56 Select the correct statements from the following.

A. Enzyme urease which catalyses the hydrolysis of urea was shown to be non-protein in nature.

B. The combination of an apoenzyme and a cofactor is known as the holoenzyme.

C. Vitamins A, D, E and K are stored in liver but not in adipose tissues.

D. The rates at which different enzymes catalyse their reactions are the same.

E. The particles in nucleus of the cell, responsible for heredity are called chromosomes.

Choose the correct answer from the options given below.

(a) A, B and E (b) A and D
(c) B, C and D (d) A, C and E

57 Which of the following is correct statement?

A. Starch is polymer of α-glucose.

B. Lactose is commonly known as invert sugar.

C. Proteins are composed of only one type of amino acid.

D. The enzymes which catalyse the oxidation of one substrate with simultaneous reduction of another substrate are named as oxidoreductase enzyme.

E. Osteomalacia deficiency is deficiency disease of vitamin D.

Choose the correct answer from the options given below.

(a) B, C and D only (b) B and E only
(c) A and E only (d) A, D and E only

58 Which of the following statement is incorrect?

A. The process of manufacturing an identical copy of a DNA molecule is called replication.

B. Testosterone is responsible for preparing the uterus for implantation of fertilised egg.

C. The process in which information contained in RNA is used to manufactures proteins is called transcription.

D. The process in which information from DNA is used to manufacture RNA is called translation.

E. Hormones released by gonads are responsible for development of secondary sex characters.

Choose the correct answer from the options given below.

(a) B, C and D (b) B and E
(c) A and E (d) B and D only

Species Selection Type Questions

59 Consider the following saccharides.

(i) Galactose (ii) Lyxose (iii) Ribose
(iv) Deoxyribose (v) Xylose (vi) Arabinose
(vii) Sucrose

How many of them are pentose sugar?

(a) 4 (b) 5 (c) 6 (d) 3

60 Consider the following 3-letter symbol of amino acids.

(i) Gln (ii) Glu (iii) Tyr
(iv) Arg (v) Cys

How many of them are neutral amino acid in nature?

(a) 3 (b) 4 (c) 2 (d) 1

61 Consider the following amino acids.

(i) Alanine (ii) Threonine (iii) Histidine
(iv) Cysteine (v) Leucine (vi) Tyrosine
(vii) Aspartic acid

How many of them are non-essential amino acids?

(a) 4 (b) 3 (c) 5 (d) 6

62 Consider the following 3-letter symbol of amino acids.

(i) Ala (ii) Lcu (iii) Ser (iv) Pro
(v) Met (vi) Thr (vii) Cys

How many of them are primary amine?

(a) 5 (b) 4 (c) 3 (d) 6

63 Consider the following enzymes.

(i) Lipase (ii) LDH
(iii) Alcohol dehydrogenase (iv) Amylase
(v) Proteases

How many of them are hydrolases in nature?

(a) 3 (b) 1 (c) 2 (d) 4

64 Consider the following enzymes.

(i) Maltose (ii) Diastase (iii) Amylose
(iv) Fructose (v) Lipase

How many enzymes are used to convert starch into maltose?

(a) 4 (b) 1 (c) 2 (d) 3

65 Consider the following hormones.

(i) Epinephrine (ii) Thyroxine (iii) Dopamine
(iv) Norepinephrine (v) Testosterone (vi) Oxytocin
(vii) Adrenaline

How many of them are the amino acids derivative?

(a) 5 (b) 2
(c) 3 (d) 4

66 Consider the following base.

(i) Adenine (ii) Uracil (iii) Thymine
(iv) Cytosine (v) Guanine

How many of them is/are a bicyclic nitrogenous base?

(a) 4 (b) 3 (c) 1 (d) 2

67 Consider the following vitamins.

(i) Thiamine (ii) Cobalamine (iii) Riboflavin
(iv) Pantothenic acid (v) Ascorbic acid (vi) Pyridoxine
(vii) Aspartic acid

How many of them are vitamin 'B'?

(a) 6 (b) 4 (c) 2 (d) 5

Matching Type Questions

68 Match the following columns.

	Column I		Column II
A.	D-sorbitol	1.	Anomeric carbon
B.	L-ascorbic acid	2.	A disaccharide
C.	Glycoside	3.	A sugar lactone
D.	C-1 of glucose	4.	Sugar alcohol

Codes

	A	B	C	D		A	B	C	D
(a)	4	3	2	1	(b)	3	1	4	2
(c)	2	4	1	3	(d)	3	4	2	1

69 Match the following columns.

	Column I		Column II
A.	Globular protein	1.	Protein with the tertiary structure in which it normally occurs in living systems.
B.	Zwitter ion	2.	Protein that is usually water soluble having a hydrophilic exterior and hydrophobic interior and an overall rounded shape.
C.	Fibrous protein	3.	A protein that is water insoluble, very tough and has a long shape.
D.	Native protein	4.	Overall a neutral molecule but migrates to cathode or anode depending on pH.

Codes

	A	B	C	D		A	B	C	D
(a)	2	4	3	1	(b)	3	4	1	2
(c)	4	1	2	3	(d)	1	3	4	2

70 Match the following columns.

	Column I		Column II
A.	Hydrophilic	1.	A carbon atom bonded to four different groups and therefore able to form enantiomers.
B.	Chiral carbon	2.	A biomolecule that produces amino acids and other biomolecules or inorganic substances upon hydrolysis.
C.	Hydrophobic	3.	Refers to *R* groups that do not interact readily with water due to their non-polar nature.
D.	Conjugated protein	4.	Refers to *R* groups which form H-bonds with water because of their polarity.

Codes

	A	B	C	D		A	B	C	D
(a)	1	4	2	3	(b)	2	3	4	1
(c)	3	4	1	2	(d)	4	1	3	2

71 Match the following enzymes given in Column I with the reactions they catalyse given in Column II.

	Column I (Enzymes)		Column II (Reactions)
A.	Invertase	1.	Decomposition of urea into NH_3 and CO_2
B.	Maltase	2.	Hydrolysis of maltose into glucose
C.	Pepsin	3.	Hydrolysis of cane sugar
D.	Urease	4.	Hydrolysis of proteins into peptides

Codes

	A	B	C	D		A	B	C	D
(a)	4	1	3	2	(b)	3	2	4	1
(c)	3	4	2	1	(d)	2	4	1	3

72 Match the following columns.

	Column I		Column II
A.	Thymine	1.	Pyrimidine base
B.	Thiamine	2.	Enzyme
C.	Insulin	3.	Hormone
D.	Pepsin	4.	Vitamin B_1

Codes

	A	B	C	D		A	B	C	D
(a)	1	4	3	2	(b)	2	3	1	4
(c)	2	3	4	1	(d)	3	1	2	4

73 Match the vitamins given in Column I deficiency disease they cause given in Column II.

	Column I (Vitamins)		Column II (Disease)
A.	Vitamin A	1.	Pernicious anaemia
B.	Vitamin B_{12}	2.	Increased blood clotting time
C.	Vitamin D	3.	Xerophthalmia
D.	Vitamin K	4.	Osteomalacia

Codes

	A	B	C	D
(a)	4	3	1	2
(b)	3	1	4	2
(c)	2	4	3	1
(d)	4	2	1	3

Final Check Through PYQs

Module-I Carbohydrates

1 The reagents with which glucose does not react to give the corresponding tests/products are *[NEET 2024]*

A. Tollen's reagent

B. Schiff's reagent

C. HCN

D. NH_2OH

E. $NaHSO_3$

Choose the correct options from the given below.

(a) B and C

(b) A and D

(c) B and E

(d) E and D

2 Sucrose on hydrolysis gives *[NCERT (New) Pg. 287, NEET 2020]*

(a) β-D-glucose + α-D-fructose

(b) α-D-glucose + β-D-glucose

(c) α-D-glucose + β-D-fructose

(d) α-D-fructose + β-D-fructose

3 The reaction of concentrated sulphuric acid with carbohydrates ($C_{12}H_{22}O_{11}$) is an example of *[NCERT (New) Pg. 283, NEET 2020]*

(a) dehydration

(b) oxidation

(c) reduction

(d) sulphonation

4 Which of the following statements is not true about glucose? *[NCERT (New) Pg. 283, NEET 2020]*

(a) It is an aldohexose.

(b) It contains five hydroxyl groups.

(c) It is a reducing sugar.

(d) It is an aldopentose.

5 Which one given below is a non-reducing sugar? *[NCERT (New) Pg. 287, NEET 2016, Phase I]*

(a) Lactose (b) Glucose

(c) Sucrose (d) Maltose

6 The correct corresponding order of names of four aldoses with configuration given below.

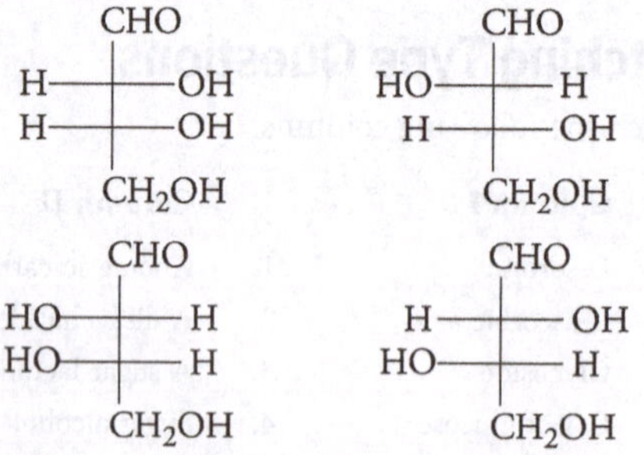

respectively, is *[NEET 2016, Phase II]*

(a) L-erythrose, L-threose, L-erythrose, D-threose

(b) D-threose, D-erythrose, L-threose, L-erythrose

(c) L-erythrose, L-threose, D-erythrose, D-threose

(d) D-erythrose, D-threose, L-erythrose, L-threose

7 D-(+)-glucose reacts with hydroxyl amine and yields an oxime. The structure of the oxime would be *[NCERT (New) Pg. 283, AIPMT 2014]*

(a) 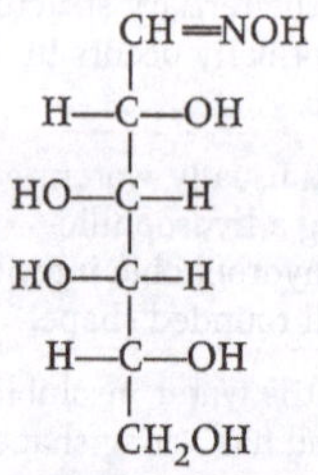

(b) 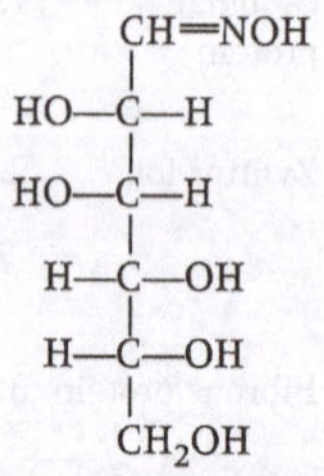

(c) 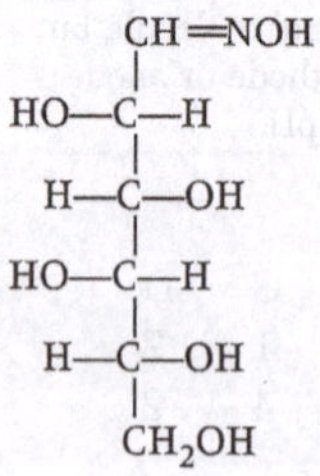

(d) 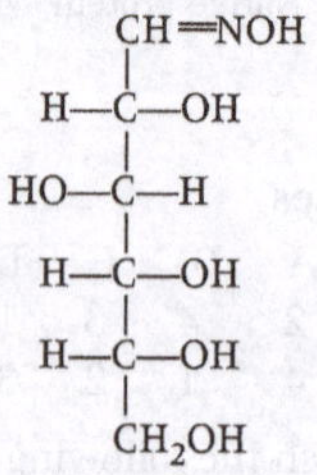

Module-II Proteins

8 Which of the following is a basic amino acid? *[NCERT (New) Pg. 290, 291, NEET (Sep.) 2020]*
(a) Alanine (b) Tyrosine
(c) Lysine (d) Serine

9 Which structure(s) of proteins remain(s) intact during denaturation process? *[NCERT (New) Pg. 293, Odisha, NEET 2019]*
(a) Both secondary and tertiary structure
(b) Primary structure only
(c) Secondary structure only
(d) Tertiary structure only

10 The non-essential amino acid among the following is *[NCERT (New) Pg. 292, NEET (National) 2019]*
(a) leucine (b) alanine (c) lysine (d) valine

11 Which of the following compounds can form a Zwitter ion? *[NCERT (New) Pg. 292, NEET 2018]*
(a) Benzoic acid (b) Acetanilide
(c) Aniline (d) Glycine

12 In a protein molecule various amino acids are linked together by *[NCERT (New) Pg. 292, NEET 2016, Phase I]*
(a) β-glycosidic bond (b) peptide bond
(c) dative bond (d) α-glycosidic bond

Module-III Enzyme, Hormones, Vitamins and Nucleic Acids

13 Given below are two statements.
Statement I A unit formed by the attachment of a base to 1′-position of sugar is known as nucleoside.
Statement II When nucleoside is linked to phosphorus acid at 5′-position of sugar moiety, we get nucleotide.
In the light of the above statements, choose the correct answer from the options given below *[NEET 2023]*
(a) Both Statement I and Statement II are false.
(b) Statement I is true, but Statement II is false.
(c) Statement I is false, but Statement II is true.
(d) Both Statement I and Statement II are true.

14 The incorrect statement regarding enzymes is *[NEET 2022]*
(a) like chemical catalysts enzymes reduce the activation energy of bio processes.
(b) enzymes are polysaccharides.
(c) enzymes are very specific for a particular reaction and substrate.
(d) enzymes are biocatalysts.

15 The RBC deficiency is deficiency disease of *[NCERT (New) Pg. 296, NEET 2021]*
(a) vitamin B_2
(b) vitamin B_{12}
(c) vitamin B_6
(d) vitamin B_1

16 Deficiency of which vitamin causes osteomalacia? *[NCERT (New) Pg. 296, NEET (Oct.) 2020]*
(a) Vitamin A (b) Vitamin D
(c) Vitamin K (d) Vitamin E

17 The correct statement regarding RNA and DNA, respectively is *[NCERT (New) Pg. 299, NEET 2016, Phase I]*
(a) The sugar component in RNA is ribose and the sugar component in DNA is 2′-deoxyribose.
(b) The sugar component in RNA is arabinose and the sugar component in DNA is ribose.
(c) The sugar component in RNA is 2′-deoxyribose and the sugar component in DNA is arabinose.
(d) The sugar component in RNA is arabinose and the sugar component in DNA is 2′-deoxyribose.

18 The central dogma of molecular genetics states that the genetic information flows from *[NCERT (New) Pg. 300, NEET 2016, Phase II]*
(a) amino acids → proteins → DNA
(b) DNA → carbohydrates → proteins
(c) DNA → RNA → proteins
(d) DNA → RNA → carbohydrates

19 Which of the following hormones is produced under the condition of stress which stimulates glycogenolysis in the liver of human beings? *[NCERT (New) Pg. 300, AIPMT 2014]*
(a) Thyroxin (b) Insulin
(c) Adrenaline (d) Estradiol

Answers

Step up Practice 1

1 (d)	2 (a)	3 (a)	4 (c)	5 (d)	6 (d)	7 (d)	8 (b)	9 (c)	10 (c)
11 (d)	12 (d)	13 (d)	14 (c)	15 (b)	16 (a)	17 (a)	18 (a)	19 (d)	20 (d)
21 (a)									

Step up Practice 2

1 (d)	2 (b)	3 (d)	4 (a)	5 (d)	6 (d)	7 (a)	8 (a)	9 (c)	10 (b)
11 (b)	12 (a)	13 (d)	14 (d)	15 (a)	16 (c)	17 (c)	18 (c)	19 (b)	

Step up Practice 3

1 (d)	2 (d)	3 (c)	4 (d)	5 (b)	6 (d)	7 (c)	8 (d)	9 (b)	10 (c)
11 (b)	12 (d)	13 (d)	14 (a)	15 (d)	16 (d)	17 (a)	18 (d)	19 (a)	20 (d)
21 (a)	22 (c)	23 (b)	24 (a)	25 (c)	26 (a)	27 (b)	28 (d)	29 (c)	

Gearing up for NEET

1 (a)	2 (c)	3 (c)	4 (b)	5 (c)	6 (d)	7 (d)	8 (c)	9 (c)	10 (d)
11 (d)	12 (c)	13 (a)	14 (d)	15 (c)	16 (d)	17 (a)	18 (c)	19 (a)	20 (c)
21 (d)	22 (b)	23 (d)	24 (b)	25 (a)	26 (c)	27 (d)	28 (b)	29 (d)	30 (c)
31 (d)	32 (a)	33 (b)	34 (a)	35 (b)	36 (b)	37 (c)	38 (a)	39 (a)	40 (a)
41 (b)	42 (d)	43 (d)	44 (d)	45 (a)	46 (c)	47 (b)	48 (c)	49 (d)	50 (d)
51 (b)	52 (b)	53 (b)	54 (d)	55 (a)	56 (a)	57 (d)	58 (d)	59 (b)	60 (a)
61 (a)	62 (d)	63 (a)	64 (c)	65 (d)	66 (d)	67 (d)	68 (a)	69 (a)	70 (d)
71 (b)	72 (a)	73 (b)							

Final Check through PYQs : Module-I

1 (c)	2 (c)	3 (a)	4 (d)	5 (c)	6 (d)	7 (d)

Final Check through PYQs : Module-II

8 (c)	9 (b)	10 (b)	11 (d)	12 (b)

Final Check through PYQs : Module-III

13 (b)	14 (b)	15 (b)	16 (b)	17 (a)	18 (c)	19 (c)

Hints and Solutions

Step up Practice 1

1 (*d*) Maltose is a disaccharides instead of monosaccharides.

2 (*a*) The bond connecting the two monosaccharides, i.e. (α-D-glucose and α-D-glucose) in maltose is an α-1,4-glycosidic linkage.

3 (*a*) Both Statement I and Statement II are false.

Their corrected form are :

Deoxyribose $C_5H_{10}O_4$ is a carbohydrate because it follows $C_5(H_2O)_2$ formula and exist as polyhydroxy carbonyl compound whose cyclic structure is as shown below.

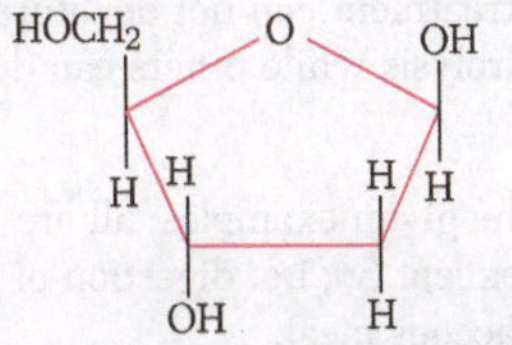

β-2-deoxyribose

Most of the carbohydrates have general formula $C_x(H_2O)_y$. But all the compounds which fit into this formula may not be classified as carbohydrates.

4 (*c*)

5 (*d*) A sugar is classified as a D-isomer if the hydroxyl group on the chiral carbon farthest from the carbonyl points to the right.

6 (*d*) The common reducing reactions of monosaccharides are due to the presence of a carbonyl group, usually on the C-1 carbon atom.

7 (*d*) Among the given match, only (d) is correctly matched according to the classification while other are incorrect. Their corrected match are

- α-D-glucose + α-D-glucose $\Rightarrow$ Maltose – Reducing sugar
- α-D-glucose + β-D-fructose $\Rightarrow$ Sucrose – Non-reducing sugar
- It is β-D-galactose instead of β-D-fructose then, β-D-galactose + β-D-glucose $\Rightarrow$ Lactose – Reducing sugar

8 (*b*) Among the given saccharides, only two, i.e. (ii) and (v) are not disaccharides while other, i.e. (i), (iii) and (iv) are disaccharides.

- Glycogen – Polysaccharides
- Fructose – Monosaccharides

9 (*c*) Carbon adjacent to oxygen atom in the cyclic structure of glucose or fructose is known as anomeric carbon. In the given structure, '*a*' and '*b*' are present at adjacent to oxygen atom. Both carbons differ in configuration of the hydroxyl group.

10 (*c*) Among the given match, (c) is not correctly matched with their characteristic.

Its corrected match is :

Carbohydrates – store the glycogen in animals.

11 (*d*) Among the given match, only (d) is correctly matched while other are incorrect.

Their corrected match are

- Glycogen – Polysaccharides
- Allose – Monosaccharides
- Cellulose – Polysaccharides

12 (*d*) Both Statement I and Statement II are true.

13 (*d*) Among the given match, product (d) is correctly matched with the given reaction.

Its corrected match is :

$$\text{Glucose} \xrightarrow{Br_2/\text{Water}} \text{(Gluconic acid), i.e.} \begin{bmatrix} COOH \\ | \\ (CHOH)_4 \\ | \\ CH_2OH \end{bmatrix}$$

14 (*c*) Among the given statements, all are correct except statement (c) about monosaccharides.

Its corrected form is :

The two different cyclic forms of a particular monosaccharide are called anomers.

15 (*b*) The molecular formula is similar in case of both glucose and fructose, i.e. $C_6H_{12}O_6$.

16 (*a*) Among the given saccharides, only two (ii) and (iv) are hexose sugar while other are pentose sugar.

17 (*a*) Cyclic structures of monosaccharides which differ in structure at C-1 are known as anomers.

Here, I and II are anomer because they differ from each other at C-1 only.

18 (*a*) D and L configuration are relative configuration decided by relating structure of given saccharide with D or L-glyceraldehyde.

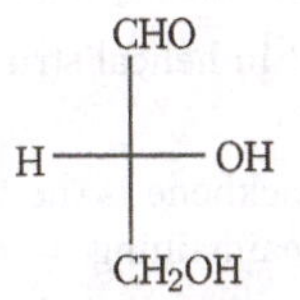

(+) Rotation

(I)

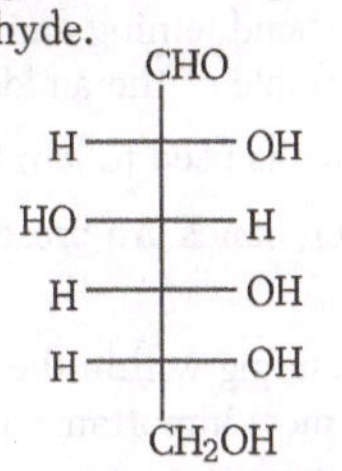

(+) Rotation

(II)

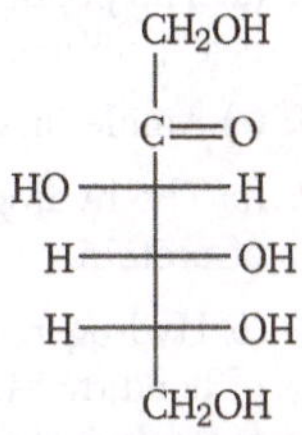

(–) Rotation

(III)

When —OH at lowest asymmetric carbon is written at right hand side, it is represented as D-configuration and when —OH is written on left hand side, it is represented as L-configuration.

19 (*d*) 20 (*d*)

21 (*a*) The structure of sucrose is

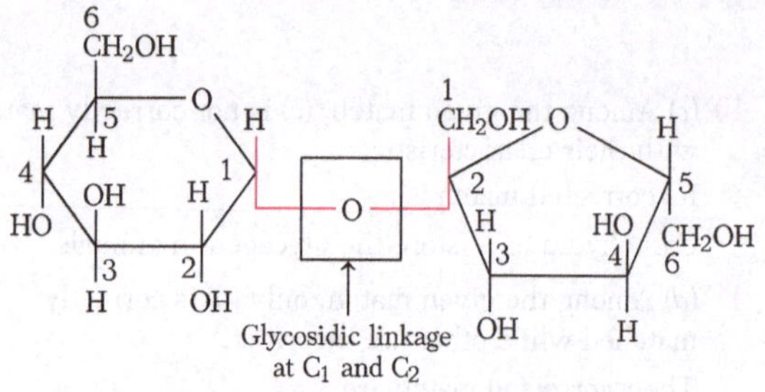

(Sucrose)

Step up Practice 2

1. (*d*) Members of amino acids are the building blocks of proteins.
2. (*b*) Two functional groups that are present in all amino acids are the carboxyl group and the amine group.
3. (*d*) Both Statement I and Statement II are true.
4. (*a*) In the given tetrapeptide, the N-terminal amino acid is Ala and C-terminal amino acid is Leu.
5. (*d*) Among the given match, (d) is correct while other are incorrect.
   Their corrected form are
   - Histidine – Essential basic amino acid
   - Asparagine – Non-essential acidic amino acid
   - Methionine – Essential neutral amino acid
6. (*d*) Among the given amino acids, (d) is correctly match according to their classification while other are incorrect. Their corrected match are
   - Proline – a secondary amino acid
   - Serine – a chiral amino acid
   - Leucine – a primary amino acid
7. (*a*) Both Statement I and Statement II are false. Their correct form are
   Glycine must not be taken through diet because it can be synthesised in our body and a non-essential amino acid.
8. (*a*) The peptide bond joining amino acids into proteins is a specific example of the amide bond.
9. (*c*) Amide linkage is used to join two amino acids.
10. (*b*) The hydrogen bonds are present in helical structure of protein.
11. (*b*) Hydrogen bonding within the backbone is the type of bond that is most important in maintaining secondary structure of a protein.
12. (*a*) The amino acid sequence of a protein is known as its primary structure.
13. (*d*) Collagen is an example of a fibrous protein.
14. (*d*) Among the given examples, insulin is not an example of fibrous protein, although it is a globular protein.
15. (*a*) In primary structure of proteins, each polypeptide in a protein has amino acids linked with each other in a specific sequence. This type of structure is known as primary structure of proteins.
16. (*c*) Secondary structure of protein denotes the shape in which a long polypeptide chain exists. The secondary structure exist in two type of structure, i.e. α-helix and β-pleated structure.
    In α-helix structure, a polypeptide chain forms all possible hydrogen bonds by twisting into a right handed screw with —NH group of each amino acid residue hydrogen bonded to $>C=O$ of adjacent amino acid, which form a helix.
17. (*c*) Enzyme treatment can not denature proteins without hydrolysis while others can do.
18. (*c*)
19. (*b*) Among the given examples, all are the examples of denaturing except (v), i.e. digestion of a non-proteinaceous meal.

Step up Practice 3

1. (*d*)
2. (*d*) When substrate molecules occupy all of the active sites in the enzyme, which is available for a particular reaction, then the enzyme is called saturated enzyme.
3. (*c*)
4. (*d*) Both Statement I and Statement II are true.
5. (*b*) The enzyme which hydrolyses triglycerides to fatty acids and glycerol is called lipase.
6. (*d*) Both Statement I and Statement II are true.
7. (*c*)
8. (*d*) Poisons such as heavy metal ions or insecticides can disrupt enzyme function by covalent modification.
9. (*b*) Hormones are produced in the endocrine system.
10. (*c*)
11. (*b*) Among the given match, (b) is correctly match.
12. (*d*) Steroids hormone actually enters the target cell.
13. (*d*) Among the given statements, statement (d) is incorrect regarding polypeptide hormones.
14. (*a*) Among the given hormones, only two, i.e. (i) and (iv) are steroids in nature.
15. (*d*) Both Statement I and Statement II are true.
16. (*d*) Vitamin B_{12} can be stored in our body and belongs to B group vitamins, because it is not water soluble.

17. (*a*) Vitamin B_1 is most closely associated with carbohydrate metabolism.

18. (*d*) Among the given match, (d) is incorrect while other are correctly match with the given diseases.

Its correct matched is :

Vitamin B_{12} – Pernicious anaemia

19. (*a*) Among the given vitamins, only three, i.e. (i), (ii) and (iii) are fat soluble vitamins.

20. (*d*) A vitamin is a small organic molecule obtained from the diet and necessary for good heatlh.

21. (*a*) Anti-haemorrhagic factor is vitamin K.

22. (*c*) Nucleotides is the repeating unit in nucleic acids.

23. (*b*) Nucleic acids are polymer of nucleotides in which nucleic acids are linked together by phosphodiester linkage.

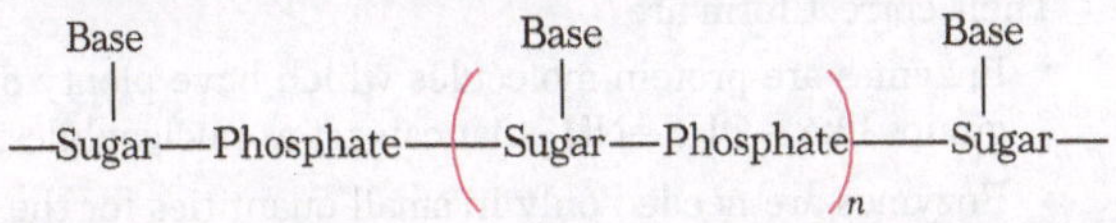

24. (*a*)

25. (*c*) Among the given match, (c) is correctly match to its complementary strand.

As, T-C-G-A ⟶ A-G-C-T

26. (*a*) A sequence of three nucleotides in messenger RNA makes a codon for an amino acid.

27. (*b*)

28. (*d*) Among the given bases, (d) is not correctly match according to their presence.

Its corrected match is :

Thymine – DNA

29. (*c*) Statement I is false but Statement II is true. The correct of Statement I is :

Nucleotides are joined together by phosphodiester linkage between 5′ and 3′ carbon atoms of the pentose sugar.

Gearing up for NEET

1. (*a*) The structure of glucose is

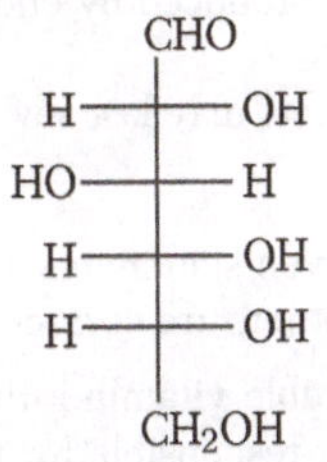

Glucose consists, 1 primary and 4 hydroxyl groups respectively.

2. (*c*) The reaction proceeds as

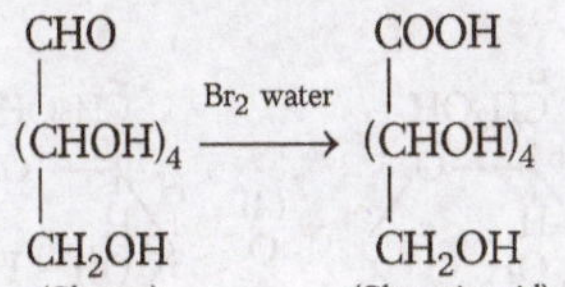

(Glucose) (Gluconic acid)

3. (*c*) Sucrose is the structure of 1-α-D-glucosyl-2-fructose.

Structure of sucrose is shown as

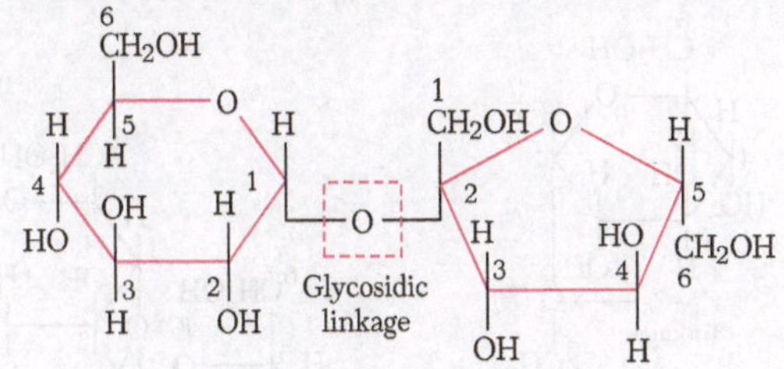

(α-D-glucose) (Sucrose) (β-D-fructose)

4. (*b*) A hemiacetal linkage consists of a carbonyl group that is also bonded to a hydroxyl group.

5. (*c*) Anomers have different configuration at C-1. If OH is present at right side anomeric carbon is known as α-form and if OH is present at left side of anomeric carbon is known as β-form

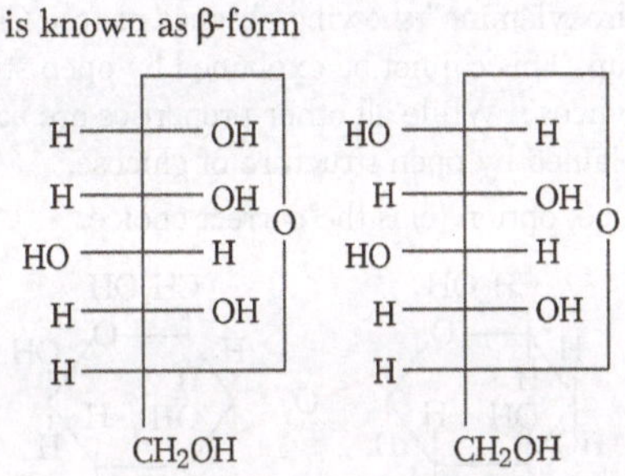

α-D-form β-D-form

6. (*d*) Sucrose is not a reducing sugar because its disaccharide bond is a 1,2-anomeric link.

7. (*d*) Sucrose on hydrolysis gives D-(+)-Glucose [i.e. dextrorotatory] and D-(–)-fructose [i.e. laevorotatory].

8. (*c*) Numbering of glucose starts from adjacent carbon of O-atom to the other carbon atom ending at last CH_2OH group as shown below :

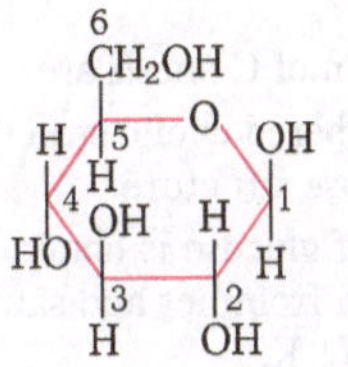

In this way, numbering for the disaccharides can be done as :

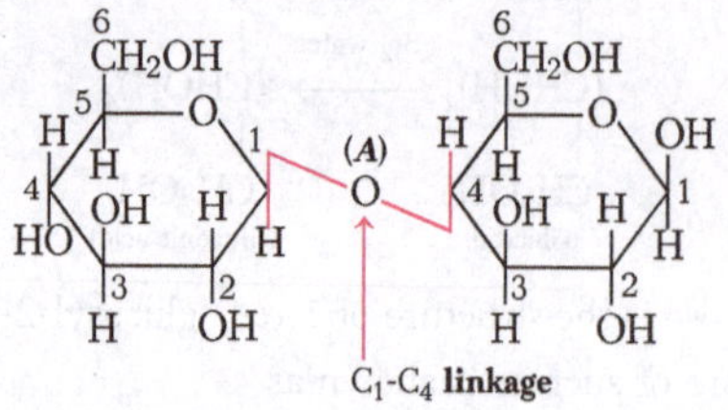

(I)

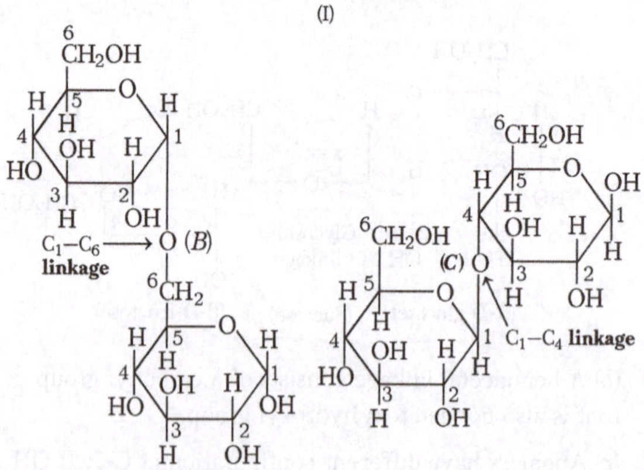

(II) (III)

9. (c) "Pentaacetate of glucose does not react with hydroxylamine" showing absence of free CHO group. This cannot be explained by open structure of glucose. While all other properties are easily explained by open structure of glucose.
Hence, option (c) is the correct choice.

10. (d)

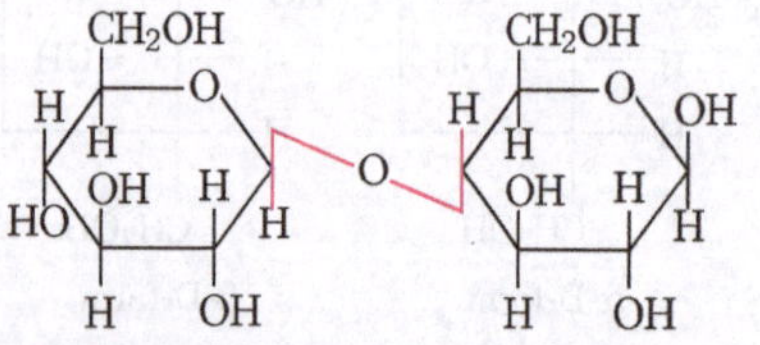

This structure represents sucrose in which α-D-fructose is attached to each other by C_1—C_2 glycosidic linkage.
Since, reducing groups of glucose and fructose are involved in glcosidic bond formation, this is considered as non-reducing sugar.

11. (d) Among the given statements, only C and E are incorrect while other statements A, B and D are correct.
The correct form of C and E are
- The six membered cyclic structure of glucose is called pyranose structure.
- The β-form of glucose is obtained by crystallisation from hot and saturated aqueous solution at 371 K.

12. (c) Among the given match, only (c) is correctly match about serum albumin.

13. (a) Among the given statements, (a) is incorrect while other are correct about peptide bond.

14. (d) There are 12 different tripeptides can be formed from one molecule each of the amino acids, tyrosine, valine and alanine.

15. (c) The isoelectric point of an amino acid is the pH at which it exists in Zwitter ion form.

16. (d) 17. (a)

18. (c) Enzymes functions as catalysts by lowering the value of the activation energy.

19. (a) The part of an enzyme that is formed of protein is called apoenzyme.

20. (c)

21. (d) Among the given statements, only B, C and D are correct while A and E are incorrect about enzymes.
Their correct form are
- Enzymes are protein molecules which have plenty of groups like $-OH$, $-NH_2$ that can act as nucleophiles.
- Enzymes are needed only in small quantities for the progress of a reaction.

22. (b) Among the given match, (b) is not correctly match according to their classification.
Its correct match is:
Epinephrine – Amino acid derivatives

23. (d)

24. (b) Androgens are a specific type of steroid whose main function is to promote development of secondary male sex characteristics.

25. (a) 26. (c) 27. (d) 28. (b)

29. (d) Among the given statements, statement (d) is not correct about hormones.
Its correct form is :
Hormones are very specific and affect everything from blood sugar to blood pressure, growth and fertility, sex drive, metabolism and even sleep.

30. (c) Among the given statements, only B, C and E are correct for hormones while A and D are incorrect.
Their correct form are
- Hormones are produced by endocrine glands in the body.
- Hormones effects may last several hours or days.

31. (d)

32. (a) Among the given statements, (a) is incorrect about vitamins while others are correct.

33. (b) The water soluble vitamin rather than B is vitamin 'C' which deficiency responsible for the scurvy (bleeding gums) disease.

34. (a) Among the given statements, statement (a) is correct about vitamin A, B and D while other are incorrect.

Their correct form are

Vitamin C is water soluble and can not be stored in our body, whereas vitamins A and D are fat soluble and they are stored in liver and adipose.

35. (*b*) The sequence in the structure of nucleic acid is phosphate group + pentose + base.

36. (*b*)

37. (*c*) The new strand of RNA from the given strand of DNA, i.e. 'AATGCCTA' will be 'GGACGGAU'.

38. (*a*) The major function of nucleic acids is storage and transfer of genetic information.

39. (*a*)

40. (*a*) **Nucleoside** species formed by the attachment of a base to 1′ position of sugar is known as nucleoside. The sugar carbon are numbered as 1′, 2′, 3′, ...to distinguish them from bases.

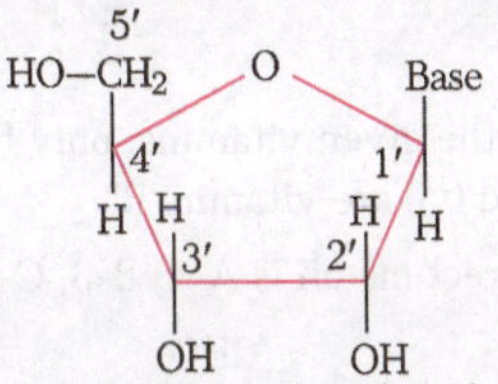

Structure of nucleoside

Nucleotide species formed by attachment of phosphoric acid to nucleoside at 5′ position of sugar nucleotide.

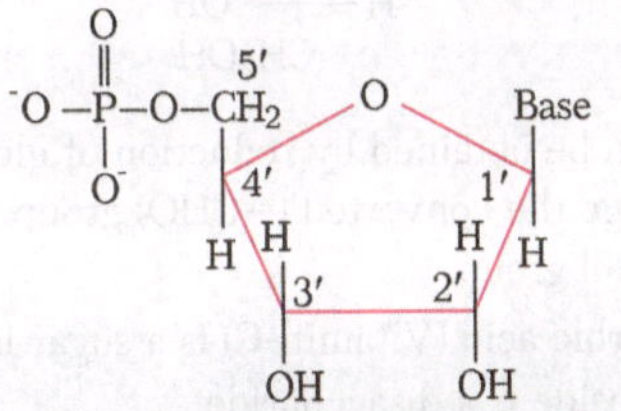

Structure of nucleotide

Dinucleotides are formed by phosphodiester linkage between 5′ and 3′ carbon atoms of the pentose sugar.

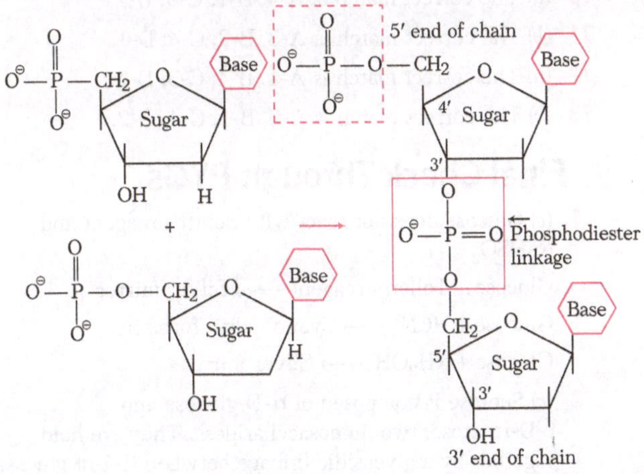

41. (*b*)

42. (*d*) A is false but R is true.

The correct form of A is :

Despite having the aldehydic group, glucose does not give Schiff's test and it does not form the hydrogen sulphite addition product with $NaHSO_3$.

43. (*d*) A is false but R is true.

The correct form of A is :

Glucose gets oxidised to gluconic acid on reaction with a mild oxidising agent like bromine water.

44. (*d*) A is false but R is true.

The correct form of A is :

The amino acid 'Asp' is known as 'Aspartic acid' which is an acidic amino acid.

45. (*a*) Both A and R are true and R is the correct explanation of A.

46. (*c*) A is true but R is false.

The correct form of R is :

Secondary and tertiary structures are held together by weak bonds and primary structure is made of a strong dipeptide linkage.

47. (*b*) Statement I is true but Statement II is false.

Its correct form is :

In D-(+)-glucose, '(D)' represents the configuration of glucose whereas '(+)' represents dextrorotatory nature of glucose.

48. (*c*) Statement I is incorrect but statement II is correct.

The correct form of statement I is :

In maltose structure, α-(1-4) glycosidic linkage is present.

49. (*d*) Both Statement I and Statement II are true.

50. (*d*) Both Statement I and Statement II are true.

51. (*b*) Statement I is true but Statement II is false.

Its correct form is :

Active sites of enzymes hold the substrate molecule in a suitable position.

52. (*b*) Statement I is true but statement II is false.

Its correct form is :

Thyroxine produced in the thyroid gland is an iodinated derivative of amino acid tyrosine.

53. (*b*) Statement I is true but Statement II is false.

Its correct form is :

RNA molecules are of three types i.e. *m*-RNA, *r*-RNA and *t*-RNA.

54. (*d*) Among the given statements, only B and C are incorrect while the other statements A, D and E are correct.

The correct form of B and C are given as

- Pyran is a cyclic organic compound with one oxygen atom and five carbon atom in the ring.
- When our body needs glucose, enzymes break the glycogen down to glucose.

55. (*a*) Among the given statements only A, B and D are correct while the statements C and E are incorrect.

Their correct form are :

- When the polypeptide chains run parallel and are held together by hydrogen and disulphide bonds, then fibre-like structure is formed.
- The primary structure of proteins arise when each polypeptide in a protein has amino acids linked with each other in a specific sequence.

56. (*a*) Among the given statements, only A, B and E are correct while the statements C and D are incorrect.

Their correct form are

- Vitamin A, D, E and K are stored in liver and adipose (fat storing) tissues.
- The rates at which different enzymes catalyse their reactions are different in nature.

57. (*d*) Among the given statements, only A, D and E are correct while the other statements B and C are incorrect.

Their correct form are

- Lactose is commonly known as milk sugar.
- Proteins are composed many type of amino acid.

58. (*d*) Among the given statements, only B, D are incorrect while the others, i.e. A, C and E are correct.

Their correct form are

- Progesterone is responsible for preparing the uterus for implantation of fertilised egg.
- The process in which information from DNA is used to manufacture RNA is called replication.

59. (*b*) Among the given saccharides, only five, i.e. (ii), (iii), (iv), (v) and (vi) are pentose sugar while other are hexose sugar.

Pentose sugar contain five carbon atoms and hexose contain six carbon atoms.

60. (*a*) Among the given, 3-letter symbol of amino acids, only three, i.e. (i), (iii) and (v) are neutral amino acid while others, i.e. Glu. (Glutamic acid) $\rightarrow$ Acidic Arg. (Arginine) $\rightarrow$ Basic amino acids.

61. (*a*) Among the given amino acids, only four, i.e. (i), (iv), (vi) and (vii) are non-essential amino acids.

The amino acids, which can synthesised in the body are known as non-essential amino acids.

62. (*d*) Among the given 3-letter symbol of amino acids, all are primary amine except one, i.e. (iv) which is a secondary amine.

63. (*a*) Among the given enzymes, only three, i.e. (i), (iv) and (v) are hydrolases in nature.

Hydrolase enzyme are those enzyme which break down proteins with the help of water.

64. (*c*) Among the given enzymes, only two, i.e. (ii) and (iii) are used to convert starch into maltose.

65. (*d*) Among the given hormones, only four, i.e. (i), (ii), (iv) and (vii) are the amino acids derivative.

66. (*d*) Among the given base, only two, i.e. (i) and (v) are a bicyclic nitrogenous base.

Structure of adenine and guanine are respectively as follows

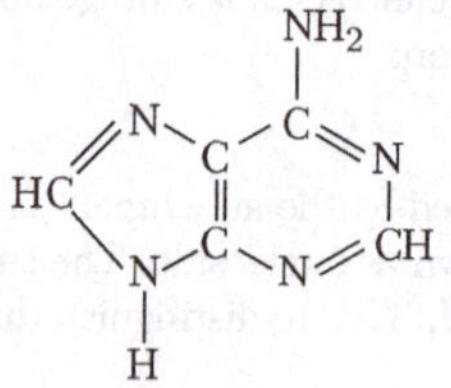

(*A*)

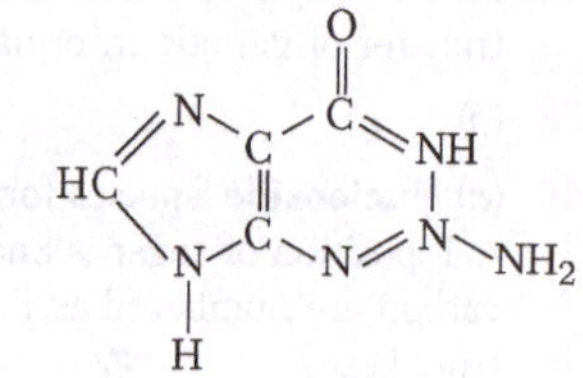

(*G*)

67. (*d*) Among the given vitamins, only five, i.e. (i), (ii), (iii), (iv) and (vi) are vitamin 'B'.

68. (*a*) The correct match is A-4, B-3, C-2, D-1.

- D-sorbitol, i.e. 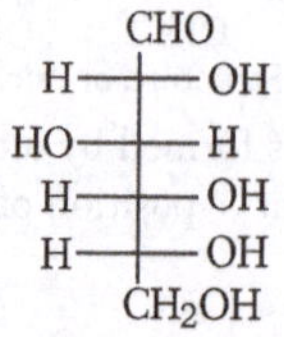 is a sugar alcohol.

It can be obtained by reduction of glucose, which change the converted (–CHO) group to a primary alcohol group.

- Ascorbic acid (Vitamin-C) is a sugar lactone.
- Glycoside is a disaccharide.
- C-1 of glucose is an anomeric carbon.

69. (*a*) The correct match is A-2, B-4, C-3, D-1.

70. (*d*) The correct match is A-4, B-1, C-3, D-2.

71. (*b*) The correct match is A-3, B-2, C-4, D-1.

72. (*a*) The correct match is A-1, B-4, C-3, D-2.

73. (*b*) The correct match is A-3, B-1, C-4, D-2.

Final Check Through PYQs

1. (*c*) Glucose does not react with Schiff's reagent and $NaHSO_3$.

Glucose + Tollen's reagent $\longrightarrow$ Silver mirror

Glucose + HCN $\longrightarrow$ Cyanohydrin formation

Glucose + NH_2OH $\longrightarrow$ Silver mirror

2. (*c*) Sucrose is composed of α-D-glucose and β-D-fructose, two monosaccharidess. They are held together by a glycosidic linkage between C-1 of glucose and C-2 of fructose respectively.

$$\text{Sucrose} \xrightarrow{\text{Hydrolysis}} \alpha\text{-D-glucose} + \beta\text{-D-fructose}$$

3. (*a*) Conc. H_2SO_4 removes water, i.e. dehydrates carbohydrates into carbon (black residue) or charred sugar.

$$C_{12}H_{22}O_{11} \text{ or } C_{12}(H_2O)_{11} \xrightarrow[-11H_2O]{\text{Conc. } H_2SO_4} \underset{\text{(Black)}}{12\,C}$$

4. (*d*) Glucose is an aldohexose (made of six carbon atoms) and it is a reducing sugar containing five —OH groups. Hence, option (d) is incorrect statement.

Glucose is a hexose.

$$\underbrace{HO—CH_2}_{\text{One } 1^\circ\text{—OH group}}—\underbrace{(CHOH)_4}_{\text{Four } 2^\circ\text{—OH group}}—\underbrace{CH{=}O}_{\text{Aldehyde group}}$$

5. (*c*) Sucrose is non-reducing sugar because reducing part of glucose ($—\overset{O}{\overset{\|}{C}}—H$) and fructose ($>C=O$) are involved in glycosidic linkage.

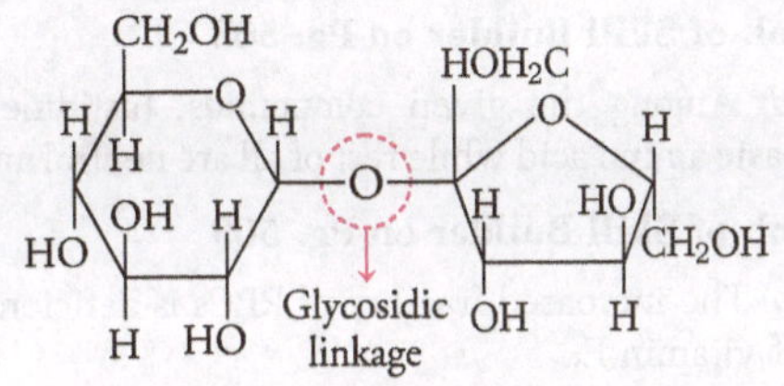

While, lactose, glucose and maltose are reducing sugars.

6. (*d*)

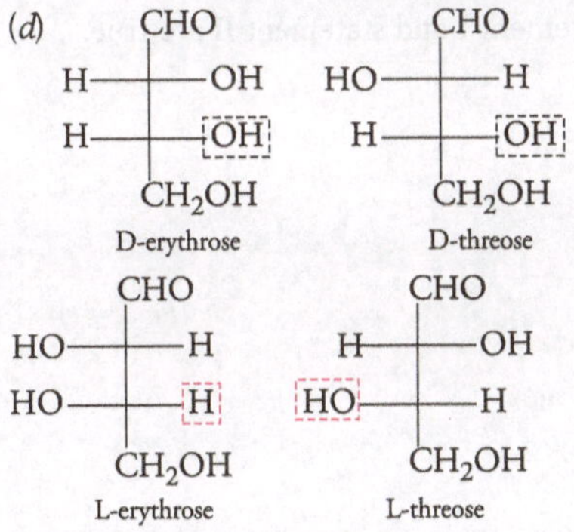

Thus, the correct option is (d).

7. (*d*) D-(+)-glucose contains aldehydic group which reacts with hydroxyl amine (NH_2OH) to yield an oxime. The complete reaction is

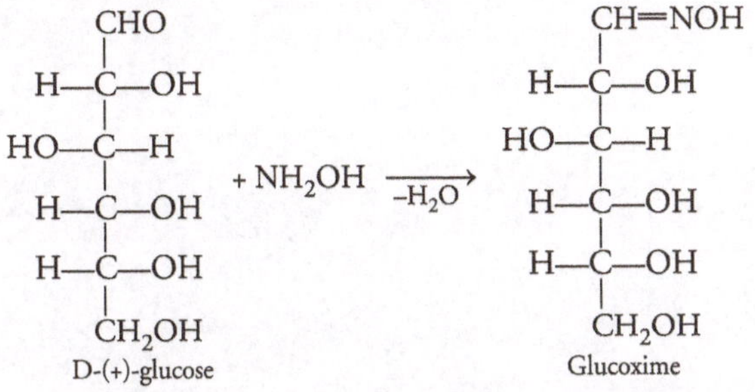

8. (*c*) (a) Alanine $\Rightarrow CH_3—CH\begin{cases}NH_2\\COOH\end{cases}$

(b) Tyrosine $\Rightarrow$

$HO—C_6H_4—CH_2—CH\begin{cases}NH_2\\COOH\end{cases}$

(c) Lysine $\Rightarrow H_2N—(CH_2)_4—CH\begin{cases}NH_2\\COOH\end{cases}$

(d) Serine $\Rightarrow HO—CH_2—CH\begin{cases}NH_2\\COOH\end{cases}$

Since, lysine contains more number of $—NH_2$ groups as compared to —COOH groups, hence it is a basic amino acid.

9. (*b*) Denaturation of proteins destroys secondary and tertiary structure while primary structure remain unaffected.

10. (*b*) The amino acids that can be synthesised in our body and hence are not essentially required in our diet are called non-essential amino acids.

e.g. Glycine, alanine, serine, proline, cysteine, glutamine, tyrosine, aspartic acid, glutamic acid, asparagine.

11. (*d*) Among the given options, only glycine ($H_2N—CH_2—COOH$) is an amino acid which contains both acidic (acquiring negative charge) and basic group (acquiring positive charge).

Glycine can form a Zwitter ion because it behaves like salts rather than simple amines or carboxylic acids. In aqueous solution, the carboxyl group can lose a proton and amino group can accept a proton giving rise to a dipolar ion known as Zwitter ion.

$$H—\underset{\overset{+}{N}H_3}{\overset{H}{\overset{|}{\underset{|}{C}}}}—COO^-$$

Zwitter ion

12. (*b*) Two amino acids in a protein are linked by a peptide bond. e.g. Glycylalanine is formed when carboxyl group of glycine combines with the amino group of alanine.

$$H_2N—CH_2—CO\,\boxed{OH + H}_2N—\underset{\underset{\text{Alanine}}{CH_3}}{CHCOOH} \xrightarrow{-H_2O} H_2N—CH_2—\underset{\text{Peptide linkage}}{\boxed{CO—NH}}—\underset{CH_3}{CH}—COOH$$

Glycylalanine (Gly-Ala)

13. (*b*) Statement I is true while Statement II is false. The correct form of Statement II is : When nucleoside is linked to phosphoric acid at 5′-position of sugar moiety, we get nucleotide.

14. (*b*) The incorrect statement about enzymes is option (b) because enzymes are protein in nature and comprised of amino acids that are linked together in one or more polypeptide chains. Rest all other given options are correct.

15. (*b*) When body is affected by anemia, it does not have enough RBC's which is result of deficiency of vitamin B_{12}. Vitamin B_{12} is important for production of RBC's.

16. (*b*) Deficiency of

Vitamin A causes—Xerophthalmia

Vitamin D causes—Osteomalacia and rickets

Vitamin E causes—Fragility of RBCs

Vitamin K causes—Increase in blood clotting time

Hence, option (b) is correct.

17. (*a*) In DNA, two helically twisted strands connected together by steps. Each strand consists of alternating molecules of deoxyribose at 2′-position and phosphate groups.

On the other hand, in RNA, the pentose sugar has an identical structure with deoxyribose sugar except that there is an —OH group instead of —H on carbon atom 2′.

Hence, it is only called ribose.

18. (*c*) The central dogma of molecular genetics states that

$$\text{DNA} \xrightarrow{\text{Transcription}} \text{RNA} \xrightarrow{\text{Translation}} \text{Protein}$$

Thus, option (c) is correct.

19. (*c*) Adrenaline hormones increases pulse rate and controls blood pressure. It releases glucose from liver glycogen and fatty acids from fats in emergency.

Skill Builder

- **Sol. of Skill Builder on Pg. 493**

(*b*) Maltose, cellobiose and lactose are reducing sugar.

- **Sol. of Skill Builder on Pg. 495**

(*a*) A. Glucose $(C_6H_{12}O_6) \xrightarrow{NaBH_4}$ Sorbitol (Chiral)

B. Glucose $\xrightarrow{(CH_3CO)_2O}$ Glucose pentaacetate (chiral)

C. Glucose $\xrightarrow{NH_2OH}$ Glucose oxime (chiral)

D. Glucose $\xrightarrow[\text{reagent}]{\text{Seliwanoff's}}$ No product

E. Glucose $\xrightarrow[\text{reagent}]{\text{Seliwanoff's}}$ No product

- **Sol. of Skill Builder on Pg. 503**

(*d*) Among the given compounds, histidine (His) is a basic amino acid while rest of all are neutral amino acids.

- **Sol. of Skill Builder on Pg. 509**

(*a*) The increased fragility of RBCs is deficiency disease of vitamin E.

- **Sol. of Skill Builder on Pg. 511**

(*d*) Both statement I and statement II are true.

For deeper insight
Scan the QR Code

Chapter 12

Principles Related to Practical Chemistry

Learning Objectives

Module-I

- Dry Test
- Wet Test
- Analysis of Acidic Radicals
- Analysis of Basic Radicals

Module-II

- Acid-Base Indicators
- Acid-Base Titration
- Redox Titration
- Mohr's Salt
- Potash Alum

Module-III

- Detection of Functional Groups
- Preparation of Organic Compounds (Acetanilide, *p*-nitroacetanilide, Aniline Yellow, Iodoform)
- Chemical Principles Involved in Some Important Experiments
- Enthalpy of Neutralisation of Strong Acid and Strong Base
- Preparation of Lyophilic and Lyophobic Solutions
- Kinetic Study of Reaction of Iodide Ion with Hydrogen Peroxide at Room Temperature

Chapter Overview with NEET Connection

This chapter deals with experimental aspects of physical, organic, inorganic and analytical chemistry. This chapter is added in NEET 2024 syllabus for the first time. So, it holds an important weightage from the exam perspective.

The basics of practical chemistry have already included in the purification of organic compounds and the basics of preparation of inorganic compounds like Mohr's salts is already covered in coordination compounds.

So, a grip over these chapters are prerequisite for better understanding of principles of practical chemistry.

Introduction

The practical chemistry chapter is related to the study of concerned substance, material or compound under specific experimental conditions.

Basically, chemical analysis is done to determine the composition of the substance/compound which are manufactured or occur naturally. This analysis is usually done in two steps, i.e. qualitative and quantitative analysis.

The principle of **qualitative analysis** is to identify the sample components, whereas the principle of **quantitative** analysis is to calculate the relative amount of these components.

Apart from this, we will also study about the experiments related to physical chemistry like the kinetics study of reactions, different types of enthalpies and preparation of sols.

Module 1

Principle of Qualitative Salt Analysis

- Dry Test
- Wet Test
- Analysis of Acidic Radicals
- Analysis of Basic Radicals

Qualitative salt analysis is a method of analytical chemistry that aims to find the chemical composition of inorganic compounds. It mainly focused on detecting ions in an aqueous solution.

The solution is treated with various reagents to test for various reactions characteristic of certain ions, which may cause colour change, solid formation or any other visible change.

The qualitative inorganic analysis can be broadly studied in two categories

- Preliminary or dry test carried out on solid samples.
- Wet reactions involving dissolved samples and reagent solutions.

Preliminary or Dry Tests

Use about the presence of possible radicals in the mixture. It includes

1. Physical examination
2. Effect of heating
3. Solubility of salts
4. Flame test
5. Charcoal cavity test
6. Cobalt-nitrate test
7. Borax bead test
8. Microcosmic salt bead test
9. Sodium carbonate bead test

Physical Examination of Salt or Mixture

In physical examination of colour, smell, density etc., of the salt or mixture are observed.

Observation		Inference
A. Colour of the Substance		
(i)	**Blue**, whose aqueous solution is also blue	Hydrated salts of Cu^{2+} (except CO_3^{2-} and Cl^-)
(ii)	**Colourless** substance	Transition metal ions absent (except some salts of Mn^{2+})
(iii)	**Green**, whose aqueous solution is also green	Salts of Ni^{2+}
(iv)	**Dark green**, whose aqueous solution is also dark green, but becomes light on dilution	Salts of Cr^{3+}
(v)	**Yellow-green**, aqueous solution is light green or almost colourless	Salts of Fe^{2+}
(vi)	**Yellow-brown**, aqueous solution is yellow	Salts of Fe^{3+}
(vii)	**Violet-pink**, whose aqueous solution is pink	Salts of cobalt.
(viii)	**Black** substance	CuO, NiO, SnO, FeS, CuS, HgS, PbS, NiS, CoS, $CuBr_2$, Ag_2S, Cu_2S, MnO_2, Fe_3O_4, FeO, Co_3O_4, Ni_2O_3 etc.
(ix)	**Brown** substance	CdO, PbO_2, SnS, Bi_2S_3, $MnCO_3$ (pale brown), $CuCrO_4$, SnS.
(x)	**Yellow** substance	Bi_2O_3, CdS, SnS_2, As_2S_3, PbI_2 Chromates, As_2S_5, AgI etc.
(xi)	**Red** substance	Cu_2O, HgO, Pb_3O_4, HgI_2 etc.
(xii)	**Orange** substance	$Cr_2O_7^{2-}$ salts, Sb_2S_3 etc.
(xiii)	**Green** substance	K_2MnO_4, carbonate or chloride of Cu^{2+}
(xiv)	**Light pink**	Hydrated Mn^{2+} salts.
(xv)	**Purple**	Permanganates and some Cr^{3+} salts
B. Odour of the substance		
(i)	Ammonical smell	NH_4^+ salts
(ii)	Vinegar like smell	Acetates
(iii)	Like smell from rotten eggs.	S^{2-} salts
C. Density		
(i)	Mixture of salts is heavy	Salts of Hg and Pb
(ii)	Mixture of salts is light	Salts of Zn, Al, Bi, Ca, Ba, Sr, Mg etc. (Chiefly carbonates)

Effect of Heating

Take the given substance in a clear, dry test tube and heat it first gently and then strongly. Observe the changes takes place upon heating.

S.No.	Observation		Inference
(i)	Substance melts		Salts of alkali metals chlorides of Hg, Ag and Pb and salts having water of crystallisation
(ii)	Substance cracks		$Pb(NO_3)_2$, $Ba(NO_3)_2$, NaCl and Kl
(iii)	Substance swells		Alums, salts of phosphates and borates
(iv)	**Colour of residue obtained after heating**		
	Hot	Cold	
	Yellow	White	Zn salts
	Brown	Yellow	Salts of Pb, Bi or Sn
	Red or black	Brown	Cd salts
	White	Blue	Cupric salts ($CuSO_4$)
	Blue	Blue-red	$CoCl_2$
	Green	Dark-red	$CoBr_2$
	Violet	Dark-red	CoI_2
	Yellow	Green	Ni salts
	Green	Violet	Cr salts
	Black (non-fusible)	Black	CuO, MnO_2, NiO
	Dark red brown	Light brown (non-fusible)	Fe_2O_3
	Dark orange red	Light orange red	HgO
(v)	**Substance sublimes on heating and colour of sublimate is**		
	White		$HgCl_2$, Hg_2Cl_2, As_2O_3, $AlCl_3$, Sb_2O_3, halides of NH_3
	Yellow		As_2S_3 and HgI_2 etc.
	Greyish black		Sulphides of Hg, Sb, As
	Yellow, blue or violet vapours		I_2
	Grey (having garlic odour)		As
(vi)	**Observation of gases evolved**		
	A. Colourless and odourless gas		
	Which supports the combustion of burning match stick (O_2)		Nitrates of Na and K
	Which turns the lime water milky (CO_2).		CO_3^{2-} or $C_2O_4^{2-}$ salts
	B. Colourless, odorous gas		
	Smell of ammonia (NH_3)		Ammonium salts
	Smell of burning sulphur (SO_2)		Sulphite and thiosulphate
	Smell of rotten eggs (H_2S)		Sulphide salts
	Pungent smelling gas and forms white fumes with NH_3		Hydrated chloride salts
	C. Coloured, odourless gas		
	Brown gas which turns starch iodide paper blue (NO_2)		Bromide salts
	Violet gas which turns starch paper blue		Iodide salts
	Yellow-green gas which decolourised the litmus paper		Chloride salts

Solubility of Salts

S.No.	Type of the salts	Observation
(i)	Nitrates and nitrites	All metal salts are soluble in water
(ii)	Acetates	All metal acetates are soluble in water
(iii)	Chlorides	All common chlorides are soluble in water except AgCl, Hg_2Cl_2 and $PbCl_2$.
(iv)	Bromides	All common bromides are soluble in water except AgBr, Hg_2Br_2,$PbBr_2$ and $HgBr_2$
(v)	Iodides	All common iodides are soluble in water except AgI, Hg_2I_2, HgI_2 and PbI_2
(vi)	Sulphides	All common sulphides are insoluble in water except sulphides of group I and group II metals and ammonium ion
(vii)	Carbonates	All common carbonates are insoluble in water except carbonates of group I and $(NH_4)_2CO_3$
(viii)	Sulphates	All common sulphates are soluble in water except $PbSO_4$, Hg_2SO_4, $BaSO_4$, $CaSO_4$ and Ag_2SO_4 which are sparingly soluble
(ix)	Phosphates	All common phosphates are insoluble in water except phosphates of group I and $(NH_4)_3PO_4$
(x)	Hydroxides	All common metal hydroxides are insoluble in water except group I hydroxides and $Ba(OH)_2$, $Sr(OH)_2$ and some group II hydroxides such as $Ca(OH)_2$

Flame Test

This test is based on the fact that in a state of high ionisation of chloride some of the cations impart characteristic colour of the flame, as the cations absorb energy from the flame and transmit the same as light of characteristic colour.

In this test a platinum wire dipped in salt paste and conc. HCl is taken near the mouth of flame having oxidising zone and the colour imparted by salt is observed.

Colour	Cation
Golden yellow	Na^+
Violet	K^+
Brick red	Ca^{2+}
Apple-green	Ba^{2+}, Mo^{2+}
Crimson red	Sr^{2+}
Blue	Cu^{2+}, As^{3+}, Sb^{3+}, Bi^{3+}

Mentor's TIP

Always remember! while performing flame tests.

- Wire must be cleaned with conc. HCl and it must be pure.
- Be and Mg do not impart colour to flame due to high ionisation energy.

Charcoal Cavity Test

In this test, salt is fused with anhydrous Na_2CO_3 or oxidising fusion mixture in a cavity on charcoal block in reducing flame. Reactions yield metal oxides. Some metal oxides are reduced to metal by action of carbon present in reducing flame while some form incrustation on cold parts of charcoal block.

The fusion reactions may be represented as given below :

$$CuCl_2 + Na_2CO_3 \longrightarrow CuCO_3 + 2NaCl$$

$$CuCO_3 \longrightarrow CuO + CO_2\uparrow$$

$$CuO + C \longrightarrow Cu + CO\uparrow$$

The conclusions can be made through the following table.

S.No.	Sample bead	Crust	Inference
(i)	Greyish white soft bead which marks paper.	Brown which turns yellow on cooling	Pb^{2+}
(ii)	White-brown bead	Orange which turns yellow on cooling	Bi^{3+}
(iii)	Smell of ammonia	Red	NH_4^+
(iv)	–	Black precipitate	Fe^{3+}, Co^{2+}, Mn^{2+}

Cobalt Nitrate Test

This test is performed only when a white, infusible mass is obtained in charcoal cavity test.

It is based on the fact that some metal oxides form coloured double oxides when heated with cobalt oxide in oxidising flame. To perform this test, white infusible mass obtained in charcoal cavity test is taken in charcoal cavity with cobalt nitrate and mixture is heated in oxidising flame.

Conclusions can be made by the following table.

S. No.	Observation	Composition	Inference
(i)	Blue residue	$CoO \cdot Al_2O_3$	Al^{3+}, PO_4^{3-}, BO_3^{3-}
(ii)	Green residue	$CoO \cdot ZnO$	Zn^{2+}
(iii)	Pink-dirty residue	$CoO \cdot MgO$	Mg^{2+}
(iv)	Bluish-green residue	$CoO \cdot Sn$	Sn^{2+}

Cobalt nitrate should not be used in excess otherwise black coloured cobalt oxide (Co_3O_4) may be formed. In presence of this black coloured oxide, it is difficult to identify other colours.

Borax-Bead Test

Some substance gives coloured bead when heated with borax bead on platinum loop. Colour of bead gives idea of the substance (transition metal in its compound).

The reactions taking place may be represented as

$$Na_2B_4O_7 \cdot 10H_2O \xrightarrow[-10\,H_2O]{\Delta} Na_2B_4O_7 \longrightarrow \underbrace{2NaBO_2 + B_2O_3}_{\text{Glassy borax bead}}$$

(Mixture of sodium metaborate and boric anhydride)

This borax bead forms coloured bead with metal salts.

e.g. $$CuSO_4 \xrightarrow{\Delta} CuO + SO_3$$

$$CuO + B_2O_3 \xrightarrow{\Delta} \underset{\substack{\text{Copper (II) metaborate} \\ \text{(green when hot and} \\ \text{blue when cold)}}}{Cu(BO_2)_2}$$

The colour of bead is different in oxidising and reducing flames, e.g. coloured copper metaborate may be reduced to colourless cuprous metaborate or to metallic copper.

$$2Cu(BO_2)_2 + C \longrightarrow 2\,CuBO_2 + B_2O_3 + CO\uparrow$$

$$2Cu(BO_2)_2 + 2C \longrightarrow \underset{\text{(Red)}}{2Cu} + 2B_2O_3 + 2CO\uparrow$$

Results have been summarised in table.

Oxidising flame		Reducing flame		Metal
Hot	Cold	Hot	Cold	
Green	Blue	Colourless	Brown-red	Copper
Brown-yellow	Pale-yellow	Green	Green	Iron
Yellow	Green	Green	Green	Chromium
Blue	Blue	Blue	Blue	Cobalt
Violet	Amethyst	Colourless	Colourless	Manganese
Violet	Raddish-brown	Grey	Grey	Nickel

Microcosmic Salt Bead Test

Microcosmic salt bead test is also used to identify the transition metal in its salt. Microcosmic salt, i.e. $Na(NH_4)HPO_4 \cdot 4H_2O$ when strongly heated give sodium metaphosphate ($NaPO_3$) which on reaction with transition metal oxide (obtained from salt) gives coloured bead.

$$Na(NH_4)HPO_4 \cdot 4H_2O \xrightarrow{\Delta} \underset{\text{Transparent bead}}{NaPO_3} + 5H_2O\uparrow + NH_3\uparrow$$

$$NaPO_3 + CoO \longrightarrow \underset{\substack{\text{Blue bead} \\ \text{[Sodium cobalt(II) phosphate]}}}{NaCoPO_4}$$

Results have been summarised in table.

Oxidising flame	Reducing flame	Metal
Green when hot, blue when cold	Colourless when hot, red when cold	Copper
Yellowish-or reddish-brown when hot, yellow when cold	Yellow when hot, colourless to green when cold	Iron
Green, hot and cold	Green, hot and cold	Chromium
Violet, hot and cold	Colourless, hot and cold	Manganese
Blue, hot and cold	Blue, hot and cold	Cobalt
Brown, hot and cold	Grey when cold	Nickel

Sodium Carbonate Bead Test

The sodium carbonate bead is prepared by fusing a small quantity of sodium carbonate on a platinum wire loop in the Bunsen flame, a white, opaque bead is produced.

If this is moistened, dipped into a little KNO_3 and then into a small quantity of a manganese compound and the whole mass heated in the oxidising flame, a green bead of sodium manganate (Na_2MnO_4) is formed.

$$MnO + Na_2CO_3 + O_2 \xrightarrow{\Delta} \underset{\substack{\text{(Sodium manganate)} \\ \text{Green bead}}}{Na_2MnO_4} + CO_2\uparrow$$

A yellow bead is obtained with chromium compounds, due to formation of sodium chromate (Na_2CrO_4).

$$2Cr_2O_3 + 4Na_2CO_3 + 3O_2 \xrightarrow{\Delta} \underset{\substack{\text{(Sodium manganate)} \\ \text{Yellow bead}}}{4Na_2CrO_4} + 4CO_2\uparrow$$

Wet Tests

Wet tests includes the dissolving of a salt (or mixture) into water so as to bring it in solution form and is analysed for acid and basic radicals. In the analysis of inorganic salt mixture, first acid radicals are analysed and then basic radicals.

Concept ladder
A salt consists of two parts known as radicals. The positively charged part of a salt (cation) which has been derived from a base is termed basic radical and the negatively charged part of the salt (anion) which has been derived from an acid is termed acidic or acid radical.

Analysis of Acid (Anion) Radicals

Most of these salts are acted upon by dil. H_2SO_4 or dil. HCl and concentrated H_2SO_4. In each case, a gas is liberated which is characteristic of the particular acidic radical.

Group I This group consists of radicals which are detected by dil H_2SO_4 or dil. HCl. e.g. SO_3^{2-} sulphite, CO_3^{2-}-carbonate, S^{-2} sulphide, NO_2^--nitrite.

Group II This group consists of radical which are detected by concentrated H_2SO_4. e.g. Cl^--chloride, Br^--bromide, I^--iodide, NO_3^--nitrate.

Group III The radicals which do not give any characteristic gas with dil. and conc. H_2SO_4. e.g. SO_4^{2-} sulphate, PO_4^{3-}-phosphate, BO_3^{2-}-borate, F^--fluoride.

Analysis of First Group Anions

Acidic radicals or anions of first group when treated with dil. H_2SO_4 (group reagent) evolve gases with characteristic colour and smell. On the basis of action of these gases anions are identified.

I. Test for CO_3^{2-}

The test for carbonate ion can be carried out as

S.No.	Experiment	Observation	Inference
1.	Take mixture in a dry test tube and add dil. HCl or H_2SO_4. Warm gently	Brisk effervescence with the evolution of colourless and odourless gas (CO_2)	may be CO_3^{2-}
2.	Pass the evolved gas into lime water [$Ca(OH)_2$]	Lime water turns milky	CO_3^{2-} confirmed
3.	Pass excess lime water to the evolved gas	Milkiness disappears	CO_3^{2-} confirmed

Reactions Involved in the Test of Carbonate (CO_3^{2-})

(i) $Na_2CO_3 + 2HCl \longrightarrow 2NaCl + H_2O + \underset{\text{Colourless odourless gas}}{CO_2\uparrow}$

(ii) $Ca(OH)_2 + CO_2 \longrightarrow \underset{\text{Calcium carbonate (milky)}}{CaCO_3\downarrow} + H_2O$

(iii) $CaCO_3 + H_2O + CO_2 \text{ (excess)} \longrightarrow \underset{\text{Calcium bicarbonate (colourless)}}{Ca(HCO_3)_2}$

Soluble carbonate gives white precipitate of silver carbonate with silver nitrate.

$$2Ag^+ + CO_3^{2-} \longrightarrow \underset{\text{White ppt.}}{Ag_2CO_3\downarrow}$$

- The precipitate is soluble in nitric acid and in ammonia. The precipitate becomes yellow or brown upon addition of excess reagent owing to the formation of silver oxide, the same happens if the mixture is boiled.

$$Ag_2CO_3\downarrow \xrightarrow{\Delta} Ag_2O\downarrow + CO_2\uparrow$$

- Aqueous carbonate solution is alkaline due to hydrolysis (with H_2O).

$$CO_3^{2-} + 2H_2O \longrightarrow H_2CO_3 + 2OH^-$$

- Alkaline solution turns pink when a drop of phenolphthalein is added to it. If CO_2 (liberated from the reaction of given carbonate with dil. H_2SO_4) is passed into above pink-coloured solution, then it is decolourised by HCO_3^- formed with CO_2.

$$CO_2 + CO_3^{2-} + H_2O \longrightarrow 2HCO_3^-$$

II. Test for Sulphide ion (S^{2-})

The analysis for sulphide ions is carried out as

S.No.	Experiment	Observation	Inference
1.	Take mixture in a dry test tude and add. Dil. HCl and H_2SO_4 and warm gently	A colourless gas (H_2S) with smell of rotten eggs evolved	S^{2-} may be present
2.	Take filter paper dipped in lead acetate on the mouth of the tube	Filter paper turns black due to formation of PbS	S^{2-} confirmed
3.	Add solution of sodium nitroprusside to the original salt solution of the mixture	Purple colour is observed	S^{2-} confirmed

Reactions Involved in the Test of Sulphide (S^{2-}) Ion

$$Na_2S + H_2SO_4 \longrightarrow H_2S\uparrow + Na_2SO_4$$

$$H_2S + (CH_3COO)_2Pb \longrightarrow \underset{\text{Black}}{PbS\downarrow} + 2CH_3COOH$$

$$Na_2S + \underset{\text{Sodium nitroprusside}}{Na_2[Fe(CN)_5NO]} \longrightarrow \underset{\text{Purple}}{Na_4[Fe(CN)_5NOS]}$$

III. Test for Nitrite Ion (NO_2^-)

The analysis for nitrite ions (NO_2^-) is carried out as

S.No.	Experiment	Observation	Inference
1.	Take mixture in a dry test tube and add dil. HCl. Warm gently	Brown fumes (NO_2) with pungent odour are evolved	NO_2^- may be present
2.	Take filter paper dipped in (starch + KI) solution, on the mouth the test tube	The evolved gas turns filter paper blue	NO_2^- confirmed
3.	Add 2-3 drops of KI and starch solution in the test tube	Deep blue or violet colour appears	NO_2^- confirmed

Reactions Involved in the Test of NO_2^- Ion

$$2NaNO_2 + H_2SO_4 \longrightarrow Na_2SO_4 + 2HNO_2$$

$$3HNO_2 \longrightarrow HNO_3 + 2NO\uparrow + H_2O$$

$$2NO + O_2 \text{ (air)} \longrightarrow \underset{\text{Brown fumes}}{2NO_2\uparrow}$$

$$2KI + H_2SO_4 + 2HNO_2 \longrightarrow K_2SO_4 + 2H_2O + 2NO + I_2$$

$$I_2 + \text{Starch} \longrightarrow \text{Blue colour}$$

Concept ladder

NO_2^- ion can be also detected by carrying out the following test.

- When the cold nitrite solution is added carefully to a saturated solution of iron (II) sulphate acidified with acetic acid or conc. sulphuric acid, a brown ring due to the compound $[Fe\cdot NO]SO_4$ is formed at the junction of two liquids.

$$NO_2^- + CH_3COOH \longrightarrow HNO_2 + CH_3COO^-$$

$$3HNO_2 \longrightarrow H_2O + HNO_3 + 2NO$$

$$Fe^{2+} + SO_4^{2-} + NO \longrightarrow [Fe\cdot NO]SO_4 \text{ or } [Fe(H_2O)_5\cdot NO]SO_4$$

- NO_2^- in CH_3COOH solution on treatment with thiourea forms SCN^- which gives red colour with $FeCl_3$ and HCl.

$$\underset{\text{Thiourea}}{(NH_2)_2CS} + HNO_2 \longrightarrow N_2 + H^+ + SCN^- + 2H_2O$$

$$FeCl_3 + SCN^- \longrightarrow \underset{\text{Blood red}}{Fe(SCN)_3} + Cl^-$$

IV. Test for Sulphite Ion (SO_3^{2-})

The test for sulphite ion can be carried out as

S.No.	Experiment	Observation	Inference
1.	Take the mixture in a dry test tube and add dil. HCl/H_2SO_4. Warm gently	A colourless gas with pungent smell of burning sulphur	SO_3^{2-} may be present
2.	Pass the evolved gas into acidified $K_2Cr_2O_7$ solution.	Gas turns acidified $K_2Cr_2O_7$ solution green	SO_3^{2-} confirmed

Reactions Involved in the test of Sulphite Ion

$$Na_2SO_3 + H_2SO_4 \xrightarrow{\Delta} Na_2SO_4 + H_2O + SO_2$$

$$Cr_2O_7^{2-} + 3SO_2 + 2H^+ \longrightarrow \underset{\text{(Green)}}{2Cr^{3+}} + 3SO_4^{2-} + H_2O$$

Concept ladder

Acidified $KMnO_4$ solution is also decolourised by SO_3^{2-} ion.

$$5SO_3^{2-} + \underset{\text{Dark pink}}{2MnO_4^-} + 6H^+ \longrightarrow \underset{\text{Colourless}}{2Mn^{2+}} + 5SO_4^{2-} + 3H_2O$$

Analysis of Second Group Anions [Cl^-, Br^-, I^-, NO_3^-]

The acidic radicals or anions of second group gives no response with dilute acids but with concentrated acids (conc. H_2SO_4 is the group I reagent), they evolve gases with characteristic colour and odour. Thus, they can be identified by using concentrated acids.

I. Test for Chloride Ion (Cl^-)

The test for Cl^- ion can be carried out as

S.No.	Experiment	Observation	Inference
1.	Heat the mixture with 1-2 mL conc. H_2SO_4 in a dry test tube	A colourless, pungent gas (HCl) is evolved	Cl^- may be present
2.	Bring a glass rod dipped in NH_4OH near the mouth of test tube	White dense fumes of NH_4Cl is evolved	Cl^- confirmed
3.	Heat of mixture with conc. H_2SO_4 and MnO_2 in a dry test tube	Greenish-yellow (Cl_2) pungent gas is evolved	Cl^- confirmed
4.	**Chromyl chloride test**		
	Heat the mixture with solid $K_2Cr_2O_7$ and conc. H_2SO_4. Now collect these vapours in a test tube containing NaOH followed by acidification with acetic acid and add lead acetate solution.	Orange yellow vapours of chromyl-chloride (CrO_2Cl_2) are evolved. A yellow ppt. of lead chromate is formed	Cl^- confirmed

Reactions Involved in the Test of Chloride (Cl^-)

(i) $NaCl + H_2SO_4 \longrightarrow NaHSO_4 + \underset{\text{Pungent smelling gas}}{HCl\uparrow}$

(ii) $HCl + NH_4OH \longrightarrow \underset{\text{White fumes}}{NH_4Cl\downarrow} + H_2O$

(iii) $2NaCl + MnO_2 + 3H_2SO_4 \longrightarrow$

$$2NaHSO_4 + MnSO_4 + 2H_2O + \underset{\text{Yellowish green}}{Cl_2\uparrow}$$

(iv) **Chromyl chloride test**

$4NaCl + K_2Cr_2O_7 + 3H_2SO_4 \longrightarrow$

$$\underset{\substack{\text{Chromyl chloride}\\\text{(orange yellow gas)}}}{2CrO_2Cl_2} + 2Na_2SO_4 + K_2SO_4 + 3H_2O$$

$$CrO_2Cl_2 + 4NaOH \longrightarrow \underset{\text{Yellow}}{Na_2CrO_4} + 2NaCl + 2H_2O$$

$(CH_3COO)_2Pb + Na_2CrO_4 \longrightarrow$

$$\underset{\text{Yellow}}{PbCrO_4\downarrow} + 2CH_3COONa$$

Mentor's TiP

If a mixture contains chlorates then **chromyl chloride test** for chloride anion is not performed because chlorates on reaction with H_2SO_4 form chlorine dioxide gas which dissolves in H_2SO_4 and form highly explosive orange yellow solution.

$$2KClO_3 + 3H_2SO_4 \longrightarrow 2ClO_2\uparrow + ClO_4^- + 3SO_4^{2-} + 4H^+ + 3K^+ + H_2O$$

II. Test for Bromide Ion (Br^-)

The test for Br^- ion can be carried out as

S.No.	Experiment	Observation	Inference
1.	Heat the mixture with 1-2 mL conc. H_2SO_4 in a dry test tube	A colourless, pungent gas (HBr) or sometimes brown fumes are evolved	Br^- may be present
2.	Heat the mixture with MnO_2 and conc. H_2SO_4	Red brown vapour of Br_2 evolved	Br^- confirmed
3.	To the solution of mixture in dil. HNO_3, add $AgNO_3$ solution	A pale yellow ppt. of AgBr is formed (hardly soluble in NH_4OH)	Br^- confirmed

Reaction Involved in the Test of Bromide (Br^-)

(i) $NaBr + \underset{\text{Conc.}}{H_2SO_4} \longrightarrow NaHSO_4 + HBr\uparrow$

$$2HBr + H_2SO_4\,(\text{conc.}) \longrightarrow 2H_2O + SO_2\uparrow + \underset{\text{Reddish brown}}{Br_2\uparrow}$$

(ii) $2NaBr + MnO_2 + 3H_2SO_4 \longrightarrow$

$$2NaHSO_4 + MnSO_4 + 2H_2O + \underset{\text{Reddish brown}}{Br_2\uparrow}$$

(iii) $NaBr + AgNO_3 \longrightarrow \underset{\text{Pale yellow}}{AgBr\downarrow} NaNO_3$

$$AgBr + 2NH_4OH \longrightarrow \underset{\substack{\text{Diammine}\\\text{silver (I)}\\\text{bromide}}}{[Ag(NH_3)_2]Br} + 2H_2O$$

Concept ladder

Br^- ion can be also detected by **Layer test.**

Mixture + Cl_2 water (add carefully) + $CHCl_3$ $\xrightarrow{\text{Shake}}$ yellowish orange colour in $CHCl_3$ layer [CS_2 or CCl_4 can be taken instead of $CHCl_3$]

$$2NaBr + Cl_2 \longrightarrow 2NaCl + \underset{\substack{\text{Orange yellow}\\ \text{soluble in } CHCl_3}}{Br_2}$$

In case of iodide ion, violet colour of I_2 in $CHCl_3$ layer is obtained.

$$2NaI + Cl_2 \longrightarrow 2NaCl + I_2 \text{ (violet)}$$

III. Test for Iodide Ion (I^-)

The test for iodide ions can be carried out as

S.No.	Experiment	Observation	Inference
1.	Heat the mixture with 1-3 mL conc. H_2SO_4 in a dry test tube	Dark violet fumes (I_2) are evolved	I^- may be present
2.	Heat the mixture with MnO_2 and conc H_2SO_4	Violet vapours in excess are evolved	I^- may be present
3.	Take a paper dipped in starch solution on the mouth of test tube	Paper turns blue	I^- confirmed
4.	To the solution of mixture in dil. HNO_3, add $AgNO_3$ solution	A yellow ppt. of AgI is formed (insoluble in NH_4OH)	I^- confirmed

Reactions Involved in the Test of Iodide (I^-)

(i) $NaI + \underset{\text{Conc.}}{H_2SO_4} \longrightarrow HI + NaHSO_4$

$H_2SO_4 + 2HI \longrightarrow \underset{\substack{\text{Violet}\\ \text{vapours}}}{I_2\uparrow} + SO_2 + 2H_2O$

(ii) $2NaI + MnO_2 + 2H_2SO_4 \longrightarrow I_2\uparrow + 2NaHSO_4 + MnSO_4 + 2H_2O$

(iii) I_2 + Starch $\longrightarrow$ Blue colour

(iv) $NaI + AgNO_3 \longrightarrow \underset{\text{Yellow}}{AgI\downarrow} + NaNO_3$

IV. Test for Nitrate Ion (NO_3^-)

The test for NO_3^- ion can be carried out as

S.No.	Experiment	Observation	Inference
1.	Heat the mixture with 1-2 mL conc H_2SO_4 in a dry test tube	Pungent light brown gas (NO_2) is evolved	NO_3^- may be present
2.	Heat the mixture with copper turnings and conc H_2SO_4	Deep brown fumes (NO_2) in excess are evolved	NO_3^- may be present
3.	Ring test to the solution of mixture in cold and dil. HCl, add freshly prepared solution of $FeSO_4$. Shake well gradually and add conc H_2SO_4 by the sides of test-tube	A brown ring of $FeSO_4 \cdot NO$ is formed at the junction of two liquids	NO_3^- confirmed

Reactions Involved in the Test of Nitrate (NO_3^-)

(i) $NaNO_3 + \underset{\text{Conc.}}{H_2SO_4} \longrightarrow NaHSO_4 + HNO_3$

$4HNO_3 \longrightarrow \underset{\text{(Brown fumes)}}{4NO_2\uparrow} + O_2\uparrow + 2H_2O$

(ii) $3Cu + 8HNO_3 \longrightarrow 3Cu(NO_3)_2 + 2NO\uparrow + 4H_2O$

$2NO + O_2 \longrightarrow 2NO_2\uparrow$

(iii) **Ring test**

$6FeSO_4 + 2HNO_3 + 3H_2SO_4 \longrightarrow 3Fe_2(SO_4)_3 + 4H_2O + 2NO\uparrow$

$FeSO_4 + NO \longrightarrow \underset{\substack{\text{Ferrous nitroso}\\ \text{sulphate}\\ \text{(brown ring)}}}{FeSO_4{\cdot}NO} \text{ or } [Fe(H_2O)_5NO]SO_4$

Concept ladder

The colour is due to charge transfer. This complex formally contains Fe (+I) and NO^+ since, Fe(II) gains one electron from NO which changes to NO^+. Its magnetic moment is 3.87 BM confirming the presence of three unpaired electrons. Nitrites gives the brown colour before H_2SO_4 is added.

$NO \longrightarrow NO^+ + e^-$

$Fe^{2+} + e^- \longrightarrow Fe^+$ ($3d^7 4s^0$, but not $3d^6 4s^1$)

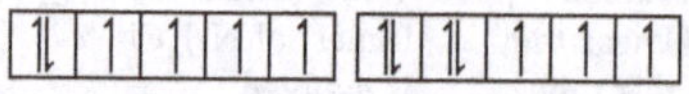

The ring test is unreliable in the presence of bromide, iodide, nitrite, chlorate and chromate, hence must be removed before ring-test of NO_3^- is performed.

3. Analysis of Third Group Anion (SO_4^{2-})

Third group radical is identified on the basis of precipitate obtained.

Tests for Sulphate (SO_4^{2-})

The test for SO_4^{2-} ion can be carried out as

Radical or anion	Experiment	Observation	Inference
Sulphate (SO_4^{2-})	In the solution of mixture, add $BaCl_2$ solution.	A curdy white ppt. ($BaSO_4$) is formed (insoluble in all conc acids)	May be SO_4^{2-} present
	In the solution of mixture, add lead acetate solution.	White ppt. of $PbSO_4$ is formed.	SO_4^{2-} confirmed

Reactions Involved in the above Test of Sulphate (SO_4^{2-})

- $Na_2SO_4 + BaCl_2 \longrightarrow \underset{\text{White}}{BaSO_4\downarrow} + 2NaCl$
- $(CH_3COO)_2Pb + Na_2SO_4 \longrightarrow \underset{\text{White}}{PbSO_4\downarrow} + 2CH_3COONa$

Analysis of Basic Radicals

Basic radicals, i.e. cations are classified into six groups on the basis of their behaviour against some reagents (group reagent). Classification is based on whether a cation reacts with these reagents by the formation of precipitate or not. Classification of basic radicals into groups based on K_{sp} values of the respective precipitates.

Group	Basic radicals	Group reagent	Precipitate as	Explanation
I	Ag^+, Hg_2^{2+} (I), Pb^{2+}	Dil. HCl, cold	Chlorides (AgCl, Hg_2Cl_2, $PbCl_2$)	K_{sp} values of chlorides are low, hence precipitated. Others have higher K_{sp} values hence, not precipitated.
II	Cu^{2+}, Cd^{2+}, Pb^{2+}, Hg, (II), Bi^{3+}, Sb^{3+}, Sn^{2+}, As^{3+}	H_2S gas in presence of dil. HCl	Sulphides (CuS, As_2S_3 etc.)	K_{sp} values of sulphides are low hence, precipitated by low $[S^{2-}]$ ion. HCl (with common H^+ ion) decreases ionisation of H_2S which gives low $[S^{2-}]$. Hence, II group sulphides are precipitated. Others with higher K_{sp} values are not precipitated here.
III	Al^{3+}, Cr^{3+}, Fe^{3+}	NH_4OH in presence of NH_4Cl	Hydroxides, $Al(OH)_3$ etc.	K_{sp} values of $Al(OH)_3$ etc are low. NH_4Cl (with common NH_4^+ ion) decreases ionisation of NH_4OH giving low $[OH^-]$. Hence, group III hydroxides are precipitated.
IV	Zn^{2+}, Ni^{2+}, Mn^{2+}, Co^{2+}	H_2S in ammoniacal medium	Sulphides (ZnS, NiS etc.)	K_{sp} values of sulphides of group IV are high hence, precipitation takes place in higher $[S^{2-}]$. Basic medium increases ionisation of H_2S, thus increasing $[S^{2-}]$ hence, precipitation of group IV sulphides.
V	Ca^{2+}, Ba^{2+}, Sr^{2+}	$(NH_4)_2CO_3 + NH_4Cl$	Carbonates ($CaCO_3$, $BaCO_3$) etc.	K_{sp} values of carbonate are less than that of group IV (Mg^{2+}) hence precipitation before Mg^{2+}.
VI	Mg^{2+}, (Na^+, K^+) also included	$NH_4OH + Na_2HPO_4$ (only for Mg^{2+})	White ppt ($MgHPO_4$)	—
0 (zero)	NH_4^+	Dil. NaOH, Δ	NH_3 gas is involved	—

Preparation of Original Solution

To prepare the original solution (OS), the following solvents tried or used one after the other in the systematic order. It means, if the salt does not dissolve in a particular solvent, even on heating and try the next one. This solution must be transparent and should not have any suspended particles. List of solvents are given below

Distilled water (cold, hot), Dilute HCl (cold, hot), Conc. HCl (cold, hot)

Mentor's TiP

Dil. HNO_3 or H_2SO_4 cannot be used in place HCl. The reason is H_2SO_4 causes the precipitation of Pb^{2+}, Ba^{2+}, Sr^{2+}, Ca^{2+} as insoluble sulphates whereas, HNO_3 is an oxidising agent and can bring about the oxidation of H_2S to give yellow precipitate of S in the second group.

Analysis of Group I Cations

- In cold original solution, dilute HCl is added drop by drop. Formation of white precipitate indicates the presence of group I cations. Cations of group I are precipitated as chlorides like AgCl, $PbCl_2$ and Hg_2Cl_2.
- If no precipitate is formed, the group I cations are absent.
- Precipitates are separated and the filterate is kept for analysis of group II.
- Among these chlorides, only $PbCl_2$ is soluble in hot water and thus, separated.
- AgCl is soluble in aqueous ammonia as $[Ag(NH_3)_2]Cl$ (diammine silver chloride)
- Hg_2Cl_2 gives black coloured compound ($HgNH_2Cl$) with NH_3.

$$Hg_2Cl_2 + 2NH_3 \longrightarrow \underset{\text{Black}}{HgNH_2Cl} + Hg + NH_4Cl$$

The confirmatory tests for Pb^{2+} are given below

Test	Procedure	Observation and inference	Chemistry involved
Test for Pb^{2+}			
(i) Potassium chromate solution	$PbCl_2$ ppt. dissolves (in hot water) + Add K_2CrO_4 solution	Yellow ppt. of $PbCrO_4$ is formed which is soluble in NaOH but insoluble in CH_3COOH	$\underset{\text{Hot}}{PbCl_2} + K_2CrO_4 \longrightarrow \underset{\text{Yellow ppt.}}{PbCrO_4\downarrow} + 2KCl$
(ii) Potassium chromate solution	$PbCl_2$ ppt dissolves (in hot water) + Add KI solution	Yellow ppt of lead iodide is obtained, it confirms the presence of Pb^{2+} ions	$\underset{\text{Hot}}{PbCl_2} + 2KI \longrightarrow \underset{\text{Yellow ppt.}}{PbI_2\downarrow} + 2KCl$
(iii) Sodium hydroxide solution	Dissolve $PbCrO_4$ in hot NaOH solution	Pb^{2+} ions give a white ppt of lead hydroxide. This ppt is soluble in excess of NaOH and form ions of tetrahydroxidoplumbate(II)	$\underset{\text{White}}{Pb^{2+}} + 2OH^- \longrightarrow \underset{\text{White ppt.}}{Pb(OH)_2\downarrow}$ $Pb(OH)_2 + 2OH^- \longrightarrow \underset{\text{Soluble}}{[Pb(OH)_4]^{2-}}$ $PbCrO_4 + 4NaOH \longrightarrow \underset{\text{Sodium tetrahydroxido plumbate (II)}}{Na_2[Pb(OH)_4]} + Na_2CrO_4$

Concept ladder

AgCl dissolves in NH_4OH and forms diamminesilver(I) chloride. When HI is added to complex solution, a yellow ppt. is obtained and it is the test for Ag^+ ion which is a cation of group I.

$$AgCl + 2NH_4OH \longrightarrow \underset{\text{diamminesilver(I) chloride}}{[Ag(NH_3)_2]Cl} + 2H_2O \xrightarrow{KI} \underset{\text{Yellow ppt.}}{AgI\downarrow} + KCl + 2NH_3$$

Analysis of Group II Cations

Group IIA Hg^{2+}, Pb^{2+}, Bi^{3+}, Cu^{2+}, Cd^{2+}

Group IIB As^{3+}, Sb^{3+}, Sn^{2+}, Sn^{4+}

Group reagent H_2S gas in presence of dil. HCl

Procedure Pass H_2S gas in presence of dil. HCl through solution from which group-I is removed.

Observation	Sulphides of IIA and IIB
Yellow ppt.	CdS, As_2S_3, SnS_2
Brown ppt.	SnS
Orange ppt.	Sb_2S_3
Black ppt.	HgS, PbS, Be_2S_3, CuS

The confirmatory tests for Cu^{2+} are as follows

Test for Cu^{2+}	Black ppt. of CuS is taken in the test tube and add HNO_3.	Blue coloured solution is obtained which indicates the presence of Cu^{2+}.	$\underset{\text{Black ppt.}}{3CuS} + 8HNO_3 \longrightarrow \underset{\text{Soluble (blue)}}{3Cu(NO_3)_2} + 2NO + 3S + 4H_2O$
	Blue solution obtained above is divided into 3 parts.		
	(i) Add CH_3COOH and $K_4[Fe(CN)_6]$ to first part	Chocolate brown ppt. is formed, confirming Cu^{2+}	$Cu(NO_3)_2 + 2CH_3COOH \longrightarrow (CH_3COO)_2Cu + 2HNO_3$ $2(CH_3COO)_2Cu + K_4[Fe(CN)_6] \longrightarrow \underset{\text{Chocolate brown ppt.}}{Cu_2[Fe(CN)_6]} + 4CH_3COOK$
	(ii) Add aqueous NH_3 (excess) in second part of the blue solution	Deep blue solution is obtained, confirming Cu^{2+}	$Cu^{2+} + \underset{\text{Excess}}{4NH_3} \longrightarrow \underset{\text{Deep blue}}{[Cu(NH_3)_4]^{2+}}$
	(iii) Add KSCN is the third part of the blue solution	Black ppt. is obtained confirming Cu^{2+}	$Cu(NO_3)_2 + 2KSCN \longrightarrow \underset{\text{Black ppt.}}{Cu(SCN)_2\downarrow} + 2KNO_3$

Analysis of Group III Cations

Group basic radicals Fe^{+3}, Al^{+3}, Cr^{+3}

Group reagent $NH_4OH + NH_4Cl$

Procedure - Take salt, add few drops of concentrated HNO_3 and boil the solution and then add NH_4Cl and NH_4OH slowly.

Observation	
$Fe(OH)_3$	Reddish brown precipitate
$Cr(OH)_3$	Green precipitate
$Al(OH)_3$	White precipitate

The confirmatory tests of Fe^{3+} and Al^{3+} are as follows

	Procedure	Observational Inference	Chemistry Involved
Test for Fe^{3+} ion	Reddish brown ppt. of ferric hydroxide is dissolved in HCl. Divide the solution into two parts.	Ferric chloride is obtained.	$Fe(OH)_3 + 3HCl \longrightarrow FeCl_3 + 3H_2O$
	(i) Ferric chloride solution is treated with potassium ferrocyanide solution.	Prussian blue precipitate is obtained due to the formation of ferri ferrocyanide, confirming Fe^{3+} ion.	$4FeCl_3 + 3K_4[Fe(CN)_6] \longrightarrow \underset{\text{Prussian blue ppt. (ferri ferrocyanide)}}{Fe_4[Fe(CN)_6]_3\downarrow} + 12KCl$
	(ii) Potassium thiocyanate is added to $FeCl_3$ solution.	Blood red colouration is obtained (due to the reaction between Fe^{3+} and thiocyanate ions). It confirms the presence of Fe^{3+} ion.	$FeCl_3 + 3NH_4SCN \longrightarrow \underset{\text{red}}{Fe(SCN)_3} + 3NH_4Cl$
Test for Al^{3+} ion	Add NaOH to $AlCl_3$ solution	White gelatinous precipitate of aluminium hydroxide is produced. It is soluble in excess of NaOH due to sodium meta-aluminate formation.	$AlCl_3 + 3NaOH \longrightarrow Al(OH)_3\downarrow + 3NaCl$ $\underset{\text{White ppt.}}{Al(OH)_3} + NaOH \longrightarrow \underset{\text{Sodium meta-aluminate}}{NaAlO_2} + 2H_2O$
Lake test	White ppt. of $Al(OH)_3$ ↓ dissolved in dilute HCl ↓ Add 2-3 drops of blue litmus solution ↓ Add NH_4OH dropwise	$AlCl_3$ is formed ↓ A blue precipitate is obtained. The reason is : $Al(OH)_3$ adsorbs blue colour from the solution and forms insoluble adsorption complex known as lake. Hence, a blue mass floating in the colourless solution is obtained. Therefore, this test is called lake test.	$NaAlO_2 + 4HCl \longrightarrow AlCl_3 + NaCl + 2H_2O$ $AlCl_3 + 3NH_4OH \xrightarrow{\Delta} \underset{\text{(adsorbent)}}{Al(OH)_3\downarrow} + 3NH_4Cl$

Analysis of Group IV Cations

Group basic radicals Ni^{2+}, Co^{2+}, Mn^{2+}, Zn^{2+}

Group reagent H_2S gas in the presence of NH_4Cl and NH_4OH

Procedure

(i) Take salt solution and pass H_2S gas in presence of NH_4Cl and NH_4OH or take the filtrate of group III and concentrate it by heating, then add NH_4OH and pass H_2S gas.

(ii) Pass more amount of H_2S when precipitate is formed.

Observation	
NiS	Black precipitate
CoS	Black precipitate
MnS	Light pink a coloured precipitate
ZnS	White precipitate

Test	Procedure	Observation and inference	Chemistry involved
Test for Ni^{2+}	Dissolves NiS in *aqua-regia* ↓ Evaporate it to dryness ↓ Extract the dried mass with H_2O ↓ Add NH_4OH in excess ↓ Add few drops of dimethyl glyoxime solution	A rose red ppt. of Ni-DMG complex is obtained.	$3NiS + \underset{Aqua\text{-}regia}{[2HNO_3 + 6HCl]} \longrightarrow 3NiCl_2 + 2NO + 3S + 4H_2O$ $NiCl_2 + 2NH_4OH + \underset{(DMG)}{\begin{matrix} H_3C—C=N—OH \\ \vert \\ H_3C—C=N—OH \end{matrix}} \longrightarrow$ 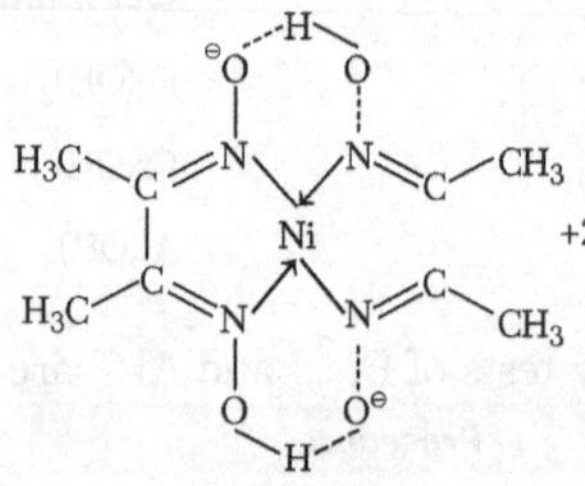 $+2NH_4Cl + 2H_2O$ Rose red colour complex (stable).
Test for Zn^{2+}	(i) Dissolve white ppt of ZnS in dil. HCl ↓ Add NaOH ↓ Dissolve it in excess of NaOH ↓ Pass H_2S gas in solution	$ZnCl_2$ solution is formed White gelatinous ppt of $Zn(OH)_2$ soluble in excess of NaOH forming $NaZnO_2(aq)$.	$ZnS + 2HCl \longrightarrow ZnCl_2 + H_2S$ $ZnCl_2 + 2NaOH \longrightarrow Zn(OH)_2\downarrow + 2NaCl$ $Zn(OH)_2 + 2NaOH \longrightarrow \underset{\text{Sodium zincate}}{Na_2ZnO_2} + 2H_2O$
Potassium ferrocyanide test	(ii) Treat $ZnCl_2$ with potassium ferrocyanide	A white ppt. of zinc ferrocyanide is obtained.	$2ZnCl_2 + K_4[Fe(CN)_6] \longrightarrow \underset{\text{Zinc ferrocyanide}}{Zn_2[Fe(CN)_6]}\downarrow + 4KCl$

Analysis of Group V Cations

Group basic radicals (Ba^{2+}, Sr^{2+}, Ca^{2+})

$$\text{Filtrate of group IV} \xrightarrow[\text{(ii) } NH_4OH,\ (NH_4)_2CO_3]{\text{(i) Boil of } H_2S} \text{White ppt.}$$

$BaCO_3$, $CaCO_3$, $SrCO_3$ appear as white ppt.

Flame test Perform flame test with these group ppt.

Apple green flame-Ba^{2+}

Crimson red-Sr^{2+}

Brick red-Ca^{2+}

Dissolve the ppt. in CH_3COOH

The confirmatory tests for Ba^{2+} and Ca^{2+} ions are as follows

Test	Procedure	Observation and inference	Chemistry involved
Test for Ba^{2+}	Dissolved barium carbonate in acetic acid ↓ Treat it with potassium chromate	Barium acetate is formed ↓ A yellow ppt. of barium chromate is produced	$BaCO_3 + 2CH_3COOH \longrightarrow (CH_3COO)_2Ba + H_2O + CO_2$ $(CH_3COO)_2Ba + K_2CrO_4 \longrightarrow \underset{\text{Yellow ppt.}}{BaCrO_4}\downarrow + 2CH_3COOK$

Test for Ca^{2+}	Dissolve calcium carbonate in acetic acid ↓ Add ammonium oxalate ↓ White ppt acidified with dil. CH_3COOH ↓ Add $KMnO_4$ solution and HCl	Calcium acetate is formed ↓ White ppt of calcium oxalate is formed ↓ Pink colour of $KMnO_4$ disappears confirming Ca^{2+}	$CaCO_3 + 2CH_3COOH \longrightarrow (CH_3COO)_2Ca\downarrow + H_2O + CO_2\uparrow$ $(CH_3COO)_2Ca + \underset{\text{Ammonium oxalate}}{(NH_4)_2C_2O_4} \longrightarrow \underset{\text{White ppt}}{(COO)_2Ca\downarrow} + 2CH_3COONH_4$ $5(COO)_2Ca + \underset{\text{Pink}}{2KMnO_4} + 16HCl \longrightarrow 5CaCl_2 + \underset{\text{Colourless}}{2MnCl_2} + 10CO_2\uparrow + 8H_2O + 2KCl$

Analysis of Group VI Cation (Mg^{2+})

The confirmatory test for Mg^{2+} ion is as follows

Test	Procedure	Observation and inference	Chemistry involved
Test for Mg^{2+}	The filtrate of group (V) is made alkaline by adding NH_4OH ↓ Add disodium hydrogen phosphate (Na_2HPO_4)	White precipitate of $Mg(NH_4)PO_4$ is obtained.	$Mg^{2+} + Na_2HPO_4 + NH_4OH$ ↓ $\underset{\text{Magnesium ammonium phosphate (white ppt)}}{Mg(NH_4)PO_4}\downarrow + 2Na^+ + H_2O$

Analysis of Group Zero Cation (NH_4^+)

Ammonium salts are decomposed by alkali and NH_3 is liberated which can be identified by the following methods:

Test	Procedure	Observation and inference	Chemistry involved
Test for NH_4^+	Add 1-2 mL NaOH in salt ↓ Heat it	Smell of ammonia gas is evolved due to the formation of ammonium chloride, it is visible as dense white fumes. When comes in contact with HCl wetted glass rod. It confirms the presence of NH_4^+ ions.	$(NH_4)_2SO_4 + 2NaOH \longrightarrow Na_2SO_4 + 2NH_3 + 2H_2O$ $NH_3 + HCl \longrightarrow \underset{\text{White fumes}}{NH_4Cl}$
	Treat the aqueous solution of ammoniam salt with **Nessler's reagent.**	A red or brown precipitate or colour is obtained due to the formation of iodide of Millon's base	$2K_2HgI_4 + 3KOH + NH_3 \longrightarrow$ 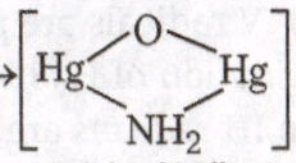 $I + 7KI + 2H_2O$ Iodide of Million's base (brown ppt.)

NEET Close-up

Example Similar to PYQ Asked in NEET 2024

Given below are certain cations using inorganic qualitative analysis, arrange them in increasing group number from 0 to VI.

A. Pb^{2+} B. Cr^{3+} C. Zn^{2+} D. NH_4^+ E. Ba^{2+}

Choose the correct answer from the options given below.

(a) C, B, A, D, E
(b) D, A, B, C, E
(c) B, E, A, D, C
(d) A, C, E, D, B

Sol. (*b*) Basic radical Group number

A. $Pb^{2+} \longrightarrow$ I and II (A)
B. $Cr^{3+} \longrightarrow$ III
C. $Zn^{2+} \longrightarrow$ IV
D. $NH_4^+ \longrightarrow$ Zero
E. $Ba^{2+} \longrightarrow$ V

Hence, the correct order is D, A, B, C, E.

Skill Builder

Given below are certain cations. Using inorganic qualitative analysis, arrange them in increasing group number from 0 to VI.

A. Fe^{3+} B. Ni^{2+} B. Sr^{2+}
D. Cu^{2+} E. Ca^{2+}

Choose the correct answer from the options given below.

(a) A, B = C, D, E
(b) C, D, E, A = B
(c) D, A, B = E, C
(d) D, A, B, C = E

For more practice Refer for Q.8 in Gearing up for NEET.

STEP UP Practice 1

1 Which metal salt gives a violet coloured bead in the borax bead test ?
(a) Cu^{2+} (b) Al^{3+} (c) Mn^{2+} (d) Co^{2+}

2 Borax bead test of salt (M) is performed, violet colour of the bead is obtained under oxidising flame. What is the oxidation state of the cation present in salt (M) ?
(a) + 7 (b) + 4
(c) + 2 (d) + 5

3 Which of the following cations is correctly matched according to the colour given in flame test ?
(a) $Cu^{2+} \longrightarrow$ Violet (b) $Ca^{2+} \longrightarrow$ Brick red
(c) $Ba^{2+} \longrightarrow$ Golden yellow (d) $Sr^{2+} \longrightarrow$ Green

4 Consider the following statements.
Statement I In charcoal cavity test, first metallic oxides is formed followed by metallic carbonates.
Statement II The metallic oxides formed in this test is reduced to metals by the action of carbon present in reducing flame.
In the light of the above statements, choose the most appropriate answer from the option given below :
(a) Both Statement I and Statement II are false.
(b) Statement I is true but Statement II is false.
(c) Statement I is false but Statement II is true.
(d) Both Statement I and Statement II are true.

5 Sometimes, yellow turbidity appears on passing H_2S gas even in the absence of group II radicals. This is because of
(a) sometimes group III radicals are precipitated as phosphates
(b) group IV radicals are precipitated as sulphides
(c) the oxidation of H_2S into S gas by some acid radicals
(d) group III radicals are precipitated as hydroxides

6 Consider the following compounds.
(i) Sodium acetate (ii) Sodium chloride
(iii) Sodium nitrate (iv) Sodium hydrogen phosphate
(v) Sodium hydroxide
How many of them give(s) a precipitate with cold $Pb(NO_3)_2$ solution but not with $Ba(NO_3)_2$?
(a) 1 (b) 3 (c) 3 (d) 4

7 Which of the following cations is correctly matched with the given group ?
(a) $Zn^{2+} \longrightarrow$ Group IV (b) $NH_4^+ \longrightarrow$ Group V
(c) $Mg^{2+} \longrightarrow$ Zero group (d) $Ni^{2+} \longrightarrow$ Group V

8 An aqueous solution of colourless metal sulphate 'M' gives a white precipitate with NH_4OH. This was soluble in excess of NH_4OH. On passing H_2S through this solution, a white ppt. is formed. The metal in the salt 'M' is
(a) Ca (b) Ba
(c) Al (d) Zn

9 Which reagent can be used to identify nickel ion ?
(a) Resorcinol (b) Dimethyl glyoxime
(c) Diphenyl benzidine (d) Potassium ferrocyanide

10 A white sodium salt dissolves readily in water to give a solution which is neutral to litmus. When silver nitrate solution is added to the solution, a white precipitate is obtained which does not dissolve in dil. HNO_3. The anion could be
(a) CO_3^{2-} (b) Cl^- (c) SO_4^{2-} (d) S^{2-}

11 The gas liberated on treating a mixture of two salts with dil. H_2SO_4 turns lime water milky and turbidity disappears with the passage of excess of gas. The aqueous solution of mixture gives white crystalline ppt. with cold NaCl solution. The filtrate gives a black precipitate, when H_2S is passed into it. The aqueous solution of mixture on heating gives reddish brown gas and when treated with ammonium hydroxide and excess of disodium hydrogen phosphate gives a white crystalline precipitate. The mixture contains
(a) $CO_3^{2-}, Pb^{2+}, NO_3^{2-}, Mg^{2+}$ (b) $CO_3^{2-}, Pb^{2+}, NO_3^{2-}, Ca^{2+}$
(c) $CO_3^{2-}, Pb^{2+}, Cl^-, Mg^{2+}$ (d) $CO_3^{2-}, Pb^{2+}, Cl^-, Ca^{2+}$

12 The best way to ensure complete precipitation from saturated $H_2S(aq)$ of a metal ion M^{2+}, as its sulphide, $MS(s)$, is to
(a) add on acid (b) increase $[H_2S]$ in solution
(c) raise the pH (d) heat the solution

13 X is a colourless salt giving following reactions:

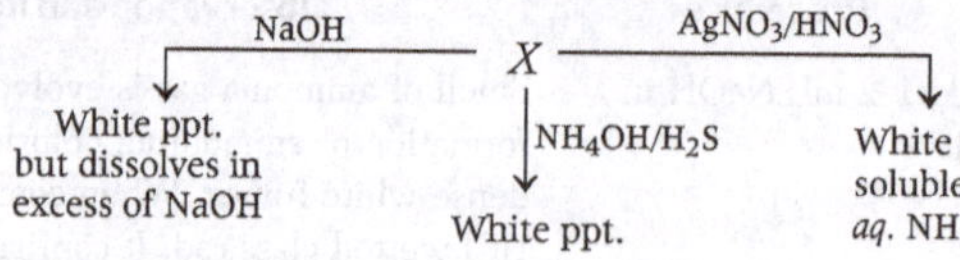

X can be
(a) $AlCl_3$ (b) $ZnCl_2$
(c) $Zn(CH_3COO)_2$ (d) $ZnBr_2$

14 Consider the following statements
Statement I Dissolve a white ppt. of $CaCO_3$ in acetic acid, heat it gently and then add ammonium oxalate solution in excess, appearance of a grey ppt. confirms the presence of Ca^{2+} cation.
Statement II Addition of NH_4OH and dimethyl glyoxime to $NiCl_2$, a cherry red precipitation confirms the presence of Ni^{2+} cation.
In the light of the above statements, choose the most appropriate answer from the option given below :
(a) Both Statement I and Statement II are false.
(b) Statement I is true but Statement II is false.
(c) Statement I is false but Statement II is true.
(d) Both Statement I and Statement II are true.

15 A salt gives violet vapours when treated with conc. H_2SO_4, it contains,
(a) Cl^- (b) Br^- (c) I^- (d) NO_3^-

16 The solution of sodium meta-aluminate on boiling with ammonium chloride gives a white precipitate of
(a) Al_2O_3 (b) $AlCl_3$
(c) $Al(OH)_3$ (d) $NaAl(OH)_4$

Module 2

Chemistry Involved in Titration, Preparation of Inorganic Compounds

• Acid-Base Indicators • Acid-Base Titration • Redox Titration • Mohr's salt • Potash Alum

Chemistry Involved in Titration

Titration is a common method of a quantitative chemical analysis. It is used to determine the unknown concentration of a known compound (analyte). As volume measurements play a key role in titration, it is also called **volumetric analysis.**

Terminologies Related to Titration

(i) **Titrant** It is a substance (as a reagent solution of precisely known concentration) that is added in titration.

(ii) **Titration volume** During the process of titration, the volume of titrant reacted is called as titration volume.

(iii) **Standard solution** A solution containing a precisely known concentration of an element or substance is called as standard solution. These are of two types, i.e. primary standard solution and secondary standard solution.

(a) **Primary standard solution** If concentration of substance can be known simply by dissolving its known amount in a given volume of solution. Then the solutions formed as primary standard solutions, e.g. oxalic acid, potassium dichromate.

(b) **Secondary standard solution** When concentration of solution can be determined by standardisation against primary standard solution. Such solutions are called secondary standard solution, i.e. H_2SO_4, $KMnO_4$ etc.

(c) **Equivalence point and End point** It is the volume of added titrant at which the number of equivalents of titrant is equal to the number of equivalents of analyte. It indicates the theoretical completion of reaction.

End point is the point of completion of the reaction indicated by suitable indicator.

Mentor's TiP

The volume of titrant at the end point is larger than the volume of titrant at the equivalence point.

Acid-Base Indicators

A substance that changes colour in response to a chemical change. An acid-base indicator changes colour depending on the pH. Thus, these are the substances which possess one colour, in acid solution and different colour in alkaline medium.

The acid-base indicator basically indicates the end point of the titration by changing colour. Some common indicators, their colours and the pH range in which they change colour are given in the following table:

pH Range and Colours of Some Common Indicators

S.No.	Indicator	pH range	Colour in acid solution	Colour in alkaline solution
1.	Thymol blue	1.2-2.8	Red	Yellow
2.	Bromophenol blue	3.1-4.6	Yellow	Purple
3.	Methyl orange	3.1-4.5	Red	Yellow
4.	Methyl red	4.2-6.3	Red	Yellow
5.	Bromothymol blue	6.0-7.5	Orange	Blue
6.	Phenol red	6.4-8.2	Yellow	Red
7.	Thymol blue (base)	8.1-9.6	Yellow	Blue
8.	Phenolphthalein	8.0-9.8	Colourless	Pink
9.	Thymophthalein	9.3-10.5	Colourless	Blue
10.	Alizarin yellow	10.1-12.1	Yellow	Lilac

Acid-Base Titration

(Neutralisation Method of Analysis)

Acid-base titrations involves a neutralisation reaction between an acid and a base in which acid reacts with equivalent amount of base.

The reaction is characterised by a rapid change in pH near the equivalence point, which is detected by the colour change of indication that occurs at the end point. It is a common method of determining the amount of acids, bases or salts of weak bases or acids in an unknown sample.

The analysis can be done by neutralisation method which may be grouped in two general classes.

- Determination of acid or base or their anhydride in a sample by titrating with a standard solution of base or acid.
- Determination of salts of weak acids or bases by titrating with a standard solution of a strong base or acid.

The titration of a very weak base with strong acid and a titration of a very weak acid with strong base can not be performed because a sharp end point cannot be observed for them. Usually when an acid is too weak to be titrated with a standard base, a salt of acid can be titrated with standard acid solution. e.g. Carbonic acid cannot be titrated by sodium hydroxide quantitatively, but sodium carbonate can be titrated by hydrochloric acid or sulphuric acid.

$$CO_3^{2-} + 2H^+ \longrightarrow H_2O + CO_2$$

Indicators in Acid-Base Titrations

S.No.	Acid-base titrations	Indicators
1.	Strong acid *vs* strong base	Bromothymol blue, phenolphthalein methyl orange, thymophthalein
2.	Strong acid *vs* weak base	Methyl orange, methyl red, bromocresol green
3.	Weak acid *vs* strong base	Phenolphthalein, thymophthalein
4.	Weak acid *vs* weak base	Phenol red

Redox Titrations

Redox reactions are based on reduction-oxidation reaction between an oxidising and a reducing agent. Thus, the concentration of reducing agents like Fe^{2+} (present in Mohr's salt) H_2O_2, $CaOCl_2$, MnO_2 can be determined by using suitable oxidising agents like $KMnO_4$, $K_2Cr_2O_7$ in acidic or basic or neutral medium. e.g. Fe^{2+} is oxidised to Fe^{2+} by MnO_4^- which in turn is reduced to Mn^{2+} in acidic medium.

$$5Fe^{2+} + MnO_4^- + 8H^+ \longrightarrow Mn^{2+} + 5Fe^{3+} + 4H_2O$$

In all cases, $N_1V_1 = N_2V_2$

But $M_1V_1 \neq M_2V_2$

$$\text{Equivalent weight} = \frac{\text{molecular weight}}{\text{total change in ON}}$$

$$= \frac{\text{molecular weight}}{\text{number of electrons gained or lost}}$$

Some examples of redox titrations are as follows

(i) Titration of Oxalic Acid *vs* $KMnO_4$

The titration of oxalic acid *vs* $KMnO_4$ is a redox titration in which the concentration of oxalic acid (reducing agent) is determined by titrating it with a standard solution of an oxidising agent, $KMnO_4$.

Such reactions are accompained by the change in valency of ions. In these titrations oxidation and reduction take place simultaneously, i.e. while one substance is being oxidised, the other one will be reduced.

$$\underset{\text{Oxidising agent}}{2KMnO_4} + 3H_2SO_4 \longrightarrow K_2SO_4 + 2MnSO_4 + 3H_2O + 5[O]; \left(E_{KMnO_4} = \frac{M}{5}\right)$$

$$5\underset{\text{Reducing agent}}{\begin{vmatrix} COOH \\ COOH \end{vmatrix}} + 5[O] \longrightarrow 5H_2O + 10CO_2\uparrow; \left(E_{H_2C_2O_4} = \frac{M}{2}\right)$$

$KMnO_4$ acts as a self indicator for end point detection.

Mentor's TiP

- Titration with $KMnO_4$ is carried out in the presence of HCl or H_2SO_4 but not in the presence of conc. HNO_3 because it is a strong oxidising agent and hence, interfere with oxidising action of $KMnO_4$.
- In $KMnO_4$ *versus* oxalic acid titration, the oxalic acid solution is heated with dil. H_2SO_4 up to 70-80°C.

(ii) Titration of Mohr's Salt *vs* $KMnO_4$

The titration of Mohr's salt $[FeSO_4 \cdot (NH_4)_2SO_4 \cdot 6H_2O]$ *versus* $KMnO_4$ (acts as an oxidising agent) is also a redox titration.

In this titration, the active constituent of ferrous ammonium sulphate (Mohr's salt) is ferrous sulphate, which is oxidised to ferric sulphate by acidified (with dil. H_2SO_4) potassium permanganate as follows

$$2KMnO_4 + 3H_2SO_4 \longrightarrow K_2SO_4 + 2MnSO_4 + 3H_2O + 5[O]; \left(E_{KMnO_4} = \frac{M}{5}\right)$$

$$[2FeSO_4 + H_2SO_4 + [O] \longrightarrow Fe_2(SO_4)_3 + H_2O] \times 5$$

$$2KMnO_4 + 8H_2SO_4 + 10FeSO_4 \longrightarrow K_2SO_4 + 2MnSO_4 + 5Fe_2(SO_4)_3 + 8H_2O$$

$$\left(E_{FeSO_4} = \frac{M}{1} = E_{\text{Mohr's salt}}\right)$$

$KMnO_4$ acts as self indicator for end point detection. This titration is carried out at room temperature because Mohr's salt is oxidised by air on heating. Sulphuric acid should be present in excess otherwise a brown precipitate (due to the formation of MnO_2) will be formed.

Concept ladder Back titration is sometimes necessary to add an excess of the standard titrant and then, determine the excess amount by back titration with a second titrant. Back titrations are useful in case of precipitation reactions or when the reaction between the analyte and titrant is very slow or when the analyte is an insoluble solid.

Example 1 *Oxalic acid ($H_2C_2O_4$) is found in many plants. If 48.0 mL of 0.02 M $KMnO_4$ solution is required to titrate 1.00g of $H_2C_2O_4$ to the equivalence point. What is the percent by mass of $H_2C_2O_4$ in the sample?*

Sol. Moles of $KMnO_4$ present in 48.0 mL of 0.02 M $KMnO_4$ are

$$= 0.02 \times 48.0$$

$$= 0.96 \times 10^{-3} \text{ mol/KMnO}_4$$

$$2MnO_4^- + 5C_2O_4^{2-} + 16\,H^+ \longrightarrow 10CO_2 + 2Mn^{2+} + 8H_2O$$

∴ Number of moles of pure $C_2O_4^{2-}$, reacted

$$= \frac{5}{2} \times 0.96 \times 10^{-3}$$

$$= 2.4 \times 10^{-3} \text{ mol}$$

Thus, mass of pure oxalic acid $= 2.4 \times 10^{-3} \times 90$

$= 0 \cdot 216$ g in 1.0 g impure oxalic acid

∴ Percentage purity = 21.6 %

Example 2 *Amount of oxalic acid present in a solution can be determined by its titration with $KMnO_4$ solution in the presence of H_2SO_4. The titration gives unsatisfactory result when carried out in the presence of HCl why?*

Sol. The titration of oxalic acid by $KMnO_4$ in the presence of HCl gives unsatisfactory result because HCl is a better reducing agent than oxalic acid and HCl reduces preferably MnO_4^- to Mn^{2+}.

Preparation of Inorganic Compounds

Preparation of Mohr's salt and potash alum given below.

Mohr's Salt

Mohr's salt is chemically ferrous ammonium sulphate hexahydrate [$FeSO_4 \cdot (NH_4)_2SO_4 \cdot 6H_2O$]. As the name suggests, it is a double salt therefore, it is prepared from solutions of ferrous sulphate and ammonium sulphate. When saturated solutions (ferrous sulphate and ammonium sulphate) are mixed together, evaporated and cooled, light green crystals of Mohr's salt are obtained.

$$(NH_4)_2SO_4 + FeSO_4 + 6H_2O \longrightarrow \underset{\text{Mohr's salt}}{FeSO_4 \cdot (NH_4)_2SO_4 \cdot 6H_2O}$$

During the preparation of ferrous sulphate solution in boiling water, dilute H_2SO_4 in small amount is also added to boiling water to prevent the hydrolysis of ferrous sulphate, i.e. to prevent conversion of ferrous sulphate into ferrous hydroxide.

Potash Alum

Chemically potash alum is $K_2SO_4 \cdot Al_2(SO_4)_3 \cdot 24H_2O$. It is also a double salt. Potash alum is prepared by dissolving of saturated solution of K_2SO_4 and $Al_2(SO_4)_3$ in equimolar ratio in small amount of water containing some drops of conc. H_2SO_4. On cooling potash alum separates as colourless crystals.

$$K_2SO_4 + Al_2(SO_4)_3 + 24H_2O \longrightarrow K_2SO_4 \cdot Al_2(SO_4)_3 \cdot 24H_2O$$

Example 3 *Alum is found to contain hydrated monovalent cation $[M(H_2O)]^+$, trivalent cation $[M'(H_2O)_6]^{3+}$ and sulphate $[SO_4^{2-}]$. What will be the ratio of these ions in the alum?*

Sol. The general formula for potash alum is $[KAl(SO_4)_2 \cdot 12H_2O]_2$, therefore, the ratio of $[M(H_2O)]^+$, $[M'(H_2O)_6]^{3+}$ and $[SO_4^{2-}]$ is 1 : 1 : 2.

STEP UP Practice 2

1 Which is incorrect about primary standard ?
(a) They are stable in air.
(b) They exist in highly pure state.
(c) They readily dissolve in water.
(d) It is titrated against secondary standard.

2 In the titration of sodium carbonate with hydrochloric acid taken in burette, the indicator used is
(a) phenolphthalein for first equivalence point and methyl orange for second equivalence point
(b) methyl orange for first equivalence point and phenolphthalein for second equivalence point
(c) either methyl orange or phenolphthalein for both equivalence points
(d) phenol red for both equivalence points

3 Consider the following statements.

Statement I Carbonic acid cannot be titrated by sodium hydroxide quantitatively.

Statement II The titration of Na_2CO_3 *vs* HCl is a neutralisation titration which involves the neutralisation of an acid with a base.

In the light of the above statements, choose the most appropriate answer from the options given below.
(a) Both Statement I and Statement II are false.
(b) Statement I is true but Statement II is false.
(c) Statement I is false but Statement II is true.
(d) Both Statement I and Statement II are true.

4

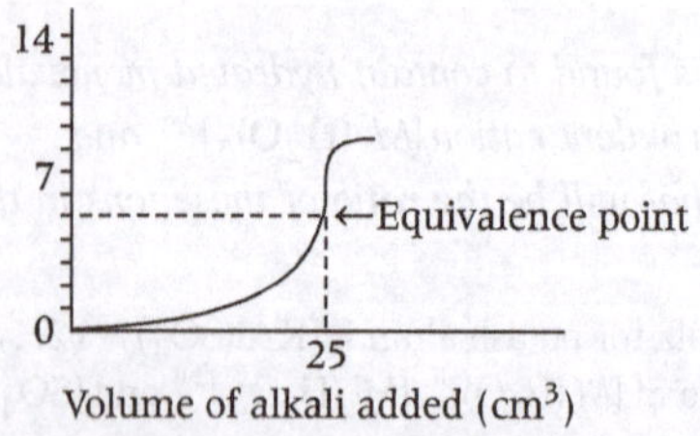

The graph represents titration curve for
(a) strong acid with strong base
(b) weak acid with strong base
(c) strong acid with weak base
(d) the weak acids only

5 Which of the following is correctly matched regarding the equivalent mass of $KMnO_4$ in $KMnO_4$ titration in acidic medium ? [M = molar mass of $KMnO_4$]
(a) Equivalent mass of $KMnO_4 \longrightarrow M$
(b) Equivalent mass of $KMnO_4 \longrightarrow \frac{M}{5}$
(c) Equivalent mass of $KMnO_4 \longrightarrow \frac{M}{2}$
(d) Equivalent mass of $KMnO_4 \longrightarrow \frac{M}{3}$

6 A solution of 10 mL of $\frac{M}{10}$ $FeSO_4$ is titrated with $KMnO_4$ solution in acidic medium, the amount of $KMnO_4$ used will be
(a) 4 mL of 0.1 M
(b) 3 mL of 0.1 M
(c) 10 mL of 0.5 M
(d) 10 mL of 0.02 M

7 Consider the following relations,
(i) $M_{KMnO_4} \times V_{KMnO_4} = 5 \times M_{\text{Mohr's salt}} \times V_{\text{Mohr's salt}}$
(ii) $M_{KMnO_4} = \frac{M_{\text{Mohr's salt}} \times V_{\text{Mohr's salt}}}{V_{KMnO_4}}$
(iii) $V_{KMnO_4} = \frac{M_{\text{Mohr's salt}} \times V_{\text{Mohtr's salt}}}{5 \times M_{KMnO_4}}$
(iv) $V_{\text{Mohr's salt}} = \frac{M_{\text{Mohr's salt}} \times V_{KMnO_4}}{M_{KMnO_4}}$
(v) $M_{\text{Mohr's salt}} = \frac{5 \times M_{KMnO_4} \times V_{KMnO_4}}{V_{\text{Mohr's salt}}}$

How many of them is (are) correct in case of titration of Mohr's salt with $KMnO_4$?
(a) 2
(b) 4
(c) 1
(d) 3

8 Which of the following will oxidise 126 g of oxalic acid ($H_2C_2O_4 \cdot 2H_2O$) in acidic medium ?
(a) 1/3 mole of $K_2Cr_2O_7$
(b) 2 mole of $K_2Cr_2O_7$
(c) 1/3 mole of $KMnO_4$
(d) 5/2 mole of $KMnO_4$

9 In the titration of oxalic acid *vs* potassium permanganate, potassium permanganate acts as
(a) external indicator
(b) self indicator
(c) reductant
(d) auto-catalyst

10 In the titration of $KMnO_4$ with oxalic acid in acidic medium, $KMnO_4$ acts as
(a) an oxidising agent
(b) a reducing agent
(c) an amphoteric
(d) a base

11 Which of the following indicators is used in $KMnO_4$ titrations ?
(a) Methyl orange
(b) Alizarine yellow R
(c) Reducing agent used in titration acts as self-indicator
(d) $KMnO_4$ as a self-indicator

12 Consider the following statements.

Statement I In the preparation of Mohr's salt, sulphuric acid should not be present in excess otherwise a brown precipitate will be formed.

Statement II Mohr's salt is oxidised by air on heating.

In the light of the above statements, choose the most appropriate answer from the option given below.
(a) Both Statement I and Statement II are false.
(b) Statement I is true but Statement II is false.
(c) Statement I is false but Statement II is true.
(d) Both Statement I and Statement II are true.

13 Select the correct match regarding the reaction of Mohr's salt.

(a) 1 mole of Mohr's salt $\longrightarrow$ 2 moles of $KMnO_4$

(b) 1 mole of Mohr's salt $\longrightarrow \frac{1}{2}$ mole of $KMnO_4$

(c) 1 mole of Mohr's salt $\longrightarrow$ 5 moles of $KMnO_4$

(d) 1 mole of Mohr's salt $\longrightarrow \frac{1}{5}$ mole of $KMnO_4$

14 Equivalent mass of Mohr's salt (as a reducing agent) is [M = molar mass of Mohr's salt]

(a) $\frac{M}{3}$ (b) $\frac{2}{5}M$

(c) M (d) $\frac{M}{6}$

15 During the preparation of standard solution of Mohr's salt few drops of conc. H_2SO_4 are added

(a) to make the solution acidic

(b) to neutralise the basic impurities

(c) to prevent the hydrolysis of Mohr's salt

(d) to make the solution neutral

16 Consider the following substances.

(i) Ammonium sulphate (ii) Dil. Sulphuric acid

(iii) Ferrous sulphate (iv) Copper sulphate

(v) Sodium hydroxide

How many of them is(are) used in the preparation of Mohr's salt ?

(a) 2 (b) 4 (c) 1 (d) 3

Module 3

Qualitative Analysis of Organic Compounds and Chemical Principles Involved in Some Important Experiments

- Detection of Functional Groups
- Preparation of Organic Compounds Acetanilide, *p*-nitroacetanilide, Aniline Yellow, Iodoform
- Chemical Principles Involved in Some Important Experiments
- Enthalpy of Neutralisation of Strong Acid and Strong Base
- Preparation of Lyophilic and Lyophobic Solutions
- Kinetic Study of Reaction of Iodide Ion with Hydrogen Peroxide at Room Temperature

Qualitative Analysis of Organic Compounds

The major steps involved in the characterisation of an organic compound are

Detection of special elements (N, S, halogens and P), present in organic compounds.
[Refer : Volume-I, Chapter-13, Module-2]

Detection of Functional Groups Present in Organic Compounds

Elemental detection shows the presence or absence of different elements. On the basis of the present elements, corresponding functional group test is carried out. Organic compounds are classified into different classes based on the presence of functional groups.

The identification of functional group depends basically on the correct determination of the elements. The chemical tests of individual functional groups can be summarised as

1. Carboxylic Group (—COOH) Tests

Carboxylic acids are represented by the general formula RCOOH. Its presence can be detected by the following tests :

(i) **Litmus paper test** If blue litmus paper is dipped in the aqueous solution of an organic compound, the change in colour of blue litmus paper to red shows the presence of carboxylic group.

(ii) **Sodium bicarbonate test** In a test tube take a little quantity of the compound and then, a saturated solution of sodium bicarbonate is added to it.

The formation of a brisk effervescence of CO_2 confirms the presence of carboxylic, —COOH group in the compound.

(iii) **Ester formation** A small quantity of organic compound taken in a test tube is heated with ethyl alcohol and conc. H_2SO_4. The solution is cooled and poured in another tube containing water. A fruity odour (due to formation of an ester) indicates the presence of carboxylic group.

$$R\text{—COOH} + C_2H_5OH \xrightarrow[\text{Conc. } H_2SO_4]{\Delta} \underset{\text{(Fruity odour)}}{RCOOC_2H_5} + H_2O$$

2. Alcoholic Group (—OH) Tests

[–OH attached to aliphatic chain of C-atoms (sp^3)]

The presence of alcoholic group is confirmed by the following tests

(i) **Sodium metal test** A small amount of organic compound is taken in a test tube and a thin slice of sodium metal is added to the test tube. A brisk effervescence of H_2 gas shows the presence of alcoholic group in the compound. The H_2 gas can be tested by bringing a fire match near to it, the gas will burn with a pop sound indicating that the reaction is completed.

$$2ROH + 2Na \longrightarrow 2RONa + H_2\uparrow$$

(ii) **Ester test** The compound is heated with acetic acid in the presence of conc. sulphuric acid. A fruity smell indicates the formation of ester.

$$R\text{—OH} + CH_3COOH \xrightarrow{\text{Conc. } H_2SO_4} CH_3COOR + H_2O$$

(iii) **Ceric ammonium nitrate test** Add a few drops of ceric ammonium nitrate to an aqueous solution of organic compound. The red colouration indicates the presence of alcoholic group in the compound.

$$2R\text{—OH} + (NH_4)_2Ce(NO_3)_6 \longrightarrow 2NH_4NO_3 + \underset{\text{Red complex}}{[(ROH)_2Ce(NO_3)_4]}$$

This test is useful when the compound contains less than ten C-atoms.

(iv) **Lucas test** This test is used to distinguish between primary, secondary and tertiary alcohols. Around 2 mL of organic compound is treated with 8 mL of Lucas reagent [prepared by dissolving 32 g of anhyd. $ZnCl_2$ in 20 mL of conc. HCl] and shake the mixture at 20°C.

- Immediate formation of turbidity confirms the presence of **tertiary alcohol.**
- Formation of turbidity after 4-5 minutes confirms the presence of **secondary alcohol.**
- No turbidity formation confirms the presence of **primary alcohol.**

3. Phenolic Group (Ph—OH) Tests

[–OH attached to benzene nucleus, i.e. phenyl group]

The presence of phenolic group is confirmed by the following tests.

(i) **Ferric chloride test** A few drops of neutral ferric chloride ($FeCl_3$) is added to aqueous solution of an organic compound. The formation of violet colour shows the presence of phenolic group in the compound

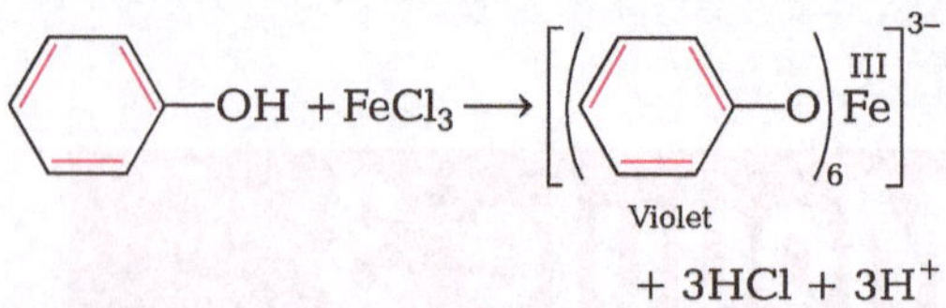

This test is also given by enols.

(ii) **Liebermann's nitroso reaction** A little amount of compound is fused with a crystal of $NaNO_2$ in a test tube. The mixture is cooled and around 1 mL of conc. H_2SO_4 is added to it. A deep green to blue solution is formed which changes to red when poured in a large excess of water. This red solution again changes to deep green or blue if made alkaline with NaOH. This green or blue colouration confirms the phenolic group in the compound.

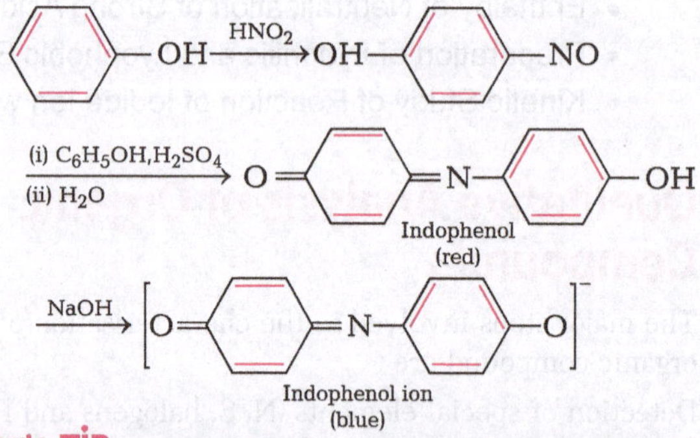

Mentor's Tip

Nitrophenols do not respond to $FeCl_3$ test as well as Liebermann's nitroso reaction.

4. Carbonyl Group (>C=O) Tests

To test the presence of carbonyl group in an organic compound Brady's reagent (Dinitrophenyl hydrazine, DNP) is used. Carbonyl compounds give orange, yellow or red coloured crystalline products with 2, 4-dinitrophenyl hydrazine.

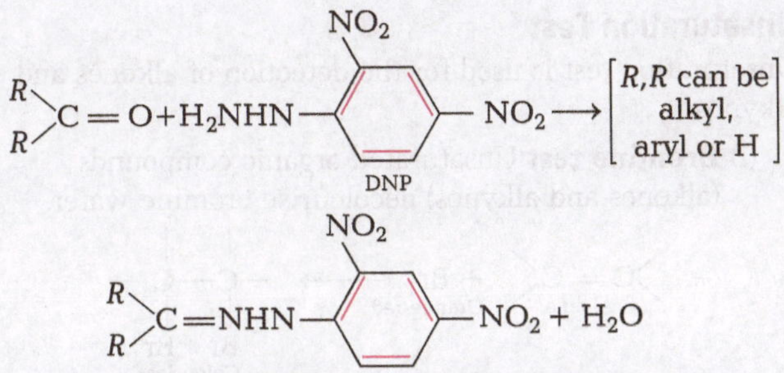

2,4-dinitrophenylhydrazine (yellow/orange/red ppt.)

After confirming the presence of carbonyl group in the compound, individual tests are carried out whether, aldehydic group (—CHO) or ketonic group ($>C=O$) is present in the given compound.

Tests for Aldehydic Group (—CHO)

(i) **Tollen's reagent test** [silver mirror test] A little quantity of the compound is taken in a test tube and than, nearly 2 mL of freshly prepared Tollen's reagent is added to the test tube. Shake, warm and allow the contents to stand for 2-3 minutes. The formation of silver mirror or a grey ppt confirms the presence of an aldehydic group in the compound.

$$2Ag(NH_3)_2OH + RCHO \longrightarrow \underset{\text{Silver mirror}}{2Ag\downarrow} + 3NH_3 + H_2O + RCOO^-NH_4^+$$

(ii) **Fehling's solution test** A mixture of equal amounts of Fehling's solution A[aqueous solution of $CuSO_4$] and Fehling's solution B[alkaline solution of sodium potassium tartarate] and a few drops of organic compound are taken in a test tube and boiled for the few minutes. Formation of red ppt. shows the presence of an aldehyde in the compound.

$$2CuO + RCHO \longrightarrow \underset{\text{Red ppt.}}{Cu_2O\downarrow} + RCOOH$$

Concept ladder

- Both aliphatic and aromatic aldehydes reduce Tollen's reagent.
- Aromatic aldehydes like benzaldehyde does not reduce Fehling's solution. Benzaldehyde is confirmed by malachite green test.
- Both the above tests (Tollen's reagent and Fehling's solution are given by reducing sugars.

(iii) **Schiff's reagent test** Add 5-6 drops of organic compound to around 2 mL of Schiff's reagent (*p*-rosaniline hydrochloride dye dissolved in water and its red or pink colour decolourised by passing SO_2). Shake the contents vigorously.

After some time, formation of a deep red, pink or violet colour indicates the presence of an aldehydic group.

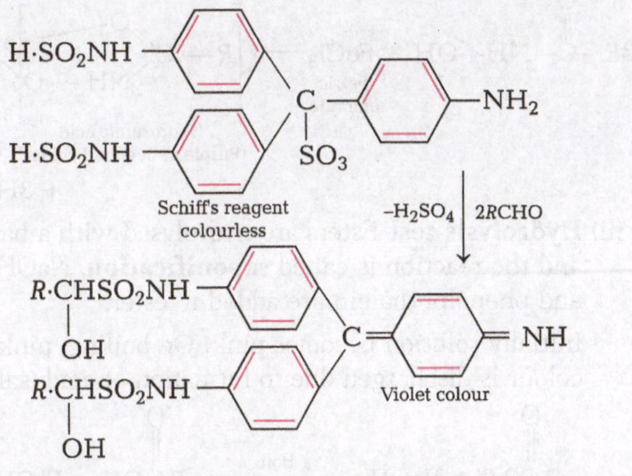

(iv) **Benedict's solution test** The compound is boiled with 2-3 mL of Benedict solution [alkaline solution of Cu^{2+} ions complexed with citrate ions] for a few minutes. Appearance of a red ppt. confirms the presence of aliphatic aldehydes.

Tests for Ketonic Group ($>C=O$)

(i) **Sodium nitroprusside test** 0.2 cc of aqueous solution of compound or 0.1 g of solid compound is added to 2 cc of sodium nitroprusside $[Na_2[Fe(CN)_5NO]$ solution and then it is made alkaline with 2-3 drops of NaOH solution.

The formation of red or purple colouration confirms the presence of ketone.

Mentor's TiP

Benzophenone does not respond to this test.

(ii) **Iodoform test** This test is useful for the identification of methyl ketones. The compound is heated with iodine and potassium hydroxide. The formation of a pale yellow precipitate confirms the presence of methyl ketones.

$$CH_3—CO—R + 3I_2 + 4KOH \xrightarrow{\Delta} RCOOK + \underset{\text{Yellow ppt.}}{CHI_3\downarrow} + 3KI + 3H_2O$$

5. Ester Group ($R-\overset{\overset{\large O}{\|}}{C}—OR$) Tests

(i) **Hydroxamic acid test** Esters react with hydroxyl amine (NH_2OH) to give hydroxamic acid, which complexes with Fe(III) to give a purple or deep red colour.

$$\underset{\text{Ester}}{R\overset{\overset{O}{\|}}{C}OR'} + NH_2OH \longrightarrow \underset{\text{Hydroxamic acid}}{R\overset{\overset{O}{\|}}{C}NHOH} + R'OH$$

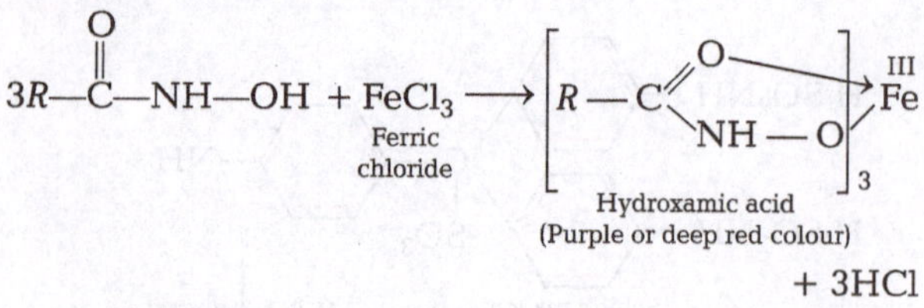

(ii) **Hydrolysis test** Esters are hydrolysed with a base and the reaction is called **saponification.** NaOH and phenolphthalein are added to ester.

Initially solution becomes pink. On boiling, pink colour is discharged due to formation of acid (salt).

$$\underset{\text{Pink}}{\underbrace{R\overset{O}{\overset{\|}{C}}OR' + NaOH}} \xrightarrow[\text{Saponification}]{\text{Boil}} \underset{\text{Colourless}}{\underbrace{R\overset{O}{\overset{\|}{C}}ONa + R'OH}}$$

Phenolphthalein is pink in basic medium and colourless in acidic medium.

6. Amide Group ($-\overset{O}{\overset{\|}{C}}-NH_2$) Tests

Amides are decomposed by alkali solution liberating NH_3 which yields white fumes with HCl.

(i) $R-\overset{O}{\overset{\|}{C}}-NH_2 + NaOH \xrightarrow{\Delta} R-\overset{O}{\overset{\|}{C}}-ONa + NH_3\uparrow$

(ii) $NH_3 + HCl \longrightarrow \underset{\text{White fumes}}{NH_4Cl}$

7. Amino Group Tests

Amino group is present in primary amines as $R—NH_2$ or $Ar—NH_2$, secondary amines as $R—NH—R$ and tertiary amines as $R-\underset{R}{\underset{|}{N}}-R$.

> **Concept ladder**
>
> Amino group test is used to distinguish between primary, secondary and tertiary amines by using the Nitrous acid test ($NaNO_2$ + dil. HCl $\xrightarrow{10°C}$ HNO_2).
>
> According to this test,
>
> - Formation of brisk effervescence shows the presence of **aliphatic primary amine.**
>
> $$\underset{\text{Primary name}}{R-NH_2} + HNO_2 \longrightarrow \underset{\text{Alochol}}{ROH} + H_2O + \underset{\text{Nitrogen}}{N_2\uparrow}$$
>
> - Formation of an oily dark coloured liquid indicates the presence of **secondary amine.**
>
> $$\underset{\text{Secondary amine}}{R_2NH} + HNO_2 \longrightarrow \underset{\text{Nitroso compound (oily)}}{R_2N\cdot NO} + H_2O$$
>
> - No reaction indicates the presence of **aliphatic tertiary amine** while production of green or brown colour indicates the presence of **aromatic tertiary amines.**

Unsaturation Test

Unsaturation test is used for the detection of alkenes and alkynes.

(i) **Bromine test** Unsaturated organic compounds (alkenes and alkynes) decolourise bromine water.

$$\underset{\text{Alkene}}{>C=C<} + \underset{\text{Orange-red}}{Br_2} \longrightarrow \underset{\text{Colourless}}{-\underset{Br}{\underset{|}{C}}-\underset{Br}{\underset{|}{C}}-}$$

$$-C\equiv C- + Br_2 \longrightarrow -\underset{Br}{\underset{|}{C}}=\underset{Br}{\underset{|}{C}}- \xrightarrow{Br_2} \underset{\text{Colourless}}{-\overset{Br}{\overset{|}{\underset{Br}{\underset{|}{C}}}}-\overset{Br}{\overset{|}{\underset{Br}{\underset{|}{C}}}}-}$$

(ii) **Baeyer's test** Unsaturated organic compounds also decolourise cold and alkaline potassium permanganate (Baeyer's reagent).

$$\underset{\text{Violet}}{2KMnO_4} + H_2O \longrightarrow 2KOH + 2MnO_2 + \underset{\text{Colourless}}{3(O)}$$

$$\begin{matrix}CH_2\\ \|\\ CH_2\end{matrix} + H_2O + O \longrightarrow \begin{matrix}CH_2OH\\ |\\ CH_2OH\end{matrix}$$

$$CH\equiv CH + 4(O) \longrightarrow \underset{\text{Oxalic acid}}{\begin{matrix}COOH\\ |\\ COOH\end{matrix}}$$

Preparation of Organic Compounds

Preparation of some organic compounds acetanilide, *p*-nitro acetanilide, aniline yellow and iodoform are discussed below

1. Acetanilide

The IUPAC name of acetanilide is N-phenylethanamide. Acetanilide is structurally represented as

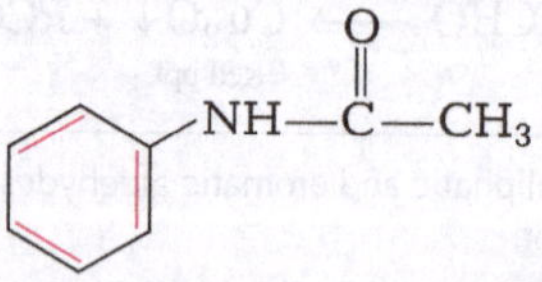

Acetanilide is prepared by the direct acetylation of aniline. The acetylation is carried out by acetyl chloride in the presence of an organic base like pyridine which removes HCl formed during the reaction and shifts the equilibrium in the forward direction.

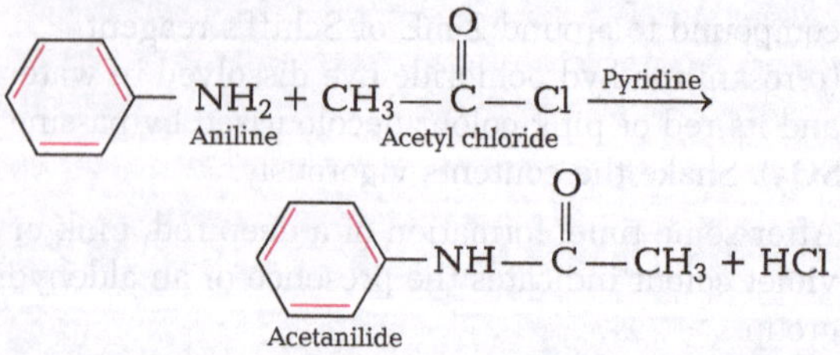

Acetanilide is also prepared when acetylation is carried out with acetic anhydride in the presence of few drops of concentrated H_2SO_4 or acetic acid that acts as a catalyst.

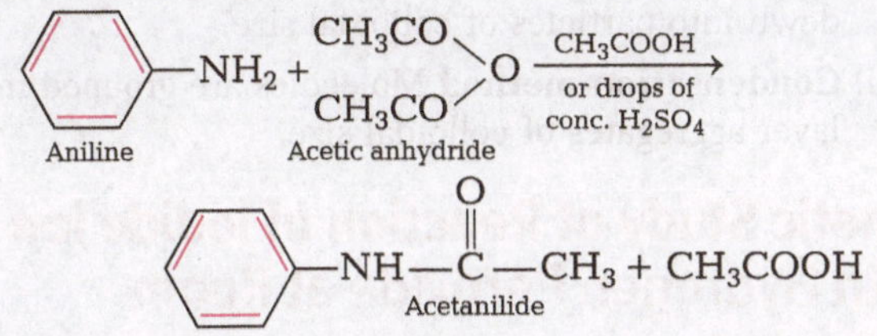

Concept ladder During the preparation of acetanilide from aniline and acetic anhydride a small amount of zinc is added to the reaction mixture for preventing the oxidation of aniline and to reduce the coloured impurities present in aniline during the reaction.

2. *p*-nitroacetanilide

Its IUPAC name is 4-nitro-N-phenyl ethanamide. Structurally, it is represented as

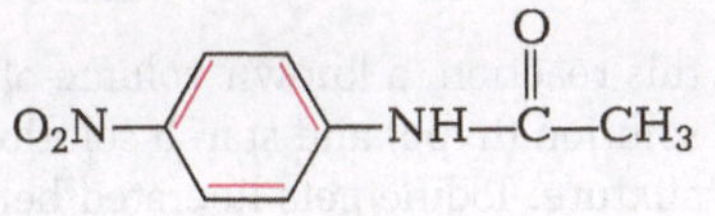

It is prepared by the nitration of acetanilide. Acetanilide is dissolved in glacial acetic acid. Concentrated H_2SO_4 is added to it with vigorous stirring.

Temperature of reaction mixture should be maintained below 10°C. Now add fuming HNO_3 drop by drop with regular stirring. It gives *p*-nitro acetanilide along with a little amount of *o*-isomer. In this process, fuming HNO_3 in the presence of conc. H_2SO_4, gives nitronium ion (NO_2^+) which attacks on acetanilide to form *p*-nitro acetanilide through the cyclopentadienyl cation (intermediate) formation.

(i) $HNO_3 + H_2SO_4 \longrightarrow \underset{\text{Nitronium ion}}{NO_2^+} + H_2O + HSO_4^-$

(ii)

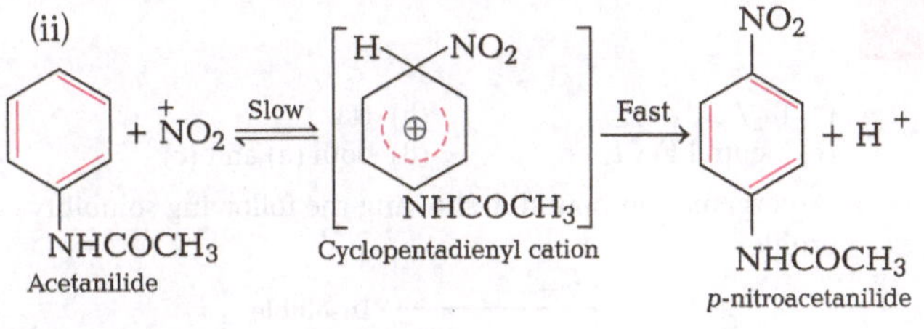

(iii) $H^+ + HSO_4^- \longrightarrow H_2SO_4$

3. Aniline Yellow

Chemically it is known as *p*-aminoazobenzene. Structurally, it is represented as

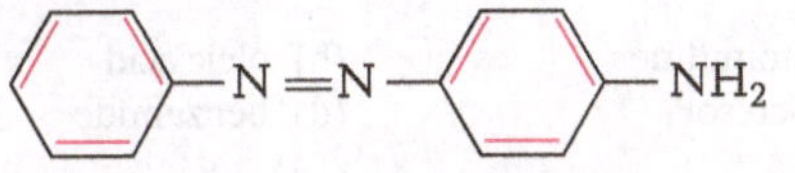

It is prepared by the rearrangement of diazoamino benzene. Diazoamino benzene needed for the preparation of aniline yellow is obtained by the coupling reaction of benzene diazonium chloride with aniline carried out at 273-278 K in fairly acidic medium.

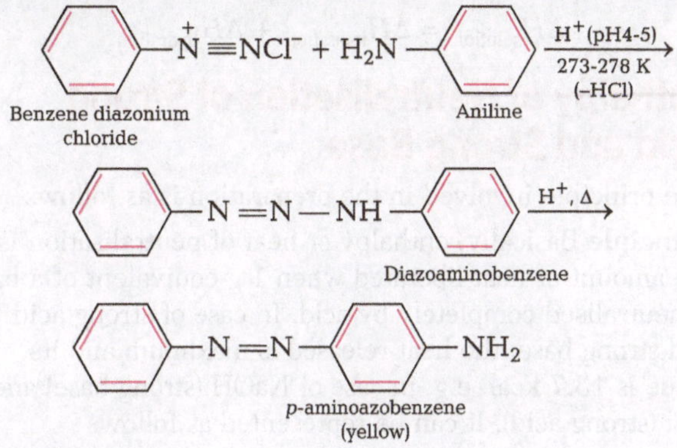

4. Iodoform

It is chemically called triodomethane. Structurally, it is represented as CHI_3. It is prepared from acetone. When acetone is heated with potassium iodide and sodium hypochloride, iodoform as a yellow precipitate is obtained.

$$NaOCl + KI \longrightarrow \underset{\text{Sodium hypoiodite}}{NaOI} + KCl$$

$$\underset{\text{Acetone}}{CH_3{-}\overset{\overset{\large O}{\|}}{C}{-}CH_3} + NaOI \longrightarrow CI_3{-}\overset{\overset{\large O}{\|}}{C}{-}CH_3$$

$$\xrightarrow{NaOH} CH_3CO\overset{-}{O}\overset{+}{N}a + \underset{\substack{\text{Iodoform} \\ \text{(yellow ppt.)}}}{CHI_3\downarrow}$$

Chemical Principles Involved in Some Important Experiments

The chemical principles involved in some important experiments are as follows

Enthalpy of solution of $CuSO_4$

The principle involved in the experiment is as follows

Principle The enthalpy of solution of $CuSO_4$ can be determined by dissolving a known amount of salt in a measured volume of water in a calorimeter. The rise or fall in temperature is recorded as ΔH. It can be calculated as

$$\Delta H = \frac{(W - w) \times \Delta T \times M}{m}$$

where, W = water equivalent of calorimeter

w = mass of water taken

M = molar mass of solute

m = mass of solute, $\Delta T = T_{\text{final}} - T_{\text{initial}}$

The dissolution of solute in a solvent is exothermic or endothermic depending upon the nature of solute. If heat is absorbed, enthalpy changes comes with **positive sign** and if heat is evolved, enthalpy changes comes with **negative sign.**

$$\Delta H_{\text{solution}} = \Delta H_{\text{ionisation}} + \Delta H_{\text{hydration}}$$

Enthalpy of Neutralisation of Strong Acid and Strong Base

The principle involved in the preparation is as follows

Principle Basically, enthalpy or heat of neutralisation is the amount of heat liberated when 1 g equivalent of a base is neutralised completely by acid. In case of strong acid and strong base, the heat released is maximum and its value is 13.7 kcal. e.g. in case of NaOH (strong base) and HCl (strong acid). It can be represented as follows

$$HCl + NaOH \longrightarrow H_2O + 13.7\ \text{kcal}$$

As both of these are strong, they get dissociated completely and the reaction is precisely expressed as,

$$H^+ + OH^- \longrightarrow H_2O + 13.7\ \text{kcal}$$

Preparation of Lyophilic and Lyophobic Solutions

The principle involved in the preparations is as follows

Principle The main concern in the preparation of colloidal solutions is that the dispersed particles must be within the size range of 1mμ – 300mμ. Lyophilic sols are easily prepared as colloidal materials like starch, gelatin, acacia etc., when added to water, they swell up and spontaneously break into particulates of matter of colloidal range.

However, lyophobic sols, need special techniques of preparation. There are basically two methods.

(i) **Dispersion method** Coarser of aggregates are break down into particles of colloidal size.

(ii) **Condensation method** Molecules are grouped into layer aggregates of colloidal size.

Kinetic Study of Reaction of Iodide Ion with Hydrogen Peroxide at Room Temperature

The principle involved in this experiment is mentioned below:

Principle The rate of reaction between H_2O_2 and I^- ions can be studied by considering different concentrations of iodide ions. In the presence of an acid, this reaction occurs as follows,

$$2H_3O^+ + 2I^- + H_2O_2 \longrightarrow 4H_2O + I_2$$

$$2I^- + H_2O_2 + 2H^+ \longrightarrow I_2 + 2H_2O$$

To maintain this reaction, a known volume of sodium thiosulphate solution (hypo) and starch solution is added to the reaction mixture. Iodine gets liberated here and reacts readily with sodium thiosulphate solution and gets reduced to I^- ions.

$$I_2 + 2S_2O_3^{2-} \longrightarrow S_6O_6^{2-} + 2I^-$$

When thiosulphate gets completely consumed, the liberated iodine reacts with starch solution to give blue coloured complex.

$$I_2 + \text{Starch} \longrightarrow \text{Blue coloured complex.}$$

STEP UP Practice 3

1 A compound liberates CO_2 with $NaHCO_3$ and also gives colour with neutral $FeCl_3$ solution. The compound can be

(a) 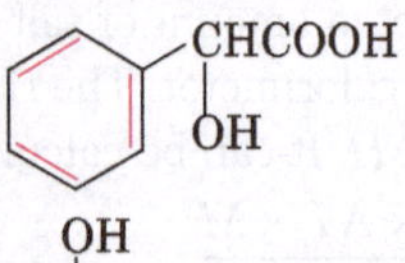

(b) 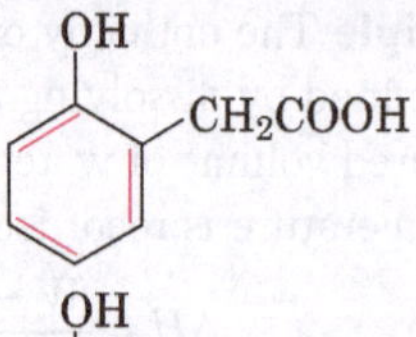

(c) 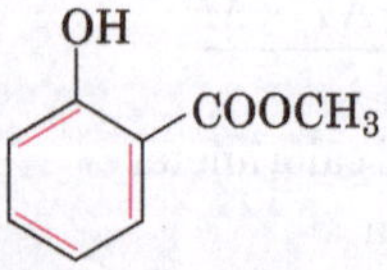

(d) 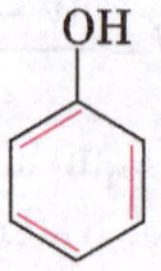

2 Phenol can be distinguished from ethanol by the reactions with

(a) Br_2/CCl_4 (b) Na

(c) neutral $FeCl_3$ (d) both (a) and (c)

3 An organic compound X showing the following solubility profile,

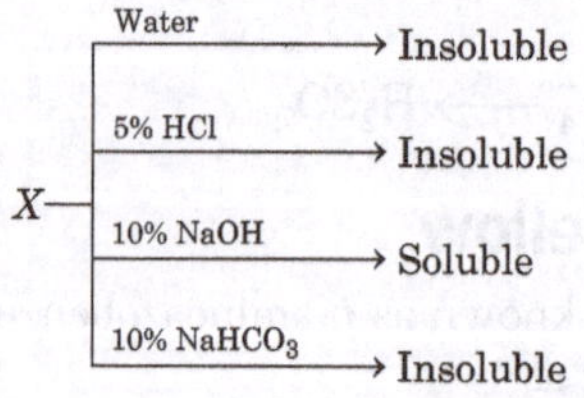

X is

(a) o-toluidine (b) oleic acid

(c) m-cresol (d) benzamide

4 Consider the following statements.

Statement I Nitrophenol does not respond to $FeCl_3$ test as well as Liebermann's nitroso reaction.

Statement II Phenol on heating with phthalic acid in presence of conc. H_2SO_4 gives pink coloured compound called phenolphthalein.

In the light of the above statements, choose the most appropriate answer from the options given below :

(a) Both Statement I and Statement II are false.
(b) Statement I is true, but Statement II is false.
(c) Statement I is false, but Statement II is true.
(d) Both Statement I and Statement II are true.

5 Consider the following tests.

(i) Ferric chloride test (ii) Carbylamine test
(iii) Litmus test (iv) Liebermann's nitroso test
(v) Phthalein test

How many of them is/are not given by phenols ?

(a) 3 (b) 2 (c) 1 (d) 4

6 The reagent which does not react with both, acetone and benzaldehyde is

(a) sodium hydrogen sulphite (b) phenyl hydrazine
(c) Fehling's solution (d) Grignard reagent

7 In organic analysis, the reagent 2, 4-dinitrophenyl hydrazine is used for the detection of which of the following functional groups ?

(a) Alcohol (b) Acid (c) Aldehyde (d) Amines

8 Compound '*A*' reacts with $CHCl_3$ and KOH and gives offensive smelling compound. Compound '*A*' can be

(a) quaternary aliphatic amine (b) primary aromatic amine
(c) secondary amine (d) tertiary amine

9 Which of the following product is not correctly matched regarding the given reaction ?

(a) Aniline $\xrightarrow[H_2SO_4,\,15°C]{\text{Conc. } HNO_3 + \text{ conc.}}$ o (2%)-and p(51%)-nitroanilines

(b) Aniline $\xrightarrow[\text{Conc. } H_2SO_4,\,15°C]{\text{Conc. } HNO_3 +}$ m-nitroaniline (47%)

(c) Aniline $\xrightarrow[\text{Conc. } H_2SO_4,\,15°C]{\text{Conc. } HNO_3 +}$ a black tarry matter

(d) Aniline $\xrightarrow[\text{Conc. } H_2SO_4,\,15°C]{\text{Conc. } HNO_3 +}$ no reaction

10 Choose the correct match regarding anilides

(a) Anilides $\longrightarrow$ N-phenyl derivative of amide of an acid
(b) Anilides $\longrightarrow$ N -acetyl derivative of amide of an acid
(c) Anilides $\longrightarrow$ N-phenyl derivative of aniline
(d) Anilides $\longrightarrow$ N-ethyl derivative of aniline

11 Consider the following statements.

Statement I p-nitroacetanilide is prepared by direct acetylation of aniline.

Statement II Acetanilide is prepared by the nitration of acetanilide.

In the light of the above statements, choose the most appropriate answer from the option given below.

(a) Both Statement I and Statement II are false.
(b) Statement I is true, but Statement II is false.
(c) Statement I is false, but Statement II is true.
(d) Both Statement I and Statement II are true.

12 Choose the correct match regarding the application of acetanilide in medicine.

(a) Acetanilide $\longrightarrow$ Hypnotic
(b) Acetanilide $\longrightarrow$ Antiseptic
(c) Acetanilide $\longrightarrow$ Antipyretic
(d) Acetanilide $\longrightarrow$ Antimalarial

13 Consider the following compounds ,

(i) CH_3CHO (ii) CH_3COCH_3 (iii) HCHO
(iv) 2-propanol (v) Propanal

How many of them can not be used in the preparation of iodoform ?

(a) 3 (b) 4 (c) 2 (d) 1

14 An organic compound give positive iodoform and Tollen's tests. The organic compound is

(a) CH_3CH_2OH (b) $CH_3CH_2CH_2CHO$
(c) CH_3CHO (d) CH_3COCH_3

NEET Exclusive EXTRA BYTES

- Calcium salts give colour immediately while barium or strontium salts, give colour after sometime.
- Chlorides of Hg, Sn and Sb do not give chromyl chloride test due to the presence of higher covalent nature.
- Chromyl chloride test is performed in dry test tube because CrO_2Cl_2 is water soluble and gives chromic acid, so gas will not come out.
- Precipitation of second group sulphides in qualitative analysis is carried out with H_2S in the presence of HCl and not nitric acid as HNO_3, a strong oxidant, will oxidise H_2S to give colloidal sulphur. Thus, precipitation of group-II sulphides will not occur.
- For removal of H_2S, CH_3COOH must not be added in excess because in its excess, $(NH_4)_2S$ may be formed which may be oxidised to SO_4^{2-} and $BaSO_4$, $SrSO_4$ and $CaSO_4$ may get precipitated.

GEARING UP FOR NEET

1 Formation of which compound, among the following is not a confirmatory test of Pb^{2+} ions
(a) lead chromate (b) lead nitrate
(c) lead sulphate (d) lead iodide

2 Microcosmic salt and borax are used in the identification of cations by dry tests. They are respectively
(a) $NaBO_2$ and Na_2PO_3
(b) $NaNH_4HPO_4 \cdot 4H_2O$ and $Na_2B_4O_7 \cdot 10H_2O$
(c) $NaPO_3$ and $NaBO_2$
(d) $Na_2B_2O_2$ and $NaNH_2HPO_3$

3 On addition of conc. H_2SO_4 to a chloride salt, colourless fumes are evolved but in case of iodide salt, violet fumes come out. This is because
(a) H_2SO_4 reduces HI to I_2 (b) HI is of violet colour
(c) HI gets oxidised to I_2 (d) HI changes to HIO_3

4 In the detection of group II acid radicals, the salt containing chloride is treated with concentrated sulphuric acid and a colourless gas is liberated. The name of the gas is
(a) hydrogen chloride gas (b) chlorine gas
(c) sulphur dioxide gas (d) nitrogen gas

5 For the given aqueous reactions which of the statements is false?

$$KI + K_3[Fe(CN)_6] \xrightarrow{\text{Dil. } H_2SO_4} \text{brownish yellow solution.}$$
$$\downarrow ZnSO_4$$
$$\text{Colourless solution} \longleftarrow \text{(White ppt. + brownish yellow filtrate)}$$

(a) The first reaction is a redox reaction.
(b) White ppt. is $Zn_3[Fe(CN)_6]_2$.
(c) Addition of filtrate to starch solution gives blue colour.
(d) White ppt. is soluble in NaOH solution.

6 To an aqueous solution of a mixture contains Br^- and I^-, on passing Cl_2 gas and adding $CHCl_3$, the organic layer will be
(a) violet (b) reddish brown
(c) black (d) red

7 An aqueous solution of a substance gives a white precipitate on treatment with dilute hydrochloric acid, which dissolves on heating. When hydrogen sulphide is passed through the hot acidic solution, a black precipitate is obtained. The substance is a
(a) Zn^{2+} salt (b) Cu^{2+} salt (c) Ag^+ salt (d) Pb^{2+} salt

8 Given below are certain cations. Using inorganic qualitative analysis, arrange them in increasing group number from 0 to VI.
A. Mn^{2+} B. Al^{3+} C. Pb^{2+} D. Mg^{2+} E. Cu^{2+}

Choose the correct answer from the options given below.
(a) A, B, C, D, E (b) D, A, C, E, B
(c) C, E, B, A, D (d) B, C, A, D, E

9 While titrating dilute HCl solution with aqueous NaOH, which of the following will not be required?
(a) Burette
(b) Pipette and distilled water
(c) Clamp and phenolphthalein
(d) Bunsen burner and measuring cylinder

10 The indicator used in the titration of acetic acid with sodium hydroxide for quantitative estimation is
(a) phenolphthalein
(b) methyl orange
(c) phenol red
(d) a mixture of methyl red and methyl orange.

11 Consider a titration of potassium dichromate solution with acidified Mohr's salt solution using diphenylamine as indicator. The number of moles of Mohr's salt required per mole of dichromate is
(a) 2 (b) 1 (c) 4 (d) 6

12 The essential condition for an indicator to be used in a titration is
(a) $pK_{In} = pK_a - pK_b$ of solution at equivalence point
(b) $pK_{In} = pK_b$ of solution at equivalence point
(c) $pK_{In} = pH$ of solution at equivalence point
(d) $pK_{In} = pK_a + pK_b$ of solution at equivalence point

13 The difference between titrant and titrate is
(a) that titrant is a solution of an accurately known concentration whereas a titrate is the substance whose concentration is to be determined by titration
(b) that titrant is a solution of unknown concentration whereas titrate is a solution of known concentration
(c) that one is titrated against the other
(d) that one is the reactant and the other is the product

14 Why HCl is not used to make the medium acidic in oxidation reaction of $KMnO_4$ in acidic medium?
(a) Both HCl and $KMnO_4$ act as oxidising agent.
(b) $KMnO_4$ oxidises HCl into Cl_2 which is also an oxidising agent.
(c) $KMnO_4$ is a weaker oxidising agent than HCl.
(d) $KMnO_4$ acts as a reducing agent in the presence of HCl.

15 When $KMnO_4$ solution is added to oxalic acid solution, the decolourisation is slow in the beginning but becomes instantaneous after sometime because
(a) CO_2 is formed as the products
(b) reaction is exothermic
(c) MnO_4^- catalyses the reaction
(d) Mn^{2+} acts as an auto-catalyst

16 Phenolphthalein is an indicator for acid-base titration, it exists as
(a) benzenoid form in acid and quinonoid form in basic solution
(b) quinonoid form in acid and benzenoid form in basic solution
(c) quinonoid form in both
(d) benzenoid form in both

17 The titration of Mohr's salt *vs* $KMnO_4$ is an example of redox titration. In this titration, $KMnO_4$ oxidises only ferrous salt to the ferric salt (no effect on other ions) but we can not use ferrous sulphate in place of Mohr's salt because
(a) it is less stable than Mohr's salt
(b) in air it is oxidised to ferric sulphate
(c) in air it loses water of crystallisation
(d) All of the above

18 Which of the following statements are correct ?
A. Fe^{3+} gives brown colour with potassium ferricyanide.
B. Fe^{2+} gives brown colour with ammonium thiocyanate.
C. Fe^{2+} gives blue precipitate with potassium ferricyanide.
D. Fe^{3+} gives red colour with potassium sulphocyanide.
E. Fe^{3+} gives black precipitate in charcoal cavity test.

Choose the correct answer from the options given below :
(a) A, B, D (b) B, C and D only
(c) B, C and E (d) C, D and E only

19 When a pinch of sodium bicarbonate is added to carboxylic acid, brisk effervescence is produced. This effervescence is produced due to evolution of
(a) H_2 gas (b) CO gas (c) CO_2 gas (d) N_2 gas

20 Nitation of aniline is achieved by
(a) direct treatment with nitration mixture under reflux
(b) using fuming HNO_3
(c) acetylation followed by nitration and subsequent hydrolysis
(d) using dil. H_2SO_4 in cold water

21 In the preparation of *p*-nitroacetanilide from aniline, nitration is not done by nitrating mixture (a mixture of conc. H_2SO_4 and conc. HNO_3) because
(a) on nitration it gives *o*-nitroacetanilide
(b) it gives a mixture of *o*-and *p*-nitroaniline
(c) $—NH_2$ group gets oxidised
(d) it forms a mixture of *o*-and *p*-nitroacetanilide

22 In case of weak acid and strong base, the heat of neutralisation is less than 13.7 kcal because some part of heat is utilised in
(a) dissociation of base (b) association of base
(c) dissociation of acid (d) association of acid

23 During the preparation of acetanilide from aniline a small amount of zinc is added to the reaction mixture because
(a) zinc induces the precipitation
(b) zinc prevents the reduction of aniline during the reaction
(c) zinc reduces the coloured impurities in the aniline and also prevents its oxidation during the reaction
(d) zinc forms a white crystalline complex with aniline

24 Which of the following statements is wrong about aniline yellow?
(a) It is carcinogenic.
(b) It is also called *p*-aminoazobenzene.
(c) It is an acid dye.
(d) It is also called 4-phenylazoaniline.

25 An organic compound '*A*' burns with a sooty flame. It is negative towards Tollen's reagent test and positive for Brady's reagent test. The compound '*A*' is
(a) acetophenone
(b) acetone
(c) salicylic acid
(d) benzaldehyde

26 The methods used for the preparation of lyophilic and lyophobic sols are respectively
(a) oxidation
(b) dissolution in water and peptisation
(c) peptisation and oxidation
(d) reduction

Assertion-Reason

Directions (Q. Nos. 27 to 29) Given below are two statements, one is labelled as Assertion (A) and the other is labelled as Reason (R).
(a) Both A and R are true and R is the correct explanation of A.
(b) Both A and R are true but R is not the correct explanation of A.
(c) A is true but R is false.
(d) A is false but R is true.

27 **Assertion** (A) If a mixture contains chlorates, chromyl chloride test for chloride anion will not be performed.
Reason (R) Chlorates on reaction with dil. H_2SO_4 form chlorine dioxide gas which dissolves in H_2SO_4 and forms highly explosive violet solution.

28 **Assertion** (A) In the preparation of acetanilide, small amount of zinc is added.
Reason (R) Zinc is added to prevent the reduction of aniline and to reduce the coloured impurities.

29 **Assertion** (A) Phenol on heating with phthalic acid in the presence of conc. H_2SO_4 gives pink coloured compound phenolphthalein.
Reason (R) Pink colour of phenolphthalein in alkaline medium is due to the formation of ions.

Statement Type Questions

Directons (Q. Nos. 30 to 32) In the light of the above statements, choose the correct answer from the options given below.

(a) Both Statement I and Statement II are false.
(b) Statement I is true, but Statement II is false.
(c) Statement I is false, but Statement II is true.
(d) Both Statement I and Statement II are true.

30 **Statement I** The identification of Ni^{2+} is carried out by dimethyl glyoxime in the presence of NH_4OH.

Statement II The dimethyl glyoxime is a bidentate neutral ligand.

31 **Statement I** For acid-base titration, a weak acid or weak base is used as an indicator.

Statement II Determination of acid or base or their anhydride in a sample by titrating with a standard solution of base or acid.

32 **Statement I** 2,4-dinitrophenyl hydrazine is used for the detection of amines functional groups.

Statement II A yellow or orange precipitate separates out in the case of compound containing amine group due to the formation of respective hydrazones.

33 Which of the following statements is not correct ?

A. An acidified solution of $K_2Cr_2O_7$ liberates iodine from iodides.
B. In acidic medium, dichromate ions are converted to chromate ions.
C. $(NH_4)_2Cr_2O_7$ on heating undergo exothermic decomposition to give Cr_2O_3.
D. Potassium dichromate is used as a titrant for estimation of Fe^{2+} ions.
E. Oxalic acid *vs* $KMnO_4$ titration is carried out in the presence of conc. HNO_3.

Choose the correct answer from the options given below.

(a) A and C only
(b) C and E only
(c) B and D only
(d) B and E only

34 Select the incorrect statements from the following.

A. In $KMnO_4$ *vs* oxalic acid titration, the oxalic acid solution is heated with dilute. H_2SO_4 upto 50-60°C.
B. In $KMnO_4$ *vs* oxalic acid titration, oxalic acid is a reducing agent and $KMnO_4$ is an oxidising agent.
C. Oxalic acid *vs* $KMnO_4$ titration is carried out in the presence of conc. HNO_3.
D. In oxalic acid *vs* $KMnO_4$ titration, $KMnO_4$ acts as self indicator for end point detection.
E. Oxalic acid *vs* $KMnO_4$ titration is an example of neutralisation reaction.

Choose the correct answer from the options given below.

(a) B, C and D only
(b) B and D only
(c) A, C and E only
(d) D and E only

35 Select the correct statements from the following

A. Add 2-3 drops of KI and starch solution in the test tube then a deep blue or violet colour appears which confirms the presence of NO_2^- anion.
B. When filter paper dipped in lead acetate over the mouth of test tube, filter paper turns green due to the formation of PbS which confirms the presence of S^{2-} ion.
C. Take a glass rod dipped in NH_4OH near the mouth of test tube, white dense fumes of NH_4Cl evolved which confirms the presence of Cl^- ion.
D. If a mixture contains chlorates, chromyl chloride test for chloride anion should not be performed.
E. A paper dipped in starch solution on the mouth of test tube, paper turns blue which confirms the presence of I^- ion.

Choose the correct answer from the options given below.

(a) A and B only
(b) A, C, D and E
(c) B, C and E only
(d) A, C and E only

36 Select the incorrect statements from the following :

A. In sodium bicarbonate test, formation of brisk effervescence shows the presence of —CHO group.
B. Benzoic acid treated with sodium bicarbonate forms sodium benzoate.
C. Heat a small quantity of carboxylic acid with ethyl alcohol and a little dil. H_2SO_4 forms ester with a fruity smell.
D. Dip blue litmus paper in the aqueous solution or suspension of the compound turns red indicates the presence of an acid.
E. When propanoic acid reacts with ethanol, it forms ethyl propanoate and CO_2.

Choose the most appropriate answer from the options given below.

(a) B and E only
(b) C and D only
(c) A, C and E only
(d) B, C and E only

37 Select the incorrect statements from the following.

A. Starch sol can be prepared by the condensation method as it is an intrinsic colloid.
B. In condensation method, increase in size of the solute particle to colloidal size which may be affected by hydrolysis, oxidation, reduction or double decomposition.
C. Arsenious sulphide sol can be prepared by the dispersion method.
D. In condensation method, hydrolysis, oxidation etc., all the reactions are performed in such a way that these result in the formation of insoluble products.
E. In dispersion method, reduction in size of the coarse particle to colloidal size by grinding, shaking, use of an electric arc.

Choose the correct answer from the options given below.

(a) A and C only
(b) D, C and E only
(c) A and E only
(d) B, D and E only

Species Selection Type Questions

38 Consider the following indicators.

(i) Bromothymol blue (ii) Methyl red
(iii) Phenolphthalein (iv) Methyl orange
(v) Phenol red (vi) Thymophthalein
(vii) Bromocresol green

How many of them are used in strong acid *vs* strong base titrations ?

(a) 3 (b) 4 (c) 6 (d) 5

39 Consider the following compounds.

(i) Carboxylic acids (ii) Alcohols (iii) Formic acid
(iv) Phenols (v) Propionic acid

How many of them does not turn blue litmus to red ?

(a) 4 (b) 2 (c) 3 (d) 1

40 Consider the following compounds.

(i) 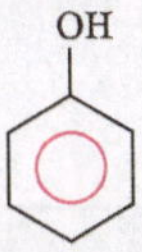

(ii) 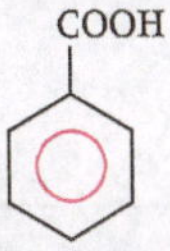

(iii) HCOOH (iv) 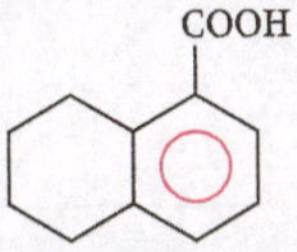

(v) 

The total number of compounds, which will produce brisk effervescence with aqueous sodium bicarbonate solution is

(a) 5 (b) 4 (c) 3 (d) 2

41 Among the following samples of acid and base.

(i) 100 mL of 1M NaOH and 100 mL of 1 M HCl
(ii) 100 mL of 2 M KOH and 100 mL of 1M H_2SO_4
(iii) 100 mL of 1 M CH_3COOH and 100 mL of 1 M NaOH
(iv) 100 mL of 0.5 M KOH and 100 mLof 0.5 M HNO_3
(v) 100 mL of 1 M HCOOH and 100 mL of 1 M NaOH

The total number of samples, which have same enthalpy of neutralisation is/are

(a) 2 (b) 4
(c) 3 (d) 5

Matching Type Questions

42 Match Column I with Column II.

Column I (Metal ion)	Column II (Group in qualitative analysis)
A. Fe^{3+}	1. Group-V
B. Ca^{2+}	2. Group-IV
C. Zn^{2+}	3. Group-II
D. Cu^{2+}	4. Group-III

Codes

(a) A-3, B-4, C-2, D-1
(b) A-2, B-4, C-1, D-3
(c) A-4, B-3, C-2, D-1
(d) A-4, B-1, C-2, D-3

43 Match Column I with Column II.

Column I (Test method)	Column II (Reagent)
A. Carbylamine test	1. C_2H_5OH and conc. H_2SO_4/Δ
B. Lucas test	2. $CHCl_3$ and alc. KOH
C. Ester test	3. $C_6H_5SO_2Cl/Aq.$ KOH
D. Hinsberg's test	4. Conc. HCl and $ZnCl_2$ (anhyd.)/20°C

Codes

(a) A-2, B-4, C-1, D-3
(b) A-3, B-4, C-1, D-2
(c) A-2, B-1, C-4, D-3
(d) A-3, B-1,C-2, D-4

44 Match Column I with Column II.

Column I	Column II
A. Intrinsic colloids	1. Neutralisation reaction of HCl and NaOH
B. Semipermeable membrane	2. Hydrophobic sol
C. Extrinsic colloids	3. Hydrophilic sol
D. Arrhenius theory of ionisation	4. Cellophane paper

Codes

(a) A-2, B-1, C-3, D-4 (b) A-3, B-1, B-2, D-4
(c) A-2, B-4, C-3, D-1 (d) A-3, B-4, C-2, D-1

45 Match Column I with Column II.

Column I (Cations/Anions)	Column II (Group number)
A. NO_3^-	1. III
B. Sr^{2+}	2. VI
C. SO_4^{2-}	3. II
D. Mg^{2+}	4. V

Codes

	A	B	C	D
(a)	2	4	3	1
(b)	3	4	1	2
(c)	3	1	4	2
(d)	4	3	2	1

Final Check Through PYQs

1 During the preparation of Mohr's salt solution (Ferrous ammonium sulphate), which of the following acid is added to prevent hydrolysis of Fe^{2+} ion? *[NEET 2024]*
(a) Dilute hydrochloric acid
(b) Concentrated sulphuric acid
(c) Dilute nitric acid
(d) Dilute sulphuric acid

2 Given below are certain cations. Using inorganic qualitative analysis, arrange them in increasing group number from 0 to VI. *[NEET 2024]*

A. Al^{3+} B. Cu^{2+} C. Ba^{2+} D. Co^{2+} E. Mg^{2+}

Choose the correct answer from the options given below.
(a) B, A, D, C, E (b) B, C, A, D, E
(c) E, C, D, B, A (d) E, A, B, C, D

Answers

Step up Practice 1

1 (c)	2 (c)	3 (b)	4 (c)	5 (c)	6 (a)	7 (a)	8 (d)	9 (b)	10 (b)
11 (a)	12 (c)	13 (b)	14 (c)	15 (c)	16 (c)				

Step up Practice 2

1 (d)	2 (a)	3 (d)	4 (c)	5 (b)	6 (d)	7 (a)	8 (a)	9 (b)	10 (a)
11 (d)	12 (c)	13 (d)	14 (c)	15 (c)	16 (d)				

Step up Practice 3

1 (b)	2 (d)	3 (c)	4 (b)	5 (c)	6 (c)	7 (c)	8 (b)	9 (d)	10 (a)
11 (a)	12 (c)	13 (d)	14 (c)						

Gearing up for NEET

1 (b)	2 (b)	3 (c)	4 (a)	5 (b)	6 (a)	7 (d)	8 (c)	9 (d)	10 (a)
11 (d)	12 (c)	13 (a)	14 (b)	15 (d)	16 (a)	17 (d)	18 (d)	19 (c)	20 (c)
21 (c)	22 (c)	23 (c)	24 (c)	25 (a)	26 (b)	27 (c)	28 (c)	29 (d)	30 (d)
31 (d)	32 (a)	33 (d)	34 (c)	35 (b)	36 (c)	37 (a)	38 (d)	39 (d)	40 (c)
41 (c)	42 (d)	43 (a)	44 (d)	45 (b)					

Final Check through PYQs

1 (d)	2 (a)

Hints and Solutions

Step up Practice 1

1. (*c*) Mn^{2+} gives violet coloured bead in borax bead test.
2. (*c*) Manganese give violet coloured bead in + 2 oxidation state, i.e. it is present as Mn^{2+}.
3. (*b*) Among the given matches, (b) is correctly matched while others are incorrect.

   Their correct matches are

   $$Cu^{2+} \longrightarrow \text{Blue}$$
   $$Ba^{2+} \longrightarrow \text{Apple-green}$$
   $$Sr^{2+} \longrightarrow \text{Crimson red}$$

4. (*c*) Statement I is false but Statement II is true.

   Its correct form is :

   In charcoal cavity test, first metallic carbonate is formed followed by formation of metallic oxide.
5. (*c*)
6. (*a*) Among the given compounds, only one, i.e. (ii) gives a precipitate with $Pb(NO_3)_2$ but not with $Ba(NO_3)_2$.

   $$Pb(NO_3)_2 + 2NaCl \longrightarrow PbCl_2\downarrow + 2NaNO_3$$

   $BaCl_2$ is soluble in water.
7. (*a*) Among the given cations, (a) is correctly matched with the given group while others are incorrectly matched.

   Their correct matches are,

   $$NH_4^+ \longrightarrow \text{Zero group}$$
   $$Mg^{2+} \longrightarrow \text{Group VI}$$
   $$Ni^{2+} \longrightarrow \text{Group IV}$$

8. (*d*)
9. (*b*) Dimethyl glyoxime can be used to identify nickel ion.
10. (*b*) NaCl is a salt of strong acid and strong base, hence, on dissolution it will give neutral solution. As white ppt. is obtained by the addition of $AgNO_3$ to the solution of Na salt, it can be of AgCl.

    Further, AgCl is also insoluble in HNO_3. Hence, the anion is Cl^-.

    $$NaCl + AgNO_3 \longrightarrow AgCl\downarrow + HNO_3$$

11. (*a*) 12. (*c*)
13. (*b*) The reaction proceeds as follows

    (X) $ZnCl_2$

    $ZnCl_2 \xrightarrow{NaOH} Zn(OH)_2\downarrow + 2NaCl$ (White ppt. but dissolved in excess of NaOH)

    $ZnCl_2 \xrightarrow{NH_4OH/H_2S} ZnS$ (White ppt.)

    $ZnCl_2 \xrightarrow{AgNO_3/HNO_3} Zn(NO_3)_2$ (White ppt. soluble in *aq.* NH_3)

14. (*c*) Statement I is false but Statement II is true.

    Its correct form is :

    Dissolves the white ppt. of $CaCO_3$ in acetic acid, and heat it gently then add ammonium oxalate solution in excess, appearance of white ppt. confirmed the presence of Ca^{2+} cation.
15. (*c*) The reaction proceeds as follows

    $$2KI + 2H_2SO_4 \longrightarrow 2KHSO_4 + 2HI$$
    $$2HI + H_2SO_4 \longrightarrow \underset{\text{(Violet vapour)}}{I_2\uparrow} + SO_2 + 2H_2O$$

16. (*c*) The reaction proceeds as follows

    $$\underset{\text{(Sodium meta-aluminate)}}{NaAlO_2} + NH_4Cl + H_2O \xrightarrow{\Delta} NaCl + \underset{\text{(White gelatinous)}}{Al(OH)_3\downarrow} + NH_3$$

Step up Practice 2

1. (*d*) Among the given statements, (d) is incorrect because secondary standard is titrated against primary standard and not *vice-versa.*
2. (*a*) In the titration of sodium carbonate with hydrochloric acid first equivalence point appears at pH of about 8.3, hence, phenolphthalein is used as an indicator for first equivalence point. Whereas, second equivalence point appears at an pH of about 3.9, hence, methyl orange is used as an indicator for second equivalence point. It is also called double titration.
3. (*d*) Both Statement I and Statement II are true.
4. (*c*) The given graph represents titration curve for strong acid with weak base.
5. (*b*) In $KMnO_4$ titration, $KMnO_4$ is reduced as

   $$MnO_4^- + 8H^{2+} + 5e^- \longrightarrow Mn^{2+} + 4H_2O$$
   $$\text{Eq. mass} = \frac{\text{Mol. mass}}{\text{No. of electrons gain or lost}} = \frac{M}{5}$$

6. (*d*) $MnO_4^- + 5Fe^{2+} + 8H^+ \longrightarrow 5Fe^{3+} + Mn^{2+} + 4H_2O$

   Hence, 1 mole of $KMnO_4$ is required to titrate 5 moles of $FeSO_4$.

   $$\text{Moles of } FeSO_4 \text{ titrated} = 10 \text{ mL} \times \frac{M}{10} = 1 \text{ milimoles}$$
   $$= 10^{-3} \text{ mol}$$

   5 mol Fe^{2+} reacts with 1 mol $KMnO_4$

   10^{-3} mol Fe^{2+} reacts with $\frac{1}{5} \times 10^{-3}$ mol

   $$= 0.2 \times 10^{-3} \text{ mol} = 10 \text{ mL of } 0.02 \text{ M}$$

   Hence, option (d) is correct.

7. (*a*) Among the given relations, only two, i.e. (iii) and (v) are correct in case of titration of Mohr's salt with $KMnO_4$.

8. (*a*) 126 g of oxalic acid $= 1$ mol of $H_2C_2O_4 \cdot 2H_2O$

$$2MnO_4^- + 5C_2O_4^{2-} + 16H^+ \longrightarrow 2Mn^{2+} + 10CO_2 + 8H_2O$$

1 mole of oxalate ion requires $= 2/5$ mol of $KMnO_4$

$$Cr_2O_7^{2-} + 3C_2O_4^{2-} + 14H^+ \longrightarrow 2Cr^{3+} + 6CO_2 + 7H_2O$$

1 mole of oxalate ion requires $= 1/3$ mol of $K_2Cr_2O_7$.

9. (*b*) In the titration of oxalic acid *vs* $KMnO_4$, $KMnO_4$ acts as an oxidant as well as a self indicator.

$$2KMnO_4 + 3H_2SO_4 \xrightarrow[\text{(auto-catalyst)}]{} K_2SO_4 + 2MnSO_4 + 3H_2O + 5[O]$$

$$5\begin{array}{l} COOH \\ | \\ COOH \end{array} + 5[O] \longrightarrow 5H_2O + 10CO_2\uparrow$$

10. (*a*)

11. (*d*) $KMnO_4$ acts as a self indicator in $KMnO_4$ titrations.

12. (*c*) Statement I is false while the Statement II is true.

The correct form of Statement I is :

In the preparation of Mohr's salt, sulphuric acid should be present in excess otherwise a brown precipitate will be formed.

13. (*d*)
$$2KMnO_4 + 8H_2SO_4 + 10FeSO_4(NH_4)_2SO_4 \cdot 6H_2O \longrightarrow K_2SO_4 + 2MnSO_4 + 5Fe_2(SO_4)_3 + 10(NH_4)_2SO_4 + 68H_2O$$

It is obvious from above equation that 10 moles of Mohr's salt will react with 2 moles of $KMnO_4$.

Thus, one mole of Mohr's salt will react with $\frac{2}{10} = \frac{1}{5}$ mole of $KMnO_4$.

14. (*c*) Moht's salt $(FeSO_4 \cdot (NH_4)_2SO_4 \cdot 6H_2O)$ is oxidised as

$$Fe^{2+} \longrightarrow Fe^{3+} + e^-$$

$$\text{Eq. mass} = \frac{\text{Mol. mass}}{\text{No. of electrons gained or lost}} = \frac{M}{1} = M$$

15. (*c*) During the preparation of standard solution of Mohr's salt, few drops of conc. H_2SO_4 is added to prevent the hydrolysis of Mohr's salt.

16. (*d*) Among the given substances, only three, i.e. (i), (ii) and (iii) are used in the preparation of Mohr's salt.

Step up Practice 3

1. (*b*) The compound liberates CO_2 with $NaHCO_3$, so it contains — COOH group and it also gives colour with neutral $FeCl_3$ solution, so it also contains a —OH group directly attached to the benzene ring (i.e. phenol).

Hence, the structure of the compound is

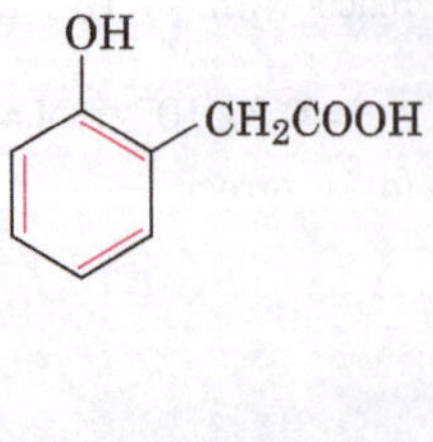

2. (*d*) Aqueous or alcoholic solution of phenol with excess of bromine water gives a yellowish white precipitate.

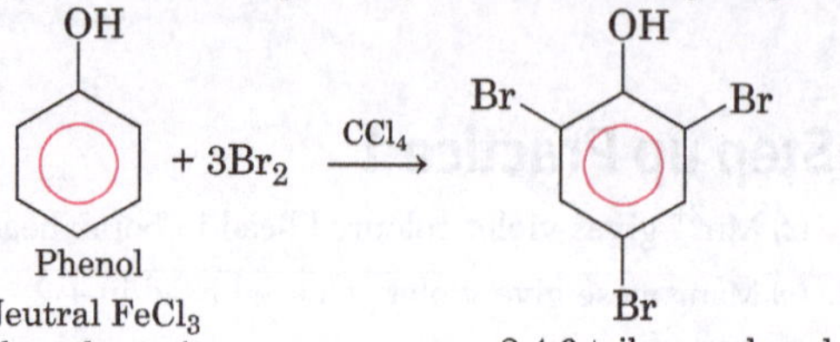

In aliphatic compounds of alcohol has no reaction with bromine water and neutral $FeCl_3$ as well.

3. (*c*) *m*-cresol is the given organic compound that shows the following solubility profile.

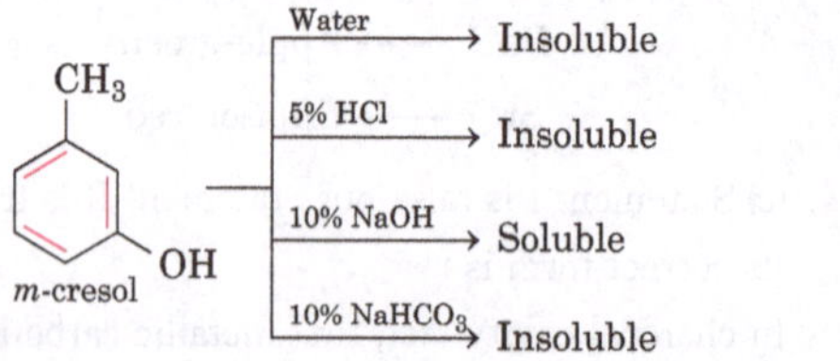

m-cresol on reaction with 10% NaOH forms 3-methyl sodium phenoxide ion.

4. (*b*) Statement I is true but Statement II is false.

Its correct form is :

Phenol on heating with phthalic acid, in presence of conc. H_2SO_4 gives colourless compound called phenolphthalein.

5. (*c*) Among the given test, only one, i.e. (ii) is not given by phenols because carbylamine test is given by primary amines.

6. (*c*) Benzaldehyde does not reduce Fehling's solution (a distinction from other aldehydes).

Acetone (ketone) also does not give any test with Fehling's solution.

7. (*c*) 2,4-DNP test is used for the detection of aldehydes.

8. (*b*) $RNH_2 + CHCl_3 + 3KOH \longrightarrow RNC + 3KCl + 3H_2O$

(where, R may be alkyl or aryl group)

9. (*d*) Aniline cannot undergo direct nitration. Since, HNO_3 is a strong oxidising agent, it oxidises aniline to a black tarry matter and $PhNH_2$ also gets protonated.

10. (*a*) Anilides are generally N-phenyl derivative of amide of an acid.

11. (*a*) Both Statement I and Statement II are false.

Their correct forms are

- *p*-nitroacetanilide is prepared by the nitration of acetanilide.
- Acetanilide is prepared by direct acetylation of aniline by using the mixture of equal volumes of acetic anhydride and acetic acid.

12. (*c*) Acetanilide is used as an antipyretic.

13. (*d*) Among the given compounds, all can be used in the preparation of iodoform except (iii), i.e. formaldehyde because only those compounds which contain either $CH_3-\underset{|}{\overset{}{C}}H-$ (with OH) group or $CH_3-\underset{\|}{C}-$ (with O) group on reaction with iodine and sodium hydroxide (alkali) yield iodoform.

$$CH_3-\underset{\displaystyle OH}{\underset{|}{CH}}- \quad \text{group or} \quad CH_3-\underset{\displaystyle O}{\underset{\|}{C}}-$$

14. (*c*) The compound which contains —CHO group, gives positive Tollen's test and the compound with $CH_3-\underset{\displaystyle O}{\underset{\|}{C}}-$ group gives positive iodoform test.

Thus, the structure of the compound should be $CH_3-\underset{\displaystyle H}{\underset{|}{C}}=O$.

Gearing up for NEET

1. (*b*) $Pb(NO_3)_2$ is a water soluble colourless compound. Hence, formation of lead nitrate compound is not used as a confirmatory test of Pb^{2+} ions.

2. (*b*) **3.** (*c*) **4.** (*a*)

5. (*b*) The reactions proceed as follows

$$K_3\overset{+3}{[Fe(CN)_6]} + 2K\overset{-1}{I}\,(\text{excess}) \xrightarrow{\text{Dil. } H_2SO_4} K_4\overset{+2}{[Fe(CN)_6]} + \underset{\substack{\text{Brownish yellow}\\ \text{solution}}}{K\overset{-1,0}{I_3}\,(KI + I_2)}$$

$$ZnSO_4 \longrightarrow \underset{\text{White ppt.}}{K_2Zn[Fe(CN)_6]} + I_3^-$$

$$\Rightarrow \underset{\substack{\text{Brownish}\\ \text{yellow}\\ \text{filtrate}}}{I_3^-} \longrightarrow \underset{\substack{\text{Turns starch}\\ \text{solution blue}}}{I_2} + I^-$$

$\Rightarrow K_2Zn[Fe(CN)_6]$ reacts with NaOH as,

$$K_2Zn[Fe(CN)_6] + 4NaOH \longrightarrow [Zn(OH)_4]^{2-} + [Fe(CN)_6]^{4-}$$

$\Rightarrow$ Thus in the given reactions the white ppt. is $K_2Zn[Fe(CN)_6]$.

6. (*a*) When chlorine is added, it will displace bromine from bromide and iodine from iodide.

Also, bromine will displace iodine from iodide. The iodine will be present in the organic layer will appear violet.

$$\Rightarrow \quad Cl_2 + 2Br^- \longrightarrow 2Cl^- + Br_2$$

$$Cl_2 + 2I^- \longrightarrow 2Cl^- + I_2$$

$$\Rightarrow \quad Br_2 + 2I^- \longrightarrow 2Br^- + I_2$$

7. (*d*) $PbCl_2$ is soluble in hot water but insoluble in cold water.

$$Pb^{2+} + 2HCl \xrightarrow{\Delta} \underset{(aq)}{PbCl_2} \xrightarrow{H_2S} \underset{\text{(black ppt.)}}{PbS\downarrow}$$

8. (*c*)

Basic radical		**Group number**
A. Mn^{2+}	$\longrightarrow$	IV
B. Al^{3+}	$\longrightarrow$	III
C. Pb^{2+}	$\longrightarrow$	I and II A
D. Mg^{2+}	$\longrightarrow$	VI
E. Cu^{2+}	$\longrightarrow$	II A

Thus, the corrct order is C, E, B, A, D.

9. (*d*)

10. (*a*)

11. (*d*) The reaction proceeds as follow

$$\underset{\text{(Mohr's salt)}}{6FeSO_4 \cdot (NH_4)_2SO_4 \cdot 6H_2O} + K_2Cr_2O_7 + 7H_2SO_4$$
$$\longrightarrow K_2SO_4 + Cr_2(SO_4)_3 + 3Fe_2(SO_4)_3 + 6(NH_4)_2SO_4 + 43H_2O$$

So, six moles of Mohr's salt is required for one mole of dichromate ion.

12. (*c*) For an indicator to be used, pK_{In} = pH of solution at equivalence point.

13. (*a*)

14. (*b*) Because $KMnO_4$ oxidises HCl into Cl_2 which is also an oxidising agent.

$$2Cl^- \longrightarrow Cl_2 + 2e^-] \times 5$$

$$MnO_4^- + 8H^+ + 5e^- \longrightarrow Mn^{2+} + 4H_2O] \times 2$$

15. (*d*) The reaction proceeds as follows,

$$5C_2O_4^{2-} + \underset{\text{Purple}}{2MnO_4^-} + 16H^+ \longrightarrow \underset{\substack{\text{Colourless}\\ \text{(auto-catalyst)}}}{2Mn^{2+}} + 8H_2O + 10CO_2$$

In this reaction, Mn^{2+} acts as an auto-catalyst.

16. (*a*) Phenolphthalein is colourless in acid solution (benzenoid form) and pink in alkali (basic) solution (quinonoid form).

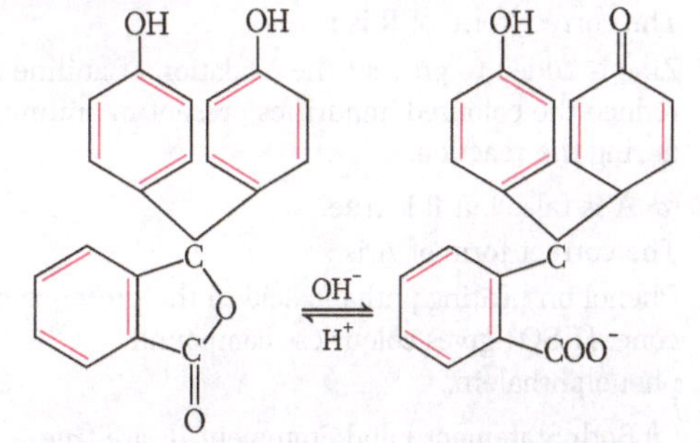

Colourless (acidic medium) benzenoid form

Red (alkaline medium) quinonoid form

17. (*d*)

18. (*d*) Among the given statements, only C, D and E are correct while A and B are incorrect.

Their correct forms are

- Fe^{2+} gives blue colour (Turnbull's blue) with potassium ferricyanide.
- Fe^{3+} gives red colour with ammonium thiocyanate.

19. (*c*) When a pinch of sodium bicarbonate is added to carboxlic acid following reaction takes place.

$$\underset{\text{Carboxylic acid}}{RCOOH} + \underset{\text{Sodium bicarbonate}}{NaHCO_3} \longrightarrow RCOONa + CO_2\uparrow + H_2O$$

Large amount of CO_2 gas is released in the reaction which producres brisk effervescence.

20. (*c*) **21.** (*c*)

22. (*c*) In case of weak acid and strong base, the heat of neutralisation is less than 13.7 kcal because some part of heat is utilised in dissociation of the weak acid.

23. (*c*)

24. (*c*) It is a basic dye.

25. (*a*) Since, given compound '*A*' burns with sooty flame therefore, it must be an aromatic compound. Again when it reacts with Brady's reagent (acidic 2, 4-dinitrophenyl hydrazine solution), it yields orange precipitate. Therefore, it must be aldehyde or ketone. But ketone does not perform Tollen's reagent test, therefore, it must be a ketone. Hence, '*A*' is acetophenone.

26. (*b*) Dissolution in water and peptisation methods are used for the preparation of lyophilic and lyophobic sols respectively.

27. (*c*) A is true but R is false.

The correct form of R is :

Chlorates on reaction with conc. H_2SO_4 form chlorine dioxide gas which dissolves in H_2SO_4 and form highly explosive orange yellow solution.

28. (*c*) A is true but R is false.

The correct form of R is :

Zinc is added to prevent the oxidation of aniline and to reduce the coloured impurities present in aniline during the reaction.

29. (*d*) A is false but R is true.

The correct form of A is :

Phenol on heating phthalic acid in the presence of conc. H_2SO_4 gives colourless compound phenolphthalein.

30. (*d*) Both Statement I and Statement II are true.

31. (*d*) Both Statement I and Statement II are true.

32. (*a*) Both Statement I and Statement II are false.

Their correct form are :

- 2,4-dinitrophenyl hydrazine is used for the detection of aldehyde and ketone group.
- A yellow or orange precipitate separates out in case of compound containing carbonyl group due to the formation of respective hydrazones.

33. (*d*) Among the given statements, only B and E are incorrect while the other statements are correct.

Their correct forms are

- In acidic medium, dichromate ions gets reduced to Cr^{3+} ions.
- Oxalic acid *vs* $KMnO_4$ titration is carried out in the presence of H_2SO_4.

34. (*c*) Among the given statements, only A, C and E are incorrect while the statements B and D are correct.

The correct form of statements A, C and E are :

- In $KMnO_4$ *vs* oxalic acid titration, the oxalic acid solution is heated with dilute H_2SO_4 upto 70-80°C.
- Oxalic acid *vs* $KMnO_4$ titration is carried out in the presence of H_2SO_4.
- Oxalic acid *vs* $KMnO_4$ titration is an example of redox reaction.

35. (*b*) Among the given statements, A, C, D and E are correct while the statement B is incorrect.

The correct form of B is :

When filter paper dipped in lead acetate over the mouth of test tube, filter paper turns black due to the formation of PbS, which confirms the presence of S^{2-} ion.

36. (*c*) Among the given statements, A, C and E are incorrect while the statements B and D are correct.

The correct forms of Statements A, C and E are :

- In sodium bicarbonate test, formation of brisk effervescence shows the presence of —COOH group.
- On heating a small quantity of carboxylic acid with ethyl alcohol and a little conc. H_2SO_4 forms ester with a fruity smell.
- When propanoic acid reacts with ethanol it forms ethyl propanoate and H_2O.

37. (*a*) Among the given statements, A and C are incorrect while B, D and E are correct.

The correct forms of Statement A and C are:

- Starch sol is an intrinsic colloid and can be prepared by warming with suitable solvent (water).
- Arsenious sulphide sol can be prepared by the condensation method.

38. (*d*) Among the given indicators, only five, i.e. (i), (ii), (iii), (iv) and (vi) are used in strong acid *vs* strong base titrations.

39. (*d*) Among the given compounds, only one i.e, (ii) does not turn blue litmus to red because alcohols do not possess acidic character.

40. (*c*) Among the given compounds, only three compounds (ii), (iii) and (iv) will produce brisk effervescence with aqueous sodium bicarbonate solution.

41. (*c*) Among the given samples of acid and base only three samples (i), (ii) and (iv) have same enthalpy of neutralisation.

42. (*d*) The correct match is A-4, B-1, C-2, D-3.

43. (*a*) The correct match is A-2, B-4, C-1, D-3.

44. (*d*) The correct match is A-3, B-4, C-2, D-1.

45. (*b*) The correct match is A-3, B-4, C-1, D-2.

Final Check Through PYQs

1. (*d*) Dilute H_2SO_4 does not act as an oxidising agent which prevent oxidation of Fe^{+2} into Fe^{+3} while concentrated H_2SO_4 will oxidise Fe^{+2} into Fe^{+3}.

2. (*a*)

	Basic radical	Group number
A.	Al^{3+}	III
B.	Cu^{2+}	II A
C.	Ba^{2+}	V
D.	Co^{2+}	IV
E.	Mg^{2+}	VI

Hence, the correct order is B, A, D, C, E.

Skill Builder

- **Sol. of Skill Builder Pg. 545**

(*d*)

	Basic radical	Group number
A.	Fe^{3+}	III
B.	Ni^{2+}	IV
C.	Sr^{2+}	V
D.	Cu^{2+}	II (A)
E.	Ca^{2+}	V

Hence, the correct order is D, A, B, C = E.

Practice Test 01

Important Instructions

- The test of 1 hour duration and contains 50 Multiple Choice Questions (four options with a single correct answer) from Chemistry.
- There are 50 questions in each subject, divided into **two Sections** : Section A and Section B.
  (a) **Section A** contains 35 questions in each subject and all questions are compulsory.
  (b) **Section B** contains 15 questions from each subject out of which 10 questions are to be attempted.
- Each question carries 4 marks. For each correct response, the candidate will get 4 marks. For each incorrect response, one mark will be deducted from the total score.

Section-A (Q. No. 1 to 35)

1. The osmotic pressure of 5% (mass/volume) solution of cane sugar at 150°C (molecular weight of sugar $=342\text{ g mol}^{-1}$) is
(a) 4.55 atm (b) 3.55 atm (c) 2.65 atm (d) 5.07 atm

2. Which of the following statements are incorrect?
A. The anion is named first in both positively and negatively charged coordination entities.
B. The ligands are named in an alphabetical order before the name of the central atom/ion.
C. Name of all the cationic ligands ends with -o.
D. If the complex ion is a cation, the name of the metal ends with suffix -ate.
E. The neutral complex molecule is named similar to that of the complex cation.
Choose the most appropriate answer from the options given below.
(a) A, C and D (b) B, C and D (c) C and E (d) B, D ane E

3. Acetic acid react separately with the following alcohols. The rate of esterification is highest for
(a) CH_3OH (b) C_2H_5OH (c) $(CH_3)_2CHOH$ (d) $(CH_3)_3COH$

4. Match Column I with Column II.

	Column I		Column II
A.	Concentration *vs* time for zero order reaction	1.	$\frac{E_a}{R}$
B.	Half-life period *vs* initial concentration for zero order reaction	2.	$-k$
C.	Logarithm of rate constant *versus* reciprocal of temperature	3.	$\frac{1}{2k}$
D.	Half-life period *vs* initial concentration for 1st order reaction	4.	zero

Codes

	A	B	C	D		A	B	C	D
(a)	3	2	1	4	(b)	2	3	1	4
(c)	4	3	1	2	(d)	1	2	3	4

5. Which of the following statements are correct?
A. Lowering of vapour pressure takes place only in ideal solution.
B. Addition of non-volatile solution to a solvent decreases the vapour pressure of the solvent.
C. Relative lowering of vapour pressure depends only upon the concentration of the solvent.
D. Solvent with higher boiling points have higher vapour pressure at a given temperature.
E. For a solution containing several non-volatile solutes, the relative lowering of vapour pressure depends on the sum of mole fraction of different solution.
Choose the correct answer from the options given below.
(a) A and C (b) B and E
(c) A, C and D (d) B, D and E

6. An aqueous solution of 2% non-volatile solute exert a pressure of 1.004 bar at normal boiling point of the solvent. The molar mass of solute is
(a) 36.38 g mol^{-1} (b) 41.35 g mol^{-1}
(c) 54.35 g mol^{-1} (d) 64.35 g mol^{-1}

7. Which of the following is a major product of given reaction?

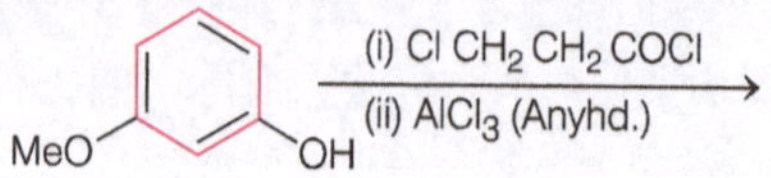

(a) 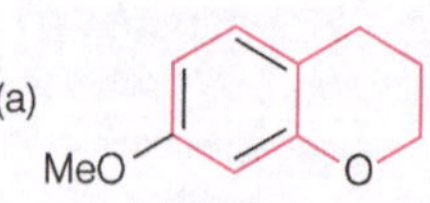

(b) 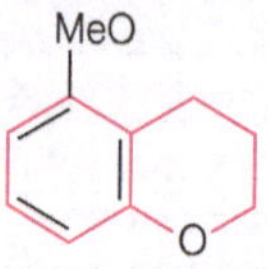

(c) 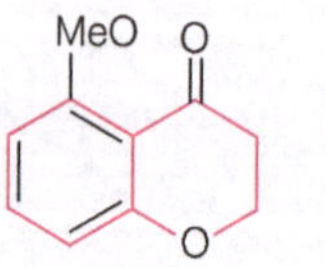

(d) 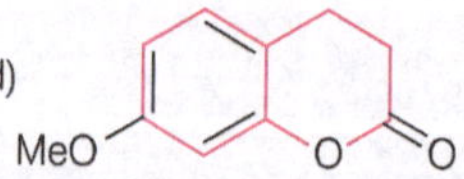

8. The number of moles of AgCl precipitated when excess of $AgNO_3$ is added to 1 mole of $[Cr(NH_3)_4Cl_2]Cl$ is
(a) zero (b) 1.0
(c) 3.0 (d) 2.0

9. Which of the following factors may be regarded as the main cause of lanthanoids contraction?
(a) Poor shielding of one of 4*f* electron by another in the subshell.
(b) Effective shielding of one of 4*f* electron by another in the subshell.
(c) Poor shielding of 5*d* electrons by 4*f* electrons.
(d) Greater shielding of 5*d* electrons by 4*f* electrons.

10. Reactivity of alkyl halides towards nucleophillic substitution reactions decreases in the order :
(a) $C_2H_5F > C_2H_5Cl > C_2H_5Br > C_2H_5Cl$
(b) $C_2H_5Cl > C_2H_5Br > C_2H_5I > C_2H_5F$
(c) $C_2H_5Br > C_2H_5I > C_2H_5F > C_2H_5Cl$
(d) $C_2H_5I > C_2H_5Br > C_2H_5Cl > C_2H_5F$

11. Choose the incorrect statement from the following.
(a) XeO_3 has four σ and four π-bonds.
(b) The hybridisation of Xe in XeF_4 is sp^3d^2.
(c) Among the noble gases, the occurrence (percent by weight) of argon is highest in air.
(d) Liquid helium is used in cryogenic liquids.

12. The interhalogen ICl is more reactive than I_2. This is because,
(a) I—Cl bond is weaker than I—I bond. Consequently I—Cl bond breaks easily to form halogen atoms which readily bring about the reaction.
(b) I—Cl bond is polar and thus is more reactive than the non-polar I—I bond.
(c) There is a large difference in size of the atoms which provides instability to the molecule and consequently, it is more reactive than I_2.
(d) None of the above

13. The spin only magnetic moment of $[MnBr_4]^{2-}$ is 5.9 BM. The geometry of complex is,
(a) square planar
(b) tetrahedral
(c) square pyramidal
(d) trigonal pyramidal

14. Given below are two statements, one is labelled as Assertion (A) and other is labelled as Reason (R).
Assertion (A) Equivalent conductivity of a weak electrolyte at infinite dilution can be found by Kohlraush law.
Reason (R) Kohlraush law is applicable only to weak electrolytes.
In the light of the above statements, choose the correct answer from the options given below.
(a) Both A and R are true but R is not the correct explanation of A.
(b) A is true but R is false.
(c) A is false but R is true.
(d) Both A and R are true and R is the correct explanation of A.

15. Given below are hydrides of group 15 element. Arrange them in decreasing order of basic strength.
A. NH_3 B. PH_3 C. AsH_3 D. SbH_3
Choose the most appropriate answer from the options given below.
(a) A, B, C and D (b) D, B, C and A
(b) C, A, B and D (d) A, B, D and C

16. Titanium shows magnetic moment of 1.73 BM. in its compound. What is the oxidation number of Ti in the compound?
(a) +2 (b) +3
(c) +4 (d) +1

17. Which of the following complexes exists as a pair of enantiomers?
(a) *trans*-$[Co(en)_2Cl]^+$
(b) $[Co(NH_3)_4Cl_2]^+$
(c) $[Co(P(C_2H_5)_3)ClBr]$
(d) $[Cr(en)_3]^{3+}$

18. Which of the following method cannot be used to prepare *n*-propyl iodide from *n*-propyl alcohol?
(a) $CH_3CH_2CH_2OH + HI \xrightarrow{\Delta}$
(b) $CH_3CH_2CH_2OH + KI + H_2SO_4 \xrightarrow{\Delta}$
(c) $CH_3CH_2CH_2OH \xrightarrow[\Delta]{Pu/I_2}$
(d) $CH_3CH_2CH_2OH + KI + H_3PO_4 \xrightarrow{\Delta}$

19. The tendency of 3*d* metal ions to form stable complexes is due to their
(a) variable oxidation state
(b) strong electronegative nature
(c) high charge/size ratio and vacant *d*-orbitals
(d) very low ionisation energy

20. Which of the following alkyl bromides will give rearranged product under $S_N1$reaction?
(a) 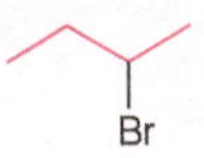

(b) 

(c) 

(d) 

21. The expected spin only magnetic moments for $[Fe(CN)_6]^{4-}$ and $[FeF_6]^{3-}$ are
(a) 1.73 and 1.73 BM
(b) 1.73 and 5.92 BM
(c) 0.0 and 1.73 BM
(d) 0.0 and 5.92 BM

22. To prepared 3-ethyl-3-pentanol, which of the following pairs of reactants should be used?
(a) $CH_3CH_2COCH_3$ and $CH_3CH_2CH_2MgBr$
(b) $CH_3CH_2COCH_2CH_3$ and CH_3CH_2MgBr
(c) $CH_3CH_2CH_2COCH_2CH_3$ and CH_3MgBr
(d) $CH_3CH_2CH_2COCH_3$ and CH_3CH_2MgBr

23. What would happen when a solution of potassium chromate is heated with an excess of dilute nitric acid?
(a) Cr^{3+} and $Cr_2O_7^{2-}$ are formed.
(b) $Cr_2O_7^{2-}$ and H_2O are formed.
(c) CrO_4^{2-} is reduced to +3 state of Cr.
(d) CrO_4^{2-} is oxidised to +7 state of Cr.

24. The structure of the compound that gives a tribromo derivative on treatment with bromine water is

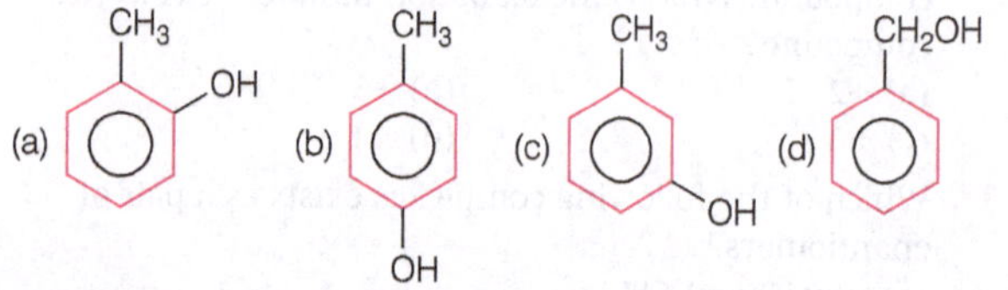

25. Match Column I with Column II.

Column I	Column II
A. Non-ideal solution showing positive deviation	1. *n*-hexane + *n*-heptane
B. Non-ideal solution showing negative deviation	2. Carbon tetrachloride + Benzene
C. Solution showing abnormal molar mass	3. Chloroform + Benzene
D. Ideal solution	4. Acetic acid + Benzene

Codes

	A	B	C	D
(a)	1	2	3	4
(b)	2	3	4	1
(c)	1	3	4	2
(d)	2	4	3	1

26. The reaction,

$$2C_2H_5OH \xrightarrow[413\text{ K}]{\text{conc. } H_2SO_4} (C_2H_5)_2O + H_2O$$

is an example of
(a) electrophilic substitution reaction
(b) nucleophilic substitution $S_N1$reaction
(c) E_2 elimination reaction
(d) nucleophilic substitution S_N2 reaction

27. Given below are two statements.
Statement I The rate of reaction is accelerated by presence of catalyst.
Statement II The presence of catalyst increases the activation energy barrier.
In the light of the above statements, choose the correct answer from the options given below.
(a) Both Statement I and Statement II are false.
(b) Statement I is true but Statement II is false.
(c) Statement I is false but Statement II is true.
(d) Both Statement I and Statement II are true.

28. Which of the following cannot be used to oxidise primary alcohols to aldehydes?
(a) CrO_3 in anhydrous medium.
(b) Pyridinium chlorochromate.
(c) $KMnO_4$ in acidic medium.
(d) Heating in presence of Cu at 573 K.

29. 4-methylacetophenone on heating with alkaline $KMnO_4$ followed by hydrolysis with dil. H_2SO_4 gives
(a) toluene (b) acetophenone
(c) terephthalic acid (d) phthalic acid

30. Select the correct statements from the following
A. Primary aliphatic amines form highly unstable alkyl diazonium salts.
B. Benzene diazonium chloride is prepared by the nitration of aniline with nitrous acid at 273-278 K.
C. Benzene diazonium fluoroborate is water soluble and stable at room temperature.
D. In Sandmeyer reaction, halide ion (Cl^-) can be easily introduced in the benzene ring in the presence of Cu(I) ion.
E. The azo products are often colourless.
Choose the correct answer from the option given below
(a) A, B, C and D (b) A, B and D
(c) C and E (d) B, C, D and E

31. Ethanol on reaction with alkaline $KMnO_4$ gives *X* which reacted with methanol in the presence of an acid gives a sweet compound *Y*. *X* and *Y* respectively are
(a) acetaldehyde and acetone
(b) acetic acid and methyl acetate
(c) formic acid and methyl formate
(d) ethylene and ethyl methyl ether

32. In the following binary liquid mixtures, how many mixtures shows negative deviation?
(i) Ethanol and acetone
(ii) Benzene and toluene
(iii) Acetone and chloroform
(iv) Acetone and carbon disulphide
(v) Phenol and aniline
(vi) Bromoethane and chloroethane
(vii) *n*-hexane and *n*-heptane
(a) 4 (b) 3 (c) 1 (d) 2

33. Select the correct statements from the following.
A. Threonine, amino acid can be synthesised in the body.
B. Proteins are condensation polymer of α- and β-amino acid.
C. Naturally occurring amino acid have L-configuration.
D. Amino acids which can not be synthesised in the body are known as essential amino acid.
Choose the correct answer from the option given below.
(a) B and D (b) C and D (c) A, B and C (d) A and C

34. The final product (*Y*) in the given reaction is

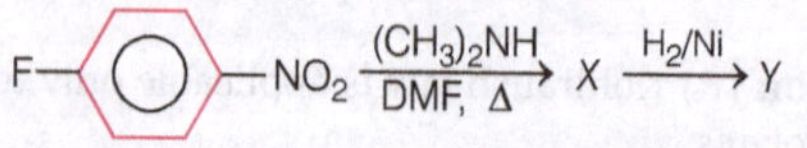

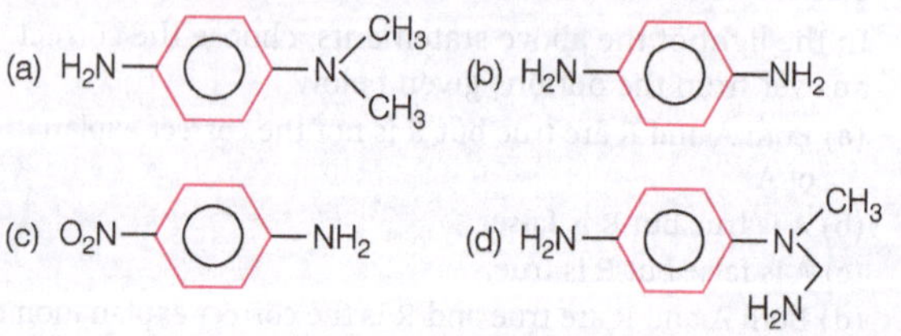

35. The solubility in water of $C_6H_5NH_2$(I), $(C_2H_5)_2NH$ (II) and $C_2H_5NH_2$(III) increases in the order.

(a) II < III < I (b) I < II < III
(c) III < II < I (d) II < I < III

Section-B (Q. No. 36 to 50)

36. Among the following samples of acid and base

(i) 100 mL of 1 M NaOH and 100 mL of 1 M HCl
(ii) 100 mL of 2 M KOH and 100 mL of 1 M H_2SO_4
(iii) 100 mL of 1 M CH_3COOH and 100 mL of 1 M NaOH
(iv) 100 mL of 0.5 M KOH and 100 mL of 0.5 M HNO_3
(v) 100 mL of 1 M HCOOH and 100 mL of 1 M NaOH

The total number of samples, which have same enthalpy of neutralisation is/are

(a) 1 (b) 4
(c) 3 (d) 5

37. In the given reaction, the product *Y* is

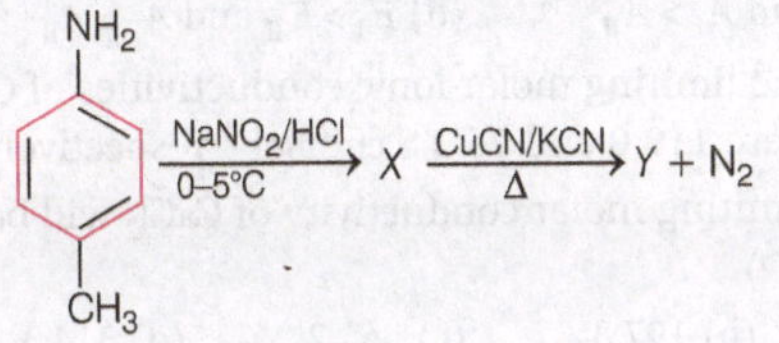

(a) 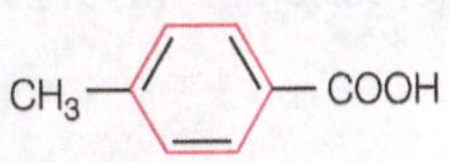

(b) 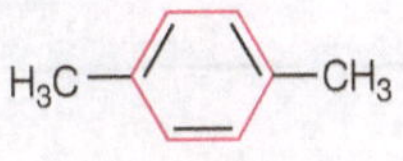

(c) 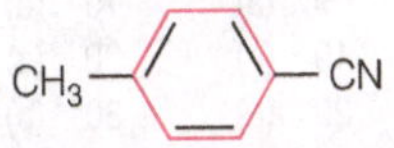

(d) 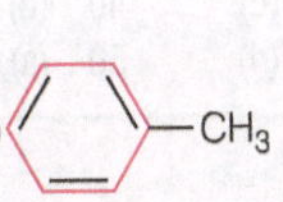

38. Given below are two statements.

Statement I H_2O is the only hydride of group 16, which is liquid at ordinary temperature.

Statement II In ice, each oxygen atom is surrounded by two covalent bonds and two hydrogen bonds.

In the light of the above statements, choose the correct answer from the options given below.

(a) Both Statement I and Statement II are false.
(b) Statement I is true but Statement II is false.
(c) Statement I is false but Statement II is true.
(d) Both Statement I and Statement II are true.

39. Which of the following reactions of glucose can be explained only by its cyclic structure?

(a) Glucose forms in cyanohydrin with HCN.
(b) Glucose react with hydroxylamine to form an oxime.
(c) Pentaacetate of glucose does not react with hydroxylamine.
(d) Glucose is oxidised by nitric acid to gluconic acid.

40. Which of the following is not an essential amino acid?

(a) Valine (b) Leucine
(c) Lysine (d) Alanine

41. Given below are two statements. One is labelled as Assertion (A) and other is labelled as Reason (R).

Assertion (A) $[Pt(en)_2Cl_2]^{2+}$ complex ion shows total number of three isomers.

Reason (R) $[Pt(en)_2Cl_2]^{2+}$ complex ion has an octahedral geometry.

In the light of above statements, choose the correct answer from the options given below

(a) Both A and R are true but R is not the correct explanation of A.
(b) A is true but R is false.
(c) A is false but R is true.
(d) Both A and R are true and R is the correct explanation of A.

42. Match Column I with Column II.

Column I (Complex)	Column II (O.N. of metal)
A. $Ni(CO)_4$	1. +1
B. $[Fe(H_2O)_5NO]^{2+}$	2. Zero
C. $[Co(CO)_5]^{2-}$	3. −1
D. $[Cr_2(CO)_{10}]^{2-}$	4. −2

Codes

	A	B	C	D
(a)	2	1	4	3
(b)	3	2	1	4
(c)	4	3	2	1
(d)	1	4	3	1

43. Consider the following reaction and identify the product *Y*.

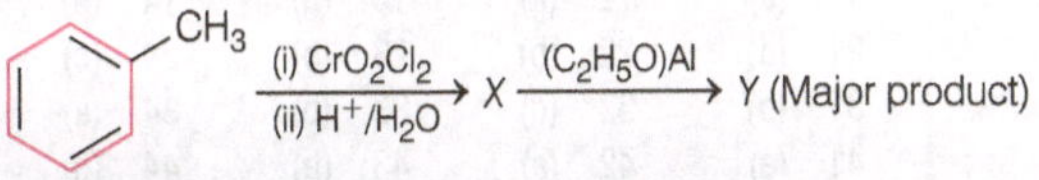

(a) 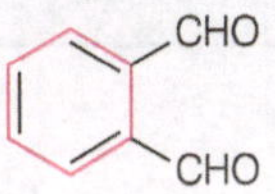

(b) 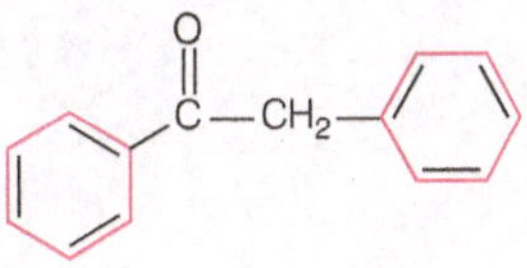

(c) 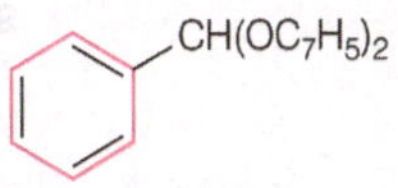

(d) 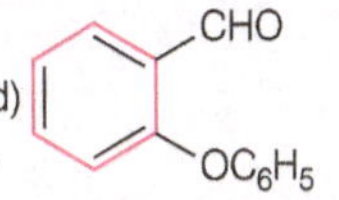

44. Select the incorrect statement

(a) The osmotic pressure (π) of a solution is given by the equation, $\pi = MRT$, where *M* is the molarity of solution.
(b) The correct order of osmotic pressure of 0.01 M aqueous solution of each compound is $BaCl_2 > KCl > CH_3COOH >$ sucrose.

(c) Raoult's law states that the vapour pressure of a component over a solution is proportion to its mole fraction.
(d) Two sucrose solutions of same molarity prepared in different solvents will have the same freezing point depression.

45. The hormone that helps in the conversion of glucose into glycogen is
(a) cortisone
(b) norepinephrine
(c) adrenaline
(d) insulin

46. If the molar conductivities (in S cm^2mol^{-1}) of NaCl, KCl and NaOH at infinite dilutions are 126, 150 and 250 respectively, the molar conductivity of KOH (in S cm^2mol^{-1}) is
(a) 2132 (b) 126
(c) 234 (d) 274

47. Which of the following aldehyde/ketone reacts with benzaldehyde in presence of dil. NaOH to form cinnamaldehyde?
(a) Acetaldehyde
(b) Acetophenone
(c) Acetone
(d) Formaldehyde

48. Consider the reaction, $2A + B \longrightarrow$ Products
When concentration of *B* alone was doubled, the half-life did not change. When the concentration of *A* alone was doubled, the rate increased by two times. The unit of rate constant for this reaction is
(a) unitless (b) mol $L^{-1}s^{-1}$
(c) s^{-1} (d) L $mol^{-1}s^{-1}$

49. The Arrhenius plots of two reactions I and II are shown graphically. The graph suggests that

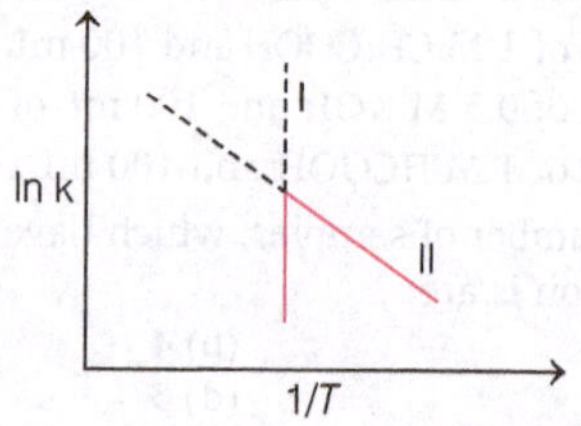

(a) $E_I > E_{II}$ and $A_{II} > A_I$ (b) $E_{II} > E_I$ and $A_{II} > A_I$
(c) $E_{II} > E_I$ and $A_I > A_{II}$ (d) $E_I > E_{II}$ and $A_I > A_{II}$

50. Given that the limiting molar ionic conductivities of Ca^{2+} and Cl^- ions are 119.0 and 76.3 S cm^2mol^{-1} respectively at 298 K. The limiting molar conductivity of $CaCl_2$ will be (in S cm^2mol^{-1})
(a) 271.6 (b) 197.3 (c) 563.2 (d) 314.3

Answers

1 (d)	2 (a)	3 (a)	4 (b)	5 (b)	6 (b)	7 (d)	8 (b)	9 (a)	10 (d)
11 (a)	12 (a)	13 (b)	14 (b)	15 (a)	16 (b)	17 (d)	18 (b)	19 (c)	20 (c)
21 (d)	22 (b)	23 (b)	24 (c)	25 (b)	26 (d)	27 (b)	28 (c)	29 (c)	30 (b)
31 (b)	32 (d)	33 (b)	34 (a)	35 (b)	36 (c)	37 (c)	38 (d)	39 (c)	40 (d)
41 (a)	42 (a)	43 (b)	44 (d)	45 (d)	46 (d)	47 (a)	48 (d)	49 (d)	50 (a)

For deeper insight
Scan the QR Code

Class 11th & 12th (Complete Syllabus)

Practice Test 02

Important Instructions

- The test of 1 hour duration and contains 50 Multiple Choice Questions (four options with a single correct answer) from Chemistry.
- There are 50 questions in each subject, divided into **two Sections** : Section A and Section B.
  (a) **Section A** contains 35 questions in each subject and all questions are compulsory.
  (b) **Section B** contains 15 questions from each subject out of which 10 questions are to be attempted.
- Each question carries 4 marks. For each correct response, the candidate will get 4 marks. For each incorrect response, one mark will be deducted from the total score.

Section-A (Q. No. 1 to 35)

1. H_2S acts only as a reducing agent while SO_2, can act both as a reducing and oxidising agent because
(a) S in H_2S has −2 oxidation state.
(b) S in SO_2 has oxidation state +4.
(c) hydrogen in H_2S is more positive than oxygen in SO_2.
(d) oxygen is more negative in SO_2.

2. Which of the following statement is incorrect about the elements/compounds of group 14?
(a) Silicones are polymeric organosilicon compounds.
(b) SiF_4 has tetrahedral shape.
(c) Pb^{2+} is less stable than Sn^{2+}.
(d) Mg_2C_3 is an allylide type of ionic carbide.

3. ΔH and ΔS for the reaction,

$$Ag_2O(s) \longrightarrow 2Ag(s) + \frac{1}{2}O_2(g)$$

are 30.56 kJ/mol and 66.0 J/K/mol respectively.
The temperature at which the free energy change for the reaction will be zero is
(a) 463 K (b) 354 K
(c) 483 K (d) 20 K

4.

Given data	Bond enthalpy
$N\equiv N$	945 kJ mol^{-1}
H—H	436 kJ mol^{-1}
N—H	391 kJ mol^{-1}

The enthalpy change of the reaction will be

$$N_2(g) + 3H_2(g) \longrightarrow 2NH_3(g)$$

(a) −89 kJ/mol (b) −93 kJ/mol
(c) −105 kJ/mol (d) 105 kJ/mol

5. Which one of the following has tetrahedral structure?
(a) SO_2 (b) SO_3
(c) SO_4^{2-} (d) SO_3^{2-}

6. For the energy levels in an atom, which one of the following statement is correct?
(a) There are seven principal electron energy level.
(b) The second principal energy level has four sub-energy level and contains a maximum of six electrons.
(c) The principal energy level *N* can have a maximum of 32 electrons.
(d) The 4*s* sub-energy level has higher than 3*d* sub-energy level.

7. The rate constant, the activation energy and the Arrhenius parameter of a chemical reaction at 25°C are $3\times10^{-14}\,s^{-1}$, 104.4 kJ mol^{-1} and $6.0\times10^{14}\,s^{-1}$ respectively. The value of rate constant at $T\rightarrow\infty$ is
(a) infinity
(b) $3.6\times10^{30}\,s^{-1}$
(c) $2.0\times10^{18}\,s^{-1}$
(d) $6.0\times10^{14}\,s^{-1}$

8. The correct statement regarding the following energy diagrams is

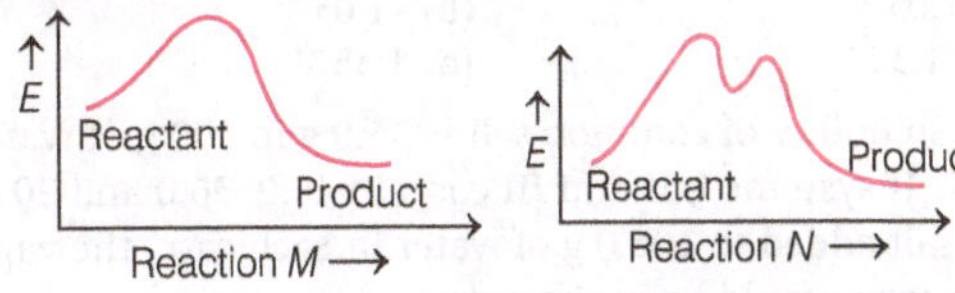

(a) reaction *M* is faster and less exothermic than reaction *N*.
(a) reaction *M* is slower and less exothermic than reaction *N*.
(c) reaction *M* is faster and more exothermic than reaction *N*.
(d) reaction *M* is slower and more exothermic than reaction *N*.

9. Given below are two statements.
Statement I N_3^- is weaker base than NH_2^-.
Statement II The lone pair of electrons of N atom in N_3^- is in a sp^2-orbital while in NH_2^-, it is in a sp^3-orbital.

In the light of above statements, choose the correct answer from the options given below.
(a) Both Statement I and Statement II are false.
(b) Statement I is true but Statement II is false.
(c) Statement I is false and Statement II is true.
(d) Both Statement I and Statement II are true.

10. Match Column I with Column II.

Column I (Buffer solution)	Column II (pH)
A. 0.1 M CH_3COOH + 0.01 M CH_3COONa	1. 5.8
B. 0.01 M CH_3COOH + 0.1 M CH_3COONa	2. 3.8
C. 0.1 M CH_3COOH + 0.1 M CH_3COONa	3. 7.0
D. 0.1 M CH_3COONH_4	4. 4.8

Codes

	A	B	C	D		A	B	C	D
(a)	2	1	4	3	(b)	1	2	4	3
(c)	2	1	3	4	(d)	3	1	4	2

11. Select the correct statements regarding crystallisation from the following.
A. Crystallisation technique is based on the difference in solubilities of compound and the impurities in a suitable solvent.
B. The impure compound is dissolved in a solvent in which it is sparingly soluble at higher temperature.
C. The solution is diluted to get a nearly saturated solution.
D. On cooling the solution, the impure compound crystallises out.
E. For the purification of solid organic compounds, the crystallisation technique can be used.
Choose the correct answer from the options given below.
(a) A, B and C (b) B, C and E (c) A, B and E (d) C, D and E

12. Determine the standard reduction potential for the half cell reaction,

$$Cl_2 + 2e^- \longrightarrow 2Cl^-$$

Given, $Pt^{2+} + 2Cl^- \longrightarrow Pt + Cl_2,\ E°_{cell} = -0.15\ V$

$Pt^{2+} + 2e^- \longrightarrow Pt,\ E° = 1.20\ V$

(a) 1.05 V (b) −1.05 V
(c) −1.35 V (d) 1.35 V

13. The solubility of common salt is 36.0 g in 100 g of water at 20°C. If systems I, II and III contain 40.0, 36.0 and 20.0 g of the salt added to 100.0 g of water in each case, the vapour pressures would be in the order
(a) I < II < III (b) I > II > III
(c) I = II > III (d) I = II < III

14. The freezing point of solution made by dissolving 1.1 g of $CoCl_3 \cdot 6NH_3$ (molecular weight = 267) in 100 g H_2O is −0.29°C. How many moles of solute particles exist in solution for each mole of solute introduced? ($K_f = 1.86°C/m$)
(a) 3 (b) 2 (c) 1 (d) 4

15. Given below are two statements.
Statement I Fructose does not contain an aldehyde group but still reduces Tollen's reagent.
Statement II In presence of a base, fructose undergoes a rearrangement to form glucose and mannose.
In the light of above statements, choose the correct answer from the options given below.
(a) Both Statement I and Statement II are false.
(b) Statement I is true but Statement II is false.
(c) Statement I is false but Statement II is true.
(d) Both Statement I and Statement II are true.

16. Which of the following is the major product (X) of the reaction ?

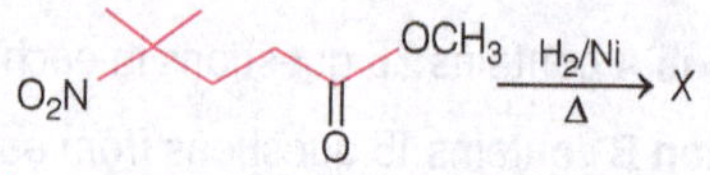

(a) 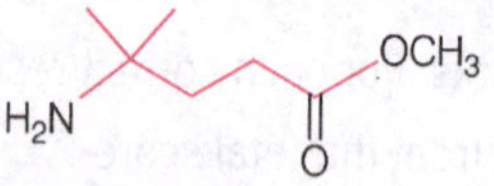

(b) 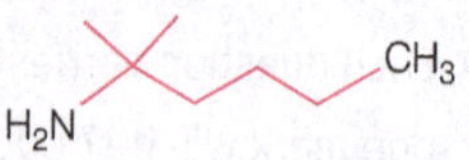

(c) 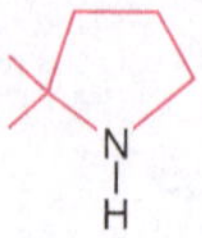

(d) 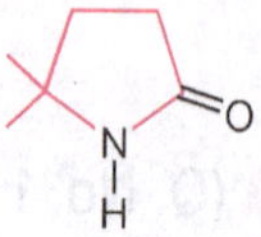

17. In nitrogen family, the H—M—H bond angle in the hydrides gradually becomes closer to 90° on going from N to Sb. This shows that gradually
(a) the basic strength of hydrides increases.
(b) almost pure p-orbitals are used for M—H bond.
(c) the bond energies of M—H bond increases.
(d) the bond pairs of electrons become nearer to the central atom.

18. How many lone pairs of electrons are present on Xe in $XeOF_4$?
(a) 4 (b) 3
(c) 1 (d) 2

19. The conductivity of 0.001028 mol L^{-1} acetic acid is 4.95×10^{-5} S cm^{-1}. Calculate its dissociation constant if Λ_m° for acetic acid is 390.5 S cm^2 mol^{-1}.
(a) 1.78×10^{-5} mol L^{-1} (b) 0.178×10^{-5} mol L^{-1}
(c) 0.0178×10^{-5} mol L^{-1} (d) 2.87×10^{-5} mol L^{-1}

20. Which of the following statements are incorrect about element X, Y and Z having atomic number 19, 37 and 55 respectively?
A. Their ionisation potential would increases with increasing atomic number.
B. Y would have an ionisation potential between those X and Z.
C. Z would have highest ionisation potential.
D. X would have the highest negative value of $\Delta_{eg}H$.
E. X would have high electronegativity value on Pauling scale than Y.
Choose the correct answer from the options given below
(a) C, D and E (b) A, B and C
(c) A, C and E (d) B, C and D

21. Consider the properties given below.

A. Enthalpy B. Entropy C. Gibbs free energy
D. Heat E. Work

The number of properties that depends upon the initial and final states of system is

(a) A and D (b) B and E
(c) A, B and C (d) B, D and E

22. Consider the following compounds/species:
$[Al(H_2O)_3Cl_3]$, PF_5, N_2O_5, CO_2, CH_4, N_2H_4, PCl_5
The number of compounds having equal value of covalency and oxidation number is,

(a) 2 (b) 3 (c) 4 (d) 5

23. Select the incorrect statements from the following.

A. In the primary batteries, the reaction occur only once and after use over a period of time battery becomes dead.
B. In mercury cell, zinc-mercury amalgam and a paste of HgO and carbon is used as cathode and anode respectively.
C. In lead storage battery during the discharge phase, sulphuric acid is formed as product in overall cell reaction.
D. A nickel-cadmium cell has shorter life than the lead storage cell.
E. Fuel cell are galvanic cells that are designed to convert the energy of combustion into electrical energy.

Choose the correct answer from the given options below.

(a) A and E (b) B, C and D
(c) A, B, C and D (d) C, D and E

24. For the square planar complex [*Mabcd*] (where, *M* is central metal and *a*, *b*, *c* and *d* are monodentate ligands), the number of possible geometrical isomers are

(a) 2 (b) 1
(c) 4 (d) 3

25. Given below are two statements. One is labelled as Assertion (A) and other is labelled as Reason (R).

Assertion (A) The IUPAC name for the compound; $NCCH_2CH_2COOH$ is 3-cyano propanoic acid.

Reason (R) COOH is considered as substituent group while CN is considered as the principal functional group.

In the light of above statements, choose the correct answer from the options given below.

(a) Both A and R are true but R is not the correct explanation of A.
(b) A is true but R is false.
(c) A is false but R is true.
(d) Both A and R are true and R is the correct explanation of A.

26. In the following reactions, the number of reactions in which K_p is less than K_c?

(i) $N_2O_4(g) \rightleftharpoons 2NO_2(g)$
(ii) $2HI(g) \rightleftharpoons H_2(g) + I_2(g)$
(iii) $2SO_2(g) + O_2(g) \rightleftharpoons 2SO_3(g)$
(iv) $N_2(g) + O_2(g) \rightleftharpoons 2NO(g)$
(v) $N_2(g) + 3H_2(g) \rightleftharpoons 2NH_3(g)$

(a) 3 (b) 2 (c) 4 (d) 5

27. Match Column I with Column II.

Column I (Radiation)	Column II (Wavelength)
A. X-rays	1. 30 m
B. Cosmic rays	2. 1 mm
C. Radiowaves	3. 10^{-5} nm
D. Microwaves	4. 1 nm

Codes

	A	B	C	D		A	B	C	D
(a)	4	3	1	2	(b)	1	2	3	4
(c)	2	3	1	4	(d)	3	4	1	2

28. Match Column I with Column II.

Column I (Metal ion)	Column II (Number of unpaired electrons)
A. V^{2+}	1. 1
B. Ti^{3+}	2. 4
C. Fe^{3+}	3. 3
D. Mn^{3+}	4. 5

Codes

	A	B	C	D		A	B	C	D
(a)	1	2	3	4	(b)	3	1	4	2
(c)	4	2	1	3	(d)	1	3	2	4

29. In the following sequence of reaction, the product (*Z*) is,

$$CH_3CH_2CH_2Br \xrightarrow[\text{(alc)}]{KOH} (X) \xrightarrow{HBr} (Y) \xrightarrow{KOH(aq)} (Z)$$

(a) propene (b) propyne
(c) propan-1-ol (d) propan-2-ol

30. In the reaction.

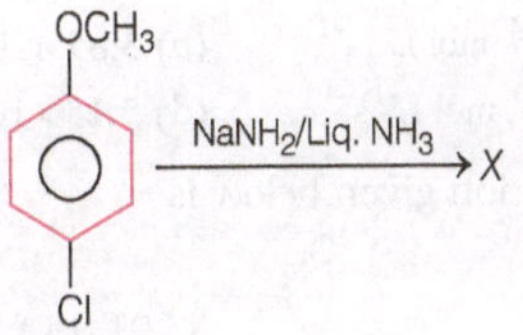

The major product *X* is,

(a) 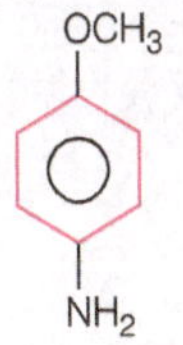

(b) 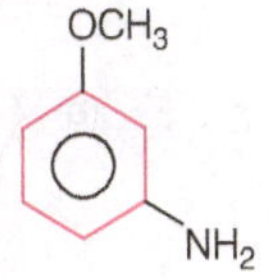

(c) 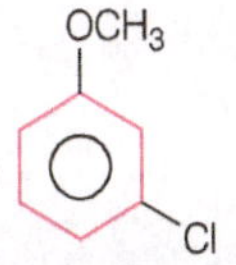

(d) 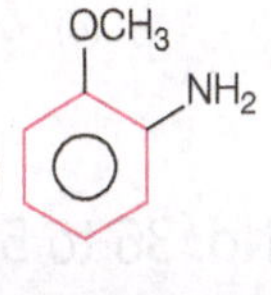

31. Which of the following statements are correct?

A. The decomposition of gaseous ammonia on a hot platinum surface is a first order reaction at high pressure.
B. For first order reaction, $t_{1/2}$ is independent of initial concentration of the reacting species.

C. A plot between ln [R] and t for a first order reaction gives negative slope.

D. If concentration of the reactant is doubled, half life period remains same in the zero order reaction.

E. For a first order reaction, $t_{1/2}$ is independent of initial concentration of the reacting species.

Choose the correct answer from the options given below.

(a) C, D and E (b) A, B and E
(c) A, C and D (d) B, C and E

32. Knowing that the chemistry of lanthanoids (Ln) is dominated by its +3 oxidation state, which of the following statement is incorrect?

(a) Due to large size of Ln (III) ions, the bonding in its compounds is predominantly ionic in character.
(b) The ionic size of Ln (III) decrease in general with increasing atomic number.
(c) Ln (III) compounds are generally colourless.
(d) Ln (III) hydroxide are mainly basic in character.

33. The standard reduction potential at 298 K for the following half cell reactions are given below.

$$Zn^{2+}(aq) + 2e^- \longrightarrow Zn(s);\ E° = -0.762\ V$$
$$Cr^{3+}(aq) + 3e^- \longrightarrow Cr(s);\ E° = -0.740\ V$$
$$2H^+(aq) + 2e^- \longrightarrow H_2(g);\ E° = 0.0\ V$$
$$Fe^{3+}(aq) + e^- \longrightarrow Fe^{2+}(aq);\ E° = 0.77\ V$$

Which is strongest reducing agent?

(a) $Cr(s)$ (b) $Zn(s)$ (c) $H_2(g)$ (d) $Fe^{2+}(aq)$

34. The reaction, $N_2O_5\ (\text{in } CCl_4) \longrightarrow 2NO_2 + \frac{1}{2}O_2(g)$ is first order with respect to N_2O_5 with rate constant $6.25 \times 10^{-4}\ s^{-1}$. What is the value of rate of reaction when $[N_2O_5] = 1.25\ mol\ L^{-1}$?

(a) $7.81 \times 10^{-4}\ mol\ L^{-1}s^{-1}$ (b) $3.85 \times 10^{-4}\ mol\ L^{-1}s^{-1}$
(c) $6.35 \times 10^{-3}\ mol\ L^{-1}s^{-1}$ (d) $5.15 \times 10^{-5}\ mol\ L^{-1}s^{-1}$

35. X in the reaction given below is

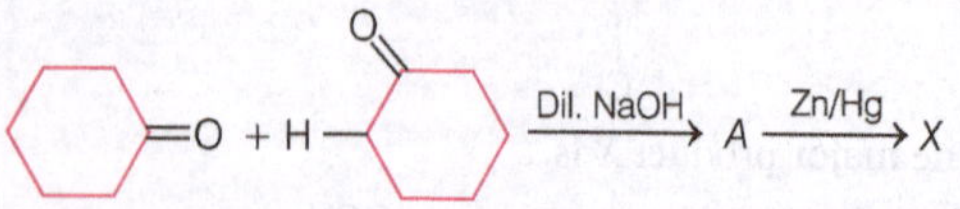

(a) 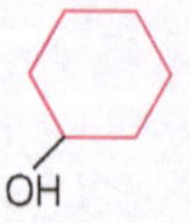

(b) 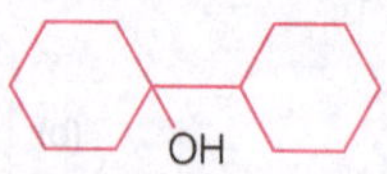

(c) 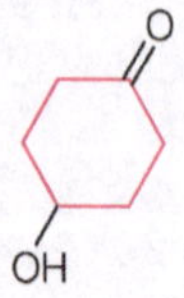

(d) 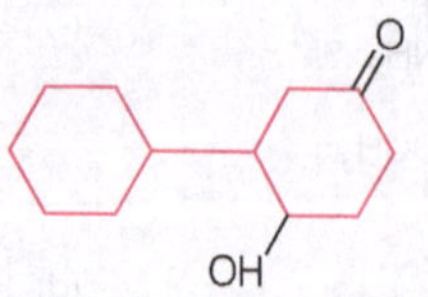

Section-B (Q. No. 36 to 50)

36. Final product of the following reaction.

$$CH_3C \equiv CCH_2CH_3 \xrightarrow[\text{(ii) Hydrolysis, (iii) } H_2O_2]{\text{(i) } O_3}$$

(a) $CH_3COOH + CO_2$ (b) $CH_3COOH + HOOCCH_2CH_3$
(c) $CH_3CHO + CH_3CH_2COOH$ (d) $CH_3COOH + CH_3COCH_3$

37. In the following reaction, A is

$$A \xrightarrow{\text{Bromination}} B \xrightarrow{NaNO_2/HCl} C \xrightarrow[C_2H_5OH]{\text{Boiling}} \textit{Sym}\text{-tribromobenzene}$$

(a) benzoic acid (b) salicylic acid
(c) phenol (d) aniline

38. Peptides are composed of amino acids joined by amide bond. Which of the following statements is not correct?

(a) Amide groups are more resistant to hydrolysis than similar ester groups.
(b) $p\pi$ - $p\pi$ resonance stabilises the amide bond.
(c) Stable conformation of peptides are restricted to those having planar amide groups.
(d) Amide groups do not participate in hydrogen bonding interactions.

39. A student prepared a standard solution of sodium oxalate by weighing 3.2 g of the dry anhydrous salt, dissolving it in distilled water and making the solution upto 500 mL. Molarity of the sodium oxalate solution is

(a) 0.04776 M (b) 0.07644 M (c) 0.09446 M (d) 0.06447 M

40. 112 mL of NO_2 at STP was liquified, the density of the liquid being $1.15\ g\ mL^{-1}$. What will be the volume and the number of molecules in liquid NO_2.

(a) 0.10 mL and 3.01×10^{22} (b) 0.20 mL and 3.01×10^{21}
(c) 0.20 mL and 6.02×10^{23} (d) 0.40 mL and 6.02×10^{21}

41. From the given data below.

$$NH_3(g) + 3Cl_2(g) \longrightarrow NCl_3(g) + 3HCl(g);\ -\Delta H_1 \quad ...(i)$$
$$N_2(g) + 3H_2(g) \longrightarrow 2NH_3(g);\ -\Delta H_2 \quad ...(ii)$$
$$H_2(g) + Cl_2(g) \longrightarrow 2HCl(g);\ \Delta H_3 \quad ...(iii)$$

The heat of formation of $NCl_3(g)$ in term of ΔH_1, ΔH_2 and ΔH_3 is

(a) $\Delta H_f = -\Delta H_1 - \frac{\Delta H_2}{2} - \frac{3}{2}\Delta H_3$

(b) $\Delta H_f = \Delta H_1 + \frac{\Delta H_2}{2} - \frac{3}{2}\Delta H_3$

(c) $\Delta H_f = \Delta H_1 - \frac{\Delta H_2}{2} + \frac{3}{2}\Delta H_3$

(d) None of the above

42. The hybridisation of atomic orbitals of nitrogen in NO_2^+, NO_3^- and NH_4^+ are

(a) sp, sp^2 and sp^3 respectively (b) sp, sp^3 and sp^3 respectively
(c) sp^2, sp and sp^3 respectively (d) sp^2, sp^3 and sp respectively

43. If S_1, S_2, S_3 and S_4 are the solubilities of AgCl in water, in 0.01 M $CaCl_2$, in 0.01 M NaCl and in 0.05 M $AgNO_3$ respectively at a certain temperature, the correct order of solubilities is

(a) $S_1 > S_2 > S_3 > S_4$ (b) $S_1 > S_3 > S_2 > S_4$
(c) $S_1 > S_2 = S_3 > S_4$ (d) $S_1 > S_3 > S_4 > S_2$

44. In which of the following pairs, there is highest difference in the oxidation number of underlined elements?

(a) $\underline{N}O_2$ and $\underline{N}_2O_4$ (b) $\underline{P}_2O_5$ and $\underline{P}_4O_{10}$
(c) $\underline{N}_2O$ and $\underline{N}O$ (d) $\underline{S}O_2$ and $\underline{S}O_3$

45. Lassaigne's test for the detection of nitrogen fails in

(a) $NH_2CONHNH_2 \cdot HCl$ (b) NH_2NH_2HCl
(c) NH_2CONH_2 (d) $C_6H_5NHNH_2HCl$

46. Which of the following statement is true?

(a) *tert*-butoxide is a stronger base as well as stronger nucleophile than ethoxide.

(b) *tert*-butoxide is a weaker base but stronger nucleophile than ethoxide.

(c) *tert*-butoxide is stronger base, but weaker nucleophile than ethoxide.

(d) *tert*-butoxide and ethoxide are equally strong bases as well as strong nucleophiles.

47. Match Column I with Column II.

Column I (Reaction)	Column II (Name of reaction)
A. $CH_3CH_2CH_2Cl \xrightarrow[\Delta]{NaI,\ Acetone} CH_3CH_2CH_2I$	1. Hunsdiecker reaction
B. $CH_3CH_2Cl \xrightarrow[\Delta]{Hg_2F_2} CH_3CH_2F$	2. Fittig reaction
C. $RCOOAg \xrightarrow[\Delta]{Br_2/CCl_4} RBr$	3. Finkelstein reaction
D. $C_6H_5Br \xrightarrow{Na,\ \Delta} C_6H_5—C_6H_5$	4. Swarts reaction

Codes

	A	B	C	D		A	B	C	D
(a)	3	4	1	2	(b)	4	3	2	1
(c)	1	3	4	2	(d)	2	3	4	1

48. Given below are two statements. One is labelled as Assertion (A) and other is labelled as Reason (R).

Assertion (A) Oxidation of toluene as well as ethylbenzene with $KMnO_4$ gives benzoic acid.

Reason (R) Both toluene and ethylbenzene are more reactive than benzene towards electrophilic substitution reaction.

In the light of above statements, choose the correct answer from the options given below.

(a) Both A and R are true but R is not the correct explanation of A.

(b) A is true but R is false.

(c) A is false but R is true.

(d) Both A and R are true and R is the correct explanation of A.

49. Following are the isomers of molecular formula for C_5H_{12}

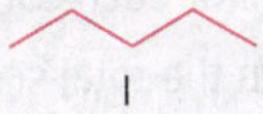
I

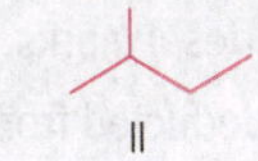
II

III

Decreasing order of their boiling point is

(a) I > II ≡ III (b) I > II > III

(c) II > I > III (d) III > I > II

50. Action of *R*MgX with vinyl chloride gives

(a) alkane (b) alkyne

(c) alkene (d) aromatic hydrocarbon

Answers

1 (c)	2 (c)	3 (a)	4 (b)	5 (c)	6 (c)	7 (d)	8 (c)	9 (d)	10 (a)
11 (c)	12 (d)	13 (d)	14 (d)	15 (d)	16 (d)	17 (b)	18 (c)	19 (a)	20 (c)
21 (c)	22 (b)	23 (b)	24 (d)	25 (b)	26 (b)	27 (a)	28 (b)	29 (d)	30 (b)
31 (d)	32 (c)	33 (b)	34 (a)	35 (b)	36 (b)	37 (d)	38 (d)	39 (a)	40 (b)
41 (a)	42 (a)	43 (b)	44 (d)	45 (b)	46 (c)	47 (a)	48 (a)	49 (b)	50 (c)

For deeper insight
Scan the QR Code

Class 11th & 12th (Complete Syllabus)

Practice Test 03

Important Instructions

- The test of 1 hour duration and contains 50 Multiple Choice Questions (four options with a single correct answer) from Chemistry.
- There are 50 questions in each subject, divided into **two Sections** : Section A and Section B.
  (a) **Section A** contains 35 questions in each subject and all questions are compulsory.
  (b) **Section B** contains 15 questions from each subject out of which 10 questions are to be attempted.
- Each question carries 4 marks. For each correct response, the candidate will get 4 marks. For each incorrect response, one mark will be deducted from the total score.

Section-A (Q. No. 1 to 35)

1. 100 g of liquid *A* (molar mass 140 g/mol) was dissolved in 1000 g of liquid *B* (molar mass 180 g/mol). The vapour pressure of pure liquid *B* was found to be 500 torr. If the total vapour pressure of solution is 475 torr, the vapour pressure of pure liquid *A* is

(a) 210.3 torr (b) 147.6 torr
(c) 118.2 torr (d) 280.7 torr

2. The major product of the following reaction is

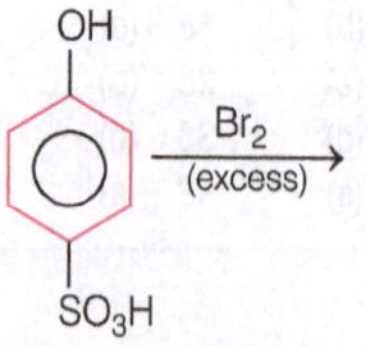

(a)
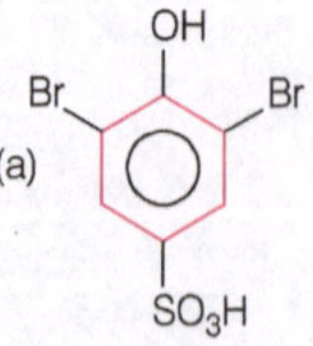

(b)
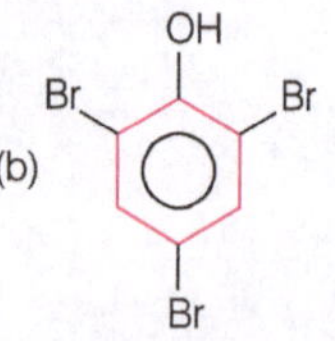

(c)
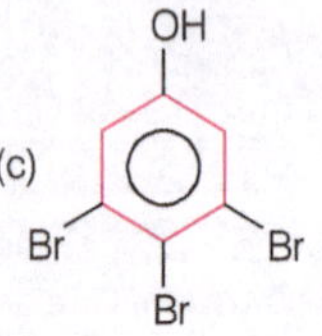

(d)
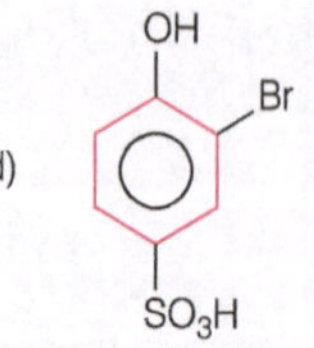

3. 0.50 g of an organic compound was Kjeldahlised and the NH_3 evolved was absorbed in 50 mL of 0.5 M H_2SO_4. The residual acid required 60 cm^3 of 0.5 M NaOH. The percentage of nitrogen in the organic compound is

(a) 56 (b) 38
(c) 17 (d) 40

4. Identify the reagents in the following transformations,

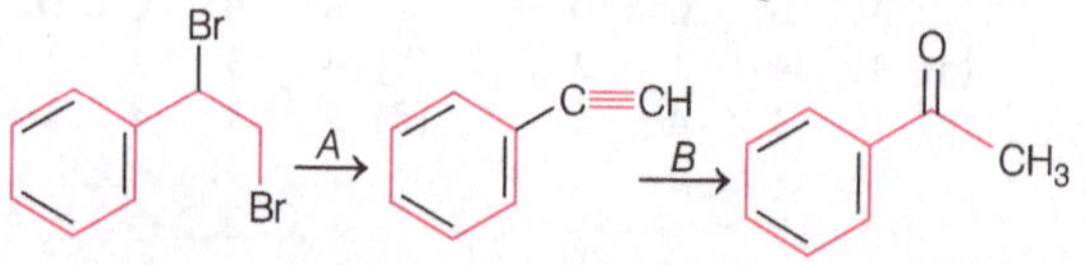

(a) Alc. KOH and H_2O, H_2SO_4, $HgSO_4$
(b) Alc. KOH and $KMnO_4$ / H^+
(c) $NaNH_2$ and H_2O, $HgSO_4$, H_2SO_4
(d) $NaNH_2$ and $KMnO_4$ / H^+

5. The major product formed when 3, 3-dimethylbutan-2-ol is heated with conc. sulphuric acid is

(a) 2, 3-dimethyl-2-butene
(b) 2, 3-dimethyl-1-butene
(c) 3, 3-dimethyl-1-butene
(d) *cis* and *trans* isomers of 2, 3-dimethyl-1-butene

6. If the molar conductivities (in S cm^2 / mol) of NaCl, KCl and NaOH at infinite dilution are 126, 150 and 250 respectively, the molar conductivity of KOH (in S cm^2 / mol) is

(a) 432 (b) 126 (c) 234 (d) 274

7. Which of the following statement regarding the molecularity of a reaction is wrong?

(a) It is the number of molecules of the reactant and taking part in a single step chemical reaction.
(b) It is calculated from the reaction mechanism.
(c) It may be either a whole number or fractional.
(d) It depends on the rate determining step in the reaction.

8. Consider the following sequence of reaction.

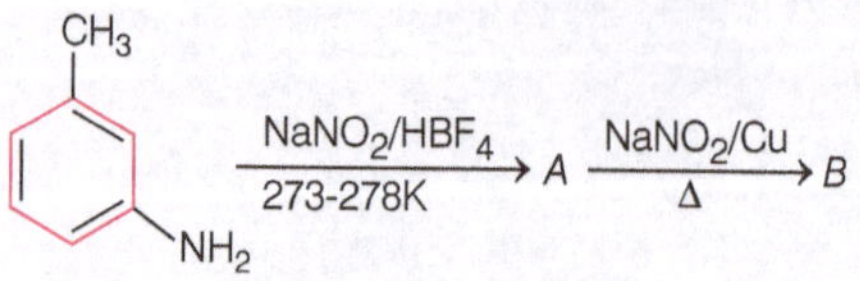

Compounds A and B respectively are

(a) 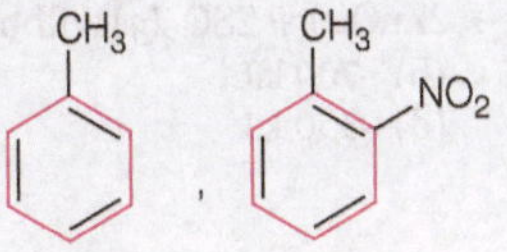

(b) 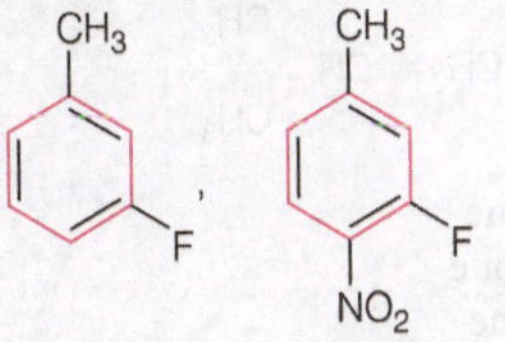

(c) 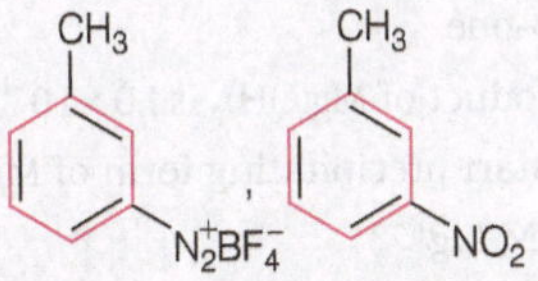

(d) 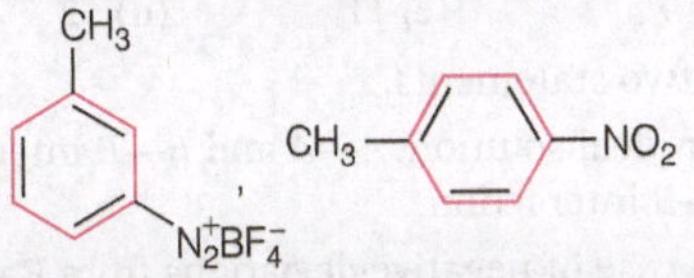

9. Osmotic pressure of urea solution at 10°C is 500 mm. The solution is diluted with temperature raised to 25°C till osmotic pressure becomes 131.6 mm. The solution is diluted

(a) 2 times (b) 2.5 times
(c) 4 times (d) 3.6 times

10. Enantiomers have

(a) identical melting point/boiling point but different refractive indices.
(b) identical melting/boiling point and refractive indices but rotate plane polarised light in opposite directions but to the same extent.
(c) different refractive index and rotate plane polarised light in the same direction but to different extent.
(d) different melting/boiling point but rotate plane polarised light in different directions but to the same extent.

11. The oxidation of SO_2 by O_2 to SO_3 is an exothermic reaction. The yield of SO_3 will be maximum if

(a) temperature is increased and pressure is kept constant
(b) temperature is reduced and pressure is increased
(c) both temperature and pressure is increased
(d) both temperature and pressure is decreased

12. Given that $E^\circ_{K^+/K} = -2.93$ V, $E^\circ_{Fe^{2+}/Fe} = -0.44$ V,
$E^\circ_{Zn^{2+}/Zn} = -0.76$ V, $E^\circ_{Cu^{2+}/Cu} = 0.34$ V

Based on the given data, which of the following is the strongest reducing agent?

(a) K^+ (b) Zn^{2+}
(c) Cu (d) Fe

13. Which is the correct statement about $Cr_2O_7^{2-}$ structure?

(a) It has neither Cr—Cr bonds nor O—O bonds.
(b) It has two Cr—Cr bonds and six O—O bonds.
(c) It has no Cr—Cr bonds and five O—O bonds.
(d) It has one Cr—Cr bond and six O—O bonds.

14. Which of the following statement is incorrect?

(a) Due to large size of the Zn (III) ions the bonding in their compounds is predominantly ionic in character.
(b) The ionic size of Ln (III) decrease in general with increasing atomic number.
(c) Ln (III) compounds are generally colourless.
(d) Ln (III) hydroxides are mainly basic in character.

15. $t_{1/4}$ can be taken as the time taken for the concentration of a reactant to drop to 3/4 of its initial value. If the rate constant for a first order reaction is k, then $t_{1/4}$ can be written as

(a) $\frac{0.85}{k}$ (b) $\frac{0.59}{k}$ (c) $\frac{0.29}{k}$ (d) $\frac{0.70}{k}$

16. Match Column I with Column II.

Column I (Equations)	Column II (Type of processes)
A. $K_p > Q$	1. Non spontaneous
B. $\Delta G^\circ < RT \ln Q$	2. Equilibrium
C. $K_p = Q$	3. Adiabatic
D. $Q = 0$	4. Spontaneous

Codes

	A	B	C	D		A	B	C	D
(a)	1	2	3	4	(b)	2	4	1	3
(c)	4	1	2	3	(d)	3	4	2	1

17. The hormones used by athletes to increase the mass and strength of muscles is/are

(a) estrogens (b) gestogens
(c) androgens (d) both estrogens and androgens

18. The pair of compounds in which both the metals are in the highest possible oxidation state is

(a) $[Fe(CN)_6]^{3-}$, $[Co(CN)_6]^{3-}$ (b) CrO_2Cl_2, MnO_4^-
(c) TiO_2, MnO_2 (d) $[Co(CN)_6]^{3-}$, MnO_2

19. Match Column I with Column II.

Column I	Column II
A. Beilstein test	1. Sulphur
B. Sodium nitroprusside	2. Carbon
C. Leibig's method	3. Nitrogen
D. Kjeldahl's method	4. Chlorine

Codes

	A	B	C	D		A	B	C	D
(a)	2	3	4	1	(b)	4	1	2	3
(c)	3	1	2	4	(d)	1	2	4	3

20. Which of the following reaction sequence will convert?

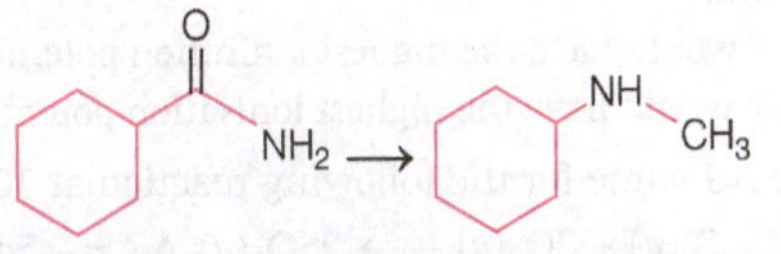

(a) Carbylamine, Hoffmann bromamide, reduction with H_2/Pd
(b) Reduction amination, Hoffmann bromamide reaction, carbylamine reaction.

(c) Reduction with $LiAlH_4$, carbylamine reaction, Hoffmann bromamide reaction.
(d) Hoffmann bromamide reaction, carbylamine reaction, reduction with H_2/Pd.

21. Match Column I and Column II.

Column I (Ions)	Column II (Spin magnetic moment)
A. Co^{3+}	1. $\sqrt{8}$ BM
B. Cr^{3+}	2. $\sqrt{35}$ BM
C. Fe^{3+}	3. $\sqrt{24}$ BM
D. Ni^{2+}	4. $\sqrt{15}$ BM

Codes

	A	B	C	D		A	B	C	D
(a)	3	4	2	1	(b)	2	1	4	3
(c)	4	1	3	2	(d)	1	3	2	4

22. Given below are two statements.
Statement I 2-pentanol and 3-pentanol cannot be distinguished by iodoform test.
Statement II 2-pentanol and 3-pentanol both are secondary alcohols.
In the light of above statements, choose the correct answer from the options given below.
(a) Both Statements I and II are false.
(b) Statement I is true but Statement II is false.
(c) Statement I is false but Statement II is true.
(d) Both Statements I and II are true.

23. *p*-cresol reacts with chloroform in alkaline medium give a compound *A* which add hydrogen cyanide form another compound *B*. This latter compound on acidic hydrolysis gives chiral carboxylic acid. The structure of carboxylic acid is

(a) 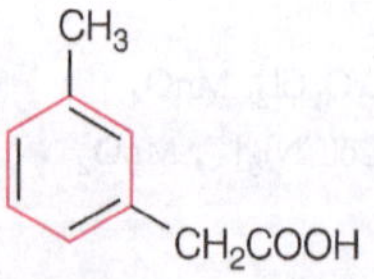

(b) 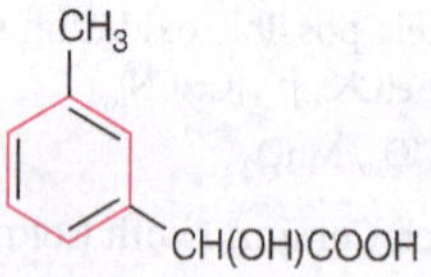

(c) 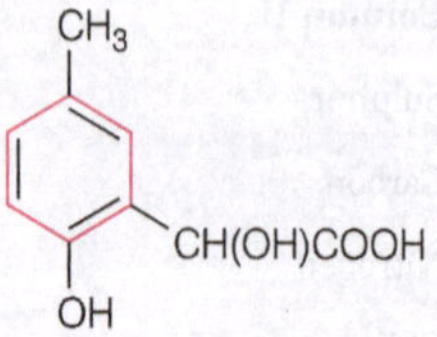

(d) 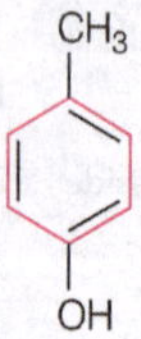

24. Elements *X*, *Y* and *Z* have atomic numbers 19, 37 and 55 respectively, which of the following statement is true about them?
(a) Their ionisation potential would increase with increasing atomic number.
(b) *Y* would have an ionisation potential between those of *X* and *Z*.
(c) *Z* would have the highest ionisation potential.
(d) *Y* would have the highest ionisation potential.

25. The ΔG value for the following reaction at 300° as given

$$S_2(g) + 2O_2(g) \longrightarrow 2SO_2(g); \Delta G = -544 \text{ kJ}$$
$$2Zn(s) + S_2(g) \longrightarrow 2ZnS(s); \Delta G = -273 \text{ kJ}$$
$$2Zn(s) + O_2(g) \longrightarrow 2ZnO(s); \Delta G = -480 \text{ kJ}$$

The ΔG for the reaction

$$2ZnS(s) + 3O_2(g) \longrightarrow 2ZnO(s) + 2SO_2(g)$$ will be

(a) –731 kJ (b) –700 kJ
(c) –260 kJ (d) –350 kJ

26. The IUPAC name of

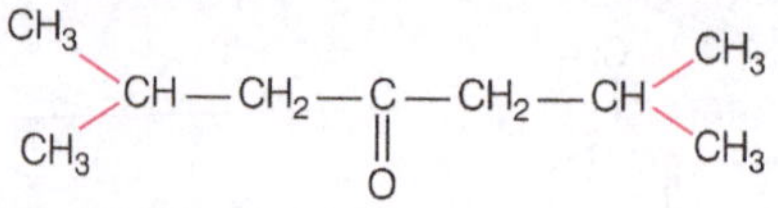

(a) 4, 2-dimethylhexan-4-one
(b) 2, 6-dimethylheptan-4-one
(c) 4, 4-dimethylhexan-4-one
(d) 2, 6-dimethylheptan-3-one

27. At 25°C, the solubility product of $Mg(OH)_2$ is 1.0×10^{-11}. At what pH will Mg^{2+} ions start precipitating form of $Mg(OH)_2$ from a solution of 0.001 M Mg^{2+}?
(a) 10 (b) 7 (c) 11 (d) 12

28. Given below are two statements.
Statement I For ideal solution, *A*—*A* and *B*—*B* interaction are similar to *A*—*B* interaction.
Statement II In case of negative deviations from Raoult's law, *A*—*A* forces are stronger than *A*—*B* and *B*—*B* forces.
In the light of above statements, choose the correct answer from the options given below.
(a) Both Statement I and Statement II are false.
(b) Statement I is true but Statement II is false.
(c) Statement I is false but Statement II is true.
(d) Both Statement I and Statement II are true.

29. Choose the incorrect statement with respect to given reaction

$$\overset{VI}{3MnO_4^{2-}} + 4H^+ \longrightarrow \overset{VII}{2MnO_4^-} + \overset{IV}{MnO_2} + 2H_2O$$

(a) The reaction shows disproportionation of an oxidation state (VI) in MnO_4^{2-}.
(b) Here, the oxidation state of manganese in one of the products MnO_4^- increases to (VII) and in the other product MnO_2 decreases to (IV).
(c) Manganese (VI) here becomes unstable relative to manganese (VII) and manganese (VI) in acidic medium.
(d) One mole of MnO_4^{2-} is converted into two moles of MnO_4^- and 1/3 mole of MnO_2.

30. The enthalpies of formation of $Al_2O_3(s)$ and $Fe_2O_3(s)$ are –1670 kJ/mol and –834 kJ/mol respectively. What is the enthalpy change for the reaction?

$$Fe_2O_3(s) + 2Al(s) \longrightarrow Al_2O_3(s) + 2Fe(s)$$

(a) 2405 kJ/mol (b) –2405 kJ/mol
(c) –836 kJ/mol (d) 800 kJ/mol

31. Which of the following is correct electronic configuration of the singly positive nitrogen molecular ion
(a) $\sigma 1s^2 \sigma^* 1s^2 \sigma 2s^2 \sigma^* 2s^2 \pi 2p_x^2 = \pi 2p_y^2 \sigma 2p_z^1$
(b) $\sigma 1s^2 \sigma^* 1s^2 \sigma 2s^2 \sigma^* 2s^2 \sigma 2p_z^2 \pi 2p_x^2 = \pi^* 2p_y^1$
(c) $\sigma 1s^2 \sigma^* 1s^2 \sigma 2s^2 \sigma^* 2s^2 \sigma 2p_z^1 \pi 2p_x^2 = \pi 2p_y^1$
(d) $\sigma 1s^2 \sigma^* 1s^2 \sigma 2s^2 \sigma^* 2s^2 \sigma 2p_z^2 \pi 2p_z^2$

32. Which of the following is correctly arranged in order of increasing weight?

(a) 0.625 of Fe < 0.0105 equivalent of $H_2C_2O_4 \cdot 2H_2O$ < 6.0×10^{21} atom of Zn < 0.006 g atom of Ag.

(b) 0.625 g of Fe < 6.0×10^{21} atom of Zn < 0.006 g atom of Ag < 0.0105 equivalent of $H_2C_2O_4 \cdot 2H_2O$.

(c) 0.0105 equivalent of $H_2C_2O_4 \cdot 2H_2O$ < 0.006 g atom of Ag < 6.0×10^{21} atom of Zn < 0.625 g of Fe.

(d) 0.0105 equivalent of $H_2C_2O_4 \cdot 2H_2O$ < 0.625 g of Fe < 0.006 g atom of Ag < 6.0×10^{21} atoms of Zn.

33. Chlorine is prepared in the laboratory by treating manganese dioxide (MnO_2) with aqueous HCl according to reaction.

$$4HCl(aq) + MnO_2(g) \longrightarrow 2H_2O(l) + MnCl_2(aq) + Cl_2(g)$$

How many gram of HCl will react with 5.0 g of manganese dioxide?

(a) 4.2 g HCl (b) 2.4 g HCl (c) 8.4 g HCl (d) 3.6 g HCl

34. Consider the following halogen containing compounds.

(i) CH_3Cl (ii) CCl_4 (iii) CH_2Cl_2

(iv) $CHCl_3$ (v) 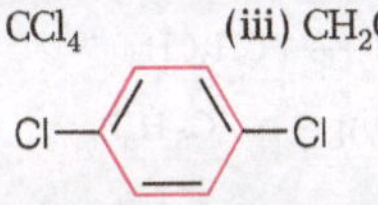

The number of compounds with a net zero dipole moment.

(a) 2 (b) 3 (c) 4 (d) 5

35. The increasing order of Coupling of diazonium salts of following species take place in order.

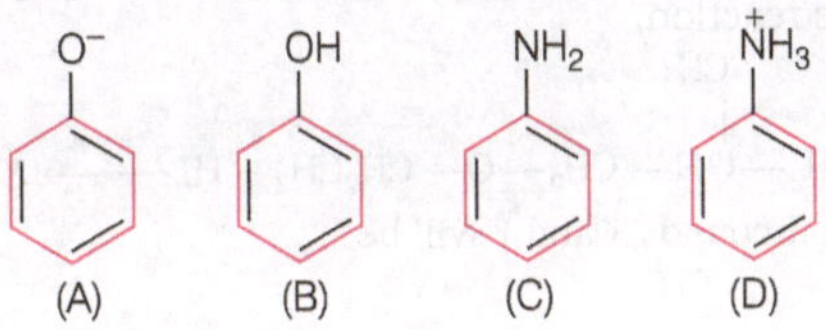

(a) D, B, C, A (b) D, C, B, A (c) A, B, C, D (d) B, D, A, C

Section-B (Q. No. 36 to 50)

36. Consider the following statements about protein denaturation :

A. During denaturation, the 2° (secondary) and 3° (tertiary) structures of proteins are not destroyed.

B. The 1° (primary) structure of a protein is destroyed during denaturation.

C. Curdling of milk, caused by lactic acid formed by bacteria, is an example of protein denaturation.

D. Denaturation typically causes a loss of a protein's biological (physiological) activity.

E. In most standard denaturation processes, the primary structure (covalent backbone) remains intact.

Which of the above statements are incorrect?

(a) (A) and (C) (b) (A) and (B)
(c) (A), (B) and (C) (d) (B), (C) and (E)

37. Select correct statements from given statements.

A. Raoult's law states that the vapour pressure of a component over a binary solution of volatile liquid is directly proportional to its mole fraction.

B. Two sucrose solutions of the same molarity prepared in different solvents will have the same depression in freezing point.

C. The correct order of osmotic pressure of 0.01 M solution of each compound is $BaCl_2 > KCl > CH_3COOH >$ glucose.

D. In the equation, osmotic pressure, $\pi = MRT$, M is molarity of solution.

E. The molecular weight of NaCl determined by colligative property measurement is less than the theoretical molecular weight.

Choose the correct answer from the options given below.

(a) A, B and D (b) B, C and D
(c) A, C, D, E (d) B, C, D, E

38. Among the given complexes, which one of the following is an inner orbital complex as well as diamagnetic in behaviour?

(a) $[Co(NH_3)_6]^{3+}$ (b) $[Zn(NH_3)_6]^{2+}$
(c) $[Cr(NH_3)_6]^{3+}$ (d) $[Ni(NH_3)_6]^{2+}$

39. Which of the following is the stronger reducing agent among the following oxyacids of phosphorus?

(a) Hypophosphorus acid
(b) Phosphorus acid
(c) Hypophosphoric acid
(d) Pyrophosphorus acid

40. Given below are two statements, one is labelled as Assertion (A) and other is labelled as Reason (R).

Assertion (A) *p*-phenol sulphonic acid on treating with Br_2 water gives 2, 4, 6-tribromophenol.

Reason (R) Sulphonic acid is a good leaving group.

In the light of above statements, choose the correct answer from the options given below.

(a) Both A and R are true but R is not the correct explanation of A.
(b) A is true but R is false.
(c) A is false but R is true.
(d) Both A and R are true and R is the correct explanation of A.

41. For the reaction $2A + B \rightarrow A_2B$, rate $= k[A][B]^2$ with $k = 2 \times 10^{-6}$ mol^{-2}L^{2}s^{-1}. The reaction was started with $[A] = 0.1$ mol/L and $[B] = 0.2$ mol/L. The rate of reaction when $[A]$ is reduced to 0.06 mol/L will be

(a) 3.89×10^{-9} mol L^{-1}s^{-1}
(b) 5.29×10^{-9} mol L^{-1}s^{-1}
(c) 2.59×10^{-9} mol L^{-1}s^{-1}
(d) 7.32×10^{-9} mol L^{-1}s^{-1}

42. Which set of terms correctly identifies the carbohydrate shown?

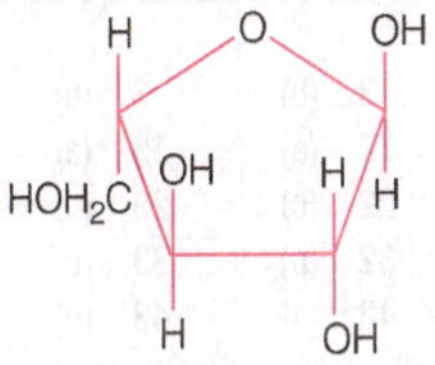

(i) Pentose (ii) Aldose (iii) Ketose
(iv) Pyranose (v) Furanose

Choose correct option from the given below options.

(a) (i), (ii) and (v)
(b) (ii) and (iv)
(c) (i), (iii) and (v)
(d) (ii) and (v)

43. An electrochemical cell is setup as follows
Pt (H_2, 1 atm) | 0.1 M HCl || 0.1 M acetic acid | (H_2, 1 atm) Pt
EMF of this cell will not be zero because
(a) the temperature is constant
(b) the pH of 0.1 M HCl and 0.1 M acetic acid is not same
(c) acids used in two compartments are different
(d) EMF of a cell depends on molarities of acids used

44. Consider the following statements
A. The order of a reaction is an experimental quantity.
B. The order is applicable only for elementary reactions.
C. The rate constant for a first-order gaseous reaction will have the unit atm s^{-1}.
D. The half-life of a reaction decreases with an increase in temperature.
Which of the above statements are correct?
(a) (B) and (C) (b) (A) and (B)
(c) (A) and (D) (d) (C) and (D)

45. In the following reaction sequence.

$$CH_3CH=CH_2 \xrightarrow[\text{(ii) } H_2O_2/OH^-]{\text{(i) } B_2H_6/THF} X \xrightarrow[\text{(ii) } CH_3I]{\text{(i) NaOH}} Y$$

The structure of product (Y) is
(a) $CH_3CH_2CH_2OCH_3$ (b) $(CH_3)_2CH-OCH_3$
(c) $CH_3CHOHCH_3$ (d) $CH_3CHOHCH_2OH$

46. Match Column I and Column II.

Column I (Compound)	Column II (Number of lone pairs)
A. BrF_5	1. 2 occupying axial position
B. ICl_4^-	2. 1 occupying equatorial position
C. ClF_3	3. 1 occupying axial position
D. SF_4	4. 2 occupying equatorial position

Codes

	A	B	C	D		A	B	C	D
(a)	3	1	4	2	(b)	3	4	1	2
(c)	4	3	2	1	(d)	2	1	4	3

47. The increasing order of stability of the following radicals is
(a) $(CH_3)_2\dot{C}H < (CH_3)_3\dot{C} < (C_6H_5)_2\dot{C}H < (C_6H_5)_3\dot{C}$
(b) $(C_6H_5)_3\dot{C} < (C_6H_5)_2\dot{C}H < (CH_3)_3\dot{C} < (CH_3)_2\dot{C}H$
(c) $(C_6H_5)_3\dot{C}H < (C_6H_5)_2\dot{C} < (CH_3)_3\dot{C} < (CH_3)_2\dot{C}H$
(d) $(CH_3)_2\dot{C}H < (CH_3)_3\dot{C} < (C_6H_5)_3\dot{C} < (C_6H_5)_2\dot{C}H$

48. Consider the following statements.
A. The principal quantum number n is a positive integer with value $n = 1, 2, 3, \ldots$
B. The azimuthal quantum number l for a given n (principal quantum number) can have values as $l = 0, 1, 2, \ldots, n$
C. Magnetic orbital quantum number m_l for a particular l (azimuthal quantum number) has $(2l + 1)$ values.
D. $\pm 1/2$ are the two possible orientations of electron spin.
E. For $l = 7$, there will be a total 14 orbitals.
Which of the above statement(s) are correct?
(a) A, B and C (b) A, B, D and E
(c) A, C and D (d) B, C and D

49. Match Column I with Column II.

Column I (Conversion)	Column II (Reagent)
A. $CH_3COAg \longrightarrow CH_3COOCH_3$	1. Br_2
B. $CH_3CH=CH_2 \longrightarrow BrCH_2CH=CH_2$	2. I_2
C. $CH_3CH_2Cl \longrightarrow CH_3CH_2F$	3. NBS
D. $C_6H_5COOAg \longrightarrow C_6H_5Br$	4. Hg_2F_2

Codes

	A	B	C	D		A	B	C	D
(a)	1	3	2	4	(b)	2	4	1	2
(c)	2	3	4	1	(d)	3	1	2	4

50. In the reaction,

$$CH_3CH_2-CH(CH_3)-CH_2-O-CH_2CH_3 + HI \xrightarrow{\text{Heated}} X + Y$$

The compounds X and Y will be
(a) $CH_3CH_2CH(CH_3)-CH_2OH + CH_3CH_2-I$
(b) $CH_3CH_2-CH(CH_3)-CH_2I + CH_3CH_2OH$
(c) $CH_3-CH_2-CH(CH_3)-CH_3 + CH_3CH_2OH$
(d) $CH_3CH_2-CH(CH_3)-CH_2OH + CH_3CH_3$

Answers

1 (d)	2 (b)	3 (a)	4 (c)	5 (a)	6 (d)	7 (c)	8 (c)	9 (c)	10 (b)
11 (b)	12 (a)	13 (a)	14 (c)	15 (c)	16 (c)	17 (c)	18 (b)	19 (b)	20 (d)
21 (a)	22 (c)	23 (c)	24 (b)	25 (a)	26 (b)	27 (a)	28 (b)	29 (d)	30 (c)
31 (a)	32 (b)	33 (c)	34 (a)	35 (a)	36 (b)	37 (c)	38 (a)	39 (a)	40 (a)
41 (a)	42 (a)	43 (b)	44 (c)	45 (a)	46 (a)	47 (a)	48 (c)	49 (c)	50 (a)

For deeper insight
Scan the QR Code